ELGAR COMPANION TO NEO-SCHUMPETERIAN ECONOMICS

330.1 H
R

BPP College

Library & Information Service

BPP

REFERENCE USE ONLY

Not to be removed from the library

D1330673

Elgar Companion to Neo-Schumpeterian Economics

Edited by

Horst Hanusch

Professor and Chair in Economics,
University of Augsburg, Germany

Andreas Pyka

Professor in Economics
University of Bremen, Germany

Edward Elgar
Cheltenham, UK • Northampton, MA, USA

© Horst Hanusch and Andreas Pyka 2007

All rights reserved. No part of this publication may be reproduced, stored in a retrieval system or transmitted in any form or by any means, electronic, mechanical or photocopying, recording, or otherwise without the prior permission of the publisher.

Published by
Edward Elgar Publishing Limited
Glensanda House
Montpellier Parade
Cheltenham
Glos GL50 1UA
UK

Edward Elgar Publishing, Inc.
William Pratt House
9 Dewey Court
Northampton
Massachusetts 01060
USA

A catalogue record for this book
is available from the British Library

Library of Congress Control Number: 2006934128

ISBN 978 1 84376 253 9 (cased)

Printed and bound in Great Britain by MPG Books Ltd, Bodmin, Cornwall

Contents

PART 4   NEO-SCHUMPETERIAN MACRO DYNAMICS:
         GROWTH AND DEVELOPMENT

4.1   Growth

Contributors

Zoltan J. Acs, Professor of Economics, University of Baltimore, Baltimore, MD, USA

Peter M. Allen, Professor, School of Management, Cranfield University, Bedfordshire, UK

Esben S. Andersen, Associate Professor, Department of Business Studies, Aalborg University, Denmark

Cristiano Antonelli, Professor of Economics, Department of Economics, University of Turin, Italy

W. Brian Arthur, Citibank Professor, Santa Fe Institute, Santa Fe, NM, USA

David Audretsch, Director, Max Planck Institute of Economics, Jena, Germany

Mie Augier, Assistant Professor, Department of Organization and Industrial Sociology, Frederiksberg, Denmark, and Stanford University, Stanford, CA, USA

Markus Balzat, Assistant Professor, Economics Department, University of Augsburg, Germany

Siegfried Berninghaus, Professor, Institute for Economic Theory and Operations Research, University of Karlsruhe (TH), Germany

Thomas Brenner, Research Associate, Evolutionary Economics Group, Max Planck Institute of Economics, Jena, Germany

Uwe Cantner, Professor of Economics, Economics Department, Friedrich-Schiller-University Jena, Germany

Bo Carlsson, E. Mandell DeWindt Professor of Industrial Economics, Case Western Reserve University, Cleveland, OH, USA

Philip Cooke, Professor and Director, Centre for Advanced Studies, Cardiff University, Wales, UK

Christian Cordes, Research Associate, Evolutionary Economics Group, Max Planck Institute of Economics, Jena, Germany

Richard H. Day, Professor of Economics, Department of Economics, University of Southern California, Los Angeles, CA, USA

Elias Dinopoulos, Professor of Economics, Department of Economics, University of Florida, Gainesville, FL, USA

Mark Dodgson, Professor and Director, Technology and Innovation Management Centre, University of Queensland Business School, Brisbane, Qld, Australia

Kurt Dopfer, Professor of Economics and Director of the Institute of Economics, University of St. Gallen, Switzerland

Giovanni Dosi, Professor, Laboratory of Economics and Management, Sant' Anna School of Advanced Studies, Pisa, Italy

Gunnar Eliasson, Professor, Research leader, Department of Industrial Economics and Management, The Royal Institute of Technology (KTH), Stockholm, Sweden

Georg Erdmann, Professor, Technical University Berlin, Germany

Jan Fagerberg, Professor, Centre for Technology, Innovation and Culture, University of Oslo, Norway

Giorgio Fagiolo, Assistant Professor, Department of Economics, University of Verona, Italy, and Laboratory of Economics and Management, Sant' Anna School of Advanced Studies, Pisa, Italy

Dominique Foray, Professor of Economics of Innovation, College of Management, Polytechnique Fédérale de Lausanne, Switzerland

John Foster, Professor and Head of School of Economics, The University of Queensland, Brisbane, Qld, Australia

Chris Freeman, Emeritus Professor, SPRU – Science and Technology Policy Research, The Freeman Centre, University of Sussex, Brighton, UK

Koen Frenken, Assistant Professor, Urban and Regional Research Centre Utrecht (URU), Utrecht University, The Netherlands

Jean-Luc Gaffard, Professor, University of Nice, Sophia Antipolis, OFCE, and Institut Universitaire de France, France

Thomas Grebel, Associate Professor, Economics Department, University of Augsburg, Germany

Marc Gruber, Assistant Professor, College of Management of Technology, Ecole Polytechnique Fédérale de Lausanne, Switzerland

Hariolf Grupp, Professor, Institute of Economic Policy Research (IWW), Karlsruhe University, and Fraunhofer Institute for Systems and Innovation Research (ISI), Karlsruhe, Germany.

Werner Güth, Professor and Director Strategic Interaction Group, Max Planck Institute of Economics, Jena, Germany

John Hagedoorn, Professor of Strategy and International Business, Department of Organization and Strategy, and MERIT, Maastricht, The Netherlands

Hardy Hanappi, Professor and Head of Research Unit Economics, Deputy Head of the Institute for Mathematical Methods in Economics, University of Technology, Vienna, Austria

Horst Hanusch, Professor, Economics Department, University of Augsburg, Germany

Ernst Helmstädter, Emeritus Professor, Department of Economics, Westphalian University of Münster, Germany, and Research Professor, Institute for Work and Technology, Science Centre of North-Rhine Westphalia, Gelsenkirchen, Germany

Ken-ichi Imai, Senior Fellow Emeritus, Institute of International Studies, Stanford University, and Emeritus Professor, Hitotsubashi University, Kunitachi, Japan

Alfred Kleinknecht, Professor of Economics, TU Delft, Faculty of Technology, Policy and Management, The Netherlands

Jackie Krafft, CNRS researcher, GREDEG, University of Nice, Sophia-Antipolis, Valbonne, France

Jens J. Krüger, Assistant, Economics Department, Friedrich-Schiller-University Jena, Germany

Witold Kwasnicki, Professor of Economics, Institute of Economic Sciences, University of Wroclaw, Poland

Jacques Lesourne, Member of the Board of Directors of IDEI, Former Professor at the CNAM (Centre National des Arts et Métiers), Paris, France

Brian J. Loasby, Emeritus and Honorary Professor, Department of Economics, University of Stirling, Scotland, UK

Bart Los, Assistant Professor, Faculty of Economics and Groningen Growth and Development Centre, University of Groningen, The Netherlands

Francisco Louçã, Professor, Faculty of Economics and Management, Technical University of Lisbon, Lisbon, Portugal

Bengt-Åke Lundvall, Professor, Department of Business Studies, Aalborg University, Denmark

Franco Malerba, Professor of Industrial Economics, Bocconi University, Milan, Italy

John A. Mathews, Graduate School of Management, Macquarie University, Sydney, NSW, Australia

Maureen McKelvey, Professor in Technology Management, Department of Industrial Dynamics, Chalmers University of Technology, Gothenburg, Sweden

J. Stanley Metcalfe, Stanley Jevons Professor of Political Economy and Cobden Lecturer, Director of the ESRC Centre for Research on Innovation and Competition, The University of Manchester, UK

C.W.M. Naastepad, Economics of Innovation, Delft University of Technology, The Netherlands

Richard R. Nelson, George Blumenthal Professor of International and Public Affairs, Business and Law, Columbia University, New York, USA

Jan Nill, Institute for Ecological Economic Research (IÖW), Berlin, Germany

Bart Nooteboom, Professor, Faculty of Economics and Business Administration, Tilburg University, The Netherlands

Luigi Orsenigo, Professor of Industrial Organization, University of Brescia, and Deputy Director, CESPRI, Bocconi University, Milan, Italy

Michael Peneder, Austrian Institute of Economic Research, Vienna, Austria

Carlota Perez, Visiting Senior Research Fellow at Cambridge Endowment for Research in Finance, Judge Institute, Cambridge University, UK, and Honorary Research Fellow at SPRU – Science and Technology Policy Research, University of Sussex, UK

The late **Mark Perlman**, formerly University Professor of Economics, Emeritus, University of Pittsburgh, PA, USA

Andreas Pyka, Chair for Economic Theory, University of Bremen, Germany

Fritz Rahmeyer, Professor, Economics Department, University of Augsburg, Germany

Nadine Roijakkers, Researcher, Eindhoven Centre for Innovation Studies, Eindhoven University of Technology, The Netherlands

Christian Sartorius, Senior research fellow, project coordinator, Fraunhofer Institute for Systems and Innovation Research (ISI), Karlsruhe, Germany

Pier Paolo Saviotti, Université Pierre Mendès France, INRA/SERD, Grenoble, France, and Directeur de Recherche, Institut National de la Recherche Agronomique, GREDEG, University of Nice, Sophia-Antipolis, France

Nicole Schall, Research Associate, Centre for Advanced Studies, Cardiff University, Wales, UK

F.M. Scherer, Aetna Professor Emeritus, John F. Kennedy School of Government, Harvard University, Cambridge, MA, USA

Hermann Schnabl, Associate Professor, Department of Microeconomics, University of Stuttgart, Germany

Fuat Şener, Associate Professor, Economics Department, Union College, New York, USA

Horst Siebert, AGIP Professor in International Economics, Johns Hopkins University, and President-Emeritus, Kiel Institute for World Economics, Germany

Yuichi Shionoya, Professor Emeritus, former President Hitotsubashi University; National Institute of Population and Social Security Research, Tokyo, Japan

Gerald Silverberg, Senior Research Fellow, MERIT, Maastricht University, The Netherlands

Paul Stoneman, Research Professor, Warwick Business School, University of Warwick, UK

Mauro Sylos Labini, Research Fellow, S. Anna School of Advanced Studies, Pisa, Italy

David J. Teece, Mitsubishi Bank Professor of International Business and Finance, Director, Institute of Management, Innovation, and Organization Haas Business and Public Policy Group, Economic Analysis and Policy Group, University of California at Berkeley, CA, USA

A. Roy Thurik, Professor of Economics and Entrepreneurship, Erasmus University Rotterdam, The Netherlands, and Professor of Entrepreneurship, Free University, Amsterdam; scientific advisor, EIM Business and Policy Research, Zoetermeer, The Netherlands; and Research Professor of Entrepreneurship, Growth and Public Policy, Max-Planck-Institut of Economics, Jena, Germany

Bart Verspagen, Professor of Economics, Eindhoven University of Technology, The Netherlands

Marco Vivarelli, Professor, Catholic University of Piacenza, Italy; CSGR-Warwick University, UK; and Max Planck Institute of Economics, Jena, Germany

Matthias Weber, Austrian Research Centers, Vienna, Austria

Claudia Werker, Research Fellow, The Evolutionary Economics Group, Max-Planck-Institute for Economics, Jena, Germany

Paul Windrum, Reader in Strategic Innovation and Management, Manchester Metropolitan University Business School, Manchester, UK

Ulrich Witt, Director Evolutionary Economics Group, Max-Planck-Institute of Economics, and Professor of Economics, Department of Economics, University of Jena, Germany

Stefan Zundel, Professor, Department of Economics, Lausitz University of Applied Sciences, Lausitz, Germany

Acknowledgements

We thank Senate Hall for allowing us to reprint the text of the article 'A model of the entrepreneurial economy' by David Audretsch and Roy Thurik, which was originally published in the *International Journal of Entrepreneurship Education*, **2**(2), 2004, pp. 143–66. Some minor changes have been made.

Introduction
Horst Hanusch and Andreas Pyka

Without doubt, economics is the science which focuses on economic welfare and the means to its increase. This can be stated as a goal for all schools in economics, among the most important being the Classical, the Keynesian and the Neoclassical school, as well as the neo-Schumpeterian approach, about which this *Companion* deals. But the angle of analysis differs sharply among these various approaches. One of the decisive differences can be found in the emphasis which is put on the different levels of economic analysis and their particular interrelatedness.

Owing to the dominance of the Neoclassical school in the 20th century, the approach of a micro foundation of macroeconomics has wide appeal. The aggregation from micro to macro becomes possible because of the idea of representative households and firms. Although this approach may seem convincing thanks to its analytical stringency, its mechanistic design may lead to difficulties when it comes to the analysis of dynamic phenomena endogenously caused by the economic system.

Neo-Schumpeterian economics, by contrast, seeks to get a grip on these dynamic phenomena of economic reality. In order to do this, between the micro and the macro level of economic analysis the important meso level is considered (e.g. Dopfer, Foster and Potts, 2004). It is the meso level of an economic system in which the decisive structural and qualitative changes take place and can be observed.

To understand the processes driving the development at the meso level, neo-Schumpeterian economics puts a strong emphasis on knowledge, innovation and entrepreneurship at the micro level. Innovation is identified as the major force propelling economic dynamics. In this emphasis on innovation, the major difference in the neo-Schumpeterian approach with respect to alternative economic approaches can be identified. Generally, one may say that novelty, i.e. innovation, is the core principle underlying the neo-Schumpeterian approach. Innovation competition takes the place of price competition as the coordination mechanism of interest. Of course, prices are also of significance, but, concerning the driving forces of economic development, they are not central. Whereas prices are basic concerning the adjustment to limiting conditions, innovations are responsible for overcoming previous limiting conditions and – as in economic reality, everything has an end – setting new ones.

The challenges for neo-Schumpeterian economics

The raison-d'être of neo-Schumpeterian economics is the prevailing trans-formations of economies, which persist at the macro, the meso and the micro levels. However, although the transformations are very visible at the macro level, they cannot be analysed or understood on this level (e.g. Carlsson and Eliasson, 2003). The sources of these qualitative changes instead can be found in the industry dynamics at the meso level (e.g. Saviotti and Pyka, 2004), yet the dynamic potential of industries is propelled by the creation of novelties and entrepreneurial decisions at the micro level of the economy.

Consider, for example, the transformation of economies with respect to employment shares towards service industries which has led to the so-called 'Fourastier Hypothesis'. This by no means can be explained by referring to the proportional growth of existing industries. Instead new industries emerge again and again throughout the history of capitalism, driving out existing ones or at least changing considerably their relative weights. The emergence of the new industries is driven by innovation and tested by entre-preneurial action.

Perhaps the most severe transformation the industrialized world has undergone is the current one, caused by the increased importance of knowl-edge, in particular scientific knowledge relevant for production activities combined with an increasing internationalization of business. For many years now, knowledge intensification and globalization have been widely considered to be the most important challenges with which industrialized and industrializing economies are confronted (e.g. Pyka and Hanusch, 2006). In addition, severe qualitative changes in the sectoral composition, in the relevant competences and in the institutional settings lead to catching-up and leapfrogging processes which affect the international com-petitiveness of nations and regions, and confronts established companies with major technological and organizational transformation processes.

These qualitative changes can immediately be traced back to developments going on at the meso or industry level. The underlying industrial dynamics are characterized by a crucial transformation of the nature of competition. Especially in technological intensive industries such as biotechnology-based industries and information and communication technologies, owing to the high degree of complexity of the underlying knowledge base, competition no longer takes place between single companies only, but often occurs between networks of actors, where new knowledge is created and diffused collectively. Most importantly, firms often no longer compete in a price dimension only, as competition in innovation has taken the dominant role.

Accordingly, competition and cooperation are simultaneously guiding the decisions of economic actors. Whereas traditional manufacturing firms are forced by the ongoing globalization to become ever larger, either through own growth or by mergers and acquisitions on an international basis, and are acting in an environment of strong price competition, they are at the same time intensively engaged in a competition for innovation. To cope with the pressure stemming from complex modern innovation processes, they are obliged to search for possibilities of collaboration with small and new entrepreneurial and technological intensive start-up companies. In knowledge-intensive industries, we often observe the co-existence of small entrepreneurial firms, shaping technological development and contributing strongly to technological progress, and large established companies performing their business in routinized ways.

By emphasizing the decisive role of entrepreneurial business formation and the emergence of new industries, we are already hinting at the processes at the micro level of the economy underlying all these development processes. Innovations, affecting potentially the composition of sectors, are born at the micro level. New ideas paired with well developed absorptive capacities of entrepreneurs, who are well connected to their own financial and scientific/ technological networks, lead eventually to wide and fast diffusion of novelty and thus to new industries (e.g. Grebel, Pyka and Hanusch, 2003). As a prerequisite for a prolific creation of a new industry, of course, consumers also have to be aware of the new commodities and services offered.

Knowledge generation and diffusion processes stand behind innovation. Thus, an examination of knowledge in general and knowledge dynamics in particular is absolutely necessary in neo-Schumpeterian economics. The simplified treatment of knowledge as a public good, such as is a concern in neoclassical economics, is intellectually no longer profitable. Instead, the tacit, local, and complex character of knowledge are emphasized. This is the subject of many of the contributions to this *Companion*.

By focusing on the generation and dissemination of new knowledge, from the point of view of knowledge dynamics, severe non-linearities enter the neo-Schumpeterian economic system, decisively affecting the dynamics of the sectoral development as well as the sectoral composition of an economy. As a consequence, neo-Schumpeterian economics has rid itself of the concept of a representative agent. Heterogeneous agents with varying competences and capabilities, industries at very different stages of maturity, and institutional frameworks differing between sectors, regions and nations co-exist, enriching strongly the complexity of the economic systems under analysis. The changes going on at the macro level of the economy then are not only the aggregates of the changes at the meso level. Several emergent properties and non-linearities have to be considered, e.g. unbalanced growth processes, catching-up, leapfrogging as well as forging-ahead etc. become part of the economic reality.

The intellectual roots of neo-Schumpeterian economics

In order to analyse the innovation-driven development of economic systems, neo-Schumpeterian economics draws on several intellectual roots. Obviously, first and foremost we must consider the huge legacy of Joseph Alois Schumpeter (Hanusch, 1999). Schumpeter was among the first authors to stress the important role of innovation in his *Theory of Economic Development* (1912). There, he not only described economic development as the disruption of the regular circular flow caused by the introduction of novelties, but he also dedicated a large part of his presentation to the description of the entrepreneur, as the economic actor who kicks off economic development. In his later book, *Capitalism, Socialism and Democracy* (1942) – following the developments of his time – he updated his ideas of entrepreneur-initiated development with the consideration of large research and development (R&D) departments of industrial firms where innovation had become a routine occupation.

Only rarely considered in the postwar period, in the early 1980s Schumpeter's theories were rediscovered in *Evolutionary Economics*, which has to be considered as the second intellectual source of neo-Schumpeterian economics. Obviously, the scope of this introduction does not allow a sound appreciation of the important impact of evolutionary economics. Instead, the reader is referred to, among others, Dopfer (2001, 2005), Hodgson, Samuels and Tool (1994), Silverberg (1988) and Witt (2003).

Evolutionary economics deals with dynamic developments taking place in historical time and therefore allows for path dependencies and irreversibilities. The major focus of evolutionary economics lies in the emergence and diffusion of novelties which are driven by creation, selection and retention, the crucial forces of every evolutionary theory dealing with either biological or cultural evolution. The outcome of evolutionary processes is determined neither ex ante nor as the result of global optimizing, but rather is due to true uncertainty underlying all processes of novelty generation, and so allows for openness towards future developments, a feature of evolutionary theories which makes them ideal for analysing innovation processes. Not surprisingly, in evolutionary economic theories, learning and the cognition of economic actors are central. Boundedly rational actors learn and experimentally search in uncertain and permanently changing environments. The feature of path dependency corresponds well with the cumulative nature of building up competences. Additionally, innovation is considered as a process spurred collectively by many different actors. Heterogeneity of actors is an important source of novelty (e.g. Saviotti, 1996).

The emphasis on the interaction between agents in knowledge generation and diffusion processes in evolutionary economics relates to a third strand of literature which has to be considered an intellectual root of neo-Schumpeterian economics, namely 'Complexity economics'. Pathbreaking work in this area has been done by, among others, Kirman (1989) and Arthur (1994). (For a review of most recent applications of complexity approaches in the domains of neo-Schumpeterian economics, see Frenken 2006.) Social systems share many commonalities with complex systems. Within the last 20 years, complexity sciences have developed tools to describe and analyse complex systems which are increasingly applied to socio-economic phenomena.

It is easy to show that innovation-driven neo-Schumpeterian economies are perfect examples of complex systems, as defined e.g. by John Casti (2001). On this approach, simple systems are characterized by few interactions and feedbacks, whereas complex systems show close and frequent interactions of components, combined with negative as well as prominent positive feedback effects. Whereas in simple systems one finds centralized and hierarchical decision processes, complex systems have strongly decentralized structures. Furthermore, simple systems are decomposable. Complex processes, on the other hand, are irreducible, i.e. neglecting a single part has severe consequences for understanding them. Finally, whereas the behavior of simple systems can be predicted, the behavior of complex systems is – owing to non-linearities caused by interaction and feedbacks – fundamentally unpredictable. It is clear that all features of complex systems can readily be found in neo-Schumpeterian economies. Most strikingly, the unpredictability of the complex system's behavior – with respect to innovation one can speak of truly uncertain outcomes – qualifies complexity approaches for the analysis and understanding of neo-Schumpeterian economies.

Another intellectual source for neo-Schumpeterian economics lies in those approaches dedicated to *change and development*. Although long run capitalistic development has been on the agenda of economics since the contributions of Kuznets, Clark and Schumpeter in the early decades of the 20th century, because of the strong dominance of short term equilibrium analysis of mainstream neoclassical economics this tradition went out of vogue until the early 1990s, by which time a new interest in the laws of motion and industry development re-emerged, formulating stylized facts of so-called 'industry life cycles' (eg. Utterback and Abernathy, 1975; Gort and Klepper, 1982; Jovanovic and McDonald, 1994; Klepper, 1997).

Finally, neo-Schumpeterian economics has an important source of inspiration in the mainly descriptive approaches of *systems theory*. Here, learning and the building up of competences is considered as an interactive and collective process. Besides economic actors – basically firms – institutional actors such as universities and other public research laboratories as well as the institutional frameworks and governance structures shape the innovation process taking place in national (e.g. Nelson, 1993; Lundvall, 1988), sectoral (e.g. Malerba, 2002, 2005), regional (e.g. Cooke, 2002) as well as corporate innovation systems (e.g. Cantwell, Dunning and Janne, 2004) and are important in determining their performance.

The hallmarks of neo-Schumpeterian economics
What are the distinctive marks of the neo-Schumpeterian approach in economics? As already stated above, neo-Schumpeterian economics considers the introduction of novelties as the decisive characteristic of capitalistic organized economies. By its very nature, innovation, and in particular technological innovation, is the most important and visible form of novelty. Therefore, it is not very surprising that neo-Schumpeterian economics today is most appealing in studies of innovation and learning behavior at the micro level of an economy, in studies of innovation-driven industry dynamics at the meso level, and in studies of innovation-determined growth and international competitiveness at the macro level of the economy. The contributions of this *Companion* will deal almost exclusively with these areas.

From a general point of view, however, the future developmental potential of socio-economic systems, i.e. *innovation* in a very broad sense, encompassing technological innovation as well as organizational, institutional and social innovation, has to be considered as the *normative principle* of neo-Schumpeterian economics. Instead of allocation and efficiency within a certain set of constraints, neo-Schumpeterian economics is concerned with the conditions for and consequences of a removal and overcoming of these constraints limiting the scope of economic development. Thus, neo-Schumpeterian economics is concerned with all facets of open and uncertain developments in socio-economic systems.

What are the consequences of this normative basis in innovation for economic analysis in a neo-Schumpeterian spirit? Most scholars labelling themselves as neo-Schumpeterians probably would agree on the three constitutive elements following this normative commitment:

1. *Qualitative change* affects all levels of the economy, and so we must consider not only structural changes but also the removal of constraints inhibiting development under the status quo and allow for development under new circumstances.
2. Qualitative changes do not appear continuously in time but correspond to the idea of *punctuated equilibria* encompassing periods of smooth and regular development as well as periods of radical change.
3. Finally, these processes show strong non-linearities and positive feedback effects which are responsible for *pattern formation* and other

forms of spontaneous structuring, i.e. they are not completely erratic, even if the innovative success by its very nature is characterized by strong uncertainty.

Although very visible at the industry level, qualitative change is happening at all levels and domains of an economy. A comprehensive neo-Schumpeterian approach therefore also has to consider transformation processes on, e.g., the public and the monetary sides of an economy. In the concluding chapter of this *Companion*, 'A roadmap to comprehensive neo-Schumpeterian economics', we highlight the impact of the innovation orientation on other areas of economies. The bulk of contributions of this *Companion*, however, are restricted to neo-Schumpeterian economics of the real side, that realm of neo-Schumpeterian economics which without doubt has to be considered as the most developed.

The structure of the *Companion*
The final part of this introduction is dedicated to a brief presentation of the *Companion*'s structure and the various contributions of the particular sections. By compiling the topics of the subsections, we paid attention to a broad covering of the relevant fields and consciously allowed for some redundancies when the topics showed different dimensions. We are convinced that the contributions to the *Companion* give an informed and sophisticated overview on the stage of development in neo-Schumpeterian economics, as well as pointing to important directions for future research.

From Schumpeter's universal social science to neo-Schumpeterian thinking
Part 1 of the *Companion* following this introduction is entitled 'From Schumpeter's universal social sciences to neo-Schumpeterian thinking' and deals with the broad intellectual heritage of Joseph A. Schumpeter. The various contributions deal with different aspects of Schumpeter's impact on neo-Schumpeterian economics. Horst Hanusch and Andreas Pyka start with a short biography of Schumpeter, followed by Mark Perlman who introduces the intellectual sources which framed Schumpeter's ideas of economic methodology. Along this line, Yuichi Shionoya outlines the concept of Schumpeterian universal social science in his contribution. Kurt Dopfer reasons on the impact of Schumpeter on meso economics. In the English translation of Schumpeter's *Theory of Economic Development*, one chapter of the German version was excluded. John Mathews corrects this error. Zoltan Acs, also drawing on the lost chapter of Schumpeter's *Theory of Economic Development*, outlines a synthesis between entrepreneurship and philanthropy as a model for capitalistic organized societies. Matthias Weber in his chapter makes an important nexus between Schumpeterian

reasoning and the sociology of innovation, which has to be considered an important branch of modern innovation research. Part 1 closes with a chapter by Chris Freeman and his reflections on the Schumpeterian renaissance that has taken place in the last two decades.

Neo-Schumpeterian meso dynamics: theory
The following two sections introduce the major research program of neo-Schumpeterian economics of the real side of an economy, highlighting the most important concepts and approaches applied to the analysis of meso dynamics, both theoretically and empirically. Part 2 starts with contributions summarized under the heading 'Essentials of innovation processes', subdivided into subsections on the subjects of innovation processes ('Entrepreneurship, firms and networks'), the object of innovation processes ('Knowledge and competencies') and 'Innovation processes and patterns'.

Entrepreneurship, firms and networks   In Chapter 9, Thomas Grebel introduces the reader to modern approaches, allowing a profound discussion of the complex actor who plays such an important role in neo-Schumpeterian economics. In Chapter 10, Fritz Rahmeyer composes an evolutionary theory of the firm, allowing us to conceive firms as separate units between the entrepreneurial actor and the industry. Marc Gruber then takes a management perspective, analysing the processes of new venture generation. Mark Dodgson in his contribution highlights the important role of technological collaborations in modern innovation processes. The strategic dimensions of technological alliances are outlined by Nadine Roijakkers and John Hagedoorn in Chapter 13. Finally, David Audretsch and Roy Thurik introduce a model of entrepreneurial economics, which is better suited for knowledge-intensive economies than the widely used managerial approaches.

Knowledge and competencies   As already mentioned above, it is knowledge which stands behind innovation. The concept of knowledge accordingly plays an important role in neo-Schumpeterian economics and has generated a great deal of attention in the last few years. This is the focus of the section entitled 'Knowledge and competencies'. Dominique Foray introduces the concepts of tacit and codified knowledge, a subtle but important distinction with significant consequences for the analysis of knowledge generation and diffusion processes. Similarly, Cristiano Antonelli distinguishes between the concepts of global technological progress and the important notion of localized technological progress. Both concepts are responsible for a decisive difference in the treatment of technological spillovers in neo-Schumpeterian economics. Whereas in Neoclassical economics, owing to the perception of knowledge as a public good, i.e. as codified knowledge which is globally applicable, technological spillovers are treated as incentive-reducing only, in Neo-Schumpeterian economics the idea-creating impacts of spillovers are emphasized because of the detailed consideration of the intricacies of the underlying knowledge. In Chapter 17, on competencies and capabilities, Mie Augier and David Teece show the consequences this changed view on knowledge has for understanding learning processes and the building up of competences in firms. In a similar vein, Brian Loasby applies these concepts to the important question of firm organization. Ernst Helmstädter then leaves the actor's and firm's perspective when highlighting the role of knowledge in a neo-Schumpeterian economy. Ulrich Witt and Christian Cordes outline the consequences of the cognitive framework of neo-Schumpeterian economics for the dynamics to be observed on the industry level.

Innovation processes and patterns The chapter of Ulrich Witt and Christian Cordes leads to the final subsection in Part 2, 'Innovation processes and patterns'. Giovanni Dosi and Mauro Sylos Labini open this subsection with a contribution on technological trajectories and technological paradigms. Although, because of the uncertainty inseparable from innovation, economic agents can no longer follow any optimal path in their innovation endeavors, this does not mean that innovation processes are erratic. Instead, specific patterns of technological evolution emerge as prevailing technological visions and concepts. The cumulativeness of learning processes guides innovative actions. In Chapter 22, Franco Malerba emphasizes the symbiotic nature of technological progress and firms' R&D strategies which leads to certain technological regimes. Another form of emerging structures is emphasized by Andreas Pyka's chapter on innovation networks. Innovation networks are considered as constellations which evolve thanks to the collaborative R&D strategies of the actors involved in innovation processes. The last chapter in this subsection, by Paul Stoneman, applies the concept of pattern formation and self-organization to the domain of the diffusion of innovation.

Modelling industry dynamics Not very surprisingly, neo-Schumpeterian economics relies on new tools when it comes to the construction of models. The section 'Modelling industry dynamics' deals with methodologies and instruments able to cope with the requirements of dynamic and innovation-driven processes. Chapter 25, by Witold Kwasnicki gives a broad overview on the development of different classes of economic models employed in modelling neo-Schumpeterian dynamics. In a similar vein, the contribution of Paul Windrum introduces the important classes of simulation models in the neo-Schumpeterian context. As the phenomena of interest are dynamic processes, including different forms of non-linearities, and are composed of heterogeneous populations of actors, analytical techniques are not very promising. By applying numerical approaches, the possibilities of modelling are dramatically extended. Stan Metcalfe introduces the concept of replicator dynamics, a frequently applied and powerful tool in the analysis of evolutionary processes. Replicator dynamics are used for the study of development processes of populations composed e.g. of firms. These development processes encompass both selection as a representation of competition and growth spurred by innovative success. The chapter by Luigi Orsenigo deals with a particular class of simulation models, namely history-friendly models. Within neo-Schumpeterian economics, history-friendly models are used for the modelling of the development of specific industries, thereby focusing on their particularities. This class of simulation models is significant for its closeness to empirical analysis. The final contribution in this section, by Andreas Pyka and Giorgio Fagiolo, deals with a class of simulation models which only recently have been applied in neo-Schumpeterian economics, but very likely show the strongest potential, namely agent-based models. Modellers generally have to wrestle with an unavoidable trade-off between the demands of a general theoretical approach and the descriptive accuracy required to model a particular phenomenon. Agent-based models have shown themselves to be well adapted to this challenge, basically by shifting outwards this trade-off.

Neo-Schumpeterian meso dynamics: empirics
The first subsection deals with tools and concepts allowing for measuring industry dynamics. The challenge for the empirical strands of Neo-Schumpeterian economics lies in the necessity to investigate and analyse dynamic processes which most often concern intangible knowledge and contain a great deal of qualitative information.

Measuring industry dynamics   In their chapter, Uwe Cantner and Jens Krüger introduce empirical tools which allow us to cope with these challenges, in particular dealing with heterogeneity, which is a prerequisite as well as a consequence of every innovation process. Hariolf Grupp deals with science and technology indicators constructed from patent information. In many cases, patents are the only information available, and so a good understanding of the scope of their explanatory power is essential for empirical investigations. Michael Peneder offers an industry classification and taxonomy approach, which may be considered an empirical attempt to identify technological patterns and regimes. The particular focus of Neo-Schumpeterian economics on innovation and dynamic processes propelled by heterogeneous agents demands the application of tools so far not applied in economics. An attempt to rectify this is made by Koen Frenken in his chapter, where he introduces the important concept of entropy statistics. In the contribution by Thomas Brenner, a particular methodology to identify local industrial clusters is introduced. The idea of clusters as self-organized regional competence agglomerations enjoys enormous popularity both in theory and in politics. To get an empirical grip on innovation clusters is an essential precondition to improving our understanding of the underlying complex processes. The final contribution in this subsection, by Bart Los and Bart Verspagen deals with the important question of measuring technological spillovers. Los and Verspagen give an overview on the different possibilities to tackle this interesting problem empirically and offer a helpful taxonomy of the various spillover measures.

Case and industry studies   Owing to the severe problems and difficulties of the empirical measurement of neo-Schumpeterian dynamics, case and industry studies are frequently used to improve our understanding. Nelson and Winter (1982) coined the notion of 'appreciative theorizing' to describe this important strand of literature within empirical neo-Schumpeterian economics. Chapter 36, by Ken-ichi Imai, deals with the Japanese innovation system and gives a detailed description of the economic as well as institutional developments shaping the multifaceted transformation of Japan's economy. Maureen McKelvey's case study deals with the example par excellence of knowledge-based economies, namely biotech-based industries. In a similar vein, Jackie Krafft's case study covers the telecommunication industry. Both chapters show the huge advantage of case studies, which highlight the particularities of specific industries including a great deal of qualitative information. Paul Windrum's case study deals with innovation in service industries, a part of the economy that is of increasing importance with respect to employment, value creation and much more. However, it is perhaps also the most heterogeneous sector, as it encompasses knowledge-intensive business services as well as fast food restaurants. Paul Windrum's case study is a perfect example of the possibilities of case studies in tackling complex issues. The final case study, by Alfred Kleinknecht and C.W.M. Naastepad, is an example of the investigation of a particular national policy strategy, namely the employment strategy of the Netherlands in the 1990s.

Neo-Schumpeterian macro dynamics: growth and development
A crucial interest of neo-Schumpeterian economics lies in the analysis of the conditions and consequences of economic development. This section

focuses on more quantitative studies of growth and a more qualitative orientation towards economic development.

Growth   F.M. Scherer opens this section with his chapter on Schumpeter
and the micro foundations of economic growth. He closely investigates the
representation of firms' R&D activities in growth models. In the same tradition, Elias Dinopoulos and Fuat Şener provide an exposition of the scale-
effects property in the context of neo-Schumpeterian growth models in
their chapter on endogenous growth. In particular, they outline the distinct
solutions to the scale-effects problem, discuss implications and offer an
assessment of scale-invariant neo-Schumpeterian growth models. Jan
Fagerberg then considers the international dimension in offering a
Schumpeterian perspective on the technology-driven dynamics of growth
and trade, allowing an explanation of dispersed national developments
responsible for catching-up and falling-behind processes in economic
development. In analysing macroeconomic dynamics, the question of labor
replacement versus labor creation has played an important role in economics since David Ricardo's famous chapter on machinery in his 1817
book *Principles of Political Economy and Taxation*. Marco Vivarelli gives
an overview of this still open question, and considers as well the various
compensation mechanisms found in the literature. In the last chapter of this
section, John Foster introduces macro-econometric modelling of neo-
Schumpeterian dynamics, and suggests an empirical agenda that has the
capacity to highlight the relevance and importance of neo-Schumpeterian
economics. In particular, the empirical agenda focuses on the core of neo-
Schumpeterian economics, namely on the innovation-related sources of
economic growth.

Development   The section on economic development is introduced by
Richard Day's contribution, in which he emphasizes the important role of
out-of-equilibrium economics for development. Contrary to Schumpeter,
who started his analysis of development in a state of equilibrium (circular
flow), Day begins in an out-of-equilibrium situation in which the dynamics
result from adaptive economizing of the agents. The contribution of Esben
Sloth Andersen deals with demand, a topic which only recently has come on
the agenda of neo-Schumpeterian economics (e.g. Witt, 2001). Andersen
stresses three major points as to why this has to be changed: obviously,
demand represents the core force of selection which gives direction to neo-
Schumpeterian dynamics; additionally, firms' innovative activities relate,
directly or indirectly, to the structure of expected and actual demand;
finally, the demand side represents the most obvious way of turning to the
much-needed analysis of macro-evolutionary change of the economic

system. The next three contributions deal with long waves, the Kondratieff cycles Schumpeter was so fascinated by in his *Business Cycles* of 1939. Long waves can be considered as an analytical framework for the analysis of long run qualitative change. In this sense, Francisco Louçã focuses attention on the recurrent phenomena of long waves in different cycles. Recurrent phenomena provide justification for cycles, since in the case of only unique features of particular technological breakthroughs, cycles would not be evident. Carlota Perez emphasizes the important co-evolutionary relationship of long term development of the real and the financial sectors of an economy. In the last contribution to the long wave debate, Gerald Silverberg shows how long waves fit into an overarching theory of neo-Schumpeterian economic dynamics, thereby addressing theoretical as well as empirical issues. Paolo Saviotti's chapter on qualitative change has to be considered central neo-Schumpeterian economics. He shows that, without the focus on qualitative phenomena, long run economic development is perfectly misunderstood. In the last chapter of this section, Richard Nelson summarizes neo-Schumpeterian reasoning on growth and development and offers some important issues for the agenda of future neo-Schumpeterian research.

Neo-Schumpeterian economics and the systemic view
As mentioned above, approaches from systems theory are an important intellectual source of neo-Schumpeterian economics. This section is dedicated to the systemic view. Bo Carlsson begins with a survey of the rich literature on innovation systems from a neo-Schumpeterian angle. Then Bengt-Åke Lundvall elaborates on the the lines of development of the most prominent concept stemming from systems theory, namely national innovation systems. In Chapter 55, Hermann Schnabl draws on input–output analysis in order to get a formal grip on these systems. In the following chapter, Phil Cooke and Nicole Schall apply the system concept at the regional level, introducing the important concept of regional innovation systems. Markus Balzat and Horst Hanusch close this section with a chapter summarizing the fundamentals of national innovation systems relevant from a neo-Schumpeterian perspective.

Research and technology policy
Considering neo-Schumpeterian dynamics has important consequences for policy making. Basically, the benchmark in the sense of a welfare optimal solution got lost, while concepts such as enabling infrastructures, platform technologies and R&D networks etc. have aroused attention. This section of the *Companion* deals with neo-Schumpeterian innovation and technology policy. Stan Metcalfe opens with his contribution on innovation policy for knowledge-based economies. The chapter of Horst Siebert then takes the

macro-economic perspective, investigating the conditions furthering and hindering economic growth and focusing on the example of Germany. Georg Erdmann, Jan Nill, Christian Sartorius and Stefan Zundel derive theoretical conditions for effective policy strategies dependent of time. Hardy Hanappi closes the section with a chapter on macroeconomic policy dealing with conceptual and theoretical issues of policy on and for the macro-level in a Neo-Schumpeterian perspective.

The impact of neo-Schumpeterian thinking on different fields
The last part of the *Companion*, Part 7 containing invited contributions, deals with important topics that cannot be allocated to other subjects, but that nonetheless are more or less relevant for the whole body of neo-Schumpeterian economics. Jacques Lesourne opens with a chapter on game theory and the particular role of evolutionary game theory for neo-Schumpeterian economics. In a similar vein, Bart Nooteboom extends the concept of transaction costs in order to make it applicable in the context of learning and innovation processes. Chapters 64 and 65, by JeanLuc Gaffard and Gunnar Eliasson, respectively, investigate the role of neo-Austrian approaches in neo-Schumpeterian economics. Siegfried Berninghaus and Werner Güth introduce the reader to experimental economics, which is of significant importance for neo-Schumpeterian economics, e.g. when it comes to the formulation of alternative behavioral assumptions. Brian Arthur then deals with the important subject of complexity economics. As stated above, complexity economics is an essential intellectual source of inspiration for neo-Schumpeterian economics. The same holds for the following chapter, by Peter Allen, dealing with self-organization, pattern formation, emergent phenomena and phase transitions, which are constitutive features of neo-Schumpeterian economic systems and core concepts in neo-Schumpeterian economics. Besides the time dimension, innovation processes have an important geographical dimension. Claudia Werker considers the neo-Schumpeterian perspective in regional economics and economic geography in the penultimate chapter.

A roadmap to comprehensive neo-Schumpeterian economics
The *Companion* concludes with a final chapter by the editors in which they develop a guideline for a comprehensive neo-Schumpeterian approach which has to encompass not only the real side of the economy, but also financial markets and the role and impact of the state. In this sense, neo-Schumpeterian economics has to consider the co-evolutionary processes between the different economic domains in order to offer a powerful alternative to the economic mainstream for the analysis of economies and their future developmental potentials.

References

Arthur, W.B. (1994), *Increasing Returns and Path Dependence in the Economy*, Ann Arbor, MI: University of Michigan Press.

Cantwell, J.A., Dunning, J.H. and Janne, O. (2004), 'Towards a technology-seeking explanation of U.S. direct investment in the United Kingdom', *Journal of Innovation Management*, **10**(1), 5–20.

Carlsson, B. and Eliasson, G. (2003), 'Industrial dynamics and economic growth', *Industry and Innovation*, **10**(4), 435–56.

Casti, J. (2001), 'Introduction to complex systems', Exystence working paper (www.complexityscience.org).

Cooke, P. (2002), *Knowledge Economies*, London: Routledge.

Dopfer, K. (2001) (ed.), *Evolutionary Economics – Program and Scope*, Boston, Dordrecht, London: Kluwer Academic Publishers.

Dopfer, K. (2005), *The Evolutionary Foundations of Economics*, Cambridge, UK: Cambridge University Press.

Dopfer, K., Foster, J. and Potts, J. (2004), 'Micro–meso–macro', *Journal of Evolutionary Economics*, **14**, 263–79.

Frenken, K. (2006), 'Technological innovation and complexity theory', *Economics of Innovation and New Technology*, **15**(2), 135–55.

Gort, M. and Klepper, S. (1982), 'Time paths in the diffusion of product innovations', *Economic Journal*, **92**, 630–53.

Grebel, T., Pyka, A. and Hanusch, H. (2003), 'An evolutionary approach to the theory of entrepreneurship', *Industry and Innovation*, **10**(4), 493–514.

Hanusch, H. (1999) (ed.), *The Legacy of Joseph Alois Schumpeter*, 2 vols, Cheltenham, UK and Northampton, MA, USA: Edward Elgar.

Hodgson, G.M., Samuels, W.J. and Tool, M.R. (1994) (eds), *The Elgar Companion to Institutional and Evolutionary Economics*, Aldershot, UK and Brookfield, USA: Edward Elgar.

Jovanovic, B. and McDonald, G. (1994), 'The life cycle of a competitive industry', *Journal of Political Economy*, **102**, 322–47.

Kirman, A. (1989), 'The intrinsic limits of modern economic theory: the emperor has no clothes', *Economic Journal*, **99**(395), 126–39.

Klepper S. (1997), 'Industry life cycles', *Industrial and Corporate Change*, **6**(1), 145–81.

Lundvall, B.-Å. (1988), 'Innovation as an interactive process: from user–producer interaction to the National Innovation Systems', in Dosi, G., Freeman, C., Nelson, R.R., Silverberg, G. and Soete, L. (eds), *Technical Change and Economic Theory*, London: Pinter Publishers.

Malerba, F. (2002), 'Sectoral systems of innovation and production', *Research Policy*, **31**(2), 247–64.

Malerba, F. (2005), 'Sectoral systems of innovation: a framework for linking innovation to the knowledge base, structure and dynamics of sectors', *Economics of Innovation and New Technology*, **14**(1–2), 63–82.

Nelson, R.R. (1993) (ed.), *National Innovation Systems: A Comparative Analysis*, Oxford: Oxford University Press.

Nelson, R.R. and Winter, S.G. (1982), *An Evolutionary Theory of Economic Change*, Cambridge, MA and London: Harvard University Press.

Pyka, A. and Hanusch, H. (2006) (eds), *Applied Evolutionary Economics and the Knowledge-Based Economy*, Cheltenham, UK and Northampton, MA, USA: Edward Elgar.

Ricardo, D. (1817), *Principles of Political Economy and Taxation*, London, New York: J.M. Dent & Sons.

Saviotti, P.P. (1996), *Technological Evolution, Variety and the Economy*, Cheltenham, UK and Brookfield, USA: Edward Elgar.

Saviotti, P.P. and Pyka, A. (2004), 'Economic development by the creation of new sectors', *Journal of Evolutionary Economics*, **14**(1), 1–36.

Schumpeter, J.A. (1912), *Theorie der wirtschaftlichen Entwicklung*, Leipzig: Duncker & Humblot.

Schumpeter, J.A. (1939), *Business Cycles: A Theoretical, Historical, and Statistical Analysis of the Capitalist Process*, 2 vols, New York: McGraw-Hill.

Schumpeter, J.A. (1942), *Capitalism, Socialism, and Democracy*, New York: Harper and Bros.
Silverberg, G. (1988), 'Modelling economic dynamics and technical change: mathematical approaches to self-organisation and evolution', in Dosi, G., Freeman, C., Nelson, R.R., Silverberg, G. and Soete, L. (eds), *Technical Change and Economic Theory*, London, New York: Pinter Publishers.
Utterback, J. and Abernathy, W. (1975), 'A dynamic model of process and product innovation', *Omega*, 639–56.
Witt, U. (2001) (ed.), 'Economic growth – what happened on the demand side?', special issue, *Journal of Evolutionary Economics*, **11**(1).
Witt, U. (2003), *The Evolving Economy – Essays on the Evolutionary Approach to Economics*, Cheltenham, UK and Northampton, MA, USA: Edward Elgar.

PART 1

FROM SCHUMPETER'S UNIVERSAL SOCIAL SCIENCES TO NEO-SCHUMPETERIAN THINKING

1 Schumpeter, Joseph Alois (1883–1950)
Horst Hanusch and Andreas Pyka

1 A short biography[1]

Joseph Alois Schumpeter was born on 8 February 1883 in Triesch (today: Trest) in South Moravia. After a short period in Graz (Austria), he and his mother moved to Vienna where he enrolled at university in 1901. Having finished his studies in Vienna, he spent a short period at the London School of Economics. He then left Europe, as Swedberg anecdotally mentions in his outstanding biography on Schumpeter (1991), in order to accept a job opportunity as an advisor to an Arabian princess in Cairo, Egypt. There he not only earned a small fortune, but also wrote his habilitation thesis 'Wesen und Hauptinhalt der theoretischen Nationalökonomie'. Upon his return to Vienna and the Austro-Hungarian Empire, he submitted this book to the University of Vienna, where it was successfully accepted. Later he was appointed as the youngest professor in economics in Czernowitz (today Chervotsy in the Ukraine). In 1911, he moved to the University of Graz. During this period, Schumpeter finished his most important book, *The Theory of Economic Development*, which was published by the end of 1911.

After World War I and the decline of the Austrian monarchy, which for him as well as for many intellectuals in those days was a rather bitter experience, Schumpeter's interest changed from academics to policy. First, he worked in a so-called 'commission for the socialization of the German coal industry' before he accepted a position as Austrian Minister of Financial Affairs in the government of Karl Renner in 1919. His political career was far from successful, and was rather short: only a few months after his appointment, Schumpeter has to confess to himself that his achievements as an Austrian politician could best be labelled a mess, so finally he had to retreat. However, after his political activities, Schumpeter did not return to academia, but instead tried his best working for private companies. In 1921 he became a member of the board of executives of a small bank in Vienna. Again, Schumpeter was anything but successful. In the mid-1920s, the bank went bankrupt and Schumpeter lost his whole fortune, ending up with enormous debts. Supported by Arthur Spiethoff, Schumpeter finally returned to his scientific roots and became a professor at the University of Bonn in 1925.

After an extremely difficult period – within only a few months Schumpeter's young wife passed away in childbirth and his mother died – Schumpeter finally decided to leave Europe once more and to accept an offer from Harvard University in Cambridge, Massachusetts. In the United States, Schumpeter, as a well recognized scientist, became president of the Econometric Society, and eventually the first non-American citizen to hold the position of president of the American Economic Association. In 1950, Schumpeter suffered a stroke and passed away at his home in Taconic, Connecticut.

2   Joseph Alois Schumpeter's œuvre

Schumpeter's scientific heritage is immense. In his bibliography, Massimo Augello (1990) lists 30 books and educational pamphlets and more than 260 scientific papers and book reviews. Schumpeter's personal opinion regarding human accomplishments is quite applicable to himself: the third decade within a life span is of outstanding importance because one's major new ideas are created between the ages of 20 and 30. Later, the individual returns to these ideas and develops them further but does not really add many significant changes to the original concepts.

Schumpeter's œuvre can be divided into three separate parts. His first field may be summarized under the heading 'methodological and economic–historical work'. In the middle of the so-called 'older Methodenstreit' within German economics, the debates between Gustav von Schmoller in Berlin and Carl Menger in Vienna, Schumpeter took the position of the theoretical school and defended the position of deductive reasoning held by the so-called 'marginal triumvirate', namely Jevons in Cambridge, Walras in Lausanne and Menger in Vienna. In his habilitation thesis of 1908, 'Das Wesen und der Hauptinhalt der theoretischen Nationalökonomie', Schumpeter clearly favored the theoretical school. However, already in this early book we find the typical dichotomy Schumpeter used in his later work between statics and dynamics, and equilibrium and disequilibrium. Furthermore, already the young Schumpeter dedicated his time to the history of economics and in 1914 published his *Epochen der Dogmen- und Methodengeschichte*. This small book has to be considered the forerunner of his unfinished and posthumously published masterpiece *History of Economic Analysis* (1954). The ambitious aim of this book was an analysis of the development of economics, from ancient Greece until the late 1940s.

Schumpeter's second preoccupation was social and institutional change in capitalistic organized societies. Here too, the roots for his later well recognized book, *Capitalism, Socialism and Democracy*, of 1943 – which was the basis for his famous presidential address at the annual meeting of the American Economic Association in 1950, 'The march into socialism' – can be traced back to a publication from 1918, *Die Krise des Steuerstaates (Crisis of the Tax State)*. Especially in this work, Schumpeter's visionary capabilities and his ability to reason beyond the borders of economics become obvious. Furthermore, in the chapter 'Socialism and Democracy', Schumpeter foresaw the realm of a new political economy, practically twenty years before it emerged as an independent literature. He developed his own theory of democracy as opposed to traditional approaches. There, democracy was considered as an intrinsic value which is also fundamental for welfare economics. In his approach, the democratic system is instead a kind of coordination mechanism, similar to the market mechanism. Markets coordinate individual needs via price competition and democracies coordinate social needs via competition for voters.

From today's perspective, the most important part of Schumpeter's œuvre is his *Theory of Economic Development*, published in 1912. The central ideas were already published in an article, 'Über das Wesen der Wirtschaftskrisen (The Nature of Economic Crisis)' which appeared in 1910. His theory of economic development has to be considered as the core of Schumpeterian thinking. It is also the major reason for the renaissance of his ideas, which began in the 1980s. In his voluminous theoretical and empirical study, *Business Cycles*, of 1939, Schumpeter again drew on his ideas formulated in his early research.

3 Schumpeter's impact on modern economics

Without doubt, the ideas concerning economic development are the most central ones in Schumpeter's œuvre. They have to be considered as an early design of a framework as opposed to traditional neoclassical approaches. Neoclassical thinking focuses on the optimal allocation of resources and the adaptations following exogenous shocks, such as demographic change, changing preferences etc. Thus, neoclassical theory establishes an unending circular flow characterized by static equilibrium. Schumpeter, however, uses a completely different notion of development, very close to evolutionary thinking (although he did not use the analogy to biological evolution in his early work): 'Economic development has to be considered as a process generated within the economic system . . . I was deeply convinced . . . that there must be a source of energy within the economic system which endogenously destroys every equilibrium state which might be reachable' (Schumpeter, cited from the famous preface of the Japanese translation of his *Theory of Economic Development*, own translation). Accordingly, Schumpeter is much less concerned with adaptation after exogenous shocks, but focuses on the endogenous forces of development processes, which shows the quantitative dimension and, even more importantly, a qualitative dimension. Nevertheless, one has to mention that some authors claim (see Hodgson, 1993) that Schumpeter's opinion concerning neoclassical equilibrium theory was at least ambivalent. He was a strong admirer of Léon Walras, whom he personally visited in Switzerland in 1908.

However, in the same year that he met Walras, Schumpeter (1908, p. 573) clearly states that he considered the concept of an economic equilibrium to be in no case a stable and unchangeable situation: 'Economic development and all the important sources of disturbance of equilibrium states lead away from equilibrium without showing any tendency of returning to it' (own translation).

In a way, Schumpeter may be seen to have anticipated the basic constituencies of our conception of neo-Schumpeterian economics: all economic variables are in a process of permanent change. The continuous minor development processes are interrupted from time to time by discontinuous major changes 'like e.g. the development from stage-coaches to railways' (own translation) (Schumpeter, 1912, p. 93). For that reason, traditional equilibrium-oriented approaches following classical mechanics cannot be applied; economic development is understandable only in irreversible, i.e., historical time. Thus, besides certain tendencies to reach an equilibrium state, important factors leading to disequilibria have to be considered.

As a major source of endogenously created economic development Schumpeter identifies *new combinations*. This was his notion for innovations successfully penetrating markets. He also used a broad definition of innovation encompassing not only technological innovation, such as product and process innovation, but also the discovery of new resources, the development of new markets, as well as new organizational designs of economic processes (Schumpeter, 1934, p. 66).

The new combinations are introduced by dynamic businessmen, the *entrepreneurs*, who are the central economic agents in Schumpeter's construct of ideas. In the description of an entrepreneur, a certain closeness to elite theories stemming from German philosophy of the late 19th century cannot be denied (e.g., F. Nietzsche). An entrepreneur does not resemble the *static agent* of a neoclassical world, but is a resourceful, visionary person who is eager for power and economic success, willing to bear incalculable risks. Such a person is always dissatisfied in situations which come close to a neoclassical equilibrium. Through the introduction of novelties, he wants to fulfil his dreams of founding a private empire driven by the wish of being successful because of success and the pleasure to design and to manage. These ambitions will result in extraordinary profits, or, in the terminology of Schumpeter, profits as index for success (Schumpeter, 1934, p. 93). This way, entrepreneurs disturb the prevailing order and constitute the kernel of unbalanced developments.

The appearance of entrepreneurs does not necessarily happen only in capitalist-organized societies. However, Schumpeter convincingly shows that capitalist societies are best suited for introducing innovations because of the well developed institutions of the capital markets. Thus, for Schumpeter, the actors in capital and loan markets play an important role in the processes of economic development. Monetary expansion and the creation of credit are necessary prerequisites for a successful market penetration of novelties and the accompanying reallocation by entrepreneurial action: 'The essential function of credit in our sense consists in enabling the entrepreneur to withdraw the producers' goods which he needs from their previous employments, by exercising a demand for them, and thereby to force the economic system into new channels' (Schumpeter, 1934, p. 106).

It is inescapable that, in Schumpeter's understanding, the functions of markets have to change. It is no longer price competition only, but, following his ideas of development, quality competition, driven by innovations and imitations of economic actors, takes over the leading role. In other words, profit opportunities are signalled not exclusively by market prices and market structures but also by the creativity and daringness of entrepreneurial actors which change the relative scarcity in an economic system.

The activities of entrepreneurs are not equally distributed in time but appear in swarms that lead to wave-like developments, i.e. a cyclical structure in economic development. In his later book, *Business Cycles* (1939), Schumpeter addressed the questions of economic ups and downs in detail. Again he repeated the notion of the endogeneity of the sources of economic development (Schumpeter, 1939, p. v): 'Cycles are not, like tonsils, separable things that might be treated by themselves, but are, like the beat of the heart, of the essence of the organism that displays them.' As a theoretical construct of his historically framed analysis, Schumpeter referred to three overlapping cyclical movements, shown in Figure 1.1. Of course he emphasized the artificial character of this construct, which is nevertheless didactically helpful.

Of course in Schumpeter's reasoning, the central element and source of cyclical behavior are endogenously generated innovations within the economic system. To begin with, Schumpeter refers to the concept of *long waves* of Kondratieff. Long waves or Kondratieff cycles are long lasting cycles of a length of approximately 60 years, which are triggered by radical innovations. Examples are the railways, electrification or cars with combustion engines. These long run developments are overlapped by so-called 'Juglar cycles' with a length of approximately 10 years. These cycles are caused by major innovations within the technological and scientific framework of the radical innovation, e.g. the discovery of a new chemical compound in the pharmaceutical industry or the introduction of the dynamo in the electricity industry. Juglar cycles again are overlapped by so-called 'Kitchen cycles' with a length of approximately 40 months, which are caused by the investment strategies of firms, the depreciation of capital stocks, as well as warehousing.

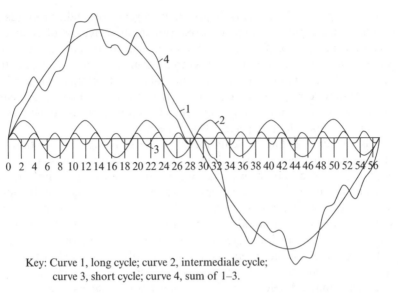

Key: Curve 1, long cycle; curve 2, intermediale cycle;
curve 3, short cycle; curve 4, sum of 1–3.

Source: *Business Cycles*, 1939, p. 213.

Figure 1.1   Schumpeter's overlapping cycles

Concerning his ideas on competition, already ideas which would appear later in *Capitalism, Socialism and Democracy* are apparent: instead of the competitive capitalism pushed forward by creative entrepreneurs, the idea of a so-called 'trustified capitalism', where large firms and their institutionalized research laboratories generate innovations systematically, is shown to be of increasing importance. Affected by his impressions of the US economy, Schumpeter concludes, 'innovation itself is being reduced to routine. Technological progress is increasingly becoming the business of trained specialists who turn out what is required and make it work in predictable ways' (Schumpeter, 1943, S.132).

These developments are accompanied by significant changes in property rights and contract law: on the one hand, the immediate relationship between the entrepreneur and production capital is lopped. On the other hand, the owners of the capital stock are increasingly led by speculative expectations. Consequently, the typical interests and concerns of capital owners on the real business side disappear. This leads Schumpeter, although following a different line of reasoning, to a similar conclusion as the one of Karl Marx, namely a compulsory transition to a socialistic-organized economy. Generally, Schumpeter admired the economic and sociological œuvre of Marx (Schumpeter, 1943, SS. 9–44). Following

Schumpeter, one has only to displace the omnipresent political ambitions in Marx's work in order to get the brilliant contribution to theoretical economics of a great economist. However, contrary to Marx, for Schumpeter, the failure of the capitalistic regime is not responsible for its disappearance, but rather its extraordinary success in generating economic growth and development is to blame.

4 Schumpeter's heritage

Against the background of the recent interest in technological progress and innovation in the economic discipline, it might appear astonishing that it took until the middle of the 1980s for the economics community to rediscover the ideas of Schumpeter (for a detailed analysis on the impact of Schumpeter's intellectual legacy, see Hanusch, 1999). In addition, we might point out that in this period the foundation of the International Joseph Alois Schumpeter Society took place.

Essentially two reasons are responsible for the reserved interest in Schumpeter and his work. First and also very much regretted by Schumpeter himself, his ideas took a backseat to those of his contemporary John Maynard Keynes. Keynes's theories of the removal of macroeconomic imbalances and of potential means of stabilizing the circular flow were fascinating the economics community and politicians until the middle of the 1970s. The second reason for the early neglect lies in the early stage of development in mathematics. Only with the development of the theory of dynamic systems as well as numerical techniques could these obstacles be surmounted. Especially within evolutionary economics, the attempts to formalize Schumpeter's ideas have increased tremendously in recent years. Therefore, one can state without doubt that there has been a significant increase in the impact and role of Schumpeter's intellectual heritage (the Age of Schumpeter, Schumpeterian Renaissance) for modern economics since the 1980s.

Note

1. A detailed and authoritative biography is written by Wolfgang Stolper (1994), one of the many students of Schumpeter who belongs to the group of the best-known economists of the 20th century.

References

Augello, M.M. (1990), *Joseph Alois Schumpeter, A Reference Guide*, Berlin: Springer.

Hanusch, H. (1999), *The Intellectual Legacy of Joseph A. Schumpeter*, Cheltenham, UK and Northampton, MA, USA: Edward Elgar.

Hodgson, G.M. (1993), *Economics and Evolution: Bringing back Life into Economics*, Cambridge: Polity Press.

Schumpeter, J.A. (1908), *Das Wesen und der Hauptinhalt der theoretischen Nationalökonomie*, reprinted Berlin: Duncker & Humblot, 1970.

Schumpeter, J.A. (1910), 'Über das Wesen der Wirtschaftskrisen, Zeitschrift für Volkswirtschaftslehre', *Sozialpolitik und Verwaltung*, **19**, 271–325.

Schumpeter, J.A. (1912), *Die Theorie der wirtschaftlichen Entwicklung. Eine Untersuchung über Unternehmergewinn, Kapital, Kredit, Zins und den Konjunkturzyklus*; 8th edn, Berlin: Duncker & Humblot, 1993.

Schumpeter, J.A. (1914), 'Epochen der Dogmen- und Methodengeschichte', *Grundriß der Sozialökonomik, I. Abteilung: Wirtschaft und Wirtschaftswissenschaft*, Tübingen.

Schumpeter, J.A. (1918), 'Die Krise des Steuerstaates', *Zeitfragen aus dem Gebiet der Soziologie*, **4**.

Schumpeter, J.A. (1934), *The Theory of Economic Development – An Inquiry into Profits, Capital, Credit, Interest and the Business Cycle*, English trans. Redvers Opie, Cambridge, MA: Harvard University Press.

Schumpeter, J.A. (1939), *Business Cycles. A Theoretical, Historical, and Statistical Analysis of the Capitalist Process*, New York, London:.

Schumpeter, J.A. (1943), *Capitalism, Socialism, and Democracy*, reprinted New York: Allen & Unwin, 1976.

Schumpeter, J.A. (1949), 'The march into socialism', *American Economic Review*, **40**, SS. 446–569.

Schumpeter, J.A. (1954), *History of Economic Analysis*, herausgegeben von New York: Elizabeth Boody Schumpeter, new edn 1994, London: Routledge.

Stolper, W. (1994), *Joseph Alois Schumpeter. The Public Life of a Private Man*, Princeton, NJ: Princeton University Press.

Swedberg, R. (1991), *Joseph A. Schumpeter. His Life and Work*, Cambridge: Polity Press.

2 Schumpeter's views on methodology: their source and their evolution

Mark Perlman

An explanatory introduction

In spite of the fact that his first book, the 1908 *Das Wesen und der Hauptinhalt der theoretischen Nationalökonomie* (hereafter *DWHN*), appears to deal principally with economic methodology as seen by the Viennese and by Gustav Schmoller's German students, Schumpeter expressed his own views on that topic openly and sincerely for the first time in his third book, the 1914a *Epochen der Dogmen- und Methodengeschichte* (*EDM*). By then he had broken with his quondam mentor, Eugen von Böhm-Bawerk.[1] The book, however was star-crossed; the news of its publication was swept up by the fury of the outbreak of World War I. Those few who read it recognized a masterpiece. But only aficionados of economic methodology and the history of thought who read in German had access to it until it was finally translated into English some 40 years later, in 1954, and appeared as *Economic Doctrine and Method* (Schumpeter, 1954b). As that was the same year when Schumpeter's massive chef-d'œuvre *The History of Economic Analysis* (*HEA*) was also published, *EDM*'s ill-fated star persisted, and the book remains neglected. Yet, in my opinion, for anyone who believes in instrumentalism, its predictions were the best he ever made.

The *EDM*'s themes were the desirability of incorporating mathematics into economic theory, the idiocy of wasting effort fighting over schools and methods, and the need to develop a dynamic general equilibrium mathematics. By contrast the themes of the 1954a volume were far more numerous, as well as intricate in description, and involved in principle but not always by example all of the techniques[2] associated with each of the following: economic history, economic statistics, economic theory, economic sociology, political economy, and the various applied sub-fields.

If the 1914 book was a highly polished, but small, true gem, the 1954a effort was a far larger 'Kohinoor-type diamond', still somewhat uncut as well as unpolished. From the standpoint of historical longevity few books look as good after about 90 years as *EDM*. Contrastingly from the standpoint of monumental polymathic achievements, no single work in the field of the history of economic thought yet produced can begin to rival *HEA*.

But the polished perfection of his earlier conclusion says a great deal about the man: his inherent genius (revealed in the speed of his preparation); his arrogant audacity in saying eventually everything that was on his mind; his need to meet the *Habilitation* requirements of his university (the University of Vienna at a time when its economics department was dominated by two brothers-in-law, Friedrich von Wieser and Eugen von Böhm-Bawerk); his incredible capacity for working long hours and taking mountains of shorthand notes; his need to organize professional alliances to further his career ambitions; his 'Tourette Syndrome-like' capacity for blurting out accurate but cutting remarks; and his amazing capacity to become perhaps half as cynically wise in his old age as he had been cleverly brash in his youth.

The truth is that Schumpeter was never what he seemed. His family background was not what he let on. After his father's death, his widowed mother married a retired senior officer in the Austrian Army's Quartermaster Corps. Though that marriage eventually ended in a divorce, during its better years young Joseph was admitted to the aristocratic Theresianum, the *grande école* of Vienna; without his mother's alliance, temporary as it was, that likely would not have happened. We will return to this point in the last section.

Throughout his life Schumpeter implied (and was even known to have stated falsely) that his stepfather was a Field Marshal, that he was part of the aristocracy, and that his mathematical training was advanced.[3] Better yet there are myriad legends about *bons mots* associated with his contacts with the famous and the mighty, most of which should be credited to Schumpeter himself. Doubtless many had a kernel of truth, but like appetites the taste for embellishment comes with the telling. Whatever else, he is the source of more anecdotes than any other economist I can recall.

In his years at the Theresianum, Schumpeter acquired inter alia a knowledge of Greek, Latin, French, Italian, and Spanish. He also read widely in history and literature. He had some knowledge of graphic arts and music. His knowledge of mathematics, however, in spite of his suggestions to the contrary, was limited. Mastering logic is not the same thing as mastering the more advanced forms of algebra and the calculus.

Schumpeter's subsequent student years *in economics* at the university were astoundingly short. After two years taking only courses in law, his first exposure to economics lectures was in 1903. By 1908 (in a mere five years) he had completed the whole curriculum and gained his *Habilitation*, meaning that in those five years he had become fully qualified to hold a principal chair in economics. In those years he had also managed to study economic institutions according to the Gustav Schmoller empirical pattern, had absorbed if not by rote a capacity for reciting perfectly the whole canon of the Carl Menger tradition emphasizing overall economic analysis (logical modeling), and had read a bit in mathematical economics, becoming something of a Walras enthusiast – a choice that a more politic student might have hidden, given Carl Menger's legacy of eschewing mathematical representation. To top it off he had defended successfully his *Habilitationschrift*, entitled *Das Wesen und der Hauptinhalt der theoretischen Nationalökonomie* (*DWHN*), which managed to present seriously both sides of the classic Menger–Schmoller *Methodenstreit* in the guise of offering an apparently persuasive argument to Schmollerites why there was merit in Menger's analytical approach.

We will return to this aspect of the chapter shortly, but the immediate issue is to describe very briefly its purpose and its tortuous locus. Any six-part essay requires a roadmap. Rather than describe Schumpeter's fully evolved perceptions of methodology at the end of his life (for that is what Professor Yuichi Shionoya has done so magnificently that I doubt that anyone will ever improve on it), I have chosen to trace how his methodology evolved and how at different times very competent scholars have described well different facets of that picture.

The first of the six sections deals with the various meanings of *economic methodology*, once a relatively simple idea but by now a real morass of opinions. The second traces the development over time of Schumpeter's vision of what economic theory and methodology encompassed.

Three sections follow, each dealing with a particular effort to identify some aspect of Schumpeter's methodology: first, a 1951 essay by Professor Fritz Machlup, also a product of the University of Vienna but of one generation later; second, a set of ideas largely worked out by a very well-read sociologist, Professor Richard Swedberg, relating to Schumpeter's perceptions of economic sociology as the root from which his rapidly growing methodological vine eventually sprung, and, third, an innovational effort by Professor Yuichi Shionoya to use Schumpeter's vision to create a new holistic 'economic philosophy', of which economic methodology must be an inherent element.

Finally, the last section offers some of my own concluding remarks reflecting not the Schumpeterianism that is so popular today, but the reasons behind much of the negatively critical view of Schumpeter's work during the last third of his life when he was a member of the Harvard faculty. Why was a man who was so open to all sorts of knowledge so blind when it came to learning anything about American economics and economic institutions?

1 The meanings of methodology

When he was writing the 1914 book (*EDM*) his overriding theme was the need for coupling intellectual curiosity with intellectual tolerance. For pre-World War I Vienna this was clearly something of a novelty because Mengerism[4] (as per the Menger–Schmoller *Methodenstreit*) was an undisputable article of local pedagogical faith – a faith that not only separated the holy 'model-building-analytical Vienna economics', from the Great Satan (i.e. the history-of-institutions-based 'Berlin economics') but by means of ignoring everything else put Marshallian and Walrasian economics well beyond the Pale. Schumpeter's 1914 articulated belief was that each method had its own merits and could be successfully applied to different kinds of problems.

The traditional basic question of methodology relates to what a theory, a hypothesis, a generalization, or even a discipline is supposed to do. Somewhat better focused, the question becomes why should what has been offered be considered intellectually serious? In the case of a theory, why should it be believed?

Some argue (as did Schumpeter) that a theory ought to offer a useful prediction (a doctrine known as *instrumentalism*, which was canonized in the fields of physics and chemistry). Pure and simple instrumentalism makes no claim to describing accurately the process by which the outcome is realized; it merely justifies itself by its results. The test of the pudding is in the eating!

Others argue that a theory is really a short-cut to understanding the process involved with little or no attention given to what a theory might or might not predict. This perception of a theory is seemingly less demanding and asks (not so simply, by the way) the theorist to list all the factors that might affect the outcome without necessarily identifying which will be the more and which the less dominating in every or even in the usual circumstances. Here the test of the theorist is how well he comprehends everything that may be involved.

Still others see in methodology a reflection of the history of the great central discipline, philosophy. Karl Pribram offers *in extensio* the claim that there are but two methodologies, both of Hellenic origin, in the history of economics: Platonic essences, and Aristotelian empirical observations as well as Natural Law (Pribram, 1983). I would go a bit further by adding to his list the efforts of various Church Fathers e.g. St Augustine and St Thomas Aquinas, to meld Roman as well as Hellenic thought with Jewish and Christian Biblical thinking.

The emergence of Augustinian theology, which became canon soon after Augustine's death, was not without its fights, and when it came to be accepted it was neo-Platonism not traditional Platonism that became orthodoxy. Plato had argued that Truth could only be an abstraction, and he included mathematics as potential Truth. Augustine, who stands as the principal Church Father during the last centuries of the Old Roman

Empire, held that Truth, namely the Church's Holy Mysteries (e.g. the Eucharist) could not be perceived through mathematics. Accordingly, Absolute Truth (the Godhead) was perceivable only in the abstract, not including mathematical thinking.

When early in the 13th century Averröes' Latin translations (from Arabic) of much of Aristotle's work became available, a new intellectual movement entered the canonical fray. From the ecclesiastical standpoint the 'innovators' were two Dominicans, teaching initially at the University of Paris: Albertus Magnus (a German count) and his star student, Thomas Aquinas (coming from a prominent Italian family). They advanced their belief that God's magnificence could also be grasped through the senses – or, to put their point in its broadest context – they noted that Aristotle had taught that beside the laws passed by men there were Natural Laws (which must have come from God, even if not explicitly listed in the Bible). Therefore empiricism was not to be scorned; one should appreciate what the senses revealed for they were instruments which the Godhead employed to enrich His world.

Karl Pribram's *A History of Economic Reasoning* traces this dichotomy through centuries until well after World War II (Pribram, 1983). He argues that the line of Plato–Augustine–the Franciscans–Descartes–Kant and even the Bolsheviks can be contrasted with the line of Aristotle–Aquinas–Francis Bacon-Hegel and post-WWII American free trade policy. But such quick grouping misses much of the story.

Fate played its own tricks on Roman Catholic Doctrine. European nationalism started developing in the 14th century and by the time of Martin Luther (1483–1546) schismatic movements could no longer be repressed in much of Northern Europe. Among the more reform-minded Englishmen were the Puritans who reinterpreted Holy Scripture to suit their beliefs, one of which came from the last verses of the Book of Daniel. That verse (Daniel xii, 10)[5] stressed that all men would have to be educated before the Second Coming. Influenced by this belief coming from his Puritan mother, Francis Bacon, a jurist (Lord Chancellor) and a natural philosopher laid out in several essays his rejection of Porphyry's *quadrivium and trivium* and preached a personal (do-it-yourself) systematic version of Aristotelian empiricism (his innovation was termed by him 'the scientific method'). It became one of the two modern foundations of natural science.

About two decades later René Descartes, a French professional soldier, a conventional Roman Catholic believer, and actually one of history's mathematical geniuses, became taken with Platonic thought and reincorporated along with the traditional Augustinian credo Plato's faith in mathematics and in abstract modeling. The result, leading eventually to Cartesian modeling (i.e. incorporating algebra with geometry) then became as the popular form of Platonic Truth, a version of Science. Indeed, it has served until very recently as the principal foundation of the physical sciences.

The 17th century was an era of great intellectual changes. Recall: (1) Bruno was burned in 1600, yet, even though (2) Francis Bacon published his *Novum Organon* in 1620, (3) Galileo was so frightened by Bruno's fate that he recanted in 1632; (4) Decartes published his *Discours de la Méthode* in 1637 and (5) Thomas Hobbes, a quondam royalist switched sides and published *The Leviathan* in 1651, which became the root from which virtually all systematic non-theological treatments of the source of government power stem. The full shift occurred when (6) in 1662 the re-throned Charles II (of England, Scotland and Ireland) became the Patron of the Royal Society and gave it such cachet that anything it accepted as scientific was effectively shielded from all theological condemnation. In 62 years the Church had lost its monopoly on Truth.

The scientific method after Bacon and Descartes came to be efforts at fusing the two systems. The 18th century exemplar was Isaac Newton, whose work on the physics of light articulated the idea of a 'Crucial Test', namely the empirical verification of a logical model. The enduring value of Bacon and Descartes' ideas played out 'successfully' in the growth of theoretical physics and chemistry – 'successfully' because the Newtonian theories of equilibrium holding the universe together now have been superseded through the very methods that Newton advocated.

The 18th century was the time of gentlemanly leisure, a condition which led not only to widespread wagering (gambling) but also to a large number of mathematical discoveries with regard to probability theory (the several generations of the Swiss Bernoulli family are famous in this regard). At the same time, the Enlightenment Movement created its own new Gospel, namely that science was 'superior' to theology because its assertions were 'provable', whereas religious belief was not; even worse, many of the philosophers of the Enlightenment thought that religious beliefs could be no more than frightening superstitions.

As one would expect in 'the world of the intellect' there were several types of negative reactions to the Enlightenment's anti-religion 'liberating' message. By the end of the 18th century these reactions included not only those of the Roman Catholic authorities but also the reactions of several national cultures.

In the case of Britain the reaction was a profound philosophical skepticism, but one phrased largely in 'practical' terms. As already mentioned, Thomas Hobbes published in 1651 *The Leviathan*, a treatise positing that governments were not ordained by God but by every man's presumed fear of every other man. His reasoning was Cartesian, and in no time there were several major efforts (mostly predicated on some limited empirical observation) that his conclusion of boundless interpersonal fear was not the only reason for social organization. The massive literature 'disproving Hobbes' contains the foundations of modern economics as well as modern democratic theory (cf. Perlman and McCann, 1998).

The German response to the Enlightenment was on a broader scale, i.e. a variety of Romantic (as in nationalistic) philosophical writings and the development of several popular sociological (i.e. both idealistic and material) political movements. In the main there were two philosophical approaches that were immediately incorporated into the world of scientific thinking, the transcendental static thinking of Emmanuel Kant and the more applicable evolutionary ideas of Georg Hegel. Kant's thinking was in line with the eternal Truths stemming from Plato's influence, while Hegel's thinking focused not on eternal Truths (as such) but on an Aristotelian dialectic explaining how a thesis (a synthesis from an earlier period) was challenged by an antithesis resulting eventually in a new synthesis, which became the revised thesis, and the process went on indefinitely. Hegelians were not looking for Truth; they were seeking the principles underlying evolution.

Kant and Hegel were only two of the more recognized Romantic philosophers of the 18th and 19th centuries. Others followed. I would cite Nietzsche's assertion that truth was a matter of perspective, his point being that there was not necessarily a Truth but many truths, the latter involving not only different values but also different ways of demonstrating one's values.

By 1900, the topic of Scientific Truth became a matter of intense debate, particularly in Vienna: could science ignore religion, could science ignore other cultural traditions, could science ignore perspectivalism?

We now come to the critical point of this discussion of economic methodology. This combination of philosophical matrices, all of which Schumpeter had studied as a Theresianum student, was coupled with historical studies emphasizing the changing nature of capitalism and industrial society. When he went to the University of Vienna, what the professors (particularly Wieser and Böhm-Bawerk) wanted to stress was the absolute correctness of the neo-Platonic model-building method as they interpreted the Carl Menger legacy. The seminar course he took with Böhm-Bawerk was particularly strident in that two of the other students, Otto Bauer and Rudolf Hilferding, were leading Marxists and in that capacity apparently matched their professor with sharp language.[6] Tradition has it that Schumpeter also participated vigorously, but it was less than clear which side, if either, he favored.

Britain and America went down a different path, cleaving to a more single-minded foundation and holding less concern about methodological questions. The growing interest in democratic self-government put principal emphasis on the philosophy of self-government and personal responsibility for economic welfare. The dominant cultural choice lay in Jeremy Bentham's Utilitarianism, even as later modified by John Stuart Mill and William Stanley Jevons. Bentham's 'buzzword' was 'The Greatest Good for the Greatest Number', no doubt a fine phrase but one assuming that one can sum individuals' goods as against their 'bads.'

Space limitations preclude any discussion of Utilitarianism except to stress a tangential point that what made Schumpeter so important to virtually all British and American 20th century-trained economists was that his approach to economics was devoid of utilitarian underpinnings. Here was an author whose vision of economics was conceptually very different from the ones that they already knew, particularly Smith, Ricardo, Jevons, Marshall, Pigou, and Maynard Keynes.

Developments in physics and chemistry in Britain and America focused more than most realized on the utilitarian consequences of scientific advance. Within the fraternity of the leading British economists, some form of utilitarianism was the foundation of all their work: John Stuart Mill's 'masterpieces', the (1843) *System of Logic* and his (1848) *Principles of Political Economy*; William Stanley Jevons's anti-Mill (1874) *Principles of Science*; John Neville Keynes's (1891) *The Scope and Method of Political Economy* as well as Appendices C ('The Scope and Method of Economics') & D ('Uses of Abstract Reasoning in Economics') of Alfred Marshall's *Principles of Economics* (see the 1920 8th edition) were considered the main texts on the appropriateness of various methods, particularly induction and deduction, with intuition coming off very badly.

Methodology got less local attention in American universities, in part because either the John Stuart Mill ethical utilitarianism or the Marshallian tradition were observed in most graduate departments, and where one or the other was not (i.e. the loci of institutional economics) the lines between economics and sociology were rather blurred, and the sociologists rather than the economists were the ones interested in the topic. What did surface, however, was a general conviction that physics, with its quantifiable characteristics, its logical structure, and its history of theory correctly predicting empirical outcomes, offered the preferable paradigm for the development of a scientific economics. The exemplar for economic analysis was Paul Samuelson's *Foundations of Economic Analysis* (1947).

This situation for economists generally continued unchanged until Milton Friedman's classic *Essays in Positive Economics* was first published (Friedman, 1953). Its message was 'pure and simple' instrumentalism: one used the model that predicted outcomes best; in his case the model of pure competition predicted the price and quantity outcomes of American automobile sales far better than the model of imperfect competition (one which better suited the theoretical assumptions describing the industry). It was also an era when econometrics was becoming the mainstay in the graduate economics student's diet, and it became canon to write a dissertation trying to devise a model that predicted accurately whatever phenomenon one studied, irrespective of what a historian might have thought ought to be included.

At this point one should mention the strange lack of impact of Thomas Kuhn, whose *The Structure of Scientific Revolutions* became something of the canonical foundation for studies of the history and philosophy of science: Kuhn explicitly doubted whether economics was sufficiently onto-logical to qualify as a regular science (Kuhn, 1962, but cf. Backhouse, 1996). However, most economists are like young people in love; they remain deaf to all advice.

In 1977 I asked Mark Blaug to write a survey of economic methodology for the Cambridge Series surveying recent developments in economic thought; the resulting book, *The Methodology of Economics or How Economists Explain* (Blaug, 1980, and a second edition in 1992) became an unexpected best-seller. Juxtaposed to Blaug's essentially Popperian beliefs (falsificationism) is the work of Professor D. McCloskey (McCloskey, 1985), who argues (as she notes that I did even earlier (Perlman, 1978)), that economists are not scientists but advocates; the real name of the operation is 'rhetoric' i.e. what method of presentation maximizes persuasion.

The current fluidity of economic methodology as a sub-discipline is further exemplified in an interesting book by Sheila Dow (1985) whose view is that the more descriptive term is mode of thought rather than method, the difference being the variety of factors within the scope of the author's approach from which the method(s) is/are derived. A more recent and also fascinating article by Victoria Chick, 'Theory, method, and mode of Keynes's *General Theory*' bears this approach out with a nicely complex set of box-diagrams (Chick, 2003, pp. 308, 311).

To summarize: methodology has held several meanings, clearly includ-ing but certainly not limited to theory based on instrumentalism; theory based on understanding; philosophical foundations, especially the contrast between logic and empiricism; British and American Utilitarianism and its progeny; and contemporary concerns regarding culture, perspectivalism, paradigms, and rhetoric. The field remains active with much repetition (that even more than the acrimony), as well as a readable journal.

We now move on to Schumpeter's own methodological evolution, and how it was seen by three different perceptive thinkers, Fritz Machlup, Richard Swedberg, and Yuichi Shionoya. It is Professor Yuichi Shionoya's effort to argue from the specific to the general (using Schumpeter's writings) that suggests the lines or form of a new economic philosophy.

2   The locus of Schumpeter's thinking

Schumpeter has had no small number of biographers, with a particularly fine recent biographical essay by Horst Hanusch (1999). I have tended to rely most strongly on a longer scholarly work by Richard Swedberg (1991) and on a rather gossipy and comprehensive (two-volume) survey of 'Schumpeter-warts-and-all' by Loring Allen (1991). This is not to slight two very careful consciously interpretive biographies by Eduard März (1983) and Wolfgang Stolper (1994). The principal virtue of Swedberg's account is its precision and its steady focus on the record.

While still an undergraduate at the University of Vienna, Schumpeter was already publishing papers. Of these, one in 1906 was a summary of Léon Walras's work (Schumpeter, 1906) wherein a remarkably brash young man was endorsing the use of mathematics, a method which Carl Menger had explicitly discouraged. Yet, for all of his independence of mind while he was a student, Schumpeter entertained a tight definition of what economics was about. It was focused entirely on an abstraction, a topic totally devoid of any psychological, political, sociological, or moral underpinnings or overtones. 'Political economy' was the 'flawed' version of the subject, not one that was devoid of interest but one which the younger Schumpeter thought could never achieve the status of a true science.

Most important, however, was Schumpeter's *Habilitationschrift* (*DWHN*) which we have already noted was a summary of the Menger–Schmoller *Methodenstreit* in a form that was for a Böhm-Bawerk protégé even-handed regarding the Schmoller historical approach to a degree approaching his master's limit; it was also framed consciously to fit his variation into the Walrasian framework. Suffice it to note here that relatively soon thereafter he seems to have dropped the book; indeed he chose to take no copy with him when he moved to Harvard. Why did he lose interest? Some say it was because he had begun to believe that partial static equilibrium models (he was the coiner of the term 'methodological individualism') were comparatively sterile. My own hunch (and it can be only that) is his recollection of the genesis of the book.

He had been overtly courting Böhm-Bawerk's approval, and he suited the manuscript to the taste of the customer. When he and Böhm-Bawerk eventually broke in 1913 over an argument in his second book, he came to regard the memory of his kowtowing with personal chagrin. Nonetheless it is a competent job, was well reviewed,[7] and compares favorably even with Marshall's *Principles* because of his extended treatment of general equilibrium analysis.

His second book, the 1912[8] *Theorie der wirtschaftlichen Entwicklung* (*TWE*), brought him his great fame, insofar as it introduces his 'vision', one which may start with the Physiocrat's static circular flow but goes far beyond into the realm of innovations that are financed by modern credit capitalism. Quite aside from the book's merits was its immediate impact. He had asserted that in a static economy there need logically be no interest (i.e. a rate of zero). It was this point with which Böhm-Bawerk took such vehement exception that, when Schumpeter refused to recant, Böhm-Bawerk became irate and is said to have asserted that Schumpeter had no future in Austrian academia. Thus Schumpeter lost his patron (cf. Samuelson, 1981). Even worse, Böhm-Bawerk died suddenly in 1914, and Schumpeter was gentleman enough to write a euphonious eulogy observing all the niceties of *nil nisi bonum*.

With the loss of Böhm-Bawerk's patronage and the likely prospect of no further advancement in Austria, Schumpeter turned to form something of an alliance with Max Weber. Space precludes much of a discussion of Weber, an economist and sociologist who by this time had recovered his health after a long period of nervous instability. Around 1912, already a professor of economics at the University of Munich, Weber proposed a massive encyclopedic study of the field of economics,[9] the first volume of which contained three essays: one by Wieser on economic theory, one by Karl Bucher (a moderate Schmollerite) and a third section on the history of economic thought, to be Schumpeter's contribution. The resulting manuscript became *EDM* and was, as Schumpeter recalled, the third part of his 'sacred decade of intellectual fertility'.

EDM was written with several purposes in mind.[10] First, he was doing it as a favor to Weber as part of the larger project. Second, he wanted to stress his belief that arguing over proper method and the supremacy of one school of economic thought over another was, at best, sheer provincialism and, at worst, a fearful waste of talent. Third, he thought that the future of economics lay in its mathematization, generally, and its capacity to develop a theory of dynamic general equilibrium, specifically.

To put the matter bluntly, Schumpeter turned his back on the Viennese *Genossenschaft*, on Menger's disdain for mathematics, and on total concentration on economic statics. As Schumpeter always wrote for a purpose, I have held that, of all of his books, this was the one where he scored highest from a straightforward instrumentalist standpoint (Perlman, 2002). Unfortunately the book's actual publication was just as World War I commenced, and it went largely unnoticed except by aficionados of the history of economic thought who were fluent in German (it was not translated into English until 1954).[11]

During World War I, Schumpeter remained at Graz; the official explanation was that, as a professor, he should remain at his teaching post. But his ideas were changing. Prior to *EDM* his perception of economics was philosophically 'pure', i.e. he thought 'pure' economics could be separated from 'impure' political economy. But after writing *EDM* he ventured increasingly into the more exciting fields of political economy, publishing in 1918 'The

Crisis of the Tax State'; in 1919 'On the Sociology of Imperialism', and eventually in 1927 'Social Classes in an Ethnically Homogenous Environment'. I see these moves as not only an abandonment of the concept of subject-purity, but a continuing effort to ally himself with the empirical Weberian legacy. Put another way, the fence between pure economics and political economy (something he once held as definitional) was developing many holes, then even large gaps. The boy-wonder was now maturely facing a man's problems.

By 1917, Schumpeter was playing Austrian national politics with an eye to getting some ministry. In time he did become Minister of Finance in a Socialist government but was eased out when he was suspected of some political disloyalty. He then turned to business and became an officer of the Biedermann Bank, where for a time he prospered. Eventually not only did the Bank fail, but his personal fortune was wiped out and he was burdened with considerable personal debt. So saddled, he was then lucky to get a professorship in Bonn. In time he sought to succeed Schmoller in Berlin, and when that plan failed he decided to move to Harvard.[12]

During the 1920s he worked on a book on the theory of money. He seems consciously to have been racing Maynard Keynes, whose (1930) *A Treatise on Money* foreclosed Schumpeter's publishing his comparable manuscript.[13]

At Harvard his first big project was a two-volume study carrying an unfortunate title, *Business Cycles: A Theoretical, Historical, and Statistical Analysis of the Capitalist Process*.[14] Kuznets savaged it in a long essay in the *American Economic Review*; Kuznets pointed out profound flaws in Schumpeter's use of both historical and statistical data. Moreover, by the time the book appeared, Keynes had again trumped him with his (1936) *General Theory of Employment, Interest, and Prices*. And finally everything was overtaken by the outbreak of World War II. Schumpeter sided with Germany, particularly after Germany invaded the Soviet Union.[15] That allegiance destroyed much of the affection from his students and colleagues. The result was months of personal depression, even despair.

He retreated into a bitter personal isolation and turned to writing. In 1942, his *Capitalism, Socialism, and Democracy* was rushed into publication; the book went through two revisions and a third, enlarged edition of 1950. As it turned out this book became his most popular work. If anything it was far more Weber-sociological than economic.

Five years or so after the war he was elected President of the American Economic Association, a timely honor. He died at the end of January 1950 within a month of giving his presidential address.

After his death the great event was the publication in 1954 of his unfinished *History of Economic Analysis* (HEA, Schumpeter, 1954a), as edited by his widow, aided by Gottfried von Haberler, Arthur W. Marget, Paul M. Sweezy, Richard M. Goodwin, Alexander Gerschenkron[16] and several others.[17]

This is the crowning achievement in his treatment of economic methodology. In the first part he explains that true methodological skill requires a knowledge of economic history, economic statistics, economic theory, economic sociology, political economy and the literature of the various applied sub-fields. This is the principal point of his great effort. For 'Schumpeter the Wise' (no longer 'Schumpeter the Clever'), economic methodology presumes an understanding of everything to do with any economic aspect of the social sciences.

The book is a polymathic masterpiece. When I was asked to write a new Introduction (Schumpeter, 1954a [1994]) to a 1994 printing I spent a fair amount of time going over Schumpeter's judgments about writers and writings. I could find no instance where he had tilted his interpretation nor, except for his contempt for virtually all things American, had he purposely omitted any materials. Kurt Dopfer used a phrase, 'participant–observer', to describe how an author can try to accommodate his subject's every nuance or even whim. And in *HEA* Schumpeter achieved just that.

The book is not without its critics. Frank Knight thought he slighted the influence of Protestantism. Mark Blaug thought that he promised more than he had delivered. My judgment is that his capacity for understanding all the variations and nuances of belief that one can find in a writing is Schumpeter's great contribution to Methodology. While I will return to this point at the end of the chapter, his appreciation of contributions frequently did not extend to how well the author pulled it off. Kuznets was appalled at the carelessness of his historical focus; others (Frisch and Tinbergen) were amazed at his mathematical clumsiness. And all of his students could never understand his aversion to American institutions and political theories. Briefly put, his polymathic knowledge seems to have been unchallengeable, but care in checking the relevance or accuracy of what he had read seems to have occasionally escaped his attention.

3 Machlup's 1951 essay on Schumpeter's methodology

The May issue of the 1951 *Review of Economics and Statistics* contained 15 essays memorializing Schumpeter, who had died in January 1950. These essays plus five more were published as *the* Memorial volume under the auspices of the *Review* shortly afterwards (Schumpeter, 1951a). 'Schumpeter's Economic Methodology' by Fritz Machlup appears both in the journal issue and in the later collection.

Machlup's essay outlined
Machlup opens the essay with the observation that, like many economists, the younger Schumpeter, who strongly advocated mathematical methods, in his maturity seemed to turn to endorsing historical methods; it was in

keeping with his sentiments in his first (1908) book, that 'there was no contradiction between the historical and the abstract approaches, and that the
only difference was in their interest for different problems'(Machlup, 1951,
p. 95). Machlup then quotes with evident approval Schumpeter's view that
methodological debates were generally sterile. In Machlup's words,

> I submit that, with his superior understanding of general epistemology and sci-
> entific method and his extensive learning and reading in many fields of knowl-
> edge, he could not stand the methodological nonsense that was continually
> advertised by the various 'authorities' in the field. When others reiterated their
> bigoted patter, Schumpeter could not help coming back with his own message,
> which urged methodological tolerance and was intolerant only of illiteracy and
> intolerance itself. (Ibid.)

Although Machlup noted that Schumpeter's commitment to methodological individualism was limited to *economics*, not *politics*, he eschewed all criticism of the inherent ignoring of political methodological individualism, a
point clearly missing from all of Schumpeter's presentation in the various
editions of his *Capitalism, Socialism, and Democracy*. Why Machlup chose
this route, given that he was a thorough Hayekian, seems to be simply Fritz's
applying the rule of *nil nisi bonum* in memorial volumes.

Nevertheless it weakened his 1951 article and reveals a major blind
spot in Schumpeter's work, for if there was any single point that separated Schumpeter's work from mainstream American thinking it was
Schumpeter's clear aversion to the history of British utilitarianism and its
impact on American socio-economic-politico developments. Machlup also
pussyfooted around the topic of Schumpeter's wild assessment of the
futures of capitalism and socialism, an assessment that it seems to me clearly
showed major limitations in Schumpeter's thinking – quite possibly in
Schumpeter's reading, since nowhere is there mention of James Madison or
the American Institutionalists as a school, much less any mention of John
R. Commons who of them all may have influenced American institutions,
themselves, the most.[18]

Finally, Machlup's interest was confined to Schumpeter's tolerance for
different methods; Machlup did not examine whether Schumpeter used
these methods successfully.

The mathematics–statistics–econometrics aspect
Two papers in the eventual 1951 Memorial Volume were written by Jan
Tinbergen and by Ragnar Frisch. They are respectful to the point of express-
ing heartfelt affection. Yet both essays contain some stunning criticisms.

Tinbergen, after noting the leadership that Schumpeter had taken in
founding the Econometric Society, expresses his consternation when he read

and found virtually no evidence of econometric analysis in Schumpeter's (1939) *Business Cycles*. Moreover,

> one finds a mental attitude vis-à-vis econometric work which is not only rather critical, but to some extent alien to it.
>
> The space devoted to typical econometric research in this one-thousand-page book is relatively small. The place given to the description of facts, to a somewhat primitive chart-reading, and to institutional considerations is much larger. The treatment, even of theoretical points, is quite different from the econometric habit of a rigorous subdivision according to the relations discussed. (Tinbergen, 1951, p. 59)

Possibly because of this perhaps unanticipated criticism, the editors included in the published volume an essay by another of Schumpeter's colleagues in the founding of the Econometric Society, Ragnar Frisch. If such was the plan, the outcome may have been unanticipated.

Frisch admits his amazement in discovering that Schumpeter's mathematical skills were extremely limited; he covers that embarrassment by extolling Schumpeter's mathematical imagination, not an unimportant point, but one which gives the lie to the ending of Arthur Smithies' wonderful eulogy, quoted here in full:

> Towards the end of the summer of 1945, he (Schumpeter) made a (n) . . . appraisal:
> 'Looking back on these months and on the weeks that are still left, and looking back on my life in the process, three things stand out,
> '(1) Always the same mistakes committed, and the same type of strength and weakness displayed.
> '(2) The story might be written in terms of lost opportunities (though that stands out in retrospect: there were those that were seized and used promptly enough).
> '(3) Yet there is no regret – if I had used every one of those opportunities I should not have done a better job of it all – perhaps even the contrary, for success up to the hilt with any one of them would have stuck me in the particular line and not only narrowed me but landed me in uncomfortable situations . . . Ease me gently to my grave.'
> And the entry concludes:
> 'Never grudge the time (a) to think, (b) *for a bit of math*. (Smithies, 1950, p. 23, emphasis added)

The historical aspect

On two occasions Simon Kuznets, whom Vibha Kapuria-Foreman and I characterized in a memorial essay, 'An economic historian's economist' (Perlman, 1996), wrote two analytically devastating essays on Schumpeter's work. The first, which became his 1924 Master's Essay at Columbia and which brought him enthusiastic sponsorship by Wesley Clair Mitchell is a careful exposition of Schumpeter's system as revealed in his 1908 and 1912 books. It is unpublished but is carefully summarized in Perlman (2001). His major criticisms are two.

First, the data do not lend themselves to a two-phase business cycle (employed in the 1912 volume); even more basic to this point is Kuznets's argument that business cycle analysis must be in the Baconian tradition (facts first, then generalization, then rechecking with new facts, then refining the generalization, etc. etc.), not the Cartesian (purely intellectualized) tradition, which Kuznets implies came to Schumpeter from his Menger and his Marxian training.

Second, Kuznets, even as a student, criticized Schumpeter's perception of what a theory was supposed to be. Schumpeter, he opined, thought a theory was a perfect predictive model; he (Kuznets) thought a good theory could only be 'a shortcut to understanding'.

As against these criticisms Kuznets grants that Schumpeter's insights were marvelous.

Kuznets's later review of Schumpeter's *Business Cycles* (Kuznets, 1940) is phrased extraordinarily deferentially, but for all that totally devastatingly. Again those criticisms are summarized in my 2001 article; the major point is that Schumpeter's reliance upon historical material is invariably second-hand, and his authorities were often careless or just plain wrong.

It is these criticisms of Schumpeter's work which became the foundations of my own reservations. Part of my empirical heritage is a distrust of intellectual excogitation: it is too easy to construct models as substitutes for empirical reality with the result that one is building 'castles in the air'.

The psychological switch
Although never admitting it explicitly, in his methodological work Schumpeter came to replace his methodological economic individualism with a methodological economic institutionalism. This switch is accepted pretty much without comment in the opening chapters of his (1954) *HEA*. It first becomes slightly apparent in his third book (Schumpeter, 1914a), one designed in part to weld his relationship with Max Weber, whose historical approach was predicated on a sociological analysis of economic decision making. Many of the essays written between that time and his 1942 *CSD* are strong evidence that his commitments were broadening; I would cite his highly appreciative essay on Gustav Schmoller as the clearest example of that change taking place.[19] In both editions of his *CSD* where he exposes his underlying appreciation of the Marxian materialist dialectic, the change seems to me to have been complete.

Economic methodological individualism, a term used frequently by Schumpeter throughout his life, is accordingly less descriptive of his thinking after fairly early on. However, his use of it to describe much modern economic analysis, including specifically the thinking in the body of Marshall's *Principles*, remains appropriate. It just ceased to describe his own work.

On a later occasion Fritz Machlup identified what he thought were the six basic propositions of the Menger–Austrian School tradition (Machlup, 1982):

a. Methodological economic individualism, but not methodological political individualism,
b. Methodological subjectivism (what I would call epistemic foundations),
c. The use of marginal analysis in economic theory, but only after the epistemic foundations had been revealed as prices,
d. The concept of using utility seen as subject to diminishing returns,
e. The use of opportunity cost as a decision-making technique,
f. The incorporation of time in round-about production techniques and in explanations of consumer behavior.

To these I would add

g. Some concern that models based on perfect competition should also be accompanied by models based on imperfect competition (the latter seen principally not as the result of inadequate information but as the result of restrictions in the factor markets).

In my view Schumpeter abandoned a good bit of that Viennese legacy. He was never totally comfortable with methodological individualism because he developed a taste for Walrasian general equilibrium early on, and he had little or no interest in political individualism. By the time he had finished his second book, his concept of time was no longer Böhm-Bawerkian, but he never worked it out along the lines that Hayek or Shackle chose to follow. In the case of epistemic foundations, in later years Schumpeter reversed his earlier alignment (effectively opposing psychology as a necessary consideration in economic analysis) and came to see the importance of institutions in shaping individual preferences. And his Marxist leanings precluded his belief in the propriety of assuming perfect competition since he had accepted the idea that capitalism inevitably led to oligopolistic market structures.

Unfortunately Machlup based his 1951 article completely on the Menger–Viennese view of method and used as his evidence mostly Schumpeter's first book, the one that Schumpeter seems to have later disinherited. And to a lesser degree Machlup adverted to the tolerance found in *EDM*, which I, myself, think that Fritz seriously undervalued (cf. Perlman, 2002, particularly pp. 292–4). Although Machlup's essay contained much unqualified praise, Machlup (as I have already noted) erroneously claimed that Schumpeter was unwilling to consider the contributions of scientific psychology; Machlup was writing in total ignorance of what was in the burgeoning *HEA* manscript.[20] I believe that, as he delved into his final projects dealing with the development of erudite knowledge in all fields, Machlup came to appreciate Schumpeter's erudition all the more.

4   Richard Swedberg's view of Schumpeter's methodology

Richard Swedberg's study of Schumpeter's work is of a current breadth and depth possibly matched only by Professor Shionoya. Yet Swedberg's approach is quite different. Swedberg, quite aside from his fine scholarly qualities, comes to Schumpeter from the standpoint of a sociologist. Economists as a fraternity have tended to view sociologists as intellectual inferiors, and the current misconception is that sociologists want to ape economists. Such is clearly not the whole case. What separates the two disciplines is mostly the 'mainline economist' view that economics should be confined to only the most direct problems of the production and distribution of goods and services (generally as measured in money or quantities, and invariably individual but occasionally social as well). This 'narrowness' has been of relatively recent origin, since it was somewhat alien to Alfred Marshall's and Arthur Pigou's opinion, to say nothing of both Clarks – John Bates and John Maurice. But the impact of Pareto's insistence upon the premise of rationality (and full knowledge) and Samuelson's *Foundations of Economic Analysis* seemingly confirmed the narrower definition. Sociologists, on the other hand, also have their specialists, but the rigidity of disciplinary development seems to me (not a 'mainline economist') less evident.

Swedberg is a sociologist whose numerous works on the boundaries between the two disciplines are comprehensively thoughtful – both descriptive and analytical (cf. Swedberg, 1990). Besides publishing several books focused on economic sociology generally (Swedberg, 1996) and on Max Weber's work specifically (Swedberg, 1998; Weber, 1999), he has used Joseph Schumpeter's career and writings to point up his case (Swedberg, 1991).

Scholars like Professor Swedberg have used the evolution of the work of a particular economist to show how his perception of economic processes was enriched by breaking away from what many 'mainline' economists consider economic theories' necessary (sacred) premise: logical studies of (1) the efficient creation of products and services, and (2) how logic can be used to explain the reasons for the distribution of the factor rewards. Swedberg's task has not been made any easier by the decision of some major economists (e.g. Vilfredo Pareto) to insist that any deviation makes the writer a sociologist. No one can doubt Pareto's great works in economics (e.g. his 1896–7 *Cours d'économie politique* and his 1906 *Manuale d'économie politique*, but in my judgment his greatest work which he insisted was not economics was his voluminous *1916 Trattato di sociologia generale* which Talcott Parsons translated and published in 1935 under the imaginative title of *Mind and Society*. Just as cats can look at kings, I can assert that Pareto's well-known inflexibility should be ignored and economists ought to study all economic activities, even those not capable of formal display (i.e. not predicated on logic or formulatable mathematically).

Nor has Swedberg's task been made easier by very well-known economists who are not model-oriented but empirical studies-oriented. Accordingly, their scorning of the necessary assumption of logic, instead of merely saying that on rare occasions it was truly a useful technique. Wesley Clair Mitchell and John R. Commons and their students had grave doubts about the usefulness of any ideas or theories that were not derived one way or another from systematic observation. And the fact that these purportedly 'heterodox' but nonetheless acknowledged economic giants created bases for legislative and other types of social change further muddied the waters. I recall Jacob Viner asking me if I could think of any contribution of the Commons School to economics. My reply was such social legislation as encouraged unionism and provided universal social insurance. 'That,' said Viner, 'Is not economics!' – strange reaction from the man who claimed that economics was what economists did when they chose to call it economics.

Swedberg takes up Schumpeter's work starting really with the 1912 *TWE* to show how during the next decade and a half he made important excursions off that once-worshiped straight and narrow conventional economics path. Unlike Machlup, Swedberg sees the principal picture from the standpoint of Schumpeter's writings during the period 1918 through all of the 1920s. And after his decade of brilliance (the first three books) he moved ever closer to wanting to enrich economic analysis with something involving an institutional dimension.

Schumpeter's arrangement with Max Weber involved something of a meeting of the minds. Weber thought Schmoller's views on the importance of economic institutions somewhat extreme, not so much in their own terms but as seen in the way he exercised his grip on appointments in German universities. In practice Weber's interest in institutions went far beyond what even the most liberal interpretation could call economics-tinged. He was fascinated by bureaucratic complexities, by the roles of religious credos and fervor, by built-in prejudices and what Nietzsche would have called perspective judgments.

Schumpeter was clearly looking for alliances, and one with Weber certainly had its natural advantages. But Schumpeter's interest focused clearly on only those institutions which seemingly had a direct link to the traditional two foci of economics: the problems of production and the problems of distribution; albeit he focused more on macro than on micro, on dynamics rather than on statics.

All authors intent upon showing how Schumpeter was broadening his focus point to either three or four essays written during the period: 'The Crisis of the Tax State' (Schumpeter, 1918); 'Imperialism and Social Classes' (Schumpeter, 1919); 'Gustav v. Schmoller und die Probleme von heute' (Schumpeter, 1926), and 'The Instability of Capitalism' (Schumpeter, 1928). Each of these essays touches on his developing a sense of economic sociology, i.e. a sociology overlapping economics.

All are interesting, but the single untranslated one (dealing with Schmoller) I find the most revealing because it is there that I sense his most comfortable stance. He had really come to accept the greater power of historical studies over the power of Mengerian analysis. Perhaps the easiest underlying explanation was that the analytical approach had not tackled economic dynamics. However, it seems to me that Swedberg, a sociologist, is understandably far more impressed with the other three essays, perhaps because they help define Schumpeter's economic sociology (Swedberg, 1991, pp. 94–107).

From Swedberg's standpoint, Schumpeter's methodology evolved from a reasonably broad compromise among the Mengerian, the Walrasian, and the Schmoller approaches, to a Schumpeterian fusion of economic institutionalism, economic dynamics, and those aspects of sociology which were politically vital at particular times. From one standpoint Swedberg credits Schumpeter with developing an integrated economic institutionalism where the avowed purpose is to avoid intellectual provincialism in the name of Occam's Razor. From another standpoint Swedberg points to Schumpeter's economic sociology as the best, perhaps the only real, fusion of what we know about the dynamics of market societies.

5   Professor Yuichi Shionoya's version

Professor Shionoya has written extensively on Schumpeter's methodology – indeed on all of his work. In truth he is the master of the subject. In all, I cite about a dozen of his works in English; he has also published in Japanese and German.

Insofar as I am aware, Shionoya's tracing of the development of Schumpeter's thinking is in much greater detail with considerably more neutral insight than that of any other writer. Unlike Machlup (and to a limited extent me) neither Swedberg nor Shionoya could have ever met

Schumpeter, and those with whom they have had discussions about him were generally his students or colleagues. The immediate consequence is that their assessments of his work seem to me to be relatively free of the bias of his personality – a factor which clearly influenced Machlup and to a lesser extent myself.[21]

In Shionoya's view, Schumpeter came onto the Viennese intellectual scene when interest in scientific methodology was beginning to peak. The precursors of logical positivism, Ernst Mach, Henri Poincaré, and Pierre Maurice Duheim, had been something of a rage. But logical positivism had inherited the scene when Schumpeter's first book *DWHN* was conceived and written. Shionoya's first point is that even then Schumpeter thought that argument about methodology was a clear waste of time. He quotes Schumpeter's words:

> Like many specialists (of the natural sciences) in our time, I am convinced that the contentions of 'schools' are true in *ways* for which are meant and *for the purposes intended*.
>   Each method has its concrete areas of application, and it is useless to struggle for universal validity. We shall emphasize over and over again that a discussion of methods had meaning only in relation to pratical scientific works. (Shionoya, 1990, p. 192; see citation in Hanusch, 1999, p. 278)

Yet Shionoya stresses that Schumpeter was at least in good part an instrumentalist, albeit (as we have seen) not of the pure and simple variety. Schumpeter saw the historical approach (method?) as descriptive, and the analytical as predictive. Schumpeter, according to Shionoya, had a streak of pragmatism.

> While [historical] description does no more than make a catalogue of facts, a theory undertakes the transformation of facts, not for any far-reaching or mysterious purpose but only for a better summary of facts. *A theory constructs a scheme for facts; its aim is to give a brief representation to an immense amount of facts and to achieve as simply and as completely as possible what we call understanding.* (Italics in original; quoted by Shionoya, 1990, p. 210 and also found in Hanusch, 1999 p. 296).

In sum, Schumpeter's instrumentalism was applied to the differentiation between theoretical and historical hypotheses. If we follow the common practice in labeling as 'historicism' an approach which emphasizes the historical method in economics, we can argue that his instrumentalism rejects historicism from static economics. Considering that the instrumentalist postion was mainly taken by natural scientists, it is his unique adaptation that the social scientist Schumpeter, in introducing instrumentalism into economics, paid attention to differences between theoretical and historical hypotheses. To avoid misunderstanding, it should be noted that he never rejected historicism but only separated it from the domain of economic theory. The separation of theory and history on the basis of instrumentalism was his own methodological solution to the *Methodenstreit*. (Shionoya, 1990, pp. 211–12; also found in Hanusch, 1999, pp. 297–8)

Shionoya's paper, 'Taking Schumpeter's Methodology Seriously' (Shionoya, 1992), started his construction of a 'new' field, economic philosophy. Shionoya argues that Schumpeter had begun to construct a systematic framework involving first the sociology of a science, second the methodology of a science, and third the history of a science. By this time Shionoya was referring to all of Schumpeter's works, not mostly to *DWHN* as before. Shionoya speculates that Schumpeter chose to drop the final chapter of *TWE* in the second edition because even in the 1920s he felt embarrassed somewhat by his digression into a general philosophic framework; upon reflection the chapter seemed to him to be too sociological (ibid., p. 346). Shinoya proceeds to a fascinating insight about creative self-consciousness, generally, but derived in good measure from his perception of Schumpeter's own hesitancies: one starts with *statics*, then turns to *dynamics*, and finally there is the problem of fitting one's thought into 'all areas of social life' (ibid., p. 348). Shionoya speculates that the principal value of *CSD* is as an example of trying to make that last jump.

   In this vein, Schumpeter's methodological system is synthesized by seven propositions:

a.   Hypotheses are excogitated.
b.   Theories are not intended to be cognitively descriptive and should not be put directly to a simple test of true or false.
c.   Theories at most are 'merely instruments for . . . description'.
d.   Theories involve efforts to describe facts simply *but completely* (emphasis added).
e.   Effort is wasted in trying to justify hypotheses as a direct avenue to the truth.
f.   'The purpose of hypotheses is to produce a theory fit to facts, and thus they are evaluated by their practical success.'
g.   Facts can exist aside from theories, but 'for any set of observed facts there may be several different theories' (Shionoya, 1992, pp. 353–4).

   Building upon this foundation Shionoya develops a somewhat non-Friedman perception of instrumentalism in that he uses the seven foregoing hypotheses, flanking the sixth with all the others – somewhat like Churchill's statement that 'in war the Truth is so precious it must be thoroughly surrounded with a full complement of lies'.

   Shionoya's two major treatments, indeed polished gems, are his *Schumpeter and the Idea of Social Science: A Metatheoretical Study*

(Shionoya, 1997) and a more recent (and as yet unpublished) paper, 'What is Economic Philosophy: Its Scope and Tasks', given at the meeting of the History of Economics Society, July 2003. The book is not so much an intellectual biography, albeit developed and presented along the lines of the 1992 paper, but an effort to give something of a Kantian intellectual form to what I would call Institutional Economics as it was taught at Wisconsin in my youth. Although it has a basic chronological sequence, its chronology is mixed with foci on specific aspects of Schumpeter's intellectual experiences. There are eleven chapters. In the first, 'The Plan of the Book', Shionoya very nicely shows how the tenth chapter 'History of Science' combines 'Scientists and Social Conditions' (Chapter 2); 'Problems and Methods' (Chapter 3); 'The Sociology of Science' (Chapter 4); 'The Methodology of Science' (Chapter 5); 'Economic Statics' (Chapter 6); 'Economic Dynamics' (Chapter 7); 'The Methodology of Economic Sociology' (Chapter 8); 'Economic Sociology' (Chapter 9). There is a final chapter, 'Value Judgements and Political Economy' (Chapter 11).

The book is really a product of Shionoya's exhaustive knowledge of Schumpeter's writings and Shionoya's 'excogitated' (i.e. Kantian-type) institutionalism. In that sense its virtue, compared to Commons's and Veblen's efforts to explain institutionalism, is that it can be relatively easily grasped. Commons's and Veblen's approach was empirical and the framework was too frequently omitted or often hidden by factual details coming from the law or from customary practices in the product and factor marketplaces.

Finally, Shionoya has in the unpublished paper gone on to the next step, an effort to make the Schumpeterian intellectual experience, viewed as an historical panorama, the basis for developing something new and heretofore missing, a full economic philosophy with a range of methods, coherent structures, and even what has been problematic since the abandonment of Scholasticism – a place for ethics, albeit more akin to Rawlsism than to Revelation.

6 Some concluding remarks

There are several things peculiar to Schumpeter which all students should realize. First, he was both brilliant and clever enough to construct an artificial highly original persona. I have already mentioned that he was never what he 'seemed to be.' In many senses he spent most of his life without a true national identity. He was not the Austrian aristocrat he claimed to be; his ties to Germany were never very evident; and he lacked any interest in American political and economic institutions. The topic of his attitude towards Jews is, I believe, generally mishandled. Wolfgang Stolper's insistence that he was not anti-Semitic seems to me to overlook the history of the times. By the standards of pre-World War I, he was not seen as particularly anti-Semitic; by the standards of pre-World War II his lack of open and uncompromising support for an appointment for Samuelson at Harvard suggests that his position can only be explained by anti-Semitism.

Second, of his many contributions I would think four stand out.

First, after incorporating the Walrasian system into the going feud between the historical approach and the analytical approach to economics, he turned his back on economic statics and thereafter concentrated not on economic dynamics or even business cycles (as he wished he could do) but on the evolution of the capitalist system.

Second, had Max Weber survived, the two of them might have created an institutionalist approach to economics that would have seriously rivaled the British and American Marshall–Pigou–Maynard Keynes 'mainline' tradition.

Third, Schumpeter's principal venture into economic sociology, *CSD*, in spite of its seeming continued popularity, hid its principal contribution, namely the nature of the creative response as the great contribution of private capitalism.

Finally, he stands alone as the great polymath authority in the history of economic thought. And fortunately for us, Yuichi Shionoya has constructed an excogitated institutionalist system that does Schumpeter such credit as he deserves.[22] I venture the guess that Schumpeter's polymathic achievement will be respected but not inspected, and that Schumpeter's achievement will have been revealed to most economists through Shionoya's work.

Notes

1. This chapter is dedicated to Professor Dr. Horst Hanusch, who has done so much to transform the Schumpeter tradition into a sturdy platform upon which he and others have erected numerous fascinating intellectual edifices.
2. A technique is essentially the equivalent of a method. Methodology, by way of contrast, traditionally involves explanations of why one uses one technique rather than another. Put bluntly, methodology involves choosing the right arrow from one's quivers.
3. Apparently other economists have embraced similar duplicities. Alfred Marshall always inflated his father's career and never mentioned that he had been imprisoned for embezzlement. However, Marshall's knowledge of math was valid; he was a Sixth Wrangler.
4. Mengerism was taught in the purported tradition of Carl Menger (as interpreted by his two students, Friedrich von Wieser and his brother-in-law, Eugen von Böhm Bawerk). Within the past decade or two several writers, including Erich Streissler and many others, have demonstrated that these two were quite selective in their 'fashioning' Mengerism – indeed, Menger was much more Austrian historical institution- minded than they admitted. The topic is thoroughly reconsidered and resynthesized in a number of essays, particularly one by Karl Mitford (1990) and then rebutted by Laurence H. White (1990) in a volume edited by Bruce Caldwell (1990). I tend to accept Streissler's interpretation but have to admit that *What Menger Really Meant* is becoming as fashionable as *What Marx Really Meant* a century ago.
5. Many shall purify themselves and be refined, making themselves shining white, but the wicked shall continue in wickedness and none of them shall understand; *only the wise leaders shall understand*' (emphasis added).

6. Böhm-Bawerk favored the sharp riposte; when it was directed against scholars like John Bates Clark, it was seen as bad manners and ignored. Students in the Böhm-Bawerk seminar were not allowed to ignore the thrusts; apparently the two Marxians gave as good as they got.
7. Nevertheless it has never been translated into English.
8. The copyright date is 1912; the book, however, was available for sale in 1911.
9. Weber, like Schumpeter with the Wieser–Böhm-Bawerk mode, was too original to fit into the Schmoller Prussian system, and set out to create a more universalist handbook of economics embracing both the theoretical and historical approaches current at the time. The Weberian project originally involved many volumes, but most appeared after Weber's untimely death.
10. I am inclined to agree with Professor Viner that the framework of this study was filched from the brilliant book on the same topic by Luigi Cossa, whose handling of the subject had been so admired by William Stanley Jevons that he agreed to translate an earlier version into English. Cossa, flattered by such attention from so great a figure, reedited the book for the occasion.
11. While it was clearly dwarfed by HEA it enjoyed a polish and a comprehensiveness that the unfinished HEA lacked. It remains very much worth reading.
12. This decade (from 1917 until 1928) was one personal disaster following another involving not only repeated blows to his professional reputation but also deaths within his immediate family: in a few weeks his mother, his second wife, and his new-born son. These apparently affected his own religiosity, and he became devout in a rather strange way, reporting daily to his dead mother and second wife.
13. It was published some 20 years after his death (Schumpeter, 1970).
14. I have held elsewhere that, had the subtitle been the main title and vice versa, the criteria for judging the book might have worked to Schumpeter's advantage (Perlman, 2003).
15. Several of Schumpeter's students who were being called up for military service have commented to me how embarrassed they were to pay a farewell call on their teacher and hear him say, 'You are fighting the wrong enemy' (the right one being the Soviet Union).
16. Mrs Alexander Gerschenkron seems to have been the key figure in the project since she was able to transcribe his archaic Austrian shorthand notes.
17. In the period between his death and the appearance of the magisterial *HEA*, Mrs Elizabeth Boody Schumpeter and the Oxford Press arranged the publication of a set of his essays on individuals, not including the one on von Schmoller, but adding at the suggestion of his close friend and colleague, Gottfried von Haberler, three short essays on G.F. Knapp, Friedrich von Wieser, and Ladislaus von Bortkiewicz (Schumpeter, 1954c).
18. Schumpeter's total lack of both knowledge about and interest in American history is a major theme in David McCord Wright's essay in the 1951 memorial (Wright, 1951). I have treated elsewhere Schumpeter's ambivalence regarding Wesley Clair Mitchell (Perlman, 1997).
19. This respectful tone was not always present in other pieces he had written.
20. By the time my friendship with Machlup developed (1955–82), it was just after he had read the *HEA*, and his admiration for Schumpeter was even greater than is evident in his 1951 essay. Had Machlup known what Schumpeter had already written as the first two chapters of the *History of Economic Analysis* (but published only posthumously in 1954) where he reversed that judgement, his article would have been even totally laudatory. It focused on, and he seemed to respect him largely for, mostly his work in methodology, based as it was on his vast reading, note taking, capacity for recall, and verbalized intellectual tolerance.

Briefly put, insofar as I can recall my many conversations with Machlup about Schumpeter, I cannot recall any strongly positive remarks other than his respect for the range of Schumpeter's erudition and its impact on his judgments that methodology was not for beginners, that methodological partisanship was worse than ridiculous, and that Schumpeter, a man of incredibly wild statements, was also more than significantly capable of true wisdom. Nonetheless it was Machlup who was at the time asked to write the essay, most probably because Fritz was the one who was recognized as the principal student of economic methodology.

21. Machlup had been the butt of too many of Schumpeter's clever (?) jibes to have liked
     him. I met him only twice. At the first meeting he questioned me pointedly, 'Does your
     father assign CSD in his [famous] Wisconsin course, "Capitalism & Socialism"?' His
     aggressive tone led me to lie: I said that it was on the reading list (it was not). My second
     encounter was at the Columbia University Memorial Service for Wesley Clair Mitchell,
     where he went out of his way to snub the usual *nil nisi bonum* rule reserved for such occa-
     sions (cf. Perlman, 1997, pp. xxvi–xxix).
22. By 'excogitated' I mean an institutionalism that emanates from a set of Platonic essences;
     the more usual variety comes from Aristotelian (and, more properly Francis Bacon's)
     cognitive empirical generalizations. True some philosophers (e.g. John Dewey) were
     principally empiricist, but the great majority have been Platonic realists. Of these
     latter, few have ever regarded institutionalism as more than a hodge-podge of national
     arrangements.

References

Allen, Loring (1991), *Opening Doors: The Life & Work of Joseph Schumpeter*, two vols:
    Volume One *Europe*; Volume Two *America*, with a Foreword by Walt W. Rostow, New
    Brunswick, NJ: Transaction.
Backhouse, Roger, E. (1996), 'Vision and progress in economic truth: Schumpeter after Kuhn',
    in Laurence S. Moss (ed.), *Joseph A. Schumpeter: Historian of Economics*, London:
    Routledge, pp. 21–32.
Blaug, Mark ([1980] 1992), *The Methodology of Economics or How Economists Explain*, New
    York: Cambridge University Press.
Caldwell, Bruce (ed.) (1990), 'Carl Menger and his legacy in economics: annual supplement
    to the *History of Political Economy*', vol. 22, Durham and London: Duke University
    Press.
Chick, Victoria (2003), 'Theory, method, and mode of thought in Keynes's *General Theory*',
    Journal of Economic Methodology, **10**, 307–27.
Dow, Sheila (1985), *Macroeconomic Thought: A Methodological Approach*, New York: Oxford
    University Press.
Friedman, Milton (1953), 'The methodology of positive economics', in Milton Friedman
    (ed.), *Essays in Positive Economics*, Chicago, IL: Chicago University Press, pp. 3–43.
Hanusch, Horst (1999), *The Legacy of Joseph A. Schumpeter*, two vols, Cheltenham, UK and
    Northampton, MA, USA: Edward Elgar.
Jevons, William Stanley ([1874] 1920), *The Principles of Science: A Treatise on Logic and
    Scientific Method*, London: Macmillan.
Keynes, John Maynard (1930), *Treatise on Money*, London: Macmillan.
—— (1936), *The General Theory of Employment, Interest, and Money*, London: Macmillan.
Keynes, John Neville (1891), *The Scope and Method of Political Economy*, London:
    Macmillan.
Kuhn, Thomas (1962), *The Structure of Scientific Revolutions*, Chicago, IL: University of
    Chicago Press.
Kuznets, Simon (1940), 'Review of Joseph Alois Schumpeter's *Business Cycles: A Theoretical,
    Historical, and Statistical Analysis of the Capitalist Process*', *American Economic Review*,
    30, 257–71.
Machlup, Fritz (1951), 'Schumpeter's economic methodology', in Joseph Schumpeter, (1951),
    pp. 95–101.
—— (1982), 'Austrian economics', in Douglas Greenwald (ed.), *Encyclopedia of Economics*,
    New York: McGraw-Hill.
—— (1984), *Knowledge, Its Creation, Distribution, and Economic Significance*, vol. III, *The
    Economics of Information and Human Capital*, Princeton: Princeton University Press.
Marshall, Alfred ([1890] 1946), *Principles of Economics*, 8th edn, originally published 1920,
    London: Macmillan and Company.
März, Eduard (1983), *Joseph Alois Schumpeter – Forscher, Lehrer und Politiker*, Munich: R,
    Oldenbourg Verlag.

McCloskey, D. (1985), 'The rhetoric of economics', *Journal of Economic Literature*, **21**, 481–517.

Mitford, Karl (1990), 'Menger's methodology', in B. Caldwell, 1990, pp. 215–39.

Perlman, Mark (1978), 'Review, *Knowledge and Ignorance in Economics* by Terrence Hutchison', *Journal of Economic Literature*, **16**, 582–5.

—— (1996), *The Character of Economic Thought, Economic Characters, and Economic Institutions*, Ann Arbor: University of Michigan Press.

—— (1997), 'Introduction to the 1997 edition', in J.A. Schumpeter, 1954c, pp. vii–xli.

—— (2001), 'Two Phases of Kuznets's interest in Schumpeter', in Steven G. Medema (ed.), *Economics, Broadly Considered*, London and New York: Routledge, pp. 128–41.

—— (2002), 'Schumpeter and schools of economic thought', in Günther Chaloupek, Alois Guger, Ewald Nowatny and Gerhard Schwödiauer (eds), *Ökonomie in Theorie und Praxis: Festschrift für Helmut Frisch*, Berlin: Springer, pp. 279–96.

—— (2003), 'Career disagreements: Simon Kuznets's relationships with Joseph Alois Schumpeter and Arthur Frank Burns', in Christian Scheer (ed.), *Studien zur Geschichte der ökonomischen Theorie XXII: Ideen, Methoden und Entwicklungen der Dogmengeschichte (Schriften des Vereins für Socialpolitik,* Neue Folge 115/XXII), Berlin: Duncker & Humblot.

Perlman, Mark and Charles R. McCann, Jr (1998), *Pillars of Economic Thought: Ideas and Traditions*, Ann Arbor: University of Michigan Press.

Pribram, Karl (1983), *A History of Economic Reasoning*, Baltimore: Johns Hopkins University Press.

Samuelson, Paul A. (1947), *Foundations of Economic Analysis*, Cambridge, MA: Harvard University Press.

—— (1981), 'Schumpeter as an economic theorist', in H. Frisch (ed.), *Schumpeterian Economics*, Boston: Praeger, pp. 1–27.

Schumpeter, Joseph A. (1906), 'Über die mathematische Methode der theoretischen Ökonomie', *Zeitschrift für Volkswirtschaft, Socialpolitik und Verwaltung*, **15**, 30–49.

—— (1908), *Das Wesen und der Hauptinhalt der theorischen Nationalökonomie*, Leipzig: Duncker & Humblot.

—— (1912), *Theorie der wirtschaftlichen Entwicklung*, Leipzig: Duncker & Humblot.

—— (1914a), *Epochen der Dogmen- und Methodengeschichte*, Tübingen: J.C.B. Mohr, translated in 1954 by R. Aris (see Schumpeter, 1954b).

—— (1914b), 'Eugen von Böhm-Bawerk, 1851–1914', *Zeitschrift für Volkswirtschaft Sozialpolitik und Verwaltung*, **23**, 454–528.

—— (1918), 'Die Krise des Steuerstaates', translated into English in *International Economic Papers*, **6** (1954), 5–38.

—— (1919), 'Zur Soziologie der Imperialismus', *Archiv für Sozialwissenschaft und Sozialpolitik*, **6**, 1–39, 275–310, translated into English as *Imperialism and Social Classes*, in J.A.Schumpeter (1991), *The Economics and Sociology of Capitalism*, edited by R. Swedberg, Princeton: Princeton University Press.

—— (1926), 'Gustav V. Schmoller und die Problem von heute', *Schmollers Jahrbuch für Gesetzgebung, Verwaltung und Volkswirtschaft*, **50**, 337–88.

—— (1927), 'Die socialen Klassen im ethnissch homogenen Milieu', *Archiv für Sozialwissenschaft und Sozialpolitik*, **57**, 1–67, translated into English as *Imperialism and Social Classes*, in J.A. Schumpeter (1991), *The Economics and Sociology of Capitalism*, edited by R. Swedberg, Princeton: Princeton University Press..

—— (1928), 'The instability of our economic system', take given at the meeting of the British Association for the Advancement of Science.

—— (1939), *Business Cycles: A Theoretical, Historical, and Statistical Analysis of the Capitalist Process*, two vols, New York: McGraw-Hill.

—— ([1942] 1947), *Capitalism, Socialism, and Democracy*, 2nd edn, New York: Harper and Bros.

—— (1951), *Essays of J.A. Schumpeter*, edited by Richard V. Clemence, Cambridge: Addison-Wesley Press.

—— ([1954a] 1994), *History of Economic Analysis*, with a new introduction by Mark Perlman, New York: Oxford University Press.

Schumpeter, Joseph A. ([1914] 1954b), *Economic Doctrine and Method*, translated by R. Aris, New York: Oxford University Press.
—— ([1954c] 1997), *Ten Great Economists: From Marx to Keynes*, with an Introduction by Mark Perlman, London: Routledge.
—— (1970), *Das Wesen des Geldes*, edited with an Introduction by Fritz Karl Mann, Göttingen: Vandenhoeck und Ruprecht.
Shionoya, Yuichi (1990), 'Instrumentalism in Schumpeter's economic methodology', *History of Political Economy*, **22**(2), 187–222; reprinted in H. Hanusch, 1999, vol. 2, pp. 273–308.
—— (1992), 'Taking Schumpeter's methodology seriously', *Entrepreneurship, Technological Innovation, and Economic Growth: Studies in the Schumpeterian Tradition*, Ann Arbor: University of Michigan Press, pp. 343–62.
—— (1997), *Schumpeter and the Idea of Social Science: A Metatheoretical Study*, London and New York: Routledge.
—— (2003), 'What is economic philosophy: its scope and tasks', paper given at the meeting of the History of Economics Society, July.
Smithies, Arthur (1950), 'Memorial: Joseph Alois Schumpeter', 1883–1950, in S.E. Harris (ed.), *Schumpeter, Social Scientist*, Cambridge, MA: Harvard University Press.
Stolper, Wolfgang (1994), *Joseph A. Schumpeter: The Public Life of a Private Man*, Princeton: Princeton University Press.
Swedberg, Richard (ed.) (1990), *Economics and Sociology: Redefining their Boundaries: Conversations with Economists and Sociologists*, Princeton: Princeton University Press.
—— (1991), *Schumpeter: A Biography*, Princeton: Princeton University Press.
—— (ed.) (1996), *Economic Sociology*, Cheltenham, UK and Brookfield, USA: Edward Elgar.
—— (1998), *Max Weber and the Idea of Economic Sociology*, Princeton: Princeton University Press.
Tinbergen, Jan (1951), *Econometrics*, London: Allen & Unwin.
Weber, Max (1999), *Essays in Economic Sociology*, edited by Richard Swedberg, Princeton: Princeton University Press.
White, Laurence H. (1990), 'Restoring an "Altered" Menger', in B. Caldwell, 1990, pp. 349–58.
Wright, David McCord (1951), 'Schumpeter's political philosophy', in Joseph A. Schumpeter, 1951, pp. 130–35.

3 Schumpeterian universal social science
Yuichi Shionoya

1 Evolution of mind and society

Joseph Schumpeter is well-known for his two works *Theorie der wirtschaftlichen Entwicklung* (1912) and *History of Economic Analysis* (1954) among others. The former book represented a breakthrough in overcoming the limitations of neoclassical economic statics; it was a unique attempt of economic dynamics identifying the fundamental phenomenon of economic development with the innovations of entrepreneurs. Schumpeter won his immortal reputation with this single book. Although his idea of economic development was disregarded in the Age of Keynes during the third quarter of the twentieth century, it has stimulated the rise of modern evolutionary economics in recent decades, when people's concern has shifted from the short-run to the long-run economic problem. The latter book, published posthumously, was Schumpeter's *tour de force*, which demonstrated that he was perhaps the last of the great polymaths in the history of economics. It was soon accepted as the most authoritative work in the field. Over 50 years after the publication, nothing has taken its place and nothing has equaled it in terms of scale and insight.

Why was Schumpeter interested in both the development of economy and that of economics? One might argue, it is little wonder that an economist has an interest in the history of economics. For Schumpeter, however, the history of economics was not merely the hobby of an erudite scholar; there was a deeper reason for his interest in the history of economics. For him, the developments of society and economy, on the one hand, and the developments of thought and science, on the other, were two aspects of the same evolutionary process. As he was engaged in the development of economy, so was he interested in the history of economic doctrines. In his idea of social science, both developments are social phenomena to which parallel treatments are applied, and he tried to shed light on the interrelationship between mind and society. Schumpeter's interest in both economic development and scientific development was not accidental. He identified the social sciences in the form of eighteenth-century moral philosophy with the 'sciences of mind and society' (1954, p. 141) and characterized especially Giambattista Vico's work as 'an evolutionary science of mind and society' (ibid., p. 137). This idea delineates the nature of Schumpeter's view of social science, which I call a universal social science (Shionoya, 1997).

For Schumpeter, the theory of economic development and the history of economics merely represent two branches of a universal social science that are directly concerned with the evolution of mind and society. His whole work, in fact, covered much wider disciplinary branches. It is argued that his wide-ranging work comprises a system of substantive theory and that of metatheory. Generally speaking, while substantive theory addresses certain natural and social phenomena and covers a variety of particular sciences, metatheory is a reflection on theories and includes the philosophy of science (or the methodology of science), the history of science, and the sociology of science. For instance, economic theory investigates economic behavior, processes, and institutions, while meta economic theory addresses economic theories from the perspectives of philosophy, history, and sociology.

From this viewpoint, Schumpeter's work in the field of substantive theory, on the one hand, consists of three branches: economic statics, economic dynamics, and economic sociology. While the former two belong to the ordinary scope of economics, the latter one is addressed to an economy institutionally embedded in a society. In other words, economic sociology deals with interactions between economy and society. On the other hand, Schumpeter worked in the field of metatheory about economics, too, which also includes three branches: economic methodology, the history of economics, and the sociology of economics. Economic methodology is concerned with the static structure and rules of science applied to economics; the history of economics deals with historical development of economic theories; and the sociology of economics concerns scientific activities of economists as social phenomena.

Thus these two systems are parallel in viewing the economy, on the one hand, and economics, on the other, from the viewpoints of, first, static structure, second, dynamic development, and third, their activities in a social context. In Schumpeter's idea of a universal social science, a set of substantive theories is matched with another set of metatheories with a parallel structure of three layers. Thus I call Schumpeter's universal social science a 'three-layered, two-structure approach to mind and society'.

The two systems are linked together by the sociological dimension in which both economy and knowledge are treated in the social context. He intended this concept to replace Marx's social theory based on the economic interpretation of history. Whereas Marx's theory, another version of a universal social science, addressed the relationship between social relations of production (substructure) and a system of ideology (superstructure), stressing the unilateral influences of the former on the latter, Schumpeter paid attention to the bilateral interaction between economy and ideas. His system of social science should be understood against this broad perspective, in which evolutionary economics of innovation is only a part of Schumpeterian evolutionism of mind and society.

Besides Marx, the most direct impulse toward a universal social science was an insight Schumpeter gained by reflection on the *Methodenstreit* between theory and history at the end of the nineteenth century and the research program of the German Historical School, especially of Gustav von Schmoller. Adopting the German Historical School's viewpoint of historical development as a global process, Schumpeter regarded Schmoller's approach as the prototype of economic sociology and argued that economic sociology or institutional analysis of economic history would realize the synthesis of theory and history (Schumpeter, 1926).

The ambitious aim Schumpeter cherished throughout his academic life was a 'comprehensive sociology'. Comprehensive sociology is an approach to social phenomena as a whole and is supposed to be a synthesis of interactions between every single area and all others in a society. Its core idea is the *Soziologisierung* of all social sciences (Schumpeter, 1915). In the light of this goal, he only dealt with two sociologies, i.e. economic sociology and the sociology of science, which may be regarded as his strategic version of a comprehensive sociology. Instead of attempting sociological approaches to every single area of the humanities and social sciences and synthesizing them into a comprehensive system, Schumpeter depended on the dichotomy between real, social fields including economy, on the one hand, and ideal, cultural fields including science, on the other, in accordance with the idea of the contemporary German sociology of culture. By putting both fields in a global social context, it was possible to inquire into an essential interaction between mind and society and the resultant evolutionary process.

2 Fundamental ideas

So much for the structure of the Schumpeterian system. Now I will set out the fundamental ideas characterizing the substance of the system, referring to his publications. There are three important ideas: (1) the methodology of instrumentalism, (2) the relationship between economic statics and dynamics, and (3) evolutionary economic sociology.

(1) Schumpeter's first book, *Das Wesen und der Hauptinhalt der theoretischen Nationalökonomie* (1908) recapitulated the theoretical essence and the methodological foundation of neoclassical economics established by the Marginalist Revolution in the 1870s. He adapted the scientific methodology of Ernst Mach's instrumentalism to Walras's general equilibrium theory (Shionoya, 1990a). Instrumentalism is the view that theories are not descriptions of reality but instruments for deriving useful results and are neither true nor false. He defined science as tooled knowledge. Therefore, the

realism of assumptions in a corpus of theories does not matter. His view of instrumentalism is more flexible and pragmatic than the current conception in that the usefulness of theories is not limited to predictability but includes not only the generation of predictions but also the classification, organization, and explanation of observable phenomena and guides for action.

Schumpeter was also influenced by Mach's phenomenology, according to which science should not indulge in a metaphysical speculation that assumes the essence behind phenomena, and it should reject the notion of causality, which attributes phenomena to some ultimate cause. Mach argued that one should address only functional relationships between elements that are found in the phenomenal world through sensual experiences. Walras's general equilibrium model conceptualizes the world in terms of general interdependence between prices and quantities of goods and factors of production. Schumpeter discovered in Walras's theory the best case for the application of phenomenalism, and this is the reason why he admired Walras so much.

Schumpeter's instrumentalist methodology aimed partly at a contribution to the solution of the *Methodenstreit* by making a distinction and a separation between theoretical and historical methods. According to this methodology, it is of no use to quarrel about the superiority of historical and theoretical methods because they are tools designed for different purposes. Instrumentalism was first developed by Schumpeter to lay a foundation for neoclassical economics but later functioned as an anchor in his attempt to construct a universal social science. In the field of economic sociology, the integration rather than the separation of theory and history is conceived as research agenda, because it is necessary to formulate historical phenomena by theoretical hypotheses. His methodological work can be compared to Max Weber's theory of ideal type, which was another solution to the *Methodenstreit*.

(2) For Schumpeter, a general equilibrium in economic statics was the logic of an economy that formulated the consequences of the adaptive behavior of economic agents responding to their exogenously given circumstances. He regarded economic statics as the Magna Carta of economic theory in the sense that economics should be established as an exact and autonomous science. Economic statics is concerned with the process of circular flow, in which the economy repeats itself year after year, with its size and structure remaining constant under given conditions. According to Schumpeter, economic growth through an increase in population and capital can be explained by economic statics because these changes are exogenous. Although often misunderstood, economic statics, in his view, is not an abstract, unrealistic construction but explains real forces in an economic process.

In sharp contrast with economic statics, Schumpeter constructed economic dynamics or theory of economic development in *Theorie der wirtschaftlichen Entwicklung*. He defined economic development by reference to three elements: its cause (innovation), its carrier (entrepreneurship), and its means (bank credit). Economic development is the destruction of circular flow or 'creative destruction' when entrepreneurs introduce innovations, including new products, new techniques, new markets, new sources of supply and new organizations. His basic idea of evolutionism was that both the cause of changes in an economic system and the response mechanism to those changes must be endogenous; thus he regarded the entrepreneurial activity of innovation as the cause of economic development and the formulation of business cycles as the process of absorbing the impact of innovation with a response mechanism. Since economic development is conceived as the destruction of equilibrium, it cannot be an object of scientific inquiry unless it is linked epistemologically with some mechanism of restoring order. Whatever destructive forces of innovation may emerge in the economy, markets can be relied on to adapt to them and absorb their effects in order to establish new equilibrium. In this sense, Schumpeter emphasized that economic dynamics should be accompanied by, and based on, economic statics.

Underlying the distinction between statics and dynamics is the distinction between the conceptions of man: the hedonistic man and the energetic man. The former is the mass of the people; the latter is the leader. The entrepreneur is a special kind of leader in the economic domain. The leader as the carrier of innovations in a particular area of social life is in marked contrast to the majority of people who only take adaptive or routine actions. Schumpeter believed that such a contrast exists not only in economy but also in science, the arts, politics, and so on. He applied the statics–dynamics dichotomy to various aspects of social life as the fundamental idea of a universal social science.

(3) Economic dynamics was merely a midpoint in social studies toward a universal social science, because even if both innovation and response mechanism that are requisite for economic development are explained endogenously within an institutional framework, the capitalist economic system is exogenously given. Moreover, the occurrence of the entrepreneurial activity of technological change cannot be explained by his theory; it remains in a 'black box' that is exogenous to the economic system. Inquiries concerning the black box of innovations were left to Schumpeterian economists after World War II. Schumpeter found in economic sociology a way out of the difficulty. The evolution of capitalism, in his view, must be explained in terms of the changing relationship between the economic and non-economic domains, or between mind and society. The general idea of the

evolution of a society as a whole through the interrelations among areas where different sorts of innovations occur was first shown in Chapter 7 of the first edition of his *Theorie der wirtschaftlichen Entwicklung*. Although he kept this idea, since this chapter was omitted from subsequent editions, the idea has been little known (Shionoya, 1990b).

Early in his academic life in the 1910s, Schumpeter began sociological studies and focused on a theory of social class that would serve as the crucial link between the concept of leadership in various areas of social life, on the one hand, and the overall concept of civilization or the *Zeitgeist*, on the other. The work was published much later as 'Die sozialen Klassen in ethnisch homogenen Milieu' (1927). This sociological link became the key to his famous thesis of failing capitalism in *Capitalism, Socialism and Democracy* (1942), the most widely read book among his writings. In this book Schumpeter fully developed evolutionary economic sociology to address the interaction between economic and non-economic areas with an intermediary of social class theory. Rejecting the view that capitalism would fall because of its economic failure, he presented a provocative thesis that the very success of capitalism in economic terms would erode its social and moral foundations by changes in the ethos of social classes. Thus capitalist economic development driven by the innovation of entrepreneurs will in the long run make the *Zeitgeist* of the society anticapitalistic and this in turn will gradually create a social atmosphere in which it is more difficult for innovations to occur. He emphasized that his thesis of failing capitalism was not a historical prediction but a theoretical deduction based on a universal social science.

Schumpeter summarized the above description of evolutionary economic sociology by introducing the concept of 'institution'. He defined economic sociology as 'a sort of generalized or typified or stylized economic history' (1954, p. 20). It is the concept of an institution that can generalize, typify, or stylize the complexities of economic history. In his view, the concept of institution is intended to achieve the synthesis of theory and history in that, while it is a means of generalizing historical events, it is limited owing to its historical relativity. It can be conceived as a compromise between the generality meant by theory and the individuality meant by history. Thus, economic sociology consists of an analysis of institutions that are exogenously given to economic theory and is identified with the fourth basic method of economics besides theory, statistics, and history.

It is the core proposition of institutional economics that institutions and individuals constitute an action–information loop. Institutions are social norms, consisting of law, morality, and customs. Institutions offer information on normative rules to individuals, and actions of individuals, in turn, provide institutions with habitual behaviors. While the former process is concerned with individuals embedded in a society complying with a given static order, the latter process can involve dynamic deviations from customs and routines. Schumpeter sometimes called the institutional totality simply the *Zeitgeist* that exists outside the economy. Therefore, the action–information loop between institutions and individuals presents another picture of the interaction between economic and non-economic areas, in addition to the interaction through social classes. Institutional economics and economic sociology provide complementary approaches to the goal of a comprehensive sociology.

3   Rhetoric, vision and ideology

Now I will bring in some philosophical categories to explore implications of Schumpeter's metatheoretical reflection on the discipline of economics. Philosophy is critical thinking of a systematic kind about knowledge and consists of three major branches: epistemology (or methodology), ontology (or metaphysics), and axiology (or ethics), each branch being concerned with 'method, existence, and value' of knowledge, respectively. Correspondingly, economic philosophy as a particular branch of philosophy would cover economic methodology, economic ontology, and economic ethics. Thus we have a system of meta economic theory (i.e. economic methodology, the history of economics, and the sociology of economics) and a system of economic philosophy (i.e. economic methodology, economic ontology, and economic ethics). Both systems are reflections on economic knowledge including economic theory and economic thought. The system of metatheory overlaps with the system of economic philosophy at the branch of economic methodology.

A short remark in terms of these concepts on the contemporary state of economic methodology and science theory will be useful to elucidate an aspect of Schumpeter's contributions to a universal social science. After the reign of logical positivism was over, the philosophy of science remarkably shifted its interests from the static and normative rules of scientific activities to the historical and sociological aspects of science actually occurring in scientific forums and laboratories. In this respect, Schumpeter's work in the history and the sociology of science is to be noted.

Although Schumpeter did not work directly on a system of economic philosophy, his extensive work on the history and the sociology of science is interpreted as relevant to important aspects of economic philosophy. In terms of the tripartite branches of philosophy, the current transformation of economic methodology will necessitate the tripartite transformation or extension of philosophical approaches to economic knowledge 'from methodology to rhetoric', 'from ontology to vision' and 'from ethics to ideology'. This new set of notions or their mixture (i.e. rhetoric, vision, and ideology) may be labeled 'economic thought'. Under the rule of logical positivism these notions were regarded as elements of prescientific or unscientific activities that should be removed from science, but have survived under the guise of obscure notions such as economic thought or economic philosophy distinct from economic analysis and have been stored in the history of economics. Schumpeter was unique in taking these notions seriously in his metatheoretical reflection of economic knowledge. Although he distinguished between economic thought and economic theory, or between vision and model, he did not mean that each stage is independent of the other, or that economic thought and vision must be removed from the consideration of the philosophy of science. He emphasized instead that vision influences model, and tried to take out some solid factors from the black box of the prescientific process.

It is argued that economic thought includes political claims about economic issues, on the one hand, and basic ideas and conceptions underlying economic theory, on the other. The former is 'ideology', the latter is 'vision'. In economic thought ideology and vision are inseparably related to each other and supported by the methods of 'rhetoric', although they include some elements of economic analysis. The structure of economic thought in terms of 'rhetoric, vision, and ideology' is parallel to that of traditional philosophy in terms of 'epistemology, ontology, and ethics'. Both structures represent different levels of approaches to the three aspects of economic knowledge, i.e. 'method, existence, and value'.

Among the four sets of notions relating to economic knowledge (i.e. substantive economic theory, meta economic theory, economic philosophy, and economic thought), the elements most characteristic of Schumpeter are economic sociology, instrumentalist methodology, and rhetoric. The discussion of this combination will further clarify the nature of the scope and method of Schumpeter's universal social science (Shionoya, 2004).

On the ontological level, realism maintains that what actually exists in any area of thought is a fixed structure independent of our beliefs and statements. In contrast, anti-realism claims that what we call reality is nothing but a conceptual construct. In economics, one cannot but deal with the unobservable non-material or non-physical world, which includes mental entities such as wants, intentions, beliefs, values, meanings, expectations, etc. and social relations such as equilibrium, competition, externalities, classes, conventions, institutions, etc. Scientific realism in social science insists on the reality of these things. Without worrying about the reality of entities on the ontological level, instrumentalists using its view of science oppose realism on the epistemological level and avoid fruitless debates on the reality and truthfulness of assumptions concerning unobservable entities. They emphasize the practical purposes of science. This was the basic methodological standpoint of Joseph Schumpeter.

From the standpoint of instrumentalism, there is no real issue about ontology because metaphysical propositions are not capable of being tested. It will suffice to say that social objects of studies are posited by the vision of social scientists. Schumpeter's famous article 'Science and Ideology' (1949) discussed the paramount importance of vision as a prescientific act. Vision, consisting of metaphysical propositions, provides a quarry from which hypotheses can be derived. Without them we would not know what it is that we want to know.

Schumpeter's conception of ideology includes not only political claims but also preconceptions prevailing in science and society. For him, because scientific work takes place in a socially continuous process, vision is shaped by ideology. Particularly, in addressing an unexplored field of economic sociology, Schumpeter relied on the literary tools of rhetoric (i.e. antithesis, metaphor, and paradox) to articulate his vision for the formulation of assumptions and hypotheses (Shionoya, forthcoming). They are indispensable to the conveyance of empirical or intuitive knowledge in the form of vision. He admitted that the role of vision is significant in the study of long-term process of change because theoretical formulation and its justification in this field are so difficult that vision must remain as vision. In order that vision may become socially shared knowledge, it must be presented through the tool of rhetoric. No other methods were available. Schumpeter is well-known for his vivid rhetoric. For him, rhetoric was not a figure of speech but a tool of thought.

References

Schumpeter, Joseph Alois (1908), *Das Wesen und der Hauptinhalt der theoretischen Nationalökonomie*, Leipzig: Duncker & Humblot.
—— (1912), *Theorie der wirtschaftlichen Entwicklung*, Leipzig: Duncker & Humblot; English translation: *The Theory of Economic Development*, Cambridge, MA: Harvard University Press, 1934.
—— (1915), *Vergangenheit und Zukunft der Sozialwissenschaften*, Leipzig: Duncker & Humblot.
—— (1926), 'Gustav v. Schmoller und die Probleme von heute', *Schmollers Jahrbuch*.
—— (1927), 'Die sozialen Klassen in ethnisch homogenen Milieu', *Archiv für Sozialwissenschaft und Sozialpolitik*; English translation: *Imperialism and Social Classes*, New York: Augustus M. Kelly, 1951.
—— (1942), *Capitalism, Socialism and Democracy*, New York: Harper & Brothers, 3rd edn, 1950.
—— (1949), 'Science and ideology', *American Economic Review*, **39**(2), 346–59.
—— (1954), *History of Economic Analysis*, New York: Oxford University Press.
Shionoya, Yuichi (1990a), 'Instrumentalism in Schumpeter's economic methodology', *History of Political Economy*.
—— (1990b), 'The origin of the Schumpeterian research program: a chapter omitted from Schumpeter's *Theory of Economic Development*', *Journal of Institutional and Theoretical Economics*.

Shionoya, Yuichi (1997), *Schumpeter and the Idea of Social Science: A Metatheoretical Study*, Cambridge: Cambridge University Press.

—— (2004), 'Scope and method of Schumpeter's universal social science: economic sociology, instrumentalism, and rhetoric', *Journal of the History of Economic Thought*, September.

—— (forthcoming), 'Joseph Alois Schumpeter: the economist of rhetoric', in Jürgen Backhaus (ed.), *The Founders of Modern Economy: Maastricht Lectures in Political Economy*, Cheltenham, UK and Northampton, MA, USA: Edward Elgar.

4 The pillars of Schumpeter's economics: micro, meso, macro

Kurt Dopfer

1 Introduction

This chapter attempts a fresh look at Schumpeter's theoretical edifice. The purpose is not to give a comprehensive or complete account; magisterial works providing exactly this already exist, such as those by Wolfgang Stolper (1994), Richard Swedberg (1991), Mark Perlman and Charles McCann (1998) and Yuichi Shionoya (1997). Instead, we investigate the theoretical corpus of Schumpeter's economics with a view to its possible and actual influence on the construction of a modern Neo-Schumpeterian programme. We shall, on the one hand, briefly highlight the generic architecture of economics as inspired by Schumpeter's work, and, on the other hand, discuss Schumpeter's specific theoretical positions against this background. Turning to the latter, not only do we draw on Schumpeter's theoretical work directly but we also try to achieve a deeper understanding of his theory by looking at the way in which he criticises competing positions, in particular those of classical and neoclassical economics. This will provide us with an idea of what Schumpeter thought a good theory to be.

The main proposition of this chapter is that Schumpeter launched a revolution along a trajectory from micro to meso, and, with less distinction, from meso to macro. It is argued that his inspiration was the introduction into economics – from the standpoint of contemporary economics – of a *micro–meso–macro* framework.[1] For the micro, Schumpeter put the energetic entrepreneur centre stage. Not only did he introduce the term 'methodological individualism' but, more importantly, he drew a clear line of distinction between the neoclassical *Homo oeconomicus*, who only reacted to given opportunities, and the energetic innovative individual, who engaged actively in changing these opportunities. The consequences of this theoretical position were far-reaching. Sketched briefly, a novelty represents an idea that can be actualised by many agents. The theoretical body received, therefore, a qualitative element (an idea) and a numerical specification of its actualisation (a population). Thus micro cannot be aggregated into macro, since qualities cannot be added up and the individual agent has to be treated as a distinct member of a population. What emerges is a meso unit that gives micro its distinct position, and that constitutes the building block for the construction of macro. In this view, the course of formulating the theory is not from micro to macro but – with no short cut possible – from micro to meso, and from there to macro.

Schumpeter's major contribution was, as we shall see, in the theoretical exposition of micro and meso. He entertained a grand vision, as laid down, for instance, in his *Capitalism, Socialism and Democracy* (Schumpeter, 1942), but he failed to provide a clear theoretical exposition that would show how the meso components of the economic system are dynamically coordinated, or how the 'circular flow' is structured, and how, in this way, economic development occurred as a process of structural change. It is interesting that the body of contemporary Neo-Schumpeterian contributions essentially mirrors Schumpeter's original research programme. There is a wealth of important contributions on micro and meso but less so on macro, as it emerges as a complex structure from the dynamic interplay of micro and meso and as it changes incessantly over time 'from within' (Hanusch and Pyka, 2005).

2   Coordination and change

All sciences resemble one another in that they deal, on the one hand, with relationships among elements and, on the other hand, with the behaviour of the whole over time. Economics is no exception, and, at its most fundamental, the questions of economics are how the economic activities of many individuals are coordinated and how the economy changes over time.

The birth of modern economics in the second half of the nineteenth century was largely a response to two grand revolutions, and the general questions of coordination and change received a particular historical mark. The first revolution was a *politico-economic* one, and gave individuals high degrees of freedom in their operations. The founders of the discipline had a natural curiosity with respect to the theoretical treatment of coordination under conditions of a free, rather than regulated, market economy (as had prevailed in the *ancien régime*). The other revolution was *technological–industrial*. Epochal inventions, such as the steam engine and the mechanical loom, led to a path of unprecedented economic growth and broad structural change. Both the bourgeois–liberal and the technological–industrial revolution set the stage for economics as a modern science. In a metaphoric nutshell, economists gained interest in the 'invisible hand' (Adam Smith) and, in the forces that changed by 'creative destruction', the economy 'from within' (Schumpeter).

The two great disciplinary questions provided the inspiration for various theoretical answers. From the point of view of the history of theory development, we can distinguish broadly between classical and neoclassical economics.

3   The received doctrines

Dealing with Schumpeter's assessment of classical and neoclassical economics, it is appropriate to recognise that he took his position to be a yardstick for the assessment of the work of others. He missed few opportunities to make it clear that a theory that failed to acknowledge the central role of the entrepreneur was fundamentally flawed.

Using this lens, Schumpeter brought the works of the classical economists into particularly sharp focus. The proponents of the classical doctrine worked with aggregate resource magnitudes, and they proposed looking for objective laws in their relationships. The activities of individuals had no role to play in this objective machinery, and were at best epiphenomena, explained by, but not explaining, the aggregate relationships. Schumpeter, for one thing, objected to the view that all economic development was bound to terminate in a secular stationary state. In this way, David Ricardo and Thomas Malthus conceived economic development as a process whereby population increases led to decreasing marginal returns from agriculture, collapsing eventually into the stationary state of a secular subsistence equilibrium. This 'dismal vision' enjoyed a revival in the works of the stagnationists of the times, who held – confirming the predictive conjectures of their classical precursors – that 'the capitalist system has spent its powers, . . . that our economy is, amid convulsions, settling down to a State of Secular Stagnation' (Schumpeter, 1954/1986, p. 570). Contemporary authors such as Alvin Hansen failed, in Schumpeter's view, to recognise that individuals had the power eventually to counter the alleged immanent objective forces, and that these could never force the system into a secular stationary state.

Schumpeter's objectivist critique was not targeted specifically at the stagnationists but included all strands of the classical canon. His critique did not concern the particular direction of the developmental course, or the differences in weight given to its determining factors, but merely the notion that economic change could be explained on the basis of objective laws. The nature of those laws was irrelevant; that is, they could be associated either with entropic forces or with new ideas and knowledge growth. For Schumpeter, the essential point was that development was always propelled by the 'agens' of the entrepreneur, and that 'in technical or organisational progress there is no autonomous momentum which carries in itself a developmental law, which would be due to progress in our knowledge. [. . .] There is no automatic progress' (1912, p. 480). It is impossible to understand Schumpeter's disregard of Adam Smith's work unless one realises that his criticism was not aimed at the categories of the proposed determinants as such but, rather, at their presumed objective nature. From his antiobjectivist platform, Schumpeter issued an indictment of several authors, such as Friedrich List, but the central target was Smith. There is 'nothing original' in his writings, Schumpeter says, except that,

> nobody, either before or after A. Smith, ever thought of putting such a burden upon division of labour. With A. Smith it is practically the only factor in economic progress. [. . .] Technological progress, 'invention of all those machines' – and even investments – is induced by it and is, in fact, just an incident of it . . . Division of labour itself is attributed to an inborn propensity to truck and its development to the gradual expansion of markets – the extent of the market at any point of time determining how far it can go. It thus appears and grows as an entirely impersonal force, and since it is the great motor of progress, this progress too is depersonalised. (1954/1986, p. 188)

Schumpeter highlighted innovations as the central driving force of development, and Smith analogously emphasised the power of innovations unlike any other classical writer, but still no other economist of that strand had to suffer a comparable disregard. It was, arguably, precisely this close congeniality that prompted Schumpeter to take Smith's work as an exemplar for demonstrating the essential difference between his and the classical approach.

4   Methodological individualism

Neoclassical economics ushered in a wind of change. In Schumpeter's view, it introduced a major innovation by acknowledging that the individual agent was central to the formation of economic theory. Its pioneers, such as Léon Walras, William Stanley Jevons, Heinrich Gossen and Vilfredo Pareto, understood that a proper theoretical account of economic phenomena was inconceivable on the basis of objective laws, but was bound to be premised on an understanding of individual cognition and behaviour. Schumpeter did not merely endorse this view but also made a significant contribution to its methodological underpinnings. Inspired by the writings of Carl Menger, he introduced into the project the concept of 'methodological individualism' (Heertje, 2004). He gave a term to what already united the neoclassical writers and what made them distinct with respect to their classical precursors.

The question that arises is whether Schumpeter actually belongs to the neoclassical camp. After all, he is usually considered to represent a major heterodox figure of contemporary economics. A look at the origins of the concept provides us with the essential cue. The neoclassical economists set out to solve the problem of Smith's 'invisible hand'. Their problem was static, and Pareto's construal of *Homo oeconomicus* was designed to serve this purpose. *Homo oeconomicus* only reacts to opportunities, but in no way changes them. Schumpeter's theoretical problem, in turn, was not static, but dynamic. *Homo oeconomicus* was designed to solve the problems of static analysis, and, because it was successful in doing so, it proved inherently inappropriate for solving the dynamic problem.

It is here that Schumpeter's entrepreneur enters the scene. Methodological individualism can thus be interpreted as having two distinct components: one that deals with passive (reactive) individual behaviour, and another that deals with (pro)active individual behaviour. There is, in this way,

passive methodological individualism, and
active methodological individualism

While Schumpeter did not introduce this distinction explicitly, he left no doubt in his writings that neoclassical economics was flawed because it featured only passive methodological individualism – ignoring its active counterpart. Schumpeter was not just an innovator with regard to the concept of methodological individualism; he also completed it.

5 Meso economics

This was only the beginning of the story, however. In Schumpeter's interpretation, the active individual was not active simply in terms of ongoing operations under given conditions, but also – and decisively – in terms of changing these conditions. Most significantly, the active agent changes the conditions by introducing into the system a new idea. Naturally, not all ideas are economically relevant, and we must distinguish analytically between those ideas that are relevant and those that are not. We consider as relevant those ideas that can serve as a basis for economic operations. We call an idea useful for economic operations a generic idea or generic rule (Dopfer, 2005; Dopfer and Potts, 2007). A generic rule – say, technology – can, *qua* idea, often be actualised. The idea imposes no limitations on the frequency of its physical actualisation. There is 'one-ness' in the rule, but 'many-ness' in its actualisations.

The process of actualising a rule (Y) follows a distinct historic logic over time, with an inception ($1/n$, $(n-1)/n$), an unfolding (Y/n, $(n-Y)/n$) and a termination (n/n, $0/n$). There is, therefore, 'first-ness' ($1/n$) in the adoption of a new rule. The first adoption of a rule (the innovation) must be distinguished from its first occurrence (the invention). Schumpeter emphasised in all his works that the major task of the generically active agent – the entrepreneur – lies in the carrying out of new combinations in the market and not in finding new ideas. The energetic entrepreneur is followed by a swarm of imitating, generically passive adopters (Y/n). The process settles down in a (temporarily) stable pattern of relative adoption frequency, whereby all adopters who wanted to adopt the rule have actually adopted it (n/n, and $0/n$, if competing rule X is eliminated). We shall provide this abstract skeleton with some empirical flesh when discussing Schumpeter's contribution based on the notion of the meso trajectory (Section 7).

At this juncture it is important to recognise that Schumpeter's thoughts had a subversive nature, in that they were capable of challenging the foundations of economics. In abstract attire, there is one-ness of idea, and many-ness of physical actualisations. Ontologically, there is bimodality. This yields an elementary analytical unit with two distinct components. One is structural; the other processual. As idea, meso represents a component of a (macro) structure. It relates to other ideas in its mode of quality. As physical actualisation, meso unfolds in time (and space). The structural component, if expressed in a temporal context, must be conceived of as the process component stated in terms of the historical logic proposed. The macro structure is to be viewed, if actualised, as being composed of structure-specific process components.

Neoclassical economics does not specify a comparable elementary unit for the theoretical elucidation of structure and process. Its mono-modality leads to a uniform micro unit that can be aggregated and disaggregated in its qualitatively unspecified quantities *ad libitum*. It lacks a qualitative specification (an idea or rule) and a numerical specification (a population of adopters). It can, therefore, serve neither as a structure component nor as a process component. At this point, the question may arise whether other, notably classical and Marshallian, approaches provide a meso unit with the stated properties. As it happens, the two approaches do indeed resemble the meso unit sketched. It is also the case, however, that they lack the essential features that relate to the bimodality of the construal, and as a consequence it is preferable to refer to them as quasi- or proto-meso approaches.

6   Proto-meso: classical economics and Alfred Marshall

Classical economics approaches meso with its concepts of natural and actual price. The natural price is the market price under 'normal circumstances', towards which the prices of all commodities are continuously gravitating. Particular circumstances may keep the actual market price above the natural price. We may interpret this such that these particular circumstances represent the introduction of a novelty, and the entrepreneur has (as the monopolist) an innovation rent. The actual price would then differ initially from the natural price. Subsequently, there would be a tendency for the actual price to gravitate towards the natural price. This is a good approximation of what can indeed be observed in real economies. The classical economists interpreted this differently, however. They were prepared to regard factors such as natural disasters, governmental price regulations or organised monopoly power as particular circumstances causing a price deviation, but they did not make any systematic reference to technical (or other) innovations. The natural price represents a static datum, defined by the market form of competition. This market form is not itself an emergent property of a meso process. Furthermore, individuals are not introduced into the theory, and in fact are not required given the objective 'law of gravity'. Nonetheless, the dynamics of meso can be explained only on the basis of a process of interactions among individuals, and not in terms of a commodity aggregate attracted by a centre of gravitation. The defects of the theoretical construct show up, essentially, in two ways. On the one hand, there is no explanation of the dynamics of market forms, which figured prominently in Schumpeter's work (for example, Schumpeter, 1912/1934). On the other hand, the classical model fails to tackle adequately major aspects of the meso process, such as diffusion, macroscopic adoption, selection and path dependence.

Another important case of quasi-meso is provided by Marshall's distinction between short- and long-run demand and supply schedules. Marshall introduced time into analytical processes, and showed how equilibria shift over time because of certain factors. These include economies of scale internal to an industry, demand shifts, and classical factors such as population and capital accumulation. Again, though, technological progress does not figure as a key factor. There is no systematic assumption about an initial innovation that evolves along a technological or other knowledge trajectory. A difference with regard to the classical canon exists, however, in that Marshall did employ methodological individualism. This provides an explanatory potential, but, again, when specifying the concept, he introduced the construct of the 'representative firm'. An account of meso relies crucially on the premise of the heterogeneity of agents. Schumpeter's distinction between the entrepreneur and the 'statische Wirte' (for example, managers) is an exemplar for this essential kind of heterogeneity in meso. As a consequence, Marshall failed to explain the meso process, and his analysis eventually drew on classical factors and the operant notions of elasticities and shifting schedules. There are objective determinants on the one side, and shifting quantities on the other, but no generic process. Marshall had an evolutionary vision, and, from everything that we know about his life, he was frustrated when he attempted to match it to his actual work.

7 Schumpeter's meso trajectory

The meso unit inspired by Schumpeter's work constitutes both a structural component and a process component. The structural component must be brought into analytical perspective by relating it to other structural components and by then combining them into a structured whole. Schumpeter's contribution to the integration of the meso component into a macro structure is discussed in the next section. Here we discuss Schumpeter's contribution to meso as a process component.

A novel idea or rule is viewed as being physically actualised along a three-phase trajectory. To facilitate the discussion, we may further subdivide each of the phases, and specify the trajectory on the basis of six (sub-) phases. Turning to the initial analytical outline, the three phases are: origination; adoption; retention. In the first phase, origination, the distinction is between the creation and the discovery of a new idea; in the next phase, adoption, it is between the initial and the many following adoptions; and in the terminal phase, retention, the distinction is between the stabilising and destabilising forces determining the generic rule regime. The six-phase dynamic was originally introduced as a schema for a comparative theory study that included neoclassical, Austrian and evolutionary/Schumpeterian economics (Dopfer, 1993). In the following, the discussion is confined to the contribution that Schumpeter made to the theoretical elucidation of the six trajectory phases. These can be summarised as follows.

I   **Origination**
     Sub-phase 1:   creation of novel idea, innovative potential
     Sub-phase 2:   search, discovery and recognition process, microscopic selection
II   **Adoption**
     Sub-phase 3:   first adoption, chaotic environment, bifurcation, uncertain outcome
     Sub-phase 4:   macroscopic adoption of 'seed', selective environment, path dependence
III **Retention**
     Sub-phase 5:   retention of adopted 'seed', meta-stability of actualisation process
     Sub-phase 6:   existing regime as breeding ground for novel potential(s), link to phase I

Schumpeter's key contribution lies in his analysis of sub-phases 2, 3 and 4. The *locus classicus* of his analysis is phase II. In sub-phase 3 (the first stage of adoption) the entrepreneur puts a new combination into practice, changing the environment by initiating a new meso trajectory, which eventually gains momentum in sub-phase 4 (the second stage). The latter is, generally, a population process, which can be specified theoretically in various ways. Schumpeter focused on the dynamics of capitalist market forms, such as monopoly, oligopoly and competition, and discussed their welfare and societal consequences. Neo-Schumpeterian economics has an explicit population core, from which diffusion, selection, path dependence and related models can be developed and the original market dynamic integrated. A further link is from Schumpeter's adoption phase II to the second stage of origination (sub-phase 2), which displays entrepreneurial activities with regard to the search and discovery of new ways of doing things.

The lacunae in Schumpeter's work are sub-phases 1, 5 and 6. In all his work Schumpeter emphasised that it is not the creation but the carrying out of new ideas that is relevant for coping with the phenomenon of economic development. 'There are always changes in an economy, and we are not closer to the exhaustion of possibilities today than we were in the stone age' (1912, p. 161). While this is a reasonable conjecture, it does not provide us with an appropriate micro foundation for a theory of a knowledge-based economy in which the creation of knowledge is a pivotal factor and requires theoretical recognition. The lack of explication for sub-phase 1 is a major theoretical shortcoming in Schumpeter's work (Witt, 2002).

The second lacuna refers to phase III, which, essentially, deals with institutional factors. Schumpeter refers to institutions and related factors occasionally, as when arguing that habits, once 'hammered in', become 'as firmly rooted in ourselves as a railway embankment in the earth' (Loasby, 1999), but he fails to deal with phase III systematically. Significantly, meso builds on the notion of circularity between individual and population. The trajectory dynamic unfolds not as a diffusion of a single valued variable but, rather, as a process in which individuals interact with an emergent population in a self-reinforcing way. Thorstein Veblen analysed this process on the basis of his concept of circular and cumulative causation. Schumpeter, instead, stressed the significance of the linear causality principle (Schumpeter, 1912), which poses various problems when dealing with meso. Not only is a population an aggregate of individual behaviours but, frequently, it also becomes an (order) parameter that feeds back to individual behaviour. The application of the linear causality principle excludes a broad range of models subsumed under the term 'path dependence', and following this principle would narrow down the scope of a Neo-Schumpeterian programme drastically.

8   The generic architecture of the economy

While this critique may be justified, however, it cannot distract from Schumpeter's principal merit: laying the foundations of meso.

Given its bimodality, macro emerges in this framework as a two-storey structure. It is composed of a '*deep*' level, of ideas or generic rules, and a '*surface*' level, of their physical actualisations. The critical task of theory making in this framework is the translation of meso into the thus defined macro.

How did Schumpeter deal with the task of explaining coordination and change at the two levels? A theoretical account of the 'deep' level of coordination and change refers, essentially, to the division of knowledge and labour. It is remarkable not only that Schumpeter explicitly rejects the essential message of chapters 1 and 2 of Smith's *Wealth of Nations* (Section 3) but also that he largely fails to make any attempt to deal with the problem of coordination and change at the 'deep' generic level.

The 'surface' level of the actual process can be associated with Schumpeter's concept of 'circular flow'. He borrowed this concept from the classical economists, and employed it in the first two chapters of his *The Theory of Economic Development* (1912/1934). In the first chapter he provides an impressive *tour d'horizon* of classical theories and identifies a host of factors determining the system's stationarity. He views stationarity as an equilibriated flow defined in terms of persistency in the parameter of generic variables and as recurrent resources flow. In the second chapter the entrepreneur enters the stage, destroying the equilibrium of the circular flow and propelling economic development.

Schumpeter emphasises in general that economic development is a qualitative process involving structural change. The question arises, therefore, of how structure is dealt with in the circular flow that defines the macro state of the system, whether it be stationary or non-stationary (developmental). Having failed to integrate meso at the deep level, Schumpeter's analysis has no counterpart at the surface level, where meso unfolds in the actual emergence of a new macro structure. Classical economists gave the circular flow a rich texture, with productive and consumptive activities embedded in the matrix of social classes. In contrast, Schumpeter leaves in limbo the structure of the circular flow. It remains basically unstructured. As a consequence, economic development can be viewed only in an implicit manner, as a process involving the destruction of existing economic structures, or as incessant structural change.

There was, however, Walras's general equilibrium theory, which Schumpeter ranked as the Magna Carta of economics as a discipline (Schumpeter, 1952/1997). He referred to it on various occasions when dealing with coordination issues, but it was evident that a theory that treats the generic variables, such as technology and institutions, exogenously could not explain the coordination and change of these variables.

It must be considered a major deficiency of Schumpeter's work that he failed to furnish any immediate insights as to how the theoretical step from meso to macro is to be accomplished. He entitled Chapter 7 of his *Theory of Economic Development* (1912) 'The economy as a whole', but nonetheless hardly addressed there the issue of meso trajectories as they combine, in a process of self-organisation, into macro structure and as they incessantly change 'from within'. Instead of dealing with this issue further, he dispensed altogether with Chapter 7 in later (including the English-language) editions.

9 Conclusion

In mainstream economics, aggregation and disaggregation are mirror procedures – or, as Paul Samuelson says in his textbook, you can start either with micro or with macro as you see fit. In the Schumpeterian programme, meso is central. Meso serves as both structural component and process component, explaining generic structure and generic change. To rely in this programme only on micro and macro is rather like having Hamlet without the prince. Schumpeter made the cast complete by laying the foundations and by contributing theoretically to meso.

Acknowledgements

I gratefully acknowledge comments and suggestions by Georg D. Blind, Patrick Baur, Charles McCann, Stuart McDonald, Joseph Clark, Peter Fleissner, John Foster, Jason Potts, Andreas Pyka, Mike Richardson, Markus Schwaninger and Ulrich Witt.

Note

1. The concept of *meso* assumes an intermediate position in the distinction between *micro* and *macro*, and hence presumes that distinction. The micro–macro distinction became popular after the publication of Keynes's *General Theory*, in which he demonstrated that the aggregates of individual decisions (micro) of a Walrasian or similar (neo)'classical' equilibrium was consistent with various states of the system when defined in terms of aggregates of other (macro) variables, in particular employment, income and money volume. The present-day proponents of the so called 'new' classical macroeconomics view the problem differently, but the important point here is that the established distinction between microeconomics as dealing with Walras-type decision variables and macroeconomics as dealing with the aforementioned aggregate variables has survived, and is serving as a powerful taxonomic device and classifier for textbooks and teaching curricula in the discipline. This dichotomy did not exist at the time when Keynes was alive and when Schumpeter wrote his essay on Keynes. Schumpeter suggested using either the term 'monetary analysis' or 'income analysis' for what today is called macroeconomics, arguing that '(s)ince the aggregates chosen for variables are, with the exception of employment, monetary quantities or expressions, we may also speak of monetary analysis, and, since national income is the central variable, of income analysis' (Schumpeter, 1952/1997, p. 282). It is evident that the usage of the terms 'microeconomics' and 'macroeconomics' is a mere convention, and that we could employ with equal vindication Schumpeter's terminology, or a similar one, to denote appropriately the distinction between the two sets of variables. Evolutionary economists see no necessity to follow the conventional terminology and usually refer, when talking about *micro*economic analysis, to firms, households or behavioural routines and, when talking about *macro*economic analysis, to the division of labour and knowledge or static and dynamic relationships between aggregate magnitudes. The term '*meso*' emerges as constituent concept, as we shall see, from an evolutionary perspective that defines micro and macro in this way.

Bibliography

Alcouffe, A. and T. Kuhn (2004), 'Schumpeterian endogenous growth theory and evolutionary economics', *Journal of Evolutionary Economics*, **14**, 223–36.
Andersen, E.S. (1994), *Evolutionary Economics: Post-Schumpeterian Contributions*, London: Pinter.
Brette, O. and C. Mehier (2005), 'Veblen's evolutionary economics revisited through the "micro-meso-macro" analytical framework: the stake for the analysis of clusters of innovation', paper presented at the *EAEPE Conference, Bremen*, 10–12 November.
Dopfer, K. (1993), 'The generation of novelty in the economic process: an evolutionary concept', *Entropy and Bioeconomics*, ed. J.C. Dragan, E.K. Seifert and M.C. Demetrescu, Milan: Nagard, pp. 130–53.
Dopfer, K. (ed.) (2005), *The Evolutionary Foundations of Economics*, Cambridge: Cambridge University Press.
Dopfer, K., J. Foster and J. Potts (2004), 'Micro–meso–macro', *Journal of Evolutionary Economics*, **14**, 263–79.
Dopfer, K. and J. Potts (2007), *The General Theory of Economic Evolution*, London and New York: Routledge.
Encinar, M.-I. and F.-F. Munoz (2006), 'On novelty and economics: Schumpeter's paradox', *Journal of Evolutionary Economics*, **16**, 255–77.
Fagerberg, J. (2003), 'Schumpeter and the revival of evolutionary economics: an appraisal of the literature', *Journal of Evolutionary Economics*, **13**, 125–59.
Foster, J. (2000), 'Competitive selection, self-organisation and Joseph A. Schumpeter', *Journal of Evolutionary Economics*, **10**, 311–28.
Graca Moura, M. da (2003), 'Schumpeter on the integration of theory and history', *European Journal of Economic Thought*, **10**(2), 279–301.
Hanusch, H. (ed.) (1988), *Evolutionary Economics: Applications of Schumpeter's Ideas*, Cambridge: Cambridge University Press.
Hanusch, H. and A. Pyka (2005), 'Principles of Neo-Schumpeterian economics', *Discussion Paper no. 278*, University of Augsburg.
Heertje, A. (1988), 'Schumpeter and technical change', *Evolutionary Economics: Applications of Schumpeter's Ideas*, ed. H. Hanusch, Cambridge: Cambridge University Press.
Heertje, A. (2004), 'Schumpeter and methodological individualism', *Journal of Evolutionary Economics*, **14**, 153–6.
Hodgson, G.M. (1993), *Economics and Evolution: Bringing Life back into Economics*, Cambridge: Polity Press.
Holland, J.H., K.J. Holyoak, R.E. Nisbett and P.R. Thagard (1986), *Induction. Processes of Inference, Learning and Discovery*, Cambridge, MA: MIT Press.
Loasby, B. (1999), *Knowledge, Institutions and Evolution in Economics*, London and New York: Routledge.
Mathews, J.A. (2002), 'Introduction: Schumpeter's lost chapter', *Industry and Innovation*, **9**(1–2), 1–6.
Metcalfe, J.S. (1998), *Evolutionary Economics and Creative Destruction*, London and New York: Routledge.
Nelson, R.R. and S.G. Winter (1982), *An Evolutionary Theory of Economic Change*, Cambridge, MA: Harvard University Press.
Perlman, M. and C.R. McCann (1998), *The Pillars of Economic Understanding*, vol. I, *Ideas and Traditions*, Ann Arbor: Michigan University Press.
Rosenberg, N. (2000), *Schumpeter and the Endogeneity of Technology: Some American Perspectives*, London and New York: Routledge.
Schefold, B. (1986), 'Schumpeter as a Walrasian Austrian and Keynes as a classical Marshallian', *The Economic Law of Motions: A Marx–Keynes–Schumpeter Centennial*, ed. H.J. Wagener and J.H. Drukker, Cambridge: Cambridge University Press.
Schumpeter, J.A. (1912), *Theorie der wirtschaftlichen Entwicklung*, Leipzig: Duncker & Humblot [revised English edition, without chapter 7, 1934; chapter 7, in English, in *Industry and Innovation* (2002) **9**(1/2), 91–142].

Schumpeter, J.A. (1939), *Business Cycles: A Theoretical, Historical and Statistical Analysis of the Capitalist Process*, New York: McGraw-Hill.
Schumpeter, J.A. (1942), *Capitalism, Socialism and Democracy*, New York: Harper & Brothers.
Schumpeter, J.A. (1952/1997), *Ten Great Economists: From Marx to Keynes*, London: Routledge.
Schumpeter, J.A. (1954/1986), *History of Economic Analysis*, London: Routledge.
Shionoya, Y. (1997), *Schumpeter and the Idea of Social Science: A Metatheoretical Study*, Cambridge: Cambridge University Press.
Stolper, W.F. (1994), *Joseph Alois Schumpeter*, Princeton, NJ: Princeton University Press.
Swedberg, R. (1991), *Schumpeter: A Biography*, Princeton, NJ: Princeton University Press.
Winter, S.G. (1984), 'Schumpeterian competition in alternative technological regimes', *Journal of Economic Behaviour and Organization*, **5**, 287–320.
Witt, U. (2002), 'How evolutionary is Schumpeter's theory of economic development', *Industry and Innovation*, **9**(1–2), 7–22.

5 Reflections on Schumpeter's 'lost' seventh chapter to the *Theory of Economic Development*
John A. Mathews

Joseph Alois Schumpeter burst onto the world economic stage in the early years of the 20th century, creating a lasting challenge to the orthodoxy of his peers. Born in 1883, the year of the death of Karl Marx, he died in 1950, leaving behind an astonishing body of work with which the world of economics is still seeking to come to terms. As a young man, before he turned 30, he had published three major texts that made him world famous. 'What is more unheard of,' asked his contemporary, Arthur Spiethoff, 'a 25-year-old and a 27-year-old who stirs at the foundations of the discipline, or a 30-year-old who writes its history?'[1]

Schumpeter's first book, based on his Habilitation thesis completed by the young student at the University of Vienna, was a bold attempt to bring the new concepts of marginal and equilibrium analysis into German-speaking economics, where the emphasis was on historical and institutional analysis. This work, *Das Wesen und der Hauptinhalt der theoretischen Nationalökonomie* (The Essence and Principal Contents of Economic Theory) published in 1908, when Schumpeter was not yet 25, remains untranslated into English. In the next book, published in 1912, but whose theses were sketched in an article published in 1910, Schumpeter outlined an even bolder framework for a dynamic, evolutionary approach to economic theory. This work, entitled *Theorie der wirtschaftlichen Entwicklung* (The Theory of Economic Development), departed radically from the conventional economic framework, dubbed the static, 'circular flow' and instead proposed a source of developmental novelty internal to the economic process, and carried through in the form of entrepreneurial initiative. This was turned into the core of a comprehensive theory of the workings of the capitalist economy, encompassing profits, interest, credit, cyclical fluctuations and the rise and fall of industries. This book was capped by a third, on the history of economic doctrines, entitled *Epochen der Dogmen- und Methodengeschichte* (Economic Doctrine and Method: An Historical Sketch). This work traced the various lines of development of economic reasoning, and looked ahead to a future where economic issues would be analysed as much from a dynamic as from a static perspective. All this had been accomplished by the time he turned 30. By the eve of the First World War, the world of economics lay at Schumpeter's feet.

Then, as is well known, he turned away from academic achievement, to seek his fortune first in politics (rising to be short-lived Minister of Finance in the socialist post-war government of Austria in 1919) and then in business, as chairman of a Viennese bank. Both careers ended ignominiously: he was dismissed from his position in the government, and was wiped out financially by the crash of 1924, which saw him forced to resign from his position of chairman at the bank, and burdened with many personal debts. By 1925 he was back in academic life, now with a professorship of public finance at the University of Bonn, an appointment that created a sensation in the German-speaking world of economics.[2] But Schumpeter was by now a much more cautious man, and in the second German edition of his 1912 book, which he published in 1926, he made a very significant change: he dropped the far-reaching seventh chapter.

It is this seventh chapter, lost to the world after Schumpeter's decision to drop it from his second edition (which then formed the basis of the English translation published only in 1934) that provides the focus of this study.[3] The chapter, entitled *Das Gesamtbild der volkswirtschaft* (The economy as a whole) provides a fascinating missing 'chapter' in Schumpeter's thought, previously inaccessible to the English-speaking world. The chapter, clearly written in haste late in 1911 to catch a printing deadline, sketches a highly original summation of his model of economic development, where transformation is generated from internal dynamics represented by entrepreneurial initiative – in contrast to the prevailing doctrines, which saw change in economic circumstances, and growth, as responding to external stimuli, such as population growth, or technological innovation, or the opening up of new geographic markets. In this broad framework, which he dubbed 'dynamic' in contrast to the 'static' mainstream and classical doctrine, he made the first clear distinction between static and dynamic analysis, and demonstrated how the static analysis is accurate at any point in time, but completely misleading if applied over a period of time. He went further, and stretched his framework to encompass the socio-economic totality, arguing that the same principle of entrepreneurial initiative could account for evolutionary change in all sectors of the social system, from politics, to the arts, to science itself. He saw this, quite explicitly, as laying down a sketch of a unified approach to the development of the social sciences. Little wonder that Schumpeter's book had created something of a sensation.

Hence the great interest in this first English translation of Schumpeter's 'lost' seventh chapter: it allows us to see his life work as in a sense a working out of the lines first sketched in this youthful masterpiece. As he accommodated to the world of English-speaking economics, Schumpeter apparently felt it prudent to keep this chapter locked away in a 'bottom drawer' – drawing on it extensively in his later writings, in a way that remained unsuspected by scholars with access only to his English language works, or to the second and third German editions of his 1912 book (which had quickly become a rarity). The second German edition of *The Theory of Economic Development* (*TED*) contained an extensively reworked chapter 2, which reflected the content of the dropped chapter 7. But this was not available in English until 1934. The first intimations to the English-speaking world of Schumpeter's revolutionary approach were his 1927 and 1928 articles, 'The explanation of the business cycle' (published in *Economica*, Dec. 1927) and 'The instability of capitalism' (published in the *Economic Journal*, Sept. 1928).[4] Apart from a couple of earlier pieces, these were the major articles that established Schumpeter's reputation in English, paving the way to a chair at Harvard in 1932. These articles are widely viewed as early intimations of his later works, namely *Business Cycles* (1939) and *Capitalism, Socialism and Democracy* (1942). With the benefit of the translation of chapter 7, we can now see these instead as reworkings of chapters 6 and 7 of his 1912 book, elaborated and extended and brought to an English-speaking audience.

The present chapter provides reflections on Schumpeter's overall schema and in particular his 1912 vision as outlined in *TED* and its seventh chapter. It seeks to identify the major theoretical innovations introduced by Schumpeter in his 1912 work, and how these came to form a body of hypotheses that can be called the 'Schumpeterian schema'. The critical reception of this schema, and its continuing relevance to industrial analysis, is developed. The main contribution of the chapter is a defence of the evolutionary character of the Schumpeterian schema (despite his own disavowals and much criticism by others) and analysis of his framework from the perspective of modern Darwinian analysis, complexity theory, and 'bottom up' intelligent agent simulation. The chapter closes with a review of Schumpeter's 1912 vision of a unified social science, and its relevance to modern evolutionary social science perspectives.

Schumpeter's 1912 book and the 'lost' seventh chapter

Schumpeter had published his first book (not yet translated into English) as a way of announcing his arrival as a serious economist. It did not offer any new framework or model, but was a discursive treatment of current trends in economic theory. In particular, his aim was to shock German political economy with its traditional focus on institutional and historical treatment, at the expense of abstract economic reasoning, with his fresh focus on the new, mathematical reasoning, using equilibrium and marginalist principles. It is perhaps because these principles became so completely accepted in the wider world of economics that Schumpeter never felt the need to have his youthful exposition translated into English; perhaps it would have been a source of embarrassment to see his early gushings revealed to a wider English-speaking world.

His second book was a quite different affair. This was a mature and breathtakingly ambitious sketch of a dynamic economic framework that could create 'development' (we would now say 'evolutionary dynamics') through its own internal workings, rather than waiting for outside shocks or stimuli to move it onto new trajectories. In retrospect I would argue that we can see at least five major theoretical innovations in Schumpeter's second book, that had no counterparts in the contemporary work in economics, and which resonate still as challenges to the discipline. These were innovations that he would spend the rest of his life elaborating and pursuing.

Statics v. dynamics

The title 'The theory of economic development' announced a new departure in economic theorizing. Schumpeter paid his dues to the classic expression of political economy (whether in its classical or neoclassical, Marshallian format), arguing that in terms of static adjustment to a new situation, the economic framework left out nothing of importance. Economic subjects would take stock of a new arrangement of capital, for example, or new distribution of consumer wants, and make changes accordingly, through the mediation of prices and adjustments to production functions. But his point was that this mechanism did not account for secular change, which needed to operate according to different, open-ended, evolutionary principles. (He avoided the use of the term 'evolutionary' for fear of being branded a holistic, German reactionary – but this is what he meant.) Even when the classics discussed long-run developments, as Malthus, Ricardo or Mill did in relation to the falling rate of profit, for example, Schumpeter demonstrated that they were operating a static framework merely extended in time; it was not a framework that contained fresh sources of dynamic adjustment within it. It was his central goal in the 1912 book to erect a dynamic framework that would stand alongside the static framework, complementing it but not displacing it. This vision of economic analysis, as a fusion of dynamic analysis over time but static analysis at any point in time, was absolutely unique to Schumpeter, and stands as one his greatest accomplishments. He termed the static framework the 'circular flow' (*Kreislauf*) and devoted the first chapter of *TED* to its exposition, again returning to the point in the abandoned seventh chapter.[5]

Internal development v. external shock

Where then was the source of dynamic change to come from? Schumpeter closely followed the newest trends in economic theorizing, and in particular followed the work of the leading American political economists, including John Bates Clark, Frank Fetter and Irving Fisher. Clark in particular had published pathbreaking books in 1899 and 1907, which exercised great influence on the young Schumpeter. In the 1907 work, Clark treated economic dynamics, and traced economic change to any one of five external forces: an increase in population; an increase in capital; new techniques, or progress in methods of production; progress in economic organization of society; and emergence of new consumer wants. This was Schumpeter's starting point.[6] He felt that it was incomplete for economic science to be so dependent on external forces, and so he posited instead an internal source of variation, and insisted that it was only economic change that was grounded in this internal source, that could properly be called 'economic development'. Again, it is clear that he is talking in open-ended evolutionary terms here, and is making a fundamental Darwinian point that an evolutionary system has to have within it the seeds for its own change (variation) or it cannot evolve. This was a fundamental departure, found only in Schumpeter and not in any of the classics, apart from Marx. For Marx, the seeds of change were to be found in the proletariat. But Schumpeter focused on the real engine of change, namely the investment behaviour of capitalists and the innovative activity of entrepreneurs, and located the source of change in the entrepreneurial function. This was a momentous breakthrough.

Entrepreneurship and the role of credit
The entrepreneur, or more widely the economic function of entrepreneurship, was the centrepiece of Schumpeter's 1912 book. Certainly he was not the first to talk about entrepreneurs. Discussion went all the way back to Richard Cantillon, who in the 18th century provided a strikingly modern definition of entrepreneurship, and, in Schumpeter's time, theorists such as Clark in the USA had developed sophisticated accounts of entrepreneurial profit, capital, wages, and interest. Schumpeter's own Austrian predecessor, Albert Schäffle, discussed entrepreneurship in a way that is clearly anticipatory of Schumpeter's formulation,[7] but it was Schumpeter who took over this terminology, and made it the centrepiece of a new conception of 'economic development' or open-ended evolutionary change. And he linked entrepreneurship to a fundamental institutional feature of capitalism, namely the provision of credit.

This is where he offered original formulations. First, he insisted that the entrepreneur should be distinguished from the capitalist who advanced credit; the capitalist would take his reward in the form of interest, and in this sense would bear the financial risk of the enterprise failing.[8] Second, the entrepreneur would not be required to have a source of savings as his departure point; Schumpeter thereby banished 'savings' as a major factor involved in economic dynamics, and with it other 'funds' such as the classical doctrine of the wages fund (to which he devotes an inordinately long discussion in the seventh chapter, designed to bury the wages fund doctrine forever). Third, the existence of sources of credit – such as bank loans, or equity contributions, or, in the 1990s, venture capital – enables the entrepreneur to enter the markets for capital goods and factor services *like any other firm*, thereby disturbing whatever equilibrium might exist within the 'circular flow'; this was Schumpeter's critical insight, that brought the entrepreneur onto a par with all the existing economic actors, but acting as a source of disturbance to equilibrium. Fourth, the entrepreneur does not have to be an inventor, but simply a source of 'recombinations' of existing production services, e.g. new techniques of production, or new approaches to marketing, or new ways of organizing. Fifth, and for good measure, Schumpeter made the entrepreneur and his borrowing of funds the source of interest, denying that interest could be earned in the static 'circular flow' where all activities are matched to existing demands. (This was the comment that infuriated his Austrian contemporaries, such as his teacher, E. von Böhm-Bawerk, and his lifelong rival, Ludwig von Mises.)[9] Sixth, although Schumpeter was much attracted to the figure of the entrepreneur as a leader, who breaks the mould and sets new directions, he was always aware that it is basically an economic function that is being carried out, by an individual, or by a firm, or – in later writings – by a giant firm occupying an industry monopoly position. Schumpeter was always clear that it was the *function* that took precedence over the *person* of the entrepreneur. Finally, and this was surely the most brilliant coup of all, Schumpeter made entrepreneurial action the source of business cycles, thereby 'closing' his system in the most profound and satisfying way.

Business cycles created by internal development and entrepreneurship
As against the prevailing Austrian doctrine that viewed the business cycle as a monetary phenomenon, whereby credit expands in excess of the demand by investment, and contracts just when demand is accelerating, Schumpeter rested cycles of business fluctuation on activities in the real economy, through the agency of entrepreneurial action. This was another major innovation in economic theory. Against the widespread view that saw business cycles as phenomena triggered by external disturbance (such as variations in crop supplies, or weather patterns etc) or by monetary phenomena (not linked to actual production) Schumpeter instead grounded them in his theory of economic development. He argued, in effect, that economic development is internally generated, by entrepreneurial action, and as such *it has to be cyclical in character*. In the 1912 book the cycle traced out is what he later referred to as the 'first approximation', namely a wave process that

goes through four phases, of upswing, recession, depression (overshoot) and recovery. In modern parlance, Schumpeter made business cycles the principal 'emergent phenomena' of his dynamic system, in a way that anticipates much later developments in the theory of complex adaptive systems.

The economy as part of a complex social order
Schumpeter went to great lengths in the 1912 book, and especially in the seventh chapter, to establish the economic domain in its widest scope – the 'economy as a whole' – in an even wider social context. Like his German contemporary, Max Weber, Schumpeter was really an early exponent of 'economic sociology' and saw the future development of the discipline very much along these lines. Whereas Weber treated economic phenomena at some length in his treatises, such as *Economy and Society*, he could never be said to have added anything particularly novel in the exposition, which is perhaps one reason why Weber's economic sociology never really caught on in a big way. But with Schumpeter the matter is entirely different. Vividly, in bold brush strokes, in the seventh chapter, he outlined the framework of a dynamic economic sociology, where again the driving force is entrepreneurship. In just a few sentences, he sketched what such an approach would look like. This too was a fundamentally novel way of viewing 'the economy as a whole' in its wider social setting.

The abandonment of the seventh chapter
Why then, did Schumpeter drop this innovative chapter from the second edition, and never refer to it again in his own published work? There is no clear or easy answer to this question. Schumpeter himself never referred to the matter, so we can only speculate as to his motive. Perhaps he saw it as too precocious, too bold, and not appropriate for a more mature man of the world who by now aspired to a professorship at Harvard (which he secured in 1932). Perhaps he was bemused by the fact that it attracted most attention in the early reviews, and was praised in particular by reviewers who used his broader framework to argue against the analytical approach to economics that Schumpeter had espoused in his first book. Perhaps he felt that it held him as hostage to a too bold and demanding programme of research that he could never realistically hope to substantiate.

One possibility that ought to be seriously considered is that Schumpeter came to disagree with the framework outlined in the seventh chapter – as he came to disagree with his own first book (which perhaps explains why it was never translated). But this seems most definitely *not* to be the case. If there is one thread that connects the life work of Schumpeter, it is the strenuous contention that economic change is driven by internal dynamics arising from entrepreneurial initiative. Certainly he changed his mind concerning the character of entrepreneurship as such, moving to see it as being embodied in large firms rather than in heroic individuals, in his later 1942 exposition, *Capitalism, Socialism and Democracy*. He fleshed out the cyclical fluctuations aspect of the framework at great length in his 1939 work, *Business Cycles*, but this did not depart from the 1912 work in fundamentals. Thus there is a thread that connects the work of Schumpeter from 1912 to 1942 and beyond; let us call this the Schumpeterian 'schema'.

Schumpeter: an 'Austrian' or a 'German'
Erik Reinert (2002) makes the striking point that Schumpeter, when viewed against the backdrop of German political economy, is less original than he otherwise appears to be. His work is saturated with then-current debates in the German and Austrian traditions. There is much to reflect on in this observation. Schumpeter, although an Austrian by birth, and a Viennese in his intellectual formation, never sought to identify himself as an 'Austrian' economist alongside contemporaries like Ludwig von Mises, Friedrich Hayek and others. On the contrary, he sought to identify himself with a wider world of German and European scholarship and, as noted above, with the best current trends in English-speaking economics and social science, particularly those emanating from the USA. But through all this, Schumpeter was immersed in German scholarship and intellectual traditions, drawing intensively from Kant, Nietzsche, Weber and Sombart, so much so, that he rarely felt the need to refer to them explicitly.[10] Schumpeter was more a 'German' than an 'Austrian', but through his schema of the economy as a whole, he became a truly cosmopolitan theorist.

Evolutionary dimensions to the Schumpeterian schema
On the face of it, the 1912 book is not a promising place to start with a description of Schumpeter's schema as 'evolutionary'. His own words are quite emphatic and definitive. He states, after asking whether his framework could be described as 'evolutionary':

> the evolutionary idea is now discredited in our field, especially with historians and ethnologists . . . To the reproach of unscientific and extra-scientific mysticism that now surrounds the 'evolutionary' ideas, is added that of dilettantism. With all the hasty generalizations in which the word 'evolution' plays a part, many of us have lost patience. (1912/1983, pp. 57–8).

This attitude is understandable when we consider the state of evolutionary thinking in the early years of the 20th century, when Schumpeter was writing. The neo-Darwinian synthesis had not yet been effected, awaiting the rediscovery of Mendel's laws of genetics; there were rampant appeals to 'vitalism' and 'organicism' that were somehow irreducible to other principles; and there was the looming presence of social Darwinism, eugenics and strong beliefs in a capitalistic 'natural' order. Schumpeter clearly wanted none of this, so he saw it as expedient to discard any label of 'evolutionary' and concentrate instead on what he called 'development'.

But his schema is saturated with what we would today call open-ended, evolutionary dynamics. The state of play regarding evolutionary dynamics is very different in 2002 from what it was in 1912 when Schumpeter's book appeared. Today there is an understanding of the breadth and scope of evolutionary dynamics, and there is a general, conceptual framework of Darwinian processes that has application in biological systems, but also in many others, including social and economic systems. Darwinian processes of variation followed by selection and retention are now recognized in a vast array of domains, from individual development to the acquisition of behavioural routines, and from the evolution of languages, through evolution of conceptual thinking, to evolution of technologies, organizations, institutions and laws.[11] For example in the development of the individual person, it is now suggested that the nervous system and brain develop along Darwinian lines (or through the operation of what Calvin calls a neural 'Darwin machine').[12] Experiments in cat brain and ocular development have found for example that there is no set template of neural connections between the eye and the visual cortex, but instead there is a proliferation of potential connections followed by their selection by the weight or preponderance of visual stimuli actually experienced by the growing cat. Thus it is the visual environment that 'selects' the pattern of visual neural–cortical connections that is best 'adapted' to it.

In this context, of evolutionary thought becoming the benchmark across the entire social and biological domain, including new areas such as artificial life and artificial economies, Schumpeter's schema is admirably evolutionary in spirit. There has long been controversy over whether Schumpeter can be considered an 'evolutionary' theorist. The belated publication of the seventh chapter, in my view, puts the matter beyond doubt. Schumpeter was an evolutionary thinker, through and through.

Witt (2002) approaches this same question, and answers it firmly in the affirmative. By sketching an abstract outline of what an 'evolutionary' approach looks like, and then demonstrating how Schumpeter's schema fits in with this outline, he resolves the vexed question of whether Schumpeter is an 'evolutionary' theorist or not.[13] I am in unreserved agreement with Witt on this point.

As in any evolutionary system, there needs to be a source of variation, a source of selection (possibly utilizing different vehicles) and a source or mechanism of retention. Schumpeter provided all of these in his 1912 book. Entrepreneurial recombinations provide the source of *variation*; it is the existence of the credit system that guarantees that entrepreneurs are able to effect the new combinations when they see an opportunity.[14] Market-based competition provides the *selection* mechanism; there are more variations than needed, and so there has to be some whittling down, accomplished through the selective pressures of price, differentiation and innovation.[15] New variations selected by the market are retained through entrepreneurs building firms around these new combinations, and growing the firms, or replicating them through national and international expansion. It is the continuity of firms, and their capacity to sustain innovation, that is the fundamental *retention* mechanism in the capitalist economy.[16]

Now Schumpeter did not himself use these terms, but they are clearly what he had in mind. They are the appropriate terms to use in the present context, where there is widespread appeal to, and concordance with, the evolutionary framework. Nelson and Winter (1982) introduced their pioneering analysis of evolutionary economic processes by making the argument that selective pressures operate on firms in terms of variations in their underlying capabilities and routines (and, by extension, resources). This was a completely novel way of viewing inter-firm dynamics. It dispensed with neoclassical fantasies such as that firms adjust instantaneously to changes in commercial conditions, e.g. changes in prices, by adjusting their production functions. Instead Nelson and Winter argued that firms respond to changes in conditions through the medium of their routines, which can be varied only slowly and with difficulty. They modelled evolutionary dynamics in terms of random variations in firms' routines, tracing out the selective pressures subsequently felt over hundreds of repeated iterations. Thus the ingredients of an evolutionary approach in economics are now reasonably well-defined.[17] The Schumpeterian schema is entirely consistent with this, and indeed provides the appropriate framework for its further development.

The modern view then is to see evolutionary processes in general terms with applications in the world of biology, of behaviour, of individual development and development of such systems as the immune or nervous systems, and in the world of ideas, laws, institutions and business processes. Thus it is no longer a case of describing a biological process and then using biological 'analogies' in the business world. It is the evolutionary process itself which can be seen as primary, as an abstraction, and then applied in different settings, be they biological, developmental, human social or economic. The characteristic feature of this view is to see the evolutionary dynamics in terms of 'replicator–interactor' dynamics – terms popularized by Dawkins.[18] This is all admirably reflected in Schumpeter's 1912 book and his schema.

Schumpeter in the light of modern agent-based modelling
One of the problems with Schumpeter's schema has been the difficulty of 'incorporating' it within the corpus of the neoclassical mathematical

economic system, with general equilibrium at its core. Indeed it never fitted, and because Schumpeter himself did not supply the needed mathematical apparatus, no-one else did, and the Schumpeterian alternative languished in favour of its more rigorous, static rival. The Schumpeterian schema was slowly whittled down to a few key 'Schumpeterian' assumptions that fitted within the neoclassical framework, such as the 'Schumpeterian hypothesis' that innovation can be facilitated better by large monopolies than by smaller competitors. Even if these hypotheses did fit with the spirit of the Schumpeterian system, they in no way captured its breadth. Occasional efforts to develop an economic dynamics (see Day, 1994) have generally focused on the macro economy rather than on micro behaviour at the level of individual economic agents, where Schumpeter's insights really have to be located. So such efforts have been sporadic and yielded little. The great impetus to Schumpeterian thinking came from Nelson and Winter, whose pathbreaking book in 1982 unleashed a wave of new modelling and generated new insights into the construction of firms, and their routines, and their satisficing behaviour.[19]

But the situation may be changing strongly in Schumpeter's favour. I refer to the rise of intelligent agent-based systems modelling, or what has been fortuitously called 'bottom up' social science.[20] The critical breakthrough has of course been the increase in computing power, and the impact on social science thinking of the breakthroughs in complexity and artificial life. Now there are several examples of 'agent-based computational economics' (ACE) or simulation of artificial economies, where Schumpeterian insights can be embodied in agents' behavioural rules, and Schumpeterian emergent behaviour can be captured. Arthur (1995) is an early example of the application of agent-based modelling to economic phenomena, but the decisive breakthrough came with Epstein and Axtell (1996) and their book, *Growing Artificial Societies: Social Science from the Bottom Up*. This is a first demonstration of the power of simple agent-based models, in this case a Swarm-model called *Sugarscape*, both to generate emergent behaviour (such as flocking) and to cross disciplinary boundaries in a fresh approach to a 'unified' social science.

Recent papers give a taste of what is to come.[21] Bruun and Luna (2000) and Bruun (2004) construct a mini-version of a Schumpeterian world, with production and credit, and entrepreneurs creating new firms by having access to credit, where some firms grow and others fall into bankruptcy depending on their ability to satisfy consumer demand. The interesting thing about this model is that it generates non-predetermined *cyclical behaviour*. This, in my submission, is what makes the model Schumpeterian.[22] Computer-based simulations, over thousands of iterations, of complex worlds of mutually interacting intelligent agents, or 'artificial economies', which generate emergent behaviour in the form of cyclical phenomena, do promise to capture both the reflexivity and 'bottom up' character of agent-based reasoning, as well as the emergent phenomena predicted by verbal descriptions, all in a rigorous and reproducible fashion in the context of a particular system. Of course much debate will ensue as to the adequacy of the representational system employed, and the techniques employed. But this promises to provide a fascinating way forward, and the ultimate field of application of the Schumpeterian schema. It is yet another reason why the Schumpeterian schema is today seen with such excitement; it resonates with the tools of investigation now available.

Schumpeter's schema and a unified social science
Finally we turn to Schumpeter's most radical – but sketchy – contribution in the 'lost' seventh chapter of *TED*. The concluding pages of the seventh chapter of the 1912 book outline a bold research programme for a unified social science. For reasons best known to himself, Schumpeter kept these musings secret from the English-speaking world, and never referred to them again in German, either. The only scholar who has examined them from the perspective of a wider social science, is Professor Shionoya.[23] His study provides the benchmark for analyses of Schumpeter's wider aims.

Let us outline Schumpeter's argument in his own words, deleting much of the extraneous commentary that adds length but not incisiveness to his exposition. He starts by introducing the notion that there are several areas of social life each of which has its own autonomy and its own social actors; these may or may not overlap, but in each case there is a concreteness to their social activities. Some comments are interpolated in italics.

[2002, p. 135] For the process of development described above, there are . . . noticeable analogies to other areas of social life . . . Take as examples the areas of politics, of art, of science, of social life, of moral considerations, etc. . . . Here one has to observe that the distinction between those areas of social life lies not simply in a mere abstraction. . . . On the one hand, we find in each of those areas people whose main activity lies in this area. In the area of the economy we find those people who belong to the economic professions . . . workers, industrialists, merchants, farmers etc. . . . In the area of art, one also meets well-defined individuals, in whose activity the development and any given state of the arts consists. . . . The same is true in the area of politics. . . . to those areas we distinguished from one another, real groups of people correspond who are in general different from each other. . . . [*Schumpeter captures the relative autonomy of these activities in a nice pair of metaphors.*] No machine is built according to political principles, and no picture is painted according to the law of marginal utility. . . . Thus, this separation is . . . not simply an abstraction; one and the same individual can be active in different areas. . . . [*Thus Schumpeter establishes the concrete reality of people being located within different social spheres, and their relative autonomy. He now wants to demonstrate how similar principles to those found in static economics can account for adjustments within each of these autonomous areas.*]

At any particular point of time each of these areas of social life comes under the shaping influence of data which are analogous to those which determine an economy, at any point of time, in accordance with the formulations of the static theory. . . . The problem to be solved is only to show again, in each single case, how this relationship works in its context, and then to present the essence of it in a precise general treatment. [*This is, incidentally, an excellent one-line summary of Schumpeter's vision of method in the social sciences.*] The first problem is a historical one, the second a theoretical one. Up to the present it has only satisfyingly been solved for the field of economics. [*This is grossly unfair to Schumpeter's sociological contemporaries, particularly Weber.*] . . . To select an example: the art of a time is a child of the time. The geographic environment, the circumstances which one can describe as the character of a people or similarly, the social structure, the economic situation, the ruling ideas concerning what is grand and desirable, and what is low and despicable – those aspects form art at any particular point in time. The modern historian attempts to show this in some detail. [*So much for statics; Schumpeter now wishes to demonstrate that dynamic behaviour cannot be based on responses to external factors alone. He does so by continuing with the analogy of art.*]

. . . It strikes one as obvious that there are particular forces at work in the area of artistic creation, that it conforms in the course of its development not only passively to outer influences but that there is more to it than simply being dragged along by the changes in the environment. [*He goes on to describe how the field of artistic expression develops its own rules, each to its time and place, and how these can be linked more or less directly – with greater or lesser determinacy – to the circumstances of each.*]

The conception of each area [*of social life*] as a result of the other fields is replaced by the conception of the whole state of social life . . . But with this the theory of development loses foundations. For the transition from one state to the other can only follow according to the static rules. [*In this way he sets up the basic contradiction, which can only be resolved by entrepreneurial intervention – as done already at length for the case of the economy.*]

Thus our conception is unsatisfying in this respect as well. So now we come to the last step on our explanatory journey. There is a further analogy between what we presented first for the field of economics, and the processes in the other areas of social life. It is concerned with the mechanism of development, with that relatively autonomous development which is characteristic of every single field of social life. [*Thus he subjects the entire scope of social processes to an open-ended, evolutionary treatment.*] . . . Now, these groups [*of concrete persons*] in each area may be divided into two clearly distinguished groups – just as in the case of economically active persons. . . . In each field there are statically disposed individuals and there are leaders. The former are characterized by doing in essence what they have learnt to do . . . The latter by contrast are characterized by their perception of what is new; they change the outmoded frame of their activity, as well as the given data of their area. . . . We observe these differences in art, in science, in politics. . . . Everywhere these two types are very clearly demarcated, letting those spirits stand out who create new directions of art, new 'schools', new parties. [*Schumpeter now sums up.*] We always find this analogy between the behavior of the majority in these areas including the economy. This behavior consists, on the one hand, in the copying, recognition of, and adaptation to, a given state of affairs of materialistic and idealistic nature; and, on the other hand, the behavior of a [*new direction-setting*] minority in these areas such as that of the economy. The characteristic of this behavior lies herein, *that it is oneself who changes the given state of affairs.*

Our analogy emerges also in the manner in which the new gets pushed through. The mere thought is not sufficient and is never pushed through 'on its own' . . . The history of science shows this in a drastic way. In this process . . . the new thought will be picked up by a forceful personality and, because of the influence that personality possesses, be pushed through. This personality does not have to be the creator of the thought, just as little as the entrepreneur for instance does not have to be the inventor of the new method of production which he introduces. Here, as everywhere else, the leader is characterized by the energy of the act and not that of the thought.[24] . . . A new thought would virtually *never be experienced as a new reality* [*author's italics*] without the activity of a leader, with whom one has to reckon, whom one has to recognize, to whom one has to adjust. [*Thus entrepreneurship is generalized across to all fields of social life, as the vehicle of 'development' or, as we would say, of evolutionary dynamics. Finally Schumpeter emphasizes that the leader's work is not driven by adaptation to the given, but by creation of the new – to which the system then adapts.*]

[*The new idea*] never happens as a response to present or revealed needs. The issue is always to obtrude the new . . . Its acceptance is always a case of compulsion being exercised on a reluctant mass . . . Any area of social life has doubtlessly its own means and levers for pushing through the new. One need not exaggerate the analogy. But the basic line is the same. [*This completes the exposition of social entrepreneurship. The final point is to establish the interconnections of all the areas of social life.*]

There is only one question left. How is it possible that despite this relative autonomy of each single field there is only one underlying and large truth . . . [*namely*] that every element of every area is at any point of time in a relationship with every element of every other area – that all states of all areas mutually determine each other and belong to each other. Let us call the totality of these areas the *social culture* of a nation and the basic underlying idea of all its developments the *social development of culture*. Then we can pose the question as to how it can be explained – according to our conception – that the social culture of a nation is at any point in time a unity and that the social development of culture of any nation always shows a uniform tendency?[25]

At this point, Schumpeter is more or less exhausted, and rapidly rounds off his exposition, and the 1912 book as a whole. He does so, no doubt brimming with plans as to how to execute this dazzling vision of a unified social science. But as noted above, his ambitions took him in other directions, towards politics and business, and it was only when these ambitions had been frustrated that he returned to scholarship, in a German university. By then he had lost most of his earlier *brio*, and was much more cautious in developing and expounding research programmes.

The point I wish to make is simple and straightforward. In this brief passage, of no more than ten pages in the German original (with considerable padding that I have eliminated in the above extracts), Schumpeter anticipated the entire programme of Darwinian or evolutionary approaches to the social sciences. What is today called evolutionary linguistics, evolutionary psychology, evolutionary anthropology, evolutionary culture (and mimetics), evolutionary epistemology – all these areas of current social scientific activity, that are the leading edge, the avant-garde of our time, all were anticipated by Schumpeter, as a dazzling 28-year-old, in 1912.

To summarize Schumpeter's vision in 1912, he saw each area of social life as having its relative autonomy – autonomous actors, autonomous processes of adjustment, autonomous instigators of change – and its own internal dynamics, or what we would now call its own open-ended evolutionary dynamics. But each of these areas also created the 'external' conditions for the other areas, in a complex system of mutual dependence. They would thus co-evolve in a vast process of mutual interdependence.

The evolutionary approaches to the social sciences provide the best possible fulfilment of Schumpeter's vision of a unified social science. The evolutionary approaches dispense with the idea that there is a fixed pattern to social structures and processes, laid down either by functional necessity or by innateness, and that instead there is a more or less constant process of variation, selection and retention going on, that accounts for creative adaptation. But as far as I am aware, no evolutionary theorist has sought to go as far as Schumpeter in insisting on the interdependence, and mutual conditioning, of the different areas of social life – including that of the business world and economics. So in this sense, Schumpeter's vision remains still the most radical vision of what the social sciences can achieve.

But to bring such a vision to fruition would require the most awesome of scientific undertakings. If the Schumpeterian approach is acknowledged as the best available account of capitalist dynamics, then it should be made the foundation of all studies in microeconomics, macroeconomics, evolutionary economics, developmental economics, and above all in practical, business-oriented economics and competitive strategy – as well as providing a framework for all the social sciences, from anthropology, through sociology, to evolutionary psychology. Just to enunciate such a programme is to identify how great is the resistance to it, in terms of intellectual inertia, and how far we are from a unified approach to the social sciences. But if ever there was a candidate for such a unifying mission, it is surely the Schumpeterian schema.

Notes

1. Cited in Schumpeter (1912/1934/1983), p. ix.
2. These details are elaborated in the admirable biography of Schumpeter published by Professor Richard Swedberg (1991), a work which combines the personal, political and intellectual strands in the story of J.A.S.

3. The chapter, 'The economy as a whole' (*Das Gesamtbild der volkswirtschaft*), is translated into English and published for the first time in a special issue of the journal *Industry and Innovation*, **9** (1/2), 2002. See Backhaus (2002) and Schumpeter (1912/2002).
4. Both articles are republished in Schumpeter's collected essays, Clemence (1951/1989).
5. Note that his fellow Austrian and contemporary, and lifelong rival, Ludwig von Mises, used the same duality of static v. dynamic aspects in his system, as elaborated much later in *Human Action* (written in the 1930s and published in 1940). Von Mises, and the wider Austrian school, use the terminology 'evenly rotating economy' for what Schumpeter had described as a 'circular flow'.
6. See Schumpeter (1912/2002, p. 99); and see Shionoya (1997, p. 162), for a discussion.
7. Balabkins (2000) discusses Schäffle's contribution, and its possible source for Schumpeter's 1912 formulation.
8. The foremost US economist of the period, J.B. Clark, in his 1899 work *The Distribution of Wealth* (in which he developed a marginal productivity theory of distribution), spelt out many of the positions on entrepreneurial profit, and how it forms the source from which interest and wages are paid, that were taken up by Schumpeter: 'It is clear, on the face of the facts, that the two static incomes – those, namely, of the laborer and of the capitalist – are paid to them by the *entrepreneur,* who receives and sells the product of their joint industry. In the cotton mill, it is the hirer of capital and of labor who puts the goods on the market and from the proceeds pays the workmen and the owners of capital. If he pays first to the capitalists what the final productivity law, as applied to capital, calls for, he has a remainder out of which he must pay wages; and now it is the final productivity law that decides what he must pay as wages. If there is anything left on his hands after the two payments are made, it is a profit; and the terms *profit* and *residual income* are thus synonymous' (Clark, 1899, ch. XIII, p. 30).
9. See von Mises' comment on Schumpeter's suggestion, that obviously still rankles, in his 1940 text, *Human Action*, p. 530: 'It has been asserted that in the imaginary construction of the evenly rotating economy no interest would appear [Ref. to Schumpeter, 1912]. However, it can be shown that this assertion is incompatible with the assumptions on which the construction of the evenly rotating economy is based.' Of course, it all depends on how profits are defined.
10. It can be demonstrated that Schumpeter drew important ingredients of his work from these authors. From Kant, I argue that Schumpeter drew an important parallel with his own concept of entrepreneurship. In his *Critique of Pure Reason*, Kant had laid out a stunning intellectual structure that sought to account for the knowability of the world, and to preserve space for human action and its moral foundations. He argued that science could trace all phenomena to their causes – but that humans could initiate new chains of causality through their own moral autonomy and free will. The parallels with the autonomy of the entrepreneur are striking. From Nietzsche, Schumpeter drew on the notions of 'leader' and 'superman' as ideal of his heroic entrepreneur. From Weber he drew his notions of economic sociology, while from Sombart he drew extensively on the institutional and historical discussion of capitalism, and indeed drew his notion of 'creative destruction' directly from Sombart (Reinert, 2002). It was Schumpeter's genius that knitted these various strands together.
11. On Darwinian processes in general, see recent reviews such as those by Cziko (1995), Plotkin (1993) and Dawkins (1983).
12. See Calvin (1996) for an overview of this perspective.
13. There is a considerable literature on this question; see, for example, Hodgson (1993).
14. The parallel with genetic recombination, and in particular the exchange of genetic material between microorganisms, is striking.
15. It is well known that market processes, as described in English political economy of the early 19th century (Malthus, Ricardo) provided a key analog of competitive selection for Darwin; yet market processes have resisted an evolutionary treatment themselves, with important exceptions such as Alchian (1950) and Nelson and Winter (1982).

16. Retention is captured in such notions as the 'stickiness' of routines and the resources uti-
     lized by firms, a point emphasized in the pathbreaking text on evolutionary economics
     produced by Nelson and Winter (1982).
17. For excellent introductions, see Dosi and Nelson (1994) or Metcalfe (1998); Langlois and
     Everett (1994) provide an illuminating discussion informed by a reading of the current
     evolutionary debates in the biological sciences. Andersen (1994), Hodgson (1993) or
     Witt (1992) provide expositions of the evolutionary approach to economics from
     different perspectives, while Vromen (1995) provides an extended comparison of evolu-
     tionary schools of thought. The modern field was essentially started by Nelson and
     Winter (1982).
18. See Dawkins (1983) for his fundamental contributions to the elaboration of replica-
     tor–interactor dynamics at the genetic level. These have been discussed at the cultural
     level in terms of 'mimetic' processes, involving *memes* instead of genes; see Blackmore
     (1999) for a comprehensive discussion. In this context, economic evolution operates at
     another level of replicator–interactor dynamics again, one that proceeds much faster
     than either genetic or mimetic evolution, and independently of both.
19. Even here there have been limits to the Schumpeterian insights, and the modelling has
     been very abstract; in the 20 years since publication of the Nelson and Winter book, one
     can hardly say that there are strong schools of 'NW' modelling under way.
20. The phrase comes from Epstein and Axtell (1996).
21. See Bruun (2004) and Grebel, Pyka and Hanusch (2004) for a recent discussion of these
     issues.
22. This is just a first step, utilizing the now considerable library of software routines called
     Swarm, and which promises to become a bedrock discipline of social scientific investi-
     gation in the future. It offers a 'third way' between mathematical equations (always
     insufficient to capture the real complexity and reflexivity of the social world) and verbal
     descriptions (like those of Schumpeter) which contain insights but cannot subject them
     to testing in any rigorous way.
23. See the article on the seventh chapter, by Shionoya (1990) and the later book-length
     exposition of Schumpeter's quest for a unified social science: Shionoya (1997). These
     texts are fundamental to the appreciation of the Schumpeterian opus.
24. Note the tantalizing anticipation here of later social accounts of scientific change, par-
     ticularly that of Kuhn (1962) and his notion of 'paradigm shifts' as driving scientific
     development. To my knowledge, Kuhn was never aware of Schumpeter's prior discus-
     sion of this issue.
25. This final passage is rendered by Shionoya (1997, p. 40) as follows: 'In spite of the rela-
     tive independence of all areas, why is there such an important truth – indeed the truth
     which we cannot so much prove exactly as perceive – that every element in every area, at
     any time, is connected with every element in every other area, that all situations in all
     areas determine each other and depend on each other? If we call the aggregate of these
     areas the *social culture* of a nation and the totality of its development *sociocultural devel-
     opment*, we can ask: how does our approach explain that the social culture of a nation
     at any given time is a unity and the sociocultural development of a nation always has a
     unifying tendency?'

References

Alchian, A.A. 1950. Uncertainty, evolution, and economic theory, *Journal of Political
    Economy*, **58**, 211–21.
Andersen, E.S. 1992. The difficult jump from Walrasian to Schumpeterian analysis, paper pre-
    sented to International Schumpeter Society conference, Kyoto, 19–22 Aug.
Andersen, E.S. 1994/1996. *Evolutionary Economics: Post-Schumpeterian Contributions.*
    London: Pinter Publishers.
Arthur, W.B. 1995. Complexity in economics and financial markets, *Complexity*, **1** (1), 20–25.
Backhaus, J. 2002. Presentation of Schumpeter's 'lost' seventh chapter of *The Theory of
    Economic Development, in Industry and Innovation*, **9** (1/2), 91–2.

Balabkins, N. 2000. J.A. Schumpeter at the University of Czernowitz 1909–1911: Possible sources of inspiration for his innovator? Paper delivered to 13th Heilbronn Symposium in Economics and the Social Sciences, on Joseph Alois Schumpeter, Heilbronn, June.

Blackmore, S.J. 1999. *The Meme Machine.* Oxford: Oxford University Press.

Bruun, C. 2004. The economy as an agent-based whole: simulating Schumpeterian dynamics, *Industry and Innovation,* **10** (4), 475–92.

Bruun, C. and Luna, F. 2000. Endogenous growth with cycles in a Swarm economy: fighting time, space and complexity. In F. Luna and B. Stefansson (eds), *Economic Simulations in Swarm: Agent-Based Modelling and Object Oriented Programming.* Dordrecht and London: Kluwer Academic.

Calvin, W.H. 1996. *The Cerebral Code: Thinking a Thought in the Mosaics of the Mind.* Cambridge, MA: MIT Press.

Clark, J.B. 1899/1908. *The Distribution of Wealth: A Theory of Wages, Interest and Profits.* New York: The Macmillan Company.

Clark, J.B. 1907. *Essentials of Economic Theory.* New York: Macmillan.

Clemence, R.V. (ed.) 1951/1989. *Essays on Entrepreneurs, Innovations, Business Cycles, and the Evolution of Capitalism, by Joseph A. Schumpeter.* With new introduction by Richard Swedberg. New Brunswick, NJ: Transaction Publishers.

Cziko, G. 1995. *Without Miracles: Universal Selection Theory and the Second Darwinian Revolution.* Cambridge, MA: MIT Press.

Dawkins, R. 1983. Universal Darwinism: In D.S. Bendall (ed.), *Evolution from Molecules to Men.* Cambridge: Cambridge University Press.

Day, R.H. 1994. *Complex Economic Dynamics. Vol. 1: An Introduction to Dynamical Systems and Market Mechanisms.* Cambridge, MA: MIT Press.

Dosi, G. and Nelson, R.R. 1994. An introduction to evolutionary theories in economics, *Journal of Evolutionary Economics,* **4,** 153–72

Epstein, J.M. and Axtell, R. 1996. *Growing Artificial Societies: Social Science from the Bottom Up.* Washington, DC: Brookings Institution Press, and Cambridge, MA: The MIT Press.

Grebel, T., Pyka, A. and Hanusch, H. 2004. An evolutionary approach to the theory of entrepreneurship, *Industry and Innovation,* **10** (4), 493–514.

Hodgson, G. 1993. *Economics and Evolution.* Cambridge, UK: Polity Press.

Kuhn, T. 1962. *The Structure of Scientific Revolutions.* Chicago, IL: University of Chicago Press.

Langlois, R. and Everett, M. 1994. What is evolutionary economics? In L. Magnusson (ed.), *Evolutionary and Neo-Schumpeterian Approaches to Economics.* Boston and Dordrecht: Kluwer Academic.

Metcalfe, J.S. 1998. *Evolutionary Economics and Creative Destruction: Graz Schumpeter Lectures, 1.* London: Routledge.

Nelson, R.R. and Winter, S.G. 1982. *An Evolutionary Theory of Economic Change.* Cambridge, MA: The Belknap Press of Harvard University Press.

Plotkin, H. 1993. *Darwin Machines and the Nature of Knowledge.* Cambridge, MA: Harvard University Press.

Reinert, E.S. 2002. Schumpeter in the context of two canons of economic thought, *Industry and Innovation,* **9** (1/2), 23–40.

Schumpeter, J.A. 1912/1934/1983. *The Theory of Economic Development: An Inquiry into Profits, Capital, Credit, Interest, and the Business Cycle.* Trans. from the German by Redvers Opie. With an Introduction by John E. Elliott. New Brunswick, NJ: Transaction Publishers.

Schumpeter, J.A. 1912/2002. The economy as a whole (Das Gesamtbild der volkswirtschaft): The 'lost' seventh chapter to *The Theory of Economic Development,* trans. by Ursula Backhaus, *Industry and Innovation,* **9** (1/2), 93–145.

Schumpeter, J.A. 1927. The explanation of the business cycle, *Economica,* (Dec.), 286–311 (reprinted in Clemence, 1989, pp. 21–46).

Schumpeter, J.A. 1928. The instability of capitalism, *Economic Journal,* (Sept.), 361–86 (reprinted in Clemence, 1989, pp. 47–72).

Schumpeter, J.A. 1935. The analysis of economic change, *Review of Economic Statistics*, (May), 2–10 (reprinted in Clemence, 1989, pp. 134–49).

Schumpeter, J.A. 1939. *Business Cycles: A Theoretical, Historical and Statistical Analysis of the Capitalist Process*. New York: McGraw-Hill.

Schumpeter, J.A. 1942. *Capitalism, Socialism, and Democracy*. New York: Harper Bros.

Shionoya, Y. 1990. The origin of the Schumpeterian research programme: a chapter omitted from Schumpeter's 'Theory of Economic Development', *Journal of Institutional and Theoretical Economics*, **146** (2), 314–27.

Shionoya, Y. 1997. *Schumpeter and the Idea of Social Science*. Cambridge: Cambridge University Press.

Swedberg, R. 1991. *Schumpeter: A Biography*. Princeton, NJ: Princeton University Press.

Thomas, B. 1991. Alfred Marshall on economic biology, *Review of Political Economy*, **3** (1), 1–14.

von Mises, L. 1940/1959. *Human Action*. London: William Hodge.

Vromen, J. 1995. *Economic Evolution. An Enquiry into the Foundations of 'New Institutional Economics'*. Cambridge: Cambridge University Press.

Witt, U. 1992. Evolutionary concepts in economics, *Eastern Economic Journal*, **18**, 405–19.

Witt, U. 2002. How evolutionary is Schumpeter's theory of economic development? *Industry and Innovation*, **9** (1/2), 7–22.

6 'Schumpeterian capitalism' in capitalist development: toward a synthesis of capitalist development and the 'economy as a whole'

Zoltan J. Acs

I Introduction

As is evident from this volume, and many other publications, Schumpeter experienced a renaissance in the last few decades of the twentieth century. This was in large part due to the technological revolution, especially in America, that rediscovered the importance of entrepreneurship and innovation in the *Theory of Economic Development* ([1911] 1934) (*TED*). However, despite this renaissance of Schumpeterian thought, Schumpeter has remained hostage to *Capitalism, Socialism and Democracy* (1950 [1942]) (*CSD*), with its emphasis on the large corporation and the state. Therefore no acceptable theory of the economy as a whole has emerged.

CSD is in fact a theory of the economy as a whole. The reason that Schumpeter never returned to the 'lost' seventh chapter is that at the time he was writing *CSD* in the early 1940s, the institutions of economic development were on a fundamentally different track than they are today. This was the world of 'Schumpeterian capitalism', the transition from capitalism to socialism, where the entrepreneurial function as well as the entrepreneurial class would disappear. The large corporation, by taking over the entrepreneurial function, not only makes the entrepreneur obsolete, but also undermines the sociological and ideological functions of capitalist society.

This is so obvious that I am surprised that scholars even debate this point (Acs, 1984). This leaves us with an interesting question, 'How would Schumpeter close the model of capitalist development given what has happened to the institutional structure of society since his death?' With the ascendance of market economies all over the world, what Audretsch and I call 'The emergence of the entrepreneurial society' (Acs and Audretsch, 2001), *CSD* offers very little that fits the modern world. We suggest that the starting point of this synthesis should be the 'lost' chapter 7, 'The Economy as a Whole', from the first edition of the *TED*. The point of chapter 7 is to connect the entrepreneur to the economic development of society as a whole. According to Schumpeter ([1911] 2002:130):

If one takes those circumstances into account, then one sees the traces of steel in the types of the entrepreneur clearly enough in the social structure. It is not only an economic, but also a social process of reorganization that takes its origin from him. The social pyramid does not consist in economic building blocks . . . His position as entrepreneur is tied to his performance and does not survive his energetic ability to succeed. His position as entrepreneur is essentially only a temporary one, namely, it cannot also be transmitted by inheritance: a successor will be unable to hold on to that social position, unless he inherits the lion's claw along with the prey . . . One cannot speak in the same sense of a class of entrepreneurs and not ascribe to it quite the same social phenomena as one can of those groups, where one finds the same people and their successors remaining in the same position for a long time. Certainly, all those who are entrepreneurs at a certain point of time, will find themselves in situations which have so much in common with entrepreneurial challenges that it suggests alignment of behavior of their self consciously and coherently acting together. But in the case of the entrepreneur this alignment of behavior is much less emphasized and it leads much less to the formation of common dispositions and to a common set of customs and general cultural environment than in the case with other 'classes' . . . Then we can pose the question as to how it can be explained – according to our conception – that the social culture of a nation is at any point in time a unity and that the social development of culture of any nation always shows a uniform tendency.

In this chapter we offer a model of economic development of society as a whole that is consistent with the early edition of Schumpeter's *TED* by placing the entrepreneur at the centre of economic development and focusing on his role in economic development. In this interpretation we cast the USA as the first new nation, the product of a shift in human character and social role that produced the English Revolution and modern American civilization. It was the working out of this new character type, the agent, who possessed unprecedented new powers of discretion and self-reliance yet was bound to collective ends by novel emerging forms of institutional authority and internal restraint (Hickman, 1998).[1] The agent is responsible for the entrepreneurship–philanthropy nexus through which development occurred. Through philanthropy much of the new wealth created historically has been given back to the community to build up the great social institutions *that have a positive feedback on future economic growth and stability*. For example, John D. Rockefeller gave back 95 per cent of his wealth before he died.

II The entrepreneurship–philanthropy nexus
It is widely recognized that much of the success of the American economy in recent years, and historically, is due to its entrepreneurial spirit. Individual initiative and creativity, small business and wealth creation are indelible parts of the American spirit. As a result of the recent technological revolution both the general public and government officials are keenly aware of the role

of the entrepreneur in job and wealth creation and economic growth (Hebert and Link, 1989). This crucial role of the entrepreneur in economic development has fostered efforts by government at all levels to promote entrepreneurship (Hart, 2003).[2] This view is consistent with Schumpeter's early view of entrepreneurship in the *TED* and in *Business Cycles*, however it is inconsistent with much of *CSD* (Mathews, 2002: 3).

However, what is increasingly recognized is that there is another crucial component of American economic, political and social stability. Writing in 1957, Merle Curti advanced the hypothesis that 'philanthropy has been one of the major aspects of and keys to American social and cultural development' (Curti, 1957: 353). To this we would add that philanthropy has also been crucial to economic development. Further, when combined with entrepreneurship, the two become a potent force in explaining the long-run dominance of the American economy. We suggest that if we do not analyse the entrepreneurship–philanthropy nexus, we can understand neither how economic development occurred nor what accounts for American economic dominance.

Philanthropy and economic prosperity is not a new idea. In *Corruption and the Decline of Rome*, Ramsay MacMullen (1988) discusses how charitable foundations were partly responsible for the flourishing of Rome, and their decline coincided with the loss of the empire. The roots of American philanthropy can be found in England in the period from 1480 to 1660. By the close of the Elizabethan period, 'it was generally agreed that all men must somehow be sustained at the level of subsistence' (Jordan, 1961: 401). Though the charitable organizations at the beginning of this period in England were centred on religion and the role of the Church, by the close of the sixteenth century, religious charities comprised only 7 per cent of all charities (ibid.: 402).

How is this philanthropic behaviour explained? According to Jordan, there was the partly religious and partly secular sensitivity to human pain and suffering in sixteenth-century England (ibid.: 406). Doubtless, another important motivating factor was Calvinism, which taught that 'the rich man is a trustee for wealth which he disposes for benefit of mankind, as a steward who lies under direct obligation to do Christ's will' (ibid.: 406–7).

The real founders of American philanthropy were the English men and women who crossed the Atlantic to establish communities that would be better than the ones they had known at home (Owen, 1964). The Puritan leader John Winthrop forthrightly stated their purpose in the lay sermon, 'A Model of Christian Charity', in which he preached on the ship *Arabella* to the great company of religious people voyaging from the old world to New England in the year 1630 (Bremner, 1960: 7). These Puritan principles of industry, frugality and humility had an enduring impact on America (Tocqueville [1835] 1996).

Beginning with the Puritans who regarded excessive profit making as both a crime and a sin (and punished it accordingly), there is a long history of Americans who have questioned the right of people to become rich. In view of the popular prejudice against ostentatious enjoyment of riches, the luxury of doing good was almost the only extravagance the American rich of the first half of the nineteenth century could indulge in with good consciences (Tocqueville [1835] 1996). To whatever extent it is true that donating was the only luxury allowed the rich in the first half of the nineteenth century, things had certainly changed by the second half of the century when Carnegie, Mellon, Duke *et al.* were making their fortunes.

One of the greatest nineteenth-century philanthropists was George Peabody. Peabody, a man of modest beginnings, through canny investment gained a fortune and through impeccable honesty gained a reputation for flawless integrity. He developed a philosophy of philanthropy. Two considerations seem to have been most influential in his philanthropies. One was a deep devotion to the communities in which he was reared or in which he made his money. The other was a secular vision of the Puritan doctrine of the stewardship of riches; his desire, in the simplest terms, was to be useful to mankind. In his lifetime, he donated over $8 million to libraries, science, housing, education, exploration, historical societies, hospitals, churches and other charities (Parker, 1971: 209).

Peabody's most enduring influence, however, lies in the precedents and policies formulated by the Peabody Education Fund Trustees. This fund not only paved the way for subsequent foundation aid to the South after the Civil War but also influenced the operational patterns of subsequent major foundations including John D. Rockefeller's Education Board, the Russell Sage Foundation and the Carnegie Foundation. The thesis that George Peabody was the founder of modern educational foundations was best expressed in the *Christian Science Monitor* (as cited in Parker, 1971: 208):

> George Peabody was in fact the originator of that system of endowed foundations for public purposes which has reached its highest development in the United States . . . It is interesting to consider the many ways in which the example set by [George Peabody] has been followed by visioned men of means in the United States . . . In a sense the Peabody Fund was not the only monument to George Peabody, for the example he set has been followed by a host of other Americans.

Andrew Carnegie exemplified the ideal Calvinist. Carnegie put philanthropy at the heart of his 'gospel of wealth' (Hamer, 1998). For Carnegie, the question was not only, 'How to gain wealth?' but, importantly, 'What to do with it?' 'The Gospel of Wealth' (*The Economist*, 1998) suggested that millionaires, instead of bequeathing vast fortunes to heirs or making benevolent grants by will, should administer their wealth as a public trust during life (Carnegie, 1889). Both Carnegie (at the time) and Jordan (as a historian) suggest that a key motive for philanthropy is social order and harmony. It is plausible that philanthropists like Carnegie took a longer-term approach and realized that their interests necessitated assisting the worthy poor and disadvantaged: enlightened self-interest as opposed to altruism.

In the USA, much of the new wealth created historically has been given back to the community, to build up the great social institutions *that have a positive feedback on future economic growth* (Myers, 1907). For example, it was precisely the great private research universities of Stanford, MIT, Johns Hopkins, Carnegie-Mellon, Duke and Chicago, among others, that were created over a century ago by American philanthropy that played such a critical role in the recent American successes (*The Economist*, 4 October 1997).

We suggest that American philanthropists – especially those who have made their own fortunes – create foundations that, in turn, contribute to greater and more widespread economic development through opportunity, knowledge creation and entrepreneurship. This was Andrew Carnegie's hope when he wrote about 'the responsibility of wealth' over a century ago, and it still inspires entrepreneurs today, though they usually express it in terms of a duty to 'give something back' to the society that helped make their own success possible. The founders of modern American philanthropy tried to provide answers to problems that were national in scope, at a time when national governments were weak.

The American model of entrepreneurship and philanthropy in the nineteenth century was followed by a period of progressivism (increasing role of government) in the early twentieth century and then World War I. Though the period of the 1920s was one of technological change and prosperity, underlying economic problems resulted in the collapse of the world economy into the Great Depression of the 1930s. This period, together with that of World War II, changed the role of the government and the philanthropic activities of the entrepreneur. It is not our point here to argue that the role of philanthropy was to provide social welfare – health insurance, social security, unemployment insurance. Indeed, the rise of the state in the twentieth century was in some ways a rise of social welfare provided by government.

This function, however, is distinct from the pure function of philanthropy that arises from issues of wealth. The rise of the welfare state with its high marginal taxes, high inheritance taxes, antitrust laws, and the abolition of private property in some societies, tried to eliminate the role of private wealth altogether. In fact, in a socialist state the only role for philanthropy might be religious giving. What is interesting is that in the USA the rise of the welfare state did not coincide with a decline in philanthropy. In fact, according to a study by the National Bureau of Economic Research (Dickinson, 1970) total private domestic philanthropy as a percentage of Gross National Product between 1929 and 1959 increased from 1.7 per cent to 2.3 per cent, respectively. It averaged 2.1 per cent during the period. This figure is not significantly different from the 2.5 per cent that Americans contributed to philanthropic causes in 2003. According to the Johns Hopkins non-profit sector project, this figure is the highest in the world, followed by Spain, Britain and Hungary.[3] In the USA, almost 80 per cent of donations are made by individuals. Why did Americans continue to fund philanthropy at least at a constant level even as the Federal Government stepped into the business of social security? According to *Newsweek* (29 September 1997: 34):

> There's no escaping the brutal truth: the nation famous for capitalism red in tooth and claw, the epicenter of the heartless marketplace, is also the land of the handout. It's not really such a paradox. Both our entrepreneurial economic system and our philanthropic tradition spring from the same root: American individualism. Other countries may be content to let the government run most of their schools and universities, pay for their hospitals, subsidize their museums and orchestras, even in some cases support religious sects. Americans tend to think most of these institutions are best kept in private hands, and they have been willing to cough up the money to pay for them.

We have suggested that American philanthropists created foundations that in turn contributed to greater and more widespread economic prosperity by investing in the future of America. Therefore, what differentiates American capitalism from all other forms of capitalism (Japanese, French, German, and Scandinavian) is its historical focus on both the creation of wealth (entrepreneurship) and the reconstitution of wealth (philanthropy).[4] Philanthropy remains part of an implicit social contract stipulating that wealth beyond a certain point should revert to society (Chernow, 1999). Individuals are free to accumulate wealth; however, wealth must be invested back into society to expand opportunity (Acs and Dana, 2001).

Though it has been recognized that the philanthropists of the nineteenth century made possible the basis for wealth creation and social stability, this has not been quantified and placed within the framework of private and social costs and benefits (America, 1995). Take as an example the difficulty in calculating the ex post benefits of the creation of the University of Chicago by the Rockefeller family. The number of Nobel Prize winners at the University of Chicago is one measure of the social benefits that have been reaped by the Rockefeller family investment. Certainly, there was no immediate private benefit to the Rockefeller family, since the contributions occurred several generations later.

The entrepreneurship–philanthropy nexus has not been fully understood by either economists or social scientists, in part owing to a narrow view of self-interest as a fundamental institution of capitalism. Recently, Jeffrey Sachs has articulated a position by which to judge our philanthropic activities based on past accomplishments. According to Sachs, writing in *The Economist*, creating opportunity for future generations is about creating knowledge today, and the model to study is the Rockefeller Foundation.

> The model to emulate is the Rockefeller Foundation, the pre-eminent development institution of the 20th century, which showed what grant aid targeted on knowledge could accomplish. Rockefeller funds supported the eradication of hookworm in the American South; the discovery of the Yellow Fever vaccine; the development of penicillin; the establishment of public-health schools (today's undisputed leaders in their fields) all over the world; the establishment of medical facilities in all parts of the world; the creation and funding of great research centers such as the University of Chicago, the Brookings Institution, Rockefeller University, and the National Bureau of Economic Research; the control of malaria in Brazil; the founding of the research centers that accomplished the green revolution in Asia; and more. (*The Economist*, 24 June 2000: 83)[5]

In 'Schumpeterian capitalism' wealth creation, wealth ownership and wealth distribution were in part left up to the state. However, in an entrepreneurial society it is individual initiative that plays a vital role in propelling the system forward. Entrepreneurial leadership is the mechanism by which new combinations are created, new markets are opened up and new technologies are commercialized that are the basis for prosperity. In an entrepreneurial society, entrepreneurship plays a vital role in the process of wealth creation and philanthropy plays a crucial role in the reconstitution of wealth. The execution of this as we have argued earlier in the chapter was based on the development of a new character type possessing unprecedented new powers of discretion and yet bound to collective ends. This interpretation is also consistent with Schumpeter's chapter 7.

This model of entrepreneurial capitalism, despite the unequal distribution of wealth, with its sharp focus on entrepreneurship and philanthropy should be encouraged. Rather then constraining the rich through taxes, we should allow the rich to campaign successfully for social change through the creation of opportunity. In the past the fight against slavery had some very wealthy backers. If we shut off the opportunities for wealthy individuals to give back their wealth we will also shut off the creation of wealth, which has far greater consequences for an entrepreneurial society.

However, these views of giving back are not universally shared even in the USA. The rich have retreated from facing up to the challenge of how to reconstitute their wealth (*Fortune*, 2 February 1998: 88). Such views are not really fashionable among scholars of philanthropy and more than a few of the professionals who staff foundations. For example, a book recently published by the MIT Press on American foundations argues that they mostly serve as vehicles for advancing the economic and social interests of their benefactors (Dowie, 2001). At an American Assembly meeting a few years ago, the participants (most of whom were professionals who worked for foundations and other non-profit groups) produced a statement calling on philanthropists to do more to redistribute their wealth from the 'haves' to the 'have nots'. Carnegie would have been appalled since he thought that, by fostering greater economic opportunities, philanthropists could prevent such redistributive schemes.

III   Conclusion
In this chapter we have suggested that a theory of economic development based on the early edition of *TED* that includes the 'lost' chapter 7 represents a viable option on how to bridge the gap between economic development and the economy as a whole. We suggest that the relationship between entrepreneurship and philanthropy may provide the institutional foundation for building a Schumpeterian theory of society as a whole.

Notes
1. One could argue that the recent antitrust case against Microsoft was as much about anti-competitive behaviour as about violating this social contract.
2. For a longer version of this argument see Acs and Phillips (2002). Also see Acs and Audretsch (2001) for a statement on the emergence of the entrepreneurial society and Acs, Carlsson and Karlsson (1999).
3. See Salamon and Anheier (1999).
4. For a statement on the nature and logic of capitalism, see Robert L. Heilbroner (1985). Of course it is precisely the institutional framework that differs from country to country and not necessarily the logic of the system. For a discussion of the different institutional frameworks see Michael Porter (2000), on Japan see Wolfgang Streech and Kozo Yamamura (2002), on France see Jonah D. Levy (1999) and on Sweden see Acs and Karlsson (2002) and the working paper by Henreksen and Jakonsson (2000).
5. For a theory of knowledge in economic growth, see Arrow (1962) and Romer (1990). For an application to the regional and global economy see Acs (2000).

References
Acs, Zoltan J., 1984, *The Changing Structure of the U.S. Economy*, New York: Praeger.
Acs, Zoltan J., 2000, *Regional Innovation, Knowledge and Global Change*, London: Pinter.
Acs, Zoltan J. and David B. Audretsch, 2001, 'The emergence of the entrepreneurial society', Swedish Foundation for Small Business, Stockholm, Sweden, May.
Acs, Zoltan J. and Leo P. Dana, 2001, 'Two views of wealth creation', *Small Business Economics*, **16** (2), 63–74.

Acs, Zoltan J. and Charlie Karlsson, 2002, 'Institutions, entrepreneurship and firm growth: the case of Sweden', special issue of *Small Business Economics*.

Acs, Zoltan J. and Ronnie J. Phillips, 2002, 'Entrepreneurship and philanthropy in American capitalism', *Small Business Economics*, **19** (3), 189–204.

Acs, Zoltan J., B. Carlsson and C. Karlsson, 1999, 'The linkages among entrepreneurship, SMEs and the macroeconomy', in Z. Acs, B. Carlsson and C. Karlsson (eds), *Entrepreneurship, Small & Medium-Sized Enterprises and the Macro Economy*, Cambridge: Cambridge University Press, pp. 3–44.

America, Richard, F., 1995, *Philanthropy and Economic Development*, Westport: Greenwood Press.

Arrow, K.J., 1962, 'Economic welfare and the allocation of resources for invention', in Richard Nelson (ed.), *The Rate and Direction of Inventive Activity*, Princeton: Princeton University Press, pp. 609–26.

Bremner, Robert, H., 1960, *American Philanthropy*, Chicago: University of Chicago Press.

Carnegie, Andrew, 1889, 'Wealth', *North American Review*, June.

Chernow, Ron, 1999, *Titan: The Life of John D. Rockefeller Sr*, New York: Vintage.

Curti, Merle, 1957, 'The history of American philanthropy as a field of research', *The American Historical Review*, **62** (2), 352–63.

Dickinson, Frank, G., 1970, *The Changing Position of Philanthropy in the American Economy*, National Bureau of Economic Research, New York: Columbia University Press.

Dowie, Mark, 2001, *American Foundations*, Cambridge: MIT Press.

The Economist, 'The knowledge factory', 4 October 1997, pp. 1–22.

The Economist, 'The gospel of wealth', 30 May 1998, p. 19.

The Economist, 'Sachs on globalization', 24 June 2000, pp. 81–3.

Fortune, 'Most generous Americans', 2 February 1998, p. 88.

Hamer, J.H., 1998, 'Money and the moral order in late nineteenth and early twentieth-century American capitalism', *Anthropological Quarterly*, **71**, 138–50.

Hart, David, 2003, 'The emergence of entrepreneurship policy: governance, start-ups, and growth in the knowledge economy', manuscript, Center for Business and Government, Kennedy School of Government, Harvard University.

Hebert, Robert F. and Albert N. Link (1989), 'In search of the meaning of entrepreneurship', *Small Business Economics*, **1** (1), 39–50.

Heilbroner, Robert, 1985, *The Nature and Logic of Capitalism*, New York: Harper and Row.

Henreksen, Magnus and Ulf Jakonsson, 2000, 'Where Schumpeter was nearly right – the Swedish model and capitalism, socialism and democracy', working paper no. 370, Stockholm School of Economics.

Hickman, Larry A. (1998), *Reading Dewey: Interpretations for a Postmodern Generation*, Indianapolis: Indiana University Press.

Jordan, W.K., 1961, 'The English background of modern philanthropy', *The American Historical Review*, **66** (2), 401–8.

Levy, Johah D., 1999, *Tocqueville's Revenge: State, Society and Economics in Contemporary France*, Boston: Harvard University Press.

MacMullen, Ramsay (1988), *Corruption and the Decline of Rome*, New Haven: Yale University Press.

Mathews, John A., 2002, 'Introduction: Schumpeter's "lost" seventh chapter', *Industry and Innovation*, **9** (1–2), 1–6.

Myers, Gustavus, 1907, *History of Great American Fortunes*, New York: The Modern Library.

Newsweek, 'The land of the handout', 29 September 1997, pp. 34–6.

Owen, David, 1964, *English Philanthropy 1660–1960*, Cambridge: The Belknap Press of Harvard University.

Parker, George F., 1971, *Peabody*, Vanderbilt: Vanderbilt University Press.

Porter, E. Michael, 2000, *Can Japan Compete?*, London: Macmillan Press.

Romer, Paul, 1990, 'Increasing returns and long run growth', *Journal of Political Economy*, **94**, 1002–37.

Salamon, Lester M., Helmut K. Anheier and Associates, 1999, 'The emerging sector revisited', The Johns Hopkins University Institute for Policy Studies Center for Civil Society Studies.

Schumpeter, Joseph A., [1911] 1934, *The Theory of Economic Development*, Cambridge: Harvard University Press.
Schumpeter, Joseph A., [1911] 2002, 'The economy as a whole: the seventh chapter of Schumpeter's The Theory of Economic Development', trans. Ursula Backhaus, *Industry and Innovation*, **9**, 93–145.
Schumpeter, Joseph A., [1942] 1950, *Capitalism, Socialism and Democracy*, New York: Harper and Row.
Streech, Wolfgang and Kozo Yamamura, 2002, *The Origins of Nonliberal Capitalism: Germany and Japan in Comparison*, New York: Cornell University Press.
Tocqueville, Alexis de, [1835] 1996, *Democracy in America*, New York: Harper and Row.

7 The neo-Schumpeterian element in the sociological analysis of innovation
Matthias Weber

1 Introduction

At about the same time that neo-Schumpeterian economics started to play a prominent role in the analysis of technological change and innovation, the conceptual foundations for interpreting the emergence of new technologies also became a major issue in sociological research (social studies of technologies).[1] This was certainly not a pure coincidence, but reflected a widespread discontent with the still prevailing approach for dealing with the relationship between innovation and technological change, on the one hand, and economic and social change on the other. So neo-Schumpeterian economics emphasized its rejection of basic principles of neoclassical economics, i.e. in particular the assumed fully rational and optimizing behaviour of actors and the belief in the equilibrium model of a social optimum if only free markets were ensured by appropriate institutional settings. In social studies of technology, the belief in scientific and technological determinism was a strongly opposed approach. Neither was it a coincidence that the basic concepts used in economics as well as in sociology drew on similar intellectual sources. As will be shown in this contribution, important lines of thought are highly compatible with one another, even if the respective research interests in both disciplines tend to emphasize different aspects of the same phenomenon. After all we may see a reunification of sociological and economic perspectives on technological change, or at least a potential to link them to each other.

The relationship between social studies of technology and neo-Schumpeterian economics must also be seen in the wider context of a more fundamental change in perspective in the social and economic sciences aiming to overcome the dominant, but oversimplified, way of dealing with sources, conditions and impacts of technological change. Similar insights to those in neo-Schumpeterian economics and the social studies of technology were also addressed in a number of other disciplines: regional economics and economic geography (Storper and Scott, 1992; Scott and Storper, 1986; Pyke and Sengenberger, 1992), sociological economics (Granovetter and Swedberg, 1992), business economics (Nonaka and Takeuchi, 1995), institutional economics (Hodgson, 1988) and political sciences (Mayntz and

Scharpf, 1995). This fundamental reorientation of the social and economic sciences with respect to the role of technological change is thus involving a broad spectrum of disciplines, but the two disciplines that primarily addressed this contribution stand out in terms of their ground-laying and pervasive impact.

Coming back to the sociological perspective, the main inspirations for reconceptualizing technological change can be traced back to four main influences:

1. Detailed historical studies of technologies and their emergence shed a new light on the subtle factors and mechanisms by which processes of technological change are determined. They highlighted the importance of studying the economic, social, institutional and political context in which new technologies emerge and thus broadened the range of factors regarded as relevant for shaping new technology.
2. These and other empirical insights nurtured the widespread discontent with the way science and technology were conceptualized in the context of social and economic analysis. Not only were the oversimplified scientific–technological determinist models of innovation and technological change and the rational, optimizing actor model in neoclassical economics rejected, but also the general underestimation of the importance of technology for socioeconomic development was criticized.
3. Earlier conceptual and empirical contributions on the evolution of science, for instance under the headlines of Social Studies of Science (SSS) and Sociology of Scientific Knowledge (SSK), were important precursors for the sociological interpretation of technological change. With science being increasingly seen as a social endeavour, the development of which needs to be explained on the basis of social interactions (Merton, 1973), the application of similar arguments with respect to technology was evident.
4. The concept of scientific paradigms, arguing that scientific change is characterized by phases of comparative stability and fast transformation (Kuhn, 1962), exerted a strong influence on later interpretations of the patterned character of technological change. It found its way into evolutionary economics as well as into sociology, using a wide range of different concepts (see in particular Dosi, 1982; Dosi and Sylos Labini, Chapter 21 in this volume).

Although evolutionary economics and social studies of technologies (SST) were thus inspired by a number of similar sources and both contributed to a broadening of the range of factors that are considered relevant for the emergence of new technological trajectories, they are quite distinct in the emphasis they put on certain aspects of technological change and innovation. As regards the social studies of technologies perspective, two main orientations need to be highlighted. First of all, the microfoundations of processes of technological change were analysed in much detail, i.e. the range of actors considered and their interactions. Apart from scientists, engineers and developers, also users, consumers and even wider audiences of stakeholders have been recognized as relevant actors. In other words, the context of usage has been increasingly taken into account as an important locus of technology shaping. Secondly, the importance of social, cultural and institutional structures has been brought to the forefront. These two dimensions of sociological analysis reflect established and often antagonistic behaviouralist and structuralist traditions in sociological research. In the context of sociological research on technological change, (co-) evolutionary and multi-level approaches have been developed that aim to bridge the gap between these two traditions.[2]

In order to be able to deal with a quite broad range of factors relevant to innovation, a large part of the sociological literature has put the emphasis on the study of individual technologies and their embedding in institutional, organizational and other social conditions. Case study-based research methods were frequently used as a means to underpin empirically the conceptual and heuristic value of the rather general guiding approaches in SST for explaining processes of sociotechnical change. Several different levels of analysis have been addressed, ranging from individuals to laboratories and industries or to wider societal and cultural transformations.

The main conceptual frameworks or schools of thought that inspired the empirical work emerged in the 1980s. The term 'social studies of technology' (SST) will be used subsequently to capture the different lines of thought that have emerged over the past two decades in order to deal with innovation and technological change from a sociological perspective.[3] In spite of their distinct differences, they shared several basic arguments and should thus not be seen as entirely disconnected from each other (see also Russell and Williams, 2002; Rohracher, 1998):

1. A first comprehensive collection of critical research work was edited by MacKenzie and Wajcman (1999, first edition 1985) on *The Social Shaping of Technology*. It emphasized the importance of social categories such as the influence of particular political, economic or cultural interests and values for explaining the emergence of new technologies and innovation.
2. The social constructivist approach (SCOT – social construction of technology) builds extensively on the sociology of scientific knowledge

(SSK), focusing on the processes by which 'closure' of debates among different relevant social groups and convergence of the different interpretations that are assigned to a technology are achieved (Pinch and Bijker, 1984). These processes also go hand in hand with the stabilization of social practices and institutional settings.

3. Actor network theory (ANT) aims to overcome the distinction between the 'social' and the 'technical' in order to build a new social theory that assigns an equally important role to both. It concentrates on the strategies and decisions of key actors, for instance at the level of the research labs or in policy. The proponents of this approach are particularly interested in the ways networks of technologies and actors are built and how they stabilize one another (Callon, 1987, 1992; Latour, 1991). Actor networks are seen as being composed of material and non-material elements, with technical elements playing an equally important role as actors in the emerging network that constitutes a technology. In other words, technical and non-technical elements are treated symmetrically as 'actants' in a network.

4. The large technical systems approach (LTS) as developed by Hughes (1983) emphasizes equally the sociotechnical nature of innovation, but concentrates on their systemic character as particularly apparent in infrastructure systems. He stresses the key role played by 'system-builders' for the emergence of a system, but assigns also a major role to technological 'momentum' and systemic interdependencies for determining the course of the emergence of an LTS. Hughes and his successors (e.g. Mayntz and Hughes, 1988; Summerton, 1994; Coutard, 1999) were thus able to point to a broad range of social *and* technological barriers to innovation.

Obviously, synthesizing the work on the social studies of technology in four main research strands is an oversimplification. First of all, the differences between these lines of research have blurred over the past decade, and the mutual recognition of the different schools has increased. Secondly, there are several lines of research that cannot be easily subsumed under any of the three main lines. For instance, the concept of 'actor-centred institutionalism' was developed in order to deal more adequately with the political factors that contribute to the shaping of technology (Mayntz and Scharpf, 1995). It amalgamates elements of the different schools mentioned, but draws also on work from other disciplines, in particular political sciences. While thus being related to the four aforementioned strands, it would be hard to subsume it under any one of them. Similarly, the approach of sociotechnical constituencies as suggested by Molina (1993) has borrowed ideas from the earlier schools and put them in a wider context. Still, the four basic lines reflect major differences in perspective as well as still ongoing key debates within the social studies of technology.

In spite of some important differences between the aforementioned schools of sociological thought on new technology and innovation, they all share a number of key positions that will be worked out in further detail in the subsequent sections: the socially shaped character of technologies; the embeddedness of technology in local and historical settings; the systemic and configurational character of technology and society; and the interpretation of the dynamics of sociotechnical change.

The emphasis put on these four issues may differ across the different schools of thought, but they reflect widely shared convictions within the community of SST researchers. Moreover, the intention is to highlight differences and similarities between the understanding of these key elements in SST and the corresponding interpretation in the neo-Schumpeterian economics of innovation. Obviously, the two research traditions focus on different objects of analysis; neo-Schumpeterian economics tends to look at innovation in general terms, whereas SST focuses also on the constitution of the 'content' of technology (Williams and Edge, 1996). Still, understanding the complementarities and similarities between both lines of investigation can be fruitful for increasing the awareness of the limitations of each of the approaches.

2   The socially shaped character of technology

A basic conviction of all SST work is that technological change is not driven by any inherent scientific or technical logic, but to a significant extent determined by the particular social contexts in which a technology is produced and used, and from which it cannot be dissociated. Moreover, the process of social shaping is not restricted to the invention and innovation phase, but extends well into the actual diffusion phase where contexts of application are regarded as important sources of learning and shaping of technologies. The recognition that technologies continue to be in the making during their diffusion is a feature that is also mirrored in neo-Schumpeterian economics. However, SST goes much further in underlining that societal choices are made about the substance and the direction of technological change, and that these – often normative – choices are the result of negotiation processes between different social groups and actors, using market as well as non-market interactions.

Whereas neo-Schumpeterian economics tends to put the behaviour of firms and research organization within their institutional contexts at the centre-stage of innovation analysis, SST research considers a broader range of actors and their influence on technological choices, ranging from individual end-users of innovations to the wide spectrum of policy actors shaping the framework conditions for innovations. It looks deeply into the specific motivational structures of actors and their interactions at the micro level (e.g. processes of networking and coalition building).

Also the range of factors of influence regarded as relevant for driving technological change is broader than from a neo-Schumpeterian perspective. It comprises for instance the (collective) visions and expectations that guide individual technology decisions, the power relations, the structure of coalitions, cultural characteristics, and the creativity and values of individuals. These and other issues are usually considered in less detail in evolutionary economics, but are of central importance in SST.

Such a differentiated view of the potential influences on technological change and innovation requires an empirically driven approach for capturing individual decision behaviour. It is clearly difficult to reconcile with the model-oriented approach that dominates economics and that emphasizes the need for simplification and generalization. This is most obvious for rationalist models in mainstream neoclassical economics where technological change is regarded as an externally given set of options from which rational individuals can derive their choices. While also stressing the need for generalization, the (neo-) Schumpeterian approach to innovation has already started to open up the 'black box of innovation' (Rosenberg, 1982) and is thus much closer to the assumptions of SST research. The notion of 'appreciative theorizing' has been introduced (Nelson and Winter, 1982) by leading neo-Schumpeterian economists to underline their departure from the mainstream. More recently, the 'history-friendly models' as discussed by Orsenigo (in this volume) represent a compromise between generalized formal models on the one hand and empirical concreteness on the other.

There is ample evidence of similarities between neo-Schumpeterian Economics and SST as regards the socially shaped character of technology and innovation. For instance, already Schumpeter's emphasis on the key role of the entrepreneur for bringing about innovation is not only a cornerstone in neo-Schumpeterian research, but also compatible with Hughes's (1983) concept of system builders. The notion of satisficing and routinized behaviour as introduced by Nelson and Winter (1982), while aiming at generalization, is rooted in sociological and historical analyses of decision-making processes in firms. Also the contingent and unpredictable nature of sociotechnical change is stressed in both SST research and neo-Schumpeterian economics, though with different emphases. In neo-Schumpeterian economics, innovation (in particular innovation of a radical nature) is seen as being subject to a high degree of unpredictability, resulting mainly from technological and economic uncertainties and interdependence. Sociological analysis confirms these determinants of unpredictability, but in addition stresses also the role of social processes and interdependencies (i.e. processes of coalition and network building, the emergence of guiding visions and expectations, the role of formal and informal power relations, the impact of cultural characteristics or the role of values), thus opening up an even broader space of possible contingencies.

Overall, in spite of sharing a number of basic assumptions regarding the key characteristics of technological change and innovation, SST considers a broader range of social factors and processes, and looks at them more deeply. Neo-Schumpeterian economics has tended to concentrate on firms and research organizations and their institutional environment. However, there are promising fields of research emerging that attempt to combine insights from neo-Schumpeterian economics and SST, for instance in the context of the analysis of the interactions of actors in networks and their contribution to the generation of new knowledge (Pyka and Windrum, 2003).

3 The embeddedness of technology in local and historic contexts

A second characteristic of SST research is the focus on technologies rather than firms as the main unit of innovation analysis, with the emphasis being put on the 'embeddedness' of technology in actor constellations, local contexts and historical settings. This perspective is a direct implication of the socially shaped character of technology, because social settings differ in time and space. Similar ideas have been raised in neighbouring disciplines; for instance notions of 'innovative style' (Kline, 1991) and 'innovative milieu' (Camagni, 1995) have been suggested to capture this localized and historic character of innovation processes and the conditions determining their diffusion.

The localized character of innovation is also recognized in neo-Schumpeterian economics, building in particular on the recognition that knowledge, skills and their interpretation by different actors (e.g. users and producers) tend to be local and cumulative. Here, the emphasis is put on different mechanisms responsible for this localized and cumulative character of knowledge and learning. For instance, increasing returns to scale (Arthur, 1988), network externalities (David, 1985; Katz and Shapiro, 1994), tacitness (Dosi, 1988) and the orienting function of mental frameworks, paradigms and guideposts (Dosi, 1982; Sahal, 1985) have been stressed. In the context of systems approaches, the embeddedness of local interactions and innovation processes in national, regional and sectoral institutional contexts plays a major role (Lundvall, 1992; Nelson, 1993; Edquist, 1997; Malerba, 2004; Johnson and Jacobsson, 2000). Especially Lundvall (1992) stresses the role of institutional settings for framing the learning processes between users and suppliers of technology during the innovation process. Regional innovation systems approaches recognize also the spatial and cultural proximity as relevant elements of the economic analysis of innovation, thus drawing the attention of the local and regional 'tissue' in which innovations are embedded (Braczyk *et al.*, 1998). Innovation systems approaches have been widely used in recent years as a heuristic device for designing and evaluating research, technology and innovation policies at different levels.

These and other conceptual ideas are also reflected in SST research. For instance, the notions of 'technological momentum' (Hughes, 1983, 1987) and 'technological frame' (Bijker, 1995) capture certain facets of Dosi's techno-logical paradigms and of Sahal's technological guideposts, but they have been criticized within SST for having a too deterministic flavour. Similarly, while scarcely using the term 'innovation system', several of the basic ingre-dients of this heuristic approach are also central to SST research, such as e.g. knowledge and skills, interactive learning processes, institutional settings, etc. SST goes beyond these concepts by taking further aspects into account for determining the local and historic embeddedness of technology. The specificities of different types of knowledge and skills, the practices of use as well as the meanings and values attached to technologies exert a strong influence on the process of shaping and give rise to technological path-dependencies; the practices of users extend also well into early phases of innovation beyond their contribution to the selection and purchase of inno-vations; scientific and technological infrastructures are regarded as of major importance; and so on. In general, by expanding the perspective further downstream (i.e. towards the use, diffusion and appropriation of technolo-gies) and further outside the traditional concerns of sociological analysis (i.e. to regulation, policy, infrastructures), SST covers a broad and rich spectrum of aspects of embedding (cf. Russell and Williams, 2002, pp. 78f.).

The embeddedness of technologies has a number of important implica-tions for their assessment. If the impacts of new technology depend to a large extent on the context and the local conditions of deployment, a general and objective assessment of the technological impacts is not possi-ble any more. This insight has severe implications for policy, namely that highly generalized policy measures, either in support of innovation and technological shaping or with the aim of preventing negative impacts, are inappropriate for dealing with local and historic conditions. The approach of Constructive Technology Assessment addresses specifically this problem of local embeddedness and aims at establishing locally adapted mecha-nisms of technology assessment (Rip *et al.*, 1995).

It can thus be concluded that, in spite of many similarities, SST research covers a broader range of contextual influences of the process of technolog-ical change than neo-Schumpeterian economics, but a growing convergence between both disciplines can be observed.

4   The systemic and configurational character of technology and society

The relationship between the social and the technical has always been one of the most contentious issues between the different schools of thought within SST. The key question is dealing with the degree of autonomy that can be assigned to technological change. In other words, a technology can either be reduced to a result of social interaction, or be regarded as something with an inherent logic of its own. Although the different streams of SST are united by their rejection of scientific and technological determinism, it seems hard to deny that technical artefacts and infrastructures impose rigidities and constraints on the further shape and diffusion of technologies.

Obviously, it would be too simple to reduce this question to the dichotomy between the social and technical. Most researchers tend to stress the integrated systemic and configurational character of society–technology interactions or relations (Rohracher, 2000; Russell and Williams, 2002, p. 51), where technology and society are not just regarded as separate though interacting entities, but rather as tightly interwoven parts of the same process of change. Technological entities always integrate social and technical elements; they co-evolve and cannot be dissociated from one another. Several different concepts are used to describe this phenomenon, ranging from 'seamless web' (Hughes, 1986), 'entrenchment' (Collingridge, 1980) and 'socio-technical ensembles' (Bijker, 1993) to 'socio-technologies' (McLoughlin, 1999) and 'technostructures' (Rammert, 1995), not forgetting 'large technical systems' (Hughes, 1983). Perhaps the most far-reaching approach with respect to conceptualizing the relationship between the social and the technical is actor-network theory (ANT) which rejects the idea of separate but interacting domains very explicitly; no analytical a priori distinction is made between actors and technologies which are both 'actants' in a network, though with distinct characteristics. Both the social and the technical are seen as essential and mutually dependent processes of change in society, with technical actants giving stability to the more volatile social tissue (Callon, 1987; Latour, 1991). Guided by ANT, empirical work on electric vehicles demonstrated very powerfully the necessity – and ability – of engineers and planners to imagine integrated sociotechnical visions of the world (Callon, 1980, 1987), as did the example of 'heterogeneous engineering' in the case of sailing ship construction and navigation techniques in the 15th century (Law, 1987).

Most explicit in the use of the systems concepts is obviously the work on Large Technical Systems (LTS) (Hughes, 1983; Mayntz and Hughes, 1988; Summerton, 1994; Coutard, 1999). Systems approaches have often been criticized for a number of reasons: ambiguity of system delimitations, too much emphasis on the stability and entrenchment of systems, too little attention to conflict as a source of change, etc. Other concepts like sociotechnical configurations are now often used to capture some of the essential features of systems approaches, thus avoiding the aforementioned criticism. In contrast to the innovation systems approaches that have become very popular in neo-Schumpeterian economics since the early 1990s, LTS and related work take into account both the institutional and organizational context of technology as well as the systemic character of technology in its own right.

Thanks to the emphasis put on the specific and empirically observable interests, objectives and values of a very broad range of actors, SST is probably better equipped for dealing with a broad spectrum of social conflicts than neo-Schumpeterian approaches that tend to follow a more reductionist, model-oriented approach, be it in an appreciative or a history-friendly way. As a consequence, questions regarding the direction of innovation and technological change can be addressed more concisely within an SST framework, for instance in the context of the debates on innovation and sustainable development. Still, the simplicity and versatility of (in particular) the innovation systems perspective, which is more focused on firms' interaction at the micro level and the influence of institutional structures at the macro level, has turned out to be much more effective in terms of shaping policy agendas.

5   The dynamics of technological change from a sociological perspective
The interpretation and explanation of the dynamics of technological change has always been one of the key themes of SST research. Also in this respect, SST shares with evolutionary economics the criticism of linear and descriptive models of change and underlines the importance of explaining dynamics on the basis of underlying interrelationships and mechanisms (i.e. what is often called 'microfoundations').

Subsequently, different levels of sophistication of looking at the dynamics of technological change will be addressed, starting with predominantly descriptive approaches for capturing the overall dynamics of change. The following three sections will look at the main phases of dynamics that are often referred to in the SST literature, even if different headlines are used.[4] The most recent development is the analysis of technology dynamics as a multi-level phenomenon, which will be addressed in the last section.

5.1   Descriptive technology and innovation dynamics
First of all, and in spite of the necessity to go beyond mere descriptions of the patterns of change, it is indispensable to take a phenomenological look at the macrodynamics of change. Similar concepts as in neo-Schumpeterian economics have been used in SST to capture the observation

that technological change, while being inherently open, proceeds along certain pathways or trajectories. The concept of trajectories is widely used in both neo-Schumpeterian economics and SST to describe the comparatively stable development process of a technology. Whereas neo-Schumpeterian economists tend to use evolutionary metaphors and models to explain the emergence of trajectories (Nelson and Winter, 1982), some SST researchers have coined the term 'quasi-evoluationary' in order to stress the conscious and often strategic coupling between variation, selection and stabilization (Schot, 1992).

These types of approaches are not uncontested because they tend to have a deterministic flavour and overemphasize the macroscopic patterning while neglecting the underlying fluidity at the micro level. In order to capture the specificity of technological developments at the level of individual technologies, the notion of innovation journeys has been introduced. It stresses the openness of technological change and points to the fact that the originally intended shape and use of a technology may change completely in the course of its evolution, and in particular as a result of new forms of usage (Rip and Schot, 2002).

With hindsight, technological trajectories may often look like steady and even linear processes of improvement, but in fact they emerged from a pattern of meandering and branching, with phases of accelerated change and slow change, characterized by many dead ends that were tested in vain. This implies that there are options available where individual and collective actions can be taken in order to make choices between the branches to take, even if there may only be short windows of opportunity when a technology is still sufficiently malleable to influence its course of development (Erdmann, Nill, Sartorius and Zundel, in Chapter 60 of this volume; Sartorius and Zundel, 2005).

Technological trajectories tend to be rather stable as long as they are embedded in what some have called 'technological paradigms' (Dosi, 1982; Dosi and Sylos Labini, Chapter 21 in this volume) or – as a less constraining way of guidance – technological frames (Bijker, 1995) to describe how search and innovation routines are guided. These concepts have later on been broadened beyond even the reach of technologies by referring to the technological or sociotechnical regime as framing and orienting processes of technological change. A technological regime can be defined as 'the coherent complex of scientific knowledge, engineering practices, production process technologies, product characteristics, skills and procedures, established user needs, regulatory requirements, institutions and infrastructures' (Rip and Kemp, 1998). A shift in technological regime can give rise to the emergence of new trajectories, and thus the abandonment of others.

These attempts to interpret sociotechnical change in terms of evolutionary concepts have been important steps forward in terms of understanding technology dynamics, but as ex post rationalizations they do not have much predictive power for individual cases of emerging technologies. In some cases it may even be hard to identify any macroscopic regularities at all, because there is no clear settlement of technological trajectories but rather an ongoing process of change and local adaptation, driven by contradictions and tensions between various potential trajectories and paradigms in design and implementation (Fleck *et al.*, 1990).

This shortcoming of descriptive approaches to technology and innovation dynamics can be found in both neo-Schumpeterian economics and SST. In general, however, SST research tends to emphasize the diversities, contingencies and underlying interactions that characterize technological change rather than aggregate regularities. In neo-Schumpeterian economics, the desire to generalize findings beyond the reach of individual cases seems to be more pronounced, but it implies that the relevance of these generalizations for individual cases is rather limited. However, the empirical contributions of SST and neo-Schumpeterian economics have equally contributed to our improved understanding of technological change.

In order to discuss some of the concepts specific to SST in this respect, we will have a look at three main phases of sociotechnical change that can be frequently observed when studying individual trajectories from an SST perspective: early creation and negotiation; alignment, stabilization and closure; and appropriation and use. In reality, there is obviously no clear-cut distinction between these phases, and neither do they necessarily follow sequentially after each other. They rather take place in parallel, if not to say that sociotechnical change moves back and forth between them, However, it is nevertheless useful for analytical purposes to represent the aggregate process by these distinct phases, in order to systematize the underlying mechanisms and networks of actors that characterize each of them.

5.2   Early creation and negotiation

The early phase of technological change is characterized by a high degree of openness and interpretative flexibility of the artefacts and technologies in question (Pinch and Bijker, 1984), i.e. their content, meaning and usage are still malleable. In this phase, to use the evolutionary metaphor, variety is generated and different alternative designs are suggested and tested. Beyond the incremental advancement of existing trajectories, the role of visionary thinkers and outsiders regarding the established communities should not be underestimated for giving new impulses and generating ideas that have the potential to initiate the emergence of a new paradigm.

This early stage is also crucial for breaking up existing arrangements that stabilize the incumbent technology or system. Breaking up established structures and entering the stage tends to be very hard for new emerging technologies. The role of fuzzy and sometimes over-optimistic expectations can play a very important role in generating promises and visions about what a new technology could potentially deliver (van Lente, 1993). Mokyr (1990) speaks of 'hopeful monstrosities' that still need to be shaped in terms of design and possible patterns of use in order to check and understand their potential. 'Hypes' and the creation of hypes can be instrumental for ensuring sufficient R&D funding in this initial phase, but they entail the risk of later disappointments if the promises do not hold.

Overarching 'Leitbilder' can play an important role in focusing expectations and efforts to make them more tangible. By amalgamating visionary projections with a pragmatic assessment of what seems feasible, 'Leitbilder' represent a concrete and realistic image of the future that can serve as an orientation for concrete decisions to shape technologies. As such, they can also be used to mediate between different decision arenas with their respective time horizons and codes (policy, research, industry, etc.) and thus to support negotiation processes between them (Dierkes, Hoffmann and Marz, 1992).

The phase of early creation and negotiation thus requires building up momentum in two respects. First of all, it requires defining the 'sociotechnical core' (Weyer, 1997), i.e. to anticipate technical and social configurations that could work, for instance by envisaging new forms of individual or societal demand and thus developing an understanding of the possible functions a new technology could play. Learning spaces or niches need to be developed that serve as arenas of development. This is the more important as early protection of a niche tends to be granted only if the functions and demands that are supposed to be met with a new technology can be successfully articulated in research proposals.

Secondly, support needs to be generated within the wider constituency that is needed to promote and support a technology, including also policy-making and lobbying organizations. The formation of networks is particularly crucial in this respect; i.e. the building of alliances with actors in the different realms that are relevant for the success and later entrenchment of a technology (i.e. policy, users, industry, research, etc.).

5.3   Alignment, stabilization and closure

This is the phase when first major (collective) choices are made and the technology in question is adapted to different possible social contexts of application. Several concepts have been conceived to describe this process of establishing more stable relationships between society and technology.

Some underline the stabilization and entrenchment of a technology in context (Collingridge, 1980), or its role as a catalyst of social change rather than as a driver (Sorensen, 2002). Others stress the need for the translation of roles and functions in the course of the joint transformation of a sociotechnical entity or actor network (Callon, 1992), or the importance of building alliances and sociotechnical constituencies in order to support the emergence of a technology (Molina, 1993). In the end, the process of alignment and stabilization leads to different types of interdependencies between actors, organizations, technologies, infrastructures and institutions. For instance, standardization can play an important role as a mechanism to achieve (or counteract) alignment (Schmidt and Werle, 1998). Similarly, new visions and paradigms can be important means to guide processes of social alignment. Infrastructures represent very powerful enablers and reinforcements of entrenchment, especially when requiring major amounts of investment. Finally, social practices with respect to a new technology are critical for its emergence, because they are directly linked to its adoption (or rejection). In this fluid situation, power and influence can be decisive in tipping the balance in favour of one technological trajectory and against another alternative.

A typical dilemma in this context is how to avoid too early alignment and maintain competition between alternatives until processes of learning have advanced sufficiently the state of knowledge to allow making well-informed choices. Strategic Niche Management has been suggested as an approach to open up such protected learning spaces as a means to enable both learning processes and alignment. It also helps avoid immediate competition of an emerging technology with the established and well-entrenched sociotechnical system, a situation that is unlikely to turn out successfully for the newcomer technology (Hoogma *et al.*, 2002; Weber *et al.*, 1999). Not only is a new technology in an infant state likely to present several problems and failures, entailing the risk of losing credibility, but also the so-called 'sailing ship effect' (i.e. the further improvement of the incumbent technology once it is threatened by new alternatives) needs to be taken into account.

At a certain moment in time, the fluid process of entrenchment leads to at least a temporary closure of open debates and negotiations. Standards are set, actor networks constituted, social practices established and the main stabilizing mechanisms have exerted their influence and contributed to the creation of comparatively stable interdependencies and 'lock-ins'. In the end, technology and the social are interwoven and embedded in economic, social and technological contexts, as well as in cultural and symbolic practices. Obviously, in many, closure is never achieved, but a technology remains in an infant state of making and falls into oblivion.

5.4   Appropriation and use

The diffusion of technology is not just the result of the adoption of a given artefact, but is often paralleled by a profound transformation of the technology in question once it is put to use in a social context. This transformation refers not only to a change or improvement of the technology to make it better fit given user requirements, but must be conceived more broadly as a process of domestication (Lie and Sorensen, 1996). A technology obtains a role in a social setting, and not just the initially intended and inscribed meanings. It can play very different roles (not the least depending on the diverse range of users) and acquire new meanings that lead to new commitments and identities in the context of use. These processes of decontextualization/disembedding and recontextualization/re-embedding are crucial for making a technology flexible and thus enabling its adaptation and wider diffusion into new contexts other than the ones it was initially meant for (Weyer, 1997; Rip and Schot, 1999).

The importance of the context of use and appropriation for giving technology a meaning can be well exemplified by the case of information and telecommunication technology, where user requirements often do not pre-exist but are the result of a joint learning process (see Williams and Edge, 1996; Cawson, Haddon and Miles, 1995). This learning process has a much broader scope than user–supplier relationships addressed in the national systems of innovation literature where mainly the fairly well defined requirements of industrial users have been considered (Lundvall, 1992). In SST, social learning puts the emphasis on the development and the articulation of demand and subsequently on the specification of contexts of use as a central locus of innovation, for instance by means of experiments with users (Russell and Williams, 2002, p. 75; Rip and Schot, 2002).

The emphasis put on appropriation and use has major implications for the ability to anticipate technological development and assess its impacts; rather than technology forecasting it becomes necessary to 'anticipate on the contextualization' of innovations (Rip and Schot, 1999). Similarly, the ex ante assessment of technological impacts can only be of limited help as long as the possible contextualizations are unknown.[5]

5.5   Multi-level and policy-oriented approaches

The classic dichotomy between micro- and macro-level analysis, between structure and agency as the main determinants of sociotechnical change, has been a source of fierce debates in both economics and sociology for decades. Meso-level approaches that focus, for instance, on styles of innovation, technological niches, innovation networks or sectoral innovation systems (Green *et al.*, 1998; Kemp, Schot and Hoogma, 1998; DeBresson and Amesse, 1991; Malerba, 2004) were an attempt to bridge the gap, but, at least from the perspective of SST, they turned out to be too narrow to capture the broad spectrum of determinants recognized as important.

Moreover, a growing interest can be observed in making constructive use of the insights from SST as well as from neo-Schumpeterian economics, aiming to guide and inform the development of policy strategies and the shaping of sociotechnical change. These constructive approaches can take different forms: first of all, process-oriented approaches have been designed that build on the active involvement of a range of actors and stakeholders in forward-looking decision-making processes (Rip, Misa and Schot, 1995; Brown, Rappert and Webster, 2000). Secondly, tools and guidelines have been developed to support innovation management strategies that incorporate insights from SST (for instance, de Laat, 1996; Weber *et al.*, 1999).

Finally, multi-level approaches have been developed in recent years that take local settings as well as structural conditions into account for explaining technology and innovation dynamics (and thus bridge the gap between macro and micro). For instance, the literature on transitions and transition management has been quite influential in academic as well as in policy debates (Rotmans *et al.*, 2001; Kemp and Rotmans, 2005). It amalgamates insights from neo-Schumpeterian economics as well as from SST. Central to this framework are two main interests. First of all, it aims to understand long-term processes of emergence and transformation of technological regimes, but secondly also to guide and organize collective processes of decision making. It has started to be adopted in policy with respect to the role of innovation for sustainable development. Because of the pervasiveness of sociotechnical transitions, innovation is regarded as a distributed phenomenon that depends on decisions and inputs from a wide spectrum of social loci and actors (Kuhlmann, 2001). Transition management relies strongly on learning processes in technological niches as well as on networking and institutional change at the level of technological regimes, both set within in a sociotechnical landscape of comparatively stable socioeconomic and cultural context conditions (see Geels, 2002; Kemp and Rotmans, 2005; Rip and Kemp, 1998). Multi-level perspectives like the transitions framework stress the need for intervention at different levels simultaneously: advancing technological niches while shaping regimes in order to contribute to an adjustment of the sociotechnical transitions.

Within meso- and multi-level approaches, networking and learning are regarded as central mechanisms of coordination that facilitate adaptability and learning on the one hand, and the entrenchment and stabilization of technology on the other by interconnecting distributed agents. These insights have also led to first joint attempts between SST researchers and neo-Schumpeterian economists to model the dynamics of innovation networks, based on self-organization and self-referential concepts (Pyka and

Küppers, 2002; Pyka, in Chapter 23 of this volume). This kind of inroad is of particular interest insofar as it allows merging micro-level (i.e. micro-economic or behavioural) and macro-level (i.e. macroeconomic or structural) determinants of technological change into multi-level simulation models. At the moment, these approaches, inspired by complex systems research, either formally or metaphorically, are still in their infancy, but represent an interdisciplinary promise for better capturing innovation dynamics.

While using a different terminology, SST accounts of innovation dynamics are thus quite similar to those in neo-Schumpeterian economics, at least in conceptual terms. In both disciplines the balance between stabilizing and selecting forces on the one hand and contingent, variety-creating forces on the other is regarded as crucial for determining innovation dynamics. However, the detailed mechanisms taken into consideration are more variegated in SST than in economics, where the interest in the generalization of findings based on conceptual and empirical models, but also using formal and simulation models, is more advanced. For instance, path-dependencies and lock-ins have been modelled mathematically in economics, but they have also been analysed in great detail in SST in terms of stabilizing mechanisms that lead to entrenchment and closure, taking into account a very rich spectrum of aspects ranging from technological interdependencies to cultural issues. Once entrenchment and stabilization mechanisms have worked out and closure is achieved, they exert a selective force by excluding incompatible options, very similar to the mechanisms of lock-in and path-dependency that have been modelled in neo-Schumpeterian economics (e.g. Arthur, 1988). Probably most distinctive of SST in terms of interpreting dynamics is the emphasis on contextualization as a decisive influence shaping the actual content of a technology, a quality that has also attracted increasing attention to evolutionary modelling, but usually simplified into fitness landscapes or market environments. However, as mentioned before, this observation reflects the basic difference in research interests between SST and neo-Schumpeterian economics, where the former puts more emphasis on the specificities of individual historic and local settings and the latter aims more at generalizations for explaining dynamics.

6   Conclusions: the joint contribution of social studies of technology and neo-Schumpeterian economics to reorienting innovation research

The sociological perspectives on technological change introduced in this contribution share with neo-Schumpeterian thinking the conviction that innovation and new technology are not the deterministic result of scientific and technological push factors, nor can they be derived directly from market needs. Rather, they emerge in response to a wide range of social, technological, economic, political and other wider environmental factors. It could also be shown that the two perspectives differ in many respects, but these differences should not be interpreted in terms of conflicts but rather in terms of potential for complementarities and cross-fertilization. In this sense, the often cited convergence between SST and neo-Schumpeterian economics misses the point. One should rather say that both frameworks are overlapping and have their specific strengths. Those features that distinguish SST are summarized below.

The first main strength of SST consists of the broad range of factors and determinants that have been captured in a wide variety of case histories. Whereas SST tends to develop a highly sophisticated conceptual vocabulary as a means of generalization, in neo-Schumpeterian economics middle-range generalizations and theories with some prescriptive power are more common. This characteristic of SST is particularly useful to capture the influence of users on the shaping of new technology and the role of institutional, cultural and political factors. SST thus allows for a very detailed analysis of the changing shape of new technology from its early inception to its application.

The second main strength must be seen in the fact that the social studies of technology have probably made the most far-reaching attempts to understand the detailed behaviour of individuals and groups of individuals, and how it determines innovation dynamics. It puts the emphasis on the detailed mechanisms and specificities, on the diversity and contingency of sociotechnical change rather than on regularities. In neo-Schumpeterian economics, on the contrary, generalized models of behaviour are applied to guide research (firms, routines, satisficing behaviour, etc.), an approach that is geared towards seeking generalization in view of better innovation performance. It is thus better equipped to capture aggregate regularities, whereas SST tends to call these regularities into question (e.g. the stability of company boundaries). Also in this respect, the two strands could be seen as complementary to one another. In other words, 'while the techno-economic patterns it depicts can be taken as an appropriate summary for the aggregate effects of structured incentives or of routine procedures and transactions, SST [here 'Social Shaping of Technology', MW] in effect seeks to demonstrate how and to what extent the microeconomic mechanisms this work posits actually operate in specific cases' (Russell and Williams, 2002, p. 44). In other words, the strength of SST to capture detailed and differentiated accounts of case histories is a weakness from the perspective of generalization. The ability to generalize at an intermediate level of aggregation in turn is a strength of neo-Schumpeterian economics.

A third important strength must be seen in the ability of SST to deal with a wide variety of types of social conflicts about the substance of new technologies, thus going beyond the scope of most economic analysis. This becomes most obvious with respect to the direction of sociotechnical change, for instance in terms of environmental or sustainability objectives attached to innovation. By recognizing the socially shaped character of innovations, a rationale for giving innovation a direction can be derived, even if the direction to choose may be highly controversial. At least, the existence of these underlying conflicts of interest about the direction of technological change is explicitly part of the analytical framework of SST. Not surprisingly, social shaping research has been quite influential in putting onto the policy agendas issues of sustainability and innovation, i.e. abandoning the growth orientation of most innovation research coming from (also neo-Schumpeterian) economics.

Fourth, multi-level frameworks based on concepts like strategic niche management and transition management have made a significant step forward in SST from purely analytical insights towards providing orientation and advice for policy. Based on a comprehensive conceptual framework, which takes into account a wide range of determinants and dynamic (stabilizing and reinforcing) mechanisms, policy approaches have been developed that rely strongly on network building, experimentation in niches, learning processes and contextualization in a long-term perspective. As such, this research and policy analysis stream represents a strong blending of sociological and evolutionary thinking, with the aim of modernizing policy steering and coordination.

Finally, as a consequence of the broader range of aspects taken into account in SST, also a broader range of levers is made available for shaping technological innovation: science and technology, mental frameworks and expectations, organizational settings, cultural frameworks, application contexts, social practices, power relations etc. open up a multitude of inroads to influence processes of technology creation, stabilization, closure and use.

These particular strengths of SST as compared with neo-Schumpeterian economics must be seen in relation to the different research interests that the two disciplines pursue. Whereas neo-Schumpeterian economics tends to look at innovation with the intention of generalizing findings into appreciative or history-friendly theories, and increasingly also into mathematical and simulation models, SST focuses on the constitution of the 'content' of technology (Williams and Edge, 1996). Recognizing these differences in focus may help us to perceive the complementarities between the two lines of investigation as well as the limitations and specific advantages of each of the approaches.

Both research strands thus made important complementary contributions to the change in perspective on the role of innovation and technological change for processes of social–economic change within the broad spectrum of social and economic sciences. Thanks to their fundamental nature, both SST and neo-Schumpeterian economics have inspired a rethinking in other disciplines and provided the basic elements for incorporating a more elaborated view of innovation and new technology into existing conceptual frameworks, if not to say for triggering the development of new frameworks. This is not to say that they were the only sources of inspiration for this change in perspective, but by putting innovation and new technology at the heart of analysis, they provided deep new insights on which other disciplines could build.

Notes

1. The author would like to thank Andreas Pyka, Harald Rohracher and Bernhard Truffer for constructive comments on earlier drafts of this contribution.
2. See for instance the work on technological or sociotechnical regimes (Rip and Kemp, 1998), notions that have inspired research work in neo-Schumpeterian economics as well. Also Schot (1992) borrows elements from neo-Schumpeterian economics when introducing his idea of quasi-evolutionary models.
3. It is not always easy to distinguish clearly the main lines of thought within SST, especially because there has been a tendency towards convergence between them. The different sides have come to recognize and integrate the respective contributions in their own lines of research. This is reflected, for instance, in the breadth of contribution covered by the second edition of MacKenzie and Wajcman's book, *The Social Shaping of Technology* (1999). As a consequence, the label 'social shaping of technology' is sometimes used as an overarching headline now. However, in this contribution the more neutral term 'social studies of technology' is used.
4. See for instance Russell and Williams (2002) or Weyer (1997) who speaks of 'generation of the socio-technical core', 'stabilization' and 'decontextualization'.
5. This leads to the well-known Collingridge (1980) dilemma which argues that attempts to control a technology in an early development phase fail because its final shape and contextualization cannot be predicted; once it has become entrenched, however, it is not open anymore to any attempt at control.

References

Arthur, W.B. (1988), Competing technologies: an overview, in G. Dosi *et al.* (eds), *Technical Change and Economic Theory*, London: Pinter, pp. 590–607.
Bijker, W.E. (1993), Do not despair: there is life after constructivism, *Science, Technology & Human Values*, **18**(1), 113–38.
Bijker, W.E. (1995), *Of Bicycles, Bakelite and Bulbs: Towards a Theory of Sociotechnical Change*, Cambridge, MA: MIT Press.
Braczyk, H.-J., Cooke, P. and Heidenreich, M. (eds) (1998), *Regional Innovation Systems*, London: UCL Press.
Brown, N., Rappert, B. and Webster, A. (eds) (2000), *Contested Futures: A Sociology of Prospective Science and Technology*, Aldershot: Ashgate.
Callon, M. (1980), The state and technical innovation: a case study of the electric vehicle in France, *Research Policy*, **9**, 358–76.
Callon, M. (1987), Society in the making: the study of technology as a tool for sociological analysis, in W.E. Bijker, T.P. Hughes and T. Pinch (eds), *The Social Construction of Technological Systems. New Directions in the Sociology and History of Technology*, Cambridge, MA: MIT Press, pp. 83–103.
Callon, M. (1992), The dynamics of techno-economic networks, in R. Coombs, P.P. Saviotti and V. Walsh (eds), *Technological Change of Company Strategy. Economic and Sociological Perspectives*, London: Academic Press, pp. 72–102.

Camagni, R. (1995), The concept of innovative milieu and its relevance for public policies in European lagging regions, *Papers in Regional Science*, **74**, 317–40.

Cawson, A., Haddon, L. and Miles, I. (1995), *The Shape of Things to Consume: Delivering Information Technology into the Home*, Aldershot: Avebury.

Collingridge, D. (1980), *The Social Control of Technology*, London: Pinter.

Coutard, O. (ed.) (1999), *The Governance of Large Technical Systems*, London: Routledge.

David, P. (1985), Clio and the economics of QWERTY, *American Economic Review*, **75**, 332–7.

DeBresson, C. and Amesse, F. (1991), Networks of innovators: a review and introduction to the issue, *Reseach Policy*, **20**, 363–79.

De Laat, B. (1996), 'Scripts for the future. Technology foresight, strategic evaluation and sociotechnical networks: the confrontation of script-based scenarios', PhD thesis, University of Amsterdam.

Dierkes, M., Hoffmann U. and Marz, L. (1992), *Leitbild und Technik. Zur Entstehung und Steuerung technischer Innovationen*, Berlin: Edition Sigma.

Dosi, G. (1982), Technological paradigms and technological trajectories: a suggested interpretation of the determinants and directions of technological change, *Research Policy*, **11**, 147–62.

Dosi, G. (1988), Sources, procedures and microeconomic effects of innovations, *Journal of Economic Literature*, **26**, 1120–71.

Edquist, C. (ed.) (1997), *Systems of Innovation. Technology, Institutions and Organizations*, London: Pinter.

Fleck, J., Webster, J. and Williams, R. (1990), The dynamics of IT implementation: a reassessment of paradigms and trajectories of development, *Futures*, **22**, 618–40.

Geels, F.W. (2002), Technological transitions as evolutionary reconfiguration processes: a multi-level perspective and a case-study, *Research Policy*, **31**, 1257–74.

Granovetter, M. and Swedberg, R. (eds) (1992), *The Sociology of Economic Life*, Boulder, CO: Westview.

Green, K., Walsh, V., Coombs, R. and Richard, A. (1998), Differences in 'styles' of technological innovation: an introduction, *Technology Analysis and Strategic Management*, **25**, 403–7.

Hodgson, G.M. (1988), *Economics and Institutions. A Manifesto for a Modern Institutional Economics*, Oxford: Polity Press.

Hoogma, R., Kemp, R., Schot, J. and Truffer, B. (2002), *Experimenting for Sustainable Transport. The Approach of Strategic Niche Management*, London: EF&N Spon.

Hughes, T.P. (1983), *Networks of Power: Electrification of Western Society, 1880–1930*, Baltimore, MD: Johns Hopkins University Press.

Hughes, T.P (1986), The seamless web: technology, science, etcetera, etcetera, *Social Studies of Science*, **16**, 281–92.

Hughes, T.P. (1987), The evolution of large technical systems, in W.E. Bijker, T.P. Hughes and T.J. Pinch. (eds), *The Social Construction of Technological Systems*, Cambridge, MA: MIT Press, pp. 51–82.

Johnson, A. and Jacobsson, S. (2000), The diffusion of renewable energy technology: an analytical framework and key issues for research, *Energy Policy*, **28**, 625–40.

Katz, M. and Shapiro, C. (1994), Systems competition and network effects, *Journal of Economic Perspectives*, **8**, 93–115.

Kemp, R. and Rotmans, J. (2005), The management of the co-evolution of technical, environmental and social systems, in K.M. Weber and J. Hemmelskamp (eds), *Towards Environmental Innovation Systems*, Berlin: Springer, pp. 33–54.

Kemp, R., Schot, J. and Hoogma, R. (1998), Regime shifts to sustainability through processes of niche formation: the approach of strategic niche management, *Technology Analysis and Strategic Management*, **10**, 175–95.

Kline, S. (1991), Styles of innovation and their cultural basis, *Chemtech*, August, pp. 473–80.

Kuhlmann, S. (2001), *Management of Innovation Systems. The Role of Distributed Intelligence*, Antwerp: Maklu-Uitgevers.

Kuhn, T. (1962), *The Structure of Scientific Revolutions*, 2nd edn, Chicago, IL: University of Chicago Press.

Latour, B. (1991), Technology is society made durable, in J. Law (ed.), *A Sociology of Monsters: Essays on Power, Technology and Domination*, London: RKP, pp. 103–31.

Law, J. (1987), Technology and heterogeneous engineering: the case of Portuguese expansion, in W.E. Bijker, T.P. Hughes and T.J. Pinch (eds), *The Social Construction of Technological Systems*, Cambridge, MA: MIT Press, pp. 111–34.

Lie, M. and Sorensen, K.H. (eds) (1996), *Making Technology our Own? Domesticating Technology into Everyday Life*, Oslo: Scandinavian University Press.

Lundvall, B.-Å. (ed.) (1992), *National Systems of Innovation. Towards a Theory of Innovation and Interactive Learning*, London: Pinter.

MacKenzie, D. and Wajcman, J. (eds) (1999), *The Social Shaping of Technology*, 2nd edn, Buckingham: Open University Press.

Malerba, F. (ed.) (2004), *Sectoral Systems of Innovation. Concepts, Issues and Analyses of Six Major Sectors in Europe*, Cambridge: Cambridge University Press.

Mayntz, R. and Hughes, T.P. (eds) (1988), *The Development of Large Technical Systems*, Frankfurt a.M.: Campus.

Mayntz, R. and Scharpf, F.W. (eds) (1995), *Gesellschaftliche Selbstregulierung und politische Steuerung*, Frankfurt a.M.: Campus.

McLoughlin, I. (1999), *Creative Technological Change: the Shaping of Technology and Organisations*, London: Routledge.

Merton, R.K. (1973), *The Sociology of Science. Theoretical and Empirical Investigations*, Chicago, IL: University of Chicago Press.

Mokyr, J. (1990), *The Lever of Riches*, Oxford: Oxford University Press.

Molina, A. (1993), In search of insights into the generation of techno-economic trends: micro- and macro-constituencies in the microprocessor industry, *Research Policy*, **22**, 479–506.

Nelson, R.R. (ed.) (1993), *National Innovation Systems: a Comparative Study*, Oxford: Oxford University Press.

Nelson, R.R. and Winter, S.G. (1982), *An Evolutionary Theory of Economic Change*, Cambridge, MA: Bellknap Press.

Nonaka, I. and Takeuchi, H. (1995), *The Knowledge-creating Company: How Japanese Companies Create the Dynamics of Innovation*, New York: Oxford University Press.

Pinch, T. and Bijker, W.E. (1984), The social construction of facts and artefacts: or how the sociology of science and the sociology of technology might benefit each other, *Social Studies of Science*, **14**, 399–444.

Pyka, A. and Küppers, G. (eds) (2002), Innovation Networks. Theory and Practice, Cheltenham, UK and Northampton, MA, USA: Edward Elgar.

Pyka, A. and Windrum, P. (2003), The self-organisation of strategic alliances, *Economics of Innovation and New Technology*, **12**, 245–68.

Pyke, F. and Sengenberger, W. (eds) (1992), *Industrial Districts and Local Economic Regeneration*, Geneva: International Institute for Labour Studies.

Rammert, W. (1995), Technology within society, parts I and II, in T. Cronberg and K. Sörensen (eds), *Similiar Concerns, Different Styles? Technology Studies in Western Europe*, COST Report, Brussels: European Commission, pp. 161–238.

Rip, A. and Kemp, R. (1998), Technological change, in S. Rayner and E.L. Malone (eds), *Human Choice and Climate Change*, vol. 2, Columbus, OH: Battelle Press, pp. 327–99.

Rip, A. and Schot, J. (1999), Anticipation on contextualisation: loci for influencing the dynamics of technological development, in D. Sauer and C. Lang (eds), *Paradoxien der Innovation. Perspektiven sozialwissenschaftlicher Innovationsforschung*, Frankfurt a.M.: Campus.

Rip and Schot (2002), Identifying *loci* for influencing the dynamics of technological develop- ment, in K.H. Sorensen and R. Williams (eds), *Shaping Technology, Guiding Policy: Concepts, Spaces and Tools*, Cheltenham, UK and Northampton, MA, USA: Edward Elgar, pp. 155–72.

Rip, A., Misa, T. and Schot, J. (eds) (1995), *Managing Technology in Society: the Approach of Constructive Technology Assessment*, London: Pinter.

Rohracher, H. (1998), Technology policy – would social studies of technology make a difference?, *Schriftenreihe des Interuniversitären Forschungszentrums für Technik, Arbeit und Kultur* (IFZ), Heft 27, Graz.

Rohracher, H. (2000), Converging paradigms? Economic and sociological concepts of technical change and economic policy, *Veda, Technika, Spolecnost* (Science, Technology, Society), **IX**(XXII), pp. 5–26.

Rosenberg, N. (1982), *Inside the Black Box. Technology and Economics*, Cambridge: Cambridge University Press.

Rotmans, J., Kemp, R. and van Asselt, M. (2001), More evolution than revolution. Transition management in public policy, *Foresight*, **3** (1), 15–31.

Russell, S. and Williams, R. (2002), Social shaping of technology: frameworks, findings and implications for policy, with glossary of social shaping concepts, in K.H. Sorensen and R. Williams (eds), *Shaping Technology, Guiding Policy. Concepts, Spaces and Tools*, Cheltenham, UK and Northampton, MA, USA: Edward Elgar, pp. 37–132.

Sahal, D. (1985), Technology guideposts and innovation avenues, *Research Policy*, **14**, 61–82.

Sartorius, C. and Zundel, S. (eds) (2005), *Time Strategies, Innovation and Environmental Policy*, Cheltenham, UK and Northampton, MA, USA: Edward Elgar.

Schmidt, S. and Werle, R. (1998), *Coordinating Technology: Studies in the International Standardisation of Telecommunications*, Cambridge, MA: MIT Press.

Schot, J. (1992), Constructive technology assessment and technology dynamics: the case of clean technologies, *Science, Technology and Human Values*, **17**, 36–56.

Scott, A. and Storper, M. (eds) (1986), *Production, Work, Territory: The Geographical Anatomy of Industrial Capitalism*, Boston: Allen and Unwin.

Sorensen, K.H. (2002), Social shaping on the move? On the policy relevance of the social shaping of technology perspective, in K.H. Sorensen and R. Williams (eds), *Shaping Technology, Guiding Policy. Concepts, Spaces and Tools*, Cheltenham, UK and Northampton, MA, USA: Edward Elgar, pp. 19–36.

Storper, M. and Scott, A. (1992), *Pathways to Industrialization and Regional Development*, London: Routledge.

Summerton, J. (ed.) (1994), *Changing Large Technical Systems*, Boulder, CO: Westview.

van Lente, H. (1993), *Promising Technology: the Dynamics of Expectations in Technological Developments*, Delft: Eburon.

Weber, K.M., Hoogma, R., Lane, B. and Schot, J. (1999), *Experimenting with Sustainable Transport Innovations: a Workbook for Strategic Niche Management*, Sevilla/Enschede: IPTS/University of Twente.

Weyer, Johannes (1997), Konturen einer netzwerktheoretischen Techniksoziologie, in J. Weyer, U. Kirchner, L. Riedl and J.F.K. Schmidt (eds), *Technik, die Gesellschaft schafft*, Berlin: Edition Sigma, pp. 23–52.

Williams, R. and Edge, D. (1996), The social shaping of technology, *Research Policy*, **25**, 865–99.

8 A Schumpeterian renaissance?
Chris Freeman

I Introduction

This chapter endeavours to address three main questions. First, has there actually been a 'Schumpeterian renaissance'? Second, if so, which of the main features of this renaissance have been especially influential? Finally, which of these features has been particularly contested and what has been the outcome of these debates?

Early work on the economics of invention and innovation often commented on the lack of attention to these topics in the mainstream literature, or indeed, in any of the published literature, e.g. Jewkes *et al.* (1958) or Rogers (1962). In his book *Diffusion of Innovations* (1962), Rogers reported that he could find only one study of diffusion of industrial innovations in the economics literature and as late as 1973, in a major survey article, Kennedy and Thirlwall still complained at the lack of attention to innovation.

The same complaint certainly could not be made today and this is indeed one indication that there has been a Schumpeterian renaissance in the late twentieth century, continuing to this day. Rogers (1986) himself in his later work on diffusion of innovations commented on the rapid proliferation of studies in this field in the 1970s and 1980s. A more general indication of the upsurge of interest in the economics literature as well as in the related management literature is provided by the appearance of a number of new journals in the 1980s and 1990s (Table 8.1). This change is also evident in the numbers of papers dealing with Schumpeterian topics in such major journals as the *Economic Journal*, *The American Economic Review*, the *Journal of Economic Literature* and the *Harvard Business Review*.

In the period just after his death, much of the literature concentrated on one rather narrow aspect of Schumpeter's legacy – the role of large monopolistic firms in innovation (see Kamien and Schwartz, 1975, for a summary of this debate). This was sometimes erroneously construed as Schumpeter's main contribution to economics and described as the Schumpeterian theorem. As with several similar debates, it has been largely resolved by various contributors to the Schumpeterian renaissance, who have shown that in the early phases of a technological revolution typically many small firms compete, although one or a few of these may enjoy temporary monopolistic positions and earn exceptionally high profits.

Table 8.1   The Schumpeterian heritage: journals dealing mainly with innovation and management of innovation

Title	Date of inception
Technological Forecasting and Social Change	1965
Research Policy	1971
Science and Public Policy	1973
Economics of Innovation and New Technology	1980
Structural Change and Economic Dynamics	1989
Journal of Evolutionary Economics	1991
Industrial and Corporate Change	1991
Industrial Innovation	1993
Technovation	1980
International Journal of Technology Management	1983
Technology Analysis and Strategic Management	1988
International Journal of Innovation Management	1997
International Journal of Entrepreneurship and Innovation	1999

Recent evidence has confirmed abundantly Schumpeter's theory of 'bandwagon' effects in which these high profits are eroded and competed away by new entrants, not before, however, some of them have grown into very large successful firms. In the later stages of rapid diffusion, these profits may confer exceptional advantages in market power, incremental innovation and scale of R&D, as has evidently been the case with Microsoft, to take only one example from recent history. An evolutionary view of changing technology and market structure resolves many such problems despite the complexities of the turbulent competitive struggles and occasionally of government intervention. Attention to the high degree of uncertainty about the outcome of such struggles and depth of empirical analysis of their evolution has been one of the main achievements of the Schumpeterian renaissance.

Schumpeter's main point that competition from the new or improved product, process or organization is a more devastating form of competition than non-innovative competition has been abundantly confirmed, absorbed and disseminated by numerous case studies of management in almost every industry. (See, for example, Crépon *et al.* (1998) for a statistical approach to productivity gains from innovation, or Christensen and Rosenbloom (1995) for the case of competition *between* innovative firms.) So, too, has his point that there are phases in this struggle when large monopolies do enjoy some advantages, despite the persistent dogmatic insistence of some of his critics that they are always harmful to technical progress and economic efficiency. Perhaps the stronger evidence of the Schumpeterian renaissance is in the attention paid to management of innovation in management courses, schools and textbooks (see, for example, Tidd *et al.*, 1997, and Porter, 1990, for competition in innovation between nations). Lundvall (2004) has reported that Google came up with 5000 references to 'national systems of innovation'.

Historians still wrestle with the definition and evaluation of the Renaissance in Italy six centuries ago, so that it is hardly surprising that the contemporary evaluation of the Schumpeterian renaissance is controversial. Bibliometric evidence, although it is quite persuasive of a considerable growth of interest in some of Schumpeter's main ideas, does not in itself demonstrate that any of his ideas became dominant in the economics profession, nor which of his ideas have had the greatest influence beyond this profession.

Consequently, the viewpoint of this chapter is a purely personal one and certainly would not claim to be definitive. It is however based on about 50 years of research and discussion from the time of Schumpeter's death (1950) until the present day. This has been sufficient to convince this author that Schumpeter's central ideas – that innovation is the crucial source of effective competition, of economic development and the transformation of society – have become very widely accepted. They were, of course, neither original to Schumpeter, nor unusual for Germany in the nineteenth and twentieth centuries. Reinert (1995, 2002) has argued convincingly that they were actually quite widespread among German economists both before and during the *Methodenstreit*. Schumpeter himself acknowledged his debt both to Marx and to Schmoller, while other ideas, such as the expression 'Creative Destruction' have been traced to Sombart.

The formulation of the young Marx and Engels in their exuberant *Communist Manifesto* (1848) has scarcely been improved upon by either Schumpeter or his followers, as a succinct summary of some of the most significant features of capitalist economies:

> The bourgeoisie cannot exist without constantly revolutionising the instruments of production and thereby the relations of production and with them the whole relations of society . . . Constant revolutionising of production, uninterrupted disturbance of all social conditions, everlasting uncertainty and agitation, distinguish the bourgeois epoch from all earlier ones.

Despite their total disagreement on the source and role of profit and ownership under capitalism, Schumpeter derived his theory of the erosion of profit margins during diffusion of innovations also from Marx.

It should be noted that Schumpeter took the side of Menger in the *Methodenstreit* and repeatedly during his lifetime insisted on the value of

Walrasian equilibrium theory (Freeman and Louçã, 2001: 43–4). This has caused some of his biographers and critics to describe his theory and indeed his whole life as a paradox (Allen, 1991: 4). Nevertheless, it is quite understandable that Rosenberg (1994: 41) should insist on his point that Schumpeter made a more radical challenge to neoclassical orthodoxy than any other twentieth-century economist. Although his work was indeed paradoxical, the renaissance of his influence in the last 20 years has certainly not been based on equilibrium theory but on his evolutionary dynamics. Several recent authors have emphasized that Schumpeter's method was a pluralistic combination of the historical institutional perspective of Schmoller with the use of formal analytical techniques (Ebner, 2000; Shionoya, 1991). This combination is believed to be in the tradition of Schmoller himself. The discussion is partly semantic but, be this as it may, the Schumpeterian renaissance derives from his evolutionary ideas. And as Dahmen (1984) put it: 'Schumpeterian dynamics is characterised by its focus on economic transformation' (p. 25).

II Influential features of the Schumpeterian Renaissance
However, the Schumpeterian renaissance has not simply been based on a more widespread recognition of the importance of innovation. Although this was certainly a major feature of most of Schumpeter's work, if it had been the only one, then others would deserve more credit than him. His distinctive contribution was based on his recognition of some special features of the innovative process in the evolution of capitalist societies, notably the clustering of innovations and the explosive growth of new firms and industries based on these clusters. He described this evolution as a succession of industrial revolutions and it is the recognition of this historical process which has characterized the Schumpeterian renaissance, just as Dahmen (1984) foresaw in his theory of structural change and development blocks.

The clustering of inventions and innovations, of the inputs and the outputs of research and development activities, has been apparent from all the work on measurement of scientific and technical activities which has proliferated since Schumpeter's death. Early work was mainly concerned with the measurement of inputs into innovative projects and indirect measures of inventive output, especially patent statistics, which had of course been available for centuries but seldom used much by economists until the proceedings of the first major conference on 'The rate and direction of inventive activity' became available. This conference was a herald of the Schumpeterian renaissance and was followed by a brilliant demonstration by Schmookler (1966) of the use of patent statistics for economic analysis. He maintained that the appearance of clusters of patents in various industries after major productive investment in those industries demonstrated that invention and innovation were generally demand-led and not technology-led. This initiated a fruitful debate among Schumpeterians, even though the most influential paper concluded that Schmookler's interpretation of clustering was mistaken (Mowery and Rosenberg, 1979) since the clustering measured the numerous follow-through inventions of the rapid diffusion phase of innovation rather than the crucial original inventions and innovations.

This debate and several others in the 1960s and 1970s also began to make use of the newer statistics of science and technology which were becoming available, culminating in the systematic measurement of innovations themselves (Arundel *et al.*, 2003). Before these most recent developments surrogate measures of innovative activities, such as R&D statistics, provided a valuable additional impetus to the new wave of Schumpeterian research in such areas as the relationship between innovation and economic growth, innovations and international trade performance or innovations and profitability.

Even long before official innovation surveys, much painstaking work on individual industries had already provided convincing evidence of clustering and explosive growth directly related to these clusters (e.g. Hufbauer, 1966). On a broader canvas, historians too had used economic statistics to confirm some of Schumpeter's points, especially on the growth of leading industries in technological revolutions (Table 8.2). In the most recent period the semiconductor industry and the computer industry in several countries both had growth rates which far exceeded those of other industries. As in previous revolutions, this rate was several times more rapid than the average growth rate of industrial output (Table 8.2).

This last point reminds us that the actual course of events in the real economy has probably been more persuasive than any theoretical arguments

Table 8.2   Estimated growth rates of leading industries and firms in technological revolutions

Industry	Period	Growth rate per annum
Cotton (UK)	1770–1801	8%
Railways (UK)		
Freight	1837/46–1866/74	13%
Passengers		9%
Steel (USA)	1880–1913	11%
Automobiles (USA)		
Ford Model-T	1908–1927	14%

Source: Author's estimates based on data in Freeman and Louçã (2001).

or historical statistics. The effects of the diffusion of information and communication technology (ICT) have been so obvious to almost everyone that it has become quite difficult for opponents of Schumpeter's theory of successive technological revolutions to sustain their argument, at least in this case. The successive spurts of innovation and growth in the electronics industry, the telecommunication industry, the computer industry and the Internet have made the ICT revolution a commonplace and the expressions 'information society' and 'knowledge economy' have passed into general use (e.g. Castells, 1996, 1997, 1998). The numerous books and papers on this topic are testimony to the Schumpeterian renaissance, whether or not they acknowledge his direct or indirect influence.

Whilst there are relatively few people who would be ready to defend the proposition that there has not been an ICT revolution, surprisingly there are still a few who cling to the notion that there never was an industrial revolution in Britain in the first place, although the evidence of contemporary observers, of artists and writers, of artefacts and of economic statistics is almost as strong as in the contemporary revolution. However, some of the most authoritative and best-known historians have used and defended an essentially Schumpeterian framework, particularly with respect to the first industrial revolution (Hobsbawm, 1962, 1964; Landes, 1969, 1993). The compelling evidence of the industrial statistics is discussed in Freeman and Louçã, 2001: 24–31. Schumpeter himself confronted early exponents of the idea that there never was an industrial revolution and whilst conceding that there was a little substance in their ideas, nevertheless gave them a clear if gentle rebuff (Schumpeter, 1939, vol. 2: 253–5).

Whilst to speak of a 'Schumpeterian renaissance' does imply that the general spirit of his work and his main ideas have become a significant influence on the general climate of ideas, it certainly does not imply that every one of his propositions and theories have been accepted. Nor is that what he himself would have wished. On the contrary, he was quite emphatic that he did not want a 'school' of disciplined followers, but expected that further research on innovation, while enriching and reinforcing some of his ideas, would falsify others. This has indeed been the general outcome of the Schumpeterian renaissance, which has usually been marked by a lack of dogmatism and a readiness to accept the evidence of new empirical research studies.

An example of this spirit is the reassessment of the role of incremental innovation by most scholars in the Schumpeterian renaissance. Schumpeter himself drew a sharp distinction between 'entrepreneurs' who were responsible for innovations, as acts of 'will not intellect', and managers who were 'mere' imitators. He did however recognize that, during the diffusion of an innovation, further significant improvements could be made in both product and process, as well as financial and organizational innovations, necessary for opening new markets and introducing the product to new countries. Thus, he remarked with respect to the automobile that it would never have diffused so widely if it had remained the same product as at its inception, and if it had not transformed its own environment. Moreover, his strictly functional definitions of 'entrepreneurs', 'capitalists', 'owners' and the 'mere head or manager of a firm' (Schumpeter, 1939, vol. 1: 102–9) left room for the designation of any individual as an entrepreneur (innovator). In his terminology, an entrepreneur might have any official job title and he himself argued that the leaders of R&D groups in the large German electrical firms were 'entrepreneurs' in his sense of the word. The function could be temporary in the course of a career so that the same individual could be innovator, manager, owner or capitalist, sequentially or all together.

Researchers in the Schumpeterian renaissance have made use of his definitions to distinguish the role of a 'product champion' (Schon, 1973) as the individual who struggles to push an innovation through to its launch against various obstacles, by an 'act of will'. Other researchers, for example, Project SAPPHO (Rothwell, 1992; Freeman, 1994) made a distinction between 'technical innovators' and 'business innovators' and examined the role of each in various industries. In some industries, the same person often performed both functions; in others, they were usually different people with the 'business innovator' being that person in the management and organizational structure who acted as the champion for the technical innovator.

All of this was very much in Schumpeter's tradition, but the results of research demonstrated increasingly that the role of incremental innovations was extraordinarily important and that users of innovation played a key role in this process of incremental improvement. Schumpeter's remarks about the automobile would apply even more to the computer and to other products of the earlier revolutions as well (see, for example, Mowery and Nelson, 1999).

Studies such as that of Hollander (1965) on the source of productivity gains in the rayon industry, in successive generations of Du Pont plants showed that incremental process innovations were just as important as incremental product innovations. These perceptions were further enhanced by the research of Lundvall and his colleagues at Aalborg on user-producer interactions and innovations (Lundvall, 1985). Arrow's (1962) seminal paper on the economic implications of learning by doing and the Aalborg work on learning by user–producer interaction led to the general acceptance of these ideas by the economics profession and management theorists. Lundvall himself extended his theory to the study of another sphere of influence of the Schumpeterian renaissance – the 'national system of innovation' (see Chapter 54 of the present work).

So influential was the evidence of the empirical research on innovation that it led some scholars to argue for the abandonment of the distinction between incremental innovations and more radical innovations, as well as between innovations and their diffusion (Silverberg, 2002) and between invention and innovation. However, even though these boundaries are difficult to draw, Schumpeter's distinctions have proved valuable in conceptual terms, especially in relation to inventions.

III   The Outcome

Already during his lifetime, Schumpeter's theory of business cycles was strongly contested (Kuznets, 1940) and he was disappointed by the reception accorded to what he thought of as his major contribution to economic theory – his two volumes on business cycles (1939). During the Schumpeterian renaissance his work on this topic has continued to be the subject of heated controversy. As is well known, it was Schumpeter who introduced the expression 'Kondratieff cycles' into the literature to designate those long-term fluctuations in economic growth which the Russian economist, Nikolai Kondratieff had identified and analysed in the 1920s. Schumpeter's contribution was to explain these cycles in terms of successive technological revolutions. Unfortunately, he failed to analyse satisfactorily either the timing and the phases of the technological revolutions or the timing of the related, but necessarily later, phases of the associated business cycles. Treating them as synchronous has led to a great deal of confusion.

Since his death, while his theory of successive technological revolutions has been very influential, his attempt to defend the nature and periodicity of the Kondratieff cycle has encountered continuous strong criticism (e.g. Solomou, 1987; Rosenberg and Frischtak, 1984; and see Louçã and Reijnders (1999) for a set of papers on the statistical debate). Although it has been prolonged and sometimes heated, this debate has also been an important part of the Schumpeterian renaissance and has led to some fruitful outcomes as well as to the refutation of some of Schumpeter's own ideas about business cycles. In the early days of the econometrics movement, Kondratieff was welcomed into the Econometric Society and his work was taken very seriously by leaders of the movement, such as Frisch and Tinbergen, as well as by Schumpeter. Partly because of Schumpeter's efforts, his work gave a lasting impetus to qualitative and historical research on long-term fluctuations in economic development, as well as the purely quantitative analysis which preoccupied many of his critics.

The same is true of Schumpeter's own work on business cycles despite the heavy criticism which it has encountered. In their discussion of the numerous contributions to long wave theory, Freeman and Louçã (2001)

Table 8.3   Three types of analysis of long-term economic fluctuations

Model analysis	Statistical and econometric analysis		Historical analysis
	Kondratiev Oparin Kuznets Imbert Dupriez		Trotsky
	Duijn	Mandel	Maddison
Forrester	Kleinknecht	SSA	
Sterman	Menshikov	Gordon	Regulation Schools
Mosekilde	Hartman	Aglietta	
	Metz	Boyer	Freeman
Mensch	Reijnders		Pérez
	Ewijk	Reati	Tylecote
	Zwan	Kuczynski	Fayolle
Silverberg		Shaikh	
		Entov	Bosserelle
		Poletayev	
		Moseley	
	(others: Sipos, Chizov, Craig/Watt, Glismann, Taylor, Nakicenovic, Marchetti)		(others: Braudel, Wallerstein, Modelski)

Source: Freeman and Louçã (2001), p. 97.

distinguish three main streams of analysis: model analysis, statistical and econometric analysis and historical analysis (Table 8.3). Whilst they themselves believe that a synthesis of the historical approaches is likely to be the most fruitful for evolutionary economics, they nevertheless emphasize the positive stimulus which the whole Schumpeterian debate on business cycles has given to economic theory as well as to the elucidation of appropriate statistical techniques in the analysis and modelling of economic fluctuations.

Recent new work with the Cambridge Growth Model suggests that there may still be valuable results to be achieved by a synthesis of the various techniques shown in Table 8.3. This work further indicates the increasing need to integrate the environmental dimension with long-term analysis of this kind. This could help to remedy a major weakness of the Schumpeterian renaissance: lack of sufficient attention to this dimension of economic and structural change.

Finally, there has been a major positive development arising from the recent Schumpeterian work on long wave analysis: new work on financial capital and technological revolutions (Perez, 2002). The work of Perez not only makes a major contribution to the resolution of several of the major problems arising in the prolonged debate about the timing of 'technological revolutions' and business cycles, it also provides for the first time a set of ideas which fill one of the major gaps in the Schumpeterian renaissance: the role of credit creation in Schumpeterian evolution. Neither Schumpeter nor the neo-Schumpeterians had hitherto related the evolution of credit creation to the evolution of new technologies (see Perez, 2002, and Chapter 49 of the present work).

Conclusions

Like Fagerberg (2003), this chapter concludes that the 'Schumpeterian renaissance' has been a real phenomenon. Its main feature has been the resurgence of ideas about innovation, including industrial revolutions. Although it has led to heated debates, these have themselves been a constructive contribution of the renaissance and have enriched evolutionary theory in economics. Fagerberg was justified in his view that the ideas of the 'neo-Schumpeterian' evolutionary economists, although departing in some respects from Schumpeter's own ideas, were nevertheless strongly influenced by the Schumpeterian renaissance.

References

Allen, R. (1991). *Opening Doors: The Life and Work of Joseph Schumpeter* (2 vols). New Brunswick: Transaction Books.

Arrow, K.J. (1962). Economic welfare and the allocation of resources for invention, in R. Nelson (ed.), *The Rate and Direction of Innovative Activity: Economic and Social Factors*. Washington, DC: National Bureau of Economic Research.

Arundel, A., Boodoy, C., Hollanders, H., Nesta, L. and Patel, P. (2003). *The Future of the European Innovation Scoreboard (EIS)*. Policy Benchmarking Workshop, Luxembourg, 24 Feb.

Castells, M. (1996, 1997, 1998). *The Information Age: Economy, Society and Culture* (3 vols). Oxford: Blackwell.

Christensen, C.M. and Rosenbloom, R.S. (1995). Explaining the attacker's advantage: technological paradigms, organisational dynamics and the value network, *Research Policy*, **24**: 233–59.

Crépon, B.E., Duguet, E. and Mairesse, J. (1998). Research, innovation and productivity: an econometric analysis at the firm level, *Economics of Innovation and New Technology*, **7**: 115–58.

Dahmen, E. (1984). Schumpeterian dynamics: some methodological notes, *Journal of Economic Behaviour and Organisation*, **5**: 25–34.

Ebner, A. (2000). Schumpeter and the 'Schmollerprogramm' integrating theory and history in the analysis of economic development, *Journal of Evolutionary Economics*, **10**: 355–72.

Fagerberg, J. (2003). Schumpeter and the revival of evolutionary economics: an appraisal of the literature, *Journal of Evolutionary Economics*, **13**(2): 125–59.

Freeman, C. (1994). The economics of technical change: a critical survey, *Cambridge Journal of Economics*, **18**: 463–514.
Freeman, C. and Louçã, F. (2001). *As Time Goes By*. Oxford: Oxford University Press.
Hobsbawm, E. (1962). *The Age of Revolution*. London: Weidenfeld and Nicolson.
Hobsbawm, E. (ed.) (1964). *Labouring Men*. London: Weidenfeld and Nicolson.
Hollander, S. (1965). *The Sources of Increased Efficiency: A Study of DuPont Rayon Plants*. Cambridge, MA: MIT Press.
Hufbauer, G.C. (1966). *Synthetic Materials and the Theory of International Trade*. London: Duckworth.
Jewkes, J., Sawers, D. and Stillerman, J. (1958). *The Sources of Invention*. London: Macmillan.
Kamien, M.I. and Schwartz, N.L. (1975). Market structure and innovation, *Journal of Economic Literature*, **13**: 1–37.
Kennedy, C. and Thirlwall, A.P. (1983). *Technical progress, Surveys of Applied Economics*, vol. 1. London: Macmillan.
Kuznets, S. (1940). Schumpeter's business cycles, *American Economic Review*, **30**: 257–71.
Landes, D. (1969). *The Unbound Prometheus: Technological and Industrial Development in Western Europe from 1750 to the Present*. Cambridge: Cambridge University Press.
Landes, D. (1993). The fable of the dead horse: or the industrial revolution revisited, in J. Mokyr (ed.), *The British Industrial Revolution*. Boulder, CO: Westview Press.
Louçã, F. and Reijnders, J. (1999). *The Foundations of Long Wave Theory* (2 vols). Cheltenham, UK and Northampton, MA, USA: Elgar.
Lundvall, B.-Å. (1985). Product innovation and user–producer interaction, *Industrial Development Research Series*, vol. 31. Aalborg: Aalborg University Press.
Lundvall, B.-Å. (2004). 'Introduction' to C. Freeman, Technological infrastructure and international competitiveness, *Industrial and Corporate Change*, **13**(3): 531–9.
Marx, K. and Engels, F. (1848). *Manifesto of the Communist Party*. Republished in many editions, e.g. in Marx, Selected Works, vol. 1, Moscow, 1935.
Mowery, D.C. and Nelson, R.R. (eds) (1999). *Sources of Industrial Leadership: Studies of Seven Industries*. Cambridge: Cambridge University Press.
Mowery, D.C. and Rosenberg, N. (1979). The influence of market demand upon innovation: a critical review of some recent empirical studies, *Research Policy*, **8**: 102–53.
Perez, C. (2002). *Technological Revolutions and Financial Capital: The Dynamics of Bubbles and Golden Ages*. Cheltenham, UK and Northampton, MA, USA: Edward Elgar.
Porter, M. (1990). *The Competitive Advantage of Nations*. New York: Free Press, Macmillan.
Reinert, E.S. (1995). Competitiveness and its predecessors: a cross-national perspective, *Structural Change and Economic Dynamics*, **6**: 223–42.
Reinert, E.S. (2002). Schumpeter in the context of two canons of economic thought, *Industry and Innovation*, **9**: 23–39.
Rogers, E.M. (1962). *Diffusion of Innovations*. New York: Free Press of Glencoe.
Rogers, E.M. (1986). Three decades of research on the diffusion of innovations: progress, problems, prospects. Paper at the DAEST Conference, Venice, April.
Rosenberg, N. (1994). Joseph Schumpeter: radical economist, in Y. Shinoya and M. Perlman (eds), *Schumpeter in the History of Ideas*. Ann Arbor, MI: University of Michigan Press, pp. 41–57.
Rosenberg, N. and Frischtak, C.R. (1984). Technological innovation and long waves, *Cambridge Journal of Economics*, **8**: 7–24.
Rothwell, R. (1992). Successful industrial innovation: critical factors for the 1990s, *R&D Management*, **22**(3): 221–39.
Schmookler, J. (1966). *Invention and Economic Growth*. Cambridge, MA: Harvard University Press.
Schon, D.A. (1973). Product champions for radical new innovations, *Harvard Business Review*, **5**, March/April.
Schumpeter, J.A. (1939). *Business Cycles: A Theoretical, Historical and Statistical Analysis of the Capitalist Process*. (2 vols). New York: McGraw-Hill.
Shionoya, Y. (1991). Schumpeter on Schmoller and Weber: a methodology of economic sociology, *History of Political Economy*, **23**: 193–219.

Silverberg, G. (2002). The discrete charm of the bourgeoisie: quantum and continuous per-spectives on innovation and growth, *Research Policy*, **31**(8–9): 1275–91.

Solomou, S. (1987). *Phases of Economic Growth, 1850–1979: Kondratieff Waves and Kuznet Swings*. Cambridge: Cambridge University Press.

Tidd, J., Bessant, J. and Pavitt, K. (1997). *Managing Innovation: Integrating Technological, Market and Organisational Change*. Chichester: Wiley.

PART 2

NEO-SCHUMPETERIAN MESO DYNAMICS: THEORY

2.1
Essentials of Innovation Processes

2.1.1
Entrepreneurship, firms and networks

9 Neo-Schumpeterian perspectives in entrepreneurship research
Thomas Grebel

1 Introduction

What makes a successful entrepreneur? A question which has often been asked in practice as in theory. Be it to rate founders of new businesses to decide over possible funding or be it the attempt to model entrepreneurial behavior in economic theory. His importance for an economy's prosperity has always been emphasized. Entrepreneurs found firms and create jobs. This is why policy making in practice tries to take measures to foster entrepreneurial behavior. To track the profile of an entrepreneur in general and a successful entrepreneur specifically, we come across a challenging venture. A lot of different concepts have been developed. And, as always, it is a matter of perspective. Some authors approach their concept focusing on the factor distribution of income; some take the route from the market process; others associate the entrepreneur with the firm and, last but not least, there are concepts that center on the heroic Schumpeter vision of the entrepreneur (Casson, 1990).

Obviously, a clear-cut definition of the entrepreneur has not been established yet. The reason may be that there is no unique characteristic that distinguishes entrepreneurs from non-entrepreneurs and it is rather exogenous factors that determine success; or it may possibly be the case that we have not found the right tools to investigate the specificities of an entrepreneur. Mainstream economic theory has neglected the entrepreneur for quite some time. In the pursuit of efficiency and optimal behavior in a presumed deterministic world, the methodological trajectory led away from the entrepreneur as a central figure in economic theorizing. Heterodox approaches have resurrected the discussion about the entrepreneur and strive to unravel the mystery that surrounds him.

The objective of this chapter is to trace briefly the history of the entrepreneur in the literature. Some basic concepts will be mentioned. Furthermore, methodological issues will be addressed to give an idea about the difficulties of doing research in entrepreneurship. Finally, some remarks on future research will be stated.

2 The history of the entrepreneur in economic literature

2.1 Early economics

The entrepreneur experienced ups and downs in the economic literature. Before the neoclassical era he was perceived as the central figure, the pivotal point of economic development. Richard Cantillon (1755) called the entrepreneur an *undertaker*, a person that does not flinch from engaging in uncertain business ventures. He buys and produces goods for a certain price to sell it later on at a yet unknown price. His disposition to face uncertainties makes him an entrepreneur. François Quesnay (1888) added the importance of capital which renders possible any entrepreneurial action in the first place. Furthermore, *property rights* make the entrepreneur an independent owner of a business. Without a granted right of ownership there would not be an incentive to engage in business. In the mid-1840s, Jean-Baptiste Say (1845) developed the most comprehensive concept of entrepreneurship at that time (see Figure 9.1). The entrepreneur uses the ideas of a *philosopher*, that is, new knowledge which has not yet been applied in the economy to produce a new product. To do this the entrepreneur employs workers, capital and natural resources to actualize the new knowledge into a tradable good. Thus, the entrepreneur decisively influences the production sector in the economy. He starts the economic transformation process and, doing this, he also introduces novelty into the economic system. Even more, he decides the income distribution among the providers of production factors distributing the resulting revenues, generated by the

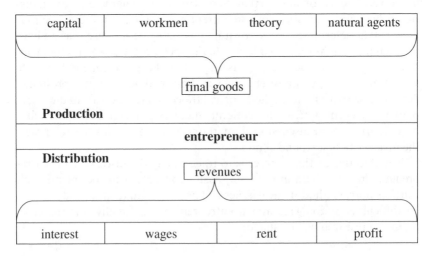

Figure 9.1   The entrepreneur as the central agent of the economic world

sales of such goods: the capitalist receives interest, the worker wages and the owners of land get paid their rent.[1] Say put emphasis on entrepreneurial aspects in economic theory which were gradually neglected with the arrival of the neoclassical era.

2.2 Neoclassical economics

In the 18th century the entrepreneur almost disappeared from the economic literature. The prevailing need among economists to reduce inconsistencies in their mostly verbal economic theories, called for an adequate methodological framework to analyze economic phenomena consistently. With the introduction of the Newtonian mechanics into economics, the ground for the neoclassical era was prepared. The mathematics applied in physics to describe general laws and axioms in nature, offered many improvements in economic thinking and modeling. But mathematics did not only ensure consistency in theorizing: mathematical approaches always end up in a unique and thus deterministic result, provided the researcher has the right touch. Moreover, this important characteristic also called for a specific ontological base of economic behavior. Unique results in formal theorizing required also unique economic behavior of the agents investigated. This created an economic man with perfect rationality that always makes optimal decisions which eventually lead to equilibrium. The *homo oeconomicus* was born. And along with it, the entrepreneur lost his right to exist, because what would make the entrepreneur first among equals? And if so, how could an economic agent superior to a *homo oeconomicus* be reconciled with this methodological approach? The critique on neoclassical theory is well known and therefore should not be overemphasized at this point. The imponderability of modeling entrepreneurial behavior has long been discussed and opened up different strands of economic research.

2.3 Heterodox economics and the Schumpeterian entrepreneur

The revival of this discussion about the entrepreneur was taken up by various heterodox economists in the 20th century.[2] Some have become renowned for explicitly processing an entrepreneurial concept. To use an example, Frank Knight (1921), working on the concept of uncertainty, attached the capacity and willingness of *business men* to cope with *uncertainty* as a principal feature to the entrepreneur. Entrepreneurs make predictions about consumer needs and bear the uncertainty of coordinating the production process in order eventually to sell a tradable good.

Israel Kirzner developed a comprehensive concept of the entrepreneur that originated from the Austrian tradition. In Austrian economics knowledge plays an important role in the market process. All economic actors are involved in a learning process and not before all agents have acquired the relevant knowledge does equilibrium become possible. According to Kirzner, the entrepreneur is an actor who is one step ahead in this learning process. Kirzner describes the entrepreneur as a person 'who buys in one market in order to sell, possibly at a considerably later date, in a second market' (Kirzner, 1973, p. 172). Therefore, the entrepreneur needs to have more knowledge about markets than others. The entrepreneur learns *spontaneously* about the possibility to make profits. He participates in the market process and is alert to arbitrage opportunities, and moreover, he is the first to make use of such opportunities. Therefore, the entrepreneur of Kirzner fulfills a specific function within the market process. Using arbitrage opportunities he reallocates resources and gradually reduces inefficiency in the market, which will eventually lead to equilibrium. In other words, Kirzner's entrepreneur is an arbitrageur and equilibrator.

The most popular conceptualization of the entrepreneur was developed by Joseph A. Schumpeter. Obviously there are similarities to Kirzner's concept of the entrepreneur but Schumpeter took another route of argumentation to get to his concept. Schumpeter challenged, as did many other economists, formal theorizing. But Schumpeter was the first who linked his criticism on methodology closely to his concept of the entrepreneur: he criticized the circular flow of an economic system and outlined the deficiencies of a static concept incapable of explaining the underlying dynamics of a continuously developing and changing economy. The economic process would come to a standstill. As a matter of fact, economies change over time and there is something which prevents the occurrence of equilibrium. And this driving force which renders the economic process a continuous ever-changing process is novelty. A *homo oeconomicus* would not bring along such a change, since perfect rationality and optimal behavior induce a static state of equilibrium without any incentive to deviate from decisions made. This disruptive endogenous element of novelty Schumpeter (1911) called *innovation*. It disrupts any economic equilibrium and prevents a standstill. Hence, innovation cannot be an exogenous element which falls as 'manna from heaven'. It is initiated by a passionate heroic economic actor, an actor which would not be satisfied with a static state of equilibrium. This economic actor Schumpeter called the *entrepreneur*. With this concept Schumpeter takes a pre-eminent position in the entrepreneurship literature as well as in heterodox economics.

The entrepreneur becomes the core element of Schumpeter's dynamics of economic change. The entrepreneur carries out new combinations; he introduces new products, new production methods, new markets, new materials and new organizations. He innovates whereas others just follow along the lines to imitate the innovator. Schumpeter labels the entrepreneur as a leader and almost characterizes this leader as an antipode to the *homo oeconomicus*, or, as Schumpeter puts it: 'It is therefore, more by will than by intellect that the leaders fulfill their function, more by "authority," "personal weight," and so forth than by original ideas.'[3]

The entrepreneur breaks up traditional structures and challenges existing habits with

> the dream and the will to found a private kingdom, usually, though not necessarily, also a dynasty. (. . .) Then there is the will to conquer: the impulse to fight, to prove oneself superior to others, to succeed for the sake, not of the fruits of success, but of success itself. (. . .) Finally, there is the joy of creating, of getting things done, or simply of exercising one's energy and ingenuity. (Schumpeter, 1911, p. 93)

Schumpeter fleshed out the concept of a heroic economic actor with a passionate personality contrasting a mere economizing *homo oeconomicus*. Doing this, he opened up many links to other disciplines such as sociology, organization theory, psychology, anthropology and business management.[4] Aside from that, Schumpeter worked on his vision of entrepreneurship and innovation to a further extent. He also considered innovativeness and entrepreneurship on the firm and network level. Thus, he initiated a research field that has become known as neo-Schumpeterian economics.

Because of its interdisciplinary approach it is eclectic and therefore it is not easy to delimit. Nevertheless, in order to find possible prospects of further entrepreneurship research, an attempt should be made. In the following, we will address some of the promising theories that may shed some light onto the future research on entrepreneurship.

3 Building blocks of neo-Schumpeterian entrepreneurship research

Schumpeter's entrepreneurship concept stresses the dynamic aspect of the economic process by introducing innovation as an endogenous element into economic theory. As a consequence Schumpeter asks for a different methodological treatment to allow for economic change. This is what makes the Schumpeterian concept unique.

Hébert and Link (1982) collected different themes of entrepreneurship concepts in literature.[5] Some of those concepts describe a static perspective, whereas others rather focus on subordinate aspects of entrepreneurial behavior. The Schumpeterian idea of the entrepreneur appears to be the most promising one, since it suggests going beyond pure economic aspects of entrepreneurship.[6] The entrepreneur as an innovator, as someone who brings along technological and economic change, has to deal with true uncertainty. He makes boundedly rational decisions not based on complete information and therefore his motivation cannot be explained neglecting psychological, sociological and other non-economic aspects.

In the following we will try to outline the basics of neo-Schumpeterian entrepreneurship research. As already pointed out, neo-Schumpeterian economics, or evolutionary economics, is an eclectic approach and the suggestions made will not be exhaustive.

3.1   Psychology, sociology and culture

Let us start with one of the most original Schumpeterian ideas, an idea that also concerns the most controversial aspect of the entrepreneur, that is, psychological and sociological aspects.

Personal characteristics or so-called 'traits' are probably the most convincing aspect of entrepreneurship, at least from an intuitive perspective. We usually associate a successful entrepreneur with someone who excels in his motivational drive, the need to achieve success and a high esteem of his work.[7] Unfortunately, empirical results on traits research have not succeeded in coming up with a unique profile of a stereotypical, successful entrepreneur. The results are mixed.[8] One would even presume that traits do not matter at all.

Moreover, taking a look at sociology, those theories are based on the observation of social behavior. They try to find the nature of entrepreneurial behavior in simply looking at social behavior and cultural norms. In other words, the focus is shifted away from the individuals' level, emphasizing the individuals' social context. One might conclude that the fact of being an entrepreneur becomes less and less a matter of birth but a matter of one's social environment. And, once more, empirical results are mixed.

There is something to both views but considering each by itself, the stereotype of an entrepreneur cannot be detected:

> If trait research had been successful, it could only serve as a basis for selecting the right leader. If behavioral studies were successful, the critical behavioral determinants of leadership could be taught to people. (Short and Dunn, 2002, p. 3)

Does this mean that we have to discard all existing approaches? Although a unique causality between economic, psychological or sociological and entrepreneurial behavior cannot be identified, this does not mean that these approaches do not matter at all. Research on entrepreneurship has to take into account the complexity of all possible determinants that induce entrepreneurship. Traits may not be a unique determinant which is crucial for an individual's entrepreneurial actions but they will definitely increase an individual's propensity to entrepreneurial behavior given a certain economic, sociological and cultural background. The social and cultural background of an economic actor will have an impact on the individual's decision making. Individuals who are convinced they have a higher impact on others (i.e. individuals with a high degree of self-efficacy), a high staying power and a positive overall self-evaluation will have a higher affinity for entrepreneurial behavior than others given a specific context.[9]

3.2 Social networks, social capital

Above we saw that the social context plays an important role. The economic process consists of interaction, be it on the market, in firms, or elsewhere. Entrepreneurial action such as opening up a firm involves the interaction of a potential entrepreneur with members of his social network. Parents may support his child's decision to found a firm. Friends may provide funds. In general the entrepreneur may balance his personal deficiencies by persuading some members of his social network either to support or even to join his venture.[10] He may have the power to influence others for his cause by having the ability to evaluate others (social perception), to adapt to certain social institutions (social adaptability), to communicate effectively (expressivness), so that he leaves a positive impression (impression management) with other economic actors (business partners, customers, etc.).[11]

In a pure economic perspective those aspects have often been neglected since they are associated with other scientific disciplines. Neo-Schumpeterian economics, however, tries to incorporate hitherto non-economic aspects into economic theories. In particular entrepreneurial behavior asks for additional tools to investigate the nature of economic behavior. The psychology of actors and their social context may offer insights into their economic behavior. Social networks offer access to resources, provided their members have a common supportive attitude. Moreover, the extent to which someone will be able to make use of those resources within the social network will depend on the potential entrepreneur's social capital.[12]

There is a pool of concepts originating in social psychology and sociology which offer new aspects to the research on entrepreneurship and need to be synthesized further in a Schumpeterian sense.

3.3 Knowledge

Aside from broadening the perspective on the entrepreneur via psychological and sociological aspects, the focus of modern entrepreneurship research has also to be put on the role of entrepreneurial resources. One of the most important resources for successful entrepreneurial behavior is knowledge, a resource which may also be found within the entrepreneur's social context, and this resource is gaining more and more importance as we talk about knowledge-based economies.

3.3.1 Basic knowledge requirements for an entrepreneur Obviously, the entrepreneur always had to have high cognitive capabilities. The ability to analyze complex problems and to organize the actualization of solutions, combined with the sustaining willingness to be successful, requires sophisticated cognitive abilities. Becker (1993) and Schultz (1971) stress the role of human capital and suggest that it has a positive impact on economic success; the more human capital within a firm the more successful a firm will be. Even more so will human capital be important to the entrepreneur as the leader of the economic transformation process.[13] Knowledge about the specificities of a business itself, of management and business administration and especially about technology and its potential is the basic requirement to run a business successfully.[14] However, with an increasing dynamics in the evolution of knowledge, the challenges in entrepreneurial endowments change, too.

3.3.2   Traditional aspects of knowledge dynamics   In traditional industries as well as in knowledge-based economies the stock of knowledge was and still is a crucial element of competitive advantage. The same holds for the creation of new knowledge. In contrast to modern knowledge-based economies, however, it was possible that the founding entrepreneur had all the relevant knowledge to start up a business all by himself; even more, it used to be possible that the knowledge base of the future could be enhanced simply within the firm.

3.3.3   Modern aspects of knowledge dynamics   With the emergence of knowledge-based economies, the creation and the management of knowledge has experienced a dramatic change. The generation of knowledge is no longer confined to single actors but, on grounds of its growing complexity, knowledge is dispersed among economic actors and requires new forms to manage and generate new knowledge. This also induces major changes in the requirements of capabilities of the entrepreneur. As a consequence, the complexity of knowledge is also a reason why most firms are founded by more than just one individual. Hence, entrepreneurs have to be able to collect and connect the knowledge of various actors, and this implies even more the entrepreneur's capability to exploit the potential of his social network.

Moreover, since the rate of knowledge creation and its complexity is increasing, organizational structures have to change, too. It is not only the process of establishing new firms which offers new challenges in entrepreneurial behavior, but also the management of knowledge on a corporate level.

3.3.4   Knowledge and entrepreneurship at the corporate level   Schumpeter expanded his vision on innovation and therewith his concept of entrepreneurship in his later works. As already mentioned, he shifted his focus from the individual to the firm level. Because of the complexity of the innovation process he stressed the task of firms to organize the innovation process within the firm. Obviously, this draws off some attention from the entrepreneur as an individual. His specific profile becomes less important provided that the organizational structure of the firm is adequate to exploit the personnel's innovative potential. The founding entrepreneur may even be replaced by some professional manager from outside that may not exactly match a stereotypical Schumpeterian entrepreneur. Furthermore, innovation will no longer be the outcome of a single individual's efforts; rather the innovation process will be spread over the whole firm and it will be institutionalized so that R&D departments take over the creation of innovation.

The literature on the knowledge-based theory of the firm gives us further insights into the nature of innovation, i.e. the nature of creating new knowledge in firms. A lot of neo-Schumpeterian thoughts can be found in works such as Penrose (1959), who sees a firm as a collection of resources, which pursues its productive opportunities in the context of a set of endowments of human and real capital using existing capabilities. Once the generation of knowledge is spread among several actors, communicational skills become important. In order to communicate all actors need the appropriate capabilities to understand each other so that they can make use of the knowledge of others. Eliasson (1990) labels those capabilities 'receiver competence', whereas Cohen and Levinthal (1989) incorporate the concept of 'absorptive capacities' of firms. All these aspects substantiate the characteristics of understanding, creating and managing knowledge as a base to fostering entrepreneurship at the firm level.

3.3.5 Financial capital and entrepreneurship Entrepreneurs who seek to start a business very often face capital constraints. In case they do not have a sound financial background, they need to find possible sources of financial funds. Financial funds signify the catalyst of almost any business process. With the assumption of perfect capital markets, an entrepreneur could obtain money from the capital market. Irrespective of the entrepreneur's own personal finances, viable business ideas would always meet the adequate provision of capital. Nevertheless, as evidence shows, with increasing wealth of the entrepreneur, the barriers to actualize one's business ideas shrink.[15] The offspring of entrepreneurs – as corresponds to the remarks on sociological and cultural aspects above – rather tend to be entrepreneurs than those of others.

Apart from that, a shortage of financial funds at the starting of a firm can have a negative effect on its future competitiveness. The financial base determines the firm in its organizational structure, scale and scope. This may, for example, restrict a firm's capacity to penetrate markets, to do research and development and, last but not least, to keep up with other more well-endowed competitors; hence a lack of financial funds can leave a disadvantaged imprint on the firm (Stinchcombe, 1965).

Sources of financial funds are manifold. Some entrepreneurs may have their own private funds; others may find financial support within their social network, others, though less frequent, may be bank-financed. However, one of the most important sources of financial funds is venture capital. Start-up firms that are backed by venture capital show a higher level of performance than others.[16] They introduce more radical innovation and exert more aggressive market strategies.[17] Each dollar spent on R&D by venture capital-backed firms induces more patents compared to other firms.[18] As this empirical evidence shows, venture capital spurs entrepreneurship on a large scale. Of course, it is not only the provision of financial capital that causes this positive effect. Venture capitalists give professional support to young innovative firms and also offer managerial expertise and specific technological knowledge.

4 Conclusion

It has become obvious that the research on entrepreneurship does not only challenge purely economic aspects of entrepreneurial behavior: the entrepreneur cannot be a mere economizer within a static world where true uncertainty is absent. Nor can the entrepreneur behave irrationally; such a concept would render scientific research senseless. We have to take into account all possible aspects that determine entrepreneurial behavior. Decisions based on bounded rationality involve also non-economic aspects such as psychological and sociological ones. Personal traits alone will not decide whether someone will be an entrepreneur or not, but they will increase a person's propensity to make entrepreneurial decisions. Likewise, an individual's social context will not be the exclusive determinant but it will increase the likelihood of entrepreneurial behavior. Social networks will constitute a pool of relevant resources to facilitate entrepreneurial actions. To no lesser extent the role of (venture) capital as a catalyst of entrepreneurial behavior has to be taken into account.

Aside from that, the increasing complexity of modern economies necessitates a higher rate of economic interaction. Today's knowledge-based economies are characterized by a dynamic technological progress. The generation of knowledge is no longer a one-man show but involves the cooperation of many different actors. This requires cognitive capabilities that enhance the diffusion and thus the understanding of knowledge to pave the way for entrepreneurship and innovation. Receiver competencies and absorptive capacities become a crucial element of economic and technological change in a world of imperfect knowledge. Self-evidently, considering the entrepreneur as the pivotal actor in this process, he has to have superior knowledge and capabilities to coordinate and lead the dynamics of economic and technological change.

To gain more insights into entrepreneurship, we need to investigate phenomena which cannot be adequately discussed within a general equilibrium framework. Some economic processes do not simply follow a deterministic path but nevertheless will influence entrepreneurial behavior such as the diffusion of knowledge as well as social network dynamics.[19] Neo-Schumpeterian economics offers a lot of ideas about how research on entrepreneurship can be enhanced. It will be our task to assemble all the bits and pieces to complete the toolbox of neo-Schumpeterian economics and to unravel the mystery of the entrepreneur.

Notes

1. Other classical economists such as Adam Smith and David Ricardo put their focus rather on other economic phenomena. They recognized the importance of the entrepreneur in the economy but in principle neglected this subject matter.
2. For a comprehensive survey on concepts of entrepreneurs, see for example Hébert and Link (1982).
3. Schumpeter (1934, p. 88).
4. Compare Swedberg (2004) or, in detail, see Schumpeter (1950).
5. Hébert and Link (1982, p. 152), the 12 themes in short: the entrepreneur as a risk-taker, as a source of financial funds, as decision maker, as industrial leader, as manager or superintendent, as organizer or coordinator, as owner of a business, as an employer of production factors, as contractor, as arbitrageur, as allocator of resources, and last but not least as an innovator.
6. Compare Grebel (2004).
7. Compare Schumpeter (1911), Weber (1965), McClelland (1961).
8. See Gartner (1989).
9. Compare Baron (2000).
10. See, for example, Aldrich and Zimmer (1996), Birley (1985) and Granovetter (1973) for a basic inquiry.
11. See, for example, Nahapiet and Ghoshal (1998).
12. See Portes (1998) for an overview.
13. Compare Brüderl *et al.* (1996).
14. See Kakati (2003).
15. Compare Holtz-Eakin *et al.* (1994), Meyer (1990) and Evans and Leighton (1989).
16. See Hellmann and Puri (2002).
17. See Hellmann and Puri (2002).
18. See Kortum and Lerner (2000).
19. For further details see Grebel (2004) and Grebel *et al.* (2003).

References

Aldrich, H.E. and Zimmer, C. (1996), Entrepreneurship through social networks, in H.E. Aldrich (ed.), *Population Perspectives on Organizations*, Uppsala: Acta Universitatis Upsaliensis, pp. 13–28.

Baron, R.A. (2000), Psychological perspectives on entrepreneurship: cognitive and social factors in entrepreneurs' success, *Current Directions in Psychological Science*, **9** (1), 15–18.

Becker, G.S. (1993), *Human Capital, A Theoretical and Empirical Analysis with Special Reference to Education*, Chicago: University of Chicago Press.

Birley, S. (1985), The role of networks in the entrepreneurial process, *Journal of Business Venturing*, **1**, 107–17.

Brüderl, J., Preisendörfer, P. and Ziegler, R. (1996), *Der Erfolg neugegründeter Betriebe – eine empirische Studie zu den Chancen und Risiken von Unternehmensgründungen*, Berlin: Duncker & Humblot.

Cantillon, R. (1755), Essai sur la nature du commerce en général (reprint 1931).

Casson, M. (1990), *Entrepreneurship*, Cheltenham, UK and Northampton, MA, USA: Edward Elgar.

Cohen, W.M. and Levinthal, D.A. (1989), Innovation and learning: the two faces of R&D, *Economic Journal*, **99**, 569–96.

Eliasson, G. (1990), The firm as a competent team, *Journal of Economic Behavior and Organization*, **19**, 273–98.

Evans, D.S. and Leighton, L. (1989), Some empirical aspects of entrepreneurship, *American Economic Review*, **79** (3), 519–35.

Gartner, W.B. (1989), Who is an entrepreneur? is the wrong question, *Entrepreneurship Theory and Practice*, **13** (4), 47–68.

Granovetter, M.S. (1973), The strength of weak ties, *American Journal of Sociology*, **78**, 1360–80.

Grebel, T. (2004), *Entrepreneurship – a New Perspective*, London: Routledge.

Grebel, T., Pyka, A. and Hanusch, H. (2003), *Industry and Innovation*, **10** (4), 493–514, December.

Hébert, R.F. and Link, A.N. (1982), *The Entrepreneur: Mainstream Views and Radical Critiques*, 2nd edn, New York: Praeger.

Hellmann, T. and Puri, M. (2002), Venture capital and the professionalization of start-up firms: empirical evidence, *The Journal of Finance*, **57** (1), 169–97.

Holtz-Eakin, D., Joulfaian, D. and Rosen, H.S. (1994), Sticking it out: entrepreneurial survival and liquidity constraints, *Journal of Political Economy*, **102** (1), 53–75.

Kakati, M. (2003), Success criteria in high-tech new ventures, *Technovation*, **23**, 447–57.

Kirzner, I.M. (1973), *Competition and Entrepreneurship*, Chicago: University of Chicago Press.

Knight, F.H. (1921), *Risk, Uncertainty and Profit*, New York: Houghton Mifflin.

Kortum, S. and Lerner, J. (2000), Assessing the contribution of venture capital to innovation, *Rand Journal*, **31** (4), 674–92.

McClelland, D.C. (1961), *The Achieving Society*, New York: Van Nostrand Reinhold.

Meyer, B. (1990), Why are there so few black entrepreneurs?, NBER working paper no. 3537. National Bureau of Economic Research, Cambridge, MA.

Nahapiet, J. and Ghoshal, S. (1998), Social capital, intellectual capital, and the organizational advantage, *Academic Management Review*, **23**, 242–66.

Penrose, E. (1959), *The Theory of the Growth of the Firm*, Oxford: Basil Blackwell.

Portes, A. (1998), Social capital: its origins and applications in modern sociology, *Annual Review of Sociology*, August, **24**, 1–24.

Quesnay, F. (1888), Oeuvres économiques et philosophiques, Aalen: Scientia-Verlag (reprint Frankfurt, 1965).

Say, J.-B. (1845), *A Treatise on Political Economy*, 4th edn, Philadelphia: Grigg & Elliot.

Schultz, T.W. (1971), *Investment in Human Capital*, New York: Free Press.

Schumpeter, J.A. ([1911] 1934), *The Theory of Economic Development* (trans. Redvers Opie, 1934), London: Transaction Publishers.

Schumpeter, J.A. (1950), *Capitalism, Socialism, and Democracy*, 3rd edn, New York: Harper and Brothers.

Short, L. and Dunn, P. (2002), The search for a theory of entrepreneurship, University of Louisiana.

Stinchcombe, A.L. (1965), Social structures and organizations, in J.G. March (ed.), *Handbook of Organizations*, Chicago: Rand McNally.

Swedberg, R. (2004), *Joseph A. Schumpeter: The Economics and Sociology of Capitalism*, Princeton: Princeton University Press.

Weber, M. (1965), *The Protestant Ethic and the Spirit of Capitalism*, London: Unwin University Books.

10 From a routine-based to a knowledge-based view: towards an evolutionary theory of the firm
Fritz Rahmeyer

1 Introduction

One of the central subjects of evolutionary economics, especially in the line of thought of Nelson and Winter, for their part based on Marshall and Schumpeter, is the analysis of entrepreneurial innovation activities and the evolution of markets and industries. But a theory of the individual firm beneath the level of the industry as a population of firms is only fragmentary. It is the object of this chapter to reduce this gap and to lay more emphasis on the firm instead of the industry. To this end, at first, some necessary comments concerning the idea of evolution and its adequacy for economic reasoning are made (section 2). Next, alternative theories of the firm in the fields of industrial and institutional economics will be scrutinized (section 3). As the building block of an enlarged evolutionary theory of the firm, a resource-based view in dynamic form presents itself. Knowledge, both as an input to and an output of production, is the most important resource and gives reason for a knowledge-based view of the firm (section 4). The broadening of the currently existing behavioural evolutionary approach, resulting from findings of the field of Business Strategy, opens up a more active role, enabling the firm to gain a sustained competitive advantage. In addition, it leads to an *intended* heterogeneity among firms concerning market performance and internal organizational structure.

2 Evolution in nature and society: fact, forms, theory

Evolution as an endogenously emerging historical process denotes a mainly gradual and irreversible change of an organic or a socioeconomic system when compared to its initial state. In economic thought, there is still no agreement concerning the content and adequacy of this idea and especially its theoretical foundation. For obvious reasons, this concept may first of all be put forward analogous to the neo-Darwinian theory of biological evolution. Reasoning by analogy is a method of scientific cognition and means the transfer of theoretical ideas between scientific disciplines in order to solve problems (see Cohen, 1993, p. 13). Thus a close transferability need not exist (see Niman, 1994, p. 364; also Dosi and Nelson, 1994, p. 155). The building blocks of a neo-Darwinian theory of evolution[1] are the constrained emergence of variety among the individuals of a species, occurring undirected and by chance, their advantage or disadvantage concerning the survival and replication rate of genes by means of natural selection of organisms as the physical characteristic of an individual and the retention of those characteristics that are best adapted to the environment. Each individual in a population is unique and, when compared to the average, it will either be favoured or at a disadvantage (population thinking; see Mayr, 1984, p. 38). The result of the selection process is a directed change inside a population. It does not go off purposefully but opportunistically as well as coincidentally and does not lead to a perfect adaptation. So, on the one hand, evolution requires the emergence of diversity and in this way change while, on the other hand, it destroys variety and gives rise to a directed and structured course. It is the result of a two-stage process, characterized by chance (creation of variety) and necessity (adaptation of individuals), constituting a dynamic equilibrium between adapted individuals and their given environment. Basically it takes place by a gradual but not an erratic change of a population. Besides the emergence and natural selection of diversity among the units of a population, a genetic evolutionary explanation also comprises the more regular development of the individual organisms in the population, the latter, unlike the former, dependent on the environment. From a historical point of view, Darwin took up basic elements of English Political Economy for the formation of his theory of evolution, such as the law of population as a natural force and the idea of the division of labour in growing markets (see Schweber, 1985). For him, Classical Political Economy was a branch of evolutionary biology (see Depew and Weber, 1995, p. 2).

To put forward a socioeconomic theory of evolution, functional counterparts for all elements of biological evolution in the economic sphere must be found. For that, information, knowledge and behavioural rules as units of variation are looked upon analogously to a pool of genes into which novelty flows and which are selected for application and diffusion in the form of technical artefacts, production engeneering and entrepreneurial activities as phenotypes in firms and markets on a competitive basis. Selection takes place at various stages as a hierarchical process (see Mokyr, 1991, p. 128). To generalize, it is the basic idea of a possible, albeit only weak, reasoning by analogy between biological and economic evolution, but going beyond merely speaking in images, that the origin, application and storage of scientific and technical knowledge, giving rise to economic and organizational innovations and change, may be interpreted as a simultaneous endogenous process of the emergence and reduction of diversity, caused in the end by the need for the creation and combination of scarce productive resources. Economic evolution includes both change and regularity, so the explanation of the emergence, selection and retention of human knowledge is in the forefront of evolutionary economics (see Herrmann-Pillath, 2002, p. 22). Economically usable knowledge has the properties of a public good. Its production is not given exogenously, but is the result of invention and discovery as economic forces, whose returns must be appropriated as well as exploited (see Foray, 2004, p. 14).

Now, there are a considerable number of important differences between the biological theory of evolution and an evolutionary approach to economic change regarding the emergence and selection of variety as evolutionary mechanisms. To mention the most important ones:

a. Socioeconomic novelties come into being not only by happenstance, but also to a high degree intentionally and for the purpose of altering the environment (see Winter, 1975, p. 103; Ramstad, 1994, p. 84; McKelvey, 1996, p. 23). But irrespective of purposeful human activities, their result is mostly unknown.
b. Selection of economic variety within a population of individuals is the consequence of human activities, too (artificial selection). The respective units of variation and the environment interact with one another. An evolutionary theory may comprise ' "blind" and "deliberate" processes' (Nelson and Winter, 1982, p. 11).
c. Technical and economic evolution runs faster and frequently more progressively than biological evolution.
d. Accumulated experience, knowledge and behavioural rules will be transmitted to the next generation.

So socioeconomic evolution takes place parallel to or even above all in accordance with the model of Lamarck (see Nelson and Winter, 1982, p. 11; Saviotti and Metcalfe, 1991). According to that theory, evolution is an exclusively vertical phenomenon, the continuous internal development of an organism or a technical artefact or product in the direction of a higher complexity and perfection in adaptation to environmental demands. At the same time, the retention of acquired features passes to the next generation through transmission. Variety is the result of adaptation to the external environment, but for Darwin it is both a precondition and the result of variation and selection. For the reasons mentioned above, Witt (inter alia 2001, p. 48) pleads for the elaboration of a more generalized and independent, instead of a Neo-Darwinian, theory of evolution, one whose focus of interest is useful, unforeseeable economic and technical knowledge and innovations and their origin, dissemination and consequences.

Despite these differences between biological and economic evolution concerning the dominant evolutionary modes of operation, a comparable causal structure for describing and explaining organic and socioeconomic change is discernible. It exists in the theoretical conception of the emergence of variety in different forms, its reduction by competition and the retention of selected variety accompanied by the transmission of acquired characteristic features. A simultaneous result is the internal development of individual organisms (evolution and development). 'Evolutionary theory is a manner of reasoning in its own right, quite independently of the use made of it by biologists . . . What matter are variety, selection and development – not the natural world' (Metcalfe, 2005, p. 420). In addition, by self-organization in the form of interactions between the units of analysis among themselves and with the environment, new economic structures may emerge unpredictably, but without human design or government intervention. To summarize, economic evolution comprises both Darwinian and Lamarckian integral parts (see Fleck, 2000, p. 265; Hodgson, 2001, p. 114). For this view, the term 'Universal Darwinism' (see Hodgson, 2002, p. 269) was coined,[2] in which Neo-Darwinism is the more detailed theory with a higher element of explanation (see Hodgson, 2001, p. 116; Knudsen, 2001, p. 122).

3   Survey of theories of the firm

On an evolutionary, behaviourist view, it is the purpose of a theory of the firm to describe and explain internal practices and activities in enterprises and in markets. Both are organized by rules and structures of business (see Schneider, 1997, p. 55). Regarding the latter, in addition to market structure, these contain all the capabilities, including the provision of resources, which offer an explanation for the heterogeneity between firms concerning their internal growth and their organization and strategy (ibid., p. 60; also Dosi and Marengo, 1994, p. 158). The courses of activities inside a firm concern its birth, existence and passing. Individual firms will affect these activities, relevant to scale and scope of production, the carrying out of innovations, and the internal restructuring of its organization, through their own unique efficiency. A theory of the firm in this way must explain the dissimilarities in the levels of success among enterprises ('why firms succeed or fail'; Porter, 1991, p. 95). Simultaneously, the firm is a self-contained and developing entity in its own environment, deliberately utilizing and building resources, while also being a part of the evolution of its population within an industry. At the level of the firm and the industry, it is subjected to the pressure of internal and external selection, in its entirety or its separate activities. The manifestations of evolution, on different levels, happen at the same time (see Foss, 2001, p. 328; Rathe and Witt, 2001, p. 337). From an evolutionary point of view, there is no representative firm.

Currently there is no unified theory of the firm, either in economics or in management strategy (see Garrouste and Saussier, 2005, p. 194). Economics mainly deals with market performance and its determining factors, while strategic management looks into allocation and coordination within the firm. Structuring competing theories, which give priority to different aspects of firms, in broad agreement with the literature, technological, institutional and efficiency-oriented theories are distinguished (see Winter, 1988; Williamson, 1990b; Conner, 1991; Spulber, 1992; Chandler, 1992; Knudsen, 1995; Teece, Pisano and Shuen, 1997). They integrate characteristics of competitive markets, business strategies and organizational structures. The main dividing line exists between institutional and efficiency-oriented theories.

3.1 Technological theories

Among the technological theories, there are the standard neoclassical theory and the one typical of industrial organization. In neoclassical theory, the firm is characterized by its production and cost function. Subject to this restriction, it maximizes its profits for which it has complete information concerning supply and demand, resulting in the 'optimal product-market price' (Kay, 1997, p. 9). This expresses the optimum performance in decision making, exchange as its main field of activity, the market as the mode of coordination, and prices as the only way of gaining competitive advantage. Firms exist to combine completely mobile and freely available factors of production and choose from among efficient production schemes. They all have access to the same knowledge of production. So the neoclassical theory of the firm represents a theory of market allocation, but not a detailed model of an individual firm (see Demsetz, 1988, p. 143; Spulber, 1992, p. 543).

According to industrial economics, besides their production and cost functions, and in that industrial structure, firms are also characterized by their competitive strategies (see Spulber, 1992, p. 569). Their internal structure is again unspecified. Business or corporate profits result from determinants of market structure (industry effects), but not at the firm level (positioning effect). Including Porter's idea of the 'competitive forces', that builds a bridge between industrial organization and strategic management, both elements of market structure and market conduct, in the end preferences and production techniques, as well as competitive advantages at the firm level, have an effect on firm and market performance. 'A general model of strategic choice must include both environmental analyses (of threats and opportunities) and organizational analyses (of strengths and weaknesses)' (Barney, 1997, p. 53). As the main criticism of the technology-oriented theories of the firm, the argument is raised regarding their predominantly static orientation and the inadequate consideration and processing of information and knowledge (for the latter, see O'Brien, 1984, p. 53).

3.2   Institutional theories

On an organizational or institutional view, the purpose of a theory of the firm is to explain the existence and the boundaries of firms, and their internal organizational structure (see Holmstrom and Tirole, 1989, p. 65; also Foss, 2005a, p. 24). Different approaches of these theories have the assumption in common that coordination of individual economic activities does not only take place in markets, but also in enterprises as hierarchically structured organizations. The main subjects are contractual relations and incentive conflicts among the owners of productive factors and – as the connecting link – property rights. As an explanation, both asymmetric information, even uncertainty[3] (Knightian view) as well as bounded rationality, asset specifity and opportunism resulting in transaction costs (Coasian view) are taken for granted (see Rumelt, Schendel and Teece, 1991, p. 13; Foss 2000, p. XXX). Knowledge about the manufacturing process is assumed to be the same for all firms, but not so regarding their internal organization. To this end, the shaping of institutional arrangements in organizations on a contractual basis for the efficient use of information and the protection of their overall performance is considered. Organizational problems are of such a form as making a contract to manage internal relationships. In this connection, economically relevant contracts are always incomplete. Especially notable is the fact that the purchase of knowledge and entrepreneurial capabilities is not completely contractable (see Hodgson, 1998, p. 183). Learning of individuals and organizations is neglected. The (ex ante) formation of incentive, control and information systems to guarantee the performance of the tasks of an agent in accordance with the principle, assuming asymmetric information before and after the making of a contract, is in the forefront. Technologically the firm is again looked upon as a production function. The competitive process is not taken into consideration.

Transaction costs economics, as a part of institutional economics, works on the assumptions of bounded rationality, of opportunism of market competitors or contracting parties, and of asset specificity of exchange between the participants (see Williamson, 1990a, p. 34). Contracts between competitors are necessarily incomplete because of limitations of knowledge and must be renegotiated continually. They must correspondingly allow for adaptation as new situations later arise (ex post consideration). To resist opportunistic behaviour after specific assets have been invested, the firm is organized as a governance structure (ibid., p. 18), showing incentive and adaptation qualities. But it is not only a production or a cost function: 'governance is the means by which to infuse order, thereby to mitigate conflict and to realize . . . mutual gain from voluntary exchange' (Williamson, 2002, p. 180). Firms and markets are alternative modes of the organization of production and exchange. Consequently they may be looked upon as adapting and reshaping organizations reacting to economize on transaction costs in a world of bounded rationality and incomplete information. The relative level of transaction costs determines the size and scope of a firm, and thereby its boundaries. By comparison, the production process of a firm is not included in the consideration. Dynamic aspects such as learning and technical innovations are not taken into account concerning the decision in favour of markets or firms, too (see Hodgson, 1998, p. 188). To summarize, in institutional theories, nearly all problems of economic organization originate from conflicts resulting from individual incentives either in advance of drafting a contract or afterwards by organizing a governance structure (see Foss, 1999, p. 732; 2005a, p. 32). Neither theory comes with an answer regarding firm heterogeneity and a dynamic perspective on the boundaries of the firm, except for transaction costs.

3.3   *Efficiency-based theories*
Among this category of theories, the static resource-based view of the firm and the advanced process-oriented 'dynamic capability approach' are included (see Williamson, 1991, p. 76; Teece, Pisano and Shuen, 1997, p. 510). The former is positioned by Barney (2001, p. 644) against Porter's approach of explaining competitive advantage in the tradition of Industrial Economics as the result of market power on product markets. Both variants contend that firms are not merely organizations characterized by a bundle of contracts or transactions. They mainly exist because they are looked at as being able to employ and build a bundle of specific resources and capabilities for their own use, in order to cope with economic and technical change and with uncertainty and to generate and appropriate value. These will increase in the passage of the industrial process by means of knowledge and innovation activities. Thus internal managerial activities, unlike external factors, the former resulting as well from interactions between firms, are taken into account to explain competitive advantage.[4] The firm with its internal structure is a goal-directed operating organization of common human activities, actively changing its environment, and also a social and historical unit. It is not only an entity capable of adapting to environmental influences (see Foss, 1996, p. 471). With regard to its available specific resources and both competences for their employment, among others organizational routines as vehicles of internal coordination and practical knowledge, the firm by its own decree will be

lastingly heterogeneous, in contrast to its competitors. In the tradition of Marshall and Schumpeter, gradual as well as major innovation activities are the promoters of economic evolution. Following mainly Foss (1993, p. 132; but also Hodgson, 1998, p. 180; Foss, Knudsen and Montgomery, 1995, p. 4), in particular the dynamic capability approach may be categorized as a hitherto missing element of evolutionary economics. The focus of interest of an evolutionary theory of the firm in an ontogenetic, developmental reflection is the process of manufacturing, but not pure exchange, contractual relations or transaction costs, but first of all learning of individuals and organizations as a problem-solving activity, resulting in new knowledge and capabilities. Its central question from a business strategy point of view is: why do efficient, successful firms differ in their own discretion (see Nelson, 1991, p. 61; Dosi and Marengo, 1994, p. 158; Carroll, 1993, p. 242)? Efficiency does not mean optimality of market performance but best possible interaction with and adaptation to the environment.

New directions in alternative theories of the firm complement or even take the place of the 'optimal product-market price' as the central category of neoclassical theory. The following elements in various combinations are considered (see Kay, 1997, p. 10):

a.   bounded rationality and satisficing as alternative behavioural assumptions to optimization (Simon);
b.   resources in factor markets instead of predominantly goods in product markets (Penrose);
c.   firms and hybrid institutions as complementary institutional arrangements to markets (Coase, Williamson);
d.   innovations instead of prices as the most important competitive activity (Schumpeter).

From this point of view, '. . . the firm . . . is a hierarchically organized collection of resources making imperfect decisions in which technological change is typically the critical strategic variable' (ibid., p. 29).

4   Evolutionary approach to a theory of the firm

4.1   *Principles of a behavioural theory of the firm*
The subject of an evolutionary perspective in economics may be defined as describing and explaining endogenously, but also exogenously emerging, undetermined and irreversible technical, economic and organizational change, especially the creation and diffusion of new knowledge and technical innovations, and thereby both the blind and guided genesis of variety and as well its purposeful selection on the market. Forces of persistence retain

continuity in respect to which features will survive in the selection process (see Nelson, 1995, p. 56). Besides, evolutionary change is seen as the result of the self-organization of complex systems, for instance, in the context of market coordination (see Witt, 1996, p. 709; Foster and Metcalfe, 2001, pp. 2,14).

In contrast to the technological and institutional theories, evolutionary economics is directed to the real, observable behaviour of enterprises. In it, the industrial process, instead of exchange and contracting, is at the centre of attention. Firms, above all, are carriers of production techniques and productive knowledge. Knowledge about the manufacturing process is necessarily incomplete, unequally distributed and able to be appropriated to a different degree. Concerning the behavioural rule of firms, the evolutionary approach rejects the assumption of optimality. Instead of conscious optimized decision making, Nelson and Winter (1982, p. 15), on the basis of bounded rationality of the competitors, work from the assumption of the rule-bound behaviour of routines to characterize the process 'of how things are done' in business firms and organizations more generally' (Winter, 1986, p. 152; 1988, p. 175). Inherently rigid 'standard operating procedures' (Cyert and March, 1963, p. 101), which are founded on past experience, serve as the basis for organizational routines (see Pierce, Boerner and Teece, 2002, p. 87). Their result is like that of intended rationality, long lasting and predictable. Besides, both authors use a non-reductionist method of analysis, conceding enterprises as purposefully behaving organizations an independent importance, separated from the basic individual actors ('individual behavior as a *metaphor* for organizational behavior'; Nelson and Winter, 1982, p. 72).[5] In addition, learning and the creation of knowledge is regarded as a social, not only an individual, process.

The organizational routines of the firm for employing productive resources, comparable to skills of individuals, include its repetitive hierarchically structured behaviour in manufacturing, investment, search and innovation activities (see ibid., pp. 16,73). In this, knowledge, experience and competence regarding both production and organization that to a high degree are of a local and specific nature are accumulated. Routines create continuity and reinforce the internal stability of the firm (see Winter, 1975, p. 101). They do not have to result in optimal outcomes, but are adapted to the respective environment.[6] In the view of Nelson and Winter (1982, p. 14) organizational routines are comparable to genes as units of variation in nature, as much as firms to organisms as their phenotypes. The frequency of successful routines will increase as a result both of the (external) selection process within a population of firms and within the individual firm over the period of its development, the latter being of a more purposeful kind. Intended and problem-oriented processes of learning and searching, to be directed at seeking profits, which occur cumulatively and path-dependently, based on failures in the past, can change behavioural routines gradually and with some delay. The introduction of technical and organizational innovations into the market is intended to improve the adaptability of firms in case of an unsatisfactory market performance and to open up new activities (for the latter, see Winter, 1975, p. 105; Witt, 1996, p. 712). In contrast to optimal adaptation, a variety of routines of firms will occur, driving evolutionary change (see Metcalfe, 1995, p. 471). Corresponding to their specific routines, firms will differ for efficiency reasons in the level of unit costs and profits. Modifications of routines impede the transmission and retention of invariable rules and are in conflict with evolution in nature. Thereby the explanation of stability and persistence of firm behaviour will also be affected. In this evolutionary understanding, firms in the end are regarded as knowledge-based organizations capable of learning and transformation, or even as 'repositories of productive knowledge' (Winter, 1988, p. 175). They are in their entirety or their individual essential parts such as routines, resources (see Aldrich, 1999, p. 40) subject to selection in the market, and show an irregular, internal path of development. Undeniably, besides their routine and learning activities, the persistent profitability of enterprises also depends on their internal organization, for instance the existing control and incentive mechanisms. In this way, they give rise to transaction costs (see Vromen, 1995, p. 109), as 'the institutional structure of production' (thus Coase, 1988, p. 47).[7]

4.2   Resource-based view of the firm
In broadening the basic behavioural approach of evolutionary economics for management theories concerning business strategy, firms will be characterized through three relatively stable attributes (see Nelson, 1991, p. 67; 1994, p. 233). They may increasingly lead to intended, chosen, permanent inter- and intra-industrial heterogeneity regarding their market performance and the provision of resources. These attributes are, first, their market strategy and internal organizational structure and, second, their specific competences and capabilities, particularly for utilizing and for creating scarce productive resources and carrying out innovation activities as central parts of corporate and competitive strategy. Resources must be selected, capabilities built (so Makadog, 2001, p. 389).

Strategy comprises the long-term objects of an enterprise and its incurred commitments, based on its given internal resources.[8] Structure includes the organization of a firm with regard to its environment to achieve its objects. Both elements decide the core competences of a firm, referring mainly to technology and production in order to obtain sustained competitive advantage. They change only slowly as a consequence of bounded rationality and its given hierarchy of routines.

The capabilities of an enterprise for the formation and growth of resources and its competences for their deployment supplement, and above all modify, its operating routine activities. They are regarded as a 'higher-level routine' (Winter, 2003, p. 991) and so serve as a basis for the deliberate development of successful that is value creating strategies. '[T]he capabilities discussion provides a bridge between the predominantly descriptive concerns of evolutionary theory and the prescriptive analysis of firm strategy' (Dosi, Nelson and Winter, 2000, p. 12). Capabilities and competences, as well as the decision-making rules, determine the competitive strength of a firm (see Dosi and Teece, 1998, p. 301). They arise from cumulative entrepreneurial search, learning and innovation processes, and from knowledge transmission. As with routines, they are characterized by continuity and delayed change.

In this broadening of the basic behavioural model, the firm, following Penrose (1959, p. 24), is looked upon as a bundle of productive physical and human resources (stocks), capable of internal development, whose produced heterogeneous results (flows) are able to be used for manufacturing purposes in different ways. The unique bundles of resources and services, coordinated by means of administrative decision making, create its capabilities. 'The business firm . . . is both an administrative organization and a collection of productive resources' (ibid., p. 31). These, for their part, induce the productive output of the resources (ibid., p. 78). Learning in the course of the manufacturing process will result in persistent corporate growth and, in this way, extends the capabilities of the firm concerning manufacturing and organization. Corporate growth will result in surplus firm-specific resources, for instance human capital, as a result of its growing experience, for which no efficient market exists. They make possible an expansion of production in previous and in new business activities, which again lead to innovations in knowledge and resources in enterprises. As a consequence of the indivisibility of productive factors, the different possible uses and the new development of resources and productive services, a firm will not be able to attain a state of long-term equilibrium. To sum up, resources may be defined as specific productive factors, obtained in markets, modified and refined through the ability of the company's management, employees or external specialists into characteristic features of the firm for the purpose of its competitiveness (see Schneider, 1997, p. 60).[9]

So firms, in the form of their provision of resources as input factors which are valuable and in short supply, and the supply of services, show qualities of both coherence and heterogeneity. Their existence, and their horizontal and vertical boundaries, may be justified as an aggregation of such basic units (bundle of routines, pool of resources, nexus of contracts), for which an internal organization compared to market coordination produces a comparative advantage with regard to generating individual skills, organizational routines, valuable resources and, at last, competitive advantages compared with rivals (see Williamson, 1999, p. 1096; Granstrand, 1998, p. 467; Madhok, 2002, p. 536). As their individual types, tangible, physical and also intangible resources, such as human capital, technical knowledge and organizational resources (for example corporate management), are distinguished (see Barney, 1991, p. 101; Bamberger and Wrona, 1996, p. 132). The former are subject to wear, the latter, as a result of indivisibilities, show a partly unlimited usage, perhaps via appropriation and exploitation through individuals and organizations. Increasing returns in use again result in path-dependency. In contrast to tradable productive input factors, resources are not completely movable and so show less value in any different use. They are difficult to imitate and substitute, if this is indeed possible. Owing to incomplete information, their expected value for a firm exceeds their market price. In addition, they can be protected against rivals by creating limits to competition (also called 'isolating mechanisms'; Rumelt, 1984, p. 567) comparable to barriers to entry (for characteristics of resources, see Barney, 1991, p. 105; Peteraf, 1993, p. 180). The sort of resources to be employed arises out of their competitive environment in product markets. On this functional definition, firms are interpreted as 'integrated clusters of core competencies' for the coherent employment of resources (see Teece et al., 1994, p. 23; Dosi and Teece, 1998, p. 296). They exist beyond market structure and competitive strategies.

A qualitatively different and scarce supply of valuable resources gives reason for a permanent (Ricardian) efficiency rent. Firms at the same time have to absorb the generated rent and to convert it by investment activities into internal growth (fitness). The effect may be an increase in size and market share possessed by successful firms. Not all firms of a population need to behave uniformly concerning their fitness in the form of internal growth and financing of innovations, especially if they are not able to realize and use their available opportunities equally. The relative position of a firm inside its industry (firm characteristics) gains in importance in explaining the relative corporate success compared with the attractiveness of the industry as a whole or its environment (industry characteristics). So the resource-based or efficiency-based approach must be categorized as a complement rather than exclusively a substitute for the firm in industrial economics (see Conner, 1991, p. 143; Bamberger and Wrona, 1996, p. 141). That is why in its static version it disregards the environment as well as the internal organization of an enterprise. Both the internal strengths and the weaknesses of a firm and external threats and opportunities of the product and factor markets simultaneously determine corporate success, not merely the supply of resources or the environment. Altogether, the resource-based or efficiency-based view assigns a more active role to firms than merely the adaptation to a given environment or its change. In this way, it broadens the original behavioural theory of the firm.

The resource-based view starts at a given provision of heterogeneous and imperfectly mobile resources of firms. It neglects to explain how new resources are created and already existing ones integrated, or how the resource base is broadened (so-called 'dynamic capabilities'; see Teece, Pisano and Shuen 1997, p. 510; Eisenhardt and Martin, 2000, p. 1107; Spanos and Lioukas, 2001, p. 924). It also remains an open question how the intra-industrial heterogeneity among firms with regard to the initial accumulation of valuable resources will come about (see Noda and Collis, 2001, p. 899). If the personal knowledge of individuals and the collective knowledge of organizations, the latter being stored in their technologies and management as their carrier ('organizations know more than what their contracts can say' (Kogut and Zander, 1992, p. 383), is looked at as the central resource to improve decision making and the internal control of enterprises, then its creation, application and dissemination is the most important task of the firm and its management resources (see Mahoney, 1995, p. 97). Technical and organizational knowledge is especially applied in transforming tangible input into the production of goods. Equally, it leads to competence and capability building and therefore is a prerequisite for generating, extending and using a bundle of resources. Merely insignificant differences among firms concerning their adopted strategy and their market conditions may increase as the result of diverging, self-reinforcing interactions, for instance increasing returns in production and use, or of local learning and experience. Converging forces of imitating corporate success and management decisions may influence the pursued path of a firm and reduce differences in its development. The emergence of knowledge, techniques, rules set off both by external factors such as new scientific discoveries and by internal learning, the valuation of technical artefacts, products, organizations and their activities by external as well as internal selection, together with retention and diffusion of confirmed new knowledge and more effective routines and capabilities, describe an evolutionary process of knowledge creation and transmission (for which see Zollo and Winter, 2002, p. 343). The newly created knowledge contributes to the necessary diversity for the continuation of the evolutionary process.[10] In the terms of March (1991, p. 71), the growth of knowledge and thereby technical innovations are the result of a balance 'between the exploration of new possibilities and the exploitation of old certainties'. The two activities compete for resources so that a balance between them must be found according to the intention of a firm. Penrose's theory of firm growth may be looked at as an attempt to show regularities in the internal development of a firm. Unlike the static resource-based approach, following the dynamic capability view, the persistent success of firms depends on their interrelation with the environment, for instance their technological opportunities and appropriability requirements, not on exclusively internal conditions. But transaction costs resulting from activities concerning the formation and employment of resources, and the appropriation and protection of their created rent, are not included in the analysis (see Foss 2005a, p. 103; 2005b, p. 549). In the end, economic, technological and organizational evolution is both the result of an unintentionally occurring market selection as a result of environmental pressure and of voluntary, purposeful entrepreneurial activities, which are founded on acquired knowledge (see Vanberg, 1996, p. 693). As with Winter (1995, p. 151): 'It is in addressing the dynamics of resource exploitation that one finds the strongest complementarities between the resource-based view and evolutionary economics.'

4.3 Knowledge-based view of the firm

On this interpretation as a knowledge-generating, knowledge-integrating and knowledge-using organization, the activities of a firm, aside from coordination, are characterized by learning, innovation and organizational change as a dynamic process (see Eliasson, 1994, p. 179). These reproduce and raise its knowledge level, intentionally and deliberately, accompanied by mistakes and costs, and replace in evolutionary reasoning the optimization of resource allocation in the technology-oriented theories of the firm. Learning and production of knowledge happen in different organizational ways: first, internal to the firm through scientific research and development and the innovation of new products and manufacturing processes (R&D competition), and through gaining experience on the part of employees in manufacturing (doing, using); second, through the purchase and commercial use of external knowledge from the science and technology sectors, that is, universities or research laboratories, or from rivals or customers and suppliers, for instance by means of reverse engineering, fluctuation of R&D personnel, or from R&D cooperation with competing firms in different forms (see Malerba, 1992, p. 847; Antonelli, 1999, p. 247). The common pool of knowledge will increase in this way and serve as a basis for positive externalities for further creating and exploiting knowledge.

Internal and external sources of knowledge are complementary. Internally created knowledge and its dissemination inside the firm will not cause transaction costs to the same extent as purchasing external knowledge. Knowledge transfer between firms is an especially important reason for incomplete contracts. Furthermore, the acquisition and use of the mostly product-specific and firm-specific knowledge from learning and experience is made available to a greater extent than in the case of technical knowledge acquired through formal R&D activities. This is of a more public nature, and to an even greater degree more difficult to appropriate. Positive externalities of this latter kind of knowledge are abundant, acting in this way as an incentive to cooperate with rivals. As a consequence, patent protection to acquire property rights may decrease in importance, compared to gaining lead time and secrecy (see Lewin et al., 1987, p. 793). In the case of an at least partial exclusion of the proceeds of knowledge production, temporary (Schumpeterian) monopoly quasi-rents will arise (see Peteraf, 1993, p. 180) and make possible the financing of R&D expenditures. Knowledge and innovations emerge as a result of both market incentives and technological opportunities. Against that, the huge amounts of costs of R&D investments and the uncertainty regarding their technical and economic results will bring disadvantages as well. From a management point of view, this gives reason for a participation in different forms of research cooperation to get access to external resources. But the acquisition and utilization of external knowledge requires an 'absorptive capacity' of the recipient firms, based on accumulated knowledge in the past and resulting from their own learning and research activities (see Cohen and Levinthal, 1990, p. 128). As a result, the production of knowledge and innovations is not an individual entrepreneurial activity, but more and more has become a collective and specialized process, in that a multitude of private and public contributors are involved, who interact positively by means of both creation and exploitation of spillover effects (see Pyka, 1999, p. 71).

In addition, knowledge consists in both a more tacit, implicit and more codified, explicit form. The former is stored in individuals and organizations and is especially the result of experience, not formalized and hardly transferable in and among enterprises. Its proceeds are able to be privately appropriated to a high degree, so that enterprises have a common knowledge base. Explicit knowledge is stored in codebooks, patents and computer software and is more easily divisible and exchangeable (see Grant, 1996, p. 111; Antonelli, 1999, p. 244; Argote, 1999, p. 71). The codification of knowledge is the result of an economic decision concerning its costs and benefits, but not of inherent characteristic features of the different forms of knowledge (see Cowan, David and Foray, 2000, p. 240). The possibility of appropriating implicit, often also localized, knowledge will diminish in the course of the life cycle of a technology. At the same time, its chances of codification and its more even distribution among firms will increase (see Saviotti, 1998, p. 850).

By combining the different sources and forms of learning and knowledge, the following possibilities of differentiating knowledge in firms will arise (see Antonelli, 1999, p. 245):

a. internal implicit knowledge, obtained especially through realization of practical experience (learning, using);
b. external implicit knowledge, through appropriation from the collective innovation system;
c. internal explicit knowledge, as a result of in-house research and development activities;
d. external explicit knowledge, required from formal R&D cooperation.

These individual kinds of knowledge complement one another, too. Enterprises, according to industries and the attained phase of the life cycle of their products, are integrated into a network of internal and external knowledge, with resulting spillover effects. Nonaka and Takeuchi (1997, p. 74) give priority to the creation and extension of knowledge by articulating implicit knowledge in an explicit form, what they call 'externalization'. Different forms of scattered productive knowledge can be integrated and utilized inside a firm more efficiently than by contracting between individuals on the market, especially in the case of tacit knowledge. So a reason for its existence is provided (see Demsetz, 1988, p. 157; Grant, 2003, p. 208; Foss, 2005a, p. 37): 'we proposed that a firm be understood as a social community specializing the speed and efficiency in the creation and transfer of knowledge' (Kogut and Zander, 1996, p. 503). An increasing specialization and distribution of knowledge supports the emergence of cooperation between them. Because of this, the horizontal and vertical boundaries of a firm will be increasingly blurred. But, as a consequence of opportunistic behaviour concerning the necessary disclosure of its own research activities, cooperation may not be stable.

Firms with their individual activities differ from one another with regard to their sources and processing of information and productive knowledge. Also for this reason they show a technical and organizational diversity, according to their technological path taken, their level of unit production costs, the different capabilities in converting new knowledge into new organizational routines, innovations and internal growth. They develop internally, as regards their resources and capabilities, on the basis of their business strategy,[11] and they or their individual activities are subject to selection in the competitive market place. As a result, both market and organizational structure will be permanently altered.

Following the dynamic capability, knowledge-based view, the firm, aside from being a pure 'exchange structure' to impose incentives and control on individuals internally, is a social, knowledge-creating and knowledge-applying 'productive unit' (for this distinction, see Knudsen, 1995, p. 214; also Spulber, 1992, p. 566; Langlois and Foss, 1999, p. 213). It coordinates and integrates dispersed and specialized knowledge regarding the employment of resources of different participants and in different forms (see Hayek, 1945, p. 519) and on this basis can simultaneously create new knowledge. This applies to all activities of the firm. Knowledge is stored and accumulated in individual persons and with that in organizations with their hierarchically structured routines and capabilities. It is subject to the selection in the market and competition process (see Foss 1997, p. 317; Dosi and Teece, 1998, p. 282). Together with its stock of knowledge and its capabilities, the organizational structure of the firm must evolve. So the evolutionary dynamic capability approach of developing and using knowledge and resources in an integrated way includes the production process and the organizational structure of an enterprise, requiring an integration of theories of Organizational Economics and Strategy Research such as the resource-based and knowledge-based view of the firm (see Foss, 2005a, p. 50). In that way it may contribute to both the explanation of internal firm organization and its strategy to resist competitive pressure and to attain sustained competitive advantage.

5   Concluding remarks

The relation between evolutionary economics and business strategy in the version of a resource-based and a dynamic-capability view of the firm may be looked at from two different starting points. On the one hand, evolutionary economics is intended for the broadening of the static resource-based approach towards a behavioural, process-oriented variant, to explain the creation of new resources and capabilities for their use. On the other hand, the resource-based view and especially its extension in the form of the knowledge-based view, are promising candidates to close a gap within the framework of evolutionary economics. In this way, industry dynamics as the evolution of a population of firms is supplemented by a more detailed characterization regarding the development of individual firms. This second approach is looked into here. The heterogeneity of firms as the result of rent-generating resources, first and foremost knowledge, is emphasized. Knowledge is created, intentionally and blindly, converted into innovations which are subjected to the selection pressure of the market, but are also adaptable to changes in its environment. Confirmed productive knowledge is preserved and grows in the course of evolution. By considering the internal conditions of success, such as resources and capabilities, in addition to their routines, evolutionary economics will be completed by normative aspects of strategic management. But, all in all, neither is the emergence of rent-generating activities explained as yet in a satisfactory manner, nor will a unified theory of the firm be constructed, but more likely a hybrid one will emerge, being composed of different technological, institutional and efficiency-based elements.

Notes

1. For the origin of the synthetic evolutionary biology, see Mayr (1984, p. 454) and Depew and Weber (1995, p. 299).
2. 'Darwinism includes not only specific theories that explain particular biological mechanisms, but also a general theory that applies to all open, complex and evolving systems, irrespective of the particular mechanisms of inheritance or replication' (Hodgson, 2002, p. 273).
3. Knight (1921, p. 271) regards the existence of a firm as a result of 'the reduction of the uncertainty in individual judgments and decisions' (p. 293) that is shared between owners and employees. Besides, a firm makes possible a greater flexibility in case of uncertainty than forming individual contracts between individuals on the market. In contrast to Knight, Coase (1937, p. 400) is of the following opinion: 'We can imagine a system where all advice or knowledge was bought as required.'
4. 'economizing is more fundamental than strategizing – or, put differently, that economy is the best strategy' (Williamson, 1991, p. 76).
5. For a critique of this scientific approach that conflicts with methodological individualism, see Foss (2003, p. 196). As he sees it, too little attention is devoted to individual decision making (p. 198).
6. 'no such thing as a universal best practice can possibly exist. There can only be local "best" solutions' (Becker, 2004, p. 652).
7. 'The fact that incentives are not taken into account is a drawback shared by all the evolutionary theories of the firm' (Garrouste and Saussier, 2005, p. 186).
8. Following Porter (1991, p. 102), the firm is regarded as a bundle of activities, aiming at its adaptation to the environment and also their formation. The shaping of a market strategy will occur on the basis of the available provision of resources that is assumed to be equal for all firms (see also Spanos and Lioukas, 2001, p. 908).
9. But there is not yet a unified definition of what resources and capabilities exactly are. See for that critique Duschek (2002, p. 50), Bromiley and Fleming (2002, p. 329). Teece, Pisano and Shuen (1997, p. 516) prefer the term 'firm specific assets' instead of resources.
10. 'the growth of our knowledge is the result of a process closely resembling what Darwin called "natural selection", that is, the *natural selection of hypotheses*' (Popper, 1972, p. 261).
11. For a life cycle model of business organization emphasizing the role of the entrepreneur who is constrained by his/her flexible 'business conception', see Witt (2000, p. 736).

References

Aldrich, H. (1999), *Organizations Evolving*, London, Thousand Oaks, CA, New Dehli: Sage.
Antonelli, C. (1999), 'The evolution of the industrial organisation of the production of knowledge', *Cambridge Journal of Economics*, **23**, 243–60.
Argote, L. (1999), *Organizational Learning: Creating, Retaining and Transferring Knowledge*, Boston, Dordrecht, London: Kluwer.
Bamberger, I. and T. Wrona (1996), 'Der Ressourcenansatz und seine Bedeutung für die Strategische Unternehmensführung', Zeitschrift für betriebswirtschaftliche Forschung, H.2, 130–53.
Barney, J. (1991), 'Firm resources and sustained competitive advantage', *Journal of Management*, **17**, 99–120.
Barney, J. (1997), *Gaining and Sustaining Competitive Advantage*, Reading, MA: Addison-Wesley.
Barney, J. (2001), 'Resource-based *theories* of competitive advantage: a ten-year retrospective on the resource-based view', *Journal of Management*, **27**, 643–50.
Becker, M. (2004), 'Organizational routines: a review of the literature', *Industrial and Corporate Change*, **13**(4), 643–77.

Bromiley, P. and L. Fleming (2002), 'The resource-based view of strategy: a behaviourist critique', in M. Augier and J. March (eds), *The Economics of Choice, Change and Organization, Essays in Memory of Richard M. Cyert*, Cheltenham, UK and Northampton, MA, USA: Edward Elgar, pp. 319–36.

Carroll, G. (1993), 'A sociological view on why firms differ', *Strategic Management Journal*, **14**, 237–49.

Chandler, A.D. (1992), 'What is a firm? A historical perspective', *European Economic Review*, **36**, 483–92.

Coase, R. (1937), 'The nature of the firm', *Economica*, **4**, 386–405.

Coase, R. (1988), 'The Nature of the Firm: influence', *Journal of Law, Economics, and Organization*, **4**(1), 33–47.

Cohen, B. (1993), 'Analogy, homology and metaphor in the interactions between the natural sciences and the social sciences, especially economics', in N. de Marchi (ed.), *History of Political Economy*, **25**, Annual Supplement: Non-Natural Social Science, pp. 7–44.

Cohen, W. and D. Levinthal (1990), 'Absorptive capacity: a new perspective on learning and innovation', *Administrative Science Quarterly*, **35**, 128–58.

Conner, K. (1991), 'A historical comparison of resource-based theory and five schools of thought within industrial organization economics: do we have a new theory of the firm?', *Journal of Management*, **17**, 121–54.

Cowan, R., P. David and D. Foray (2000), 'The explicit economics of knowledge codification and tacitness', *Industrial and Corporate Change*, **9**, 211–53.

Cyert, R. and J. March (1963), *A Behavioral Theory of the Firm*, Englewood Cliffs, NJ: Prentice-Hall.

Demsetz, H. (1988), 'The Theory of the Firm revisited', *Journal of Law, Economics, and Organization*, **4**, 141–61.

Depew, D. and B. Weber (1995), *Darwinism Evolving*, Cambridge, MA: MIT Press.

Dosi, G. and L. Marengo (1994), 'Some elements of evolutionary theory of organizational competences', in R. England (ed.), *Evolutionary Concepts in Contemporary Economics*, Ann Arbor: University of Michigan Press, pp. 157–78.

Dosi, G. and R.R. Nelson (1994), 'An introduction to evolutionary theories in economics', *Journal of Evolutionary Economics*, **4**, 153–72.

Dosi, G. and D. Teece (1998), 'Organizational competencies and the boundaries of the firm', in R. Arena and Ch. Longhi (eds), *Markets and Organization*, Berlin: Springer, pp. 281–301.

Dosi, G., R. Nelson and S. Winter (2000), 'Introduction: the nature and dynamics of organizational capabilities', in G. Dosi, R. Nelson and S. Winter (eds), *The Nature and Dynamics of Organizational Capabilities*, Oxford, New York: Oxford University Press, pp. 1–22.

Duschek, S. (2002), *Innovation in Netzwerken*, Wiesbaden: Deutscher Universitätsverlag.

Eisenhardt, K. and J.A. Martin (2000), 'Dynamic capabilities: what are they?', *Strategic Management Journal*, **21**, 1105–21.

Eliasson, G. (1994), 'The Theory of the Firm and the Theory of Economic Growth', in L. Magnusson (ed.), *Evolutionary and Neo-Schumpeterian Approaches to Economics*, Boston, Dordrecht, London: Kluwer, pp. 173–201.

Fleck, J. (2000), 'Artefact↔activity: the coevolution of artefacts, knowledge and organization in technological innovation', in J. Ziman (ed.), *Technological Innovation as an Evolutionary Process*, Cambridge: Cambridge University Press, pp. 248–66.

Foray, D. (2004), *The Economics of Knowledge*, Cambridge, MA: MIT Press.

Foss, N. (1993), 'Theories of the firm: contractual and competence perspectives', *Journal of Evolutionary Economics*, **3**, 127–44.

Foss, N. (1996), 'Knowledge-based approaches to the theory of the firm: some critical comments', *Organization Science*, **7**, 470–76.

Foss, N. (1997), 'Evolutionary and contractual theories of the firm: how do they relate?', *Rivista Internazionale di Scienze Sociali*, **105**, 309–37.

Foss, N. (1999), 'Research in the strategic theory of the firm: "Isolationism" and "Integrationism"', *Journal of Management Studies*, **36**, 725–55.

Foss, N. (2000), 'The theory of the firm. An introduction to themes and contributions', in N. Foss. (ed.), *The Theory of the Firm: Critical Perspectives on Business and Management*, Vol. 1, London: Routledge, pp. XV–LXI.

Foss, N. (2001), 'Evolutionary theories of the firm: reconstruction and relations to contractual theories', in K. Dopfer (ed.), *Evolutionary Economics: Program and Scope*, Boston: Kluwer, pp. 319–55.

Foss, N. (2003), 'Bounded rationality and tacit knowledge in the organizational capabilities approach: an assessment and a re-evaluation', *Industrial and Corporate Change*, **12**(2), 185–201.

Foss, N. (2005a), *Strategy, Economic Organization, and the Knowledge Economy. The Coordination of Firms and Resources*, Oxford, New York: Oxford University Press.

Foss, N. (2005b), 'Resources and transaction costs: how property rights economics furthers the resource-based view', *Strategic Management Journal*, **26**, 541–53.

Foss, N., C. Knudsen and C. Montgomery (1995), 'An exploration of common ground: integrating evolutionary and strategic theories of the firm', in C. Montgomery (ed.), *Resource-Based and Evolutionary Theories of the Firm: Towards a Synthesis*, Boston: Kluwer, pp. 1–17.

Foster, J. and J. Metcalfe (2001), 'Modern evolutionary economic perspectives', in J. Foster and J. Metcalfe (eds), *Frontiers of Evolutionary Economics*, Cheltenham, UK and Northampton, MA, USA: Edward Elgar, pp. 1–16.

Garrouste, P. and S. Saussier (2005), 'Looking for a theory of the firm: future challenges', *Journal of Economic Behaviour and Organization*, **58**, 178–99.

Granstrand, O. (1998), 'Towards a theory of the technology-based firm', *Research Policy*, **27**, 465–89.

Grant, R. (1996), 'Toward a knowledge-based theory of the firm', *Strategic Management Journal*, **17** (Winter Special Issue), 109–22.

Grant, R. (2003), 'The knowledge-based view of the firm', in D. Faulkner and A. Campbell (eds), *The Oxford Handbook of Strategy*, vol. I, Oxford: Oxford University Press, pp. 197–221.

Hayek, F.A. (1945), 'The use of knowledge in society', *The American Economic Review*, **35**, 519–30.

Herrmann-Pillath, C. (2002), *Grundriß der Evolutionsökonomik*, Munich: Fink.

Hodgson, G. (1998), 'Competence and contract in the theory of the firm', *Journal of Economic Behaviour and Organization*, **35**, 179–201.

Hodgson, G. (2001), 'Is social evolution Lamarckian or Darwinian?', in J. Laurent and J. Nightingale (eds), *Darwinism and Evolutionary Economics*, Cheltenham, UK and Northampton, MA, USA: Edward Elgar, pp. 87–120.

Hodgson, G. (2002), 'Darwinism in economics: from analogy to ontology', *Journal of Evolutionary Economics*, **12**, 259–81.

Holmstrom, B. and J. Tirole (1989), 'The theory of the firm', in R. Schmalensee and R. Willig (eds), *Handbook of Industrial Organization*, vol.1, Amsterdam: North-Holland, pp. 61–133.

Kay, N. (1997), *Pattern in Corporate Evolution*, Oxford: Oxford University Press.

Knight, F. (1921), *Risk, Uncertainty and Profit*, New York, Boston: Houghton, Mifflin.

Knudsen, C. (1995), 'Theories of the firm, strategic management, and leadership', in C. Montgomery (ed.), *Resource-based and Evolutionary Theories of the Firm: Towards a Synthesis*, Boston, Dordrecht, London: Kluwer, pp. 179–217.

Knudsen, T. (2001), 'Nesting Lamarckian within Darwinian explanations: necessity in economics and possibility in biology?' in J. Laurent and J. Nightingale (eds), *Darwinism and Evolutionary Economics*, Cheltenham, UK and Northampton, MA, USA: Edward Elgar, pp. 121–59.

Kogut, B. and U. Zander (1992), 'Knowledge of the firm, combinative capabilities, and the replication of technology', *Organization Science*, **3**, 383–97.

Kogut, B. and U. Zander (1996), 'What firms do? Coordination, identity, and learning', *Organization Science*, **7**, 502–18.

Langlois, R. and N. Foss (1999), 'Capabilities and governance: the rebirth of production in the theory of economic organization', *Kyklos*, **52**, 201–18.

Lewin, R., A. Klevorick, R. Nelson and S. Winter (1987), 'Appropriating the returns from industrial research and development', *Brookings Papers an Economic Activity*, Special Issue on Microeconomics, 783–820.

Madhok, A. (2002), 'Reassessing the fundamentals and beyond: Ronald Coase, the transaction cost and resource-based theories of the firm and the institutional structure of production', *Strategic Management Journal*, **23**, 535–50.

Mahoney, J. (1995), 'The management of resources and the resource of management', *Journal of Business Studies*, **33**, 91–101.

Mahoney, J. and J. Pandian (1992), 'The resource-based view within the conversation of strategic management', *Strategic Management Journal*, **13**, 363–80.

Makadog, R. (2001), 'Toward a synthesis of the resource-based and dynamic-capability views of rent creation', *Strategic Management Journal*, **22**, 387–401.

Malerba, F. (1992), 'Learning by firms and incremental technical change', *The Economic Journal*, **102**, 845–59.

March, J. (1991), 'Exploration and exploitation in organizational learning', *Organization Science*, **2**, 71–87.

Mayr, E. (1984), *Die Entwicklung der biologischen Gedankenwelt*, Berlin: Springer.

McKelvey, M. (1996), *Evolutionary Innovations. The Business of Biotechnology*, Oxford: Oxford University Press.

Metcalfe, J.S. (1995), 'The economic foundations of technology policy: equilibrium and evolutionary perspectives', in P. Stoneman (ed.), *Handbook of the Economics of Innovation and Technical Change*, Cambridge, MA: Blackwell, pp. 409–512.

Metcalfe, J.S. (2005), 'Evolutionary concepts in relation to evolutionary economics', in K. Dopfer (ed.), *The Evolutionary Foundations of Economics*, Cambridge: Cambridge University Press, pp. 391–430.

Mokyr, J. (1991), 'Evolutionary biology, technological change and economic history', *Bulletin of Economic Research*, **43**, 127–49.

Nelson, R. (1991), 'Why do firms differ, and how does it matter?', *Strategic Management Journal* (Special Issue Winter), **12**, 61–74.

Nelson, R. (1994), 'The role of firm difference in an evolutionary theory of technical advance', in L. Magnusson (ed.), *Evolutionary and Neo-Schumpeterian Approaches to Economics*, Dordrecht: Kluwer, pp. 231–42.

Nelson, R. (1995), 'Recent evolutionary theorizing about economic change', *The Journal of Economic Literature*, **33**, 48–90.

Nelson, R. and S. Winter (1982), *An Evolutionary Theory of Economic Change*, Cambridge, MA: Belknap Press.

Niman, N. (1994), 'The role of biological analogies in the theory of the firm', in Ph. Mirowski (ed.), *Natural Images in Economic Thought*, Cambridge: Cambridge University Press, pp. 360–83.

Noda, T. and D.J. Collis (2001), 'The evolution of intraindustry firm heterogeneity: insights from a process study', *Academy of Management Journal*, **44**, 897–925.

Nonaka, I. and H. Takeuchi (1997), *Die Organisation des Wissens*, Frankfurt/Main: Campus Verlag.

O'Brien, D. (1984), 'The evolution of the theory of the firm', in F. Stephen (ed.), *Firms, Organization and Labour*, New York: St. Martin's Press, pp. 25–62.

Penrose, E. (1959), *The Theory of the Growth of the Firm*, Oxford: Blackwell.

Peteraf, M. (1993), 'The cornerstones of competitive advantage: a resource-based view', *Strategic Management Journal*, **14**, 179–91.

Pierce, J., C. Boerner and D. Teece (2002), 'Dynamic capabilities, competence and the behavioural theory of the firm', in M. Augier and J. March (eds), *The Economics of Choice, Change and Organization, Essays in Memory of Richard M. Cyert*, Cheltenham, UK and Northampton, MA, USA: Edward Elgar, pp. 81–95.

Popper, K. (1972), 'Evolution and the tree of knowledge', in K. Popper, *Objective Knowledge. An Evolutionary Approach*, Oxford: Clarendon Press, pp. 256–84.

Porter, M. (1991), 'Towards a dynamic theory of strategy', *Strategic Management Journal*, **12**, 95–117.

Pyka, A. (1999), 'Der kollektive Innovationsprozeß', *Volkswirtschaftliche Schriften*, Heft 498, Berlin: Duncker & Humblot.
Ramstad, Y. (1994), 'On the nature of economic evolution: J.R. Commons and the metaphor of artificial selection', in L. Magnusson (ed.), *Evolutionary and Neo-Schumpeterian Approaches to Economics*, Dordrecht: Kluwer, pp. 65–121.
Rathe, K. and U. Witt (2001), 'The nature of the firm – static versus development interpretations', *Journal of Management and Governance*, **5**, 331–51.
Rumelt, R. (1984), 'Towards a strategic theory of the firm', in R. Lamb (ed.), *Competitive Strategic Management*, Englewood Cliffs, NJ: Prentice-Hall, pp. 557–70.
Rumelt, R., D. Schendel and D. Teece (1991), 'Strategic management and economics', *Strategic Management Journal*, **12**, 5–29.
Saviotti, P. (1998), 'On the dynamics of appropriability of tacit and of codified knowledge', *Research Policy*, **26**, 843–56.
Saviotti, P. and J. Metcalfe (1991), 'Present development and trends in evolutionary economics', in P. Saviotti and J. Metcalfe (eds), *Evolutionary Theories of Economic and Technological Change*, Chur, Switzerland: Harwood Academic, pp. 1–30.
Schneider, D. (1997), *Betriebswirtschaftslehre, Band 3: Theorie der Unternehmung*, Munich, Vienna: Oldenburg.
Schweber, D. (1985), 'The wider British context in Darwin's theorizing', in D. Kohn (ed.), *The Darwinian Heritage*, Princeton, NJ: Princeton University Press, pp. 35–69.
Spanos, Y. and S. Lioukas (2001), 'An examination into the causal logic of rent generation: contrasting Porter's competitive strategy framework and the resource-based perspective', *Strategic Management Journal*, **22**, 907–34.
Spulber, D. (1992), 'Economic analysis and management strategy: a survey', *Journal of Economic and Management Strategy*, **1**, 535–75.
Teece, D., R. Rumelt, G. Dosi and S. Winter (1994), 'Understanding corporate coherence: theory and evidence', *Journal of Economic Behaviour and Organization*, **23**, 1–30.
Teece, D., G. Pisano and A. Shuen (1997), 'Dynamic capabilities and strategic management', *Strategic Management Journal*, **18**, 509–33.
Vanberg, V. (1996), 'Institutional evolution within constraints', *Journal of Institutional and Theoretical Economics*, **152**, 690–96.
Vromen, J. (1995), *Economic Evolution. An Inquiry into the Foundations of New Institutional Economics*, London, New York: Routledge.
Williamson, O. (1990a), *Die ökonomischen Institutionen des Kapitalismus*, Tübingen.
Williamson, O. (1990b), 'A comparison of alternative approaches to economic organization', *Journal of Institutional and Theoretical Economics*, **146**, 61–71.
Williamson, O. (1991), 'Strategizing, economizing, and economic organization', *Strategic Management Journal*, **12** (Special Issue Winter), 75–94.
Williamson, O. (1999), 'Strategy research: governance and competence perspectives', *Strategic Management Journal*, **20**, 1087–1108.
Williamson, O. (2002), 'The theory of the firm as a governance structure: from choice to contract', *The Journal of Economic Perspectives*, **16**(3), 171–95.
Winter, S. (1975), 'Optimization and evolution in the theory of the firm', in R. Day and T. Groves (eds), *Adaptive Economic Models*, New York: Academic Press, pp. 73–118.
Winter, S. (1986), 'The research program of the behavioural theory of the firm: orthodox critique and evolutionary perspective', in B. Gilad and S. Kaish (eds), *Handbook of Behavioural Economics, vol. A: Behavioural Microeconomics*, Greenwich, CT: JAI, pp. 151–88.
Winter, S. (1988), 'On Coase, competence, and corporation', *Journal of Law, Economics, and Organization*, **4**, 163–80.
Winter, S. (1995), 'Four Rs of profitability: rents, resources, routines, and replication', in C. Montgomery (ed.), *Resource-Based and Evolutionary Theories of the Firm: Towards a Synthesis*, Dordrecht: Kluwer, pp. 147–78.
Winter, S. (2003), 'Understanding dynamic capabilities', *Strategic Management Journal*, **24**, 991–5.
Witt, U. (1996), 'A "Darwinian Revolution" in economics?', *Journal of Institutional and Theoretical Economics*, **152**, 707–16.

Witt, U. (2000), 'Changing cognitive frames – changing organizational forms: an entrepreneurial theory of organizational development', *Industrial and Corporate Change*, **9**(4), 733–55.

Witt, U. (2001), 'Evolutionary economics: an interpretative survey', in K. Dopfer (ed.), *Evolutionary Economics: Program and Scope*, Dordrecht: Kluwer, pp. 45–88.

Zollo, M. and S. Winter (2002), 'Deliberate learning and the evolution of dynamic capabilities', *Organization Science*, **13**, 339–51.

11 Managing the process of new venture creation: an integrative perspective
Marc Gruber

1 Entrepreneurship: business creation and management style

Schumpeter (1946) viewed the entrepreneur as a creator of disequilibrium in the marketplace, who is able to recognize and exploit market opportunities before others and reaps the profits for his acts of creative destruction. Though there is no consensus amongst scholars on how to define the terms 'entrepreneur' and 'entrepreneurship', the contemporary literature largely shares the understanding that entrepreneurship entails a process which starts with the discovery of an opportunity that can be capitalized on by *creating a new organization* (Bygrave, 1997). In a more encompassing perspective the term 'entrepreneurship' has also been applied to the pursuit of a business opportunity by an *existing business*, drawing attention to the fact that entrepreneurial management is nowadays also considered to be a distinctive *management style*. However, it was only some decades ago that entrepreneurship was regarded as an inevitable stage businesses had to get through on their way to professional management, and not as an end in itself (Sahlman *et al.*, 1999). This perception has changed owing not only to public acknowledgment of the important macroeconomic roles new and small businesses fulfill, but also to an increasing dynamism in the business environment which causes opportunities to emerge quickly and therefore calls for quick and nimble (i.e., entrepreneurial) actions by almost all economic actors, irrespective of their age and size (McGrath and MacMillan, 2000).

This chapter focuses on the narrower understanding of entrepreneurship, i.e., the process of seizing an opportunity by creating a *new* organization. The purpose of this chapter is to develop an integrative perspective on managing the process of new venture creation, thereby following MacMillan and Katz's (1992) call for more comprehensiveness in entrepreneurship theory and modeling. Hence, in order to depict current knowledge and to gain fresh insights, a novel framework is applied which is based on systems theory and distinguishes challenges in new venture management on a normative, a strategic and an operational level. However, before we turn to this discussion, the specific characteristics of new venture management are outlined.

2 Characteristics of new venture management

New ventures have distinct characteristics that distinguish them from larger, more established firms and which shape the challenges entrepreneurs face when building a new organization. In particular, the newness and small size of these firms, the high degree of uncertainty of their endeavor as well as the dynamics of their (competitive) environment challenge entrepreneurs in the pursuit of their business opportunities. Table 11.1 gives an overview of these characteristics and outlines key challenges associated with them.

In their management activities, entrepreneurs have to deal with the typical day-to-day business operations and in parallel have to build a company, i.e. transform their business idea into a viable organization.[1] In order to develop a deeper understanding of the challenges associated with the evolution and growth of new ventures, researchers have designed models that depict the development of these firms and identify various stages of their growth (see Table 11.2). Greiner (1972/1998) developed the most widely cited model which also builds the basis for the models of Churchill and Lewis (1983) and Scott and Bruce (1987). Greiner identifies five stages of growth and turbulent transitions. He argues that, as a company grows, each evolutionary period causes its own period of revolution that has to be resolved by adequate managerial acts such as the delegation of tasks. Building on the model of Greiner, Churchill and Lewis (1983) explicitly focus on the development of small firms. In particular, they recognize that growth is not the only goal that can be pursued, and instroduce stages of stability into the model. The Scott and Bruce (1987) model represents a further refinement of these arguments and considers additional factors such as the industry.

Though these models give valuable insights on the various tasks entrepreneurs face during the early development of their businesses, they typically fail to differentiate between tasks which are operational in nature and tasks which have strategic importance for the new venture. Yet such distinctions are elementary for the effectiveness and efficiency of management, as research has repeatedly shown (Porter, 1996). In addition, most of these models put their focus on the 'hard', tangible factors of management and neglect the fact that the development of soft factors such as the culture of the firm plays an important role for new venture success (Schein, 1983). Hence, in the following section we propose a framework for managing the process of new venture creation which addresses these shortcomings by applying a more comprehensive, integrative perspective.

3 New venture creation: an integrative framework

The preceding discussion of the characteristics of new ventures and their environment depicted the challenges entrepreneurs typically face when creating a new organization. In order to establish an organizational entity

Table 11.1   Characteristics and challenges of new venture management
(Gruber, 2004)

Characteristics	Challenges for new ventures	Authors
Newness of the firm	• new ventures usually do not not have the access, links, experience, reputation as well as legitimacy of older firms, making it necessary to establish credibility and trust • they must rely to a high degree on social interactions among strangers • entrepreneurs cannot build on previous firm-specific experience	Stinchcombe (1965) Freeman/ Carroll/ Hannan (1983) Romanelli (1989)
Small size of the firm	• lack of human and financial resources • limited ability to survive during unfavorable conditions • high likelihood that critical skill gaps are encountered • lack of resources restricts the amount of (market) power a firm can exercise, disadvantage in negotiations	Aldrich/Auster (1986) Birch (1987) SBA (1983) McGrath (1996) Pleitner (1995)
Uncertainty and turbulence	• superior way of doing business unknown • fundamental rules for conducting business have yet to be determined • high likelihood of suboptimal decisions, which may have fatal consequences for a small firm with limited resources • competitive structure of the industry is changing, relationships with suppliers, distributors etc. are unstable	Knight (1921) Kirzner (1973) Anderson and Zeithaml (1984) Tushman and Anderson (1986)

successfully, entrepreneurs have to deal with these challenges in a comprehensive way, and have to bring along a diverse set of capabilities. For instance, Kao (1989) outlines an entrepreneur's job description which includes creative, operational/managerial, interpersonal and leadership tasks.

Table 11.2 Synopsis of influential growth models (Gruber, Harhoff and Tausend, 2003)

Model	Stage 1	Stage 2	Stage 3
Steinmetz (1969)	Idea generation and product development	New levels in the hierarchy, specialization and formalization	
Greiner (1972/ 1998)	Growth through creativity	Crisis of leadership and growth through direction	Crisis of autonomy and growth through delegation
Churchill/ Lewis (1983)	Obtaining customers, delivering product or service contracted for	Generate revenues and control expenses	Further growth or disengagement
Scott/Bruce (1987)	Developing a commercially acceptable product, obtaining customers, economic production	Control revenues and expenses, expand customer base and align firm structure	Co-ordination and delegation, managed growth, ensuring resources
Kazanjian/ Drazin (1990)	Idea generation and product development	Optimizing product and processes, distribution	Efficiency, optimizing profitability

In the following discussion a structured, multidimensional approach to the management of the new venture creation process is adopted by distinguishing a normative, strategic and operational level of venture management – a comprehensive perspective which is based on systems theory[2] and which has proved to be valuable for understanding firms in an integrative way (Bleicher, 1999; Gruber, 2000). In detail, these levels can be described as follows:

- At the *normative level*, management lays down the general, mid- to long-term goals of a firm and defines the basic codes of behavior as well as generally accepted company norms and principles, thereby establishing the identity, culture and structure of the company.
- At the *strategic level*, the firm focuses on establishing favorable prerequisites for achieving above normal returns by developing valuable resources and capabilities, by positioning its own activities relative to the competition, by bundling its strengths, and by developing suitable strategies for gaining as well as sustaining competitive advantages;

all within the normative guidelines of the firm (Bleicher, 1999; Schwaninger, 1994; Bowman, 1974).
- At the *operational level*, the firm deals with the execution of strategies within the normative scope of the firm (Bleicher, 1999; Ulrich and Krieg, 1974).

In addition to distinguishing these dimensions of management, three stages of new venture development are considered in our framework, namely a *pre-founding stage* (including opportunity identification), a *founding stage* (including incorporation and market entry), and an *early development stage* (including market penetration).

Building on this generic discussion, Table 11.3 gives an overview of key normative, strategic and operational tasks of new venture management in the pre-founding, founding and early development stage of organizational evolution.

As this framework shows at the *normative level*, one of the core challenges in the pre-founding stage of a new venture is the definition of a company vision and its values. It is basically up to the founders to develop a vision for the future development of their company, yet they have to take into account that these long-term goals (1) define the guide lines for all other decisions, and (2) influence the perceptions various actors in the environment will have of the emerging firm. For example, if the founders conclude that they want to remain independent and follow a low-growth strategy, they will not be prime candidates for venture capital financing.

Corresponding to the definition of a company vision, the core values of the firm have to be defined. In practice, this often happens implicitly, e.g., when founders discuss how to tackle certain problems or argue about venture strategies and in the process arrive at a common understanding of their values. These core values as well as the vision of the company impact the gradual development of a company culture. As reported by several studies, a market orientation is found to be of particular importance for the success of new ventures. For example, Raffa and Zollo (1995) and Roberts (1991) found that firms that were quick in adopting a market orientation achieved a higher performance level than firms that did not.[3] As the firm evolves and more and more employees join the organization, its culture has to be fostered and its vision shared in order to avoid drifting into a heterogeneous entity and losing orientation and focus.

Entrepreneurs also face important normative tasks such as the definition of new roles and the institutionalization of an organizational structure. Also, strategic alliances as well as measures to establish credibility and trust can be regarded as key challenges at the normative level, helping the firm to establish itself as a respected organizational entity.

Table 11.3 *Normative, strategic and operational challenges of new venture management*

	Pre-founding stage	Founding stage	Early development stage
Normative level	■ Defining company vision and values	■ Sharing of company vision and values in firm ■ Forming of organizational culture ■ Building credibility/trust ■ Definition of roles	■ Sharing of company vision and values in firm ■ Fostering of organizational culture ■ Building credibility/trust ■ Refining organizational structure
			→ t
Strategic level	■ Opportunity recognition and market identification ■ Conception of business model and identification of competitive advantage	■ Market entry strategy ■ Resource building ■ Strategic alliances	■ Growth strategy ■ Replicating resources ■ Sustaining competitive advantage / erecting barriers to market entry
			→ t
Operational level	■ Business intelligence ■ Networking	■ Business intelligence ■ Networking ■ Presentations and negotiations ■ Market tests	■ Business intelligence ■ Networking ■ Management of personnel ■ Customer relationship management
			→ t
	↓ Founder(s)	↓ Team	↓ Organization

Thus, by defining these fundamental characteristics of the new venture, normative management is able to make major contributions to overcoming the liabilities of newness. As the firm evolves into a larger and more mature entity, also liabilities of smallness are gradually overcome; however, the risk of becoming inert must be addressed in the process.

As a new venture progresses from the pre-founding stage to the early development stage, major tasks at the *strategic level* include market identification, the development of a business model and a market entry strategy. Market entry typically represents a major milestone, as revenues allow new ventures to enter a more favorable resource-dependence position (Schoonhoven, Eisenhardt and Lyman, 1990). The ability of a firm to gain and sustain its competitive advantage in the marketplace is closely linked to its resource base. While classical economic theory has a very broad understanding of the term 'resources' (cf. Ricardo, 1817), strategic management mainly focuses on those key resources which enable a firm to achieve sustainable competitive advantages in the marketplace (Leonard-Barton, 1992; Dierickx and Cool, 1989). According to Amit and Schoemaker (1993) strategically valuable resources have characteristics such as scarcity, low tradability, inimitability, limited substitutability, appropriability and durability. As new ventures typically start out with very limited strategic resources, they need to replicate these resources in order to be able to grow. However, due to the very characteristics of strategically valuable resources, firms sometimes face severe problems in this replication process (Szulanski and Winter, 2002; Dierickx and Cool, 1989).

An equally challenging task for a new venture is to sustain its competitive advantage, even in the face of more established, resource-rich corporations going after the same target segment. When the new venture is a pioneer or an early mover in the market, one possibility is to erect barriers to market entry for potential new competitors. In a comprehensive literature study, Karakaya and Stahl (1989) identified 19 different market-entry barriers such as access to distribution channels, incumbent's cost advantages or customer switching costs. However, the consideration of pioneering advantages has to be complemented by consideration of a laggard's disadvantages and careful analysis of a new venture's ability to erect entry barriers or to overcome them. Narasimhan and Zhang (2000) observe that new ventures often race into a market only to avoid the disadvantages of entering late, rather than being able to capture pioneering advantages.

Another factor influencing the sustainability of competitive advantage is environmental turbulence. In order to achieve congruence with the requirements of a changing business environment and to sustain its advantage, a new venture should foster so-called 'dynamic capabilities' which are elementary for renewing its competences (Teece, Pisano and Shuen, 1997). As firms progress through the various stages of development, more and more knowledge and experience is gathered on internal operations and on the environment, reducing the initial uncertainty and allowing the firm to refine its initial strategy.

At the *operational level*, there are numerous tasks which have to be carried out in order to implement the strategy of the new firm. For instance, tasks such as business intelligence or networking are important throughout all three stages of development, while presentations for financial investors, market tests of the product and the management of customer relationships become important at various stages of development. Owing to environmental uncertainty, operational management in new ventures can be very turbulent at times (Macdonald, 1985).

Looking at the overview in Table 11.3, it is obvious that entrepreneurs need to manage a new venture with much anticipation. Especially in firms that have to rush to market in order to capture first-mover advantages, the duration of these stages is compressed (Greiner, 1972/1998), posing further challenges to the founders. For instance, with new employees joining the rapidly growing firm on a daily basis, fostering a strong culture and common vision is a major challenge at the normative level (Gruber and Harhoff, 2002). Developing a market entry strategy and engaging in supportive strategic alliances within a short time frame are critical challenges at the strategic level of a high-growth venture. Taking into account the scope and complexity of these tasks, it is evident that the time for setting up a successful new venture cannot be shortened arbitrarily.

From a managerial perspective it has also to be stressed that normative, strategic and operational tasks complement each other. Entrepreneurs who neglect certain tasks will face problems in establishing a successful company. Thus, these tasks have to be addressed in a well-orchestrated manner, making it necessary to manage 'hard factors' and 'soft factors' simultaneously. Considering these comprehensive managerial challenges it is not surprising that venture capitalists typically attribute higher importance to the quality of the management team than to the quality of the venture idea during the venture evaluation process.

4   Conclusion

This chapter studies the creation of new ventures from a comprehensive management perspective. We propose a novel framework which distinguishes a normative, strategic and operational dimension of new venture management. This multidimensional perspective is based on systems theory and has already proved to be of value for understanding larger corporations as well as small and medium-sized enterprises in a comprehensive and integrative way. As it also allows conceptualizing transformation processes in firms (Bleicher, 1999), we believe that it can serve as a fruitful approach for studying a wide range of phenomena in the field of entrepreneurship.

As the preceding discussion has shown, there are distinct challenges an entrepreneurial team has to master in order to establish the emerging firm as a viable entity. While some tasks are quite obvious in new venture management (e.g., the process of developing and launching an offering), others in many cases are not priorities in the minds of overburdened entrepreneurs (e.g., fostering a beneficial company culture), yet are likely to have a profound impact on the overall ability to succeed in the marketplace and to establish the firm as a viable economic actor. Hence, the framework presented can also have practical applications, e.g., in teaching a comprehensive understanding of new venture management.

Notes

1. In the process, many firms never arrive at becoming established entities. As evidence from business mortality statistics shows, discontinuance rates can be as high as 70 per cent in the first five years depending on the industry under study (Yoon and Lilien, 1985; Timmons, 1999; Cooper and Bruno, 1977).
2. For a thorough discussion of systems theory and its application in planning see, e.g., Ackoff (1970), Gälweiler (1986), Ulrich and Krieg (1974) and Schwaninger (1994).
3. Narver and Slater (1990) define market orientation as the 'organization culture that most effectively creates the necessary behaviors for the creation of superior value for buyers and, thus, superior performance for the business'.

References

Ackoff, R.L. (1970), *A Concept of Corporate Planning*, New York: Wiley.
Aldrich, H. and Auster, E. (1986), Even dwarfs started small: liabilities of age and size and their strategic implications, in L. Cummings and B. Staw (eds), *Research in Organizational Behavior*, Greenwich: JAI, pp. 165–98.
Amit, R. and Schoemaker, P.J.H. (1993), Strategic assets and organizational rent, *Strategic Management Journal*, 33–46.
Anderson, C. and Zeithaml, C.A. (1984), Stage of product life cycle, business strategy, and business performance, *Academy of Management Journal*, 5–24.
Birch, D. (1987), *Job Creation in America*, New York: Free Press.
Bleicher, K. (1999), *Das Konzept integriertes Management*, 5th edn, Frankfurt am Main: Campus Verlag.
Bowman, E.H. (1974), Epistemology, corporate strategy and academe, *Sloan Management Review*, 35–50.
Bygrave, W.D. (1997), The entrepreneurial process, in W.D. Bygrave (ed.), *The Portable MBA in Entrepreneurship*, New York and Chichester: Wiley, pp. 1–26.
Churchill, N.C. and Lewis, V.L. (1983), The five stages of small business growth, *Harvard Business Review*, May–June, 30–50.
Cooper, A.C. and Bruno, A.V. (1977), Success among high-technology firms, *Business Horizons*, 16–22.
Dierickx, I. and Cool, K. (1989), Asset stock accumulation and sustainability of competitive advantage, *Management Science*, 1504–11.
Freeman, J., Carroll, G.R. and Hannan, M.T. (1983), The liability of newness: age dependence in organizational death rates, *American Sociological Review*, 692–710.
Gälweiler, A. (1986), *Unternehmensplanung*, Frankfurt/New York: Campus Verlag.

Greiner, L. (1972/1998), Evolution and revolution as organizations grow, *Harvard Business Review*, March–April 1972, 37–46 (also: *HBR* May–June 1998, 55–66).

Gruber, M. (2000), *Der Wandel von Erfolgsfaktoren mittelständischer Unternehmen*, Wiesbaden: DUV/Gabler.

Gruber, M. (2004), Marketing in new ventures: theory and empirical evidence, *Schmalenbach Business Review*, **1**, 164–99.

Gruber, M. and Harhoff, D. (2002), Generierung und nachhaltige Sicherung komparativer Wettbewerbsvorteile, in U. Hommel and T. Knecht (eds), *Wertorientiertes Start-up Management*, Stuttgart: Frankfurter Allgemeine Buch, pp. 320–34.

Gruber, M., Harhoff, D. and Tausend, C. (2003), Finanzielle Entwicklung junger Wachstumsunternehmen, in A.-K. Achleitner and A. Bassen (eds), *Controlling für junge Unternehmen*, Stuttgart: Schaeffer-Poeschel, pp. 27–50.

Kao, J.J. (1989), *Entrepreneuship, Creativity & Organization*, Englewood Cliffs, NJ: Prentice-Hall.

Karakaya, F. and Stahl, M.J. (1989), Barriers to entry and market entry decisions in consumer and industrial goods markets, *Journal of Marketing*, **2**, 80–91.

Kazanjian, R. and Drazin, R. (1990), A stage-contingent model of design and growth for technology-based new ventures, *Journal of Business Venturing*, **5**, 137–50.

Kirzner, I. (1973), *Competition and Entrepreneurship*, Chicago, IL: University of Chicago Press.

Knight, F.H. (1921), *Risk, Uncertainty and Profit* (1971 reprint), New York: Houghton Mifflin.

Leonard-Barton, D. (1992), Core capabilities and core rigidities: a paradox in managing new product development, *Strategic Management Journal*, 111–25.

Macdonald, R.J. (1985), Strategic alternatives in emerging industries, *Journal of Product Innovation Management*, 158–69.

MacMillan, I.C. and Katz, J.A. (1992), Idiosyncratic milieus of entrepreneurial research: the need for comprehensive theories, *Journal of Business Venturing*, 1–8.

McGrath, R.G. (1996), Options and the entrepreneur: toward a strategic theory of entrepreneurial behavior, working paper, Columbia University, New York.

McGrath, R.G. and MacMillan, I. (2000), *The Entrepreneurial Mindset – Strategies for Continuously Creating Opportunity in an Age of Uncertainty*, Boston, MA: Harvard Business School Press.

Narasimhan, C. and Zhang, J.Z. (2000), Market entry strategy under firm heterogeneity and asymmetric payoffs, *Marketing Science*, **4**, 313–27.

Narver, J.C. and Slater, S.F. (1990), The effect of a market orientation on business profitability, *Journal of Marketing*, **4**, 20–35.

Pleitner, H.J. (1995), Das Unternehmerbild aus unterschiedlichen Perspektiven der Gründung, in J. Mugler and K.-H. Schmidt (eds), *Klein- und Mittelunternehmen in einer dynamischen Wirtschaft: Ausgewählte Schriften von Hans Jobst Pleitner*, Berlin: Duncker & Humblot, pp. 90–99.

Porter, M. (1996), What is strategy?, *Harvard Business Review*, Nov.–Dec., 61–78.

Raffa, M. and Zollo, G. (1995), Marketing strategies of small innovative software companies, in G.E. Hills, D.F. Muzyka, G.S. Omura and G.A. Knight (eds) *Research at the Marketing/Entrepreneurship Interface – Proceedings of the UIC Symposium on Marketing and Entrepreneurship*, Chicago, IL: University of Illinois, pp. 205–25.

Ricardo, D. (1817), *Principles of Political Economy and Taxation*, London: J.M. Dent & Sons.

Roberts, E.B. (1991), Strategic transformation and the success of high-technology companies, *International Journal of Technology Management*, 59–80.

Romanelli, E. (1989), Environments and strategies of organization start-up: effects on early survival, *Administrative Science Quarterly*, 369–87.

Sahlman, W.A., Stevenson, H.H., Roberts, M.J. and Bhidé, A. (eds) (1999), *The Entrepreneurial Venture*, Boston, MA: Harvard Business School Press.

SBA – Small Business Administration (1983), *The State of Small Business: A Report of the President*, Washington, DC: US Government Printing Office.

Schein, E.H. (1983), The role of the founder in creating organizational culture, *Organizational Dynamics*, Summer, 13–28.

Schoonhoven, C.B., Eisenhardt, K.M. and Lyman, K. (1990), Speeding products to markets: waiting time to first product introductions in new firms, *Administrative Science Quarterly*, 177–207.

Schumpeter, J.A. (1946), *Kapitalismus, Sozialismus und Demokratie*, Berne: Francke Verlag.

Schwaninger, M. (1994), *Managementsysteme*, Frankfurt am Main: Campus Verlag.

Scott, M. and Bruce, R. (1987), Five stages of growth in small business, *Long Range Planning*, **20** (3), 45–52.

Steinmetz, L. (1969), Critical stages of small business growth, *Business Horizons*, Feb., 29–35.

Stinchcombe, A.L. (1965), Social structure and organizations, in J.G. March (ed.), *Handbook of Organizations*, Chicago, IL: Rand McNally & Co., pp. 153–93.

Szulanski, G. and Winter, S. (2002), Getting it right the second time, *Harvard Business Review*, January, 62–9.

Teece, D.J., Pisano, G. and Shuen, A. (1997), Dynamic capabilities and strategic management, *Strategic Management Journal*, 509–33.

Timmons, J.A. (1999), *New Venture Creation – Entrepreneurship for the 21st Century*, Boston/London: Irwin/McGraw-Hill.

Tushman, M.L. and Anderson, P. (1986), Technological discontinuities and organizational environments, *Administrative Science Quarterly*, 439–65.

Ulrich, H. and Krieg, W. (1974), *St. Galler Management-Modell*, Berne: Haupt Verlag.

Yoon, E. and Lilien, G.L. (1985), New industrial product performance: the effects of market characteristics and strategy, *Journal of Product Innovation Management*, 134–44.

12 Technological collaboration
Mark Dodgson

Introduction

Collaboration between firms, once believed unambiguously to be characteristic of anti-competitive cartels and monopolistic behaviour, is now, in
the fields of research and technology, positively associated with industrial
dynamism and innovation. Firms actively collaborate in their technological activities – through joint ventures, strategic alliances, joint R&D contracts, and various innovation networks – despite the possibility of the loss
of proprietary assets, and the probability of shared returns from these
investments. Government policies for industry and technology promote
collaboration – by means of sponsored consortia, directives to public
research institutions, and tax and financial incentives – despite any residual
concerns over its anti-competitive and market-distorting potential.[1]

Essentially, collaboration is nowadays recognized as an important
feature in the generation and diffusion of technology and, by extension,
industrial development. It is a common feature of the research environment
and industry in most industrialized and industrializing nations, and in
Europe is a central element of pan-national industry policy.

Technological collaboration involves shared commitment of resources
and risk by a number of partners to agreed complementary aims. Vertical
collaboration occurs throughout the chain of production, from the provision of raw materials, through the production and assembly of parts, components and systems, to their distribution and servicing. Horizontal
collaborations occur between partners at the same level in the production
process. Firms may be comparatively more reluctant to form horizontal
collaborations as these may lead to disputes over ownership of their outcomes, such as intellectual property rights, or to direct competition between
collaborating firms.

The collaboration phenomenon has received widespread academic attention. There have, for example, been a number of special editions of academic journals published on the subject.[2] Since Project SAPPHO,[3] the
importance to innovators of external collaboration with users and other
sources of technology has been recognized (Rothwell *et al.*, 1974).
Empirical studies have examined the increasing scale and range of collaborative activity around the world (Hagedoorn, 2002; Sakakibara and
Dodgson, 2003). Economists, public policy analysts, geographers, and

management academics have analysed and explained the motives, conduct and significance of collaborations, attempting to learn how governments, regions and firms can improve their outcomes.

A selection of the wide range of analyses of the motivations for, and conduct of, collaboration is presented here, albeit with a distinctive Schumpeterian bias. Collaboration is viewed as an activity within an economy characterized by dynamic adaptation, rather than static efficiencies: where the basis of industrial activity and competitiveness is creativity, change and innovation in organization and technology. It is with this perspective that the questions are posed of why, given their potential downside, firms collaborate in their technological activities, and governments encourage them to do so.

Macro-level analyses
Macro-level analyses examine a range of structural reasons for collaboration. At its broadest level, political economists contend that the general propensity towards cooperation is influenced by different kinds of business systems (or capitalisms): the ways in which firms relate to one another, to their employees, government and to financial systems (Dore, 2000; Hall and Soskice, 2001). These business systems provide a context in which, for example, firms relate to one another within the chain of production along a continuum of spot-trading to 'obligational contractual relations' (Sako, 1992).

Researchers within an innovation and knowledge systems perspective argue how collaboration is influenced by differences in the institutional make-up of nations, specifically in their science and technology infrastructure, and in the quality of social relationships between, for example, users and suppliers (Lundvall, 1992). The contention here is that, as industry becomes more knowledge-intensive, the science and technology system shifts to a more complex, socially distributed, and diverse, structure of knowledge production activities (Gibbons *et al.*, 1994). Foster and Metcalfe (2001) describe the value of innovation systems which produce specialized knowledge and combine increasingly wide types of knowledge, and refer to Richardson's (1972) prescient observation about the increasing complementarity and increasing dissimilarity of relevant knowledge bases. Geographers bring spatial issues to bear in the combinatorial benefits of regions, clusters or, more broadly, an 'associational economy' (Cooke and Morgan, 2000).

Other structural considerations here include the intellectual property legal frameworks supporting the capacity to appropriate innovations; and the level of competition in the specific industry. There is some evidence to suggest, for example, that collaboration is a feature of more competitive industries (Eisenhardt and Schoonhoven, 1996).

Technological change affects the propensity to collaborate. Technology itself, particularly through the medium of vastly more powerful, fast, cheap and secure information and communications technology, has facilitated greater collaboration. The increasing depth, breadth and speed of relationships between science and technology have required greater integration of public- and private-sector participants in their production (Meyer-Krahmer and Schmoch, 1998).

Rapidly changing and disruptive technologies create many uncertainties for business firms. A number of analyses of collaboration link it with uncertainties in the generation and early diffusion of new technologies (Freeman, 1991). The product life-cycle model of Abernathy and Utterback (1978), for example, implies a cyclical role for collaboration based on uncertainty. Thus, in early stages of development, there are periods of high interaction between organizations with many new entrant companies possessing technological advantages over incumbent firms, and extensive collaboration between firms until a 'dominant design' emerges in a technology. As the technology matures, uncertainty declines and collaborative activity recedes. Collaboration brings a variety of inputs to bear to advantage when resolving problems associated with uncertainty (Klein, 1977).

At first sight, analysis of collaboration with a strictly Schumpeterian perspective fits best with the Mark I, creative destruction, entrepreneur-based model of innovation, rather than the Mark II, creative accumulation, large firm-based model. Schumpeter's entrepreneur, the vehicle for seeing innovative 'new combinations' and 'getting things done' was not autarkic. He was a collaborator: the combiner of diverse functions and activities, ranging from the invention itself to the source of the finance capital. In contrast, Schumpeter's 'business teams of trained specialists' were simple processors of predictable, routine innovation without need for external collaborative inputs. The contemporary empirical truth lies in the 'dynamic complementarity' of both models (Dodgson and Rothwell, 1994). The behavioural or creative advantages of Schumpeter's entrepreneur complements the large-scale, routinized (and hence introspective), activities of the large firm.

Micro-level analyses
At a micro level, from the perspective of firm competitiveness, collaboration can be analysed as having both *economizing* and *strategizing* benefits. Firms can be driven by both objectives, but economizing motivations imply a degree of certainty in outcomes, and often greater homogeneity amongst partners. Strategizing objectives, in comparison, imply more exploratory activities, and commonly more heterogenous partners.

Firms may collaborate in order to reduce or share costs and prevent duplication of effort. In neoclassical analysis, economizing through collaboration is a means to set cost-sharing and/or output-sharing rules for the participants in an R&D project in order to correct market failures which would otherwise prevent firms from conducting the socially optimum level of R&D (see Sakakibara, 1997).

From an institutional economics perspective, firms select collaboration (or 'quasi-vertical integration') as a governance structure, compared to the alternatives of market transactions (such as arm's length contracting or mergers and acquisitions), or hierarchies (internalization), because of transaction costs advantages. Defining and maintaining the relevance of contracts in uncertain, and often exploratory, environments is costly, if at all feasible. Mergers and acquisitions are commonly irreversible. Vertical integration precludes the benefits of effective trading amongst specialists. In contrast, collaboration provides a mechanism whereby close linkages among different organizations enable the development of sympathetic systems, procedures, and vocabulary which may reduce transaction costs. Additionally, collaboration may also allow partners to 'unbundle' discrete technological assets for transfer (Mowery, 1988) and may address the difficulty of valuing technological knowledge by providing a means of exchange that does not necessarily rely on price.

By taking a perspective that emphasizes the importance of information for innovation, markets provide only the one signal, price, which limits information accumulation, and provides little knowledge of technological developments. Hierarchies create routines that can lead to introspection and predictability in signals (DiMaggio and Powell, 1983). Collaboration provides a far richer form of information provision and exchange, and helps overcome bounded rationality problems.

The strategizing motivations for collaboration range from the objectives of competitor exclusion through raised entry barriers, technical standard setting or locking in key players, to a means of improving technological competencies, skills and learning. Our focus is on the latter objectives, although we shall move beyond neoclassical analysis of collaboration providing a vehicle to internalize the externality created through spillovers of research outcomes, to a Schumpeterian or, more particularly, Penrosian, analysis which emphasizes the process of resource and capability building through knowledge accumulation and purposive learning.

Our particular concern is with technological competences, although in the course of their realization these are inseparable from organizational concerns. Of importance here is the way in which in multi-product firms, the firm might wish to draw on outside knowledge to a greater extent by combining in-house technological competences and external technological acquisitions to help serve their markets. Essentially, given the increased complexity and systemic nature of technological innovations, there is a growing need to possess, or have access to, multiple technological competences (Granstrand, Patel and Pavitt, 1997).

The primary mechanism for the development of technological competences remains in-house R&D. However, as Cohen and Levinthal (1989) have demonstrated, a company's own R&D increases its capability to learn from others. Firms that invest in R&D benefit more from collaboration than firms that do not, which may add to their motivation to learn from partners. Furthermore, experiential learning makes firms better collaborators. Hence in collaborations formed with strategizing objectives, what is important is not only the output of the project, but also the process of knowledge accumulation, or learning.

Learning and trust

There is a substantial literature which places learning centrally in its analysis of collaboration (Dodgson, 1993a). In this view, learning is necessary to comprehend and respond to the changes occurring in industrial and technological systems, and produces the competences that provide sustainable competitive advantage. These approaches suggest that learning provides motive for, and desired outcomes from, collaboration. Collaboration also assists firms' internal constraints to learning. An external orientation assists firms to overcome the organizational introspection described in the management and organization theory literature, and applicable to firms' R&D groups. External links can bring new knowledge into the firm of a specific, project-based nature. They also can enable firms to reconsider their existing ways of doing things: be it in R&D organization or the implementation of new technology. Collaboration provides an opportunity to observe novelty through the approaches of partners, can stimulate reconsideration of current practices, and can be an antidote to the 'not-invented-here-syndrome'. Learning vicariously also can help prevent the repetition of mistakes and collaboration can provide opportunities for 'higher level' learning (Argyris and Schon, 1978).

Learning is exchanged not only between the partners in a particular collaborative project, but also between the broader networks of participating firms (what Freeman (1991) calls 'networks of innovators').

The management and organization literature on collaboration describes the considerable operational problems in meeting the objectives of partners. The quality of relationships between partner firms has obvious implications for the outcomes of technological linkages. Numbers of studies show how effective collaboration and learning between partners depend on high levels of trust.

A variety of reasons can be suggested for high trust facilitating effective collaboration, both horizontal and vertical (Dodgson, 2000). The first

relates to the sort of *knowledge* being transferred. It may be tacit, uncodified and firm-specific. It is, therefore, not readily transferable, requiring
dense, reliable and continuing communication paths. Furthermore, it is
often *proprietorial* and commercially valuable. What is being exchanged is
the kind of knowledge and skills which are not easily replicated or purchased by competitors and thus can provide important elements of a firm's
defining competencies and competitiveness. Collaborators are not only
expected to share trust in each other's ability to provide valid and helpful
responses to uncertainty, but also are expected not to use this information
in ways which may prove disadvantageous to partners.

A second reason relates to time scale of successful inter-firm links.
Trust facilitates continuing relationships between firms (Arrow, 1975).
Continuity is valuable because the objective of inter-firm links may change
over time, in line, for example, with changing or new market and technological opportunities. Furthermore, it is only within a long-term horizon
that reciprocity in collaboration can occur. At any one time, one partner
will be a net gainer in a collaboration. The disincentive to cut and run is
based on the view of future gains which can only be achieved through continuity of collaboration. Trust mitigates against opportunistic behaviour, as
does fear of mistrust on the part of future new partners, should a firm
behave in such a manner.

A third reason for the advantages of high trust in collaboration reflects
the high management cost of such linkages. Selecting a suitable partner and
building the dense communications paths through which tacit knowledge
can be transferred has considerable management costs, both real and
opportunity. These costs are increased when consideration of interpersonal
trust is extended to interorganizational trust. Trust between partner firms
is commonly analysed by means of relationships between individuals.
Given the problems of labour turnover and the possibilities of communications breakdowns on the part of particular managers, scientists and engineers, to survive, trust relationships between firms have to be general as well
as specific to individuals. It has to be engrained in organizational routines,
norms and values. Interorganizational trust is characterized by community
of interest, organizational cultures receptive to external inputs, and widespread and continually supplemented knowledge among employees of the
status and purpose of the links (Dodgson, 1993b). Such features are not
costless, and, having made the effort to build such strong relationships,
jeopardizing them through a lack of trust is not a sensible option.

Conclusions
There are anti-competitive and strategic dangers associated with collaboration. Technological collaboration can be anti-competitive, by excluding

certain firms, or raising entry barriers, or operating in the form of cartels which antitrust legislation prevented in the past. Such anti-competitiveness can occur in vertical as well as horizontal collaborations. Also there may be strategic dangers from firms which overly rely on externally sourced rather than internally generated technology. Without internal technological competencies there can be no 'receptors' for external technology, nor capacity for building the technological competences which provide the basis for firms' technology strategies (and which provide the basis for attracting potential partners).

Nonetheless, collaboration remains an important component of contemporary industry. Partners in collaboration can obtain mutual benefits that they could not achieve independently. It enables them to share costs and risks, increase the scale and scope of activities, enhance their ability to deal with complexity, and assist in dealing with uncertainties associated with technological and market changes. Compared to other forms of governance regime, collaboration is more flexible, and under certain circumstances is more efficient in the transfer and coalescence of information and knowledge.

Notes

1. In the USA, it was Ronald Reagan's 1984 National Cooperative Research Act, 70 years after the introduction of Woodrow Wilson's sweeping antitrust legislation, that removed the risk of prosecution for firms collaborating in R&D.
2. See, for example, *Research Policy*, **20**(5) (1991) and, for more recent examples, *Managerial and Decision Economics*, **24** (2003), and *Technology Analysis and Strategic Management* (2003).
3. A study of success and failure in innovation carried out at the Science Policy Research Unit (SPRU), University of Sussex, UK.

References

Abernathy, W. and J. Utterback. 1978. Patterns of industrial innovation. *Technology Review*, **80**: 40–47.
Argyris, C. and D. Schon. 1978. *Organizational Learning: Theory, Method and Practice*. London: Addison-Wesley.
Arrow, K. 1975. Gifts and exchanges, in E. Phelps (ed.), *Altruism, Morality and Economic Theory*. New York: Russell Sage.
Cohen, W. and D. Levinthal. 1989. Innovation and learning: the two faces of R&D. *Economic Journal*, **99**: 569–96.
Cohen, W. and D. Levinthal. 1990. Absorptive capacity: a new perspective on learning and innovation. *Administrative Science Quarterly*, **35**: 128–52.
Cooke, P. and K. Morgan. 2000. *The Associational Economy: Firms, Regions, and Innovation*. Oxford: Oxford University Press.
DiMaggio, P. and W. Powell. 1983. The iron cage revisited: institutional isomorphism and collective rationality in organizational fields. *American Sociological Review*, **48**: 147–60.
Dodgson, M. 1993a. Learning, trust and technological collaboration. *Human Relations*, **46**: 77–95.
Dodgson, M. 1993b. Organizational learning: a review of some literatures. *Organization Studies*, **14**: 375–94.

Dodgson, M. 2000. *The Management of Technological Innovation: An International and Strategic Approach*. Oxford: Oxford University Press.

Dodgson, M. and R. Rothwell. 1994. Innovation and size of firm, in M. Dodgson and R. Rothwell (eds), *The Handbook of Industrial Innovation*, Aldershot, UK and Brookfield, USA: Edward Elgar.

Dore, R. 2000. *Stock Market Capitalism: Welfare Capitalism: Japan and Germany versus the Anglo-Saxons*. Oxford: Oxford University Press.

Eisenhardt, K. and C. Schoonhoven. 1996. Resource-based view of strategic alliance formation: strategic and social effects in entrepreneurial firms. *Organization Science*, 7: 136–50.

Foster, J. and J. Metcalfe. 2001. *Frontiers of Evolutionary Economics*. Cheltenham, UK and Northampton, MA, USA: Edward Elgar.

Freeman, C. 1991. Networks of innovators: a synthesis of research issues. *Research Policy*, **20**: 499–514.

Gibbons, M., C. Limoges, H. Nowotny, S. Schwartzmann, P. Scott and M. Trow. 1994. *The New Production of Knowledge: The Dynamics of Science and Research in Contemporary Societies*. London: Sage.

Granstrand, O., P. Patel and K. Pavitt. 1997. Multi-technology corporations: why they have 'distributed' rather than 'distinctive core' competencies. *California Management Review*, **39**: 8–25.

Hagedoorn, J. 2002. Inter-firm R&D partnerships: an overview of major trends and patterns since 1960. *Research Policy*, **31**: 477–92.

Hall, P. and Soskice, D. (eds). 2001. *Varieties of Capitalism: The Institutional Foundations of Comparative Advantage*. Oxford: Oxford University Press.

Klein, B. 1977. *Dynamic Economics*. Cambridge, MA: Harvard University Press.

Lundvall, B.-Å. 1992. *National Systems of Innovation*. London: Pinter.

Meyer-Krahmer, F. and U. Schmoch. 1998. Science-based technologies: university–industry interactions in four fields. *Research Policy*, **27**: 835–51.

Mowery, D. 1988. *International Collaborative Ventures in US Manufacturing*. Cambridge, MA: Ballinger.

Richardson, G.B. 1972. The organisation of industry. *Economic Journal*, **82**: 883–96.

Rothwell, R., C. Freeman, A. Horley, V. Jervis, Z. Robertson, and J. Townsend. 1974. SAPPHO updated – project SAPPHO, phase II. *Research Policy*, **3**: 258–91.

Sakakibara, M. 1997. Heterogeneity of firm capabilities and cooperative research and development: an empirical examination of motives. *Strategic Management Journal*, **18**: 143–64.

Sakakibara, M. and M. Dodgson. 2003. Strategic research partnerships: empirical evidence from Asia. *Technology Analysis and Strategic Management*, special edition.

Sako, M. 1992. *Prices, Quality and Trust: How Japanese and British Companies Manage Buyer–Supplier Relations*. Cambridge: Cambridge University Press.

13 Strategic and organizational understanding of inter-firm partnerships and networks

Nadine Roijakkers and John Hagedoorn

Introduction

Standard market transactions of unrelated companies and, full or partial, integration by means of mergers and acquisitions were, until recently, considered by many as the only stable forms of interaction between companies. Most observers viewed inter-firm partnerships, where companies can maintain their independence but, at the same time, share some of their activities with others, as a relatively unstable and temporary aspect of company behaviour. The upsurge in inter-firm partnerships in the 1980s, however, stimulated scholars to develop a number of theories explaining inter-firm collaboration as a more lasting characteristic of companies in many industries. In the 1980s and 1990s, a large number of interesting contributions emerged on the formation, evolution, operation, and outcomes of inter-firm partnerships and interorganizational networks. The background against which most scholars have studied this variety of issues reflects a mix of theoretical perspectives, methodological approaches, and distinct foci in terms of industrial background, modes of cooperation, and international patterns (Axelsson and Easton, 1992; Badaracco, 1991; Contractor and Lorange, 1988a, 1988b, 2002; Doz and Hamel, 1998; Gomes-Casseres, 1996; Grabher, 1993; Harrigan, 1985; Jarillo, 1993; Lewis, 1990; Lorange and Roos, 1992; Nohria and Eccles, 1992; Pfeffer and Salancik, 1978; Porter, 1990).

Within the range of theoretical approaches and methodologies used, we can distinguish two broad-based, diametrically opposed, approaches to the study of inter-firm partnerships: a strategic management view and an interorganizational perspective (Gulati *et al.*, 2000; Hagedoorn and Osborn, 2002; Osborn and Hagedoorn, 1997). Whereas the strategic approach stresses such issues as independence, the use of detailed contracts, and the crucial role of opportunism in partnerships, the interorganizational approach emphasizes the more positive aspects of alliances, such as complementarity, the development of interorganizational trust, and mutual gain. While a complete review of 20 years of research in this field is beyond the scope of the current chapter, we do intend to provide a thorough

Table 13.1   Main characteristics of the two most important perspectives on inter-firm collaboration

Theoretical premises	Strategic management view	Interorganizational view
Main purpose of the firm	Competition	Cooperation
Organization of the industry	Stand-alone, go-it-alone companies	Networked, highly integrated companies
Characteristics of inter-firm partnerships	Firm-oriented	Partner- or network-oriented
	Independence	Interdependence
	Internalization of core activities such as R&D	Specialization, complementarity, and network-level coordination
	Short-term, oriented towards fulfilling immediate corporate needs	Long-term
	Opportunism, unequal power balance	Interorganizational trust
	Contracts	Informal controls
	Promotion of self-interest	Strive for mutual gain

discussion of these different approaches with reference to their particular understanding of the purpose of the firm, the organization of industries, and the specific features characterizing inter-firm partnerships (see Table 13.1).

A strategic management view

The strategic management view of inter-firm collaboration has been instrumental to the study of inter-firm partnership and networks (Contractor and Lorange, 1988a, 1988b, 2002; Gulati *et al.*, 2000; Hagedoorn and Osborn, 2002; Osborn and Hagedoorn, 1997). A basic research issue that is being dealt with from this perspective is what type of relationship companies should maintain with their suppliers, customers, competitors, or other organizations in their competitive environment. Although a number of researchers were already struggling with this complex question some decades ago (Hymer, 1960; MacMillan and Farmer, 1979; Pfeffer and Salancik, 1978; Warren, 1967), most contributions to this field began to appear more recently. In answering this question, researchers have typically chosen to view companies as autonomous entities, striving for competitive advantage either from the unique set of skills and capabilities they possess internally (e.g. Barney, 1986, 1991) or from externally located industry sources (e.g. Porter, 1980, 1985). We can label this particular perspective 'strategic' because most of these scholars share the presumption that companies are atomistic actors, competing for profits against each other in a 'hostile' market environment. The underlying assumption that it is best for companies to be primarily competitive in their relationships with others is what clearly differentiates this view from the other perspective, the inter-organizational perspective on firms and the nature of their relations (see Table 13.1).

Researchers employing a strategic view generally agree that all types of inter-firm relationships are largely competitive in nature (Badaracco, 1991; Doz and Hamel, 1998; Hamel, 1991; Hamel *et al.*, 1989; Harrigan, 1985; Perlmutter and Heenan, 1986; Porter, 1990; Porter *et al.*, 1990; Prahalad and Hamel, 1990; Reich and Mankin, 1986). Drawing on central concepts from neoclassical economics, they argue that individuals, and the companies they form, are primarily motivated by self-interest and that competition is therefore an important feature of the industrial landscape. In other words, with a strategic view, companies are assumed to be complex organizations of individuals with multiple, partially conflicting interests and/or goals where all companies need to compete to further their immediate, firm-specific needs. Whereas established companies will consistently strive to enhance their competitive advantage vis-à-vis rivals with the aim of earning superior profits, new entrants and manufacturers of substitute products will attempt to strengthen their competitive position in order ultimately to replace existing firms (Porter, 1980, 1985). In such a competitive environment, each company should try to obtain a high level of market power, enabling it to deal effectively with competitive threats as well as capitalize on some of the most relevant commercial opportunities. The most powerful companies, in this respect, are the ones that remain independent agents and interact with other companies only through arm's length market transactions (see also Table 13.1). By 'going-it-alone' these companies can avoid becoming overly dependent on specific other firms in their environment, which enhances their effective market power in relation to these companies (Hamel, 1991; Hamel *et al.*, 1989; Porter *et al.*, 1990; Reich and Mankin, 1986).

A large number of researchers within this strategic management view began to recognize the extensive use of inter-firm partnerships by predominantly large, established companies in the 1980s. To the extent that specific modes of inter-firm collaboration, such as equity-based partnerships, would compromise the independence and market power of the companies involved, these inter-firm relations were viewed as a second-best option to performing certain tasks independently (Bettis *et al.*, 1992; MacDonald, 1995; Porter, 1990; Porter *et al.*, 1990; Reich and Mankin, 1986). As Porter

(1990) has so clearly pointed out, inter-firm partnerships are hardly ever an optimal solution, because no company can rely on others for skills and capabilities that are critical to its competitive position. In this respect, most observers tended to regard a prominent form of inter-firm collaboration, i.e. R&D partnerships, with substantial suspicion, for two main reasons. First, R&D constitutes a core activity for most high-tech companies and, as such, it was not often considered a sound basis for inter-firm collaboration. Second, inter-firm R&D partnerships are often subject to the hazard of opportunism (Harrigan, 1985, 1988). Owing to the ultimately competitive nature of these relationships, partners will be tempted to serve their own interests to the detriment of others, by manipulating, bargaining, or the use of power to achieve results (see also Table 13.1). Inter-firm collaboration, it was therefore concluded, is a form of competition that is negatively related to the long-term survival prospects of companies (Bettis *et al.*, 1992; Hendry, 1995; MacDonald, 1995; Reich and Mankin, 1986; Sapienza, 1989). While a highly competitive environment stimulates companies to continuously improve themselves and innovate, inter-firm partnerships would merely lead to mediocrity and competitive weakness (Porter *et al.*, 1990).

As some contributions were thus highly cautionary in nature and focused on the numerous problems involved in managing partnerships and networks, others described the circumstances under which it would be beneficial for companies to engage in cooperation (Badaracco, 1991; Bleeke and Ernst, 1991; Dussauge *et al.*, 2000; Dyer, 1996; Dyer and Ouchi, 1993; Hamel, 1991; Hamel *et al.*, 1989; Kanter, 1994; Lewis, 1990; Nishiguchi, 1994; Ohmae, 1989; Parkhe, 1991; Prahalad and Hamel, 1990). These authors also acknowledge that inter-firm partnerships are fraught with substantial problems and risks, but, unlike some of the contributions described in the above, they view these partnerships as a potentially useful tool for improving the firm's competitive position. By selecting a specific alliance option and crafting each partnership to serve immediate corporate needs, managers can use inter-firm partnerships to further the competitive interests of their firms (see also Table 13.1). Hamel *et al.* (1989), for instance, argue that companies can substantially benefit from inter-firm partnerships with competitors to the extent that they are able to gain access to their partner's knowledge and skills. However, Hamel *et al.* (1989) do caution managers that the use of inter-firm partnerships should be based on a sound understanding of what is to be learned from specific partners. A well-developed capacity to learn and strong defences against their partner's probing of their skills and technologies remain necessary.

As many authors recognized the risk of surrendering crucial competitive knowledge, researchers began to propose that short-term partnerships be based on detailed contracts, stipulating the expected behaviour of partners and the preferred outcomes of the agreement (Kawasaki and MacMillan, 1986). In this line of research, specific modes of cooperation, such as contractual agreements, are thus characterized by their strengths and weaknesses in helping companies ward off competitive threats and to capitalize on opportunities to improve their competitive advantage in relation to other firms (Bleeke and Ernst, 1991; Doz and Hamel, 1998; Dyer, 1996; Dyer and Ouchi, 1993; Hamel, 1991; Hamel *et al.*, 1989; Kanter, 1994; Teece, 1992; Williamson, 1986).

Although the strategic management view was clearly dominating partnership research in the 1980s, researchers increasingly considered this view inadequate for explaining the partnering behaviour of a large number of companies that were embedded in dense networks of interfirm relations. This ultimately led to the development of the interorganizational perspective of interfirm collaboration, which we will discuss in the next section.

An interorganizational perspective

As pointed out in the preceding section, the basic assumption underlying most of the relevant theoretical and empirical work in strategic management is that companies are primarily motivated by self-interest and that, therefore, competition drives interaction between companies. Researchers applying an interorganizational perspective, however, do not seem to share this particular view of companies and the nature of their relations. Instead, they tend to characterize inter-firm relationships as a dynamic, constantly evolving process where companies adopt a mix of both competitive and cooperative postures in their relationships with other firms. In the interorganizational perspective, it is argued that companies are embedded in dense, tightly connected networks of interorganizational relations (see Table 13.1). In such a network, the interests and goals of the participating companies are hardly ever totally conflicting or fully aligned. In their relations towards other firms in their environment, therefore, companies must find an optimal balance between competitive and cooperative behaviour, depending on the prevailing circumstances. In some situations, companies may find it more beneficial to create long-term, trustful partnerships while under different circumstances they may view an aggressive, competitive posture as a more suitable approach. Whereas researchers employing a strategic view thus adopt a rather atomistic view of companies, where inter-firm collaboration is regarded as just another competitive tool, most scholars taking an interorganizational perspective see inter-firm partnerships and interorganizational networks as an alternative way of dealing with other companies (Axelsson and Easton, 1992; Burt, 1992; Ciborra, 1991;

Contractor and Lorange, 1988b, 2002; Galaskiewicz and Zaheer, 1999; Gomes-Casseres, 1996; Grabher, 1993; Granovetter, 1985; Gulati, 1998; Gulati *et al.*, 2000; Hagedoorn, 2002; Hakansson and Johansson, 1993; Jarillo, 1993; Johansson and Mattsson, 1987; Larson, 1992; Lorenzoni and Baden-Fuller, 1995; Miles and Snow, 1992; Powell *et al.*, 1996; Ring and van de Ven, 1992; Thorelli, 1986).

The main theoretical premise underlying the interorganizational perspective is that great benefits may accrue to those companies that intentionally embed themselves in dense networks of long-term collaborative relationships with other companies (Axelsson and Easton, 1992; Barley *et al.*, 1992; Chung *et al.*, 2000; Ciborra, 1991; Gomes-Casseres, 1996; Gulati, 1999; Lorenzoni and Baden-Fuller, 1995; Lyles, 1988, 1994; Powell and Brantley, 1992; Powell *et al.*, 1996). Specifically, in the interorganizational perspective, it is argued that companies can substantially benefit from taking part in a cooperative network to the extent that the network is able to accomplish more than any of the individual partners can achieve independently. The related notion that most companies are willing to accept a relatively high level of interdependence for mutual gain towards common goals gained prominence particularly in the technology and organizational learning views of inter-firm collaboration (Auster, 1992; Baum *et al.*, 2000; Ciborra, 1991; Contractor and Lorange, 1988b, 2002; Kale *et al.*, 2000; Hagedoorn, 1993, 2002; Osborn and Baughn, 1990; Teece, 1989; Yli-Renko *et al.*, 2001).

In these literatures, innovative output is considered one of the most prominent outcomes of inter-firm partnerships from which cooperating companies can all benefit. Indeed, researchers studying a number of positive outcomes of inter-firm collaboration, such as learning and innovation, for the most part have often argued that embeddedness in a highly integrated network of equity-based partnerships enables companies to respond effectively to radical changes in their technological environment (see also Table 13.1). To the extent that these changes require the development of a whole new set of technological skills and capabilities, inter-firm partnerships with other, specialized companies are an important part of a learning process for high-tech firms, a process in which they actively search for new opportunities in a network setting of a multitude of inter-firm partnerships (Ciborra, 1991; Hagedoorn, 2002). The companies in such knowledge networks tend to align their research strategies, or even develop their strategies jointly, in an effort to accrue network-wide benefits, such as those pertaining to common access to complementary, specialized technological knowledge, to the advantage of all network partners (Best, 1990; Chung *et al.*, 2000; Jarillo, 1993). The fact that strategic coordination takes place within networks has led several researchers to describe them as an organizational form that exists at a higher level of aggregation than individual companies where the network (also sometimes referred to as group, clique, or constellation) as a whole may compete against other networks or build up collaborative relationships where appropriate (Gomes-Casseres, 1994, 1996; Powell, 1990; Thorelli, 1986).

Another important stream of interorganizational research related to the technology and interorganizational learning views comes under the heading of interorganizational trust. In the interorganizational perspective, trust in relationships between companies is viewed as an important element in understanding the nature of inter-firm partnerships and interorganizational networks (Gulati, 1995; Hakansson and Johansson, 1993; Herrigel, 1993; Johansson and Mattsson, 1987; Kale *et al.*, 2000; Lazerson, 1993; Ring and van de Ven, 1992; Saxton, 1997; Staber, 1998; Zaheer *et al.*, 1998). In fact, at the core of the interorganizational perspective, we find an understanding of inter-firm collaboration where the interaction between companies is based on interorganizational trust and mutual adaptation (see also Table 13.1). To the extent that two or more companies have shared interests and common goals, they are likely to engage in inter-firm collaboration where they adapt to each other's demands within a number of long-term, trustful partnerships (Johansson and Mattsson, 1987). Several authors within this research tradition have argued that interorganizational trust is so basic to any partnership and any network relation that, without trust, a number of positive outcomes of inter-firm collaboration, such as innovation, will not emerge if trust does not play an important role in these collaborative relationships between companies. In this respect, interorganizational trust in a group of cooperating companies, that are more or less 'equals' in terms of their (market) power, size and the level of complementarity in their knowledge base, is an important precondition for the occurrence of interorganizational learning and innovation (Ciborra, 1991; Hagedoorn, 1993; Lyles, 1988, 1994; Mowery *et al.*, 1998; Mytelka, 1991).

References

Auster, E., 1992, The relationship of industry evolution to patterns of technological linkages, joint ventures, and direct investment between US and Japan, *Management Science*, **17**, 1–25.

Axelsson, B. and Easton, G., 1992, *Industrial Networks: a New View of Reality*, Chichester, Wiley.

Badaracco, J., 1991, *The Knowledge Link: how Firms Compete through Strategic Alliances*, Boston, Harvard Business School Press.

Barley, S., Freeman, J. and Hybels, R., 1992, Strategic alliances in commercial biotechnology, in N. Nohria and R. Eccles (eds), *Networks and Organizations: Structure, Form, and Action*, Boston, Harvard Business School Press, pp. 311–47.

Barney, J., 1986, Strategic factor markets: expectations, luck, and business strategy, *Management Science*, **32**, 1231–41.

Barney, J., 1991, Firm resources and sustained competitive advantage, *Journal of Management*, **17**, 99–120.

Baum, J., Calabrese, T. and Silverman, B., 2000, Don't go it alone: alliance network composition and startups' performance in Canadian biotechnology, *Strategic Management Journal*, **21**, 267–94.

Best, M., 1990, *The New Competition: Institutions of Industrial Restructuring*, Cambridge, Polity.

Bettis, R., Bradley, S. and Hamel, G., 1992, Outsourcing and industrial decline, *Academy of Management Executive*, February, 7–22.

Bleeke, J. and Ernst, D., 1991, The way to win in cross-border alliances, *Harvard Business Review*, November/December, 127–35.

Burt, R., 1992, *Structural Holes: the Social Structure of Competition*, Cambridge, Harvard University Press.

Chung, S., Singh, H. and Lee, K., 2000, Complementarity, status similarity, and social capital as drivers of alliance formation, *Strategic Management Journal*, **21**, 1–22.

Ciborra, C., 1991, Alliances as learning experiments: cooperation, competition, and change in high-tech industries, in L. Mytelka (ed.), *Strategic Partnerships and the World Economy*, London, Pinter Publishers, pp. 51–77.

Contractor, F. and Lorange, P., 1988a, Why should firms cooperate? The strategy and economics basis for cooperative ventures, in F. Contractor and P. Lorange (eds), *Cooperative Strategies in International Business*, Lexington, Lexington Books, pp. 3–30.

Contractor, F. and Lorange, P. (eds), 1988b, *Cooperative Strategies in International Business*, Lexington, Lexington Books.

Contractor, F. and Lorange, P. (eds), 2002, *Cooperative Strategies and Alliances*, Amsterdam, Elsevier.

Doz, Y. and Hamel, G., 1998, *Alliance Advantage: the Art of Creating Value through Partnering*, Boston, Harvard Business School Press.

Dussauge, P., Garrette, B. and Mitchell, W., 2000, Learning from competing partners: outcomes and durations of scale and link alliances in Europe, North America and Asia, *Strategic Management Journal*, **21**, 99–126.

Dyer, J., 1996, Specialized supplier networks as a source of competitive advantage: evidence from the auto industry, *Strategic Management Journal*, **17**, 271–91.

Dyer, J. and Ouchi, W., 1993, Japanese-style partnerships: giving companies a competitive edge, *Sloan Management Review*, Fall, 51–63.

Galaskiewicz, J. and Zaheer, A., 1999, Networks of competitive advantage, in S. Andrews and D. Knoke (eds), *Research in the Sociology of Organizations*, Greenwich, JAI Press, pp. 237–61.

Gomes-Casseres, B., 1994, Group versus group: how alliance networks compete, *Harvard Business Review*, July/August, 62–74.

Gomes-Casseres, B., 1996, *The Alliance Revolution: the New Shape of Business Rivalry*, Cambridge, Harvard University Press.

Grabher, G. (ed.), 1993, *The Embedded Firm*, London, Routledge.

Granovetter, M., 1985, Economic action and social structure: the problem of embeddedness, *American Journal of Sociology*, **91**, 481–501.

Gulati, R., 1995, Does familiarity breed trust? The implications of repeated ties for contractual choice in alliances, *Academy of Management Journal*, **38**, 85–112.

Gulati, R., 1998, Alliances and networks, *Strategic Management Journal*, **19**, 293–317.

Gulati, R., 1999, Network location and learning: the influence of network resources and firm capabilities on alliance formation, *Strategic Management Journal*, **20**, 397–420.

Gulati, R., Nohria, N. and Zaheer, A., 2000, Strategic networks, *Strategic Management Journal*, **21**, 203–15.

Hagedoorn, J., 1993, Understanding the rationale of strategic technology partnering: interorganizational modes of cooperation and sectoral differences, *Strategic Management Journal*, **14**, 371–85.

Hagedoorn, J., 2002, Inter-firm R&D partnerships: an overview of major trends and patterns since 1960, *Research Policy*, **31**, 477–92.

Hagedoorn, J. and Osborn, R., 2002, Inter-firm R&D partnerships: major theories and trends since 1960, in F. Contractor and P. Lorange (eds), *Cooperative Strategies and Alliances*, Amsterdam, Elsevier, pp. 517–42.

Hakansson, H. and Johansson, J., 1993, The network as a governance structure, in G. Grabher (ed.), *The Embedded Firm*, London, Routledge, pp. 35–51.

Hamel, G., 1991, Competition for competence and inter-partner learning within international strategic alliances, *Strategic Management Journal*, **12**, 83–102.

Hamel, G., Doz, Y. and Prahalad, C., 1989, Collaborate with your competitors and win, *Harvard Business Review*, January/February, 133–9.

Harrigan, K., 1985, *Strategies for Joint Ventures*, Lexington, Lexington Books.

Harrigan, K., 1988, Joint ventures and competitive strategy, *Strategic Management Journal*, **9**, 141–58.

Hendry, J., 1995, Culture, community, and networks: the hidden cost of outsourcing, *European Management Journal*, **13**, 193–200.

Herrigel, G., 1993, Power and the redefinition of industrial districts: the case of Baden-Wuerttemberg, in G. Grabher (ed.), *The Embedded Firm*, London, Routledge, pp. 227–52.

Hymer, S., 1960, The international operations of national firms: a study of foreign direct investment, Cambridge, MIT Press.

Jarillo, J., 1993, Strategic networks: creating the borderless organization, Oxford, Butterworth-Heinemann.

Johansson, J. and Mattsson, L., 1987, Inter-organizational relations in industrial systems: a network approach compared with the transaction-cost approach, *International Studies of Management and Organization*, **17**, 34–48.

Kale, P., Singh, H. and Perlmutter, H., 2000, Learning and protection of proprietary assets in strategic alliances: building relational capital, *Strategic Management Journal*, **21**, 217–37.

Kanter, R., 1994, Collaborative advantage: the art of alliances, *Harvard Business Review*, July/August, 96–108.

Kawasaki, S. and MacMillan, J., 1986, The design of contracts: evidence from Japanese sub-contracting, mimeo, University of Western Ontario.

Larson, A., 1992, Network dyads in entrepreneurial settings: a study of the governance of exchange relationships, *Administrative Science Quarterly*, **37**, 76–104.

Lazerson, M., 1993, Factory or putting out? Knitting networks in Modena, in G. Grabher (ed.), *The Embedded Firm*, London, Routledge, pp. 203–26.

Lewis, J., 1990, *Partnerships for Profit: Structuring and Managing Strategic Alliances*, New York, Free Press.

Lorange, P. and Roos, J., 1992, *Strategic Alliances: Formation, Implementation and Evolution*, Oxford, Blackwell Publishing.

Lorenzoni, G. and Baden-Fuller, C., 1995, Creating a strategic center to manage a web of partners, *California Management Review*, **37**, 146–63.

Lyles, M., 1988, Learning among JV-sophisticated firms, in F. Contractor and P. Lorange (eds), *Cooperative Strategies in International Business*, Lexington, Lexington Books, pp. 301–16.

Lyles, M., 1994, The impact of organizational learning on joint venture formations, *International Business Review*, **3**, 459–67.

MacDonald, S., 1995, Too close for comfort?: the strategic implications of getting close to the customer, *California Management Review*, **37**, 8–27.

MacMillan, K. and Farmer, D., 1979, Redefining the boundaries of the firm, *Journal of Industrial Economics*, **27**, 277–85.

Miles, R. and Snow, C., 1992, Causes of failure in network organizations, *California Management Review*, Summer, pp. 53–72.

Mowery, D., Oxley, J. and Silverman, B., 1998, Technological overlap and inter-firm cooperation: implications for the resource-based view of the firm, *Research Policy*, **27**, 507–23.

Mytelka, L. (ed.), 1991, *Strategic Partnerships and the World Economy*, London, Pinter Publishers.

Nishiguchi, T., 1994, *Strategic Industrial Sourcing: the Japanese Advantage*, New York, Oxford University Press.

Nohria, N. and Eccles, R. (eds), 1992, *Networks and Organizations: Structure, Form, and Action*, Boston, Harvard Business School Press.

Ohmae, K., 1989, The global logic of strategic alliances, *Harvard Business Review*, **67**, 143–54.
Osborn, R. and Baughn, C., 1990, Forms of inter-organizational governance for multinational alliances, *Academy of Management Journal*, **33**, 503–19.
Osborn, R. and Hagedoorn, J., 1997, The institutionalisation and evolutionary dynamics of inter-organizational alliances and networks, *Academy of Management Journal*, **40**, 216–78.
Parkhe, A., 1991, Inter-firm diversity, organizational learning, and longevity in global strategic alliances, *Journal of International Business Studies*, **22**, 579–601.
Perlmutter, H. and Heenan, D., 1986, Cooperate to compete globally, *Harvard Business Review*, **64**, 136–62.
Pfeffer, J. and Salancik, G., 1978, *The External Control of Organizations*, New York, Harper and Row.
Porter, M., 1980, *Competitive Strategy: Techniques for Analysing Industries and Competitors*, New York, Free Press.
Porter, M., 1985, *Competitive Advantage*, New York, Free Press.
Porter, M., 1990, *The Competitive Advantage of Nations*, London, Macmillan.
Porter, M., Enright, M. and Tendi, P., 1990, The competitive advantage of nations, *Harvard Business Review*, **68**, 73–93.
Powell, W., 1990, Neither market nor hierarchy: network forms of organization, *Research in Organizational Behaviour*, **12**, 295–336.
Powell, W. and Brantley, P., 1992, Competitive cooperation in biotechnology: learning through networks?, in N. Nohria and R. Eccles (eds), *Networks and Organizations: Structure, Form, and Action*, Boston, Harvard Business School Press, pp. 366–94.
Powell, W., Koput, K. and Smith-Doerr, L., 1996, Inter-organizational collaboration and the locus of innovation: networks of learning in biotechnology, *Administrative Science Quarterly*, **41**, 116–45.
Prahalad, C. and Hamel, G., 1990, The core competence of the corporation, *Harvard Business Review*, May/June, 79–91.
Reich, R. and Mankin, D., 1986, Joint ventures with Japan give away our future, *Harvard Business Review*, **64**, 78–86.
Ring, P. and van de Ven, A., 1992, Structuring cooperative relationships between organizations, *Strategic Management Journal*, **13**, 483–98.
Sapienza, A., 1989, R&D collaboration as a global competitive tactic: biotechnology and the ethical pharmaceutical industry, *R&D Management*, **19**, 285–95.
Saxton, T., 1997, The effects of partner and relationship characteristics on alliance outcomes, *Academy of Management Journal*, **40**, 443–61.
Staber, U., 1998, Inter-firm cooperation and competition in industrial districts, *Organization Studies*, **19**, 701–24.
Teece, D., 1989, Profiting from technological innovation: implications for integration, collaboration, licensing, and public policy, *Research Policy*, **15**, 285–305.
Teece, D., 1992, Competition, cooperation and innovation: organizational arrangements for regimes of rapid technological progress, *Journal of Economic Behavior and Organization*, **18**, 1–25.
Thorelli, H., 1986, Networks: between markets and hierarchies, *Strategic Management Journal*, **7**, 37–51.
Warren, R., 1967, The inter-organizational field as a focus for investigation, *Administrative Science Quarterly*, **12**, 396–419.
Williamson, O., 1986, *Economic Organization*, New York, New York University Press.
Yli-Renko, H., Autio, E. and Sapienza, A., 2001, Social capital, knowledge acquisition, and knowledge exploitation in young technology-based firms, *Strategic Management Journal*, **22**, 587–613.
Zaheer, A., McEvily, B. and Perrone, V., 1998, Does trust matter? Exploring the effects of inter-organizational and interpersonal trust on performance, *Organization Science*, **9**, 141–59.

14 The models of the managed and entrepreneurial economies

David Audretsch and Roy Thurik

Acknowledgement: the present paper benefited from a visit by Roy Thurik to Bloomington in the framework of the BRIDGE (Bloomington Rotterdam International Doctoral and Graduate) program in April 2003. Comments by Ingrid Verheul and two anonymous are gratefully acknowledged. We thank Senate Hall for allowing us to reprint the text of the article 'A model of the entrepreneurial economy' by David Audretsch and Roy Thurik, which appeared in the *International Journal of Entrepreneurship Education* in 2004. Some minor changes have been made.

1 Introduction

Robert Solow (1956) was awarded a Nobel Prize for identifying the sources of growth – the factors of capital and labor. These were factors best utilized in large-scale production. Throughout the first three-quarters of the last century, the increasing level of transaction costs (Coase, 1937) incurred in large-scale production dictated increasing firm size over time. Certainly, statistical evidence points towards an increasing presence and role of large enterprises in the economy in this period (Caves, 1982; Teece, 1993; Brock and Evans, 1989). This development towards large-scale activity was visible, not just in one country, but in most of the OECD countries. In this same period, the importance of entrepreneurship and small business seemed to be fading. Although it was recognized that the small business sector was in need of protection for both social and political reasons, there were few that made this case on the grounds of economic efficiency.

Romer (1986), Lucas (1988, 1993) and Krugman (1991) discovered that the traditional production factors of labor and capital are not sufficient in explaining growth and that knowledge instead has become the vital factor in endogenous growth models. Knowledge has typically been measured in terms of R&D, human capital and patented inventions (Audretsch and Thurik, 2000, 2001). Many scholars have predicted that the emergence of knowledge as an important determinant of growth and competitiveness in global markets would render new and small firms even more futile. Conventional wisdom would have predicted increased globalization to present an even more hostile environment to small business (Vernon, 1970).

Caves argued that the additional costs of knowledge activity that would be incurred by small businesses in a global economy 'constitute an important reason for expecting that foreign investment will be mainly an activity of large firms' (Caves, 1982, p. 53). As Chandler (1990, p. 78) concluded: 'to compete globally you have to be big'. Furthermore, Gomes-Casseres (1997, p. 33) observed that 'students of international business have traditionally believed that success in foreign markets required large size'. In a world that became dominated by exporting giant firms, global markets, global products and global players became the focus of interest. Small firms were thought to be at a disadvantage vis-à-vis larger firms because of the fixed costs of learning about foreign environments, communicating at long distances, and negotiating with national governments.

Despite these counteracting forces, entrepreneurship has emerged as the engine of economic and social development throughout the world.[1] The role of entrepreneurship has changed dramatically, fundamentally shifting between what Audretsch and Thurik (2001) introduced as the model of the managed economy and that of the entrepreneurial economy. In particular, Audretsch and Thurik (2001) argue that the model of the managed economy is the political, social and economic response to an economy dictated by the forces of large-scale production, reflecting the predominance of the production factors of capital and (unskilled) labor as the sources of competitive advantage. By contrast, the model of the entrepreneurial economy is the political, social and economic response to an economy dictated not just by the dominance of the production factor of knowledge – which Romer (1990, 1994) and Lucas (1988) identified as replacing the more traditional factors as the source of competitive advantage – but also by a very different, but complementary, factor they had overlooked: entrepreneurship capital, or the capacity to engage in and generate entrepreneurial activity. It is not straightforward that knowledge or R&D always spills over owing to its mere existence (Audretsch and Keilbach, 2004).

The purpose of this chapter is to discuss the distinction between the models of the managed and entrepreneurial economies and to explain why the model of the entrepreneurial economy may be a better frame of reference than the model of the managed economy when explaining the role of entrepreneurship in the contemporary, developed economies. This is done by contrasting the most fundamental elements of the managed economy model with those of the entrepreneurial economy model. Building upon Audretsch and Thurik (2000, 2001), Audretsch et al. (2002) and Thurik and Verheul (2003), 14 dimensions are identified as the basis for comparing models of the entrepreneurial and the managed economy. The common thread throughout these dimensions is the more important role of new and small enterprises in the entrepreneurial economy model (as compared to that of the managed economy). Understanding the distinction between the models of the entrepreneurial and managed economies is vital for entrepreneurship education explaining why the causes and consequences of entrepreneurship differ in the managed and the entrepreneurial economies (Wennekers *et al.*, 2002; Thurik *et al.*, 2002). This suggests that the conditions for, and aspects of, teaching entrepreneurship under the model of the entrepreneurial economy may not be the same as under the managed economy model. While the paradigm prevalent across the management curricula was a response to managing production in the managed economy model, the model of the entrepreneurial economy dictates new approaches.

2   The era of the managed economy

Throughout the first three-quarters of the last century large enterprise was clearly the dominant form of business organization (Schumpeter, 1934). The systematic empirical evidence, gathered from both Europe and North America, documented a sharp decrease in the role of small business in the postwar period. This was the era of mass production when economies of scale seemed to be the decisive factor in dictating efficiency. This was the world described by John Kenneth Galbraith (1956) in his theory of countervailing power, where the power of 'big business' was balanced by that of 'big labor' and 'big government'. This was the era of the man in the gray flannel suit and the organization man, when virtually every major social and economic institution acted to reinforce the stability and predictability needed for mass production (Piore and Sabel, 1984; Chandler, 1977).[2] Stability, continuity and homogeneity were the cornerstones of the managed economy (Audretsch and Thurik, 2001). Large firms dominated this economy. Large corporations in the managed economy are described in *The Economist* (22 December 2001, p. 76): 'They were hierarchical and bureaucratic organizations that were in the business of making long runs of standardized products. They introduced new and improved varieties with predictable regularity; they provided workers with life-time employment; and enjoyed fairly good relations with the giant trade unions.' In organization studies this modernism is referred to as Fordism.[3]

Small firms and entrepreneurship were viewed as a luxury, as something Western countries needed to ensure a decentralization of decision making, obtained only at the cost of efficiency. A generation of scholars, spanning a broad spectrum of academic fields and disciplines, has sought to create insight into the issues surrounding this perceived trade-off between economic efficiency on the one hand and political and economic decentralization on the other (Williamson, 1968). These scholars have produced a large number of studies focusing mainly on three questions: (i) What are the gains to size and large-scale production?, (ii) What are the economic and welfare implications of an oligopolistic market structure; i.e., is economic performance promoted or reduced in an industry with just a handful of large-scale firms?, and (iii) Given the overwhelming evidence that large-scale production and economic concentration are associated with increased efficiency, what are the public policy implications?

This literature has produced a series of stylized facts about the role of small business in the postwar economies of North America and Western Europe:

- *Small businesses were generally less efficient than their larger counter-parts.* Studies from the United States in the 1960s and 1970s revealed that small businesses produced at lower levels of efficiency than larger firms (Weiss, 1976, 1964; Pratten, 1971).
- *Small businesses were characterized by lower levels of employee compensation.* Empirical evidence from both North America and Europe found a systematic and positive relationship between employee compensation and firm size (Brown *et al.*, 1990; Brown and Medoff, 1989).
- *Small businesses were only marginally involved in innovative activity.* Based on R&D measures, small businesses accounted for only a small amount of innovative activity (Chandler, 1990; Scherer, 1991; Acs and Audretsch, 1990; Audretsch, 1995).
- *The relative importance of small businesses was declining over time in both North America and Europe* (Scherer, 1991).

3   The emergence of the entrepreneurial economy

Given the painstaking and careful documentation that large-scale production was driving out entrepreneurship, it was particularly startling and seemingly paradoxical when scholars first began to document that (what had seemed like) the inevitable demise of small business, began to reverse itself from the 1970s onwards. Loveman and Sengenberger (1991) and Acs and Audretsch (1993) carried out systematic international analyses examining the re-emergence of small business and entrepreneurship in North America and Europe. Two major findings emerged from these studies. First, the relative importance of small business varies largely across countries, and, secondly, in most European countries and North America the importance of small business increased from the mid-1970s. In the United States the average real GDP per firm increased by nearly two-thirds between 1947 and 1989 – from $150 000 to $245 000 – reflecting a trend towards larger enterprises and a decreasing importance of small firms. However, within the subsequent seven years it had fallen by about 14 per cent to $210 000, reflecting a sharp reversal of this trend and the re-emergence of small business (Brock and Evans, 1989). Similarly, small firms accounted for one-fifth of manufacturing sales in the United States in 1976, but by 1986 the sales share of small firms had risen to over one-quarter (Acs and Audretsch, 1993).

The reversal of the trend away from large enterprises towards the re-emergence of small business was not limited to North America. It was also seen in Europe. For example, in the Netherlands the business ownership rate (business owners per workforce) fell during the postwar period, until it reached the lowest point of 0.081 in 1984 (Verheul *et al.*, 2002). The downward trend was subsequently reversed, and a business ownership rate of 0.104 was reached by 1998 (ibid.). Similarly, the employment share in manufacturing of small firms in the Netherlands increased from 68.3 per cent in 1978 to 71.8 per cent in 1986. In the United Kingdom this share increased from 30.1 per cent in 1979 to 39.9 per cent in 1986; in (Western) Germany from 54.8 per cent in 1970 to 57.9 per cent by 1987; in Portugal from 68.3 per cent in 1982 to 71.8 per cent in 1986; in the North of Italy from 44.3 per cent in 1981 to 55.2 per cent in 1987, and in the South of Italy from 61.4 per cent in 1981 to 68.4 per cent in 1987 (Acs and Audretsch, 1993). A study of EIM (2002) documents how the relative importance of small firms in Europe (19 countries), measured in terms of employment shares, continued to increase between 1988 and 2001. See Figure 14.1 for the development of the entrepreneurship rates (=business ownership rates) in a selection of countries taken from van Stel (2003). Some U-shape can be observed for these countries. The upward trend of the entrepreneurship rate is leveling off in such countries as the UK and the US.[4] In the UK this may be due to policy measures favoring incumbent growth businesses rather than start-ups

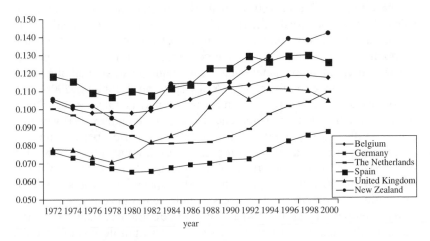

Figure 14.1   Entrepreneurship rates (business owners per workforce) in six OECD countries

(Thurik, 2003). In the US this may be due to the high level of economic development and to shake-out of industries that are in a more advanced stage than elsewhere in the area of modern OECD countries.[5]

As the empirical evidence documenting the re-emergence of entrepreneurship increased, scholars began to look for explanations and to develop a theoretical basis. Early explanations (Brock and Evans, 1989) revolved around six hypotheses regarding the increased role of small firms:

- Technological change reduces the importance of scale economies in manufacturing.[6]
- Increased globalization and the accompanying competition from a greater number of foreign rivals render markets more volatile.
- The changing composition of the labor force, towards a greater participation of women, immigrants, young and old workers, is more conducive to smaller than to larger enterprises, owing to the greater premium placed on work flexibility.
- A proliferation of consumer demand away from standardized and mass-produced goods towards tailor-made and personalized products facilitates small producers serving niche markets.
- Deregulation and privatization facilitate the entry of new and small firms into markets previously protected and inaccessible.
- The increased importance of innovation in high-wage countries reduces the relative importance of large-scale production, fostering entrepreneurial activity instead.

Audretsch and Thurik (2001) explain the re-emergence of entrepreneurship in Europe and North America on the basis of increased globalization, which has shifted the comparative advantage towards knowledge-based economic activity. They discuss the consequences for economic performance: entrepreneurship capital may be a missing link in explaining variations in economic performance (Audretsch and Keilbach, 2004). An alternative and wider view of this missing link may be that it is the institutional fabric that makes the difference between high and low performance. For example, Saxenian (1994) attributes the superior performance of Silicon Valley to a high capacity for promoting entrepreneurship. While the traditional production factors of labor and capital, as well as knowledge capital, are important in shaping output, the capacity to harness new ideas by creating new enterprises is also essential to economic output.

While entrepreneurs undertake a definitive action, i.e., they start a new business, this action can not be viewed in a vacuum devoid of context. Rather, as Audretsch et al. (2002) show, entrepreneurship is shaped by a number of forces and factors, including legal and institutional as well as social factors. The study of social capital and its impact on economic decision making and behavior dates back to classic economics and sociology literature where it is argued that social and relational structures influence market processes (Granovetter, 1985). Thorton and Flynne (2003) and Saxenian (1994) argue that entrepreneurial environments are characterized by thriving supportive networks that provide the institutional fabric linking individual entrepreneurs to organized sources of learning and resources. Studying networks located in California's Silicon Valley, Saxenian (1990, pp. 96–7) emphasizes that it is the communication between individuals that facilitates the transmission of knowledge across agents, firms, and industries, and not just a high endowment of human capital and knowledge in the region:

> It is not simply the concentration of skilled labor, suppliers and information that distinguish the region. A variety of regional institutions – including Stanford University, several trade associations and local business organizations, and a myriad of specialized consulting, market research, public relations and venture capital firms – provide technical, financial, and networking services which the region's enterprises often cannot afford individually. These networks defy sectoral barriers: individuals move easily from semiconductor to disk drive firms or from computer to network makers. They move from established firms to startups (or vice versa) and even to market research or consulting firms, and from consulting firms back into startups. And they continue to meet at trade shows, industry conferences, and the scores of seminars, talks, and social activities organized by local business organizations and trade associations. In these forums, relationships are easily formed and maintained, technical and market information is exchanged, business contacts are established, and new enterprises are conceived . . . This decentralized and fluid environment also promotes the diffusion of intangible technological capabilities and understandings.

Such contexts generating a high propensity for economic agents to start new firms can be characterized as being rich in entrepreneurship capital. Other contexts, where the start-up of new firms is inhibited, can be characterized as being weak in entrepreneurship capital.[7]

Entrepreneurship capital exerts a positive impact on competitiveness and growth in a number of ways. The *first* way is by creating knowledge spillovers. Romer (1986), Lucas (1988, 1993) and Grossman and Helpman (1991) established that knowledge spillovers are an important mechanism underlying endogenous growth. However, they shed little light on the actual mechanisms by which knowledge is transmitted across firms and individuals. Insight into the process of knowledge diffusion is important, especially since a policy implication commonly drawn from new economic growth theory is that, owing to the increasing role of knowledge and the resulting increasing returns, knowledge factors (e.g., R&D) should be publicly supported. It is important to recognize that also the mechanisms for spillovers may play a key role and, accordingly, should serve as a focus for public policy enhancing economic growth and development.[8]

The literature identifying mechanisms creating knowledge spillovers is sparse and remains underdeveloped. However, entrepreneurship is an important area where transmission mechanisms have been identified.[9] This will be explained below.

Cohen and Levinthal (1989) suggest that firms develop the capacity to adapt new technology and ideas developed in other firms and are therefore able to appropriate some of the returns accruing to investments in new knowledge made externally (i.e., outside their own organization). This view of spillovers is consistent with the traditional knowledge production function, where firms exist exogenously, and then make (knowledge) investments to generate innovative output. Audretsch (1995) proposes a shift in the unit of observation away from exogenously assumed firms towards individuals, such as scientists, engineers or other knowledge workers, i.e., agents with endowments of new economic knowledge. When the focus is shifted from the firm to the individual as the relevant unit of observation, the appropriability issue remains, but the question becomes how can economic agents with a given endowment of new knowledge best appropriate the returns from that knowledge? Albert O. Hirschman (1970) argues that, if voice proves to be ineffective within incumbent organizations, and loyalty is sufficiently weak, a knowledge worker may exit the firm or university where the knowledge is created in order to create a new company. In this spillover process the knowledge production function is reversed. Knowledge is exogenous and embodied in a worker and the firm is created endogenously through the worker's effort to appropriate the value of his knowledge by way of innovative activity. Hence, entrepreneurship serves as a mechanism by which knowledge spills over from the source to a new firm in which it is commercialized. There is a considerable history of people who only started their firms after large firms were uninterested in the innovation. This applies particularly to competence-destroying industries. Chester Carlsson started Xerox after his proposal to produce a new copy machine was rejected by Kodak. Steven Jobs started his Apple Computer after his proposal to produce a new personal computer was turned down by Xerox.

A *second* way in which entrepreneurship capital generates economic growth is through augmenting the number of enterprises and increasing competition. Jacobs (1969) and Porter (1990) argue that competition is more conducive to knowledge externalities than is local monopoly.[10] With local competition Jacobs (1969) is not referring to competition within product markets as has traditionally been envisioned within the industrial organization literature, but rather to the competition for new ideas embodied in economic agents. Not only does an increase in the number of firms enhance the competition for new ideas, but greater competition across firms also facilitates the entry of new firms specializing in a particular new product niche. This is because the necessary complementary inputs are more likely to be available from small specialist niche firms than from large, vertically integrated producers. Feldman and Audretsch (1999) as well as Glaeser *et al.* (1992) found empirical evidence supporting the hypothesis that an increase in competition in a city, as measured by the number of enterprises, is accompanied by higher growth performance of that city.[11]

A *third* way in which entrepreneurship capital generates economic output is by providing diversity among firms (Cohen and Klepper, 1992). Not only does entrepreneurship capital generate a greater number of enterprises, it also increases the variety of enterprises in a certain location. A key assumption of Hannan and Freeman (1989) in the population ecology literature is that each new organization represents a unique formula.[12] There has been a series of theoretical arguments suggesting that the degree of diversity, as opposed to homogeneity, will influence the growth potential of a location.

The theoretical basis for linking diversity to economic performance is provided by Jacobs (1969), who argues that the most important sources of knowledge spillovers are external to the industry in which the firm operates and that cities are a source of considerable innovation because here the diversity of knowledge sources is greatest (Audretsch and Feldman, 1996; Jaffe *et al.*, 1993). According to Jacobs (1969) it is the exchange of complementary knowledge across diverse firms and economic agents that yields an important return on new economic knowledge. He develops a theory emphasizing the argument that the variety of industries within a geographic environment promotes knowledge externalities and, ultimately, innovative activity and economic growth. In this environment entrepreneurship capital can contribute to growth and development by injecting diversity and serving as a conduit for knowledge spillovers, leading to increased competition. The entrepreneurial economy is characterized by a high reliance on this third role of entrepreneurship capital.[13]

4 Contrasting the entrepreneurial and managed economy models
The era of the managed economy is being supplanted by the emergence of the entrepreneurial economy. This suggests two contrasting models with a differing role of entrepreneurship. The model of the managed economy revolves around the links between stability, specialization, homogeneity, scale, certainty and predictability on the one hand and economic growth on the other. By contrast, the model of the entrepreneurial economy focuses on the links between flexibility, turbulence, diversity, novelty, innovation, linkages and clustering on the one hand and economic growth on the other. The

models of the managed and the entrepreneurial economy can be compared, distinguishing between different groups of characteristics, including underlying forces, external environment characteristics, internal or firm characteristics and policy characteristics.

4.1   Underlying forces

The first group of characteristics contrasts the forces underlying the models of the entrepreneurial and managed economy: localization versus globalization; change versus continuity; and jobs *and* high wages versus jobs *or* high wages.

In the model of the managed economy production results from the inputs of labor and capital (Solow, 1956). Geography provides a platform to combine (mobile) capital with (immobile) lower-cost labor (Kindleberger and Audretsch, 1983). In the model of the entrepreneurial economy knowledge is the dominant factor of production. The comparative advantage in the knowledge economy is dependent on innovative activity. Knowledge spillovers are an important source of this innovative activity. Hence, in the model of the entrepreneurial economy local proximity is important, with the region being the most important locus of economic activity, as knowledge tends to be developed in the context of localized production networks embedded in innovative clusters.

While the model of the managed economy focuses more on *continuity* (Chandler, 1977), the model of the entrepreneurial economy provokes and thrives on *change*. Although innovation is present under the conditions of both change and continuity, the locus of innovative activity differs. A distinction can be made between incremental and radical innovations. Innovations are considered incremental when they are compatible with the core competence and technological trajectory of the firm (Teece *et al.*, 1994). By contrast, a radical innovation can be defined as extending beyond the boundaries of the core competence and technological trajectory of the firm. In the model of the managed economy change is absorbed within a given technological paradigm, the average firm excels at incremental innovation. By contrast, in the model of the entrepreneurial economy, the capacity to break out of the technological lock-in imposed by existing paradigms is enhanced by the ability of economic agents to start new firms. Thus, incremental innovative activity along with diffusion plays a more important role in the model of the managed economy. While often requiring large investments in R&D, this type of innovative activity generates incremental changes in products along the existing technological trajectories. In the entrepreneurial economy model, the comparative advantage of the high-cost location demands innovative activity earlier in the product life cycle and which is of a more radical nature.

One of the most striking policy dilemmas in the model of the managed economy is that unemployment can be reduced only at the cost of lower wages. In the model of the entrepreneurial economy high employment can be combined with high wages and a low wage level does not imply high employment.[14] An indication of the absence of a trade-off between high wages and employment is the fact that, although corporate downsizing has been rampant throughout the OECD countries, there is a wide variance in unemployment rates. Audretsch *et al.* (2002) show that economies of OECD countries exhibiting characteristics in conformity with the entrepreneurial economy model have been more successful at creating new jobs to compensate for jobs lost in the process of corporate downsizing. Small firms in general, and new ventures in particular, are the engine of employment creation.[15] Under the model of the managed economy the job creation by small firms is associated with lower wages. However, the growth of new firms may generate not only greater employment, but also higher wages. New firm growth ensures that higher employment does not come at a cost of lower wages, but rather the opposite – higher wages. Hence, while small firms generate employment at a cost of lower wages in the model of the managed economy, in the entrepreneurial economy model small firms may create both more jobs and higher wages.[16]

4.2 External environment

The second group of characteristics contrasts the external environment characteristics of the models of the managed and the entrepreneurial economies. Turbulence, diversity and heterogeneity are central to the model of the entrepreneurial economy. By contrast, stability, specialization and homogeneity are the cornerstones in the model of the managed economy.

Stability in the model of the managed economy results from a homogeneous product demand, resulting in a low turnover rate of jobs, workers and firms. The model of the entrepreneurial economy is characterized by a high degree of turbulence. Each year many new firms are started and only a subset of these firms survives. Nelson and Winter (1982) argue that the role of diversity and selection is at the heart of generating change. This holds for both the managed and the entrepreneurial economy model. However, what differs in these models is the management and organization of the process by which diversity is created as well as the selection mechanism. In the model of the managed economy research activities are organized and scheduled in departments devoted to developing novel products and services. The management of change fits into what Nelson and Winter (1982) refer to as the firm's routines. The ability of existing businesses to manage the process of change pre-empted most opportunities for entrepreneurs to start new firms, resulting in a low start-up rate and a stable industrial structure. In the model of the entrepreneurial economy the process of generating new ideas, both within and outside R&D laboratories, creates a turbulent environment with many opportunities for entrepreneurs to start new firms based upon different and changing opinions about different and changing ideas.

A series of theoretical arguments has suggested that the degree of *diversity* versus *specialization* may account for differences in rates of growth and technological development. While specialization of industry activities is associated with lower transaction costs and, therefore, greater (static) efficiency, diversity of activities is said to facilitate the exchange of new ideas and, therefore, greater innovative activity and (dynamic) efficiency. Because knowledge spillovers are an important source of innovative activity, diversity is a prerequisite in the model of the entrepreneurial economy where lower transaction costs are preferably sacrificed for greater opportunities for knowledge spillover. In the model of the managed economy, there are fewer gains from knowledge spillovers. The higher transaction costs associated with diversity yield little room for opportunities in terms of increased innovative activity, making specialization preferable in the model of the managed economy.

Whereas the trade-off between diversity and specialization focuses on firms, that between *homogeneity* and *heterogeneity* focuses on individuals. There are two dimensions shaping the degree of homogeneity versus heterogeneity. The first dimension refers to the genetic make-up of individuals and their personal experiences (Nooteboom, 1994) and the second dimension refers to the information set to which individuals are exposed. The model of the managed economy is based on homogeneity, that of the entrepreneurial economy on heterogeneity. In a heterogeneous population communication across individuals tends to be more difficult and costly than in a homogeneous population: transaction costs are higher and efficiency is lower. At the same time, new ideas are more likely to emerge from communication in a heterogeneous than in a homogeneous world. Although the likelihood of communication is lower in a heterogeneous population, communication in this environment is more prone to produce novelty and innovation. The lower transaction costs resulting from a homogeneous population in the model of the managed economy are not associated with high opportunity costs because knowledge spillovers are relatively unimportant in generating innovative activity. However, knowledge spillovers are a driving force in the model of the entrepreneurial economy, offsetting the higher transaction costs associated with a heterogeneous population.

4.3   How firms function

The third group of characteristics contrasts firm behavior of the models of the managed and the entrepreneurial economy: control versus motivation;

firm transaction versus market exchange; competition and cooperation as substitutes versus complements; and scale versus flexibility.

Under the model of the managed economy labor is considered as indistinguishable from the other input factors, as long as management is able to extract a full day's worth of energy for a full day's pay (Wheelwright, 1985). It is considered homogeneous and easily replaceable. In the managed economy model firms organize their labor according to the principles of *command and control*. Management styles emphasize the maintenance of tasks through direct forms of employee control. Under the model of the entrepreneurial economy, the command and control approach to labor is less effective as the comparative advantage of the advanced industrialized countries tends to be based on new knowledge. *Motivating* workers to facilitate the discovery process and implementation of new ideas is more important than requiring an established set of activities from knowledge workers. Management styles emphasize the nurturing of interpersonal relationships facilitating rather than supervising employees. In the entrepreneurial economy model the focus of activities is on exploring new abilities, rather than exploiting existing ones. Hence, under the model of the entrepreneurial economy, motivating employees to participate in the creation and commercialization of new ideas is more important than simply controlling and regulating their behavior. The distinction between controlling and motivating employees can be traced back to, and corresponds with, McGregor's (1960) Theory X and Y, autocratic versus democratic decision making (Lewin and Lippitt, 1938), task-oriented versus interpersonal oriented styles (Blake and Mouton, 1964) and transactional versus transformational leadership (Bass *et al.*, 1996).[17] It has also been suggested that controlling versus motivating employees can be viewed as more masculine versus more feminine management styles (Van Engen, 2001), although a recent study by Verheul (2003) suggests that women are more control-oriented than men when managing employees.

Dating back to Coase (1937), and more recently to Williamson (1975), an analytical distinction can be made between *exchange via the market* and *intra-firm transactions*. Both Coase and Williamson emphasize that uncertainty and imperfect information increase the cost of intra-firm transactions. As Knight (1921) argued, low uncertainty, combined with transparency and predictability of information, make intra-firm transactions efficient relative to market exchange. In the managed economy model, where there is a high degree of certainty and predictability of information, transactions within firms tend to be more efficient than market exchange. By contrast, in the entrepreneurial economy model market transactions are more efficient because of the high uncertainty. Since the mid-1970s the economic arena has become increasingly uncertain and unpredictable (Carlsson, 1989; Carlsson and Taymaz, 1994), as witnessed by a decrease in both mean firm size and the extent of vertical integration and conglomeration.

While models of *competition* generally assume that firms behave autonomously, models of *cooperation* assume linkages among firms. These linkages take various forms, including joint ventures, strategic alliances, and (in)formal networks (Gomes-Casseres, 1996, 1997; Nooteboom, 1999). In the model of the managed economy competition and cooperation are viewed as substitutes. Firms are vertically integrated and primarily compete in product markets. Cooperation between firms in the product market reduces the number of competitors and reduces the degree of competition. In the model of the entrepreneurial economy firms are vertically independent and specialized in the product market. The higher degree of vertical disintegration under the model of the entrepreneurial economy implies a replacement of internal transactions within a large vertically integrated corporation with cooperation among independent firms. At the same time, there are more firms, resulting in an increase in both the competitive and the cooperative interface. The likelihood of a firm competing or cooperating with other firms is higher in the entrepreneurial economy model.

Under the model of the managed economy costs-per-unit are reduced through expanding the scale of output, or through exploiting economies of *scale*. In product lines and industries where a large scale of production translates into a substantial reduction in average costs, large firms will have an economic advantage, leading to a concentrated industrial structure. The importance of scale economies has certainly contributed to the emergence and dominance of large corporations in heavy manufacturing industries, such as steel, automobiles, and aluminum (Chandler, 1977). The alternative source of reduced average costs is *flexibility* (Teece, 1993), characterizing the entrepreneurial economy model. Industries where demand for particular products is shifting constantly, require a flexible system of production that can meet such a whimsical demand.

4.4   Government policy

The final group of contrasting dimensions of the models of the entrepreneurial economy and the managed economy refers to government policy, including the goals of policy (enabling versus constraining), the target of policy (inputs versus outputs), the locus of policy (local versus national) and financing policy (entrepreneurial versus incumbent).

Under the model of the managed economy public policy towards the firm is essentially constraining in nature. There are three general types of public policy towards business: antitrust policy (competition policy), regulation, and public ownership. All three of these policy approaches restrict the firm's freedom to contract. Under the model of the managed economy the relevant policy question is: How can the government withhold firms from abusing their market power? The entrepreneurial economy model is characterized by a different policy question: How can governments create an environment fostering the success and viability of firms? Whereas the major issues in the model of the managed economy are concerns about excess profits and abuses of market dominance, in the model of the entrepreneurial economy the issues of international competitiveness, growth and employment are important. In the managed economy model, the emphasis is constraining market power through regulation, whereas the focus in the entrepreneurial economy model is on stimulating firm development and performance through enabling policies.[18]

Another governmental policy dimension involves targeting selected *outputs* in the production process versus targeting selected *inputs*. Because of the relative certainty regarding markets and products in the model of the managed economy, the appropriate policy response is to target outcomes and outputs. Specific industries and firms can be promoted through government programs. Whereas in the model of the managed economy production is based on the traditional inputs of land, labor and capital, in the entrepreneurial economy model it is mainly based on knowledge input. There is uncertainty about what products should be produced, how and by whom. This high degree of uncertainty makes it difficult to select appropriate outcomes and increases the likelihood of targeting the wrong firms and industries. Hence, the appropriate policy in the model of the entrepreneurial economy is to target inputs, and in particular those inputs related to the creation and commercialization of knowledge.

The locus of policy is a third dimension on which the models of the managed and entrepreneurial economy can be compared. Under the model of the managed economy the appropriate locus of policy making is the national or federal level. While the targeted recipients of policy may be localized in one or a few regions, the most important policy-making institutions tend to be located at the national level. By contrast, under the model of the entrepreneurial economy, government policy towards business tends to be decentralized and regional or local in nature. This distinction in the locus of policy results from two factors. First, because the competitive source of economic activity in the model of the entrepreneurial economy is knowledge, which tends to be localized in regional clusters, public policy requires an understanding of regional–specific characteristics and idiosyncrasies. Secondly, the motivation underlying government policy in the entrepreneurial economy is growth and the creation of jobs (with high pay), to be achieved mainly through new venture creation. New firms are usually small and pose no oligopolistic threat in national or international markets. In the model of the entrepreneurial economy no external costs (in the form of higher prices) are imposed on consumers in the national economy as is the case in the model of the managed economy. The promotion of local economies imposes no cost on consumers in the national economy. Hence, local intervention is justified and does not result in any particular loss incurred by agents outside the region.

Finally, financing policies vary between the two models. Under the model of the managed economy, the systems of finance provide the existing companies with just liquidity for investment.[19] Liquidity is seen as a homogeneous input factor. The model of the entrepreneurial economy requires a system of finance that is different from that in the model of the managed economy. In the model of the managed economy there is certainty in outputs as well as inputs. There is a strong connection between banks and firms, fostering growth. In the entrepreneurial economy model certainty has given way to uncertainty requiring different (or differently structured) financial institutions. In particular, the venture and informal capital markets, providing finance for high-risk and innovative new firms (Gaston, 1989; Gompers, 1999), play an important role in the model of the entrepreneurial economy. In this model, liquidity loses its homogeneous image and is often coupled with forms of advice, knowledge and changing levels of involvement.

Storey (2003) has painstakingly documented examples of policies predicted by the entrepreneurial model such as access to loan finance and equity capital, access to markets, administrative burdens, managed workspace, university spin-offs, science parks, stimulating innovation and R&D and training in small firms. See Storey (2003, Table 3).

5   Conclusions

The model of the managed economy seems to characterize most economies throughout the first three-quarters of the previous century. It is based on relative certainty in outputs (mainly manufactured products) and inputs (mainly land, labor and capital). The twin forces of globalization have reduced the ability of the managed economies of Western Europe and North America to grow and create jobs. On the one hand, there is the advent of new competition from low-cost, but relatively highly-educated and skill-intensive, countries in Central and Eastern Europe as well as Asia. On the other hand, the telecommunications and computer revolutions have drastically reduced the cost of shifting not just capital but also information out of the high-cost locations of Europe and into lower-cost locations around the globe. Taken together, these twin forces of globalization imply that economic activity in high-cost locations is no longer compatible with routinized tasks. Rather, globalization has shifted the comparative advantage of high-cost locations to knowledge-based activities, and in particular, intellectual search activities. These activities cannot be costlessly transferred around the globe. Knowledge as an input into economic activity is inherently different from land, labor and capital. It is characterized by high uncertainty, high asymmetries across people and high transaction costs. An economy where knowledge is the main source of comparative advantage is more consistent with the model of the entrepreneurial economy.

This chapter has identified 14 dimensions that span the difference between the models of the entrepreneurial and managed economies and provide a framework for understanding how the entrepreneurial economy fundamentally differs from the managed economy. Building upon Audretsch and Thurik (2001) these contrasting models provide a lens through which economic events can be interpreted and policy measures formulated. Using the wrong lens leads to the wrong policy choice. For example, under the model of the managed economy, firm failure is viewed negatively, representing a drain on society's resources. In the model of the managed economy, resources are not invested in high-risk ventures. In the model of the entrepreneurial economy, firm failure is viewed differently, i.e., as an experiment, an attempt to go in a new direction in an inherently risky environment (Wennekers and Thurik, 1999). An externality of failure is learning. In the model of the entrepreneurial economy the process of searching for new ideas is accompanied by failure. Similarly, the virtues of long-term relationships, stability and continuity under the model of the managed economy give way to flexibility, change, and turbulence in the model of the entrepreneurial economy. What is a liability in the model of the managed economy is, in some cases, a virtue in the model of the entrepreneurial economy.

Notes

1. See Carree and Thurik (2003) for a literature survey spanning different strands.
2. See Whyte (1960) and Riesman (1950) for a description of the gray flannel suit and the organization man.
3. Early contributions of organization studies have shown that changes in the external organization affect the type of organization that is successful. For instance, Lawrence and Lorsch (1967) show that the more homogeneous and stable the environment, the more formalized and hierarchical the organization.
4. See van Stel (2003) or Verheul *et al.* (2002) for precise data and figures of the US development.
5. See also Kwoka and White (2001) who observe that, despite its importance in absolute and relative terms, the small business sector accounts for a diminishing share of US private sector activity. In van Stel (2003) it can be observed that the entrepreneurship rate in countries like Japan and France has dropped over a long period including the 1990s.
6. The influence of technological change on the shaping of business conditions has been widely discussed elsewhere in the late 1980s. See Piori and Sabel (1984) and Tushman and Anderson (1986).
7. While this may seem like a tautology, we are using the concept of entrepreneurial capital to characterize locations exhibiting a high degree of entrepreneurial capital.
8. For instance, see Scarpetta *et al.* (2002) where a firm-level database for ten OECD countries is used to present empirical evidence on the role that policy measures and institutions

in product and labor markets play for firm dynamics and productivity. Moreover, different features of entrant and exiting firms across countries are observed.
9.   As Audretsch and Feldman (1996) point out, knowledge spillovers occur in the context of networks and clusters.
10. An anonymous referee pointed out that saying that competition is more conducive to knowledge externalities than a local monopoly is not the same as that new firms create more knowledge externalities.
11. See also Acs (2002) who hints at the dual causality between the growth of cities and that of the number of firms.
12. As opposed to the organizational ecology approach of Hannan and Freeman, institutional theorists in organization studies also point to strong pressures on new firms to conform (DiMaggio and Powell, 1983).
13. A different view on the role of knowledge and its spillovers is offered in the 'systems of innovations' approach (Nelson, 1993).
14. An anonymous referee pointed out that, clearly, the trade-off between involuntary unemployment and wages requires a *ceteris paribus* condition: if the productivity of workers increases then both employment and wages can increase.
15. Carree and Thurik (1999) show that a higher share of small business in European manufacturing industries leads to higher growth of value added in the subsequent years.
16. See Acs *et al.* (2002) and Scarpetta *et al.* (2002) for illustrating data material.
17. An anonymous referee refers to Ackroyd and Thompson (1999) for some entertaining examples on the subject within UK firms.
18. As an anonymous referee pointed out: enabling one section in society may entail constraining other sections. For instance, a major policy issue for small businesses in the UK is how government can withhold banks from abusing power in the market from small business banking, thereby fostering an environment in which small businesses can succeed.
19. See Hughes and Storey (1994), Storey (1994), Reid (1996) and the special issue of *Small Business Economics* devoted to European SME Financing (Cressy and Olofsson, 1997).

References

Ackroyd, S. and P. Thompson, 1999, *Organizational Misbehaviour*, London: Sage Publications.
Acs, Z.J., 2002, *Innovation and the Growth of Cities*, Cheltenham, UK and Northampton, MA, USA: Edward Elgar.
Acs, Z.J. and D.B. Audretsch, 1990, *Innovation and Small Firms*, Cambridge, MA: MIT Press.
Acs, Z.J. and D.B. Audretsch, 1993, Conclusion, in Z.J. Acs and D.B. Audretsch (eds), *Small Firms and Entrepreneurship; an East–West Perspective*, Cambridge, UK: Cambridge University Press.
Acs, Z.J., F.R. Fitzroy and I. Smith, 2002, High-technology employment and R&D in cities: heterogeneity vs specialization, *Annals of Regional Science*, **36** (3), 373–86.
Audretsch, D.B., 1995, *Innovation and Industry Evolution*, Cambridge, MA: MIT Press.
Audretsch, D.B. and M.P. Feldman, 1996, R&D spillovers and the geography of innovation and production, *American Economic Review*, **86** (3), 630–40.
Audretsch, D.B. and M. Keilbach, 2003, Entrepreneurship capital and economic performance, *Regional Studies*, **38** (8), 949–59.
Audretsch, D.B. and A.R. Thurik, 2000, Capitalism and democracy in the 21st century: from the managed to the entrepreneurial economy, *Journal of Evolutionary Economics*, **10**, 17–34.
Audretsch, D.B. and A.R. Thurik, 2001, What is new about the new economy: sources of growth in the managed and entrepreneurial economies, *Industrial and Corporate Change*, **19**, 795–821.
Audretsch, D.B., M.A. Carree, A.J. van Stel and A.R. Thurik, 2002, Impeded industrial restructuring: the growth penalty, *Kyklos*, **55** (1), 81–97.
Audretsch, D.B., A.R. Thurik, I. Verheul and A.R.M. Wennekers (eds), 2002, *Entrepreneurship: Determinants and Policy in a European–US Comparison*, Boston/Dordrecht: Kluwer Academic Publishers.

Bass, B.M., B.J. Avolio and L.E. Atwater, 1996, The transformational and transactional leadership style of men and women, *Applied Psychology*, **45**, 5–34.

Blake, R.R. and J.S. Mouton, 1964, *The Managerial Grid*, Houston: Gulf Publishing Company.

Brock, W.A. and D.S. Evans, 1989, Small business economics, *Small Business Economics*, **1** (1), 7–20.

Brown, C. and J. Medoff, 1989, The employer size-wage effect, *Journal of Political Economy*, **97** (5), 1027–59.

Brown, C., J. Hamilton and J. Medoff, 1990, *Employers Large and Small*, Cambridge, MA: Harvard University Press.

Carlsson, B., 1989, The evolution of manufacturing technology and its impact on industrial structure: an international study, *Small Business Economics*, **1** (1), 21–38.

Carlsson, B. and E. Taymaz, 1994, Flexible technology and industrial structure in the U.S., *Small Business Economics*, **6** (3), 193–209.

Carree, M.A. and A.R. Thurik, 1999, Industrial structure and economic growth, in D.B. Audretsch and A.R. Thurik (eds), *Innovation, Industry Evolution and Employment*, Cambridge, UK: Cambridge University Press, 86–110.

Carree, M.A. and A.R. Thurik, 2003, The impact of entrepreneurship on economic growth, in Z.J. Acs and D.B. Audretsch (eds), *Handbook of Entrepreneurship Research*, Boston/Dordrecht: Kluwer Academic Publishers, 437–72.

Caves, R., 1982, *Multinational Enterprise and Economic Analysis*, Cambridge: Cambridge University Press.

Chandler, A.D., 1977, *The Visible Hand: The Managerial Revolution in American Business*, Cambridge, MA: Harvard University Press.

Chandler, A.D., 1990, *Scale and Scope: The Dynamics of Industrial Capitalism*, Cambridge, MA: Harvard University Press.

Coase, R.H., 1937, The nature of the firm, *Economica*, **4** (4), 386–405.

Cohen, W.M. and S. Klepper, 1992, The trade-off between firm size and diversity in the pursuit of technological progress, *Small Business Economics*, **4** (1), 1–14.

Cohen, W.M. and D. Levinthal, 1989, Innovation and learning: the two faces of R&D, *Economic Journal*, **99** (3), 569–96.

Cressy, R.C. and C. Olofsson, 1997, European SME financing: an overview, *Small Business Economics*, **9** (2), 87–96.

DiMaggio, P.J. and W. Powell, 1983, The iron cage revisited: institutional isomorphism and collective rationality in organizational fields, *American Sociological Review*, **48**, 147–60.

EIM, 2002, *SMEs in Europe*, Report submitted to the Enterprise Directorate General by KPMG Special Services, Zoetermeer: EIM Business & Policy Research.

Feldman, M.P. and D.B. Audretsch, 1999, Innovation in cities: science-based diversity, specialization and localized monopoly, *European Economic Review*, **43**, 409–29.

Galbraith, J.K., 1956, *American Capitalism: The Concept of Countervailing Power*, Boston: Houghton Mifflin Co.

Gaston, R.J., 1989, The scale of informal capital markets, *Small Business Economics*, **1** (3), 223–30.

Glaeser, E., H. Kallal, J. Sheinkman and A. Schleifer, 1992, Growth in cities, *Journal of Political Economy*, **100**, 1126–52.

Gomes-Casseres, B., 1996, *The Alliance Revolution: The New Shape of Business Rivalry*, Cambridge, MA: Harvard University Press.

Gomes-Casseres, B., 1997, Alliance strategies of small firms, *Small Business Economics*, **9** (1), 33–44.

Gompers, P., 1999, *The Venture Capital Cycle*, Cambridge, MA: MIT Press.

Granovetter, M.S., 1985, Economic action and social structure: the problem of embeddedness, *American Journal of Sociology*, **91** (3), 481–510.

Grossman, G.M. and E. Helpman, 1991, *Innovation and Growth in the Global Economy*, Cambridge, MA: MIT Press.

Hannan, M.T. and J. Freeman, 1989, *Organizational Ecology*, Cambridge, MA: Harvard University Press.

Hirschman, A.O., 1970, *Exit, Voice, and Loyalty*, Cambridge, MA: Harvard University Press.
Hughes, A. and D.J. Storey, 1994, *Finance and the Small Firm*, London: Routledge.
Jacobs, J., 1969, *The Economy of Cities*, New York: Vintage Books.
Jaffe, A., M. Trajtenberg and R. Henderson, 1993, Geographic localization of knowledge spillovers as evidenced by patent citations, *Quarterly Journal of Economics*, **63**, 577–98.
Kindleberger, C.P. and D.B. Audretsch (eds), 1983, *The Multinational Corporation*, Cambridge, MA: MIT Press.
Knight, F.H., 1921, *Risk, Uncertainty and Profit*, New York: Houghton-Mifflin.
Krugman, P., 1991, *Geography and Trade*, Cambridge, MA: MIT Press.
Kwoka, J.E. and L.J. White, 2001, The new industrial organization and small business, *Small Business Economics*, **16** (1), 21–30.
Lawrence, P. and J. Lorsch, 1967, *Organization and Environment*, Cambridge, MA: Harvard University Press.
Lewin, A. and R. Lippitt, 1938, An experimental approach to the study of autocracy and democracy: a preliminary note, *Sociometry*, **1**, 292–300.
Loveman, G. and W. Sengenberger, 1991, The re-emergence of small-scale production; an international comparison, *Small Business Economics*, **3** (1), 1–37.
Lucas, R.E., 1988, On the mechanics of economic development, *Journal of Monetary Economics*, **22**, 3–39.
Lucas, R.E. Jr, 1993, Making a miracle, *Econometrica*, **61** (2), 251–72.
McGregor, D., 1960, *The Human Side of Enterprise*, New York: McGraw-Hill.
Nelson, R.R. (ed.), 1993, *National Innovation Systems: A Comparative Analysis*, Oxford, UK: Oxford University Press.
Nelson, R.R. and S.G. Winter, 1982, *An Evolutionary Theory of Economic Change*, Cambridge, MA: Harvard University Press.
Nooteboom, B., 1994, Innovation and diffusion in small firms, *Small Business Economics*, **6**, 327–47.
Nooteboom, B., 1999, *Inter-Firm Alliances; Analysis and Design*, London: Routledge.
Piore, M.J. and C.F. Sabel, 1984, *The Second Industrial Divide: Possibilities for Prosperity*, New York: Basic Books.
Porter, M., 1990, *The Comparative Advantage of Nations*, New York: Free Press.
Pratten, C.F., 1971, *Economies of Scale in Manufacturing Industry*, Cambridge: Cambridge University Press.
Reid, G.C., 1996, Financial structure and the growing small firm: theoretical underpinning and current evidence, *Small Business Economics*, **8** (1), 1–7.
Riesman, D., 1950, *The Lonely Crowd: A Study of the Changing American Character*, New Haven: Yale University Press.
Romer, P.M., 1986, Increasing returns and long-run growth, *Journal of Political Economy*, **94** (5), 1002–37.
Romer, P.M., 1990, Endogenous technological change, *Journal of Political Economy*, **98**, 71–101.
Romer, P.M., 1994, The origins of endogenous growth, *Journal of Economic Perspectives*, **8** (1), 3–22.
Saxenian, A., 1990, Regional networks and the resurgence of Silicon Valley, *California Management Review*, **33**, 89–111.
Saxenian, A., 1994, *Regional Advantage*, Cambridge, MA: Harvard University Press.
Scarpetta, S., Ph. Hemmings, T. Tressel and J. Woo, 2002, The role of policy and institutions for productivity and firm dynamics: evidence from micro and industry data, OECD Economics Department working paper 329, Paris: OECD.
Scherer, F.M., 1991, Changing perspectives on the firm size problem, in Z.J. Acs and D.B. Audretsch (eds), *Innovation and Technological Change: An International Comparison*, Ann Arbor: University of Michigan Press, 24–38.
Schumpeter, J.A., 1934, *The Theory of Economic Development*, Cambridge, MA: Harvard University Press.
Solow, R., 1956, A contribution to the theory of economic growth, *Quarterly Journal of Economics*, **70**, 65–94.

Storey, D.J., 1994, *Understanding the Small Business Sector*, London: Routledge.

Storey, D.J., 2003, Entrepreneurship, small and medium-sized enterprise and public policies, in Z.J. Acs and D.B. Audretsch (eds), *Handbook of Entrepreneurship Research*, Boston/Dordrecht: Kluwer Academic Publishers, 473–511.

Teece, D.J., 1993, The dynamics of industrial capitalism: perspectives on Alfred Chandler's 'Scale and Scope', *Journal of Economic Literature*, **31**, 199–225.

Teece, D.J., R. Rumelt, G. Dosi and S. Winter, 1994, Understanding corporate coherence: theory and evidence, *Journal of Economic Behavior and Organization*, **23** (1), 1–30.

Thorton, P.H. and K.H. Flynne, 2003, Entrepreneurship, networks and geographies, in Z.J. Acs and D.B. Audretsch (eds), *Handbook of Entrepreneurship Research*, Boston/Dordrecht: Kluwer Academic Publishers, 401–36.

Thurik, A.R., 2003, Entrepreneurship and unemployment in the UK, *Scottish Journal of Political Economy*, **50** (3), 264–90.

Thurik, A.R. and I. Verheul, 2003, The relationship between entrepreneurship and unemployment: the case of Spain, in E. Genesca, D. Urbano, J.L. Capelleras, C. Guallarte and J. Verges (eds), *Creacion de Empresas. Entrepreneurship*, Barcelona: Servei de Publicacions de la UAB, 521–47.

Thurik, A.R., A.R.M. Wennekers and L.M. Uhlaner, 2002, Entrepreneurship and economic growth: a macro perspective, *International Journal of Entrepreneurship Education*, **1** (2), 157–79.

Tushman, M.L. and Ph. Anderson, 1986, Technological discontinuities and organizational environments, *Administrative Science Quarterly*, **31** (3), 439–65.

Van Engen, M., 2001, Gender and Leadership: a contextual perspective, unpublished doctoral dissertation, Tilburg University, the Netherlands.

Van Stel, A.J., 2003, COMPENDIA 2000.2: a harmonized data set of business ownership rates in 23 OECD countries, EIM Research Report H200302, Zoetermeer: EIM Business and Policy Research.

Verheul, I., 2003, Commitment or control? Human resource management in female- and male-led businesses, Strategic Study B200206, Zoetermeer: EIM Business and Policy Research.

Verheul, I., A.R.M. Wennekers, D.B. Audretsch and A.R. Thurik, 2002, An eclectic theory of entrepreneurship: policies, institutions and culture, in D.B. Audretsch, A.R. Thurik, I. Verheul and A.R.M. Wennekers (eds), *Entrepreneurship: Determinants and Policy in a European–US Comparison*, Boston/Dordrecht: Kluwer Academic Publishers, 11–82.

Vernon, R., 1970, Organization as a scale factor in the growth of firms, in J.W. Markham and G.F. Papanek (eds), *Industrial Organization and Economic Development*, Boston: Houghton-Mifflin, 47–66.

Weiss, Leonard W., 1964, The survival technique and the extent of sub-optimal capacity, *Journal of Political Economy*, **72** (3), 246–61.

Weiss, Leonard W., 1976, Optimal plant scale and the extent of suboptimal capacity, in R.T. Masson and P.D. Qualls (eds), *Essays on Industrial Organization in Honor of Joe S. Bain*, Cambridge, MA: Ballinger.

Wennekers, A.R.M. and A.R. Thurik, 1999, Linking entrepreneurship and economic growth, *Small Business Economics*, **13** (1), 27–55.

Wennekers, A.R.M., L.M. Uhlaner and A.R. Thurik, 2002, Entrepreneurship and its conditions: a macro perspective, *International Journal of Entrepreneurship Education*, **1** (1), 25–64.

Wheelwright, S.C., 1985, Restoring competitiveness in U.S. manufacturing, *California Management Review*, **27**, 113–21.

Whyte, W.H., 1960, *The Organization Man*, Harmondsworth, Middlesex: Penguin.

Williamson, O.E., 1968, Economies as an antitrust defense: the welfare trade-offs, *American Economic Review*, **58** (1), 18–36.

Williamson, O.E., 1975, *Markets and Hierarchies: Analysis and Antitrust Implications*, New York: The Free Press.

2.1.2
Knowledge and competencies

15 Tacit and codified knowledge
Dominique Foray

For a long time economic analysis equated knowledge to information. Based on this amalgam, economic analysis adopts a particular approach to knowledge and information; i.e. the universe can be described by a finite (but very large) set of states to which probabilities can be assigned (Laffont, 1989). Knowledge improves when the probability of a particular state is estimated more accurately. Knowledge can therefore be expressed by a vector of probabilities relating to a predetermined set of states. Of course there is a huge practical advantage in adopting this type of approach, but it still does not enable us to grasp phenomena as important as learning and cognition.

In the new neo-Schumpeterian conception (Nelson & Winter, 1982; Loasby, 1989; Dosi, 1996; Steinmueller, 2000; Cowan *et al.*, 2000), knowledge has something more than information: knowledge – in whatever field – empowers its possessors with the capacity for intellectual or physical action. What we mean by knowledge is fundamentally a matter of cognitive capability. Information, on the other hand, takes the shape of structured and formatted data that remain passive and inert until used by those with the knowledge needed to interpret and process them. The full meaning of this distinction becomes clear when one looks into the conditions governing the reproduction of knowledge and information. While the cost of replicating information amounts to no more than the price of making copies (i.e. next to nothing, thanks to modern technology), reproducing knowledge is a far more expensive process because cognitive capabilities are not easy to articulate explicitly or to transfer to others. Knowledge reproduction has therefore long hinged on the 'master–apprentice' system (where a young person's capacity is moulded by watching, listening and imitating) or on interpersonal transactions among members of the same profession or community of practice. These means of reproducing knowledge may remain at the heart of many professions and traditions, but they can easily fail to operate when social ties unravel, when contact is broken between older and younger generations and when professional communities lose their capacity to act in stabilizing, preserving and transmitting knowledge. In such cases, reproduction grinds to a halt and the knowledge in question is in imminent danger of being lost and forgotten.

Therefore the reproduction of knowledge and the reproduction of information are clearly different phenomena. While one takes place through learning the other takes place simply through duplication. Mobilization of a cognitive resource is always necessary for the reproduction of knowledge, while information can be reproduced by a photocopy machine.

As observed by Steinmueller (2002), by failing to differentiate between knowledge and information, economics, a discipline that often has an imperialistic attitude towards the other social sciences, has, quite surprisingly, left a vast field open to other disciplines. This field consists of the subjects 'learning' and 'cognition', two central themes in our conception of knowledge.

A further complication is the fact that knowledge can be codified: so articulated and clarified that it can be expressed in a particular language and recorded on a particular medium. Codification hinges on a range of increasingly complex actions such as using a natural language to write a cooking recipe, applying industrial design techniques to draft a scale drawing of a piece of machinery, creating an expert system from the formalized rules of inference underlying the sequence of stages geared to problem solving, and so on. As such, knowledge is detached from the individual, and the memory and communication capacity created is made independent of human beings (as long as the medium upon which the knowledge is stored is safeguarded and the language in which it is expressed is remembered). Learning programmes are then produced that partially replace the person who holds and teaches knowledge.

When knowledge is differentiated from information, economic problems relating to the two can be distinguished. Where knowledge is concerned, the main economic problem is its reproduction (problem of learning), while the reproduction of information poses no real problem (the marginal cost of reproduction is close to 0). The economic problem of information is essentially its protection and disclosure, i.e. a problem of public goods. However, the codification of knowledge creates an ambiguous good. This good has certain properties of information (public good) but its reproduction as knowledge requires the mobilization of cognitive resources.

1   The reproduction of tacit knowledge

1.1   *Tacit knowledge*
An essential aspect of knowledge which makes its reproduction difficult is pointed out by Polanyi (1966) who introduced us to the concept of tacit knowledge. Tacit knowledge cannot be expressed outside the action of the person who has it. In general, we are not even aware of the fact that we have such knowledge, or else we simply disregard it: 'We can know more than we can tell' (Polanyi, 1966, p. 4). We can use the example of the rugby player who tries to describe all the gestures and know-how required to score a goal. At the end of a long description, the player concludes: 'If you tried

to write down exactly, with absolute certainty, everything you do when you kick a ball between two posts, it would be impossible, you'd still be here in a thousand years. But you just need to have done it once and your body and mind have the exact formula, ready to be repeated' (interview with J.Webb, British journalist, quoted in Mangolte, 1997; our translation). It is only when the player is prompted to describe in detail what he does that he becomes aware of all the gestures he made and the intentions he had 'without thinking'.

For this very reason, tacit knowledge is a good that is difficult to make explicit for transfer and reproduction (von Hippel, 1994, 1998).

1.2   Three modes of reproduction

The reproduction of knowledge primarily involves the composition, delivery and use of a script, that is, a 'set of rules similar to those given to an actor who is asked to improvise on a particular theme' (Weizenbaum, 1976). Three main forms of elaboration and transmission of scripts can be distinguished (Figure 15.1).

Form (a) consists in demonstration which takes place primarily in the context of relations between master and apprentice or teacher and learner.

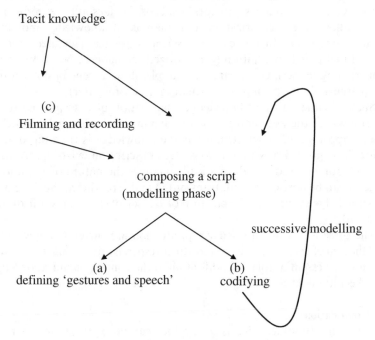

Figure 15.1   Three forms of reproduction of tacit knowledge

The teacher lays down a set of rules which he or she transmits to the learner through gestures and speech (Perriault, 1993).

Form (b) is that of codification, in which the script is detached from the person in possession of the knowledge, with a view to inscribing it in a medium. This form may require successive modelling phases and the mobilization of languages other than natural language. In form (b) the script may be imperfect (e.g. the operating manual for a machine) but it has the virtues of a public good (it is a non-rival good which can be copied and distributed at a very low cost).

Both forms (a) and (b) imply the elaboration and presentation of the script, a phase in the modelling of tacit knowledge (Hatchuel & Weil, 1995). It is a difficult and costly process. Take, for example, a tennis teacher who wants to transmit his knowledge. Whether he wants to write a book or provide teaching on the court, he has to create a model consisting of breaking down the gesture into micro-movements.

Codification (form (b)) would probably require additional modelling phases, although not necessarily. For instance, codification of a cooking recipe would involve knowledge modelling very similar to that required for its demonstration.

Form (c) consists of an audiovisual recording of the action. The recording of voices and images provides a means for facsimile reproduction, which allows the memorization and analysis of knowledge mobilized during that action. In this case, the script is not really created, but the subject matter is there, faithfully memorized, available to be worked on in constructing the script (one can, for example, show a scene in slow motion or enlarge a photo to study a particular mechanism better).

Such a sequence (tacit knowledge, elaboration of a script, reproduction) involves the key moment of the dynamics of knowledge which is the composition of a script. Even if the knowledge is then reproduced through demonstration and if no written description exists, a script has been elaborated and this dramatically changes the nature of the knowledge. It can be now expressed, transmitted and reproduced. Socialization of knowledge starts with the creation of the script (in whatever form this is taken).

The three forms of knowledge reproduction are currently all available, and the aim of this chapter is to study their respective developments in order to show the essential role of codification in the context of our knowledge-based economies.

2   Codification

Scripts can be codified; that is to say, they can be expressed in a particular language and recorded on a particular medium. Consequently, it is detached from the individual, and the memory and communication capacity created is made independent of human beings.

Although it involves high fixed costs, codification also enables agents to perform a number of operations at a very low marginal cost (Cowan & Foray, 1997). It reduces the costs and improves the reliability of storage and memorization. As long as the medium remains legible and the code has not been forgotten, codified scripts can, theoretically, be stored and retrieved indefinitely. Other aspects of transmission – such as transport, transferral, reproduction and even access and search – are functions whose costs always decrease with codification. Because codified script is easy to reproduce, the number of copies can be multiplied. This makes it easier to retrieve and transport (Simon, 1982).

A second aspect of codification relates to the fact that codified script is similar to a commodity. It can be described and defined more specifically in terms of intellectual property. When knowledge is codified it becomes transferable, independently of the transfer of other resources such as people in whom tacit knowledge is embedded. This improves the efficiency of knowledge market transactions (Arora *et al.*, 2001).

A lesser effect concerns the impact of codification on spatial organization and the division of labour. The ability to codify script enables firms to externalize knowledge production and to acquire larger quantities of knowledge at a given cost. It is no longer necessary to develop knowledge internally, for it can be bought. This effect is at the root of the growing trend towards outsourcing in many industries. Not only is the production of elements and components externalized; even their design can be bought.

2.1   Systems of codification

As in any situation of demonstration of tacit knowledge (form a), its codification (form b) involves the composition of a script, expressed in natural language. But the process of inscription in a medium external to the individual requires the mobilization of tools and additional structures.

Codification results in the formulation of a message imprinted on a base or medium. This process involves the mobilization of imprinting tools and techniques. From the invention of writing to its mechanization and from copyists to the electronic printer, progress in printing technologies has been enormous. Codification can also require additional modelling phases (apart from the initial composition of the script) and the mobilization of artificial languages, especially when the knowledge concerned is complex.

Basically, knowledge codification has two functions. The first is the function of storage and 'transfer' that permits signalling over time and space and provides humans with marking, mnemonic and recording capabilities

(Foray & Hargreaves, 2003). When codifying became common, as Goody (1977: 37) writes, 'no longer did the problem of memory storage dominate man's intellectual life'. This function is examined in subsection 2.2.

Traditional forms of codified knowledge had unique properties related to their use of symbolic representation. The ability to manipulate symbolic representations to reorder, juxtapose, visualize, and manipulate provides a basis for transforming the knowledge they represent. This is the second function of literacy and knowledge codification, discussed in subsection 2.3; it is the basis for their second order effects. As we shall see, the second order effects may dominate the first order effects, partly because of the forces favouring new types of codification activities.

2.2   The 'visible' function: creating memory, communication and learning programmes

The codification of a certain kind of knowledge (know-how) generates new opportunities for knowledge reproduction. For example, a written recipe is a 'learning programme' enabling people who are not in direct contact with those who possess the knowledge, to reproduce it at a 'lower' cost. Goody (1977: 143) writes: 'The written recipe serves in part to fill the gap created by the absence of Granny, Nanna or Mémé (who has been left behind in the village, or in the town before last).'

'In part' is the important term here. Naturally, codification mutilates knowledge. Getting the written recipe does not totally eliminate the learning costs. What is expressed and recorded is not complete knowledge; it is a learning programme that helps to reproduce knowledge. When a young technician receives a user's manual, he or she is not directly given knowledge on 'how to run the machine'. That said, the manual is helpful and will serve to reduce the costs of knowledge reproduction.

In many cases, when technicians have 'learned to learn' and are dealing with a more or less standard machine, knowledge reproduction becomes almost instantaneous and assumes characteristics close to those of information reproduction. In more complex cases, however, the codified knowledge, while certainly useful, will provide only partial assistance. Knowledge reproduction will then occur through training, practice and simulation techniques (aircraft pilots, surgeons).

The other aspect of the first function of codification concerns the locus of power in social institutions. Once again, Goody (ibid.) offers acute observations. Codification depersonalizes knowledge. The written recipe acquires independence from those who teach it. It becomes more general and universal. It reduces the relation of subordination between master and apprentice: the latter can learn when he or she has decided to do so and does not need to wait until the master is willing to teach.

The important aspect of this initial function is economic. Once a recipe has been written, it can be disseminated at a very low cost or even virtually free of cost, owing to new information technologies. This means that, although the production cost of the first copy (basically, the codification cost) may be very high, the cost of all subsequent copies will rapidly decrease so that the codified knowledge can be reproduced and disseminated ad infinitum. It is clearly the codification of knowledge that changes the conditions of its circulation and that constitutes the condition on which advances in information technology can serve to improve that circulation until it is almost perfect.

It must be noted that in our contemporary context, the recording of voices and images provides a means of 'facsimile' reproduction (referred to as form (c) in Figure 15.1). As such, facsimile recording involves no 'higher level' codification of the structure or meaning of the recording. The important new ICT-based features that permit 'illustration' of these recordings, their deeper, second order inscription, suggest new possibilities for the transmission of and distant access to all kinds of knowledge, far beyond the traditional forms of codified knowledge and written instructions.

There is, thus, a sort of convergence (of course, far ahead of us) between various kinds of knowledge in terms of marginal cost of storage and transfer. In this sense, the traditional forms of codified knowledge are losing their singularity as a category of knowledge that is more appropriate than others for achieving the operations of storage and transfer at low marginal costs.

2.3 The invisible function

This is why it is important to consider the second function, the ability to manipulate symbolic representations by their reordering, juxtaposition, visualization and manipulation. This is what makes codification unique compared to simple facsimile representation. Because the second function allows consideration of the cognitive processes and capacities of the audience, it provides reproduction methods which are far more powerful than those that facsimile recordings can achieve.

In particular, codification makes it possible to arrange and examine knowledge in different ways. Even in traditional forms of codification, a vast array of symbolic representations is encompassed by this second function of codification. The creation of lists, tables, formulae, blueprints and virtual models are cases of progressively more complex symbolic codification. A 'simple' list could not be created without some kind of codification. Likewise, tables open the path towards taxonomic and hierarchical structures (Slaughter, 1985). While such structures can be created by oral means, they do not work well as tools for the extension and re-ordering of knowledge. Tables and formulae, which are the basis for mathematical constructions, become meaningful when they can be visualized and manipulated in a space. These capabilities are inherent in codification and essentially absent in facsimile recording.

Codification provides a spatial device to screen and classify information, opening new opportunities for the modelling or representation of knowledge, a condition for rapid knowledge production and accumulation.

2.4   Codification has two facets

Codification has always had two facets: it is a state in which knowledge (the script) is presented, and it is a tool for constructing new knowledge. The trend described above shows that the second aspect (codification as a creative tool) tends to play an increasingly decisive role.

2.5   Direct and indirect costs of codification and the endogenous nature of economic choices

We have considered the effects of codification at length, regarding learning, memory and communication capacities as well as cognitive dynamics.

Codification costs depend on the adaptation of existing languages and models to the type of knowledge to be codified. When this infrastructure exists, direct costs of codification are reduced to those of printing (writing and other). They diminish very fast with the evolution of information technologies. When no infrastructure exists, the fixed costs are immense and will often be borne by several generations (Konrad & Thum, 1993).

There are also indirect costs of codification. At least three kinds of issue concern such indirect costs. The first involves the fragility of digital memory. We will address this issue in the final section, as one of the most interesting problems raised by the knowledge economy.

The second issue pertains to the problem of organizing information in storage units, which can generate substantial costs (see Steinmueller, 2000, for an analysis and overview of this problem). If the net benefits of codification increase, we are likely to find ourselves faced with more of it, or at least want to have useful access to more of it. This demands as yet unknown organizational abilities or technologies. How to enter knowledge or information into our non-mental memories (both data-entry and data-storage technology) becomes more important in our codification activities and in their economics.

The third issue concerns the organizational rigidity that codification can generate while increasing communication and transaction efficiency. Codification can become a source of 'lock-in' to obsolete conceptual schemes and to the technological and organizational systems built around them. Because of the investments needed to create both codified knowledge and a community of users of it, a certain amount of path dependence will emerge. It can be difficult to switch from one mode of operation to a different one which better suits both internal and external contemporary realities (Arrow, 1974).

Of course costs and benefits will explain the decision to codify only in the case of codifiable knowledge (Cowan & Foray, 2001; Cowan *et al.*, 2000). The economic question is therefore the following: how do economic agents decide whether or not to codify 'codifiable but not yet codified knowledge'? This is where price considerations come in. A computer technician may choose either to codify his or her knowledge in the form of a manual or expert system and then to exploit its dissemination, or else to keep it tacit so that users carry on buying the technician's repair services. In such a case, a set of factors influences the demand for codification, including institutional arrangements affecting the structure of incentives for codification activities. They also concern the state of technology, which determines codification costs. This position on the endogenous nature of boundaries between tacit and codified knowledge and the importance of economic determinants is in fact very similar to that of Nelson and Winter (1982).

If, instead, we take the case of tacit, non-codifiable knowledge (considering the state of printing, modelling and language technologies), for example knowledge concerning the recognition of a perfume, there is obviously no possible choice or discussion on costs. For the firm, the only way of managing knowledge is by resorting to the internal labour market. If this firm has a vision of its future it will be able to allocate resources to an R&D programme for developing the complex tools to make this knowledge codifiable in the long term (what is in fact happening is the development of an artificial nose capable of recognizing and analysing smells). But in the short term the knowledge remains tacit, without that being the consequence of an economic choice.

Thus the economic analysis of the choice to codify concerns only that which is codifiable in a given historical context. This 'codifiability' depends on the existence of appropriate languages, printing technologies and modelling capabilities for the knowledge under consideration.

3 Current transformations in the economics of knowledge reproduction

3.1 The uncertain evolution of reproduction by demonstration

This mode of reproduction – the master prepares and presents the script to his apprentice – predominated for a long time. Its efficiency depended on a sufficiently large and stable population of 'masters' who retained, and in many cases captured, the tacit knowledge. In large companies and in industrial clusters it was the internal labour market which for a long time had the function of memorizing, transferring and accumulating knowledge (Lam,

2000). Some centuries before, the craft guild played the same role (Epstein, 1998). The stability of employees and their mobility in a clearly delimited area are essential elements in such a system of memorization, accumulation and transfer of knowledge. A sort of community of fate which linked the expert to the firm according to a principle of life employment implied that the employee had to devote the last part of his or her professional life to the transmission of know-how. For example, large companies used to bring in a replacement two years before an engineer was due to retire, so that the transmission of expertise took place smoothly between teacher and learner. In such cases, the conditions were propitious for ensuring that the professional community itself took care of the memorization and transmission of knowledge from one generation to the next.

Internal labour markets, however, are approaching a state of crisis in which increasing externalization, turnover and mobility are making traditional methods of knowledge management, based upon localization of tacit skills transfer, ever more uncertain.

Today young engineers often arrive just a week before their predecessors leave. As a result, other ways of transmitting expertise have to be found, for those based on the teacher–learner relationship no longer function. Furthermore, the evolution of these labour markets, from broadly defined jobs and continuous careers towards narrowly defined jobs and stratified careers, is making the accomplishment of knowledge management functions by these markets more difficult (Lam, 2000).

3.2   Advantages and shortcomings of facsimile reproduction
In the first analysis, the advantages of technical reproducibility (form (c) on Figure 15.1) are obvious. It affords a mode of memorization and learning which seems better than codification. Making a film on a traditional craft technique allows people to store and to have access to interesting knowledge. The creation of this information is subject to increasing returns in the sense that there are high fixed costs to produce the first copy and very low marginal costs to produce and diffuse additional copies. But this is a first degree of codification that does not involve any generation of new knowledge structures and representations. This form of knowledge representation has shortcomings even compared to the more primitive instruction manual. Although the user may be able to memorize individual components more rapidly by viewing visual representations, a simple visual representation will provide little or no cognitive structure for understanding the information, whereas all but the very worst instruction manuals are capable of delivering such clues.

Exchanging images or learning by images are pleasant and useful activities but an increasing use of this mode of knowledge representation could limit cognitive advances obtained via representations based on the codification of scripts.

3.3 Current transformations in codification

The new information and communication technologies (ICT) have had a decisive impact by substantially expanding the fields of codifiability and increasing the profitability of codification. ICT have three effects on the codification of knowledge: effects on the process of codification, on its outcomes, and on incentives to codify.

First, by generating progress in printing techniques (computers and printers, graphics software, etc.) they reduce the cost of codification of simple knowledge. Second, by requiring the formulation of new languages (for artificial intelligence) and substantially increasing the capacity to model complex phenomena, they allow the codification of more and more complex knowledge (expertise). As noted above, these developments give codification ever-greater importance in terms of the creation of new knowledge and automation of more or less routine procedures. The evolution of the 'blueprint,' previously a method of codifying knowledge about dimensions and relationships among the components of an artefact, is a good case in point (Foray & Steinmueller, 2003). Blueprints involve graphical expression and a limited amount of writing. Most of the blueprints created in the 1980s involved the skills of a 'draughtsperson', capable of rendering design ideas through the use of 'multiview orthographic projection'. The transformation of blueprints into artefacts or artefacts into blueprints involved a considerable repertoire of skills, many of which were not scripted in any explicit fashion, but acquired through experience. Thus, the blueprint of that time was an 'incomplete' script for the reproduction of an artefact. Over a 20-year period the meaning of the term 'blueprint' has evolved considerably. Contemporary engineering diagrams are capable of incorporating precise information about curvature, sufficient data to allow the visual representation of the artefact from any viewing angle, and the possibility of additional information allowing virtual simulation of the artefact's performance under various environmental conditions. Furthermore, it is possible to link 'blueprint' data for some artefacts to fabrication equipment able to create the artefact from the blueprint and to digitize the surfaces and dimensions of artefacts in order to create a blueprint.

The third effect concerns incentives: by providing a medium for a new electronic communication infrastructure, ICT enhance the economic value of codification since codified knowledge can circulate easily on these networks.

These effects can help to introduce dynamic interdependence between the growth of ICT capacities and the increase in resources allocated to codification. ICT raise the value of codified knowledge, which increases private incentives to codify knowledge and results in an expansion of the codified knowledge base. This can, in turn, affect the supply and demand of ICT, and so on. A virtuous circle of positive feedback is established.

It is, however, advisable to qualify this view of the impact of technological progress on the value of codification (see above, our discussion on costs).

Conclusion: codification at the heart of the advent of knowledge-based economies

As argued, there is a general trend towards the increasing codifiability of knowledge (Abramovitz & David, 1996; David & Foray, 2002). This trend, however, is largely unbalanced. Technological change related to the evolution of ICT has varying impacts on the codifiability of different types of knowledge (Cowan, 2001).

Our study on current changes in the different modes of reproduction of knowledge confirms what Steinmueller (2000) has said: 'codification has become the very essence of economic activity'. In this respect we think of the prime importance not only of the visible function of codification (memory, communication and learning) but also of its invisible function – the other side of the coin – which induces and facilitates the elaboration of new cognitive devices (from the table to the formula) and, as such, is a potent tool for abstraction and intellectual creation.

References

Abramovitz, M. and David, P. [1996], 'Technological change, intangible investments and growth in the knowledge-based economy: the US historical experience', in D. Foray and B.-Å. Lundvall (eds), *Employment and Growth in the Knowledge-based Economy*, OECD, Paris.

Arora, A., Fosfuri, A. and Gambardella, A. [2001], *Markets for Technology*, MIT Press.

Arrow, K.J. [1974], *The Limits of Organization*, Norton.

Cowan, R. [2001], 'Expert systems: aspects of and limits to the codifiability of knowledge', *Research Policy*, **30**.

Cowan, R. and Foray, D. [1997], 'The economics of knowledge codification and diffusion', *Industrial and Corporate Change*, **6**(3).

Cowan, R. and Foray, D. [2001], 'On the codifiability of knowledge: technical change and the structure of cognitive activities', in P. Petit (ed.), *Economics and Information*, Kluwer Academic Publishers.

Cowan, R., David, P.A. and Foray, D. [2000], 'The explicit economics of knowledge codification and tacitness', *Industrial and Corporate Change*, **9**(2).

David, P.A. and Foray, D. [2002], 'An introduction to the economy of the knowledge society', MERIT Research Memorandum Series, 2001-041, University of Maastricht.

Dosi, G. [1996], 'The contribution of economic theory to the understanding of a knowledge-based economy', in D. Foray and B.-Å. Lundvall (eds), *Employment and Growth in the Knowledge-based Economy*, OECD, Paris.

Epstein, S.R. [1998], 'Craft guilds, apprenticeship, and technological change in preindustrial Europe', *The Journal of Economic History*, **58**(3).

Foray, D. and Hargreaves, D. [2003], 'The development of knowledge of different sectors: a model and some hypotheses', *London Review of Education*, **1**(1).

Foray, D. and Steinmueller, W.E. [2003], 'The economics of knowledge reproduction by inscription', *Industrial and Corporate Change*, **12**(2).

Goody, J. [1977], *The Domestication of the Savage Mind*, Cambridge University Press.

Hatchuel, A. and Weil, B. [1995], *Experts in Organizations: a Knowledge-based Perspective on Organizational Change*, de Gruyter.

Konrad, K. and Thum, M. [1993], 'Fundamental standards and time consistency', *Kyklos*, **46**(4).

Laffont, J.J. [1989], *The Economics of Uncertainty and Information*, MIT Press.

Lam, A. [2000], 'Tacit knowledge, organisational learning and societal institutions: an integrated framework', *Organizational Studies*, **21**(3).

Loasby, B. [1989], *The Mind and Method of the Economist*, Edward Elgar.

Mangolte, P.A. [1997], 'La dynamique des connaissances tacites et articulées: une approche sociocognitive', *Economie Appliquée*, vol. L, 2.

Nelson, R.R. and Winter, S. [1982], *An Evolutionary Theory of Economic Change*, The Belknap Press of Harvard University Press.

Perriault, J. [1993], 'The transfer of knowledge within the craft industries and trade guilds', in A. Berthelet and J. Chavaillier (eds), *The Use of Tools by Human and Non-Human Primates*, Clarendon Press.

Polanyi, M. [1966], *The Tacit Dimension*, Doubleday.

Simon, H. [1982], *Models of Bounded Rationality: Behavioural Economics and Business Organization*, vol.2, MIT Press.

Slaughter, M.M. [1985], *Universal Languages and Scientific Taxonomy in the Seventeenth Century*, Cambridge University Press.

Steinmueller, W.E. [2000], 'Will new information and communication technologies improve the "codification" of knowledge?', *Industrial and Corporate Change*, **9**(2).

Steinmueller, W.E. [2002], 'Networked knowledge and knowledge-based economies', *International Journal of Social Sciences*, **171**, March.

Von Hippel, E. [1994], 'Sticky information and the locus of problem solving: implications for innovation', *Management Science*, **40**(4).

Von Hippel, E. [1998], 'Economics of product development by users: the impact of "sticky" local information', *Management Science*, **44**(5).

Weizenbaum, J. [1976], *Computer Power and Human Reason*, W.H. Freeman.

16 Localized technological change
Cristiano Antonelli

1 Introduction

Technological change cannot be treated like the exogenous fall of manna from heaven. Technological change is endogenous to the economic process and it is the prime factor of continual change as it is the result of the pressure of economic forces both on the demand and the supply side. Technological change, however, cannot be treated like the customary result of routine activities: total factor productivity growth measures confirm that technological change yields results that are far larger than any rational calculations based upon marginal productivity might consider.[1]

The need to combine into a homogenous framework the endogenous understanding of the dynamics by means of which technological (and organizational) change is introduced in the economic system, with the elements of surprise and the unknown that necessarily characterize it, has always proved challenging for economic analysis.

The localized technological progress approach provides an attempt to solve the puzzle by building upon different traditions of analysis: the bounded rationality and limited knowledge framework for understanding individual decision making, the inducement approach, the economics of learning and the economic analysis of irreversibility. The key point is that firms are induced to change their routines and their technologies when a mismatch between plans and actual conditions emerges. Such an innovative reaction is made necessary and shaped by the burden of irreversibility. At the same time it is made possible, and yet constrained, by the dynamics of learning and the effects of limited knowledge and bounded rationality.

The localized approach provides a framework to analyzing technological change as the endogenous and induced outcome of an out-of-equilibrium self-sustaining dynamics that takes place in a set of highly specific and contextual circumstances. To do this it integrates different strands of literature in order to overcome the criticisms and shortcomings of each of them. The rest of the chapter is organized as follows. A simple exposition of the process mechanism is presented in section 2. The basic ingredients of the localized approach are identified in section 3. Section 4 presents the multidimensional analysis of the localized approach. The implications in terms of path-dependent complex dynamics are highlighted in section 5. The conclusion summarizes the main results and puts them in perspective.

2 The process

The introduction of technological innovations is the result of the creative reaction of firms, induced by changes in product and factor markets, that firms are not able to cope with, by means of movements in the given technical space. The creative reaction of firms is possible especially when an appropriate environment favors it, although constrained in a limited multidimensional space by the effects of irreversibility, limited information and learning processes that reduce their mobility.

In this approach, technological change is the outcome of the creative reaction to the failure to meet the expected levels of aspiration and the mismatch between expectations and actual facts. It is made possible by the continual efforts of accumulation of competence and technological knowledge and the eventual introduction of innovations by existing agents rooted in a well defined set of scientific, technical, geographic, economic and commercial circumstances.

Firms are viewed as learning agents, which do not limit the scope of their action to adjusting prices to quantities and vice versa. They are also able to change intentionally their technology, as well as their strategies. The introduction of innovation, however, is risky and agents are reluctant to innovate. Innovative behavior is solicited and induced by emerging discrepancies between plans and reality when performances fall below the expected levels of satisficing thresholds.

Sheer resilience in any given condition engenders actual losses or results below subjective expectations. The constraints imposed by irreversibility and limited knowledge about alternative techniques in the existing range of options reduce the scope for traditional substitution and make it expensive and resource-consuming. The search for new routines and new technologies is now activated.

Technological change is primarily the result of the valorization and implementation of underlying learning processes, in doing as well as in using and in interacting, that are localized into the specific context of action of each economic agent. Technological change, moreover, is also influenced by strategic decision making of agents which try and maximize their profits and do necessarily take into account the product and factor markets in which they are based. Finally, and consistently, the rate and the direction of technological change are influenced by the specific set of circumstances, as they are perceived by decision makers, at each point in time.

The efforts and the outcomes of the introduction of new routines and new technologies are confronted with the opportunity costs of resilience and the costs of switching, i.e. the costs of facing the constraints raised by irreversibility and limited knowledge. The firm will implement its adjustment by means of a mix of technical changes, consisting in movements in the existing space of techniques and products, and technological and organizational innovations, consisting in the actual modification of the space of techniques and products. The composition of the mix will depend upon the relative costs of technical changes with respect to technological (and organizational) ones.

Technological change is introduced by firms as a creative response to the mismatch between expectations and plain facts: hence technological change is generated in out-of-equilibrium conditions. The larger the discrepancies are between the expectations of each agent and its actual conditions, the faster are the rates of introduction of new technologies. The introduction of new technologies by each agent in turn, however, engenders new discrepancies between the expectations of any other agent and their actual market conditions. Hence technological change feeds technological change and out-of-equilibrium conditions further reproduce out-of-equilibrium outcomes.

Firms can react to the mismatch between expectations and actual conditions by means of the introduction of localized technological changes only if the specific context of action provides appropriate opportunities for the introduction of new technologies. Localized technological change in turn can engender an actual increase of total factor productivity levels, with respect to any other technique that belongs to the existing space of techniques, or simply make it possible for firms to be as productive as in the equilibrium technique. The specific contextual conditions, internal to each firm, each region, each industry, each institutional context and each scientific and technological field, play a major role in assessing the actual technological opportunities for each firm. The costs of innovative activities as well as their outcome are highly contextual and contingent on the specific set of circumstances in which the action of firms is embedded.

Innovation is the possible result of the creative reaction of a firm only when the surrounding environment is conducive to favoring the introduction of new technologies. The localization into technological commons, such as technological districts, professional communities, industrial sectors and 'filières', where other firms carry on complementary innovation and share substantial portions of the relevant technological knowledge, is a key factor in assessing the actual innovative capability of firms.

In less favorable contexts firms are obliged to face the discrepancy between expectations and actual conditions just by means of technical adjustments, bearing all the costs engendered by irreversibility and limited knowledge. Technological change is slower as well, as the gaps are smaller between expectations and actual conditions: the system can converge towards more stable and static equilibria with lower opportunities for growth.

Proximity in geographical and knowledge space among learning agents able to react to the failure of their aspiration levels, by means of the shared access and participation in a collective knowledge base and the eventual introduction of complementary innovations, is an essential condition to activate the failure inducement mechanism of technological change, to overcome the reluctance to change and to convert the isolated reaction of dispersed agents to adverse market conditions into the collective introduction of systemic innovations. Innovation is a highly contextual outcome, conditional on the occurrence of a large number of necessary conditions (Antonelli, 2006a, 2006b).

3 The basic ingredients

The notion of localized technological change is the result of the selective merging of quite distinct strands of literature: the notion of bounded rationality, the induced technological change approach, the economics of learning and the economics of knowledge, the economics of irreversibility. The analysis of bounded rationality, the notion of satisficing behavior and the distinction between substantive and procedural rationality introduced by Herbert Simon provide the basic context for the analysis. The action of economic agents is characterized by relevant search and information costs: agents do not control all the information about all the techniques available at each point in time on the existing maps of isoquants. Quite obviously agents are myopic for they are unable to foresee all the possible consequences of their actions and cannot anticipate correctly all the possible technologies that any other agent is trying and introducing at each point in time. Agents, however, are able to organize rationally the sequence of actions when facing changes and alterations in their plans. Finally, agents behave on the basis of their own subjective perceptions of the environment and are especially sensitive to the subjective definition of internal satisfaction (Simon, 1982).

When the levels of aspirations are not realized, agents take into consideration the introduction of innovations, which is the result of the deception and dissatisfaction of agents that can overcome their reluctance to innovate only in a specific context of complementary circumstances. The notion of failure-inducement elaborated in the behavioral approach complements and integrates the induced technological change approach (March and Simon, 1958; Antonelli, 1989, 1990).

Prospect theory as developed by Kahneman and Tversky (1979, 1992) provides important elements for understanding the process by means of which firms are pushed to innovate. Prospect theory assigns an important role to gains and losses, rather than by revenue levels in assessing the decision making. The reflection effect, a key component of the prospect theory, suggests that risk aversion is strong when gains are considered. Risk-seeking behavior, however, emerges when losses are taking place: the more agents are exposed to frustration, the less risk-adverse they are and actually they become more and more ready to accept high levels of uncertainty. The search for new technologies and the introduction of product, process and organizational innovations is likely to take place, with accelerated rates, when frustration and actual losses are encountered by agents, dissatisfied with the current state of their business.

The analysis of Paul David on the effects of irreversibility of physical and human capital, as well as reputation and market relations, contributes the understanding of the factors of localization. Following Paul David, a distinction between irreversibility and quasi-irreversibility can be made. When irreversibility applies, agents cannot overcome the effects and are bound to keep using the production factors in place; they cannot change their location, their customers or their suppliers. Irreversibility takes place when no change can be made to a given context. Irreversibility lies at the heart of traditional, textbook microeconomics: the theory of costs, the theory of the firm and the theory of the market are all short-term theories. As is well known, the very definition of 'short-term' in microeconomics impinges upon the notion of irreversibility. When an amount of capital has been chosen it cannot be changed swiftly. Only in the long term does capital become a flexible input. As a consequence firms can change the levels of output, but incur a reduction of technical efficiency and an increase in average costs. In turn the positive slope of the supply curve is a direct consequence of the short-term shape of the average and marginal costs. In turn the theory of the market is fully based upon short-term analysis and hence upon the assumption of 'rigid' irreversibility (David, 1975).

When quasi-irreversibility applies instead, agents are rooted by an irreversibility which limits their mobility and requires dedicated resources to be handled: constrained adjustment is possible. The introduction of new technologies is induced to overcome the limits of irreversibility. The case of quasi-irreversibility emerges when a given constraint caused by the irreversible elements can be modified, by means of creative reaction and the introduction of localized technological changes.

According to the traditional induced technological change approach, the introduction of new technologies is determined by the conditions of the factors markets. Specifically, a distinction has to be made between the models of induced technological change which focus the changes in factors prices and the models of induced technological change which stress the static conditions of factors markets. In the first approach, following Hicks and Marx, firms are induced to change their technology when the price of a production factor increases (Hicks, 1932). The change in factor prices acts as a powerful inducement mechanism, which explains both the rate and the direction of introduction of new technologies. The change in factor prices in fact induces firms to introduce new technologies, which are specifically directed to save on the factor that has become more expensive. The introduction of new technologies complements the standard substitution process, i.e. the technical change consisting in the selection of new techniques, defined in terms of factor intensities, on the existing isoquants. In this case technological change is considered an augmented form of substitution: technological change complements technical change.

This approach to the induced technological change differs from the static version, elaborated by Kennedy, von Weiszacker and Samuelson, according to which firms introduce new technologies in order to save on the production factors that are relatively more expensive. In this second approach the levels of factor price matter instead of the rates of change. This approach has shown a major limitation of the former. From simple algebraic calculation it is in fact clear that firms have an incentive to introduce labor-intensive technologies, in labor-abundant and capital-scarce regions and countries, even after an increase in wages. The Kennedy–von Weiszacker–Samuelson approach, however, is severely limited from the dynamic viewpoint. It is no longer clear when and why firms should innovate. Consistently, only the direction of technological change can be induced, rather than the rate (McCain, 1974; Binswanger and Ruttan, 1978; Ruttan, 1997, 2001).

Both approaches, as is well known, have been often criticized using the Salter argument, according to which firms should be equally eager to introduce any kind of technological change, either labor- or capital-intensive, provided it makes it possible to reduce production costs and increase efficiency. Localized technological change builds upon the dynamic approach to the inducement mechanism and is able to neutralize the Salter argument, by integrating the economics of learning and the economics of irreversibility (Salter, 1960; Nordhaus, 1973).

The localized technological change approach elaborates an augmented induced innovation mechanism by integrating the economics of learning and the economics of irreversibility. According to the traditional induced technological change approach, the introduction of new technologies is determined by the conditions of factors markets (Antonelli, 2003a). Changes in product markets, however, also induce technological changes. As a matter of fact, the localized technological approach elaborates a framework where all changes, in the factor markets, in aggregate demand, as in the post-Keynesian tradition, and in the specific product markets of each firm, brought about by Schumpeterian rivalry among firms, induce the creative reaction of firms constrained by irreversibility but endowed with creativity.

The separation of these levels of analysis has been much to the detriment of the actual understanding of the dynamics of technological change (Momigliano, 1975). The separate appreciation of the role of capitalistic rivalry, or demand-pull or factor markets inducement, in fact is not sufficient to grasp the actual factors of the continual growth of productivity.

The analysis of the inducement mechanism, elaborated in the localized technological change approach, is expanded so as to integrate the changes in both the factor and the product markets. Not only do the changes in the factor markets induce the innovative reaction of firms, but also all the changes in the expected levels of the demand for their products. Firms have made plans and built irreversible production capacities for expected levels of output. When the demand for the products of the firm changes, the firm, once again, is exposed to switching and information costs. Elaborating on this argument, both the demand-pull analysis and Schumpeterian rivalry become part of the augmented inducement mechanism. Innovative reaction in fact is now induced not only by changes in factor markets, but also by the macroeconomic pressure of aggregate demand as in the demand-pull tradition of analysis (Schmookler, 1966) and by changes in the demand curve of each firm, determined by the rivalry among firms within each industry, as in the Schumpeterian tradition (Scherer, 1984, 1992).

An important ingredient of the localized technological change approach is provided by the critical assessment of the microeconomic implications of the debate upon the classification of technological change and the early economics of growth, at the aggregate level, that took place in the late 1930s (Robinson, 1937; Asimakopulos and Weldon, 1963; Besomi, 1999). The traditional classification of technological change, whether neutral, labor or capital saving, had been elaborated in the analysis of economic growth within a single and homogeneous economic system. In a different context, one where many different firms compete in global product markets and have access to different factor markets, the application of that classification of technological change yields surprising results. When technological change is neutral, i.e. it can be expressed by a generalized shift of the map of isoquants towards the origin, the new technology is always better than the previous one: each technique of the new map is in fact more efficient than the previous one. When technological change, however, is biased so that its geometric representation consists in a new map of isoquants with a change in their slopes, the new isoquants are likely to intersect the old ones. This is especially clear when technological change is incremental. The intersection is most relevant when the new technology consists only in the introduction of a bias, with no shift effects. When an isoquant that belongs to the new technology intersects the equivalent isoquant that belongs to the old one, technological change no longer consists of new techniques that are 'always' superior to the old ones. It becomes clear, instead, that the new technology is only locally superior: it is superior for some techniques and inferior for others: technological change is local.[2]

The economics of learning makes a major contribution to understanding the dynamics of localized technological change. Here the basic building block is provided by the Arrovian analysis of learning as the key factor in the increase of efficiency. New technologies are, mainly, the result of learning processes that consist in the accumulation of experience and tacit knowledge and are strictly defined and circumscribed by the technical context of activity. Agents learn by handling well-defined product and by using well-defined machines. Learning is inherently localized in a narrow technical context (Arrow, 1962a).

As a matter of fact, Edith Penrose (1952, 1959) had anticipated the Arrovian notion of learning and qualified the firm, its organization and its routines, as the privileged actor in the learning process. The firm precedes the production function as its primary activity consists in the generation of new technological knowledge. Each firm, as is well known, learns and builds up new capabilities and eventually discovers new possible applications for production factors and competences that are found within its own boundaries. According to Edith Penrose, in other words, innovative firms are successful when they try and make the most effective use of production factors that are not only locally abundant, but also internally (within their own boundaries) abundant. The bottom-up approach to understanding the dynamics of knowledge finds here the first input and in so doing it stresses the role of technological knowledge, acquired by means of localized learning processes, as the primary input in the generation of new knowledge at large, together with the scientific advances made available by the scientific community and the acquisition of external knowledge spilling into the atmosphere (Antonelli, 2006a).

The analysis of learning has been subsequently stretched and sharpened by the insight of Anthony Atkinson and Joseph Stiglitz (1969) who elaborated further upon the key role of learning in the generation of new technologies and introduced the strong hypothesis that technological change can take place only in a limited technical space, defined in terms of factor intensity. Technological change is localized because it has limited externalities and affects only a limited span of the techniques, contained by a given isoquant, that are identified by the actual context of learning. In other words technological change can only take place where firms have been able to learn: the localization here is strictly defined in terms of factor intensity and with respect to the techniques in place at each point in time.

In the analyses of Penrose and Atkinson–Stiglitz, technological change is localized and constrained by organizational routines, but it is the automatic result of learning without any intentional and explicit effort. The inducement context, characteristic of the localized technological change approach, makes it possible to overcome this major limitation. The analysis of the specific context in which learning provides the opportunity for the eventual and intentional action of introduction of new technologies and innovation remains the element of strength.

The economics of learning contributes to the economics of knowledge and paves the way to understanding the broader notion of localized technological knowledge. The notion of learning and localized technological knowledge in fact makes it possible to stress the role of knowledge as a joint product of the economic and production activity. Agents learn how, when, where and what, also and, mainly, out of their experience, accumulated in daily routines. The introduction of new technologies is heavily constrained by the amount of competence and experience accumulated by means of learning processes in specific technical and contextual procedures. Agents, in this approach, can generate new knowledge only in limited domains and fields where they have accumulated sufficient levels of competence and experience. A strong complementarity must be assumed between learning, as a knowledge input, and other knowledge inputs such as R&D laboratories, within each firm (Arrow, 1962b, 1969; Lamberton, 1971; Loasby, 1999).

A second and most important complementarity takes place in the localized technological knowledge approach between internal and external knowledge. Firms can generate new knowledge and hence eventually introduce new technologies, only when and if they are able to take advantage of external knowledge. No firm can rely exclusively on its own internal knowledge, either tacit or codified, whether it is the result of learning processes or of formal research and development activities. The notion of knowledge cumulability and complementarity between external and internal knowledge is central in the understanding of the localized technological knowledge (Antonelli, 1999a, 2001, 2003a).

The relationship between external and internal knowledge becomes a key issue. Neither can firms generate new knowledge relying only on external or internal knowledge as input. With an appropriate ratio of internal to external knowledge instead, internal knowledge and external knowledge inputs enter into a multiplicative production function. Both below and above the threshold of the appropriate combination of the complementary inputs the firm cannot innovate (Antonelli, 2006b).

Localized technological change combines the inducement mechanism with the economic implications of learning and irreversibility in a unique analytical system. Firms are characterized both by learning capabilities and by bounded rationality and limited knowledge. Necessarily, firms make plans and consequently decide actions, which are partly irreversible.

All discrepancy between expected market conditions, now including both factors and products markets, and planned decisions should be the cause of technical changes; that is, changes in the existing space of techniques, consisting in either substitutions on a given isoquant or changes from one isoquant to another, or both. All changes in the existing space of techniques, however, engender specific costs due to the irreversibility of the production factors as well as to the information costs that are necessary in order to operate the new desired techniques. Switching costs prevent standard adjustments realized by means of substitution or mere change in input levels. Localized learning provides the opportunity to introduce technological changes. Firms exposed to the discrepancy between plans and actual market conditions, limited in their mobility by limited knowledge and irreversibility, are induced to take advantage of the localized knowledge accumulated by means of learning processes and introduce technological innovations in a limited technical space.

Localized technological change is endless and fully endogenous. Firms cannot anticipate all the possible innovations introduced by any other firm in the economic system. And yet any discrepancy between plans and actual market conditions is likely to induce the localized introduction of new technologies, which in turn are the cause of new discrepancy between expectations and actual market conditions for other firms.

4 The multidimensional scope

Localized technological change reflects the pervasive role of irreversibility, externalities, information asymmetries and bounded rationality and interdependence as well as the amount of creativity each agent is able to express as a way to solve specific and contextual problems arising in the daily management of its business. Hence technological change is necessarily localized in a multidimensional space, that is, deeply rooted in the context of characteristics which define the activity of each agent.

Technological change is localized in historical time, in technical space, in the knowledge space, in technological systems, in the structural conditions of each economic system, in geographic space and, in the space of product characteristics, technological change is localized in firms. The analysis has investigated the variety of processes by means of which technological change is localized in the historical, technical, technological, structural, institutional, regional, knowledge and organizational spaces highlighting how and why the introduction of innovation is conditional on the effects of proximity.

Localized technological change is primarily localized in historical time. Each technological innovation and each element of technological knowledge and competence can be understood only as a step in a historical sequence of the cumulative introduction of technological innovations and other bits of technological knowledge. Technological change is characterized by path dependence in that it can be analyzed effectively only when the effects of cumulability and irreversibility are put in context. Cumulability plays a key role in the production of knowledge and in the integration of the new production factors into the existing production process. Irreversibility is an essential characteristic of fixed capital, both tangible and intangible. The fixed and irreversible capital can be changed only at a cost and this affects the scope of any further innovative choice. The introduction of new technologies that are complementary to the existing ones becomes a clear constraint and incentive (Antonelli, 1999a, 2001).

Technological change is localized in technical space, that is the space defined in terms of factor intensity, by the essential role of learning in building the competence and the technological knowledge that is necessary to introduce new technology and increase the efficiency of the production process (Atkinson and Stiglitz, 1969; David, 1975). Learning is essentially localized in a limited technical space and as such it cannot be applied easily elsewhere. Antonelli (1994, 1995) has further developed this notion of localized technological change, emphasizing the role of irreversibilities in fixed and immaterial capital stocks and the related switching costs and coupling its effects with the local dimension of learning originally highlighted by Atkinson and Stiglitz (1969) and further stressed by Stiglitz (1987). As a result it seems clear that technological innovations are introduced within technical corridors identified by the original technical localization of innovating agents and defined by barriers to mobility originated by switching costs and learning opportunities.

Technological change is localized in the gales of technological systems activated by technological indivisibilities, complementarities and interdependencies among technologies. The efficiency of each technology is greatly enhanced by the availability of the other complementary and interdependent technologies. Firms induced to innovate are pushed to direct their innovative efforts towards the introduction of new technologies that are complementary to others so as to take advantage of typical network externalities in their dynamic form (David, 1987; David and Bunn, 1988; Antonelli, 2001).

Technological change is localized into knowledge space. High levels of vertical and horizontal indivisibility characterize knowledge space. Each unit of knowledge has high levels of complementarity and cumulability with other units that are ordered vertically across historic time. Horizontal complementarity across different fields of origin is also relevant and can be defined in terms of complexity. Finally, each unit of technological knowledge can be applied, as well as different fields of application: the notion of fungibility is important in this context. The production of knowledge relies on the continual recombination of existing bits of knowledge. The characteristics of such indivisibilities are most relevant and make it possible to identify the commons of knowledge. The borders of such commons of specific knowledge and competence become a powerful factor of specialization in well-defined technological fields. Good access conditions to the knowledge commons and good communication channels among learning agents make easier for firms the introduction of innovations as a response to unexpected declines in performances (Antonelli, 2003a).

Technological change is localized in geographic space by the proximity between learning agents, because of the pervasive role of scientific communication and technological spillover. Proximity in geographic space interacts with proximity in knowledge space. Regional proximity favors the generation of new knowledge on three counts: (i) it helps to reduce knowledge transaction costs, (ii) it facilitates the division of scientific and technological labor and hence increases efficiency in the generation of new knowledge, and (iii) it makes it possible to accelerate the circulation of knowledge and hence to capitalize on knowledge externalities (Griliches, 1992).

Proximity in geographic space helps increasing trust among trade partners and reduces the scope for opportunistic behavior. Consequently proximity favors the emergence of local markets for technological knowledge, qualified systems of knowledge interactions, higher levels of specialization and division of labor in the generation of new knowledge, hence higher levels of general efficiency in the generation of new knowledge and in the introduction of technological innovations.

The localization in a technological district and the membership of professional and epistemic communities makes easier the access to local knowledge commons, hence increases the effects of local knowledge externalities and increases the probability of introduction of successful innovations. The quality of the local scientific infrastructure and the connectivity of the communication channels in place between the academic and the business community add strong elements to understanding the key role of technological districts in localizing technological change from a geographical viewpoint (Antonelli, 2001).

Technological change is localized in the economic structure of each economic system by local endowments, intermediary markets and hence factors costs. The structure of relative prices reflects the local endowments and the vertical organization of the economic system. It reflects in fact the vertical relations among industries along the 'filières' within the input–output matrix. The characters and types of the market structures in each given layer have powerful effects downstream in terms of relative factor prices. The effects of technological innovations vary according to the interplay between the direction of technological change, defined in terms of the marginal efficiency of each production factor, and the local structure of relative factor prices. Composition effects, that is the consequences of relative factor prices for each possible direction of technological change, have powerful consequences in terms of total factor productivity growth. The endowments of each region and the structure of relative prices within each industrial system become a powerful factor in explaining the differentiated effects of the introduction of the same technology across economic systems. Composition effects may account for the delays in adoption of incremental and biased technologies. By the same token, however, composition effects are a powerful inducement mechanism to select and focus the factor intensity of the new technologies. Firms located in a labor-abundant region have a clear incentive to introduce labor-intensive technologies, for they make it possible to make the most intensive use of the more abundant and hence cheaper local production factors. The analysis of localized technological change has shown that changes in the levels of factors price can be considered the prime mechanisms of inducement, and hence the determinant of the rate of change. The actual direction of the new technologies being introduced, however, is determined by the relative abundance of the production factors in the local factor markets (Antonelli, 2003a).

The analytical framework introduced by Lancaster (1971) proves to be especially fertile and productive, to accommodate the analysis of the innovation process in the space of product characteristics. The Lancastrian approach in fact can be easily used as a tool to stretch the localized technological change approach to analyze the role of proximity in the space of product characteristics and assess the choice between product and process innovations. It seems clear that product innovation is more localized the more specific and localized is the process of accumulation of competence and the more relevant is the latter in the generation of technological knowledge and the more dispersed the distribution of firms in the product space (Antonelli, 2004).

Finally, it is clear that technological change is localized within firms. Firms differ in many relevant ways: the vintage of irreversible factors, the competitive context, the factors markets, the location and the communication channels in place with the external environment, the organization and the structure of decision making, the learning procedures, the portfolio of products and the knowledge fields where competence is based, the composition of human capital. Each firm as a consequence follows its own path in reacting to the mismatches and introducing technological innovations. Elaborating on the legacy of Edith Penrose and Ronald Coase, it seems clear that not only the dynamics of accumulation of technological knowledge matters, but also the dynamics of competence in managing the governance mechanisms – including both transaction and coordination activities – as determined by the generation of organizational knowledge and the introduction of organizational innovations, play an important role. Governance mechanisms are no longer viewed as the result of the static combination defined by given levels of coordination and transaction costs, but as the result of dedicated activities affected by the rates of accumulation of competence and organizational knowledge. Next to the production function a corporate function where alternative governance mechanisms are considered and assessed needs to be used to analyze the firm. The interplay between technological and organizational innovations, based upon technological and organizational learning, respectively, shapes the growth path of the firm and defines the sequence of technological innovations that each firm can generate and introduce successfully (Antonelli, 1999b, 2001: 111–45, 2003a).

The logic of localized technological change applies to understanding the diffusion and the selection of new technologies as well. Each new technology is localized and as such reflects the specific conditions of innovators as well as each firm being localized in its specific context of action. The factors of localization in fact help to explain why firms may delay the adoption of some technologies. Firms will select the new technologies that fit better with their own highly specific and idiosyncratic context of operation. New technologies may happen to be superior for some firms and in some circumstances and inferior for others (David, 1985; Antonelli, 2006a).

5   Complex system dynamics and path dependence

Localized technological change, as determined and shaped by irreversibility, is inherently path-dependent. New technologies in fact must be introduced in order to cope with the discrepancy between plans and actual market conditions that irreversibility prevents adjustment to, by means of standard substitution. Yet they can change the course of actions, modifying the effects of irreversibility, although within a narrow and limited space of alternatives, defined by the effects of switching costs and learning.

The distinction between past-dependence and path-dependence is crucial in this context. Irreversibility is a source of past-dependence if no action may modify and integrate the effects of irreversibility. Irreversibility engenders path-dependence when and if specific and intentional actions may take place and modify the course of sequential events, albeit in a narrow and limited region. Irreversibility is the cause of technological change because switching costs limit the possibility for firms to react to changes in their markets by means of traditional substitution on existing isoquants. The introduction of innovation is necessary in order to adjust to the new market conditions and yet save on switching costs. Irreversibility is also at the origin of the localized introduction of innovations because it shapes the corridors of introduction of the new technologies and prevents the radical – chaotic – change of technical coefficients.

The implications of the economics of localized technological change for the dynamics of the system are most important. The system is inherently complex and dynamic. There is no such thing as a stable attractor towards which the elements of the system are eventually induced to converge. Endogenous technological change in fact is the vector of continual change and development. When the dynamics of technological change is based upon ubiquitous and automatic processes of learning, as is the case in the new growth theory, a clear sequence of attractor points can be identified and even predicted. When the variety of agents is assumed, creativity matters, and its effects are not based upon automatic and ubiquitous learning processes, however, the dynamics of the system risks becoming unpredictable and non-intelligible: system dynamics acquires all the characteristics of a chaotic process. The mix of irreversibility, local externalities and creativity, upon which the economics of localized technological change is based, is crucial in this context. Localized technological change provides system dynamics with elements of intelligibility, and even limited predictability. Irreversibility and local externalities in fact characterize the likelihood that creativity will take place and shape its effects. Irreversibility drives creativity, as an extreme form of reactivity. Local externalities and in general the local context of learning and interaction shape the actual scope of creativity and qualify its effects. Local externalities assess the effects of creativity, whether it consists of actual total factor productivity effects, or simply of technical changes that do not increase overall efficiency levels. Irreversibility and local externalities define the context in which creativity takes place and exerts its effects. The economics of localized technological change and path-dependence provides the economics of complex dynamics with new tools to understand, if not predict, economic development (Taylor, 2001).

At the system level the dynamics exerted by the mix of irreversibility, local externalities and creativity acquires all the characteristics of path-dependence. Path-dependence is the relevant analytical result, at the aggregate level, of the dynamics generated by localized technological change at the microeconomic level. Creativity and endogenous change in fact take place because of the effects of irreversibility and bear the characteristics of the local context of learning and interacting in which the action of a variety of agents takes place. Path-dependence is a form of constrained chaotic behavior where past defines at each point in time the basic ingredients of change and hence its direction.[3]

6 Conclusion

Localized technological change integrates a variety of complementary approaches so as to provide a powerful analytical framework able to accommodate in a rational procedural explanation the introduction of the unknown and of surprise.

Firms are reluctant to change their behavior and their routines: innovation is difficult and risky. Firms are induced to introduce new technologies when a number of conditions are met: when satisficing thresholds are not met, the levels of aspiration are not realized, because of a mismatch between plans and actual product and factor markets; when limited knowledge and irreversibility matter and limit the scope of substitution and technical change within the existing space of techniques; when learning and accumulated competence provide the opportunity to generate new technological knowledge, albeit in a limited technological space; when knowledge interactions and knowledge spillovers, within limited regional spaces, make external knowledge available and hence innovative activities possible and more productive; when technological complementarities with other parallel new technologies increase the stream of benefits stemming from the introduction of a new technology within a technological system; and when the distribution of rival products and customers' preferences favor the introduction of product innovations, albeit in the proximity of existing product lines.

Technological innovations are introduced when a number of forces are at play and a highly qualified set of sequential conditions favor the positive outcome. Consequently, technological change is the conditional and unpredictable result of a systemic context of opportunities and constraints. Technological change is endogenous to the working of the economic system as it is induced by all changes in factors and products markets myopic firms are unable to foresee, and localized by the effects of irreversibility, limited knowledge and learning. Localized technological change is the result of out-of-equilibrium conditions and is the cause of out-of-equilibrium conditions. In such conditions no convergence towards a stable equilibrium point can take place. To the contrary, an endless and path-dependent process of endogenous change is the result of the interplay between local mistakes and creativity, myopia and surprise (Antonelli, 2006c and 2007).

Notes

1. I acknowledge the comments and suggestions of many as well as the financial support of the European Union Directorate for Research, within the context of the Integrated Project EURODITE (Regional Trajectories to the Knowledge Economy: A Dynamic Model) Contract no. 006187 (CIT3), in progress at the Fondazione Rosselli.
2. Let us consider the case of the introduction of a new 'biased' technological change. We can now confront the old and the new technologies as expressed by two production functions:

1) $Y_1 = A_1 K^{a1} L^{b1}$
2) $Y_2 = A_2 K^{a2} L^{b2}$

where $a1$ differs from $a2$ and hence $b1$ differs from $b2$. A simple logarithmic transformation makes it possible to identify the intersection:

3) $\log A_1 / A_2 = (a1 / a2) \log K + (b1 / b2) \log L$.

3. According to Mark Taylor (2001:142–3), 'it is possible to identify the following characteristics of complex systems: 1. Complex systems are [composed] of many different parts, which are connected in multiple ways. 2. Diverse components can interact both serially and in parallel to generate sequential as well as simultaneous effects and events. 3. Complex systems display spontaneous self-organization, which complicates interiority and exteriority in such a way that the line that is supposed to separate them becomes undecidable. 4. The structures resulting from spontaneous self-organization emerge from but are not necessarily reducible to the interactivity of the components or elements in the system. 5. Though generated by local interactions, emergent properties tend to be global. 6. Inasmuch as self-organizing structures emerge spontaneously, complex systems are neither fixed nor static but develop or evolve. Such evolution presupposes that complex systems are both open and adaptive. 7. Emergence occurs in a narrow possibility space lying between conditions that are too ordered and too disordered. This boundary or margin is the "edge of chaos" which is always far from equilibrium'.

References

Antonelli, C. (1989), A failure-inducement model of research and development expenditures: Italian evidence from the early 1980s, *Journal of Economic Behavior and Organization*, **12**, 159–80.

Antonelli, C. (1990), Induced adoption and externalities in the regional diffusion of new information technology, *Regional Studies*, **24**, 31–40.

Antonelli, C. (1994), Localized technological changes: a model incorporating switching costs and R&D expenses with endowment advantages, in M. Perlman and Y. Shionoya (eds), *Innovation in Technology Industries and Institutions: Comparative Perspectives. Studies in Schumpeterian Economics*, Ann Arbor, University of Michigan Press.

Antonelli, C. (1995), *The Economics of Localized Technological Change and Industrial Dynamics*, Boston, Kluwer.

Antonelli, C. (1999a), *The Microdynamics of Technological Change*, London, Routledge.

Antonelli, C. (1999b), The organization of production, *Metroeconomica*, **50**, 234–59.

Antonelli, C. (2001), *The Microeconomics of Technological Systems*, Oxford, Oxford University Press.

Antonelli, C. (2003a), *The Economics of Innovation, New Technologies and Structural Change*, London, Routledge.

Antonelli, C. (2003b), Knowledge complementarity and fungeability: implications for regional strategy, *Regional Studies*, **39**, 595–606.

Antonelli, C. (2004), Localized product innovation. The role of proximity in the Lancastrian product space, *Information Economics and Policy*, **16**, 255–74.

Antonelli, C. (2006a), Diffusion as a process of creative adoption, *Journal of Technology Transfer*, **31**, 211–26.

Antonelli, C. (2006b), The system dynamics of collective knowledge: from gradualism and saltationism to punctuated change, *Journal of Economic and Organizaton Behavior*, **62**, 215–36.

Antonelli, C. (2006c), Path dependence, localized technological change and the quest for dynamic efficiency, in C. Antonelli, D. Foray, B. Hall and E. Steinmueller (eds), *Frontiers in the Economics of Innovation. Essays in Honour of Paul David*, Cheltenham, UK and Northampton, MA, USA, Edward Elgar.

Antonelli, C. (2007), *The Path-dependent Complexity of Localized Technological Change: Ingredients, Governance and Processes*, forthcoming, London, Routledge.

Arrow, K.J. (1962a), The economic implications of learning by doing, *Review of Economic Studies*, **29**, 155–73.

Arrow, K.J. (1962b), Economic welfare and the allocation of resources for invention, in R.R. Nelson (ed.), *The Rate and Direction of Inventive Activity: Economic and Social Factors*, Princeton, Princeton University Press for N.B.E.R.

Arrow, K.J. (1969), Classificatory notes on the production and transmission of technical knowledge, *American Economic Review*, **59**, 29–35.

Asimakopulos, A. and Weldon, J.C. (1963), The classification of technical progress in models of economic growth, *Economica*, **30**, 372–86.

Atkinson, A.B. and Stiglitz, J.E. (1969), A new view of technological change, *Economic Journal*, **79**, 573–8.

Besomi, D. (1999), Harrod on the classification of technological progress. The origin of a wild-goose chase, *BNL Quarterly Review*, **208**, 95–118.

Binswanger, Hans P. and Ruttan, Vernon W. (1978), *Induced Innovation. Technology Institutions and Development*, Baltimore, The Johns Hopkins University Press.

David, P.A. (1975), *Technical Choice Innovation and Economic Growth*, Cambridge, Cambridge University Press.

David, P.A. (1985), Clio and the economics of QWERTY, *American Economic Review*, **75**, 332–7.

David, P.A. (1987), Some new standards for the economics of standardization in the information age, in P. Dasgupta and P. Stoneman (eds), *Economic Policy and Technological Performance*, Cambridge, Cambridge University Press.

David, P.A. and Bunn, J. (1988), The economics of gateway technologies and network evolution: lessons from electricity supply history, *Information Economics and Policy*, **3**, 165–202.

Griliches, Z. (1992), The search for R&D spillovers, *Scandinavian Journal of Economics*, **94**, 29–47.

Hicks, John, R. (1932), *The Theory of Wages*, London, Macmillan.

Kahneman, D. and Tversky, A. (1979), Prospect theory: an analysis of decision under risk, *Econometrica*, **47**, 263–91.

Kahneman, D. and Tversky, A. (1992), Advances in prospect theory: cumulative representation of uncertainty, *Journal of Risk and Uncertainty*, **5**, 297–323.

Lamberton, D. (ed.) (1971), *Economics of Information and Knowledge*, Harmondsworth, Penguin.

Lancaster, K. (1971), *Consumer Demand: A New Approach*, New York, Columbia University Press.

Loasby, B.J. (1999), *Knowledge Institutions and Evolution in Economics*, London, Routledge, for Graz Schumpeter Lectures.

March, J.G. and Simon, H.A. (1958), *Organizations*, New York, John Wiley and Sons.

McCain, R.A. (1974), Induced bias in technical innovation including product innovation in a model of economic growth, *Economic Journal*, **84**, 959–66.

Momigliano, F. (1975), *Economia industriale e teoria dell'impresa*, Bologna, IL Mulino.

Nordhaus, William, D. (1973), Some skeptical thoughts on the theory of induced innovation, *Quarterly Journal of Economics*, **87**, 209–19.

Penrose, E.T. (1952), Biological analogies in the theory of the firm, *American Economic Review*, **42**, 804–19.

Penrose, E.T. (1959), *The Theory of the Growth of the Firm*, 1st and 3rd edns, Oxford, Basil Blackwell (1959) and Oxford University Press (1995).

Robinson, J. (1937), The classification of inventions, *Review of Economic Studies*, **6**, 139–42.

Ruttan, V.W. (1997), Induced innovation evolutionary theory and path dependence: sources of technical change, *Economic Journal*, **107**, 1520–29.

Ruttan, V.W. (2001), *Technology Growth and Development. An Induced Innovation Perspective*, Oxford, Oxford University Press.

Salter, W.E.G. (1960), *Productivity and Technical Change*, Cambridge, Cambridge University Press.

Scherer, F.M. (1984), *Innovation and Growth: Schumpeterian Perspectives*, Cambridge, MIT Press.

Scherer, F.M. (1992), *International High-technology Competition*, Cambridge, Harvard University Press.

Schmookler, Jacob (1966), *Invention and Economic Growth*, Cambridge, Harvard University Press.

Simon, H.A. (1982), *Models of Bounded Rationality: Behavioral Economics and Business Organization*, Cambridge, MIT Press.

Stiglitz, J.E. (1987), Learning to learn, localized learning and technological progress, in P. Dasgupta and P. Stoneman (eds), *Economic Policy and Technological Performance*, Cambridge, Cambridge University Press, pp. 125–53.

Stiglitz, J.E. (2002), Information and the change in the paradigm in economics, *American Economic Review*, **92**, 460–502.

Taylor, M.C. (2001), *The Moment of Complexity. Emerging Network Culture*, Chicago, University of Chicago Press.

17 Competencies, capabilities and the neo-Schumpeterian tradition
Mie Augier and David J. Teece

1 Introduction

There is wide agreement that Joseph Schumpeter's ideas helped initiate or at least energize many developments in twentieth-century economics.[1] These include evolutionary economics, organization theory, the theory of techno-logical change, and, of course, entrepreneurship. Various neo-Schumpterian traditions have also emerged in the field of business and corporate strategy. The business firm has been conceptualized by strategy scholars as consist-ing of bundles or 'portfolios' of fixed assets and (production) competen-cies/capabilities.[2] In recent years these ideas have become integrated into theories of the firm and economic organization. Indeed, the competences and capabilities tradition has garnered wide currency and is now generally accepted (Teece, 1982, 1986; Rumelt, 1984; Dosi *et al.*, 2000; Winter, 2000, 2003; Teece and Pisano, 1994; Teece *et al.*, 1997; Teece, 2006).[3]

There are both static and dynamic versions of the competences and capa-bilities tradition. Whereas the lineage of static versions of the capabilities framework can be traced to Ricardo, the lineage of dynamic versions can be attributed to Schumpeter (Teece *et al.*, 1997, 2002). Scholars in strategic management, organizational theory, organizational economics, sociology, and innovation studies have embraced the dynamic version of capabilities with considerable enthusiasm.

This chapter sketches the history of the development of the ideas under-lying modern approaches to competencies and (dynamic) capabilities.[4] In addition to providing a coherent framework for studying strategic manage-ment under conditions of uncertainty, rapid technological change and ambi-guity, the dynamic capabilities framework is also well suited to the analysis of learning, thereby facilitating the integration of economic, organizational, and strategic issues (Levinthal and March, 1993; Zollo and Winter, 2002).

2 Antecedents and brief history

2.1 Introduction

The field of strategic management has in recent years leveraged off theories of economic organization in general and theories of the firm in particular.

This was not always so. When Rumelt (1984) identified 'a strategic theory of the firm' and pronounced that the study of business strategy must take off from economic theories of the firm, the linkages between economic theories of the firm and strategic management were either weak or non-existent. Tensions existed and in many respects still remain, between the neoclassical theory of the firm and strategic management. This is because of the cavalier treatment in economics of know-how, the static focus of neoclassical theory, and the strong behavioral assumptions around (hyper)rationality embedded in neoclassical theory (Teece and Winter, 1984; Teece, 1984; Simon, 1993).

Over the past 50 years, some progress had been made in the social sciences to help craft more realistic foundations for the theory of the firm. For instance, the ideas of Simon, Cyert and March on 'bounded rationality', opportunistic behavior, and routines were significant inputs for the emerging perspectives of transaction cost economics and evolutionary economics. Further, it had long been in the tradition of neo-Schumpeterian economists to emphasize innovation, technological change, and evolution. And in the mid-1980s, strategy scholars began to realize the usefulness of these developments in understanding firm behavior. For example, Teece (1984) argued that the evolutionary ideas of Nelson and Winter would help in providing a theory of the firm's distinctive competencies. Routines could be thought of as the skills of the organization, and the firm as an entity with a limited range of capabilities based on its available routines and physical assets. The emphasis in this emerging literature on routines introduces the idea of path dependency; a firm's capabilities are defined very much by where it has been in the past and what it has done; and its current performance is a function of engrained repertoires (Dosi, 1988; Teece, 1984; March, 1994). Path dependencies and established technological trajectories shape the opportunities faced by firms.[5]

In order to position neo-Schumpeterian ideas on competences and capabilities, we summarize below relevant theories in organizational economics/theories of the firm. Our purpose is to compare and contrast them to dynamic capabilities.

Dynamic capabilities refer to the particular (non-immitability) capacity firms have to shape, reshape, configure and reconfigure those assets so as to respond to changing technologies and markets. Dynamic capabilities, therefore, relate to the firm's ability to adapt in order to generate and exploit internal and external *firm-specific competences,* and to address the firm's *changing environment* (Teece *et al.,* 1997). As Collis (1994) and Winter (2003) note, one element of dynamic capabilities is that they govern the rate of change of ordinary capabilities.[6] If a firm possesses resources/competences but lacks dynamic capabilities, it has a chance to make a competitive return for a short period, but superior returns cannot be sustained It may earn Ricardian (quasi)-rents, but such quasi-rents will be competed away, often rather quickly. It cannot earn Schumpeterian rents because it has not built the capacity to be continually innovative. Nor is it likely to be able to earn monopoly (Porterian) rents since these require exclusive behavior or strategic manipulation (Teece, 2006).

An illustration of some of the issues involved in the dynamic capability framework is found in the story of the British pop group, Spice Girls. The group made pop-history in the late 1990s with their successes (being the first female group to win nine number one hit-singles – only Elvis, Cliff Richard, Madonna and the Beatles ever had more). The band was the result of two entrepreneurial and innovative management gurus (Bob and Chris Herbert) who in 1994 handpicked the five members to sing in a team at first called 'Touch' (the band name and the manager were changed in 1996). After a few years of success, the band broke up and the individual band members tried to pursue solo careers. However, none of them was able to replicate the success of the band as a team (or organization), and pop-industry experts commented that only if the band got together again would they be able to return to the success of previous years. In other words, it was the dynamic orchestration of individual skills and knowledge in the organization of the band that created the success. Once apart, their individual capabilities were no longer productive. The solo careers of several of the Spice Girls ended abruptly.

2.2 Relationship to transaction cost theory[7]

The transactions cost approach is widely accepted as a framework for understanding economic organization. This perspective sees markets and hierarchies as alternative mechanisms for organizing transactions. In order to economize on transaction costs, production is frequently required to be organized in firms. Transaction cost economics builds on the assumptions of bounded rationality and opportunism (Williamson, 1975, 1985). Contractual efficiency is impaired when switching costs have to be incurred to change suppliers. In such circumstances, vertical integration is likely to be superior according to transaction cost analysis.[8]

There is much utility and exploratory power in the transaction cost framework. However, the contractual scheme upon which it is built deals with existing resources and does not examine how new resources are discovered, how they are accumulated, and how firms learn. The structure and behavior of the modern business firm cannot be fully explained by appealing to transaction costs alone. The focus for the 'main case' in transaction cost economics is governance – i.e. how things should be organized. This is an important element of management; but it is not the main concern of management scholars or practitioners. While it is important to have the right governance, it is of equal (if not greater) importance to make the right investment choices, select the right assets to 'govern', and establish the correct business model. Superior organizational capabilities require not just astute initial asset selection; they also require continuous reconfiguration and improvement. The transaction cost framework, by contrast, is primarily about asset or value protection, not value creation.[9]

Williamson clearly recognizes that, even in the world of transaction cost economics, governance costs are not the only costs that are relevant to the firm. 'Production costs' are mentioned, but not analyzed deeply. However, much lies within 'production costs' that economists and management scholars need to understand. They include not just operational issues, but strategic issues too. Some production-related issues are operational – such as the establishment of flexible procurement, enabling the firm to take advantage of changing competitive pricing – and some highly strategic, such as whether or not to invest in a new plant, whether to advance a new generation of products now, later, or never. Clearly, the performance of a business is going to be very significantly impacted by production and investment choices, as well as by governance choices.[10]

In short, the (dynamic) capabilities framework suggests that the scope of the firm cannot be explained just by transaction cost considerations. Rather, asset selection (internalization) decisions must also make reference to complementarities and cospecialization for reasons of scope economies, and appropriability (Teece, 2006).

The complementarity between transaction cost economics and dynamic capabilities has been recognized by Williamson, Teece and Winter.[11] Williamson notes that transaction cost and internal firm perspectives 'deal with partly overlapping phenomenon, often in complementary ways' (1999, p. 1098). Indeed, the very first empirical study to show the predictive power of asset specificity in setting firm boundaries (Monteverde and Teece, 1982) also showed that even greater predictive power was associated with cospecialization or 'systems integration' causing Teece (1990) to observe that 'in order to fully develop its capabilities, transaction cost economics must be joined with a theory of knowledge and production' (p. 59; also see Winter, 1988).[12] As a result, scholars began looking elsewhere to develop more robust theories of the firm. Behavioral and evolutionary economics has been recognized as another source of useful insights.

2.3   Relationship to the behavioral theory of the firm
The behavioral theory of the firm is a more dynamic perspective than transaction cost theory. It was not intended as a theory of strategy; but several insights from the behavioral perspective are used in both the resource-based view (Barney, 1991) and dynamic capability theory (Teece et al., 2002).

The behavioral theory is built around a political conception of organizational goals, a bounded rationality conception of expectations, an adaptive conception of rules and aspirations, and a set of ideas about how the interactions among these factors affect decisions in a firm (Cyert and March, 1963). Whereas goals in neoclassical theory are pictured as given alternatives each with a set of consequences attached, goals within behavioral theory are pictured as reflecting the demands of a political coalition, changing as the composition of that coalition changes. Thus, the theory treats the demands of shareholders, managers, workers, customers, suppliers, and creditors as components of the operational goals of a firm. At the same time, not all goals are salient at all times. Rather, specific goals are evoked by the presence of coalition members in the decision neighborhood, by the divisional organization of the firm, and by the recognition of particular problems. Aspirations with respect to each dimension of the goals were pictured as changing in response to the experience of the organization and its components as well as the experience of others to whom they compare themselves. Thus, it is the dynamic nature of aspirations which enables the generation of new decision alternatives. Therefore, the firm must engage in active search and imagination to create sustainable strategic opportunities (Winter, 2000).

In the behavioral view, agents have only limited rationality, meaning that behavior in organizations is intendedly rational: neither emotive nor aimless (March and Simon, 1958). Since firms are seen as heterogeneous, boundedly rational entities that have to search for relevant information, expectations in the behavioral theory are portrayed as the result of making inferences from available information, involving both the process by which information is made available and the processes of drawing inferences. Since information is costly, it is generated by search activity. The intensity of search depends on the performance of the organization relative to aspirations and the amount of organizational slack (March and Simon, 1958, pp. 47–52). The direction of search is affected by the location (in the organization) or search activity and the definition of the problem stimulating the activity. Thus, the search activity of the organization both furthers the generation of new alternative strategies, and facilitates the anticipation of uncertain futures.

Decision making in the behavioral theory is seen as taking place in response to a problem, through the use of standard operating procedures and other routines, and also through search for an alternative that is acceptable from the point of view of current aspiration levels for evoked goals. Choice is affected, therefore, by the definition of a problem, by existing rules (which reflect past learning by the organization), by the order in which alternatives are considered (which reflects the location of decision making in the organization and past experience), and by anything that affects aspirations and attention.[13]

Cyert and March (1963) emphasized the uniqueness in firms; organizations and organizational actors differ in terms of their aspirations, their knowledge, and their decisions. In terms of relevance to strategy, the most basic contribution of the behavioral theory of the firm is the importance of firm heterogeneity (Teece *et al.*, 2002). Winter (2000) also uses the ideas on satisficing and dynamic aspiration levels to suggest an ecological and evolutionary perspective in which learning is a dynamic capability. Dynamic capability theory builds on behavioral ideas of adaptation and dynamic character of expectations and goals (ibid.).

2.4 *Relationship to evolutionary ideas of the firm (and strategy)*

The evolutionary theory of the firm goes back to (at least) Alfred Marshall's construction of the industry equilibrium, which combined a population of firms in disequilibrium with industry-level supply–demand equilibrium, frequently using biological analogies.[14] A representative firm is hypothesized to bridge the dynamic analysis of firm level and the static industry level; 'firms rise and fall,' Marshall said, 'but the representative firm remains always of the same size' (1925, p. 367).

Many ideas significant for the development of the evolutionary view were also introduced by Joseph Schumpeter. For instance, although the idea of rules-based or bounded rationality became associated with Simon (1955) and March and Simon (1958) (and then later embedded in Nelson and Winter, 1982), Schumpeter was early to recognize that bounded rationality is necessary for a theory of innovation and dynamics:

> The assumption that conduct is prompt and rational is in all cases a fiction. But it proves to be sufficiently near to reality, if things have time to hammer logic into men. Where this has happened, and within the limits in which it has happened, one may rest content with this fiction and build theories . . . Outside of these limits our fiction loses its closeness to reality. To cling to it there also as traditional theory does, is to hide an essential thing and to ignore a fact which, in contrast with other deviations of our assumption from reality, is theoretically important and the source of the explanation of phenomena which would not exist without it. (Schumpeter, 1934, p. 80)

Evolutionary ideas also surfaced during the profit maximization debate in economics involving Fritz Machlup, Milton Friedman (1953), Armen Alchian (1950, 1953) and Edith Penrose (1952, 1953). The debate (concerning, among other things, the role of intentionality in economic selection and the use of a population of heterogeneous firms as a basis for selection) led to the formal evolutionary work by Winter (1964, 1971, 1975).[15]

Despite these prominent predecessors, an evolutionary view of the firm was not developed until decades later. In what was first intended to be entitled 'a Neo Schumpeterian Theory of the Firm', Nelson and Winter (1982) integrated insights from Schumpeter with ideas from Armen Alchain, Friedrich Hayek and Cyert and March (1963).[16]

The firm in their view is seen as a profit-seeking entity whose primary activities are to build (through organizational learning processes) and exploit valuable knowledge assets. Firms in this view also come with 'routines' or 'competencies', which are recurrent patterns of action which may change through search and learning. Routines will seldom be 'optimal' and will differ among agents and behaviors cannot be deduced from simply observing the environmental signals (such as prices) that agents are exposed to. This variety drives the evolutionary process since firms articulate rent-seeking strategies on the basis of their routines and competencies and competition in the product market constitutes an important part of the selection environment of confronting firms.

In order to fully understand these (and related) issues and their implications for theories of the firm and strategic management, scholars have appealed to the idea of firms as knowledge-bearing and learning entities; and a notion of the firm as endogenously creating its productive opportunity set. This line of thought was provided by Edith Penrose (1959), who was the first to argue that the firm is a repository of capabilities and knowledge and that learning is central to firm growth, and to provide a theory of firms that explicitly makes room for issues relating to the production and exploitation of productive knowledge. Productive knowledge is often related to other organizational (material) assets.[17] The firm, she said, is 'both an administrative organization and a collection of productive resources, both human and material' (ibid., p. 320). The services rendered by these resources are the primary inputs into a firm's production processes and are firm-specific in the sense that they are a function of the knowledge and experience that the firm has acquired over time. When services that are currently going unused are applied to new lines of business, these services also function as a growth engine for the firm. Learning enables the organization to use its resources more efficiently. As a result, even firms that maintain a constant level of capital may nevertheless be able to grow as services are freed for new uses as a result of organizational learning.[18]

3 The evolving dynamics of organizational capabilities

Because firms face strategic decisions on the basis of past history, it is natural to view questions relating to the development of strategy and competences in an evolutionary setting (Simon, 1993; Winter, 2000). The most recent chapter in the history of competencies and capabilities is the dynamic capabilities approach, which seeks to provide a coherent (and evolutionary) framework, which can both integrate existing conceptual and empirical knowledge and facilitate prescription. First outlined in Teece and Pisano (1994) and elaborated in Teece *et al.* (1997), a paper which had circulated for seven years as a working paper,[19] the dynamic capabilities approach builds upon the theoretical foundations provided by Schumpeter (1934), Penrose (1959), Williamson (1975, 1985), Cyert and March (1963), Rumelt (1984), Nelson and Winter (1982), Teece (1982) and Teece *et al.* (1997). In particular, it is consistent with the Schumpeterian view that the emergence of new products and processes results from new combinations of knowledge. In a similar vein, it is argued in the dynamic capabilities approach that competitive success arises from the continuous development and reconfiguration of firm-specific assets (Teece and Pisano, 1994; Teece *et al.*, 1997). Whereas Penrose and the resource-based scholars recognize the competitive importance of firm-specific capabilities, researchers of the dynamic capabilities approach attempt to outline specifically how organizations develop and renew internal competencies. Thus, the latter approach is concerned with a subset of a firm's overall capabilities, namely, those that allow firms to create new knowledge and to disseminate it throughout the organization.

The dynamic capability perspective follows Hayek (1945) (and the behavioral and evolutionary theorists) in emphasizing that coordination as an economic problem only occurs because of change. In a static environment a short period of 'set up' would be required to organize economic activity; but absent change in consumer tastes or technology, economic agents (both traders and managers) would sort out the optimal flows of goods and services (together with methods of production). Thereafter, there would be no need for their services.

Now introduce change. If there were a complete set of forward and contingent claims markets, adjustments would occur automatically; absent a complete set of futures and contingent claims markets, there is the need for economic agents to engage in trading activities, and for managers/entrepreneurs to 'integrate, build, and reconfigure internal and external competences to address rapidly changing environments' (Teece *et al.*, 1997). Coordinating and adapting effectively to changing environments (Cyert and March, 1963) is an element of a firm's dynamic capabilities. Barnard (1938) and Richardson (1960) were early to develop these themes.

Chester Barnard's view of the firm was that it was fundamentally a structure to achieve coordination and adaptation. But as Williamson (1990) observes, Barnard did not compare the firm to markets in terms of their coordinative or adaptive capabilities. One key difference is that the firm achieves coordination and adaptation with respect to non-traded or thinly traded assets; the market on the other hand enables rapid adaptation with respect to assets which are actively traded in thick markets (Teece, 2006).

However, dynamic capabilities involve much more than 'coordination' and 'adaptation', and the functions of the (strategic) manager go beyond what Barnard and Williamson have identified. In particular, coordination and adaptation do not convey very well notions such as proactive search, selection and subsequent implementation of particular courses of action critical to firms' business strategies. Nor do they convey the importance of asset alignment, opportunity identification, and access to critical cospecialized assets. These are all critical elements of management's dynamic capabilities, and are important to value creation.

Put another way, the need for firms to have dynamic capabilities stems from what can be thought of as 'market failures'.[20] The 'market failure' at issue is not due just to high transaction costs and contractual incompleteness.[21] Rather, it is associated with the non-existence of certain markets and the need to identify, align, adapt, and coordinate activities and assets, especially complementary assets.

Complementarities frequently exist amongst assets used in the firm, and frequently exist with assets outside the firm. These complementarities are easy to manage when markets are thick, as standard purchase and sale agreements or term contacts ought to suffice. But when markets are thin, or non-existent, alignment is not necessarily achieved by trades. It is the job of the (strategic) manager to decide what investments are to be made and what assets are to be purchased and how complementarities are to be achieved. Inside the firm, the strategy manager can ensure that new task boundaries are created and existing ones ignored. Under guidance from the strategy manager, the ability of (complementary) asset owners to block innovation can be eliminated through acquisition, or worked around through additional investment.

G.B. Richardson (1960) has remarked upon the information problems associated with achieving coordination and investment decisions. However, his focus is on industry-level coordination of investment. He identified situations where limited information about competitors' investment decisions may impede efficient investment. This is not the focus here. The essential coordination task identified in the dynamic capabilities framework is internal to the firm, though it may well involve strategic alliances with other firms too.

Needless to say, the proficient achievement of the necessary coordination is by no means assured inside the firm. Decision makers need information on changing consumer needs and technology. Such information is not always available or, if it is available, is likely to be incomplete, or highly subjective (Casson, 2000, p. 119; Simon, 1993). Managers are of course decision makers and they must collect information, analyze it, synthesize it, and act upon it inside the firm. Situations are dealt with in many ways, sometimes by creating rules, which specify how the organization will respond to the observations made (March and Simon, 1958). If this path is chosen, then rules may become codified and routinely applied (Casson, 2000, p. 129) whenever certain changes are detected.[22] However, such rules need to be periodically revised for the firm to have dynamic capabilities.

In some circumstances, new information and new situations may be best dealt with by forming a new firm (Knight, 1921).[23] Those who discover the new information, and can figure out the appropriate response, need not be the same individual(s) who start a new enterprise; but given the absence of a well functioning market for information about new market opportunities, the discoverer and the enterprise founder may need to be one and the same.

The coordinating and resource allocating capabilities featured in dynamic capabilities shape markets, as much as markets shape firms (Chandler, 1990; Teece, 1993; Simon, 1991). Put simply, firms and markets coevolve. Hence, while the need for asset coordination and orchestration and associated investment choices may be the fundamental problem which the firm's dynamic capabilities help address, the firm's dynamic capabilities – particularly its ability to introduce new products and services into the market – not only shapes markets; it also requires firm-level responses by competitors, suppliers, and sometimes customers.

The emergence/development of markets is thus important for strategic management. Elsewhere (Teece,1998) the emergence of intermediate product markets was identified as a major leveler in competition, enabling more specialist firms to compete and provide a limited kind of innovation, called 'autonomous innovation'. There are parts of the value chain which ought to be outsourced when well functioning intermediate (product) markets exist.[24]

4   Research agenda implications

'Competencies' and 'capabilities' are seductive concepts. They are significant parts of many modern theories of organization and strategic management; yet there is considerable confusion about the precise nature of the concepts (Dosi *et al.*, 2000). Recent contributions have clarified the key ideas somewhat (Winter, 2003; Eisenhardt and Martin, 2000; Teece, 2006). The full implications for a research agenda are still to be explored; however, we can outline at least the following important implications for research theory of the firm and strategic management; and for issues relating to entrepreneurship/leadership.

4.1   Strategic management and the theory of the firm

Ronald Coase was well aware that economists have neglected the role of management in the theory of the firm when he noted that 'economists have tended to neglect the main activity of the firm, running a business' (1988, p. 38). There is no role for the manager in the economic theory of the firm. Although Williamson claims that the role of management is 'significant' in transaction cost economics (1999, p. 1101), his support for the assertion makes reference to the emphasis in transaction cost economics on the adaptive properties of organization, and recognition that management can exercise 'fiat'. This is clearly inadequate. In the dynamic capabilities framework, management plays distinctive roles in selecting and/or developing routines, making investment choices, and in orchestrating non-tradable assets. This is a more robust role for management than transaction cost economics has so far afforded.

But whatever differences may exist in transaction cost economics with respect to the role of the manager, they pale next to models of the neoclassical firm in economics where managers and the management function have been blotted out.[25] As Baumol puts it:

> Obviously, the entrepreneur has been read out of the model. There is no room for enterprise or initiative. The management group becomes a passive calculator that reacts mechanically to changes imposed on it by fortuitous external developments over which it does not exert, and does not even attempt to exert, any influence. One hears of no clever ruses, ingenious schemes, brilliant innovations, of no charisma or of any of the other stuff of which outstanding entrepreneurship is made; one does not hear of them because there is no way in which they can fit into the model. (Baumol, 1968, p. 67)

Winter, as well as Teece (1984) likewise observed that entrepreneurship had been suppressed in the theory of the firm. Serious questions are raised with respect to the value of neoclassical models in management theory, management education, and, by implication, management practice.

4.2   Strategic management and entrepreneur- (and leader-)ship

It is important to understand the role of management in the dynamic capabilities framework advanced above. If, as Winter (2003) and others suggest, dynamic capabilities are defined mainly around high-level routines, perhaps the role of (strategic) management is reduced and relegated to selecting new routines. Certainly, if innovation becomes truly a routine in large firms, then the manager/intrapreneur has a modest role to play after the routines are in place. The framework presented above suggests a bigger role because it also references asset selection and asset orchestration as a part of dynamic capabilities.

In an economic system, principals and/or their agents must design and implement processes to manage change, must direct the reinvestment of cash flow, and must configure asset portfolios, including allocating resources between exploitation and exploration (March, 1991, 1994). They must also stand ready to reconfigure them as circumstances change. In a strict evolutionary view of the world, there is no specific agent and no hierarchy responsible for regulating the evolutionary process (Cohendet *et al.*, 2000).

However, in a less evolutionary view of the world, there is room for a managerial and entrepreneurial function. The manager/entrepreneur need not be an individual; in the modern corporation it is a function. As Schumpeter (1949) noted: 'The entrepreneurial function may be and often is filled cooperatively – in many cases, therefore, it is difficult or even impossible to name an individual that acts as "the entrepreneur"' (pp. 71–2).

The manager/entrepreneur must articulate goals, set culture, build trust, and play a critical role in the key strategic decisions. Clearly the role of the entrepreneur and the manager overlap to a considerable extent. As Simon (1991) recognized:

> Especially in the case of new or expanding firms, the entrepreneur does not face an abstract capital market. He or she exerts much effort to induce potential investors to share the company's views (often optimistic) about its prospects. This executive is much closer to Schumpeter's entrepreneur than to the entrepreneur of current neoclassical theory. Whether the firm expands or contracts is determined not just by how its customers respond to it, but by how insightful, sanguine and energetic its owners and managers are about its opportunities. (p. 31)

The manager/entrepreneur plays a key role in achieving asset selection and the 'coordination' of economic activity, particularly when complementary assets must be assembled. The manager/entrepreneur can bargain and negotiate and buy or sell or swap investments/assets, orchestrate internal assets (intrapreneurship) and transact with the owners of external assets (entrepreneurship). He is likely to have strong skills in working out new 'business models', which define the architecture of new businesses (Chesbrough and Rosenbloom, 2002). The astute performance of this function will help achieve what Porter (1996) calls 'strategic fit', not just with internally controlled assets, but with the assets of alliance partners.[26] The manager/entrepreneur can also shape learning processes with the firm. These are not functions which can be achieved by markets divorced from managers/entrepreneurs.

Thus the entrepreneur/manager function in the dynamic capabilities framework is in part Schumpeterian (the entrepreneur introduces novelty and seeks new combinations) and in part evolutionary (the entrepreneur endeavors to promote and shape learning). Whether intrapreneur or entrepreneur, the function senses new opportunities and leads the organization forward to seize them. The entrepreneur/manager must therefore lead. These are roles not recognized by economic theory; but these roles are the essence of dynamic capabilities and are critical to the theory of strategic management.

5 Conclusion

Several decades with evolutionary theory has brought shifting focus on several fronts. Not only have areas such as economics, management and strategy become enriched with evolutionary ideas, but also concepts such as routines, competencies, capabilities and learning rose from neglected subfields to attain near parity with old concepts of organization and management theory; and ideas on competences and capabilities have begun to emerge as viable complements not only of neoclassical economics, but also much of transaction cost theory (Dosi, 2004). Most of this new discussion takes place within the analytical framework of evolutionary (and neo-Schumpeterian) theory, broadly speaking.

Such a framework invites research on entrepreneurship, organizational learning and the role of the manager/leader of the firm. The dynamic capability view sets off from several evolutionary ideas and sees the firm as an incubator and repository for difficult to replicate assets; and technological and knowledge assets are central. Distinctive processes support the creation, protection, and augmentation of firm-specific assets and competences. These assets and competences reflect both individual skills and experiences as well as distinctive ways of doing things inside firms. To the extent that such assets and competences are difficult to imitate and are effectively deployed and redeployed in the marketplace (reflecting dynamic capabilities), they can provide the foundations for competitive advantage.

Dynamic capability was intended in the beginning as a set of ideas around flexibility, adaptability, integration, disintegration, etc. Increasing focus on changing knowledge assets, technology, etc. has spurred increasing focus on organizational change and how environments and histories of business firms shape organizational forms, practices and competencies. As a result, the dynamic capability perspective seeks to explore how changes in the world are likely to result in changes in business firms, and how organizations can improve and survive by developing and positioning dynamic capabilities.

The dynamic capability perspective is still developing; we may even see it as 'pre-paradigmatic', in Thomas Kuhn's terminology. As a theoretical perspective, the dynamic capability framework offers an integrative methodology and perspective in which several theoretical traditions are used as tools for analyzing the dynamics of business organizations. Understanding and utilizing ideas from different traditions – transaction cost theory, evolutionary economics and behavioral theory – provides a unique intellectual platform for dynamic capabilities. Such an integrative approach is also consistent with Schumpter's view on using theories from the past as well as from the present to analyze economic growth and change:

> The time may have come . . . to co-ordinate and to organize [different past the-oretical traditions] work by means of comprehensive 'programs' and to provide, for the use of the individual research worker, orderly schemata of possible prob-lems. It is here, and in its instrumental capacity, not as a master but as a servant of historical research, that theory may prove useful. (Schumpeter, 1947, p. 9)

The future relevance of competences and capabilities within strategic man-agement will depend on whether future developments in the field will bring us closer to an empirically relevant paradigm, which can accommodate and address issues relating to the dynamics of the business enterprise. This in turn will depend on the ability of the scholars and ideas within strategic management to work together and for the research program to accommo-date an interdisciplinary vision, and to be disciplined (March, 1996). Such an interdisciplinary, yet disciplined vision is the first step toward realizing a coherent program in strategic management; and we may see the dynamic capability program as taking the first important steps toward establishing a coherent and rigorous research program in strategic management. By integrating ideas from other traditions, the dynamic capability program sets a research agenda for future studies in strategic management. Future areas of research include (but are not limited to) the nature of the firm, strategic management and entrepreneurship and leadership.

Notes

1. Comments from and discussions with Giovanni Dosi, James March and Sid Winter are gratefully acknowledged; as is the skillful assistance of Patricia Lonergan in completing this contribution.
2. Although the idea and terminology of organizations as bundles of competencies dates back to Oskar Morgenstern (1951), the more well known originator of the term was Philip Selznick (1957). Selznick introduced the idea of a firm's 'distinctive competence'; and Prahalad and Hamel (1990) popularized the idea of the 'core competencies' of the organization. For a discussion of some of these developments, see Dosi *et al.*, (2000).
3. Richardson (1972) relied on Edith Penrose's (1959) idea of the firm as a collection of resources yielding various productive services. As Richardson (1972, p. 888) noted: 'It is convenient to think of industry as carrying out an indefinitely large number of activities, activities related to the discovery and estimation of future wants, to research, develop-ment, and design, to the execution and co-ordination of processes of physical transfor-mation, the marketing of goods, and so on. And we have to recognize that these activities have to be carried out by organizations with appropriate capabilities, or, in other words, with appropriate knowledge, experience, and skills.'
4. For a history of the field of strategy in general, see Rumelt *et al.*, (1994). The present chapter focuses more narrowly on the history of (dynamic) capabilities and competen-cies within strategic management. More specific discussions of the nature of dynamic capabilities are found in Winter (2003) and Teece (2006).
5. Many writers have pointed to Schumpeter's ideas of 'creative destruction' underlying the modern emphasis on technological change. However, it is worth noting that Schumpeter

did not reserve the term for just technological change; for him, it was useful for analyzing many areas of the economy. As he noted: 'This concept covers the following five cases: (1) The introduction of a new good – that is one with which consumers are not yet familiar – or of a new quality of a good. (2) The introduction of a new method of production, that is one not yet tested by experience in the branch of manufacture concerned, which need by no means be founded upon a discovery scientifically new, and can also exist in a new way of handling a commodity commercially. (3) The opening of a new market, that is a market into which the particular branch of manufacture of the country in question has not previously entered, whether or not this market has existed before. (4) The conquest of a new source of supply of raw materials or half-manufactured goods, again irrespective of whether this source already exists or whether it has first to be created. (5) The carrying out of the new organization of any industry, like the creation of a monopoly position (for example through trustification) or the breaking up of a monopoly position' (Schumpeter, 1934, p. 66).

6. For the particulars on the specific nature of different types of dynamic capabilities, see Teece (2006).

7. Parts of this section draw on Teece (2006).

8. The link between transaction cost economics and strategy was present already when Williamson (1975) demonstrated the relevance of transaction cost ideas to issues of corporate strategy (such as efficient firm boundaries); and the Chandler–Williamson M-form hypothesis quickly became a key insight in the strategic management field, in particular after being supported by a number of empirical studies, beginning with Armour and Teece (1978).

9. The way in which governance (choice of firm boundary) issues do come into play in strategic management is well illustrated in Teece (1986), where there is extensive discussion of complementary assets and whether or not these should be internalized. Deciding whether to 'own' or 'rent' (i.e. integrate or outsource) complementary assets depends on whether the assets were available in competitive supply. A concern to focus on is the distribution of gains (and losses) between the innovator and the owners of the complementary assets. Williamson also explores appropriability through ex post recontracting. However, the appropriability issues of most concern to business managers do not come from a pure form of what Williamson calls 'the fundamental transformation'. With this transformation, an ex ante large numbers bargaining situation is transformed into a small numbers situation after idiosyncratic irreversible investment assets are deployed, and recontracting hazards result. Rather, it is simply that technological innovation changes the demand for certain inputs (resources) and their complements. The entity that can cleverly bargain to obtain a 'long' position in those assets on favorable terms will be able to appropriate a greater share of the gains from innovation. Put differently, in Teece (1986), it is asset selection based on value creation that shapes firm boundary selection issues – not just the minimization of transaction costs.

10. For instance, Langlois (1992) highlights the case of the diesel electric locomotive, where in the 1920s, Charles Kettering had developed advanced lightweight diesel technology at the GM Labs. The earliest use was in submarines. Alfred P. Sloan, GM's Chairman, saw the possibility of applying the technology to make diesel electric locomotives. (Steam power was, at the time, completely dominant.) GM needed capabilities resident in the locomotive manufacturers, and at Westinghouse Electric. As Langlois notes: 'The three sets of capabilities might have been combined by some kind of contract or joint venture. But the steam manufacturers – Alco, Baldwin, and Lima – failed to cooperate. This was not, however, because they feared hold-up in the face of highly specific assets. Rather, it was because they actively denied the desirability of the diesel and fought its introduction at every step. General Motors was forced to create its own capabilities in locomotive manufacture' (p. 115).

11. For other relevant and informative – although perhaps a bit more skeptical – discussions of the complementarity between transaction cost theory and capability ideas, see Dosi and Marengo (2000) and Dosi (2004).

12. Various studies have now shown that competences/cospecialization also play a role in the make or buy decision (Walker and Weber, 1984; Jacobides and Hitt, 2001).
13. Within this framework, four concepts were developed. The first is the quasi-resolution of conflict, the idea that firms function with considerable latent conflict of interests but do not necessarily resolve that conflict explicitly. The second is uncertainty avoidance. Although firms try to anticipate an unpredictable future insofar as they can, they also try to restructure their worlds in order to minimize their dependence on anticipation of the highly uncertain future. The third concept is problemistic search, the idea that search within a firm is stimulated primarily by problems and directed to solving those problems. The fourth concept is organizational learning. The theory assumes that firms learn from their own experiences and the experiences of others.
14. As Marshall explains in his 'Principles': 'we may read a lesson from the young trees in the forest as they struggle upwards through the benumbing shade of their older rivals. Many succumb on the way, and a few only survive; those few become stronger with every year, they get a larger share of light and air with every increase of their height, and at last in their turn they tower above their neighbors. One tree will last longer in full vigor and attain a greater size than another; but sooner or later age tells on them all. And as with the growth of trees, so was it with the growth of business as a general rule before the great recent development of vast joint-stock companies, which often stagnate, but do not readily die' (Marshall, 1925, pp. 315–16). For excellent discussions of Marshall's evolutionary ideas, see the work of Brian Loasby (1976, 1989).
15. In contrast to the position of Friedman and others, evolutionary theory emphasizes that selection does *not* always lead to efficient outcomes because firms operate in a context or environment of other firms. 'In fact,' Nelson and Winter write, 'there is good reason to expect the opposite, since selection forces may be expected to be "sensible" and to trade off maladaptation under unusual or unencountered conditions to achieve good adaptations to conditions frequently encountered. In a context of progressive change, therefore, one should not expect to observe ideal adaptation to current conditions by the products of evolutionary change' (1982, p. 154).
16. The title, 'Towards a Neoschumpeterian Theory of the Firm' was the title of Winter's first working paper, written at the RAND Corporation (Winter, 1968), which became the main basis of the Nelson and Winter collaboration, leading to Nelson and Winter (1982).
17. As Penrose writes: 'For physical resources the range of services inherent in any given resource depends on the physical characteristics of the resource, and it is probably safe to assume that at any given time the known productive services inherent in a resource do not exhaust the full potential of the resource . . . The possibilities of using services change with changes in knowledge . . . there is a close connection between the type of knowledge possessed by the personnel in the firm and the services obtainable from its material resources' (1959, p. 76).
18. Teece's paper on the multiproduct firm (Teece, 1982) was the first to apply Penrose's ideas to strategic management issues. He focused on her observation that human capital in firms is usually not entirely 'specialized' and can therefore be (re)deployed to allow the firm's diversification into new products and services. He also used Penrose's view that firms possess excess resources which can be used for diversification. Later, Wernerfelt (1984) cites Penrose for 'the idea of looking at firms as a broader set of resources . . . [and] the optimal growth of the firm involves a balance between exploitation of existing resources and development of new ones'.
19. This explains why references to dynamic capabilities began before the publication of this paper. In the early to mid-1990s, the working paper versions were quoted. See for instance Mahoney and Pandian (1992).
20. The use of the term 'market failure' is only relative to the theoretical norm of absolute static and dynamic efficiency. Of course, a (private) enterprise economic system as a whole achieves an efficient allocation of resources, as strategic managers and the organization they lead are an inherent part of the economic system. However, the framework does highlight the fact that management systems and corporate governance must function well for a private enterprise market-oriented system to function well.

21. To the extent that transaction costs are relevant, it is of the dynamic variety (see Langlois, 1992).
22. Casson argues that rule making is entrepreneurial, but that rule implementation is routine, and is characterized by managerial and administrative work.
23. Frank Knight was (probably) the first to argue a distinct entrepreneurial theory of the firm (Langlois and Cosgel, 1993). In particular, Knight thought of entrepreneurs as possessing different judgments (and different capacities for judgments) and acting upon (and profiting from) genuine uncertainty and unpredictability: 'it is true uncertainty which by preventing the theoretically perfect outworking of the tendencies of competition gives the characteristic form of "enterprise" to economic organization as a whole and accounts for the peculiar income of the entrepreneur' (Knight, 1921, p. 232).
24. The creation of intermediate markets is not readily explained by asset specificity concerns, as implied by transaction cost economics. The absence of standards, or simply the decisions by incumbent firms to size production so as to avoid the need to sell intermediate products are possible explanations for the enigma of markets for intermediate inputs.
25. Consider the nature of the model of the firm. In its simplest form, the theoretical firm must choose among alternative values for a small number of well-defined variables; price, output, perhaps advertising outlay. In making this choice management is taken to consider the costs and revenues associated with each candidate set of values, as described by the relevant functional relationships, equations, and inequalities. Explicitly or implicitly the firm is then taken to perform a mathematical calculation which yields optimal (i.e., profit-maximizing) values for all of its decision variables and it is these values which the theory assumes to be chosen, which are taken to constitute the business decision. There matters rest, forever or until exogenous forces lead to an autonomous change in the environment. Until there is such a shift in one of the relationships that define the problem, the firm is taken to replicate precisely its previous decisions, day after day, year after year.
26. As Porter (1996) notes, 'strategic fit among many activities is fundamental not only to competitive advantage but also to sustainability of that advantage. It is harder for a rival to match an array of interlocked activities than it is merely to imitate a particular sales force approach, match a process technology, or replicate a set of product features.' (p. 73), [and] 'when activities complement each other, rivals will get very little benefit from imitation unless they successfully match the whole system – frequent shifts in positioning are costly – strategy is creating a fit among a company's activities. The success of strategy depends on doing many things well – not just a few in an integrating among them. If there is not fit among activities, there is no distinctive strategy and little sustainability' (p. 77).

References

Alchian, A. (1950), Uncertainty, evolution, and economic theory, *Journal of Political Economy*, **58**, 211–22.
Alchian, A. (1953), Biological analogies in the theory of the firm: comment, *American Economic Review*, **43**(4), 600–603.
Armour, H. and D.J. Teece (1978), Organizational structure and economic performance: a test of the multidivisional hypothesis, *The Bell Journal of Economics*, **9**(2), 106–22.
Barnard, C. (1938), *The Functions of the Executive*, Harvard University Press.
Barney, J. (1991), Firm resources and sustained competitive advantage, *Journal of Management*, **17**(1), 99–120.
Baumol, W. (1968), Entrepreneurship in economic theory, *American Economic Review*, **58**(2), 64–71.
Casson, M. (2000), An entrepreneurial theory of the firm, in N. Foss and V. Mahnke (eds), *Competence, Governance, and Entrepreneurship*, Oxford University Press.
Chandler, A.D. (1990), *Scale and Scope*, Belknap Press.

Chesbrough, H.W. and R.S. Rosenbloom (2002), The role of the business model in capturing value from innovation: evidence from Xerox Corporation's technology, *Industrial and Corporate Change*, **11**(3), 529–55.

Coase, R.H. (1988), The nature of the firm: origin, meaning, influence, *Journal of Law, Economics, and Organization*, **4**(1), 3–47.

Cohendet, P., P. Llerena and L. Marengo (2000), Is there a pilot in the evolutionary firm?, in N. Foss and V. Mahnke (eds), *Competence, Governance, and Entrepreneurship*, Oxford University Press.

Collis, D.J. (1994), Research note: how valuable are organisational capabilities?, *Strategic Management Journal*, **15**, 143–52.

Cyert, R. and J.G. March (1963), *A Behavioral Theory of the Firm*, Prentice-Hall.

Dosi, G. (1988), Sources, procedures and microeconomic effects of innovation, *Journal of Economic Literature*, **26**, 1120–70.

Dosi, G. (2004), A very reasonable objective still beyond our reach: economics as an empirically disciplined social science, *Models of a Man: Essays in Memory of Herbert A. Simon*, MIT Press.

Dosi, G. and L. Marengo (2000), The tangled discourse between transaction cost economics and competence-based views of the firm, in N. Foss and V. Mahnke (eds), *Competence, Governance, and Entrepreneurship*, Oxford University Press.

Dosi, G., R.R. Nelson and S.G. Winter (2000), Introduction, in G. Dosi, R.R. Nelson and S.G. Winter (eds), *The Nature and Dynamics of Organizational Capabilities*, Oxford University Press.

Eisenhardt, K. and J.A. Martin (2000), Dynamic capabilities: what are they?, *Strategic Management Journal*, **21**, 1105–22.

Friedman, M. (1953), The methodology of positive economics, *Essays in Positive Economics*, University of Chicago Press.

Hayek, F.A. (1945), The use of knowledge in society, *Individualism and Economic Order*, University of Chicago Press.

Jacobides, M.G. and L.M. Hitt (2001), Vertical scope revisited: transaction costs versus capabilities and profit opportunities in mortgage banking, working paper 01-17, Financial Institution Center, Wharton School, University of Pennsylvania.

Knight, F. (1921), *Risk, Uncertainty and Profit*, Houghton Mifflin.

Langlois, R. (1992), Transactions-cost economics in real time, *Industrial and Corporate Change*, **1**(1), 99–127.

Langlois, R. and M. Cosgel (1993), Frank Knight on risk, uncertainty, and the firm, *Economic Inquiry*, **31**, 456–65.

Levinthal, D. and J.G. March (1993), The myopia of learning, *Strategic Management Journal*, **14**, 95–112.

Loasby, B. (1976), *Choice, Complexity and Ignorance*, Oxford University Press.

Loasby, B. (1989), *The Mind and Method of the Economist*, Edward Elgar.

Mahoney, J. and R. Pandian (1992), The resource-based view within the conversation of strategic management, *Strategic Management Journal*, **13**(5), 363–80.

March, J.G. (1991), Exploration and exploitation in organizational learning, *Organization Science*, **2**, 71–87.

March, J.G. (1994), *A Primer on Decision Making*, Free Press.

March, J.G. (1996), A scholar's quest, *Stanford Graduate School of Business Magazine*.

March, J.G. and H.A. Simon (1958), *Organizations*, Wiley.

Marshall, A. (1925), *Principles of Economics*, Macmillan.

Monteverde, K. and D.J. Teece (1982), Supplier switching costs and vertical integration in the U.S. automobile industry, *The Bell Journal of Economics*, **13**(1), 206–13.

Morgenstern, O. (1951), Prolegomena to a theory of organization, *RAND Research Memorandum, RM 5438*, The RAND Corporation.

Nelson, R. and S.G. Winter (1982), *An Evolutionary Theory of Economic Change*, Belknap Press.

Penrose, E. (1952), Biological analogies in the theory of the firm, *American Economic Review*, **42**, 804–19.

Penrose, E. (1953), Biological analogies in the theory of the firm: rejoinder, *American Economic Review*, **43**(4), 603–9

Penrose, E. (1959), *The Theory of the Growth of the Firm*, Blackwell.
Porter, M. (1996), What is strategy?, *Harvard Business Review*, November–December.
Prahalad, C. and G. Hamel (1990), The core competence of the corporation, *Harvard Business Review*, May–June.
Richardson, G.B. (1960), *Information and Investment*, Oxford University Press.
Richardson, G.B. (1972), The organization of industry, *Economic Journal*, **82**(327), 883–96.
Rumelt, R. (1984), Towards a strategic theory of the firm, in R.B. Lamb (ed.), *Competitive Strategic Management*, Prentice-Hall.
Rumelt, R., D. Schendel and D.J. Teece (1994), Introduction, *Fundamental Issues in Strategy*, Harvard Business School Press.
Schumpeter, J. (1934), *The Theory of Economic Development*, Harvard University Press.
Schumpter, J. (1947), Theoretical problems of economic growth, *Journal of Economic History*, **7**, 1–9.
Schumpeter, J. (1949), Economic theory and entrepreneurial history, in Harvard University Research Center in Entrepreneurial History (ed.), *Change and the Entrepreneur*, Harvard University Press, pp. 63–84.
Selznick, P. (1957), *Leadership in Administration: A Sociological Interpretation*, Harper and Row.
Simon, H.A. (1955), A behavioral model of rational choice, *Quarterly Journal of Economics*, **69**, 99–118.
Simon, H.A. (1991), Organizations and markets, *Journal of Economic Perspectives*, **5**, 25–44.
Simon, H.A. (1993), Strategy and organizational evolution, *Strategic Management Journal*, **14**, 131–42.
Teece, D.J. (1982), Towards an economic theory of the multiproduct firm, *Journal of Economic Behavior and Organization*, **3**, 39–63.
Teece, D.J. (1984), Economic analysis and strategic management, *California Management Review*, **26**(3), 87–110.
Teece, D.J. (1986), Profiting from technological innovation, *Research Policy*, **15**(6), 285–305.
Teece, D.J. (1990), Contributions and impediments of economic analysis to the study of strategic management, in J. Frederickson (ed.), *Perspectives on Strategic Management*, Harper Business.
Teece, D.J. (1993), The dynamics of industrial capitalism: perspectives on Alfred Chandler's *Scale and Scope*, *Journal of Economic Literature*, **31**, 199–225.
Teece, D.J. (1998), Capturing value from knowledge assets: the new economy, market for know how, and intangible assets, *California Management Review*, **40**(3), 55–79.
Teece, D.J. (2006), Explicating dynamic capabilities, working paper.
Teece, D.J. and G. Pisano (1994), The dynamic capabilities of firms: an introduction, *Industrial and Corporate Change*, **3**(3), 537–56.
Teece, D.J. and S.G. Winter (1984), The limits of neoclassical theory in management education, *American Economic Review*, **74**(2), 116–21.
Teece D.J., L. Pearce and C. Boerner (2002), Dynamic capabilities, competence, and the behavioral theory of the firm, in M. Augier and J.G. March (eds), *The Economics of Choice, Change and Organization: Essays in Honor of Richard M. Cyert*, Edward Elgar.
Teece, D.J., G. Pisano and A. Shuen (1997), Dynamic capabilities and strategic management, *Strategic Management Journal*, **18**(7), 509–33.
Walker, G. and D. Weber (1984), A transaction cost approach to make-or-buy decisions, *Administrative Science Quarterly*, **29**(3), 373–92.
Wernerfelt, B. (1984), A resource-based view of the firm, *Strategic Management Journal*, **5**, 171–80.
Williamson, O.E. (1975), *Markets and Hierarchies: Analysis and Antitrust Implications*, The Free Press.
Williamson, O.E. (1985), *The Economic Institutions of Capitalism*, The Free Press.
Williamson, O.E. (1990), Chester Barnard and the incipient science of organization, in O.E. Williamson (ed.), *Organization Theory: From Chester Barnard to the Present and Beyond*, Oxford University Press.
Williamson, O.E. (1999), Strategy research: governance and competence perspectives, *Strategic Management Journal*, **20**, 1087–1108.

Winter, S.G. (1964), Economic 'natural selection' and the theory of the firm, *Yale Economic Essays*, **4**(1), 225–72.

Winter, S.G. (1968), Towards a neo-Schumpterian theory of the firm, RAND Research Memorandum, The RAND Corporation.

Winter, S. (1971), Satisficing, selection and the innovating remnant, *Quarterly Journal of Economics*, **85**, 237–61.

Winter, S.G. (1975), Optimization and evolution in the theory of the firm, in R. Day and T. Groves (eds), *Adaptive Economic Models*, Academic Press.

Winter, S.G. (1988), On Coase, competence, and the corporation, *Journal of Law, Economics, and Organization*, **4**(1), 163–80.

Winter, S.G. (2000), The satisficing principle in capability learning, *Strategic Management Journal*, **21**, 981–96.

Winter, S. (2003), Understanding dynamic capabilities, *Strategic Management Journal*, **24**(10), 991–5.

Zollo, M. and S. Winter (2002), Deliberate learning and the evolution of dynamic capabilities, *Organizational Science*, **13**(3), 339–51.

18 Firm organization
Brian J. Loasby

In none of his writings on economic development does Schumpeter give explicit attention to the organization of firms. Although this is not yet among the leading topics in neo-Schumpeterian theory, it seems to be increasing in prominence, and to deal with it economists have either turned to other sources or created their own treatment, which is sometimes a re-creation of earlier work. It would therefore be misleading to represent neo-Schumpeterian analyses of firm organization as a direct filiation of Schumpeter's ideas. It is nevertheless possible to identify sufficient cues in Schumpeter's exposition to indicate coherence within the neo-Schumpeterian agenda.

Defining economic development as 'the carrying out of new combinations', Schumpeter (1934, p. 66) lists five cases: new goods, new methods of production, new markets, new sources of supply, and new organizations of industry. Now the concept of 'new combinations' implies the organization of ideas and activities, and that provides our theme: organization as a process, as a framework for this process, and as a structure of relationships and behaviour that result from it. Schumpeter himself immediately observes that new combinations are usually embodied in firms; but instead of considering how this is done he emphasizes that these are usually new firms which displace existing firms. Thus the disruptive character of capitalist enterprise crowds out the analysis of either the development or the structure of these new businesses. When he later gave a major role to innovation carried out within existing large-scale businesses he presented this revised view in the context of the stimulus to innovation from the ever-present threat of supersession (as with Marx), and so the organization of the innovative process within each firm was still submerged (Schumpeter, 1943).

Nor does Schumpeter consider in any detail the content of innovations. His fifth case, 'the carrying out of the new organization of any industry', must surely entail restructuring the firms within that industry, especially in his example of 'the creation of a monopoly position'; but firm organization as the subject of innovation, like firm organization as a means to innovation, remains unexamined. It is therefore no surprise that his third category, 'the opening of a new market', also receives no attention as an organizational process, although the creation or modification of market institutions is often necessary even when new markets are not the primary focus of innovation, and the creation or modification of market institutions typically requires an appropriate organization of the firms that contribute to this process. (The most spectacular example of the latter is the rise of supermarkets where, as the name implies, firms are themselves markets.) Thus by reading Schumpeter we may be made aware of the importance of firm organization as both the subject and the instrument of innovation, but we are also implicitly warned to look elsewhere for appropriate analyses of either.

Very similar conclusions may be drawn from Schumpeter's treatment of knowledge, uncertainty, and human cognition. His theoretical system is based on a sharp distinction between the circular flow of economic activity and the process of economic development, the former being assigned to Walras and the latter to himself. This has been very effective in designating a protected space for Schumpeterian economics, but at some cost in analytical coherence and the development of its research programme. The argument by which Schumpeter defines this protected space entails an immanent criticism of Walrasian reasoning, especially in its subsequent neo-Walrasian form which relies on the pure rationality of all agents: 'The assumption that conduct is prompt and rational is in all cases a fiction. But it proves to be sufficiently near to reality, if things have time to hammer logic into men. Where this has happened, and within the limits in which it has happened, one may rest content with this fiction and build theories upon it' (Schumpeter, 1934, p. 80). Schumpeter's argument anticipates Friedman's famous defence of equilibrium theorizing, and even implicitly relies on a (non-biological) evolutionary winnowing of inefficient behaviour. It may easily be extended to include Lionel Robbins's view that the organization of firms is of no interest to economists, because these selective forces ensure allocative efficiency; organization, like money, simply conceals the fundamentals, and so does an analytical focus on either.

Such reasoning implies that we need no theory to explain change; the economy adapts to any variation in circumstances. Schumpeter claimed that this was indeed Walras's view; and it is implicit in all equilibrium theories which ignore or trivialize the problems of equilibration, and which therefore can accommodate only the most exiguous theory of the firm. However, Schumpeter bases the distinctive role of the entrepreneur on the great difficulty of change; and in order to do so he must deny the sufficiency of assuming conduct to be prompt and rational. Indeed he declares that what actually sustains the coordinated activity of the circular flow is 'knowledge and habit . . . as firmly rooted in ourselves as a railway embankment in the earth' (ibid., p. 84). Moreover, like each railway embankment, the knowledge and habits of every individual and every group are adjusted to particular local circumstances; this is clear from Schumpeter's exposition though he does not draw explicit attention to it.

He even supplies a good economic argument for this reliance on 'automatic' behaviour rather than 'rationality' by drawing attention to the dramatic reduction in mental effort that results. Cognition is a resource which is very scarce in relation to its possible uses, and its allocation is therefore crucial.

Schumpeter does not observe that the treatment of cognition as a free good in standard economics installs a fundamental incoherence at its heart. For him, the significance of this means of economizing cognition is the triple barrier to entrepreneurship that it produces: the extraordinary effort required to work out a scheme of innovation, the need to escape from deeply embedded modes of thinking and acting, and the task of inducing many other people to make the changes that are necessary. (These are all problems of organization, cognitive or interpersonal.) That is why Schumpeter insists on the 'special quality' of entrepreneurship, and perhaps also why he emphasizes motives that do not appear in standard preference functions: founding a private kingdom, achieving conspicuous success, and the joy of creativity. This emphasis on the psychology of the entrepreneur matches the psychological obstacles to innovation; human agency is matched with context. Both take us beyond standard economics, for costless cognition leaves little room for psychology, or for entrepreneurship.

To the difficulties of entrepreneurship which result from the prevalence of routine (and the limited mental capacity which it economizes) Schumpeter adds the uncertainty that necessarily accompanies any venture beyond what is familiar. Even if 'new combinations' connect what already exists the entrepreneur is unlikely to have detailed knowledge of all these components, and even less likely to foresee all their interactions. But Schumpeter appears to evade the implications of uncertainty for the innovative process by asserting that 'the success of everything depends upon intuition, the capacity of seeing things in a way which afterwards proves to be true' (ibid., p. 85). Though this may serve as a retrospective account of successful entrepreneurship, it excludes entrepreneurial failure by definition; more importantly, it gives a misleading account of innovative processes, in which even successful outcomes typically differ from what was originally intended, and diverts attention from the role of organization in these processes. This is particularly important for the Schumpeter II version of innovation which emphasizes the role of the large firm.

We may accept Schumpeter's (1934, p. 85) assertion that 'one can give no particular account of the principles by which' the entrepreneurial vision is formulated; indeed, the impossibility of specifying any procedure for ensuring success is a necessary condition for entrepreneurship, as Frank Knight had pointed out between the original and revised versions of what became *The Theory of Economic Development*. We can go further by citing Chester

Barnard's (1938, p. 305) warning against 'imputing logical reasoning to men who could not or cannot base their actions on reasoning'. However, though we cannot provide any 'particular account' we can state some general psychological principles. There is a good deal of evidence that human beings are not particularly good natural logicians; and this is not surprising in evolutionary terms when we recognize (as Barnard pointed out) that a complete set of appropriate premises is rarely available. By contrast human beings are notably adept at imposing patterns on phenomena and developing patterns of actions which are well matched to these classification systems; these pattern-making capabilities seem to be inherent in the structure of the human brain, and their application to each person's environment is facilitated by the slow development of both mental and physical skills as that person grows to maturity.

Such developmental processes, which supplement genetic programming, explain the locally appropriate routine behaviours which are so essential to Schumpeter's analysis. A crucial exaptation of local individual pattern making is its extension from actual phenomena to ideas of phenomena not directly experienced; indeed precisely such a sequence was postulated by Alfred Marshall (Raffaelli, 2003). If we forgo any claims that conjectures about either actual or potential phenomena turn out to be correct, then we have a general account of the mental processes which may deliver ideas for 'new combinations': an account, moreover, which suggests ways in which such ideas may be encouraged, and even what sorts of ideas may tend to be encouraged in particular environments (for general-purpose entrepreneurship is as dubious a model as general-purpose problem solving). Among these environments, organizations deserve particular attention, for they too are systems for pattern making and economizing on cognition.

From this brief survey we may conclude that Schumpeter offers us important cues for improving our analyses of economic development. The first is that innovation rests on novel connections, a cue that links Schumpeter to Adam Smith (and especially to Smith's account of 'combining together the powers of the most distant and dissimilar objects'). The second is the role of organization in the development of any projected innovation; this links Schumpeter to Alfred Marshall's proposition that organization aids knowledge, and to Penrose's definition of a firm as a pool of resources within an administrative framework. The third cue, to the implications of human cognition, directs us to Herbert Simon's emphasis on the scarce resource of attention and the importance of predetermined decision premises in defining problems and the search for solutions. The dual role of automatic processes in Schumpeter's theory provides cues to Marshall, especially as interpreted by Raffaelli (2003), to Simon and to Nelson and Winter's focus on routines as the content as well as the context of innovation, which may itself be derived from Simon by way of Cyert and March (1963), and to Gigerenzer and Selten's (2001) exposition, also influenced by Simon, of domain-specific procedural rationality. All these ideas may also be related to Schumpeter's explanation of what actually supports a well-coordinated economy.

Thus there is a substantial body of thought about firm organization which is compatible with Schumpeter's general account and provides much of the detail which it lacks. It shows not only why organization matters for explaining economic development but how it matters; neither of these questions is answered by equilibrium growth theory. The organization of the brain makes the best of human cognitive powers by assigning most activities to domain-specific routines, thus allowing highly selective attention to the creation of new connections; and the application of these principles to the interpersonal organizations that we call firms matches human capabilities and makes innovation possible both within firms and through inter-firm relations.

In order to act intelligently, individuals must impose order and simplify decision making by decomposing systems into quasi-independent domains, developing routines which release cognitive resources for creativity: there may be too many degrees of freedom as well as too few. Adam Smith showed, first in explaining the development of science and then in explaining the growth of productivity, how specialization on particular problem areas or particular activities encourages the growth of domain-specific knowledge; and we now know how the structure of the human brain, and its potential for developing networks of connections, makes this possible. To take advantage of this potential it is necessary for people to differ in their areas of specialization, and also to develop ways in which the differentiated knowledge produced by these specialisms may be effectively integrated. Conceiving new ways of integrating knowledge is the entrepreneurial function; and though Schumpeter initially focuses on the entrepreneurial personality he recognizes that this function may be distributed across people, most obviously in the large corporation. The entrepreneurial corporation is itself a major example of a Schumpeterian 'new combination', and of particular importance because it is a device for generating further 'new combinations'. Chandler (1962, 1990) has analysed both.

Firms are differentiated clusters of internally differentiated knowledge and skill, appropriate to particular sets of activities, although the boundaries of these sets are always conjectural; in this ambiguity of scope lies both danger and the possibility of applications not yet thought of. They constitute epistemic communities which develop, interpret and apply 'knowledge that', and communities of practice which develop and apply 'knowledge how'. These communities may be thought of as systems which reduce transaction costs, if these are broadly defined to include all the costs of establishing a reliable basis for interacting, such as the costs of achieving compatability of interpretations and procedures (often more problematic than compatability of incentives) and assurance of the specific competence of those with whom one is dealing. These costs should be thought of as investments in social and organizational capital that constitute distinctive knowledge frameworks. Thus organization mitigates the limitations of individual cognition by the asymmetric distribution of knowledge; that this may cause some incentive problems reminds us that there are always opportunity costs. As Penrose so clearly explained, firms generate resources, and these provide reserves or options which may then be deployed in productive services to exploit opportunities which are imagined within the firm. Penrose (1959, p. 36) explicitly relates this sequence to Schumpeter's conception of the entrepreneur, who is however described as 'too dramatic a person for our purposes'; although distinguishing, like Schumpeter, between entrepreneurship and management, she notes, like Marshall, that managerial activities often suggest the basis for entrepreneurial conceptions.

The division of labour within each firm creates a distributed process of localized learning, which needs to be appropriately coordinated if it is to be effectively used; and since any system of coordination must itself respect the scarcity of cognitive resources, and the limited capacity of any individual for communicating and absorbing knowledge which has been developed within different contexts, the scope of any firm must also be restricted. Conventional attempts to produce a theoretical explanation of the firm focus on the boundaries that separate internal from market transactions; and bounded rationality is invoked only to generate incentive problems, at the expense of the logically prior issues of knowledge and attention. Especially, but not only, if the objective is to locate the firm within a theory of innovation, we need to look inside the firm, as Penrose insisted; but we also need to look at the connections between firms.

Organizational design prescribes where (and therefore how) problems are to be defined, who should deal with them by what processes and using what premises, and what kinds of solutions are likely to be acceptable; by embedding the assumptions which support domain-specific routines it shapes the generation of novelty and provides an internal selection environment. (The interaction between automaticity and creativity is crucial.) Thus different organizations tend to generate different outcomes. Simon envisaged organizational design as a problem of decomposition, and produced an evolutionary argument for believing that natural systems would usually be quite highly decomposable; this leads us to expect that people will develop locally-sufficient heuristics. However, active intervention by humans may violate natural decompositions, and the implicit assumptions of decomposability on which we rely mean that we may pay insufficient attention to this danger. Since we have no direct access to the full description of any real-world system, even if we have created it, there is no way of ensuring that a system is correctly defined before we attempt to decompose it; any decomposition that is manageable by humans must be coarser than the phenomena that it attempts to encompass.

Moreover, any organization has to cope with a range of problems which ideally require different decompositions; and so organizational design is always an option of difficulties, and may lead to the misspecification of problems and misattributions of causality. These fallacies of decomposition, though important, are a pathology of the imperfect specifications that are necessary for the functioning of any organization which is capable of dealing with uncertainty – and therefore of managing innovation. Insistence on strict conformity to definitions of responsibility and prescribed channels of communication, though economizing on cognition and formally appropriate within a system which is as fully specified as an Arrow–Debreu equilibrium, is likely to be very unhelpful, especially when trying to produce innovations or to respond to innovations that have been introduced by others. (This is an amplification of Schumpeter's proposition that the impact of change is predominantly disruptive.) Thus whatever the standard arrangements, there must be scope for alternatives, which themselves may have formal standing, for example in guidelines for the creation and management of project teams. Informal organization is an essential component of any evolving business, since new knowledge can be neither deduced nor prescribed. The foundational treatment is Burns and Stalker's (1961) empirically based analysis of mechanistic and organic systems.

These principles also apply to relationships between firms, where joint ventures serve as the counterpart to project teams as devices to deal with particular sets of problems while preserving the distinctive structures which are believed to be still appropriate to the major activities of each. The combination is likely to be difficult and costly, and so justifiable only by prospects of exceptional gains. New organizations are often more effective in promoting new combinations, but every innovation is carried by continuity, which an existing business can supply if the appropriate elements can be identified. Often the relevant continuity is provided by the movement of individuals or groups from established businesses to new enterprises, a pattern which can sometimes be kept within the corporate family by the sponsorship of quasi-independent new ventures.

As Knight observed, our classification systems are based on apparently relevant similarities while ignoring apparently irrelevant differences; but judgments of relevance, and especially of its boundaries, are conjectural.

Reclassification is an important trigger of innovation. The principle that related effort should be coordinated and unrelated effort segregated was once believed to imply organization by function; but experience with diversification eventually persuaded Du Pont's senior management that research, production and marketing were much more closely related within each of their increasingly distinctive product areas than were any of these functions across products. Richardson's distinction between similarity and complementarity as dimensions of relatedness helps to guide the application of this principle, though it is still necessary to investigate the kinds and degrees of similarity and complementarity, and to recognize that there will not always be a straightforward solution.

Contracts of employment include the right to give and the willingness to accept direction within some range. Knight argued that people are willing to accept direction in exchange for some protection from uncertainty, and this argument can be extended by recognizing that we can economize on cognition by gaining access to knowledge and skills developed through the division of labour between specialisms and by learning from others within one's own specialism. Both processes, which operate across as well as within hierarchies, and may be informal as well as formal, rely on the willingness to accept information, instructions, and goods from others without question, except in special circumstances. This implies an acknowledgment that other people know best in particular respects; and this psychological propensity seems to underlie Barnard's proposition that authority is accepted rather than imposed. Although in some cases there are strong pressures to accept, there are many ways of evading or undermining the power of command, even in military organizations; and successful businesses depend on cooperation which cannot be enforced.

Since the acceptance of authority, though potentially highly efficient, is also dangerous, there are good reasons to seek some assurance about the quality of what is being provided. Firms supply the regularity of contact which can provide the basis for such assessments, and for initial judgments on members of the firm not previously encountered. But similar considerations apply to dealings with other firms, and the establishment of a sound basis for assessment is an important reason for developing external linkages. Closely complementary but dissimilar activities provide the strongest example, where integration within a single business is ruled out by the absence of internal competence, including the competence to understand how to manage disparate activities within a single framework. Thus, even when specific assets are to be committed, access may be better than control. In general, analyses of firm organization should include external organization, formal and informal; this may extend to industrial districts or even to national systems of innovation.

An important consequence of inter-firm relationships is that the knowledge base of a firm may need to be significantly wider than is needed for its own production. Evidence from patenting shows that large technology-based companies conduct substantial research within the technological fields of their suppliers, and these activities are not reduced when suppliers are invited to take a larger share in design; it appears that, even if interfaces become more standardized, firms believe that they need to know a good deal about the possibilities open to their collaborators in order to manage their own programmes of innovation. The increasing importance of system integrators is accompanied by a similar disparity between the range of activities and the range of knowledge; and so the relationship between the distribution of knowledge and the currently fashionable principles of modularity and a clear focus on core competences is an attractive research area.

If organization provides structure for processes of economic development, then structures must be more stable than processes. However, organizational change is an important route to knowledge, which stimulates further organizational change (this is Marshall's and Young's principle of increasing return). This is a process of trial and error, for no-one can be certain what will turn out to be true; and so heterogeneity across firms is an important principle of neo-Schumpeterian economics. It is to be found in the organization of individual minds and in the organization of firms.

References

Barnard, C.I. (1938), *The Functions of the Executive*, Cambridge, MA: Harvard University Press.
Burns, T. and G.M. Stalker (1961), *The Management of Innovation*, London: Tavistock.
Chandler, A.D. (1962), *Strategy and Structure*, Cambridge, MA: MIT Press.
Chandler, A.D. (1990), *Scale and Scope*, Cambridge, MA: Belknap Press.
Cyert, R.M. and J.G. March (1963), *A Behavioral Theory of the Firm*, Englewood Cliffs, NJ: Prentice-Hall.
Gigerenzer, G. and R. Selten (eds) (2001), *Bounded Rationality: The Adaptive Toolbox*, Cambridge, MA: MIT Press.
Penrose, E.T. (1959), *The Theory of the Growth of the Firm*, Oxford: Basil Blackwell.
Raffaelli, T. (2003), *Marshall's Evolutionary Economics*, London: Routledge.
Schumpeter, J.A. (1934), *The Theory of Economic Development*, Cambridge, MA: Harvard University Press.
Schumpeter, J.A. (1943), *Capitalism, Socialism and Democracy*, London: Allen and Unwin.

19 The role of knowledge in the Schumpeterian economy
Ernst Helmstädter

He was quite the opposite of those celebrated scholars who rarely make an error and who instill in their best students an inferiority complex. Schumpeter's very imperfections gave hope and drive to his students. (Paul A. Samuelson, see Recktenwald, 1988:9)

Introductory remarks

In the first part of the chapter, I shall consider the Schumpeterian economy as it is reflected in Schumpeter's own writings over the several phases of more than four decades of his scientific activity. In other words, we are dealing with the – indeed undervalued – role of knowledge in Schumpeterian economics. In the second part, I shall proceed to a stylized Schumpeterian economy. Introducing knowledge into this model, I propose to start with Hayek's division of knowledge issue (1937, 1945) and to combine it with the methodology of New Institutional Economics (NIE), which has been directed to the division of labor. Using this setting, the knowledge issue seems to introduce itself into the Schumpeterian economy. The final part discusses further approaches to the introduction of knowledge into the evolutionary context. It will be shown that there are no obstacles to an integration of these perspectives under the 'knowledge sharing approach', as I call my own proposal (Helmstädter, 2003).

Since innovations play the main role in Schumpeter's world of the developing economy, it would be surprising if there should not be found a link to knowledge. As Schumpeter himself taught us, innovations, before they enter the economy, may go through an inventive phase. No question, *inventions* can be seen as a link between *new knowledge* and *innovations*. However, Schumpeter never literally spoke of economically useful knowledge in general! Instead, he wrote much about *scientific* knowledge, even about the knowledge of the economics discipline and about the methodological approach to be applied. But the knowledge that simply belongs to innovations did not seem of specific interest to him. Thus, the question arises as to how we may find a plausible connection between knowledge for innovation and the Schumpeterian innovative economy. Indeed, our task will be to establish such a connection under the auspices of the knowledge based economy we speak about today.

1   Looking for knowledge in Schumpeter's most important monographs

We shall now take a look at the five large monographs which constitute Schumpeter's literary legacy to our discipline. Our question will be: did the author tell us anything in his writings – from the first monograph, *Das Wesen und der Hauptinhalt der theoretischen Nationalökonomie* (1908), to the posthumously published *History of Economic Analysis* (1954) – about the role of innovations inducing knowledge? Obviously, we can only answer this question by giving an outline of the characteristic features during the quite different phases of his writings.

Wesen und Hauptinhalt deals with the state of affairs of our discipline, as the young author saw it at the beginning of the 20th century in Vienna. His main subject is directed towards Economics as 'eine in sich geschlossene autonome Provinz des Reichs des Wissens' (523; a closed autonomous province of the empire of knowledge, E.H.), in contrast to an exact discipline (524). His aim is to turn the traditionally overcome discipline into an exact system (527) in which one proceeds with exact thinking (563). That means giving up the widely applied psychologisms, and using mathematical reasoning and empirical research; furthermore, it requires us to leave behind the static notion of the economic model and to consider economic processes and developments, in other words, to introduce a so-called 'energetic' (621) approach as opposed to the traditional logical one or – in general – to consider a dynamic approach to economics.[1]

What Schumpeter announced at the end of his first monograph was presented by him four years later in *Die Theorie der wirtschaftlichen Entwicklung* (first German edition of 1912). It was a very successful book that has been modified through five German editions (Stolper, 1988: 36). These revisions generally had the form of abbreviations – the first German edition amounted to 548 pages, the abridged and revised second edition (1926) to 369 and the American edition (1934), based on the second German edition, to only 245 pages (Stolper, 1988:37; Swedberg, 1994:331).

In Schumpeter's view, the driving force of economic development and, literally, its hero is none other than the entrepreneur. He pushes through innovations, he is the epitome of leadership. These great leaders, who are able to blow up the barriers of the prevailing restrictions in any societal sector, are not limited to the economic field, but belong to politics and the arts as well. 'Auf jedem Gebiete gibt es statisch disponierte Individuen und Führer' (542; In every sector one finds statically predisposed individuals and leaders, E.H.). 'So gut wie nie würde ein neuer Gedanke ohne die Tätigkeit eines Führers als eine Realität empfunden werden' (544; Almost never would a new idea be seen as reality without the action of a leader, E.H.)

What are the skills of an entrepreneur? He pushes forward innovations that he creates by new combinations of already known elements. Thus, what is new comes out of the entrepreneurial capacity to combine existing feasibilities. This activity certainly needs some ingenious talent, but not real knowledge. Nevertheless, the elements may, at least partly, consist of inventions with embodied knowledge. Because there are no shortages of inventions, knowledge does not play a restrictive role at all. The scarce factor is the capability to unite given elements in a new combination and to promote actual innovations. This is what entrepreneurs actually do.

It is not by accident that knowledge does not matter in Schumpeter's settings. In the following statement, Schumpeter *expressis verbis* contradicts once more the mainstream judgment of his time: 'Es ist die Auffassung, daß in diesem technischen und organisatorischen Fortschritt ein selbständiges Moment liegt, das sein Entwicklungsgesetz in sich selbst trägt und wesentlich auf dem Fortschritte unseres Wissens beruht' (480; One can take the view that during this technical and organizational progress, a specific momentum is included that holds its law of development in itself and is essentially based on the progress of our knowledge. E.H.). Schumpeter's statement against the mainstream thinking of the discipline makes clear that inventions and knowledge are not to be seen as the driving force of economic development, and therefore are of no interest for Schumpeter. It holds even that inventions are to be taken not as the *cause* but as the *effect* of development (479).

As Streissler (1989:29–33, 1994) has repeatedly shown, Schumpeter found the original figure of the entrepreneur as an innovator and leader in the writings of his teacher, Friedrich von Wieser,[2] as well as in the German literature of a former time. Schumpeter himself stressed that the German historic school of economic thinking made one of the best contributions to the dynamic aspects of economic development (617).

What Schumpeter had in mind, when he denied the innovative influence of inventions and new knowledge, finds a very detailed expression in the empirical evidence presented in his *Business Cycles* (1939), where he speaks about the first Kondratieff cycle (1767–1842) (Chapter VI). There he refers to two different types of new events. We may call them *original inventions* and *applied novelty*. It may be useful to add these notions (included in parenthesis) in Schumpeter's following texts just to illustrate Schumpeter's meaning under the different connections:

- 'We hold . . . that the influence exerted was not in the direction of initiating new (*original inventions*, E.H.) – economic, political, artistic, and so on – creations' (233, footnote 1).
- 'The cotton textile industry was the new leader, according to our terminology, but was not new (*original inventions*, E.H.) in the sense of common parlance' (271).

- 'But if invention is not the core of the matter, neither is objective opportunity. Study of our period shows us again that "doing the thing" – the actual setting up new production functions (*applied novelty*, E.H.) – is a distinct phenomenon' (272).
- 'The New Men and the New Firms stand out so well in this case because the industry itself was new (*applied novelty*, E.H.) as . . . the industries that carry Kondratieff upswings' (273).

We notice that everything depends on the new men and their new firms that things get done.

In the fourth book, *Capitalism, Socialism and Democracy* (1942) the scenario changes somehow from men to processes. If compared to the notion of perfect competition of the neoclassical theory, the entrepreneur is the actor in the process of a new type of competition. When Schumpeter introduces this process, he first speaks of a process of qualitative change, later of a process of industrial mutation, and finally of a process of Creative Destruction: 'This process of Creative Destruction is the essential fact of capitalism' (83). As a further illustration of this process, Schumpeter adds a time dimension: the perennial gale of creative destruction (84). Later we only find once more the notion of perennial gale (88) and, twice times that of the process of creative destruction (104, footnote 24, 1943).[3] In spite of the scarce mentioning of the notion of creative destruction in Schumpeter's original work, it has received most attention in the secondary literature. Presumably it is the most cited conceptual invention of Schumpeter.

In my view, however, it is an ill-formulated notion. By asking what is cause and what is effect, we must ascertain that a creative innovation is obviously the cause, and the so-called destruction of an old production function is the effect. Thus, in fact, Schumpeter should have spoken of *destructive creation*. But this sequence of the dual notion does not sound as well as it does the other way around. We may ask, what urges us at all to stigmatize the motive power of economic development by characterizing it as a kind of destruction? Innovations bring about more and better products, which increase productivity. Destructions by innovations should be understood as a normal outcome of selection by the competitive process. To give the specific type of competition which Schumpeter had in mind a name, it is enough to speak of 'dynamic competition'. We shall come back to this issue later in more detail.

There are some other processes mentioned in *Capitalism, Socialism and Democracy* which are hostile to capitalist development: the obsolescence of the entrepreneurial function, the destruction of the protecting strata, the destruction of the institutional framework of the capitalist society (131–42). Under the heading of a 'growing hostility' (143–55), Schumpeter mentions the group of intellectuals as a specific phenomenon of the capitalist society: 'Unlike any other type of society, capitalism inevitably and by virtue of the very logic of its civilization creates, educates and subsidizes a vested interest in social unrest' (146). Here one group of the knowledge sector appears on the wrong side of capitalist development, the knowledge of intellectuals as the enemy, not as a power, of development.

Where Schumpeter speaks of the 'obsolescence of the entrepreneurial function' he also mentions a certain type of knowledge that influences technical progress: 'Technical progress is increasingly becoming the business of teams of trained specialists who turn out what is required and make it workable in predictable ways' (132). What else can these specialists be but 'knowledge workers'?

So far, we have looked for the role of knowledge in Schumpeter's writings under the heading of innovations. There is still another means to an understanding of the knowledge complex in an economy: the theory of division of labor. In the history of economic thought, we find two authors in direct succession to Adam Smith (1723–1790) who himself spoke about knowledge in connection with division of labor: Heinrich von Storch (1766–1835; see Rentrup, 1989; Schumann, 2003) and Charles Babbage (1791–1871), both only briefly mentioned in Schumpeter's *History of Economic Analysis*.

In this book, Schumpeter makes a few remarks about the division of labor (187f.) as Adam Smith saw it. He even attacks Adam Smith by saying that there 'is nothing original about it', but 'nobody, either before or after Adam Smith, ever thought of putting such a burden upon division of labor'. What really disturbs Schumpeter is the theory of development embodied in Adam Smith's division of labor: 'With A. Smith it is practically the only factor in economic progress.' This is exactly the point which Heinrich von Storch (1819) sees as the greatest originality of Adam Smith: 'Smith . . . hat dargetan, dass die Arbeitstheilung das Erzeugniß zugleich in hohem Grade vermehrt, und daß hierin ihr größerer Nutzen besteht, weil sie dadurch eine Quelle des Überflusses an allen Hervorbringungen der Arbeit wird' (3rd vol., 6: Smith . . . has explained that the division of labor lets production increase to a high degree, and this is its greatest advantage, because it becomes a source of affluence in all products of labor, E.H.).

Nevertheless, Heinrich von Storch himself criticizes Adam Smith for not going far enough in his analysis of the division of labor. The reason, in Storch's opinion: Adam Smith only saw material goods and physical labor. He should also have taken into account 'inner goods' as well as 'nonphysical labor'. By 'inner goods' Storch understands 'alle unkörperlichen Früchte der Natur und der Arbeit, in denen der Mensch eine Nützlichkeit findet und welche das moralische Eigentum desselben bilden können' (2nd vol., 341: all non-physical fruits of nature and labor, where human beings may find benefits and which can constitute their moral property, E.H.). As an example, he refers to 'our capabilities and everything that directly serves for its development and completeness' (2nd vol., 342). One of these inner goods is knowledge! As the division of physical labor allows for the increase in the production of material output, the division of non-physical labor leads to the development and completeness of inner goods. Though this may sound strange to our ears, it introduces for the first time the aspect of the division of knowledge. Storch deals with this theme in the second volume of his work about societal education: 'Die Lehre von der geselligen Bildung [civilization] hat die Gesetze darzustellen, nach denen die inneren Güter in einem Volke hervorgebracht, angesammelt und verzehrt werden' (2nd vol., 337: The lesson of societal education [civilization] concerns the inner goods in a society, how they are produced, accumulated and consumed, E.H.). By the way, Storch's ideas about the inner goods can also be seen as a first approach to *Institutional Economics*.

Charles Babbage approaches the division of knowledge issue more directly. The XXth chapter of his *Economy of Machinery* (1st edn 1832) considers the division of mental labor (191–202) and the XXXVth chapter deals with 'the future prospects of manufactures, as connected with science' (379–92). Schumpeter (*History of Economic Analysis*, 541f.) acknowledges the work of Babbage almost enthusiastically, but does not even mention his specific conception of the division of mental labor. Babbage's basic idea refers to the identical way in which a machine as well as mental labor work go ahead step by step (Brödner, 1999:XXII).

One may wonder why Schumpeter in his *History of Economic Analysis* sheds only a little light on the problem of the division of labor. My answer is that he must have seen the division of labor issue in a certain neighborhood to the static state of an economy. Indeed, only under such circumstances can the division of labor be completed. As we have already seen, the distance to this final state was no source of progress for Schumpeter, at least not a permanent one.

We should keep in mind the specific Schumpeterian type of an economy in which development is occurring. Schumpeter's developing economy is opposed to the 'Kreislaufwirtschaft' (1912:1–102) and the 'organisch wachsende Wirtschaft' (1911:474). The Kreislaufwirtschaft is an economy in a static state and, if it expands slowly and steadily, it may even grow organically near the stationary state. (By the way, Schumpeter's 'organisch wachsende Wirtschaft' is quite comparable to Gustav Cassel's 'gleichmäßig fortschreitende Wirtschaft' [Cassel, 1923:27–34].) However, Schumpeter's developing economy is not based on steadiness, but on discontinuity. The innovations he has in mind are innovations 'of the first ... order of magnitude' (*Business Cycles*, 94). They cause structural breaks and 'unstabilize the economic world' (138).

Looking for knowledge as a source of economic progress, our tour d'horizon through Schumpeter's great monographs could not find comments on the importance of this factor. In connection with innovations, the scarce factors for him are not inventions and knowledge, but the activities of innovating entrepreneurs. That may have been specifically true during the first Kondratieff cycle (1767–1842). Later on, as the entrepreneurial function becomes more and more obsolete, technical progress increasingly goes over to the hands of 'business teams and trained specialists' (see above) in large enterprises. In Schumpeter's view, the capitalist process surrounds itself with 'crumbling walls'.

The second possible access route to knowledge as a source of economic progress, the division of labor issue, seems blocked for Schumpeter, because he finds no potential of progress in that issue. We shall propose exactly this approach, and hope to be able to add to Schumpeter's true understanding of a developing economy as a new cornerstone, the division of knowledge.

2   The skeleton of a neo-Schumpeterian knowledge-based economy

2.1   *The most important stylized fact: dynamic competition*
The basis of the developing economy à la Schumpeter has to be seen in the light of the Schumpeterian type of competition. Schumpeter formally called it a new type of competition, compared to the old fashioned 'perfect competition'. Within the competitive process of the new type, new products, new production processes and new kinds of organizations compete with old ones. Competition is not only price-oriented but quality-oriented. The markets are in permanent motion, more or less far away from equilibrium. Innovative firms lead the way, followed by imitating firms. The old neoclassical model of a 'representative firm' does not hold anymore. Markets are characterized by heterogeneity. Let us call the underlying type of competition 'Dynamic Competition', keeping in mind that nothing else is meant but 'creative destruction', Schumpeter's unhappy romantic dramatization of this type of competition.

To illustrate this competitive process, we may refer to the so-called 'Barone curve' (Barone, 1935, 1st edn. 1908; Helmstädter, 1990). Figure 19.1 shows a market diagram with the demand curve and the supply curve, which is the horizontal sum of the marginal cost curves of all supplying firms. Near to the ordinate, the most advanced firm A with its average and marginal cost function MA and MC is inserted. We assume that the firm maximizes its profit by taking the price p^* as given and therefore choosing point Q, where p^* equals the firm's marginal costs. The vertical projection

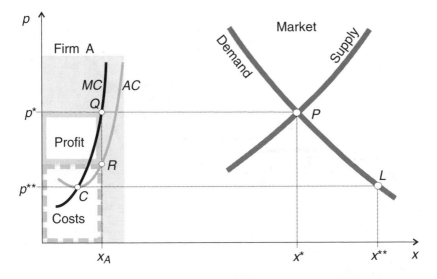

Figure 19.1

of point Q to the abscissa marks the supply x_A of firm A. The point R shows the amount of the average cost, when the firm produces the amount of x_A. The corresponding profit and costs of the firm A are shown by the corresponding rectangles.

We assume now that three additional firms are suppliers to this market. Nevertheless, we neglect the possible oligopolistic behavior of the four firms and maintain the mentioned maximizing rule, which holds strictly only under 'perfect competition'. Figure 19.2 presents all four firms, A, B, C and D, according to their increasing average costs. Leaving aside the single cost curves and only showing the different average costs leads to the inserted step-like curve, the so called 'Barone curve'. Above this curve the different profits are indicated. Firm E, the marginal supplier, makes a loss, because its average cost is higher than the price p^*. On the abscissa, the supplied amounts x_A, x_B, x_C and x_D are shown. The step function of the Barone curve differentiates the turnover at this market into the differential profits and costs of the four firms. Figure 19.2 shows also the profit slope of this market.

If no innovation occurs, no additional firms would enter the market and the demand function would not change. The market would then expand to its final long-run equilibrium at point L'' of Figure 19.3. At this point, every surviving firm would use the best equipment. It is further assumed that the optimal outputs of the four firms would be equalized, as would be the profits. In this case, the Barone curve runs flat. We see that the long-run equilibrium under perfect competition, L, has been approached but not really

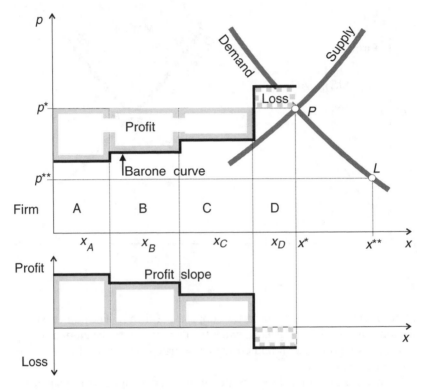

Figure 19.2

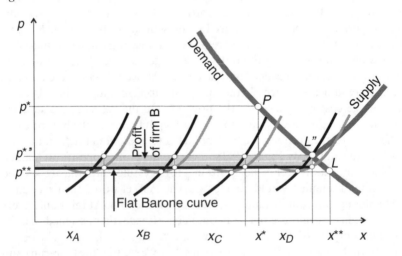

Figure 19.3

reached. If the four firms demonstrate oligopolistic behavior, the equilibrium point would lie even farther away from L.

What does the model of the Barone curve teach us with respect to Schumpeter's dynamic competition? First, it demonstrates the diffusion of benchmark equipment, which may have been introduced by a process innovation. The market develops as long as the best technique is not yet used by all supplying firms. In other words: as long as the Barone curve is steep, the market expands. The final flatness of the Barone curve indicates that no further expansion will occur.

So far, our example refers to the market for a homogeneous good. Schumpeter's dynamic competition takes also into account qualitative changes on the product side. Such product innovations can also be considered under the auspices of the market diagram à la Barone. One has only to define the x-axis in a suitable way for heterogeneous goods that are near substitutes in a common market. That would mean that the qualitatively different products had to be quantitatively transformed in relation to a certain standardized good. Product innovations of a leading firm would make the Barone curve steeper and would stimulate the expansion of the market by diffusion of the product of higher quality and end in a flat Barone curve if no further innovation happened. This second interpretation of the Barone curve is only mentioned here to show that the Barone scheme is not restricted to the market for homogenous goods, as is often assumed. In other words, if Schumpeterian dynamic competition includes quality competition, the Barone curve must not be given up.

The Barone scheme illustrates a market in a short-run disequilibrium. The order of the suppliers reflects their competitiveness at a given moment of time. The next moment may show a different situation. This depends on the entrepreneurial competencies of the supplying firms.

The realized differential profit of a market period is an indicator of the existing potential to expand, even if no further innovations occur. Depending on a continuing flow of further innovations, the market can develop permanently: this is the state of 'restless capitalism' (Metcalfe, 2002b:4).

There is no question that different markets of an economy will never have the same potential to grow. Some markets may even shrink. Whether an economy grows depends on whether there exists a sufficient number of developing markets. Schumpeter spoke about such a developing economy in his *Theorie der wirtschaftlichen Entwicklung* (chap. 7, 463–548). The simulation models of Nelson and Winter (1982) and Elliason (1988, 1992) describe the market structure by inclining firm profitability functions, quite compatible with Barone curves. Thus, introducing this diagrammatic form does not say anything new with respect to the market structure in an evolutionary economy of Schumpeter's style. The scheme may only help to deliver an easily comprehensible instrument of demonstration. In either case, the diagram refers to the most important stylized fact of a Schumpeterian economy: dynamic competition.

2.2 Introducing knowledge

Having introduced Schumpeter's dynamic competition, it is possible (and we may say even recommended) to introduce the issue of *knowledge*, as it has to do with competition, according to Hayek a generic search process. A national economy consists of numerous competitive markets. By their interactions, which have to be considered as the process of division of labor, the system of relative prices gets discovered. It was Hayek (1937) who rightly understood this result as a specific kind of economic knowledge that can only emerge out of a competitive market economy. That means that the division of labor is accompanied by a specific process of *division of knowledge*.

Hayek's argument stands at the top of the famous debate about rational calculation under socialism. It states that, under socialist conditions, the process of the division of knowledge cannot happen. This process combines the 'fragments of knowledge existing in different minds' (Hayek, 1937:52) to the advantage of the society. 'Knowledge in this sense is more than what is usually described as skill, and the division of knowledge of which we here speak more than is meant by the division of labour.' What is meant by knowledge is 'the knowledge of alternative possibilities of action of which [a person, E.H.] makes no direct use' (Hayek, 1937:50, n.l). Thus, we may speak of the working knowledge of the competitive agents. This knowledge belongs to 'the particular circumstances of time and place' under which economic decisions must be made (Hayek, 1945:524). 'The price system [operates, E.H.] as a kind of machinery for registering change, or a system of telecommunication which enables producers to watch merely the movement of a few pointers . . . in order to adjust their activities to changes of which they may never know more than is reflected in the price movement' (Hayek, 1945:527).

Division of knowledge (DK) is analogous to division of labor (DL) with respect to the advantages of specialization. The analogy holds further with respect to the necessity of combining the fragmented activities for the societal use of dispersed knowledge (DK) or exchange activities (DL). But the contents and the modes of the included human interactions are different, which necessarily means that different institutions must be taken into account.

The New Institutional Economics (NIE) originally dealt with the institutions under the DL aspect:[4] transactions. Of main interest is the exchange of goods and services. Sometimes the notion of transaction is extended e.g. to 'political transactions', which necessarily causes difficulties. According to

Williamson (1996:58, 379), transactions are defined as follows: 'A transaction occurs when a good or a service is transferred across a technically separable interface.' What is said here about goods and services is not transferable to knowledge interactions. When a transaction occurs, an interface guarantees that, during this period, the seller and the buyer cannot both be the owner of the thing in question, and it is equally impossible that during this period neither owns it. If an interaction between a teacher and a student were successful, a certain piece of knowledge might be shared and both agents would have it at their disposal from that time on. If the aforementioned definition of a transaction holds, knowledge sharing cannot be understood as a transaction.

There are further basic differences between the institutions of knowledge sharing and the exchange of goods and services. Exchange presupposes private property and allows special payment of the price for a good or service. Knowledge, specifically codified knowledge, is generally useful for the society as a public good. The society pays for it by general payment.

The input of new knowledge by a firm in most cases occurs by employing an additional knowledge worker. Here, the firm pays for such knowledge it hopes to get in the future by general payment according to the necessarily incomplete employment contract. There is no possibility of buying knowledge piece by piece by special payment.

Things are different in the case in which a firm buys the rights of a patent. Here a special price is given and special payment is possible in the same way as in other service transactions. Special payment is one important precondition for the interaction mode of economic competition. General payment needs another interaction mode: non-economic competition or cooperation. Non-economic competition combines a set of competitive interactions. Best known is 'reputation competition' or 'status competition' that governs scientific communities (Helmstädter, 2004).

Taking the knowledge worker's employment contract as an example, we may say that salary is one element of the circumstances under which a knowledge worker prefers to work. Cultural surroundings, the social situation inside the organization and outside contacts play important roles. Knowledge workers compete for recognition in their community. The rank by reputation or status competition matters for future chances, monetary ones included.

With these few remarks it should be obvious that knowledge interactions with their specific institutions are included in the DL process, which is interconnected with a DK process. Let us refer to the kind of knowledge that emerges out of both processes as 'endogenous knowledge'. It contains the price system, the knowledge of the 'circumstances of time and place' under which it currently holds, the working experience of the participating competitors, perhaps even some new technical insight. This endogenous knowledge is tacit or implicit knowledge, to use the usual terminology. It is dispersed through the society and given only in fragments to the single competitors. By its very nature, this type of endogenous knowledge cannot be a public good.

The economy also has at its disposal exogenous new knowledge. This is the knowledge which comes from the research and development and the education sectors. These sectors are somehow connected with the economy, but not directly included in the DL process. However, they are a generic part of the DK process and its institutions. Now, we can say that the total DK process produces endogenous and exogenous new knowledge. Everywhere that specialization allows increased efficiency and interactions of specialists must bring about a societal benefit.

Exogenous knowledge may be called a resource because it enters the economy from outside, while endogenous knowledge is the outcome of the competitive economic process itself, not its input. For the innovative strategies, both kinds of knowledge must get suitably mixed.

Having discussed the main knowledge searching and sharing issues in connection with the Schumpeterian economy, it may be useful to assemble them in a summary list (Table 19.1).

I would like to call the approach behind the items of the summary list, for the sake of simplicity, the 'knowledge sharing approach'. Knowledge sharing has to be considered as the basic subject matter of knowledge interactions, in the same way as transactions are the subject matter of exchange. Both activities follow their own institutions and create institution costs as opportunity or output costs.[5] It is usual to call the institution costs of exchange transaction costs. In the same way, the institution costs of knowledge sharing could be called knowledge sharing costs. But in both cases, institutions are the subject that has to be optimized to minimize the costs. To my mind, it sounds plausible to state that New Institutional Economics in general deals with institution costs.

One last remark seems necessary: what has been said so far as to the knowledge sharing approach stands at the very beginning of knowledge as a subject in economics, even if in the history of economic thought we can find important starting points. What we are still missing is a foundation of a specific branch of the economic knowledge issue. To my mind, it should be an integrated part of evolutionary and new institutional economics.

3   Further approaches to bringing knowledge into the Schumpeterian economy

Having outlined the perspectives of the knowledge sharing approach, I shall show how this approach fits into some further proposals about a

Table 19.1   Knowledge sharing aspects in a neo-Schumpeterian economy

	Subject	Authors or discipline
I	Starting point: dynamic competition in the Schumpeterian developing economy	Schumpeter (Barone)
The issues for further consideration		
II	Division of physical labor lets knowledge increase	Adam Smith
III	Division of mental labor as a specific type of interaction	Von Storch, Babbage
IV	Division of knowledge included in the division of labor: the competitive search process finds out dispersed tacit knowledge	Hayek
V	The division of knowledge process of the R&D and education sector creates codified knowledge as a resource. Mode of interaction: reputation competition and co-operation; subject of interactions: knowledge searching and sharing. Knowledge-sharing institutions as a new branch of NIE	New Institutional Economics
VI	Applications and empirical research: knowledge policy, knowledge management, case studies about innovation processes in firms and regions*	Policy, empirical research

* Section VI indicates empirical applications about knowledge sharing. For more information see Helmstädter (1999, 2003).

'modern Schumpeterian agenda' (Metcalfe, 2002a:1), as proposed at the eighth conference of the International Schumpeter Society in Manchester in 2001 (see *Journal of Evolutionary Economics*, 12(1–2), March 2002). At this conference, the Schumpeter prize was given to Brian J. Loasby for his fundamental work on *Knowledge, Institutions and Evolution in Economics* (1999). This book assembles the items of interest that I am dealing with in this chapter. Thus, a comparison with Loasby's approach may be of interest. I would like to refer also to the conference contributions of J. Stanley Metcalfe, Richard R. Nelson and John A. Mathews. They asked the following questions about knowledge and institutions under evolutionary perspectives: Which kind of 'knowledge growth framework' is adequate to 'restless capitalism'?, how can we combine the institutional and evolutionary scenarios?, and what is the role of knowledge under the 'resource-based view'?

3.1   *Brian J. Loasby's monograph on knowledge creation*

What the proposed knowledge sharing approach means becomes clearer when it is confronted with Loasby's alternative approach to knowledge in economics. This may be called the 'knowledge creation approach'.

The knowledge sharing approach does not discuss knowledge creation itself. The notion of knowledge sharing implies that the knowledge to be shared already exists. The same is true with respect to the central issue of knowledge interactions. These can only happen if one participating agent already possesses some knowledge which his counterpart wishes to share. All this means that the knowledge sharing approach deals with the diffusion or dissemination of knowledge. For a society whose growth of knowledge depends on specialization, this issue is of greatest importance. Besides, one may add that the dissemination leads by further specialization to further knowledge creation. Under societal aspects, specialization and dissemination build a complex combination.

But there are other ways to demonstrate that the knowledge sharing approach, even if it refers only to already existing knowledge, should not be regarded as inferior to the creation approach. Similar disseminations happen in our brain: pre-existing structures of human brains create novelty by routines, as Loasby (2003:106) refers to:

> An established neural network supports routines of behaviour and rules for con-ceptualising and resolving problems, and it strives to preserve its own coherence, even by denying the validity of information. . . . What novelties are possible for any person at any point of time depends on the pre-existing structure and the history of past adaptations; but these constraints are rarely sufficent to be of much help in predicting novelty, except in a negative sense.

Thus, novelties cannot spring from an inadequate individual neural network and unsuitable experience. One may say that novelty is shaped by pre-existing conditions, although not by strong restrictions. The difference with respect to the dissemination aspect does not seem too large: an existing individual neural structure disseminates a kindred novelty. If novelties are embodied in existing structures, what makes them really new? I would not wish to go more deeply into this question. My argument here is directed only to the possible difference between dissemination and the creation of knowl-edge. It does not seem too great, such that neither could be compared.

In his knowledge monograph, Loasby (1999) refers to 'economic systems in which knowledge is seriously incomplete, fallible, and dispersed, but capable of improvement and coordination' (10). The basic issue of the book is '*epistemological*': '*what can we know?*' (1), the first of Kant's three funda-mental questions. The intention is 'to focus on a particular set of economic consequences of uncertainty' (2).

All these questions must be included within the purview of economic knowledge. The knowledge sharing approach must be supplemented by the knowledge creation approach, with perhaps some further considerations (see the contributions of Kubon-Gilke, 2003, and Bünstorf, 2003). The question can only be whether the knowledge sharing approach can be understood as a common framework for the complexity of the world of knowledge in the economy and society.

3.2   Which kind of 'knowledge growth framework' is adequate to 'restless capitalism'?

Here, we simply have to ask, first, what makes knowledge grow? The obvious answer seems to be: specialization. So we are immediately confronted with the division of knowledge process. From specialization also follows 'microdiversity' (Metcalfe, 2002a:3), which increases the chances of finding new knowledge under the conditions of an 'extreme micro heterogeneity of the underlying inventive process' (10). Metcalfe asks the question how to coordinate such a process and rightly stresses that 'not all the relevant co-ordinating institutions fall into the market category' (7). This is a point about which an additional remark may be made.

J. Stanley Metcalfe calls his proposal a 'market-based approach' (9). This can be understood as comprising a variety of interaction processes with different kinds of competition, up to and including pure cooperation. Thus, under the auspices of the knowledge sharing approach, I would stress the interaction issue. The notion of interaction is strictly reserved for interactions of individuals. This notion allows a variety of individual coordinating modes, including several types of sanctions that can be applied. For specific market interaction processes, economic competition holds if specific payment and full monetary sanctions are given. Inside the division of knowledge process normally general payment holds. This follows from the fact that knowledge is not payable piece by piece. Between interacting knowledge workers often monetary payment is just impossible. This does not mean, however, that there is no mutual remuneration at all. What we have to keep in mind is the variety of interaction processes that are convenient for knowledge sharing. We still do not know very much about these processes.

3.3   How can we combine the institutional and evolutionary scenario?

Richard R. Nelson asks how to bring institutions into an evolutionary economic growth framework. He notes that both 'camps share a central behavioral premise that human action and interaction needs to be understood largely as the result of shared habits of action and thought' (19). The epitome of actions that promote innovations lies in the complex process of division of knowledge. To understand innovation systems (Metcalfe,

2002a:13), one has to take into consideration the knowledge sharing inter-actions and their specific institutions. Thus, according to the knowledge sharing approach, we should add to the division of labor process, which is the basis of the New Institutional Economics, its dual process of the division of knowledge. Everything can happen in Nelson's world.

What Richard R. Nelson says about the aim of institutions is completely compatible with the knowledge sharing approach. He recommends we understand institutions 'not so much as "constraints" on behavior, as some analysts do, but rather as defining effective ways to get things done when human cooperation is needed' (22). This specifically is true for human inter-action in the division of knowledge process.

Nelson's distinction between physical and social technologies is of particular interest (22). As an illustration, he refers to two very successful innovations as new social technologies: mass production in the last decades of the 19th century in the US and the production of synthetic dyestuffs in Germany and England since the late 1860s. The first example, that of US mass production, used not only new technologies and routines but also involved social technologies. 'The need for professional managers [also, E.H.] pulled Business Schools into being' (24), 'new institutions grew up rapidly in the new world' (24f.). By contrast, the synthetic dyestuff example represents 'the rise of the first science based industry' (24). Different sets of institutions have been applied by British and German firms. One problem has been the supply of academic chemists with the help of government funding for universities: 'For a variety of reasons the supply of German chemists initially is [has been, E.H.] much greater than the supply of British chemists' (26).

The last example demonstrates that there exists a deep connection between public and private actions inside the division of knowledge process. This is one of its differences from the division of labor process.

3.4   What is the role of knowledge under the 'resource-based view'?
The third article to which I would like to refer sees the field of economics not from the usual perspective of output and exchange of goods and services, but rather from an input perspective, directed to non-natural resources. The article by John A. Mathews seems to be written under the auspices of 'mergers and acquisitions' experienced over recent decades. As with the success of a professional soccer team, buying experienced players from outside is sometimes more efficient than trying to improve the available ones. A firm can successfully buy a set of already known and tried resources from a competing firm to capture 'competitive dynamics' (Mathews, 2002:29).

What is meant by resources? 'Resources include tangible entities such as production systems, technologies, machinery, as well as intangibles like brands, or property rights such as landing rights for an airline or bandwidth for a telecommunication company' (32). A footnote (32, n.3), referring to two other authors, adds 'difficult-to-trade knowledge assets and assets complementary to them, such as its reputational and relational assets'. In my opinion, there is no doubt that knowledge assets belong to the resources Mathews has in mind. This becomes clear in Mathew's further explanations, when he refers to the question how firms experience their own resources. According to Mathews, the resource stock provides services – in my understanding, knowledge services – for the production of goods and services. How good the services are is to be discovered by a learning process, 'where the outcome depends on the management's knowledge, experience and capacity for imaginative experiment' (35). In his remarks about clusters, Mathews refers to 'science-driven clusters like Research Triangle Park in North Carolina, or the Hsinchu district in Taiwan where all the country's major IT and semiconductors activities are co-located' (46f.). His final conclusion is that 'clusters constitute a form of economic organization where resources are shared between firms locally' (47). Surely, we can easily define these resources as implicit knowledge that can only be shared by face-to-face interaction.

Whatever may be the activities of the reconfiguration or recombination of those resources, they build the 'competence' (32) of a firm, which actually is to be understood as a knowledge qualification. In this connection, I would like to make one last remark that refers to the Austrian capital theory. John A. Mathews mentions this issue (33) only casually with respect to the non-equilibrium dynamic character of this conception. But in my opinion, resource economics can easily be seen as a process of roundabout production à la Böhm-Bawerk. Physical as well as human resources prepare the final output. More and more meta work (= knowledge work) is needed to prepare and execute production work. A new Austrian capital theory should take this change of the composition of capital into consideration. Human capital deepening can be understood today as a process by which more knowledge work gets applied to steadily increase the output of the final goods and services of the society.

These comments on some alternative ways to handle knowledge in an evolutionary economy have been made to show how these stimulating contributions in the field of evolutionary economics may be subsumed easily under the proposed knowledge sharing approach. So far the comments may have given an indication of the usefulness of that approach to serve as a framework for the complex knowledge issues with which neo-Schumpeterian economics seems to be confronted.

Notes

1. The sharpness of Schumpeter's attacks against Austrian mainstream economics at this time can be seen nowhere better than in the 24-page review which Friedrich von Wieser (1911) as one of the attacked authors and Schumpeter's teacher wrote three years after the publication of *Wesen und Hauptinhalt*.
2. 'Schumpeter's "creative entrepreneur" is evidently a subspecies of his teacher's idea of the "great man" in history' (Streissler, 1994:35).
3. Here Schumpeter refers to the psychological ability of a socialist society to 'fulfil important functions in the process of creative destruction'.
4. For simplicity, I neglect here the governance issue of NIE.
5. The criticism by the neoclassical economists of NIE denies the necessity of specific transaction costs. This argument is right for transaction input costs, but not for transaction output costs (opportunity costs).

References

Babbage, Charles (1993), 1st edn 1832, *On the Economy of Machinery and Manufactures*, London: Routledge/Thoemess Press.
Barone, Enrico (2. durchges. Aufl. 1935), 1st edn 1908, *Grundzüge der theoretischen NationalÖkonomie*, Berlin: Bonn.
Brödner, Peter (1999), Charles Babbage – Ein Vordenker der Moderne, in Charles Babbage (1st edn 1832), *Die Ökonomie der Maschine*, Berlin: Kulturverlag Kadmos, XV–XXVIII.
Bünstorf, Guido (2003), Processes of knowledge sharing: from cognitive psychology to economics, in Ernst Helmstädter (ed.), *The Economics of Knowledge Sharing. A New Institutional Approach*, Cheltenham, UK and Northampton, MA, USA: Edward Elgar, pp. 74–98.
Cassel, Gustav (1923), first edn 1918, *Theoretische Sozialökonomie*, Erlangen Leipzig: A. Deichertsche Verlagsbuchhandlung.
Eliasson, Gunnar (1988), Schumpeterian innovation, market structure, and the stability of industrial development, in Horst Hanusch (ed.), *Evolutionary Economics. Applications of Schumpeter's Ideas*, Cambridge: Cambridge University Press, pp. 151–99.
Eliasson, Gunnar (1992), The MOSES-Model – database and applications, The Industrial Institute for Economic and Social Research, Research Report no. 40, Stockholm, 5–135.
Hayek, Friedrich A. von (1937), Economics and knowledge, *Economica*, 4(13), 33–54.
Hayek, Friedrich A. von (1945), The use of knowledge in society, *American Economic Review*, XXXV(4), 519–30.
Helmstädter, Ernst (1990), Ein makroökonomisches Rahmenmodell der evolutorischen Ökonomik, in Ulrich Witt (ed.), *Studien zur Evolutorischen Ökonomik I*, Schriften des Vereins für Socialpolitik Band 195/1, Berlin: Duncker & Humblot, pp. 163–82.
Helmstädter, Ernst (1999), Arbeitsteilung und Wissensteilung – Ihre institutionenökonomische Begründung, in P. Brödner, E. Helmstädter and B. Widmaier (eds), *Wissensteilung. Zur Dynamik von Innovation und kollektivem Lernen*, Munich and Mering: Rainer Hampp Verlag, pp. 33–54.
Helmstädter, Ernst (2003), The institutional economics of knowledge sharing: basic issues, in E. Helmstädter (ed.), *The Economics of Knowledge Sharing. A New Institutional Approach*, Cheltenham, UK and Northampton, MA, USA: Edward Elgar, pp. 11–38.
Helmstädter, Ernst (2004), Wirtschaft und wissen. Die institution der wissensteilung als aufgabe der ordnungspolitik, *ORDO*, Bd. **55**, 37–76.
Kubon-Gilke, Gisela (2003), Motivation, learning, knowledge sharing and division of labour, in E. Helmstädter (ed.), *The Economics of Knowledge Sharing. A New Institutional Approach*, Cheltenham, UK and Northampton, MA, USA: Edward Elgar, pp. 51–73.
Loasby, Brian J. (1999), *Knowledge, Institutions and Evolution in Economics*, London: Routledge.
Loasby, Brian J. (2003), The cognitive basis of institutions: an evolutionary aspect, in E. Helmstädter (ed.), *The Economics of Knowledge Sharing. A New Institutional Approach*, Cheltenham, UK and Northampton, MA, USA: Edward Elgar, pp. 99–116.

Mathews, John A. (2002), A resource-based view of Schumpeterian economic dynamics, *Journal of Evolutionary Economics*, **12**(1–2), March, 29–54.

Metcalfe, J. Stanley (2002a), Introduction to the special issue: change, transformation and development, *Journal of Evolutionary Economics*, **12**(1–2), March, 1.

Metcalfe, J. Stanley (2002b), Knowledge of growth and the growth of knowledge, *Journal of Evolutionary Economics*, **12**(1–2), March, 3–15.

Nelson, Richard R., Winter, Sidney G. (1982), *An Evolutionary Theory of Economic Change*, Cambridge, MA and London: Belknap Press.

Recktenwald, H.C., Scherer, F.M. and Stolper, W.F. (1988), *Schumpeters monumentales Werk – Wegweiser für eine dynamische Analyse*, Düsseldorf: Verlag Wirtschaft und Finanzen.

Rentrup, Konrad (1989), *Heinrich von Storch, das 'Handbuch der Nationalwirtschaftslehre' und die Konzeption der 'inneren Güter'*, Heidelberg: Physica-Verlag.

Schumann, Jochen (2003), Human capital, knowledge and knowledge sharing: a view from the history of economic thoughts, in E. Helmstädter (ed.), *The Economics of Knowledge Sharing. A New Institutional Approach*, Cheltenham, UK and Northampton, MA, USA: Edward Elgar, pp. 119–26.

Schumpeter, Joseph A. (1908), *Das Wesen und der Hauptinhalt der theoretischen Nationalökonomie*, Leipzig: Duncker & Humblot, reprinted in W. Engels (ed., 1991), Faksimile-Edition 'Klassiker der Nationalökonomie', Düsseldorf: Verlag Wirtschaft und Finanzen.

Schumpeter, Joseph A. (1912), *Die Theorie der wirtschaftlichen Entwicklung*, Leipzig: Duncker & Humblot, reprinted in W. Engels (ed., 1988), Faksimile-Edition 'Klassiker der NationalÖkonomie', Düsseldorf: Verlag Wirtschaft und Finanzen.

Schumpeter, Joseph A. (1939), *Business Cycles. A Theoretical, Historical and Statistical Analysis of the Capitalistic Process*, 2 vols, New York and London: McGraw-Hill.

Schumpeter, Joseph A. (1947), 1st edn 1942, *Capitalism, Socialism, and Democracy*, London: George Allen & Unwin, rev. 2nd edn.

Schumpeter, Joseph A. (1954), *History of Economic Analysis*, ed. and introduced by Elizabeth Body Schumpeter, London: Allen & Unwin/New York: Oxford University Press.

Stolper, W.F. (1988), Schumpeter's Theorie der wirtschaftlichen Entwicklung – Eine kritische Exegese, in H.C. Recktenwald *et al.* (eds), *Schumpeter's monumentales Werk – Wegweiser für eine dynamische Analyse*, Düsseldorf: Verlag Wirtschaft und Finanzen, pp. 35–73.

Storch, Heinrich (1819), *Handbuch der National-Wirtschaftslehre*, 3rd vol., aus dem Französischen mit Zusätzen von D. Karl Heinrich Rau, Hamburg: Perdes und Besser.

Streissler, Erich (1989), Der Unternehmer in der deutschen Nationalökonomie des 19. Jahrhunderts, in B. Gahlen, B. Meyer and J. Schumann (eds), *Wirtschaftswachstum, Strukturwandel und dynamischer Wettbew-erb. Ernst Helmstädter zum 65. Geburtstag*, Berlin: Springer Verlag, pp. 17–33.

Streissler, Erich (1994), The influence of German and Austrian economics on Joseph A. Schumpeter, in Y. Shionoya and M. Perlman (eds), *Schumpeter in the History of Ideas*, Ann Arbor, MI: University of Michigan Press, pp. 13–38.

Swedberg, R. (1994), English original edn 1991, *Joseph A. Schumpeter. Eine Biographie*, Aus dem Englischen übersetzt von Johannes G. Pankau, Stuttgart: Klett-Cotta.

Wieser, Friedrich von (1911), Das Wesen und der Hauptinhalt der theoretischen Nationalökonomie. Kritische Glossen, Jahrbuch für Gesetzgebung, Verwaltung und Volkswirtschaft im Deutschen Reich, **XXXV**, 2, Leipzig; reprinted in Friedrich A. von Hayek (ed., 1929), *Friedrich Freiherr von Wieser, Gesammelte Abhandlungen*, Tübingen: J.C.B. Mohr (Paul Siebeck), pp. 10–34.

Williamson, Oliver E. (1996), *The Mechanics of Governance*, New York/Oxford: Oxford University Press.

20 Selection, learning and Schumpeterian dynamics: a conceptual debate
Ulrich Witt and Christian Cordes

1. Introduction

The relevance of Darwinian thought for economics is a controversial issue since Darwin's (1859) *Origin of the Species* started to attract the economists' attention. Schumpeter explicitly denied Darwin's explanatory model of evolution in nature had any relevance for economics. Instead, he emphasized the role which innovations and entrepreneurship play for endogenous economic change, i.e., the changes emerging from within the economy. The motivation for his reservations concerning biological metaphors and analogies becomes apparent in the seventh chapter of his *Theory of Economic Development* (which was omitted from later editions and has only recently been made available in English; cf. Schumpeter, 2002). In this chapter, he dealt with the heuristic analogy to classical mechanics and gravitating (equilibrating) systems which played a constitutive role in the neoclassical economic theory of his time. He argued that the analogy was mistaken and had obscured much of the interesting phenomena of real world economic problems, particularly those related to economic change. Dissatisfaction with this state of affairs was a major reason for working out his own theory of an entrepreneurship-centered economic development (Witt, 2002). Under such conditions it did not seem to make much sense to seek the questionable benefits of yet another schematic analogy – this time one informed by evolutionary biology.

In the neo-Schumpeterian approach to economic development this assessment has changed fundamentally. Schumpeter's themes – innovation, industry competition, and growth – are conceptualized in terms of metaphors borrowed from Darwinian thought (Nelson and Winter, 1982). In particular, here the selection metaphor is considered to be the distinguishing principle of evolutionary economics (cf. Dosi and Nelson, 1994; Nelson, 1995). In part, Schumpeter himself contributed to the conditions under which such a reorientation could take place. In his later, equally influential book (Schumpeter, 1942) he made a remarkable turnaround. He no longer believed in the path-breaking role of pioneering entrepreneurs who carry out major innovations and thus drive waves of economic development and growth. Instead, Schumpeter directed his interest to the conduct of the large, modern trusts. These trusts' bureaucratic teams of trained specialists, he now claimed, carry out innovations as routine work. The really important implication for him was that the incessant innovativeness of these trusts embraced monopolistic practices as a necessary concomitant Schumpeter (1942, ch. 8).

The 'Schumpeterian competition' hypothesis, as this conjecture was soon labeled, deviated significantly from the predominant model of perfect competition. This fact stirred an intense debate on the relationships between market structure and innovativeness (cf. Baldwin and Scott, 1987, for a survey). However, the theoretical underpinnings of the conjectured relationship between market structure and innovativeness were rather weak.[1] The neo-Schumpeterian approach launched by Nelson and Winter (1982) tried to fill the gap with an evolutionary dynamics. Their approach is a synthesis of Schumpeter's (1942) ideas and two further elements: the behavioral theory of the firm suggested by the Carnegie school (March and Simon, 1958; Cyert and March, 1963) and a loose analogy to the concept of natural selection (Nelson and Winter, 1980). Schumpeter had argued that, in modern trusts, entrepreneurial decisions, including those on innovations, were made in specialized departments. But he had left open how these organizational units actually operate and interact. Following the ideas of the Carnegie school, Nelson and Winter suggested that the behavior of those units and their interactions are based on organizational routines. Production planning, calculation, price setting, and even the allocation of R&D funds all follow organizational routines. An evolutionary dynamics is added to this interpretation by claiming that the routines are subject to selection.

The concept of selection-driven industrial dynamics is now widely used in the neo-Schumpeterian camp (Andersen, 1994; Kwasnicki, 1996; Cantner and Pyka, 2001; Becker, 2004; Lazaric and Raybaut, 2005). Moreover, it has recently been argued that selection among firm routines can be subsumed as a special case to the principles of 'Universal Darwinism' (which is an abstract reduction of the Darwinian theory of evolution; cf. Hodgson, 2002; Knudsen, 2002). Yet, as will be claimed in this chapter, Schumpeter's reservations about biological analogies and metaphors and his consistent abstinence with respect to their use still deserve scrutiny. The concept of selection is a case in point. Where it is not clearly stated what specific economic processes are supposed to bring about 'economic natural selection', the biological metaphor may be more misleading than productive (cf. Winter, 1964, for a thorough criticism of the older literature). Concepts other than that of selection may be more appropriate for representing the Schumpeterian dynamics of innovations and their diffusion. The purpose of the present chapter is to elucidate and discuss exemplarily this problem in order to strengthen the conceptual underpinnings of Schumpeterian dynamics.

The chapter proceeds as follows. Section 2 takes a closer look at processes and units of selection in biological evolution. The findings are contrasted with the conditions characteristic of cultural evolution of which economic evolution is a part. Section 3 outlines the role of social–cognitive learning, a core element of cultural and economic evolution in the context of the firm organization and its development over time. Section 4 extends the discussion to the cognitive underpinnings of Schumpeterian innovation dynamics, especially with regard to entrepreneurship and industry life cycles. Section 5 offers concluding remarks.

2.   Selection and the evolutionary process

In biological evolution, variation is supplied mainly by mutations and recombinations of parental genes, i.e., genetic crossover in every generation, both of which provide the 'raw material' for natural selection (Mayr, 1991, p. 88). An essential attribute of any selection argument is the stability of selective characteristics and environment over time. Natural selection is an *a posteriori* phenomenon.[2] Therefore, a prerequisite for natural selection to produce systematic change is a certain degree of inertia on the part of the environment and the unit of selection. Furthermore, according to the central dogma of molecular biology, no information contained in the properties of the somatic proteins could be transferred to the nucleic acids of DNA (Dawkins, 1983; Mayr, 1991, p. 120). The phenotype does not pass information to the genotype. Thus, there are two features that enable selection to become a systematically shaping force in natural evolution: an environment changing relatively slowly compared to intergenerational genetic adaptation and the absence of a systematic feedback between phenotype and genotype.

Economic processes, in contrast, operate in an environment that is characterized by many variables that change rapidly and simultaneously. Moreover, economic agents are endowed with the cognitive capabilities that allow them to anticipate and avoid selection threats. Their proactive behavior may often mean that very rapid adjustments are made, many of them deliberately planned innovations. This is pertinent, particularly where the successful market diffusion of one innovation entails increasing pressure on the competitors which may trigger the entrepreneurial search for an innovative response. If it were assumed that, in the economic domain, there is something comparable to natural selection, what would this mean? It would have to be assumed that the economic analogue to phenotypes competes for differential reproductive success, resulting in changes of the composition of the economic analogue to the gene pool (cf., e.g., Knudsen,

2004, who substitutes phenotype–genotype distinction for one between 'interactors' and 'replicators'). These assumptions already raise a first interpretative problem without addressing the difficulties of the analogues for the phenotypes and the gene pool. Given the lack of inertia just described, it is doubtful whether that kind of selection would indeed have time enough to develop a systematically shaping influence.

A second problem that arises relates to the question of whether there are any reasonably well suited analogues to phenotypes and genotypes or gene pools. Since Nelson and Winter's (1982) seminal work, the organizational routines of the firms in an industry have often been interpreted as the analogue to the genotype. The corresponding analogue to phenotypes would then be the specific operations resulting from the routines (cf., e.g., Hodgson and Knudsen, 2004). If the analogy holds, differential success of the operations should automatically feed back to the population of routines in the industry (if there were sufficient time). How does this happen? By existing firm organizations varying their sizes? By differential entry and exit dynamics (in which cases very high competitive pressure would have to be assumed)? Or is the reason observational learning and imitation behavior? In that case, the firm's capacity to anticipate, and probably cure, deficiencies in its performance would be decisive. This would mean that there is not only 'external' selection at the level of market competition, but simultaneously something like 'internal' selection at the level of the firm's decision making. The question then is whether 'internal' selection can indeed be assumed to follow the logic of differential success.

It has been argued that any 'internal', decision-based selecting among routines itself follows routines, only higher ones.[3] Yet this may be less plausible than it appears at first sight. 'Internal' selection is likely to depend on aspiration levels, hypothesis formation, and insight on the part of those individuals involved in the higher routines. As a consequence, when involved in the same higher routine at different times or places, people with different attitudes, opinions, and aspirations may bring about rather different developments. Indeed, organizational routines refer to the *form* of interactions in the organization, including the form of communicating information. They may constrain the amount and, perhaps, even the quality of information thus processed. But organizational routines do not determine the meaning or cognitive *content* of the information. To deal with the latter, an analysis that differs qualitatively from what can be expressed in terms of organizational routines is therefore necessary. People follow intentions, conceptions, and conjectures that may, in the same situation, differ dramatically from one person to another.[4] People observe, learn, and gain insight. These cognitive activities are no less a source of regular and predictable features in business behavior, and they may be no less significant and specific for the organization in which people work. But the changes occurring at this level follow a logic different from that of genetic selection processes. The notion of mental 'selection' processes would therefore be misleading.[5] Human goal-directed behavior renders the functioning of the three mechanisms, selection, variation, and inheritance, interdependent rather than independent. Moreover, purposeful human action can give rise to 'directional' change in economic evolution.

Of course, in economic evolution people do choose between alternatives, products, behaviors, ideas, etc. – processes one could call 'selection'. But these processes are a kind of 'one-off' selection, because they do not trigger progressive evolution (Dawkins, 1983). They do not involve replication or the succession of generations, both of which are prerequisites for cumulative selection processes that give rise to adaptive complexity. A consumer's or an entrepreneur's choice represents an act of subset selection, i.e., she or he picks out a subset from a set according to a criterion of preference (see Price, 1995). In the Darwinian concept of natural selection, offspring are not subsets of parents but, thanks to genetic recombination, new entities. Furthermore, Darwinian natural selection is not carried out by intelligent agents who do the selecting. Natural or Darwinian selection does not refer to an abstract and general process, it refers to a domain-specific process tied to specific premises.

3.   Social–cognitive learning, coordination and firm growth

In the neo-Schumpeterian approach to innovations, industry competition, and growth, the Darwinian principle of natural selection is, as a heuristic device, often attributed a key role. Analogies to the principle and Darwinian thought more generally are often also considered to be the core of an evolutionary approach to economics. However, the usefulness of invoking natural selection as a metaphor for conceptualizing processes of economic change is debatable. The reasons have been highlighted in the previous section. To interpret selection as a generic, domain-unspecific principle which covers all evolutionary processes including economic evolution (as in the recent pleas for Universal Darwinism), does not solve any of the problems, but rather seems to raise additional questions. How, then, do Darwinian thought and economic evolution relate? A few remarks on this question may help to clarify the basis of an evolutionary approach to economics.

The Darwinian theory is, of course, relevant for economics in a very basic sense. The human species is, after all, a result of natural (Darwinian) evolution. However, this relevance does not directly affect the analytic concepts of economic theorizing. Natural evolution has shaped the ground, and still defines the constraints, for man-made, or cultural, evolution. The historical process of economic evolution can therefore be conceived as emerging from, and being embedded in, the constraints shaped by evolution in nature. Darwinian theory explains the origins of economic evolution in human phylogeny and fosters the understanding of the lasting influence on behavior of innate elements, dispositions, and programs that are results of the forces of natural selection and which impose limitations on economic evolution (Witt, 2003, ch. 1). From this perspective, the biologically evolved foundations of social cognition, learning, and reasoning directly enable and affect cultural evolution together with its own modes of transmission and its much faster pace (cf. Cordes, 2004).

Evolutionary selection has established a set of cognitive devices that participate in generating human behavior (cf., e.g., Singer, 2000). The key adaptation has been the one that enabled humans to understand other individuals as intentional agents like themselves – a capability necessary for reproducing another's behavioral strategies (Tomasello, 1999). This unique cognitive skill of human beings underlies behavioral patterns such as joint attentional activities, discourse skills, learning to use tools, the creation and use of conventional symbols, and the participation in and creation of complex social organizations and institutions. The species-unique aspects of human cognition are socially constituted. This means that human social organization is an integral part of the process that resulted in the special characteristics of human cognition. The sophisticated human skills of social cognition, such as imitative learning, do not just mimic the surface structure of an observed behavior. They also involve reproduction of an instrumental act understood intentionally. Humans do not just copy the behavioral means, they also reproduce the intended end to which the behavioral means were applied.

The partly innate, partly learned behavioral repertoire is the basis on which economic evolution and, thus, innovations, industrial dynamics, and growth rest. Social–cognitive learning is a crucial element here (Bandura, 1986, ch. 2). It allows for fidelity of transmission and diffusion of behaviors and information among the members of a population that are not feasible in genetic transmission (see Kruger *et al.*, 1993). It also enables humankind to accumulate a multitude of modifications in the course of socioeconomic evolution and to pool collective cognitive resources both contemporaneously and over historical time. By means of cumulative cultural evolution, the modifications to artifacts and the techniques contributed by one agent or group of individuals stay in place until, at some future date, further refinements are delivered, perhaps by other individuals. These again remain in existence until yet another instance of progress occurs.[6] In this way, the evolution of technology rests on the collective learning process. The conscious separation of goals and means serves to identify the method or strategy of tool use as an independent behavioral entity. Humans realized that natural objects could be changed in shape and be manipulated in order to obtain artifacts, tools, and eventually machinery. Darwinian concepts explain the origins of the human adaptation for culture and the lasting influence of certain evolved cognitive traits. They cannot, however, do justice to cultural evolution in general, and to economic evolution in particular, both of which follow their own rules.[7]

An approach oriented towards the diffusion of new knowledge offers a conceptual basis for analyzing systematic features of both organizational change at the firm level and changes at the industry level. Let us turn to the firm level first. As Penrose (1959) claimed long ago, the developmental potential of firm organizations is constrained by the cognitive limitations of its employees. The human cognitive apparatus faces constraints that entail selective information processing on the basis of discriminative attention processes which influence the diffusion of information and the accumulation of firm-specific knowledge. Cognitive cues are employed to discriminate among different kinds of information and are themselves organized into more complex systems called cognitive frames. Starting from a set of innate cues, associative chains, enabled by the innate capability of associative learning, create more and more complex sets of frames.

Elsewhere it has been argued that an entrepreneur can take advantage of these cognitive dispositions by introducing a 'business conception' as a cognitive frame (Witt, 1998). Such a conception can furnish the employees with a shared cognitive framework that directs the limited resource of human attention. In this way, a firm's organization can attain a higher degree of cognitive coherence among its members, which affects the interpretation of information, the coordination of dispersed knowledge, and individual endeavor, as well as the motivation to contribute to a common goal instead of focusing on private interests. Cognitive commonalities emerge from, for example, communication and observational learning from social models of behavior. In order to implement a business conception as a cognitive frame that is socially shared within the firm organization, it is necessary for the entrepreneur to be able to exert some cognitive leadership. A sufficiently frequent face-to-face interaction then raises the chances of making employees adopt the entrepreneurial business conception as a shared cognitive frame. The frequency of face-to-face interactions declines, however, as the size of the firm organization grows. At a certain point, cognitive coherence is no longer spontaneously achieved.

Firms can react in several ways to this challenge to, and sometimes even serious crisis in, their growth process (Witt, 2000). An often observed move is bureaucratization. A formalized regime of a detailed, hierarchical instructing and monitoring of the employees' actions is introduced. It replaces the culture of cooperation, delegation, and informal coordination encouraging initiative and creativity that prevailed before. Alternatively, a subdivision of entrepreneurship can be tried. In that case, entrepreneurially talented employees must be identified[8] who are capable of exerting entrepreneurial cognitive leadership inside subdivisions of the growing firm. It is then necessary to coordinate this group of entrepreneurial peers on an overarching business conception. Despite their different structures, organizational cultures, and degrees of cognitive coherence in their employees' actions, the two alternative regimes do not necessarily differ in short-run efficiency and profitability. However, a divided entrepreneurship regime is more conducive to keeping employees highly motivated and to eliciting creative problem solving behavior. The long-term growth potential of a firm with such a regime may therefore be significantly higher than that of bureaucratized firms relying on tight monitoring.

4. Cognitive underpinnings of industrial dynamics

The processes of social–cognitive learning also play a key role in the innovation-driven industry evolution. According to Schumpeter (1934), the first entrepreneurs entering a market and carrying through a 'new combination' enjoy a temporary monopoly (cf. Saviotti and Pyka, 2004). Therefore, these most talented, 'pioneering' entrepreneurs are able to earn 'promoter's profits'. The success of their business conceptions, strategies, and behaviors is observed by other agents. Less pioneering entrepreneurs start to imitate the business conception of the first movers and also enter the market. Thus, pioneering innovators become 'social models of behavior' (Bandura, 1986, ch. 2). Their attitudes, values, and modes of action are copied with some variation, a process that is based on the above-mentioned human faculty of taking the perspective of others and of understanding the means they choose to reach their goals.

Diffusion of the social model induces a 'swarm-like' appearance of entrepreneurs that marks the beginning of the life cycle of a new industry, i.e., a rapid rise in the number of entrants (Klepper, 1996). During the life cycle of an industry, another factor that contributes to an increase in the number of firms is the occurrence of spin-offs (cf., e.g., Klepper and Sleeper, 2002). An employee may be dissatisfied with the current operations of the firm, either because a sound business conception is lacking or because the employee disapproves of the existing one. After observing the firm's performance in a given competitive environment, the employee may have thought up his own and, at least subjectively, more appealing business conception. If such agents then found their own start-up enterprise, they can partly rely on the knowledge base they have previously acquired in their old firm.

In the course of imitation processes, the 'promoter profits' of the pioneering entrepreneurs are competed away and the innovation eventually becomes routine, possibly coupled with a lock-in of a dominant product design (Abernathy and Utterback, 1978). Firms then increase their attention to the production process, invest more in capital-intensive methods of production, and expand in size and output (Klepper, 1996). This often means routinization of tasks whose execution can be easily supervised so that a bureaucratic monitoring regime for running the firm organization may be quite effective. Since, as mentioned, tight monitoring tends to curb creativity and the intrinsic motivation for problem solving on the part of the employees, effective control may, however, come at the cost of a declining (only very costly, bureaucratically produced) innovative capacity. In a market environment with a rapid pace of innovation, diffusion by imitation, and corresponding competitive pressure on less innovative firms, static efficiency is not sufficient – the very point of the Schumpeterian competition hypothesis.

At this point, if not earlier, a characteristic period of 'shake out', i.e., a decline in the number of firms in the industry, occurs (Klepper, 1997), in the life cycle of an industry. This is caused by exits and mergers and acquisitions of the existing firms. Here, too, the driving force is entrepreneurial action. Again, this is usually based on a business conception of how, by integrating previously independent organizations and their activities, economic advantages can be realized through economies of scale, critical size, or more capital-intensive production methods.[9] The integration usually requires major organizational restructurings. If a regime of divided entrepreneurship is tried, conveying the business conception that guides these restructurings to the peer group of entrepreneurial managers and making them adopt it is an enormous challenge for the superior entrepreneur's cognitive leadership.

Innovations – new ideas, entrepreneurial imaginings, inventions, and commercial opportunities – occur in unevenly distributed ways over the life cycle of an industry. Relatively little is known so far about their sources, except that these are not the result of 'blind variation' (as Universal Darwinists, following Campbell, 1987, often claim). Even though innovations are the crucial element in Schumpeter's theory, he showed no interest in their sources. He simply assumed that technological and commercial novelty as such is abundantly available common knowledge (Schumpeter, 1934, p. 88). What counted for him was only the pioneering carrying out of 'new combinations' which, even though they were already widely known, nobody had dared as yet to realize. In a more encompassing view, the understanding of the endogenous emergence and diffusion of novelty requires hypotheses about both inventiveness and innovativeness. It is a fact that the human mind can intuitively grasp the meaning of novelty. Even though the very act of assigning meaning to newly generated novelty is not explicable, the motivations for human creative behavior can be analyzed. Such an analysis can help in explaining where, and when, novelty is more likely to emerge (cf. Witt, 2005).

These brief considerations of the sources of cultural or economic novelty point to evident differences when compared to the conditions under which genetic novelty emerges in biological evolution (for an early statement, cf. Alexander, 1981). The human mind is capable of suppressing meaningless novelty and of evaluating the significance of others *ex ante*, whereas each genetic novelty is physically expressed by biochemical processes and evaluated, in a more costly way, *ex post* by natural selection. Furthermore, in nature the causes of genetic variations are not only independent of the causes of natural selection: variations do not occur in a response to the needs of the organism (Mayr, 1991, p. 143). Because of the enormous complexity of the molecular processes of genetic recombination they are usually also considered random. In contrast, in cultural evolution in general, and in economic evolution in particular, the causes of novelty generation are not independent of the wants and longings of individuals. An entrepreneur may, for example, strive to avoid 'selection pressure', to enjoy a temporary monopoly, or to follow a general achievement motivation (McClelland, 1961). Meeting the needs of the agents is a crucial driving force behind the introduction of variation, i.e., the design of novelty.[10] The interaction between 'selection' and variation or novelty is at the core of industrial economics. Firms find ways to influence the competitive process and to pre-empt its effects. If they see their performance deteriorating relative to that of other firms, they usually react by deliberately seeking to improve it. Hence, there is a feedback between the kind and intensity of the competitive process and the generation of new ways of economic action which contributes to the fact that cultural change has outpaced genetic change.

5. Conclusions

In this chapter it has been argued that the differences between the way evolution works in nature and the way cultural, not least economic, evolution works are significant. This is obvious, if, for example, the process of natural selection is compared to the imitative knowledge diffusion processes in the economic sphere where cognition and social learning play a key role. Metaphors from, and analogy constructions to, the domain of biology – even the very abstract ones which refer to the principles of variation, selection, and retention – may therefore not be as useful as many of their proponents claim. This thesis accords with Schumpeter's reservations in this regard. As an alternative, a conceptual foundation for Schumpeterian, evolutionary dynamics has been advocated in which the cognitive influences and social learning processes are put at center stage. This is a more direct way of inquiring into the role of innovations and entrepreneurship than doing so via biological metaphors and analogies. It is a key, it has been contended, to a proper conceptualization of, on the one hand, organizational development and growth and, on the other hand, industrial dynamics.

Notes

1. Static game-theoretic models of 'innovation races' (e.g. Reinganum, 1985) that were designed to provide a theoretical foundation did not do justice to the notion of innovation and in their portrayal of the industry nothing was evolving.
2. Darwin (1859, ch. 4), Lewontin (1970), Mayr (1991, p. 87). There are two kinds of selection: first, there is natural selection for general viability that improves adaptedness and, second, there is sexual selection, both of which lead to greater reproductive success (Mayr, 1991, p. 164).
3. Note that such routines would have to operate on an even longer time scale in order to be able to assess and exchange lower organizational routines. In that case, the condition of an invariant market environment that would allow a discrimination to be made between the higher routines is even harder to meet.
4. Artifacts with similar purposes, for instance, can be designed to very different specifications and chosen for very different reasons (Ziman, 2000, p. 7).
5. Limiting the analysis to the level of organizational routines alone, while abstracting from the role of intentions, conceptions, and conjectures, i.e., the cognitive content, is therefore likely to exclude important determinants of industrial change. A significant example is the role of entrepreneurship. As has been argued elsewhere (Witt, 1998), this role is cognitive in nature – the conceiving, implementation, and enforcement of a business conception that provide the cognitive orientation on which the firm members can be coordinated. It is therefore perhaps no accident that entrepreneurship is rarely mentioned in the neo-Schumpeterian approach. Yet business conceptions are genuinely entrepreneurial accomplishments. They are needed to create and shape a firm. Consequently, they may inspire the design of organizational routines without themselves being organizational routines.
6. In anthropology this phenomenon is termed 'ratchet effect' (Tomasello, 1999).
7. With reference to hypotheses from evolutionary psychology, Cordes (2005a) has argued that there are specialized psychological mechanisms that have evolved during human phylogeny to solve cognitive problems linked to the making and using of tools. These mechanisms indicate considerable content sensitivity, also with respect to the observational learning of how to apply tools, and play a role in directing attentional processes. Thus, innate cognitive dispositions contribute to information which will be subject to profound contemplation, what information will easily diffuse within a population of agents, and whether it will become an input to creative, e.g., entrepreneurial, activity. Such a bias influences culturally engendered and institutionalized attitudes toward, for example, productive and useful work, the compliance with certain cultural norms, or the aesthetic sense for appreciating skill and dexterity.
8. As Penrose (1959) argued, their availability is a major bottleneck in the firms' growth.
9. The reason that a business venture is available for acquisition or merger may sometimes be related to a firm's development as outlined in the previous section. A start-up may have been able to expand under a founder entrepreneur until eventually it faces the above-mentioned growth-induced coordination crisis. Under such conditions, the founder entrepreneur may be unable, or unwilling, to make the transition to the necessary new organizational regimes. Instead, she or he may wish to cash in on the founding success and put the venture up for sale.

10.   'Design' indicates purpose. For its maker a variant's features are bound to be correlated with their intended purpose (Khalil, 1995; Ziman, 2000, p. 7). In a similar vein, Cordes (2005b) has argued that the motivation to avoid physical effort beyond a variable individual level of adaptation shapes the direction of human technological creativity.

References

Abernathy, W.J. and Utterback, J.M. (1978), 'Patterns of industrial innovation', *Technology Review*, **80**(7), 40–47.

Alexander, R.D. (1981), 'Evolution, culture, and human behavior: some general considerations', in R.D. Alexander and D.W. Tinkle (eds), *Natural Selection and Social Behavior*, New York: Chiron Press, pp. 509–20.

Andersen, E.S. (1994), *Evolutionary Economics – Post-Schumpeterian Contributions*, London: Pinter.

Baldwin, W.L. and Scott, J.T. (1987), *Market Structure and Technological Change*, Chur: Harwood Academic Publishers.

Bandura, A. (1986), *Social Foundations of Thought and Action*, Englewood Cliffs, NJ: Prentice-Hall.

Becker, M.C. (2004), 'Organizational routines: a review of the literature', *Industrial and Corporate Change*, **13**(4), 643–77.

Campbell, D.T. (1987), 'Blind variation and selective retention in creative thought as in other knowledge processes', in G. Radnitzky and W.W. Bartley (eds), *Evolutionary Epistemology, Theory of Rationality, and the Sociology of Knowledge*, La Salle, IL: Open Court, pp. 91–114.

Cantner, U. and Pyka, A. (2001), 'Classifying technology policy from an evolutionary perspective', *Research Policy*, **30**(5), 759–75.

Cordes, C. (2004), 'The human adaptation for culture and its behavioral implications', *Journal of Bioeconomics*, **6**(2), 143–63.

Cordes, C. (2005a), 'Veblen's "instinct of workmanship", its cognitive foundations, and some implications for economic theory', *Journal of Economic Issues*, **39**(1), 1–20.

Cordes, C. (2005b), 'Long-term tendencies in technological creativity: a preference-based approach', *Journal of Evolutionary Economics*, **15**(2), 149–68.

Cyert, R.M. and March, J.G. (1963), *The Behavioral Theory of the Firm*, Englewood Cliffs, NJ: Prentice-Hall.

Darwin, C. (1859), *On the Origin of the Species by Means of Natural Selection*, London: J. Murray.

Dawkins, R. (1983), 'Universal Darwinism', in D.S. Bendall (ed.), *Evolution from Molecules to Men*, Cambridge: Cambridge University Press, pp. 403–25.

Dosi, G. and Nelson, R.R. (1994), 'An introduction to evolutionary theories in economics', *Journal of Evolutionary Economics*, **4**, 153–72.

Hodgson, G.M. (2002), 'Darwinism in economics: from analogy to ontology', *Journal of Evolutionary Economics*, **12**, 259–81.

Hodgson, G.M. and Knudsen, T. (2004), 'The firm as an interactor: firms as vehicles for habits and routines', *Journal of Evolutionary Economics*, **14**(3), 281–307.

Khalil, E.L. (1995), 'Neo-classical economics and neo-Darwinism: clearing the way for historical thinking', in G.M. Hodgson (ed.), *Economics and Biology*, Aldershot, UK and Brookfield, US: Edward Elgar, pp. 548–98.

Klepper, S. (1996), 'Entry, exit, growth, and innovation over the product life cycle', *American Economic Review*, **86**(3), 562–83.

Klepper, S. (1997), 'Industry life cycles', *Industrial and Corporate Change*, **6**(1), 145–81.

Klepper, S. and Sleeper, S.B. (2002), 'Entry by Spinoffs', *Papers on Economics & Evolution*, 0207.

Knudsen, T. (2002), 'Economic selection theory', *Journal of Evolutionary Economics*, **12**, 443–70.

Knudsen, T. (2004), 'General selection theory and economic evolution: the price equation and the replicator/interactor distinction', *Journal of Economic Methodology*, **11**(2), 147–73.

Kruger, A.C., Ratner, H.H. and Tomasello, M. (1993), 'Cultural learning', *Behavioral and Brain Sciences*, **16**, 495–552.
Kwasnicki, W. (1996), *Knowledge, Innovation and Economy – An Evolutionary Exploration*, Cheltenham, UK and Brookfield, USA: Edward Elgar.
Lazaric, N. and Raybaut, A. (2005), 'Knowledge, hierarchy and the selection of routines: an interpretative model with group interactions', *Journal of Evolutionary Economics*, **15**(4), 393–421.
Lewontin, R. (1970), 'The units of selection', *Annual Review of Ecology and Systematics*, **1**, 1–18.
March, J.G. and Simon, H.A. (1958), *Organizations*, New York: Wiley.
Mayr, E. (1991), *One Long Argument: Charles Darwin and the Genesis of Modern Evolutionary Theory*, Cambridge, MA: Harvard University Press.
McClelland, D.C. (1961), *The Achieving Society*, New York: The Free Press.
Nelson, R.R. (1995), 'Recent evolutionary theorizing about economic change', *Journal of Economic Literature*, **23**, 48–90.
Nelson, R.R. and Winter, S.G. (1980), 'Firm and industry response to changed market conditions: an evolutionary approach', *Economic Inquiry*, **28**, 179–202.
Nelson, R.R. and Winter, S.G. (1982), *An Evolutionary Theory of Economic Change*, Cambridge, MA: Belknap Press of Harvard University Press.
Penrose, E.T. (1959), *The Theory of the Growth of the Firm*, Oxford: Basil Blackwell.
Price, G.R. (1995), 'The nature of selection', *Journal of Theoretical Biology*, **175**, 389–96.
Reinganum, J.F. (1985), 'Innovation and industry evolution', *Quarterly Journal of Economics*, **100**(1), 81–99.
Saviotti, P.P. and Pyka, A. (2004), 'Economic development by the creation of new sectors', *Journal of Evolutionary Economics*, **14**, 1–35.
Schumpeter, J.A. (1934), *The Theory of Economic Development*, Cambridge, MA: Harvard University Press.
Schumpeter, J.A. (1942), *Capitalism, Socialism and Democracy*: New York, Harper & Brothers.
Schumpeter, J.A. (2002), 'The economy as a whole – seventh chapter of the Theory of Economic Development', *Industry and Innovation*, **9**(1/2), 93–145.
Singer, W. (2000), 'Response synchronization: a universal coding strategy for the definition of relations', in M.S. Gazzaniga (ed.), *The New Cognitive Neurosciences*, Cambridge, MA: MIT Press, pp. 325–38.
Tomasello, M. (1999), 'The human adaptation for culture', *Annual Review of Anthropology*, **28**, 509–29.
Winter, S.G. (1964), 'Economic "natural selection" and the theory of the firm', *Yale Economic Essays*, **4**, 225–72.
Witt, U. (1998), 'Imagination and leadership – the neglected dimension of an evolutionary theory of the firm', *Journal of Economic Behavior and Organization*, **35**, 161–77.
Witt, U. (2000), 'Changing cognitive frames – changing organizational forms: an entrepreneurial theory of organizational development', *Industrial and Corporate Change*, **9**(4), 733–55.
Witt, U. (2002), 'How evolutionary is Schumpeter's theory of economic development?', *Industry and Innovation*, **9**(1/2), 7–22.
Witt, U. (2003), *The Evolving Economy – Essays on the Evolutionary Approach to Economics*, Cheltenham, UK and Northampton, MA, USA: Edward Elgar.
Witt, U. (2005), 'On novelty and heterogeneity', in T. Lux, S. Reitz and E. Samanidou (eds), *Non-linear Dynamics and Heterogeneous Interacting Agents*, Berlin: Springer, pp. 123–38.
Ziman, J. (2000), 'Evolutionary models for technological change', in J. Ziman (ed.), *Technological Innovation as an Evolutionary Process*, Cambridge: Cambridge University Press, pp. 3–12.

2.1.3
Innovation processes and patterns

21 Technological paradigms and trajectories*

Giovanni Dosi and Mauro Sylos Labini

Introduction

It is well recognized that the accumulation of knowledge and the related evolution of technology are fundamental drivers of socioeconomic change. However, beyond such general agreement, the social sciences still face subtle and controversial issues concerning the detailed understanding of what Richard Nelson calls the evolution of human know-how (Nelson, 2003).

More specifically, intricate puzzles concern 'what ultimately determines what . . .'. For example, as discussed at greater length in Dosi, Orsenigo and Sylos Labini (2005), is it resource accumulation that primarily fosters the exploration of novel innovative opportunities, or, conversely, does innovation drive capital accumulation? Do new technological opportunities emerge mainly from some extra economic domain ('pure science') or are they primarily driven by economic incentives? Should one assume that the institutions – however defined – supporting technical change are sufficiently adaptive to adjust to whatever economic inducement emerges from market interactions; or, conversely, are they inertial enough to shape the rates and directions of innovation and diffusion?

A first major issue concerns the identification of possible invariances in the patterns of technological search and knowledge accumulation, together with discrete differences across sectors and industries. Relatedly, a general question regards what one may call the *degrees of plasticity* of technological changes vis-à-vis economic and social drivers as distinct from the inner momentum that technology-specific opportunities happen to provide. Pushing it to caricatured extremes, what are the constraints to what 'money can buy'? Conversely, are there hard 'natural' boundaries to what social dynamics may 'negotiate'?

In any case, the revealed economic impact of technological innovation has to be understood and explained in a broader context, linking the elements of a microeconomic theory of innovation to the macroeconomic patterns of socioeconomic change.

---

* This work draws upon a longer essay (Dosi, Orsenigo and Sylos Labini, 2005), to which the reader is also referred for much more thorough background references.

Paradigms and trajectories: some basic features

In order to begin to answer the foregoing questions, a variety of concepts have been put forward over the last couple of decades to characterize the nature of innovative activities:[1] technological regimes, paradigms, trajectories, salients, guidepost, dominant design and so on. These concepts are highly overlapping in that they try to capture a few common features of the procedures and direction of technical change. Let us consider some of them. The notion of technological paradigm, which shall for the time being serve as our yardstick is based on a view of technology grounded on three fundamental ideas.

First, it suggests that any satisfactory description of 'what is technology' and how it changes must also embody the representation of the specific forms of knowledge on which a particular activity is based and can not be reduced to a set of well-defined blueprints. It primarily concerns problem-solving activities involving, to varying degrees, tacit forms of knowledge embodied in individuals and organizational procedures.

Second, paradigms entail specific heuristics and visions of 'how to do things' and how to improve them, often shared by the community of practitioners in each particular activity (engineers, firms, technical society, etc.), i.e. they entail collectively shared cognitive frames (Constant, 1980).

Third, paradigms often also define basic templates of artifacts and systems, which over time are progressively modified and improved. These basic artifacts can be described in terms of some fundamental technological and economic characteristics. For example, in the case of an airplane, the basic attributes are described not only and obviously in terms of inputs and production costs, but also on the basis of some salient technological features such as wing-load, take-off weight, speed, distance it can cover, etc. What is interesting here is that technical progress seems to display patterns and invariances in terms of these product characteristics. Examples of technological invariances of this kind can be found e.g. in semiconductors, agricultural equipment, automobiles and a few other micro technological studies (Sahal, 1981; Saviotti, 1996). The exponential growth of transistor-per-cheap and clock speed in microprocessor – the so-called Moore's law – is probably the most famous and popularized example of invariance: over the last 30 years, no matter what the relative price dynamics and the appropriability conditions, it has remained surprisingly steady. Recently, Frenken, Saviotti and Trommetter (1999), searching for sound empirical measures of variety, have proposed an interesting empirical account as to the way in which different artifacts follow relatively stable patterns in the space of their basic characteristics: the driving forces behind these patterns, it is suggested, are the scope of the specific technology (the range of services it can perform), but also the rate of advance of the relevant knowledge necessary to produce them. In general, the notion of techno-logical trajectories is associated with the progressive realization of the inno-vative opportunities underlying each paradigm, which can in principle be measured in terms of the changes in the fundamental technoeconomic characteristics of artifacts and production processes.[2] The core ideas involved in this notion are the following:

a. Each particular body of knowledge (each paradigm) shapes and con-strains the rates and direction of technical change, if a first rough approximation, irrespective of market inducements.
b. Technical change is partly driven by repeated attempts to cope with technological imbalances which it itself creates.[3]
c. As a consequence, one should be able to observe regularities and invariances in the pattern of technical change which hold under different market conditions (e.g. under different relative prices) and the disruption of which is mainly correlated with radical changes in knowl-edge bases (in paradigms).

The concepts of paradigms and trajectories are also in tune with the rather general supposition, by now widely acknowledged in the innovation literature, that learning is *local* and *cumulative*. 'Locality' means that the exploration and development of new techniques and product architectures is likely to occur in the neighborhood of the techniques and architectures already in use (Atkinson and Stiglitz, 1969; David, 1975; Antonelli, 1995). 'Cumulativeness' stands for the property that current technological devel-opments often build upon past experiences of production and innovation, proceed via sequences of specific problem solving junctures (Vincenti, 1990), and in a few circumstances also lead to microeconomic serial corre-lations in successes and failures. This is what Paul David, citing Robert Merton, citing The New Testament, calls the Matthew Effect: 'For unto every one that hath shall be given, and he shall have abundance: but from him that hath not shall be taken away even that which he hath.' Note that 'cumulativeness' at the micro level provides robust support for those inter-firm asymmetries in performances which one increasingly finds in diverse longitudinal databases, while industry-wide, region-wide and country-wide factors of cumulativeness in learning dynamics are good candidates for the explanation of why industries, regions and countries tend systematically to differ in both technological and economic performances.

The robustness of notions such as technological trajectories is of course a primarily empirical question. Be that as it may, fundamental issues regard the carriers, the fine-grained processes and the driving factors underlying the observed patterns of technological change.

Technological paradigm and the patterns of technological discovery
The notion of technological paradigm is clearly an attempt to characterize the structure of technological knowledge and its accumulation over
time. It happens that such a notion has become part of a larger analytical
perspective trying to interpret economic change as an evolutionary
process (cf. Nelson and Winter, 1982; Dosi *et al.*, 1988). However a
distinct stream of investigation, under the heading of *evolutionary epistemology*, has invoked evolutionary processes in order to account for
knowledge dynamics themselves. The term was coined by Donald
Campbell (1974) in his generalization of Popper's falsificationist philosophy of science to knowledge processes at all biological, psychological and
social levels. Drawing on the theories of biological evolution, Campbell
addresses knowledge dynamics with the spectacles of *blind variation and
selective retention.*[4] Rather controversial issues here include the following:
How close should the analogy be with biological evolution? And, more
specifically, to what extent are knowledge variations 'blind'? What are the
fundamental units which undergo an evolutionary process? What does
'selection' precisely mean and how does it operate in the arena of knowledge accumulation?

In this respect, we suggest that the 'blindness' issue may well be a false
problem. Even if the processes of search (in both domains of science and
technology) are highly structured by the pre-existing bodies of knowledge,
improvements and discoveries are always full of unexpected events and surprises. In the case of new technological knowledge, innovation almost by
definition implies the achievement of results that are beyond well specified
and well understood *ex ante* options.[5]

Conversely, our inclination is *not* to draw too close an analogy between
biological and social evolution. For example, we are generally rather
skeptical of analogies such as those suggested by Richard Dawkins
(1983) between genes and cultural 'memes' – whatever they are.[6] In addition, we are even more skeptical about *misuses* of the biological analogy,
trying to explain the efficiency or even the evolutionary optimality of
a particular body of knowledge and cultural traits on the grounds of
their purported beneficial value in terms of survival and environmental
adaptation.

Be that as it may, in this domain of analysis of the dynamics of knowledge one is only beginning to link technology centered investigation with
the broader field of studies addressing the nature and dynamics of cognitive structures and learning processes for some discussion of these issues,
cf. Dosi, Marengo and Fagiolo (2005) and, focused in particular on the fascinating question as to why human know-how has evolved so unevenly in
different fields, cf. Nelson (2003).

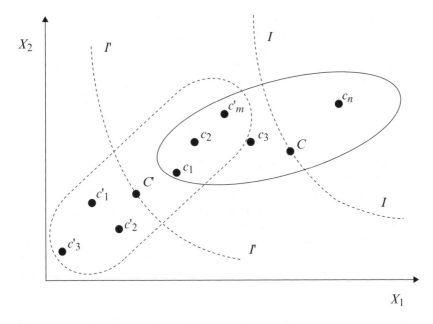

Figure 21.1 Distribution of micro coefficients

Paradigms, trajectories and the theory of production[7]

Paradigms and trajectories have important implications for any theory of production seeking to be sufficiently abstract in order to grasp some basic general features of technology and of production processes, and at the same time to be in tune with the microeconomic evidence. The story we suggest runs as follows.

In general, micro coefficients are distributed somewhat as depicted in Figure 21.1, where the combinations of two inputs necessary to produce the same unit of output are represented. We show at two different points of time (the two sets depicted) the single techniques/firms ($c_1, c_2, \ldots, c_n$) and ($c_1', c_2', \ldots, c_n'$), and their mean values over any industry, C and C'. The basic features of the distribution of techniques and their dynamics are the following:

1. At any point in time there are likely to be one or very few best practice techniques (e.g. c_1) which dominate, irrespective (or within reasonably wide ranges) of relative prices.
2. Different agents are characterized by persistently diverse techniques. Even if they are informed about the existence of superior ones they simply do not know how to implement them. Pushing the argument

further, even if firms were given all the blueprints of the best practice technique, performance and thus revealed input coefficients might still differ widely.

3. Over time (let us say at t') the dynamic of firms' technical coefficients in each particular activity is the joint result of the process of imitation/ diffusion of the best practice techniques and of the search for new ones. The processes are driven and constrained by the relevant technological paradigms (and potentially influenced by relative prices).

4. Moreover, the aggregate evolution of observed input coefficients is shaped by (i) selection (e.g. variation of market shares given and mortality patterns) and (ii) the entry of new firms.

5. Changes over time of the best practice techniques themselves highlight rather regular paths (i.e. trajectories) both in the space of input coefficients and also in the space of the core technical characteristics of outputs. Changes in the relative prices, in a first approximation, do not induce substitution among 'technical blueprints' already known to the firms. Rather, they affect both the direction of imitation and the adoption of innovation by the firms themselves.

Note that, in this story, no mention has been made of notions such as 'production functions'. Of course, one can always draw some imaginary 'isoquants' through C, C', C'' etc, together with the lines depicting relative prices at t, t', t'' . . ., and then undertake the usual estimations, separating 'interfactoral substitution' from the so-called 'technological progress'. However, if our story is correct, such an exercise does not shed any new light on the process of change of the coefficients, but rather obscures its actual drivers.

In our definition of trajectory, it is appropriate to expand the space over which technologies are described, in order to include, in addition to input requirements (i.e. the economic definition of techniques in the incumbent production theory), the core characteristics of processes and artifacts. The general conjecture here is that in this higher dimensional space trajectories and 'punctuated' discontinuities are associated with progress upon and changes in knowledge bases, artifact templates and search heuristics. In this respect, Saviotti and Metcalfe (1984) have distinguished between 'technical' and 'service' characteristics of products. The first can be directly manipulated by producers and describes the internal structure of the technology (e.g. wing span). The second are variables that also users take into account in their adoption or purchasing decision (e.g. speed).[8] Admittedly, while the above distinction may be useful for analytical purposes, it is not always easy to apply in empirical studies (e.g. is fuselage length imposed by the internal structure of the technology or by the needs of airlines?).

Our discussion so far has primarily focused upon some general feat-ures of technological knowledge, production processes and their revealed technoeconomic outcomes. In turn, note that a good deal of 'economi-cally useful' technological knowledge is nowadays mastered by business firms, which even undertake in some countries a small but not negligible portion of the research aimed at a more speculative understanding of physical, chemical and biological properties of our world (i.e. they under-take 'basic science').[9] Given that, how does the foregoing interpretation of technological knowledge relate to the structure and behavior of firms themselves?

Technology, capabilities and theory of the firm
Possibly one of the most exciting intellectual enterprises developed over the last decade has involved the interbreeding between the evolutionary eco-nomics research program (largely evolutionary inspired), technological innovation studies and an emerging competence/capability-based theory of the firm. The roots lie in the pioneering organizational studies of Herbert Simon, James March and colleagues (Simon, 1969; March and Simon, 1993; Cyert and March, 1992; March, 1988) and in the equally pioneering explorations of the nature and economic implications of organizational routines of Nelson and Winter (1982) (including follow-up studies such as those discussed in Teece, Pisano and Shuen, 1997; Dosi, Nelson and Winter, 2000; Dosi, Coriat and Pavitt, 2000, the Special Issue of *Industrial and Corporate Change*, 2000, edited by Mie Augier and James March; Montgomery, 1995; and Foss and Mahnke, 2000). It is intuitive enough that business firms 'know how to do certain things' – things such as building automobiles and computers – and know that these are performed with different efficacies and revealed performances. In turn, as one sees in Dosi, Nelson and Winter (2000) and Dosi, Faillo and Marengo (2003), organiza-tional knowledge is in fact a fundamental link between the social pool of knowledge/skills/discovery opportunities, on the one hand, and the rates/direction/economic effectiveness of their exploration/development/exploitation on the other.

Distinctive organizational competences/capabilities bear importance also in that they persistently shape the destiny of individual firms, in terms, of for example, profitability, growth, probability of survival, and, at least equally as important, their distribution across firms shapes the patterns of change of broader aggregates such as particular sectors or whole countries. In this respect, capability-based theories of the firm may be considered as a sort of projection of knowledge dynamics, dis-cussed earlier, into the space of organizational traits and organizational behaviors.

Technoeconomic paradigms: from micro technologies to national systems of innovation and production

So far, we have discussed paradigms, trajectories or equivalent concepts mainly at the microtechnological level. A paradigm-based theory of innovation and production (we have argued) seems to be highly consistent with the evidence on the patterned and cumulative nature of technical change and also with the evidence on microeconomic heterogeneity and technological gaps. Moreover, it directly links with those theories of production in economics which allow for dynamic increasing returns (from A. Young and Kaldor to recent and more rigorous formalized on path-dependent models of innovation diffusion), whereby the interaction between micro decisions and some forms of learning or some externalities produces irreversible technological paths and lock-in effects with respect to technologies which may well be inferior, on any measure, to other notional ones, but still happen to be dominant – loosely speaking – because of the weight of their history (Arthur, 1989; David, 1985; Dosi and Bassanini, 2001).

The upside of the same story is that a world of knowledge-driven increasing returns is much less bleak than conventional economic theory has been preaching: there always are (partly) 'free lunches', offered by ever-emerging opportunities for technological, organizational and institutional innovation. However, there is nothing automatic in the economic fulfillment of the notional promises offered by persistent and widespread learning processes. Indeed the fulfillment of such promises ultimately depends upon matching/mismatching patterns between technological knowledge, the structure and behaviors of business organizations and broader institutional set-ups.

The steps leading from a microeconomic theory of innovation and production to more aggregate analyses are clearly numerous and complex. A first obvious question concerns the possibility of identifying relatively coherent structure and dynamics at broader levels of observation. Indeed, historians of technology (T. Hughes, B. Gilles and P. David, among others) highlight the importance of technological systems, in the terminology of this chapter, structured combination of *micro* technological paradigms.[10]

Diverse but overlapping streams of inquiry have recently focused on systems of innovation at the levels of sectors, regions and nations.[11] The analysis of such systems happens to occur, in the literature, from different angles.

One such analysis focuses upon the specificities of national institutions and policies supporting directly or indirectly innovation, diffusion and skills accumulation (by way of illustration, think of the role of university research and of military/space programs in the US 'national system' or of training institutions in the German one).[12]

A second approach emphasizes the importance of user–producer relations and the associated development of a collective knowledge base and commonly shared behavioral rules and expectations.[13]

Third, Patel and Pavitt, among others, have stressed the links between national patterns of technological accumulation and the competencies and innovative strategies of a few major national companies.[14]

Fourth, a few scholars have began to analyze the institutional and organizational specificities of sectoral systems of innovation, production and competition (Malerba and Orsenigo, 1996; Marsili, 2001).

At an even higher level of generality, Freeman and Perez (1988), Freeman and Louçã (2001) and Perez (2002) have used the notion of *technoeconomic paradigms* as a synthetic definition of macro-level systems of production, innovation, political governance and social relations. For example, they identify broad phases of modern industrial development, partly isomorphic to the notion of 'regimes of socio-economic "Regulation"' suggested by the mainly French macroinstitutionalist literature (Aglietta, 1976; Boyer, 1988a, 1988b; see also Coriat and Dosi, 1998a).

In an extreme synthesis, both perspectives hold, first, that one may identify rather long periods of capitalist development distinguished according to specific engines of technological dynamism and their modes of governance of the relationships amongst the major social actors (e.g. firms, workers, banks, collective political authorities, etc.) and, second, that the patterns of technological advancement and those of institutional changes are bound to be coupled in such ways as to yield recognizable invariances for quite long periods in most economic and political structures. Just to provide an example, one might roughly identify, over the three decades after World War II, across most developed economies, some 'Fordist/Keynesian' regimes of socioeconomic 'regulation', driven by major innovative opportunities of technological innovation in electromechanical technologies, synthetic chemistry, forms of institutional governance of industrial conflict, income distribution and aggregate demand management. Analogously, earlier in industrial history, one should be able to detect some sort of archetype of a 'classical/Victorian regime' driven in its growth by the full exploitation of textile manufacturing and light engineering mechanization, relatively competitive labor markets, politically driven effort to expand privileged market outlets, etc.[15]

These general conjectures on historical phases or regimes are grounded on the importance in growth and development of specific combinations among technological systems and forms of socioeconomic governance. More specifically, on the technological side, the notions of technoeconomic paradigms predict that growth in each phase is driven by the exploration of distinct sources of technological knowledge with a highly pervasive scope of application across multiple activities and products, such as, in the past, steam engine technologies and, later, electricity, or, nowadays, information and communication technologies.[16]

A complementary, somewhat more 'cross-sectional', exercise concerns the identification of national socioeconomic regimes with distinctive embedding mechanisms of technological learning within national systems of innovation, production and governance.

So, even if micro paradigms present considerable invariances across countries, the ways they are combined in broader national systems of innovation display, we suggest, a considerable variety, shaped by county-specific institutions, policies and social factors. The hypothesis here is that evolutionary microfoundations are a fruitful starting point for a theory showing the way in which technological gaps and national institutional diversities jointly reproduce themselves over rather long spans of time, in ways that are easily compatible with the patterns of incentives and opportunities facing individual agents, even when they might turn out to be profoundly suboptimal from a collective point of view (on what one may call the political economy of diverse technoeconomic paradigms).[17]

Notes

1. Interpretations of technical change and a number of historical examples may be found in Freeman and Soete (1997), Freeman (1994), Rosenberg (1994), Nelson and Winter (1982), Hughes (1983), David (1975), Saviotti (1996), Pavitt (1999), Dosi (1984), Basalla (1988), Constant (1980) and Ziman (2000), among others. (For partial surveys see Dosi, 1988, and Freeman, 1994.)
2. Incidentally, note that the notion of dominant design is well in tune with the general idea of technological paradigms but the latter does not necessarily imply the former. A revealing case are pharmaceuticals technologies which involve specific knowledge bases, specific search heuristics, etc. (i.e. the strong mark of paradigms) without any hint at dominant design. Molecules, even when aimed at the same pathology, might have quite different structures: in that space, one is unlikely to find similarities akin to those linking even a Volkswagen Beetle 1937 and a Ferrari 2000. Still, the notion of 'paradigm' holds in terms of underlying features of knowledge bases and search processes.
3. This is akin to the notion of reverse salient (Hughes, 1983) and technological bottlenecks (Rosenberg, 1976); to illustrate, think of increasing the speed of a machine tool, which in turn demands changes in cutting materials, which leads to changes in other parts of the machine.
4. More precisely, his framework rests on three basic ideas: (i) the principle of blind variation and selective retention, (ii) the concept of a vicarious selector (i.e. knowledge that has been retained and is already in memory directs further research in a not-blind way) and (iii) the organization of vicarious selectors as a nested hierarchy.
5. For example, Vincenti (1990), describing the way in which engineers explore and achieve new designs, vividly clarifies the tension between purposeful search and 'blind' trials.
6. See Ziman (2000) and Hodgson (1993) for critical discussions of the analogies and differences among models of biological, cultural and socioeconomic evolution.
7. This section largely draws from Cimoli and Dosi (1995).
8. Incidentally, such an approach may be considered an adaptation to technological innovation of the approach used by Lancaster (1966) to propose a 'new' consumer theory.
9. See Pavitt (1991), Rosenberg (1990).

10. See for example the fascinating reconstruction of the emerging system of electrification and electrical standards in David (1991), taken as an insightful guidance also for contemporary diffusion of ICT systems.
11. For a broad review see Freeman (1995).
12. In this vein, see especially the contribution of Nelson (1993).
13. See in particular, the works in Lundvall (1992).
14. See Patel and Pavitt (1997) and for some qualifications Cantwell (1989) and (1997).
15. For more on this, see Coriat and Dosi (1998b).
16. A sort of reduced form of such a notion of technoeconomic paradigms comes – especially in the north American literature – under the heading of 'general purpose technology' (see Bresnahan and Trajtenberg, 1995).
17. See, from different angles, Soskice (1997), Boyer and Hollingsworth (1997), Amable, Barré and Boyer (1997), Hall and Soskice (2001), Crouch and Streeck (1997), Kogut (1993), Lazonick (2002) and Aoki (2001).

References

Aglietta, M. 1976. *A Theory of Capitalist Regulation: The US Experience*, London: Verso.
Amable B., R. Barré and R. Boyer. 1997. *Les systèmes d'innovation à l'ère de la globalisation*, Paris: Economica.
Antonelli, C. 1995. *The Economics of Localized Technological Change and Industrial Dynamics*, Boston, MA: Kluwer Academic Publishers.
Aoki, M. 2001. *Towards a Comparative Institutional Analysis*, Cambridge, MA: MIT Press.
Arthur, W.B. 1989. 'Competing technologies, increasing returns, and lock-in by historical events', *Economic Journal*, **99**, 116–31.
Atkinson, A.B and J.E. Stiglitz. 1969. 'A new view of technological change', *The Economic Journal*, **79**(315), 573–8.
Basalla, G. 1988. *The Evolution of Technology*, Cambridge: Cambridge University Press.
Boyer, R. 1988a. 'Technical change and the theory of "regulation"', in G. Dosi *et al.* (eds), *Technical Change and Economic Theory*, London: Pinter Publishers, pp. 67–94.
Boyer, R. 1988b. 'Formalizing growth regimes within a regulation approach. A method for assessing the economic consequences of technological change', in G. Dosi *et al.* (eds), *Technical Change and Economic Theory*, London: Pinter Publishers, pp. 608–30.
Boyer, R. and J.R. Hollingsworth. 1997. *Contemporary Capitalism: The Embeddedness of Institutions*, Cambridge: Cambridge University Press.
Bresnahan, T.F. and M. Trajtenberg. 1995. 'General purpose technologies "Engines of Growth"?', *Journal of Econometrics*, **65**, 83–108.
Campbell, D. 1974. 'Evolutionary epistemology', in P.A. Schilpp (ed.), *The Philosophy of Karl Popper*, vol.14, LaSalle, IL: Open Court Publishing Company.
Cantwell, J.A. 1989. *Technological Innovation and Multinational Corporations*, Oxford: Basil Blackwell.
Cantwell, J.A. 1997. 'The globalization of technology: what remains of the product cycle model?', in D. Archibugi and J. Michie (eds), *Technology, Globalisation and Economic Performance*, Cambridge: Cambridge University Press, pp. 172–97.
Cimoli, M. and G. Dosi. 1995. 'Technological paradigms, patterns of learning and development: an introductory road map', *Journal of Evolutionary Economics*, **5**, 243–68.
Constant, E.W. 1980. *The Origins of the Turbojet Revolution*, Baltimore, MD: Johns Hopkins University Press.
Coriat, B. and G. Dosi. 1998a. 'The institutional embeddedness of economic change. an appraisal of the "evolutionary" and the "regulationist" research programs', in K. Nielsen and B. Johnson (eds), *Institutions and Economic Change*, Cheltenham, UK and Lyme, USA: Edward Elgar.
Coriat, B. and G. Dosi. 1998b. 'Learning how to govern and learning how to solve problems. On the co-evolution of competences, conflicts and organizational routines', in A. Chandler, P. Hagström and Ö. Sölvell (eds), *The Dynamic Firm*, Oxford/New York: Oxford University Press.

Crouch, C. and W. Streeck. 1997. *Political Economy of Modern Capitalism*, London: Sage.

Cyert, R.M. and J.G. March. 1992. *A Behavioral Theory of the Firm*, 2nd edn, Oxford: Blackwell Business.

David, P.A. 1975. *Technical Choice, Innovation and Economic Growth*, Cambridge, MA: Cambridge University Press.

David, P.A. 1985. 'Clio and the economics of QWERTY', *American Economic Review*, **75**, 332–7.

David, P. 1991. 'Computer and dynamo. The modern productivity paradox in a not too distant mirror', in OECD (ed.), *Technology and Productivity. The Challenge for Economic Policy*, Paris: OECD, pp. 315–47.

Dawkins, R. 1983. *The Extended Phenotype: The Gene as a Unit of Selection*, Oxford: Oxford University Press.

Dosi, G. 1984. *Technical Change and Industrial Transformation*, London: Macmillan.

Dosi, G. 1988. 'Sources, procedures and microeconomic effects of innovation', *Journal of Economic Literature*, **26**, 1120–71.

Dosi, G. and A. Bassanini. 2001. 'When and how chance and human will can twist the arms of Clio: an essay on path-dependence in a world of irreversibilities', in R. Garud and P. Karnoe (eds), *Path-Dependence and Creation*, Mahwah, NJ: Lawrence Erlbaum Associates.

Dosi, G., B. Coriat and K. Pavitt. 2000. 'Competences, capabilities and corporate performance', Final Report Dynacom Project (http://www.sssup.it/~LEM/Dynacom/files/DFR.pdf).

Dosi, G., M. Faillo and L. Marengo. 2003. 'Organizational capabilities, patterns of knowledge accumulation and governance structures: an introduction', LEM Working Paper no. 11, Pisa.

Dosi, G., L. Marengo and G. Fagiolo. 2005. 'Learning in evolutionary environments', in K. Dopfer (ed.) (2005), *Evolutionary Foundations of Economics*, Cambridge: Cambridge University Press.

Dosi, G., R.R. Nelson and S. Winter. 2000. *The Nature and Dynamics of Organizational Capabilities*, Oxford: Oxford University Press.

Dosi, G., L. Orsenigo and M. Sylos Labini. 2005. 'Technology and the economy', in N.J. Smelser and R. Swedberg (eds), *The Handbook of Economic Sociology*, 2nd edn, Princeton, NJ: Princeton University Press.

Dosi, G., C. Freeman, R.R. Nelson, G. Silverberg and L. Soete. 1988. *Technical Change and Economic Theory*, London/New York: Pinter Publishers.

Foss, N.J. and V. Mahnke. 2000. *Competence, Governance, and Entrepreneurship: Advances in Economic Strategy Research*, Oxford/New York: Oxford University Press.

Freeman, C. 1994. 'The economics of technical change: a critical survey', *Cambridge Journal of Economics*, **18**, 1–50.

Freeman, C. 1995. 'The national system of innovation in historical perspective', *Cambridge Journal of Economics*, **19**(1), 5–24.

Freeman, C. and F. Louçã. 2001. *As Time Goes By: The Information Revolution & the Industrial Revolutions in Historical Perspective*, Oxford: Oxford University Press.

Freeman, C. and C. Perez. 1988. 'Structural crises of adjustment: business cycles and investment behaviour', in G. Dosi *et al.* (eds), *Technical Change and Economic Theory*, London: Pinter Publishers.

Freeman, C. and L. Soete. 1997. *The Economics of Industrial Innovation*, London: Francis Pinter.

Frenken, K., P.P. Saviotti and M. Trommetter. 1999. 'Variety and niche creation in aircraft, helicopters, motorcycles and microcomputers', *Research Policy*, **28**(5), 469–88.

Hall, P. and D. Soskice. 2001. *Varieties of Capitalism – The Institutional Foundations of Comparative Advantage*, Oxford: Oxford University Press.

Hodgson, G.M. 1993. *Economics and Evolution: Bringing Life Back into Economics*, Cambridge: Polity Press, and Ann Arbor, MI: University of Michigan Press.

Hughes, T.P. 1983. *Networks of Power: Electrification in Western Society 1880–1930*, Baltimore, MD: Johns Hopkins University Press.

Kogut, B. 1993. *Country Competitiveness: Technology and Organization of Work*, Oxford: Oxford University Press.

Lancaster, K.J. 1966. 'A new approach to consumer theory', *Journal of Political Economy*, **74**, 132–57.

Lazonick, W. 2002. *American Corporate Economy*, London: Routledge.

Lundvall, B.-Å. 1992. *National Systems of Innovation: Towards a Theory of Innovation and Interactive Learning*, London: Pinter Publishers.

Malerba, F. and L. Orsenigo. 1996. 'The dynamics and evolution of industries', *Industrial and Corporate Change*, **5**, 51–88.

March, J.G. 1988. *Decision and Organization*, Oxford: Basil Blackwell.

March, J.G. and H. Simon. 1993. 'Organizations revisited', *Industrial and Corporate Change*, **2**(3), 299–316.

Marsili, O. 2001. *The Anatomy and Evolution of Industries: Technological Change and Industrial Dynamics*, Cheltenham, UK and Northampton, MA, USA: Edward Elgar.

Montgomery, C.A. 1995. *Resource-based and Evolutionary Theories of the Firm*, Dordrecht: Kluwer.

Nelson, R.R. 1993. *National Systems of Innovation*, Oxford: Oxford University Press.

Nelson, R.R. 2003. 'On the uneven evolution of human know how', *Research Policy*, **32**, 909–22.

Nelson, R.R. and S.G. Winter. 1982. *An Evolutionary Theory of Economic Change*, Cambridge, MA: The Belknap Press of Harvard University Press.

Patel, P. and K. Pavitt. 1997. 'The technological competencies of the world's largest firms: complex and path-dependent, but not much variety', *Research Policy*, **26**(2), 141–56.

Pavitt, K. 1991. 'What makes basic research economically useful?', *Research Policy*, **20**(2), 109–19.

Pavitt, K. 1999. *Technology Management and Systems of Innovation*, Cheltenham, UK and Northampton, MA, USA: Edward Elgar.

Perez, C. 2002. *Technological Revolutions and Financial Capital. The Dynamics of Bubbles and Golden Ages*, Cheltenham, UK and Northampton, MA, USA: Edward Elgar.

Rosenberg, N. 1976. *Perspectives on Technology*, Cambridge, MA: Cambridge University Press.

Rosenberg, N. 1990. 'Why do firms do basic research (with their money)?', *Research Policy*, **19**, 165–74.

Rosenberg, N. 1994. *Exploring the Black Box: Technology, Economics and History*, Cambridge: Cambridge University Press.

Sahal, D. 1981. *Recent Advances in the Theory of Technological Change*, New York: Addison-Wesley.

Saviotti, P. 1996. *Technological Evolution, Variety and the Economy*, Cheltenham, UK and Brookfield, USA: Edward Elgar.

Saviotti, P.P. and J.S. Metcalfe 1984. 'A theoretical approach to the construction of technological output indicators', *Research Policy*, **14**(3), 141–51.

Simon, H.A. 1969. *Science of the Artificial*, Cambridge, MA: MIT Press.

Soskice, D. 1997. 'German technology policy, innovation, and national institutional frameworks', *Industry and Innovation*, **4**, 75–96.

Teece, D.J., G. Pisano and A. Shuen. 1997. 'Dynamic capabilities and strategic management', *Strategic Management Journal*, **18**(7), 509–33.

Vincenti, W.G. 1990. *What Engineers Know and How They Know It: Analytical Studies from Aeronautical History*, Baltimore, MD: The Johns Hopkins University Press.

Ziman, J. 2000. *Technological Innovation as an Evolutionary Process*, Cambridge: Cambridge University Press.

22 Schumpeterian patterns of innovation and technological regimes

Franco Malerba

1 Introduction[1]

The structure and organization of innovative activities greatly differs across sectors. In certain sectors innovative activities are concentrated among a few major innovators while, in others, innovative activities are distributed among several firms. In some sectors large firms do the bulk of innovative activities while in others small firms or new innovators may be quite active.

This difference in the structure of innovative activities may be related to a fundamental distinction widely studied by Schumpeter. Schumpeter identified two major patterns of innovative activities, one characterized by 'creative destruction' with technological ease of entry and a major role played by entrepreneurs and new firms in innovative activities, and the other by 'creative accumulation' (using the label proposed by Keith Pavitt) with the prevalence of large established firms and the presence of relevant barriers to entry for new innovators. Of course, these two different structures of innovative activities are very stylized and a lot of sectors present intermediate forms in the structure of their innovative activities. But for conceptual and analytical purposes it is important here to focus on these two archetypical ways.

In recent years, Schumpeterian and evolutionary research have first of all verified the presence of these two distinct forms of relationship between market structure and innovation and, while recognizing the dynamic endogenous relationship between market structure and innovation, have also related them to some rather invariant features (with respect to relative prices and incentives mechanisms) of learning and knowledge accumulation: *technological (learning) regimes*. The notion of technological regime provides a synthetic representation of some of the most important economic properties of technologies and of the characteristics of the learning processes that are involved in innovative activities.

Section 2 discusses the features and the empirical evidence of the relationship between market structure and innovation in Schumpeterian and evolutionary perspectives, identifying the two distinct patterns of innovative activities. Section 3 examines the notion of technological regimes in general and then it focuses on opportunity, appropriability, cumulativeness and knowledge base conditions. Section 4 analyses the relationship between technological regimes and Schumpeterian patterns of innovative activities. Finally, in section 5, some basic lessons and future research directions are examined.

2 Schumpeterian patterns of innovation

Schumpeter identified two different basic forms of innovation and market structure. The first one, labelled subsequently *Schumpeter Mark I*,[2] was proposed in *The Theory of Economic Development* (1934). This pattern of innovative activity is characterized by 'creative destruction' with technological ease of entry and a major role played by entrepreneurs and new firms in innovative activities. New entrepreneurs come in a sector with new ideas and innovations, launch new enterprises which challenge established firms and continuously disrupt the current ways of production, organization and distribution, thus wiping out the quasi-rents associated with previous innovations. The second one, labelled subsequently *Schumpeter Mark II*, was proposed in *Capitalism, Socialism and Democracy* (1942). In this work Schumpeter discussed the relevance of the industrial R&D laboratory for technological innovation and the key role of large firms. This pattern of innovative activity is characterized by 'creative accumulation' (using Keith Pavitt's words) with the prevalence of large established firms and the presence of relevant barriers to entry for new innovators. With their accumulated stock of knowledge in specific technological areas, their competencies in R&D, production and distribution and their relevant financial resources, large firms create major barriers to entry to new entrepreneurs and small firms.[3]

Recent research has clearly shown that, during the evolution of industries, changes may occur in the Schumpeterian patterns of innovations. Early in the history of an industry, a Schumpeter Mark I pattern may be present. When technology is changing very rapidly, uncertainty is very high and barriers to entry are very low, new firms are the major innovators and are the key elements in industrial dynamics. When the industry develops and eventually matures and technological change follows well-defined trajectories, Schumpeter Mark II patterns may emerge. Economies of scale, learning curves, barriers to entry and financial resources become important in the competitive process. Thus, large firms with monopolistic power come to the forefront of the innovation process (Utterback and Abernathy, 1975; Gort and Klepper, 1982; Klepper, 1996). In the presence of major technological and market discontinuities, however, a Schumpeter Mark II pattern of innovative activities may be replaced by a Schumpeter Mark I. In this case, a rather stable organization characterized by incumbents with monopolistic power is displaced by a more turbulent one with new firms using a new technology or focusing on a new demand (Henderson and Clark, 1990; Christensen and Rosenbloom, 1995).

The empirical verification of these two archetypes has been at the centre of the economics of innovation ever since its inception. The older tradition framed the issue in terms of what has been called the 'market structure and innovation' approach (Kamien and Schwartz, 1982). Here, the focus was on testing the relationship between the rate of innovation and firm size, on the one hand, and the rate of innovation and monopoly power, on the other. It is now widely acknowledged that the results obtained within this framework failed to recognize the mutual causation between innovation, market structure and firm size. Rather, these variables are best thought of as endogenously codetermined (Dasgupta and Stiglitz, 1980; Nelson and Winter, 1982).

Malerba and Orsenigo (1995, 1996) have explored the empirical question of which (if any) of the two Schumpeterian models of innovation can be actually observed in the data, using a wider notion of the Schumpeterian patterns of innovation. Patterns of innovative activities have been analysed on the basis of a set of indicators which attempt to capture some of the essential features of the two Schumpeterian 'models'.[4] Specifically, Malerba and Orsenigo used the following indicators: concentration and asymmetries (captured by the Herfindhal index) among firms; size of the innovating firms; change over time in the hierarchy of innovators and relevance of new innovators as compared to established ones (called also 'technological entry'). The first two sets of indicators (concentration and firm size) have been conventionally used in the traditional discussions of the so-called 'Schumpeterian hypotheses': they are meant to measure whether innovative activities tend to be concentrated in a few firms or are evenly distributed across a large number of firms and whether large firms or small firms are the main source of innovation in any particular technological class. The other two sets of measures aim to shed light on the degree of 'stability' and 'creative accumulation' or 'dynamism' and 'creative destruction' in the organization of innovative activities. In particular, these indicators try to identify dimensions related to the role of new innovators and the stability in the list of main innovators over time.

Indeed, consistent relationships exist between these indicators,[5] and the relationships between the various indicators of the patterns of innovative activities[6] are actually related to the two archetypical Schumpeterian models. These models also discriminate significantly between technological classes. Schumpeter Mark I technological classes are to be found especially in the 'traditional' sectors, in mechanical technologies, in instruments and in the white electric industry. Conversely, most of the chemical and electronic technologies are characterized by the Schumpeter Mark II model. Cross-country comparisons of the Schumpeterian patterns of innovation show that these patterns of innovative activities are technology-specific: strong similarities are observed in the same technological class across countries. Thus the sector-specificity of the patterns of innovative activities emphasizes two major points: some features of the technological environments are common to groups of industries and they are to some extent invariant with respect to the institutional environment. However country differences persist, and are sometimes quite significant as a result of the working of either specific institutional factors related to national systems of innovation or of the presence of a firm or an industry with a peculiar history.

3 Technological regimes

This contribution proposes that the specific ways sectoral innovative activities are organized can be related to the nature of the relevant *technological (learning) regime*. A technological regime is defined by the specific combination of technological opportunities, appropriability of innovations, cumulativeness of technical advances and the properties of the knowledge base underpinning firms' innovative activities. The notion of technological regime provides a synthetic way of representing some of the most important economic properties of technologies and of the characteristics of the learning processes that are involved in innovative activities. Thus, it identifies some fundamental structural conditions that contribute to defining the requisite competencies, the incentives and the dynamic properties of the innovative process.

The notion of technological regime dates back to Nelson and Winter (1977, 1982) who suggested that the dynamics of innovation and market structure is driven by processes of market selection and the nature of technology, which differs greatly across sectors. Technological regimes set the boundaries of what can be achieved in firms' problem solving activities and identify also the 'natural trajectories' along which solutions to these problems can be found. Nelson and Winter (1982) and Winter (1984) identify two different basic technological regimes according to the relevant knowledge base: an entrepreneurial regime in which the knowledge base is related to science and is non-cumulative and universal (thus facilitating the entry of new firms), and a routinized regime which is more cumulative and internal to the industry (thus facilitating the innovation by established firms). After Nelson and Winter, various authors – Gort and Klepper (1982), Cohen and Levin (1989) and Audretsch (1997) among others – have pointed out that, more than firm size or demand, opportunity and appropriability conditions appear as the most relevant factors affecting the dynamics of market structure and innovation. Levin *et al.* (1985) and Levin *et al.* (1987) have introduced specification of measures of appropriability and opportunity in the analyses of the relationship between market structure and innovation. The insertion of very rough proxies of opportunity and appropriability conditions significantly improved the performance of econometric exercises which followed an otherwise conventional approach (Cohen and Levin, 1989).[7, 8]

Within this line of research, Malerba and Orsenigo (1990, 1993) have proposed that a technological regime is a particular combination of some fundamental properties of technologies: opportunity and appropriability conditions; degrees of cumulativeness of technological knowledge; and characteristics of the relevant knowledge base. Let us briefly discuss these basic dimensions.

Technological opportunities reflect the likelihood of innovating for any given amount of money invested in search. High opportunities provide powerful incentives to the undertaking of innovative activities and denote an economic environment that is not functionally constrained by scarcity. In this case, potential innovators may come up with frequent and important technological innovations.[9] Four basic dimensions of opportunity can be identified: *level, pervasiveness, sources* and *variety*.

- *Level*   High opportunities provide powerful incentives to the undertaking of innovative activities, because they determine a high probability of innovating for a given amount of resources invested in search.
- *Variety*   In some cases, high levels of opportunity conditions are associated with a potentially rich variety of technological solutions, approaches and activities. This is particularly so in the early stages of an industry life cycle.[10]
- *Pervasiveness*   In the case of high pervasiveness, new knowledge may be applied to several products and markets, while in the case of low pervasiveness new knowledge may apply only to a few (eventually one) products and markets.
- *Source*   The sources of technological opportunities markedly differ among technologies and industries. As Freeman (1982), Rosenberg (1982) and Nelson (1993), among others, have shown, in some industries opportunity conditions are related to major scientific breakthroughs in universities. In other sectors, opportunities to innovate may often come from advancements in R&D, equipment and instrumentation, as well as from endogenous learning. In still other sectors, external sources of knowledge in terms of suppliers or users may play a crucial role.

Appropriability of innovations summarizes the possibilities of protecting innovations from imitation and of reaping profits from innovative activities.

It is possible to identify two basic dimensions: level and means of appropriability.

- *Level* Sectors can be ranked according to high or low appropriability conditions (Levin *et al.*, 1987). High appropriability means the existence of ways to protect innovation successfully from imitation. Low appropriability conditions denote an economic environment characterized by the widespread existence of externalities (ibid.).[11]
- *Means of appropriability* Firms utilize a variety of means in order to protect their innovations, ranging from patents, to secrecy, continuous innovations and the control of complementary assets (Levin *et al.*, 1987; Teece, 1986). The effectiveness of these means of appropriability largely differ from industry to industry, thus affecting the level as well as the nature of knowledge externalities.

Cumulativeness of technical advances is related to the fact that today knowledge and innovative activities form the base and the building blocks of tomorrow's innovations: an innovation generates a stream of subsequent innovations, which are a gradual improvement on the original one, or create new knowledge which is used for other innovations in related areas. High levels of cumulativeness are therefore typical of economic environments characterized by continuities in innovative activities and increasing returns. As a consequence, innovative firms are more likely to continue to innovate in specific technologies and along specific trajectories than non-innovative firms are. Three different sources of cumulativeness can be identified:

- *Learning at the technology level* The generation of new technological knowledge builds upon what has been previously done. The cognitive nature of learning processes and past knowledge constrains current research, but also generates new questions and new knowledge.
- *Organizational sources* Cumulativeness might be generated by the establishment of R&D facilities at a fixed cost, which then produce a relatively stable flow of innovations. More generally, however, cumulativeness is likely to be originated by firm-specific technological and organizational capabilities, which can be improved only gradually over time and thus define what a firm can do now and what it can hope to achieve in the future.
- *Success breeds success* Finally, the notion of cumulativeness can be related to the Schumpeterian intuition that critical market feedbacks link R&D investment, technological performance and profitability (Schumpeter, 1942). For instance, persistence may be simply the

outcome of 'success-breeds-success' processes like those used in Nelson and Winter (1982) models: innovative success yields profits that can be reinvested in R&D, thereby increasing the probability to innovate again.

Relatedly, cumulativeness may be observed at various levels of analysis: technology, firm, sector (in case of low appropriability conditions and within industry knowledge spillovers) and region (in case of low appropriability conditions and spatially localized knowledge spillovers).

The properties of the knowledge base relate to the nature of knowledge underpinning firms' innovative activities. Two major characteristics of the knowledge base may be identified: the nature of knowledge and the means of knowledge transmission and communication.

- *Nature of knowledge* Technological knowledge involves various degrees of specificity, tacitness, complexity and independence (Winter, 1987).[12] Some of these features of knowledge may change during the evolution of a specific sector or technology (degree of codification, independence and complexity).
- *Means of knowledge transmission* The characterization of a technology according to each of the dimensions of the nature of knowledge strongly affects the ways firms can effectively get access to the relevant knowledge.[13]

4 The relationship between technological and Schumpeterian patterns of innovative activities

4.1 The theoretical relationships
Malerba and Orsenigo (1990, 1997) and Breschi *et al.* (2000) have explored theoretically the effects of technological regimes in terms of opportunity (OPP), cumulativeness (CUM), appropriability (APP) conditions and properties of the knowledge base on the sectoral patterns of innovative activities. In particular, three dimensions of Schumpeterian patterns of innovation have been examined: the rate of concentration of innovative activities among firms, the degree of stability in the hierarchy of innovative firms and the technological entry and exit (i.e. the relevance of new innovators in an industry).

In Breschi *et al.* (2000) an econometric analysis is conducted concerning the relationship between the specific patterns of innovative activities in a given industry and the prevailing technological regime, as measured by the specific values of technological opportunities (OPP), appropriability of innovations (APP), cumulativeness of technical advances (CUM), and properties of knowledge base related to basic sciences (generic knowledge) (KBA) and to applied sciences (specific knowledge) (KAP). Here the theoretical discussion and the empirical analysis in Breschi *et al.* (2000) is presented. The relationships between technological regimes and sectoral patterns of innovation can be summarized in the following way.

Technological entry and exit (ENTRY)   *Ceteris paribus*, high technological opportunities tend to favour the technological entry of new innovators. In fact, by raising the expected returns of R&D high opportunity conditions increase the incentives to engage in innovative search. Conversely, conditions of low technological opportunities limit innovative entry and restrict the innovative growth of successful established firms. As previous theoretical models (Winter, 1984; Jovanovic, 1982) have shown, higher opportunities provide potential entrants with an ample pool of available scientific and technological knowledge, thus affecting entry in a positive way. *Ceteris paribus*, technological entry and exit are high if cumulativeness is low. In this case, in fact, would-be innovators are not at a major disadvantage with respect to incumbent firms, as discussed in Winter (1984). Finally, a knowledge base of a generic type related to basic sciences should be negatively related to entry, because firms need to have already accumulated absorptive capabilities in order to integrate and use generic knowledge. On the contrary, a knowledge base of a specific type related to applied sciences is going to be positively related with entry, because new innovators may profit from the availability of specialized knowledge (Cohen and Levinthal, 1989).

Concentration of innovative activities (CONC)   The impact of technological opportunities on the concentration ratio of innovative activities may depend on the interactions between opportunity, appropriability and cumulativeness conditions. In particular, if high technological opportunities make big technological leaps likely and these advantages are reinforced in subsequent rounds of innovative activity by high appropriability and cumulativeness conditions, concentration of innovative activities will increase. However, high technological opportunities allow for the entry of new innovative firms, thereby reducing concentration. The opposite holds for low opportunity conditions. Existing theoretical models support both these conjectures. From Nelson and Winter (1982), Jovanovic and Lach (1988), Winter (1984), Iwai (1984a, 1984b) and Dosi *et al.* (1995) among others, ambiguous effects of technological opportunities on concentration are expected.

Ceteris paribus, by limiting the extent of knowledge spillovers and by allowing successful innovators to maintain their innovative advantages, high degrees of technological appropriability are expected to result in a relatively higher level of concentration of innovative activities. Conversely, by determining a wider diffusion of the relevant knowledge across firms, low appropriability conditions are more likely to lead to the presence of a large population of innovators. Also theoretical models, such as Nelson and Winter (1982) and Jovanovic and Lach (1988), point to this relationship: higher appropriability of innovations in fact allows greater advantages to innovators and leads to a greater concentration of innovative activities. Similarly, from Winter (1984) one would expect that, *ceteris paribus*, the relationship between cumulativeness of technical advances and concentration is positive: higher cumulativeness of technical advances means that existing innovative firms increasingly build upon their existing innovations and capabilities, therefore increasing the concentration of innovative activities.

Regarding the properties of the knowledge base, the availability of generic knowledge related to basic sciences can, in principle, allow a variety of different agents to engage in innovative activities. However, the access to the knowledge base and its exploitation often require the presence of absorptive capabilities by existing firms (Cohen and Levinthal, 1989; Rosenberg, 1990) and therefore costly R&D and other learning activities that tend to increase the level of innovative concentration. Conversely, specific knowledge related to applied sciences is more specialized and accessible to firms (both established and new), with a negative effect on the level of innovative concentration.

Stability in the ranking of innovators (STAB)   From Winter (1984) and Dosi *et al.* (1995), one could conjecture that the relationship between stability in the ranking of innovative firms and appropriability and cumulativeness conditions is positive: stability is high if appropriability and cumulativeness are high. In this case leading innovators maintain their top positions because they are able to innovate continuously, building on their previous innovations (high cumulativeness), and protecting their innovations from imitation (high appropriability). Existing innovators accumulate technological knowledge and capabilities that act as powerful barriers to the entry of new innovators. As opportunity conditions are concerned, in general a negative relationship may be expected; as higher opportunities favour entry and increase the likelihood of innovating, they also tend to disrupt the existing ranking of innovators. As mentioned previously, however, in conjunction with high appropriability and high cumulativeness conditions, the opposite effect may prevail.

Technological regimes and Schumpeterian patterns of innovation   The relationship between technological regimes and Schumpeterian patterns of

Table 22.1   *Expected theoretical relationships between patterns of*
             innovation and characteristics of technological regime

Pattern of innovation / Technological regime	Concentration (CONC)	Stability (STAB)	Entry and exit (ENTRY)
Opportunities (OPP)	+/−	+/−	+
Appropriability (APP)	+	+	−
Cumulativeness (CUM)	+	+	−
Generic knowledge (KBA)	+		−
Specific knowledge (KAP)	−		+

innovation could be summarized in the following way, and presented in Table 22.1, taken from Breschi *et al.* (2000).

Schumpeter Mark I (large and highly turbulent population of innovators)
High technological opportunities, low appropriability and low cumulativeness (at the firm level) conditions and a limited role of generic knowledge are more likely to lead to low degrees of concentration of innovative activities with a relatively large number of innovators, high rates of entry and high instability in the hierarchy of innovators.

Schumpeter Mark II (concentrated and rather stable population of innovators)   High appropriability and cumulativeness (at the firm level) conditions and a generic knowledge base are generally associated with high degrees of concentration of innovative activities, low rates of entry and a remarkable stability in the hierarchy of innovators. Given the above conditions, this pattern is compatible both with low and with high technological opportunities.

4.2   The empirical analysis
Breschi *et al.* (2000) have tested the relationships discussed above by using two major sources of data. First, the EP-CESPRI data base on patents applications by firms of three countries (Italy, Federal Republic of Germany and the United Kingdom) for the period 1978–91 was used for measures of sectoral patterns of innovative activities: innovative concentration, technological entry, stability of the hierarchy of innovators, and a synthetic measure of the Schumpeterian patterns of innovative activities. Second, data on industry-specific technological regimes were drawn from the PACE (Policy Appropriability and Competitiveness for European

Enterprises) questionnaire survey coordinated by the Merit Institute (The Netherlands) (Arundel *et al.*, 1995).[14] *Opportunity conditions* (OPP) are captured in terms of the scientific and technological ferment in an industry, measured by sectoral R&D intensity. *Appropriability conditions* (APP) are measured with responses to questions concerning the effectiveness of two methods used by firms to prevent competitors from copying product and process innovations: patents and secrecy.[15] *Cumulativeness conditions* (CUM) are measured by the importance of frequent technological improvements in making product innovations difficult or commercially unprofitable to imitate. The score received by this question (CUM) can therefore be assumed as a proxy of the degree to which technical advances in a given industry take place in a 'cumulative' way. Finally, one feature of the knowledge base – its generic or specific character – is captured by the role of basic (KBA) and applied (KAP) sciences in fostering innovation in an industry.[16]

The role played by technological regimes has been tested by performing regression analysis (OLS and Logit) using the various measures of Schumpeterian patterns of innovation as dependent variables. The main results show that variables related to technological regimes are individually significant at the conventional statistical level and have the expected sign. In particular, APP, CUM and KBA are significantly and positively related to the concentration ratio of innovators (CONC), and stability in the hierarchy of innovators (STA), as well as to a Schumpeter Mark II pattern, while they are negatively related to entry of innovative firms (ENTRY). An interesting result emerges in relation to the dimension of the knowledge base considered in the analysis. KBA is significantly and positively related to all above-mentioned measures of sectoral patterns of innovation, except the entry of new innovators. This result suggests that a knowledge base related to basic sciences leads to a Schumpeter Mark II pattern because firms need to have absorptive capabilities and large R&D laboratories able to transform advances in basic sciences into new products and processes. Established innovators may be better suited for these types of opportunities. On the contrary, advances in applied sciences KAP are already closer to a possible innovative exploitation and are more focused on specific applications. They may be easily 'used' by new entrants (as well as by established firms) and are therefore associated with a Schumpeter Mark I pattern of innovations. Tests of the joint significance of opportunity, appropriability and cumulativeness variables reject the null hypothesis, thus providing further confirmation of the important influence of technological regimes on Schumpeterian patterns of innovation. Finally, the ratio of the explained variance significantly increases when dummy variables are included in the specification to capture fixed-country effects, thus suggesting that the relationship between technological regimes and Schumpeterian patterns of innovation is fundamentally mediated by the specific features of each national system of innovation.

5 Conclusions

In this contribution it has been argued that the nature of technological (and organizational) learning, interacting with processes of market selection, defines specific regimes of industrial evolution, which in turn generate empirically observable regularities in the form of archetypical sectoral patterns of innovation called Schumpeter Mark I and Mark II. It has been advanced that sectoral patterns of innovation, while different across sectors, are rather invariant across countries for the same sector.

Although stylized and archetypical, these findings constitute a robust starting point for more general empirical and theoretical analyses on the factors affecting industry dynamics and, more broadly, industrial evolution. Interesting progress may take place along the following lines of research. First, an obvious direction calls for richer and more detailed empirical evidence on the links between technological regimes, patterns of innovation and industrial dynamics, following the contributions discussed above. Second, the discussion on technological regimes and Schumpeterian patterns of innovation may be linked to taxonomies of sectoral patterns of innovation, such as Pavitt (1984) and Marsili (2001). Third, technological regimes as a factor explaining patterns of innovative activities could be enriched by looking at other factors affecting innovation in sectors: non-firm organizations (universities, public research organizations, etc.), firms' relationships and networks and institutions, such as in the sectoral systems framework (Malerba, 2002, 2004). Finally, the relationship between technological regimes and patterns of innovative activities could be developed theoretically and analytically by models of industry evolution in two ways. One route is to follow Nelson and Winter (1982), Winter (1984), Jovanovic (1982), Dosi *et al.* (1995) and Klepper (1996) among others, which have incorporated some aspects and dimensions of technological regimes in their models. Newly developed models should provide specific parametrizations of variables like opportunity, appropriability, cumulativeness and knowledge base and should represent in detail the functional mechanisms linking the regime variables to technological innovation, market selection and industrial dynamics. These models should examine non-linearities and the feedbacks from innovation and market selection to technological and learning regimes, thus making the regime concept more endogenous with respect to innovation and industrial dynamics. The other route is to insert technological regimes in specific models of industry evolution, such as in history-friendly models (see Malerba *et al.*, 1999), thus examining the working of the technological regime variables in specific sectoral settings.

Notes

1. This contribution draws extensively on my long-term collaboration with Luigi Orsenigo.
2. A. Phillips (1971), Nelson and Winter (1982) and Kamien and Schwartz (1982).
3. The Schumpeterian Mark I and Mark II patterns of innovation could be labelled also 'widening' and 'deepening'. A widening pattern of innovative activities is related to an innovative base which is continuously enlarging through the entry of new innovators and to the erosion of the competitive and technological advantages of the established firms. A deepening pattern of innovation, on the contrary, is related to the dominance of a few firms which are continuously innovative through the accumulation over time of technological and innovative capabilities (Malerba and Orsenigo, 1995).
4. Malerba and Orsenigo (1995, 1996) have used patent data. First, the OTAF-SPRU data base on patents granted by the American Patent Office has been elaborated at the firm level for four European countries (Germany, France, the United Kingdom and Italy) for the period 1969–86 considering 33 technological classes (Malerba and Orsenigo, 1995). Second, a similar analysis at the firm level has been performed using a different dataset: the EPO (European Patent Office) data base on patent applications for six countries (Germany, France, the United Kingdom, Italy, United States and Japan) in the period 1978–91 (Malerba and Orsenigo, 1996). With the EP data base, patent data have been aggregated into 48 main technological classes and one residual class. These classes have been built from 12-digit subclasses of the International Patent Classification (IPC) grouping them according to the specific application of patents (EP-CESPRI classification). Economic data have been gathered on firms' size in terms of employees in 1984 for the OTAF-SPRU data base and in 1991 for the EP-CESPRI data base. Firms which are part of business groups have been treated as individual companies. The OTAF-SPRU and the EP-CESPRI datasets give remarkably consistent results. Thus, for the sake of simplicity, in what follows reference will be made only to the EP-CESPRI data base, unless otherwise specified.
5. First, correlation analysis for the various technological classes shows in all countries a positive correlation between concentration and asymmetries, stability of innovators' hierarchy and (although to a lesser extent) the size of innovating firms, and a negative correlation between these measures and entry of new innovators.
6. Principal component analysis performed for all the technological classes identifies in all countries one dominant factor which captures a large fraction of the variance and which represents quite neatly the distinction between Schumpeter Mark I and Schumpeter Mark II technological classes.
7. The notion of technological regime holds some relationship with the concepts of technological paradigms and trajectories. These latter try to capture the idea that technologies differ drastically and that their development retains a strong autonomous internal logic (Dosi, 1982, 1988).
8. In his 'bounds' approach, John Sutton (1998) claims that the relationship between market structure and innovation is constrained by the specificity of the technology in terms of the diversity of possible technological trajectories available to firms and the productivity of R&D investments along each trajectory. These concepts bear some link to the notion of different learning contexts characterizing the various sectors.
9. It should be pointed out that opportunity conditions may greatly change in the course of the evolution of industries. In several industries technological opportunities may eventually become depleted, as the literature on the industry life cycle has emphasized (Klepper, 1996). On the other hand, there are industries where opportunities are regenerated and recreated by firms' innovative activities, such as R&D.
10. As Utterback and Abernathy (1975), Dosi (1982) and Henderson and Clark (1990), among others, have pointed out, in the *pre-paradigmatic stage* of technologies, when a dominant design has not yet been defined, firms may search in various directions and

come up with different technological solutions. Later on, in the *paradigmatic stage*, when a dominant design has emerged, technical change may proceed along specific trajectories so that the variety of radically different technological solutions is reduced.

11. The particular regime of appropriability has two different effects on innovative output: an incentive effect and an efficiency effect. High appropriability levels have a strong incentive effect, which increases the R&D spending by single firms. On the contrary, high appropriability levels may reduce the possibility that other firms benefit from such technical advances, therefore reducing the positive efficiency effect of technical advances at the sectoral level (Levin and Reiss, 1988).

12. From Winter (1987) one could identify the following dimensions: (a) *generic v. specific:* in a sector the knowledge base may be of a generic nature or specific to well defined application domains; (b) *tacit v. codified*: in a sector the knowledge base underpinning innovative activities may show varying degrees of tacitness; (c) *complex v. simple*: similarly, the relevant knowledge base may show relatively high or low degrees of complexity in terms of integration of different scientific and engineering disciplines and technologies needed for innovative activities and of variety of competencies (such as R&D, manufacturing equipment, engineering and production and marketing) needed for innovative activities; (d) *independent v. system*: the knowledge relevant to innovative activities may be easily identifiable and isolated or rather it may be part of (and therefore embedded within) a larger system, and therefore difficult to decompose in 'chunks'.

13. One can argue that the more knowledge is ever-changing, tacit, complex and part of a larger system, the more relevant are informal means of knowledge transmission, like 'face-to-face' talks, personal teaching and training, mobility of personnel and even acquisition of entire groups of people. Moreover, it should also be stressed that such means of knowledge transmission are extremely sensitive to the distance among agents. On the other hand, the more knowledge is standardized, codified, simple and independent, the more relevant are formal means of knowledge communication, such as publications, licences, patents, and so on. In such circumstances, one can argue that geographical proximity does not play a crucial role in facilitating the transmission of knowledge across agents. A fundamental implication of this argument is that the nature of knowledge strongly affects the way technological opportunities and knowledge externalities are transmitted among distant firms (Breschi and Malerba, 1997).

14. The survey was based on responses (on a five-point Likert scale) from 713 R&D executives from the European Union's largest manufacturing firms on a broad range of innovation-related issues: goals of innovation, external sources of knowledge, public research, methods to protect innovations, government programmes to support innovation, and barriers to profiting from innovation. The unit of analysis was the line of business, as defined by four-digit ISIC sectors.

15. The variable APP is for each individual respondent the sum of scores received by each of these two mechanisms for either process or product innovations.

16. Survey respondents were asked to rate the importance to the progress of their unit's technological base of ten fields of basic and applied science over the past ten years. The variable KBA represents for each individual respondent the sum of scores received by the fields of basic science: biology, materials science, chemistry, medical and health, physics, chemical engineering, mathematics. The variable KAP represents instead the sum of scores received by the fields of applied science: electrical engineering, computing science and mechanical engineering.

References

Arundel, A., van de Paal, G. and Soete, L. (1995). 'Innovation strategies of Europe's largest industrial firms: results of the PACE survey for information sources, public research, protection of innovations and government programmes', Report for the SPRINT Programme, DG XIII EC, MERIT Institute, University of Limburg.

Audretsch, D. (1997). Technological regimes, industrial demography and the evolution of industrial structure, *Industrial and Corporate Change*, **6** (1).

Breschi, S. and Malerba, F. (1997). 'Sectoral innovation systems: technological regimes, Schumpeterian dynamics and spatial boundaries', in C. Edquist (ed.), *Systems of Innovation. Technologies, Institutions and Organisations*, London: Cassell.

Breschi, S., Malerba, F. and Orsenigo, L. (2000). Technological regimes and Schumpeterian patterns of innovation, *Economic Journal*, **110** (463), 388–410.

Christensen, C.M. and Rosenbloom, R. (1995). Explaining the attacker's advantage: technological paradigms, organisational dynamism and the value network, *Research Policy*, **24** (2), 233–57.

Cohen, W.M. and Levin, R.C. (1989). 'Empirical studies of innovation and market structure', in R. Schmalensee and R. Willig (eds), *Handbook of Industrial Organisation*, Amsterdam: North-Holland.

Cohen, W.M. and Levinthal, D.A. (1989). Innovation and learning: the two faces of R&D, *Economic Journal*, **99**, 569–96.

Dasgupta, P. and Stiglitz, J. (1980). Industry structure and the nature of innovative activity, *Economic Journal*, **90**, 266–93.

Dosi, G. (1982). Technological paradigms and technological trajectories. A suggested interpretation of the determinants and directions of technical change, *Research Policy*, **11**(3), 147–62.

Dosi, G. (1988), 'The nature of the innovative process', in G. Dosi, C. Freeman, R. Nelson, G. Silverberg and L. Soete (eds), *Technical Change and Economic Theory*, London and New York: Pinter, pp. 221–38.

Dosi, G., Marsili, O., Orsenigo, L. and Salvatore, R. (1995). Technological regime, selection and market structure, *Small Business Economics*, **7**, 1–26.

Freeman, C. (1982). *The Economics of Industrial Innovation*, London: Pinter.

Gort, M. and Klepper, S. (1982). Time paths in the diffusion of product innovations, *Economic Journal*, **92**, 630–53.

Henderson, R. and Clark, K.B. (1990). Architectural innovation: the reconfiguration of existing product technologies and the failure of established firms, *Administrative Science Quarterly*, **35**, 9–30.

Iwai, K. (1984a). Schumpeterian dynamics: part I: an evolutionary model of selection and imitation, *Journal of Economic Behaviour and Organisation*, **5**, 159–90.

Iwai, K. (1984b). Schumpeterian dynamics: part II: technological progress, firm growth and economic selection, *Journal of Economic Behaviour and Organisation*, **5**, 321–51.

Jovanovic, B. (1982). Selection and the evolution of industry, *Econometrica*, **50**, 649–70.

Jovanovic, B. and Lach, S. (1988). Entry, exit and diffusion with learning-by-doing, *American Economic Review*, **79** (4), 690–99.

Kamien, M.I. and Schwartz, N.L. (1982). *Market Structure and Innovation*, Cambridge: Cambridge University Press.

Klepper, S. (1996). Entry, exit, growth and innovation over the product life cycle, *American Economic Review*, **86**, 562–83.

Levin, R.C. and Reiss, P.C. (1988). Cost-reducing and demand creating R&D with spillovers, *Rand Journal of Economics*, **19**, 538–56.

Levin, R.C., Cohen, W.M. and Mowery, D.C. (1985). R&D, appropriability, opportunity, and market structure: new evidence on some Schumpeterian hypotheses, *American Economic Review, Papers and Proceedings*, **75** (2), 20–24.

Levin, R.C., Klevorick, A.K., Nelson, R.R. and Winter, S.G. (1987). Appropriating the returns from industrial research and development, *Brookings Papers on Economic Activity*, **3**, 783–820.

Malerba, F. (2002). Sectoral systems of innovation and production, *Research Policy*, **31** (2), 247–64.

Malerba, F. (2004). *Sectoral Systems of Innovation. Concepts, Issues and Analyses of Six Major Sectors in Europe*, Cambridge: Cambridge University Press.

Malerba, F. and Orsenigo, L. (1990). 'Technological regimes and patterns of innovation: a theoretical and empirical investigation of the Italian case', in A. Heertje and M. Perlman (eds), *Evolving Technologies and Market Structure*, Ann Arbor, MI: Michigan University Press.

Malerba, F. and Orsenigo, L. (1993). Technological regimes and firm behaviour, *Industrial and Corporate Change*, **2** (1), 45–71.

Malerba, F. and Orsenigo, L. (1995). Schumpeterian patterns of innovation, *Cambridge Journal of Economics*, **19** (1), 47–66.

Malerba, F. and Orsenigo, L. (1996). Schumpeterian patterns of innovation are technology specific, *Research Policy*, **25**, 451–78.

Malerba, F. and Orsenigo, L. (1997). Technological regimes and sectoral patterns of innovative activities, *Industrial and Corporate Change*, **6** (1), 83–116.

Malerba, F., Nelson, R., Orsenigo, L. and Winter, S. (1999). History friendly models of industry evolution: the case of the computer industry, *Industrial and Corporate Change*, **8** (1) 3–40.

Marsili, O. (2001). *The Anatomy and Evolution of Industries: Technological Change and Industrial Dynamics*, Cheltenham, UK and Northampton, MA, USA: Edward Elgar.

Nelson, R.R. (1993). *National Innovation Systems*, Oxford: Oxford University Press.

Nelson, R.R. and Winter, S. (1977). In search of a useful theory of innovation, *Research Policy*, **6**, 36–76.

Nelson, R.R. and Winter, S. (1982). *An Evolutionary Theory of Economic Change*, Cambridge, MA: The Belknap Press of Harvard University Press.

Pavitt, K. (1984). Sectoral patterns of innovation: towards a taxonomy and a theory, *Research Policy*, **13**, 343–73.

Phillips, A. (1971), *Technology and Market Structure: a Study of the Aircraft Industry*, Lexington, MA: D.C. Heath.

Rosenberg, N. (1982). *Inside the Black Box*, Cambridge: Cambridge University Press.

Rosenberg, N. (1990). Why do firms do basic research (with their own money)?, *Research Policy*, **19**, 165–74.

Schumpeter, J.A. (1934). *The Theory of Economic Development*, Cambridge, MA: Harvard Economic Studies.

Schumpeter, J.A. (1942). *Capitalism, Socialism and Democracy,* New York: Harper and Brothers.

Sutton, J. (1998). *Technology and Market Structure*, Cambridge, MA: MIT Press.

Teece, D.J. (1986). Profiting from technological innovation: implications for integration, collaboration, licensing and public policy, *Research Policy*, **15**, 286–385.

Utterback, J.M. and Abernathy, W.J. (1975). A dynamic model of product and process innovation, *Omega*, **3**, 639–56.

Winter, S.G. (1984). Schumpeterian competition in alternative technological regimes, *Journal of Economic Behavior and Organization*, **5**, 287–320.

Winter, S.G. (1987). 'Knowledge and competence as strategic assets', in D.J. Teece (ed.), *The Competitive Challenge: Strategies for Industrial Innovation and Renewal*, Cambridge, MA: Ballinger.

23 Innovation networks
Andreas Pyka

1 Introduction

Modern technical solutions are characterized by an increased interrelatedness between heterogeneous actors and knowledge fields. No single firm can keep pace with the development of all relevant technologies. In order to overcome knowledge bottlenecks, firms seek access to external knowledge sources, most often in bilateral research collaborations. These research collaborations encompass vertical as well as horizontal relationships between firm actors and also interinstitutional relationships between firms, on the one hand, and public research organizations and university labs, on the other hand. Through these multiple bilateral and multilateral relationships, a tight web of connections emerges which in the literature is referred to as an innovation network (e.g. Pyka and Küppers, 2002). Innovation networks have gained significant importance as a mean of co-ordination and pattern formation of industrial research and development (R&D) processes.

Although in economics the impact of technological change on economic development, progress and growth was always widely recognized, no detailed study of the emergence and diffusion of innovation, not to mention innovation networks, was performed. Even economists such as Joseph A. Schumpeter, who put innovation, or in his terms 'new combinations', at the center of his theory of economic development of 1912, attributed innovative success to the specific feature entrepreneurship of outstanding individuals in an economy. Almost 30 years later, Schumpeter (1942), inspired by the development of the American industries, identified a significant change in the organization of R&D processes in the specialized R&D laboratories of large firms (routinized innovation). A further 40 years later, another significant change has taken place in the organization of R&D. This change manifests itself in the interaction between R&D labs and other innovative actors, such as universities and public research institutes, specifically in innovation networks. Nevertheless, it took until the end of the 1980s and the beginning of the 1990s until a certain interest in the theoretical explanation of this phenomenon awakened interest in economics.

An important reason for the late interest in and the problems with the investigation of networks, and specifically innovation networks, can be seen in the difficulties the theory of the firm poses for economists (see e.g. Holmstrom and Tirole, 1989). Here, the questions 'why do firms exist?' and 'what are their boundaries?' are debated. Sidney Winter (1991, p. 179), reflecting on this problem, had to admit that the present state of the art is characterized by incoherence and contradictions.

In an economy without firms, a specific industrial sector would consist simply of isolated labor-sharing individuals connected by markets. Only the bundling and organization of several activities within a firm gives this branch its specific structure (e.g. small and medium-sized firms, large enterprises etc.). However, not only firms, but on a higher level also networks between them (and other involved actors) are decisive features of the industrial patterns we observe. In the theory of the firm, three different approaches exist, which are also used for the explanation of networks and are suitable to different degrees to explain the observed structures. In a way, in these approaches, networks are considered either as a means to minimize R&D costs, or as a means to minimize transaction costs, or as a means to create novelties.

In the first approach, the firm is seen as a functional relationship between inputs and outputs of production. This production function approach also constitutes the basis of mainstream neo-classical industrial economics. Accordingly, the questions posed are those on the optimality in the allocation of resources and the respective incentives of firm behavior. With respect to industrial innovation processes, since the early 1980s a branch of literature (new industrial economics) also analyzes the conditions and incentives of firms to engage in R&D co-operation by drawing on a game-theoretic framework.

The second approach can be traced back to Ronald Coase (1937) and no longer focuses on immediate production processes but rather on the underlying transactions. For Coase and his followers, the main reason for the existence of firms is costs which arise by using the price mechanism of markets. Therefore, firms come into being because the costs of co-ordinating the transactions via markets are higher than the costs of a hierarchical organization within a firm; in other words, there are incentives for cost saving. These considerations were later transferred to networks by Oliver Williamson (1975) and others. In this perspective, networks are an intermediate co-ordination form between the originally supposed dichotomy of hierarchy and markets.

The third strand of literature, the knowledge-based approach, differs sharply from these incentive-based approaches. Early proponents of this theory were Alfred Marshall (1920), who recognized knowledge as the decisive fact in production, and Edith Penrose (1959), who identified the knowledge base of a firm as its main asset. In the early 1980s, this approach was taken up by evolutionary economics. Here, the role of knowledge for economic development and the success of firms was explicitly recognized and constituted the cornerstone of economic analysis. In the evolutionary perspective, networks are seen as a central determinant in the industrial creation of novelty, and are therefore a decisive co-ordination mechanism. In networks, new technological opportunities are created via technological complementarities and synergies by bringing together different technological and economic competencies.

A further reason for the late interest of economics in the phenomenon of innovation networks has to be seen in the difficulties in analyzing this complex form of organization with the traditional economic toolbox. Since the end of the 1990s, however, different network typologies and their meaning for the diffusion of knowledge have been explicitly discussed, drawing on new approaches from graph theory and complexity theory. The decisive advantages of these new methodologies are the analytic and numerical tools they offer for the theoretical and empirical analysis of complex networks and their evolution. Thanks to these developments, networks in general and innovation networks in particular are taking over an increasingly important position in the economic analysis of interactions between agents.

In the following sections, first the incentive-based approaches of explaining networks are discussed, before the knowledge-based approach of evolutionary economics is introduced in detail. The final section introduces the basic ideas of modern network analysis.

2   The incentive-based approaches

The transactions costs approach and the production function approach of neo-classical new industrial economics both draw on a marginalist perspective by comparing the marginal costs and benefits of different alternatives. As chronologically the transaction costs theory offers an earlier explanation of economic and innovation networks, we start with this branch of the literature.

2.1   *Transaction costs analysis*

According to the prevailing theories of industrial organization, up to the 1980s the phenomenon of innovation networks was a surprising stylized fact. These theories predicted that transactions would occur either in markets or in hierarchically structured organizations, i.e. firms. It was Williamson (1975) who introduced a theoretical explanation in terms of transaction costs, which explains that growing firms move increasingly away from an atomistic competition, thereby internalizing the different functions and stages of production which are characterized by a high degree of uncertainty and/or specificity of assets. In these cases, bounded rationality and opportunistic behavior necessitate an integration of the respective functions within the firms. An institutional configuration aiming at an organization in networks, in the first place, was seen as unstable and inefficient because of the incurring of higher transaction costs.

However, with this approach, the growing frequency of collaborative networks in industrial reality was not explainable. To resolve the problems, two answers are possible.[1] Either networks are not more than a temporary deviation from normal behavior (markets or hierarchies), which does not last long, or networks present an additional form of industrial organization, thereby adding a new alternative to the supposed dichotomy of markets and hierarchy. In his 1985 book, Williamson admitted to the latter: 'Whereas I was earlier of the view that transactions of the middle kind were very difficult to organize and hence were unstable, on which account the bimodal distribution was more accurately descriptive, I'm now persuaded that transactions in the middle range are much more common' (Williamson, 1985). According to this view, firms are assumed to engage in co-operative relationships in order to minimize their transaction costs.

By acknowledging this, transaction costs economics now draws on a kind of continuum of possible co-ordination mechanisms, with pure market transactions on one end of the spectrum and the hierarchically organized firm on the other. In between these two extremes, so-called 'hybrid forms' are located. Which specific organizational form is chosen depends on the frequency of transactions and the importance of asset specificity, as well as on uncertainty and opportunism. In this continuum perspective, one can move from the market pole, where all necessary information is captured by market prices, towards putting-out systems, different kinds of repeated exchange, and subcontracting arrangements. Contractual relationships, either joint ventures or networks, are located close to the hierarchy pole.[2] With respect to the analysis of innovation networks, the following features of the underlying transactions are of crucial importance within transaction costs economics:[3] system interdependence, indivisibilities, asset specificity, tacitness of knowledge, market and technological uncertainties, and non-appropriability.

Although, within transaction costs economics, the phenomenon of innovation networks is discussed prominently for the first time, a decisive shortcoming of this kind of analysis cannot be neglected: transaction costs economics focuses only on cost reductions and neglects the idea-creating aspects e.g. the emergence of novelties via the organization of R&D in innovation networks. So, for example, in an empirical investigation of the information technology sector, Hagedoorn and Schakenraad (1992) identified innovation networks as a frequently used organizational form in knowledge-intensive sectors in which high uncertainty and low appropriability prevail. In transaction costs economics, this particular combination would never lead to collaborative forms but, owing to the high monitoring costs, to a hierarchical organization of the R&D process (see DeBresson and Amesse, 1991). Therefore, the criticism as well as the further development of the transaction costs approach concentrate on the assumption of opportunistic behavior, which does not allow for the development of something like mutual trust in a co-operative relationship. In this light, any kind of control mechanism in a network of firms is considered as detrimental to innovation (Mytelka, 1991). Nooteboom (1999), in his dynamic transaction costs approach, in which he also introduces elements of evolutionary economics (see below), correctly states that, in a dynamic perspective, firms have to consider their reputations as reliable partners in an industry. Opportunistic behavior would lead to a bad reputation, isolating a firm more and more in the course of time.

2.2   New industrial economics

In the field of New Industrial Economics since the early 1980s, co-operation in innovation moved to the center of interest for two reasons: on the one hand, new industrial economics by its very nature moved away from the idea of perfect competition by invoking the Structure–Conduct–Performance approach, in which, besides prices, other means of competition, i.e. marketing, R&D etc. play a role for determining firm behavior; and with the arrival of game theory as a formal tool of analysis, the explicit investigation of firm interactions becomes possible. On the other hand, the discussion was inspired by new decisions and policies concerning the possible outcomes of allowing firms to collaborate in so-called 'pre-competitive R&D', despite strong anti-trust regulation.

The majority of theoretical models analyze questions with respect to the conditions and incentives necessary for firms to engage in co-operation in R&D and the welfare properties of the different possible solutions. Building on either so-called 'non-tournament' models, in which firms are engaged in either Cournot or Bertrand competition and continuously innovate (e.g. D'Aspremont and Jacquemin, 1988), or on so-called 'patent races', in which firms compete for a single stochastically distributed innovation and the respective patent (e.g. Katsoulacos, 1988), innovation and competition are analyzed in two- or more-stage games, comparing situations of pure competition in markets and hierarchies, with collaboration only in R&D, and collaboration in R&D as well as on the markets. According to these models, collaboration in R&D seems to improve the performance of firms as well as social welfare in situations in which technological appropriability is low and technological spillovers reduce the incentives of firms to invest in costly R&D processes. Therefore, co-operative R&D is considered as a means to restore reduced R&D incentives due to low appropriability.

Another strand of literature deals with co-operative know-how exchange as a possible explanation of the empirical phenomenon of imperfect appropriability conditions i.e. technological spillovers, despite the existence of such appropriability means as patents, secrecy etc. The authors also draw on game-theoretic models, in particular the class of behavioral co-operative games. Von Hippel (1989) and Schrader (1989) invoke the classical Prisoners' dilemma to model the empirical phenomenon of free know-how exchange between firms, which they label 'informal know-how trading'.

Von Hippel (1989, p. 158) motivates his approach as follows:

> When required know-how is not available in-house, an engineer typically cannot find what he needs in publications either: much is very specialised and not published anywhere. He must either develop it himself or learn what he needs to know by talking to other specialists. Since in-house development can be time-consuming and expensive, there can be a high incentive to seek the needed information from professional colleagues. And often, logically enough, engineers in firms which make similar products or use similar processes are the people most likely to have the needed information.

And, indeed, he finds informal know-how exchange to be widespread in the sectors he is investigating:

> An engineer at an aerospace firm was having trouble manufacturing a part from a novel composite material with needed precision. He called a professional colleague he knew at a rival firm and asked for advice. As it happens, that competitor had solved the problem by experimenting and developing some process know-how involving mold design and processing temperatures, and the colleague willingly passed along this information. (Von Hippel, 1989, p. 168)

Within the game-theoretic framework, the authors are able to show that, under certain circumstances, informal knowledge exchange could become a Nash equilibrium if the game is repeated infinitely. By drawing on the work of Schelling (1973), other authors (Foray, 1995; Pyka, 1999) show that similar results can be expected when more than two players are engaged in this game, thereby transferring the results of bilateral co-operation onto multilateral cases.

3 The knowledge-based approaches

In the following sections, first, the traditional approaches are criticized and, building on this, the knowledge-based perspective of innovation processes is introduced. Finally, the significance and consequences of this evolutionary perspective for the investigation of innovation networks are stressed.

3.1 Criticism of the traditional theories

Both the neo-classical approach to new industrial economics and transaction costs analysis are controversial according to what they can contribute to the analysis of innovation networks. Mainly out of this criticism, more recent approaches draw on a knowledge-based foundation in their reasoning. Here, the future benefits from the synergetic creation of knowledge through interaction with heterogeneous actors, dynamic technological accumulation and learning are seen as the major issues of networks in innovation processes. Whereas the criticism of the transaction cost theory focuses on a significant shortcoming of this approach, namely the neglect of these technological complementarities, the criticism of the models of new industrial economics aims at the basic assumptions underlying the theory, which are fundamentally at variance with innovation processes.

It is beyond the scope of this chapter to discuss in detail the criticism made by evolutionary economics with respect to assumptions underlying the neo-classical reasoning.[4] For our purposes, it is sufficient to mention three major points evolutionary economists claim to be of great importance in the discussion of economic development processes and which are incompatible with neo-classical theory. First of all, evolutionary theory wants to explain how novelties emerge and diffuse. A specific characteristic in these processes is uncertainty, which cannot be treated adequately by drawing on stochastic distributions referring to the concept of risk. Therefore, the assumption of perfect rationality underlying neo-classical models cannot be maintained, unless the concepts of bounded and procedural rationality are invoked. Consequently, actors in evolutionary models are characterized by incomplete knowledge bases and capabilities. Closely connected, the second point concerns the important role heterogeneity and variety play in development processes. Because of the assumption of perfect rationality in neo-classical models, homogeneous actors and technologies are analyzed. Heterogeneity as a source of novelty is by and large neglected, or treated as only a temporary deviation. Finally, the third point deals with the time dimension in which learning and the emergence of novelties take place. By their very nature, these processes are truly dynamic, meaning that they occur in historical time. The possibility of irreversibility, however, does not exist in the mainstream approaches, which rely on linearity and equilibrium. As we will see below, these critical points, emphasized by the knowledge-based approach, constitute the basis for an innovation process, characterized as an evolutionary development.

With respect to the criticism of the transaction cost approach in analyzing innovation networks, there exists a quite heterogeneous literature, which shows a considerable dissatisfaction with the market/hierarchy dichotomy placing networks simply as an intermediate case between two extremes. According to this strand of the literature (e.g. Chesnais, 1996; Foray, 1991), networking should not be explained primarily in terms of transaction costs, but should rather be examined in terms of strategic behavior, appropriability and technological complementarities. This criticism can be traced back to Richardson (1972), who states that

> firms are not islands of planned co-ordination in a sea of market relations but are linked together in patterns of co-operation and affiliation. Planned co-ordination does not stop at the frontiers of the individual firm but can be effected through co-operation between firms. The dichotomy between firm and market, between directed and spontaneous co-ordination is misleading; it ignores the institutional fact of interfirm co-operation and assumes away the distinct method of co-ordination this can provide.

The crucial problem of traditional transaction costs analysis is the interpretation of organizational dynamics in terms of marginal costs.[5] By focusing on transaction costs only, as a consequence of the marginalist perspective adopted, an (implicit) perfect substitutability between internal and external knowledge sources is assumed. In this light, the characteristic features of innovation processes, such as true uncertainty, variety and irreversibility, are totally ignored.

Thus the incentive-based approaches, with their focus on cost-based and rational decisions, exclude crucial aspects of firms' strategies, which are influenced by factors lying by their very nature beyond the scope of these approaches. Also, of course cost–benefit calculations (with respect to innovation itself a problematic activity) play an important role, the firms' behavior being influenced additionally by several other factors such as learning, individual and collective motivation, mutual trust etc. It is the role of these factors which the knowledge-based approach of evolutionary economics explicitly takes into account.

3.2   Innovation processes from a knowledge-based perspective

By switching from the incentive-based perspective to the knowledge-based perspective, the evolutionary approaches have realized a decisive change in the analysis of innovation processes. In this light, innovation processes mutate from optimal cost–benefit considerations to collective experimental and problem solving processes (Dosi, 1988). The knowledge base of a firm is no longer perfect. Instead a gap between the competencies of a firm and difficulties which are to be mastered opens up (C-D gap; Heiner, 1983). There are two reasons responsible for this C-D gap in innovation processes: on the one hand, technological uncertainty introduces errors and surprises in firm behavior. On the other hand, the very nature of technological knowledge avoids an unrestricted access. Knowledge in general, and new technological know-how in particular, are no longer considered as freely available, but as local (technology-specific), tacit (firm-specific), and complex (based on a variety of technology and scientific fields). To understand and to use the respective know-how, specific competencies are necessary, which have to be built up in a cumulative process in the course of time.

Thus the technological opportunity space is restricted by the specific competencies bundled within a firm. 'It is clear that this opportunity will be restricted to the extent a firm does not see opportunities for expansion, is unwilling to react upon them, or is unable to respond to them' (Penrose, 1959, p. 32). Moreover, despite the possibility of exploiting the technological opportunities of a specific technology in the case of mastering the necessary competencies, this opportunity space is not unrestricted, but cumulatively depleted; i.e. further progress along this specific technological trajectory (Dosi, 1982) becomes increasingly difficult to achieve owing to technological bottlenecks and scientific restrictions. This, however, does not imply that progress comes to rest whenever these specific opportunities are depleted. The different technological trajectories and their technological opportunities do not co-exist unrelated, but are connected by several influencing devices and feedback mechanisms. Therefore, a single technology cannot be explained in isolation, but should be understood in a broader framework. Improvements in one technology can create totally different applications in other technologies or even totally new technological opportunities. Behind these processes of a mutual stimulation and pressing ahead of technical progress, so-called 'cross-fertilization effects' of different technologies (Mokyr, 1990) are identified.

It is obvious that an innovation process so characterized demands certain prerequisites to be fulfilled, if a firm wants to participate successfully. Because of the increased complexity of modern innovation processes, a firm has to master a great number of different knowledge fields. In order to have the necessary access to external knowledge sources, firms, besides their specific competencies, have to provide for an additional broad knowledge base, the so-called 'absorptive capacity' (Cohen and Levinthal, 1989; Cantner and Pyka, 1998) or 'receiver competence' (Eliasson, 1990) which allows them to react flexibly to external developments and external knowledge. Malerba (1992) states in this respect: 'This complexity has meant that multidisciplinary knowledge has become necessary for the generation and development of new products. In the computer industry, for example, the disciplines involved in the innovation process may range from solid state physics to mathematics, and from language theory to management science.' So-called 'go-it-alone' strategies or 'conservative' strategies, which imply that a firm relies only on its own R&D endeavors, cannot be successful in such a complex environment. Because of the systemic character[6] of present-day technological solutions, technological development necessarily becomes a complex interactive process involving many different ideas and their specific interrelationships.

3.3   Innovation networks in the knowledge-based approach

Obviously, the above characterization of innovation processes has significant impacts on the analysis of innovation networks. These networks need to be understood not only in terms of transaction costs considerations, but also in the terms of learning, path dependencies, technological opportunities, and complementary assets.[7] Networks do not only influence the co-ordination of resources, but also insert a significant impact on their creation. This has to be seen in a twofold perspective: first, the pooling of different competencies in the network of firms, of course, enhances this process of resource creation by exploiting complementary effects. However, additionally, the co-operation in networks also creates a real surplus or synergy in this process (Brousseau, 1993).

How can networks influence and contribute to the process of organizational learning? Drawing on the above features of technological knowledge (tacit, local and complex), it becomes clear that know-how characterized this way cannot be exchanged via markets (even if the 'right' incentives exist). Without a common knowledge base and shared experience, a simple know-how transfer is not possible. What is required here is the common development of this kind of knowledge. 'In this light networks represent a mechanism for innovation diffusion through collaboration and the interactive relationship becomes not only a co-ordination device to create resources, but an essential enabling factor of technical progress' (Zuscovitch and Justman, 1995). Here it is not enough just to know *what* others are doing. The firms also need to know *how* the respective technologies function and work together. To support this inter-firm learning of often long-range cumulative, tacit and local know-how, a stable and long-lasting collaborative environment is necessary.[8] Clark and Juma (1987) introduce the notion of 'evolutionary articulation', characterized by an essentially resonating feature: 'In order to achieve the status of useful knowledge it [the information] needs to undergo a process of evolutionary articulation between supplier and recipient.'

In transaction costs analysis, so-called 'asset specificities' are considered as a reason for a non-market co-ordination e.g. in innovation networks or in a hierarchical organization. The evolutionary approach, based on its knowledge foundation, goes a step further by emphasizing that a firm's opportunity space is determined by what has been done in the past. Because learning is local, history matters, i.e. the technological trajectory a firm follows is strongly path-dependent. However, firms following different technological paths and engaged in innovation networks can also experience a kind of path convergence with important consequences for their technological opportunities. In this way, innovation networks offer a possibility of overcoming the restrictions of the irreversibilities and instead build on different specific knowledge bases. With the fusion of different technological capabilities, the exploration of new opportunities becomes possible: the cross-fertilization effects. In this respect, the essential dynamic properties of innovation networks become obvious.[9] The technological as well as organizational boundaries of the firms participating in a network have to be seen in an evolutionary manner.

Besides this creation of new so-called 'extensive' opportunities (Coombs, 1988), which constitute the synergetic or surplus effect of innovation networks, complementary effects were mentioned. In this respect, it is helpful to recall that the variety of assets and competencies which a firm needs access to in order successfully to commercialize a new technology is likely to be quite large, even for only modest complex technologies.[10] Here, innovation networks prove to be a promising alternative co-ordination mechanism which allows firms to have access to the complementary assets, which otherwise would have to be built up alone – an extremely expansive and time-consuming endeavor, thus confronting small and medium-sized firms with often insurmountable difficulties.[11]

> Successful innovation requires complex forms of business organisation. Innovating organisations must form linkages to others, upstream and downstream, lateral and horizontal. Advanced technological systems do not, and cannot, get created in splendid isolation. The communication and co-ordination requirements are often stupendous, and in practice the price system alone does not suffice to achieve the necessary co-ordination. (Teece, 1986, p. 416)

Innovation networks represent such a flexible organizational device.

To summarize, within the knowledge-based approach, innovation networks are considered to have three major implications. First, they are seen as an important co-ordination device, enabling and supporting inter-firm learning by accelerating and supporting the diffusion of new technological know-how. Second, within innovation networks, the exploitation of complementarities becomes possible, which is a crucial prerequisite to master modern technological solutions characterized by complexity and a multitude of involved knowledge fields. Third, innovation networks constitute an organizational setting which opens the possibility of the exploration of synergies by the amalgamation of different technological competencies. In this way, innovation processes are fed with new extensive technological opportunities, which otherwise would not exist, or whose existence would at least be delayed.

4 New approaches in the analysis of innovation networks

One of the major difficulties in the analysis of networks is the question of how to deal with the high degree of complexity as well as their rich dynamics. Obviously, descriptive approaches quickly reach their limits when network size increases or the number of relations between the actors changes over time. Only in recent years have some new approaches, originally developed in graph theory and statistical physics (see Albert and Barabasi, 2002, for an extensive overview), become employed for the economic analysis of networks, and innovation networks in particular (see e.g Cowan, 2004).Two of the most prominent ones, scale-free networks and small worlds, are briefly discussed in this section.

Barabasi and Albert (1999) develop a general algorithm of network evolution which can easily be applied for the modeling of the evolution of innovation networks. The crucial graph theoretic variable they are looking at describes the connectivity of the nodes, measuring the number of realized connections of a single node in a network divided by the number of possible relationships. Applying the model to the evolution of innovation networks, agents e.g. firms can be considered to be the nodes of the graph and the collaborative relationships between two agents are represented by edges connecting two nodes.

If there is a sequential entry process of new agents (i.e. the graph is growing) and new agents make their choice of partners on a completely random basis, the connectivity of the agents simply follow proportionally the time of their entry: the longer the agent takes in joining the overall network, the stronger is its connectivity and no particular pattern with respect to the connectivity distribution emerges. Albert and Barabasi (2002) introduced a different logic for the potential relationships of new nodes which they labelled 'preferential attachment'. This strongly affects the observed pattern formation and can easily be transferred to the logic of innovation networks: if the probability of the new nodes to be connected with an already existing node depends on the connectivity of the already existing nodes, the networks produced by this algorithm show a skewed, scale-free distribution of their degrees. The degree is related to the connectivity and measures the absolute number of connections of a single node. See Figure 23.1.

In the evolution of innovation networks, the positive feedback via the preferential attachment mechanism seems to be absolutely plausible: new agents prefer to collaborate with agents who are well connected within the relevant population of agents i.e. with agents who are, compared to other agents, more central. Albert and Barabasi (2002) found evidence for scale-free networks and, by this, for the plausibility of their preferential attachment mechanism in many empirical networks (e.g. citation networks between scientists and hyper-links in the Internet). For innovation networks within biotechnology based industries, Powell *et al.* (2005) refer to scale-free degree distributions found in their data encompassing collaborations between biotechnology firms. Figure 23.1 shows such a scale-free innovation network within the biotechnology-based industries taken from Ebersberger, Jonard and Pyka (2005).

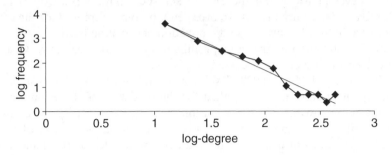

Figure 23.1   *Scale-free network of biotech collaborations*

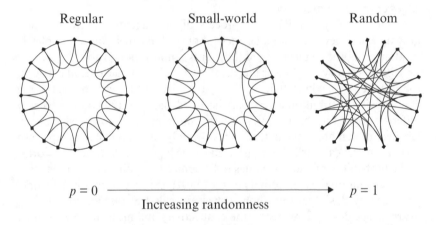

Figure 23.2   *The Watts–Strogatz model (after Watts and Strogatz, 1998)*

Of course, the innovation network architecture or typology will exert a severe influence on the creation and diffusion of new knowledge. In section 3, the importance of close and long-lasting connections between heterogeneous agents with respect to the exploration of new technological opportunities as they are emphasized within the knowledge based approaches of evolutionary economics were discussed. Watts and Strogatz (1998) introduced a class of network typologies which seems to suit perfectly this discussion of the efficacy of innovation networks. With the help of Figure 23.2, their reasoning is easily understandable.

The left-hand network is characterized by a high degree of regularity; every node is connected with its neighbors to the left and the right. Such a network with a high cliquishness is well suited for the exchange of complex

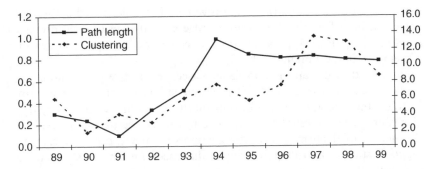

Figure 23.3   Small worlds in biotechnology collaboration networks

knowledge. The various actors are in close contact to their immediate neighbors and the close interaction allows the building up of absorptive capacities by evolutionary articulation. The right-hand network in Figure 23.2 can be characterized as a complete random network (created by 'rewiring' every node; rewiring probability p=1). Such networks show, on the one hand, a very low degree of cliquishness, but, on the other hand, a very short average path length, measuring the distance between any two nodes in the network. The average path length determines the speed of diffusion of knowledge in the network. Watts and Strogatz discovered a hybrid network architecture that combines both advantages of evolutionary articulation and high speed of knowledge diffusion, which they labeled 'small world networks' (the graph in the middle of Figure 23.2).

The small world network architecture seems to be a kind of emergent property for many real world innovation networks. Powell *et al.* (2005) discovered the combination of short path length and high degree of cliquishness for biotechnology innovation networks in the USA. In a similar vein, small worlds have been discovered in international collaboration networks in the biotechnology-based industries by Ebersberger, Jonard and Pyka (2005) shown in Figure 23.3.

5   Summary and conclusions

The aim of this chapter has been to give an overview of the development of theoretical concepts in economics to investigate innovation networks. Drawing as a starting point on the theory of the firm, it is obvious that the analysis of innovation networks is confronted with the same obstacles as economic innovation theory in general.

The difficulties can mainly be traced back to the incentive-based perspective of traditional approaches. Both the production function approach of neo-classical economics as well as transaction costs analysis view innovation networks from a too-narrow incentive-based perspective. Because of neglecting basic features of innovation processes and focusing on a cost perspective only, these approaches do not catch the essential features of present-day innovation networks.

Without drawing on the knowledge-based perspective of evolutionary economics, the crucial characteristics of innovation networks, i.e. inter-firm learning, the exploitation of complementarities, and the creation of synergies, cannot be captured. This knowledge-based perspective is supported by the motives of the firms participating in innovation networks – here, firms regularly state synergistic partnering as the reason for their engagement in co-operation.

Finally, the main concepts which modern economic innovation theory draws upon in the analysis of innovation networks were discussed. However, up to now, there has been no clear terminology, and several almost similar concepts compete. Therefore, on the research agenda of innovation economics in a neo-Schumpeterian framework there has to be the development of a common standard in the analysis of innovation networks which is also well suited for empirical investigations. A promising direction of research is opened up by network analysis coming from theoretical physics. This chapter has aimed to be a first step in this direction.

Notes

1. R. Coombs *et al.* (1996), p. 6.
2. See OECD (1992), p. 77.
3. See DeBresson and Amesse (1991), pp. 365f. and Teece (1990).
4. A major discussion can be found in, among other authors, the work of Nelson and Winter (1982), Witt (1987), DeBresson (1987), Clark and Juma (1987), Silverberg (1988) and Faber and Proobs (1990).
5. See Foray (1991), p. 395.
6. Imai and Baba (1991).
7. This list of necessary components is taken from Dosi, Teece and Winter (1992).
8. A point also stressed by Aoki (1986) as crucial for the success of Japanese firms, which are embedded in long-term networking relationships with subcontracting firms.
9. See e.g. Imai and Itami (1984).
10. Teece (1986).
11. This is also stressed by Mowery (1989): 'Technological developments in a number of industries also have increased the importance of access to new or unfamiliar technologies . . . Collaboration can provide more rapid access to technological capabilities that are not well developed within a firm and whose development may require large investment and considerable time.'

References

Albert, R. and Barabasi, A. (2002), Statistical mechanics of complex networks, *Revue of Modern Physics*, **47**, 47–97.
Aoki, M. (1986), Horizontal vs. vertical information structure of the firm, *American Economic Review*, **76**, 971–83.

Barabasi, A. and Albert, R. (1999), Emergence of scaling in random networks, *Science*, **286**, 509–12.

Brousseau, R. (1993), *L'Économie des Contrats; Technologies de l'Information et Coordination Interentreprises*, Paris: Presses Universitaires de France.

Cantner, U. and Pyka, A. (1998), Absorbing technological spillovers, simulations in an evolutionary framework, *Industrial and Corporate Change*, **7**.

Chesnais, F. (1996), 'Technological agreements, networks, and selected issues in economic theory', in R. Coombs, A. Richards, P.P. Saviotti and V. Walsh (eds), *Technological Collaboration, The Dynamics of Cooperation in Industrial Innovation*, Cheltenham, UK and Brookfield, USA: Edward Elgar.

Clark, N. and Juma, C. (1987), *Long Run Economics – An Evolutionary Approach to Economic Growth*, London: Pinter Publishers.

Coase, R. (1937), 'The nature of the firm, Economica 1937, 386–405', in G. Stigler and K. Boulding (eds), *Readings in Price Theory*, London: George Allen & Unwin.

Cohen W.M. and Levinthal D. (1989), Innovation and learning: the two faces of R&D, *The Economic Journal*, **99**, 569–96.

Coombs, R. (1988), 'Technological opportunities and industrial organization', in G. Dosi *et al.* (eds), *Technical Change and Economic Theory*, London: Pinter Publishers.

Coombs, R., Richards, A., Saviotti, P.P. and Walsh, V. (1996), 'Introduction: technological collaboration and networks of alliances in the innovation process', in R. Coombs, A. Richards, P.P. Saviotti and V. Walsh (eds), *Technological Collaboration, The Dynamics of Cooperation in Industrial Innovation*, Cheltenham, UK and Brookfield, USA: Edward Elgar.

Cowan, R. (2004), Network Models of Innovation and Diffusion, Research Memorandum, MERIT, #010, Maastricht.

Dahmèn, E. (1989), 'Development blocks in industrial economics', in B. Carlsson (ed.), *Industrial Dynamics*, Dordrecht: Kluwer Academic Publishers.

D'Aspremont, C. and Jacquemin, A. (1988), Cooperative and non-cooperative R&D in duopoly with spillovers, *American Economic Review*, **78**, 1133–7.

DeBresson, C. (1987), The evolutionary paradigm and the economics of technical change, *Journal of Economic Issues*, **21**, 751–62.

DeBresson, C. and Amesse, F. (1991), Networks of innovators: a review and introduction to the issue, *Research Policy*, **20**, 363–79.

Dosi, G. (1982), Technological paradigms and technological trajectories: a suggested interpretation of the determinants and directions of technological change, *Research Policy*, **11**, 147–62.

Dosi, G. (1988), Sources, procedures, and microeconomic effects of innovation, *Journal of Economic Literature*, **24**, 1120–71.

Dosi, G, Teece, D.J. and Winter, S.G. (1992), 'Toward a theory of corporate coherence: preliminary remarks', in G. Dosi, R. Giannetti and P.A. Toninelli (eds), *Technology and Enterprise in a Historical Perspective*, Oxford: Clarendon Press.

Ebersberger, B., Jonard, N. and Pyka, A. (2005), Small world and scale-free networks in biotech collaboration, mimeo.

Eliasson, G. (1990), The firm as a competent team, *Journal of Economic Behaviour and Organization*, **19**, 273–98.

Faber, M. and Proobs, J.L.R. (1990), *Evolution, Time, and the Environment*, Berlin: Springer.

Foray, D. (1991), The secrets of industry are in the air: industrial cooperation and the organizational dynamics of the innovating firm, *Research Policy*, **20**, 393–406.

Foray, D. (1995), 'Coalitions and committees: how users get involved in information technology standardization', in R. Hawkins, R. Mansell and J. Skea (eds), *Standards, Innovation and Competitiveness: The Politics and Economics of Technical Environments*, Aldershot, UK and Brookfield, USA: Edward Elgar.

Hagedoorn, J. and Schakenraad, J. (1992), Leading companies and networks of strategic alliances in information technology, *Research Policy*, **21**, 163–91.

Heiner, R.A. (1983), The origin of predictable behaviour, *American Economic Review*, **73**, 560–95.

Holmstrom, B. and Tirole, J. (1989), 'The theory of the firm', in R. Schmalensee and D. Willig (eds), *Handbook of Industrial Organization*, vol. 1, Amsterdam: North-Holland.

Imai, K. and Baba, Y. (1991), 'Systemic innovation and cross-border networks, transcending markets and hierachies to create a new techno-economic system', in OECD (ed.), *Technology and Productivity: The Challenge for Economic Policy*, Paris: OECD.

Imai, K. and Itami, H. (1984), Interprenetration of organization and market: Japan's firm and market in comparison with the US, *International Journal of Industrial Organization*, **2**, 285–310.

Katsoulacos, Y. (1988), On incentives and corporate policies, *Aussenwirtschaft*, June, 141–50.

Malerba, F. (1992), Learning by firms and incremental technical change, *The Economic Journal*, **102**, 845–9.

Marshall, A. (1920), *The Principles of Economics*, 8th edn, London: Macmillan Press.

Mokyr, J. (1990), *The Lever of Riches*, New York: Oxford University Press.

Mowery, D.C. (1989), Collaborative ventures between US and foreign manufacturing firms, *Research Policy*, **18**, 19–33.

Mytelka, L. (1991), *Strategic Partnerships and the World Economy*, London: Pinter Publishers.

Nelson, R.R. and Winter, S.G. (1982), *An Evolutionary Theory of Economic Change*, Cambridge, MA: Cambridge University Press.

Nooteboom, B. (1999), *Inter-Firm Alliances, Analysis and Design*, London: Routledge.

OECD (1992), *Technology and the Economy: The Key Relationships*, Paris: OECD.

Penrose, E. (1959), *The Theory of the Growth of the Firm*, Oxford: Basil Blackwell.

Powell, W., White, D., Koput, K. and Owen-Smith, J. (2005), Network dynamics and field evolution: the growth of interorganizational collaboration in the life sciences, *American Journal of Sociology*, **110**(4), 1132–205.

Pyka, A. (1997), Informal networking, *Technovation*, **17**, 207–20.

Pyka, A. (1999), *Der kollektive Innovationsprozess – Eine theoretische Analyse informeller Netzwerke und absorptiver Fähigkeiten*, Berlin: Duncker & Humblot.

Pyka, A. and Küppers, G. (eds) (2002), *Innovation Networks – Theory and Practice*, Cheltenham, UK and Northampton, MA, USA: Edward Elgar.

Richardson, G.B. (1972), The organisation of industry, *The Economic Journal*, **82**, 327.

Schelling, T. (1973), Hockey helmets, concealed weapons, and daylight saving, *Journal of Conflict Resolution*, **17**, 381–429.

Schrader, S. (1989), *Zwischenbetrieblicher Informationstransfer, Eine empirische Analyse kooperativen Verhaltens*, Berlin: Duncker & Humblot.

Schumpeter, J.A. (1912), *Theorie der wirtschaftlichen Entwicklung*; 8th edn, 1993, Berlin: Duncker & Humblot.

Schumpeter, J.A. (1942), *Capitalism, Socialism and Democracy*, London: Unwin.

Silverberg, G. (1988), 'Modelling economic dynamics and technical change: mathematical approaches to self-organization and evolution', in G. Dosi (ed.), *Technical Change and Economic Theory*, London and New York: Pinter Publishers.

Teece, D.J. (1986), Profiting from technological innovation, *Research Policy*, **15**, 286–305.

Teece, D.J. (1990), Innovation and the organization of industry, working paper no. 90–96, Consortium on Competitiveness and Cooperation, Berkeley.

Von Hippel, E. (1989), 'Cooperation between rivals: informal know-how trading', in B. Carlsson (ed.), *Industrial Dynamics*, Dordrecht: Kluwer Academic Publishers.

Watts, D. and Strogatz, S. (1998), Collective dynamics of small worlds, *Nature*, **393**, 400–403.

Williamson, O. (1975), *Markets and Hierarchies: Antitrust Analysis and Implications*, New York: The Free Press.

Williamson, O. (1985), *The Economic Institutions of Capitalism*, New York: The Free Press.

Winter, S.G. (1991), 'On Coase, competence and the corporation', in O. Williamson and S.G. Winter (eds), *The Nature of the Firm: Origins, Evolution and Development*, Oxford: Oxford University Press, pp. 179–95.

Witt, U. (1987), *Individualistische Grundlagen der evolutorischen Ökonomik*, Tübingen: Mohr Siebeck.

Zuscovitch, E. and Justman, M. (1995), 'Networks, sustainable differentiation, and economic development', in D. Batten, J. Casti and R. Thord (eds), *Networks in Action, Economics and Human Knowlege*, Berlin: Springer Verlag.

24 Technological diffusion: aspects of self-propagation as a neo-Schumpeterian characteristic
Paul Stoneman

1 Introduction

Joseph Schumpeter for many is considered to be the father of the modern analysis of technological change in economics. Schumpeter (1934) defined technological change as having three main stages (which today are much more likely than previously to be considered as interrelated). The first of these is invention (the generation of new ideas) the second innovation (the development of new ideas in to marketable products and processes) and the third is diffusion (the spread of new technology across its potential uses). This chapter is primarily concerned with the third.

Empirically it has been observed that the diffusion process takes time, often a considerable period of time (Stoneman, 2002). It is commonly noted that if one plots some percentage measure of penetration of a new technology over time then that plot is usually S-shaped, showing slow initial growth, after which growth increases up to some mid-point after which, although still positive, it starts to slow until usage approaches an asymptotic level. The shape of this diffusion curve may differ across firms, technologies, countries and industries.

There is a growing literature that attempts to explain the rationale behind these observed time profiles. Of this growing body of work, however, it is not always easy to clarify what may and may not be considered to be neo-Schumpeterian within the spirit of this volume. There are recent contributions that specifically label themselves as Schumpeterian (for example, Aghion and Howitt, 1997) but these are not necessarily inclusive or exclusive. It might be thought that the modern embodiments of Schumpeterian sentiments were more likely to be found in evolutionary economics than in neoclassical economics. However when it comes to the analysis of diffusion this is not necessarily so. The modelling and analysis of diffusion phenomena is a very eclectic field. It is not only a subject area addressed by a number of disciplines (for example, geography, marketing, and sociology all have literatures in this area as well as economics) but even within economics itself it is an area where evolutionary and neoclassical approaches have for long stood side by side, often taking quite similar approaches and providing considerable cross-fertilization. Some of the more significant landmarks in the field, e.g. Davies (1979) are essentially non-neoclassical in approach whereas some of the approaches showing more Schumpeterian sentiments, e.g. Reinganum (1981), take a typically neoclassical modelling approach. Nor does the underlying approach always matter that much; David (1969) for example provides a neoclassical contribution that yields results almost the same as those of the non-neoclassical work in Davies (1979). Moreover, although neoclassical economics has long been the dominant approach in this field, even as early as Cyert and March (1963) the limitations of assuming neoclassical type rational maximizing behaviour in a world of uncertainty were being discussed in the context of new technology adoption.

For Schumpeter, the diffusion process was seen as embodied within its economic context. Diffusion is considered to involve the birth and death of firms or at least the expansion and contraction of firms (creative destruction) and involve endogenously driven changes in factor and output prices to a significant degree. To a large extent the Schumpeterian view of the diffusion process is that it is self-propagating in that, once begun, diffusion has its own momentum. In a self-propagating process use of a technology per se generates further use of that technology and usage continues to extend even in the absence of external shocks. It is upon this characteristic of the Schumpeterian approach that we are going to concentrate. For this chapter therefore we cut through the issue of what may and what may not be labelled Schumpeterian and instead consider a particular issue in the study of diffusion. Why might diffusion be self-propagating?

This chapter will explore more fully several different approaches to the analysis of diffusion that show self-propagation and explore the mechanisms that provide it. In doing so that literature will be ignored which, in contrast, is based upon the view that, in order to continue, technological diffusion requires external stimuli. This is not to play down the importance of that literature; the factors considered therein may well be quantitatively significant. However, for present purposes such issues are put on one side. That literature can however be accessed in Stoneman (2002).

In the next section the Schumpeterian approach is discussed in more detail before the consideration of alternative self-propagating mechanisms. After a review of the different approaches, empirical relevance is addressed and a few brief policy remarks are made.

2   Self-propagating mechanisms

2.1   The Schumpeterian approach[1]
In the Schumpeterian approach to diffusion there are two basic self-propagating forces at work that drive or enable the diffusion process

(although one could probably also specify others). The scenario is that the process of diffusion of a new technology begins with innovation (from a set of accumulated inventions) by an entrepreneur seeking profits. This then leads to the initiation of the two interacting processes that lead to the growth of the use of the new technology.

1. *Emulation* The entrepreneur is profit seeking and if the new technology is superior will realize profit gains from his/her actions. These profit gains act to attract others to copy the innovator in the search for profits. The emulators in turn will be copied as they realize excess profits and as this occurs the use of new technology will continue to expand.
2. *Price changes* As imitators copy the innovator, the supply and/or price of goods on the market and the supply or the cost of inputs to production will be changed and the profitability of old technology operations will be reduced. This will either drive non-innovators from the market or encourage such innovators to change their technology as the relative profitability of switching from old to new technology changes (the mechanism also relied upon more recently by Reinganum, 1981).

The joint effect of emulation and price changes is to increase the probability that a non-adopter will switch to the new technology or that firms will enter the market using new technology. As the number of users of new technology increases the number of users still to convert to the new technology decreases and/or the potential for industry expansion through entry becomes less, implying a declining pool of potential adopters. Jointly these two effects will generate the S-shaped diffusion curve, with a slow take-off followed by faster growth and then a slowing diffusion process as usage approaches its asymptote.

2.2 *Epidemic models*

Epidemic diffusion models provide a classic example of a self-propagating diffusion mechanism. Such models are essentially predicated on the assumption that, as the number of users of a new technology increases, so the probability of a non-user adopting the technology also increases. Thus use encourages further use. However, although the probability of a non-user adopting increases with use, the number of potential converts decreases with use, the two countervailing effects, as in the Schumpeterian story, producing the commonly observed S-shaped diffusion curve.

The underlying mechanisms that produce these effects may be of several types.

1. The medical literature uses such models to represent the spread of diseases that are caught from human contact. The greater the number of infected persons the greater is the probability of a non-infected person meeting and being infected by such a person (as long as the disease is not fatal).
2. Early uses in economics argued that personal contact could spread knowledge of the existence (or performance characteristics) of a technology and the more users there are the greater is the chance of meeting a user and learning of existence or characteristics.
3. Later models in economics, e.g. Mansfield (1968), argued that as usage extends so familiarity will lead to reduced risk and uncertainty encouraging further use.

Although they have also been extensively criticized (see, for example, Davies, 1979), models built upon epidemic principles have been widely used in both Economics and Marketing (see for example, Mahajan and Wind, 1986).

2.3   Self-selection processes

The evolutionary approach to technological diffusion (see, for example, Metcalfe, 1994, 1995) provides alternative self-propagating mechanisms. A typical argument is that profits finance investment and consequently a profitable firm will invest more and grow faster than an unprofitable firm. A firm introducing a new superior technology will be more profitable than a firm either not investing in new technology or mistakenly investing in an inferior technology. Thus an early adopter of a superior technology will have greater profits than other firms, invest more than other firms and grow more than other firms, this growth leading to expansion in the share of industry output produced on the new technology (i.e. extending diffusion). Moreover, as the market share of the innovating firm increases, non-innovating firms will tend to leave the industry, reinforcing the spread of the new technology. Such a process has its own momentum.

Such processes as that just described are also considered to generate effects whereby there is survival of the fittest. Those firms with the best technologies grow, those with the worst decline and or die. The parallel with biological and ecological processes is immediate and deliberate (referring to Lotka, 1925, and Volterra, 1926, now being common). The processes are also evolutionary with the structure of the industry, the size of firms and the performance of industry and firms evolving over time through the process of competition. Perhaps it is in the work of Nelson and Winter (1982) more than most that the implications of such processes for industry structure and performance are best illustrated.

2.4 Network externalities

Over the last 20 years a growing literature has explored the issue of network externalities. Originally considered for the purposes of addressing issues relating to standards and compatability, network externalities were used to explore the competition between different versions of the same underlying basic technology (e.g. VHS vs. Beta video recording technologies); to address why the establishment of dominant standards (e.g. QWERTY) should be established in some cases and not others: and to consider whether any dominant standards established were necessarily optimal (see, for example, Arthur, 1989; David and Greenstein, 1990). The important function that network externalities play in these processes is that, as the installed base of a particular technology variant grows, so the benefits from that variant compared to other variants increases and thus there is greater likelihood that any new adopters will choose the dominant variant. Of course this also implies that, as the dominant variant has a growing installed base, the payoff to the adoption of the generic technology is also growing and so there is a self-propagating effect that will drive along the diffusion of the generic technology. Network externalities thus provide an alternative self-propagating mechanism.

There may be many types of network externalities. There are simple externalities such as one might find with telephones, the benefit of ownership growing (at least up to some point) with the total number of users. There are other such effects (see, for example, Choi, 1997) whereby network externalities essentially work by reducing uncertainty as to which technology will dominate. Alternatively network externalities may arise through the provision of complementary inputs (e.g. as the stock of hardware increases the stock of software available also increases, or infrastructure develops as the stock of the product increases). It may even be the case that some network externalities are carried over between technology generations, thereby reinforcing alternative diffusion drivers (Liikanen, Stoneman and Toivanen, 2002).

2.5 Supply-side learning

Not all self-propagating effects have to be demand-side effects. David and Olsen (1986) discuss how supply and demand interact in the diffusion process and in particular how learning by doing effects on the supply side may drive a diffusion process. As usage extends so the cumulative number of units of a technology produced increases. If it is the case that there is learning by doing on the supply side then production costs decline as cumulative production increases and greater usage will feed through into lower prices and thus further extension of use.

Further supply-side effects of this kind may also exist. For example, if network externalities or some other effects lead to standardization then it is possible that scale economies may be realized in production that will further stimulate usage. Perhaps more important, however, is the possibility that increased usage will stimulate further innovation. As the market for a new product grows and matures, and/or infrastructure is provided and/or as standardization occurs, the potential for further innovation in products and processes could increase (Utterback, 1993). As this potential is realized, so diffusion extends.

3   Empirical evidence

One may suggest numerous reasons as to why diffusion should be self-propagating, but eventually it is necessary to evaluate whether the suggestion has any empirical validity. To test the suggestion empirically, however, is not a simple matter. Self-propagation would suggest that the probability of a non-user becoming a user of a new technology in a time period would be a function of the level of usage of the technology in that time period. However, as usage extends, the number of potential converts is declining. Jointly these two effects suggest that, within time series data, one would expect to find that diffusion follows an S-shaped growth curve. Unfortunately, other factors may also generate such a pattern and thus the existence of such patterns per se is not sufficient evidence of self-propagation. Thus, although there is considerable evidence of S-shaped curves, in order to validate the relationship between current usage and extensions of usage a better approach is perhaps to use panel data sets and estimate hazard functions. If one can show directly that the probability of a non-user adopting the new technology in a time period is positively related to the number of existing users in that time period then there may well be some support for the existence of self-propagating effects. Karshenas and Stoneman (1993) found evidence that, in the adoption of CNC technology in the UK metalworking industry, even after taking account of differences between firms, price and price expectation effects, and potential order effects, there were still some remaining positive impacts of current usage on the probability of adoption. These they labelled 'epidemic effects' but they could just as simply be wider self-propagating effects.

Liikanen, Stoneman and Toivanen (2002) also find empirical evidence of network externalities in the diffusion of mobile phones. In their cross-country study they find spillovers (network externalities) between both fixed lines and mobile phones and between first- and second-generation mobile phones. Perhaps just as convincing is that many empirical studies of diffusion do find that the cost of acquiring new technology and/or the profit gain from adoption impact significantly upon the decision to adopt (Geroski, 2000). As the cost of acquisition essentially is determined by the cost of production of new technology this provides a major route through which supply-side learning may act in a self-propagating manner.

4 Policy issues

The alternative to self-propagation is that diffusion is essentially driven by a series of exogenous shocks to the system. Thus, for example, it may be that, for reasons not related to self-propagation, the cost of acquiring the new technology falls over time and as it does so the extent of usage extends. If that is the nature of the diffusion process then a continuous series of shocks is required to keep the diffusion process going or else it will stop. Of course it is possible (and probable) that any real world diffusion proves to be a mixture of both types of processes with external shocks giving occasional encouragement to self-propagating processes.

We may, however, ask whether self-propagation has any particular policy implications. There is a tendency in discussions of diffusion policy to turn immediately to discussion of instruments. That is mistaken. It is much better to ask initially why policy intervention may be necessary. The only criterion by which we may judge the need for intervention is whether, given self-propagation, the market unaided will not produce a welfare optimal outcome. Here there is a long history of literature that would argue that self-propagation is essentially the result of the existence of externalities (those externalities being of varied kinds, for example network externalities or information externalities) and the nature of externalities is such that a market failure exists and private returns to actions are (in this case) less than the social returns to those actions. Market incentives are thus suboptimal and therefore the diffusion path will be suboptimal: generally too slow. There is thus a case for intervention to speed diffusion.

That intervention may be of several kinds. It may be intervention that promotes standardization in a market and thereby speeds diffusion. It may be intervention that provides subsidies that correct market incentives. It may even be policies that stimulate information spreading. It may be policies that shift risk and stimulate diffusion in that way. In general, however, one cannot specify a detailed policy in the absence of detailed knowledge of the processes that are generating the diffusion in the particular case being considered and the market failures that are present in that particular case.

5 Conclusions

In this short chapter the issue of self-propagation in the diffusion process has been addressed. It was argued that to some degree at least the Schumpeterian approach to diffusion involves self-propagation with usage of a new technology generating further use per se. A number of alternative routes by which this result can occur have been discussed and their empirical relevance briefly addressed. In the presence of such self-propagating processes it is likely that, from a welfare point of view, diffusion will be too slow and thus the existence of such processes is also a rationale for government intervention in the process.

Note

1. The Schumpeterian approach was largely formulated as a means to explain the existence of cycles in the level of economic activity. Although these cycles are considered to be the results of the diffusion process, that process itself can be discussed with only limited reference to the analysis of cycles and thus in order to save space we have largely ignored this wider aspect of the issue.

Bibliography

Aghion, P. and Howitt, P. (1997), 'A Schumpeterian perspective on growth and competition', in D. Kreps and K. Wallis (eds), *Advances in Economics and Econometrics: Theory and Application*, Vol. 2, Cambridge: Cambridge University Press.

Arthur, W.B. (1989), Competing technologies, increasing returns and lock in by historical events, *Economic Journal*, **99**, 116–31.

Choi, J.P. (1997), Herd behavior, the penguin effect and the suppression of informational diffusion: an analysis of informational externalities and payoff interdependency, *Rand Journal of Economics*, **28**(3), 407–25.

Cyert, R.M. and March J.G. (1963), *A Behavioral Theory of the Firm*, 2nd edn, Malden, MA: Blackwell.

David, P. (1969), *A Contribution to the Theory of Diffusion*, Center for Research in Economic Growth Research Memorandum, no. 71, Stanford University.

David. P and Greenstein, S. (1990), The economics of compatability standards: an introduction to recent research, *Economics of Innovation and New Technology*, **1**, 3–42.

David, P. and Olsen, T. (1986), Equilibrium dynamics of diffusion when incremental technological innovations are foreseen, *Ricerche Economiche*, **40**(4), October–December, Special issue on Innovation Diffusion, 738–70.

Davies, S. (1979), *The Diffusion of Process Innovations*, Cambridge: Cambridge University Press.

Geroski, P. (2000), Models of technology diffusion, *Research Policy*, **29**, 603–25.

Karshenas, M. and Stoneman, P. (1993), Rank, stock, order and epidemic effects in the diffusion of new process technology, *Rand Journal of Economics*, **24**(4), 503–28.

Liikanen, J., Stoneman, P. and Toivanen, O. (2002), 'Intergenerational effects in the diffusion of new technology', a paper presented at the EARIE Conference, Madrid, 5–8 September.

Lotka A.J. (1925), *Elements of Physical Biology*, Baltimore, MD: Williams and Williams.

Mahajan, V. and Wind, Y. (1986), *Innovation Diffusion Models of New Product Acceptance*, Cambridge, MA: Ballinger.

Mansfield, E. (1968), *Industrial Research and Technological Innovation*, New York: Norton.

Metcalfe, J.S. (1994), Evolutionary economics and technology policy, *Economic Journal*, **104**, 931–44.

Metcalfe, J.S. (1995), The economic foundations of technology policy: equilibrium and evolutionary perspectives', in P. Stoneman (ed.), *Handbook of the Economics of Innovation and Technological Change*, Oxford: Blackwell, pp. 409–512.

Nelson, R. and Winter, S. (1982), *An Evolutionary Theory of Economic Change*, Cambridge, MA: Harvard University Press.

Reinganum, J. (1981), Market structure and the diffusion of new technology', *The Bell Journal of Economics*, **12**, 618–24.

Schumpeter, J.A. (1934), *The Theory of Economic Development*, Cambridge, MA: Harvard University Press.

Stoneman, P. (2002), *The Economics of Technological Diffusion*, Oxford: Basil Blackwell.

Utterback, J.M. (1993), *Mastering the Dynamics of Innovation*, Boston: Harvard Business School.

Volterra, V. (1926), Variazioni e fluttuazioni del numero di individui in specie de animali conviventi, *Memorie Accademia dei Lincei*, **2**, 31–113.

2.2
Modelling Industry Dynamics

25 Schumpeterian modelling
Witold Kwasnicki

Schumpeterian models of economic growth and industrial dynamics may also be known as evolutionary models. By using the term 'evolution' or 'evolutionary' neo-Schumpeterians indicate the importance of long-term changes and the crucial role of innovation for economic development.

In spite of general agreement on the evolutionary character of Schumpeter's theory, there is a question as to whether the theory of economic development of Joseph Alois Schumpeter can be considered as evolutionary? Two important voices in this debate are Geoffrey M. Hodgson (1997) and Matthias Kelm (1997). Ulrich Witt (2002) also clearly states that question in the title of his paper: 'How evolutionary is Schumpeter's theory of economic development?' Putting aside all the controversies it seems justifiable to separate two notions, namely the meaning of Schumpeter's original ideas and the way in which Schumpeter's work has been read in modern times. It seems that the revival of Schumpeter's ideas in the last few decades, is fully based on an evolutionary interpretation of his original ideas. One of the founders of modern evolutionary economics, Richard Nelson (1995) states directly that 'the evolutionary theories of economic growth . . . all draw inspiration from Joseph Schumpeter'.

What are the main features of evolutionary, Schumpeterian models? First of all, the models are *dynamic* ones (corresponding to the frequently mentioned words of Sidney Winter, 'Dynamics first'). To those who hold to this interpretation, the evolutionary process is a dynamic, spontaneous, historical process in which macroeconomic characteristics are the effects of activity of economic agents observed at the micro level. Next, to be called 'Schumpeterian', a model should be focused on *far-from-equilibrium analysis*. The other features which seem to be crucial to an evolutionary approach are *diversity and heterogeneity of economic agents and their behaviour*,[1] *the search for innovation based on a concept of hereditary information (knowledge)*, and *a selection process* which leads to a diversified rate of growth. Schumpeter stressed the importance of the entrepreneur in the economic process, and so one of the important questions in this context reflects the way in which decisions are made. Therefore decision-making procedures are present in almost all neo-Schumpeterian models.

Development of 'Schumpeterian modelling' has its own history. In the historical process we can distinguish three stages (Figure 25.1). The early

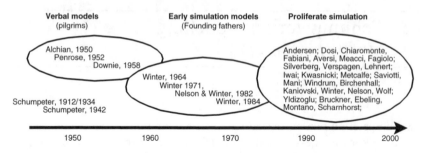

Figure 25.1   Three stages of Schumpeterian modelling

stage ('Pilgrims', mainly in the 1950s) is dominated by verbal models, three of which seem to be representative, namely Alchian (1950), Penrose (1952) and Downie (1958). The second stage, 1960s and 1970s, may be called early simulation models ('Founding fathers'), and here the representative models are Winter (1964, 1971, 1984), and Nelson and Winter (1982). Nelson and Winter's book of 1982 may be considered as the culmination of this stage and may be treated as initiating the third stage, which may be called 'Schumpeterian modelling proliferation'.

The rest of the chapter is organized as follows. In section 1 Schumpeter's ideas are outlined. This is followed by a short description of the models of Alchian and Downie. In section 3, a brief report on current neo-Schumpeterian models is presented. The chapter ends with a short description of a separate stream of modelling efforts in evolutionary economics, namely Agent-based computational economics (ACE). What we have observed in the last decade is a convergence process of formerly separate streams of modelling, i.e. neo-Schumpeterians and ACE. Within a broad research effort sometimes referred to as 'Artificial life' (A-life), Lane (1993a, 1993b) distinguishes 'artificial worlds in economics'. Some models rooted in the Schumpeterian tradition may also be classified as ACE models; two recent examples being Fagiolo and Dosi (2003) and Silverberg and Verspagen (2002). To what extent this convergence process will be continued and will give interesting results is still an open question, but it seems to be interesting to point to the possibility in this short chapter.

Schumpeterian ideas on economic development

Schumpeter formulated and presented fully matured (although still far from any formal approach and without applying any mathematical models) propositions of principles and goals of economic analysis in the evolutionary spirit. As is frequently mentioned in this book, these references appear in his 1912 *Theory of Economic Development* and in later publications (Schumpeter, 1928, 1935, 1939, 1942, 1947). In the marginalist theory, predominating at the beginning of the 20th century, the causes of development were seen in factors exogenous to economic process. One of the founders of the marginalist school, J.B. Clark (*The Distribution of Wealth*, 1894, New York, Macmillan) treated population growth, changes in consumer's attitudes, and changes of production methods as exogenous factors. This view was challenged by Schumpeter, who correctly pointed out that such factors ought to be discovered in the economic process itself. In his opinion, capitalism could never be perceived as a process at equilibrium states and could never be treated as a stationary process. The essential element of his theory is the concept of recurring structural changes, what he called 'gales of creative destruction', followed by waves of expansion and rapid growth: 'evolution is lopsided, discontinuous, disharmonious by nature . . . evolution is a disturbance of existing structures and more like a series of explosions than a gentle, though incessant, transformation' (Schumpeter, 1939, vol.1, s.102). Persons responsible for these gales of creative destruction are those introducing radical innovations, the pioneering entrepreneurs. Entrepreneurs search for new productive and trade combinations (innovations in the understanding of Schumpeter) to gain greater profit. The entrepreneurs profit flows from what Schumpeter referred to as 'temporary monopoly positions'. Profit emerges through the process of economic growth, in other words in a dynamic economy. In the opinion of Schumpeter, profit is not always the primary motivation for entrepreneurs; as frequently the entrepreneur will be motivated by artistic creation, the need for an outlet for his temperament, the desire to demonstrate his possibilities, or just an initiation of novel actions.

Schumpeter was so convinced of the evolutionary character of the capitalistic economy that in 1942 he wrote: 'The essential point to grasp is that in dealing with capitalism we are dealing with an evolutionary process. It may seem strange that anyone can fail to see so obvious a fact which moreover was long ago emphasized by Karl Marx' (Schumpeter, 1942, p.82). But it is necessary to mention that Schumpeter's understanding of the adjective 'evolutionary' is slightly different to the Darwinian or Lamarckian evolution. Economic development, as all evolutionary processes, is historical in nature, future development being determined by the pathway of changes as well as by the current state of the process. 'Every concrete process of development finally rests upon preceding development . . . Every process of development creates the prerequisites for the following' (Schumpeter, 1934, p. 64). Innovations in economic process, as mutations in biological evolution, are essential elements of development. In 1939, he wrote that economic evolution is equivalent to 'changes in the economic process brought about by innovation, together with all their effects, and the responses to them by the economic system' (Schumpeter, 1939, vol. 1, s. 86). In the opinion of

Schumpeter, those changes 'illustrate the same process of industrial mutation – if I may use that biological term – that incessantly revolutionizes the
economic structure *from within*, incessantly destroying the old one, creating
a new one. This process of Creative Destruction is the essential fact about
capitalism' (Schumpeter, 1942, p. 84).[2]

We can find elements of selection and the search for innovations in these
statements, i.e. the most essential mechanisms of evolutionary processes.
But in his later works his understanding of the evolutionary process
appears different than that in his early works.

> The term evolution may be used in a wider and in a narrower sense. In the wider
> sense it comprises all the phenomena that make an economic process non-
> stationary. In the narrower sense it comprises these phenomena minus those that
> may be described in terms of continuous variations of rates within an unchang-
> ing framework of institutions, tastes, or technological horizons, and will be
> included in the concept of growth. (Schumpeter, 1954, p. 964).

This means that, for Schumpeter, 'evolution' in the wider sense is almost the
same as 'change' and in the narrower sense is equivalent to economic
growth.

The notion that economic change comes 'from within', and not exogenously from the economic process, seems to be one of the most important
contributions of Schumpeter's theory. This notion shaped the future development of the evolutionary approach to economic analysis. Schumpeter's
approach stresses the importance of qualitative changes although it is very
difficult to encompass them in mathematical models or by any formal
approach. Qualitative changes and the generation of economic diversity
are the central categories in the long-term perspective of economic changes.
Therefore, for Schumpeter, the most interesting are those changes 'which so
displaces its equilibrium point that the new one cannot be reached from the
old one by infinitesimal steps. Add successively as many mail coaches as
you please, you will never get a railway thereby' (Schumpeter [1912] 1934,
p. 64). In 1947, he related innovation to historical and non-reversible
changes, repeating the phrase of 1912 when he wrote: 'This historic and
irreversible change in the way of doing things we call "innovation" and we
define: innovations are changes in production function which cannot be
decomposed into infinitesimal steps. Add as many mail-coaches as you
please, you will never get a railroad by so doing' (Schumpeter, 1947).

Schumpeter pointed out a very essential feature of the capitalistic
economy, this feature being in fact general for all evolutionary processes,
namely that effective development strongly depends on diversity and that
diversity is the basic source of innovation. This is the 'evolutionary engine'.
Diversity leads to diminishing the current quality of systems performance,

and so from the short-term perspective it is disadvantageous. But it is beneficial in the long-term. As Schumpeter wrote (1942, p. 83): 'A system . . .
that at *every* point in time fully utilizes its possibilities to its best advantage
may yet in the long run be inferior to a system that does so at *no* given point
in time, because the latter's failure to do so may be a condition for a level
or speed of long-run performance.'

Schumpeter is considered one of the founders of the evolutionary
approach to economic analysis, and such has been the perspective through
which his works have been approached in the last few decades. But
Schumpeter, commenting on the possibility of applying biological analogies to analysis of economic phenomena, wrote that 'no appeal to biology
would be of the slightest use' (Schumpeter, 1954, p. 789). This opinion
seems to be a constant in his thinking. To excuse Schumpeter we may
suppose that this opinion was based on a very specific, seemingly wrong,
understanding of the transmission of biological ideas to economic analysis at the beginning of the 20th century. At the beginning of the chapter on
The fundamental phenomenon of economic development, he wrote:

> Closely connected with the metaphysical preconception . . . is every search for a
> 'meaning' of history. The same is true of the postulate that a notion, a civiliza-
> tion, or even the whole of mankind, must such a matter-of-fact mind as Roscher
> assumed and as the innumerable philosophers and theorists of history in the
> long brilliant line from Vico to Lambrecht took and still take for granted. Here,
> too, belong all kinds of evolutionary thought that centre in Darwin – at least if
> this means no more than reasoning by analogy – and also the psychological prej-
> udice which consists in seeking more in motives and acts of violation than a
> reflex of the social process. But the evolutionary idea is now discredited in our
> field, especially with historians and ethologists, for still another reason. To the
> reproach of unscientific and extra-scientific mysticism that now surrounds the
> 'evolutionary' ideas, is added that of dilettantism. With all the hasty generalisa-
> tions in which the word 'evolution' plays a part, many of us have lost patience.
> (Schumpeter [1912 (1934)], pp. 57–8)

Pilgrims

Armen A. Alchian was the first economist to construct a model of economic
development directly on the basis of evolutionary ideas. Alchian searched
for the way to replace the neoclassical maximization principle with the biological concept of natural selection. The possibility of the application of
'natural selection' to describe firm behaviour was discussed by Alchian in
1950 and by Penrose two years later (Alchian, 1950; Penrose, 1952). As
Alchian argued, competition is not described by the motive of profit maximization but by 'adaptive, imitative, and trial-and-error behaviour in search
for profit' and therefore 'those who realize *positive profit* are the survivors;
those who suffer losses disappear'. Alchian's vision is clearly concordant

with the Darwinian proposition (Alchian, 1950, pp. 211–13). The work of Alchian was the first very important step toward building mathematical models of economic development on the basis of evolutionary metaphors. In one place he states that 'The economic counterparts of genetic heredity, mutations, and natural selection are imitation, innovation, and positive profits' (Alchian, 1950, p. 220). In a very suggestive way he presents the way of analysing firm behaviour in a competitive environment:

> A useful, but unreal, example in which individuals act without any foresight indicates the type of analysis available to the economist and also the ability of the system to 'direct' resources despite individual ignorance. Assume that thousands of travelers set out from Chicago, selecting their routes completely at random and without foresight. Only our 'economist' knows that on but one road are there gasoline stations. He can state categorically that travelers will *continue* to travel only on that road; as those on the other roads will soon run out of gas. Even though each selected his route at random, we might call those travelers who were so fortunate as to have picked that road wise, efficient, foresighted, etc. Of course, we would also consider them the lucky ones. (Alchian, 1950, p. 214)

Alchian did not consider one very important element of firm behaviour, namely the searching processes of competing firms for technological innovation. In similar neoclassical fashion Alchian treated technological change as coming from outside. It seems that the main aim of Alchian's article was not to show the virtues of the evolutionary approach but to point out some consequences of using the maximization principle treated as the primary motive of economic agents' actions.

Although there is no evidence that Jack Downie was influenced by Alichan's work, we can consider his model as presented in *The Competitive Process* (1958), as an extension of the model of Alchian. Two papers by Nightingale (1997, 1998) give a good overview of Downie's model. In the first paper, Nightingale states that Downie's work was 'anticipating Nelson and Winter'.

In his population-oriented model, Downie considers an industry producing a homogeneous product. One of the evolutionary and Schumpeterian features of the model is the heterogeneity of firms. The production technique selected by each individual firm influences a unique level of cost of that firm. A firm's unique character flows from the property that differences between techniques are cumulative in a sense that depends on past investments in production capacity and proprietary elements of knowledge accumulated within the firm (Downie, 1958: 81–90). Individual firm development is a stochastic process, being a result of past mistakes and also random influences. Therefore we can say that a specific process leading to the uniqueness of each firm resembles the evolutionary principle of variation. This uniqueness is transmitted from year to year but in the course of firm development the technique can be modified. Growth is a main goal of each firm, and so profit is reinvested in production capacity. The production capacity is equal to sales, which are assured by the price mechanism; namely price is set by each firm to keep sales at the production capacity level over time (ibid.: 63–7). Through the so-called 'transfer mechanism', firms experience different levels of efficiency. Each firm's profit depends on production costs, and so firms having lower costs of production gain larger profit and are able to develop much quicker than their competitors. Therefore the share of each firm changes according to the firm's specific sales growth. We can say that the average firm has the average growth rate and firms with above (below) average cost have an above (below) average growth rate. Less efficient firms withdraw from the market and more efficient firms dominate. Due to this process, in the course of time, the industry average efficiency increases. Naturally, this selection process leads to a monopoly by the most efficient firm. The monopolization occurs in a case of no innovation but, as Downie notes, a loss of a market by a less efficient firm acts as the firm's stimulus. Firms may still be profitable, but those with growth rates below that of the most efficient will attempt to improve their production techniques by some form of innovation. This process Downie calls the 'innovation mechanism'. The search for innovation is a random process and not all firms succeed in finding better techniques, although the successful firms create new best practice levels of efficiency. Therefore, we can say that we observe turbulence in shares of firms because it may happen that former losers gain advantageous techniques and regain their market position (Downie, 1958: 91–4). In Downie's theory firms do not maximize profit but are 'able to take over the business of another and . . . conduct it reasonably effectively' (ibid.: 30).

Founding fathers

Schumpeterian models, to encompass the essence of the evolutionary approach, ought to be nonlinear. In general, this requirement has not allowed for their analytical treatment. Thanks to the development of computer technology in the 1950s and 1960s, and the concurrent development of the simulation approach, it was possible to build and to analyse behaviour of evolutionary models.

The computer simulation may be considered an alternative means of economic analysis. Discontinuities of development are natural phenomena observed in socioeconomic processes and, in a sense, these discontinuities form the essence of socioeconomic systems. The search for alternative approaches of economic analysis goes in different directions, for example, applications of chaos theory, fuzzy sets theory, catastrophe theory and game theory, to name only a few. The proper application of the simulation approach to economic analysis seems to be one of the most promising means for further development and a better understanding of socioeconomic processes.

Out of three distinct evolutionary schools, namely the Austrian, institutionalist and neo-Schumpeterian, only neo-Schumpeterians widely apply formal modelling and use the simulation approach to economic analysis. Institutionalists and the Austrians prefer verbal and graphical representations of economic phenomena. Therefore it is not surprising that some institutionalists call neo-Schumpeterians 'simulationists'.

The first simulation model within the neo-Schumpeterian tradition was that of Sidney Winter, made at the beginning of the 1960s. Sidney Winter and Richard Nelson, in the 1970s and 1980s, worked out different models and summarized their efforts in the well known book, sometimes called the 'bible of evolutionary economists' (Nelson and Winter, 1982). Nelson and Winter models serve frequently as a pattern for other evolutionary models. In the Nelson and Winter (NW) models, and in almost all models of the Schumpeterian tradition, a firm is the basic unit of evolution. Nelson and Winter apply a population perspective and they postulate that it is possible to specify the space in which innovative search takes place.

The assumption of macroeconomic properties flowing from the microeconomic behaviour of economic agents (i.e. firms) is the basic reason for using simulation to investigate these models. The first model, which will be discussed shortly is the one presented in Nelson and Winter (1982, ch. 9). This model can be seen also as the first evolutionary growth model.

The state of the evolutionary process of an industry at any moment t is described by the capital stock and the behavioural rules of each firm. The state in the next moment $(t+1)$ is determined by the state in the previous moment. In this growth model firms use production techniques which are characterized by fixed labour and capital coefficients. Firms manufacture homogeneous products, so the model describes only process innovation. It is assumed that firms produce using a Leontief production function, and therefore substitution between labour and capital is not explicitly present in the model. Invention occurs as a result of firms' search activities. Firms search for new combinations of labour and capital coefficients. Changes in both coefficients are not correlated, and so a phenomenon that resembles substitution between labour and capital may be observed in the simulated process. Search activities are determined by satisfying behaviour, in a sense that a new technique is adopted only if the expected rate of return is higher than the firm's present rate of return. The search process may take two different forms: local search (mutation) or imitation. In the first case, firms search for new techniques of industrial practice. The term *local* search indicates that each undiscovered technique has a probability of being discovered which linearly declines with a suitably defined technological distance from the current technology. Imitation allows a particular firm to find techniques currently employed by other firms but not yet used in its own production process. The probability of technique imitation is proportional to its share in output. It is assumed that if a firm is engaged in search, it can use only one type of search. The selection of a search type is a random event with a fixed probability for each type. An additional source of novelty in the economy is the entry by new firms, which also search for innovation.

The rate of return on techniques is the main selection force in the NW model. A firm's investment in capital is equal to its profit, diminished by a fixed fraction, which depends on paid dividends and capital depreciation. A firm's capital stock shrinks if profit of that firm is negative. Therefore we have a second selection force which causes firms to withdraw from the market if they do not keep pace with the technological progress of its competitors.

To calibrate the model sketched above for the Solow data on total factor productivity for the United States in the first half of the 20th century, it was assumed that firms produce a homogenous product named GNP. Using that model, Nelson and Winter address the question whether these time series of the calibrated model correspond in a broad qualitative sense to the ones actually observed by Solow.

The most developed and documented NW model which deals with the evolution of the production techniques and other behavioural rules of an industry producing a homogenous product is frequently called 'Schumpeterian competition' (Nelson and Winter, 1982, ch. 12; Winter, 1984). As in the formerly sketched model, a number of firms produce a single homogenous product. Techniques used by different firms differ in output per unit of capital, i.e. in capital productivity A. All other technique factors, such as return to scale and input coefficients, are assumed to be equal for all firms. Technical change (i.e., increase of the productivity of capital) takes the form of process innovations and process imitations. Each firm chooses a technique with the highest productivity out of the three possible techniques (i.e. currently used and found through innovative and imitative processes). The probability that firms innovate or imitate depends on R&D funds determined in proportion to the level of physical capital. Profit per unit of capital is calculated by including R&D costs as ordinary cost elements. The maximum investment of a firm depends on current profit plus loans from the banks (calculated in proportion to the profit). The firm's desired investment is determined by the unit costs, a mark-up factor influenced by the market share of the firm, and the rate of depreciation. The investment process has no time-lags. By multiplying the capital stock with the new level of productivity, we have the production capacity of the firms in the industry in the next period. Product price is not firm-specific but is equal for all firms and flows from the downward-sloping demand function to balance supply and demand. The investment decision of each firm is based on the investment function, which depends on the firm's market share, price elasticity of the demand function, unit profit and bank policy.

A firm grows (or shrinks, in terms of its market share and long-run performance index) according to its profit (or loss) gained in each year (instant of time). A firm is withdrawn from the market if its capital falls below the assumed minimum capital or if its long-run performance index falls below the assumed value. Firms can imitate and innovate. Improving productivity of capital is the main aim of the innovative process.

Winter (1984) presents an interesting elaboration of search activity and entry. Firms are partitioned into two types: primarily innovative or imitative. This allows Winter to apply a notion of technological regime, depending on whether the source of technical progress is external to the firm (e.g., from public scientific knowledge bases) or from the firms' own accumulated technological capabilities. These two regimes are named *entrepreneurial* and the *routinized*. Specific parameters exogenously impose the type of investigated regime.

Proliferated simulation

Since the publication of the seminal work by Richard Nelson and Sidney Winter in 1982, evolutionary models have proliferated enormously. In this short chapter, we are not able to review neo-Schumpeterian models (reviews and surveys of evolutionary models can be found in Dosi *et al.*, 1988; Saviotti and Metcalfe, 1991; Nelson, 1995; Silverberg and Verspagen 1995a, revised version 2003; see also Kwasnicki, 2001). Here we present only short remarks on the general method of development as observed in the last two decades.

The models are rather new, most of them developed in the 1990s. Looking into the history of the Schumpterian tradition it seems possible to distinguish a few related but in some ways independent streams of modelling efforts. The first is very closely associated with the work of Nelson and Winter (1982). In that tradition, the works of Winter (1984), Jonard and Yildizoglu (1998, 1999), Winter *et al.* (2000) and Yildizoglu (2002) can be included. The other streams get inspiration from the work of Nelson and Winter, but have essential distinguishing features.

The second stream of models can be called 'Silverberg–Verspagen models'. One distinguishing feature of SV models is that technological progress is embedded in vintage capital. In the model presented in Silverberg (1985) and Silverberg *et al.* (1988), firms are self-financing using their cash and liquid interest-bearing reserves. The idea that firms rely on rather simple rules of thumb or routines rather than explicit optimization procedures is applied in models developed by Silverberg, Lehnert and Verspagen (Silverberg and Lehnert, 1993, 1996; Silverberg and Verspagen, 1994a, 1994b, 1994c, 1995b). These models can be seen as the continuation of the work initiated by Gerald Silverberg in the 1980s (Silverberg, 1985; Silverberg *et al.*, 1988). The main difference between the Silverberg and Verspagen (1995a) model and the ones presented in Silverberg (1985) and Silverberg and Lehnert (1993) is the way in which innovation is endogenized.

The third stream of models may be called 'Dosi *et al.* models', e.g., Chiaromonte and Dosi (1993), Dosi *et al.* (1993, 1994, 1995). The Dosi *et al.* approach is highly bottom-up simulation. The aim of the authors seems to be to start from basic mechanisms of industrial development without making any assumptions about the possible modelled properties of the system and to obtain the well-known features (*stylized facts*) from the co-working of these basic mechanisms of development. A similar assumption is offered by Kwasnicki in his model of industrial dynamics (Kwasnicka and Kwasnicki, 1992, 1996; Kwasnicki, [1994] 1996, 2000).

There are also numerous models that can be identified as having a 'Schumpeterian flavour'. The model presented by Andersen (1997) is based on Pasinetti's scheme of the structural economic dynamics of a labour economy with the inclusion of an evolutionary, micro-economic foundation. A proposition of Bruckner *et al.* (1989), Bruckner *et al.* (1994) applies a general *n*-dimensional birth–death transition model to describe technological development. Because of a natural limitation of space, we will only point out a selection of other existing models, e.g., Metcalfe (1993, 1994), Windrum and Birchenhall (1998), Englmann (1994), Iwai (1984a, 1984b), Nelson and Wolff (1997), Saviotti and Mani (1993).

Agent-based computational economics
Artificial life (a-life) is the name of a flourishing, multidisciplinary field of research that attempts to develop mathematical models and use computer simulations to demonstrate ways in which living organisms grow and evolve. It is hoped that in this way deeper insights into the nature of organic life will be gained, together with a better understanding of the origin of metabolic processes and in a wider sense of the origin of life. Christopher Langton, who organized the first a-life workshop at Santa Fe in 1987, coined the term 'artificial life' in the 1980s. In fact, two men have conducted very similar theoretical research under the name of self-replicating (or cellular) automata. John von Neumann, the Hungarian-born mathematician and a pioneer of computer science, and the Polish mathematician Stanislaw

Ulam in the early 1950s, had begun to explore the nature of very basic theoretical forms called self-replicating, cellular automata. Their intention was to apply this basic concept to the growth, development, and reproduction of living creatures. These theoretical, mathematical 'cells' can be used to simulate biological and physical processes by repetitively subjecting each cell to a simple set of rules; e.g., every cell has a colour that changes according to its update rules and the colours of its neighbouring cells. Von Neumann and Ulam proved that, using a rather complex set of rules, it is possible to draw an initial configuration of cells in such a way that the configuration would 'reproduce' itself. These cellular automata consist of a lattice of cells. Each cell is characterized by specific values which can change according to fixed rules. A cell's new value is calculated on the basis of its current value and the values of its immediate neighbours. It is shown that such cellular automata naturally form patterns, reproduce and 'die'.

Langton used the work of von Neumann as a starting point to design a simple a-life system that could be simulated on a computer. In 1979, he developed an 'organism' that displayed many lifelike properties. The loop-shaped 'creature' reproduced itself in such a way that, as new generations spread outward from the initial organism, they left 'dead' generations inside the expanding area. In the opinion of Langton the behaviour of these forms mimicked the real-life processes of mutation and evolution.

There are numerous examples of agent-based modelling. Biologist Tom Ray created 'agent' programs on his laptop. The aim of each agent was to make a copy of itself in memory. Ray assumed a finite lifetime of each program. He left the programs running all night and in the morning he noticed that his agents were engaging in the digital equivalents of competition, fraud and sex. When the program agents copied themselves random changes of their code occurred, and so it can be said that they mutated and evolved. Naturally, most mutations were destructive and 'died', but some changes let an agent do its job better in a sense that they consisted of fewer instructions and were able to copy themselves more quickly and more reliably and to run faster. The shorter versions replicated more quickly and very soon outnumbered their larger 'competitors'.

The a-life approach is sometime called 'agent-based modelling' to pinpoint its mathematical difference from the differential equations approach. We can write down the differential equations for interacting populations of individuals (e.g. the Lotka–Volterra equation of a prey–predator system) but we can also follow individual histories of each animal (element, agent, firm) and summarize their histories into more aggregate characteristics. Contemporary a-life researchers try to identify the distinctive behaviours of living creatures and then use them to devise software simulations that 'move, eat, mate, fight and cooperate' without incorporating those features explicitly into the modes of behaviour of these elements. The recipe for preparing a-life software (or 'silicon' species, as it is sometimes called) is rather simple: prepare an environment in which the synthetic organisms can act, create a few hundred individuals to populate it and define a set of rules for them to follow. Try to simplify the problem as much as possible while keeping what is essential. Write a program which simulates the simple rules with interactions and randomizing elements. Run the program many times with different random number seeds to attempt to understand how the simple rules give rise to the observed behaviour. Locate the sources of behaviour and the effects of different parameters. Simplify the simulation even further if possible, or add additional elements that are found to be necessary. We can summarize this approach in the following 'equation': *Agents (microlevel entities) + Environment + Dynamics = A-Life.*

In this approach, life is treated as a kind of game in which each agent struggles for existence with the mixture of chance and necessity by applying a set of basic behavioural rules. A small number of rules can generate amazingly complex patterns of behaviour, such as groups of independent agents organizing themselves into a semi-isolated group of agents. This feature makes the a-life approach a potentially powerful research tool.

The current efforts of a-life researchers are focused on searching for a so-called 'emergent hierarchical organization' (EHO). The aim of this kind of modelling is to discover whether, and under what conditions, recorded computer-simulated histories exhibit interesting *emergent properties*. (The term 'emergent properties' means that they arise spontaneously from the dynamics of the system, rather than being imposed by some external authority.) Observed order, such as the specific evolution of an industry with its initial, mature and declining phases, emerges from the aggregate of a large number of individuals acting alone and independently.

A similar approach has been applied in economic analysis, called either artificial economics or agent-based economics. The intention is very similar to that of a-life: allow for economic interactions between artificial agents initially having no knowledge of their environment but with abilities to learn, and next observe what sorts of markets, institutions and technologies develop and the way in which the agents co-ordinate their actions and organize themselves into an economy. Some models rooted in neo-Schumpeterian tradition are very close to the ACE approach.

Notes

1. Therefore it is frequently said that Schumpeterian models are based on an idea of a 'population concept', i.e., the modelled process is observed within a population of agents (e.g. firms).
2. A few decades earlier Schumpeter ([1912] 1934) expressed it as follows: 'By "development" . . . we shall understand only changes in economic life as are not forced upon it

from without but arise by its own initiative, from within' (p. 63). 'Development in our sense is a distinct phenomenon, entirely foreign to what may be observed in the circular flow or in the tendency toward equilibrium. It is spontaneous and discontinuous change in the channels of flow, disturbance of equilibrium, which forever alters and displaces the equilibrium state previously existing' (p. 64).

References

Alchian, A.A. (1950), 'Uncertainty, evolution and economic theory', *Journal of Political Economy*, **58**(June), 211–21.

Andersen, Esben Sloth (1997), 'Escaping satiation in an evolutionary model of structural economic dynamics', paper presented at the workshop on Escaping Satiation: Increasing Product Variety, Preference Change and the Demand Side of Economic Growth, Max Planck Institute for Research into Economic Systems, Jena, 11–13 December.

Bruckner, E., Ebeling, W. and Scharnhorst, A. (1989), 'Stochastic dynamics of instabilities in evolutionary systems', *System Dynamics Review*, **5**, 176–91.

Bruckner, E., Ebeling, W., Jiménez Montaño, M.A. and Scharnhorst, A. (1994), 'Hyperselection and innovation described by a stochastic model of technological evolution', in L. Leydesdorff and P. van den Besselaar (eds), *Evolutionary Economics and Chaos Theory*, London: Pinter.

Chiaromonte, F. and Dosi, G. (1993), 'Heterogeneity, competition, and macroeconomic dynamics', *Structural Change and Economic Dynamics*, **4**, 39–63.

Dosi, G., Fabiani, S., Aversi, R. and Meacci, M. (1994), 'The dynamics of international differentiation: a multi-country evolutionary model', *Industrial and Corporate Change*, **2**(3), 225–41.

Dosi, G., Fabiani, S., Freeman, C. and Aversi, R. (1993), 'On the process of economic development', Center for Research in Management, University of California at Berkeley, CCC working paper no. 93-2.

Dosi, G., Marsili, O., Orsenigo, L. and Salvatore, R. (1995), 'Learning, market selection and the evolution of industrial structures', *Small Business Economics*, **7**, 411–36.

Dosi, G., Freeman, C., Nelson, R., Silverberg, G. and Soete, L. (eds) (1988), *Technical Change and Economic Theory*, London: Pinter Publishers.

Downie, J. (1958), *The Competitive Process*, London: Duckworth.

Englmann, F.C. (1994), 'A Schumpeterian model of endogenous innovation and growth', *Journal of Evolutionary Economics*, **4**, 227–41.

Fagiolo, G. and Dosi, G. (2003), 'Exploitation, exploration and innovation in a model of endogenous growth with locally interacting Agents', *Structural Change and Economic Dynamics*, **14**, 237–73.

Hodgson, G.M. (1997), 'The evolutionary and non-Darwinian economics of Joseph Schumpeter', *Journal of Evolutionary Economics*, **7**, 131–45.

Iwai, K. (1984a), 'Schumpeterian dynamics, part I: an evolutionary model of innovation and imitation', *Journal of Economic Behavior and Organization*, **5**, 159–90.

Iwai, K. (1984b), 'Schumpeterian dynamics, Part II: technological progress, firm growth and "economic selection"', *Journal of Economic Behavior and Organization*, **5**, 321–51.

Jonard, N. and Yildizoglu, M. (1998), 'Technological diversity in an evolutionary industry model with localized learning and network externalities', *Structural Change and Economic Dynamics*, **9**(1), 35–55.

Jonard, N. and Yildizoglu, M. (1999), 'Sources of technological diversity', Cahiers de l'innovation, no.99030, CNRS, Paris.

Kelm, Matthias (1997), 'Schumpeter's theory of economic evolution: a Darwinian interpretation', *Journal of Evolutionary Economics*, **7**, 97–130.

Kwasnicki, W. ([1994] 1996), *Knowledge, Innovation, and Economy. An Evolutionary Exploration*, Wroclaw: Oficyna Wydawnicza Politechniki Wroclawskiej; 2nd edn, 1996, Cheltenham, UK and Brookfield, USA: Edward Elgar.

Kwasnicki, W. (2000), 'Monopoly and perfect competition – there are two sides to every coin', in Paolo Saviotti and Bart Nooteboom (eds), *Technology and Knowledge: From the Firm to Innovation Systems*, Cheltenham, UK and Northampton, MA, USA: Edward Elgar.

Kwasnicki, W. (2001), 'Comparative analysis of selected neo-Schumpeterian models of industrial dynamics', paper presented at the Nelson and Winter Conference in Aalborg, 12–15 June; revised version published in 2003 as 'Evolutionary models' comparative analysis. Methodology proposition based on selected neo-Schumpeterian models of industrial dynamics', *The ICFAI Journal of Managerial Economics*, **1**(2) November.

Kwasnicka, H. and Kwasnicki, W. (1992), 'Market, innovation, competition. An evolutionary model of industrial dynamics', *Journal of Economic Behavior and Organization*, **19**, 343–68

Kwasnicka, H. and Kwasnicki, W. (1996), 'Long-term diffusion factors of technological development: an evolutionary model and case study', *Technological Forecasting and Social Change*, **52**, 31–57.

Lane, D. (1993a), 'Artificial worlds in economics: part 1', *Journal of Evolutionary Economics*, **3**, 89–107.

Lane, D. (1993b), 'Artificial worlds in economics: part 2', *Journal of Evolutionary Economics*, **3**, 177–97.

Metcalfe, J.S. (1993), 'Some Lamarcian themes in the theory of growth and economic selection: provisional analysis', *Revue Internationale de Systémique*, **7**(5), 487–504.

Metcalfe, J.S. (1994), 'Competition, evolution and capital markets', *Metroeconomica*, **45**(2), June, 127–54.

Nelson R.R. (1995), 'Recent evolutionary theorizing about economic change', *Journal of Economic Literature*, **33**(1), 48–90.

Nelson, R.R. and Winter, S.G. (1982), *An Evolutionary Theory of Economic Change*, Cambridge, MA and London: Belknap Press.

Nelson, Richard R. and Wolff, Edward N. (1997), 'Factors behind cross-industry differences in technical progress', *Structural Change and Economic Dynamics*, **8**, 205–20.

Nightingale, John (1997), 'Anticipating Nelson and Winter: Jack Downie's theory of evolutionary economic change', *Journal of Evolutionary Economics*, **7**, 147–67.

Nightingale, John (1998), 'Jack Downie's competitive process: the first articulated population ecological model in economics', *History of Political Economy*, **30**(3).

Penrose, E.T. (1952), 'Biological analogies in the theory of the firm', *American Economic Review*, **42**(5), 804–19.

Saviotti, P.P. and Mani G.S. (1993), 'A model of technological evolution based on replicator dynamics', paper presented at the conference Developments in Technoogy Studies: Evolutionary Economics and Chaos Theory, University of Amsterdam, Amsterdam, 6–8 May.

Saviotti, P.P. and Metcalfe, J.S. (eds) (1991), *Evolutionary Theories of Economic and Technological Change*, Chur: Harwood Academic Publishers.

Schumpeter J.A. ([1912] 1934), *Theorie der Wirtschaftlichen Entwicklung*, Leipzig: Duncker und Humbolt, English translation, *The Theory of Economic Development*, Cambridge, MA: Harvard University Press/tlumaczenie polskie w 1960, *Teoria rozwoju gospodarczego*.

Schumpeter J.A. (1928), 'The instability of capitalism', *Economic Journal*, **XXXVIII**(151), September, 361–86.

Schumpeter, J.A. (1935), 'The analysis of economic change', *Review of Economics and Statistics*, **17**, 2–10.

Schumpeter, J.A. (1939), *Business Cycles: A Theoretical, Historical, and Statistical Analysis*, 2 vols, New York: McGraw-Hill Company.

Schumpeter, J.A. (1942), *Capitalism, Socialism, and Democracy*, New York: Harper & Row (1950, Oxford: Oxford University Press, reprinted Harper Colophon, 1975).

Schumpeter, J.A. (1947), 'The creative response in economic history', *Journal of Economic History*, **VII**(2), November, 149–59.

Schumpeter, J.A. (1954), *History of Economic Analysis*, New York: Oxford University Press.

Silverberg, Gerald (1985), '*Technical progress, capital accumulation and effective demand: a self-organisation model*', Universitat Stuttgard; published in D. Batten (ed.) (1987), *Economic Evolution and Structural Change*, Berlin/Heidelberg/New York: Springer-Verlag.

Silverberg, Gerald and Lehnert, Doris (1993),'Long waves and "evolutionary chaos" in a simple Schumpeterian model of embodied technical change', *Structural Change and Economic Dynamics*, **4**, 9–37.

Silverberg, Gerald and Lehnert, Doris (1996), ' "Evolutionary chaos": growth fluctuations in a Schumpeterian model of creative destruction', in W.A. Barnett, A. Kirman and M. Salmon (eds), *Nonlinear Dynamics in Economics*, Cambridge: Cambridge University Press.

Silverberg, Gerald and Verspagen, Bart (1994a), 'Learning, innovation and economic growth: a long-run model of industrial dynamics', *Industrial and Corporate Change*, **3**(1), 199–223.

Silverberg, Gerald and Verspagen, Bart (1994b), 'Economic dynamics and behavioral adaptation: an application to an evolutionary endogenous growth model', IIASA working paper WP-94-84.

Silverberg, Gerald and Verspagen, Bart (1994c), 'Collective learning, innovation and growth in a boundedly rational, evolutionary world', *Journal of Evolutionary Economics*, **4**, 207–26.

Silverberg, Gerald and Verspagen, Bart (1995a), 'Evolutionary theorizing on economic growth', in K. Dopfer (ed.), *The Evolutionary Principles of Economics*, Norwell, MA: Kluwer Academic Publishers.

Silverberg, Gerald and Verspagen, Bart (1995b), 'An evolutionary model of long term cyclical variations of catching up and falling behind', *Journal of Evolutionary Economics*, **5**, 209–27.

Silverberg, Gerald and Verspagen, Bart (2002), 'A percolation model of innovation in complex technology spaces', MERIT-Infonomics Research Memorandum, 2002-025.

Silverberg, G., Dosi, G. and L. Orsenigo (1988), 'Innovation, diversity and diffusion: a self-organisation model', *Economic Journal*, **98**, 1032–54.

Windrum, Paul and Birchenhall, Chris (1998), 'Is product life cycle theory a special case? Dominant design and the emergence of market niches through coevolutionary learning', *Structural Change and Economic Dynamics*, **9**, 109–34.

Winter, S.G. (1964), ' "Economic Natural Selection" and The Theory of the Firm', *Yale Economic Essays*, **4**, 225–72; reprinted in P.E. Earl (ed.) (1988), *Behavioural Economics*, 2 vols, Aldershot, UK and Brookfield, USA: Edward Elgar.

Winter, S.G. (1971), 'Satisficing, selection, and the innovating remnant', *Quarterly Journal of Economics*, **2**, May, 237–61; reprinted in Ulrich Witt (ed.) (1993), *Evolutionary Economics*, Aldershot, UK and Brookfield, USA: Edward Elgar.

Winter, S.G. (1984), 'Schumpeterian competition in alternative technological regimes', *Journal of Economic Behavior and Organization*, **5**, 287–320.

Winter, S.G., Kaniovski, Y.M. and Dosi, G. (2000), 'Modeling industrial dynamics with innovative entrants', *Structural Change and Economic Dynamics*, **11**, 255–93.

Witt, Ulrich (2002), 'How evolutionary is Schumpeter's theory of economic development?', *Industry and Innovation*, **9**, 7–22.

Yildizoglu, M. (2002), 'Competing R&D strategies in an evolutionary industry model', *Computational Economics*, **19**, 51–65.

26 Neo-Schumpeterian simulation models
Paul Windrum

1 Introduction

The use of simulation is now well-established within neo-Schumpeterian economics. Modellers have turned to simulation as a practical means of investigating complex models that are not tractable using traditional analytical techniques. The boom in simulation over the last 20 years means it is impossible to cover all the models that have been developed, or all the issues that have been raised by these models. The chapter will therefore focus its discussion on a limited number of models. The models considered are the Nelson and Winter growth model, the Silverberg–Verspagen vintage capital model, the Dosi *et al.* sector models, the Malerba *et al.*, and the Windrum–Birchenhall models. These have been selected according to two criteria: their influence in the field (e.g. a number of researchers have typically contributed to their subsequent development), and/or their ability to illustrate key issues.

Sections 2 and 3 discuss the replicator algorithm and the distinguishing features of Type 1 and Type 2 simulation models. Sections 4, 5 and 6 discuss the modelling methods and content of the early simulation models (Nelson and Winter, Silverberg–Verspagen, and Dosi *et al.*, respectively) that have established the neo-Schumpeterian modelling tradition. This enables us to identify the discernable collection of features that set neo-Schumpeterian models apart from other (e.g. neoclassical) models, and gives them a collective coherence. This coherence is shown to exist at two levels: the world in which real economic agents operate, and the set of algorithms that are used to model the behaviour of agents in this world. In particular, openended innovative search and selection form the dynamic cornerstone of neo-Schumpeterian simulation models.

Section 7 discusses the criticisms frequently levelled against the early models, and the subsequent search for new methods of simulation testing and novel modelling techniques in order to address new research questions. This paves the way for a critical appraisal of recent models by Malerba *et al.*, and Windrum-Birchenhall (section 8). In Windrum-Birchenhall the elements of the neo-Schumpeterian framework are developed. By contrast,

*   The author would like to thank Murat Yildizoglu and Gerald Silverberg for their helpful comments on an earlier draft of this chapter. The usual disclaimers apply.

Malerba *et al.* marks a potentially significant break from this framework. The chapter evaluates both their contribution to methodology and to modelling content.

2 Replicator dynamics

The selection algorithm is perhaps *the* distinguishing characteristic of the neo-Schumpeterian framework. Of those used, the replicator algorithm has been particularly popular. Part of the replicator's attraction, no doubt, is its origin: the replicator was first developed by R.A. Fisher to model natural selection in biology (Fisher, 1930). Yet this is only part of the explanation. Other selection algorithms, with equally strong evolutionary associations, exist. For instance, biased roulette wheels are widely used to model selection in genetic algorithms (GAs) and classifiers (see Goldberg, 1991; Holland *et al.*, 1989). In addition to its origin, the replicator algorithm has a number of attractive qualities. First, it is simple to implement, and offers a practical solution to a particular problem. As such, it is a very useful tool in the simulator's toolkit. Second, the algorithm is well-established within economics, e.g. evolutionary games theory. Third, a set of tractable analytical results exist for the deterministic version of the replicator (see Fundenberg and Levine, 1998; Hofbauer and Sigmund, 1998; Samuelson, 1997; Weibull, 1995; and Metcalfe's Chapter 27 in this volume). The same cannot be said for GAs and classifiers, for example, where Holland's schema theorem of selection remains a subject of great controversy.

The deterministic version of the replicator contains a powerful theorem: Fisher's fundamental theorem of natural selection (also known as 'Fisher's Law'). This states that selection, given an initially complete set of n objects (whether these be competing biological species or technologies) each with a differential level of fitness f_i, will work to reduce the number of competing objects until, in the limit, only that object with the highest relative fitness remains. A key driver of the process is a monotonic increase in the average fitness of the population $\bar{f}(x)$, which occurs as a result of objects with below average fitness being deleted from the population.

$$\dot{x}_i = x_i\left[f_i(x) - \bar{f}(x)\right] \quad i = 1,\ldots,n, \tag{26.1}$$

$$\text{where } \bar{f}(x) = \sum_{i=1}^{n} x_i f_i(x).$$

Translating Fisher's fundamental theorem into the economic domain suggests the market is a powerful selection mechanism that can evaluate the qualities of competing technologies and select that technology which is optimal for a given set of consumer preferences and production constraints. This has been investigated in formal models such as Soete and Turner (1984) and Metcalfe (1988). However, it was soon noted that Fisher's theorem is only valid for *constant* fitness functions and that very different outcomes can occur when selection is frequency-dependent, i.e. f_i is not constant but depends on market/population shares (including its own share). These outcomes include the emergence of multiple equilibria and convergence solutions that are non-optimal. For example, in sequential selection models by Arthur *et al.* (1987), and David (1997), where the population of adopters increases over time, increasing returns to adoption and path dependence can result in the selection of suboptimal technologies. Moreover, Banerjee (1992) has shown that, if decision making is strictly sequential, then even improved information will not necessarily ensure convergence to a superior technology. Meanwhile, in models by Bruckner *et al.* (1994), and Weisbuch *et al.* (2000) where the number of agents is constant in each period, frequency dependence can lead to convergence on a limiting distribution rather than a single state.

Two key modifications to the algorithm can be found in neo-Schumpeterian simulation models. The first is a consequence of an important shortcoming of the replicator: its blissful disregard of variety generation, whether through sexual reproduction in nature, or through human learning and innovation in economics. In terms of technical change, the relative fitness f_i of competing technologies will change over time as a direct consequence of firms' innovative activities, although the payoffs associated with investments in innovation will be subject to a degree of random noise. Consequently, simulation modellers incorporate a stochastic version of equation (26.1) in their models.

A second modification involves adding a parameter α $(0<\alpha<1)$ in front of the right-side of equation (26.1). This enables the modeller to adjust the strength of the replicator (e.g. in Metcalfe's 1988 analytic model, and Windrum and Birchenhall's 1998 simulation model) and, hence, the speed of selection. There are a number of reasons for doing this. First, consumers in different markets will vary with respect to their ability to collect and process information on all available products, and product innovations. Second, in circumstances where a technology space needs to be searched – i.e. the entire technology set is not initially present in the population – the probability of identifying a welfare enhancing-technology is positively related to the number of firms searching that space. Given that consumers are boundedly rational, it makes sense to temper the strength of market selection. In contrast to traditional neoclassical models with instant adjustment, the evolutionary modeller is free to adjust the speed at which market selection occurs.

3   Type 1 and Type 2 simulation models

Windrum's (1999) taxonomy distinguishes between two generic types of simulation model: 'Type 1' and 'Type 2' models. At a fundamental level, what distinguishes them are two very different views about the world in which real economic agents operate. Everything in the Type 1 world can, in principle, be known and understood. Often it is assumed that the entire set of objects in the world (e.g. techniques of production, or products) is known at the outset. The opposite is the case in the Type 2 world. Here the set is unknown, and agents must engage in an open-ended search for new objects. Associated with this distinction are important differences with regard to the types of innovative learning and adaptation that are considered, definitions of bounded rationality, the treatment of heterogeneity amongst individual agents and the interaction between these individuals, and whether the economic system is characterized as being in equilibrium or far-from-equilibrium.

Neoclassical simulation models tend to be of Type 1, reflecting a primary interest in learning that leads to improvements in allocative efficiency. Two types of learning have been investigated in Type 1 models: inferential learning based on a Bayesian updating of decision rules where there is asymmetric or imperfect information, and action/strategy learning (notably in evolutionary games). In each case, learning is conducted within an equilibrium framework, the focus of the analysis being intertemporal coordination and, where the problem arises, ways of dealing with multiple equilibria. Risk is probabilistic in these models. Agents are boundedly rational to the extent that they have limited information, and collecting and processing new information is costly. However, it is assumed that all agents are endowed with appropriate algorithms to represent the environment. Hence they can, in principle, evaluate the outcomes associated with each alternative course of action. This in turn implies an assumption regarding interactions between agents. Representative agents predominate Type 1 models. When heterogeneity is incorporated, this is done in such a way that it does not disturb the equilibrium conditions.

A criticism frequently levelled by neo-Schumpeterians at Type 1 models is the narrow sense of innovation being explored. In contrast to Type 1 models, agents in Type 2 models engage in the open-ended search of dynamically changing environments. This is due to two factors. The first is the ongoing introduction of novelty and the generation of new patterns of behaviour, which are themselves a force for learning and adaptation. Agents operate in the presence of Knightian uncertainty: they cannot know, ex ante, the outcomes of a particular course of action (Knight, 1921). For example, firms must, through experience, improve their perceptions of the relationships between R&D investment and competitiveness, and adjust their R&D activities accordingly. However, the payoffs to R&D

are not static. On the one hand, each firm engages in R&D in order to improve its relative fitness – to change the payoffs in its favour. Yet the final payoff cannot be known ex ante because rival firms are also learning and innovating. The notion of bounded rationality is thus far broader than that considered in Type 1 models. Agents not only face problems with respect to their ability to collect and process information, they must also deal with the algorithmic complexity of the problem faced and their ability to define preferences over expected actions, events and outcomes. In these models, agents are not initially endowed with an understanding of the underlying structure of the environment in which they operate but must develop a representation of the underlying structure. Further, radical innovation involves the introduction of new objects into the environment that alter this underlying structure and, hence, the payoffs associated with alternative actions.

The second factor underpinning open-ended search is the complexity of the interactions between heterogeneous agents. Interactions are non-linear and are an important determinant of the final outcome of the system. Thus, in addition to specifying the dimension of heterogeneity amongst agents and the rules that govern their individual behaviour, one must specify the rules governing the interaction between agents. The macro phenomena that emerge will differ as a consequence of the interactions that occur between the individual members and subtle differences that exist within the heterogeneous population. If multi-scale effects exist, due to a further feedback between macro phenomena and individuals' behaviour, then small initial differences will be further magnified. Notable examples include differences in levels of R&D expenditure between industries, and Moore's Law in semiconductors. In the first case, it is suggested that differential levels of investment arise and persist because individual firms frame their expenditures with reference to average industry-level expenditures (Silverberg *et al.*, 1988). In the second case, it has been suggested a doubling of the processing capability of semiconductors every 1.5 years is maintained by the self-fulfilling expectations of firms in the industry (MacKenzie, 1992; van Lente, 1993). Accepting Moore's Law as a yardstick, and fearful that rivals will achieve this improvement, firms within the industry invest greater sums in R&D to ensure the next generation of semiconductors has twice the processing capability of the previous generation. Weisbuch *et al.* (2000) observe that the presence of non-linearity and multi-scale effects such as these makes it impossible to deduce macro behaviour from the behaviour of an 'average' or 'representative' individual.

The discussion highlights an important conceptual difference in the underlying nature of Type 1 and Type 2 models. As noted, Type 1 models view the economic system as an *equilibrium structure*. In Type 2 models, by contrast, the aggregate regularities that appear are not equilibrium properties but emergent properties that arise from an *evolutionary process*: a process in which variety generation and selection interact (see Saviotti's Chapter 51 in this volume). Indeed, the interplay between novelty generation and market selection drives the economic system 'far from equilibrium' and maintains it in a non-equilibrium state. Convergence tends to be transient rather than durable. A shock to the system, e.g. a scientific discovery that prompts the development of a radical innovation, can lead to a fundamental change in the system's structure. Identifying the generic features of Type 2 models assists in focusing the discussion of neo-Schumpeterian simulation models, their similarities and differences, strengths and weaknesses, in the remaining sections of the chapter.

4   Nelson and Winter growth model

It is hard to overestimate the impact of the Nelson and Winter model on neo-Schumpeterian economics. Its publication in 1982 stimulated a whole body of simulation research and its continuing legacy is evident in two respects: first, the adoption of their approach to simulation modelling and, second, the diffusion of key elements of the model's content. A significant portion of the 1982 book is given over to the rationale for simulation and a discussion of how one should go about conducting simulation research. The authors' personal objective was to improve upon the traditional Solow one-sector growth model (Solow, 1957). To this end, they sought to develop a model whose explanatory content was greater than the Solow model, and which was more realistic in terms of its micro foundations of technical change and innovation. The latter led the authors to a consideration of the non-linear and highly stochastic interactions that occur between firms in the innovation process. Since these were not amenable to traditional analytical techniques, Nelson and Winter turned to simulation.

Having identified a need for simulation, Nelson and Winter considered how the modelling process should relate to ongoing empirical research, and introduced a two-step approach to the empirical validation of simulation models.[1] The first step involves the identification of the emergent properties (or 'stylized facts' as they called them) that the model is expected to replicate. Typically, these are industry or macro-level phenomena.[2] Having passed this first step, the second step assesses whether the model can provide further insight into economic processes. In the case of their own model, it can account for the aggregate time paths for output (GDP), capital and labour inputs, and wages (labour share in output) observed in the first half of the 20th century (step 1), and it establishes a link between firms' innovative performance and variability in firms' market shares over time (step 2). Nelson and Winter's approach to simulation modelling has become the norm amongst neo-Schumpeterian simulation modellers.

In terms of content, the key elements of the Nelson and Winter model subsequently became a de facto standard for neo-Schumpeterian simulation models. These are *heterogeneity* within a population of agents, a *selection mechanism*, and a *novelty generation mechanism* that maintains variety in the population over time. The firm is the basic unit of selection in the Nelson and Winter model. Heterogeneity in a population of firms is due to the differential productivity of the production techniques used to produce a homogeneous good. Each firm operates with just one production technique at a particular point in time, and consumer demand is assumed to be homogeneous in the model, such that demand curves are downward sloping and market price is exogenously given. Further, the homogeneous good assumption precludes improvement in relative performance through product innovation. Hence, market selection is driven by the relative efficiency of the alternative process technologies. While not explicit in this early model, a replicator dynamic is implicitly driving the selection dynamics over time. Firms using more efficient production techniques earn higher rates of profit on the standard product and so grow at differential rates over time. By contrast, firms using relatively less efficient techniques are less profitable, decline over time, and eventually die.

The third element of the model is the open-ended search for new, more efficient production techniques. Firms can improve their chances of success by replacing production techniques of below-average efficiency with techniques of above-average efficiency. The search process can take one of two forms: local search or imitation. In the first case, firms search for previously undiscovered techniques. A finite set of alternative techniques exists but firms do not initially know what this set is. Further, firms are constrained in their search for this set. Translating the set into a search space of $n \times m$ dimensions, the probability of discovering a new technique declines linearly according to the technological distance (measured in Euclidean distance) from their existing production technique. This constraint is said to reflect limited current competencies or some other form of inertia. By varying the skewness of this distance function, a labour or capital bias can be introduced into the localized search process. Imitation, the second type of search process, involves a firm adopting a technique that is already employed by another firm. The diffusion process, though it does not involve the introduction of novelty within the population, will involve an upgrading of knowledge and skills by the imitating firm. It is assumed that the probability of imitating a particular technique is proportional to the current share in output of that technique. Finally, an additional source of innovation is the flow of new market entrants in the model. In this model, firms only engage in search if their rate of return falls below a given threshold (a parameter of the model). This is one of the most notable features of the model. According to Nelson and Winter, this captures the satisficing behaviour of firms.

A number of subsequent authors have modified or extended the model. Yildizoglu (2002), for example, modifies the rules regarding investment in R&D and productive capital. In the original Nelson and Winter model, firms invest a fixed proportion of their profit in R&D. Yildizoglu compares the performance of these 'NW firms' with 'Gen firms'. Gen firms adjust their R&D expenditures by taking into account their own performance and those of rival firms. The learning procedure of these firms is modelled using a genetic algorithm (hence the name 'Gen'). Since both capital formation and future R&D activity are financed from current profit, an additional decision rule needs to be added. Yildizoglu assumes R&D investment takes priority, with capital investment equal to the remainder of profit after future R&D expenditure has been deducted. The simulation experiments that are conducted use different initial proportions of NW and Gen firms in the population. The findings indicate that Gen firms are more successful in identifying superior R&D strategies, giving them a selective advantage. As a consequence, Gen firms tend to dominate the population over time. Further, the higher technological performance of Gen firms results in a higher level of social welfare.[3]

Winter *et al.* (2000) present a stripped down version of the Nelson and Winter model that explores the impact of new entrants on technological change. In part the aim is to generate a set of formal analytical properties of the model: three theorems and one lemma are analysed for the first version of the model and two theorems and one lemma for the second version. Simulation is used to explore a third version of the model that is not amenable to formal analytical techniques. In contrast to the original Nelson and Winter model, the model assumes that innovations are solely associated with new market entrants, i.e. incumbent firms do not innovate. Hence, variety is maintained by the random arrival of new firms with higher productive efficiency. In the first version of this model, differential competitiveness is determined by capital per unit of output. By contrast, in the second version of the model, differential competitiveness is determined by labour productivity (the capital/output ratio is assumed to be constant for all firms). In the third version, differential competitiveness depends on the efficient use of both factor inputs.

Kwasnicki and Kwasnicka (1992) have extended the Nelson and Winter model to consider multi-unit firms and (a degree of) product diversity. Specifically, the assumption of a homogeneous good is replaced by a set of alternative product variants. Production techniques remain the key driver of the model but now each technique determines the quality of the good as well as the underlying cost of production. Consumers are assumed to be homogeneous and so successful firms are those that identify techniques that offer attractive quality/price combinations for a given preference set. In contrast to Winter, Kaniovski and Dosi, only existing market incumbents introduce new product/process innovations. The key strategic innovation decision for these firms is whether to search for a more efficient production technique (embodied within a plant) or, alternatively, to set up a new plant that produces a new product variant. Importantly, no knowledge constraints are placed on this latter process. This diverges from the behavioural assumptions of the original Nelson and Winter model, and is responsible for the phenomena of 'fitness jumping', the distinguishing feature of the Kwasnicki–Kwasnicka model. The combination of radical product and radical process innovation, associated with the opening of a new plant, is very powerful. Since firms in this model can instantaneously engage in any activity that improves their performance, they rapidly cluster around new production activities that are seen to be fitness-enhancing. The identification of a new, fitness enhancing activity is quickly transmitted and firms cluster around this new activity. The result is a rapid increase (jump) in the average fitness of the population.

5   Silverberg–Verspagen vintage capital framework

It is interesting to note that, while a number of researchers subsequently extended the Nelson and Winter model, their interest was in applying the model to explain industry dynamics, not macroeconomic growth. Meanwhile, those modellers investigating macro dynamics tended to follow a different track. Though their models encompass the three key elements of heterogeneity, selection and novelty generation, they typically eschew detailed firm-level descriptions in order to keep the complexity of the simulation model within manageable bounds (Verspagen, 1995). Of particular note is a group that will be collectively labelled the 'Silverberg–Verspagen framework'. The label indicates the important contributions of two of the key authors to this body of research, but the contributions of the other authors should not be overlooked. Key papers include Silverberg (1987), Silverberg *et al.* (1988), Silverberg and Lehnert (1993), Verspagen (1993), Silverberg and Verspagen (1994, 1995a, 1995b, 1996).

A distinguishing feature of this framework is that technological progress is embedded in the vintage of capital. In Silverberg *et al.* (1988) it is assumed that a single best practice technology exists at any one time, and that all current investments are made in this technology. Consequently, the capital stock in each period will comprise a set of vintages going back in time. The technological lifespan of capital equipment is defined by a specified scrapping margin that governs the oldest permissible vintage. This is related to technological obsolescence and/or wear and tear. The aggregate capital stock is then a sum or integral (in discrete or continuous time cases, respectively) over the vintages during this technological lifespan, and average technical coefficients (e.g. labour productivity and capital–output ratios) are the corresponding vintage-weighted sum or integrals. In later models the analysis is extended to allow for several (for simplicity two) 'best-practice' technological trajectories to coexist.

The basic building blocks are common to the models in this framework. The first block describes the basis of selection. Silverberg (1987), Silverberg *et al.* (1988) and Verspagen (1993) use a replicator to model selection. In the other models within this family a predator–prey algorithm is used. However, the dynamics of the predator–prey and replicator algorithms are formally related.[4] As in the Nelson and Winter model, selection is based on the differential productive efficiency of firms, though relative efficiency is here determined by the composite of vintage capital currently employed to produce a homogeneous good. Vintages of capital are distinguished by two technical coefficients: a capital coefficient (c) and a labour coefficient (a). For a given wage rate (w), the profit rate for a particular vintage is $(1-w/a)/c$. While the capital coefficient is a constant, the labour coefficient and the wage rate change over time. Labour productivity is assumed to change under the influence of technical progress. In the long run, wages tend to track labour productivity through a Philips curve. Rising real wages provide an incentive for firms to replace labour with capital. The current composition of capital can be upgraded by replacing older capital vintages with the latest vintage. This is funded by the profits generated by the current composite stock. Although the authors do not explore the link, this is reminiscent of Böhm-Bawerk's theory of interest and capital. In effect, old, less efficient capital is being transformed into newer, more efficient capital over time.[5]

The second block of the model governs the introduction of new vintages of technology and new market entrants into the system. In this open-ended Type 2 model, new capital innovations are introduced in each period. Given the fixed labour productivities of each vintage, and ever-increasing real wages over time, each vintage of capital technology will at some point be superseded by newer technologies and become unprofitable. Note that, since it is assumed that losses are financed by running down capital stocks (scrapping), those firms operating with unprofitable capital vintages will tend to decline over time. Firms are declared bankrupt, and exit the model, when their share of employment falls below a given threshold.

The third block of the model governs the innovation process. The firm's innovation strategy is characterized by their 'R&D quota'. Firms are heterogeneous with respect to their innovation strategy, which changes over time through a combination of imitation and mutation. As in the Nelson and Winter model, innovation is a search process comprising two parts: radical process innovation and imitation. While the imitation algorithm is very similar to that in the Nelson and Winter model, the algorithm modelling radical innovation differs significantly. The latter is governed by a Poisson process with a given arrival rate. The arrival rate depends on an 'innovation potential function' which has three determinants: the firm's current R&D funds, its distance from the best practice frontier, and the average R&D expenditure in the industry. These variables themselves evolve over time as a consequence of innovation and learning by the population of firms. In each period, each firm has a variable number of different types of capital, and devotes resources to a search for new types of capital. Since all firms are assumed to produce a homogenous product, the problem is to determine how much to spend on this search activity, relative to current levels of profit and sales.

A key advantage of this approach is that vintage capital stock is relatively easy to compute from empirical data. Time series generated by the models have been shown to match several characteristics observed in OECD data. There are, however, problems associated with calculating discrete-time vintage capital stocks. Notably, it can lead to awkward mathematical complications when they are embedded in a dynamic framework with endogenous scraping.

The framework is able to take into account several stylized facts about technological change and growth, notably the coexistence of alternative technologies, the exploration versus exploitation trade-off of innovation effort, the importance of innovation diffusion speed, and the characteristics of knowledge. These issues were not considered by the Nelson–Winter model or by neoclassical growth models. For example, in Silverberg and Verspagen (1994), the trajectory of the average R&D quota tends to fluctuate around a positive rate. Moreover, this is (at least for linear innovation functions) independent of the initial conditions. Hence, positive long-run growth rates are endogenously generated in the model. The evolution of the rate of technical change is characterized by a long period of slow increase followed by a sudden 'take-off' where the rate of technological change jumps and then keeps fluctuating at this high level. The take-off is also associated with a sharp decrease in market concentration. This observation nicely makes the point that the connection between R&D activity and market concentration might be characterized by coevolution rather than by causal relationships in either direction (as suggested in many models rooted in the industrial organization tradition). In Silverberg and Verspagen (1995b) the analysis is extended to cross-national growth. In a two country version of the model, complex patterns of technological convergence and divergence between the countries are generated.

6   Dosi *et al.* sector models

The models developed by Dosi and co-authors in the early to mid-1990s sought to link differential growth rates of countries to variations in the pattern of innovation found in key economic sectors (Chiaromonte and Dosi, 1993; Dosi *et al.*, 1994; Dosi *et al.*, 1995). In these models, a firm is characterized by a single labour coefficient. Firms differ with respect to their technological capabilities (in the form of labour input coefficients), and their R&D and price setting (mark-up) strategies. Unlike the Silverberg–Verspagen framework, however, these strategies do not evolve as a consequence of behavioural learning. Rather, firms' strategies are randomized at the outset and remain fixed over their lifetime.

The search space in Dosi *et al.* (1994) is similar to the Nelson and Winter model. The probability of an innovation occurring is positively related to R&D investment (which is measured by the current and a lagged number of R&D employees), with the improvement in productivity being randomly determined. By contrast, the search process in Chiaromonte and Dosi is a complicated two-dimensional space of 'technological paradigms' and labour coefficients. Firms either produce capital goods (each of which is characterized by a set of coordinates in the two-dimensional plane), or they produce a homogeneous consumption good (for which they need machines as inputs). Paradigms differ with respect to the labour coefficient required to produce a homogeneous consumption good. In the capital goods sector, the probability of identifying a new innovation is again positively related to the number of R&D workers that are employed, and the productivity gain associated with a newly identified capital good is randomly determined in the model. In the consumption good sector, firms possess a skill level for each available type of capital good. This skill level evolves by a learning process that has private and public features. It is assumed that imitation is costless and instantaneous. Hence, when a firm improves its skill in using a particular capital good, this simultaneously improves the skills of all the firms that operate that particular capital good. Labour productivity depends on the characteristics of the capital good and the firm's skill level. Firms in the consumption good sector maximize a function involving labour productivity, prices, and an order backlog, and thereby choose which capital good they wish to use.

A replicator algorithm is used to model selection in each of the papers. In Dosi *et al.* (1994), prices and exchange rates are the key variables that determine relative competitiveness. Thus the relative success of individual firms depends on labour productivity, wages and other aggregate characteristics, and behavioural variables (such as mark-up pricing rules). In Chiaromonte and Dosi (1993), relative competitiveness also depends on back orders in the previous period. In all three models, a firm will exit the sector if its market share falls below a given critical level. The number of firms is constant over time. For each firm that enters the sector, a new firm is introduced. The initial productivity of the new entrant is set equal to the current average level of productivity in the sector and the country, plus a random white noise.

The discussion of generated model outputs is rather unsystematic in Chiaromonte and Dosi (1993), and Dosi *et al.* (1994). Clear-cut relationships between particular variables and outcomes are not established, and sensitivity analysis is not reported. Indeed, Chiaromonte and Dosi (1993) provide information on just one simulation run, and Dosi *et al.* (1994) provide little information about alternative runs beyond those that are illustrated. These papers follow Nelson and Winter in putting emphasis on empirical plausibility, based on the ability of the models to generate outputs that roughly accord with stylized empirical data (in this case for GDP exports and imports). The discussion in Dosi *et al.* (1995) does go beyond the generation of stylized outputs (here S-curve diffusion patterns) to consider how alternative hypotheses about innovating firms (i.e. new market entrants, established firms or a combination thereof) and the kind of market selection can generate industrial structures with very different patterns of concentration, rates of entry and exit, stability/turbulence, and distributions of firm size. However, this paper also fails to provide information on rigorous sensitivity testing of the results.

7   Limitations of the early models

The simulation models discussed above were an important component in the establishment of a viable, neo-Schumpeterian alternative to mainstream (neoclassical) economic thought. Indeed, the explicit objective of the early models was to demonstrate the feasibility of the new approach. In this respect the models were highly successful. They were capable of generating outputs that accorded with empirically observed phenomena while simultaneously providing evolutionary neo-Schumpeterian explanations for these phenomena. Still, there remained much scope for development and, by today's standards, the early models were limited in a number of respects. First, the empirical phenomena that were specified, and with which the model outputs were compared, were rather general and did not necessarily represent a difficult test. Second, a very limited range of agents were considered – in fact, just firms – and the representations of these agents were highly stylized. Third, the models contained many degrees of freedom with respect to the outputs generated. Fourth, the authors tended not to engage in rigorous testing procedures, either of model variables, or of model outputs. Indeed, it was very common to find that authors had not engaged in any form of sensitivity analysis but rather provided illustrated outputs from just a handful of simulation runs.[6]

A number of the limitations can be traced to weaknesses in Nelson and Winter's two-step validatory procedure of model assessment. As previously discussed, this involves an assessment of whether a model generates outputs that accord with one or more empirically observed stylized facts. The procedure does not consider the nature of the selected empirical phenomena and whether these represent a sufficient test for the model, or how to go about comparing different models that are capable of generating the same or similar outputs. This parallels Brock's (1999) discussion of scaling laws in economics. Empirical regularities need to be handled with care because most of them are 'unconditional objects', i.e. they only indicate properties of stationary distributions and, hence, cannot provide information on the dynamics of the stochastic processes that generated them (ibid., p. 410). Of the models discussed in this chapter, the Silverberg–Verspagen and Dosi *et al.* models differ significantly with respect to the behaviour and learning procedures of agents, and in their causal variables. Yet both produce similar outputs – outputs that mimic some very general empirical observations regarding differential growth rates between countries, and technology leadership and catch-up. Further, the Nelson and Winter model replicated highly aggregated data on time paths for output (GDP), capital and labour inputs, and wages (labour share in output) that could equally be replicated by conventional neoclassical growth models.

A general issue faced by agent-based simulation models, that are rich with respect to the number of variables they contain, concerns the need to reduce the dimensions of the model in order to establish which of the key variables are driving the model's outputs. The early models tended not to consider methods to reduce the degree of freedom. Another issue concerns the lack of sensitivity analysis conducted on model outputs. As noted above, these often presented 'illustrative outputs' taken from a handful of simulation runs. Rarely did the authors conduct large numbers of simulation runs or systematically test the outputs for different parameter values or for different random seeds. Rather, the papers tended to emphasize the interpretation of the outputs as empirically 'plausible'.

The content of the early models has also attracted criticism. As illustrated in sections 4, 5 and 6, firms were typically the only agents to be explicitly modelled. Consumers and other agents were collectively shoehorned into an extremely opaque external 'selection environment' that was odelled via a replicator algorithm (or similar). Even the descriptions of firms' behaviour and learning procedures, and the interactions between firms, were very simple (and not that far removed from conventional neoclassical representations). Consequently, strong restrictions were imposed on the range of topics, and the types of research questions open to investigation. The role of consumers, government and other agents in the innovation process and, hence, their impact on technological change could not be addressed. Further, one could not investigate important areas of empirical research, such as product diversification, processes of vertical integration/disintegration (supply chains) and formal/informal horizontal alliances (innovation networks), services innovation, economic geography, and public sector innovation. There was a clear danger of imposing a highly conservative constraint on the continuing theoretical development within neo-Schumpetrian economics. Indeed, despite the avowed intention to break away from mainstream economic thought, the early models dealt with very conventional economic phenomena. In this respect, there is even a continuing and discernable imprint of neoclassical economics.[7] Subsequent researchers have sought to develop new research agendas and, as part of this process, have engaged in the development of models that are more amenable to these new research issues. Two examples of these later models are considered in the next section: the Malerba *et al.* model (1999, 2001) and the Windrum and Birchenhall succession model (2001, 2005).

8 Malerba *et al.* (1999, 2001) and Windrum and Birchenhall (2001, 2005) models

The series of papers by Malerba, Nelson, Orsenigo and Winter mark an important contribution to simulation modelling, a contribution that will undoubtedly influence the future direction of simulation research within neo-Schumpeterian economics. Their work opens up important methodological issues regarding simulation modelling. Malerba *et al.* put forward a 'history-friendly modelling' method as a potential solution to the problems discussed above. This method suggests that we tie down simulation models to carefully specified, empirical 'histories' of individual industries, i.e. to specific case studies for which a detailed empirical history exists. According to the authors, detailed histories serve to inform the simulation work in a number of key respects. First, the modeller is to use empirical data as a guide when specifying the representations of agents (their behaviour, decision rules and interactions) and the environment in which they operate. Second, they can assist in the identification of particular parameters on key variables (from the many variables available in the model) that are likely to have been important in generating the observed history. Third, they enable more demanding tests on model outputs to be specified. Tests may, for example, involve comparing the model's outputs with data on market concentration, rates of innovation in different phases of the industry life cycle, rates of firm entry and exit, and distributions of firm size.

The approach is attractive in its elegance and coherence, and Malerba *et al.* are among the first to propose an empirically-based approach to simulation modelling.[8] In practice, previous researchers have used historical case studies to guide the specification of agents and environment, and to identify possible key parameters. What truly distinguishes the history-friendly approach is the proposal that a model should be evaluated by comparing its output, or 'simulated trace history', with the actual history of an industry. Through a process of backward induction, it is suggested, one can arrive at the correct set of structural assumptions, parameter settings and initial conditions. Having identified the set of 'history-replicating parameters', sensitivity analysis can be conducted to establish whether, in the authors' words, 'history divergent' results are possible. The aims, then, are clear and represent an attempt to move beyond the kind of appreciative theorizing that characterized the earlier Nelson and Winter methodology.

Given its likely influence on simulation modelling in neo-Schumpeterian economics, we need to evaluate carefully the strengths and weaknesses of this approach. To illustrate, let us consider the authors' own application of the history-friendly approach. To date, two history-friendly case studies have been developed, one on the evolution of the computer industry (Malerba *et al.*, 1999, 2001, the other on the pharmaceutical/biotechnology industry (Malerba and Orsenigo, 2001). The former is the most widely known. The authors develop a multi-agent model, containing consumers and firms, to investigate sequential technological competitions. Quality is assumed to be a simple integer value. This has a number of advantages, such as enabling the analysis to be conducted within a two-dimensional quality-price space. It has the disadvantage, however, of precluding the type of detailed analysis of quality differentiation dealt with by Windrum and Birchenhall (2001, 2005). The two–dimensional quality–price space is divided by the modeller into a number of parts, of arbitrary size. Each part represents a different technology. By dividing the space into a series of compartments, a definite ordering of the space is introduced by the modellers.[9] In this particular set-up, the authors divide the space into two compartments. One (that includes the origin) contains a set of 'mainframe' designs that have lower quality/ higher price combinations than the compartment containing 'PC' designs. Note that this specification is imposed by the authors, without recourse to empirical support. What is more, it fundamentally determines the final outcome of the model: the PC compartment is clearly the attractor state in this set-up. One important consequence is that one can dispense with algorithms with which to model population selection.

The two markets are further subdivided into a large number of independent niches, or 'sub-markets'. Here a 'niche' is defined as containing one 'consumer class'. Since each class has a distinct preference set (a particular point in quality/price space), the number of potential market niches is determined by the number of consumer classes that are initialized by the modeller. The utility functions of the classes are randomized within the overall quality/price parameters of each market segment (i.e. mainframe or PC), and remain fixed thereafter. Because user preferences are initialized as fixed points in quality/price space, a particular class will not become 'active' until a minimum level of quality/price performance has been reached. Once this threshold has been reached, the value that a consumer class places on a technology design becomes an increasing function of its performance and its cheapness. The utility of a design for a particular class is given by a Cobb–Douglas function in which the exponents are measures of the extent to which the quality and price threshold requirements have been exceeded.

Consumer utility also depends on the size of network externality associated with that design (measured by its current market share). In addition, utility depends on a third factor, advertising. It is assumed that the effect of advertising expenditures on sales follows a logistic curve. Together, brand loyalty and network externalities can lead to strong lock-in effects. There is, however, a clear ordering of the various components of consumers' utility sets in this model, with the strongest weight being placed on quality/price. Hence, lock-in effects become significant when one or more companies, with very similar quality/price designs, are trying to sell to the same consumer class.

Firms' profits are gross margins on production costs, and are used in a number of ways. First, firms spend a constant fraction of their profits (set equal to 15 per cent for all firms) to repay their initial debt with investors (which is the initial debt capitalized at a current interest rate). The remainder is then invested in R&D and marketing activities. Firms are made up of sets of technological and marketing competencies, that are accumulated over time, and rules of action. These rules concern the research trajectories followed by firms, pricing decisions, R&D and marketing expenditure, the adoption of new technologies and diversification into new markets. At the beginning of a simulation run, each firm is randomly initialized with an R&D fund and a design (represented by a point in the two-dimensional quality–price space). Note that the model is set up so that the first set of products is located within the boundaries of the mainframe compartment. Through innovation, the first set of firms search this pre-specified quality/price space, and succeed or fail in developing designs that satisfy a consumer class. Later, at a given time in a simulation run, a new group of firms are created and the design space is opened up to include the PC compartment.

A new set of firms/designs is randomly distributed across this quality/price space. The survival of new firms also depends on their identifying a design that satisfies the price/quality preference of a consumer class. If the initial endowment of a new firm is exhausted before its design meets a consumer class's minimum quality–price threshold, then the firm goes bankrupt.

Firms use their R&D budgets to finance innovation activities. In the model these are divided into equal amounts over a pre-specified number of periods. The returns to R&D depend on the research direction that each firm decides to follow, and on latent 'technological opportunities'. These opportunities are defined by the outer boundary of the mainframe and/or PC compartment in quality/price space. Hence, the closer a firm gets to its pre-specified boundary (measured in Cartesian distance), the lower the return for a given level of R&D expenditure. Depending on how the boundaries of the price/quality space are set up in the model, the rates of returns to R&D investment will differ. In the published implementation of the model, the size of the mainframe price/quality space is far smaller than that of the PC price/quality space. Hence, the returns to R&D in the PC market are far greater than those in the mainframe market.

R&D expenditures generate research competencies. In the model, R&D competencies take the form of two types of engineers: those that focus on reducing production costs (and hence price) and those that focus on improving computer performance (and hence quality). The joint action of these efforts determines the innovative path, or 'technological trajectory', that a firm pursues. This choice is highly path-dependent and sensitive to initial experiences. For example, if a firm early on experiences increased profits as a consequence of quality improvements, then it will hire more staff to focus on further quality improvements. By contrast, if a firm bene-fits from improved price competitiveness, then it will increase the number of staff that focus on further cost reductions. Advertising expenditures sim-ilarly generate marketing competencies. These are, like R&D expenditures, subject to depreciation, so firms who do not have the funds to invest will experience a deterioration of their competencies and the productivity of a given volume of expenditure fall.

It is possible for old technology firms to switch to the new technology market. The incentive to switch is a function of the size of the PC market, defined in terms of sales, as compared to the mainframe market. Specifically, diversification becomes attractive when the ratio between the size of the PC market and the size of the mainframe market is bigger than a given threshold value (a parameter of the model). Again, we see that the initial specification of the boundaries of the quality/price space determines whether the mainframe or the PC market is the attractor state. The process of switching is not easy, and involves a number of steps. First, mainframe firms must recognize the need to switch. In the model, recognition is a function of the current technological position of the firm in relation to the technology frontier (i.e. the distance between the quality/price of its product and the outer boundary of the mainframe quality/price space), and of the progress realized by PC firms (measured as the distance between the outer boundary of the PC quality/price space and the quality/price position of the current best-practice PC firm).

Once a mainframe firm perceives the need to switch, it must change its competence base. In the model, adoption costs comprise a fixed cost (that is equal for all firms), and the payment of a fraction of firms' accumulated budget to the creation of a new competence base. If firms' budgets are insufficient to cover these set-up costs, then they cannot switch markets. One advantage that successful old technology firms enjoy is their large profits, which can be used to diversify into the new technology. Diversification also occurs in a very specific way. As in Kwasnicki and Kwasnicka (1992), it is assumed that firms diversify by setting up a spin-off company to produce the new technology product. Initially, the spin-off company inherits a fraction of its parent's budget, and R&D and advertising capabilities (parameters of the model). The initial PC design is implemented by taking the current average quality PC design, and adding a degree of random noise. Once created, it is assumed the spin-off company acts independently, i.e. it has a separate budget, builds its own distinct set of R&D, advertising and production competencies, and does not engage in cross-subsidies with its parent company.

The authors begin their output testing by observing the model is capable of generating output traces that mimic the stylized history of one firm, IBM. IBM came to dominate the old, transistor-based technology and continued to hold on to its large market share in mainframes when new, microprocessor technology firms entered the industry. The company continued to survive because it diversified into PCs and gained a significant (though not dominant) share of the new PC market. The authors then identify a set of key variables whose parameters determine whether 'history replicating' or 'history divergent' outputs are generated. Of the initial set of parameters that replicate the IBM story, two parameters are discussed. On the findings of 50 simulation runs, the authors suggest that the 'history replicating' pattern requires a relatively high coefficient on market share in consumer demand for mainframes, and a lower coefficient in consumer demand for PCs. The values of these coefficients represent network externalities and branding effects, suggesting consumer lock-in was greater in the mainframe market than the PC market.[10] Reducing the parameter coefficient in mainframe demand lowers market concentration. At some point, as the parameter is lowered, a dominant firm (with resources sufficient to later establish a new spin-off PC company) will no longer emerge. This is the point at which the model starts to generate 'history divergent' outputs. The second parameter investigated is the timing of the new technology. Given that it takes a certain time (i.e. iterations of the simulation model) for a dominant firm to build up the resources necessary to establish a spin-off company, replication of the IBM pattern means the new technology cannot be introduced too quickly. The timing of the new technology is thus a critical parameter.

Having discussed the model at some length, we are now in a position to consider a number of issues regarding history-friendly modelling. These will be grouped into two general categories. The first category comprises implementation issues. The second comprises methodological issues. With regard to implementation, I shall highlight five issues. First, the modelling activity is not informed by a history of the computer industry as a whole, but of one particular company, IBM. Research questions concerning the conditions under which established firms can survive a technological succession are relevant to this firm, but they are not relevant to others in the industry. For instance, the conditions under which new PC start-ups can overcome the initial supply and demand-side externalities enjoyed by the likes of IBM, HP and DEC were the relevant issues for Microsoft and Intel. So to what extent is this an empirically based model of the industry? Second, the IBM account is itself highly stylized and subjective. It does not report on detailed empirical data regarding R&D expenditure across the industry, market shares, or profitability of the company, or those of the other firms. On the demand side, the authors do not provide empirical data on the relative sizes of network externalities, or branding in the mainframe and PC markets. This raises a very important question. In practice, can we acquire the wealth of detailed data required to put the method into practice?

Examining the model, it is clear that the authors have been influenced by theoretical literature when structuring their model. For example, the specification of R&D competences, and the process by which old technology firms diversify into the new technology market are not based so much on the history of the computer industry but, rather, on the theoretical literature on dynamic competencies. There are many alternative ways for firms to switch markets without the need to set up a spin-off company: indeed, IBM did *not* do this when it entered the PC market. It is also noticeable that a number of the model's distinguishing features do not follow from the stylized IBM history but are a consequence of the two-dimensional quality–price framework. This is the reason why consumer utility functions have quality and price thresholds, and why there is a distinct ordering within these utility functions between, on the one hand, quality/price and, on the other, network externalities and branding. Further, a whole set of rather arbitrary assumptions regarding the rates of return on R&D are the product of the two-dimensional framework rather than any empirical evidence. Clearly, then, a number of other factors, besides the specific history of the computer industry, have influenced the modelling choices at various points. It would seem, therefore, that modelling choices invariably extend beyond a historical case study. There are those who would argue that a historically grounded method requires the modeller to give precedence to the historical evidence above all other considerations. But what are we to do if the evidence is incomplete, offers no guidance on a particular point, or else seems to contain alternative, competing viewpoints?

In addition to informing the specification of agents, the two-dimensional quality–price space informs the set of questions that can and cannot be posed. The final end state of the model is determined by the way in which the modeller sets up this space. In this particular set-up, there are no multiple equilibria and we know ex ante that the end state is a succession. It would be possible to manipulate the two-dimensional space into another configuration of compartments, but the fact remains that the end state is pre-specified ex ante by the modeller. This highly prescribed search space is far removed from agent-based models in which agents search complex fitness landscapes that are randomly assigned, or fitness landscapes that evolve over time as a consequence of agents' actions. This denies a whole set of other questions, relevant to the computer and other industries, being addressed. For example, the assumption that quality is a simple integer, and that consumers treat it as such, precludes a detailed investigation of how quality differentiation may affect the dynamics of sequential technological competitions. Finally, the authors do not present a rigorous sensitivity analysis of the initial seedings or the random parameter values used in the 50 simulation runs they report to have conducted. Indeed, the number of simulation runs conducted is very low by current standards.

The second set of issues concern (deeper) methodological aspects of history-friendly modelling. First, the new test procedure advocated by history-friendly modelling involves comparing the output traces of the simulated model with detailed empirical studies of the actual trace history of an economic system. However, we are still confronted by the problem of comparing individual traces of the model and reality, which does not represent an advance over the original Nelson and Winter methodology: is this model 'capable' of generating an output trace that resembles the empirically observed trace? This simulated trace may, or may not be a typical output of the model. For us to move beyond comparing individual traces, we need to know if the distribution of simulated output traces approximates the actual historical traces of the system under investigation. But this is often not possible in practice. Let us consider a simple example. Suppose the real economic system has a data-generation process that does not change over time (i.e. it is ergodic). Even if this were the case, we do not typically observe the entire distribution of all observations but rather a very limited set of observations – possibly only *one*, unique roll of the dice. The actual history of an industry that we empirically observe is only one of a set of possible worlds. So how do we know that the actual historical trace is in any sense 'typical' (statistically speaking) of the potential distribution? If we do not know this, then we have nothing against which we can compare the distributions generated by our model. We cannot determine what is typical, and what is atypical.

Second, following the previous point, how can we discuss counterfactuals in a meaningful fashion? The authors' discussion of implementing 'history replicating' and 'history divergent' simulations requires that we knowing what a 'typical' history, or some distribution, is. Yet a typical history, i.e. an invariant history that is common to all individual firms, does not exist. Hence, one must resort to some form of 'stylized' description of events. This may be a stylized description of the industry in general, or else a stylized description of a particular firm. The choice is arbitrary. Malerba *et al.* chose the latter, presenting a stylized account of IBM's past. Equally, they could have chosen Microsoft, Sun, Netscape or Hewlett Packard. However, the stylized accounts provided by these companies would be very different from that provided by IBM. Since the test procedures are highly sensitive to the particular account that is (arbitrarily) chosen, the terms of reference for 'history replicating' and 'history divergent' runs will change, as will the set of variables that are identified for sensitivity analysis. There appears to be no way out of this conundrum.

Third, a different problem concerns the ability to induce backwards the 'correct' set of structural assumptions, parameter settings, or initial conditions from a set of traces, even if we have a model that generates an appropriate distribution of output traces. Simply stated, there are in principle a great many combinations of alternative parameter settings that can produce an identical output trace. We cannot deduce which combination of parameter settings is correct, let alone the appropriate set of structural assumptions. Fourth, following the previous two issues, we are unable to use this method as the basis to select between alternative, competing explanatory models. Any number of (very different) models may be able to produce the same trace. How do we choose between them? In practice, then, the history-friendly approach is not much of an advance on 'stylized facts'.

Fifth, the method implies that we are able to construct counterfactual histories (although the authors do not themselves engage in this in their papers). For example, we need to be able to construct a world in which IBM did not enter the PC market. This poses a very serious question. Could the PC market have developed in much the same way had IBM not invented the PC? Can we meaningfully construct a counterfactual history? As Cowan and Foray (2002) discuss, it is exceedingly difficult in practice to construct counterfactual histories because economic systems are stochastic, non-ergodic, and structurally evolve over time. Finally, there is the key methodological question: to what extent can we actually rely on history to be the final arbiter of theoretical and modelling debates? To pose the question in another way, can simulations, in principle, be guided by history? In practice, it is unlikely that we will be able to appeal to history, either to bear witness or to act as a final arbiter in a dispute. This is because history itself is neither simple nor uncontested, and any attempt to develop a historically based approach to modelling faces deep level methodological problems. At one level, the contestability of history is evidenced by the ongoing debate about whether inferior quality variants can win standards battles. Leibowitz and Margolis (1990) have contested the suggestion that the QWERTY keyboard (David, 1985) and the DOS operating system (Arthur, 1988) were inferior quality variants, bringing forward data that suggest they were, in fact, superior in quality.

But the contestability of history exists at a more fundamental level. E.H. Carr, in his classic work, *What is History?* (1961), observed that history is not simply a collection of 'facts' whose meaning is recognized and agreed on by historians. The writing of history is itself a creative process in which many pieces of 'data', bequeathed to us from the past, are filtered by the historian. The historian gives prominence to some of these pieces of data. These are accorded particular status by the historian in his/her account of the past; a narrative that communicates to the reader the significance of, and the relationship between, the set of selected data. In acting thus, the historian is proposing the elevation of these particular data to the status of 'historical fact'. These are accorded the status of 'fact' by the wider community of contemporary historians, by taking the same data and using it in their historical narratives in an uncontested manner. There are a number of issues here. To begin with, the data that one begins with are themselves frequently pre-selected. Some records have been fortuitously bequeathed by the past (i.e. not destroyed) but many will be missing. Of those that exist, these will have been recorded for a particular purpose and in a particular way. They are not impartial. For example, they may be the subjective viewpoints expressed by people: those who could write, and who chose to record them. Equally, statistical data sets were (as now) constructed according to criteria that reflect certain choices and, as a consequence, have inbuilt biases. As econometricians know only too well, data that could assist in a particular discussion may simply not have been collected. Such problems exist with data from the recent past, just as they do for data from the more distant past.

Carr observed how we are keenly aware of the contestability of current events, and the construction of alternative interpretations of those events. Witness, for example, recent divisions in the United Nations on taking military action in Iraq. The same was true for events in the past. One cannot, therefore, appeal to history for a single set of incontrovertible and uncontested 'facts'. In the end, one can only provide an 'account' of history, an account that will be contestable, as well as partial. Does acknowledging the process of writing history, and its inherent limitations, automatically imply the adoption of a post-modernist position of subjective relativism? Can we not distinguish between good or bad history writing? Is any viewpoint, however ludicrous, justifiable? Certainly not. Indeed, it would be rather surprising for a Marxist historian writing during the early 1960s. The logic of Carr's reasoning leads to a call for detailed, high-quality historical studies in which the historian critically faces the given data that have been bequeathed by time. The historian should present, as best he can, the data that are currently known, highlighting contradictions between alternative sources and disputes over their interpretation. In this way, each account openly acknowledges its own limitations. Further, an account cannot be complete but is part of an unfolding sequence of writing on the subject.

The development of high-quality accounts, open to critical scrutiny, is essential to the history-friendly approach (and indeed for any other historically based methodology). It is, after all, on the basis of these accounts that guidance is taken on particular modelling choices, on parameter testing and output evaluation. In recognizing the limitations of any historical account, we simultaneously recognize the limitations of decisions based on that account. But this is a strength, not a weakness, of open academic discourse. How, then, are we to proceed? Let me suggest the following possibility. While a single 'typical' history may not exist, we may be able to draw some generalizations on the basis of a large collection of historical case studies. This is not unlike the situation that existed in pre-Darwinian biology. For many centuries botanists spent their time identifying and categorizing different species without an underpinning theory of evolution. Yet their work was an essential prerequisite for Darwin formulating his theory of speciation. So far, there are only a few examples of historically grounded simulation models, but there is a wealth of empirical studies within the neo-Schumpeterian tradition, written over the last 20 years, which can be drawn upon. Importantly, modellers embarking on this project will need to ensure that they do not constrict their models prematurely. If the models are not flexible enough to consider alterative scenarios, then we will be left with a set of models that are more, not less, incompatible with one another.

In summary, the pursuit of a historically based modelling methodology offers significant promise. Yet the methodology is not without its problems.

Clearly, reasonable expectations need to be set. Recourse to history cannot guarantee solutions for all of our modelling problems. It will not necessarily help us identify the dynamics that give rise to a set of unconditional objects, or tell us how to model the behaviour of agents, their learning routines, rules of interaction, and so on, correctly. There are, however, potential benefits to be had by trying to develop empirically based simulation models. The benefits are conditioned by the quality of the empirical and historical accounts that are developed, on the modeller's ability to recognize and handle the limitations of the method, the quality of the modelling choices that are made on the basis of available data, and (as ever) the quality of the models themselves.

As an example of how models with very different structures and assumptions can perform equally well according to the history-friendly criteria – i.e. they are equally capable of generating successions with trajectories that map on to historically observed trajectories – let us consider the Windrum and Birchenhall succession model (2001, 2005). We should note at the outset that these authors have (to date at least) not sought to engage in developing rigorous, empirically based models of particular industries but instead explore the properties of their theoretical models, using stylized facts for guidance on model set-up and on generic outputs. Windrum and Birchenhall (2005) seek to highlight key features of technological successions that were not dealt with in Malerba *et al.* and other models, notably through an unpacking of the complex variable that is 'product quality'. Additionally they address the issue of rigorous sensitivity analysis on parameter values and random seeds by taking on board insights gleaned from recent developments in econometrics.

Windrum and Birchenhall present a multi-agent framework that explicitly models populations of consumers and firms, and their interaction. The nature and direction of technological innovation is determined by the interaction of heterogeneous consumer preferences and heterogeneous firm knowledge bases at the micro level. The emergent properties of the innovation process are, in turn, an important input in the learning processes of consumers and firms, leading to changing preferences and knowledge bases. The net result is the *coevolution* of consumer preferences, firm knowledge bases and technologies over time.

In a similar fashion to Malerba *et al.*, the model is initialized with a given number of consumer groups, or 'classes', and a given number of firms (both are parameters of the model). Also, each consumer class is endowed with a single preference set. Here the similarities end. In the Windrum and Birchenhall model, each firm produces one product design and 'targets' one particular consumer class. There is no mechanism by which firms can set up spin-off companies. Firms are randomly assigned to consumer classes at the outset and the initial characteristics of the product design are randomized. Each firm has a mental model of the preferences of its target consumer class. The task facing the firm is to improve its mental model of the target preference set. This it achieves through product innovation and learning over time. Here firms take into account not only the consequences of their own past innovative activities but also the relative success/failure of their competitors' past innovative activities.

As noted, a key difference between this model and the Malerba *et al.* model is the treatment of quality. Where Malerba *et al.* treat quality as a simple integer value, and assume that the new technology is always superior in quality/price performance, Windrum and Birchenhall observe that product quality is a complex concept in its own right. Perceived quality depends on the particular set of consumer preferences that exist in the market at any given moment in time, and so is subjective, temporal and subject to change (as preferences change over time). These demand-side factors are external to the firm. Different consumer classes of users attach different priorities (weights) to the various aspects. This variety reflects the different lifestyles, interests and values of the various consumer classes. For example, supermarkets today cater for distinct classes of shoppers: vegetarians, vegans, and those who wish to purchase organic produce. These classes of consumers did not exist 20 years ago, indicating that new classes can appear and disappear within a consumer population over time. Even if we try to recast the issue in terms of technical quality, it is rare to find a particular product that is unambiguously superior to its rivals. Technically, different designs tend to excel in some aspects while being weaker in others. Further, the quality–price trade-off varies between designs because higher-quality designs are more expensive to produce.

In order to tackle the issue of product quality, the model adopts a Lancaster characteristics approach. Lancaster observed that products deliver a range of different services to the final user (Lancaster, 1971). In the model, a product is represented by a vector of service characteristics. The value of each characteristic can range between 1 and 0, according to whether it is of higher or lower quality. Both the dimensions and the quality values can differ between rival technology products. The initial set of characteristic values is randomized in the model. Through innovation, firms are able to alter the values of the product characteristics they offer their target consumers. The utility of each consumer class contains three components: direct utility provided by the quality of a particular design, indirect utility (initial income minus the price paid for the design), and a network externality component.

A replicator is used to model the selection process. In contrast to the models previously discussed, selection in this framework operates on the relative success of alternative consumer–firm couplings, as measured by the relative utility associated with each consumer class. Over time, the share of classes with above-average utilities will grow, and classes with below-average utility will decline. If there is just one firm servicing a particular consumer class, then its growth/decline directly corresponds to the growth/decline of that consumer class. If, however, more than one firm targets the same consumer class, then a firm's growth/decline additionally depends on the relative competitiveness of its products vis-à-vis rivals targeting the same consumer class.

Firms have strategies for mark-up pricing. The framework allows for these strategies to evolve as a consequence of behavioural learning (*à la* Silverberg and Verspagen), or else for mark-ups to be fixed over the lifetime of firms (*à la* Dosi *et al.*). Costs comprise two components. First, variable costs depend on the levels of service characteristics contained in the product offered. Marginal costs are a linearly increasing function of higher quality. Second, fixed costs are a function of static scale economies that depend on the size of current output. The learning task facing firms is to identify, through innovation, that combination of characteristics that is attractive to its target consumer type and maximize its target profit levels (i.e. for a given variable and fixed cost structure). The way in which firms' innovation is modelled differs significantly from the other models we have discussed. First, firms are not satisficing. They always seek to improve product performance if this increases profits. Second, the search process is modelled using a 'learning algorithm' that is a modified genetic algorithm.

The learning algorithm contains two operators, one that models imitation and one that models innovation. Imitation is modelled by a (unidirectional) 'selective transfer' operator[11] that is implemented in the following way. Firms evaluate the changes made in their rivals' product offers – i.e. changes in product characteristics and prices – in the previous period, and changes in consumer demand for those products. A firm will imitate its rivals by introducing identical features, i.e. values of characteristics, if, *ceteris paribus*, it judges that this will improve its own performance. Innovation is the second operator of the learning algorithm, and is modelled as a stochastic process. In each period, a given number of characteristics (a parameter of the model) are randomly selected, and a new value for these characteristics is randomly generated. Importantly, both innovations and imitations are subject to an internal evaluation of their potential merit prior to implementation. This involves a filtering process that is based on two criteria: technical issues (i.e. cost and design constraints) and the firm's understanding (i.e. current mental model) of the preferences of its target consumer class.

In contrast to Malerba *et al.*, the focus of Windrum and Birchenhall (2001, 2005) is the conditions under which new technology firms can displace old technology firms that enjoy large network externalities. In terms of the computer industry, the authors address themselves to issues that are relevant to new industry entrants in the PC market, such as Microsoft and Intel. The model is a two-stage model. Following an initial period in which old technology firms develop their designs and network externalities accrue, a 'technological shock' occurs in which new technology-based firms and new consumer classes enter the market. New and old technology products differ with respect to the bundles of service characteristics they offer. This is formalized in the following way. New and old technology products differ in at least one dimension; i.e. a new technology product offers at least one service characteristic that is not offered by the old technology. In addition, the old and new technologies may differ in the quality of service characteristics offered by both technologies. However, it is the difference in characteristic dimensions that is the defining property of alternative technologies. Over long historical periods, a sequence of technological successions is associated with shifting dimensions of consumption, firms' competencies and the characteristics of the technology products that are produced and consumed.

Windrum and Birchenhall (2005) conduct a sensitivity analysis for different random seeds, and on random parameter values for 22 model variables. The analysis involves the estimation of a robust statistical model of the probability of succession, given the state of the market immediately after the 'technology shock'. Both in-sample and out-of-sample predictions are taken into account. Data are drawn from 1000 runs of the simulation model. By estimating a robust statistical model, one can identify the key variables of the model that drive the observed output. Four key factors affecting the probability of a succession are identified. First, succession is more probable if gains in direct utility from higher-quality new technology goods outweigh the network utility of old technology goods. Second, sailing ship effects are possible. Old firms continue to innovate. The probability of a succession occurring depends on the relative innovative performance of old and new technology firms. Third, a trade-off exists between quality and price. A succession will not occur if cost (price) differentials favour the old technology. Consequently, increasing returns in production enjoyed by established firms are an important barrier to successful entry. The model thus generates supply-side and demand-side externalities that represent important barriers to the adoption of new technologies. The fourth factor is the relative length of time old firms have to develop their products compared with the time new firms have to develop theirs. Specifically, it is found that a succession is more likely to occur (i) the shorter the time old technology firms have to innovate and develop designs that closely match the preferences of their target consumers, and (ii) the longer new firms are given to innovate and turn their initial designs into designs that effectively meet the preferences of their target consumer classes.

Both the Malerba *et al.* and Windrum and Birchenhall models generate technological successions, yet the explanatory factors for these unconditional objects are very different. The key focus of Malerba *et al.* is how mature firms can survive by switching to the production of new technologies. This is achieved in their model through the setting up of spin-off firms. This possibility is not considered in the Windrum and Birchenhall model. In this sense, the Malerba *et al.* model is better suited to discussions of how established firms can survive technological successions. By contrast, the Windrum and Birchenhall model explores the complexity of quality, consumer variation with respect to perceived quality, and how new start-up firms can differentiate and exploit the dimensions of quality in order to overcome the increasing returns enjoyed by old technology firms. This is not possible in the Malerba *et al.* model. So, in this respect, the Windrum and Birchenhall model is better suited to discussions of new industry start-ups, such as Intel and Microsoft, who came to dominate the computer industry. In addition, the Windrum and Birchenhall model can generate non-successions, and the factors that prevent a succession occurring can be investigated. This is not possible in the Malerba *et al.* model.

Can we select between these models on the basis of their output traces and predictive content? Surely not. Each addresses a different set of issues. Further, it seems that selection cannot be made on the basis of individual firm histories (however detailed). Each model can be provided with supportive histories, drawn from a population that includes the likes of IBM and HP, on the one hand, and Intel and Microsoft on the other.

9 Conclusions

The chapter has traced the evolution of neo-Schumpeterian simulation modelling, from the Nelson and Winter growth model, and the early models that it inspired, through to recent contributions. One is struck by the rapid development that has occurred. There has been a consistent reappraisal of the boundaries of research, with respect both to the range of phenomena studied and to the content of the models. Today, modellers are investigating issues that were once considered beyond the remit of neo-Schumpeterian economics. What is more, thanks to the development of new algorithms and modelling tools, they are developing multi-agent models which have a richness and sophistication that was simply unimaginable when Nelson and Winter first began to experiment with simulation.

There has certainly been evolution, but there has also been a development of distinctive features which set neo-Schumpeterian models apart from other models, and which gives them a collective coherence. This coherence exists at two levels. First, there is a clear view about the type of world in which real economic agents operate; second, there is an identifiable set of algorithms that make up a neo-Schumpeterian simulation model. According to neo-Schumpeterians, real economic agents exist in a world that is inherently unpredictable. They cannot know the outcomes of a particular choice or course of action ex ante. This is the basic starting premise of all neo-Schumpeterian models.

Five significant aspects of this world were identified. First, agents engage in innovation, defined as the open-ended search for novelty. This can involve a search for new product designs, new techniques of production, new competencies, new tastes etc. Second, search is conducted within dynamically changing environments. Since agents cannot know or predict the outcomes of their actions, they must adapt and learn about the underlying structure of the environment in which they operate. This is complicated by the fact that agents' actions have an impact on, and change, their environment. Third, interactions between agents are non-linear. Small initial differences in a population of heterogeneous agents are magnified over time, leading to emergence of very different macro phenomena. Fourth, economic systems contain selection mechanisms that operate on variety. Novelty generated by innovative search is retained provided it is suited to its environment. Finally, the interaction of variety and selection drives the economic system far from equilibrium. The aggregate regularities that appear are not equilibrium properties but emergent properties that arise through this interaction.

In terms of code, the chapter identified three key elements in all neo-Schumpeterian simulation models: a search algorithm, a selection algorithm and a population of objects in which variation is expressed and on which selection operates. Since Nelson and Winter's growth model, the search algorithm has contained two components, one behavioural and one stochastic, in order to capture the complex nature of innovation. On the one hand, agents search their environment in a structured way, i.e. there are identifiable behaviours, organizational rules and responses. On the other hand, innovation has a stochastic component. Not only can purely random, serendipitous discoveries occur, but also the payoffs for truly radical innovations (i.e. those that are unlike anything previously introduced) cannot be predicted ex ante. Indeed, a common distinction is often made between gradual and radical innovation. Behavioural search is typically associated with incremental innovation, associated with a gradual improvement in the performance of existing objects, often drawing upon the experiences of other agents as well as one's own. By contrast, radical innovation involves the blind search of the unknown. Lessons cannot be learnt from the past or from the experience of others.

Much attention has been paid to selection algorithms, and the replicator in particular. Together, open-ended search and selection algorithms form the dynamic cornerstone of neo-Schumpeterian simulation models, and the diligence of the first simulation modellers in developing these algorithms cannot be underestimated. The third block of simulation code defines the population of objects (product designs, production techniques, competencies, tastes etc.) in which the variation generated by innovative search is expressed, and on which selection operates. This block of code also typically includes rules regarding the introduction of new objects (e.g. the arrival of new vintages of technology) and agents (e.g. new market entrants) into the system.

It was against this background that more recent modelling contributions could be considered. Two in particular were discussed in this chapter: the Malerba *et al.* model and the Windrum and Birchenhall model. Both seek to address new research questions and introduce novel modelling techniques. Windrum and Birchenhall is a multi-agent framework that contains a modified GA to model the innovation process. A replicator is used but this operates on the interactions between agents, e.g. of consumer–firm couplings. It also addresses the issue of sensitivity analysis by applying novel innovations in econometric testing. Yet the Windrum and Birchenhall framework clearly remains within the established neo-Schumpeterian tradition. By contrast, the Malerba *et al.* framework marks a significant break from that tradition because it jettisons both selection algorithms and open-ended search algorithms (which raises the question of whether it can be considered neo-Schumpeterian). The history-friendly method is an attempt to put simulation modelling on a more empirically solid foundation. This is an important move from Nelson and Winter's original method. This chapter has discussed a number of implementation and methodological concerns associated with the history-friendly method. Some are specific to the history-friendly method, others are generally applicable to all empirically based simulations (of which history-friendly modelling is one possible example). Researchers who are intent on developing this particular line of inquiry will need to address these important issues.

It is perhaps indicative of the vitality of the neo-Schumpeterian research community that Nelson and Winter, the founding fathers of neo-Schumpeterian simulation, should themselves continue to pose fundamental questions regarding methods and content. Much has been achieved over two decades, yet there is still much work to be done. For example, little or no simulation work has been conducted on the role of government and other public sector agents in the innovation process, while work has only recently begun on issues of supply chains, innovation networks, services innovation and economic geography. As these areas are addressed by the vibrant research community, the boundaries of the neo-Schumpeterian research agenda will no doubt continue to evolve, stimulating further debates about methods and content and, perhaps, even necessitating a redefinition of what constitutes a 'neo-Schumpeterian' simulation model.

Notes

1. The procedure should not be confused with sensitivity analysis. This validatory procedure merely asks whether a model can generate an output that accords with an empirically observed phenomenon. Sensitivity analysis considers the robustness of outputs by altering the values of key parameters and/or random inputs. At present there is not a generally agreed standard procedure for sensitivity analysis, either in the natural or the social sciences.
2. This is rather different to Kaldor's earlier discussion of 'stylized facts' in modelling (Kaldor, 1968, footnote, p. 177). Kaldor was referring to the use of empirical evidence to assist in the calibration of key parameter values (or ranges of values) in a model, not to the outputs generated by the model.
3. Yildizoglu (2001) has also considered the impact of agents' expectations within this model.
4. See Hofbauer and Sigmund (1998: 77–8) for a discussion of the formal relationship between the replicator dynamic and the Lotka–Volterra predator–prey equation.
5. It would be interesting to consider the implications of technological change for Böhm-Bawerk's theory of interest.
6. Notable exceptions include Silverberg and Verspagen (1994, 1995a, 1995b), and Yildizoglu (2002).
7. Kuhn (1962) and Gribbin (1984) observe the same phenomena in physics at the turn of the last century. The pioneers who played a pivotal role establishing a new scientific paradigm were nevertheless trained in the old (classical) paradigm. This restricted the range of phenomena they considered, and they carried over concepts and theories from the old paradigm (many of which were subsequently rejected).
8. Key aspects of empirically grounded simulation are to be found in Grabowski and Vernon (1987), predating Malerba *et al.* by a decade. Their simulation model of the pharmaceutical industry used empirical data on the industry to specify the relationships and parameters of the model.
9. The exception would be if the space were divided by a number of arrays emanating from the origin.
10. The authors do not provide empirical data on the relative sizes of network externalities and branding in the mainframe and PC markets, and so we cannot assess whether this was actually the case.
11. This replaces the conventional (two-way) cross-over operator of the standard genetic algorithm. While the cross-over operator may be a useful approximation for sexual reproduction, with each parent exchanging parts of their genetic material to form offspring, it is clearly inappropriate to suggest that firms must engage in two-way exchanges if one decides to imitate the other.

References

Arthur, W.B., 1988, 'Competing technologies: an overview', in G. Dosi, C. Freeman, R. Nelson, G. Silverberg and L. Soete (eds), *Technical Change and Economic Theory*, London: Pinter, pp. 590–607.

Arthur, W.B., Ermoliev, Y.M. and Kaniovski, Y.M., 1987, Path dependent processes and the emergence of macrostructure, *European Journal of Operational Research*, **30**, 294–303.

Banerjee, A., 1992, A simple model of herd behaviour, *Quarterly Journal of Economics*, **108**, 797–817.

Brock, W.A. 1999, Scaling in economics: a reader's guide, *Industrial and Corporate Change*, **8**(3), 409–46.

Bruckner, E., Ebeling, W., Jiménez-Mantaño, M.A. and Scharnhorst A., 1994, 'Hypreselection and innovation described by a stochastic model of technological evolution', in L. Leydesdorf and P. van den Besselaar (eds), *Evolutionary Economics and Chaos Theory*, London: Pinter.

Carr, E.H., 1961, *What is History?*, London: Macmillan.

Chiaromonte, F. and Dosi, G., 1993, Heterogeneity, competition, and macroeconomic dynamics, *Structural Change and Economic Dynamics*, **4**, 39–63.

Cowan, R. and Foray, D., 2002, Evolutionary economics and the counterfactual threat: on the nature and role of counterfactual history as an empirical tool in economics, *Journal of Evolutionary Economics*, **12**(5), 539–62.

David, P.A., 1985, 'Clio and the economics of QWERTY', *American Economic Review*, **75**, 332–6.

David, P.A., 1997, 'Some new standards for the economics of standardisation in the information age', in P. Dasgupta and P.L. Stoneman (eds), *The Economic Theory of Technology Policy*, Cambridge: Cambridge University Press, pp. 206–39.

Dosi, G., Fabiani, S., Aversi, R. and Meacci, M., 1994, The dynamics of international differentiation: a multi-country evolutionary model, *Industrial and Corporate Change*, **2**(3), 225–41.

Dosi, G., Marsili, O., Orsenigo, L. and Salvatore, R., 1995, Learning, market selection, and the evolution of industrial structures, *Small Business Economics*, **7**, 411–36.

Fisher, R.A., 1930, *The Genetical Theory of Natural Selection*, Oxford: Clarendon Press.

Fundenberg, D. and Levine, D.K., 1998, *Theory of Learning in Games*, Cambridge, MA: MIT Press.

Goldberg, D.E., 1991, *Genetic Algorithms*, Reading, MA: Addison-Wesley.

Grabowski, H.G. and Vernon, J.M., 1987, Pioneers, imitators, and generics? A simulation model of Schumpeterian competition, *Quarterly Journal of Economics*, **102**, 491–525.

Gribbin, J., 1984, *In Search of Schrödinger's Cat*, London: Black Swan.

Hofbauer, J. and Sigmund, K., 1998, *Evolutionary Games and Population Dynamics*, Cambridge: Cambridge University Press.

Holland, J., Holyoak, J.K. and Thagard, P.R, 1989, *Induction of Inference, Learning and Discovery*, Cambridge, MA: MIT Press.

Kaldor, N., 1968, 'Capital accumulation and economic growth', in F.A. Lutz and D.C. Hague (eds), *The Theory of Capital. Proceedings of a Conference Held by the International Economic Association*, London: Macmillan, pp. 177–222.

Knight, F.H., 1921, *Risk, Uncertainty, and Profits*, Chicago: University of Chicago Press.

Kuhn, T., 1962, *The Structure of Scientific Revolutions*, Chicago: University of Chicago Press.

Kwasnicki, W., 2001, Comparative analysis of selected neo-Schumpeterian models of industrial dynamics, Conference in Honour of Richard Nelson and Sydney Winter, Aalborg, 12–15 June.

Kwasnicki, W. and Kwasnicka, H., 1992, Market, innovation and competition, *Journal of Economic Behaviour and Organisation*, **19**, 343–68.

Lancaster, K., 1971, *Consumer Demand: A New Approach*, Columbia: Columbia University Press.

Leibowitz, S.J. and Margolis, S.E., 1990, 'Fable of the keys', *Journal of Law and Economics*, **33**, 1–25.

van Lente, H., 1993, Promising technology: the dynamics of expectations in technological developments, PhD dissertation, University of Twente, The Netherlands.

MacKenzie, D., 1992, 'Economic and sociological explanations of technological change', in R. Coombs, P. Saviotti and V. Walsh (eds), *Technological Change and Company Strategies: Economic and Sociological Perspectives*, London: Academic Press.

Malerba, F. and Orsenigo, L., 2001, Innovation and market structure in the dynamics of the pharmaceutical industry and biotechnology: towards a history friendly model, Conference in Honour of Richard Nelson and Sidney Winter, Aalborg, 12–15 June.

Malerba, F., Nelson, R.R., Orsenigo, L. and Winter, S.G., 1999, History friendly models of industry evolution: the computer industry, *Industrial and Corporate Change*, **8**(1), 3–41.

Malerba, F., Nelson, R.R., Orsenigo, L., and Winter, S.G., 2001, Competition and industrial policies in a 'history friendly' model of the evolution of the computer industry, *International Journal of Industrial Organization*, **19**, 613–34.

Metcalfe, J.S., 1988, The diffusion of innovations: an interpretative survey, in G. Dosi, C. Freeman, R. Nelson, G. Silverberg and L. Soete (eds), *Technical Change and Economic Theory*, London: Pinter.

Nelson, R.R. and Winter, S.G., 1982, *An Evolutionary Theory of Economic Change*, Cambridge, MA: Harvard University Press.

Samuelson, L., 1997, *Evolutionary Games and Equilibrium*, Cambridge, MA: MIT Press.

Silverberg, G., 1987, 'Technical progress, capital accumulation and effective demand: a self-organisation model', in D. Batten, J. Casti and B. Johansson (eds), *Economic Evolution and Structural Adjustment*, Berlin/Heidelberg/New York: Springer-Verlag.

Silverberg, G. and Lehnert, D., 1993, Long waves and evolutionary chaos in a simple Schumpeterian model of embodied technical change, *Structural Change and Economic Dynamics*, **4**, 9–47.

Silverberg, G. and Verspagen, B., 1994, Learning, innovation and economic growth: a long-run model of industrial dynamics, *Industrial and Corporate Change*, **3**(1), 199–223.

Silverberg, G. and Verspagen, B., 1995a, Evolutionary theorizing on economic growth. A survey, *MERIT Research Memoranda 2/95–017*, Maastricht, NL: MERIT; subsequently published in K. Dopfer (ed.), *The Evolutionary Principles of Economics*, Norwell, MA: Kluwer.

Silverberg, G., and Verspagen, B., 1995b, An evolutionary model of long term cyclical variations of catching up and falling behind, *Journal of Evolutionary Economics*, **5**, 209–27.

Silverberg, G. and Verspagen, B., 1996, 'From the artificial to the endogenous: modelling evolutionary adaptation and economic growth', in E. Helmstädter and M. Perlman (eds), *Behavioral Norms, Technological Progress and Economic Dynamics: Studies in Schumpeterian Economics*, Ann Arbor, MI: University of Michigan Press.

Silverberg, G., Dosi, G. and Orsenigo, L., 1988, Innovation, diversity and diffusion: a self-organisation model, *Economic Journal*, **98**, 1032–54.

Soete, L. and Turner, R., 1984, Technological diffusion and the rate of technical change, *Economic Journal*, **94**, 612–23.

Solow, R., 1957, Technical change and the aggregate production function, *Review of Economic Statistics*, **29**, 312–20.

Verspagen, B., 1993, *Uneven Growth between Interdependent Economies. The Evolutionary Dynamics of Growth and Technology*, Aldershot: Avebury.

Verspagen, B., 1995, Convergence in the world economy: a broad historical overview, *Structural Change and Economic Dynamics*, **6**, 143–66.

Weibull, J., 1995, *Evolutionary Games Theory*, Cambridge, MA: MIT Press.

Weisbuch, G., Kirman, A. and Herreiner, D., 2000, Market organisation and trading relationships, *The Economic Journal*, **110**, 411–36.

Windrum, P., 1999, Simulation models of technological innovation, *American Behavioral Scientist*, **42**, 1531–50.

Windrum, P. and Birchenhall, C., 1998, Is life cycle theory a special case? Dominant designs and the emergence of market niches through co-evolutionary learning, *Structural Change and Economic Dynamics*, **9**, 109–34.

Windrum, P. and Birchenhall, C., 2001, Modelling technological successions in the presence of network externalities, Conference in Honour of Richard Nelson and Sidney Winter, Aalborg, 12– 15 June.

Windrum, P. and Birchenhall, C., 2005, Structural change in the presence of network externalities: a co-evolutionary model of technological successions, *Journal of Evolutionary Economics*, **15**(2), 123–48.

Winter, S.G., Kaniovski, Y.M. and Dosi, G., 2000, Modelling industrial dynamics with innovative entrants, *Structural Change and Economic Dynamics*, **11**, 255–93.

Yildizoglu, M., 2001, Connecting adaptive behaviour and expectations in models of innovation: the potential role of artificial neural networks, *European Journal of Economics and Social Sciences*, **15**(3), 203–20.

Yildizoglu, M., 2002, Competing R&D strategies in an evolutionary industry model, *Computational Economics*, **19**, 51–65.

27 Replicator dynamics
Stan Metcalfe

Introduction

The concept of a replicator process is a powerful tool for the analysis of evolutionary phenomena, for it provides a rich foundation for a dynamics of development, a way of making sense of the central evolutionary theme that change is premised upon the variation, growth and decline of entities in a population. Replication fits naturally with the idea of selection as one of the principal evolutionary processes and, like all evolutionary processes, it involves the dynamics of populations. It also fits naturally with two central ideas in economic analysis, that of competition as a process of rivalry and of economic growth as a process of development. For the study of innovation-based processes a replicator dynamic is essential precisely because innovation always entails variation and its economic and social consequences are adaptive. Ideas in relation to the replicator principle are used extensively in evolutionary biology (Frank, 1998), in game theory (Vega-Redondo, 1996; Gintis, 2000) and in evolutionary economics (Nelson and Winter, 1982; Andersen, 1994; Saviotti, 1996; Metcalfe, 1998; Dosi, 2000).[1] The purpose of this chapter is to clarify the founding ideas behind the replicator dynamic and apply them to some typical problems in economic evolution.

The population method

Replicator dynamics is a method for analysing change across populations of entities, it is a dynamics grounded in diversity and it provides a foundation to the claim that evolution only occurs in the presence of variety in behaviour. It is part of the more general population method of analysis, which contrasts sharply with the methods of essentialism where the aim is to identify representative, essential characteristics of phenomena. As Sober (1984) states, variety is the natural state in evolutionary analysis and it is the operation of interfering evolutionary forces that destroys that variety. A world lacking variation within it cannot evolve; it is from this perspective lifeless. Replicator dynamics connects the concept of variety to the consequential dynamics of change to explain how populations evolve.

In its original sense in evolutionary biology, replication means the making of copies of some entity via a reproduction process. But the idea is not related to copy making per se but to differential growth or decline of the number of entities or, more generally still to the change in some index of the scale of importance of those entities in a population. In evolutionary economics such an entity would be a productive activity, the making of a product or service through some transformation process, and the index of activity would be the output of that production process over a given time interval. What matters about replication is its connection to differential growth and decline across populations and thus it is a natural tool to use in understanding growth and development as evolutionary processes. This is why the idea of replication is often twinned with the idea of interaction; it is interaction within (and between) populations that causally generates differential replication (Hull, 1988).

Defining a population and the associated activities requires a boundary to be placed around a set of entities, entities that differ in their causal dynamic properties yet are unified by membership of that population. At any point in time the population displays structure as a consequence of ordering processes and this structure is usually measured by the relative scale of the entities in the population. The scale could be the number of each entity 'alive' in the population at each date. However, we can also measure the relative importance of each entity by reference to the contribution that it makes to some index of activity across the population, and evolution is then defined as the change in the relative scales of activity over some time interval. The crucial step in this method is the delineation of the criteria by which the entities in question are to be counted as members of the population. The boundary is drawn such that the entities are engaged in a 'common' activity, the consequences of which are subject to evaluation within a 'common' selection environment. For example, if the entities are firms and their activity is the production of commodities that fit the same market purpose we expect that the particular market evaluates the activities of the firms in a uniform way to generate a pattern of differential economic returns. What is evaluated here is not the firm (the vehicle) per se but the activities they undertake (what is replicated). Indeed multi-product firms will typically be evaluated in multiple selection environments so that selection for activities is different from selection of firms (Sober, 1984). Moreover, the same population of activities viewed from the perspective of selection in the product market may draw on different factor markets for their inputs and so constitute two different subpopulations from a replication perspective. Industries in different countries competing in the same international product market but drawing on local factor markets are a frequently encountered example of a multi-layered selection process. Thus the population method offers a rich form of general evolutionary economic analysis, operating at multiple interacting levels and distinguishing between firms, industries and their activities and between activities that are selected for in different market contexts.

The population method is naturally statistical in that it deals with the relative frequency of the activities in the population from which perspective it is natural to use the change in the moments, cumulants or other statistics to characterize the evolution of the distributions of characteristics (Horan, 1995). The replicator dynamic provides the foundation for this statistical method of analysis.

Accounting for evolutionary change
Let us now make these ideas more precise. The population method is a remarkably general tool of analysis in that it provides an exhaustive way to account for all the changes that occur in a population over a time interval of length, Δt. The population consists of a set of entities, each one with its set of characteristics and for each characteristic we can define an average population value and enquire as to how this average changes over time. Four processes exhaust the possibilities of population change:

1. Pure replication of the continuing (surviving) entities that remain in the population over the interval, Δt, either in terms of changes in the number of copies of each entity, or, as here, in terms of changes in the scale of activity of each entity.
2. The entry (birth) of additional entities in that population within the time interval, Δt, each such entity having a value of the characteristics in question and making a contribution to the scale of activity.
3. The exit (death) of entities, alive in the population at the beginning of the interval Δt but departing the population within the interval, taking with it their characteristics, while making some contribution to activity while they remain active.
4. Innovations (mutations) in the characteristics possessed by the continuing entities so that they vary individually between the initial and terminal dates defining the interval.

By partitioning the population of entities into continuing entities, entrant entities and exit entities we can perform a complete analysis of the change in the population between the two dates. A pure replication process would focus exclusively on the changes in respect of the continuing entities and, indeed, this is the standard method of much evolutionary analysis. In economic terms this is not entirely satisfactory for it loses sight of extremely important processes in relation to the birth and death of firms and indeed the birth and death of entire economic activities. Innovation too at the level of activities is an essential element in economic evolution for it corresponds to a change in the characteristics of the entities and thus a change in the distribution of selective advantage in the population.

Thus, if replication, differential growth and decline of activity by the surviving entities was the only population level process at work, the method would be straightforward but, in general, this is not the case: a generalized replicator dynamic must also account for the entry and exit of activity performing entities in the time interval. Accounting for evolution in a population in the presence of the birth and death of entities therefore needs some care.

Let the first census date be at t, and the second at date $t + \Delta t$, giving a period of length Δt. Let $X(t + \Delta t)$ and $X(t)$ be the output rates across the whole population at the two census dates. Define compound growth rates such that $g\Delta t$ is the growth rate of total activity, $g_c\Delta t$ is the growth rate of the activity of the surviving firms and $g_e\Delta t$ is the growth rate of the activity of the firms that exit during the interval. Thus, for example, $X_c(t + \Delta t) = X_c(t)(1 + g_c\Delta t)$ defines the activity profile of continuing entities. Let $N(t + \Delta t)$ be the level of activity contributed by those entities that enter the population in the interval Δt. Define the entry rate, $n \cdot \Delta t$, such that $N(t + \Delta t) = n \cdot \Delta t\, X(t + \Delta t)$. Similarly, define $e \cdot \Delta t$ as the fraction of activity $X(t)$ accounted for by the entities that exit in the interval. Let $E(t + \Delta t)$ be the activity contributed by the exiting entities, whence $E(t + \Delta t) = e\Delta t \cdot X(t)(1 + g_e\Delta t)$.

It follows that

$$X(t + \Delta t) = X_c(t) + E(t + \Delta t) + N(t + \Delta t),$$

or

$$X(t + \Delta t) = X(t)\left\{ \frac{(1 - e\Delta t)(1 + g_c\Delta t) + e\Delta t(1 + g_e\Delta t)}{1 - n\Delta t} \right\}.$$

It is convenient to assume that all the exit events occur at the beginning of the interval, in which case, $g_e\Delta t = -1$, and we find that

$$\frac{(1 + g\Delta t)}{(1 + g_c\Delta t)} = \frac{(1 - e\Delta t)}{(1 - n\Delta t)}. \tag{27.1}$$

Whenever the entry rate is the same as the exit rate then the growth rate of the continuing entities is the same as the growth rate in the population as a whole. More generally, as e is greater or smaller than n, then g is greater or smaller than g_c, which accords with common sense, providing we remember that the exit and entry rates are defined as proportions of aggregate activity, not as numbers of entities.

We can now identify the replicator dynamic in respect of the continuing entities and the population as a whole. If we define $c_i(t)$ as $X_i(t) / X_c(t)$, the share of each such entity in the continuing sub-population aggregate, it follows that

$$c_i(t + \Delta t) = c_i(t) \left\{ \frac{1 + g_i \Delta t}{1 + g_c \Delta t} \right\}$$

and

$$\frac{\Delta c_i}{\Delta t} = \frac{c_i(t + \Delta t) - c_i(t)}{\Delta t} = c_i(t) \left\{ \frac{g_i - g_c}{1 + g_c \Delta t} \right\}, \quad (27.2)$$

with

$$g_c(t) = \sum c_i(t) g_i.$$

Equations (27.2) are primitive replicator dynamic relations that hold exactly for continuing entities. They tie the rate of change of the structure of the sub-population to the diversity of growth rates contained within it. If the population is to evolve it must be a population defined by growth rate diversity, which is to say nothing more than the obvious statement that evolution is a dynamic process. If entity i is to increase its share of the activity of the surviving group it is necessary and sufficient that it grow more quickly than the average for its population, $g_i > g_c$, and conversely, if i is to decline in relative importance over the interval. Notice for completeness that since $\sum c_i(t) = 1$ it follows that $\sum \Delta c_i(t) = 0$, always a useful check on the internal consistency of the replicator process.

Now define $s_i(t)$ as $X_i(t) / X(t)$, the share of a continuing activity in the total activity in the time interval, and it follows that

$$s_i(t + \Delta t) = s_i(t) \left\{ \frac{1 + g_i \Delta t}{1 + g \Delta t} \right\}$$

$$= s_i(t) \left\{ \left(\frac{1 + g_i \Delta t}{1 + g_c \Delta t} \right) \left(\frac{1 - n \Delta t}{1 - e \Delta t} \right) \right\}, \quad (27.3)$$

whence the two measures of population structure are related by

$$\frac{s_i(t + \Delta t)}{s_i(t)} = \frac{c_i(t + \Delta t)}{c_i(t)} \left(\frac{1 - e \Delta t}{1 - n \Delta t} \right). \quad (27.4)$$

If the exit and entry rates in terms of activity (not numbers of entities) coincide then the two measures of structure coincide and $g = g_c$. In general they will not, and although a continuing entity may be increasing its share in that sub-population ($g_i > g_c$) it may still be experiencing a declining share in the total population if n is sufficiently greater than e. Relations (27.2), (27.3) and (27.4) provide the elements of the replicator dynamic corrected for processes of entry and exit.

In many cases it is more transparent to work with the replicator dynamic in continuous time, in which case, letting the time interval Δt tend to zero, we can replace equations (27.1) to (27.3) with

$$g = g_c + n - e, \qquad (27.1')$$

$$\frac{dc_i}{dt} = c_i(t)(g_i - g_c), \qquad (27.2')$$

$$\frac{ds_i}{dt} = s_i(t)(g_i - g) = s_i(t)(g_i - g_c - n + e). \qquad (27.3')$$

Let us now put these ideas to work to trace the evolution in the average value of a characteristic across two generations and include the possibility of innovation by the continuing entries. Entry and exit are of course already particular kinds of innovation in the population. Suppose there is some characteristic of the entities, labelled z, and we wish to know how the average value $\bar{z}$ changes over our time interval, taking account of changes at the level of each entity and changes at the level of the population. A good example would be the evolution of average productivity in a population.[2] The answer depends on our generalized replicator process, inclusive of entry and exit, and the innovations that occur within the continuing sub-population. It follows from our definitions that

$$\bar{z}(t) = (1 - e)\bar{z}_c(t) + e\bar{z}_e(t),$$

where $\bar{z}_c(t) = \Sigma c_i(t) z_i(t)$ and $\bar{z}_e(t)$ is the average value of $z(t)$ for those entities that will exit over Δt. Similarly,

$$\bar{z}(t + \Delta t) = (1 - n)\bar{z}_c(t + \Delta t) + n\bar{z}_n(t + \Delta t),$$

where $\bar{z}_n$ is the average value of $z(t + \Delta t)$ for the entrants over the interval. The change in z then follows as

$$\Delta\bar{z} = \bar{z}(t + \Delta t) - \bar{z}(t) = (1 - n)\Delta\bar{z}_c$$
$$+ n(\bar{z}_n(t + \Delta t) - \bar{z}_c(t + \Delta t)) - e(\bar{z}_e(t) - \bar{z}_c(t)). \qquad (27.5)$$

Expression (27.5) is a complete accounting for the change in average population value of characteristic z. On the right-hand side, the first term is the replicator effect in the continuing population, adjusted for the impact of entry. The second and third terms reflect the effects of entry and exit expressed as deviations from the average value for the continuing entities at the appropriate dates.

It is the change in average value in the continuing entities that we can now express more fully taking account of the replicator dynamic. We draw here on a famous result in evolutionary analysis, the Price equation (Price, 1970; Frank, 1998; Andersen, 2004; Gintis, 2000) which decomposes the change in average value into additive effects due to selection and innovation. Thus, following the proper accounting at the two dates, we find

$$\Delta \bar{z}_c = \sum_i c_i(t + \Delta t) z_i(t + \Delta t) - \sum_i c_i(t) z_i(t)$$

$$= \sum_i \Delta c_i z_i(t) + \sum_i c_i(t + \Delta t) \Delta z_i$$

$$= \frac{1}{1 + g_c} \left\{ \sum_i c_i(t)(g_i - g_c) z_i(t) + \sum_i c_i(t)(1 + g_i) \Delta g_i \right\}$$

or

$$(1 + g_c) \Delta \bar{z}_c = C_c(g_i z_i) + E_c((1 + g_i) \cdot \Delta z_i). \tag{27.6}$$

Expression (27.6) is the famous Price equation; in which, $C_c(g_i \, z_i)$, the measure of the selection effect, is the (c_i weighted) covariance between fitness values (the growth rates g_i) and the values of z_i at the initial census date. This captures the idea that the change in the average value of the characteristic depends on how the characteristic co-varies with growth rates across the population. The second term, $E_c((1 + g_i) \cdot \Delta z_i)$, the measure of the innovation effect, is the expected value (again c_i weighted) between the growth rates and the changes in the characteristic values at the level of each entity. Notice the recursive nature of this formulation; for if the entities are also defined as sub-populations of further entities we can apply the Price equation repeatedly to each sub-population. For example, if entity i itself consists of a population of j sub-entities we can write

$$(1 + g_i) \Delta \bar{z}_i = C_{cj}(g_{ij}, z_{ij}) + E_{cj}((1 + g_{ij}) \Delta z_{ij})$$

and apply this to each of the i entities in the original population. As Andersen (2004) suggests, the Price equation 'eats its own tail', an attribute of considerable significance in the analysis of multi-level evolutionary processes. It means that we can decompose any population change into change between sub-populations and change within sub-populations in an identical fashion so that at each level of aggregation we can reflect the same forces of adaptation.

We have applied the accounting across two generations of the population and, of course, we can continue to iterate the replicator process indefinitely. As we do so the nature of the entities will change and a date may be reached when not one of the original members of the population remains alive. However, the activity continues and since the forces of selection remain the same we can continue to speak of a given population.

A special case: Fisher's fundamental theorem

One special application of (27.6) is when the characteristic z_i is taken to be the growth rate g_i for, in this case, we find that

$$(1 + g_c)\Delta g_c = V_c(g_i) + E_c((1 + g_c)\Delta g_i),$$

where $V_c(g_i)$ is the variance in the growth rates within the population of continuing entities. This first term, the selection effect, is known as Fisher's Fundamental Theorem, after its originator, the distinguished biologist and statistician R.A. Fisher (1930). Too much should not be made of it in this specific context. It is a direct consequence of defining the growth rates as we have, and it captures only the selection part of the evolution of the average growth rate. However, its significance lies in its being a very special case of a much wider principle, Fisher's Principle (Metcalfe, 1998), namely that the statistical variability within the population accounts for the rate and direction of evolutionary change – the variation cum selection view of development.[3] We show below how this principle is one of considerable power in tracking the forces of evolution in economic populations.

Thus far we have developed an accounting scheme for any evolutionary process within some arbitrary population. It is entirely neutral as to the explanation of the growth rates, innovation rates and entry and exit rates in any population, providing the framework into which more substantive theories can be located, compared and tested. What gives the scheme its content in any case is the particular explanation that causally links the characteristics of the entities to the differential growth of their scales of activity.

In using the replicator dynamic it is important to distinguish sorting processes from selection processes since both give rise to diversity in growth rates. The distinction is this. In a sorting process, the individual values, g_i, are independently determined and can vary independently of one another. In a selection process, the growth rates are mutually determined, and one cannot vary without creating some corresponding changes in the growth rates of the other entities in the population. The replicator dynamic applies to both but only in the latter case do we have a truly evolutionary process, in which change follows from order.

An economic example
To illustrate the application of the replicator dynamic method we consider here a minimalist model of competitive selection where the entities are firms, the population is defined in terms of the market selection environment and the activity in question is the production of a homogenous commodity. This simple, canonical model is defined in terms of the balanced growth of the particular market for each firm and the growth of its productive capacity. Each firm sets a price p_i, given its unit cost level h_i and the rate at which it requires profits to invest in capacity expansion. These two growth relations we write for each firm as

$$g_{iD} = g_D + \delta[\bar{p}_c - p_i], \tag{27.7}$$

and

$$g_{iS} = f[p_i - h_i],$$

with g_D, the rate of growth of the overall market and $\bar{p}_c = \Sigma c_i p_i$, the average market price. We ignore questions of entry and exit to focus on the essentials of replication. The symbol δ is the coefficient of selection in relation to demand and f is the common propensity to grow of the firms. If each firm sets a price to balance the rate of growth of its market with the rate of growth of its capacity then its 'normal' growth rate is

$$g_i = g_D + \Delta[\bar{h}_c - h_i],$$

where $\Delta = f\delta/(f + \delta)$ is the coefficient of selection and $\bar{h}_c = \Sigma c_i h_i$ is the average level of unit cost in the population. The replicator dynamic relation follows immediately as

$$\frac{dc_i}{dt} = \Delta c_i(\bar{h}_c - h_i) \tag{27.8}$$

and it contains a clear evolutionary message.

The necessary and sufficient condition for a firm to increase its market share is that its unit costs be lower than the population average. Any firm which has above average unit costs is on a trajectory of market decline. Notice that this is no longer true by the meaning of the terms but as a consequence of the theory embedded in (27.7).

Now consider the evolution of the population characteristics, specifically, the average unit cost level $\bar{h}_c$, taking account of selection and innovation. In continuous time,

$$\frac{d\bar{h}_c}{dt} = \sum \frac{dc_i}{dt}h_i + \sum c_i\frac{dh_i}{dt}.$$

Let the firms differ in their innovation rates and define $-\lambda_i$ as the proportionate innovation rate for the firm i; then

$$\frac{d\bar{h}_c}{dt} = -\Delta V_c(h_i) - \sum c_i\lambda_i h_i$$

$$= -\Delta V_c(h_i) - C_c(\lambda,h) - \bar{\lambda}_c\bar{h}_c. \tag{27.9}$$

The first term captures Fisher's Principle in this model, the second two terms account for the innovation rate in terms of the population average, $\bar{\lambda}_c = \sum c_i\lambda_i$, and the covariance between λ and h. Of course, the average innovation rate also evolves in this population and it readily follows that

$$\frac{d\bar{\lambda}_c}{dt} = -\Delta C_c(h,\lambda) + \sum c_i\frac{d\lambda_i}{dt}, \tag{27.10}$$

so how h and λ are jointly distributed across the population partially determines the evolution of the average innovation rate.

Now the covariance terms in (27.9) and (27.10) can be written differently for, if we consider the linear regression between the values of λ_i and h_i, each observation weighted by the share of that firm in population output, it follows that $C_c(h\lambda) = \beta_c V_c(h)$, where β_c is the slope of the linear regression between these characteristics. Of course, as the structure of the industry changes so the value of this regression coefficient will change.

Hence (27.9) becomes a more compact expression,

$$\frac{d\bar{h}_c}{dt} = -\Delta[1 + \beta_c]V_c(h_i) - \bar{\lambda}_c\bar{h}_c \tag{27.9'}$$

and (27.10) becomes

$$\frac{d\bar{\lambda}_c}{dt} = -\Delta\beta_c V_c(h) + \sum c_i\frac{d\lambda_i}{dt}. \tag{27.10'}$$

Thus evolution of the population average reflects the statistical relation between the contributing factors, that is to say the degree to which the different causes are correlated. Thus population evolution becomes a matter of variation and correlation. Correlation across population diversity is everything in an evolutionary process, and the replicator method allows us to uncover the deeper meanings of this claim. What this correlation is depends not only on the distribution of the characteristics across the population but quite crucially on how the activities of the entities are coordinated to produce order in the population. Change those coordinating processes and we must change the consequences for the pattern of evolution.

This simple example is not meant other than to demonstrate the population method and its link to the replicator dynamic; to demonstrate that our accounting for evolution is a framework in which to fit multiple economic theories of evolution. Note, however, the richness of even this simple account. We combine accumulation and innovation and the rate of innovation is to a degree endogenous. We have an imperfect $(0 < \delta < \infty)$ but growing product market, and we have selection that jointly depends on price setting behaviour and profitability. Moreover, adding further dimensions of firm performance, variation in product quality or variations in the propensity of firms to grow, or increasing returns can only strengthen and further enrich the argument and illustrate the dependence of evolution on variation and correlation. Particular explanations of the rate of technical progress and its distribution across firms also add to the scope for a richer theory of economic evolution. The point is that, as in all evolutionary theories of a variation selection kind, adding new sources of variation within the population including entry and exit provides more material on which selection can work (Foster and Metcalfe, 2001). This is the strength of the replicator method.

Wider issues
One significant aspect of the replicator method is that it provides a device for dealing with the dynamics that follow from variety in behaviour, dispensing completely with the need to resort to the fiction of the representative, or rather, uniform agent, a most non-evolutionary methodological device. Similarly, the replicator dynamic provides a method for approaching economic change freed from any resort to equilibrium reasoning. It depends greatly on the way activity is coordinated in a population but that is a matter of establishing order, not equilibrium. Indeed, in any knowledge-dependent activity, and economic activities are necessarily knowledge-dependent, it is to be expected that activity continually changes knowledge so that evolution is open-ended. This approach contrasts sharply with the dominant methods in economic theory for the analysis of change. In economic theory in general the standard dynamic method is to identify the attractors for a system and then enquire into the stability of the system if it deviates from this set of states. As knowledge of dynamic systems has increased, this has identified

several problems with this approach, two of which are technical and two of which are more substantive. The technical points relate to the fact that any system may possess multiple basins of attraction or that the attractors may change more quickly than the system can converge, so that the system finds itself further away from the attractor as time advances. On both counts, the very meaning of convergence is in doubt.

The more substantive issues need more comment. The first relates to the problem of not being able to ground the economic dynamics of the system when it is out of equilibrium in the same rational processes that define the attracting positions. The theory has two unrelated parts and this is clearly unsatisfactory. More fundamental still is the second point that the very process of moving towards the possible attracting states changes the very nature of those states so there cannot be equilibrium states in general, only sets of interconnected variables moving at different velocities. For knowledge-based systems the invariance of attracting states to out-of-equilibrium dynamics is not to be expected. In this context replicator dynamics provides a method to replace the distance from attractor dynamic of conventional theory with the distance from mean dynamic of evolutionary processes. In the examples above what drives the dynamic of the system is a distance from mean dynamics, in which the characteristics that causally underpin growth are distributed relative to their population means. Since the means evolve as well (Fisher's Principle), the nature of this dynamic process is always changing. In the presence of innovation and the growth of knowledge, it may never settle in a state of rest but continually discover new dimensions and spaces of activity through entry and exit. The replicator dynamic provides the basis for an open-ended analysis of evolutionary processes that combine multiple forms of innovation in populations with structural change within populations. It is a natural method to study the development of systems that are ordered, are dynamically constrained but which are never, and never could be, in a state of rest: that is to say those evolving systems that in the very process of establishing order set in train changes to that order, systems that are self-organizing and simultaneously self-transforming.

Notes

1. An excellent overview of the developmental view of economic evolution can be found in Cantner and Hanusch (2002). See also Cohen and Malerba (2001) for an assessment of the empirical content of replicator dynamics.
2. See Bartlesmann and Doms (2000) and Carlin *et al.*, (2001) for an introduction to a rapidly growing literature on the population analysis of productivity growth.
3. In fact, there is a deeper interpretation of the selection effect in the Fisher/Price accounting. It is that the rate of change of the nth cumulant of the distribution of any characteristic is proportional to the magnitude of the $(n+1)$, the cumulants. I call this 'the cumulant theorem'.

References

Andersen, E.S., 1994, *Evolutionary Economics: Post Schumpeterian Contributions*, Pinter, London.

Andersen, E.S., 2004, 'Population thinking, Price's equation and the analysis of economic evolution', *Evolutionary and Institutional Economics Review*, 1, 127–48.

Bartlesmann, E. and Doms, M., 2000, 'Understanding productivity: lessons from longitudinal data', *Journal of Economic Literature*, 38, 569–94.

Cantner, U. and Hanusch, H., 2002, 'Evolutionary economics: its basic concepts and methods. A tribute to Mark Perlman', in H. Lim, U.K. Park and G.C. Harcourt (eds), *Editing Economics: Essays in Honour of Mark Perlman*, Routledge, London.

Carlin, W., Haskel, J. and Seabright, P., 2001, 'Understanding "The essential fact about capitalism": markets, competition and creative destruction', *National Institute Economic Review*, 175, 67–84.

Cohen, W.M. and Malerba, F., 2001, 'Is the tendency to variation a chief cause of progress?' *Industrial and Corporate Change*, 10, 561–608.

Dosi, G., 2000, *Innovation, Organisation and Economic Dynamics*, Edward Elgar, Cheltenham, UK and Northampton, MA, USA.

Fisher, R.A., 1930, *The Genetical Theory of Natural Selection*, Clarendon, Oxford.

Foster, J. and Metcalfe, J.S. (eds), 2001, *Frontiers of Evolutionary Economics*, Edward Elgar, Cheltenham, UK and Northampton, MA, USA.

Frank, S.A., 1998, *Foundations of Social Evolution*, Princeton University Press, Princeton, NJ.

Gintis, H., 2000, *Game Theory Evolving*, Princeton University Press, Princeton, NJ.

Horan, B.L., 1995, 'The statistical character of evolutionary theory', *Philosophy of Science*, 61, 76–95.

Hull, D. (1988), *Science as a Process*, University of Chicago Press, Chicago, IL.

Metcalfe, J.S., 1998, *Evolutionary Economics and Creative Destruction*, Routledge, London.

Nelson, R and Winter, S., 1982, *An Evolutionary Theory of Economic Change*, Belknap, Harvard.

Price, G.R., 1970, 'Selection and covariance', *Nature*, 227, 520–21.

Saviotti, P., 1996, *Technological Evolution, Variety and the Economy*, Edward Elgar, Cheltenham, UK and Brookfield, USA.

Sober, E.S., 1984, *The Nature of Selection*, MIT Press, Boston.

Vega-Redondo, F., 1996, *Evolution, Games and Economic Behaviour*, Oxford University Press, Oxford.

28 'History-friendly' models of industrial evolution
Luigi Orsenigo*

1 Introduction

'History-friendly' models (HFM) are an approach to the construction of evolutionary models based on the formalization of the essence of appreciative theories about mechanisms and factors affecting the evolution of specific industries suggested by empirical research.

The development of HFM was inspired by the reconsideration of some basic methodological principles that underlie evolutionary economics. In particular, HFM reflect the commitment to the argument that

1. realism should be considered as an important merit of theoretical models and that the design of formal economic models ought to proceed well informed by the empirical literature on the subject matter they purport to address;
2. formal evolutionary theory can be a major help to empirical research in economics.
3. formal models play a crucial role in the development of more general theories that are capable of subsuming diverse specific instances into a compact, broad and simple conceptual framework.

In this chapter, we shall discuss first the basic methodology of HFM. Second, we shall briefly present the basic structure of a model of the evolution of the computer industry and some applications and exercises carried out on such a model. In Section 4, a brief illustration of a model of the pharmaceutical industry will be used to suggest how HFM can be used in an inductive way to progress towards broader generalizations and theories. The concluding section indicates some lines for future research.

2 The methodology of HFM

HFM are inspired by the recognition that there is often a tension between detailed, rich, empirical and historical accounts of specific phenomena and

---

* This chapter is largely based on earlier articles written jointly with Franco Malerba, Richard Nelson and Sidney Winter. However, they are not responsible for any mistakes nor do they necessarily agree with all the ideas presented in this chapter.

'general theories', almost always formalized in mathematical models. This is arguably the case in evolutionary economics, too. The evolutionary models of the 'first generation' attempted in general and primarily to explore the logic of evolutionary economic processes and to establish the usefulness of this new approach. In most case, these models were rather simple and abstract. They had as their empirical referent broad phenomena such as economic growth, the relationship between industrial structure and innovation, the diffusion processes, and other stylized facts about issues of industrial dynamics. Sometimes they had a very complex formal structure, but both the description of phenomena under observation and the internal structure of these models were highly simplified, as they concern both the kind of agents that were explicitly modelled (typically only firms) and the representation of their internal structure. Also the demand side was not usually represented in any depth.

These models were, in our assessment, tremendously successful, yet this very success raises a number of questions. First, it becomes necessary to explore further the fundamental principles of evolutionary economics that are able to explain such a large variety of phenomena. This is the realm of 'high theory', which ought to be as general, compact and parsimonious as possible. In other words, the task here is to identify and strengthen the 'hard core' of evolutionary theory. Recent work, e.g. by Sidney Winter, Giovanni Dosi and others, goes precisely in this direction (Bottazzi *et al.*, 2001; Winter *et al.*, 2000).

Second, in a strongly complementary way, one might try to impose a stronger empirical discipline on formal models, for at least two reasons. In some cases, especially as models progress in mathematical sophistication, their linkage with specific economic facts tends to become worryingly tenuous. Moreover, and more important, sometimes the empirical phenomena that the theorist tries to explain are extremely generic and not sufficiently specified or conditioned to restrictions. Thus, they can result from very different dynamic processes. Phenomena like S-shaped curves in diffusion theory or skewed firm's size distributions are typical examples of this kind of 'unconditional objects' (Brock, 1999). In these instances, it might be useful both to enrich the internal structure of the model and, above all, to increase the number and the kind of facts that one tries to explain at the same time. The imposition of a tighter 'empirical discipline' is necessarily a more demanding test for the model.

Last, but by no means least, evolutionary economics has been developing to a large extent through the construction of empirical and historical case studies. Usually these 'histories' present rich and detailed evidence and suggest powerful explanations. Actors and variables like the educational system, policies, institutions, the internal organizational structure of firms and the structure of demand play a fundamental role in these accounts. This literature is based on 'appreciative theorizing' (Nelson and Winter, 1982), i.e. non-formal explanations of observed phenomena based on specific causal links proposed by the researcher. Nelson and Winter argued that not only is appreciative theorizing a true causal theory, but it is also a fundamental and unavoidable step in any process of 'theory making'. Thus, it is dangerous to play down its methodological status, since it provides the fundamental building blocks and the understanding of the specific set of phenomena under investigation. However, it is sometimes hard to check the logical consistency of appreciative models: whether the suggested causal arguments are consistent and sufficient to provide an explanation. This is particularly the case if these appreciative models embody non-linear and path-dependent processes and a variety of agents and institutions. Moreover, these accounts are usually hard to generalize. Each history is often treated as unique, because the details and the specific observed sequence of events make difficult or controversial any claim that the particular case can be considered as an instantiation of a more general process applicable to a wider range of cases.

These remarks suggest, in our view, that in many cases there is a tension between empirical analysis of specific cases and the construction of general theories. To a large extent, this tension is unavoidable and it is a legitimate and indeed fruitful source of progress in understanding. But, possibly, it might have indeed gone too far.

Against this context, HFM try to bridge this gap. In this vein, formal models should be considered first of all as attempts at checking the consistency and the robustness of the verbal arguments that constitute the appreciative theory. Hence, HFM aim to capture the essence of the appreciative theory put forth by analysts of the history of an industry or a technology, and thus to enable its logical exploration. Often, in these cases, only a simulation model can capture (at least in part) the substance of the appreciative model. But it is worth observing that a 'history-friendly' model does not necessarily need to be based upon simulation, nor necessarily on an evolutionary approach.[1]

On the other hand, HFM might contribute to the construction of more general theories in at least two ways. First, the construction of formal models of specific industries might be useful in forcing the theorist trying to apply a general model to a specific case to recognize that often the 'devil is in the details', calling both for more realism than is sometimes the case and for stronger awareness of the distance that might exist between any 'general' theory and the issue under investigation.

Second, in a more inductive attitude, building different HFM for different industries may help the development of 'general theories' by prompting the analyst to clearly recognize what is similar and what is different between two or more sectors. As an example, at the very beginning of the development of a model, one must obviously identify the distinctive features of the industries under investigation. In all probability, then, a model built to deal with the computer industry should be different from a model of the pharmaceutical industry. But the deliberation about which features have to be different and which can be similar is a basic inductive exercise, which paves the way for subsequent generalizations. Thus a 'history-friendly' approach can allow us to tackle, in a dynamic setting, some general traditional questions of industrial economics, such as why do industries differ, what are the relationships between innovation, demand structure and market structure, what are the determinants of processes of vertical integration and specialization, etc.

In this sense, HFM try to impose a 'double' methodological discipline on evolutionary industrial organization theory: imposing formal discipline on appreciative theorizing and empirical discipline on more abstract, general theories.

3   The model of the computer industry
The first attempt at building an HFM concerned the computer industry (Malerba *et al.*, 1999). The model clearly shares the distinctive characteristics of the evolutionary approach. Agents are characterized by 'bounded rationality', i.e. they do not completely understand the causal structure of the environment in which they are set and they are unable to elaborate exceedingly complex expectations about the future. Rather, firms' and consumers' actions are assumed to be driven by routines and rules that introduce inertia in their behavior. Agents, however, can learn and are able to improve their performance along some relevant dimensions, in particular technology.

Given earlier periods' conditions, firms act and modify their performance. Specifically, profitable firms expand, and unprofitable ones shrink. Thus the model is mainly driven by processes of learning and selection. Jointly, the actions of all agents determine aggregate industry conditions, which then define the state for the next iteration of the model.

Strong non-linearities are present in this structure. They generate a complex dynamics and prevent an analytical solution of the system. Moreover, the model does not impose equilibrium conditions: on the contrary, 'ordered' dynamics emerge as the result of interactions far from equilibrium.

3.1   *The basic structure*
The history analysed in the model begins with a number of firms engaging in efforts to design a computer, using funds provided by 'venture capitalists'. Computers are designed on the basis of transistor technology. Some

firms exhaust their capital endowment without achieving a computer that meets a positive demand and so fail. Some other firms succeed and begin to sell. This way they first break into the mainframe market. Profits are used to pay back the initial debt, to invest in R&D and in marketing. Successful firms gain market shares and grow. Over time firms come closer to the technological frontier defined by transistor technology, and technical advance becomes slower.

After some time, microprocessors become exogenously available. This shifts the technological frontier, so that it is possible to achieve better computer designs. A new group of firms tries to design new computers exploiting the new technology, in the same way as happened for transistors. Some of these firms fail. Some enter the mainframe market and compete with the incumbents. Some others open up the PC market. Incumbents may choose to adopt the new technology to achieve more powerful mainframe computers. The adoption of new technology by old firms is costly and time-consuming. After they have switched to the new technology, incumbents may decide to diversify into the PC market and compete with new PC producers.

3.2 Some features of the formal structure of the model

Computers are defined by two characteristics, 'cheapness' (defined as the inverse of the price of a given computer) and 'performance' which improve over time as a consequence of firms' R&D spending. Computers can be designed using two different technologies, characterized by the type of components they embody: transistors and microprocessors. These technologies become exogenously available at different periods and they define the maximum levels of the two characteristics that can be achieved by a computer design.

Computers are offered to two quite separate groups of potential customers. One group ('large firms'), greatly values performance and wants to buy mainframes. The second group ('small users'), has less need for high performance but values cheapness. It provides a potential market for personal computers. The value that customers place on a computer design is an increasing function of its performance and its cheapness,[2] which, jointly, define the 'merit' of a particular computer to the eye of the customers.

Consumers buy a computer valuing its 'merit', compared to other products. In addition, however, markets are characterized by brand loyalty (or lock-in) effects and respond to firms' marketing policies. Moreover, there is a stochastic element in consumers' choices between different computers. Without lock-in effects or marketing, demand would be similar to a standard demand curve. It would tend to converge towards the higher-quality product, even if a positive probability of surviving for computers with lower design would always remain. The inclusion of brand loyalty and bandwagon effects introduces inertia and forms of increasing returns in market dynamics.

Firms' behavior is meant to capture elements of the theory of the firm based on 'dynamic competencies' (Winter, 1987; Dosi and Marengo, 1993; Teece and Pisano, 1994). Firms are represented by sets of technological and marketing competencies that are accumulated over time, and by rules of action. Through their R&D expenditures, firms accumulate technical capabilities and design better computers. Outcomes of R&D activities depend on the research direction each firm decides to follow (which is assumed to be firm-specific and time-invariant), on latent technological opportunities (i.e. the maximum levels of the two characteristics that can be achieved by a computer design) as well as on a probabilistic effect.

The price that firms charge on their products is obtained by adding a mark-up to production costs, which in turn are determined by the technical progress function. R&D and advertising expenditures are simply determined as constant fractions of profits (after the repayment of their debt).

An essential element of the 'dynamic competence' approach to the theory of the firm concerns the cumulative nature of firms' competencies: firms tend to improve gradually following rather rigid directions. As a consequence, competence traps and lock-in phenomena are distinctive features of this approach. In the model, existing transistor-based mainframe firms are able to switch over to microprocessor technology, but this transition takes time and money. The probability that an incumbent firm will try to switch over is a function of how much progress has been achieved by microprocessor computer designs and of the distance of a transistor firm from the frontier of technological possibilities defined by transistor technology. When adoption takes place, a firm has to pay a once and for all switchover cost. After adoption, firms have access to the new technological frontier and can innovate faster. Moreover, these companies now have the possibility to diversify, producing computers for the PC market. The incentive for diversification is a function of the size of the PC market, defined in terms of sales, as compared to the mainframe market. The old trajectory of technological progress will not be – in general – the best suited one to design PCs. As a matter of fact, IBM entered the PC market founding a completely new division. The procedures governing diversification in the model mimic the actual strategy used by IBM.

The parent company starts a new division, which inherits from the parent company a fraction of its budget and of its technical and advertising capabilities. The parent company exploits 'public knowledge' in the PC market and partly imitates PC firms. Further, it picks up randomly a new technical progress trajectory. After birth, the new division behaves exactly as a new entrant, with independent products, profits and budget.

3.3 The simulation runs

The model is able to replicate the industry history. A dominant firm (IBM) emerges relatively quickly in the mainframe market and it maintains its large market share, even after the entry of the new microprocessor-based producers. IBM then diversifies into the PC market, and gains a nontrivial, but not a dominant, share.

The parameter setting reflects the basic key assumptions of the appreciative model. Specifically, the dominant position of IBM in the mainframe market was due to significant effects of brand loyalty and consumer lock-in. This raised substantial entry barriers to new entrants. Second, by the time microprocessors became available, computer design under the old technology was reasonably advanced, and the leader, IBM, responded to the availability of the new technology pretty rapidly. Third, IBM's massive resources enabled it quickly to mount an R&D and advertising effort sufficient to catch up with the earlier entrants into the PC market. However, in the PC market lock-in and brand loyalty processes were less significant and customers were quite sensitive to the merit of the computer being offered, particularly to price.

The logic of the model has then to be tested by conducting counterfactual simulation runs. Thus a reduction of the parameter capturing brand loyalty effects in the demand function of the mainframe market lowers significantly the market's concentration. Similarly, if the time of introduction of microprocessor technology is anticipated, new firms break into the market before the emergence of a dominant firm. Hence, the process of microprocessor adoption is then slower and more costly. Facing this environment, IBM is not able to achieve a significant market share in the PC market because it must compete with firms which have already a dominant position in the new segment.[3]

3.4 Further exercises: diversification, industrial policies and experimental users

Being satisfied by the ability of the model to both reproduce the stylized history and to react appropriately to changes in the key parameters (as suggested by the theory), it becomes possible to explore new issues and questions. For example, a first exercise concerned whether and under what conditions a different diversification strategy by IBM had performed better (Malerba et al., 2001a).[4]

A further issue that has been explored through the model relates to the effectiveness of public policies under conditions of dynamic increasing returns (Malerba et al., 2001b). According to the model, the emergence of a monopolist in the mainframe market was almost inevitable, given the presence of two interacting sources of increasing returns that tend to reinforce each other: cumulativeness in firms' efforts to advance product and process technologies and brand loyalty and lock-in effects on the demand side. Within this setting, a set of simulation runs examined the effects of the timing of an intervention of an antitrust authority (AA) breaking the monopolist into two smaller companies.

Results show the fundamental relevance of the timing of the intervention in dynamic markets and suggest that it is extremely difficult to contrast the tendency towards concentration typical of markets characterized by substantial dynamic increasing returns.[5] Small initial advantages tend to grow bigger and bigger over time and catching up is almost impossible. Leaders do not only have a 'static' advantage: they also run faster than laggards. Thus, antitrust intervention might be effective in modifying the degree of concentration only in the short run. Policies of the kind are somehow designed to 'level the playing field', but this does not seem to be enough. In order to get effective and long-lasting results, some form of 'positive discrimination' might be necessary. That is to say, in the presence of strong dynamic increasing returns, policies should make competitors able to run (much) faster than the monopolist, and not just remove static disadvantages. On the other hand, even if the intervention has limited effects on the mainframe market, it produces noticeable consequences on a proximate market, i.e. the PC segment, where concentration is lower than in the standard case.[6]

A third set of simulations does not deal directly or solely with the computer industry, but with a more general issue, i.e. the role of experimental users and/or diverse preferences among potential users in forcing the successful introduction of radically new technology in an industry (Malerba *et al.*, 2003). Typically, a new technology is inferior to the old one in its early stages and it progresses only through the R&D efforts of new entrants. But, absent customers who are prepared to buy these initially inferior products, the new firms are not likely to survive and, despite the opportunities afforded by a potentially powerful new technology, the industry will stay stuck with the old.

To explore this hypothesis, various demand contexts are analysed. In a first set of runs, the bandwagon effects in the demand equation are modified in such a way that new firms trying to introduce a new technology are unable to get any significant market share in the market. As a consequence, established leaders in the market do not have the incentive to adopt the new technology. The same result occurs, though, even when the bandwagon effect is eliminated but customers are sophisticated and preferences are homogeneous, in the sense that users always buy the 'best' product currently offered in the market. Since the new technology is initially inferior to the old one, sophisticated customers continue to buy the old (currently better) designs, preventing new entrants from finding a profitable market and developing the new technology.[7]

The situation changes if a group of customers is introduced who will buy some of the products based on the new technology, simply because they are new or if there is a group of customers with very different tastes than the customers who had been buying the old products. In both cases, the new firms, and the new technology, is able to get a foothold in the industry and to grow. Established firms are now challenged by these new ones, and they change over their own practices. The result is that, down the road, products using the new technology come to dominate the market and over the long run even the old consumers may be significantly better off.

4   The model of the pharmaceutical industry

A further attempt at building an HFM concerns the pharmaceutical industry and biotechnology (Malerba and Orsenigo, 2002). The model is still largely work-in-progress and therefore only some brief comments will be reported here. This case differs drastically from computers in a number of respects. Thus, beyond its intrinsic interest, the model of pharmaceuticals might illustrate how HFM can be used in an inductive and 'comparative' perspective to generate and test hypotheses about the determinants of market structure and its evolution.

Pharmaceuticals are traditionally a highly R&D-intensive sector where, despite a series of radical technological and institutional 'shocks', the core of leading innovative firms and countries has remained quite small and stable for a very long period of time. However, different from computers, the degree of concentration has been consistently low, whatever level of aggregation is considered.

These patterns are intimately linked to two main factors: first, the nature of the processes of drug discovery, i.e. the properties of the space of technological opportunities and of the search procedures through which firms explore the space of technological opportunities. Specifically, innovation processes have been characterized for a very long time by low degree of cumulativeness and by 'quasi-random' procedures of search (random screening). Thus, innovation in one market (a therapeutic category) does not entail higher probabilities of success in another one. The second factor is the fragmented nature of the relevant markets: a drug treating hypertension is no use for those suffering from Alzheimer's.

In the model, a number of firms compete to discover, develop and market new drugs for a large variety of diseases. They face a large space of – at the beginning – unexplored opportunities. However, the search for new promising compounds is essentially random, because the knowledge of why a certain molecule can 'cure' a particular disease and of where that particular molecule can be found is limited. Thus firms explore randomly the 'space of molecules' until they find one which might become a useful drug and patent it. After discovery, firms engage in the development of the drug, without knowing how difficult, time-consuming and costly the process will be and what the quality of the new drug will be. Then the drug is sold on the market, whose notional size is defined by the number of potential patients. Marketing expenditures allow firms to increase the number of patients to whom they can gain access. At the beginning, the new drug is the only product available on that particular therapeutic class. But other firms can discover competing drugs or imitate (after patent expiration). The innovator will therefore experience a burst of growth following the introduction of the new drug, but later on its revenues and market shares will be eroded away by competitors and imitators.

The discovery of a drug in a particular therapeutic class does not entail any advantage in the discovery of another drug in a different class, except for the volume of profits they can reinvest in search and development. Moreover, the various sub-markets (therapeutic categories) that define the overall pharmaceutical industry are independent of one another also on the demand side. As a consequence, diversification into different therapeutic categories is also purely random. Hence, firms will start searching randomly again for a new product everywhere in the space of molecules. Firms' growth will then depend on the number of drugs they have discovered (i.e. in diversification into different therapeutic categories), on the size of the markets they are present in, on the number of competitors and on the relative quality and price of their drug vis-à-vis competitors. Occasionally, a firm can discover a blockbuster. But, given the large number of therapeutic categories and the absence of any form of cumulativeness in the search and development process, no firm can hope to be able to win a large market share in the overall market, but – if anything – only in specific therapeutic categories for a limited period of time. As a result, the degree of concentration in the whole market for pharmaceuticals and in any individual therapeutic category will be low. However, a few firms will grow and become large, thanks essentially to the discovery of a 'blockbuster' and to diversification.

The advent of biotechnology starts to change this picture. In the model, a first, very rough, reduced form is introduced of the cognitive processes underlying drug discovery after the molecular biology revolution. In the model, scientific knowledge allows firms to focus their search on particular areas (Nelson, 1982). Moreover, science makes new products potentially available.

On these bases, new science-based firms enter the market, trying to discover new drugs, yet these new firms are specialized in specific techniques and applications, which might prove to be dead-ends or can be successfully applied only in particular areas. Moreover, they have little funding and, even when they succeed in discovering a new drug, they do not control the resources to develop and market it.

Thus, only a few of the new biotechnology firms (NBFs) will succeed in discovering, developing and selling a new drug. Conversely, extant big pharmaceutical companies do not react immediately to the new opportunities and when they eventually adopt the new technologies they have to gradually 'learn' the new knowledge base. However, they have plenty of financial and marketing resources. Moreover, they are able – in principle – to 'screen' wider sub-sets of the search space: they are 'generalists' rather than 'specialists'. Against this background, big pharmaceutical companies and NBFs may find it profitable to strike collaborative agreements, whereby NBFs complete some specific project with additional funding provided by their large partners. The drug is then developed and (if successful) marketed by the big pharma corporation, paying a royalty to the NBF. As a consequence, a network of alliances begins to emerge.

As in the model of the computer industry, firms act following very simple rules as it concerns investment in R&D and marketing. Also the basic structure of demand is quite similar to the previous model, except, of course, that now there is a large number of independent markets. The main difference then concerns the representation of the search space in which firms conduct their innovative and imitative activities: here, the discovery of a new promising drug is totally random and there is no cumulativeness in technological advances.

Results are also encouraging. The model is actually able to replicate some of the key features of the pharmaceutical industry in these periods, especially as it concerns the low level of concentration both in the overall market and, to a lesser extent, also in each therapeutic category. Similarly, the biotechnology revolution does not change market structure substantially, despite a significant entry of new firms. A dense network of agreements between incumbents and NBFs start to develop, though. Collaborative relations allow for the survival of many NBFs and for the further growth of some incumbents, that benefit from collaboration for discovering better drugs.

Various exercises show, indeed, that it is quite difficult to increase concentration substantially in this model, unless the costs of R&D are drastically increased and technological change and marketing are made much more cumulative. Similarly, it is almost impossible, within the current structure of the model, for new biotechnology firms to displace incumbents.

Within this context, it becomes possible to start running exercises concerning e.g. the effects of alternative forms of patent protection and market regulation.

5 Conclusions

HFM, as developed so far, appear to be adequately flexible and 'powerful' to fulfil the purposes behind their creation. They capture in a stylized and simplified way the focal points of an appreciative theory about the determinants of the evolution of two industries. They are able to replicate the main events of the industry histories with a parameter setting that is coherent with basic theoretical assumptions. Changes in these parameters lead to 'alternative histories' that are consistent with the fundamental causal factors of the observed stylized facts. Furthermore, on these bases, it becomes possible to explore the effects of different hypotheses about agents' behavior, the conditions which determine the profitability of different strategies or the impact of alternative designs for industrial policies and forms of market regulation. Finally, in a more 'theoretical' attitude, HFM can be used to develop and analyse more general assumptions about the determinants of the evolution of market structures, such as the structure of demand and of the relevant technological regimes. HFM, thus, provide some original insights and suggestions for the study of the evolution of industrial structures, particularly by examining the dynamic properties of structures characterized at the same time by several sources of increasing returns.

These models are only preliminary attempts and there are many opportunities for further research along these lines. A first direction of analysis, already in progress, concerns the processes of vertical integration and specialization and the co-evolution of an upstream and a downstream industry. More generally, there is obviously ample scope for the construction of models of different industries, which can explore different histories and investigate new theoretical questions. HFM might therefore prove to be valid tools for progress at the same time towards a more general and a more empirically/historically founded theory of industry evolution and economic change.

Notes

1. For example, the model presented by Jovanovic and MacDonald (1993) could be thought of as a neoclassical antecedent of 'history-friendly' models. Much of the work by Steven Klepper goes also in the direction of building models for specific industries as a basis for further generalization. See, for instance, Klepper (2002).
2. Markets for mainframes and for PCs consist of a large number (a parameter in the model) of independent sub-markets. They are sub-groups of purchasers with identical preferences.
3. Conversely, IBM becomes able to dominate also the PC market, if the parameters measuring economies of scale in R&D and brand loyalty in the PC market are increased and when the diversification process is eased.
4. Here diversifying firms, instead of starting a totally new division, try to apply their specific 'mainframe' competencies to the PC and set up a new internal division which develops PCs following the old trajectory of technological progress and begins its activities starting from

the position reached by the parent company in the space of technological characteristics. This strategy may entail the disadvantage that the new division's trajectory of advance might fare relatively badly in a market that values more cheapness rather than performance. Conversely, the strategy based on the acquisition of new knowledge from external sources can be much more expensive and, in general, the new technological strategy of the parent company might well turn out to be a very bad one. Simulation results show that a 'competence-driven' strategy performs relatively better if the design of a PC does not require a drastic re-orientation in the competencies mix (i.e. in the trajectory of technological advance) and if the PC market were not too distant from the mainframe market.

5. When AA intervenes very early, the market becomes concentrated again very soon, because one company will quickly gain an advantage and grow by exploiting increasing returns. In the case of later intervention, the emergence of a new monopolist takes more time. Finally, if the intervention occurs after 20 years, the market will be divided into two oligopolists, who will not be able to profit any longer from the possibility of gaining market leadership, because dynamic increasing returns are limited (technological opportunities are almost depleted). Similar results were obtained in the analysis of policies supporting the entry of new firms.

6. In fact, when AA intervenes early (after 1 or 5 years), both new 'IBM children' are able to diversify into the PC market, thereby reducing concentration there. In case AA intervenes 'late' (after 10 or 20 years), only one firm will be able to diversify, but it will be smaller and the overall concentration in the PC market will decrease.

7. This result shows that, quite paradoxically, a more 'competitive' market – with little inertia in consumers' behavior – can generate more concentration than a market where inertia is greater.

References

Bottazzi, G., Dosi, G. and Rocchetti, G. (2001), 'Modes of knowledge accumulation, entry regimes and patterns of industrial evolution', *Industrial and Corporate Change*, **10** (3), 609–38.

Brock, W.A. (1999), 'Scaling in economics: a reader's guide', *Industrial and Corporate Change*, **8** (3), 409–46.

Dosi, G. and Marengo, L. (1993), 'Some elements of an evolutionary theory of organizational competence', in R.W. England (ed.), *Evolutionary Concepts on Contemporary Economics*, University of Michigan Press, Ann Arbor.

Jovanovic, B. and MacDonald, G.M. (1993), The life cycle of a competitive industry, working paper no. 4441, National Bureau of Economic Research, Cambridge, MA.

Klepper, S. (1996), 'Entry, exit and innovation over the product life cycle', *American Economic Review*, **86** (3), 562–82.

Klepper, S.(2002), 'The capabilities of new firms and the evolution of the US automobile industry', *Industrial and Corporate Change*, **11** (4), 645–66.

Malerba, F. and Orsenigo, L. (2002), 'Innovation and market structure in the dynamics of the pharmaceutical industry and biotechnology: towards a history-friendly model', *Industrial and Corporate Change*, **11** (4), 667–704.

Malerba, F., Nelson, R., Orsenigo, L. and Winter, S. (1999), 'History friendly models of industry evolution: the computer industry', *Industrial and Corporate Change*, **1**, 3–41.

Malerba, F., Nelson, R., Orsenigo, L. and Winter, S. (2001a), 'Product diversification in a "history-friendly" model of the evolution of the computer industry', in A. Lomi and E. Larsen (eds), *Dynamics of Organizations. Computational Modeling and Organization Theories*, MIT Press, Cambridge, pp. 349–76.

Malerba, F., Nelson, R., Orsenigo, L. and Winter, S. (2001b), 'Competition and industrial policies in a "history-friendly" model of the evolution of the computer industry', *International Journal of Industrial Organization*, **19**, 613–34.

Malerba, F., Nelson, R., Orsenigo, L. and Winter, S. (2003), Demand, innovation and the dynamics of market structure: the role of experimental users and diverse preferences, CESPRI working paper no. 135.

Nelson, R. (1982), 'The role of knowledge in R&D efficiency', *Quarterly Journal of Economics*, **97** (3), 453–70.
Nelson, R. and Winter, S. (1982), *An Evolutionary Theory of Economic Change*, Harvard University Press, Cambridge, MA.
Teece, D. and Pisano, G. (1994), 'The dynamic capabilities of firms: an introduction', *Industrial and Corporate Change*, **3**, 537–55.
Winter, S. (1987), 'Knowledge and competence as strategic assets', in D.J. Teece (ed.), *The Competitive Challenge*, Ballinger, Cambridge, MA, pp. 159–84.
Winter, S., Kaniovski, Y.M and Dosi, G. (2000), 'Modeling industrial dynamics with innovative entrants', *Structural Change and Economic Dynamics*, **11**, 255–93.

29 Agent-based modelling: a methodology for neo-Schumpeterian economics
Andreas Pyka and Giorgio Fagiolo

1 Introduction

The tremendous development of an easy access to computational power within the last 30 years has led to the widespread use of numerical approaches in almost all scientific disciplines. Nevertheless, while the engineering sciences focused on the applied use of simulation techniques from the very beginning, in the social sciences most of the early examples of numerical approaches were purely theoretical.

There are two reasons for this. First, since the middle of the 20th century, starting with economics, equilibrium-oriented analytical techniques flourished and were developed to a highly sophisticated level. This led to the widely shared view that, within the elegant and formal framework of linear analysis offered by neoclassical economics, the social sciences could reach a level of accuracy and stringency not previously thought to be possible.

Second, within the same period, new phenomena of structural change exerted a strong influence on the social and economic realms. Despite the mainstream neoclassical successes in shifting the social sciences to a strong mathematical foundation, an increasing dissatisfaction with this approach emerged. For example, by the 1970s, the benchmark of atomistic competition in neoclassical economics had already been replaced by the idea of monopolistic and oligopolistic structures under the heading of workable competition (e.g. Scherer and Ross, 1990). A similar development, emphasizing positive feedback effects and increasing returns to scale caused by innovation, led to the attribute 'new' in macroeconomic growth theory in the 1980s (Romer, 1990).

In addition to these stepwise renewals of mainstream methodology, an increasingly larger group claimed that the general toolbox of economic theory, emphasizing rational behaviour and equilibrium, was no longer suitable for the analysis of complex social and economic changes. In a speech at the International Conference on Complex Systems organized by the New England Complex Systems Institute in 2000, Kenneth Arrow stated that, until the 1980s, the 'sea of truth' in economics laid in simplicity, whereas since then it has become recognized that 'the sea of truth lies in complexity'. Adequate tools have therefore to include the heterogeneous composition of agents (see, e.g., Kirman, 1989, 1997b; and Saviotti, 1996), the possibility of multi-level feedback effects or interactions (Kirman, 1997a; Cantner and Pyka, 1998; Fagiolo, 1998) and a realistic representation of dynamic processes in historical time (Arthur, 1988; Marengo and Willinger, 1997). These requirements are congruent with the possibilities offered by simulation approaches. It is not surprising that within economics the first numerical exercises were within evolutionary economics, where phenomena of qualitative change and development are at the front of the research programme.

The first generation of simulation models were highly stylized and did not focus on empirical phenomena. Instead, they were designed to analyse the logic of dynamic economic and social processes, exploring the possibilities of complex systems behaviour (see also the chapters by Windrum and Kwasnicki in this volume).

However, since the end of the 1990s, more and more specific simulation models aiming at particular empirically observed phenomena have been developed, focusing on the interaction of heterogeneous actors responsible for qualitative change and development processes. Modellers have had to wrestle with an unavoidable trade-off between the demand of a general theoretical approach and the descriptive accuracy required to model a particular phenomenon. A new class of simulation models has shown itself to be well adapted to this challenge, basically by shifting outwards this trade-off: so-called agent-based models (ABMs henceforth) are increasingly used for the modelling of socioeconomic developments (see, e.g., Gilbert and Troitzsch, 1999).

Our chapter deals with the new requirements for modelling entailed by the necessity to focus on qualitative developments, pattern formation, etc. which is generally highlighted within neo-Schumpeterian economics and the possibilities given by ABMs. The chapter is organized as follows. In section 2 we examine in more detail the basic motivations underlying the emergence of the ABM paradigm and we sketch its main underpinnings. Section 3 presents the building blocks of an ABM and briefly discusses the extent to which ABMs can be employed to deal with empirical phenomena. Finally, section 4 concludes and flags open problems in the ABM research agenda.

2   Micro–macro systems, mainstream models and agent-based approaches

Generally speaking, ABMs deal with the study of socioeconomic systems that can be properly conceptualized by means of a set of 'micro–macro' relationships. In such systems, the micro level typically contains heterogeneous basic entities, the additional decomposition of which does not help in explaining the phenomena under study (e.g. firms, consumers, workers).

Repeated interactions among these entities over time induce ceaselessly changing microeconomic patterns (e.g. production and consumption levels). These micro patterns, once aggregated over the relevant set of micro entities, generate a macro dynamics for the aggregate variable of interest (e.g. GNP). The goal of ABMs is to properly describe such complicated systems and to analyse their properties. More precisely, agent-based formalizations depict decentralized economies as complex systems and try to infer their aggregate properties – in a bottom-up perspective – from interactions and behaviours of micro entities.

2.1 Mainstream models: a brief critical discussion

As briefly discussed in the introduction, the need for ABM approaches has been mostly driven by an increasing dissatisfaction with how 'mainstream' theorists model 'micro–macro' relationships. The classic reference here is the class of so-called 'micro-founded macroeconomic models' (Sargent, 1987), which became the yardstick for any representation of dynamic decentralized economies composed of agents autonomously undertaking courses of actions and decisions over time (cf. Dosi and Orsenigo, 1994, for a critical discussion).

As is well known, these models take a pragmatic and positivist perspective and solve the trade-off between analytical solvability and descriptive accuracy in favour of the former. Indeed, many oversimplifying assumptions – often considered as 'free goods' – are employed in order to derive sharp, analytical conclusions. For example, the interaction structure (i.e. the assumptions over the set of channels connecting agents and conveying information at each point in time among them) is either of a degenerate type – agents do not interact at all, as happens in models where a 'general equilibrium' microfoundation is assumed – or it can be traced back to a 'complete' network – agents interact with anyone else, as happens in micro–macro models based on a game-theoretic microfoundation. No room for intermediate and more complicated interaction patterns is left on the ground.

In a similar vein, any heterogeneity across agents (concerning e.g. agents' properties such as endowments, wealth and so on, and, more generally, behavioural rules, competencies, learning, etc.) is abolished and, whenever introduced in the model (think e.g. of the standard general equilibrium framework), its role is not even addressed (Kirman, 1989).

Moreover, agents are typically assumed to be hyperrational entities, holding rational (sometimes even technological) expectations and possessing no computational bounds. This is of course at odds with any experimental (and casual, by the way) evidence and has crucial implications in the way aggregate properties and models' outcomes are interpreted (Dosi *et al.*,

2005). In fact, the strong consistency requirements induced by hyperrationality compress any sequence of decisions made over time by the agents into a single and coherent stream of decisions made once and for all in an irreversible manner. These models can generate only equilibrium outcomes, and *only* equilibrium observations can be observed in reality.

These examples show that, in general, the dissatisfaction towards mainstream approaches can be traced back to the way in which the latter deals with some key ingredients of the modelling process as a whole, namely: (i) assumptions and modelling design; (ii) analysis of the properties of the model; (iii) generation of testable implications; (iv) model validation and rejection. Let us briefly summarize here the debate about these four issues.

Assumptions and modelling design   As argued above, mainstream models of dynamic decentralized economies employ assumptions as a 'free good'. They are considered functional to the construction of an analytically solvable model. Sometimes, a feedback process going from model solutions back to assumptions is employed, and the latter are modified to the extent they are able to allow for analytical solutions, no matter whether they still preserve some economic interpretations or not. This can generate awkward and pathological situations, where the answer to the question 'What is the economic intuition behind this result?' is 'The third derivative of the utility function is negative.'

More rigorously, we know from the impressive work in cognitive psychology and experimental economics (Kagel and Roth, 1995; Plott and Smith, 1998) that the classes of assumptions discussed above have almost no links with empirically observed patterns of micro behaviours and interactions, and that, in the case of agents' rationality, interactions, heterogeneity, etc. if any link is present, the assumptions are often *against* the evidence.

This attitude becomes even more manifest as far as innovation and uncertainty modelling is concerned. Given the restrictions imposed e.g. by the hyperrationality paradigm, it is well known that mainstream models are not able to deal with structural innovation endogenously and imperfectly introduced in the system by the agents. These innovative behaviours, which are typically driven by persistent mistakes and trial-and-error learning processes which must cope with a truly uncertain environment (Dosi *et al.*, 2005), cannot be accounted for, almost by construction. However, as we know from a huge empirical literature on innovation and technological change, innovative behaviours in the presence of true uncertainty are at the core of any growth and development process: see, among others, Freeman (1982, 1994), Rosenberg (1982, 1994), David (1975), Dosi (1988), Nelson (1995), Lundvall (1993), Granstrand (1994), Stoneman (1995), and fair parts of Dosi *et al.* (1988) and Foray and Freeman (1992).

Analysis of the properties of the model In turn, the need for sharp, analytical implications, coupled with the nature of the mathematical toolbox employed in the analysis, cf. Sargent (1987), has generated a class of models characterized by an often excessive commitment to equilibrium analysis. As already suggested, any macro property of the system has to be conceptualized as an equilibrium one. In turn, if one assumes that the model is an adequate one to address empirical problems, any real-world observation has to be interpreted as happening in equilibrium. In this way, aggregate behaviour is nothing other than a straightforward and tautological implication of the micro level: after all, individual behaviours must be coherent in equilibrium over time and agents are all the same (see, however, Kirman, 1992, and Forni and Lippi, 1997, for a discussion on the risks of interpreting aggregate outcomes in mainstream microfounded macro models).

Generation of testable implications A large part of mainstream micro–macro formalizations we are discussing here must be interpreted as toy models which provide a theoretical ground where some basic socioeconomic principles and causal chains can be better spelled out. These models do not deliver any testable implications and therefore cannot be taken to the data in order to be validated.

However, the belief of many scholars is that this critique applies more generally to the entire class of micro–macro formalizations. Whenever the model is built in order to explain or reproduce some 'stylized fact' or observable property, it is maintained, there is the feeling that the number of oversimplifying, adhoc assumptions required to get analytically solvable implications in line with the observed phenomena increases enormously with the number of facts that one would like to explain simultaneously. Examples here range from labour market dynamics, to growth and development, consumption and demand, etc.: in all these cases one often finds many simple models each addressing a separate fact in isolation, rather than more robust models explaining together many related facts (see e.g. the discussion in Fagiolo *et al.*, 2004a).

In brief, mainstream models often pay limited attention to empirical validation and joint reproduction of stylized facts. This is true not only as far as macrodynamics is concerned, but also, more dramatically, at the micro level: consider for instance the lack of micro–macro models that jointly replicate *micro stylized facts* such as firm size and growth distributions across sectors and *macro stylized facts* concerning statistical properties of aggregated growth time-series.

Model validation and rejection Mainly as a consequence of the points discussed above, mainstream micro–macro models lack a serious procedure of model development, with obsolete and weakly performing models replaced by better ones. Model performance is related here to the ability of a model in replicating and explaining (possibly many) stylized facts and observable phenomena.

The common practice is instead that of retaining as much as possible the analytical apparatus (and, with it, the main philosophical building blocks) informing mainstream, neoclassical microfounded macro models. Optimization, forward-looking rational expectations, equilibrium, representative individuals, etc. continue to form the core of these formalizations despite their often limited explicative and interpretative capabilities.

A crucial question then must be asked. As Richard Day put it in his plenary talk at the 11th Annual Symposium of the Society for Nonlinear Dynamics and Econometrics (2003): 'Can one do good science with assumptions that are clearly at odds with any empirical evidence about micro behaviour?'

This question may in our view perfectly synthesize the debate that we have been trying to sketch so far. More to the point: there seems to be a sort of pathological pessimism of neoclassical economics with respect to many ingredients which empirical evidence points at as *the* crucial ones for understanding micro–macro relationships. Our preferred example is once again innovation. Without a minimum willingness to cope with true uncertainty, innovation processes cannot be analysed. In traditional economic modelling approaches, this minimum willingness is not reproducible: economic agents always prefer 'risky' to 'uncertain' situations.

2.2   Agent-based modelling: an alternative modelling methodology
In the last 20 years, an alternative modelling strategy has been pursued by an increasingly large number of scholars, often sharing an interdisciplinary perspective drawing stimuli, inspirations and ideas from disciplines such as biology, physics, sociology, history and computer science.

Methodologically, this alternative strategy, which we have labelled 'agent-based modelling', is rooted in the use of numerical techniques and simulation analysis, which are regarded as major tools in developing and analysing this class of models (Kwasnicki, 1998; Aruka, 2001). Although simulation analysis comes in various flavours, most of them reflect Boulding's call that we need to develop 'mathematics which is suitable to social systems, which the sort of 18th-century mathematics which we use is not' (Boulding, 1991).

In a nutshell, this approach consists of a decentralized collection of agents acting autonomously in various contexts (see section 3, below, for a more detailed description). The massively parallel and local interactions can give rise to path dependency, dynamic returns and feedbacks between the two. In such an environment, global phenomena such as the development and diffusion of technologies, the emergence of networks, herd behaviour, etc. – which cause the transformation of the observed system – can be modelled adequately. This modelling approach focuses on depicting the agents, their relationships and the processes governing the transformation.

Broadly speaking, the application of an *agent–based modelling approach* offers two major advantages. The first advantage of ABMs is their capability to show how collective phenomena came about and how the interaction of the autonomous and heterogeneous agents leads to the genesis of these phenomena. Furthermore, agent-based modelling aims at the isolation of critical behaviour in order to identify agents that more than others drive the collective result of the system. It also endeavours to single out points of time where the system exhibits qualitative rather than sheer quantitative change (Tesfatsion, 2001b). In this light, it becomes clear why agent-based modelling conforms to the principles of neo-Schumpeterian economics (Lane, 1993a, 1993b). It is 'the' modelling approach to be pursued in evolutionary settings.

The second advantage of ABM, which is complementary to the first one, is a more normative one. Agent-based models are not only used to get a deeper understanding of the inherent forces that drive a system and influence the characteristics of a system. Agent-based modellers use their models as computational laboratories to explore various institutional arrangements, various potential paths of development so as to assist and guide firms, policy makers, etc., in their particular decision context.

ABM thus uses methods and insights from diverse disciplines such as complexity sciences, cognitive science and computer science in its attempt to model the bottom-up emergence of phenomena and the top-down influence of the collective phenomena on individual behaviour (Tesfatsion, 2002).

The recent developments in new programming techniques (such as object-oriented programming) and, in particular, the advent of powerful tools of computation such as evolutionary computation (for a summary of the use of evolutionary computation and genetic programming in particular, see Ebersberger, 2002) opens up the opportunity for economists to model economic systems on a more realistic (complex) basis (Tesfatsion, 2001b).

Before describing in more detail the structure of ABMs, a remark is in order. In recent years, many classes of formalizations that basically share the same philosophical and methodological underpinnings (e.g. focus on agents, heterogeneity, bounded rationality, nontrivial interaction structures, true uncertainty, etc.), but have been labelled in different ways, have emerged in both theoretical and applied literature. Evolutionary economics, agent-based computational economics, neo-Schumpeterian models and history-friendly models, to cite only a few of them, have all been addressing similar questions on the grounds of similar approaches. In what follows, we will try to discuss the common features of these classes of models, rather than the distinctive ones. In fact, we prefer to consider them as complementary approaches, rather than 'competing brands'. Of course, one has to be aware that, from a descriptive perspective, the dimensions along which these classes of models differ might also characterize in a positive way their richness and their ultimate goals. For example, evolutionary models typically stress the selection dimension of market mechanisms, while the 'Agent-based Computational Economics' (ACE) models mainly focus both on the tool used to build and analyse them (e.g. object-oriented programming) and on the open-ended, evolving nature of individual behavioural rules.

3   Agent-based models in economics

3.1   Building blocks
Irrespective of the particular label under which different classes of ABMs have become known among economics scholars, they all share a common set of qualitative assumptions that reflect their underlying modelling philosophy. In what follows, we will try to discuss the most important ones. Our goal is, first, to define the boundaries of an admittedly huge class of models (or a 'meta-model') and, second, to single out some relevant subclasses of models that can be considered instances of that meta-model, but only feature a subset of building blocks.

Bottom-up philosophy   Any satisfactory account of a decentralized economy must be addressed in a bottom-up perspective (Tesfatsion, 2002). Aggregate properties must be viewed as the outcome of micro dynamics involving basic entities (agents). This approach might be contrasted with the typical top-down nature of all mainstream micro–macro models, where the bottom level is typically compressed into the behaviour of a representative individual.

The evolving complex system (ECS) approach   Agents live in complex systems evolving through time (Kirman, 1998). Therefore, aggregate properties are seen to emerge out of repeated interactions among simple entities, rather than from consistency requirements carried through by rationality and equilibrium assumptions made by the modeller.

Heterogeneity   Agents are (or might be) heterogeneous in almost all their characteristics. The latter range from endowments and other agents' properties, all the way to behavioural rules, competencies, and rationality and computational skills.

Bounded rationality   The environment where agents are thought to live is too complex for any notion of 'hyperrationality' to be viable (Dosi *et al.*, 2005). Therefore, one might at most impute to the agents some local (both in space and time) and partial principles of rationality, e.g. a myopic optimization rule. More generally, agents are assumed to behave as boundedly rational entities with adaptive expectations. Contrary to mainstream 'neo-classical' models – where, *strictu sensu*, learning cannot take place as the agents already know everything they need to – here many forms of uncertainty can be postulated (e.g. substantive v. procedural, risky environment v. true uncertainty). Consequently, different regimes of individual and collective learning can be modelled. For example, learning on 'fixed menus' v. learning in open-ended (endogenously evolving) spaces, learning on the spaces of actions/strategies, learning on the representations of the world, learning on the space of performances, learning on the space of preferences (Dosi *et al.*, 2005).

'True' dynamics   Partly as a consequence of adaptive expectations (i.e. agents observe the past and form expectations about the future on the basis of the past), ABMs are characterized by a true, non-reversible, dynamics: the state of the system evolves path-dependently and cannot be considered as a coherent *whole* as happens in mainstream models (Marengo and Willinger, 1997).

Direct (endogenous) interactions   Agents interact directly: the decisions undertaken today by any agent directly depend, through adaptive expectations, on past choices made by subgroups of other agents in the population (Fagiolo, 1998). These subgroups are typically those who are the 'closest ones' in some socioeconomic spaces (i.e. the 'neighbours' or the 'relevant ones'). In turn, these interaction structures may change endogenously over time, as agents can decide strategically whom to interact with on the basis of expected payoffs. All that, together with heterogeneity and bounded rationality, may of course entail nontrivial aggregation processes, non-linearities and, sometimes, the emergence of structurally new objects.

Endogenous and persistent novelty   Socioeconomic systems are inherently non-stationary. Agents face 'true uncertainty', as they are only partly able to form expectations e.g. on technological outcomes. Agents can introduce endogenously, through their decisions, structural changes in technological spaces, which typically become open-ended.

Selection-based market mechanisms   Agents are typically selected against – over many different dimensions – by market mechanisms (Nelson and

Winter, 1982). This generates, e.g. in industry dynamics, additional turbulence in the system due to the entry–exit process of firms.

3.2 The basic structure of ABMs

Let us now turn to a more formal description of the basic structure of an ABM. As we did for its methodological building blocks, we will list here a very broad set of ingredients. We will then briefly comment on the flexibility of this description and we will provide some examples of existing classes of models that are in the spirit of ABM and share an increasingly larger set of building blocks.

a. *Time*: we typically model a system evolving in discrete time steps, i.e. $t = 1, 2, \ldots$

b. *Agents (or actors)*: the system is populated by a set of agents $I_t = \{1, 2, \ldots, N_t\}$. In many examples, but not necessarily all, a constant population size is assumed ($N_t = N$).

c. *Micro states (or actions)*: each agent $i \in I_t$ is characterized by a vector of L microeconomic states (or micro-variables) $\underline{x}_{i,t} = (x^1_{i,t}, \ldots, x^L_{i,t})$. These variables are fast ones, which can be endogenously modified by agents' decisions (e.g. firm's output, consumption levels, etc.)

d. *Micro-parameters*: each agent $i \in I_t$ is also characterized by a vector of H microeconomic parameters $\underline{\theta}_i = (\theta^1_i, \ldots, \theta^H_i)$. Micro-parameters are slow-variables, i.e. quantities that cannot be endogenously modified by the agents within the time-scale of the dynamic process. Therefore, θ_i typically contains information about behavioural and technological characteristics of agent i (e.g. endowments, firms' factors productivity, workers' reservation wages, consumption elasticities, etc.).

e. *Macro-parameters:* the system as a whole is instead characterized by a vector of M time-independent macro-parameters $\underline{\Theta} = (\Theta_1, \ldots, \Theta_M)$ governing the overall technological and institutional setup. Once again, $\underline{\Theta}$ are slow-variables and cannot be modified by the agents. Examples of $\underline{\Theta}$ parameters are the level of opportunities in a technological environment, the strength of unions in wage-bargaining, etc.

f. *Interaction structures*: at each t, the way in which information is channelled among agents is governed by a (directed and possibly weighted) graph G_t containing all directed links i_{jt} currently in place (i.e. open) from agent i to agent j. The existence of a directed link i_{jt} means that agent i, when he updates his micro-variables $\underline{x}_{it}$, is affected by the choices made in the past by agent j (i.e. past j's micro variables).

g. *Micro decision rules*: each agent is endowed with a set of decision rules $(\mathfrak{R}_{i,t} = \{R^b_{i,t}(\bullet \mid \bullet), b = 1, \ldots, B\}$, mapping observable variables (e.g.

past micro variables of relevant agents, micro and macro parameters, etc.) into next-period micro-variables $x_{it}+1$. Examples of such decision rules are production functions, innovation rules, consumers' demand, etc.

h. *Aggregate variables*: by aggregation (e.g. average, sum) of micro-variables, one obtains a vector of **K** macro-variables $\mathbf{X}_t = (X^1_t, \ldots, X^K_t)$ which contain all macro information relevant to the analysis of the system. Examples are: GDP, aggregate demand, unemployment, etc. Moreover, $\underline{X}_t$ can appear as arguments of $R^b_{i,t}$ as well: this is a source of feedbacks from the macro level to the micro level.

Notice that, on the basis of these broad ingredients, one can conceive a huge class of applications. Indeed, the flexibility of the agent-based approach, together with the easiness of implementing in a modular way alternative assumptions through computer programming, allows one to envisage a large spectrum of models. For example, micro decision rules can fall in the wide range whose extremes are represented by (deterministic or stochastic) best-replies rules (as in evolutionary games), routines (as employed e.g. in evolutionary and neo-Schumpeterian models, see also below) and by algorithmic, complicated, if-then rules, accounting for a large number of conditions and non-linear feedbacks (as happens in artificial-intelligence applications such as neural networks, genetic programming, etc.). Similarly, expectations can have the form of simple myopic rules (i.e. 'tomorrow will be like today') or can employ in more intelligent ways large amounts of information coming from the past (as happens in econometric-based prediction models). Different interaction structures can also be experimented with. This allows one to answer questions related to whether the properties of the networks where agents are placed (i.e. regular v. asymmetric, small-worlds, hierarchic relations; competitive v. cooperative interaction patterns, bilateral v. multilateral links, etc.) affect the aggregate properties of the system. Finally, one can compare systems where micro decision rules and networks are static, with others where agents can act endogenously and strategically over their own rules and interaction links (i.e. additional, agent-specific, meta-rules are assumed that govern how $\Re_{i,t}$ and G_t change endogenously).

As one can see, many classes of well known, recently surfacing models can be traced back to the meta-model presented above. Examples range from evolutionary games (Vega-Redondo, 1996), (local) interaction models (Fagiolo, 1998), endogenous network-formation models (Fagiolo *et al.*, 2004b, Pyka *et al.*, 2004), and Polya-urn schemes (Arthur, 1994) to more microfounded models such as industry dynamics models in the Nelson and Winter spirit, evolutionary growth models (Silverberg and Verspagen,

1994; Fagiolo and Dosi, 2003) and ACE models of market dynamics (Epstein and Axtell, 1996; Tesfatsion, 2001a, Grebel *et al.*, 2003).

3.3   The outcomes of ABMs and their analysis

Let us consider now how a system modelled as in Section 3.2 evolves through time. At each point in time, the agents, according to their decision rules, update micro-variables.

A particular updating scheme (i.e. a rule that governs how many – and who – are allowed to update their micro-variables at time t) is typically assumed. This scheme will have an asynchronous nature if only a subset of all agents (at one extreme, *only one of them*) is allowed to reconsider the state of their micro-variables. Conversely, we will postulate a parallel updating scheme if *all* agents will have the opportunity to update their micro-variables. Notice that this is a crucial assumption as far as asymmetry of information is concerned: the more the updating scheme will be asynchronous, the more agents will tend to act over different information sets (see also Page, 1997).

Suppose some choice for initial conditions about variables and parameters, both at the micro and at the macro level has been done. Then, the dynamics of $\mathbf{x}_t = (\underline{x}_{1,t}, \ldots, \underline{x}_{N,t})$ induced at the micro-level by individual updating will entail at the macro level, simply by aggregation, a dynamics over the set of macro-variables $\underline{X}_t = (\underline{X}^1_t, \ldots, \underline{X}^K_t)$.

The stochastic components possibly present in decision rules, expectations and interactions will in turn imply that the dynamics of micro and macro variables can be described by some (Markovian) stochastic process parameterized by the micro-parameters matrix $\underline{\theta} = (\underline{\theta}'_1, \ldots, \underline{\theta}'_N)$ and the macro-parameter vector $\underline{\Theta}$ (given initial conditions $\mathbf{x}_0$ and $\underline{X}_0$).

Non-linearities which are typically induced by decision rules, expectations, and interactions networks and feedbacks, may imply that it is hard to derive analytically laws of motion, kernel distributions, time-t probability distributions, etc. for the stochastic processes governing $\{\mathbf{x}_t\}$ and $\{\underline{X}_t\}$, and a fortiori the two jointly.

This implies that the researcher must often resort to computer simulations in order to analyse the behaviour of the system he/she has modelled along the lines sketched in the general framework of section 3.2. Two remarks are in order. First, in some simple cases such systems allow for analytical solutions of some kind. For example, some evolutionary games models (Vega-Redondo, 1996) allow for analytical solutions as far as equilibria and the size of their basin of attraction are concerned. Needless to say, the more one injects into the model assumptions sharing the philosophy of building blocks discussed in section 3.1, the less tractable the model turns out to be, and the more one needs to resort to computer simulations.

Second, we employ here the term 'computer simulation' in a very broad sense. As we briefly noticed in the introduction, one might indeed think of an entire range of simulation analyses. At one extreme, one might employ simulation-like exercises to find numerical solutions of dynamical problems that have some closed-form representation, e.g. in terms of systems of (partial) differential equations (see Judd, 1998; Amman *et al.*, 1996). Similarly, simulation techniques might be used to address the study of the properties of some particular test statistics or estimator in econometrics (Gourieroux and Monfort, 1996). At the other extreme, one might employ simulations in a more constructive way either to reproduce algorithmically the rules entailed by some complicated dynamic game (cf. for example, Fagiolo, 2005), or to 'grow' a society 'from the bottom up', in the spirit of object-oriented programming (cf. Epstein and Axtell, 1996; Tesfatsion, 2001a).

When studying the outcomes of ABMs, the researcher often faces the problem that the economy he/she is modelling is by definition out-of-equilibrium (Fisher, 1985). The focus is seldom on static equilibria or steady-state paths. Rather, the researcher must more often look for long-run statistical equilibria (cf. e.g. Foley, 1994) and emergent/transient (statistical) properties of aggregate dynamics (Lane, 1993a, 1993b). Such an exploration is by definition very complicated and it is made even more difficult by the fact that the researcher does not even know in advance whether the stochastic process described by its AGM is ergodic or not and, if it somehow converges, how much time it will take for the behaviour to become sufficiently stable.

Suppose for a moment that the modeller knows, e.g. from a preliminary simulation study or from some ex ante knowledge coming from the particular structure of the ABM under study, that the dynamic behaviour of the system becomes sufficiently stable after some time horizon T^* for (almost all) points of the parameter space.

Then a possible procedure that can be implemented to study the output of the ABM runs as the one synthetically depicted in Figure 29.1 (see Fagiolo and Dosi, 2003, for an example of such a procedure). Given some choice for initial conditions, micro and macro parameters (i.e. θ, Θ, x_0 and X_0), assume running our system until it relaxes to some stable behaviour (i.e. for at least $T > T^*$ time steps). Suppose we are interested in a set $S = \{s_1, s_2, \ldots\}$ of statistics to be computed on the simulated data $\{x_t, t = 1, \ldots, T\}$ and $\{X_t, t = 1, \ldots, T\}$. For example, one of the micro variables might be individual firm's output and the correspondent macro variable could then be GNP. In such a case, one could be interested in an aggregate statistics s_j like the average rate of growth of the economy over the T time-steps (e.g. quarters). For any given run $m = 1, 2, \ldots, M$, the programme will

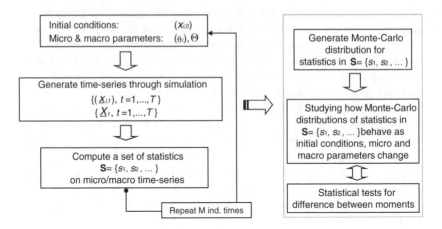

Figure 29.1   Statistical analysis of agent-based models: a suggested Monte-Carlo approach

output a value for s_j. Given the stochastic nature of the process, each run, and thus each value of s_j, will be different from the other ones. Therefore, having produced M independent runs, one has a distribution for s_j containing M observations, which can be summarized by computing e.g. its mean $E(s_j)$, its variance $V(s_j)$, etc.

Recall, however, that moments will depend on the choice for θ, Θ, $\mathbf{x}_0$ and $\underline{X}_0$. By exploring a sufficiently large number of points in the space where initial conditions and parameters are allowed to vary, and by computing $E(s_j)$, $V(s_j)$, etc. at each point, one might get a quite deep understanding of the behaviour of the system. Consider again the output example introduced above. For instance, one may simply plot $E(s_j)$, that is the Monte-Carlo mean of the economy's average growth rates, against some important macro parameters such as the level of aggregate propensity to invest in R&D. This might allow one to understand whether the overall performance of the economy increases in the model with that propensity. Moreover, non-parametric statistical tests may be conducted to check if $E(s_j)$ significantly differs in two extreme cases, e.g. high v. low propensity to invest in R&D.

3.4   Model selection and empirical validation in ABMs

From the foregoing discussion it clearly emerges that, in agent-based modelling, as in many other modelling endeavours, one often faces a trade-off between *descriptive accuracy* and *explanatory power* of the model. The more one tries to inject into the model 'realist' assumptions such as agents' heterogeneity, open-ended evolution, endogenous interactions, structural innovation, boundedly-rational behaviours, etc., the more the system becomes complicated to study and the less clear the causal relations going from assumptions to implications are. ABM researchers are well aware of this problem and have been trying to develop an effective strategy to select 'bad' from 'good' models (see e.g. Edmonds and Moss, 2004; Frenken, 2005; Werker and Brenner, 2004; and Windrum's chapter in this book).

A first set of strategies, which is typically applied in the early stages of model building, concerns the process of assumption selection. For example, one can judge a model on the basis of the 'realism' of its assumptions (Mäki, 1994), where an assumption has a higher degree of realism if it is supported by some robust experimental evidence. Alternatively, one can try to solve the trade-off between descriptive capability and explanatory power, either by beginning with the most simple model and complicating it step-by-step (i.e. the so-called KISS strategy, an acronym standing for 'Keep it simple, stupid!') or by starting with the most descriptive model and simplify it as much as possible (i.e. the so-called KIDS strategy, 'Keep it descriptive, stupid!'). A third, alternative strategy prescribes instead starting with an existing model and successively complicating it with incremental additions (this strategy might be labelled TAPAS, which stands for 'Take a previous model and add something'). In all these procedures, the crucial variable that should be able to discriminate the point at which any procedure should stop would determine the explanatory power of the model.

This is where a second set of strategies, which typically applies ex post, once a sufficiently small number of 'satisficing' models has been developed, enters the picture. This second set of strategies is indeed based on how good the model is at replicating reality. Notice that the very structure of ABMs naturally allows one to take the model to the data and validate it against observed real-world observations. Indeed, an ABM model can be thought to provide a family of data generation processes (DGPs), of which we think real-world observations are a realization.

Many approaches to empirical validation (and selection) of ABMs can in principle be taken, and the debate is very open here. For example, one might select among ABMs (and within different parameter setups of the same ABM) with respect to the number of stylized facts each of them is able jointly to replicate. A typical procedure to be followed starts with asking whether a particular model is able jointly to replicate some set of stylized facts for a given parameterization (a sort of 'exercise in plausibility'); then explore what happens when the parameter setup changes; finally, examine if some meaningful causal explanation can be derived out of that step-by-step analysis. Alternatively, one can first select among parameters by calibrating the model (e.g. by directly estimating parameters, when possible, with micro or macro data) and then judge to what extent the calibrated model is able to reproduce the stylized facts of interest.

It must be noticed, however, that the issue whether an ABM should deliver quantitative implications (and must then be judged on the grounds of its fit with real-world data) is still open. Some scholars advocate, for instance, that an ABM should be used as a 'research' tool addressing qualitative issues only: in this view, ABMs are viewed as laboratories where some simple theories, often in the form of causal relationships, can be tested (Valente, 2004). As empirical validation is no longer required, there is no need for either calibration exercises or Monte-Carlo types of explorations of the space of parameters. Indeed, in one way or the other, both types of exercises aim at selecting a preferred world (i.e. a particular DGP among the family postulated by the ABM description) and can be considered as a strategy to maximize indirectly the likelihood of a particular DGP. In other words, among the space of all parameters and initial conditions, one tries to select the one that it is assumed to generate – with the highest probability – the 'unique' observation that we have in reality. If one instead employs ABMs as generators of qualitative and causal implications only, a low-probability event generated by the model is also important (and often crucial) to understanding some casual mechanism going on in the real world. After all, the world where we live could well have been the outcome of a small probability event.

3.5   Designing agents in ABMs: beyond the basic framework

In ABMs, agents are considered as being the major driving force of evolution. As such, we regard them as the reason for the manifestation of qualitative developments going on in the system. Being the crucial component of the system, their description can go well beyond the introductory one presented above.

To begin with, one can think to implement a multi-agent approach, which assumes that agents populating the model can be divided into various categories, according to their initial endowments (availability of capital, entrepreneurial attitude, technological competencies etc.).

Accordingly, a central issue is the general design of the agents. Agents might be represented as a piece of code that has the standard attributes of intelligent agents (Wooldridge and Jennings, 1995) that is (i) *autonomy*, which means that agents operate without other agents having direct control of their actions and internal states. This is a necessary condition for implementing heterogeneity; (ii) *social ability*, i.e. agents are able to interact with other agents not only in terms of competition but also in terms of cooperation. This includes the possibility to model agents that show various forms of interaction blended from competition and cooperation; (iii) *reactivity*, with agents being able to perceive their environment and respond to it; (iv) *proactivity*, which enables the agents to take initiatives. This means that they are not only adapting to changing circumstances; rather are they engaged in goal-directed behaviour.

The above points indicate that the actors in the simulation are not only able to adapt their behaviour to a given set of circumstances but are also in a neo-Schumpeterian sense able to learn from their own experience and to modify their behaviour creatively so as to change the circumstances themselves.

In turn, decision rules (often in the form of routines) allow actors to manipulate the reality. It is not only the endowment with resources that shapes the nature of the actors, it is their individual routines that make up a large part of the actors' heterogeneity. Nelson and Winter (1982) relate routines to satisficing behaviour and bounded rationality of actors. Routinized behaviour causes some stickiness and some inertia of the system that results in some stability of the system – stability, at least to a certain degree. Furthermore, routines are not only focused on internal procedures of the actors, but they also govern external relationships with actors of the same basic group and with actors of other groups.

Finally, ABMs' micro parameters often take the form of initial endowments. Access to material and immaterial resources and their availability together with the individual experiences, make up the endowment of the agents. They combine the different components in order to realize their goals. Accordingly, endowments are the crucial assets of agents in accomplishing their tasks. Agents are typically heterogeneous in their sets of endowments. It is obvious that autonomy of agents can only be achieved with the notion of personal and individual endowment of certain factors. It is the idea of individual property rights on production factors or income that enables us to model actors acting on their sets of endowments.

4 Conclusions

In this chapter we have attempted to provide an introduction to ABMs in economics. We have begun with a discussion of the main motivations that, in recent years, led many scholars to supplement 'mainstream' (neoclassical) treatments of microfounded models of macrodynamics with alternative approaches, rooted in 'more realist' assumptions such as heterogeneity, interactions, bounded rationality, endogenous novelty, etc. After presenting the building blocks shared by this class of models, we suggested a meta structure common to (almost all) ABMs employed in economics. Finally, we examined some standard strategies used to analyse the outcomes of ABMs.

In our view, the attempt to model the aggregate dynamics of decentralized economies on the basis of a more detailed (and more realist) microfoundation such as the one postulated by ABMs is the primary requirement to pursue one of the most prominent challenges in social sciences today, namely the analysis of qualitative change. Our discussion suggests that ABMs are offering an adequate framework for this, overcoming the severe restrictions with which orthodox economic approaches are confronted. By emphasizing the role of true uncertainty and irreversibility, one is able to model qualitative development as an endogenous process driven by the agents and their interactions.

Agent-based models allow for an explicit consideration of these characteristic features, and therefore can be considered as 'the' modelling tool for the analysis of qualitative development and transformation processes. In a way, agent based models can be considered a systemic approach, allowing the consideration and integration of different social 'realities' which makes them an extremely valuable tool for the analysis of social processes which can be generally considered as multifaceted phenomena.

The field of agent-based modelling is (especially in economics, but more generally in social sciences) very far from its maturity. Many issues, especially methodological ones, are still debated, both on the model development side and on the model analysis side. Here, by way of conclusion, we will try to mention briefly some of the most crucial ones.

First, on the model building and development side, one faces a huge heterogeneity in the way agents and their behavioural and interaction rules are assumed and implemented. In the relevant literature, one often deals with many structurally different ABMs addressing very similar issues. This practice, which is ultimately caused by the flexibility of programming languages and their heterogeneity, can certainly turn out to be a plus, because it might favour a better understanding of the deep causes of a given phenomenon. However, it can also generate in the long run an inherent impossibility to compare different models and to pursue a coherent procedure of model improvement (with old and obsolete models replaced by higher-performance ones).

Second, and relatedly, an agent-based modeller confronting the KISS v. KIDS problem will often end up with an overparameterized model. In order to limit as much as possible all critiques regarding the robustness of results to different parameterizations and initial conditions, an exhaustive exploration of both parameters' and initial conditions' sets is required. But, even when the ABM has been thoroughly analysed e.g. along the lines suggested in section 3.3, some further problems arise. To begin with, how can one know for sure that the system is ergodic? And, even if it is ergodic, how can one be sure of having correctly estimated the relaxation time of our stochastic process? And, even more importantly, how can one be sure not to have neglected some truly 'emergent' properties? After all, any truly emergent property should not be totally comprehensible on the grounds of the 'alphabet', 'syntax' and 'grammar' which we employed to describe existing entities.

Third, even when the foregoing critiques have been carefully considered, an agent-based modeller should be aware of the fact that all his/her results could be heavily affected by the particular sets of behavioural and interaction rules that he/she has assumed. Those rules are often kept fixed across time. This can be justified by the observation that the rules themselves typically change more slowly than the variables which they act upon (e.g. micro and macro variables). However, in the evolutionary spirit informing ABMs, a necessary step would be that of modelling the rules themselves as endogenously changing objects. An example here concerns learning and decision rules, which can be endogenously modified by the agents along the process.

Finally, on the normative side, it must be noted that so far ABMs have almost exclusively addressed the issue of replication of stylized facts. However, ABMs can and should be employed to address policy issues as well. A need for increasingly normative-oriented ABMs delivering policy implications and out-of-sample predictions is nowadays strongly felt in the community. Thanks to the flexibility and the power of agent-based approaches, it is easy to conceive frameworks where policy experiments are carried out to evaluate the effectiveness of different policy measures (e.g., antitrust policies), for a range of different institutional setups and behavioural rules.

References

Amman, H., Kendrick, D. and Rust, J. (1996), *Handbook of Computational Economics*, Elsevier–North-Holland, Amsterdam.
Arthur, W.B. (1988), 'Competing technologies: an overview', in G. Dosi *et al.* (eds), *Technical Change and Economic Theory*, Pinter, London.
Arthur, W.B. (1994), *Increasing Returns and Path-dependency in Economics*, University of Michigan Press, Ann Arbor.
Aruka, Y. (2001), *Evolutionary Controversies in Economics: A New Transdisciplinary Approach*, Springer, Tokyo and Berlin.
Boulding, K.E. (1991), 'What is evolutionary economics?', *Journal of Evolutionary Economics*, **1**, 9–17.
Cantner, U. and Pyka, A. (1998), 'Technological evolution – an analysis within the knowledge-based approach', *Structural Change and Economic Dynamics*, **9**, 85–108.
David, P.A. (1975), *Technical Choice, Innovation and Economic Growth*, Cambridge University Press, Cambridge.
Dosi, G. (1988), 'Sources, procedures and microeconomic effects of innovation', *Journal of Economic Literature*, **26**, 126–71.
Dosi, G. and Orsenigo, L. (1994), 'Macrodynamics and microfoundations: an evolutionary perspective', in O. Granstrand (ed.), *The Economics of Technology*, North-Holland, Amsterdam.
Dosi, G., Marengo, L. and Fagiolo, G. (2005), 'Learning in evolutionary environment', in K. Dopfer (ed.), *Evolutionary Principles of Economics*, Cambridge University Press, Cambridge.
Dosi, G., Freeman, C., Nelson, R.R., Silverberg, G. and Soete, L. (1988) (eds), *Technical Change and Economic Theory*, Pinter, London.
Ebersberger, B. (2002), *Genetische Programmierung: Ein Instrument zur empirischen Fundierung ökonomischer Modelle*, DUV-Verlag, Wiesbaden.

Edmonds, B. and Moss, S. (2004), 'From KISS to KIDS: an "anti-simplistic" modelling approach', Centre for Policy Modelling, Manchester Metropolitan University, mimeo.

Epstein, J.M. and Axtell, R. (1996), *Growing Artificial Societies: Social Science from the Bottom-Up*, MIT Press and Brookings Press, Washington, DC.

Fagiolo, G. (1998), 'Spatial interactions in dynamic decentralized economies: a review', in P. Cohendet, P. Llerena, H. Stahn and G. Umbhauer (eds), *The Economics of Networks. Interaction and Behaviours*, Springer Verlag, Berlin/Heidelberg.

Fagiolo, G. (2005), 'Endogenous neighborhood formation in a local coordination model with negative network externalities', *Journal of Economic Dynamics and Control*, **29**, 297–319.

Fagiolo, G. and Dosi, G. (2003), 'Exploitation, exploration and innovation in a model of endogenous growth with locally interacting agents', *Structural Change and Economic Dynamics*, **14**, 237–73.

Fagiolo, G., Dosi, G. and Gabriele, R. (2004a), 'Matching, bargaining, and wage setting in an evolutionary model of labor market and output dynamics', *Advances in Complex Systems*, **14**, 237–73.

Fagiolo, G., Marengo, L. and Valente, M. (2004b), 'Endogenous networks in random population games', *Mathematical Population Studies*, **11**, 121–47.

Fisher, F.M. (1985), *Disequilibrium Foundations of Equilibrium Economics*, Cambridge University Press, Cambridge.

Foley, D.K. (1994), 'A statistical equilibrium theory of markets', *Journal of Economic Theory*, **62**, 321–45.

Foray, D. and Freeman, C. (1992), *Technology and the Wealth of Nations*, OECD, Paris.

Forni, M. and Lippi, M. (1997), *Aggregation and the Microfoundations of Dynamic Macroeconomics*, Clarendon Press, Oxford.

Freeman, C. (1982), *The Economics of Industrial Innovation*, Pinter, London.

Freeman, C. (1994), 'The economics of technical change', *Cambridge Journal of Economics*, **18**, 463–514.

Frenken, K. (2005), 'History, state and prospects of evolutionary models of technical change: a review with special emphasis on complexity theory', Utrecht University, The Netherlands, mimeo.

Gilbert, N. and Troitzsch, K. (1999), *Simulation for the Social Scientist*, Open University Press, Milton Keynes.

Gourieroux, C. and Monfort, A. (1996), *Simulation-based Econometric Models*, Oxford University Press, Oxford.

Granstrand, O. (ed.) (1994), *The Economics of Technology*, North-Holland, Amsterdam.

Grebel, T., Pyka, A. and Hanusch, H. (2003), 'An evolutionary approach to the theory of the entrepreneur', *Industry and Innovation*, **10**, December, 493–514.

Judd, K. (1998), *Numerical Methods in Economics*, MIT Press, Cambridge, MA.

Kagel, J.H. and Roth, A.E. (eds) (1995), *The Handbook of Experimental Economics*, vol. 1, Princeton University Press, Princeton.

Kirman, A.P. (1989), 'The intrinsic limits of modern economic theory: the emperor has no clothes', *Economic Journal*, **99**, 126–39.

Kirman, A.P. (1992), 'Whom or what does the representative individual represent?', *Journal of Economic Perspectives*, **6**, 117–36.

Kirman, A.P. (1997a), 'The economy as an interactive system', in W.B. Arthur, S.N. Durlauf and D. Lane (eds), *The Economy as an Evolving Complex System II*, Addison-Wesley, Santa Fe Institute, Santa Fe and Reading, MA.

Kirman, A.P. (1997b), 'The economy as an evolving network', *Journal of Evolutionary Economics*, **7**, 339–53.

Kirman, A.P. (1998), 'Self-organization and evolution', in F. Schweitzer and G. Silverberg (eds), *Evolution und Selbstorganisation in der Ökonomie, Selbstorganisation: Jahrbuch für Komplexität in den Natur-, Sozial- und Geisteswissenschaften*, vol. 9, Duncker & Humblot, Berlin.

Kwáśnicki, W. (1998), 'Simulation methodology in evolutionary economics', in F. Schweitzer and G. Silverberg (eds), *Evolution und Selbstorganisation in der Ökonomie,*

Selbstorganisation: Jahrbuch für Komplexität in den Natur-, Sozial- und Geisteswissenschaften, vol. 9, Duncker & Humblot, Berlin.

Lane, D. (1993a), 'Artificial worlds and economics, part I', *Journal of Evolutionary Economics*, **3**, 89–107.

Lane, D. (1993b), 'Artificial worlds and economics, part II', *Journal of Evolutionary Economics*, **3**, 177–97.

Lundvall, B.-Å. (1993), *National Systems of Innovation*, Pinter, London.

Mäki, U. (1994), 'Reorienting the assumptions issue', in R. Backhouse (ed.), *New Directions in Economic Methodology*, Routledge, London and New York.

Marengo, L. and Willinger, M. (1997), 'Alternative methodologies for modeling evolutionary dynamics: introduction', *Journal of Evolutionary Economics*, **7**, 331–8.

Nelson, R.R. (1995), 'Recent evolutionary theorizing about economic change', *Journal of Economic Literature*, **33**, 48–90.

Nelson, R.R. and Winter, S.G. (1982), *An Evolutionary Theory of Economic Change*, Cambridge University Press, Cambridge.

Page, S.E. (1997), 'On incentives and updating in agent based models', *Computational Economics*, **10**, 67–87.

Plott, C.R. and Smith, V.L. (eds) (1998), *Handbook of Experimental Economics Results*, North-Holland, Amsterdam/New York.

Pyka, A., Ahrweiler, P. and Gilbert, N. (2004), 'Simulating knowledge dynamics in innovation networks (SKIN)', Institut für Volkswirtschaftslehre der Universität Augsburg, Volkswirtschaftliche Diskussionsreihe, #267.

Romer, P.M. (1990), 'Endogenous technological change', *Journal of Political Economy*, **98**, 77–102.

Rosenberg, N. (1982), *Inside the Black Box*, Cambridge University Press, Cambridge.

Rosenberg, N. (1994), *Exploring the Black Box: Technology, Economics and History*, Cambridge University Press, Cambridge.

Sargent, T.J. (1987), *Dynamic Macroeconomic Theory*, Harvard University Press, Cambridge.

Saviotti, P.P. (1996), *Technological Evolution, Variety and the Economy*, Edward Elgar, Cheltenham, UK and Brookfield, USA.

Scherer, F.M. and Ross, D. (1990), *Industrial Market Structure and Economic Performance*, Houghton and Mifflin Company, Boston.

Silverberg, G. and Verspagen, B. (1994), 'Collective learning, innovation and growth in a boundedly rational, evolutionary world', *Journal of Evolutionary Economics*, **4**, 207–26.

Stoneman, P. (ed.) (1995), *Handbook of the Economics of Innovation and Technological Change*, Blackwell, Oxford.

Tesfatsion, L. (2001a), 'Structure, behavior, and market power in an evolutionary labor market with adaptive search', *Journal of Economic Dynamics and Control*, **25**, 419–57.

Tesfatsion, L. (2001b), 'Agent-based modelling of evolutionary economic systems', *IEEE Transactions on Evolutionary Computation*, **5**, 1–6.

Tesfatsion, L. (2002), 'Agent-based computational economics: growing economies from the bottom up', Ames, Iowa, working paper no.1, Iowa State University, Dept. of Economics.

Valente, M. (2004), 'Qualitative simulation modelling', Faculty of Economics, University of L'Aquila, L'Aquila (Italy), mimeo.

Vega-Redondo, F. (1996), *Evolution, Games, and Economic Behaviour*, Oxford University Press, Oxford.

Werker, C. and Brenner, T. (2004), 'Empirical calibration of simulation models', papers on economics and evolution # 0410, Max Planck Institute for Research into Economic Systems, Jena.

Wooldridge, M. and Jennings, N.R. (1995), 'Intelligent agents: theory and practice', *Knowledge Engineering Review*, **10**, 115–52.

PART 3

NEO-SCHUMPETERIAN MESO DYNAMICS: EMPIRICS

3.1
Measuring Industry Dynamics

30 Empirical tools for the analysis of technological heterogeneity and change: some basic building blocks of 'evolumetrics'

Uwe Cantner and Jens J. Krüger

1 Introduction

Neo-Schumpeterian and related evolutionary approaches highlight technological change and progress as major driving forces of economic development and growth. For understanding and analyzing these phenomena, a specific methodological point of view is assumed which considers technological performance and technological progress as not uniformly distributed and homogeneous across actors, which may be individuals, firms, sectors, regions or even countries. By contrast, technological performance and change are considered as heterogeneous, in that actors employ different technologies (technological variety) or they run the same technology with different performance (technological asymmetry). This variety and asymmetry is due to different inventive and innovative success of actors which in turn is related to differences of the technological knowledge used and accumulated, differences in technological opportunities, appropriability conditions, etc.

Any empirical analysis which explicitly aims at allowing for and accounting for this heterogeneity is confronted with the problem of applying appropriate measures and methods for dealing explicitly with heterogeneous technological performance and change. This chapter reviews empirical tools which are able to measure, represent and investigate the determinants of technological heterogeneity and its change within an evolutionary framework. In the following we first show how heterogeneous technological structures and their change over time can be measured by applying the nonparametric frontier function approach. This procedure relies on a specific index of total factor productivity which takes into account asymmetry in performance and variety in production functions and therefore is able to calculate local (or heterogeneous) technological advances. Second, by kernel density estimates the results obtained for technological heterogeneity and change can be visualized in the form of density plots. Third, searching for determinants of technological heterogeneity and its dynamics, quantile regression analysis is introduced which allows us to uncover relationships and dynamics beyond-the-mean.

2   Nonparametric productivity measurement

A first central problem is concerned with the measure that allows for an account of technology-related and innovation-determined heterogeneity. In the following, we suppose total factor productivity and its change over time to be valid measures. By this we postulate a number of features that this measure has to satisfy in order to fit into the framework of a neo-Schumpeterian or evolutionary approach.[1]

First of all, the measure of total factor productivity (TFP) and its change over time is a measure which is applicable to a broad range of innovative phenomena at the level of individuals, firms, sectors, regions or countries. Second, in order to account for better or worse technological performance and to give a quantitative account of these differences or asymmetries, the measure of total factor productivity should be determined by a frontier analysis where the frontier function or technology frontier is determined by the best-performing observations. All worse performing observations are at some distance from this technology frontier and this distance can be used as a measure of differential technological performance. Third, to account also for variety in production functions or output mixes the TFP measure is determined by a nonparametric procedure. Fourth, tracking this measure over time by the Malmquist productivity index allows us to take account of local technological change and to separate this from more improvements in productive efficiency.

This brief discussion results in the suggestion of an empirical procedure which differs considerably from traditional approaches to determine total factor productivity and its change. Explicitly it neither assumes a parametrically given technology (production function) which holds on average nor determines technological change as affecting all actors equally.

2.1   Technology–productivity structures

The nonparametric frontier function approach basically relies on index numbers to measure total factor productivity similar to the one used in more standard productivity analysis. In a sample of n observations for each observation $i \in \{1,...,n\}$ a productivity index h_i is defined by:

$$h_i = \frac{\mathbf{u}'\mathbf{y}_i}{\mathbf{v}'\mathbf{x}_i} \tag{30.1}$$

Here $\mathbf{y}_i$ is an s-vector of outputs and $\mathbf{x}_i$ an m-vector of inputs of observation i. The s-vector $\mathbf{u}$ and the m-vector $\mathbf{v}$ contain the aggregation weights and the prime denotes transposition.

The aggregation functions of the TFP index (30.1) for the inputs and outputs, respectively, are of a linear arithmetic type and can be determined by the nonparametric approach relying only on a minimal set of assumption; in particular, it is not to be assumed that all observations of the sample have a common identical production function.

The basic principle of the nonparametric approach is to determine the indices h_i in a way such that they can be interpreted as efficiency ratings, which implies a comparison of each observation with the relatively best observation(s). The most efficient observations of a sample are evaluated by $h_i = 1$, less efficient observations by $h_i < 1$. Comparing all observations with each other we arrive at an account of differential technological performance where the differences are quantified by the measure h_i.

The following constrained maximization problem is used to compute such an h-value for a particular observation $i \in \{1,...,n\}$:

$$\max h_i = \frac{\mathbf{u}'\mathbf{y}_i}{\mathbf{v}'\mathbf{x}_i}$$

$$\text{s.t.} \quad \frac{\mathbf{u}'\mathbf{y}_l}{\mathbf{v}'\mathbf{x}_l} \leq 1 \ (l = 1,...,n) \tag{30.2}$$

$$\mathbf{u},\mathbf{v} > 0.$$

Problem (30.2) determines h_i subject to the constraints that the h_l of all observations (including i itself) of the sample are not larger than unity and therefore bound h_i in (0,1). Moreover the elements of $\mathbf{u}$ and $\mathbf{v}$ are constrained to be strictly positive.

Since we employ linear arithmetic aggregation functions for inputs and outputs, (30.2) is a problem of fractional programming. Charnes and Cooper (1962) suggest a transformation of (30.2) into a standard linear program which can be solved with the well-known simplex algorithm. Performing this step and transforming the resulting primal to its corresponding dual problem, one arrives at the well-known Charnes, Cooper and Rhodes (1978) envelopment form of the nonparametric approach:

$$\min \theta_i$$

$$\text{s.t.} \quad \mathbf{Y}\lambda_i \geq \mathbf{y}_i$$

$$\theta_i \mathbf{x}_i - \mathbf{X}\lambda_i \geq 0, \tag{30.3}$$

$$\lambda_i \geq 0$$

where $\mathbf{Y}$ and $\mathbf{X}$ are the $s \times n$ matrix of outputs and $m \times n$ matrix of inputs of all observations in the sample, respectively. The parameter θ_i expresses the percentage level to which the inputs of observation i can be proportionally reduced, in order to have this observation producing on the production frontier representing the best-practice technologies; it is identical to h_i and is a relative measure of technological performance. Proceeding in this way and solving (30.3) for all observations in the sample, the nonparametric approach determines an efficiency or technology frontier function constructed by the best-practice observations. The efficiency rating of each observation is measured relative to this frontier.

The n-vector λ_i states the weights of all (efficient) observations which serve as reference for observation i. Efficient observations (with $\theta_i = 1$) are characterized by $\lambda_{ii} = 1$ and zero for all other elements. Grouping all observations according to their respective reference observations allows us to detect technological clusters which are distinguished by different input intensities, output intensities or input coefficients.

2.2 Technology–productivity dynamics

In order to track the productivity structure (determined by the measures introduced above), it is not valid to compare the results of consecutive periods because they are relative to different frontier functions. Consequently, to relate consecutive periods we have to compute relative measures which compare period t with $t+1$ and vice versa. The measure chosen for this purpose is the Malmquist index of productivity change. A striking and interesting feature of this index is that it can be decomposed into a measure of technological change and a measure of efficiency change, i.e. catching-up or falling behind.

The theoretical basis of the Malmquist productivity index is found in the work of Malmquist (1953) and Caves, Christensen and Diewert (1982). Färe, Grosskopf and Lovell (1994) have shown how the efficiency measure θ_i above can be used to compute the Malmquist index. Following this line of reasoning the Malmquist productivity index M_i^{t+1} states the productivity change of observation i between t and $t+1$ and is defined as follows:

$$M_i^{t+1} = \left(\frac{\theta_i^{t,t} \ \theta_i^{t,t+1}}{\theta_i^{t+1,t} \theta_i^{t+1,t+1}} \right)^{0.5} . \tag{30.4}$$

$\theta_i^{t,s}$ denotes the efficiency of observation i in period t when the frontier unction of period s serves as reference measure. Simple manipulation of (30.4) leads to the following decomposition of the Malmquist index:

$$M_i^{t+1} = \left(\frac{\theta_i^{t,t}}{\theta_i^{t+1,t+1}} \right) \left(\frac{\theta_i^{t+1,t+1} \theta_i^{t,t+1}}{\theta_i^{t+1,t} \ \theta_i^{t,t}} \right)^{0.5} = ME_i^{t+1} \cdot MT_i^{t+1} \tag{30.5}$$

The second equality in (30.5) states the decomposition of the productivity change into technological change MT_i^{t+1} and change into productive efficiency ME_i^{t+1}. Whenever $ME_i^{t+1} < 1$ ($ME_i^{t+1} > 1$) we find catching-up (falling-behind). In contrast MT_i^{t+1} indicates movements of the frontier. With $MT_i^{t+1} < 1$ ($MT_i^{t+1} > 1$) we observe technological progress (technological regress) at the frontier.

The productivity change according to (30.4) is local in the sense that it is specific to the observation under consideration. In this respect the degree of this local change depends (a) on the observation's ability to shift towards the frontier (ME_i^{t+1}) and (b) on the behavior of the frontier (MT_i^{t+1}). As to (b), the respective change is also local in the sense that for observation i it is only relevant how the part of the frontier assigned to i (by way of the elements of the λ-vector) shifts. The decomposition of the index allows us to distinguish these two movements.

3   Kernel density estimation

Once calculated one may want to have a first spot on the heterogeneity in technology or productivity levels or changes. For that, descriptive statistics have a certain appeal but even the quantification of the amount of heterogeneity in the sample by the standard deviation or the span may hide important characteristics such as multimodality. What is required is a statistical method that gives an impression of the shape of the density function of a variable while imposing only minimal a priori assumptions. The most appealing method for this task is kernel density estimation, which is a kind of smoothing of a histogram to eliminate the dependence on the bin edges (see e.g. Scott, 1992; Wand and Jones, 1995).

Kernel density methods estimate the ordinate of a density function $f(y)$ at a certain point y by a weighted average of all n data points y_i ($i = 1, ..., n$), where the weights are assumed to decrease with an increasing distance of the data points from y (and therefore decreasing relevance for the estimation of the density at y). Formally, the density at the point y is calculated by

$$\hat{f}(y) = \frac{1}{nb} \sum_{i=1}^{n} K\left[\frac{y - y_i}{b} \right]. \tag{30.6}$$

Two elements in equation (30.6) influence the resulting density estimate. The first element is the kernel function $K(w)$ which controls the weights and is assumed to satisfy the general properties of a symmetric probability density function:

$$K(w) \geq 0 \; \forall w, \int K(w)dw = 1,$$

$$\int wK(w)dw = 0 \text{ and } 0 < \int w^2 K(w)dw < \infty. \tag{30.7}$$

By construction of the kernel density estimator all continuity and differentiability properties of the kernel function carry over to the estimated density function. Common choices are the standard normal density and the functions listed in Scott (1992, p. 140). The kernel density estimate is in general rarely affected by the choice of the kernel function.

In contrast, the second element in equation (30.6), the bandwidth parameter b, has substantial influence on the density estimate. A too large value of b leads to an oversmoothed density with a possible loss of detail, whereas a too low value of b results in undersmoothing of the density which appears to be jagged and shows spurious structure. The computation of b relies on different variants of cross-validation and is discussed e.g. in Wand and Jones (1995, ch. 3). Especially in cases where the data are multi-modally distributed simpler rules-of-thumb are preferred, which tend to lead to an oversmoothed kernel density estimate.

The estimation of a whole density function rests on choosing a grid of values for y on which $\hat{f}(y)$ is computed. It has to be noted that the result of kernel density estimation is not an explicit functional form of the density, instead only a vector containing the ordinates of the density function at the chosen grid points is obtained. The whole procedure is purely nonparametric in that no assumptions about the shape of the density have to be made a priori. The outcome of such an analysis depends exclusively on the information contained in the data.

4   Quantile regression

Measurement and representation/visualization of technological heterogeneity using nonparametric methods are important parts of empirical analyses in evolutionary economics. If we want to proceed to find possible sources of heterogeneous technological structures and development it would be unfortunate if we had to rely on correlation techniques like least squares regression analysis. Even nonparametric regression methods, although at first glance well suited to evolutionary principles because of their flexibility, are not appropriate because they only estimate the mean of a dependent variable conditional on one or more explanatory variables. What is required for evolutionary empirical analyses is a regression method that provides a characterization of the entire distribution of a dependent variable given a set of explanatory variables and not just its mean.

A promising method in this respect is the approach of quantile regression, introduced by Koenker and Bassett (1978), which has the potential to uncover differences in the response of the dependent variable to changes of the explanatory variables at different points of the conditional distribution. Thereby a large amount of information about the heterogeneity of the reactions of the sample items to changes of their characteristics or their environment can be gained. In addition to these conceptual advantages, the coefficient estimates obtained with quantile regression are robust with respect to outliers in the dependent variable and in the case of nonnormal errors quantile regression estimates may be more efficient than least squares estimates (Buchinsky, 1998; Koenker and Hallock, 2001).

To understand the logic of quantile regression we first consider the case of a univariate real valued random variable y with a continuous cumulative distribution function $F(y)$. The τth, $\tau \in [0,1]$, (population) quantile of this random variable is defined as $Q_\tau(y) = \inf\{y:F(y) \geq \tau\} = F^{-1}(\tau)$. Thus, the quantile function represents the same information about the heterogeneity of the observations as does the cumulative distribution function, although in a different way. From the definition of the quantile it is clear that the calculation involves a sorting operation of the observations. The key point here is that we can replace this sorting operation by the operation of optimization. Doing so, the τth quantile can equivalently be defined as the solution to the minimization problem:

$$\min_{\xi \in \Re} E(\rho_\tau(y - \xi)), \tag{30.8}$$

where $\rho_\tau(u) = u \cdot (\tau - I(u < 0))$ denotes the 'check function' and $I(\cdot)$ represents the usual indicator function which is equal to unity if $u < 0$ and zero otherwise. Since $\rho_\tau(\cdot)$ can be interpreted as an asymmetric loss function, equation (30.8) is equivalent to straightforward minimization of expected loss:

$$E(\rho_\tau(y - \xi)) = \int_{-\infty}^{\infty} (y - \xi) \cdot (\tau - I(y - \xi < 0)) dF(y)$$

$$= (\tau - 1) \cdot \int_{-\infty}^{\xi} (y - \xi) dF(y) + \tau \cdot \int_{\xi}^{\infty} (y - \xi) dF(y) \tag{30.9}$$

with respect to the parameter ξ. Employing the integration-by-parts formula, the first-order condition of this minimization problem is

$$\frac{dE(\rho_\tau(y - \xi))}{d\xi} = -(\tau - 1) \cdot F(\xi) - \tau + \tau \cdot F(\xi) = F(\xi) - \tau = 0,$$

and its solution $\xi = F^{-1}(\tau)$ is exactly the definition of the τth quantile. If $F(\cdot)$ is strictly monotone this solution is unique. A special case of this solution is the median $F^{-1}(\frac{1}{2})$ which is the solution to the minimization of absolute expected loss (the case $\tau = 1/2$).

Replacing $F(y)$ with the empirical distribution function $F_n(y) = n^{-1}\Sigma_{i=1}^{n}I(y_i \leq y)$ for a sample of size n, $\mathbf{y} = (y_1,...,y_n)'$, the expected loss is replaced by $n^{-1}\Sigma_{i=1}^{n}\rho_\tau(y_i - \xi)$ and the minimization of the latter yields the τth sample quantile. This problem can be expressed as a linear programming problem:

$$\min_{(\xi,\mathbf{u},\mathbf{v})\in\Re\times\Re_+^{2n}} \{\tau\mathbf{e}'\mathbf{u} + (1-\tau)\mathbf{e}'\mathbf{v}|\xi\mathbf{e} + \mathbf{u} - \mathbf{v} = \mathbf{y}\}, \qquad (30.10)$$

where $\mathbf{u}$ and $\mathbf{v}$ here are n-vectors of slack variables representing the positive and negative parts of the vector of residuals and $\mathbf{e}$ is a conformable vector of ones.

Turning now to the case of linear regression, it is familiar that the solution of the least squares problem $\min_{\beta\in\Re^k}\Sigma_{i=1}^{n}(y_i - \mathbf{x}_i'\beta)^2$, where $\mathbf{x}_i$ denotes the k-vector of the explanatory variables of observation $i \in \{1,...,n\}$, allows us to estimate the conditional mean of y given $\mathbf{x}$. Koenker and Bassett (1978) show that by minimizing the sum of asymmetrically weighted (again through the check function) absolute residuals:

$$\min_{\beta\in\Re^k}\Sigma_{i=1}^{n}\rho_\tau(y_i - \mathbf{x}_i'\beta) \qquad (30.11)$$

and denoting the solution by $\hat{\beta}_\tau$, the so-called regression quantile, we can estimate the τth conditional quantile function by $\hat{Q}_\tau(y|\mathbf{x}) = \mathbf{x}'\hat{\beta}_\tau$. This is analogous to the problem of estimating a single unconditional quantile in the case $\xi = \mathbf{x}'\beta$. Varying τ between 0 and 1 one can trace the entire conditional distribution of y given $\mathbf{x}$. The marginal change $\partial\hat{Q}_\tau(y|\mathbf{x})/\partial x_{ij} = \hat{\beta}_{j\tau}$ has a similar interpretation as the coefficient estimate of a linear least squares regression.

The above minimization problem again has a computationally convenient linear programming representation (see the appendix of Koenker and Bassett, 1978):

$$\min_{(\beta,\mathbf{u},\mathbf{v})\in\Re^k\times\Re_+^{2n}} \{\tau\mathbf{e}'\mathbf{u} + (1-\tau)\mathbf{e}'\mathbf{v}|\mathbf{X}\beta + \mathbf{u} - \mathbf{v} = \mathbf{y}\}, \qquad (30.12)$$

where $\mathbf{X}$ denotes the usual $n \times k$ regression design matrix with rows $\mathbf{x}_i'$. The solution to this kind of problem is numerically straightforward by using the simplex or related algorithms.

Buchinsky (1998) demonstrates that the first-order condition of the quantile regression problem can be interpreted as a conditional moment function which fits into the GMM framework of Hansen (1982). From that insight consistency and asymptotic normality of the regression quantiles can be easily established under certain regularity conditions (for details, see Buchinsky, 1998, pp. 95ff.). Different approaches to estimate the covariance matrix of the regression quantiles and tests are discussed extensively there. Confidence intervals for the regression quantiles can be calculated by regression rank score inversion (Koenker, 1994) or computationally intensive bootstrap methods (see e.g. Buchinsky, 1998, pp. 102ff.). Both methods have good coverage properties in *iid* as well as heteroskedastic situations.

Also available for quantile regression is a goodness-of-fit statistic, proposed by Koenker and Machado (1999), which is a natural analog to R^2 in a least squares context and can be calculated by $R_\tau = 1 - \hat{V}_\tau / \tilde{V}_\tau$ for the τth regression quantile. Here, $\hat{V}_\tau = \min_{\beta \in \Re^k} \Sigma_{i=1}^n \rho_\tau(y_i - \mathbf{x}_i'\beta)$ is the minimized value of the unconstrained objective function for the τth regression quantile and $\tilde{V}_\tau = \min_{\beta_1 \in \Re} \Sigma_{i=1}^n \rho_\tau(y_i - \beta_1)$ is the minimized value of the constrained objective function for the τth regression quantile with only the intercept included as a regressor. $R_\tau \in [0,1]$ thus quantifies the explanatory power of the regression specification compared to a regression on a constant.

It is important to recognize that all computed quantities (the regression quantiles, the confidence intervals and the goodness-of-fit statistic) refer to a specific quantile τ. Calculating these quantities for a sequence of quantiles allows us to realize the promised complete characterization of the conditional distribution of y beyond the more limited information content that a traditional least squares regression provides. The regression quantiles estimate the effects of changes of the explanatory variables on the position of the respective quantiles.

Therefore, the quantile regression approach is able to uncover different effects of the explanatory variables in different parts of the support of the conditional distribution of the dependent variable. For each quantile it can be determined whether the effect of a specific explanatory variable is positive or negative and how strong this effect is compared to other quantiles. This provides a huge amount of information concerning the heterogeneity of the reactions of the sample items beyond the determination of the average reaction.

5 Conclusion

Although there exist other methods which are appealing from an evolutionary point of view, such as Markov chain methods and cluster analysis, we have presented here three tools that are well suited to measure, visualize and explain technological differences and their change over time. Especially kernel density estimation and quantile regression have a much broader applicability than just the analysis of productivity data. All three methods share the capability to obtain distribution-related information from the data that go far beyond the sole consideration of mean and variance. This qualifies them as basic building blocks that contribute to an emerging branch of empirical research for which we suggest the expressive label 'evolumetrics'.

Note

1.   For an extensive discussion of these features, see Cantner and Hanusch (2001).

References

Buchinsky, M. (1998), Recent advances in quantile regression models: a practical guide for empirical research, *Journal of Human Resources*, **33**, 88–126.
Cantner, U. and H. Hanusch (2001), 'Heterogeneity and evolutionary dynamics – empirical conception, findings and unresolved issues', in J. Foster and J.S. Metcalfe (eds), *Frontiers of Evolutionary Economics – Competition, Self-Organization and Innovation Policy*, Cheltenham, UK and Northampton, MA, USA: Edward Elgar, pp. 228–77.
Caves, D.W., L.R. Christensen and W.E. Diewert (1982), The economic theory of index numbers of the measurement of input, output and productivity, *Econometrica*, **50**, 1393–414.
Charnes, A. and W.W. Cooper (1962), Programming with linear fractional functionals, *Naval Research Logistics Quarterly*, **9**, 181–6.
Charnes, A., W.W. Cooper and E. Rhodes (1978), Measuring the efficiency of decision making units, *European Journal of Operational Research*, **2**, 429–44.
Färe, R., S. Grosskopf and C.A.K. Lovell (1994), *Production Frontiers*, Cambridge, MA: Cambridge University Press.
Hansen, L.P. (1982), Large sample properties of generalized method of moments estimators, *Econometrica*, **50**, 1029–54.
Koenker, R.W. (1994), 'Confidence intervals for regression quantiles', in P. Mandl and M. Hušková (eds), *Asymptotic Statistics*, New York: Springer, pp. 349–59.
Koenker, R.W. and G. Bassett (1978), Regression quantiles, *Econometrica*, **46**, 33–50.
Koenker, R.W. and K.F. Hallock (2001), Quantile regression, *Journal of Economic Perspectives*, **15**, 143–56.
Koenker, R.W. and J.A.F. Machado (1999), Goodness of fit and related inference procedures for quantile regression, *Journal of the American Statistical Association*, **94**, 1296–310.
Malmquist, S. (1953), Index numbers and indifference surfaces, *Trabajos de Estatística*, **4**, 209–42.
Scott, D.W. (1992), *Multivariate Density Estimation: Theory, Practice and Visualization*, New York: Wiley.
Wand, M.P. and M.C. Jones (1995), *Kernel Smoothing*, London: Chapman & Hall.

31 Typology of science and technology indicators
Hariolf Grupp

Innovation output is frequently regarded as the most important innovation statistic, although the conceptual definitions of it in the literature are far from consistent.[1] If one defines technical progress as 'the creation' of new products and as 'the transition' to new production processes, as in the neo-Schumpeterian tradition, then the emphasis is more on the procedural 'byput' than on output. It is therefore suggested that the output, byput and also input-oriented indicators be referred to collectively as 'innovation indicators'.

From the theoretical reference it becomes clear how important it is to differentiate between R&D activities and innovation stages (see Grupp, 1998, ch. 1). Input indicators are then subsets of innovation indicators accounting for resources, not for R&D expenditures alone. Further, it is important to comprehend output-oriented indices relating to R&D processes as a specific subset of all innovation indicators not necessarily leading to economic impact or progress, and to call them 'R&D results' indicators. What literature calls 'byput' or 'throughput' (Freeman, 1982, p. 8), because these measure 'attendant' or 'partial' effects of technical progress, is thus regarded as the result of R&D activities and not always as a prerequisite for innovation and progress. It is also not always sufficient for this purpose. The output-oriented measurement processes which seek to cover economically relevant innovation effects are the 'economic' indicators and should be called 'progress' indicators. Progress indicators derive from quantity or value-related or even quality-modifying effects on production, but not from achievements in R&D alone.

This chapter tries to standardize the types of innovation indicators and to point to substitutive measurement opportunities in empirical analysis of innovation processes. Describing the variety of indicators first it then focuses on two important 'byput' indicators which are so important to understand the creation or transition problem in neo-Schumpeterian analysis. These are patent statistics and the statistics of scientific publications (bibliometrics) including the statistics of citations in these documents. Generally speaking, patent indicators are equated with technology output and bibliometric indicators with science output. Validity is discussed on several levels (patent propensity, foreign extension, key patents, papers vis-à-vis patents, patent vis-à-vis literature citation etc.). The most popular indices for patent shares, patent and literature specialization and international production are passed in review, and finally the concordance problem is discussed. Do the fuzzy creation and transition processes in innovation allow us to solve the concordance problem, i.e. the matching of balancing units between science, technology and markets? If spillovers of knowledge occur, can they be traced? Overall, this chapter attempts to inform the reader on the state-of-the-art in empirical analysis of the rôle of science and technology in innovative activities.

Standardizing the types of innovation indicators: resources, R&D results and technical progress

The term 'resource indicators' which will not be examined in greater detail in this chapter (see Grupp, 1998, section 5.1) and should be regarded as a generic term embracing every possible means for measuring personnel, monetary, investive and other expenditure on research, development and innovation. These include, for instance, R&D outlays, R&D personnel statistics, investment statistics, the royalties paid, learning-on-the-job costs and many more besides.

Amongst the R&D results indicators should be all results from research and development in the direct sense; that is, irrespective of whether or not they are important for the success of innovation, market launch, and so on. The most important result indicators come from publication and patent statistics and their citations. This chapter opens with an overview of patent statistic measurements clearly showing that they are part of a long tradition in economic research and not, say, merely as an item of the scholarly studies of law. Since patent analysis is employed for various purposes (in jurisprudence, industrial management, sociological technology genesis research and so on), we will have to identify which sort of patent indicators are especially relevant for industrial and innovation economics. As explained in greater detail below, patents and scientific publications merely represent the codified part of technological and scientific knowledge placed on written record (Dasgupta and David, 1987). Furthermore, this makes the correspondence or 'concordance' problem, that is matching to or comparison with economic statistics, difficult.

Progress indicators relate not to detailed R&D activities but to the characteristics and micro- or macroeconomic effects of innovation. For some scholars, quality indicators based on product characteristics and their innovative improvement are regarded as the ideal progress indicator (see, for instance, Chapter 3 in Grupp, 1998).[2] Other progress indicators commonly encountered in the literature are those relating to the innovation

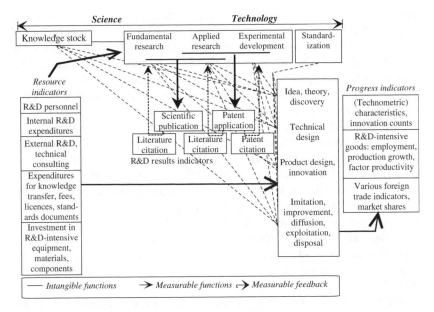

Figure 31.1   Survey of important innovation indicators and their typology

counts recorded in corporate questionnaires, measurement of high technology markets or calculation of total factor productivities and other macro- and foreign trade indicators.

Figure 31.1 is essentially a reference diagram which points to measurement possibilities and is, in this sense, still neither complete nor comprehensive but identifies the indicators conventionally used in the literature. It subdivides them fairly clearly into the three subsets proposed here. Owing to the diverse functional (and not linear, i.e. sequential!) relationships existing between R&D processes and innovation stages, the valid range of application of individual indicators often cannot be defined in precise terms. Coarse classifications spanning several validity areas and the intangible functions connecting them constitute considerable obstacles to validation.

Substitutive measurement

Meticulous definition of indicators should be preceded by careful attention to the methodological problem of innovation economics described initially. If the ideal indicator solution is seen in the determination of new or improved product characteristics then the other indicators mentioned must be regarded as substitutive indicators. Product characteristics can be quite costly to compile and corresponding time series are difficult to access. Therefore, the principle of correlative or substitutive measurement involves operationalizing other appropriately related constructs which seem to allow sufficiently accurate inferences to be drawn about progress. The subdivision in Figure 31.1 and its typology make it plain that the more traditional progress indicators do not lend themselves readily to the measurement of product quality improvement. Resource and R&D results indicators are defined in other fields of innovation measurement but not as progress variables. However, secondary effects of progress can be included with R&D indicators so that the existence of correlations cannot be excluded a priori.

Many empirical tests have shown that some innovation indicators within their defined boundaries are hardly usable for substitution, yet these nevertheless retain their validity in their own field of application (which would need to be tested for each application). The various innovation indicators in the demarcation shown in Figure 31.1 do not reflect ideal constructs; revealing this is one of the main concerns of the reference diagram.

Often, essential data is only limitedly available and investigation costs are high. Frequently valid comparison of auxiliary indicators is precluded by prohibitive investigation costs. Statistical data are not in inexhaustible supply and ultimately construction of valid substitute measurement parameters means surmounting a scarcity problem. If validation in econometric practice is out of the question, then the validity of the preferred indicator has to be deduced from theoretical plausibility considerations in which intellectual preoccupation with the various alternative indicators is a prerequisite.

Validity tests on selected indicators should ultimately reveal whether systematic errors can be graded 'small', 'moderate', 'tolerably large' or 'unacceptably large'. Their validity is then gradable successively as 'high', 'satisfactory', 'tolerable' and 'unsatisfactory' from which first, second and third-order auxiliary indicators and invalid indicators can be differentiated.

History of patenting

Treatment of the patent indicators is our starting point for discussion of R&D results indicators, for they occur more widely in neo-Schumpeterian literature than any other innovation indicator. No other innovation indicator can be traced back over comparatively long periods of time, may at the same time be disaggregated at a very low level allocatable to individual economic units, and is also precise and accurate insofar as identification of the timing of the innovation event is concerned.

In the Middle Ages, often letters with an inner seal were termed 'litterae patentes' (patent letters). They allowed the holder to make public disclosure of certain rights, privileges, titles or official functions. From this, the modern term 'patent' is derived (Machlup, 1964, cited by Kaufer, 1989, p. 1). Even today the patent is a 'property right' based on an 'officially sealed' claim. For the claim to be recognized by other competing companies all property right details claimed have to be published. The claims originally bearing the King's seal were of a non-technical sort (still today: the captain's patent). In Europe, in the fifteenth century, certain such authorizations also referred to technical or production-relevant objects, for example, to the exploitation of ore mines. The first formal patent filed in Vienna in 1474 related to 'men of great genius, apt to invent and discover ingenious devices'.[3]

Later, similar regulations appeared in other countries, for example, in England in 1623 and in France in the sixteenth century. In the USA, Massachusetts led the way in 1641 and by 1790 the whole of the United States had followed suit. In German-speaking territories, patent rights were regarded by the powers of the day as 'hoechst schaedlich' (highly detrimental), hence formalized patent rights via Napoleon's new European order first materialized in the anti-Prussian coalition, that is, in Baden, Württemberg and Bavaria (around 1825). Only accelerating industrialization and unification of Germany at that time forced the formalization of a generally valid patent law by the German Reich in 1877 (Grupp *et al.*, 2002).

In most countries, manual analysis of patent documents may date back to the year in which the respective patent legislation came into force. Machine-readable patent statistics for Germany date back to 1877, for France to 1902, for Great Britain to 1909 and for the United States to 1920 (Schmoch, 1990, p. 75).

Patents as a latent public good: three basic properties
Without property rights, technological knowledge would be public property. The inventors' competitors would be able to imitate without penalty and claim the new knowledge to be their own. If companies want to make production of technological knowledge available not entirely free of charge, they must invoke their temporary monopolistic right accorded by patenting. The patent right is therefore one of the important so-called 'property rights' or 'rights of free disposal' which play an important part in more recent developments in microeconomic theory. Other important property rights regulate access to soil or pollution of the environment. In the innovation economics context, the patent is the most important property right. Despite patent protection, the scope of which is limited not only timewise but also in terms of substance, technological externalities play a rôle so that technological knowledge is seemingly neither an entirely free public commodity nor a one hundred per cent private commodity.[4] We deal with externalities in this chapter further below.

Indicators deduced from patent statistics therefore show three qualitatively different properties which require attention in connection with the validity problem.[5] On the one hand, a patent award is a legal concept conveying to the owner the exclusive right of exploitation of a precisely defined technical knowledge for a specific period of time.[6] Award of this right is associated with fulfilment of three conditions, which vary somewhat according to the specific version of the national patent law, but virtually worldwide cover the same main aspects. Thus, an invention must have novelty, a particular quality (inventive step) and its object must be commercially applicable.

The commercial applicability criterion relates directly to the innovation process, whereas the novelty criterion has a special protective function which is involved even if a patent is not awarded. If a patent application is being published for the first time (laid open to public inspection), but is not awarded, for which various grounds can be critical, then an identical or largely identical property right cannot be refiled later.

The information function is the second qualitative property inherent in patent indicators.[7] Patent literature represents the codified part of technological knowledge which, like scientific publications, can be used by individuals other than the inventors with a view to acquiring knowledge about the progress of technological knowledge.[8] Specialists in R&D within firms scan both patent literature and scientific publications. Just like scientific publications, patent documents contain references to the prior state of the art. Since patent documents are of a legal nature, the corresponding citations are established by (mostly official) patent examiners and not by inventors. This circumstance can be used as a means of analysing progress in technology in individual cases and serves as a reference to the economic units (citations about proprietary earlier inventions of colleagues in the same company, in another company in the same country, in companies in foreign national economies, and so on).[9]

The third function relates to the output nature of a patent document. Successful R&D activity is usually followed by a patent so that the corresponding document (complete with date, inventors, holders, locations and other details) indicates the time, circumstances and locations which have yielded new R&D successes. It is this last-mentioned property of patent indicators which is used mainly in connection with innovation measurement: patent statistics as an R&D results indicator.[10]

Validity of patent statistics
First of all, it must be established which part of the inventive activity the patent definitely covers and which part of all technical inventions in practice, possibly sector-dependent, actually aspires to application.[11] Note that not all objects of innovation can be covered by patents. User software has poor patentability, whereas computer programs which are of a technical nature, that is, which control a machine or a technical plant, and even a data processor can be protected by patent law.[12] Thus patent protection exists for

all machine control programmes but not, say, for word-processing systems; these are subject to copyright (another property right). Likewise, computer architectures are safeguarded by property rights other than patents. In other areas, particularly genetic engineering, the current form of patent protection leads to legal uncertainty. Medicinal healing processes cannot be protected.

The validity range of the patent indicator may also be evaluated differently according to whether it is used as a pure R&D returns indicator or it deputizes for progress measurement. A simple graphical representation is given in Figure 31.2, where overlapping areas correspond to the order of magnitude based on true given estimates.[13]

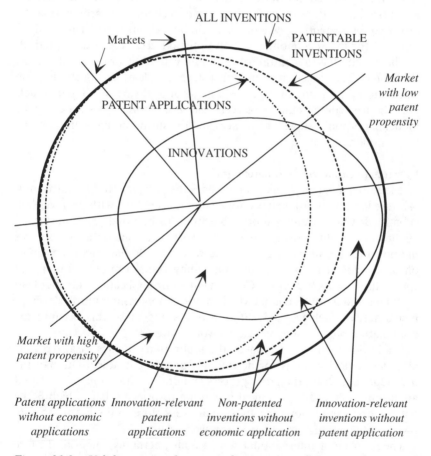

Figure 31.2   Validity range of patent indicators according to product groups (adapted from Basberg, 1987)

Patenting and innovative behaviour of competitors
Patent genesis, irrespective of whether a statistic is or is not available, affects the innovation behaviour of the market participant. Many innovation processes would take a totally different course without patent protection. Patent protection may, according to current thinking, act as the instigator of innovative activities because it helps the innovator to obtain temporary monopolistic rents. To this extent, in a market economy, the patent system can embody an aspect of knowledge allocation closely resembling allocation of traditional economic goods (Hanusch and Cantner, 1993, p. 15).[14] The literature certainly also raises a few objections, asserting that the patent system does not work in this way but allows the company to rake off protracted, exaggerated innovation rents and thus to give preference to near-to-market innovations. Thus the direction of technological progress may be distorted by patenting which, by excluding competitors, can lead to repeated and macroeconomically non-optimal R&D expenditures (ibid.).[15]

The patent has a central rôle in innovation theories of all kinds. Particularly in connection with market structures, learning effects, decision calculations and game theory, it is a major model variable. Some models are extremely complex and have been made even more sophisticated by the modelling of multi-stage patent races and the surmounting of monopolistic go-it-alone situations.

Patent application *vis-à-vis* patent grant
The fact that a patent application exists is the basis for R&D returns indicators: each person from an economic unit is accredited with the invention submitted which is understood subjectively to be novel. The unchecked application might already be known worldwide but in any case was unknown to the submitting unit, otherwise it would have used the earlier official disclosure as the basis of a know-how transfer or an imitation and spared itself the R&D effort. Consequently, the application statistics lead to double and multiple counts which, however, represent multiple developments actually achieved. Grant statistics would mask this because the examination process only recognizes world novelties.[16]

In addition to this key argument, the application statistics are also preferable on practical grounds, for, depending upon the patent legislation of the individual countries, the grant process can drag on interminably.[17] Patent applications should be arranged according to priority date, which is the date of first submission, and thus a date very close to the invention date owing to the desire to safeguard the novelty claim.

The problem of international comparability certainly comes to the fore here. Practically all countries worldwide observe an inspection period of precisely 18 months from the priority date. Incoming patent applications are thus publicized in strict entry order date (by priority date). The only exception to this is the American Patent Office.[18] There only patent grants are publicized while inventions at the application stage which are not successful in the compulsory examination process are not published individually; however country totals are statistically available per technical field. Publication date thus coincides with the grant date and does not take a fixed period of time from first filing. Furthermore, after publication, US patents can be traced to the priority date; the US peculiarities may be brought closer to international procedures in the near future.

External patenting and patent families
It has already been pointed out that the patent can also reflect the desire by a company to engage in certain markets, whence an important measurement specification for patent indicators is deduced from the foreign application scenario. Normally, an invention is applied for at the respective patent office in the territory in which the inventor is based (so-called 'domestic application'). In many countries, this is associated with the allocation of employee inventor remuneration. The priority date is thereby protected worldwide. The company then has a maximum of 12 months within which to decide whether to submit essentially equivalent foreign applications (although subject to the legal systems of other patent offices) in order to be able to claim the corresponding monopolistic rights in respect of other markets. Statistical comparison of the application equivalents for foreign markets yields information about sales strategies. Thus a further patent indicator can be deduced from the taking out of foreign applications, thus providing a proxy for identifying corporate strategies or marketing intentions.

The significance of external application has been investigated by an impressive array of literature: external patents have a higher economic value (see, for example, Griliches, 1990; Harhoff *et al.*, 1999). It can be taken as proven that companies want to stay one step ahead of the market and, hence, via external applications, erect temporary barriers to market access on various foreign markets and create a temporary distribution monopoly for their new products. External patent rights, especially for safeguarding export business in the respective country of application, are the root cause of multiple application, but direct investments can likewise be protected or domestic production by external competitors obstructed.

If the data considered are from a particular patent office in country X, then there is a measurement problem: domestic applications from X will be confused with external applications from all other countries of origin, thus highly distorting the value of the random sample. We can only eliminate this measurement problem if we think in terms of combining all external applications. The original application plus its duplicates are termed a 'patent family'. An invention with no external applications would thus have only one 'family member'; if it also is applied for in one other country, the family would consist of two members. The suggestion already made is that inventions with a large patent family should be regarded as of higher quality or value than purely domestic applications. However, the objection can also be raised that the contribution to progress of the patent cannot be estimated from the size of the family, for this, all too often, is subject to marketing and other corporate strategic considerations. For instance, it is known that European companies, owing to their particular geographical situation and high-volume trade within European countries, cover very many more (European) external markets with patent rights than, say, Japanese companies. The quality criterion for the size of patent family therefore also appears to be dictated by considerations of economic geography.

Triad technology production
In order to reduce geographic distortions in samples of valuable patents, a proper concept is that of 'triad patents'. It consists in selecting only patent families with a minimum of three members, one from the US, one from Japan and one from the European Patent Office (EPO; a regional patent authority). In the case of a domestic invention from anywhere in Europe, this means that external equivalents in the United States and Japan have to be filed such that the statistic includes the corresponding document (Grupp and Schmoch, 1999).[19]

Often, innovation research uses patent indicators for comparative analysis; that is, specializations at a particular patent office are modelled on the corresponding concept in foreign trade theory. A company or a country is given a low indicator value either if the patent activity actually is low (which would be interesting) or if the patent activity proves to be average with respect to the domestic market, but, owing to little economic interest in certain triad regions, is low in the corresponding patent office statistics. In this case the triad concept would remedy the distortion.

Do key patents exist?
From the economic theory, understandably the question is often raised as to whether large patent families (or triad patents) emanate from key inventions which cover fundamental innovations. However, the question is wrongly phrased. Just what ought to constitute a basic innovation remains largely undefined. It would be totally wrong to equate large or triad patent families with basic innovations also called radical, key or more major innovations. How could these be differentiated operationally from other patents which protect an incremental or standard innovation? The 'basic patent'

concept is often applied to genetic engineering, an area generating fundamental breakthroughs. Yet even in this spectacular R&D field, no definition of the 'basic patent' exists: many central ideas, like the manufacture of monoclonal antibodies, have contributed to a large variety of more specific patents, and catch-all applications were rejected because of lack of commercial usability. Another example is robotics. The decisive innovation of 1986, the introduction of direct drives, has been protected comprehensively by many sequentially related patent rights. The decisive factor for utilization and licensing is however the – likewise multiply protected – system integration and installation know-how (Grupp *et al.*, 1987, p. 399); a key patent cannot be defined.

The general understanding is that basic innovations do not lead to key patents but to a 'bundle' or 'swarm' of successive inventions, not necessarily forming triad families. The notion of basic innovations seems to point to special qualities in technical or scientific terms, whereas large families (triadic or otherwise) indicate true worldwide marketing strategies and higher economic value. What about other indications of the economic value of patents?

Patent claims and patent citations

A way of making the economic value of patents comparable is to count the patent claims contained therein.[20] For instance, at the American Patent Office, Japanese patents on average have fewer, German patents more, claims than the 'domestic' US patents (Tong and Frame, 1994, p. 135). It was possible to show that the export figure for France, Germany, Great Britain and Japan could be estimated in the USA with the aid of external patents from these countries submitted to the USA. At the same time, claims statistics frequently yield better estimates than straightforward patent statistics (but not in every case). The patent claim indicator cannot be detected in databanks and the scanning of random samples from documents has to be done by hand. Therefore, owing to the very substantial measurement costs, it is now virtually never used, but remains a useful concept.

Similarly, while attempting to validate patent statistics, Trajtenberg (1990) and, in a series of investigations, Harhoff *et al.* (1999) found that the economic value of patents could be measured better with a so-called 'citation weight' than with individual patent figures. Prior state of the art is researched by patent examiners during the grant process and citations to other patents are included. If a patent is mentioned very frequently as proof of a prior state of the art being exceeded, then there will be greater technological significance (once again: key character) and subsequently the innovation represents an expanding market.

However, one has to consider the extremely skewed distribution of patent value (Scherer *et al.*, 2000) and also the fact that the probability of being cited in later patents is connected with the age of the patent; very recent patents, on time grounds, have hardly had a chance to affect the current tide of technical development.

Home advantage and specialization
Clearly, economic literature has published a whole host of proposals for evaluating patent documents. As has been shown, these proposals are useful for many econometric investigations but still leave certain matters unresolved. In order to remedy the persistent shortcomings described above, one suggestion was to control for the domestic advantages of the inventor within his territory of residence. The 'domestic advantage' H for domestic applications from country X can be calculated with the aid of external patent applications in another country, Y. The term 'country' used here is tantamount to otherwise demarcated regional or institutional sets which can take domestic advantage into account (companies, groups of companies, institutions, state within countries, regions, handicapped regions within a country and so on). How to calculate H is explained in Grupp (1998, p. 156). As has been shown above, the problem can be circumvented using the triad concept. Another alternative is to calculate patent specialization.[21] The 'Specialization Indicators' are derived from only one Patent Office Y and assign fairly different values to the mix of patents involved (domestic for the applications from Y, external for all other countries respectively):

$$RTA(X,i,Y) = [P(k=X,i,Y)/\Sigma_i \, P(k,i,Y)]/[\Sigma_k \, P(k,i,Y)/\Sigma_{ik} \, P(k,i,Y)].$$
$$RPA = 100 \ln RTA$$

The RTA indicator (revealed technological advantage) is asymmetrical, unconstrained on one side and cannot be used for distance measurements. Essentially, this is possible with the RPA indicator in the absence of any poles (infinite indicator values). For distance measurements (for example, using the least squares method) a symmetrical, top and bottom-constrained, hyperbolic version is therefore advisable:[22]

$$RPA_h = 100 \, tanh \, RPA/100 = 100 \cdot (RTA^2 - 1)/(RTA^2 + 1).$$

Patent stocks
Most patent indicators measure the changes in the stock of patents in a given year or in other time periods. These reflect the growth of protected knowledge, not its current status. Owing to the cumulative nature of technical

change, it is often helpful to involve patent stocks (or potential or supply) in the analysis. This does not refer specifically to the legal validity period of the respective patent, but includes the growth of past knowledge in the innovation indicator, subject to assumptions for 'depreciation' of the knowledge status. The timespan for the patent stock involved therefore has to be judged carefully in each individual case.

Indicators for technological spillovers

Despite the close interrelationship between science and technology, it is useful to differentiate between external effects within the corporate environments (or rather technology) and in the context of the public research infrastructure (or rather science). At industrial level it has become accepted practice to characterize external effects in innovation as so-called 'technological spillovers'. In order to adhere closely to the subject of this contribution, empirical investigation of external technological effects is confined mainly to unintentional spillover effects in the narrower sense.

Jaffe (1986)[23] has not only alluded to the importance of external effects to corporate profits, but also made a convincing case in favour of the use of patent indicators for empirical investigation of this subject.[24] The principle of the method involves drawing up portfolios, for branches and individual companies, via their technological activities with the aid of patent statistics and investigating their similarities systematically. Two companies with a similar portfolio can be regarded as spillover-suspect, those with fairly diverse activity structures as non-suspect.[25] Yet the concept is based on the assumption that the patent policies of the companies considered are identical and that company strategies and patent policies average out.

An alternative concept uses patent classifications that can refer to more than one specialist area (so-called 'multiple classification').[26] Whenever there are references to more than one technical connection, the patent examiner is required to state the corresponding multiple classes (Grupp, 1996). Establishment of multiple classifications does not depend on the peculiarities of individual companies with regard to their patent behaviour.[27] The frequency of occurrence of multiple classifications can be interpreted immediately as a similarity index (ibid.). Not only the magnitude of the external effects but also their range is interesting, for example, whether it is only other companies from the same branch which benefit or whether macroeconomic effects are involved.

Measuring the science base of technology

Unlike the case of technological spillover effects, there are hardly any indicators to identify the science base of technology. The few exceptions use the circumstance that, when examining patent applications, not only do the multiple classifications need to be established but the prior state of science and technology also must be researched. In all cases, patent office officials draw on patent documents laid open to public inspection for this purpose (patent citation; see above). Occasionally, they document the former state of science and technology also by reference to scientific and not patent literature. Under what circumstances such references to 'non-patent literature' are both possible and customary is discussed in depth by Grupp and Schmoch (1992). If the frequency of such non-patent literature references in patent documents is taken to be the index for the dependence from the science basis, an indicator approach is found which is suitable for measuring the science relation.

One argument in favour of this concept for measuring the science relation is the fact that patent citations are more objective than citations from scientists in their own publications. Patent citations are checked by patent examiners; in most countries they are officials whose dealings are open to legal inspection. The citation is therefore made by reference to an established set of rules and is hardly coloured by personal behavioural idiosyncrasies. Since citations do not stem from the authors of the patent, that is, the inventors or patent attorneys, they are not subject to the anxieties that surround the questionable self-citation.[28]

This concept yields an ordinal series of sectors in regard to their science base which corresponds to survey data (Mansfield, 1991; Tijssen, 2002).[29] Econometric analyses prove that science dependence is an internal feature of technology; there are no significant technological gaps between national economies. Furthermore, Dosi *et al.* (1988, p. 1150), referring to innovation theory considerations, have pointed out that the industry-specific characteristics of the science basis are 'relatively stable timewise and between countries'.

Statistics for science output: bibliometrics

The patent application largely reflects the results of applied research and experimental development. Largely, but not exclusively, inventions arise out of a profit-oriented business ethos; however, a substantial proportion also originate from individuals and university employees and independent public research institutes.[30] Scientific results, on the other hand, are published mainly in journals; indicators relating to statistics from such publications (broken down by specialist areas, institutional origin, countries, and so on) are termed 'bibliometric indicators'.[31] Nowadays, bibliometric indicators are still nowhere near as important a research instrument for evolutionary economics as patent indicators. Bibliometric indicators are widely used in science and technology studies and in the sociology of science, whereas suggestions of economists[32] to integrate bibliometric indicators into the examination of the relationship between basic science and productivity growth have seldom been taken up.

As for patent documents, scientific publications list a number of references to earlier work (citations). In bibliometrics, no-one would deny that citation parameters are more complex to interpret than straightforward publication incidence. Certainly, citation indicators do not provide an error-free yardstick for the quality of scientific activity. Since discussion of the basics in citation analyses cannot be dealt with here, only the main aspects will be mentioned in keyword form (see Grupp and Hinze, 1994; Grupp *et al.*, 2001).

Citation frequency is dependent on many factors. These include (see, for example, Cronin, 1984; Frost, 1979; more recently David, 1994, on scientific productivity) the author's renown, the accessibility of an article which depends on its bibliographical form, the attractiveness of the field of work, the content of the article, the breadth of library reference material at the citing scientist's location etc.

Publication statistics suffer from the 'publish-or-perish' syndrome like citation statistics from the problem of self-citation. Self-citations are, on the one hand, unavoidable, because, owing to extreme specialization and differentiation in present scientific development, references can often only be found in earlier publications by the citing author or the publications of close associates. On the other hand, self-citations are a suitable way of manipulating the citation rates. A further problem is the chronological distortion of reference distribution. Reference accumulation can occur shortly after publication of the paper; however, obviously references to some publications are only made years later. Despite these objections, citation indices, while not necessarily expressing quality, certainly can reflect the impact of published results of scientific research on the future progress of research.

Papers *vis-à-vis* patents
Undeniably, patent documents like publications represent codified knowledge, that is, the formally recorded technological and scientific knowledge. The uncodified, that is, 'tacit' empirical knowledge of R&D personnel is nowhere disclosable in written form.[33] Through the patenting or publishing procedure, the tacit knowledge generates explicit information. It can be passed on (ordered, researched) in this form. Individual researchers may alternate between the two publication facilities, recording some of their R&D results in scientific publications, others in patent documents. The appearance of a scientific publication or even merely a lecture manuscript is 'detrimental to novelty' and can lead to rejection of a patent application because the subject described was already known by the manuscript.

Anyone intending to apply for a patent would therefore avoid allowing the invention to feature in any other publication prior to the priority date wherever possible.[34] Even carefully screened publications can therefore participate in the innovation race.

It is also undeniable that documents of both kinds can be the product of cooperative efforts between more fundamental researchers and company R&D personnel, the groups of authors not necessarily always being identical to the group of inventors (Noyons *et al.*, 1994).

Classification systems in science and technology
Classification systems in science and technology are bound to differ fundamentally from one another because only some of scientific activity is relevant to technology and innovation. It is now widely thought that technical relevance is lacking in the humanities and social sciences (except for analyses on technology), but also many medical and biological matters are so fundamental that they remain irrelevant to technical development at least for the foreseeable future.

Patent classification is generally used for subdividing technology and has the merit of being very finely and hierarchically divisible. It is more flexible than economic classifications; single areas of technology may (sometimes as a fraction) be assigned to product groups and hence markets.

Yet the devising of a functional relationship between markets and areas of technology which is not derived from a specific innovation project, but which is to be universally valid, would seem to be particularly unrealistic when a radical innovation is present. Such an innovation offers an across-the-board technical performance characteristic for which wide-ranging applications are expected and change of the entire characteristics bundle is imminent. Frequently, such technology is attended by expectations of substantial economic penetration.

Thus the construction of 'concordances' (matching relations of classification systems) in each case represents an attempt of a pragmatic partial solution with a shaky theoretical basis. On the other hand, overcoming the concordance problem is absolutely indispensable if a link is to be established between the multifarious occasionally disconnected innovation indicators. With the accent on the 'new techno–economic system' or the growing significance of technological fusion (Kodama, 1986), the patent classification systems or bibliometric classification principles often need to be linked by key words. The keywords can be established by technical experts.

Conclusions
Studies of measurement of technical progress are not very numerous, particularly when measured against the total number of economic research

papers. As innovation may have many discontinuous characteristics, equilibrium models time and again disclose themselves as a hindrance and – from an empirical point of view – must be supported by less than plausible assumptions. In neo-Schumpeterian innovation theory based on evolutionary economics, an attempt is made to produce models that compensate for the impossibility of closed, algebraic solutions, e.g. by the use of simulation tools, or dispense entirely with any mathematical or analytical models.

Therefore, in empirical neo-Schumpeterian research, the requirement for correspondence between empirical observables and 'appreciative' theory is confronted with the task of constructing appropriate indicators for sometimes inadequately 'tailored' theoretical constructs. If empirics were to employ uncritically newly available numeric data for econometric tests; if, in other words, measurements were carried out without any theoretical basis, the risk of false inferences would be quite large. However, the task of 'tailoring' must also be given to theory, which is often censured for playing a 'glass bead' game that allows for no relationship to actual economic realities. In this contribution we wanted to demonstrate, while very adequately meeting all theoretical requirements, how to study science and technology empirically.

If we may have given the impression that the concordance problem is far from being resolved, then this impression was intentional. The concordance problem is indicative of classification problems fundamental to the evolutionary innovation event. Overemphasis of the difficulties should not be allowed to disguise the fact that the indicators employed for single innovation projects can be used individually without being exposed to the shortcomings of the concordance problem. Definition and classification problems only come to light when various statistical data sets are combined.

Notes

1. For the economic background and the tradition of productivity measurement, see the contribution by Cantner in this volume. As far as the author is aware, the first systematic work on measuring innovation output by means of indicators was published by Freeman (1969).
2. The measurement of (technical) product characteristics was termed 'technometrics' in analogy to bibliometrics.
3. Likewise a reference to Kaufer (1989, p. 5; the original text is written in mediaeval Latin).
4. Nelson referred to technology as a 'latent public good' (Nelson, 1990); compare also von Weizsäcker (1980).
5. The following argumentation originates from Basberg (1987); see also the review article from Griliches (1990).
6. See, for example, Schmoch (1990, p. 15). The alternative to the patent as a means of protection is secrecy, extremely fast market entry plus excessive sales and service expenses and costs. Harabi (1995) discovered empirically for Swiss companies that, if patent protection is forgone, all of these alternative means of protection are used together.

7. Note the parallel between the historical background and the meaning of the word, 'be evident'.
8. Kitch (1977, passim) pointed to the important function of patents for the appropriation of technology, which became now a field of renewed emphasis in innovation research (see, among others, Grupp and Schmoch, 1999).
9. This citation function of the patent essentially is a resource indicator not a result or yield indicator. Patel and Pavitt review the citation function (1995, p. 28).
10. As early as 1854, Roscher (p. 80) listed 'discoveries and inventions' in the first place among six 'classes' of economic activities.
11. Mansfield (1986, p. 177) considers these so-called 'propensities to patent' for the United States based on a questionnaire from the early 1980s to be 50–86 per cent. As far as sector-dependence is concerned, only about 50 of all patentable inventions in the raw metal area also actually applied for patent status whereas most other branches of industry, especially chemistry, the pharmaceutical industry, machinery and electrical engineering have a propensity to patent of over 80 per cent. For large companies, the figures are even higher. For Europe, similar figures are quoted, for example, by Bertin and Wyatt (1988). Figures for Japan are available for 1993. They relate explicitly to the proportion of R&D expenditures which culminate in property rights relative to all expenditures. The protected part of the R&D expenditure varies between 45 per cent (timber products) and 89 per cent (electronic instruments) and averages 71 per cent. The 'research institute' branch protects even more intensively than manufacturing industry, specifically up to a level of 91 per cent (OECD, 1994, p. 51).
12. In the case of Japan, the proportion of protected R&D expenditures for the 'software and information services' branch is an astounding 72 per cent (OECD, 1994, p. 51).
13. Schmookler (1966, p. 49) estimates the progress-relevant part of company-specific US patents at 50–70 per cent, while Täger (1979) reckons this percentage to be approximately 80 per cent. More recent evidence available from Italy puts the proportion of patents actually used for innovation at 40–60 per cent of all applications (Archibugi, 1992, p. 359). Even if many patents deliberately ought not to be used as they are tailored exclusively to strategic purposes (obstructing of competitors) and are unconnected with the company's own innovation intentions, in this case the applicant is bound to provide certain R&D services to undergo the patent agent's public inspection procedure, otherwise patent applications would not come to public notice and protection would not be awarded.
14. According to Harabi (1991, pp. 359ff.) competitors' patents tend to increase, for the imitator, both the time and costs needed in order to imitate innovations.
15. In addition to the functions mentioned, patents can still have other entirely different ones: Harabi (1995) reports on discussions with patent lawyers according to whom companies also use patents as a means of evaluating the performance of their own R&D employees as well as for extending or retaining a known negotiating position with other companies.
16. However, determination of the value of granted patents involving retrospective examination of how long the company is prepared to pay the patent fees in order to retain property rights is an interesting application of grant statistics. The method appears to be suitable for evaluating product cycle lengths. For a review of this literature, see, for example, Schankerman and Pakes (1986) and Schankerman (1991).
17. Many patents at the application stage, to which a patent could be granted after the examination stage, are not pursued to actual grant, for example, because of short product cycles.
18. USPTO=United States Patent and Trademark Office. There, the award or grant date is called 'patent date'.
19. Henderson and Cockburn (1993) regard patents as 'important' only if they have been awarded in two or three triadic regions (p. 10).
20. 'Each claim in a patent is considered a separate and independent invention . . . each claim is, in effect, a separate patent' (Rivise, 1993, p. 100).
21. These are discussed briefly by Grupp (1994, pp. 187ff.), Patel and Pavitt (1995) and Soete and Wyatt (1983).

22. In order to make meaningful inferences, the statistical error obtained from random errors in patent statistics must be calculated. By making certain simplifying assumptions, the statistical errors D RPA_h, are:

$$DRPA_h(k, i) = \{20 \cdot RTA(k, i)/[RTA^2(k, i) + 1]\}^2 \cdot P^{-1/2}(k, i) \text{ (Grupp, 1994, 1998, p. 184).}$$

23. See also Hu and Jaffe (2003) and quotations given therein.
24. An overview is provided (Griliches, 1995, pp. 63ff.).
25. Similar empirical studies which have since appeared are summarized and discussed by Cohen and Levin (1989, pp. 1090ff.), Harhoff (1991) and Geroski (1995).
26. The International Patents Classification (IPC) comprises around 70 000 individual elements and summaries at all hierarchical stages.
27. (Griliches, 1995, p. 64) also admits that the sector concept is based on 'untenable assumptions' and 'that we do not deal with one closed industry'. He mentions the cross-classification approach with patents as an alternative model.
28. Griliches (1990, p. 1689) specifically writes: 'In that sense, the "objectivity" of such citations is greater and may contribute to the validity of citation counts as indexes of relative importance.'
29. Mansfield (1991) discovered that (in the USA) in the industrial average 15 to 19 per cent of all product and process innovations were possible not without major delay or only with substantial support from academic research. The range of mentions covers over 40 per cent in pharmaceuticals up to 2 per cent in the mineral oils sector. Tijssen (2002) found that (in Europe) some 20 per cent of the private sector's innovations turned out to be based on public sector research.
30. The percentage with no profit-motivated background may exceed 10 per cent in modern fields of technology; see Grupp and Schmoch (1992, pp. 95–115).
31. The notion of 'scientometric indicators' is likewise employed; see the handbook edited by van Raan (1988). One of the first publications to suggest quantitative measures of science originates from England (Price, 1951). The introduction of bibliometrics for progress measurement, as far as I can see, is a merit of Soviet–Ukrainian researchers (Dobrov, 1963, 1967).
32. Adams (1990); see also Wagner-Döbler (1997, p. 171).
33. Detailed demarcations are to be found in Dasgupta and David (1987), see also Gibbons *et al.* (1994) and Nightingale (2003). The seminal work is by Polanyi (1966). It should be noted that any knowledge in science and technology is tacit at the moment it is generated. It is available only in the heads of the discoverer(s) or inventor(s). The difference lies in the fact that some of this knowledge is codified later (usually not much later) if it is logged in minutes, conference papers, announcements of discoveries or inventions or journal manuscripts. Some is not written up and thus remains permanently tacit. The codification of some of this knowledge does not mean that it is easily accessible without transaction costs and would be obtainable everywhere. An access channel is required whether this be a databank, library searches or a colleague who 'knows where things stand'.
34. Certain companies take advantage of this situation in order to avoid patent application fees in minor instances. If management feels that a patent application is not worthwhile, a strategic publication is produced in order to deter companies from protecting the invention in question themselves. For further details see Grupp and Schmoch (1992).

Bibliography

Adams, J.D., Fundamental stock of knowledge and productivity growth, *Journal of Political Economy*, **98**, 672–702, 1990.

Archibugi, D., Patenting as an indicator of technological innovation: a review, *Science and Public Policy*, **19** (6), 357–68, 1992.

Basberg, B.L., Patents and the measurement of technical change: a survey of the literature, *Research Policy*, **16**, 131–41, 1987.

Bertin, G.Y. and S. Wyatt, *Multinationals and Industrial Property*, Wheatsheaf: Harvester, 1988.

Cohen, W.M. and R.C. Levin, 'Empirical studies of innovation and market structure', in Schmalensee and Willig, pp. 1059–107, 1989.

Cronin, B., *The Citation Process. The Role and Significance of Citations in Scientific Communication*, London: Taylor Graham, 1984.

Dasgupta, P.S. and P.A. David, *Information Disclosure and the Economics of Science and Technology*, New York: Macmillan, 1987.

David, P.A., 'Positive feedback and research productivity in science: reopening another black box', in Granstrand, pp. 54–89, 1994.

Dobrov, G.M., Scientific prognosis and historical–logical analysis, *Ukrainskij istorichnyj zhurnal*, **1**, 1963.

Dobrov, G.M. (ed.), *The Analysis of Trends and the Forecasting of Scientificotechnological Progress*, Kiev: Naukova Dumka, 1967.

Dosi, G., C. Freeman, R. Nelson, G. Silverberg and L. Soete (eds), *Technical Change and Economic Theory*, London: Pinter Publishers, 1988.

Freeman, C., *Measurement of Output of Research and Experimental Development*, Paris: UNESCO, 1969.

Freeman, C., *The Economics of Industrial Innovation*, London: Pinter Publishers, 1982.

Frost, C.O., The use of citations in literary research: a preliminary classification of citation functions, *Literary Quarterly*, **49** (4), 399–414, 1979.

Geroski, P., 'Markets for technology: knowledge, innovation and appropriability', in Stoneman, pp. 90–131, 1995.

Gibbons, M., C. Limoges, H. Nowotny, S. Schwartzman, P. Scott and M. Trow, *The New Production of Knowledge*, London: Sage Publications, 1994.

Granstrand, O. (ed.), *Economics of Technology*, Amsterdam: Elsevier, 1994.

Griliches, Z., Patent statistics as economic indicators: a survey, *Journal of Economic Literature*, **28**, 1661–707, 1990.

Griliches, Z., 'R&D and productivity: econometric results and measurement issues', in Stoneman, pp. 52–89, 1995.

Grupp, H. (ed.), *Dynamics of Science-Based Innovation*, Berlin: Springer, 1992.

Grupp, H., The measurement of technical performance of innovations by technometrics and its impact on established technology indicators, *Research Policy*, **23**, 175–93, 1994.

Grupp, H., Spillover effects and the science base of innovation reconsidered: an empirical approach, *Journal of Evolutionary Economics*, **6** (2), 175–97, 1996.

Grupp, H., *Foundations of the Economics of Innovation – Theory, Measurement and Practice*, Cheltenham, UK, and Lyme, USA: Edward Elgar, 1998.

Grupp, H. and S. Hinze, International orientation, efficiency of and regard for research in East and West Germany: a bibliometric investigation of aspects of technology genesis in the United Germany, *Scientometrics*, **29**, 83–113, 1994.

Grupp, H. and U. Schmoch, 'At the crossroads in laser medicine and polyimide chemistry – patent assessment of the expansion of knowledge', in Grupp, pp. 95–115, 1992.

Grupp, H. and U. Schmoch, Patent statistics in the age of globalisation: new legal producers, new analytical methods, new economic interpretation, *Research Policy*, **28** (4), 377–96, 1999.

Grupp, H., I. Dominguez-Lacasa and M. Friedrich-Nishio (eds), *Das deutsche Innovationssystem seit der Reichsgründung*, Heidelberg: Physica-Verlag, 2002.

Grupp, H., U. Schmoch and S. Hinze, International alignment and scientific regard as macro-indicators for international comparisons of publications, *Scientometrics*, **51** (2), 359–80, 2001.

Grupp, H., O. Hohmeyer, R. Kollert and H. Legler, *Technometrie – Die Bemessung des technisch-wirtschaftlichen Leistungsstandes*, Cologne: TUEV Rheinland GmbH, 1987.

Hanusch, H. and U. Cantner, Neuere Ansätze in der Innovationstheorie und der Theorie des technischen Wandels – Konsequenzen für eine Industrie- und Technologiepolitik, in Meyer-Krahmer, pp. 12–46, 1993.

Harabi, N., Einflussfaktoren von Forschung und Entwicklung in der Schweizer Industrie, *Die Unternehmung – Schweizerische Zeitschrift für betriebswirtschaftliche Forschung und Praxis*, **43**, 349–68, 1991.

Harabi, N., Appropriability of technical innovations. An empirical analysis, *Research Policy*, **24** (6), 981–92, 1995.

Harhoff, D., Strategic spillover production, vertical organization, and incentives for research and development, PhD thesis, Alfred P. Sloan School of Management (MIT), Cambridge, MA, 1991.

Harhoff, D., F. Narin, F.M. Scherer and K. Vopel, Citation frequency and the value of patented innovation, *Review of Economics and Statistics*, **81** (3), 511–15, 1999.

Henderson, R. and I. Cockburn, Scale, scope and spillovers: the determinants of research productivity in ethical drug discovery, working paper, Cambridge, MA: MIT and NBER, 1993.

Hu, A.G.Z. and A.B. Jaffe, Patent citations and international knowledge flow: the cases of Korea and Taiwan, *International Journal of Industrial Organization*, **21**, 849–80, 2003.

Jaffe, A.B., Technological opportunity and spillovers of R&D: evidence from firms' patent profiles, and market value, *American Economic Review*, **76** (5), 984–1001, 1986.

Kaufer, E., *The Economics of the Patent System*, Chur: Harwood Academic Publishers, 1989.

Kitch, E.W., The nature and function of the patent system, *Journal of Law and Economics*, **20**, 265–90, 1977.

Kodama, F., Japanese innovation in mechatronics technology: a study of technological fusion, *Science and Public Policy*, **13**, 44, 1986.

Machlup, F., *Patentwesen: Geschichtlicher Überblick*, Stuttgart: Gustav Fischer Verlag, 1964.

Mansfield, E., Patents and innovation: an empirical study, *Management Science*, **32** (2), 173–81, 1986.

Mansfield, E., Academic research and industrial innovation, *Research Policy*, **20**, 1–12, 1991.

Meyer-Krahmer, F. (ed.), Innovationsökonomie und Technologiepolitik, Heidelberg: Physica-Verlag, 1993.

Nelson, R.R., What is public and what is private about technology?, Center for Research in Management, University of California, Berkeley, 1990.

Nightingale, P., If Nelson and Winter are only half right about tacit knowledge, which half? A Searlean critique of 'codification', *Industrial and Corporate Change*, **12** (2), 149–83, 2003.

Noyons, E.C.M., A.F.J. van Raan, H. Grupp and U. Schmoch, Exploring the science and technology interface: inventor–author relations in laser medicine research, *Research Policy*, **23**, 443–57, 1994.

OECD, *Accessing and Expanding the Science and Technology Knowledge Base*, Paris: OECD, 1994.

Patel, P. and K. Pavitt, 'Patterns of technological activity: their measurement and interpretation', in Stoneman, pp. 15–51, 1995.

Polanyi, M., *The Tacit Dimension*, London: Routledge & Kegan, 1966.

Price, D.d.S., Quantitative measures of the development of science, *Archives Internationales d'Histoire des Sciences*, **14**, 85–93, 1951.

Raan, A.F.J. van, *Handbook of Quantitative Studies of Science and Technology*, Amsterdam: North-Holland, 1988.

Rivise, C.W., *Patent Applications*, Charlottesville: The Michie Company, 1993.

Roscher, W., *System der Volkswirtschaft – Grundlagen der Nationalökonomie*, Stuttgart: J.G. Cotta'sche Buchhandlung, 1854.

Schankerman, M., Les statistiques sur les renouvellements des brevets: un moyen pour mesurer la valeur de la protection par brevet ainsi que la production de l'activité inventive, *STI*, **8**, 107–32, 1991.

Schankerman, M. and A. Pakes, Estimates of the value of patent rights in European countries during the post-1950 period, *The Economic Journal*, **96**, 1052–76, 1986.

Scherer, F.M., D. Harhoff and J. Kukies, Uncertainty and the size distribution of rewards from innovation, *Journal of Evolutionary Economics*, **10**, 175–200, 2000.

Schmalensee, R. and R.D. Willig (eds), *Handbook of Industrial Organization, Volume II*, Amsterdam: Elsevier, 1989.

Schmoch, U., Wettbewerbsvorsprung durch Patentinformation – Handbuch für die Recherchenpraxis, Cologne: Verlag TÜV Rheinland, 1990.

Schmookler, J., *Invention and Economic Growth*, Cambridge, MA: Harvard University Press, 1966.

Soete, L.G. and M.E. Wyatt, The use of foreign patenting as an internationally comparable science and technology output indicator, *Scientometrics*, **5**, 31–54, 1983.

Stoneman, P. (ed.), *Handbook of the Economics of Innovation and Technological Change*, Oxford and Cambridge, MA: Blackwell, 1995.

Täger, U., Untersuchung der Aussagefähigkeit von Patentstatistiken hinsichtlich technologischer Entwicklungen, Munich: ifo-Institut, 1979.

Tijssen, R.J.W., Science dependence of technologies: evidence from inventions and their inventors, *Research Policy*, **31**, 509–26, 2002.

Tong, X. and J.D. Frame, Measuring national technological performance with patent claims data, *Research Policy*, **23**, 133–41, 1994.

Trajtenberg, M., A penny for your quotes: patent citations and the value of innovations, *RAND Journal of Economics*, **21**, 172–87, 1990.

Wagner-Döbler, R., Science–technology coupling: the case of mathematical logic and computer science, *Scientometrics*, **48** (2), 171–83, 1997.

Weizsäcker, C.C. von, *Barriers to Entry*, Berlin/Heidelberg: Springer, 1980.

32 Sectoral taxonomies: identifying competitive regimes by statistical cluster analysis
Michael Peneder

1 Introduction

More than most other economic disciplines, the neo-Schumpeterian tradition of research stresses the diverse and contingent nature of competitive behaviour. Within the confines of this paradigm, competitive performance depends on the capability to match a firm's organization and strategy to the technological, social and economic restrictions imposed by its business environment. It is in particular the notions of 'technological regimes' (Nelson and Winter, 1982; Winter, 1984; Malerba and Orsenigo, 1993, 1996) or, relatedly, of 'technological paradigms' (Dosi, 1982, 1988) and 'sectoral systems of innovation' (Malerba, 2004), which put especial emphasis on the importance of sectoral characteristics of technological change and the competitive process more generally.

Franco Malerba stresses the importance of linking the discussion on technological regimes with methodological debates about the creation of sectoral taxonomies (see his contribution to this volume). It is precisely at this point that the present chapter aims to take up the baton. The intention is to demonstrate how the generation of empirically based sectoral classifications can provide new and valuable tools for our research in the processes of industrial development.

To begin with, we can distinguish two major reasons for the creation and use of analytically based industry classifications: first, sectoral taxonomies facilitate investigations into the impact of specific characteristics of the market environment on economic activity. Substituting structural knowledge for exhaustive information about single attributes, the intractable diversity of real-life phenomena is condensed into a smaller number of salient types. Classifications thus direct our attention towards a few characteristic dimensions, according to which relative similarities or differences can be identified. They allow us to take account of heterogeneity, but simultaneously force us to be selective.

Second, from a purely practical perspective, the taxonomic approach is particulary useful when referring to data that are not easily available in a comparable format across countries or firms. The reason is that it builds upon data from those entities, which offer the best coverage of specific attributes and then produce typical profiles of the relevant variables. The resulting classification can then be applied to other data of economic activity, which are available on a broader comparable basis (for example, value added, employment, or foreign trade data).

In contrast to the prominent attention it is given in various sciences such as biology, psychology or sociology, the proper construction and use of classifications has remained underresearched within the realm of economics. We still find little or no methodological debate and a striking lack of awareness for the different approaches pursued. This chapter tries to stimulate that discussion. It starts with a summary of major classifications and their intellectual origin within the tradition of innovation research. This is followed by a discussion of major methodological issues, which begins with fairly general concepts and definitions but then focuses on a number of critical choices that have to be made during the process of statistical cluster analysis. The final section will present an illustrative example which additionally tries to give some idea about how the results from statistical cluster analyses might be validated in terms of their economic meaning.

2   The use of sectoral taxonomies
Analytically based industry classifications are frequently applied in empirical studies on competitive performance, technological development, international trade, and industrial economics. While Peneder (2003a) provides a critical survey of major classifications applied within these various fields, this section focuses on innovation-related classifications more narrowly.

2.1   Entrepreneurial v. routinized regimes
The notion of 'technological regimes' descends from the works of Joseph Schumpeter, who provided two seemingly conflicting explanations about the locus where innovation takes place. In his *Theory of Economic Development* (1911) he regarded independent entrepreneurs as the source of economic progress, but later, in *Capitalism, Socialism and Democray* (1942) he argued that innovation increasingly becomes a 'routine' task of big enterprises with large and specialized research laboratories.[1] Trying to reconcile the seeming contradiction, Schumpeter (1942) argued that the two modes correspond to different stages in the development of an economy. In his view, the 'entrepreneurial' mode (frequently labelled 'Mark 1') dominates at the earlier stages of economic development, while the 'routinized' regime ('Mark 2') gains ground at the later stages, ultimately depriving the economy of its entrepreneurial resources and defeating the capitalist system by means of its own success.

While the latter hypothesis is generally rejected, first for lack of empirical support, and second for an unwarranted determinism in its interpretation of history (Hodgson, 1993), Nelson and Winter (1982) as well as Winter (1984) made the decisive break by considering the two modes of innovation as valid characterizations of distinct technological 'regimes' that represent intrinsic differences between particular sectors (and therefore can coexist at any stages of development). As Winter (1984, p. 297) explains, 'the distinction between the two Schumpeterian regimes involves a reversal of the relative roles of innovation by entrants and established firms. An entrepreneurial regime is one that is favourable to innovative entry and unfavourable to innovative activity by established firms; a routinized regime is one in which conditions are the other way round'.[2] In the empirical applications of Audretsch (1991) or Malerba and Orsenigo (1996) sectors are therefore strictly defined in terms of characteristics that relate to the process of innovation. Of related interest, Peneder (2007a) explores the distinction between 'entrepreneurial' and 'routinized' regimes, but in contrast to the aforementioned literature defines industries according to demographic characteristics of the firm population.[3]

2.2   The Pavitt taxonomy of innovation types

Combining quantitative information with visual inspection and inductive reasoning, Pavitt (1984) created an empirical classification of sectors according to the characteristic technological paradigms among its innovating firms. The database comprises 2000 innovations in the manufacturing sector considered as being 'significant', and the corresponding innovating firms in the UK; the time span ranges from 1945 to 1979. Since the data are arguably very complex and incomplete, Pavitt refrained from a purely deductive approach with advanced statistical techniques. His taxonomy of 'sectoral technological trajectories' classifies industries as characterized either by (i) 'science-based' firms; (ii) 'production-intensive' firms, or (iii) 'supplier-dominated' firms. The second group is further subdivided into the categories of 'scale-intensive' production or 'specialized suppliers'.

Pavitt's taxonomy has been extremely influential, shaping the basic conceptual categories for a number of related classifications which followed. For example, Evangelista (2000) presents an empirical Pavitt-type sectoral classification of innovation patterns in services by means of statistical cluster analysis, while Marsili (2001) offers a detailed and updated empirical account of the various 'modal characteristics of innovative processes' in relation to sectoral systems within manufacturing.

In the 1990s, the availability of firm data from national innovation surveys induced several papers which are also related to the tradition of the Pavitt classification, but ultimately turn out to be very critical of the presumed sectoral regularities in innovation patterns. Rather than classifying industries or sectors, they focus on the distinct innovation types observed at the firm level. Although the lack of industry classifications puts them outside the immediate concern of this chapter, they need to be mentioned because they seriously challenge the use of sectoral taxonomies of innovation types more generally. For instance, Cesaratto and Mangano (1993), Arvanitis and Hollenstein (1998) and Hollenstein (2003) share a strong emphasis on the observed variety of technological behaviour within sectors that results from their empirical work with micro-data. Archibugi (2001) explicitly argues for leaving aside Pavitt's link to industries and focusing instead on the direct classification of firms.

It turns out to be one of the major virtues of the systematic collection of micro-data from the innovation surveys that one can no longer deny the great heterogeneity of behavioural patterns at the micro level. In other words, assuming that the competitive environment determines corporate strategy in its entirety (to the extent that firms are forced either to adopt optimal practices or to exit) implies an unwarranted denial of heterogeneity in competitive behaviour. However, at this point we must add that any approach which neglects market specifics conveys an equally unwarranted denial of the more systematic determinants of the firm's selection environment (including technology).

As a purely practical remark, we should also recall that industry classifications aim at serving a specific analytic purpose. They are created, for example, because they enable the transposition of partly hidden characteristics, which are otherwise not readily available in (internationally) comparable formats, and then combine them with other, more easily comparable data (as long as these can be identified by industry membership). It is difficult to find a comparably practical use for classifications which are only tied to individual patterns of behaviour. Since all analytical applications are locked into the same specific data set, one might generally prefer to run econometric estimations with the initial micro-data, where the available information is fully preserved.

3   The method of sectoral classifications

Having shown some major examples of industry classifications focusing on the field of innovation research, we may now turn to the method of creating sectoral taxonomies. We begin with some general definitions and then turn to more specific questions about the tools available from statistical cluster analysis.

3.1   General issues

The process of classification is generally defined as the ordering of cases in terms of their similarity. According to Bailey (1994), classifications themselves can be distinguished by (among others) the following characteristics: they can be labelled either as typologies or as taxonomies; monothetic or polythetic; synchronic or diachronic. The term 'typology' refers specifically to a conceptual classification, the cells of which represent type concepts rather than empirical cases. Conversely, the term 'taxonomy' refers to a classification of empirical entities based upon quantitative analysis. In this sense, one can also distinguish *monothetic* classes, in which all the cases included in a certain category are identical with respect to every relevant dimension. No exceptions or further differentiations are allowed. Such a neat and (idealized) categorization is typical of qualitative categorizations, whereas empirical classifications generally come up with *polythetic* classes. Here, the cases are not identical with respect to all variables, but rather are grouped according to the generally strongest similarity. In other words, the existence of large individual variations within the given categories of a classification is taken for granted. Finally, classifications are called *synchronic* (or phenetic), if they refer to the characteristics of an observation at a certain point in time. Conversely, classifications are called *diachronic* (or phyletic), if they are based upon characteristic patterns of change or evolution. Moreover, we generally expect that our classifications are exhaustive and mutually exclusive, thereby demanding the existence of one (but only one) appropriate class for each observation.

Two general approaches to the quantitative identification of individual observations into classes can be distinguished. A 'cut-off' procedure by which a certain discriminatory edge is defined exogenously by the researcher is the more frequently applied method. The sole advantage of this approach lies in its simplicity. In choosing not to use more powerful statistical tools, the underlying structure within the data is more or less presumed, rather than explored. Although this approach can be defended as long as the classifications are built upon one or two variables only, it is generally inadequate for the categorization of a data profile of larger dimensions. Statistical cluster analysis is the obvious alternative. It is specifically designed for classifying observations on behalf of their relative similarities with respect to a multidimensional array of variables. It is a powerful tool for the creation of sectoral taxonomies and thus deserves a more detailed discussion in the next section.

3.2 Statistical cluster analysis

Definitions and aim Statistical cluster analysis is defined as 'the art of finding groups in data' (Kaufmann and Rousseuw, 1990) such that the degree of 'natural association' (Anderberg, 1973) is (i) high among members within the same class (*internal cohesion*) and (ii) low between members of different categories (*external isolation*). In practice, internal cohesion and external separation are not definite requirements, but rather general objectives. Their fulfilment is a matter of degree and depends on the nature of the data as well as the clustering techniques applied.

Cluster analysis offers a sophisticated statistical tool for the exploration and classification of multivariate data, but it is important to acknowledge that it remains a heuristic method, which requires the researcher to make a number of choices that critically affect the final outcomes. In the following, we present a brief explanation of relevant techniques and deliberate choices that have to be made.

Measures of (dis)similarity   Once the variables are chosen, the clustering procedure starts with a given data matrix of $i = 1, \ldots, n$ observations for which characteristic attributes x are reported for $j = 1, \ldots, p$ variables. The initial data set of the dimension $n \times p$ is then transformed into a symmetric (dis)similarity matrix of dimensions $n \times n$ observations with d_{ih} being the coefficients of (dis)similarity for observations x_i and x_h.

$$
D_{n,n} =
\begin{bmatrix}
0 & \cdots & & & & 0 \\
d_{21} & 0 & \cdots & & & \\
d_{31} & d_{32} & 0 & \cdots & & \vdots \\
\vdots & & \vdots & & & \\
& \cdots & d_{ih} & \cdots & & \\
& & \vdots & & & \\
d_{n1} & d_{n2} & \cdots & & d_{n(n-1)} & 0
\end{bmatrix}
\tag{32.1}
$$

For any observations x_i, x_h and x_g with i, h and $g = 1, \ldots, n$, located within measurement space **E**, the desired formal properties of the (dis)similarity matrix $\mathbf{D}_{nn}$ are defined as follows (Anderberg, 1973, p. 99):

1. $d_{ih} = 0$ if and only if $x_i = x_h$, i.e. for all observations the distance from itself is zero and any two observations with zero distance are identical;
2. $d_{ih} >= 0$, i.e. all distances are non-negative;
3. $d_{ih} = d_{hi}$, i.e. all distances are symmetric; and finally
4. $d_{ih} <= d_{ig} + d_{hg}$, known as the triangle inequality, which states that going directly from x_i to x_h is shorter than making a detour over object x_g.

The combination of the first and second properties ensures that $\mathbf{D}_{nn}$ is fully specified by its values in the lower triangle. The fourth property establishes that E is a Euclidean space and that we can correctly interpret distances by applying elementary geometry. Any dissimilarity function that fulfils the above four conditions is said to be a *metric*.

In this spirit, the Euclidean distance e_{ih} appears to be the most natural measure of (dis)similarity, thanks to its direct application of the Pythagorean theorem:

$$euc_{ih} = \sqrt{\sum_{j=1}^{n}(x_{ij}-x_{hj})^2} \qquad 0 \le euc_{ih} < \infty. \qquad (32.2)$$

Operating with the squared differences, the Euclidean measure will, for example, rank two observations with a difference of 1 unit in the first variable and 3 units in the second variable as farther apart than two observations with a difference of 2 units in both variables. In other words, it is sensitive to outliers. Alternatively, the closely related Manhattan or 'city block distance' ascribes equal importance to any unit of dissimilarity, because it simply calculates the sum of the absolute lengths of the other two sides of the triangle:

$$cityb_{ih} = \sum_{j=1}^{p}|x_{ij}-x_{hj}| \qquad 0 \le cityb_{ih} < \infty \qquad (32.3)$$

Kaufmann and Rousseuw (1990, p. 12) use the image of a city in which the streets run vertically and horizontally to explain the peculiar name. The Euclidean measure corresponds to the shortest geometric distance 'a bird could fly' straight from point x_i to point x_h, whereas the use of the Manhattan measure is consistent with the distance that 'people have to walk' around the city blocks. Both measures in (32.2) and (32.3) fulfil the requirements of a metric.[4]

When we are interested in the 'shape' of objects rather than in the absolute size of differences, alternative measures can be more helpful. The following two measures of similarity, called 'angular separation' in (32.4) and the 'correlation coefficient' in (32.5), are most frequently used:

$$ang_{ih} = \frac{\sum_{j=1}^{p}x_{ij}x_{hj}}{\sqrt{\sum_{j=1}^{p}x_{ij}^2 \sum_{j=1}^{p}x_{hj}^2}} \qquad -1,0 \le ang_{ih} \le 1,0, \qquad (32.4)$$

$$corr_{ih} = \frac{\sum_{j=1}^{p}x_{ij}x_{hj} - (1/p)\left(\sum_{j=1}^{p}x_{ij}\sum_{j=1}^{p}x_{hj}\right)}{\sqrt{\left[\left[\sum_{j=1}^{p}x_{ij}^2 - (1/p)\left(\sum_{j=1}^{p}x_{ij}\right)^2\right]\left[\sum_{j=1}^{p}x_{hj}^2 - (1/p)\left(\sum_{j=1}^{p}x_{hj}\right)^2\right]\right]}}$$

$$-1,0 \le corr_{ih} \le 1,0 \qquad (32.5)$$

Both angular separation and the correlation coefficient measure the cosine of the angle between two vectors. The essential difference between the two is that the former is based on deviations from the origin, whereas the latter operates with deviations from the mean of the variables of an observation. As a consequence, the correlation coefficient is unaffected by mere size displacements (i.e. the uniform addition of a constant to each element). The correlation coefficient is therefore less discriminating than the angular separation measure.[5]

In addition to the above examples, the literature provides a variety of other (dis)similarity functions that are applied in statistical cluster analysis. For extensive surveys see, for example, Romesburg (1984) and Gordon (1999). The following section presents a simple numerical example plus geometric visualization that demonstrates how the choice of various measures affects the values of the final (dis)similarity matrix $\mathbf{D}_{nn}$. The example is taken from Peneder (2007b).

A numerical example   A simple numerical example can demonstrate the differences between the four (dis)similarity functions. Table 32.1 provides the values for five hypothetical objects *I* to *V* for the three variables *A*, *B* and *C*. Table 32.2 reports the calculated (dis)similarity for four different measures. Figure 32.1 offers an additional geometric visualization of the two-dimensional case, in which we only consider the variables *A* and *B*. Objects are characterized in parentheses according to their respective coordinates. The straight line between two cases corresponds to the Euclidean distance, whereas the city block distance equals the length of the connecting horizontal and vertical lines. The two rays that go from the origin to the respective cases determine the angular separation measure.

The first interesting observation is that the city block measure treats objects *II* and *III* as equally distant from *I*, whereas the Euclidean measure regards the latter as more distant. The simple reason is that we move from a quadratic to a rectangular shape. In contrast, both the angular separation

Table 32.1   A numerical example

| Objects | Numerical values of variable | | |
	A	*B*	*C*
I	4.0	2.0	1.0
II	2.0	4.0	3.0
III	3.0	5.0	3.0
IV	3.0	6.0	4.5
V	6.0	4.0	3.0

*Table 32.2   Comparing measures of (dis)similarity of the numerical
example*

Measure	Comparison of (dis)similarity between object *I* and ..			
	II	*III*	*IV*	*V*
Euclidean distance	3.46	3.74	5.41	3.46
City block distance	6.00	6.00	8.50	6.00
Angular separation	0.77	0.83	0.77	0.98
Correlation coefficient	−0.65	−0.19	−0.65	1.00

and the correlation coefficient say that, relative to *I*, *III* is more similar than
II. Secondly, for both the Euclidean and the city block distance, case *IV* is
more dissimilar to *I* than is case *III* or case *II*. However, when we apply
angular separation or the correlation coefficient, *IV* is just as similar to *I* as
is *II*, since both are located on the same ray from the origin. Finally, case *V*
is an extreme example of the differences between size- and shape-oriented
measures. Whereas *I* and *V* are clearly distant in the sense of Euclidean or
city block measures (mirroring the distance between *I* and *II*), the two cases
are highly similar in the measure of angular separation and even identical,
if we apply the correlation coefficient. The reason is that, for case *V*, we only
add a constant of two units to each of the variables. Since the correlation
coefficient is insensitive to mere size displacements, both cases are treated
as identical.Unfortunately, there is no general guideline, which establishes
the priority of one measure over another. One might choose the Euclidean
distance as the most 'natural' function, but this is only because we are
accustomed to imagining objects in Euclidean space. Kaufmann and
Rousseuw (1990), for example, recommend the city block distance instead,
because it is not sensitive to outliers. In contrast to both, angular separation and the correlation coefficient are more appropriate when we are interested in similarities in the shape of objects, rather than in the absolute size
of the differences. As a practical consideration, a cluster of objects with a
similar profile of attributes might often be easier to interpret.

In some instances, a priori conceptual considerations about the nature of
the variables and the desired properties of the classification might be a
sufficient guide in making that decision. In general, however, it is desirable
to try out more than one function and to learn how robust the results are
with respect to the variations in the concepts of measurement. However,
there are also trade-offs to consider and repeatedly increasing the number
of (dis)similarity functions inevitably leads to diminishing returns. For the
purpose of this brief overview, the four measures presented in equations

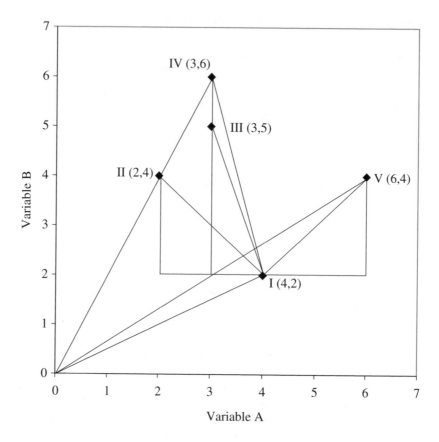

Note: The straight lines between two objects determine the Euclidean distance, the connected horizontal and vertical lines the city block distance and the two rays from the origin the angular separation measure.

Source: Peneder (2007b).

Figure 32.1   A geometric illustration of differences in (dis)similarity measures

(32.2) to (32.5) will provide a reasonable and sufficient range of functions, which allows one to take into account the robustness of the results with regard to different (dis)similarity matrices.

Clustering algorithms   The next crucial step concerns the choice of how to group objects into separate categories, i.e. we must choose what clustering algorithm to use. Again a variety of approaches is possible.[6] Among the clustering algorithms that are most widely used, we must distinguish between two general approaches. The first is the *partitioning* method, which breaks objects into a distinct number of non-overlapping groups. The most common of them, which is also applied here, is the so called 'k-means' technique. The second approach is the *hierarchical cluster analysis*, which is either divisive or agglomerative, i.e. dividing or combining hierarchically related objects into clusters. Three variations of the *agglomerative* hierarchical clustering method are used in the current analysis.

For the k-means method, the set of observations is divided by a predefined number of clusters k. For example, k nearly equal-sized segments can be formed as an initial partition. Cluster centres are computed for each group, which are the vectors of the means of the corresponding values for each variable. The objects are then assigned to the group with the nearest cluster centre. After this, the mean of the observations are recomputed and the process is repeated until convergence is reached. This is the case when no observation moves between groups and all have remained in the same cluster of the previous iteration. With this method, a critical and potentially very manipulative choice is the initial number of clusters k. In order to mitigate the inevitable degree of arbitrariness involved in that decision, I consistently apply the following self-binding rule-of-thumb: 'Choose the lowest number k that maximizes the quantity of individual clusters l which include more than 5% of the observed cases.'[7]

In contrast to the k-means method, hierarchical cluster analysis enables us to determine the boundaries between clusters at different levels of (dis)similarity. Preserving a higher degree of complexity in the output produced, hierarchical techniques require a heuristic interpretation of the surfacing patterns. Dendrograms (or 'cluster trees') support this by means of graphical representation. As with k-means cluster analysis, any of the above measures of distance can be applied. When groups with more than one object merge, various methods differ in the way they determine what the (dis)similarity between groups precisely is. The most popular and intuitively appealing choice is the *average linkage* method, whereby the average (dis)similarity between all the observations is compared for any pair of groups. Alternatively, the *complete linkage* method compares the (dis)similarity between the observations which are farthest apart, whereas the *single linkage* method takes the (dis)similarity of the nearest neighbours in any pair of groups into account.

The choice between the different linkage methods directly relates to the objectives of internal cohesion and the external isolation of clusters (mentioned at the beginning of this section). Single linkage aims only for external isolation, implying that any observation is more similar to some other object within the same cluster than to any other objects outside. Because of this property, single linkage methods frequently fail to reveal much structure within the data. The reason is that observations tend to join one common and expanding cluster, which leads to undesirable 'chaining' effects. Conversely, the complete linkage method aims at internal cohesion. This leads to compact classes, which, however, need not be externally isolated. The average linkage method avoids both extremes and seeks a compromise between the aims of internal cohesion and external isolation. As a piece of practical advice, we may follow Gordon (1999, p. 100), who recommends that, 'if it is not possible to determine a single preferred clustering procedure, it is useful to analyse data using two or more "sensible" methods of analysis and synthesize the results'. As he further explains, 'the hope is that the results are less likely to be an artefact of a single method of analysis and more likely to provide a reliable summary of any class structure that is present in the data' (ibid., p. 184).

To conclude, this methodological section has demonstrated the multitude of potentially very influential choices researchers have to make during the clustering process. In order to be credible, any classification should therefore be backed by a comprehensive documentation of the critical choices and a detailed explanation of how the graphical representations were interpreted. The next section gives a specific example of how that might be done in practice. Even though it does not directly relate to the innovation types discussed in section 2, it is of interest here, because it highlights the interaction between radical technological change and sector-specific demand for complementary human resources.

4   An illustrative example: human resources in the 'new economy'[8]

The rapid advance of new information technologies (IT) is a major cause of qualitative transformations in modern production systems. IT personnel is the fundamental category of human capital formation in the process of dissemination and adoption of computers and related equipment. It drives the progress in computer-related technologies of the IT producing sectors and enables the actual realization of productivity gains among IT user industries. The much quoted 'new economy' or 'digital revolution' also leaves some pronounced imprints on the overall formation of human capital, which we may trace in at least two dimensions. First, the structural change towards the 'new economy' favours the growth of specific computer-related occupations. Second, it tends to raise the demand for higher levels of workforce education. Together, occupational and educational attributes characterize the IT labour intensity of a firm, an industry, or the aggregate economy.

4.1   Data and the selection of variables

In the present analysis we are interested in occupational and educational characteristics of workforce composition, i.e. the share and educational level of IT labour. Data sources are the UK Labour Force Survey and the US Current Population Survey, with annual data on workforce composition available for both employment and wages. The data cover 39 sectors in the USA and the United Kingdom from 1979 until 2000. The annual data are pooled by calculating three (four) year averages from 1979 onwards. The workforce composition is represented by (i) employment and wage shares for IT labour in the total workforce and (ii) the share of personnel with higher education (university degrees) among IT labour.

Data for the different time periods enter as independent observations in the first part of the analysis, so that the initial data matrix comprises four variables and 546 observations (i.e. two countries times seven periods times 39 sectors). In order to give equal weights to all variables and eliminate the impact of specific time and country effects on the clustering process, the initial data matrix is standardized with respect to the total variation across industries for each country and year.

4.2 A three-stage clustering process

The current investigation proceeds through an elaborate three-stage clustering process, which combines *k*-means in the first and agglomerative hierarchical methods in the second and third steps of the analysis. The *k*-means method produces a first partition, which reduces the large initial data set for better use in the second step of hierarchical clustering. The second stage results in an interim classification. The third stage relies again on hierarchical clustering but uses the specific *time profile* of cluster identification in the interim classification as new variables. The sectoral taxonomy presented here is therefore a rare instance of a 'diachronic' classification.

The purpose of the first step is to condense information and segregate outlying observations into separate clusters without imposing a strong structure on the overall outcome yet. The cluster centres of the first partition are then entered as individual observations in the second step of hierarchical analysis, which is based on the average linkage method and the city block measure of distance. The other algorithms discussed in the previous methodological section were used to assess its robustness.[9] Overall, the patterns were reasonably robust and produced an interim classification of six separate categories, which represent a descending order of IT labour intensity.

In the third and final stage of the cluster analysis I transformed the data into a matrix of 39 industries as observations and the cluster identification for the respective time periods and countries as variables. Focusing only on the city block measure and assuming equal distances between classes, both average and complete linkage again produced almost identical results, whereas the single linkage method failed owing to 'chaining'. Inspection of the data and the graphical representation (not displayed here: see Peneder,

2003b) showed that the two outliers of 'computer-related services' and 'computers and office machinery' represent distinct categories within a genuinely longtailed distribution. As a consequence, the following separation into four final classes appeared to offer the most robust and consistently interpretable aggregation.

THE IT LABOUR INDUSTRY CLASSIFICATION (NACE INDUSTRY CODES IN BRACKETS)

1. *IT producer – services* (ITP/serv.): computer and related activities (72);
2. *IT producer – manufacturing* (ITP/manuf.): computers and office machinery (30);
3. *Dynamic IT user with a high and growing IT labour intensity* (ITU/high): mining and quarrying (10–14); mineral oil refining, coke and nuclear fuel (23); chemicals (24); electrical machinery and apparatus (31); radio, television and communication (32); instrument engineering (33); motor vehicles (34), other transport equipment (35), electricity, gas and water supply (40–41), air transport (62); telecommunications (642); financial intermediation (65, 67), insurance and pension funding (66), research and development (73); other business services (71, 74), Public administration and defence, incl. compulsory social security (75); education (80);
4. *Other IT user industries* (ITU/other): agriculture, forestry and fishing (1–5), food, drink and tobacco (15–16), textiles, leather, footwear and clothing (17–19), wood, products of wood and cork; pulp, paper and paper products, printing and publishing (20–22), rubber and plastics (25), non-metallic mineral products, furniture, miscellaneous manufacturing (26, 36–7), basic metals and fabricated metal products (27–8), mechanical engineering (29), construction (45), sale, maintenance and repair of motor vehicles and motor cycles (50), wholesale trade (51), retail trade (52), hotels and catering (55), railways (601), other inland transport, water transport (602–3, 61), supporting and auxiliary transport activities, activities of travel agencies (63), post and courier activities (641), real estate (70), health and social work (85), other community, social and personal services (90–93).

Source: Peneder (2003b).

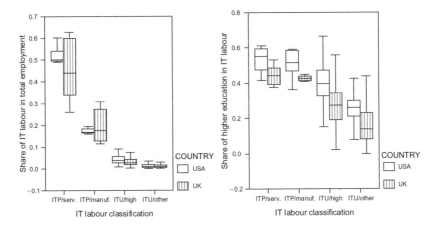

Source: Peneder (2003b).

Figure 32.2 Boxplots of workforce composition by country

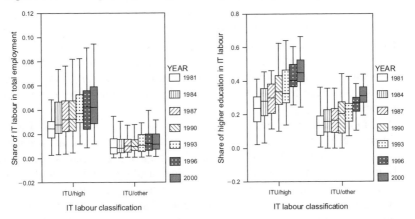

* 4-year average for the final period.

Source: Peneder (2003b).

Figure 32.3 Boxplots of workforce composition by 3-year* averages (up to indicated years)

4.3 Cluster validation

A sensible industry classification must also present interpretable structures. The boxplot charts in Figures 32.2 and 32.3 are particularly useful for that purpose, since they simultaneously display information about the shape and dispersion of the chosen attributes. The box itself comprises the middle

50 per cent of observations. The line within the box is the median. The lower end of the box signifies the first quartile, while the upper end of the box corresponds to the third quartile. In addition, the lowest and the highest lines outside the box indicate the minimum and maximum values. The observations have been split into the four different classes and are additionally separated by country.

The boxplots allow several important observations, which help to validate and interpret the cluster outcome. First, with respect to the proper identification of the separate categories, the extremely skewed distribution demonstrates why it is absolutely necessary to distinguish between IT producer and IT user industries (Van Ark, 2001). The first two groups consist only of the two outlying cases of computers and computer services. Since both are IT-producing sectors, they naturally exhibit a very high IT labour intensity. The third and the fourth category represent IT user industries. Both differ with respect to the share of persons with higher education among their IT workforce, which is much larger in the third than in the fourth group.

Second, concerning the robustness of the cluster solution with respect to differences between countries, the boxplots indicate that these hardly affect the distribution and relative order of industry groups in the chosen attribute. Similarly, with respect to the time dimension, all the four industry classes experienced a rather uniform increase in the share of higher education among IT labour and three of the four classes exhibit a similar and progressive pattern for the overall share of IT personnel in total employment over time.

Third, with respect to the particular time profile, the class of 'other IT user industries' comprises a remarkable group of sectors, for which the occupational composition of the workforce has been almost unaffected by the rapid advance of information technologies during the 1980s and 1990s (Figure 32.3). The explicit mapping of the time dimension in the third stage of the cluster analysis appears to have produced a remarkable observation, which to my knowledge has not yet received any notable emphasis in the literature on the 'new economy' phenomenon. In sharp contrast to popular belief about a more or less uniform dissemination of new information technologies in all sectors, these industries not only show no signs of catching up from low initial levels but fall further behind in terms of IT personnel. Consequently, the passage of time even appears to further reinforce the separation between the industry types instead of blurring or reversing their order.

5   Summary
Competitive performance depends on the capability to match a firm's organization and strategy to the technological, social and economic restrictions imposed by the business environment. Without denying the heterogeneity

among individual actors and firms, sectoral taxonomies stress specific characteristics of the competitive environment and their impact on economic activity. Substituting structural knowledge for exhaustive information about single attributes, the intractable diversity of real-life phenomena is thus condensed into a smaller number of salient types. This chapter first reviewed the prevalent industry taxonomies developed within the tradition of innovation research, then discussed the method of classification, putting especial emphasis on a number of critical choices that have to be made for that purpose. Finally, it presented an illustrative example that demonstrates the use and validation of statistical cluster analysis in practice.

Notes

1. Notwithstanding the inherent tension between the two concepts, both have independently developed a remarkable influence. While the emphasis on innovations by big business came to prominence as the 'Schumpeter hypothesis' in the empirical literature on *industrial organizations* (see, e.g., Scherer, 1965; Geroski, 1994; Audretsch, 1995), the earlier idea of innovation by independent entrepreneurs has increasingly become a hallmark of contemporary *entrepreneurship research* (see, e.g., Acs and Audretsch, 2003; Shane, 2004).
2. Malerba and Orsenigo (1993) more specifically characterize technological regimes in terms of opportunity, appropriability, cumulativeness, and the complexity of the knowledge base. See also the contribution of Malerba within this volume.
3. This new taxonomy is based on the interplay between 'opportunity' and the 'cost of experimentation,' where the net entry ratio serves as empirical proxy for entrepreneurial opportunity, and the turnover rate (i.e. the sum of entry and exits divided by the total firm population) indicates differences in the overall cost of experimentation.
4. They are special cases of a general dissimilarity function called the *Minkowski metric*.
5. Since correlation-type measures can take negative values, they do not strictly fulfil the above requirements of a metric. Anderberg (1973, pp. 113f.) discusses the 'limited metric character' of the correlation coefficient. However, these measures can be transformed to take values between 0 and 1 by defining $ang_{ih}{}^* = (1 + ang_{ih})/2$ and $corr_{ih}{}^* = (1 + corr_{ih})/2$ (see Gordon, 1999, p. 21).
6. Anderberg (1973, p. 23) remarked, that 'one of the most striking things about the many methods in the literature is the high degree of redundancy when applied to a set of data. The ideal would be to have a small stable of algorithms minimally duplicative among themselves but collectively representative of all the general types of classifications that might be produced by all other algorithms put together'.
7. See, for instance, Peneder (1995, 2002, 2007b). I must stress, however, that this is by no means a general convention, but only reflects personal concern about the consistency and credibility of my various cluster analyses.
8. This section briefly summarizes the work documented in Peneder (2003b).
9. Essentially identical cluster trees appear when Euclidean distances replace the city block measure, or the complete linkage method is applied instead of average linkages. Despite some differences, both angular separation and the correlation coefficient preserved a similar order of associations. The single linkage method suffered from chaining effects.

References

Acs, Z.J. and Audretsch, D.B. (2003), *Handbook of Entrepreneurship Research*, Boston: Kluwer.

Anderberg, M.R. (1973), *Cluster Analysis for Applications*, New York: Academic Press.

Archibugi, D. (2001), Pavitt's taxonomy sixteen years on: a review article, *Economics of Innovation and New Technology*, **10**, 415–25.

Arvanitis, S. and Hollenstein, H. (1998), Innovative activity and firm characteristics – a cluster analysis with firm-level data of Swiss manufacturing, paper presented at the 25th Annual EARIE Conference, Copenhagen, 27–30 August.

Audretsch, D.B. (1991), New-firm survival and the technological regime, *The Review of Economics and Statistics*, **73** (3), 441–50.

Audretsch, D.B. (1995), *Innovation and Industry Evolution*, Cambridge MA: MIT Press.

Bailey, K.D. (1994), *Typologies and Taxonomies. An Introduction to Classification Techniques*, Sage University Paper Series on Quantitative Applications in the Social Sciences, 07-102, Thousand Oaks, CA: Sage.

Cesaratto, S. and Mangano, S. (1993), Technological profiles and economic performance in the Italian manufacturing sector, *Economics of Innovation and New Technology*, **2**, 237–56.

Dosi, G. (1982), Technological paradigms and technological trajectories, *Research Policy*, **11**, 147–62.

Dosi, G. (1988), Sources, procedures, and microeconomic effects of innovation, *Journal of Economic Literature*, **26** (3), 1120–71.

Evangelista, R. (2000), Sectoral patterns of technological change in services, *Economics of Innovation and New Technology*, **9**, 183–221.

Geroski, P. (1994), *Market Structure, Corporate Performance, and Innovative Activity*, Oxford: Oxford University Press.

Gordon, A.D. (1999), *Classification*, 2nd edn, Boca Raton: Chapman & Hall.

Hodgson, G.M. (1993), *Economics and Evolution. Bringing Life Back Into Economics*, Cambridge: Polity Press.

Hollenstein, H. (2003), Innovation modes in the Swiss service sector: a cluster analysis based on firm-level data, *Research Policy*, **32**, 845–63.

Kaufmann, L. and Rousseuw, P.J. (1990), *Finding Groups in Data. An Introduction to Cluster Analysis*, New York: Wiley.

Malerba, F. (ed.) (2004), *Sectoral Systems of Innovation. Concepts, Issues and Analysis of Six Major Sectors in Europe*, Cambridge: Cambridge University Press.

Malerba, F. and Orsenigo, L. (1993), Technological regimes and firm behavior, *Industrial and Corporate Change*, **2** (1), 45–71.

Malerba, F. and Orsenigo, L. (1996), Schumpeterian patterns of innovation are technology specific, *Research Policy*, **25** (4), 451–78.

Marsili, O. (2001), *The Anatomy and Evolution of Industries. Technological Change and Industrial Dynamics*, Cheltenham, UK and Northampton, MA, USA: Edward Elgar.

Nelson, R.R. and Winter, S.G. (1982), *An Evolutionary Theory of Economic Change*, Cambridge, MA: Belknap Press.

Pavitt, K. (1984), Sectoral patterns of technical change: towards a taxonomy and a theory, *Research Policy*, **13** (6), 343–73.

Peneder, M. (1995), Cluster techniques as a method to analyse industrial competitiveness, *International Advances in Economic Research*, **1** (3), 295–303.

Peneder, M. (2002), Intangible investment and human resources, *Journal of Evolutionary Economics*, **12** (1–2), 107–34.

Peneder, M. (2003a), Industry classifications. Aim, scope and techniques, *Journal of Industry, Competition and Trade*, **3** (1–2), 109–29.

Peneder, M. (2003b), The employment of IT personnel, *National Institute Economic Review*, **184**, April, 74–85.

Peneder, M. (2007a), Firm entry and turnover: the nexus with profitability and growth, *Small Business Economics* (forthcoming).

Peneder, M. (2007b), A sectoral taxonomy of educational intensity, *Empirica* (forthcoming).

Romesburg, H.C. (1984), *Cluster Analysis for Researchers*, Belmont: Waldsworth Inc.

Scherer, F. (1965), Firm size, market structure, opportunity, and the output of patented inventions, *American Economic Review*, **55**, 1097–125.

Schumpeter, J.A. (1911), *Theorie der wirtschaftlichen Entwicklung*, 4th edn, Berlin: Duncker & Humblot.

Schumpeter, J.A. (1942), *Capitalism, Socialism and Democracy*, New York: Harper.

Shane, S. (2004), *A General Theory of Entrepreneurship*, Cheltenham, UK and Northampton, MA, USA: Edward Elgar.

Van Ark, B. (2001), The renewal of the old economy: an International comparative perspective, mimeo.

Winter, S.G. (1984), Schumpeterian competition in alternative technological regimes, *Journal of Economic Behavior and Organization*, **5** (3–4), 287–320.

33 Entropy statistics and information theory
Koen Frenken

Entropy measures provide important tools to indicate variety in distributions at particular moments in time (e.g., market shares) and to analyse evolutionary processes over time (e.g., technical change). Importantly, entropy statistics are suitable for decomposition analysis, which renders the measure preferable to alternatives like the Herfindahl index in cases of decomposition analysis. There are several applications of entropy in the realms of industrial organization and innovation studies. The chapter contains two sections, one on statistics and one on applications. In the first section, we discuss, in this order, (1) an introduction to the entropy concept and information theory, (2) the entropy decomposition theorem, (3) prior and posterior probabilities, and (4) multidimensional extensions.

In the second section, we discuss a number of applications of entropy statistics including (1) industrial concentration, (2) corporate diversification, (3) regional industrial diversification, (4) technological evolution, (5) income inequality, and (6) organization theory.

1 Entropy statistics
The origin of the entropy concept goes back to Ludwig Boltzmann (1877) and has been given a probabilistic interpretation in information theory by Claude Shannon (1948). In the 1960s, Henri Theil developed several applications of information theory in economics collected in *Economics and Information Theory* (1967) and *Statistical Decomposition Analysis* (1972).

The entropy formula
The entropy formula expresses the expected information content or uncertainty of a probability distribution. Let E_i stand for an event (e.g., one technology adoption of technology i) and p_i for the probability of event E_i to occur. Let there be n events $E_1, \ldots, E_n$ with probabilities $p_1, \ldots, p_n$ adding up to 1. Since the occurrence of events with smaller probability yields more information (since these are least expected), a measure of information h should be a decreasing function of p_i. Shannon (1948) proposed a logarithmic function to express information $h(p_i)$:

$$h\,(p_i) = \log_2\left(\frac{1}{p_i}\right),\qquad(33.1)$$

which decreases from infinity to 0 for p_i ranging from 0 to 1. The function reflects the idea that the lower the probability of an event to occur, the higher the amount of information of a message stating that the event occurred. Information is here expressed in bits using 2 as a base of the logarithm, while others express information in 'nits' using the natural logarithm.

From the n number of information values $h\,(p_i)$, the expected information content of a probability distribution, called entropy, is derived by weighing the information values $h\,(p_i)$ by their respective probabilities:

$$H = \sum_{i=1}^{n} p_i \log_2\left(\frac{1}{p_i}\right),\qquad(33.2)$$

where H stands for entropy in bits.

It is customary to define (Theil, 1972: 5):

$$p_i \log_2\left(\frac{1}{p_i}\right) = 0 \qquad \text{if} \quad p_i = 0,\qquad(33.3)$$

which is in accordance with the limit value of the left-hand term for p_i approaching zero (ibid.).

The entropy value H is non-negative. The minimum possible entropy value is zero, corresponding to the case in which one event has unit probability:

$$H_{\min} = 1 \cdot \log_2\frac{1}{1} = 0.\qquad(33.4)$$

When all states are equally probable $(p_i = 1/n)$, the entropy value is maximum:

$$H_{\max} = \sum_{i=1}^{n}\frac{1}{n}\log_2(n) = n\frac{1}{n}\log_2(n) = \log_2(n)\qquad(33.5)$$

(proof is given by Theil, 1972: 8–10). Maximum entropy thus increases with n, but decreasingly so.[1]

Entropy can be considered as a measure of uncertainty. The more uncertainty prior to the message that an event occurred, the larger the amount of information conveyed by the message on average. Theil (1972: 7) remarks that the entropy concept in this regard is similar to the variance of a random variable whose values are real numbers. The main difference is that entropy applies to qualitative rather than quantitative values and, as such, depends exclusively on the probabilities of possible events.

When a message is received that prior probabilities p_i are transformed into posterior probabilities q_i we have (Theil, 1972: 59):

$$I(q \mid p) = \sum_{i=1}^{n} q_i \log_2 \left(\frac{q_i}{p_i} \right), \tag{33.6}$$

which equals zero when posterior probabilities equal prior probabilities (no information) and which is positive otherwise.

The entropy decomposition theorem
One of the most powerful and attractive properties of entropy statistics is the way in which problems of aggregation and disaggregation are handled (Theil, 1972: 20–22; Zadjenweber, 1972). This is due to the property of additivity of the entropy formula.

Let E_i stand again for an event, and let there be n events $E_1, \ldots, E_n$ with probabilities $p_1, \ldots, p_n$. Assume that all events can be aggregated into a smaller number of sets of events $S_1, \ldots, S_G$ in such a way that each event exclusively falls under one set S_g, where $g = 1, \ldots, G$. The probability of an event falling under S_g occurring is obtained by summation:

$$P_g = \sum_{i \in S_g} p_i. \tag{33.7}$$

The entropy at the level of sets of events is:

$$H_0 = \sum_{g=1}^{G} P_g \log_2 \left(\frac{1}{P_g} \right). \tag{33.8}$$

H_0 is called the between-group entropy. The entropy decomposition theorem specifies the relationship between the between-group entropy H_0 at the level of sets and the entropy H at the level of events as defined in (33.2). Write entropy H as:

$$H = \sum_{i=1}^{n} p_i \log_2 \left(\frac{1}{p_i} \right) = \sum_{g=1}^{G} \sum_{i \in S_g} p_i \log_2 \left(\frac{1}{p_i} \right)$$

$$= \sum_{g=1}^{G} P_g \sum_{i \in S_g} \frac{p_i}{P_g} \left(\log_2 \left(\frac{1}{P_g} \right) + \log_2 \left(\frac{P_g}{p_i} \right) \right)$$

$$= \sum_{g=1}^{G} P_g \left(\sum_{i \in S_g} \frac{p_i}{P_g} \right) \log_2 \left(\frac{1}{P_g} \right) + \sum_{g=1}^{G} P_g \left(\sum_{i \in S_g} \frac{p_i}{P_g} \log_2 \left(\frac{P_g}{P_i} \right) \right)$$

$$= \sum_{g=1}^{G} P_g \log_2 \left(\frac{1}{P_g} \right) + \sum_{g=1}^{G} P_g \left(\sum_{i \in S_g} \frac{p_i}{P_g} \log_2 \left(\frac{1}{p_i/P_g} \right) \right).$$

The first right-hand term in the last line is H_0. Hence:

$$H = H_0 + \sum_{g=1}^{G} P_g H_g, \tag{33.9}$$

where:

$$H_g = \sum_{i \in S_g} \frac{p_i}{P_g} \log_2 \left(\frac{1}{p_i/P_g} \right) \qquad g = 1, \ldots, G. \tag{33.10}$$

The probability p_i/P_g, $i \in S_g$ is the conditional probability of E_i given knowledge that one of the events falling under S_g is bound to occur. H_g thus stands for the entropy within the set S_g and the term $\Sigma P_g H_g$ in (33.9) is the *average within-group entropy*. Entropy thus equals the between-group entropy plus the average within-group entropy. Two properties of this relationship follow (Theil, 1972: 22):

i. $H \geq H_0$ because both P_g and H_g are nonnegative. It means that after grouping there cannot be more entropy (uncertainty) than there was before grouping.
ii. $H = H_0$ if and only if the term $\Sigma P_g H_g = 0$ and $\Sigma P_g H_g = 0$ if and only if $H_g = 0$ for each set S_g. It means that entropy equals between-group entropy if and only if the grouping is such that there is at most one event with nonzero probability.

In informational terms, the decomposition theorem has the following interpretation. Consider the first message that one of the sets of events occurred. Its expected information content is H_0. Consider the subsequent message that one of the events falling under this set occurred. Its expected information content is H_g. The total information content becomes $H_0 + \Sigma P_g H_g$. Applications of the decomposition theorem will be discussed in the third and fourth subsections.

Multidimensional extensions
Consider a pair of events (X_i, Y_j) and the probability of co-occurrence of both events. The probabilities of the two marginal contributions are:

$$p_{i.} = \sum_{j=1}^{n} p_{ij} \qquad (i = 1,\ldots,m), \qquad (33.11)$$

$$p_{.j} = \sum_{i=1}^{m} p_{ij} \qquad (j = 1,\ldots,n). \qquad (33.12)$$

Marginal entropy values are given by:

$$H(X) = \sum_{i=1}^{m} p_{i.} \log_2\left(\frac{1}{p_{i.}}\right), \qquad (33.13)$$

$$H(Y) = \sum_{j=1}^{n} p_{.j} \log_2\left(\frac{1}{p_{.j}}\right). \qquad (33.14)$$

And two-dimensional entropy is given by:

$$H(X,Y) = \sum_{i=1}^{m}\sum_{j=1}^{n} p_{ij} \log_2\left(\frac{1}{p_{ij}}\right). \qquad (33.15)$$

The conditional entropy value measures the uncertainty in one dimension (e.g., X), which remains when we know event Y_j has occurred. It is given by Theil (1972: 116–17):

$$H_{Y_j}(X) = \sum_{i=1}^{m} \frac{p_{ij}}{p_{.j}} \log_2\left(\frac{p_{.j}}{p_{ij}}\right), \qquad (33.16)$$

$$H_{X_i}(Y) = \sum_{j=1}^{n} \frac{p_{ij}}{p_{i.}} \log_2\left(\frac{p_{i.}}{p_{ij}}\right). \qquad (33.17)$$

The average conditional entropy is derived as the weighted average of conditional entropies:

$$H_Y(X) = \sum_{j=1}^{n} p_{.j} H_{Y_j}(X) = \sum_{i=1}^{m}\sum_{j=1}^{n} p_{ij} \log_2\left(\frac{p_{.j}}{p_{ij}}\right), \qquad (33.18)$$

$$H_X(Y) = \sum_{i=1}^{m} p_{i.} H_{X_i}(Y) = \sum_{i=1}^{m}\sum_{j=1}^{n} p_{ij} \log_2\left(\frac{p_{i.}}{p_{ij}}\right). \qquad (33.19)$$

It can be shown that the average conditional entropy never exceeds the unconditional entropy, i.e., $H_X(Y) \leq H(Y)$ and $H_Y(X) \leq H(X)$, and that the average conditional entropy and the unconditional entropy are equal if and only if the two events are stochastically independent (Theil, 1972: 118–19).

The expected mutual information is a measure of dependence between two dimensions, i.e., to what extent events tend to co-occur in particular combinations. In this respect it is comparable with the product–moment correlation coefficient in the way entropy is comparable to the variance. Mutual information is given by

$$J(X,Y) = \sum_{i=1}^{m} \sum_{j=1}^{n} p_{ij} \log_2 \left(\frac{p_{ij}}{p_{i\cdot}p_{j}} \right), \tag{33.20}$$

sometimes also denoted by $M(X,Y)$ or $T(X,Y)$. It can be shown that $J(X,Y) \geq 0$ and that and $J(X, Y) = H(Y) - H_X(Y)$ and $J(X, Y) = H(X) - H_Y(X)$ (ibid.: 125–31). It can further be derived that the multidimensional entropy equals the sum of marginal entropies minus the mutual information (ibid.: 126):

$$H(X,Y) = H(X) + H(Y) - J(X,Y). \tag{33.21}$$

The interpretation is that, when mutual information is absent, marginal distributions are independent and their entropies add up to the total entropy. When mutual information is positive, marginal distributions are dependent as some combinations occur relatively more often than other combinations, and marginal entropies exceed total entropy by an amount equal to the mutual information.

2 Applications
Applications of entropy statistics were developed mainly during the late 1960s and the 1970s. Tools of entropy statistics are applied in empirical research in industrial organization, regional science, economics of innovation, economics of inequality and organization theory.

Industrial concentration
A popular application of the entropy formula in industrial organization is in empirical studies of industrial concentration (Hildenbrand and Paschen, 1964; Finkelstein and Friedberg, 1967; Theil, 1967: 290–91). Applied to a distribution of market shares, entropy is an inverse measure of concentration ranging from 0 (monopoly) to infinity (perfect competition). The measure fulfils the seven axioms that are commonly listed as desirable properties of any concentration index (Curry and George, 1983: 205):

1. An increase in the cumulative share of the ith firm, for all i, ranking firms $1, 2, \ldots i \ldots n$ in descending order of size, implies an increase in concentration.
2. The 'principle of transfers' should hold, i.e. concentration should increase (decrease) if the share of any firm is increased at the expense of a smaller (larger) firm.
3. The entry of new firms below some arbitrary significant size should reduce concentration.
4. Mergers should increase concentration.
5. Random brand switching by consumers should reduce concentration.
6. If s_j is the share of a new firm, then as s_j becomes progressively smaller so should its effects on a concentration index.
7. Random factors in the growth of firms should increase concentration.

Horowitz and Horowitz (1968) proposed an index of relative entropy by dividing the entropy by its maximum value $log_2 (n)$. In this way, one obtains a concentration index, which lies between 0 and 1. An important disadvantage of the relative entropy measure is that axiom (4) no longer holds. Mergers reduce the value of H, but also reduce the value of $log_2 (n)$. Since there may be a proportionally greater fall in $log_2 (n)$ than in H, concentration may decrease after a merger.

Though the list of axioms is also met by the more popular Herfindahl index, which is equal to the sum of squares of market shares, the entropy formula is sometimes preferred because of the entropy decomposition theorem. An early application concerns Jacquemin and Kumps (1971) who analysed (changes in) industrial concentration of European firms and sets of European firms (a group of British firms and a group of European firms belonging to the then EEC).

Corporate diversification and profitability

The decomposition property of the entropy formula has also been exploited to analyse corporate diversification and its effect on corporate growth (Jacquemin and Berry, 1979; Palepu, 1985; Hoskisson *et al.*, 1993). Let p_i stand for the proportion of a firm's total sales or production in the industry i. Entropy is computed again following (33.2) and now indicates corporate diversification. Zero entropy implies perfect specialization, while maximum entropy indicates maximum diversification.

The central question is whether diversification is rewarding for firms' profitability, and whether related diversification within an industry group or unrelated diversification across industry groups is most rewarding for corporate growth. The hypothesis holds that related diversification is more rewarding as a firm's core competencies can be better exploited in related industries. This hypothesis is in accordance with the resource-based view and the evolutionary theory of the firm that both explain growth through diversification as being motivated by utilizing excess capacity of resources (including knowledge specific to the firm) and by exploiting economies of scope (Montgomery, 1994).

Jacquemin and Berry (1979), for example, considered firms active in n 4-digit industries, which can be aggregated to G sets of 2-digit industry groups. P_g stands for the proportion of a firm's total sales or production in the 2-digit industry group g and p_i stands for the proportion of a firm's total sales or production in the 4-digit industry i. Application of (33.9) means that a firm's degree of diversification at the 4-digit level H can be decomposed into between-group diversification at the 2-digit level and the average within-group diversification at the 4-digit level. In this way, the entropy measure solves the problem of possible collinearity between 2-digit and 4-digit for Herfindahl and other indices in regression analysis (Jacquemin and Berry, 1979: 366). Collinearity is avoided with the entropy measure, as it can be perfectly decomposed in a between-group component and a within-group component. From the 1970s onwards, evidence seems to support the thesis that, where diversification generally does not increase profitability, related diversification typically has beneficial effects (Montgomery, 1994).

The entropy measure of diversification has also been applied to patent data and bibliometric data to analyse the variety in research and innovative efforts at different disciplinary, organizational or geographical units of analysis. In a patent study on environmentally friendly car technology, Frenken *et al.* (2003) used the entropy measure in two dimensions to assess whether corporate portfolios have become, on average, more varied (33.18), and, vice versa, whether technologies have become, on average, patented by a larger variety of firms (33.19). The first measure indicates the variety of technologies at each corporate level and the second measure indicates the strength of competition between firms at the level of each technology. Earlier studies applied entropy measurements on patents at the level of firms and countries (Grupp, 1990) and to bibliometric data including publication and citation distributions (Leydesdorff, 1995).

The validity of results, however, depends crucially on the construction of classification, which is used to measure the degree of relatedness between a firm's activities. Knowing the limitations of standard classifications of statistical bureaus, future research may benefit from new classifications based on more in-depth information on the nature of activities and their demand.

Regional industrial diversification
Diversification in industries has been measured by entropy at the regional level in the same way as is done for the corporate level (Hackbart and

Anderson, 1975; Attaran, 1985). In most cases, industry employment data are used to compute the shares of industries in a region. Using the entropy decomposition theorem as in (33.9), entropy values can be decomposed at a several digit-level, for example, in the first instance at the level of manufacturing and non-manufacturing and in the second instance at the level of specific manufacturing and non-manufacturing industries (Attaran, 1985).

The main interest of this regional indicator is to test whether industrial diversity reduces unemployment and promotes growth. Diversity is said to protect a region from unemployment and below-average growth rates caused by business cycles operating on supraregional levels and by external shocks (e.g., oil prices). Empirical evidence suggests that diversity indeed reduces unemployment, while evidence on the positive impact of diversity on per capita income growth is more often absent (Attaran, 1985; and see a more recent study by Izraeli and Murphy, 2003, using the Herfindhal index). The entropy measure employed in this way, however, does not capture other aspects commonly thought to affect regional employment and growth including the stage of the product life cycle of sectors present in a region.

Technological evolution
In the context of innovation studies, Saviotti (1988) proposed using entropy as a measure of technological variety. In this context, E_i stands for the probability of the event that a firm (or consumer) adopts a particular technology i. When there are n possible events $E_1, \ldots, E_n$ with probabilities $p_1, \ldots, p_n$ the entropy of the frequency distribution of technologies indicates the technological variety. Entropy can be used to indicate the emergence of a dominant design during a product life cycle in an industry (Abernathy and Utterback, 1978). A fall in entropy towards zero would indicate the emergence of such a dominant design (Frenken et al., 1999).

Technologies can often be described in multiple dimensions, i.e. as strings of product characteristics analogous to genetic strings. For example, a vehicle design with steam engine, spring suspension and block brakes may be coded as string 000, with a vehicle design with a gasoline engine, spring suspension and block brakes coded as string 100, and so on. A product population of designs then makes up a frequency distribution that can be analysed using the multidimensional extensions of the entropy.

Multidimensional entropy that captures the technological variety in all dimensions is one comprehensive variety measure. The mutual information indicates the extent to which product characteristics co-occur in the product population. The mutual information value equals zero when there is no dependence between product characteristics. The higher the value of the mutual information, the more product characteristics co-occur in 'design families'.

The relationship between variety (multidimensional entropy) and dependence (mutual information) has been analysed using (33.21), which can be rewritten, for K dimensions ($k = 1, \ldots, K$) labelled $X_1, \ldots, X_k$, as

$$\left(\sum_{k=1}^{K} H(X_k) \right) = J(X_1, \ldots, X_K) + H(X_1, \ldots, X_K).$$

From this formula, it can be readily understood that, given a value for the sum of marginal entropies ΣH_k, mutual information J can increase only at the expense of multidimensional entropy H, and vice versa. When analysing a distribution of technologies in consecutive years, the value of ΣH_k may increase, allowing both entropy and mutual information to increase *both* (though not necessarily). When entropy and mutual information rise simultaneously, a product population develops progressively more varieties through a growing number of design families, a process akin to 'speciation' in biology. This pattern has been found in data of product characteristics of early British steam engines in the eighteenth century (Frenken and Nuvolari, 2004).

Income inequality
Another application of the entropy formula as in (33.2) in economics concerns the construction of measures of income equality (Theil, 1967: 91–134; 1972: 99–109). Let p_i stand for the income share of individual i. When all individuals earn the same income, we have complete equality and maximum entropy $log_2 (n)$, and when one individual earns all income, we have complete inequality and zero entropy. To obtain a measure of income *in*equality, entropy H can be subtracted from maximum entropy to obtain

$$log_2 (n) - H = \sum_{i=1}^{n} p_i log_2 n (p_i), \tag{33.22}$$

also known as 'redundancy' in communication theory (Theil, 1967: 91–2).

Organization theory
An approach to organization theory based on the entropy concept has been developed by Saviotti (1988), who proposed using entropy to indicate the variety of possible organizational configurations of employees with a particular degree of specialization. When n individuals have the same knowledge, and this knowledge enables each individual to carry out any task in the organization, there is a maximum variety of possible organizational configurations equal to $log_2 (n)$ (maximum job rotation). By contrast, when all individuals have unique and specialized knowledge, and each task

requires a different type of knowledge, there is only one possible organization characterized by the highest degree of division of labour. The variety of possible organizational structures then equals log_2 (1) (no job rotation). The introduction of departmental boundaries, implying that job rotation is restricted to taking place within the department but not across departments, would imply that, depending on the size of departments, the entropy will lie somewhere in between the minimum and maximum value.

Note

1. In physics, maximum entropy characterizes distributions of randomly moving particles that all have an equal probability to be present in any state (like a prefect gas). When behaving in a non-random way, for example, when particles move towards already crowded regions, the resulting distribution is skewed and entropy is lower that its maximum value (Prigogine and Stengers, 1984). In the biological context, maximum entropy refers to a population of genotypes where all possible genotypes have an equal frequency. Minimum entropy reflects the total dominance of one genotype in the population (which would result when selection is instantaneous) (cf. Fisher, 1930: 39–40).

References

Abernathy, W.J. and Utterback, J. (1978) Patterns of industrial innovation, *Technology Review*, **50**, 41–7.
Attaran, M. (1985) Industrial diversity and economic performance in U.S. areas, *The Annals of Regional Science*, **20**, 44–54.
Boltzmann, L. (1877) Ueber die Beziehung eines allgemeine mechanischen Satzes zum zweiten Hauptsatzes der Warmetheorie, *Sitzungsber. Akad. Wiss. Wien, Math.-Naturwiss. Kl.*, **75**, 67–73.
Curry, B. and George, K.D. (1983) Industrial concentration: a survey, *Journal of Industrial Economics*, **31**(3), 203–55.
Finkelstein, M.O. and Friedberg, R.M. (1967) The application of an entropy theory of concentration to the Clayton Act, *The Yale Law Review*, **76**, 677–717.
Fisher, R.A. (1930) *The Genetical Theory of Natural Selection*, Oxford: Clarendon Press.
Frenken, K. and Nuvolari, A. (2004) The early development of the steam engine: an evolutionary interpretation using complexity theory, *Industrial and Corporate Change*, **13**(2), 419–50.
Frenken, K., Hekkert, M. and Godfroij, P. (2003) R&D portfolios in environmentally friendly automotive propulsion: variety, competition and policy implications, *Technological Forecasting and Social Change*, **71**(5), 485–507.
Frenken, K., Saviotti, P.P. and Trommetter, M. (1999) Variety and niche creation in aircraft, helicopters, motorcycles and microcomputers, *Research Policy*, **28**(5), 469–88.
Grupp, H. (1990) The concept of entropy in scientometrics and innovation research. An indicator for institutional involvement in scientific and technological developments, *Scientometrics*, **18**, 219–39.
Hackbart, M.W. and Anderson, D.A. (1975) On measuring economic diversification, *Land Economics*, **51**, 374–8.
Hildenbrand, W. and Paschen, H. (1964) Ein axiomatische begründetes Konzentrationsmass, *Statistical Information*, **3**, published by the statistical office of the European Communities, 53–61.
Horowitz, A. and Horowitz, I. (1968) Entropy, Markov processes and competition in the brewing industry, *Journal of Industrial Economics*, **16**(3), 196–211.
Hoskisson, R.E., Hitt, M.A., Johnson, R.A. and Moesel, D.D. (1993) Construct-validity of an objective (entropy) categorical measure of diversification, *Strategic Management Journal*, **14**(3), 215–35.

Izraeli, O. and Murphy, K.J. (2003) The effect of industrial diversity on state unemployment rate and per capita income, *The Annals of Regional Science*, **37**, 1–14.

Jacquemin, A.P. and Berry, C.H. (1979) Entropy measure of diversification and corporate growth, *Journal of Industrial Economics*, **27**(4), 359–69.

Jacquemin, A.P. and Kumps, A.-M. (1971) Changes in the size structure of the largest European firms: an entropy measure, *Journal of Industrial Economics*, **20**(1), 59–70.

Leydesdorff, L. (1995) *The Challenge of Scientometrics. The Development, Measurement, and Self-Organization of Scientific Communications*, Leiden: DSWO Press.

Montgomery, C.A. (1994) Corporate diversification, *Journal of Economic Perspectives*, **8**(3), 163–78.

Palepu, K. (1985) Diversification strategy, profit performance and the entropy measure, *Strategic Management Journal*, **6**, 239–55.

Prigogine, I. and Stengers, I. (1984) *Order Out of Chaos*, New York: Bantam.

Saviotti, P.P. (1988) Information, variety and entropy in technoeconomic development, *Research Policy*, **17**(2), 89–103.

Shannon, C.E. (1948) A mathematical theory of communication, *Bell System Technical Journal*, **27**, 379–423, 623–56.

Theil, H. (1967) *Economics and Information Theory*, Amsterdam: North-Holland.

Theil, H. (1972) *Statistical Decomposition Analysis*, Amsterdam: North-Holland.

Zadjenweber, D. (1972) Une application de la théorie de l'information à l'économie: la mesure de la concentration, *Revue d'Economie Politique*, **82**, 486–510.

34 A methodology to identify local industrial clusters and its application to Germany
*Thomas Brenner**

1 Introduction

Local clusters and industrial districts have been studied intensively in the recent economic literature. These studies mainly aim to identify the prerequisites for the development of such local systems and the specific characteristics that are responsible for their economic success. It is usually implicitly assumed that local clusters and industrial districts can be clearly identified. This means that it is assumed that local systems can be classified into two categories according to their economic situation: successful regions, labelled local clusters or industrial districts, and regions lagging behind. To this end, different approaches are discussed and the requirements for the identification of local clusters are examined.

In the literature on case studies there is usually not much discussion about the identification of local clusters. Those who conduct the case studies assume implicitly, and usually rightly so, that they have correctly identified a local cluster that they study. There are other approaches that try to identify all local clusters within a country (see Sforzi, 1990; Isaksen, 1996; Paniccia, 1998; Braunerhjelm and Carlsson, 1999). In these approaches a threshold level of the number of firms or employees in a region is arbitrarily defined, usually in relation to the size of the region. All regions in which the number of firms or employees in an industry exceeds this threshold value are said to contain a local cluster. In most of the approaches additional conditions are formulated. The most elaborated approach has been developed for Italy (see Sforzi, 1990; Sforzi *et al.*, 1997). However, even in this case the condition for the size of the industrial agglomeration is little discussed. Furthermore, the same condition is applied to all industries. What is missing is a theoretical or empirical explanation for the threshold level that is used.

At the same time, there are several works that develop theoretical models about the spatial distribution of firms with and without clustering forces and test the resulting predictions empirically (see, e.g., Ellison and Glaeser,

* I want to thank Dirk Fornahl, Ulrich Witt and the participants at the ETE-workshop in Jena for helpful comments and discussions and the German Federal Ministry for Education and Research for financial support. The usual disclaimer applies.

1997, 1999; Dumais *et al.*, 2002; Bottazzi *et al.*, 2002). These works are able to show which and to what extent industries are adequately described by different theoretical models. Agglomeration forces of some kind are proved to exist for many industries (see Ellison and Glaeser, 1997, 1999). However, these studies do not aim to identify the existing local industrial clusters and provide a list of these clusters.

This chapter develops a methodology that combines the two approaches described above. It is based on a theoretical modelling of firm locations with and without clustering forces. The modelling of clustering forces is done in such a way that the threshold in the number of firms that separates those regions containing a local cluster in a certain industry from those that do not can be examined empirically. Hence, the methodology allows the identification of the local clusters that exist in an industry and country. The methodology consists of two steps. First, the theoretical predictions can be tested with the help of empirical data. This results in information about whether the industry studied is mainly located in industrial agglomerations (this part of the methodology is similar to the approach in Ellison and Glaeser, 1997). However, in addition, the use of the methodology leads to information about the threshold that separates the number of firms in local agglomerations from the number of firms in other regions. This threshold can be used to identify all local agglomerations in an industry (this part of the methodology is similar to the approaches in Sforzi, 1990; Isaksen, 1996; Paniccia, 1998; Braunerhjelm and Carlsson, 1999).

To show the use of the developed methodology, it is applied to Germany. It is applied on the level of administrative districts and conducted for each 2-digit manufacturing industry separately. The results are used in two ways. First, they answer the question of whether clustering exists in the different manufacturing industries in Germany. Second, the threshold for the number of firms is calculated for those industries that show clustering. This number is compared to the numbers that are used in the literature. Furthermore, it allows the existing clusters to be identified.

The chapter proceeds as follows. In section 2, the theoretical framework is outlined, alternatives are discussed and predictions for the distribution of firms among regions are made. The methodology for testing these predictions is developed in section 3. In section 4 this methodology is applied to Germany and the results are discussed. Section 5 concludes.

2 Theory and predictions

There are several ways to develop a theory of clustering. Different proposals have been made in the literature. However, none of them is adequate for reaching the aims of this chapter, which seeks to establish a theoretically based prediction for the distribution of firms among regions that can be tested empirically and used for the identification of the existing local clusters in each industry.

Nevertheless, some of the approaches in the literature could be expanded so that they also enable this aim to be reached. Therefore, the different methods that might be used in this context will be discussed here. What we have to look for is a theory that makes two predictions: one for a situation without clustering and one for a situation with clustering. Both predictions should be empirically testable and comparable. Furthermore, the prediction for the situation with clustering should be such that it allows the regions that contain an industrial agglomeration to be distinguished from the other regions.

In the literature very different theoretical concepts are put forward and they differ in various factors. First, there are approaches that explicitly model space (see, e.g., Krugman, 1996; Allen, 1997; Keilbach, 2000). However, these models can only be studied by simulations. The calculation of empirically testable predictions on the basis of these models is possible but quite complex. Hence, these models are not used to identify local clusters empirically and are not adequate in the present context. The other approaches (see, e.g., Arthur, 1987; Ellison and Glaeser, 1997, 1999; Brenner, 2001; Dumais *et al.*, 2002; Fujita and Thisse, 2002; Maggioni, 2002; Bottazzi *et al.*, 2002) ignore space as a variable and consider, instead, a number of unrelated regions. As a consequence, these models describe the processes for each region separately given that alternative regions exist.

These models can be separated into those that assume a successive location of firms until all firms are founded (see, e.g., Arthur, 1987; Ellison and Glaeser, 1997) and those that assume a repeated relocation of firms among the regions (see, e.g., Brenner, 2001; Dumais *et al.*, 2002; Maggioni, 2002; Bottazzi *et al.*, 2002). In the former case a probability distribution for the location of firms is obtained. In the latter case a dynamic theory is established or a stable stationary state is calculated. If the processes are assumed to be deterministic, the stationary state is characterized by one or a few states or a deterministic development (see, e.g., Brenner, 2001; Maggioni, 2002). If the processes are assumed to be stochastic, the stationary state is characterized by a probability distribution (see, e.g., Bottazzi *et al.*, 2002).

A deterministic prediction can be expected to be rejected by data. This is because it is impossible to include all regional characteristics that influence the location of firms in the model. Hence, whether the relocation of firms is a stochastic or deterministic process cannot be answered because there is another source of fluctuations and indeterminacy: the local characteristics. The modeller can, therefore, include stochastic processes in two ways: it can be assumed that the location of firms is stochastic or it can be assumed that the local characteristics and thus the attractiveness of regions for firms is stochastic or at least not measurable, so that it has to be modelled stochastically. Both assumptions lead to a prediction in the form of a probability distribution.

Furthermore, the models in the literature differ with respect to the inclusion of regional characteristics. Several approaches include the size of regions (see, e.g., Ellison and Glaeser, 1997). More firms can be expected to be located in larger regions. However, other factors, such as the existence of universities, the geographic location or the local culture, might have similar effects. Many of the models allow for the inclusion of such factors, but there is only one approach in which many local factors, such as local prices, human capital, population density and so on, are considered (see Ellison and Glaeser, 1999).

Finally, the approaches differ with respect to whether they are used to making a prediction about the distribution of firms among regions. If predictions are made, they are usually based on theoretical assumptions about the stochastic processes that underlie the localization processes of firms (see Ellison and Glaeser, 1997; Bottazzi *et al.*, 2002).

The existing approaches and their characteristics are presented in Table 34.1. The characteristics of the approach that is taken here are given at the end of the table. Here, some motivations for the choice of the different characteristics of the approach used are given. It has already been argued above that the use of a spatial model leads to the necessity to run simulations, which is less preferable if predictions are to be tested empirically. Furthermore, a prediction of the spatial distribution of firms means that there is only one empirical data point to test the prediction for each country and industry, while a prediction for each region separately causes the existence of as many data points as there are regions. Hence, modelling each region separately is necessary for an empirical approach.

The situation is less clear with respect to relocation. Some relocation of firms certainly takes place, while many firms also keep their location although other locations might be more attractive. The real situation seems to be a mixture of the two concepts that are used in the existing approaches. One of the approaches is probably better suited to some industries while the other is probably better suited to other industries. Therefore, the question of relocation will be left open in the approach developed here. This is possible because the predictions are based on empirical findings about various distributions (see the discussion below).

With respect to stochastic processes, the optimal choice of modelling is obvious. Both the location of firms and the attractiveness of regions should be modelled in a stochastic manner. For both processes we are not able to include all relevant factors in the model because they are not obtainable at

Table 34.1   The characteristics of the models existing in the literature

Model	Object	Relocation	Stochastic processes	Regional characteristics	Predictions
Arthur (1987)	regions	no	firm preferences	—	—
Krugman (1996)	space	yes	—	—	—
Ellison & Glaeser (1997)	regions	no	location	size	theoretical
Dumais *et al.* (2002)	regions	yes	location	size	theoretical
Fujita & Thisse (2002)	two regions	equilibrium	—	—	—
Maggioni (2002)	regions	yes	none	—	theoretical
Bottazzi *et al.* (2002)	regions	yes	location	—	theoretical
approach in this chapter	regions	—	location & attrac- tiveness	size	empirical

a general level. Examples are the personal ties of founders or the influence of culture on the attractiveness of regions. It is clear that we should include as many regional characteristics in the model as possible. However, because of the lack of adequate data, usually only a few characteristics can be included. In the approach developed here, as in most approaches in the literature, only the size of the regions is considered. To reflect the excluded factors in the model, the processes have to be modelled stochastically.

The major difference between the present approach and the approaches in the literature is the use of empirical data to determine the functional form of the firm distribution among regions. Usually some assumptions are made about the characteristics of the two stochastic aspects: the location of firms and the attractiveness of regions. In the case of the location of firms the assumptions are straight forward. Each location has a certain probability of being chosen that is determined by its characteristics. The situation is less clear in the case of the attractiveness of regions. Different factors influence the attractiveness of regions. Many of them are not explicitly included in the modelling so that they have to be considered as stochastic fluctuations. This implies that assumptions have to be made about their probability distributions. For some factors this distribution can be obtained empirically. Other factors, such as culture, are difficult to address empirically.

As a consequence, it is not possible to model the fluctuations in the attractiveness of regions, caused by neglected characteristics, in a sound way. Therefore, this approach follows a concept different from those in the literature. Instead of using only one assumption about the stochastic influences, a number of different assumptions are developed on the basis of different arguments. For each of them the predictions about the firm distribution among regions are calculated and tested in the light of the available empirical data. Finally, a number of assumptions that are found to be most adequate are used for all industries. This procedure also implies that we do not have to decide whether we use a model with or without relocation. In this sense the approach that is used here is more general than the approaches in the literature. It even contains some of them.

2.1   Firm distribution among regions

According to the discussion above we have to look for different plausible assumptions about the firm distribution among regions. This means that we look for different assumptions about the mathematical form of the probability function $P(f|s)$, which describes the probability of finding f firms of the industry under consideration in a region with size s. The literature offers quite a number of different predictions of this distribution which can be used here. First, the dartboard model (see Ellison and Glaeser, 1997) predicts that the number of firms in a region is binominal-distributed if there is no clustering. This will be used as a basis for the argument here. However, this model neither considers clustering forces nor does it consider factors other than size that might influence the attractiveness of regions. Examples of such other factors that might influence the attractiveness of regions are the human capital that is available and the number of service firms.

One part of the human capital in a region is given by the number of students who are trained there. The distribution of the number of students per inhabitant is depicted in Figure 34.1 for the administrative districts in Germany. It is evident that this distribution does not have the form of a binominal distribution. Instead, the distribution in the figure seems to have the shape of an exponentially decreasing function (the exponentially decreasing function fits the data better than a hyperbolical function).

As a second example, let us examine the distribution of service firms. Legal firms, marketing firms, PR consultants, tax consultants and similar service firms are particularly important for manufacturing firms. Their distribution among the 441 regions in Germany is presented in Figure 34.2. At first glance this distribution might be interpreted as a binominal distribution. However,

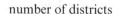

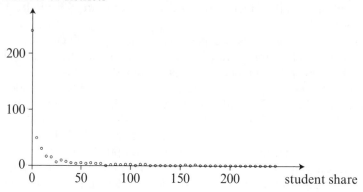

Figure 34.1   For number of students per 1000 inhabitants (horizontal axis) the number of administrative districts in Germany (vertical axis) that contain approximately this number of students is depicted

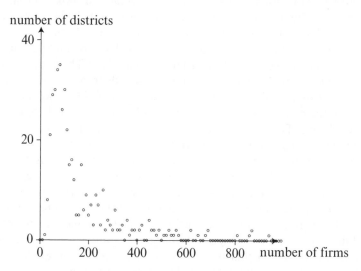

Figure 34.2   For number of service firms that provide services to other firms, e.g. legal firms, marketing firms, PR consultants and so on (horizontal axis) the number of administrative districts in Germany (vertical axis) that contain approximately this number of firms is depicted

the binominal distribution is rejected by the Kolmogorov–Smirnov test (the maximal log-likelihood value is 62464), independent of the choice of the parameters. The same does not hold for the distribution $P(n) = N \cdot n \cdot \xi^n$ where n is the number of firms found in a region, N is the normation factor given by $N = (1 - \xi)^2/\xi$ and ξ is the parameter of this distribution. This distribution is called a Boltzmann distribution here. (The specific formulation that is used here is obtained in physics under certain conditions – Maxwell's velocity distribution – for the Boltzmann distribution.) The best fit to the distribution in Figure 34.2 is reached by $\xi = 0.99075$ (the log-likelihood value is 2849).

The search for local factors that influence the firm population in a region could be continued in the above way. Further kinds of distributions might be detected. However, the more distribution functions we include in our analysis, the more complex it becomes, meaning that the empirical study takes more computer time, without necessarily increasing the insight that is obtained. Therefore, the three distributions, the binominal distribution, the exponentially decreasing distribution and the Boltzmann distribution, that have been obtained so far are used for the empirical study. It is assumed that a combination of these distributions describes the firm distribution among regions adequately if no cluster forces exist.

The binominal distribution and the Boltzmann distribution are quite similar. Therefore, the analysis has also been conducted excluding each of them once. On average the combination of the exponentially decreasing and the Boltzmann distribution does better than the combination of the exponentially decreasing and the binominal distribution. However, this result varies strongly among industries. Therefore all three distributions are included here. Mathematically we obtain

$$P_n(f|s) = (1 - \xi_3(s) - \xi_5(s)) \cdot (1 - \xi_1(s)) \cdot \xi_1(s)^f$$

$$+ \xi_3(s) \cdot \frac{[1 - \xi_2(s)]^2}{\xi_2(s)} \cdot f \cdot \xi_2(s)^f + \xi_5(s) \cdot Bn(\bar{f}, f, \xi_4(s)), \quad (34.1)$$

where $\xi_1(s)$, $\xi_2(s)$, $\xi_3(s)$, $\xi_4(s)$ and $\xi_5(s)$ are parameters and $\bar{f}$ is the total number of firms in the industry under consideration. This distribution is called the 'neutral' distribution here because it does not include the effect of any cluster forces. All parameters might depend on the size of the region, $\xi_3(s)$ and $\xi_5(s)$ determine the shares of each of the three distributions that are included in (34.1). They should characterize the industry and should not depend on the size of the region under consideration. Hence, only the other parameters are assumed to depend on the size of the region. It seems plausible that the average number of firms that are expected to be located in a region according to $P_n(f|s)$ increases linearly with the size of the region.

This should also hold for each of the three distributions separately. This can be reached by defining

$$\xi_1(s) = \frac{\xi_1 \cdot s}{1 + \xi_1 \cdot s},$$

(34.2)

$$\xi_2(s) = \frac{\xi_2 \cdot s}{2 + \xi_2 \cdot s}$$

(34.3)

and $\xi_4(s) = \xi_4 \cdot s$.

Now the situation in which local clusters occur has to be discussed. Again it is argued that we are not able to model the mechanisms that cause clustering exactly enough to calculate a mathematical distribution. Therefore, the following argument is based on the theoretical findings in Brenner (2001). There clustering is modelled in a very general way but assuming no stochastic influences. The result is that regions with an attractiveness higher than a certain value might contain a cluster. Whether they contain a cluster depends on their history, something that cannot be measured in an empirical approach like the one conducted here. The existence of a cluster in a region implies that the number of firms is much higher there (see Brenner, 2001).

With respect to the firm distribution $P(f|s)$ this implies that some of the regions that would contain quite a number of firms according to the firm distribution $P_n(f|s)$ without clustering (caused by their relative high attractiveness) will contain a much higher number of firms. Hence, the firm distribution $P_c(f|s)$ with clustering can be expected to have a similar shape to $P_n(f|s)$ but contains a number of regions with a very high number of firms. It might even be argued that the phenomenon of clustering is only empirically significant if those regions that contain a cluster can be clearly distinguished from those that do not contain a cluster. If this distinction is made on the basis of the number of firms, the firm distribution $P_c(f|s)$ has to have two maxima.

This second maximum has again to be mathematically formulated. It seems to be adequate to assume that this part of the distribution has a similar shape to the rest of the distribution. However, it has to start with a certain value of f. Therefore, an exponentially decreasing function is not an option. Since, on average, the Boltzmann distribution does better than the binominal distribution, the Boltzmann distribution is used here to describe the second maximum of the firm distribution $P_c(f|s)$. Mathematically this can be formulated as follows:

$$P_c(f \mid s) = (1 - \xi_3(s) - \xi_5(s) - \xi_8(s)) \cdot (1 - \xi_1(s)) \cdot \xi_1(s)^f$$

$$+ \xi_3(s) \cdot \frac{[1 - \xi_2(s)]^2}{\xi_2(s)} \cdot f \cdot \xi_2(s)^f + \xi_5(s) \cdot Bn(\bar{f}, f, \xi_4(s))$$

(34.4)

frequency

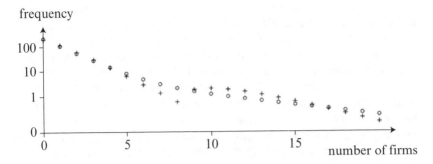

Figure 34.3 *Theoretical firm distributions among regions that result from fitting the natural distribution (circles) and the cluster distribution (crosses) to the empirical distribution of firms producing office machines*

$$+\begin{cases} \xi_8(s) \cdot \dfrac{[1-\xi_7(s)]^2}{\xi_7(s)} \cdot f \cdot \xi_7(s)^{f-\xi_6(s)} & \text{if} \quad f \geq \xi_6(s) \\[2em] 0 & \text{if} \quad f < \xi_6(s). \end{cases}$$

The first and second lines of the right-hand side are nearly identical to the neutral distribution (34.1). A second Boltzmann distribution that starts with a number of firms of $\xi_6(s)$ is added to the neutral distribution. $\xi_6(s)$, $\xi_7(s)$ and $\xi_8(s)$ are additional parameters. $\xi_8(s)$ describes the share of all regions that are described by the new part of the distribution. It should, like $\xi_3(s)$ and $\xi_5(s)$, be independent of s, so that $\xi_8(s) = \xi_8$ is assumed. The average number of firms predicted by the new part of the distribution is again assumed to increase linearly with the size of the region. This is reached by $\xi_6(s) = \xi_6 \cdot s$ and

$$\xi_7(s) = \frac{\xi_7 \cdot s}{2 + \xi_7 \cdot s}. \tag{34.5}$$

The resulting distribution is called a 'cluster' distribution. An example is presented in Figure 34.3.

3 Method of empirical analysis
Two predictions for the firm distribution among regions have been developed above. One is expected to hold for industries in which no clustering forces are present. The other is expected to hold for industries in which local

clusters exist. The parameters of both distributions can be fitted to empirical data and the resulting distributions can be tested and compared. The necessary procedure is described in the following subsections.

However, to be able to use the method that is developed here, some empirical requirements have to be satisfied. The method allows each industry or any combination of industries to be studied separately. However, the method requires information about the number of firms in the chosen industry or industries for a number of adequately chosen regions. The number of regions has to be sufficiently large to allow for statistically significant results. The analyses that have been conducted so far have shown that at least 100 regions are necessary but that more regions should be preferred. At the same time, the classification of space into regions should be chosen such that the regions match the usual extension of local clusters. This requirement is sometimes difficult to satisfy because data are often only available at a particular regional level. Furthermore, local clusters can have quite different geographic sizes.

3.1   Fitting and comparison of the two distributions

Both distributions contain a number of parameters. To fit the two theoretical distributions to reality, the parameter set that maximized the log-likelihood value is calculated. The likelihood value is the probability that the empirical situation occurs according to the theoretical distribution. The log-likelihood value is the negative logarithm of the likelihood value and is given by

$$L_n = -\ln\left[\prod_{r=0}^{N_r} P_n(f(r)|s(r))\right] \text{ and } L_c = -\ln\left[\prod_{r=0}^{N_r} P_c(f(r)|s(r))\right], \quad (34.6)$$

where N_r denotes the number of regions, $f(r)$ is the number of firms that are located in region r according to the empirical data and $s(r)$ is the size of region r. All values relate to the industry that is studied. The parameter sets that maximize L_n and L_c, respectively, have to be calculated numerically. The maximal log-likelihood values are denoted by $\hat{L}_m(i)$ and $\hat{L}_c(i)$, respectively. The respective parameter sets determine those distributions that best describe reality.

While fitting the parameters, their ranges have to be restricted. Obviously, all parameters have to be positive. Furthermore, $\xi_3 + \xi_5 \leq 1$ and $\xi_3 + \xi_5 + \xi_8 \leq 1$, respectively, has to be satisfied. In addition, the parameters, ξ_6 and ξ_8, have to be restricted in a specific way. ξ_8 determines the share of regions that contain local clusters. However, if local clusters are a specific phenomenon, they have to be the exception. We would not talk about 'local industrial clusters' if they occurred in most of the regions. Hence, the share of the regions that contain a cluster has to be small: 5 per cent is assumed to be the maximal share that is accepted here. This implies that $\xi_8 \leq 0.05$ has to be satisfied.

$\xi_6 \cdot s(r)$ determines the minimal number of firms that must be located in region r if this region is to be said to contain a local cluster. It has been argued above that this number has to be high, usually high enough so that no region would contain such a number of firms under normal conditions. For each value of ξ_6, the number of regions that can be expected without clustering to contain more than $\xi_6 \cdot s(r)$ firms can be calculated. This number is denoted by $n_{cl}(\xi_6)$ here. It will not be zero because the neutral distribution decreases exponentially and therefore never reaches a value of zero. However, according to the above argument it should be small compared to the number of regions that contain industrial clusters according to the clustering part of distribution. The condition

$$\frac{n_{cl}(\xi_6)}{N_r} < 0.2 \cdot \xi_8(i) \tag{34.7}$$

is used here.

These two conditions restrict somewhat the flexibility of the cluster distribution. Nevertheless, the neutral distribution is a special case of the cluster distribution. Therefore, the cluster distribution will always fit reality better, so that $\hat{L}_c \geq \hat{L}_n$ is satisfied for all industries.

The likelihood ratio test is used to check whether the cluster distribution describes reality significantly better than the mixed distribution. This is done for each industry separately. To this end, the value

$$\lambda = 2\ln[\hat{L}_c] - 2\ln[\hat{L}_n] \tag{34.8}$$

is calculated. λ measures this difference in the fitting of the data. Statistical theories tell us that λ can be expected to follow an χ^2-distribution if the additional term in the cluster distribution does not really improve the model (see Mittelhammer, 1996). Whether λ falls into this distribution can be tested. Hence, the hypothesis that the cluster distribution is not more adequate than the mixed distribution can be tested. If it is rejected, the industry is said to be clustering.

3.2 Checking the fit

The likelihood ratio test answers the question about which distribution describes the empirical data better. However, it does not answer the question of whether they describe the empirical data adequately. To test the adequacy of the two theoretical distributions, they are compared to the empirical distribution.

To test whether the theoretical distribution and the empirical distribution deviate from each other significantly, the Kolmogorov–Smirnov test is used. This test compares the cumulative distribution function of a theoretical and an empirical distribution. It makes a statement about the maximal distance of these two functions that should occur with a certain probability if the two distributions are identical. Hence, if the distance is too great, the hypothesis that the theoretical and the empirical distributions are identical can be rejected.

To obtain an empirical distribution, the numbers of firms for the different regions have to be compared. Hence, the empirical distribution $P_{emp}(f)$ is given by

$$P_{emp}(f) = \frac{1}{N_r} \cdot \sum_{r=1}^{N_r} \delta(f(r) = f),$$ (34.9)

where

$$\delta(f(r) = f) = \begin{cases} 1 & \text{if} \quad f(r) = f \\ \\ 0 & \text{if} \quad f(r) \neq f \end{cases}.$$ (34.10)

As a consequence, for the theoretical distribution $P_{theo}(f)$, the sum over all regions also has to be considered. It is given by

$$P_{theo}(f) = \frac{1}{N_r} \cdot \sum_{r=1}^{N_r} P_n(f \mid s(r)).$$ (34.11)

In the case of the cluster distribution, $P_n(f|s(r))$ is replaced by $P_c(f|s(r))$ in equation (34.11). The maximal distance between the theoretical and empirical cumulative distribution functions is given by

$$K = \max_x \left[\int_0^x P_{emp}(f)df - \int_0^x P_{theo}(f)df \right].$$ (34.12)

According to the Kolmogorov–Smirnov test, the theoretical distribution can be rejected at a significance level of 0.01 if $K > 1.629 \cdot \sqrt{441}$. Hence, the test provides a tool to check whether the model with or without clustering is adequately specified.

4   Application of the method to Germany

In order to demonstrate the usefulness of the method that has been developed here, it is applied to all 2-digit manufacturing firms in Germany. An application to the 3-digit manufacturing industries in Germany and an extensive discussion of the results can be found in Brenner (2004, 2006). Here, the results will only be discussed with respect to the adequacy of the modelling, the shares of the three distributions that are included in the theoretical modelling and the questions, whether and in which industries local clusters occur.

4.1 Data

The data that are used in this approach have been collected by the German Federal Institute for Labour. This institute has data on every employee who has a German social security number. Each employee is assigned to a workplace, which is a legal entity at a location. These workplaces are called *Betriebe* in the German statistics. They are usually firms. However, if a company has branches at different locations, these branches are counted as separate *Betriebe*. Branches that belong to the same legal entity and are located in the same city or town are classified as being the same *Betrieb*. The data that are used here contain the number of these *Betriebe* for each 2-digit industry and each of the 441 administrative districts in Germany for 30 June 2001. (Industries are classified according to the WZ93-classification, which is the standard classification for industries in Germany at the moment.) These numbers are used as the number of firms that exist in each region and industry. The study that is conducted here is restricted to the 23 manufacturing 2-digit industries.

4.2 Adequacy of modelling

The results of the empirical study are given in Table 34.2. According to the Kolmogorov–Smirnov test, the theoretical distribution can be rejected for both the neutral and the clustering distributions for only three of the 23 industries that are studied. In one further case one of the two distributions is rejected while the other seems to describe the empirical situation well. The remaining 19 industries seem to be adequately described by both distributions. Hence, the theoretical modelling that is chosen here seems to be adequate for describing the spatial distribution of firms in reality. The study of 3-digit industries shows an even greater adequacy (see Brenner, 2004, 2006).

4.3 Choice of distribution

Above it has been argued that it is not possible to obtain the shape of the firm distribution among regions theoretically. Therefore, three different distributions have been included in the theoretical distributions (34.1) and (34.4). It has been argued that the empirical fitting will show how relevant each of these distributions is.

The empirical results show that the Boltzmann distribution has, on average, by far the largest share in the distribution that fits reality best. On average, the Boltzmann distribution accounts for 52 per cent of the

Table 34.2　*Results of the empirical study of the 23 two-digit*
　　　　　　manufacturing industries in Germany

Industry	Share (%) of exp. Boltz. bin. distribution			K-S test: neutral cluster distribution		log-likelihood ratio	minimal size of clusters	number of clusters
food	0	92	8	2.55	40.8	0	—	—
tobacco	62	1	37	0.08*	41.2	1.8	—	—
textiles	16	56	28	0.71*	0.75*	7.5	21	2
clothing	10	51	39	0.66*	0.63*	3.0	—	—
leather	2	49	49	0.51*	0.55*	4.1	37	2
wood	62	33	5	1.24*	1.32*	0	—	—
paper	54	34	12	0.51*	0.53*	1.4	—	—
publishing & printing	0	69	31	0.95*	0.89*	0	—	—
petroleum	80	5	15	0.25*	0.20*	0.4	—	—
chemicals	3	68	28	0.92*	0.83*	0	—	—
plastics	3	83	14	0.74*	0.73*	1.1	—	—
glass etc.	1	77	22	2.42	2.40	2.5	—	—
metals	45	35	20	0.65*	0.61*	0.7	—	—
metal goods	0	74	25	1.66	1.65	1.7	—	—
machinery	0	78	22	1.28*	1.25*	0	—	—
office machines	53	0	47	0.58*	0.96*	3.7	3.7	18
electronics	3	68	29	0.58*	0.67*	0	—	—
telecommunication	46	27	27	0.90*	0.42*	0	—	—
instruments	0	47	53	1.06*	1.01*	2.3	—	—
motor vehicles	15	61	23	1.43*	0.92*	0	—	—
other vehicles	47	30	23	1.17*	1.50*	6.1	5.6	11
furniture etc.	3	90	7	1.22*	1.34*	1.4	—	—
recycling	0	71	28	1.47*	1.37*	0.7	—	—

distribution, while the exponentially decreasing function accounts for 22 per cent and the binominal distribution accounts for 26 per cent. However, these results vary strongly between industries. There are industries in which the Boltzmann distribution explains up to 92 per cent of the empirical distribution and others where the exponentially decreasing function explains up to 80 per cent of the empirical distribution. Only the binominal distribution seems to have a comparably stable share in all fitted distributions. Nevertheless, even this share varies between 5 and 53 per cent.

Hence, different factors seem to be relevant for different industries. This confirms the claim made at the beginning of the chapter that we should allow for variations among industries and that industries should be studied separately. At least for the Boltzmann distribution and the exponentially decreasing function there are industries in which these distributions should not be omitted.

4.4 Existence of local clusters

The test for the existence of local clusters is on the one hand indirect and on the other hand conservative. What we empirically test is whether the cluster distribution explains the empirical data significantly better than the neutral distribution. The cluster distribution assumes the existence of local agglomerations of the industry under consideration in a form that is predicted by theoretical models of clustering. However, there might be other reasons for the existence of such local agglomerations. Strictly speaking the existence of a special kind of local agglomeration is tested here and not the existence of local clusters. However, if local clusters exist, we would expect that the test will lead to a positive result.

At the same time, the likelihood ratio test examines whether the statement that the neutral distribution explains reality as well as the cluster distribution can be rejected. If this statement is rejected, we can be quite sure that the cluster distribution is more adequate. If the statement is not rejected, we have no clear result. The log-likelihood ratio that is presented in Table 34.2 provides some information in such a case. If the log-likelihood ratio is zero or nearly zero, it is unlikely that the cluster distribution describes reality better because its additional parameters do not improve the fit. If the log-likelihood ratio is somewhere between zero and the significant value, the situation is unclear.

For four of the 23 industries studied, the cluster distribution is shown to describe the empirical data significantly better than the neutral distribution. These are the textiles, leather, office machines and other vehicles industries. Hence, we might conclude that local industrial clusters exist in these industries. The approach taken here even allows us to determine the minimal percentage of all firms in the industry that have to be located in a region to call it a local agglomeration (see Table 34.2). Furthermore, it allows all local agglomerations to be identified:

1. **textiles**: Zollernalbkreis, Hof;
2. **leather**: Pirmasens (city), Pirmasens;
3. **office machines**: Aachen, Paderborn, Bergstraße, Darmstadt-Dieburg, Offenbach, Landau (city), Konstanz, Bad Tölz-Wolfratshausen, Dachau, Ebersberg, Freising, München, Rosenheim, Schwabach (city), Demmin, Stollberg, Suhl (city), Sömmerda;
4. **other vehicles**: Ostholstein, Plön, Schleswig-Flensburg, Emden (city), Wilhelmshafen (city), Wesermarsch, Bremerhafen (city), Bodenseekreis, Starnberg, Dahme-Spreewald, Müritz.

Besides these four industries for which local agglomerations are shown to exist, there are 11 further industries for which the log-likelihood ratio is greater than zero (see Table 34.2). In these cases the cluster distribution describes reality better than the neutral distribution, but not significantly better. Hence, there is some evidence for clustering forces in these industries.

Absolutely no evidence for clustering is found in eight industries in which the log-likelihood ratio is zero. In these industries the neutral distribution describes reality as well as the cluster distribution. These industries are food, wood, publishing & printing, chemicals, machinery, electronics, telecommunication and motor vehicles.

5   Conclusions

In this chapter various approaches to studying the distribution of firms among regions are discussed. A theoretical model is established and an empirical method for using and testing this model is developed. At the beginning of this chapter it was argued that a method is needed that can be used to investigate in which industries local clusters exist and to identify the locations of these clusters without making ad hoc assumptions about their minimal size. The empirical method that is proposed here meets both these requirements.

The method is then applied to all 2-digit manufacturing industries in Germany to show its usefulness. It is shown that the theoretical model describes the firm distribution among regions adequately for most industries. Those industries for which the existence of local agglomerations can be proved are identified and the regions in which they appear are listed.

The results show that the method that is developed here can be used to study the existence of local clusters and to identify them using empirical data on the spatial distribution of firms. The method is general and can easily be applied to different countries, different classifications of regions (as long as there is a minimum of about 100 regions) and different classifications of industries. It is able to provide a complete picture of the industries in which local clusters exist and the locations of these clusters. Data for a long period of time would even allow the emergence and change of local clusters to be studied. Hence, the method has a high potential that will, hopefully, be used extensively in further research.

References

Allen, P.M. (1997). *Cities and Regions as Self-Organizing Systems. Models of Complexity.* Amsterdam: Gordon and Breach.
Arthur, W.B. (1987). 'Urban systems and historical path dependence', in J.H. Ausubel and R. Herman (eds), *Cities and Their Vital Systems*, Washington: National Academy Press, pp. 85–97.

Bottazzi, G., Fagiolo, G. and Dosi, G. (2002). Mapping sectoral patterns of technological accumulation into the geography of corporate locations. A simple model and some promising evidence. LEM Working Paper Series 2002/21, Sant' Anna School of Advanced Studies, Pisa.

Braunerhjelm, P. and Carlsson, B. (1999). Industry clusters in Ohio and Sweden, 1975–1995. *Small Business Economics*, **12**, 279–93.

Brenner, T. (2001). Self-organisation, local symbiosis of firms and the life cycle of localised industrial clusters. Papers on Economics & Evolution #0103, Max-Planck-Institute Jena.

Brenner, T. (2004). *Local Industrial Clusters: Existence, Emergence and Evolution.* London: Routledge.

Brenner, T. (2006). An identification of local industrial clusters in Germany. *Regional Studies*, **40**, 991–1004.

Dumais, G., Ellison, G. and Glaeser, E.L. (2002). Geographic concentration as a dynamic process. *Review of Economics and Statistics*, **84**, 193–204.

Ellison, G. and Glaeser, E.L. (1997). Geographic concentration in U.S. manufacturing industries: a dartboard approach. *Journal of Political Economy*, **105**, 889–927.

Ellison, G. and Glaeser, E.L. (1999). The geographic concentration of industry: does natural advantage explain agglomeration? *American Economic Review*, **89**, 311–16.

Fujita, M. and Thisse, J.-F. (2002). *Economics of Agglomeration.* Cambridge: Cambridge University Press.

Isaksen, A. (1996). Towards increased regional specialization? The quantitative importance of new industrial spaces in Norway, 1970–1990. *Norsk Geografisk Tidsskrift*, **50**, 113–23.

Keilbach, M. (2000). *Spatial Knowledge Spillovers and the Dynamics of Agglomeration and Regional Growth.* Heidelberg: Physica-Verlag.

Krugman, P. (1996). *The Self-Organizing Economy.* Cambridge: Blackwell Publishers.

Maggioni, M. (2002). *Clustering Dynamics and the Location of High-Tech Firms.* Heidelberg: Physica-Verlag.

Mittelhammer, R.C. (1996). *Mathematical Statistics for Economics and Business.* New York: Springer.

Paniccia, I. (1998). One, a hundred, thousands of industrial districts. Organizational variety in local networks of small and medium-sized enterprises. *Organizational Studies*, **19**, 667–99.

Sforzi, F. (1990). 'The quantitative importance of Marshallian industrial districts in the Italian economy', in F. Pyke, G. Becattini and W. Sengenberger (eds), *Industrial Districts and Inter-Firm Co-operation in Italy*, Geneva: International Institute for Labour Studies, pp. 75–107.

Sforzi, F., Openshaw, S. and Wymer, C. (1997). *La procedura di identificazione dei sistemi locali del lavoro.* I sistemi locali del lavoro 1991, ISTAT.

35 Technology spillovers and their impact on productivity
Bart Los and Bart Verspagen

1 Introduction

How far do the benefits of technological activity travel? This is a question of great relevance for impact studies of technological change. To what extent do scientific activities at a university elicit commercial successes in the city or region in which it is located? Does knowledge generated in one plant cause productivity gains in other, far-away plants of a firm, even if they are located in different countries? Is the performance of banks affected positively by improvements in the products of the computer industry, or even in those of the semiconductor industry? Does knowledge emerging from an aircraft manufacturer's innovative efforts enhance the performance of automobile manufacturers? This chapter will review the increasing number of empirical approaches proposed to answer important questions like these, and will propose a classification scheme derived from theoretical perspectives.

Technological knowledge obviously has some aspects of a public good. The same piece of knowledge, an 'idea', can be used by more than one firm at the same time (non-rivalry), and once it is in the open, it is hard to exclude specific firms from using it (non-excludability). However, the public good nature of knowledge is far from complete, and significant barriers to knowledge externalities exist. To use knowledge developed by others, a firm needs specific skills, such as a general acquaintance with the technology base or even specialized knowledge. Large parts of knowledge created in a firm are tied to that firm, because it cannot be adequately described in words or numbers. The degree of such 'tacitness of knowledge' (a notion introduced by Polanyi, 1966) mainly determines whether policies aimed at learning from technology generated elsewhere will be as fruitful as policies with the objective to generate purely new knowledge.

This chapter will neither cover issues of incentives (how do knowledge spillovers affect the level of innovative activity?) and technology policy (should governments subsidize R&D projects?), nor deal with relationships between innovative efforts and variables like firm growth or employment. Instead, it gives an overview of methods to measure technology spillovers and their impact in a quantitative way.[1] It should be noted that many of the above-mentioned exemplary questions could be posed at several levels of aggregation. In many cases, however, the approaches chosen resemble each other. Our discussion will most often focus on the industry level. Wherever possible, however, we will hint at the way in which studies emphasizing technology flows within firms, among firms, among regions or among countries deal with the issue at hand.

Our survey will start from a discussion on the conceptualization of spillovers. In section 2, we discuss different types of R&D, and the types of spillovers that may arise from them. Our main typology distinguishes between 'rent spillovers' and 'knowledge spillovers'. We propose to divide the latter category into two subcategories: 'idea-creating' knowledge spillovers and 'imitation-enhancing' knowledge spillovers. After this, we will survey the work undertaken with the aim of quantifying spillovers. Here we will make a rough classification into two different streams of literature. The first, covered in section 3, is aimed at measuring the effects of 'idea-creating' spillovers only. The methods discussed here are mostly based on patent statistics, for example in the form of patent citations from one firm to the other. A different part of the literature measures the joint effects of 'idea-creating' and 'imitation-enhancing' spillovers, through productivity effects. This is covered in section 4.

2   R&D and R&D spillovers: concepts and definitions

In theory, R&D efforts might be classified into two categories: 'process-oriented' and 'product-oriented'. Process-oriented R&D aims at lowering the unit costs of producing a given type of output, keeping its quality constant. The main goal of product-oriented R&D is to produce either completely new products or higher-quality varieties of existing products. In practice, however, this distinction is rather difficult to implement, for at least two reasons. First, process innovations are often connected to product innovations, and vice versa. A typical innovation process may then involve both a new product and a way of making it, or a new process may lead not only to cheaper but also to better products. Below, we will systematically take the perspective of the innovator to discern between process-oriented and product-oriented R&D.

Despite these conceptual problems, the evidence seems to suggest that much R&D belongs to the product-oriented class, at least in developed countries. For example, Scherer (1984) reports that roughly 75 per cent of the American patents granted in 1974-6 examined by him were results of product-oriented R&D. A serious bias is likely to affect the counts, because secrecy (and hence, non-patenting) is an important way of protecting process innovations. Nevertheless, observations like this strengthen the general notion that far from all R&D is performed with the purpose of lowering costs of production.[2]

The distinction between process- and product-oriented R&D has important consequences for the type of spillovers occurring and their intensity. To the extent that process R&D is more often protected using secrecy, it is a smaller source of spillovers. On the other hand, product innovation leads to a special type of spillovers, because the goods they are embodied in are traded between firms. This has led Griliches (1979) to propose the distinction between concepts that are nowadays known as 'rent spillovers' and 'knowledge spillovers'.

2.1   Rent spillovers

When new or improved goods are traded, the benefits will generally be distributed in some way between the supplier and user. Because the supplier offers a better good than before, she will be able to command a higher price and, thus, generate a higher profit rate. However, despite the higher price, the user may experience an improved 'price–quality ratio' because prices did not increase as much as performance. A prime example of this is the market for personal computers: although over its lifespan the average computer has been greatly improved in performance, it did not become more expensive.

The division of the innovation rents between supplier and user will generally depend on market structure. A monopolist will be able to capture all rents, and could raise prices in proportion to the increase of performance if the demand curve would indicate this to be most profitable. The stronger the competition, however, the more a supplier will be forced to transfer a part of the innovation rents to the users in the form of low prices. The increased price–quality ratio leads to what is called rent spillovers. Viewed from a purely theoretical (and neoclassical) perspective, the word 'spillovers' may not be appropriate, because economic transactions are involved.

Rent spillovers cause problems with regard to output and productivity measurement. Statistical agencies apply price deflators to turn nominal output figures into real figures. As, among others, Griliches (1979) and Van Meijl (1995) have indicated, product innovations render the most common deflators unreliable, in particular if the innovating firm faces some competition or is not able to apply perfect price discrimination. The reason is that traditional methods to construct price deflators do not take quality differentials into account. To use the computer example again: without taking account of quality increase, the price for computers would have remained roughly constant over the last decade. For a user of computers, however, it is clear that he got 'more bang for the buck'. In terms of abstract measures such as 'computer power' or 'user friendliness', the price of computers declined strongly, but this is not reflected in the traditional price statistics. The resulting errors are transmitted to the measurement of productivity in industries using the innovation as an input in their production processes.

One answer to these problems has been the use of so-called 'hedonic price indices' (e.g., Griliches, 1961), or more advanced methods applying welfare functions (e.g., Trajtenberg, 1990). The hedonic method involves collecting data on a wide range of product varieties and their prices. A 'hedonic function' may then be estimated that relates product characteristics to price differentials. For example, such a function may show that an extra 100 Mhz of computer speed adds \$50 on average to the price of a computer. Using this function, the price increase of a sample of products may be decomposed into a part related to improvements in product characteristics (e.g., computers became faster), and a part of 'pure' price increase. The first of these parts may be taken as a general indication of the impact of product innovation, the second part as 'inflation'.

However, the hedonic price index does not solve all problems. It fails, for example, when entirely new products or product characteristics arise. In such a case, there is no yardstick in the form of a hedonic function. Also, the approach may be problematic if product characteristics are 'non-concatenable' (e.g., for a car driver interested in speed, two cars that can each reach 50 km/h are not equivalent to a single car that may reach 100 km/h). Hedonic price index computations also require a lot of data. Trajtenberg (1990) discusses these and other problems, and proposes a more advanced method. Under strict assumptions of utility-maximizing agents, it can deal with the problem of non-concatenable product innovations, but it does not solve and even aggravates data-related problems.

2.2   Knowledge spillovers

If knowledge is to an important extent 'codified' in publicly available sources such as patent documents, scientific and technical literature, it has public good characteristics. Such knowledge may spill over between firms even in the absence of market transactions. This is why Griliches (1979) introduced the concept 'knowledge spillovers'. Two kinds of knowledge spillover effects might be distinguished. Codified knowledge may not be perfectly protectable, which enables competitors to obtain it and to imitate the innovation subsequently. This would disturb the monopoly power the innovator would have gained (in the case of product-related knowledge) or his cost advantage over competitors (in the case of process-related knowledge). We will call these spillovers 'imitation-enhancing'. A second spillover effect, far less prominent in the microeconomic literature, can be denoted as 'idea-creating'. Existing knowledge may evoke new ideas, which can lead to innovations in other applications or fields than where the original knowledge was found.

This distinction is important from both a legal and an economic point of view. For example, patent laws would in many cases not hamper 'idea-creating' spillovers, whereas these laws are precisely intended to protect innovators against 'imitation-enhancing' spillovers. From an economic point of view, competition due to 'idea-creating' spillovers may be much less than from 'imitation-enhancing' spillovers, because the new idea may be implemented in a totally different field.

Both types of spillovers may take place through a variety of channels. In their well-known survey (conducted among hundreds of US firms) on the building of knowledge stocks, Levin *et al.* (1987) distinguished seven sources of technology. Two of them, 'acquisition of knowledge through licensing of the technology' and 'acquisition of knowledge through independent R&D' cannot (or hardly) be seen as channels of knowledge spillovers. Of the acquisition channels that relate directly to knowledge spillovers, 'reverse engineering' turned out to be the most important source of knowledge. This channel of spillovers predominantly relates to 'imitation-enhancing' spillovers.

A second channel of knowledge spillovers is the mobility of R&D employees. Especially in the United States, engineers often move from one firm to another, sometimes crossing industry borders. These mobile employees embody knowledge, which is obtained at relatively low costs by the new employer. In principle, both 'imitation-enhancing' and 'idea-creating' spillovers may be embodied in mobile employees. A firm can also obtain technology by attending technical meetings and scientific conferences, or by reading research-oriented journals. Again, the firm is likely to obtain the knowledge much more cheaply than if it were to undertake the R&D itself. Because of the voluntary nature of knowledge dissemination, the large majority of knowledge spillovers through this channel must be of the 'idea-creating' kind.

A quite different channel of spillovers is provided by patent documents. Firms are allowed to study patent documents, not only to investigate whether a new product or process is likely to be patentable or not, but also to collect relevant research information. This information may be used freely, as long as the patented product or process is not imitated. Therefore, patent documents are a potential source of 'idea-creating' knowledge spillovers. In reality patents offer far from perfect protection against imitation (see Arundel *et al.*, 1995). So patents may be a source of 'imitation-enhancing' spillovers, too.

The last channel of spillovers distinguished by Levin *et al.* (1987) is 'acquisition of knowledge through informal conversations with employees of the innovating firm'. This channel turns out to be rather important (empirically), but its consequences for the measurement of knowledge spillovers are quite vague. Actually, it is likely that this spillover channel overlaps the 'conference channel' to some extent, as both channels are characterized by interpersonal, more or less informal (unlike the 'employee mobility channel') contacts. In an inter-industry context, however, an important distinction must be noted. R&D employees will mostly visit conferences in their own field of research, and thus meet people who have similar research interests. A completely different category of researchers may be met during meetings with either suppliers of the firm's inputs or buyers of the firm's products. Such exchange of knowledge is not necessarily restricted to codified knowledge, but may also involve relatively 'tacit' knowledge. Pavitt (1984) and Von Hippel (1988) stress the importance of supplier–buyer relationships regarding innovative behaviour, but are convinced that both the importance and the main direction of this kind of knowledge spillovers vary across industries. Of course, knowledge spillovers through this channel will mostly be of the 'idea-creating' type, as they do not occur between competitors.

As will be clear by now, knowledge may be transmitted in a number of ways. It should be noted that, although the costs of obtaining knowledge from other firms will be non-zero in most cases, the spillover emerges because the receiver obtains the technology at a less than full price. Unlike rent spillovers, knowledge spillovers are real spillovers, not just a statistical redistribution of productivity gains due to competition and measurement errors.

3   Patent citation indicators of 'idea-creating' spillovers

Data drawn from patent statistics have proved to be a versatile source of empirical studies of R&D spillovers. At the same time, it must be noted that, because of the nature of patents, these methods are focused on a rather narrow subset of technology and innovation. By their nature, for example, patents almost rule out 'imitation-enhancing' spillovers. They are also focused on codified knowledge. Because the propensity to patent differs between industries, the data sources are more rich in some fields, like pharmaceuticals, than in others, like agriculture. Griliches (1990) gives an overview of the issues involved in using patent indicators in general.

Many important spillover indicators are derived from patent citation information. The main idea is that cited patents provide knowledge spillovers to citing patents, in much the same way as citations in scientific papers work. However, it must be recognized that patent citations primarily serve the legal purpose of defining the boundaries of the knowledge claimed in a patent. An important purpose of patent citations, for example, is to describe the 'state-of-the-art' in a technological field, so that the contribution of the patent may be judged by the patent examiners against this background. Patent citations may be added either by the patent examiner, in which case there is no direct evidence that the inventor knew the cited patent, or by the applicant or inventor. There are also important differences between different patent systems (e.g., the US and European patents) in terms of citation behaviour by patent examiners and applicants (Michel and Bettles, 2001). Jaffe *et al.* (1998) provide evidence supporting the use of patent citations indicators for spillovers.

Patent citations have been used to measure spillovers at different levels of analysis and types of spillovers. Jaffe *et al.* (1993) pioneered the method aiming to measure the geographical dimension of spillovers. Almeida (1996) applied the measure to sourcing of knowledge by multinational companies. Jaffe and Trajtenberg (1996) proposed to use patent citations to measure the impact of universities and public research institutes. This section will briefly review these three types of spillover studies, their theoretical 'roots' and the way in which the relevant aspects of spillovers can be measured by patent citations.

3.1   Patent citations and the geographical boundaries of spillovers

Traditionally, two factors are hypothesized to cause local concentration of certain types of knowledge building or R&D. First, there is the traditional argument about agglomeration economies that is related to the availability of common resources, such as a specialized workforce of skilled engineers, a university offering a specialized degree relevant for the type of R&D, specialized firms that can supply certain types of instruments and/or services, or even a notion such as technological culture (Saxenian, 1994). When these types of resources are important inputs into the R&D process, an emerging spatial cluster of R&D activities may provide important advantages to the 'members' of such a cluster by spillovers going around in this cluster. The second factor that may explain the spatial nature of knowledge is the tacitness of knowledge. This implies that it must be transmitted by close personal interaction as in a teacher–pupil relationship, or by a combination of codified sources, experimentation and hands-on trial-and-error applications on the knowledge-receiving end. In this case, geographical distance becomes a hindering factor for spillovers.

In terms of patent citations, the basic question then becomes whether citations are more frequent over short distances (between the citing and cited inventors) than over long distances. In order to investigate this question, Jaffe *et al.* (1993) started out with a sample of citing patent, and compared the location of the inventor of the citing patent with that of the cited patent. Their data are drawn from the US patent system, and refer to US inventors. Location is defined in terms of 'Metropolitan Statistical Areas'. A complication arises because R&D activity may be localized irrespective of spillovers, and this would increase the probability of citing and cited patent to be localized. In order to control for this, they construct a control sample, i.e., for every citing patent, they find a similar patent (in terms of technology class and invention time) that does not cite the original cited patent. They then find that the colocation of cited and citing patents is significantly larger than the colocation of cited and non-citing patents, indicating that spillovers as evidenced by patent citations are indeed locally concentrated.

Maurseth and Verspagen (2002) investigated a similar question using data on European patents in European regions (at the subnational level). They estimated the intensity of citations as a function of geographical distance between regions, as well as country-borders and language differences. They found that the intensity of patent citations decays rapidly with distance, and that national borders and language differences have a strong impact on citation intensity. Thus, the conclusion that spillovers are geographically localized seems to hold across the patent systems and innovation systems of the US and Europe.

3.2 Patent citations measuring knowledge flows in multinational companies[3]

The local nature of knowledge spillovers has important consequences for multinational companies. Although, traditionally, the R&D activities of these companies were seen as 'an important case of non-globalization' (Patel and Pavitt, 1991), i.e., the propensity to perform R&D outside the 'home' location was smaller than for activities such as production and marketing, it is now clear that also R&D activities in these companies are internationalized (LeBas and Sierra, 2002). The international business literature has identified two motives for this trend, labelled 'asset-exploiting' and 'asset-seeking'. The latter of these follows from the nation of the local nature of spillovers, and argues that companies perform R&D activities abroad in order to 'tap into' the knowledge base of the foreign location. Asset-exploiting R&D, on the other hand, builds on home-location technological strengths, and tries to 'export' these to a foreign setting by R&D aimed at customizing the product to local circumstances.

Patel and Vega (1999) propose to distinguish these two types of foreign R&D based on a measure of 'revealed technological advantage', which is essentially a specialization index based on the distribution of a company's patents over technology classes. They characterize a country's technological specialization by means of this index, and then calculate the technological specialization of foreign affiliates in a sample of multinational companies. When the specialization pattern of the foreign affiliates matches that of the host country, this is taken as evidence for asset-seeking R&D; when the specialization pattern of the foreign affiliate matches that of the home-location R&D activities of the firm, this is taken as an indication of asset-exploiting R&D. Both types of R&D are found to be relevant.

Almeida (1996) follows the example of Jaffe *et al.* (1993), focusing on the issue of firm-level spillovers, measured by patent citations in a sample of multinational corporations. His analysis again brings out the advantages of colocation for spillovers, but also points to a broader context in which these spillovers can be used. His analysis shows, for example, the use of spillovers from the US by Korean semiconductor firms. Jaffe and Trajtenberg (1999) also extend the analysis on the geographically localized nature of patent citations to the international context. Although they do not explicitly take the firm level into account, they do take time lags into account. They show that knowledge may diffuse over time to a broader geographical area, including foreign locations.

3.3   Patent citations and the impact of universities and public research institutes

Jaffe and Trajtenberg (1996) and Henderson *et al.* (1998) proposed using patent citations to measure the impact of university research. Again, from their previous work, it is clear that this impact has a strong local component. Since the Bayh–Dole Act, US universities are known to apply for more patents. Henderson *et al.* (1998) found that this upsurge in university patenting led to a decrease in the average impact of university patents in terms of their citations. Jaffe *et al.* (1998), on the other hand, find that the impact of NASA and other federal labs in the US did not decrease over time.

An obvious drawback of their method is the fact that it only considers university patents. The US is obviously a country where university patents are relatively numerous, so the patent citation indicator is perhaps not very useful outside the US. Moreover, the impact of universities may also, and perhaps most importantly, be felt by more 'basic' knowledge that cannot easily be patented because a commercial application still has to be developed. In this respect, the approach by Narin *et al.* (1997) is interesting. They propose to use citations in patents to non-patent literature as an indicator of this. This often takes the form of citations in scientific and technical papers originating from universities and public research institutes. Their finding indicates that there are large differences between technology fields with regard to the extent on which they rely on spillovers from science.

4   Spillovers in productivity studies

A vast number of studies try to assess the empirical importance of technology spillovers for productivity growth. Generally, these studies investigate a broader class of spillovers than the studies discussed in the previous section. For example, imitation-enhancing spillovers are a major part of the spillovers leading to productivity growth. It is also true, however, that difficulties exist in separating different classes of spillovers. Generally, the productivity studies start from a production function, most often an extended Cobb–Douglas specification. Not only physical capital and labour are included as production factors, but also two kinds of R&D stocks: R&D investments by the unit (firm, industry, region or country) itself and R&D obtained through spillovers from other units (so-called 'indirect' R&D). If we denote the former by R and the latter by IR, the production function looks like

$$Q_{it} = A(IR)_{it}^{\eta} K_{it}^{\alpha} L_{it}^{\beta} R_{it}^{\gamma}, \tag{35.1}$$

in which Q stands for value added, A is a constant, K indicates the stock of physical capital, L denotes employment, t is the time index and i is the unit index. If a random error factor is added, the elasticities η, α, β and γ can be estimated. Alternatively (following Solow, 1957), β can be measured as the labour share in total income (under the assumption of equilibrium in a situation of perfect competition), and with constant returns to scale with respect to capital and labour, $\alpha = 1 - \beta$. In this way, a measure for total factor productivity (TFP) is obtained, and this can be related to the changes in both R&D stocks. A third approach is to use the dual of the production function, i.e., the cost function. Changes in the costs per unit of output are regressed on changes in the prices and quantities of various inputs (see Bernstein and Nadiri, 1988). Each of these three approaches yields estimates for output elasticities with respect to indirect R&D, $(dQ/dIR)\cdot(IR/Q)$, or rates of return to indirect R&D, dQ/dIR, and these are considered to be measures for the impact of spillovers.

The most straightforward way to estimate the influence of R&D efforts in other industries is the one applied by Bernstein and Nadiri (1988). They 'simply' distinguish one indirect R&D variable for each of the (other) industries. For example, the decrease in unit costs in the US chemical industry is related to the R&D stocks of the industries that manufacture non-electrical machinery, electrical products, transportation equipment and scientific instruments. This approach lets the data speak for themselves to see which (other) industries influence the productivity of a particular industry, irrespective of the emphasis on either rent or pure knowledge spillovers. The method has one important drawback: most industry R&D stocks have risen during recent decades, which causes huge multicollinearity problems in time series analysis. Even in cross-section analysis, it is likely that multicollinearity will disturb estimation if a large number of industry R&D variables are included. Therefore, many authors have proposed using weights to construct aggregate indirect R&D investment variables (IRE):

$$IRE_j = \sum_i \omega_{ij} RE_i \quad \forall i \neq j, \tag{35.2}$$

in which i and j denote the 'spillover producing' and 'spillover receiving' units, respectively, and RE indicates R&D expenditures. Indirect R&D stocks are usually obtained by applying the 'perpetual inventory' principle to the flow variable IRE. The weights ω_{ij} are the crucial elements distinguishing the different approaches to measuring spillovers. They indicate to what extent the R&D undertaken by i may be considered to be part of the R&D stock of j. We will discuss a number of possible weighting schemes.

4.1   Unit weights

In his firm-level study emphasizing the effects of *intra*industry spillovers, Bernstein (1988) circumvents the weighting problem by setting all weights equal to one, as did Los and Verspagen (2000) in their attempt to evaluate the empirical performance of four different interindustry spillover measures. The most important disadvantage of this method is that no account is taken of the theory of spillovers, which argues that, owing to differences in technological base, appropriability, etc., the weights should in fact be very heterogeneous. The computational convenience is its main advantage. A second advantage is the fact that it takes both rent spillovers and knowledge spillovers into account. As the discussion below will show, all other methods utilize either trade statistics or 'technological activity indicators', thus a priori stressing certain categories of spillovers. The fact that, at least in Los and Verspagen (2000), unit weighted indirect R&D stocks yield the highest estimated elasticities of indirect R&D (compared to alternative measures) seems to confirm the idea that both rent spillovers and knowledge spillovers have a significant influence on productivity. Nevertheless, unit-weighted indirect R&D stocks are a very rough indicator of spilled R&D, which at best can serve as a benchmark measure for more sophisticated measures.

4.2   Weights based on transaction input and output shares

Early attempts to include spillovers in productivity analysis at the sectoral level (Brown and Conrad, 1967, Terleckyj, 1974) used trade statistics to construct industry weights ω_{ij}. Input–output tables, which classify trade flows to industry-of-origin i and industry-of-use j, are converted into tables of output coefficients, defined as the inter-industry trade flows divided by the total sales of industry i. Then, R&D weights are set equal to the output coefficients, except for the diagonal elements. To account for inter-industry investment flows, Terleckyj (1974) and Sveikauskas (1981) calculated similar output coefficients from capital flow matrices.

The output shares approach mainly emphasizes rent spillovers, because of its focus on transactions. However, it should be noted that rent spillovers can only be caused by product innovations, while many studies apply the output share weights to total R&D investment. This is mostly due to the lack of more detailed R&D investment data. But it may also be assumed that output shares indicate technological relatedness that goes beyond just rent spillovers. Under this assumption the magnitudes of pure knowledge spillovers from supplier to buyer are likely to show a positive correlation with output shares just as well as rent spillovers do. Whatever the measured direction of spillovers and the emphasis on intermediate inputs or capital input flows, output share measures primarily focus on knowledge spillovers of the 'idea-creating' kind (besides rent spillovers).

In the output shares approach, 'second-round' effects may also play a role. This occurs when spillovers are transmitted to industries down the production chain, for example, when advances in semiconductors spill over to the computer industry, and from there to the banking industry (see, e.g., Sakurai *et al.*, 1997). Wolff and Nadiri (1993), however, found these effects to be insignificant.

Input–output tables are also used to compute spillover measures in which the ω_{ij}s are defined as the input coefficients a_{ij}. These are obtained as the ratios of the money values of the deliveries from the industries i to j to the money value of j's output. Wolff and Nadiri (1993), Wolff (1997) and Jacobs *et al.* (2002) use this measure in an inter-industry context. Coe and Helpman (1995) apply a similar measure (using import weights) in their influential international spillover study. As in the case of output share-weighted measures, this measure stresses rent spillovers.

4.3 Weights based on patent and innovation output shares

Inspired by Schmookler's (1966) seminal book on the determinants of invention, Scherer (1982) pioneered another approach. First, he assigned a sample of patents granted in a certain period to an industry-of-origin, i.e., the producer of the technology described in the patent. Then, all patents were assigned to one or more industries-of-use, on the basis of information in the patent document.[4] Bearing in mind that most patents refer to product innovations, this implies that these 'patents input–output tables' describe inter-industry flows of quality improvements. Thus, estimated elasticities or rates of return of indirect R&D stocks with ω_{ij}s equal to the output coefficients of these patent tables should be considered as estimates of the productivity effects of rent spillovers rather than knowledge spillovers (see Englander *et al.*, 1988; Los and Verspagen, 2000). The only knowledge spillovers accounted for are the 'idea-creating' ones from supplier to buyer.

In this respect, the approach is comparable to the output share weights method described above.

Another measure of technological output is the number of innovations. Sterlacchini (1989) used a large innovation survey undertaken by Robson *et al.* (1988). In this survey, more than 4000 commercialized innovations (between 1945 and 1984) in the United Kingdom were assigned to an industry-of-origin (or industry-of-manufacture) and an industry-of-use. Next, he used this 'innovations input–output table' to calculate innovation share weights ω_{ij}, denoting the share of innovations of industry *i* used by industry *j*. Again, trade-related spillovers (rent spillovers and knowledge spillovers from supplier to buyer) are emphasized in these indirect technology stocks.

The main advantage of the use of innovation counts is that only significant innovations are recorded, while many patents are simply never used commercially. The most important drawback of the method is directly connected to this: only the most influential innovations are recorded in the survey, whereas many scholars stress the large productivity effects of the mass of small, incremental innovations. Moreover, only the industry that is the first user (Robson *et al.*, 1988) or the most important user (DeBresson *et al.*, 1994) is recorded as the industry-of-use, which eliminates inter-industry diffusion effects and neglects the economy-wide productivity effects of general purpose technologies. Last but not least, historical analyses are difficult because innovation data are not continually collected, as opposed to data on trade and patents.

4.4   Weights based on patent information output shares
Verspagen (1997a) derived related but different spillover measures from European Patent Office documents. In EPO documents, the knowledge described in a patent application is assigned to a single 'main patent class', and multiple 'supplementary patent classes'. The main application area of this part of the knowledge is assigned to the single main patent class, while secondary application areas are assigned to one or more supplementary patent classes. Using a concordance (broadly similar to the one devised by Johnson and Evenson, 1997) that maps patent classification codes onto manufacturing industry classes (ISIC), the industry that is most likely to have produced the knowledge was derived from the main patent class, while the industries that are most likely to benefit from the knowledge described in the patent were identified applying the same concordance to the supplementary classes, yielding a 'patent information input–output table' similar in format to the ones described above. The ω_{ij}s were then, as in many of the aforementioned methods, set equal to the output coefficients of this table.[5] These methods relate quite clearly to knowledge spillovers through patent-related

channels. Patents are interpreted as carriers of 'idea-creating' knowledge spillovers. The main disadvantage of this method is that it relates to only a very small part of the knowledge spillover channels discussed in section 2.

A second type of patent information input–output tables may be constructed using patent citations, based on the same statistics as discussed extensively in section 3 above. The patent citation share weights method has broadly the same advantages and disadvantages as the patent information share weights method. The method directly relates to 'idea-creating' knowledge spillovers (the citing patent may be considered as an idea generated by the cited patents) and implicitly assumes that each cited patent is equally relevant to the spillover receiver. Verspagen (1997b) applied his approaches to international R&D and productivity growth data to assess the importance of international technology spillovers.

4.5 Weights based on technological proximity

Setting aside some very early, relatively primitive and ill-documented research (Raines, 1968) the first spillover measure explicitly focusing on non-traded knowledge spillovers was constructed by Jaffe (1986). He argues that knowledge generated by R&D investments flows into a 'spillover pool', which is accessible to all firms. Some firms or industries benefit more from firm i's contribution to the pool than others, because not all knowledge is relevant to their R&D. To measure the part of the contribution of the ith firm that is relevant to firm j, Jaffe (1986) used a 'technological proximity' measure:

$$\omega_{ij} = \frac{\sum_{k=1}^{F} f_{ik} \cdot f_{jk}}{\sqrt{\left(\sum_{k=1}^{F} f_{ik}^2 \cdot \sum_{k=1}^{F} f_{jk}^2\right)}},$$
(35.3)

which is the cosine of two vectors consisting of the shares of the F patent classes in the 'patent portfolio' of a firm. If two firms have patented in roughly the same classes the cosine will be close to one, if the patenting activities are greatly different, the cosine will be virtually zero. Goto and Suzuki (1989) chose a similar spillover measure in their productivity study at the industry level, but used Japanese information on the shares of product classes to which the R&D of an industry is devoted, instead of patent classes. Park (1995) used the same kind of data for a study of international spillover effects. A third comparable approach can be found in Adams (1990), who used the shares of various categories of scientists in the research workforce of an industry as determinants of its position 'in technological space', while Los (2000) proposed to compute weights analogously on the basis of columns of input–output tables. In a follow-up study to his 1986 paper, Jaffe (1988) applied equation (35.3) to vectors of the shares of 19 industries in firm i's and firm j's total output. This approach was prompted by so-called 'demand-pull' theories of innovation (Schmookler, 1966), which assume that R&D and subsequent product innovations are elicited by users' wants. Firms with similar 'output compositions' were assumed to benefit from each other's knowledge.

Jaffe's (1986) spillover measure can be linked directly to one of the knowledge spillover channels discussed in the previous section, namely the imperfect protection against imitation of patents. Given this imperfection, firms with broadly the same patenting activity can learn a lot from each other's patents. The same applies to Adams's (1990) spillover measure: industries with roughly the same composition of the research staff will learn relatively much from each other, because their employees read the same professional journals, visit the same conferences, and so on. The general reasoning behind these methods, however, is that they are different measures of the same, broad variable: similarity of technological activity. A special feature of technological proximity-weighted measures is their symmetry. By definition, a 'unit of knowledge' (proxied by a dollar of R&D investment) generated by industry i is assumed to be as relevant to industry j as a unit of knowledge produced by industry j is to industry i. This assumption is logical if the emphasis is on 'imitation-enhancing' knowledge spillovers, which was the case for Jaffe's studies at the firm level. If firms i and j just try to imitate each other's innovations, symmetry of spillovers is almost guaranteed. In a context in which 'idea-creating' spillovers are paramount, the imposed symmetry is much harder to defend: why should industry i's knowledge be as relevant to the ideas of j as the other way round?

4.6   Towards a taxonomy

We have classified the technology spillover measurement methods discussed above in two ways, stressing the differences between rent spillovers and pure knowledge spillovers and between 'imitation-enhancing' and 'idea-creating' knowledge spillovers. Before presenting a table summarizing the conclusions, we will raise one more issue. When Scherer (1982) constructed his technology flow matrix, he actually constructed two of them. In the first one, a patent with two industries-of-use was recorded in two cells, both with values of 0.5. Then, output coefficients were calculated, so the cell values in each row of this first matrix add up to one. To justify the second matrix, Scherer argued that patented innovations are public goods if the number of industries-of-use exceeds one. This would imply that more than one user could use a 'unit of patented product' at a time, and the sum of R&D that generated the patented product should be attributed completely to *each* of the industries-of-use.[6] Consequently, division of the cell values by the industry-of-invention's number of patents yields row sums larger than one.

We feel that the issue of the magnitude of row sums deserves some attention with regard to knowledge spillover measures, on the basis of differences in the assumed 'specificity' of knowledge. One may either argue that some knowledge generated by unit i may be relevant for both units j and k (i.e., not very specific), or argue that a piece of knowledge is only relevant for k or j (but not both). Which fraction of knowledge is non-specific and which fraction is specific is hard to assess on the basis of statistical data only, but Scherer's two alternatives provide the extreme cases. Of the measures of knowledge spillovers discussed above, some have the property that the row sums equal one (implying specificity), whereas others have rows adding up to values larger than one (implying generality).

A completely different story holds for estimation of rates of return to R&D obtained through knowledge spillovers. These rates of return are roughly defined as the change in output as a consequence of a unit change in indirect R&D. One additional dollar of 'full generality' indirect R&D will probably yield far fewer dollars of additional output than an additional dollar of 'single industry specificity' indirect R&D (comparable in any other sense), owing to the fact that the former extra dollar is assumed to contain a lot of relevant knowledge that actually is not productive at all. The 'true' rate of return is likely to be overestimated by the 'single industry specificity' measure, because a lot of relevant knowledge that does increase output is not included in the additional dollar. Differences in the assumed specificity of spilled knowledge might be a major cause of the high variability of estimated rates of return to indirect R&D, as for example reported in Nadiri's (1993) survey. Hence we conclude that, if possible, rates of return to knowledge spillovers should be estimated using both a 'full generality' and a 'single industry specificity' knowledge spillover measure, and the results should be interpreted as lower and upper bounds for the true rate of return, respectively. Rates of return to rent spillovers should be estimated on the basis of a measure of which the rows add up to one or less, reflecting the fact that rents of innovations are not public goods and part of the rents may be captured by consumers and foreign industries.

Table 35.1 offers a taxonomy of the measurement methods discussed above. The methods are classified along two dimensions. The first one indicates whether the emphasis is on rent spillovers or on pure knowledge spillovers. The second one reflects the assumed degree of specificity of spilled knowledge. Moreover, within the class of knowledge spillover-related

Table 35.1   A taxonomy of technology spillover measures

Emphasis →	Rent spillovers	Knowledge spillovers	No a priori emphasis
assumed specificity ↓		'imposed symmetry'	'no imposed symmetry'
'single industry specificity'	transaction output share weights; patent output share weights; innovation output share weights		patent information share weights; patent citation share weights
'full generality'	transaction input share weights	technological proximity weights	unit weights

measures, the distinction between 'imposed symmetry' measures (originally designed to stress 'imitation-enhancing' spillovers between firms within an industry) and 'no imposed symmetry' measures (explicitly focusing on 'idea-creating' spillovers) is present in the table.

The classification of the input share weights measure as a 'full generality' measure may need some clarification. Contrary to the output share weights, input share weights of a given spillover-receiving industry cannot change because of changes in other industries. In principle, it is therefore possible that the weights in a row sum to more than one. The rent spillovers that are also measured by the input shares are not public at all and cannot be captured more than once, which renders the input share weights measure a doubtful method.

Notes

1. The emphasis of the survey is on methodological issues, as in Van Pottelsberghe de la Potterie (1997), which compares a very limited number of approaches, and Griliches (1992), which could not include the most recent developments. For surveys on empirical results, the interested reader should consult Mohnen (1990, 1996) and Nadiri (1993).
2. Arundel *et al.* (1995) present industry-level survey data on time spent on product R&D and process R&D, suggesting that the R&D of industries with higher R&D intensities is generally more product-oriented.
3. There is also a large literature on the impact of foreign direct investment on firm performance, which we choose not to survey here.
4. Examining some patents, Scherer (1984) had difficulties assigning 'general purpose' processes or products to specific industries-of-use. In these cases, he decided to categorize all buying industries under industries-of-use, in proportion to (trade) output shares. Johnson and Evenson (1997) propose a concordance that maps patent classification codes

assigned by the Canadian Patent Office onto industry codes, which enables them to construct their matrix without the need to examine every patent document individually.
5. Grupp (1996) followed a similar approach to determine how knowledge flows from one technological field to another (thereby omitting the mapping on an industrial classification), but did not look at productivity effects.
6. Eventually, Scherer (1982) decided to assign the industry-of-use that purchased the largest part of the industry-of-invention's output (k) a value of one and the other industries-of-use i a value of a_i/a_k, in which the as denote the purchases from the industry-of-invention.

References

Adams, J.D. (1990), 'Fundamental stocks of knowledge and productivity growth', *Journal of Political Economy*, **98**, 673–702.
Almeida, P. (1996), 'Knowledge sourcing by foreign multinationals: patent citation analysis in the U.S. semiconductor industry', *Strategic Management Journal*, **17**, 155–65.
Arundel, A., G. Van de Paal and L. Soete (1995), 'PACE report: innovation strategies of Europe's largest industrial firms', MERIT, Maastricht.
Bernstein, J.I. (1988), 'Costs of production, intra- and interindustry R&D spillovers: Canadian evidence', *Canadian Journal of Economics*, **21**, 324–47.
Bernstein, J.I. and M.I. Nadiri (1988), 'Interindustry R&D spillovers, rates of return, and production in high-tech industries', *American Economic Review (Papers and Proceedings)*, **78**, 429–34.
Brown, M. and A. Conrad (1967), 'The influence of research on CES production relations', in M. Brown (ed.), *The Theory and Empirical Analysis of Production*, New York: Columbia University Press for NBER.
Coe, D.T. and E. Helpman (1995), 'International R&D spillovers', *European Economic Review*, **39**, 859–87.
DeBresson, C., G. Sirilli, X. Hu and F. Kwan Luk (1994), 'Structure and location of innovative activity in the Italian economy, 1981–85', *Economic Systems Research*, **6**, 135–58.
Englander, A.S., R. Evenson and M. Hanazaki (1988), 'R&D, innovation and the total factor productivity slowdown', *OECD Economic Studies*, **11**, 7–42.
Goto, A. and K. Suzuki (1989), 'R&D capital, rate of return on R&D investment and spillover of R&D in Japanese manufacturing industries', *Review of Economics and Statistics*, **71**, 555–64.
Griliches, Z. (1961), 'Hedonic price indexes for automobiles: an econometric analysis of quality change', NBER Staff Report no. 3.
Griliches, Z. (1979), 'Issues in assessing the contribution of research and development to productivity growth', *The Bell Journal of Economics*, **10**, 92–116.
Griliches, Z. (1990), 'Patent statistics as economic indicators: a survey', *Journal of Economic Literature*, **28**, 1661–707.
Griliches, Z. (1992), 'The search for R&D spillovers', *Scandinavian Journal of Economics*, **94**, S29–S47.
Grupp, H. (1996), 'Spillover effects and the science base of innovations reconsidered: an empirical approach', *Journal of Evolutionary Economics*, **6**, 175–97.
Henderson, R., A.B. Jaffe and M. Trajtenberg (1998), 'Universities as a source of commercial technology: a detailed analysis of university patenting', *Review of Economics and Statistics*, **80**, 183–204.
Jacobs, B., R. Nahuis and P.J.G. Tang (2002), 'Sectoral productivity growth and R&D spillovers in The Netherlands', *De Economist*, **150**, 181–210.
Jaffe, A.B. (1986), 'Technological opportunity and spillovers of R&D: evidence from firms' patents, profits, and market value', *American Economic Review*, **76**, 984–1001.
Jaffe, A.B. (1988), 'Demand and supply influences in R&D intensity and productivity growth', *Review of Economics and Statistics*, **70**, 431–7.
Jaffe, A.B. and M. Trajtenberg (1996), 'Flows of knowledge from universities and federal laboratories: modeling the flow of patent citations over time and across institutional and geographic boundaries', *Proceedings of the National Academy of Sciences*, **93**, 12671–7.

Jaffe, A.B. and M. Trajtenberg (1999), 'International knowledge flows: evidence from patent citations', *Economics of Innovation and New Technology*, **8**, 105–36.

Jaffe, A.B., M.S. Fogarty and B.A. Banks (1998), 'Evidence from patents and patent citations on the impact of NASA and other federal labs on commercial innovation', *Journal of Industrial Economics*, **46**, 183–205.

Jaffe, A.B., M. Trajtenberg and R. Henderson (1993), 'Geographic localization of knowledge spillovers as evidenced by patent citations', *Quarterly Journal of Economics*, **108**, 577–98.

Johnson, D. and R.E. Evenson (1997), 'Innovation and invention in Canada', *Economic Systems Research*, **9**, 177–92.

LeBas, C. and C. Sierra (2002), 'Location versus home country advantages in R&D activities: some further results on multinationals' locational strategies', *Research Policy*, **31**, 589–609.

Levin, R.C., A.A. Klevorick, R.R. Nelson and S.G. Winter (1987), 'Appropriating the returns from industrial R&D', *Brookings Papers on Economic Activity*, **3**, 783–820.

Los, B. (2000), 'The empirical performance of a new interindustry technology spillover measure', in B. Nooteboom and P. Saviotti (eds), *Technology and Knowledge: From the Firm to Innovation Systems*, Cheltenham, UK and Northampton, MA, USA: Edward Elgar.

Los, B. and B. Verspagen (2000), 'R&D spillovers and productivity: evidence from U.S. manufacturing microdata', *Empirical Economics*, **25**, 127–48.

Maurseth, P.-B. and B. Verspagen (2002), 'Knowledge spillovers in Europe. A patent citation analysis', *Scandinavian Journal of Economics*, **104**, 531–45.

Michel, J. and B. Bettles (2001), 'Patent citation analysis. A closer look at the basic input data from patent search reports', *Scientometrics*, **51**, 185–201.

Mohnen, P. (1990), 'New technology and interindustry spillovers', *STI Review*, **7**, 131–47.

Mohnen, P. (1996), 'R&D externalities and productivity growth', *STI Review*, **18**, 39–66.

Nadiri, M.I. (1993), 'Innovations and technological spillovers', NBER Working Paper no. 4423.

Narin, F., K.S. Hamilton and D. Olivastro (1997), 'The increasing linkage between U.S. technology and public science', *Research Policy*, **26**, 317–30.

Park, W.G. (1995), 'International R&D spillovers and OECD economic growth', *Economic Inquiry*, **33**, 571–91.

Patel, P. and K. Pavitt (1991), 'Large firms in the production of the world's technology: an important case of non-globalisation', *Journal of International Business Studies*, **22**, 1–21.

Patel, P. and M. Vega (1999), 'Patterns of internationalisation and corporate technology: location versus home country advantages', *Research Policy*, **28**, 145–55.

Pavitt, K. (1984), 'Sectoral patterns of technical change: towards a taxonomy and a theory', *Research Policy*, **13**, 343–474.

Polanyi, M. (1966), *The Tacit Dimension*, Garden City NY: Anchor Books.

Raines, F. (1968), 'The impact of applied research and development on productivity', Washington University Working Paper no. 6814.

Robson, M., J. Townsend and K. Pavitt (1988), 'Sectoral patterns of production and use of innovations in the UK: 1945–83', *Research Policy*, **17**, 1–14.

Sakurai, N., G. Papaconstantinou and E. Ioannidis (1997), 'Impact of R&D and technology diffusion on productivity growth: empirical evidence for 10 OECD countries', *Economic Systems Research*, **9**, 81–109.

Saxenian, A. (1994), *Regional Advantage: Culture and Competition in Silicon Valley and Route 128*, Cambridge, MA: Harvard University Press.

Scherer, F.M. (1982), 'Inter-industry technology flows and productivity measurement', *Review of Economics and Statistics*, **64**, 627–34.

Scherer, F.M. (1984), 'Using linked patent R&D data to measure inter-industry technology flows', in Z. Griliches (ed.), *R&D, Patents, and Productivity*, Chicago, IL: University of Chicago Press.

Schmookler, J. (1966), *Invention and Economic Growth*, Cambridge, MA: Harvard University Press.

Solow, R.M. (1957), 'Technical progress and the aggregate production function', *Review of Economics and Statistics*, **39**, 312–20.

Sterlacchini, A. (1989), 'R&D, innovations, and total factor productivity growth in British Manufacturing', *Applied Economics*, **21**, 1549–62.

Sveikauskas, L. (1981), 'Technological inputs and multifactor productivity growth', *Review of Economics and Statistics*, **63**, 275–82.

Terleckyj, N.E. (1974), 'Effects of R&D on the productivity growth of industries: an exploratory study', National Planning Association, Washington, DC.

Trajtenberg, M. (1990), *Economic Analysis of Product Innovations*, Cambridge, MA: Harvard University Press.

Van Meijl, H. (1995), 'Endogenous technological change: the case of information technology', PhD thesis, University of Limburg, Maastricht.

Van Pottelsberghe de la Potterie, B. (1997), 'Issues in assessing the effect of interindustry spillovers', *Economic Systems Research*, **9**, 331–56.

Verspagen, B. (1997a), 'Measuring inter-sectoral technology spillovers: estimates from the European and US patent office databases', *Economic Systems Research*, **9**, 47–65.

Verspagen, B. (1997b), 'Estimating international technology spillovers using technology flow matrices', *Weltwirtschaftliches Archiv*, **133**, 226–48.

Von Hippel, E. (1988), *The Sources of Innovation*, Oxford: Oxford University Press.

Wolff, E.N. (1997), 'Spillovers, linkages, and technical change', *Economic Systems Research*, **9**, 9–23.

Wolff, E.N. and M.I. Nadiri (1993), 'Spillover effects, linkage structure and research and development', *Structural Change and Economic Dynamics*, **4**, 315–31.

3.2
Case and Industry Studies

36 The Japanese system from the neo-Schumpeterian perspective[1]
Ken-ichi Imai

Japan's transformation and the concept of entrepreneurship

The essential feature of Japan's economic system can be identified as the dynamic transformation process of industrial networks, in which entrepreneurship and innovation have played a key role. Focusing on the evolutionary process of Japan's entrepreneurship and innovation, we shall explore the essence of the Japanese system.

For that purpose, we first require a concept of entrepreneurship that emphasizes the process of changes. We start with Schumpeter's original conception of entrepreneurship. His concept of the entrepreneur as an individual who creates 'new combinations' is an effective definition of an entrepreneur, and well suited to explaining Japanese innovations (to be elaborated later).

However, Schumpeter himself did not explicitly discuss the process of transformation or change. Schumpeter's successors, the so-called 'neo-Shumpeterians', complemented this deficiency in the following ways. First, Israel Kirzner (1973) redefined entrepreneurship as 'alertness' to new opportunities, e.g., to discover a new combination of goods and services with which Schumpeter empathized. If this discovery is genuine, alertness necessarily leads to an actual implementation process in the market. Alertness is especially effective in a market disequilibrium. Therefore, this conception of entrepreneurship is highly process-oriented. Second, learning and knowledge play an important role in the neo-Shumpeterian framework. Alertness is nothing but the result of learning and knowledge. This implies that entrepreneurship is embedded in specific environments such as history and culture, and therefore depends on past processes of economic change. This in turn implies that entrepreneurs exist in their respective countries as part of the developmental path of their country.

The passage below gives a brief overview of the history of Japanese entrepreneurship, which will explain why re-embedding new economic and social relationships is important in Japan's transformation.[2]

Path dependence of Japanese entrepreneurship

The Japanese economic system before and after World War II, centered on big businesses which utilized technology imported from Europe and

America. Because this remains effective today, Japan is often viewed as salary man-centered and lacking in entrepreneurship. However, in both the pre- and post-war periods, this was not always the case.

Immediately after the Meiji Restoration, Japan invested nearly 20 per cent of its national income in constructing roads, harbors and railroads and, with this infrastructure as a basis, learned from the experience of Europe and America and quickly developed an industrial system. The people who led this industrialization learned from advanced industrialized nations (especially England), drew up blueprints for industrial development and implemented them and became known as the *zaibatsu* entrepreneurs. Whether it be Hikojirou Nakamigawa of Mitsui, or Heigoro Shoda of Mitsubishi, the *zaibatsu* organizations were created, not by individual business starters, but by entrepreneurs who were able to read the state of the world and foresee the path to capitalist industrial development. In developing economies, information needed for investment decisions is limited, with only a few people who have access. At the time, in ensuring that information and capital flowed to the necessary places, the *zaibatsu* entrepreneurs played a crucial role.

However, as the *zaibatsu* grew, they gained control of an extensive portion of the economic domain through stockholdings, manager dispatches and monopolistic purchases and sales, eventually making connections with the military and being transformed into a mechanism of monopolistic control of the nation.

At the end of World War II, the *zaibatsu* were disassembled by the US occupation forces, and high-ranking officials were purged from the business world, leaving the remaining managerial-level business elite to run the show. In the beginning, with the removal of the powerful business managers by the occupation forces, there was apprehension as to whether the reconstruction of Japanese companies was possible, but by then the first graduates of the University of Tokyo Department of Economics, Hitotsubashi University and Keio University were businessman in their 40s, and the purging of the older leaders led to a rejuvenation of the management level, and it was this shift that proved a hidden but key factor in post-war economic growth.

After the war, the crucial function which entrepreneurs demonstrated was to accelerate positive economic growth. They aggressively exchanged information with other companies on key points such as investment decisions. The young leaders, new in their positions of responsibility, needed to compensate for their lack of experience, and obtaining information on other companies allowed them to make certain adjustments in advance, decreasing uncertainty and possible dangers, which proved indispensable and advantageous to their company. The fact that they were not individualistic business starters, but were elite white-collar businessmen, allowed the smooth flow of information.

As a result of such information exchange, they came to learn that only mutual growth could adjust the conflict of interests within the group, and the incentive for growth gradually became stronger, with evaluation of growth centered on sales rather than profits. In this way, formerly loosely connected corporate groups gained motivation to grow, and when growth was realized, the performance of the group as a whole improved.

When examined in a positive light, this use of growth to adjust conflict of interests is a very clear-cut method for bringing together a network. In fact, in the period of post-war growth, expectation of mutual growth strengthened the relationships between companies, and the resulting growth in turn brought mutual trust, creating a virtuous cycle of growth.

However, when viewed with a critical eye, if companies become accustomed to this method, they can easily fall into a pattern where growth is the only thing in sight. Indeed, although corporate strategies for quantitative expansion were continuously designed, such conditions were not always given. If growth were to stop, this positive growth cycle could easily turn into a vicious downward spiral. Moreover, information exchange within corporate networks runs the risk of being corrupted by group politics. New directions for corporate activity or innovation are not easily born from this sort of information exchange, and they tend to become protective networks, like cartels. In the period of transformation following the rapid growth era, it is not surprising that cartels became a large social problem, and we cannot deny that their influence still remains today.

Transformation ignited by crisis

The turning point, that led to the conversion of the corporate groups into industrial organizations in a network model, was the oil crisis. Crisis prompts a rearrangement of relationships between companies in economic society to overcome the difficulties that they face. That is, the oil crisis prompted a reorganization of the new industrial organizations in Japan into a network model, in the same way that the dismantling of the *zaibatsu* changed the monopolistic system into the *keiretsu* system, which was at least more flexible than the *zaibatsu*.

With the advent of the oil crisis, Japanese companies began utilizing electronic technologies that were just beginning to find concrete applications for practical use in all areas of manufacturing, and they endeavored to synthesize the improved technologies to conserve energy. Leading small and medium-sized enterprises needed to rationalize and they pursued a path of specialization based on their core technologies, and in turn big businesses integrated those technologies and swiftly improved their systems. Although this division of labor was not a new phenomenon, what branded this as a network system was the fact that it crossed corporate and industrial borders. This technology transfer led to the creation of horizontal connections, and the success of this improved system attracted global attention.[3]

The technical innovation called 'mechatronics', which is a fusion of microelectronics and machine technology, is exemplary of a 'new combination' as outlined by Schumpeter, and those individuals (engineers and managers) who promoted it also suit Schumpeter's definition of an 'entrepreneur'. From this viewpoint, it is not only company founders or executives who are entrepreneurs, but rather the technical leaders who are alert to new combinations brought by electronics must also be considered as entrepreneurs. In this sense, in the mid-ranks of Japanese large companies there were many entrepreneurs and they served as reserves for new ventures, which will be discussed later.

Beginning with Schumperter's definition, and developing it as a process view of alertness to new economic opportunities, and continuous interactive actions to seize opportunities, we can truly understand the Japanese entrepreneurial process of those days.

Professor Ronald Dore (1986), who has a deep understanding of the industrial problems in Japan, skillfully described the Japanese system with the phrase 'flexible rigidity'. The transformation ignited by the oil crisis may be a typical example of flexible rigidity in the Japanese industrial system, as it responded to change 'flexibly' in respect of product manufacturing, but the relations between companies and the financial institutions remained 'rigid'. It is incorrect to assume that the main banks and their affiliates ruled over Japan, but it is evident that there was a rigidity in place that could not easily be changed.

Rigidity in the Japanese system

Japanese companies and the government took notice of the serious problems associated with this rigidity. Companies tackled them with the structural reform of their organization, employment systems, research systems, and relations with other companies, and the central and local governments aggressively pushed forward with the growth of venture businesses. However, as the phrase 'Japan's lost decade' indicates, these attempts at structural reform did not progress smoothly.

The Japanese corporate system had three inherent characteristics that could not be solved by entrepreneurship alone. First, so long as Japan operated a market-based economy, for corporations and the government to change the structure, the labor and financial markets needed to accept the changes and assist in implementing them. However, these Japanese markets had already become rigid and lacked the flexibility that was necessary for change. For example, the loaning of funds was based, not on the potential profits of a company, but on land and fixed capital that the company already owned, and the labor market could not relocate workers into places that lacked workers from places with excess labor. The kind of entrepreneurial market which exists in America was completely non-existent. To change the industrial structure, workers must be able to move, not only within a company, but to different companies, different industrial fields, in different areas, as in a 'horizontal labor market'.

Second, when technological innovation occurred with respect to a social infrastructure, i.e., communications, energy, and logistics, there was a tendency to have profound social impacts. To put it more accurately, too much attention was given to the 'creation' side of creative disruption, and too little research and policymaking was done with regard to the disruptive impact, creating a confrontation between the reformers and the Old Guard. Even economists failed to give a new persuasive theory, only trotting out old-fashioned ideas about the perceived benefits of increased competition brought about by cost cutting.

Third, simply put, the macroeconomic environment was excessively bad. When the macroeconomic growth rate fell from 3 per cent to 1 per cent, leaving aside the discussion of whether this was a temporary or long-term growth rate, the margin for reform in the private sector was drastically reduced. As discussed earlier, Japanese entrepreneurs built networks on the prerequisite of growth and adjusted only to maintain the positive flow, and, when growth stopped, falling into a downward spiral was inevitable.

These situations cannot be solved like mathematical simultaneous equations. This is because 'social embeddedness' is powerful, as sociologists Mark Granovetter and Richard Swedberg (2001) put it, and the social economic system cannot be reset easily. However, innovation can mean being 'born again' in English, and the Japanese system has had to be 'born again' quite a few times to survive. After the suffering in the 'lost decade' it is now time to be born again by a new method, which we propose later.

Evolution of Japanese innovations
For this purpose, we require a new definition of innovation. Japan's innovation system has been characterized as 'incremental innovation' in manufacturing. Japan has succeeded thus far in creating an 'innovative manufacturing system with a focus on high quality'. However, merely emphasizing manufacturing strength may be misleading. In the information age, to a large extent, quality manufacturing is based on digital design, and intensive use of digital devices. As digital technology takes center stage, the distinction between 'product' and 'information' is becoming blurred. Both are expressions of certain 'patterns' (to use Fujimoto's term) and the

difference is that, when a specific pattern is 'expressed' onto steel you get a car, but you get software when a pattern is expressed onto a computer disk or a paper (Fujimoto, 2003). The former is an expression onto a material which is difficult to write compared to the latter case, and therefore requires complementary materials, expertise and trained skills. Therefore, it requires not only digital design architecture but also continuous incremental manufacturing innovation, which differs from the radical breakthroughs in digital technology.

The architecture for automobiles, cameras, printers, and other consumer electronic products with competitive power in the global market, is of an 'integral type' which is different from the 'module-type' architecture as seen in Silicon Valley. 'Integral' architecture requires a delicate coordination among different parts and devices *interdependently* for the whole to function, while the module type allows the parts to work independently within the interface. Naturally, the module system creates an open type of industrial network, while the integral system tends to develop closed networks among a limited number of companies.

However, this difference in architecture, as it stands now, cannot continue for long. Both systems can coexist, depending on the stage of industrial maturity and basic technological and market structure of the industries. Japan is moving to adopt module systems in order to make speedy improvements, yet the core of integral systems will remain because they are vital for Japan's innovation. Integral systems do not quickly respond to rapid change, but have a special advantage in the changing environment of the middle range. Seen in the light of the comparative advantage theory of international economics, this is a natural tendency. However, Japan should adopt module systems if possible in order to be born again with an open global innovation system. The evolution of Japan's innovation system will create a workable architecture, with both modularizing and integrating essentially included.

Japan's industrial cluster
For this purpose, it is useful to reconsider Japan's industrial clusters. An industrial cluster is created in the intersection of entrepreneurship and innovation. Without entrepreneurial alertness to market opportunities, innovation does not materialize in the marketplace and clusters do not form. Without innovation, entrepreneurship alone ends in a simple expansion of traditional economic activities and fails to create a breakthrough that leads to an innovation cluster.[4]

Needless to say, the combination of entrepreneurship and innovation are diverse and multifaceted. We shall describe three actual cases in Japan, including the key points of Japanese entrepreneurship and innovation discussed above, that exemplify our proposed next-generation clusters in Japan.

First, the Aichi-Toyota Cluster is a combination of integral-type innovation and strong entrepreneurial leadership based on just-in-time products creation to meet ever-changing consumer needs. Toyota aggressively performed outsourcing, fostering reliable start-ups among its group, partially adopting a module system, and thus created a unique innovative cluster.

In general, the Japanese automobile industry is a positive example of 'flexible rigidity'. Toyota and Honda have long had their own network strategies, assigning certain design, development and production work within the company, while also flexibly outsourcing work to external companies, which allowed them to absorb the latest information technology efficiently. This flexibility is based, not on a mass productive system as in America, but on the philosophy of founder Kiichiro Toyota and his innovative idea to create products customers want, when they want them. The philosophical foundation in this tradition has been rigid in a good sense. In Honda's case, a hidden organizational innovation has become the tradition; the presidents of Honda retire from their post at a young age, unthinkable in other Japanese companies. This symbolic rule effectively allows Honda to maintain youthfulness in its technological developments. At first glance this appears to be a small issue, but without the pressure of outside forces such as the dismantling of the *zaibatsu*, the rejuvenation of leaders has been difficult in Japan and, in the aging corporate environment of Japan, the decision of Soichiro Honda to create an inner rule of rejuvenation within the company is a prime example of entrepreneurship and demonstrates decisive leadership in Japan.

Fukuoka's New Semiconductor Cluster is an example of re-embedding new relationships into old industrial networks centered around automobile factories. Key engineers who spun-off from large companies, Sony's engineers who are concentrating on 'post PC' technology and Kyushu University professors are now re-embedding new linkages for restructuring the old regional cluster.

Japanese university systems, which were firmly embedded in the old European-style system, have finally begun rapid mobilization of their human and knowledge resources. According to the Nikkei Venture Business Survey, the numbers of venture businesses started from Japanese universities exceeded 100 in the past three years. Among them, we place high hopes on the Sendai cluster surrounding Tohoku University. The university is world-famous in the field of material development using nanotechnology, which is viewed as the key to Nano-Bio-Info convergence.[5] However, supporting infrastructure such as mid-level staff and the capability of TLOs are still very weak. Strong policy assistance for the creation of new infrastructure for research universities is urgently needed. Recently in the US, a large government initiative in nanotechnology was announced. In order to help transform the Japanese system, such new infrastructure policies are desirable rather than mere calls for structural reforms within political circles, let alone retuning to traditional industrial policies.

These examples indicate that 're-embedding' is not intended to create a new blue-print and rebuild the system entirely, but rather to make change by embedding some effective elements either naturally or purposely through planning and policies, and allowing them to come into contact and interact, creating a natural wave of change. This can be the new Japanese way of creative destruction.

A unique path for new development

In the information knowledge economy, the quality of innovation depends on efficient coordination and integration of knowledge. Japan's traditional hierarchical system centering on 'Nagata-cho' (politicians) and 'Kasumigaseki' (bureaucrats) is now loosing its stronghold on power. Several networks of expert groups, including young politicians and knowledgeable bureaucrats, have begun to demonstrate their capacity to coordinate decisionmaking in the intersection of public and private domains.

For the creation of innovation clusters, those expert groups are indispensable human resources. However, in Japan there is a unique problem associated with the overconcentration in Tokyo. There is a natural tendency for the expert groups to gather together in Tokyo, especially in the center of the city. Even if they prefer living in the countryside, when a problem arises they must gather together in Tokyo to solve complex problems. The numbers of such experts in Japan are still limited, so having an office in Tokyo is necessary for efficient use of resources and to save time. Also, there is a dire lack of specialists who deal with international matters, inevitably accelerating the concentration of these professionals in Tokyo; in fact, in recent years we have seen many lawyers, accountants, patent attorneys, programmers and consultants migrating to Tokyo.

Whether this is a transitory phenomenon or a more long-run inevitable movement is a difficult problem to answer here, as it depends on both the demand side and the supply side, but the crucial question is not to do with the tendency but rather with the degree of concentration. It may be reasonable to predict the Tokyo concentration will continue for a while, but other possibilities remain.

Central to this is the location of key knowledge which has a deep impact on economic and social transformation. Usually, something new is continuously created through interactive activities in a big city like Tokyo.

Fashionable trends in town architectures, home design, apparel and foods, or new types of journalism and life styles are constantly created and recreated. Each includes some element of innovation. So far the accumulation of such incremental innovations has been an engine of Japanese economic development. But now, more profound knowledge that is deeply rooted in academic research or anchored in history and culture is critically needed. It is possible that such knowledge will be located in a cluster other than Tokyo; for example, in the Kyoto cluster. Its future is unknown but it is certain that history and culture matters in Japan's process of creative destruction.

Notes

1. This chapter is an expansion and revision of my paper 'Stability and change in the Japanese system', in *Making IT: The Rise of Asia in High Tech*, Stanford University Press, 2007.
2. A more detailed discussion can be found in Imai (1992).
3. Though this improved system flourished for a time, when the new architectural concepts emerged (architecture and modular types), further additions to this 'patchwork-type' system could not be made, thus hindering the change of systems and locking in the old system.
4. This is a central hypothesis of the Stanford Project, Regions of Entrepreneurship and Innovation (SPRIE), in which the author participated as the Japanese team leader.
5. Nano-Bio-Info convergence, in short NBI converging technology, aims to raise standards of living and improve mankind's capabilities by combining N (Nanotechnology), B (Biotechnology) and I (Information Technology).

Bibliography

Acs, Zoltan J. (ed.) 2000, *Regional Innovation, Knowledge, and Global Change*, Pinter.
Acs, Zoltan J. and Audretsch, David B. (eds), 2003, *Handbook of Entrepreneurship Research: an Interdisciplinary Survey and Introduction*, Academic Publishers.
Acs, Zoltan J., Groot, Henri L.F. de and Nijkamp, Peter (eds), 2002, *The Emergence of the Knowledge Economy: a Regional Perspective*, Springer.
Bresnahan, Timothy, Gambardella, Alfonso and Saxenian, Annalee, 2001, 'Old economy's inputs for "new economy" outcomes: cluster formation in the new silicon valleys', *Industrial and Corporate Change*, **10**(4), 835–60.
Castells, Manuel, 1989, *The Informational City: Information Technology, Economic Restructuring, and the Urban–regional Process*, Blackwell Publishers.
Christensen, Clayton M., trans. Syunpeita Tamada and Yumi Izuhara, 2001, *The Innovator's Dilemma: When New Technologies Cause Great Firms to Fail*, Harvard Business School Press.
Dore, Ronald, 1986, *Flexible Rigidities: Industrial Policy and Structural Adjustment in the Japanese Economy 1970–80*, The Athlone Press.
Feldman, P. Maryann, 1994, *The Geography of Innovation*, Kluwer Academic Publishers.
Fischer, M. Manfred, 2001, *Knowledge, Complexity and Innovation System*, Springer.
Fujimoto, Takahiro, 2003, *Competition in Creating Core Competence* (in Japanese), Chuokoron-sha.
Granovetter, Mark and Swedberg, Richard (eds), 2001, *The Sociology of Economic Life*, Westview Press.
Imai, Ken-ichi, 1992, 'Japan's corporate networks', in Shumpei Kumon and Henry Rosovsky (eds), *The Political Economy of Japan, Vol. 3: Cultural and Social Dynamics*, Stanford University Press.

Imai, Ken-ichi, 2007, 'Stability and change in the Japanese system', in Henry Rowen, Marguerite Hancock and William Miller (eds), *Making IT: The Rise of Asia in High Tech*, Stanford University Press.

Imai, Ken-ichi and Kaneko, Ikuyo, 1988, *Network Organization Theory* (in Japanese), Iwanami Shoten, Publishers.

Itami, Hiroyuki, Matsushima, Shigeru and Kikkawa, Takeo (eds), 1998, *The Essence of Industrial Amalgamation* (in Japanese), Yuuhikaku.

Kirzner, Israel, 1973, *Competition and Entrepreneurship*, University of Chicago Press.

Lee, Chong Moon *et al.*, 2000, *The Silicon Valley Edge: a Habitat for Innovation and Entrepreneurship*, Stanford University Press.

Ministry of Economy, Trade and Industry (ed.), 2001, *The Creative Transformation of Japanese Organizations* (in Japanese), Marui Press.

Shumpeter, Joseph A., 1936, *Theory of Economic Development*, Harvard University Press.

37 Biotechnology industries
M. McKelvey

1 Introduction

The biotechnology industries include economic activities and firms, which depend upon knowledge related to living organisms and biological processes. Biotechnology as a technological area builds upon a variety of every-changing knowledge bases like genetic engineering, molecular biology, protein engineering, bio-informatics, etc. This knowledge is applied to a variety of economic activities, and hence the biotech industries affect many processes, products and sectors. Examples of uses include genetically modified crops in food and agriculture; research techniques for drug discovery in pharmaceuticals; bio-remediation for environmental purposes; diagnostics and genetic testing for human health care. This chapter considers theoretical arguments and empirical evidence, in order to understand the economic dynamics of modern biotechnology from a neo-Schumpeterian perspective.[1]

To reach this objective, it is useful first to reflect on the conceptualization, which underlies this appreciative theorizing about the biotechnology industries. The perspective is fundamentally neo-Schumpeterian, as explained in other parts of the present volume and also found in McKelvey, Rickne and Laage-Hellman (2004: chs 1, 2, 3, 14) *The Economic Dynamics of Modern Biotechnology*. The economic dynamics of knowledge refers to the conceptualization that innovations and the related development of new knowledge and information go linked hand-in-hand with economic transformation. The economy changes fundamentally over time, with new products, firms and activities starting up and with existing ones being significantly modified or disappearing. Ongoing, fundamental changes in these types of scientific and technological areas affect the development of innovations, firms and other economic activities – and vice versa. Emerging technological areas and emerging industries directly and indirectly play a particularly important role in broader economic change. This dynamic process includes both formation and destruction of agents as well as changes in socio-economic incentive structure and institutions.

Biotechnology refers to a range of knowledge bases and sectors affected by living organisms and biological processes. Traditional biotechnology techniques include wine and bread-making, whereas 'modern' biotechnology usually refers to knowledge, techniques and tools developed in connection with, or after, genetic engineering techniques in the late 1970s. After this point, humans increased their control over and understanding of living organisms and biological processes. Even 'modern biotechnology' rests, however, upon a variety of more traditional knowledge bases and sectors. Moreover, traditional and modern keep shifting, as the forefront of knowledge, techniques and tools continues to develop at a rapid pace.

The biotechnology industry provides an interesting case to use empirical evidence to understand broader innovation processes and the long-term structural changes, or economic transformation. Doing so requires theoretical insight into a fundamental puzzle of the modern learning society, namely how and why the development of knowledge and of ideas in ongoing innovation processes interact with firms, markets and governments. Hence, from an appreciative theorizing perspective of neo-Schumpeterian economics, modern biotechnology can be used to probe more general and abstract issues about how and why to conceptualize the modern economy.

This chapter considers the following aspects of the biotechnology industries: (1) the global biotechnology industries, (2) science and innovation processes in biotechnology, and (3) methods and theory in appreciative theorizing.

2   The global biotechnology industries
The global biotechnology industries refer to economic activities and firms, which depend upon knowledge related to living organisms and biological processes. This section considers the definitions and operationalization of the concept of 'modern biotechnology', as related to their use and impact within the economy.

Most definitions of modern biotechnology refer back to principles of living organisms, but specify that such knowledge is put to use to meet societal needs. The OECD affects definitions and the collection of statistics in many countries, and their working definition (OECD, 2001) is 'Biotechnology is the application of scientific and engineering principles to the processing of materials by biological agents to provide goods and services.' The American industry association BIO USA (2003) defines as follows: 'New biotechnology – the use of cellular and molecular processes to solve problems or make products . . . Biotechnologies – capitalizing on the attributes of cells and biological molecules.' Similar definitions may be found within national policy agencies, industry associations, etc., around the world (OTA, 1991; VINNOVA, 2003).

Visions predict future societal impacts, including continuing development of knowledge and industrial applications. During the 1990s and the early 21st century, biotechnology has often been lifted forward as a particularly important scientific and technological area for economic development. Many financial and human capital resources have been devoted to the development of biotech during these years, through government policy, university investment, regional development agencies, etc. The biotechnology industries have a perceived economic significance as well as a perceived American leadership in science, firm formation and economic value. The lag is often perceived in terms of both quantity and breadth of scientific and economic activities as well as quality of science and size of firms (Commission of the European Communities, 2002). Since American leadership implies that the rest of the world is lagging behind, this has in turn sparked further investments in science and firms globally. Around the world, many basic scientists, policy agencies, venture capitalists, firms and others recommend further investments in these types of knowledge fields.

The global biotech industry has been developing rapidly in recent decades, although the USA seems to be leading much of the activity in firm formation, trade, venture capital and research financing. Ernst and Young (2003) reported a similar number of biotech companies in the USA and Europe, but a large difference in terms of employees and sales. In 2001, there were 1879 American biotech companies, with a total of approximately 141 000 employees and revenues exceeding $25 billion. The comparative figures for Europe were 1879 biotech companies, with approximately 34 000 employees and revenues of approximately $7.5 billion. Ernst and Young (2003) report, that following upon the declines in stock markets from 2000, global biotechnology companies are facing difficulties, such as raising capital, falling stock prices and cash shortages. Still, the Ernst and Young reports claim that more biotech companies are becoming profitable, with more than 50 companies, or 15 per cent of publicly traded American companies, having profits in at least one of the last three years. The global biotech industry has overall revenues of $41 billion and R&D expenditures of $22 billion. BIO USA (2003) reports that 155 biotechnology drugs and vaccines have been approved by the USA Food and Drug Administration as well as 370 of the same currently in clinical trials.

The OECD (2001: 9–38) compared existing international data on the biotech industries, based mainly on (official) national statistics. In terms of biotech patents, the patent applications to the USPTO increased by 15 per cent between 1990 and 2000, as compared to 5 per cent for all patents. For patents granted at USPTO and at EPO in 1990, 1997 and 2000, the same six groups top the list for biotech patents, namely, OECD, United States, European Union, Japan, Germany and United Kingdom. For venture capital invested between 1991 and 1999, $6332 billion was invested in biotechnology in the USA and approximately $2200 in the European Union. Moreover, the average size of the American venture capital investment was almost four times as large as the average investment in the European Union. In terms of trade for biologics, the USA tends to export and import more within biologics than the American average proportion within either manufactured products or advanced technology products. Approximately 1 per cent of all the USA advanced technology exports and imports were within the biologics area in 1999.

This overview provides some data and indicators of the global biotech industries. Still, questions about what biotechnology is – and where in the economy it is used and developed – matter greatly for analysis and comparisons. Many research studies and reports focus on the small start-up firms, which specialize in core biotechnology (see, further, section 4). In particular, the studies often focus on dedicated biotech firms in areas of human health care – and especially on pharmaceuticals, diagnostics and related aspects of biotech. These small start-ups are also often closely linked to university science, research-intensive and dependent upon venture capital. Hence, such studies capture firms of a specific type, often in a particular phase of firm growth.

In contrast, a broader perspective on modern biotechnology is necessary to capture all the relevant economic activities. For one, dedicated biotech firms exist in sectors other than pharmaceuticals, in a variety of other sectors. Moreover, other types of firms – which are established, large, and already sell products – also use and develop biotech. The reason why such a broader perspective is useful is that the knowledge bases of modern biotechnology have the potential to affect products, production processes and research processes in such diverse sectors as agriculture, food, environmental engineering, information technology, DNA fingerprinting, industrial biotechnology applications such as chemicals, textile, pulp and paper, etc. This range of knowledge bases and sectors within the biotechnology industries keeps expanding, as knowledge, techniques and tools keep being developed and applied. This implies that capturing the global biotechnology industries requires an understanding of both the small, start-up dedicated biotech firms as well as the large, established firm in other sectors.

Interestingly enough, the scientific/technical and economic/business literature differ in terms of the perception and definitions of modern biotechnology. Definitions matter because they affect which aspects are highlighted within the phenomena of the global biotechnology industries. There is a gap between the economic and business literature and the natural scientific, medical and engineering literature. On the one hand, the economic and business literature focuses primarily on small start-up firms and the development of a new 'sector' whereas, on the other hand, the natural scientific, medical and engineering literature increasingly starts from the assumption that modern biotechnology is an enabling (process) technology to reach other goals. The concept of an enabling technology includes the knowledge per se as well as techniques and tools. Nightingale (2000) was the first within the neo-Schumpeterian literature to argue and demonstrate that the main effects of modern biotechnology involve scale and scope within production, but particularly within research. Thereby, his analysis supports the view of biotechnology as a type of enabling technology.

When modern biotechnology is primarily defined as an enabling technology, this implies it is useful for many purposes. It is useful as a research tool, a process technique to produce existing and new products, a way to speed up existing tests as well as lower overall costs of testing and verification processes, organizing extensive data about biological processes, etc.

One way to capture the biotechnology industries is through a conceptual matrix. This conceptual matrix has one axis of 'product (sector)' and one axis of 'knowledge bases' (Brink, McKelvey, Rickne and Smith, 2004). The axis of 'product (sector)' includes a range of product and sectors, which are clearly affected by modern biotechnology. The firms included here may be small start-up firms as well as large, existing firms in various sectors, which are affected by modern biotechnology. There are sectors affected by modern biotechnology, including sectors previously listed as well as ones currently developing into businesses, like energy, sensors, bio-remediation and new materials. This expanding list implies that also in the future, new products (sectors) should be added along this axis. The axis of 'knowledge bases' refers to the variety of natural scientific, medical and technological knowledge which is relevant within the broad definition of modern biotechnology, as presented above. This axis includes a number of diverse knowledge bases, such as molecular biology, drug delivery, bio-engineering, protenomics, bio-informatics, etc. Just as for the axis of product (sector), this list is expanding over time, as the ongoing development of knowledge, tools and techniques drive this process forward.

From this perspective, the ongoing development of biotech knowledge and industry affects economic change in a variety of ways. Examples include the commercialization of basic research such as university patenting; the development of specific products like diagnostics and pharmaceutical products; the changing industrial structure between small firms, large firms and strategic alliances within a specific sector like food; the improvements of production processes and delivery of services like environmental engineering, etc. Each example could be more carefully analyzed, using the two axes of product (sector) and knowledge base. The argument would be that the driving forces are different in different sectors and parts of science and thereby such a nuance view would give a better understanding of economic change.

In summary, the global biotechnology industry is growing in importance, and it includes both dedicated biotech firms and other firms, which use and develop modern biotechnology for application in various sectors. The global biotechnology industries can be best identified and measured with a conceptual matrix, using a combination of products (sectors) and knowledge bases.

3   Science and innovation processes in biotechnology

The processes of science and innovation involve a research area, which links biotechnology as an empirical probe to the broader neo-Schumpeterian debate about the relationships between concepts, theory and empirical material. Many researchers, as well as practitioners like government policy makers, argue that biotechnology is 'high-tech' and 'science-driven'. Moreover, these types of emerging scientific and technological areas (especially and including modern biotechnology) have often been used to test and to develop further neo-Schumpeterian theory.

Claiming that modern biotechnology is 'high-tech' and 'science-driven' usually implies a clear and direct dependence upon the frontier of scientific discoveries. The empirical indicators used are often of firm expenditures on research and development and/or of interactions between scientists and firms. Even so, the assumption is often that basic science leads. These discoveries may come from a broad spectrum of fields, but generally assumed to be within natural scientific, medical and/or technological areas. This view of science stimulating innovation thereby leads analysts to focus upon issues like the impact of the size and scope of funding by private foundations and government-funded research councils as well as the quality and quantity of research results.

Various research results do suggest that basic scientists play an important role in firm formation and university commercialization through patents. Zucker, Darby and Brewer (1999) argue that certain star scientists play significant roles in both basic science and firm formation in biotechnology. These star scientists have exceptional impacts on biotech industries, given their records in patenting, publishing and starting firms. Zucker, Darby and Armstrong (2002) further emphasize the importance of market transactions and skilled scientists within commercialization in the biotechnology industries. Many case study examples can be found of the direct and clear importance of basic research for stimulating the economics of biotechnology. The first applications of genetic engineering techniques in pharmaceuticals relied heavily upon basic science (McKelvey, 1996a). Other knowledge bases developed through basic science were just as crucial for the transformation of the tomato as an input for ketchup (Harvey, Quilley and Beynon, 2003). Many companies around the world have been founded by university professors and/or hire many individuals with high-level academic degrees.

Hence, basic science as an activity and as an institution in the society can be broken down into a set of factors related to science. Many examples can be found which demonstrate that basic science clearly matters for the biotechnology industries. These are factors such as the amount and orientation of private research foundations and of government science policy, the quality of basic scientific results, the quality and quantity of trained undergraduates and of scientists, the role of key individuals in moving between basic science and firms, etc. A long list of factors has been used in the literature to explain how and why modern biotechnology has been to a large extent science-driven.

However, not all modern biotechnology is science-driven. The arguments for this statement are based on the modern view of innovation processes. Characterizing modern biotechnology as only – or even primarily – science-driven leaves us to consider it a case where the linear model holds, for example from science to technology to innovation (products). *The Handbook of Innovation* (Fagerberg, Mowery and Nelson, 2004) presents the modern view of innovation processes as uncertain, complex, changing over time, etc. Thus, in contrast to the linear model, the modern view of innovation processes does not lead to a straightforward progress from pouring in money for science, to transfer and imitation as technology, to products ready in the market. Innovation processes are clearly much more than either basic science or firm expenditure on R&D. If we accept this modern view of innovation, then we must carefully consider how science and innovation processes are related (or not) as well as which aspects of modern biotechnology are not science-driven.[2]

The chain-link model of Kline and Rosenberg (1986) stresses that science and innovation are separate but ongoing parallel processes with feedback loops. Moreover, scientific and engineering knowledge, techniques, and tools are cumulative within a broader structure of knowing, and thus science as a societal activity must be equated more broadly than only the latest scientific results. Science as a social institution includes many other aspects, such as education, industrial applications, etc. Just as concepts like 'low tech' must be reconceptualized to understand the complexity of knowledge (von Tunzelmann and Acha, 2004; Smith, 2003), so too must concepts like 'high tech' and 'science-based' be reconceptualized. Science is necessary, but not sufficient, to explain the development of the biotech industries. Moreover, over time, aspects of the knowledge base will migrate from the forefront of basic science to specific industrial applications. The firms in the biotechnology industries interact with a variety of actors and access a variety of sources of knowledge useful both for knowledge exploration and for knowledge exploitation.

A variety of empirical material has called into question the predictions that there are (and ought to be) direct links and interactions between basic science and the biotechnology industries. Many case studies of the scientific activities clearly show that not all (or maybe not even most) of the frontier of basic science necessarily leads to commercialization. In contrast to the arguments found in Zucker, Darby and Brewer (1999) and Zucker, Darby and Armstrong (2002), Gittelman and Kogut (2002) find a negative correlation between publications and patenting. This finding thus questions whether basic science really does have such a high and immediate commercial value, if a larger sample of scientists are considered. Mowery and Sampat (2004) argue that the empirical evidence does not support the argument that universities necessarily have direct effects on regional and economic development, if one looks beyond simple measures like patents, start-up firms and science parks to consider the complex ways in which universities and society interact. Although their study focuses on universities in general, the fields of biotechnology/medical and software/IT have been key areas for the commercialization of science. Mangematin *et al.* (2003) argue that, while regional linkages (including those between firms and universities) are important for firm formation, science does not explain the long-term firm performance of these regionally located firms. This type of research suggests that modern biotechnology may not be as science-driven as the first glance may suggest. Once questions related to commercialization, firm growth and performance, and industrial dynamics are considered, then the biotechnology industries can be seen to be driven by forces other than primarily basic science.

Other research suggests that the interactions among scientists and other societal actors is likely mediated by the national and regional institutional context, by specifics of sectors and by time. There are differences across Europe and across sectors. McKelvey, Orsenigo and Pammolli (2004) argue that historical national differences matter when discussing the sectoral system of innovation developing within the convergence of biotechnology and pharmaceuticals. Senker (1998) examines biotechnology in eight European countries, in comparison with the American lead. The chapters demonstrate a clear diversity in relation to national variables indicative of science, such as government policy and university–industry relationships, as well as diversity across subsectors. Other aspects also seem governed by national and regional differences. The pattern of university–industry relationships within the American context suggests strong interlinkages whereas the European patterns are less dense. This is related to industrial clustering phenomena (Swann, Prevezer and Stout, 1999). Audretsch and Stephan (1999) argue that regional spill-overs of knowledge are evident in the American context, thereby stimulating regional agglomerations. Cooke

(2001) argues that biotechnology mega-centers are developing in certain regions of the world – and indeed differently in different parts of the world. Such regions include actors involved in all parts of the value chain for pharmaceuticals as well as basic research, with implications for regional policy. Hence, differences among countries, sectors and regions matter in explaining the relative degree to which the economics of biotechnology are – or are not – science-driven.

Moreover, careful case studies of modern biotechnology, which has been directly commercialized from basic science and/or a broader application within other sectors indicate that, while basic science may be crucial, not all biotechnology is science-driven. When biotechnology is used for business activities as opposed to scientific activities, the innovation process is based on rather different goals and approach, in that the focus is on characteristics like reliability, marginal costs and marketing instead of scientific originality.

Significant innovation and creative adaptation is necessary for knowledge, techniques and tools to be useful and commercially viable, even in the application of the most basic science-driven application to an industrial context. McKelvey (1996a) details the challenges of making genetic engineering techniques useful and viable for the production of pharmaceuticals. Use in an industrial context involved both general challenges of using genetic engineering on a large scale for these new purposes as well as specific challenges relative to the firm's strategy, structure and core competencies. Since this case details both an American biotech start-up firm as well as a European pharmaceutical established firm, it is clear that some challenges were common to all actors while others related to the specificity of the firms. Harvey, Quilley and Beynon (2003) details the modification of the tomato as an input into food processes. In doing so, this book gives insight into the myriad technical, economic and broader organizational changes necessary to modify the tomato. These changes involved many actors which would not traditionally be considered 'science-driven' or 'high-tech', such as supermarkets.

In summary, this section has argued that, while basic science has been crucial for the development of modern biotechnology, many aspects of the development and economics of biotech are not directly and immediately dependent upon basic science. This proposition is based on modern theories of innovation processes in general as more uncertain and complex, but particularly upon a reconceptualization of what occurs within 'science-driven' or 'high-tech' sectors.

4 Interpreting results: methods and theory in appreciative theorizing

This section finishes by considering the theoretical implications of definitions and operationalization, thereby adding to the debate about the necessity (for appreciative theorizing to consider carefully theoretical considerations when designing empirical studies) and vice versa.

Even though the importance of the biotechnology industries is widely recognized, the international comparison of regions and countries still leaves much to be desired (OTA, 1991; OECD, 2001). That is to say, the international comparisons as well as analysis of specific regions or countries may use different definitions and may also be more or less well done and, thereby, they differ in the degree to which the results are reliable and valid. It is necessary to consider critically each report or study. The statistics collected often differ in fundamental ways because, even though analysts, researchers and policy makers often use a broad definition like the OECD one presented in section 2, these definitions then have to be operationalized in such a way as to be useful to identify and measure specific activities related to the biotech industries.

The way in which the empirical material is defined and measured matters greatly. As seen below, in the case of the biotechnology industries, these choices will affect whether one finds the theoretical results which support Schumpeter Mark I or Mark II. Therefore careful consideration of definitions and operationalization is necessary because the results will affect the interpretation of theoretical explanations. The first decision is whether to include only biotechnology firms (or dedicated biotech firms – DBFs) or whether to include DBFs as well as other firms which use and develop modern biotechnology knowledge, techniques and tools for application in various sectors.

One type of empirical study will indicate that small, new firms are of primary importance to the biotechnology industry. Assume first that only dedicated biotech firms are included in a study. A large percentage of all existing biotech firms are in a start-up phase, which means they are often smaller, younger, and more dependent on venture capital. These firms may be as small as one full time employee. A smaller percentage of the total population of biotech firms may be somewhat larger, older and have goods and service products on the market. These firms are likely in the range 50 to 200+ employees. Therefore, the relative economic importance will differ if one examines number of firms versus the total effects, even within the total population of DBFs. The first set of dedicated biotech firms will be emphasized in a study which only examines the total count of all biotech firms (or, more commonly, all biotech firms listed on the stock exchange). The second set of dedicated biotech firms will be emphasized in a study which examines the total effects of such firms, measured in terms of employees and of economic value (whether measured as stock market valuation, profits or turnover). Thus, if research looks more carefully into the total population of dedicated biotechnology firms, significant differences are visible of relevance to the theory of the firm, industry structure and economic impacts. Studies of the specific conditions for biotech firms can be found in Baum, Calabrese and Silverman (2000) and Powell *et al.* (1999).

However, even in this first type of study, biotechnology is relevant to many sectors. Depending on the study, studies of dedicated biotech firms may be restricted to only one subsector – such as pharmaceuticals – or they may include the range from pharmaceuticals, dedicated biotech firms, agriculture-food, medical technologies (devices), etc. Naturally, such choices will affect the sample, and therefore the results. Mangematin *et al.* (2003) and Lemarie, Delooze and Mangematin (2000) indicate the diverse histories of SMEs within the biotechnology industries, in various subsectors as well as in various national contexts.

A second type of empirical study will indicate that large, older firms are of primary importance to the biotechnology industry. Assume the definition includes dedicated biotech firms as well as firms which use and develop modern biotechnology in various sectors. The total population of firms will differ, given that modern biotechnology is useful in many sectors, such as pharmaceuticals, medical devices, agriculture, food, human health care and insurance. The firms developing and using biotech more generally may be extremely large, old and diversified into a range of relevant technologies and sectors. As argued in the next section, literature which includes these other types of firms often focuses on network relationships (Orsenigo, Pammolli and Riccaboni, 2001) and/or on the diversity of firms involved in innovation processes (McKelvey, 1996a; Harvey, Quilley and Beynon, 2003). For example, Valentin and Jensen (2004) demonstrate that within the food industry, large firms will be more likely to develop and capture the returns to relevant basic science, when that basic science must be combined with product/ industry specific knowledge.

As compared to the two types of studies discussed above – small start-up firms and larger established firms – a third type of empirical study focuses more explicitly on the relationships between the DBFs and other actors, such as universities, other small biotech firms, and/or the large, older firms using and developing biotech for many sectors. This line of research posits a more complex view of innovation and science processes, and it may involve studies of innovation systems, collaboration, strategic alliances, networks, etc.

This can perhaps be better understood in relation to networks and strategic alliances among different types of actors. The empirical evidence indicates a strong positive relationship between strategic alliances and innovation, especially for the small start-up biotech firm (Baum, Calabrese and Silverman, 2000; Shan, Walker and Kogut, 1994). Powell *et al.* (1999) argue that explanations of the success of the biotech firm in innovating can be related to network experience, diversity of ties and centrality in the network, for biotech firms in the period 1988–99.

Other related literature focuses on the relationships between larger and smaller firms, to answer other questions. Networks and innovation systems are one way to understand the likely effects on industrial structure as well as the relative balance of market versus other types of coordination among actors in an industry. McKelvey (1996b) argues that an innovation system approach provides an alternative theoretical framework for explaining the continuing existence of both types of firms – and especially the changing structures of relationships between small and large firms. Innovation systems thus bypass the predictions made by Cohen and Levinthal (1990) that 'competence-destroying' and 'competence-enhancing' types of knowledge will affect all firms in an industry in the same way. Orsenigo, Pammolli and Riccaboni (2001) argue that more general characteristics of knowledge help explain whether any given new knowledge base is more likely to result in DBFs and network patterns or in the large and established firms integrating them inside that organizational structure. Surviving biotech firms are more likely to have knowledge which is more generic and capable of application across a range of activities. Under other conditions and for other types of biotechnology knowledge, it is more likely that large established firms acquire the small firms and/or develop the competencies in-house.

In summary, choices about definitions and operationalization of concepts to find empirical results are clearly shown to affect the theoretical conclusions. While such considerations are important within all types of research, extra care and consideration needs to be taken for all appreciative theorizing, which helps us understand both empirical material and theoretical concepts and predictions.

Notes

1. This chapter builds, to some extent, upon previous work. See in particular McKelvey (2002), McKelvey, Orsenigo and Pammolli (2004) and McKelvey, Rickne and Laage-Hellman (2004: chs 1, 2, 3 and 14). With the usual caveats, I would also like to thank members of my research team, visiting researchers, and workshop participants at Chalmers University of Technology in 2002 and 2003.
2. This chapter claims that parts of modern biotechnology are science-driven whereas other aspects are not science-driven. This does not address the issue of change over time. Thus, a debate left for another forum is whether modern biotechnology is moving through phases of a life cycle (be they industrial, product and/or technological). In such ideas, one would argue that biotech was – or was not – moving from product to process; from radical to incremental within a dominate design, etc. Depending on the theory used, there are also related predictions about the type of firm most likely to exist and/or innovate.

References

Audretsch, D. and P. Stephan (1999). 'Knowledge spillovers in biotechnology: sources and incentives', *Journal of Evolutionary Economics*, 9 (1), 95–107.

Baum, J., T. Calabrese and B. Silverman (2000). 'Don't go it alone: alliance network composition and start-up's performance in Canadian biotechnology', *Strategic Management Journal*, **21**, 267–94.

BIO USA (2003). 'Biotechnology: a Collection of technologies' (www.bio.org).

Brink, J., M. McKelvey and K. Smith (2004). 'Definitions, methods and data to catch a moving phenomena', Chapter 2 in M. McKelvey *et al.* (eds), *The Economic Dynamics of Modern Biotechnology*, Cheltenham, UK and Northampton, MA, USA: Edward Elgar Publishing.

Cohen, W. and D. Levinthal (1990). 'Absorptive capacity: a new perspective on learning and innovation', *Administrative Science Quarterly*, **35** (1), Special Issue: Technology, Organizations, and Innovations, 123–52.

Commission of the European Communities (2002). 'Life sciences and biotechnology – a strategy for Europe', COM (2002) 27 final, 23 January.

Cooke, P. (2001). 'New economy innovation systems: biotechnology in Europe and USA', *Industry & Innovation*, **8** (3), 267–89.

Ernst & Young (2003). *Beyond Borders: The 2003 Global Biotechnology Report*, New York: Ernst & Young.

Fagerberg, J., D. Mowery and R. Nelson (eds) (2004). *The Handbook of Innovation*, Oxford: Oxford University Press.

Gittelman, M. and B. Kogut (2002). 'Does good science lead to valuable knowledge? Biotechnology firms and the evolutionary logic of citation patents', plenary paper for DRUID New Economy Conference, June (www.druid.dk).

Harvey, M., S. Quilley and H. Beynon (2003). *Exploring the Tomato: Transformations of Nature, Society and Economy*, Cheltenham, UK and Northampton, MA, USA: Edward Elgar Publishing.

Kline, S. and N. Rosenberg (1986). 'An overview of innovation', reprinted in C. Edquist and M. McKelvey (eds) (2000), *Systems of Innovation: Growth, Competitiveness, and Employment*, a two-volume reference collection, Cheltenham, UK and Northampton, MA, USA: Edward Elgar Publishing.

Lemarie, S., M.A. Delooze and V. Mangematin (2000). 'The development of biotech SMEs: the role of size, technology and market in France, Germany and the United Kingdom', *Scientometrics*, **47** (3), 541–60.

McKelvey, M. (1996a). *Evolutionary Innovations: The Business of Biotechnology*, Oxford: Oxford University Press.

McKelvey, M. (1996b). 'Technological discontinuities in genetic engineering in pharmaceuticals? Firm jumps and lock-in in systems of innovation', *Technology Analysis & Strategic Management*, **8** (2), 107–16.

McKelvey, M. (2002). 'The economics of biotechnology', *The International Encyclopedia of Business and Management* and *Handbook of Economics*, London: International Thompson Business Press.

McKelvey, M., L. Orsenigo and F. Pammolli (2004). 'Pharmaceuticals as a sectoral innovation system', in F. Malerba (ed.), *European Sectoral Systems of Innovation*, Cambridge: Cambridge University Press.

McKelvey, M., A. Rickne and J. Laage-Hellman (eds) (2004). *The Economic Dynamics of Modern Biotechnology*, Cheltenham, UK and Northampton, MA, USA: Edward Elgar Publishing.

Mangematin, V., S. Lemarie, J. Boissin, D. Catherine, F. Corolleur, R. Coronini and M. Trommetter (2003). 'Sectoral systems of innovation: SMEs' development and heterogeneity of trajectories', *Research Policy*, **32** (4), 621–38.

Mowery, D. and B. Sampat (2004). 'Universities in national innovation systems', in J. Fagerberg, D. Mowery and R. Nelson (eds), *The Handbook of Innovation*, Oxford: Oxford University Press.

Nightingale, P. (2000). 'Economies of scale in experimentation: knowledge and technology in pharmaceutical R&D', *Industrial and Corporate Change*, **9** (2), 315–59.

OECD (2001). 'Biotechnology statistics in OECD member countries: compendium of existing national statistics', STI Working Papers 2001/6, compiled by B. van Beuzekom, Paris: OECD.

Orsenigo, L., R. Pammolli and M. Riccaboni (2001). 'Technological change and network dynamics: lessons from the pharmaceutical industry', *Research Policy*, **30** (3), 485–508.

OTA (1991). 'Biotechnology in a global economy', Congress of the United States, Office of Technology Assessment, Washington, DC.

Powell, W., K. Koput, H. Smith and J. Owen-Smith (1999). 'Network position and firm performance: organizational returns to collaboration in the biotechnology industry', in S. Andrews and D. Knoke (eds), *Research in the Sociology of Organizations*, Greenwich, CT: JAI Press, pp. 129–59.

Senker, J. (ed.) (1998). *Biotechnology and Competitive Advantage: Europe's Firms and the US Challenge*, Cheltenham, UK and Northampton, MA, USA: Edward Elgar Publishing.

Shan, W., G. Walker and B. Kogut (1994). 'Interfirm cooperation and start-up innovation in the biotechnology industry', *Strategic Management Journal*, **15**, 387–94.

Smith, K. (2003). 'Growth, innovation and low tech industries', paper for the EU project 'Policy and Innovation in Low Tech – PILOT', May.

Swann, P., M. Prevezer and D. Stout (eds) (1999). *The Dynamics of Industrial Clustering: International Companies in Computing and Biotechnology*, Oxford: Oxford University Press.

Valentin, F. and R. Jensen (2004). 'Networks and appropriation in science-driven fields', in M. McKelvey, A. Rickne and J. Laage-Hellman (eds), *The Economic Dynamics of Modern Biotechnology*, Cheltenham, UK and Northampton, MA, USA: Edward Elgar.

VINNOVA (2003). *Swedish Biotechnology – Scientific Publications, Patenting and Industrial Development*, VINNOVA Analysis Paper series VA 2003:2.

Von Tunzelmann, N. and V. Acha (2004). 'Innovation in low-tech industries', in J. Fagerberg, D. Mowery and R. Nelson (eds), *The Handbook of Innovation*, Oxford: Oxford University Press.

Zucker, L., M. Darby and J. Armstrong (2002). 'Commercializing knowledge: university science, knowledge capture, and firm performance in biotechnology', *Management Science*, **48** (1), 138–53.

Zucker, L., M. Darby and B. Brewer (1999). 'Intellectual human capital and the birth of the US biotechnology enterprise', *American Economic Review*, **88** (1), 290–306.

38 Telecommunications, the Internet and Mr Schumpeter
Jackie Krafft

1 Introduction

Joseph Schumpeter is certainly one of the 20th-century economists who insisted most on the evolution and viability of capitalism. In his seminal contribution to economics, and especially in his 1912 and 1942 volumes, he largely discussed the emergence and decline of leading industries in the development of capitalist economic systems. To him, the internal dynamics of industries had a strong impact on economic growth of modern economies and, as such, was a key field of investigation (Hanusch, 1999; Metcalfe, 1997; Malerba and Orsenigo, 1996; Heertje, 1987). These assertions are clearly at the core of a timely debate. In the early 21st century, modern economies are much affected by the evolution of a specific industry, the telecommunications industry, which today includes activities such as the Internet and electronic commerce, and is also closely connected to computing, software, semiconductors and the media. This industry promised so much in terms of innovation, employment, creation of new business companies, economic development and growth, that it was generally considered as the origin of a so-called 'new economy'. In less than a couple of years, however, this industry finally turned out to be the leading factor in one of the largest industrial collapses ever observed, running more traditional industries into high turbulence and shake-out.

The purpose of this chapter is thus to understand the ups and downs of this industry, and especially to identify in Schumpeter's vision of capitalism what could be the determinants of such an evolution. In a nutshell, the chapter will investigate to what extent the key notions of Schumpeter's analysis – which include economic development and creative destruction, entrepreneurship and large firms, patterns of industry dynamics and evolution, competition as a process, and invention and innovation – can shed a new light on the evidence of the rise and decay of the telecommunications industry viewed as an exemplifying and central figure of modern economic capitalism.

2 Economic development: the complex evolution process driving the industry

Schumpeter argues that, in dealing with capitalism, we are dealing with an evolutionary process. It is by nature a form of economic change and not only never is, but never can be, stationary. In telecommunications, this argument is particularly important since there is a complex evolution process which drives the industry, and which can only be partially described within a static vision (Fransman, 2002; Antonelli, 2003).

There is first a quantitative evolution process which proceeds from the emergence of a number of new communications technologies (optical fibre, DSL, radio access, Ethernet, frame relay, ISDN, ATM) and which is also associated with an increasing demand for services (fixed and mobile telephony, Internet and online services). This quantitative evolution resulted in important industrial reconfigurations. In most industrialized countries, the historical incumbent monopoly (incumbent telecommunications operator, 'incumbent telco' hereafter) which controlled the technological infrastructure and related services was soon contested by a limited number of new entrants during partial liberalization in the 1980s. In the US, for instance, AT&T faced MCI and Sprint as new entrants; in the UK, British Telecom competed with Mercury-Cable&Wireless; and, in Japan, NTT was contested by DDI, Japan Telecom and Teleway Japan. During full liberalization in the 1990s, a larger number of new telcos entered the industry. Ex-monopolies in continental Europe such as France Telecom, Deutsche Telecom, or Telecom Italia were challenged by around 100 to 150 new competitors, among which Worldcom, GTS, Colt and Vodafone were the most aggressive. On average over the period 1998–2002, entry rates ranged between 15 to 20 per cent per year and a fierce competition in terms of new services and markets, infrastructures and technologies took place between incumbents, new entrants (from part-liberalization) and latecomers (from full liberalization).

Second, the evolution process is also qualitative since the traditional telecommunications industry, in which incumbent telcos were the key actors, was progressively transformed into a new industry, the info-communications industry, which today includes and merges companies formerly separated and undertaking activities such as computing, software, semiconductors, the Internet and electronic commerce, and the media. Beside telcos, other companies such as component and equipment suppliers (Lucent, Nortel, Alcatel, Siemens, Cisco, Nokia), Internet access providers and Internet service providers (IAPs and ISPs: Wanadoo, T-online), navigation and middleware companies (Netscape, Yahoo), and Internet content providers (ICPs: Bloomberg, Reuters, AOL Time Warner, Vivendi Universal) have emerged as major actors and contributed to shape the new industry dynamics. On the supply side, thus, the industry is becoming more and more complex, while in the meantime the demand side still expands, but at growth rates far lower than was expected. The combination of supply and demand characteristics led the telecommunications industry to experience in the early 2000s dramatic coordination failures, including overinvestment, excess capacity, downsizing, and a sharp fall in the share prices, revenue and profitability, which also diffused to user and connected industries.

What we observe is thus an industry which has faced radical transformations in a recent past, and which today attempts to survive major coordination failures (McKnight and Bailey, 1997; Bohlin and Levin, 1998; Abbate, 1999; Madden, 2003). The story to be told is complicated by the fact that this industry is composed of a large variety of companies. Some are incumbents and others new entrants; some are investing a lot in R&D and others not; some are facilities-based and others are facilities-less; some are vertically integrated while others are highly specialized; some are large, others small. The key issue to be explored within a Schumpeterian perspective is certainly to what extent these different companies will be able to survive and, further, will recover their position of economic booster.

3   Efficient allocation versus creative destruction: regulation and industry dynamics

Schumpeter's critical discussion about the static optimal allocation of resources in case of perfect competition, as opposed to the dynamic efficiency of monopolistic structures with regard to innovative activities, also contributes to reconsidering what occurred in the telecommunications industry over the last 20 years. The key problem is that, while the telecommunications dynamics is essentially driven by a creative destruction of resources in which large and small companies play a key role, regulation has essentially been oriented towards the approximation of a perfect competition situation. This gap between industry dynamics on the one hand, and regulation on the other, can be illustrated by two examples which contributed to disturbing the telecommunications industry.

The first example concerns the first wave of liberalization in the 1980s. Within the regulators' vision of the telecommunications industry, the nature of end-users' requirements was to some extent pre-established (exogenous), and liberalization was intended to favor the emergence of a less concentrated industrial structure to sustain technological efficiency. Over this period, telcos were thus induced to adjust their price below a certain average level (so-called 'price cap') determined by the regulator, the individual prices being intended to reflect costs and demand elasticities. This pricing regime was implemented to encourage companies (i) to improve their efficiency by developing profit-making incentives to decrease costs, (ii) to invest efficiently in new plants and facilities, and (iii) to develop and deploy innovative service offerings. Today, with the experience of liberalization, we know that if points (i) and (ii) were achieved, price caps did not provide firms with sufficient incentives to achieve point (iii). The rate structure generally imposes a costly, time-consuming and unnecessary burden on companies and significantly impeded the introduction of new advanced services. This point has been recurrently emphasized in regulation reports in the US and Europe since the mid-1990s.

The second example is related to the 3G auction process which occurred within the second wave of liberalization in the 1990s in most industrialized countries. For the regulators, this process of allocation of a scarce resource (the hertzien spectrum) was efficient for two major reasons (see Klemperer, 2000). First, it was supposed to improve the welfare of final customers which could access a superior technology (3G mobile phones based on UMTS technologies) with no major increases in prices in associated services. In the ideal world of competition, a rational firm is only supposed to take into account its own forward-looking costs and revenues and the likely behavior of rival firms. In this perspective, the license fee which is a sunk cost for all firms is deemed not to affect price. Second, the auction system was supposed to accelerate the rolling out of 3G mobile phones by providing telcos with adequate incentives to innovate. The costs supported by these companies could only be covered if 3G services quickly started contributing a significant amount of revenue. Here again, with the experience of the auction system, we know that the prominence of efficient allocation objectives supported by regulation had huge negative effects on the telecommunications industry dynamics. Most of the companies involved in the auction system, either directly (such as the telcos) or indirectly (such as the equipment providers and advanced service and content providers), faced major problems of indebtedness due to the effective burden of the sunk costs. Moreover, the experience of the 3G auction system also had pervasive effects concerning the technologies effectively created and diffused. Apparently, the target techno-innovation system (UMTS-driven) tends to be superseded by less advanced and competing technologies, such as the Japanese I-mode system which corresponds to a 2.5 generation of mobile phones.

Schumpeter told us that innovations led to cyclical fluctuations whose length was determined by both the character and the period of implementation of the innovations. Moreover, the combination of the use of the innovations, overinvestment, and of credit expansion going too far, was supposed to bring the upswing to an end. With this in mind, we can thus interpret the two former regulation orientations as recurrent shocks which either prevented innovation being developed, or greatly disturbed the innovation process.

4   Large companies and innovation

Schumpeter recurrently stressed his preference for monopoly and oligopoly, and thus conversely his disdain for free competition, when innovative activities are involved. Telecommunications has traditionally been an industry where large companies operate and constitute the core business. Before liberalization, natural monopolies prevailed at the national level, and though some of them were broken up with liberalization (AT&T in the 1980s, and BT in the 1990s), the development of economies of scale and network effects tends to favor large firms and oligopoly structures. This is also increasingly true in other complementary activities such as the equipment provision, the Internet end-to-end connectivity, navigation, middleware and content. But is this industry still innovative? We know that, in the old days, telecommunications were associated with large and famous research centres, such as Bell Labs in the US, CNET in France, Martlesham Laboratories in the UK. What happened to these centers in the liberalization era? Does the current industrial structure provide adequate creation and diffusion of new knowledge?

If we investigate, first, technological innovation which includes the Schumpeterian notion of a 'new combination' leading to the development of a new product, or a new method of production, we have to consider the 'upstream' part of the industry, namely the equipment suppliers and telcos. With liberalization, incumbent telcos which formerly were the main technology providers had to face fierce price competition from new entrants. In many cases, incumbents decided to delegate their R&D activity to the equipment suppliers, which thus became key actors in the industry. In a few years, the initial split of R&D expenses (on average, 15 per cent in revenue for telcos and 5 per cent for equipment suppliers) was completely reversed (thus 5 per cent in revenue for telcos and 15 per cent for equipment suppliers). Research centers which were for a long time incorporated within the telecommunications public administration were transformed into subsidiaries of incumbent telcos (Martlesham Laboratories became BT Exact Technologies, CNET became France Telecom R&D) or incorporated within equipment suppliers' structure (Bell Labs is part of Lucent). With these transformations, technological innovations were essentially delivered by equipment suppliers which became increasingly specialized in R&D, and largely favored the development of new modes of communications such as IP access and mobile telecommunications on the basis of radio access, satellite connections and optical fibres. This vertical specialization greatly stimulated the penetration of new telcos by decreasing technological barriers to entry (see Fransman, 2002).

If we now turn to organizational innovation, which is more closely related to the opening up of new markets and the reorganization of sectors of the economy (both considered as 'new combinations' by Schumpeter), the 'downstream' part of the industry, including Internet connectivity, navigation, middleware and content, provides a wide range of case studies. For instance, the end-to-end connectivity field of activity which provides customers with access to the Internet and basic applications such as e-mail and web hosting were initially developed in the early 1990s by large telcos (MCI and Sprint in the US, France Telecom Oléane in France) and major science foundations (the NSF in the US, Renater in Europe). Advanced fields of applications such as Internet browsers, search engines, directory assistance, security in data transfer, electronic payments, on-line services and broadcasting services have also been shaped by large companies such as AOL Time Warner, Microsoft, IBM, Vivendi Universal, Bloomberg and Reuters. Though some of these companies are now involved in a somewhat chaotic evolution, the pace of change in the creation of new markets, the convergence and mutation of existing markets, and to some extent the development of an Internet and mobile economy, seemed to be essentially driven by large, vertically related companies (Krafft, 2003).

5   Entrepreneurship and market process

The entrepreneur plays a central role in Schumpeter's work. He is the innovator, and the agent of economic change and development. He has a disequilibrating role in the market process by applying new combinations of factors of production, and by interrupting the circular flow of economic life which is the ongoing production of existing goods and services under existing technologies and methods of production and organization. In the 1990s, with the emerging separation in industrial organization of (i) the R&D function undertaken by equipment suppliers, (ii) the network function (wireline, wireless, mobile and IP) operated by facilities-based telcos, and (iii) the service function (connectivity, navigation, middleware, content for mobile and fixed telecommunications) provided by facilities-less companies, the rise of new entrepreneurship became a central feature of the market process in telecommunications. While a technological background was necessary to venture a new start-up in telecommunications R&D, the field of activity of equipment suppliers, this condition was not necessary for the other functions, namely the network and service function. New companies entered the industry without any technological competence, since technology was provided by equipment suppliers. Moreover, they could penetrate the market without a proprietary network, by leasing the lines and infrastructure of incumbents or other former entrants (Kavassalis and Salomon, 1997). In fact, they could gain a competitive advantage by developing new marketing services, and new but low-price applications, all strategies which were beyond the scope of the traditional experience of incumbent monopolies.

In the upturn period of the telecommunications industry, reference was thus recurrently made to the 'gifted few', the 'gurus of the new economy', such as George Soros from GTS, or Bernard Ebbers from Worldcom, pioneering in the field of new technologies, new products and new markets. These entrepreneurs initially operated in an unstable world, and were generally swimming against the tide of society which saw the telecommunications industry as a complex techno-economic system providing a limited set of applications. Quite rapidly, these new companies outperformed their incumbent competitors and registered incredibly high stock market capitalization. The total stock market value of all telecommunications companies reached the maximum level of $6500 billion in March 2000. But, at the end of 2001, nevertheless, the bubble burst and the value fell to $4000 billion. The downturn period then started, with a net diminution of new entries, the exit of existing companies including the largest ones (*Worldcom*, *GTS*), and thus high turbulence and shake-out.

Today, a new process of entry re-emerges but on somewhat different conditions. First, a technological background seems to be a prerequisite for any new start-ups, even for those which are facilities-less and operating in the service field of activities. Second, the connection to (i) large, established companies and (ii) universities and academic research institutes appears also as a precondition for performing as a business company, and especially for being financed as a start-up. The post-shake-out era of telecommunications will thus apparently be increasingly characterized by the emergence and development of innovation networks (in which companies, universities, norms and standards organisms, and even venture capitalists and financial institutions will be involved), a characteristic which was absent from the pre-shake-out period of development.

6 Destroying the old and creating the new: lessons for industry dynamics

The recession, in Schumpeter's view, is a healthy phase of restructuring, paving the way for a new burst of future innovations. The decay of capitalism is based on the vision that it is not economic failure, but rather economic success that causes major coordination failures. Is this vision helpful for understanding the recent evolution of the telecommunications industry?

On the one hand, what the Schumpeterian vision tells us is certainly that the appearance of entrepreneurs in bursts is due exclusively to the fact that the appearance of one or a few entrepreneurs facilitates the appearance of others, and that the downturn sets in as a result of smaller profit margins due to imitation. To some extent, and according to this vision, the massive entry process which occurred in the telecommunications industry in the 1990s contained in itself the promise of a period of decline. As already mentioned, the viability of a large number of companies was possible if the extent of the market was also growing in size, or at least was evolving by a multiplication of profitable niches. But this did not happen, and the rate of growth of the market at the time of its emergence is not comparable to the rate of growth of the same market at the age of maturity. Moreover, the shocks imposed on the industry, such as the 3G auction system, certainly contributed to eroding the margins of companies which were faced, on the technological side, by a radical process of change and, on the demand side, a still evolving pattern of demand in terms both of characteristics and of habits. This vision, which is a core aspect of Schumpeter's analysis, was totally neglected or superseded by mainstream conceptions which essentially focus on an ideal world of perfect predictions. The recent telecommunications history gives further evidence that this latter conception and associated equilibrium framework cannot hold when radical innovation is present.

But, on the other hand, what Schumpeter does not tell us is that creating the new does not involve necessarily destroying the old. To some extent, the new companies which entered the industry and which were supposed to outperform the incumbents did not drive these incumbent companies to exit the industry. Though some decisive attempts were made by new entrants to dominate the incumbents (in the US, for instance, Worldcom, the new entrant of a full-liberalization cohort acquired *MCI*, an entrant of a part-liberalization cohort), these are the new entrants which in the 2000s finally exited the industry and faced shake-out and turbulence more sharply. Schumpeter thus envisaged a broad dynamic qualitative analysis of the emergence, development and decline of industries, but, since he did not enter into the details of how industries change over time in terms of their structural features and forms of organization, he failed to provide a global analysis of industry dynamics. One of the complementary reasons is also certainly that, in the days he wrote, industries started from scratch with a new entrepreneur setting up a firm to introduce his invention. Then this firm was supposed to grow and to hold a monopoly position for some time, until this firm was finally imitated by new entrants which competed sharply and drove the initial firm to exit the industry. Today, and especially from what occurred in the telecommunications industry, industry dynamics seems to be quite different. Industries generally arise from the transformation of existing industries. For instance, the Internet and mobile companies did not emerged *ex nihilo*, but were from the start highly related to the traditional wireline telecommunications industry. When a shake-out occurs, firms which organized the conditions of knowledge accumulation and diffusion, such as the incumbent telecommunications companies, may survive the introduction of novelty and eventually become the leaders of the newly-born industry. As a matter of fact, incumbent telcos are today key actors in the emerging info-communications industry.

7 The process of competition

Competition was analysed by Schumpeter as a process of creative destruction the implications of which have already been mentioned in section 3. Within this notion of competition, cost and quality advantages are much more decisive than price competition, and involve a longer-term survival for companies which contribute to the economic development. But, here again, the analysis of the telecommunications industry leads to a paradox, or at least to a situation which was not envisaged by Schumpeter.

The first cohort of entrants, namely entrants coming from the first wave of part-liberalization in the 1980s, essentially engaged in a fierce rivalry in terms of price with the incumbent. The outcome of this first competitive process was thus important decreases in prices (from −30 per cent to −50 per cent for long distance and international calls; and −10 per cent to −20 per cent for local communications), accompanied by a fundamental tariff rebalancing between subscription charges and communications tariffs. Within the former monopoly situation, subscription charges were insufficient to cover the costs of a local wireline network, while domestic long distance and international tariffs were high relative to underlying costs. The second cohort of entrants, issuing from full liberalization in the 1990s, privileged a strategy of low-cost and high-quality provision of telecommunications network and services. These entrants largely contributed to (i) the elaboration of an open set of communications applications such as voice, texts, graphs, sounds, fixed images or videos; (ii) the emergence of communications between groups of users based on new patterns of infrastructures and services, mobile and Internet-oriented; (iii) the development of end-users' friendliness, reliability and safety relying on high-performance networks; and (iv) the consideration of mobility of equipment premises, end-user, services and even of different elements within the network. According to Schumpeter, we can consider these new entrants as key actors in the process of competition which occurred in telecommunications, as dynamic and innovative players compared to the first cohort of entrants which essentially behaved as imitators of the incumbents.

Within a Schumpeterian vision, the fittest new entrants of the second cohort would have then survived better than the former new entrants. The selection process which occurred in the telecommunications industry, nevertheless, led to the recomposition of a stable oligopoly, essentially composed of incumbents and entrants of the first cohort. This outcome, which is counter-intuitive, may be explained by a central element. The competition which was implemented in the telecommunications industry should have been coordinated more adequately by competitive and regulation authorities, since innovative activities were an essential part of the process.

The coordination which was effectively implemented by competitive and regulation authorities essentially concerned tariff rebalancing and interconnection fees issues, while in the meantime innovative activities characterized by the development of a qualitative change in telecommunications were left entirely to the market. This central element involved the entry of a large number of new companies which invested massively in networks and services, and resulted thus in excess capacity with incumbents still in place. The overlapping of two major technological trajectories, the one supported by incumbents and entrants of the first cohort and the other by entrants of the second cohort, would have required a deeper coordination in terms of shared infrastructure and planned investment processes, which failed to materialize in the concrete world.

8   Invention and innovation

For Schumpeter, innovation is a central feature of economic development, and this has already been mentioned in section 3. But innovations must be distinguished from inventions. The application of new combinations by entrepreneurs is possible without inventions, while inventions as such need not necessarily lead to innovations and need not have any economic consequences. This distinction is useful for understanding the changes which occurred in the industry in the age of the Internet and mobile communications (Antonelli, 2003). In fact, the research centers associated with the incumbent telcos were in the early 1980s the essential inventors of packet-switching technologies and cellular mobile systems. But clearly these inventions, which were the fruit of a high level of excellence of academic institutes which specialized in telecommunications research, did not materialize into economic development. At that time, inventions were kept within the scientific sphere, and incumbent monopolies did not consider the opportunity to transform these inventions into innovations and commercial opportunities. Part-liberalization did not introduce many changes to the fact that the telecommunications industry was more inventive than innovative.

Innovation is thus a relatively recent key feature of the telecommunications industry. First, this is because equipment suppliers now in charge of the research and development of the industry attempted more systematically and more rapidly to coordinate invention with innovation, and to provide the large number of new entrants in the full-liberalization era with adapted and commercialized technologies. Second, this is because these new entrants with a small technological background were also induced by competition to elaborate new combinations for a larger and diversified set of applications.

In the post-shake-out era, nevertheless, one may question the viability of patterns of invention or innovation since (i) research departments and subsidiaries have been involved in a considerable process of restructuring which concerns equipment suppliers and telcos, and which generally implies important budget cuts in these companies, and eventually downsizing due to the important perturbations in terms of profitability, revenues and share price; (ii) major leaders in innovative combinations for the creation of new markets and services have been much affected by the telecommunications crisis, and many of these new entrants were made bankrupt. Can we thus consider that in a near future the telecommunications industry will be a field of activity where invention and innovation are absent? The current tendency is that, despite major perturbation in this industry, invention and innovation still continue to be developed, and especially technological innovation. The development of I-mode and Wireless Lans, which are competing technological systems of the UMTS, are starting to be diffused worldwide. But an important change is nevertheless occurring: Wireless Lans were developed by companies coming from the computer industry. Thus the telecommunications industry can be considered as innovative and inventive, provided it is merged into a larger industry including now telecommunications and computer activities.

9   Conclusion

One of the main outcomes of this chapter is to show that Schumpeter is still vividly central in the understanding of the evolution of industries, and especially the telecommunications industry in which major changes occurred in terms of competition, innovation, technologies, services, incumbents and entrants. His methodology, centerd on the explanation of economic development and creative destruction issues, rather than efficient allocation and pricing issues, proves to be particularly suited to the telecommunications industrial dynamics. In the meantime, however, the complexity of this industry, and the natural evolution of modern capitalism itself, render difficult a pure application of his global and initial framework. Especially, the current re-emergence of stable oligopoly composed of incumbent companies is to some extent a key puzzle for Schumpeterian economics, which is still left unresolved.

References

Abbate, J., 1999, *Inventing the Internet*, Cambridge: MIT Press.

Antonelli, C., 2003, *The Economics of Innovation, New Technologies and Structural Change*, London: Routledge.

Bohlin, E. and Levin, S. (eds), 1998, *Telecommunications Transformation: Technology, Strategy and Policy*, Amsterdam: IOS Press.

Fransman, M., 2002, *Telecoms in the Internet Age: From Boom to Burst to . . .*, Oxford: Oxford University Press.

Hanusch, H. (ed.), 1999, *The Legacy of Joseph Alois Schumpeter*, Cheltenham, UK and Northampton, MA, USA: Edward Elgar.

Heertje, A., 1987, 'Schumpeter, Joseph Alois', *The New Palgrave*, Basingstoke: Macmillan.

Kavassalis, P. and Salomon, J., 1997, 'Mr Schumpeter on the telephone: patterns of technical change in the telecommunications industry before and after the Internet', *Communications & Strategies*, **26**, 371–408.

Klemperer, P. (ed.), 2000, *The Economic Theory of Auctions*, Cheltenham, UK and Northampton, MA, USA: Edward Elgar.

Krafft, J., 2003, 'Vertical structure of the industry and competition: an analysis of the evolution of the info-communications industry', *Telecommunications Policy*, **27**(8–9), 625–49.

Madden, G. (ed.), 2003, *Handbook on Telecommunications*, Cheltenham, UK and Northampton, MA, USA: Edward Elgar.

Malerba, F. and Orsenigo, L., 1996, 'The dynamics and evolution of industries', *Industrial and Corporate Change*, **5**(1), 51–87.

McKnight, L. and Bailey, J. (eds), 1997, *Internet Economics*, Cambridge, MA, MIT Press.

Metcalfe, S., 1997, *Evolutionary Economics and Creative Destruction*, London: Routledge.

Schumpeter, J.A., 1912, *The Theory of Economic Development*, Leipzig: Duncker & Humblot; trans. R. Orpie, Cambridge, MA: Harvard University Press, 1934; reprinted New York: Oxford University Press, 1961.

Schumpeter, J.A., 1942, *Capitalism, Socialism and Democracy*, New York: Harper & Brothers/London: George Allen & Unwin, 1976.

39 Innovation in services
Paul Windrum*

1 Introduction

Manufacturing has traditionally been viewed as the primary source of innovation and economic growth. Indeed, some commentators continue to view it as the primary source of innovation and growth. Not surprisingly, then, changes in the composition of western economies in the 1980s, consequent with a relative shift from manufacturing to services as a proportion of national GDP and employment, initially generated a lot of anxiety. This was particularly evident in the so-called 'deindustrialization' debate. Services had previously been characterized as labour-intensive sectors with little or no scope for productivity improvement. Innovation was said to be rare. Moreover, if innovation does occur, then it is primarily through investment in new capital machinery (or 'embodied innovations') developed by intermediate goods manufacturers, and that adoption is frequently due to pressure placed on service firms by manufacturers up and down the supply chain.

Despite the fatalistic predictions of some commentators, the shift towards services-based economies has not led to the relative decline of developed western nations. What is more, a more balanced view of services has emerged since the early 1990s. There is a growing appreciation that service firms are innovators in their own right, and that bilateral flows of innovation exist between services and manufacturing sectors. Computer services and telecoms, in particular, have received significant attention, as have consultancy and other knowledge-intensive business services that promote and disseminate new scientific and technological knowledge across all sectors (including manufacturing). Thanks to new research, we have a better picture of the relevance of services innovation. For example, OECD data suggest that service industries in the developed countries perform up to one-third of total private sector R&D, and account for more than 50 per cent of the total R&D embodied in the intermediate inputs and capital equipment (OECD, 2000a). Further, not only are services found to be heavy users of these new ICT technologies (Eurostat, 2001) but the economic impact of new ICTs is far more visible in services than it is in manufacturing (OECD, 2000b, 2000c).

*   The author would like to thank Ina Drejer and Anthony Arundel for their helpful comments on earlier drafts of this chapter. The usual disclaimers apply.

The broader picture of services innovation is starting to come into focus. Unfortunately, empirical research on the nature of innovation within services, and on the relationship between technological change and economic performance in services, remains limited (Cainelli *et al.*, 2002). There remains much controversy concerning the long-term social, political and economic consequences of the shift towards a services-based economy. There is also an intense, ongoing, debate regarding the salient and important aspects of services innovation at the firm level.

This chapter will discuss the multifaceted picture of innovation that has emerged in recent research in services, and the particular contributions being made by neo-Schumpeterian scholars. Important differences exist between the approach being taken by neo-Schumpeterians and by other writers. In order to highlight these differences, section 2 of the chapter will consider the three distinct approaches found in the services literature: the 'assimilation', the 'demarcation', and the 'synthesis' approach. Neo-Schumpeterians fall firmly within the last category. Section 3 develops the discussion by highlighting work conducted on each of the five dimensions of innovation discussed by Schumpeter: organizational, product, market, process and input innovation. Section 4 concludes with a summary of the main points and a look forward.

2   The assimilation, demarcation, synthesis debate

Coombs and Miles (2000) identify three distinct approaches to services innovation: the 'assimilation', the 'demarcation', and the 'synthesis' approach. The foundations of the 'assimilation approach' can be traced back to Pavitt's famous sectoral taxonomy of innovation (Pavitt, 1984). With the exception of ICT, Pavitt continued to promulgate the idea that services are 'supplier dominated', i.e. service firms are the passive recipients of innovations developed in other sectors (predominantly manufacturing), which they obtain through new capital investment or through suppliers (predominantly through pressure exerted by manufacturers up and down the supply chain). Even later, when Pavitt acknowledged the roles of computer services, telecoms and science-based services (e.g. Pavitt *et al.*, 1989), these were notable exceptions. Hence, there remained a highly conservative view regarding the innovative potential of the majority of service sectors, and the subsequent economic impact of services innovation. Innovation for most services, Pavitt argued, was prompted by the adoption of new hardware/software technologies, work practices and organizational structures that are sourced elsewhere.

In addition to an inherently conservative view regarding the capacity and impact of innovation in services, Pavitt's work left a second legacy: the view that insights gained through earlier studies of innovation in manufacturing can be translated to services. This assumes that service activities are generically the same as manufacturing activities. Theories and empirical indicators, originally developed with manufacturing in mind, are therefore equally applicable to services. Consequently, the study of services can be assimilated within a generic set of theories originally developed through the study of innovation in manufacturing. This is the underpinning methodological basis of the 'assimilation' approach. Notable examples of the approach are Barras's work on the 'reverse life cycle' in services (Barras, 1986, 1990), and the work of Evangelista (2000) and Miozzo and Soete (2001) on sectoral patterns of innovation within services. In these studies, attention is given to the importance of science and technology-based services, and to technical consultancies in innovation networks. Still, most service activities in these studies continue to be characterized as 'supplier-dominated'.

The 'demarcation approach' is the antithesis of the assimilation approach. The demarcation approach proposes that services are distinct in nature and character from manufacturing. Consequently, important differences exist between the types of innovation activities conducted in services and those conducted in manufacturing. These differences manifest themselves in, for example, an underreporting of innovation activity within services when statistical measures such as R&D staff and patent registrations/citations are applied. Formally structured 'R&D' activities are (at the firm level) more prevalent in manufacturing than in services, as is the use of patents to protect innovation, which is also relatively rare in services. These observations are now widely accepted (e.g. Eurostat, 2001), as is the call for new empirical indicators. Indeed, the issue has started to be addressed by the Community Innovation Survey (CIS), which has been developed on the basis of the OECD's *Oslo Manual* (OECD-Eurostat, 1997). The *Oslo Manual* stresses the need for new, more comprehensive measures of firms' innovation activities in order to study the relationship between technological change and economic performance in services. Since the mid-1990s, CIS surveys have included both services and manufacturing sectors, and have taken into account sources of innovation in addition to R&D. These include activities related to the design of new services, software development, the acquisition of know-how, investment in new machinery (e.g. ICT hardware) and training. The CIS is not without its limitations. Notably, it does not link innovation to commercial performance. Also, there are many aspects of innovation that are not considered by the CIS.

While the need for new measures of innovation is widely accepted, the assertion that services are fundamentally different in nature to manufacturing is far more contentious. According to the demarcation approach, completely new, *services-specific* theories of innovation are required in order to understand the nature and the dynamics of innovation in services. This is the position taken by researchers such as Gadrey *et al.* (1995), Gallouj and Weinstein (1997), Sundbo (1998), and den Hertog (2000). Notable amongst the allegedly services-specific features highlighted by these researchers is the interaction between users and service providers in the detection of new needs and in product specification, and the interaction between providers and other actors within innovation networks (e.g. suppliers and business service providers). These go beyond product and process innovation, which have been the traditional focus in manufacturing-based innovation studies. They highlight the importance of organizational, input and market innovations.

The 'synthesis approach' to services innovation is far less developed than the assimilation and demarcation approaches and (so far) has not been widely applied in empirical surveys. However, a distinct position has been outlined by Metcalfe (1998), and Drejer (2004). The objective of the synthesis approach is to take the recent insights of demarcation writers on services innovation, the insights gained in manufacturing studies, and to integrate these within a unifying neo-Schumpeterian framework. This broad framework encompasses the five dimensions of innovation discussed by Schumpeter: organizational, product, market, process and input innovation. According to this view, conventional (manufacturing-based) innovation studies privileged product and process innovation at the expense of organizational, market and input innovation, while services-based innovation studies have (re)invigorated research in these other dimensions. The aim of the neo-Schumpeterian synthesis approach is not merely to add one to the other, but to develop an integrated account that is applicable to *both* services and manufacturing, and which covers all aspects of innovative activity.

Interestingly, support for the synthesis approach can be found in work conducted by demarcation and assimilation writers. For example, Preissl (2000) and Gallouj and Weinstein (1997) from the demarcation school have recognized that types of innovation that were allegedly services-specific are also found in manufacturing. Further, the analysis by Sirilli and Evangelista (1998) of Italian innovation surveys suggests that the similarities between manufacturing and service firms are greater than the differences with respect to the strategic objectives of innovation, the propensity to innovate, sources of information used, and the barriers/enablers to innovation. Hughes and Wood (2000), two assimilation writers, report on the findings of research conducted on a sample of 576 small and medium-sized enterprises. The findings suggest that variation within manufacturing and services sectors with respect to product and process innovation is greater than the variation between the two categories.

As noted, the neo-Schumpeterian approach to services innovation is still in its infancy. The remainder of this chapter will consider the different definitions of services and services innovation currently found in the literature. This will help clarify the distinctive approach to services that is being developed by neo-Schumpeterian innovation scholars.

3 Key features of services innovation

The task of defining services proves surprisingly difficult. In the course of reviewing the literature, a number of very different definitions have been found, each highlighting a very different aspect of services. Yet each has been contested and, to date, no single, universally accepted definition of services (let alone services innovation) exists. A more positive way of viewing this is to suggest that the existence of multiple, contested definitions indicates that the phenomenon under investigation is complex in nature.

A common tactic has been to differentiate the outputs of services from those of manufacturing. For example, it has been suggested that services are concerned with the production of intangible goods. Services are things that 'can't be dropped on your foot'. Closely tied to this notion of intangibility is the proposition that services, as a consequence, cannot be stored. As Hill (1999) observes, it is certainly true that manufacturing is always concerned with the production of physical artefacts (whether final consumer products or intermediate capital goods), but it is *not* true that all services are disembodied and cannot be stored. Indeed, I would go further and state that almost all services have some form of physical aspect. Take, for example, retail and wholesale, and transport services. These sectors are concerned with the organization, storage and delivery of physical artefacts. Moreover, the service outputs of firms in these sectors depend on the use of other physical artefacts, such as shops, warehouses, containers and lorries. The advent of e-business has not changed this. On-line ordering involves the use of various physical artefacts – computers, routers, servers and cabling – while the delivery of physical goods (such as books, CDs and other consumables) involves a whole set of (physical) carriage and delivery activities. The same is true for computer software, which is frequently held up as a prima facie example of an intangible good. Further inspection reveals that all is not what it initially seems. All software depends on the arrangement of code into a particular sequence of 0s and 1s. This necessitates a physical encoding device, a physical storage device and (if it is to be used) a physical decoding device. All of these can be dropped on one's foot.

A third characteristic, found in many definitions of services, is a high degree of interaction between the user and the provider in the generation of service outputs. This has a number of potentially important implications for the character of innovation in services. Notably, it is the basis of the 'joint production thesis' developed by the demarcation school. Actually, the involvement of users in services was first discussed by Fuchs (1965), who observed that the knowledge, experience and motivation of users have a direct impact on the productivity of the provider. Fuchs took as his examples retail, banking, education and health services. The replacement of full-service provision by self-service in retailing is a clear case in point. Similarly, in banking, it matters whether the bank clerk or the customer writes out the deposit slip. In education, the contributions from, the motivation of, and the basic qualifications of students critically influence the outcome of education provision. In health care, the competences of patients with respect to describing symptoms directly affect the doctor's ability to arrive at the correct diagnosis and, hence, the correct prescription.

Much has been made of the joint production thesis by the demarcation school. Certainly, it has stimulated some interesting insights in studies of innovation in business services (see discussions by Sundbo, 1998; Boden and Miles, 2000; den Hertog, 2000; Hughes and Wood, 2000; Preissl, 2000; Windrum, 2002). But it is not true that services, by definition, require the active participation of users in their design, specification or delivery. A consideration of transport services – most obviously scheduled bus, train and aeroplane services – illustrates this. Scheduled journeys are organized, timetabled and delivered by the provider without recourse to individual customers. Indeed, the only input from the customer is the decision to turn up and pay for a particular journey. Much the same is true for other traditional services, such as retail banking and insurance. Far from being jointly produced by users and providers, retail banking and insurance products are highly standardized packages that are designed, developed and subsequently offered for sale by providers – much in the same way that mass-produced artefacts are by manufacturers. Highly standardized packages allow providers to exploit scale economies and, hence, provide services at lower prices. True, the packages offered on the market change over time in response to how well they sell, but (again) this is very similar to the way manufacturers of mass-produced artefacts operate. Certainly, it is a far cry from the picture of users and providers closely interacting in the specification, design and delivery services. It is far closer to Lundvall's notion of learning-by-interacting (Lundvall, 1988). Here the provider refines the product over time as it learns more about the user's needs and preferences. However, it is the provider who controls the specification, production and delivery of the product.

It is interesting to observe that firms in these traditional service sectors are using new ICTs to further distance the user from the provider. For example, telephone banking and insurance, and Internet banking and insurance are new business models that provide new opportunities for scale economies through the centralization of retail activities (and the consequent scaling down and closure of local branches). Opportunities to cut costs are likely to separate the user from the provider still further. For instance, there has recently been a wave of call centre relocations by large UK banks and insurance companies (to India and other lower-wage economies).

In addition to distancing the provider from the user, such geographical relocations separate the customer-facing 'front office' operations of the organization from the supporting 'back office' operations. The division of front and back offices may go hand-in-hand with an increase in the number of business sites, increasing specialization and division of labour within the organization, economies of scale and improved access to location-specific factors (i.e. human and natural resources that are unevenly distributed across the globe). Integrating activities across different nations places high demands on the information and communication structures of a firm. High-quality ICTs are thus a necessary prerequisite for the effective integration of global operations. Multinational manufacturers are well-established champions of new ICT developments. These firms are not simply large purchasers of new ICTs, they work closely with key ICT firms in order to develop new innovations that can leverage competitive advantage. If banking, insurance and other service companies become increasingly global, they will similarly become key players in the development of new ICTs.

A particular form of innovation between providers and users – 'ad hoc innovation' – has become the subject of much heated discussion. The concept was developed by demarcation writers. Gallouj and Weinstein, for example, define ad hoc innovation as the 'interactive (social) construction to a particular problem posed by a given client' (Gallouj and Weinstein, 1997, p. 549). Drejer (2004) observes that the concept is highly problematic because it describes a non-reproducible solution to a specific problem. As such, it does not conform to the normal definition of an innovation. An innovation is a novelty (i.e. something that is new to a population), that subsequently diffuses across a population. It is through the diffusion process that the innovation has an economic impact. Clearly, for diffusion to occur it must be possible to apply the innovation in different settings. This is precluded by the supposed specificity of the definition of 'ad hoc innovation'. Drejer (2004) argues that what is being described by Gallouj and Weinstein is not, in fact, innovation at all but cumulative learning. Cumulative learning is a process of continuous adaptation to small changes. This includes coming up with specific solutions to specific problems. Continuous adjustment to the needs of new customers is, Drejer argues, simply part of the day-to-day functioning of a business; it is not innovation.

In addition to provider–user interaction, research into services innovation has highlighted the importance of human resources and organizational innovation. Organizational innovation includes the development of new ways of organizing production (new management structures, supply chain relationships, strategic alliances etc.), and the development of new internal routines and work practices (i.e. 'process innovations'). Barras' work on the 'reverse life cycle' in services (Barras, 1986, 1990) is particularly notable in this respect. Barras observes that the adoption of ICTs in sectors such as banking and insurance, accounting and administration services has prompted the incremental development of 'back office' processes that aim to improve the efficiency of the service provided. As more firms in the sector adopt ICTs, so the locus of competitive advantage shifts, in the second stage of this life cycle, to the introduction of radical organizational change, with the restructuring of both back office functions and the front office in order to improve service quality with users. In the third, and final, phase of this life cycle, new products are developed. The sequence thus described is the reverse of the orthodox life cycle model, whose origins lie in case studies of manufacturing sectors.

By highlighting the significance of organizational innovation for competitive advantage and productivity, recent services research has begun to redress the imbalance of innovation studies (with its overwhelming bias towards product and process innovation). But one must be careful to avoid suggestions that organizational innovation is not important in manufacturing. It clearly is, and has long been discussed in fields such as business management, strategy and business history (Harberger, 1998). Moreover, scholars such as Chandler (1962, 1977) have long highlighted the interconnection between organizational, product and process innovation. It would seem that demarcation writers overstate the case when they suggest that organizational innovation is a unique, distinguishing characteristic of services innovation. It may, however, be the case that there is a difference in degree, with organizational change being a more prominent feature of services innovation.

Tether and Metcalfe (2003) adopt a different, and very interesting, view of service activities, one that is very much in the spirit of Georgescu-Roegen's (1971) discussion of valorization as a series of thermodynamic transformations. As Georgescu-Roegen observed, capitalist firms create economic value by bringing together material, energy, information and knowledge inputs and transforming them into goods and services. Tether and Metcalfe suggest there are three types of transformation: in the physical form of materials, energy and information, in the spatial location of these physical materials, and in their temporal availability. Different services involve different transformations. For example, hairdressers and plastic surgeons transform people; repair and maintenance services transform physical objects; banking and finance services transform information; haulage companies move things through space, while passenger transport services move people. This diversity of transformation activities helps explain why a simple definition of services does not exist.

Tether and Metcalfe locate manufacturing firms within one dimension: the physical transformation of raw materials, energy and information into physical artefacts. This conforms to conventional definitions of manufacturing. However, as we have seen, manufacturing firms are also engaged in the other forms of transformation, if to a lesser extent. The differences are not absolute but of degree, and the extent to which they differ is an empirical question. This is also the position of Drejer, who, in her review of the services literature, argues:

> The contribution from the new concepts [developed by the demarcation school] lies in the attention they direct toward the multiplicity of ways through which innovations can be carried out (i.e. different characteristics of innovation processes). (Drejer, 2004, p. 559)

Drejer goes on to argue that the various contributions to services innovation can readily be placed within Schumpeter's five dimensions of innovation: organizational, product, market, process and input.

Finally, there is the need to recognize the interaction between service and manufacturing firms within innovation networks. As noted earlier, demarcation writers have highlighted the impact of innovation in business services on manufacturing and other sectors. Business-to-business services are intermediate investments to other firms. The purchase of business services therefore affects the functioning of firms within both services and manufacturing. Citing Greenfield (1966), Drejer suggests that acknowledgement of the role played by services in economic development is not new but that empirical studies of their relative impact are. These have been investigated using input–output data from different countries. For example, Windrum and Tomlinson (1999) tested the contribution of knowledge-intensive business services (KIBS) to services and manufacturing sectors in Germany, Japan, the Netherlands and the UK, using data from 1970 to 1990. KIBS were found to have a positive impact on both service and manufacturing sectors in all four countries over the 20-year period. Similar findings have been identified in other studies, on input–output data of other countries (e.g. Drejer, 2001; Peneder *et al.*, 2003; Tomlinson, 2003).

There are three key ways in which KIBS, such as business consultants, financial services and ICT services, can have a long-term impact on client firms' productivity and performance. The first is through the provision of high-quality information on new business opportunities, new trends in the market place, and the business potential of new technologies, such as new ICTs. The second is through the outsourcing of specific inputs. This has a positive impact on productivity and competitive performance when existing in-house inputs are replaced by higher-quality, externally sourced inputs. The third impact of KIBS is as exemplars of novel business models. KIBS provide a concrete illustration of new business models and, through their ongoing relationship, introduce clients to these new ways of working and new technologies. Antonelli (1998), for example, has highlighted the role of KIBS in the diffusion of new ICTs. KIBS are leading advocates of Internet-based ICTs because these technologies enable them to interface more effectively with clients and, as a consequence, to intermediate more effectively experience, information and knowledge between clients. In this way, KIBS have become key intermediaries, improving the efficiency and speed of learning within innovation networks.

4   Summary and a look forward
The chapter has outlined the multifaceted picture of innovation that has emerged in services research. Also, it has discussed the important differences that exist between neo-Schumpeterians and other scholars in this area. Neo-Schumpeterians are developing a distinctive 'synthesis' approach: one that aims to cross-fertilize insights in organizational, product, market, process and input innovations that have been identified in services and manufacturing research. For neo-Schumpeterians, differences between services and manufacturing are ones of degree, rather than absolutes. The extent to which such differences exist is, then, an empirical issue.

On the basis of the currently available data, limited though it is, it seems that service firms tend to be more engaged in the transformation of people and goods over geographical space than manufacturing firms. By contrast, manufacturing firms tend to be more engaged in the transformation of physical materials and energy into physical artefacts than service firms. Case studies on service firms have highlighted the importance of organizational, market and input innovation. These three dimensions of Schumpeterian innovation have tended to be overlooked in studies of manufacturing. However, as we have seen, this does not mean that they are not also important in manufacturing. By bringing together and critically (re)appraising research on services and manufacturing innovation, it is possible to deepen our theoretical understanding of both domains, and to develop improved empirical research agendas.

The few large-scale comparative studies that exist (primarily based on CIS data) appear to indicate that organizational innovations are more closely tied to new product and process innovations in services than in manufacturing. In addition, the data suggest that service firms have greater difficulties than manufacturing firms in protecting their innovations through patents and copyright. Case studies have suggested the user–provider interaction tends to be stronger in services than in manufacturing, and that innovation networks tend to be more prevalent features. However, the current lack of good-quality statistical data on these issues prevents clear-cut conclusions being reached.

The neo-Schumpeterian synthesis is, in part, a critique of the assimilation and demarcation approaches. Two examples were examined in the chapter: the distinction between ad hoc learning and innovation, and the contribution of KIBS to innovation networks. The neo-Schumpeterian synthesis is also concerned with the critical reappraisal of past research in manufacturing and services. With respect to the issues addressed in this chapter, one begins to question whether certain phenomena were already present in manufacturing sectors. For instance, is the reverse life cycle really specific to services? Pilkington's invention of the float glass process is an example of a radical process innovation in manufacturing that subsequently gave rise to new glass products (Uusitalo, 1995, 1997). Is joint provider–client production specific to services? In the building industry, an architect works closely with the person(s) who commissions a new building and the two parties precisely determine the specification. Further, the innovative use of new materials and new ways of organizing construction have prompted a dramatic change in the design and scale of buildings and large engineering constructions from the Victorian era through to the present day. The same is true for manufacturing, as evidenced by the rapid change in the materials used. It seems very misleading to suggest that the link between organizational change and product/process innovation, or between new materials development and product/process innovation, is 'new' to services.

One suspects that matters have not been assisted by the caricature of manufacturing typically found in the services literature. This equates manufacturing with a version of the Fordist mass production business model in which narrowly trained, semi-skilled workers operate highly specialized capital machinery in order to mass-produce highly standardized products. This description may apply to sectors such as car fabrication but it is not, and never has been, the only type of productive organization found in manufacturing. Piore and Sabel long ago challenged this suggestion, and found it wanting (Piore and Sabel, 1984). They discuss the existence of two generic types of business model: the mass production model and the craft production model. Both can be found throughout the course of industrialized history. The craft model is based on skilled workers who produce a variety of customized goods and services. Piore and Sabel argue that neither alternative is inherently superior in terms of its efficiency. The prevalent adoption and diffusion of mass production in the 1950s and 1960s was due to a particular set of historical circumstances and the political choices made by different actors (management, unions and national/ local policy makers). This particular constellation of interests broke down in the early 1970s, reintroducing the choice between mass and craft production in many manufacturing areas.

In contrast to mass production, flexible specialization is appropriate for the production of high-quality goods that can quickly be changed (tailored) to meet rapidly changing tastes and needs in specialist markets. The model is underpinned by a reliance on skills, flexibility and networking between task-specializing firms in order to produce changing volumes and combinations of goods at high productive efficiency. Underpinning this is the development of flexible manufacturing technologies and flexible work practices that favour small batch production: 'mass customization'. Finally, where efficiency gains in mass production are predicated on economies of scale, efficiency gains in flexible specialization lie in economies of scope.

Two points can be made with respect to the demarcation, assimilation, synthesis debate discussed in the chapter. First, equating manufacturing with mass production is inappropriate. Second, equating services with flexible specialization is inappropriate. The mass production model is being applied to services as well as manufacturing. Consequently, the distinction is not between 'mass' manufacturing and 'flexible' services, and research that proceeds by comparing these two straw men is unsound.

As noted, the neo-Schumpeterian approach is still in its infancy. Looking forward, there are at least four areas that require substantial research. First, there is a clear need for a framework in which the various issues previously discussed can be brought together. Such a framework would fulfil a similar role to the sectoral taxonomies developed by the assimilation school, i.e. it would facilitate the integration of research, but it would avoid the biases inherent in these taxonomies. Secondly, there is an obvious need for more comparative research. This includes detailed firm-level case studies and the development of large-scale data sets. Third, little or no research exists on innovation in health and other 'public sector' services. A notable feature here is the number of different public and private sector organizations that interact in their design and delivery of these services, and the complexity of these interactions. The motives and drives of the public sector organizations may differ from private sector firms, but in what ways do their innovation activities differ? If differences exist, are they generic or ones of degree? How do interactions between public and private sectors affect innovation? Such questions have yet to be addressed in a serious way because innovation research has traditionally taken the firm or the sector as the relevant unit of analysis. Little attention has been given to innovation networks and concepts such as collective invention (Carlsson *et al.*, 2002). As with recent research on services, the analysis is likely to make us re-evaluate what we thought we knew about innovation in general. This, then, is a fourth area requiring substantial research effort. The neo-Schumpeterian agenda in the coming few years is certainly challenging, but the potential rewards are great.

References

Antonelli, C., 1998, 'Localized technological change, new information technology and the knowledge-based economy: the European evidence', *Journal of Evolutionary Economics*, **8** (2), 177–98.

Barras, R., 1986, 'Towards a theory of innovation in services', *Research Policy*, **15**, 161–73.

Barras, R., 1990, 'Interactive innovation in financial and business services: the vanguard of the service revolution', *Research Policy*, **19**, 215–37.

Boden, M. and Miles, I. (eds), 2000, *Services and the Knowledge-Based Economy*, London: Continuum.

Cainelli, G., Evangelista, R. and Savona, M., 2002, 'Innovation and economic performance in services: a firm level analysis', paper presented at the 12th International RESER Conference, 'The European Network of Economic and Spatial Service Research', Manchester, 26–27 September.

Carlsson, B., Jacobsson, S., Holmen, M. and Rickne, A., 2002, 'Innovation systems: analytical and methodological issues', *Research Policy*, **31** (2), 233–45.

Chandler, A.D., 1962, *Strategy and Structure*, Cambridge, MA: MIT Press.

Chandler, A.D., 1977, *The Visible Hand*, Cambridge, MA: MIT Press.

Coombs, R. and Miles, I., 2000, 'Innovation, measurement and services: the new problematique', in J.S. Metcalfe, and I. Miles (eds), *Innovation Systems in the Service Economy*, Boston: Kluwer, pp. 85–103.

den Hertog, P., 2000, 'Knowledge intensive business services as co-producers of innovation', *International Journal of Innovation Management*, **4**, 491–528.

Drejer, I., 2001, 'Business services as a production factor', CEBR Working Paper 2001–7, CEBR, Copenhagen.

Drejer, I., 2004, 'Identifying innovation in surveys of services: a Schumpeterian perspective', *Research Policy*, **33** (3), 551–62.

Eurostat, 2001, *Statistics on Innovation in Europe (Data 1996–1997)*, Luxembourg: European Communities.

Evangelista, R., 2000, 'Sectoral patterns of technological change in services', *Economics of Innovation and New Technology*, **9**, 183–221.

Fuchs, V.R., 1965, 'The growing importance of service industries', *The Journal of Business*, **38** (4), 344–73.

Gadrey, J., Gallouj, F. and Weinstein, O., 1995, 'New models of innovation – how services benefit industry', *International Journal of Service Industry Management*, **6** (3), 4–16.

Gallouj, F. and Weinstein, O., 1997, 'Innovation in services', *Research Policy*, **26**, 537–56.

Georgescu-Roegen, N., 1971, *The Entropy Law and the Economic Process*, Cambridge, MA: Harvard University Press.

Greenfield, H.I., 1966, *Manpower and the Growth of Producer Services*, Columbia, New York: Columbia University Press.

Harberger, A.C., 1998, 'A vision of the growth process', *American Economic Review*, **88** (1), 1–32.

Hill, P., 1999, 'Tangibles, intangibles, and services: a new taxonomy for the classification of output', *Canadian Journal of Economics*, **32** (2), 426–47.

Hughes, A. and Wood, E., 2000, 'Rethinking innovation comparisons between manufacturing and services: the experience of the CBR SME Surveys in the UK', in J.S. Metcalfe and I. Miles (eds), *Innovation Systems in the Service Economy: Measurement and Case Study Analysis*, Boston: Kluwer.

Lundvall, B.-Å., 1988, 'Innovation as an interactive process: from user–provider interaction to the national system of innovation', in G. Dosi, C. Freeman, R. Nelson, G. Silverberg and L. Soete (eds), *Technical Change and Economic Theory*, London: Pinter.

Metcalfe, J.S., 1998, *Evolutionary Economics and Creative Destruction*, London: Routledge.

Miozzo, M. and Soete, L., 2001, 'Internationalisation of services: a technological perspective', *Technological Forecasting and Social Change*, **67** (2), 159–85.

OECD, 2000a, *Science, Technology and Industry Outlook,* Paris: OECD.

OECD, 2000b, *A New Economy? – The Role of Innovation and Information Technology in Recent OECD Economic Growth*, Paris: OECD.

OECD, 2000c, *New Factors in Economic Growth: The Impact of ICT and Innovation*, Paris: OECD.

OECD-Eurostat, 1997, *Proposed Guidelines for Collecting and Interpreting Technological Innovation Data – Oslo Manual* (2nd edn), Paris: OECD.

Pavitt, K., 1984, 'Sectoral patterns of technological change: towards a taxonomy and a theory', *Research Policy*, **13**, 343–73.

Pavitt, K., Robson, M. and Townsend, J., 1989, 'Technological accumulation, diversification and organisation in UK companies 1945–1983', *Management Science*, **35** (1), 81–99.

Peneder, M., Kaniovski, S. and Dachs, S., 2003, 'What follows tertiarisation?: structural change and the role of knowledge-based services', presented at the 3rd European Meeting on Applied Evolutionary Economics (EMAEE), 10–12 April, Augsburg, Germany.

Piore, M.J. and Sabel, C.F., 1984, *The Second Industrial Divide: Possibilities for Prosperity*, New York: Basic Books.

Preissl, B., 2000, 'Service innovation: what makes it different? Empirical evidence from Germany', in J.S. Metcalfe and I. Miles (eds), *Innovation Systems in the Service Economy: Measurement and Case Study Analysis*, Boston: Kluwer.

Sirilli, G. and Evangelista, R., 1998, 'Technological innovation in services and manufacturing: results from Italian surveys', *Research Policy*, **27** (9), 882–99.

Sundbo, J., 1998, *The Organisation of Innovation in Services*, Cheltenham, UK and Northampton, MA, USA: Edward Elgar.

Tether, B. and Metcalfe, J.S., 2003, 'Services and services innovation', *CRIC Working Paper Series*, discussion paper no. 58, Manchester: CRIC. Printed as Tether, B. and Metcalfe, J.S., 2004, 'Systems of innovation in services', in F. Malerba (ed.), *European Sectoral Systems of Innovation*, Cambridge: Cambridge University Press.

Tomlinson, M., 2003, 'A new role for business services in economic growth', in D. Archibugi and B.-Å. Lundvall (eds), *The Globalizing Learning Economy*, Oxford: Oxford University Press.

Uusitalo, O., 1995, 'The flat glass industry: the effect of float glass on industry structure', Helsinki School of Economics and Business Administration, Helsinki.

Uusitalo, O., 1997, 'Development of the flat glass industry in Scandinavia 1910–1990: the Impact of Technological Change', *Scandinavian Economic History Review*, **3**, 276–95.

Windrum, P., 2002, 'The role of knowledge-intensive business services in e-commerce', in A. Pyka and G. Küppers (eds), *Innovation Networks: Theory and Practice*, Cheltenham, UK and Northampton, MA, USA: Edward Elgar.

Windrum, P., and Tomlinson, M., 1999, 'Knowledge-intensive services and international competitiveness: a four country comparison', *Technology Analysis and Strategic Management*, **11** (3), 391–408.

40 Flexible labour markets and labour productivity growth: is there a trade-off?
Alfred Kleinknecht and C. W. M. Naastepad

1 Introduction

Mainstream economists argue that European unemployment can be brought down by means of increased labour market flexibility, including easier hiring and firing of personnel, less trade union power and (downward) wage flexibility. They often refer to high rates of job creation in the US that clearly outperformed job growth in most of the 'rigid' economies of continental Europe. We argue that the exceptionally high job growth in the US mirrors a severe crisis in labour productivity growth. Poor labour productivity gains lead to a highly labour-intensive GDP growth. The case of the US productivity crisis is paralleled in the Netherlands that showed equally high rates of low productive and highly labour-intensive GDP growth during the 1980s and 1990s. For different reasons (and in a different institutional setting), the US and the Netherlands have achieved comparatively low wage cost pressures combined with flexible work arrangements that brought significant wage cost savings. We offer theoretical arguments of how this has damaged competence building, innovative capabilities and adoption of labour-saving process technology, thus impeding labour productivity growth.

In our introduction, we place the hype of the so-called 'New Economy' and the post-1995 rise in US labour productivity growth in the historical perspective of Kondratieff long waves in economic growth that are driven by major technological breakthroughs. We argue that US productivity growth during the second half of the 1990s fits into the framework of Kondratieff long waves and it is not exceptional by historical standards. Moreover, the resurgence of US productivity growth tends to be confined to a relatively small 'Silicon Valley' economy. The use of IT for labour productivity increases in the 'old economy' is likely to be hampered by low wage cost pressure and downward wage flexibility in highly flexible US labour markets. We document figures about the productivity crisis in the US up to the mid-1990s and in the Netherlands and offer theoretical explanations for a link between low wage pressure and low labour productivity growth.

In our conclusions, we argue that, from a Schumpeterian innovation perspective, the 'rigid' European ('Rhineland') model of labour relations has specific advantages compared to an Anglo-Saxon 'free market' model. As people stay longer in the same firm, more trust and loyalty can grow. This reduces market failure due to positive externalities. With long-lasting employment relations, there is less market failure with respect to private investment in R&D, training and other crucial assets of knowledge-intensive economies. Anglo-Saxon flexible labour relations aggravate knowledge externalities that lead private firms to invest less in knowledge than the societal optimum. Furthermore, we conclude that European unemployment can be reduced if European trade unions change their policy. The annual labour productivity gains should no longer be used for wage claims, but for shortening of the standard working week. This would help to switch from job-extensive to job-intensive growth without damaging innovation and productivity growth.

2   A new economy?

To advocates of the 'New Economy', the post-1995 acceleration of GDP (Table 40.1) and labour productivity growth (Table 40.2) in the US represents a structural break with the past. They suggest that the behaviour of the economic system has fundamentally changed. It was even argued that, thanks to diminished government regulation, increased global competition and, last but not least, the rapid rise of ICT, the classical business cycle may have ceased to exist and the trade-off between unemployment and inflation may have broken down (US Government, 2000). Accordingly, uninterrupted long-run low unemployment and non-inflationary growth was believed to be a real possibility.

Table 40.1   Gross domestic product, 1996 prices (in national currencies; average annual growth rates)

	Belgium	France	Germany*	Italy	Nether-lands	UK	EU-14**	USA	Japan
1950–60	3.0	4.6	7.7	6.1	4.6	2.7	4.5	3.5	8.8
1960–73	4.9	5.4	4.1	5.3	4.9	3.1	5.2	4.3	9.7
1973–80	2.7	2.5	2.3	3.5	2.4	1.1	2.6	2.6	3.4
1981–90	1.9	2.4	1.4	2.2	2.2	2.7	2.4	3.2	4.0
1991–2000	2.1	1.8	1.7	1.6	2.8	2.2	2.5	3.3	1.5
1991–95	1.5	1.1	1.6	1.3	2.1	1.6	1.6	2.4	1.4
1996–2000	2.8	2.5	1.7	1.8	3.6	2.8	3.5	4.1	1.6

Notes: * Rows 1–4: West Germany; row 5: united Germany.
** Excluding Luxemburg, for which no data are given in the GGDC database.

Source: Computed from Groningen Growth and Development Centre data (www.eco.rug.nl/ggdc/); see also Van Ark (2000).

An implication of this assessment is that countries with 'rigid' labour markets and highly regulated economies (like France and Germany) are advised to deregulate their economies and speed up the flexibilization of their labour markets, in order not to miss out on the 'New Economy'. Obviously, such beliefs have lost ground after the dot.com and stock market crisis during 2000–2003. But is it all nonsense? Table 40.1 shows that there was indeed a remarkable resurgence of GDP growth in a number of OECD countries during the second half of the 1990s. Was this due to 'new rules for a new economy'?

In our view, the alleged manifestations of a 'New Economy' can be interpreted in the context of Kondratieff's long wave theory formulated in the mid-1920s. According to this theory, periods of high income and productivity growth (lasting some 20–25 years) are alternating with periods of lower growth of approximately equal length. Together they form a long wave of around 40–50 years. During the prosperous phase of the long wave, the upswings of the (shorter) classical business cycles tend to be stronger, while the downswings tend to be milder. According to the long wave schedule, the period between the two World Wars was a downswing period of the long wave. The period from the end of the 1940s up to the beginning of the 1970s was an upswing, which was followed by a downswing from the early 1970s up to the early 1990s.[1] This is partly visible in the GDP growth rates in Table 40.1. Many observations of the adherents of the 'New Economy' perfectly fit into the proposition that, during the first half of the 1990s, we entered a new upswing of the Kondratieff long wave.

The explanation of a long-wave type of alternation in the speed of economic growth has often been related to the thrust-wise introduction of major new technologies. These new technologies lead to the creation of new industries that experience a long S-shaped growth cycle (empirically explored already by Kuznets, 1930). Such industry growth cycles begin with a slow and difficult introduction, followed by a steep growth and, after some time, they end in maturity. Schumpeter (1939) proposed that the points in time of the market introduction of major innovations tend to be clustered towards the end of the downswing phases of the long wave. Kuznets (1940) heavily criticized this proposition in his famous review of Schumpeter's *Business Cycles*. However, during the 1980s, theoretical and empirical evidence emerged that Schumpeter's 'cluster-of-innovation' hypothesis might be realistic.[2]

Within this Schumpeterian framework, it makes sense to argue that the recent rise in productivity and GDP growth (as visible in Tables 40.1 and 40.2) is part of a new Kondratieff upswing, set in motion by ICT as a new breakthrough technology. Empirical support for this proposition is provided by two sources. First, there is evidence for the US of a general increase in capital, especially computer and software capital. In 1995, business investment as a share of US GDP climbed above its long-term average, and it has continued upward since. As a result, capital services per hour grew faster after 1995 than before (US Government, 2000).

Second, 'input' indicators of innovation (including investments in ICT, ICT patents, intangible investments, and the technological and scientific labour potential) show a strong growth in the ICT sector in recent years; moreover, these indicators suggest that in this respect the US is leading the world (Hollander and Ter Weel, 2000). On the other hand, there exists empirical evidence that leads us to reject the proposition that recent US productivity growth has structurally increased towards historically unprecedented levels.

First, when placed in its longer-term historical context, recent US productivity growth is by no means exceptional. The growth rate of US labour productivity, when measured as GDP per hour worked, indeed increased substantially during 1996–2000, but it still remains below US achievements during the 1950s and 1960s (see Table 40.2). Second, US labour productivity growth in the second half of the 1990s is close to the EU14 average.

Third, estimates by Sichel (1999) and Jorgenson and Stiroh (1999) show that the contribution of IT capital to US output growth, though higher than in the past, is still quite low. In the period 1970–90 it was about 4.5 per cent and during the 1990s about 7–8 per cent. Jorgenson and Stiroh (1999) further show that total factor productivity growth in the 1990s did not increase despite the reported increase in IT capital.

Fourth, when examined more closely, the productivity revival in the US does not provide evidence of an economy-wide productivity growth increase. According to Gordon (2000b), the acceleration in productivity growth in the US has taken place predominantly in the computer-producing industry, and in durable manufacturing more generally, where productivity growth doubled from its 1972–95 trend. This portion of the economy, however, constitutes only 12 per cent of total GDP. In the remaining 88 per cent, once the effects of price remeasurement and of the business cycle are subtracted from the raw figures, the 'New Economy's' effects on productivity growth are surprisingly absent, and capital deepening has been remarkably unproductive (Gordon, 2000a: 4).

Outside durable manufacturing, multi-factor productivity (MFP) growth appears to have even decelerated: 'Not only has there been no spillover from the New Economy in the form of a structural acceleration in MFP growth in the rest of the economy, but there has not even been an acceleration in trend labour productivity growth in response to a massive investment boom in computers and related equipment' (Gordon, 2000a: 45–6). In other words, the US economy seems to be segmented into two,

Table 40.2   Gross domestic product per working hour, at 1996 prices (in national currencies; average annual growth rates)

	Belgium	France	Germany*	Italy	Nether-lands	UK	EU-14**	USA	Japan
1950–60	3.2	5.2	6.3	3.2	4.2	1.8	4.2	3.6	5.9
1960–73	5.5	5.1	5.0	6.7	4.5	3.6	5.7	2.6	8.4
1973–80	4.3	3.4	3.3	3.3	2.5	2.3	3.0	1.0	2.7
1981–90	2.3	2.9	1.6	2.0	1.0	2.2	2.1	1.5	3.0
1991–2000	2.4	1.3	2.4	2.0	1.1	2.2	2.2	1.6	2.0
1991–95	2.3	1.5	3.2	3.1	1.1	2.6	2.3	1.1	1.8
1996–2000	2.5	1.1	1.6	0.8	1.1	1.8	2.0	2.0	2.3

Notes: *Rows 1–4: West Germany; row 5: united Germany; **Excluding Luxemburg.

Source: Computed from Groningen Growth and Development Centre data (www.eco.rug.nl/ggdc/).

poorly integrated parts: a small but strongly growing high-tech ('Silicon Valley') sector and a large and slow growing 'old economy' sector.

It is obvious from Table 40.2 that there has been a severe crisis of labour productivity growth in the USA between 1973 and 1995. In the Netherlands, the productivity growth slowdown started in the early 1980s and still persists. In this context, one should recall that GDP could only grow by either using more labour or by making existing labour more productive. In other words, the growth rate of real GDP – by definition – equals the sum of labour productivity growth and employment growth. Hence the labour intensity (or employment elasticity) of GDP growth can be expressed as the growth of employment divided by the growth of GDP. Calculations by Auer (2000; reproduced in Table 40.3), show that there is no other country in the OECD (except for the Netherlands) that has such a high job intensity of GDP growth as the US (0.6 as compared to 0.2 for the EU on average).

More data on the labour intensity of GDP growth are given in Table 40.4. Unlike Table 40.3 (based on *jobs*), the employment elasticities in Table 40.4 are based on *hours* worked. Table 40.4 shows the US and the Netherlands as the champions of labour-intensive growth in the 1980s and 1990s. In the US, employment elasticities of GDP growth increased from almost zero in the 1950s to 0.39 in the 1960s and further to, respectively, 0.6 and 0.5 in the 1980s and 1990s. The Netherlands experienced a sharp break in the labour intensity of its GDP growth after the famous social contract of Wassenaar (1982) when trade unions voluntarily agreed upon sacrificing wage growth, relying on a trade-off between wage and job growth. After 'Wassenaar',

Table 40.3   Job intensity of economic growth, OECD, 1985–95*

Country	GDP growth (1)	Job growth (2)	Job intensity of growth = (1)/(2) (3)
Austria	2.6	0.7	0.27
Denmark	1.7	0.1	0.06
France	2.1	0.3	0.14
Germany	1.4	0.5	0.35
Ireland	5.0	1.5	0.30
The Netherlands	**2.6**	**1.8**	**0.70**
United Kingdom	2.3	0.6	0.26
EU–15	**2.0**	**0.4**	**0.20**
USA	**2.4**	**1.5**	**0.62**

Note: * Columns (1) and (2): average annual growth rates.

Source: Auer (2000).

Table 40.4   Employment elasticities, major OECD countries, 1950–2000 (1996 prices)

	B	France	G(1)	Italy	NL	UK	EU-14	USA	Japan
1950–60	−0.05	−0.13	0.19	0.48	0.10	0.31	0.07	−0.03	0.34
1960–73	−0.11	0.06	−0.22	−0.26	0.07	−0.16	−0.09	0.39	0.13
1973–80	−0.63	−0.34	−0.47	0.07	−0.05	−1.15	−0.15	0.60	0.19
1981–90	−0.22	−0.24	−0.19	0.09	0.57	0.18	0.12	0.55	0.25
1991–2000	−0.12	0.26	−0.44	−0.27	0.61	0.03	0.13	0.51	−0.35
1991–95	−0.50	−0.38	−1.00	−1.44	0.49	−0.57	−0.47	0.52	−0.26
1996–2000	0.09	0.54	0.07	0.54	0.68	0.37	0.41	0.50	−0.44

Notes: Figures are based on employment, measured in annual hours worked. Rows 1–4: West Germany; row 5: united Germany.

Source: Computed as GDP growth (from Table 40.1) minus hourly labour productivity growth (from Table 40.2) divided by GDP growth.

employment elasticities increased (from close to zero) to 0.57 in the 1980s and 0.61 in the 1990s. The Dutch Wassenaar contract was the starting point of a long period of modest wage growth. This is in contrast particularly to Germany, where wage growth and labour productivity growth remained high and employment elasticities were negative almost throughout.

One could perhaps argue that the decline of productivity growth in the Netherlands is due to a sectoral shift from high technological opportunity manufacturing to allegedly low technological opportunity services. However, such an explanation is implausible. Sectoral shifts are a long-run process, which can hardly explain a fairly sudden drop of labour productivity growth. Moreover, as the results of a shift-share decomposition analysis for the Netherlands by Naastepad and Kleinknecht (2004) show, about 90 per cent of the aggregate decline in Dutch labour productivity growth between 1970–80 and 1984–97 is due to *intrasectoral* productivity growth declines – and only the remaining 10 per cent is due to sectoral shifts.

What is striking is that as much as 37 per cent of the decline in aggregate labour productivity growth must be attributed to the decline in manufacturing productivity growth, although the share of manufacturing in aggregate GDP and employment was only about 20 per cent. The productivity growth decline in services, which account for about two-thirds of Dutch GDP and employment, contributed about 39 per cent to the aggregate labour productivity growth slowdown. These findings, and similar findings by van Ark and de Haan (1999) and van Schaik (2002), imply that the Dutch productivity crisis cannot be attributed to a rise in importance of sectors which are low-productive 'by nature', or to problems in a few isolated services sectors. In our view, the general productivity growth decline must have something to do with low wage pressure and flexible labour relations. Theoretical arguments about this will be discussed in the remainder of our chapter.

2 How does labour market flexibility hamper innovation and productivity growth?

2.1 Wages, labour productivity and innovation

Above we saw that, in the Netherlands and the USA, low labour productivity growth was paralleled by a highly labour-intensive GDP growth. It is our hypothesis that, in the Netherlands, the policy of 'loonmatiging' (often poorly translated into English as 'wage moderation' or 'wage restraint') has played an important role in bringing about this result. 'Loonmatiging' was voluntarily adopted by Dutch trade unions. According to estimates by Naastepad and Kleinknecht (2004), Dutch real wage growth declined from 4.4 per cent per annum during the period 1970–80 to only 0.3 per cent per year during 1984–97. Dutch wage increases were much more modest than the EU average: during the 1980s, Dutch wages declined by about 3.5 per cent per year relative to the average wage level in eight major OECD countries and, during the 1990s, Dutch relative wages continued to decline (by 0.3 per cent per year). Dutch trade unions followed the principle that 'Jobs are more important than wage increases.' In the USA, wage cost savings were achieved by Reaganomics that broke the power of trade unions and

Table 40.5   Decomposition of growth rates of relative unit labour cost (RULC): The Netherlands and the USA compared to a benchmark group of eight OECD countries

Period		NL	USA
1971–80	Growth of unit labour costs (relative to benchmark group):	2.2	−4.8
	Relative contribution to RULC growth (adding up to 100%) by:		
	Wage growth	−32.2%	73.7%
	Change of exchange rate	146.7%	51.0%
	Labour productivity growth	−14.5%	−24.7%
1981–90	Growth of unit labour costs (relative to benchmark group):	−2.7	1.1
	Relative contribution to RULC growth (adding up to 100%) by:		
	Wage growth	129.7%	−26.4%
	Change of exchange rate	−18.6%	70.5%
	Labour productivity growth	−11.1%	55.9%
1991–2000	Growth of unit labour costs (relative to benchmark group):	−1.4	1.9
	Relative contribution to RULC growth (adding up to 100%) by:		
	Wage growth	20.5%	16.6%
	Change of exchange rate	105.1%	85.6%
	Labour productivity growth	−25.6%	−2.25%

Notes:
Average export market shares for each decade served as weighting factors.
The benchmark group covers eight countries that take approximately 75% of OECD trade:
Japan, France, Germany, Italy, UK, Belgium, USA and Netherlands.

Source: Authors' calculations. Country-wide data on nominal wage growth, labour productivity growth and export shares are from European Commission (2000). Nominal exchange rates are from OECD (2000b).

thereby achieved labour market flexibility (including easier hiring and firing of personnel and downward wage flexibility).

Table 40.5 illustrates that, during the 1970s and 1980s in the US (and during the 1980s and 1990s in the Netherlands), wages contributed importantly to a favourable growth of relative unit labour costs (relative to OECD benchmark countries). It is also important to note that, during the named periods, in both countries, labour productivity growth contributed *negatively* to the development of relative unit labour costs.

Various parts of economic theory suggest that a positive (causal) relationship between real wage rates and labour productivity exists, notably the following:

1. In standard neoclassical theory, an increase in the relative price of labour leads profit-maximizing firms to substitute capital for labour, shifting along a given production function (representing the current state of technology), until the marginal productivity of labour equals the given real wage. Causality in this argument runs from relative factor prices to choice of technique and hence productivity.

2. According to the theory of induced technological change, a higher relative wage rate increases the labour-saving bias of newly developed technology (Hicks, 1932; Kennedy, 1964; Ruttan, 1997).

3. In the Schumpeterian theory of creative destruction, one can argue that innovating firms (compared to their non-innovative counterparts) can live better with an aggressive wage policy by trade unions and with rigid labour markets, as they possess market power. Their market power is due to monopoly rents from unique product and process knowledge that acts as an entry barrier to their markets (Geroski, Machin and van Reenen, 1993; Kleinknecht, Oostendorp and Pradhan, 1997). Higher real wage growth thus enhances the Schumpeterian process of creative destruction in which innovators compete away non-innovators. Conversely, weak wage growth and flexible labour relations protect weak firms and low-quality entrepreneurs and increase the likelihood of their survival. While this is favourable for employment in the short run, it leads to a loss of innovative dynamism in the long run (Kleinknecht, 1998).

4. In demand-driven models of technical change (Schmookler, 1966; for a recent survey and empirical support, see Brouwer and Kleinknecht, 1999), higher effective demand raises innovative activity. Almost parallel is the Kaldor–Verdoorn argument about a positive impact of demand on labour productivity. Both imply that wage restraint or downward wage flexibility will impede innovation as far as it leads to a lack of effective demand.

5. Within an endogenous growth framework (e.g. Foley and Michl, 1999: 288–98), a profit-maximizing firm's decision to invest in (labour productivity increasing) R&D, can be shown to depend on the share of wages in total costs. The higher the wage share, the more profitable it becomes to devote resources to increasing the productivity of labour.

6. According to recent research in management and industrial relations, workers can be motivated to provide above-normal effort through

incentives that express the commitment of the firm to its workforce (Akerlof, 1982). These incentives include high base wages and employment security. When adopted as part of a cluster of organizational and management practices (including decentralization of decision making and extensive training), these incentives have significant effects on innovation, productivity growth and financial performance (Appelbaum *et al.*, 2000, Gratton *et al.*, 1999, Gratton, 2000; Huselid, 1995; Michie and Sheehan, 1999; Pfeffer, 1995, 1998).

A common element in all theories is that they propose – through various channels – a positive causal relation between real wage growth and labour productivity growth. Naastepad and Kleinknecht (2004) attempt to evaluate empirically the effects of real wage growth restraint on the Dutch labour productivity growth slowdown after 1984 within the following growth accounting model (a 'hat' denotes an average annual growth rate):[3]

$$\hat{\lambda} = \hat{\gamma} + \sigma \Pi \left[\frac{\hat{w}}{r} \right] - \psi \Pi \Delta a + \left[\frac{h-1}{h} \right] \hat{x}, \qquad (40.1)$$

where $\hat{\lambda}$ = labour productivity growth (per hour), $\hat{\gamma}$ = TFP growth, w = real wage (per hour), r = the rental price of capital, $\hat{x}$ = real GDP growth, Δa = the average annualized increase in the average age of the capital stock, σ = the elasticity of capital–labour substitution, Π = the CES production function share of capital in output,[4] ψ = the 'vintage effect' coefficient, and h = the scale parameter; if $h>1$ ($h<1$), the production function exhibits increasing (decreasing) returns to scale. Equation (40.1) states that labour productivity growth is a function of the following factors:

1. (unexplained) TFP growth $\hat{\gamma}$;
2. the growth rate of capital intensity, which in turn is assumed to depend on the change in relative factor price growth [$\hat{w}/r$] and on the substitution elasticity σ;
3. a 'vintage effect', which is operationalized as the negative impact on productivity growth of a rise in the average age of the capital stock Δa. In turn, as argued above, the change in the average age of capital depends negatively on real wage growth;
4. real GDP growth $\hat{x}$, where the coefficient $(h-1)/h$ is the so-called 'Kaldor–Verdoorn' coefficient (which is economically meaningful only if $h>1$). Real GDP growth, in turn, may depend positively on real wage growth. If this is the case, then a decline in real wage growth will not only reduce GDP growth, but, through the Kaldor–Verdoorn effect, also the rate of growth of labour productivity.

Naastepad and Kleinknecht (2004) estimate econometrically the substitution elasticity, the vintage effect, and the Kaldor–Verdoorn coefficient and next use their estimates to explain the decline in Dutch labour productivity growth (per hour) between 1970–80 and 1984–97. According to their growth accounting results, the policy-engineered decline in real wage growth in the Netherlands contributed to the slowdown in Dutch labour productivity growth through the following channels:

1. a decline in capital-intensity growth (i.e. the substitution of labour for capital) over time, to which about 62 per cent of the productivity slowdown between 1970–80 and 1984–97 must be attributed;
2. a rise in the average age of the Dutch capital stock (the vintage effect), which explains about 19 per cent of the Dutch productivity growth slowdown; and
3. a decline in real GDP growth, which, through the Kaldor–Verdoorn relation, explains another 8 per cent of the Dutch post-1984 productivity growth decline.

Accordingly, real wage growth moderation, when all these channels are combined, must be held responsible for as much as 90 per cent of the decline in Dutch labour productivity growth between 1970–80 and 1984–97. Underlying these findings is a Schumpeterian process, in which weak wage growth protects weak firms and low-quality entrepreneurs and increases the likelihood of their survival (Kleinknecht, 1998).

2.2 Market failure due to flexibilization of labour relations

Flexibilization of labour relations is another factor that reduces wage cost pressure. On the one hand, one could argue that flexible hiring and firing and a high labour turnover might favour a firm's innovation performance: firms can more easily replace unproductive workers with more productive ones and a larger inflow of fresh people may enrich the pool of a firm's innovative ideas and open up new networks. On the other hand, highly flexible labour also has its disadvantages. If labour can be easily hired and fired, the risk of temporary fluctuations in production volumes is shifted from the firm to the employees. While yielding substantial wage costs savings,[5] flexible labour relations (often of short duration and with frequent job changes), are likely to lead to a loss of trust and loyalty, and to diminish the dedication to work. In other words, such flexibility will diminish social capital, forcing firms to invest more money in monitoring and control. Moreover, the so-called 'hold up' problem may become more relevant: as labour relations are (expected to be) of shorter duration, employers and employees may be more reluctant to invest in the labour relation. Such investments may be held up if the expected duration of the labour contract is short (see Akerlof, 1982; Agell, 1999).

For example, the employer may hesitate to invest in the training of flexible workers, but the employees themselves may also invest less in firm-specific knowledge, networks, trust etc. High external mobility of people increases the probability that one cannot (fully) appropriate the benefits of such investment. This 'hold up' effect will have a negative influence on the quality of products and services. Moreover, if labour turnover is high, there will be problems of knowledge transfer from quitting to new people; an organization's historical memory may become weaker. But a loss of trust and loyalty will also enhance the leaking of knowledge and trade secrets to competitors, which may discourage investments in R&D and innovation. In other words, high (external) flexibility enhances positive externalities. As a consequence, market failure will become more pervasive. This implies that e.g. investments in R&D by individual firms may be (far) below the societal optimum. While such factors do not do much harm in a knowledge-extensive 'Hamburger Economy', they may be quite damaging for the innovation potential of knowledge-intensive firms.

A high labour turnover may be particularly harmful for firms with a 'routinized' (as opposed to an 'entrepreneurial') innovation regime. A routinized innovation regime depends on continuous historical accumulation of knowledge (including 'tacit knowledge') that is a source of successful incremental innovation. In such a regime, a firm's technological competencies crucially depend on the type of knowledge it happened to accumulate in its past history (Dosi, 1988). Obviously, the continuity in knowledge accumulation will require a certain stability and continuity of staff members. Moreover, the quality of a firm's services may also suffer from a high personnel turnover since frequent changes of personnel may cause problems of information transfer between people leaving the firm and people coming in. A firm's historical memory may become weaker.

Our argument that the flexibilization of labour relations itself might have a negative impact on innovation and productivity growth is supported by a large microeconometric literature. For example, empirical studies of HRM practices and of industrial relations suggest that 'high trust' cooperative labour relations lead to higher productivity growth (see Huselid, 1995; Delaney and Huselid, 1996; Appelbaum *et al.*, 2000; Lorenz, 1992, 1999; Fernie and Metcalf, 1995; Laursen and Foss, 2003). Likewise, results from (controlled) economic experiments indicate that protection against dismissal may enhance productivity performance, as secure workers will be more willing to cooperate with management in the development of the production process and in disclosing their (tacit) knowledge for the firm (see Gächter and Falk, 2002). And our argument is also in line with the results of microeconometric studies on the probability to innovate by Michie and Sheehan (1999, 2003).

A recent study for the Netherlands is Kleinknecht *et al.* (2006), which estimated the impact of internal ('functional') forms of flexibility and of external ('numerical') forms of flexibility (i.e. high shares of people on temporary contract or a high turnover of personnel) on (i) wage costs, and (ii) sales growth among Dutch firms. Their indicator of internal flexibility measures the percentage of personnel that changed their function or department within the firm. Such flexibility can be taken as a proxy for functional (other than numerical or external) flexibility. Such functional flexibility may be more typical for 'Rhineland' rather than for 'Anglo-Saxon' labour relations. The main findings of Kleinknecht *et al.* (2006) can be summarized as follows:

1   External (numerical) forms of flexibility
- Both firm-level as well as individual worker-level wage equations (with controls for age, education, sector etc.) show that *numerical* forms of flexibility yield substantial savings on a firm's wage bill, while *functional* flexibility does not.
- While yielding savings on wage bills, numerical flexibility leads to higher job growth, but does *not* translate into higher sales growth.
- The latter point suggests that numerical flexibility appears to be related to lower labour productivity growth (the effects being slightly different for innovating versus non-innovating firms): firms that have a high turnover of personnel do not realize significantly higher sales growth, and the same holds for firms that employ high shares of personnel on truly temporary contracts (without a perspective of tenure). Seemingly, advantages from lower wage costs are more or less compensated by losses on various forms of social capital: an increased turnover of workers with short-run commitments leads to diminished trust, loyalty and identification with the firm, creates 'hold-up' problems and leads to increased market failure due to easier leaking of knowledge (i.e. positive externalities).

2   Internal (functional) forms of flexibility
- Such flexibility is associated with significantly higher sales and employment growth, in spite of paying higher wages. The effect of internal flexibility on sales growth is highly significant among firms that perform some R&D, and it is weakly significant among non-R&D performers. By handling internal and functional (other than external or numerical) flexibility, innovators invest in trust and loyalty of their personnel, which is favourable to the accumulation

of (tacit) knowledge and reduces the leaking of knowledge to competitors.

This analysis of firm-level and worker-level data supports the view that wage bill saving flexibilization of labour markets may indeed create lots of jobs, but that this is likely to happen at the expense of labour productivity growth, raising serious doubts about the long-run sustainability of a low-productivity–high-employment growth path. Our microeconometric conclusions have an important *macroeconomic* implication: if it is true that flexibilization goes at the expense of labour productivity growth, then it must be the case that labour productivity growth is lower (higher) in countries in which labour markets are relatively 'flexible' ('rigid'). The reason for such a macroeconomic pattern to prevail is that the major dimensions of labour market regulation, most notably the strictness of employment protection legislation, are inherently national and systemic, covering all sectors and all regions; hence, because all firms are affected, aggregate productivity growth must also be affected.

Buchele and Christiansen (1999) and Naastepad and Storm (2005) provide robust empirical evidence of a statistically significant and positive association between labour market regulation (including employment protection and wage regulation) and labour productivity growth. The latter study, using data for a panel of 20 OECD countries during the period 1984–97, finds – in line with the literature – that major structural characteristics of labour markets tend to vary together: for example, countries having below-average employment protection, feature relatively large earnings inequality, weaker workers' rights, and closer supervision of employees. On the other hand, countries in which employment protection is stronger also have stronger workers' rights, which require less direct supervision and result in smaller earnings differentials.

Controlling for the effects on productivity growth of capital-intensity growth and of real GDP growth, Naastepad and Storm find that those OECD countries in which the strictness of employment protection legislation is below-average (above-average), are experiencing below-average (above-average) labour productivity growth. This is in line with the conclusions of Buchele and Christiansen (1999). Using slightly different indicators and highly aggregated macro data, the latter demonstrate that the Anglo-Saxon model may be strong in creating employment, but weak in labour productivity growth, while the opposite holds for the Rhineland model: 'We have argued . . . that while more highly regulated European style labor market institutions may inhibit employment growth, they also promote productivity growth. And while less regulated US style labor markets may promote employment growth, they also inhibit productivity growth' (ibid.: 323). The evidence from these macroeconometric studies thus corroborates the findings from our microeconometric (firm-level) analysis.

3   Policy implications

Summarizing the above, more flexible labour markets and the reduction of wage cost pressure do lead to a higher job growth, but they are likely to do so at the expense of innovation and labour productivity growth. One should remember that an economy can grow only in two ways: either (1) by working more hours or (2) by producing more value added per hour worked (i.e. by technical change). Hence a low growth of GDP per hour worked (i.e. low labour productivity growth) in the Netherlands and in the US coincides with a high growth of numbers of hours worked per unit of GDP growth. The impressive rates of job growth in the two countries are the 'flip' side of a crisis of labour productivity growth. Why should we be concerned about this low-productivity–high-employment growth path?

First, the six theoretical arguments mentioned above suggest that low productivity growth is essentially caused by a lack of modernization of capital stock, i.e. by a slow speed of adoption of labour-saving technology and associated learning processes. In the long run, such a lack of modernization will make an economy vulnerable. Technologically backward factories are the first to be closed down in times of prolonged recessions.

Second, the highly labour-intensive growth path may lead to labour scarcity. For example, around the year 2000, the Netherlands had achieved full employment. In response to reaching full employment (and a tight labour market), wages in the Netherlands went up. While trade unions still tried to keep wage increases modest, employers paid many people above the level determined in collective wage agreements negotiated by trade unions. Scarcity of labour forced them to do so. This brought the low-productivity–high-employment growth path into danger. In the short run, wage increases were not matched by corresponding labour productivity growth and this contributed to a deteriorating foreign trade position. In principle, such a problem might become relevant for every development model that competes on low factor costs rather than on quality and innovation: if successful, certain factors of production will become scarce; scarcity will drive up factor prices and the model becomes self-destroying.

Finally, the examples of the US and the Netherlands may be of broader relevance. Numerous mainstream economic think-tanks again and again propagate the belief that achieving more flexible labour markets should solve the European unemployment problem. This often includes a plea for reduction of wage costs by easier hiring and firing, by bashing trade unions, and by greater (downward) wage flexibility. One should realize that, here again, there is no free lunch. The examples of the US and the Netherlands show that flexibilization of labour markets and sacrificing wage increases indeed have led to higher job growth, but this job growth was hardly due to higher overall GDP growth. It came mainly from lower GDP growth *per hour worked*, which required many more hours to be worked. While such employment creation looked successful in the short run, mainstream economists still poorly recognize the long-run structural problem involved.

The employment elasticities in Table 40.4 indicate that there have been periods (1980s and 1990s) when GDP growth contributed only modestly to the growth of labour hours in Europe. In the 1960s and 1970s, labour productivity growth was even so high that high rates of GDP growth were accompanied by a slightly *negative* growth of total labour hours in various countries. In principle, such a jobless (or even job-destroying) growth does not need to be a problem. If a high speed of labour-saving technical change allows the production of more value added with little extra (or even diminishing) labour input, it is an almost natural solution to use labour productivity gains for a collective shortening of standard working hours, rather than for wage increases. In other words, if trade unions want to reduce European unemployment, they may choose to keep real wages constant and use labour productivity gains for the financing of reduced standard labour hours. In principle, this does not need to cost the firms more money than keeping labour hours constant and increasing real wages.

This calls for a Social Pact between trade unions and employers. Such a pact might commit both parties to using large parts of the annual labour productivity gains for the financing of reduced labour times rather than for increased real wages. This would imply that, without sacrificing labour productivity growth, we would obtain a much more labour-intensive growth path. This approach would be a more intelligent solution to the unemployment problem than the Dutch and US way: creating jobs by reducing wage cost pressures and thereby giving negative incentives to labour-saving technical change.

Finally, during economic downturns, economies on the low-wage–low-productivity path are vulnerable with respect to plant closures. One should note that lack of modernization of equipment (which is at the heart of the productivity crisis) causes factories in those countries ranking high on the list of plants to be closed down (or being moved to low-wage countries) in periods of prolonged crisis. Moreover, in future years, it might well turn out that European economies, because of rigid labour markets and high wage pressure, prove superior in exploiting the labour-saving potential of ICT equipment in their 'old economy'.

Notes

1. For econometric explorations of time series that support this time scheme, see Metz (1993) and Reijnders (1992).
2. For a summary of discussions and of various pieces of evidence, see Kleinknecht (1990).
3. Equation (40.1) can be derived from a CES production function (homogeneous of degree *h*), assuming profit maximization by firms. See Naastepad and Kleinknecht (2004) for the derivation.
4. In algebra:

$$\Pi = \left[\frac{(1 - \delta)\,(k/l)^{-\rho}}{\delta + (1 - \delta)\,(k/l)^{-\rho}} \right],$$

where *k* = the capital stock (in real terms) and *l* = number of hours worked; ρ measures the substitutability of capital and labour.
5. For econometric evidence, see the wage equations estimated by Kleinknecht *et al.* (2006).

Bibliography

Agell, J. (1999), On the benefits from rigid labour markets: norms, market failures, and social insurance, *The Economic Journal*, **109** (453), F143–64.

Akerlof, G.A. (1982), Labour contracts as a partial gift exchange, *Quarterly Journal of Economics*, **97**, 543–69.

Appelbaum, E., T. Bailey, P. Berg and A.L. Kalleberg (2000), *Manufacturing Advantage. Why High-Performance Work Systems Pay Off*, Ithaca: Cornell University Press.

Auer, Peter (2000), *Employment Revival in Europe. Labour Market Success in Austria, Denmark, Ireland and the Netherlands*, Geneva: ILO.

Brouwer, E. and A. Kleinknecht (1999), Keynes plus? Effective demand and changes in firm-level R&D: an empirical study, *Cambridge Journal of Economics*, **23** (3), 385–91.

Buchele, R. and J. Christiansen (1999), Employment and productivity growth in Europe and North America: the impact of labour market institutions, *International Review of Applied Economics*, **13** (3), 313–32.

Delaney, J.T. and M.A. Huselid (1996), The impact of human resource management practices on perceptions of organizational performance, *The Academy of Management Journal*, **39** (4), 949–69.

Dosi, G. (1988), Sources, procedures and microeconomic effects of innovation, *Journal of Economic Literature*, **26**, 1120–71.

European Commission (2000), *European Economy 69. The EU Economy: 1999 Review*, Brussels: Commission of the European Communities, Directorate-General for Economic and Financial Affairs.

Fernie, S. and D. Metcalf (1995), Participation, contingent pay, representation and workplace performance: evidence from Great Britain, *British Journal of Industrial Relations*, **33** (3), 379–415.

Foley, Duncan K. and Thomas R. Michl (1999), *Growth and Distribution*, Cambridge, MA: Harvard University Press.

Gächter, S. and A. Falk (2002), Reputation and reciprocity: consequences for the labour relation, *Scandinavian Journal of Economics*, **104** (1), 1–27.

Geroski, P.A., S. Machin and J. van Reenen (1993), The profitability of innovating firms, *Rand Journal of Economics*, **24**, 198–211.

Gordon, Robert (2000a), 'Interpreting the "One Big Wave" in US long-term productivity growth', mimeo, 22 April, Northwestern University, NBER and CEPR, downloadable (http://www.econ.northwestern.edu/).

Gordon, Robert (2000b), Does the 'New Economy' measure up to the great inventions of the past?, *Journal of Economic Perspectives*, **14** (4), 49–74.

Gratton, L. (2000), *Living Strategy. Putting People at the Heart of Corporate Purpose*, London: Prentice-Hall.

Gratton, L., V. Hope Hailey, P. Stiles and C. Truss (1999), *Strategic Human Resource Management. Corporate Rhetoric and Human Reality*, Oxford: Oxford University Press.

Hicks, J.R. (1932), *The Theory of Wages*, London: Macmillan.

Hollander, H. and B. ter Weel (2000), Nederland? Kennisland!, *Economisch Statistische Berichten*, **85** (4264), 424–6.

Huselid, Mark A. (1995), The impact of human resource management practices on turnover, productivity, and corporate financial performance, *Academy of Management Journal*, **38** (3), 635–72.

Jorgenson, Dale W. and Kevin L. Stiroh (1999), Information technology and growth, *American Economic Review, Papers and Proceedings*, 109–15.

Kennedy, Charles (1964), Induced bias in innovation and the theory of distribution, *Economic Journal*, **74**, 541–7.

Kleinknecht, A. (1990), Are there Schumpeterian waves of innovations?, *Cambridge Journal of Economics*, **14**, 81–92.

Kleinknecht, A. (1998), Is labour market flexibility harmful to innovation?, *Cambridge Journal of Economics*, **22**, 387–96.

Kleinknecht, A.H., R.H. Oostendorp and M.P. Pradhan (1997), 'Patronen en economische effecten van flexibiliteit in de Nederlandse arbeidsverhoudingen – een exploratie op basis van OSA vraag- en aanbodpanels' (in Dutch), *Voorstudies en achtergronden*, V99, The Hague: Wetenschappelijke Raad voor het Regeringsbeleid.

Kleinknecht, A., R. Oostendorp, M. Pradhan and C.W.M. Naastepad (2006), Flexible labour, firm performance and the Dutch job creation miracle, *International Review of Applied Economics*, **20** (2), 171–87.

Kuznets, S. (1930), *Secular Movements in Production and Prices*, Boston: Houghton Mifflin.

Kuznets, S. (1940), Schumpeter's business cycles, *American Economic Review*, **30**, 157–66.

Laursen, K. and N.J. Foss (2003), New human resource management practices, complementarities, and their impact on innovation performance, *Cambridge Journal of Economics*, **27** (2), 243–63.

Lorenz, E.H. (1992), Trust and the flexible firm: international comparisons, *Industrial Relations*, **31** (3), 455–72.

Lorenz, E.H. (1999), Trust, contract and economic cooperation, *Cambridge Journal of Economics*, **23** (3), 301–16.

Metz, R. (1993), 'A re-examination of long waves in aggregate production series', in A. Kleinknecht, E. Mandel and I. Wallerstein (eds), *New Findings in Long-Wave Research*, London: Macmillan, pp. 80–119.

Michie, J. and M. Sheehan (1999), HRM practices, R&D expenditure and innovative investment: evidence from the UK's 1990 Workplace Industrial Relations Survey (WIRS), *Industrial and Corporate Change*, **8** (2), 211–33.

Michie, J. and M. Sheehan (2003), Labour market deregulation, 'flexibility' and innovation, *Cambridge Journal of Economics*, **27** (1), 123–43.

Naastepad, C.W.M. and A. Kleinknecht (2004), The Dutch productivity slowdown: the culprit at last?, *Structural Change and Economic Dynamics*, **15** (1), 137–63.

Naastepad, C.W.M. and S. Storm (2005), Labour relations and productivity growth in a panel of 20 OECD countries (1984–1997), mimeo, Delft University of Technology.

OECD (1999), *Employment Outlook*, Paris: OECD Publications.

OECD (2000a), *National Accounts of OECD Countries*, Paris: OECD Publications.

OECD (2000b), *Main Economic Indicators, OECD Compendium*, Paris: OECD Publications.

OECD (2003), *The Sources of Economic Growth*, Paris: OECD Publications.

Pfeffer, J. (1995), *Competitive Advantage through People. Unleashing the Power of the Work Force*, Boston: Harvard Business School Press.

Pfeffer, J. (1998), *The Human Equation. Building Profits by Putting People First*, Boston: Harvard Business School Press.

Reijnders, J.P.G. (1992), 'Between trends and trade cycles: Kondratieff long waves revisited', in A. Kleinknecht, E. Mandel and I. Wallerstein (eds), *New Findings in Long-Wave Research*, London: Macmillan, pp. 15–44.

Ruttan, Vernon W. (1997), Induced innovation, evolutionary theory and path dependence: sources of technical change, *The Economic Journal*, **107** (444), 1520–29.

Salverda, W. (2005), 'The Dutch model: magic in a flat landscape?' in U. Becker and H. Schwartz (eds), *Employment Miracles*, Amsterdam: Amsterdam University Press, pp. 39–64.

Schmookler, J. (1966), *Invention and Economic Growth*, Cambridge, MA: Harvard University Press.

Schumpeter, J.A. (1939), *Business Cycles* (2 vols), New York: McGraw-Hill.

Sichel, D.E. (1999), Computers and aggregate economic growth: an update, *Business Economics*, April, 19–24.

Stiroh, Kevin (1999), Is there a new economy?, *Challenge*, **42** (4), 82–101.

US Government (2000), *Economic Report of the President*, Washington: US Government Printing Office and http://www.access.gpo.gov/eop/.

Van Ark, B. (2000), 'De Nederlandse productiviteits paradox', *Economische Statistische Berichten*, 1 December, 974–6.

Van Ark, B. and J. de Haan (1999), 'Miracle or not? Recent trends in the growth performance of the Dutch economy', in P.A.G. van Bergeijk, J. van Sinderen and B.A. Vollaard (eds), *Structural Reform in Open Economies*, Cheltenham, UK and Northampton, MA, USA: Edward Elgar, pp. 157–79.

Van Schaik, A.B.T.M. (2002), Gaat de produktiviteitsgroei omhoog?, *Economisch Statistische Berichten*, **87** (4355), 292–3.

Verdoorn, P.J. (1949), Fattori che regolano lo sviluppo della produttività del lavoro, *L'Industria*, **1**, 3–10.

PART 4

NEO-SCHUMPETERIAN MACRO DYNAMICS: GROWTH AND DEVELOPMENT

4.1
Growth

41 Schumpeter and the micro-foundations of endogenous growth
F. M. Scherer

Beginning in the late 1980s, a 'new' essentially macroeconomic theory of economic growth began to materialize. As characterized in a memoir by one of its founders (Romer, 1994), the new theory distinguished itself from neoclassical theories 'by emphasizing that economic growth is an endogenous outcome of the economic system', and not simply the result of superior technology descending like manna from heaven, to be exploited at will by one and all.

One premise of the new endogenous growth theory is that newly-discovered knowledge spills over to facilitate technological innovations by the profit-seeking firms that invest in them and which, by securing patent protection on details of the innovations, even if not on the facilitating knowledge, earn what are hoped to be supranormal profits from them. A curiosity of the new theory is that, despite placing so much emphasis on the facilitating role of knowledge as a basis for subsequent innovations, it largely ignores the vast stock of knowledge contributed over previous decades on technological innovation and its essentially endogenous character. It in effect purports to reinvent the endogenous innovation wheel. This, as an old curmudgeon who participated in laying the earlier theoretical foundations, I recognize, may come from ignorance of previous scholars' contributions. But it ought to be taken into account by historians of thought attempting to survey the advance of economic theory during the 20th century. In this chapter I attempt at least in a limited way to set matters straight and to identify some of the persisting puzzles.

Schumpeter's pioneering role

Proponents of 'new' endogenous economic growth theories do acknowledge, typically in a cursory way, one predecessor: Joseph A. Schumpeter.[1] From the time of his *Habilitationsschrift* (1912), Schumpeter argued correctly that innovation, and in particular technological innovation, is one of the main driving forces underlying economic growth. In the English translation of his classic (1934, p. 60), Schumpeter acknowledges his intellectual debt to Karl Marx and criticizes John Stuart Mill's view that technological improvement 'is something which just happens and the effects of which we

671

have to investigate, while we have nothing to say about its occurrence *per se*'. Thus, technological change does not occur exogenously, or as one of the 'given' conditions in an economy. Rather, innovation is a profit-seeking activity carried out by business firms and, in particular, entrepreneurial business firms. In modern language, it is endogenous. In his later popularization (1942, p. 110), Schumpeter makes the point even more bluntly:

> Was not the observed [economic growth] performance due to that stream of inventions that revolutionized the technique of production rather than to the businessman's hunt for profits? The answer is in the negative. The carrying into effect of these technological novelties was of the essence of that hunt. And even the inventing itself . . . was a function of the capitalist process which is responsible for the mental habits that will produce invention. It is therefore quite wrong – and also quite un-Marxian – to say, as so many economists do, that capitalist enterprise was one, and technological progress a second, factor in the observed development of output; they were essentially one and the same thing or, as we may also put it, the former was the propelling force of the latter.

In other chapters of his 1942 book, Schumpeter advanced an additional set of hypotheses sharply at odds with the position he took in 1914. The 1912 book argued that innovations arose most frequently through new firms entering from outside the mainstream of economic activity. However, he asserted in 1942 that the most likely innovators in a world of complex and costly modern technology were well-established firms, and indeed, those that not only anticipated obtaining new monopoly power as a result of patents or other elements of 'monopolistic strategy' (p. 102) following their innovations, but those that enjoyed some degree of monopoly power before, and as a basis for, making investments in innovation. This claim spawned a vast literature on which I shall be able here to draw only a few limited insights.

Schumpeter provides in his various books little of what today would pass for a rigorously specified economic theory. A small part of that gap will be addressed here. More importantly, his theoretical 'vision' does not make clear how, in their profit-seeking innovative efforts, entrepreneurs choose which potential avenues of technological change they will pursue and which they will ignore. In other words, his theory lacks a clear statement of how the 'invisible hand' guides innovation efforts. One might analogize firms' innovative efforts to the search for still-undiscovered oil deposits. The opportunities are put there by nature; firms merely need to find them and perfect the means of exploiting them. But such a model would sooner or later run into diminishing marginal returns, which are clearly inconsistent with the Schumpeterian vision. Thus it remained for later scholars to elaborate the entrepreneurial search mechanism and explain why technological change might be self-regenerating.

Early builders on the Schumpeterian vision

One theoretical track initiated by J.R. Hicks (1932) asked how changes in wages induce technological changes in the factor bias of production functions. Most of the substantial literature on this point, excepting perhaps Fellner (1961), emerged after the contributions that will be reviewed here, so it will be given short shrift.[2]

The first known contribution that provided a fully articulated view of how market forces influence innovative efforts was a 1959 article by Richard R. Nelson (1959). Two major themes are stated in the first two paragraphs and elaborated both conceptually, with careful recognition of precursor authors, and with extensive case study evidence, in the remainder of the article. To paraphrase the first two paragraphs:

> Invention is strongly motivated by perceived profit opportunities. Demand and cost factors play major roles with the state of scientific knowledge significantly affecting the cost and hence the profitability of invention. . . . second, . . . invention . . . is an activity often carried on under conditions of great uncertainty.

George Stigler once said that 'It's all in Adam Smith.' Smith in fact had important things to say about the precursors of modern industrial research and development laboratories. However, for the roots of endogenous innovation theory, one can justifiably say that 'it's all in Nelson'.

The 'demand factors' examined in Nelson's contribution went beyond prior authors' vague notions of 'need' as inducements to technological innovation. The role of demand was suggested in tentative form by Jacob Schmookler (1954) and then elaborated by him (1966) into a conceptualization supported by an ambitious analysis of patent data.[3] Among other things, in his 1966 book Schmookler showed how supply- and demand-side influences interacted to induce technological changes and how the uneven distribution of technological knowledge and capabilities affected the industrial loci from which entrepreneurs responded to demand-side stimuli.

Neither Nelson nor Schmookler formulated an explicit economic model of how demand and supply influenced, separately or together, the allocation of resources to technological innovation. It is here that I creep into the picture. As an extension of my work modelling the allocation of resources to the development of new weapons systems, I began systematic research in 1963 on how market structure affected the pace of innovation – a classic Schumpeterian theme. My work was supported by a grant from the Inter-University Committee on the Economics of Technological Change, funded in turn by the Ford Foundation, and was enriched by discussions in 1964 and 1965 between Schmookler and myself in the off-hours at committee meetings, usually held in Cambridge or Princeton.[4] Schmookler stressed the importance of demand and I the role of supply-side (knowledge-side) advances. It was Schmookler who provided the synthesizing metaphor, one adopted previously in a different context by Alfred Marshall: just as it took two blades of a pair of scissors to cut paper, so both supply (knowledge base) and demand changes affected the profitability of technological innovations and hence the pace at which they were undertaken.

Following similar concepts applied to weapons R&D, my main theoretical model viewed business firms' investment in research and development as a capital investment problem. Under it, firms attempted in any given project to maximize the discounted surplus of quasi-rents $v(t)$ less R&D costs $C(t)$, with the key novelty being the assumption that the quasi-rents depended in fairly intricate ways on the timing of rivals' competing innovations. Footnote 11 to the resulting article (Scherer, 1967) stated:

> Continuous exogenous technological progress can be represented by an additional term $-\lambda t$ in the exponent of [the R&D cost term]. Developments made worthwhile mainly because of a shift in the time–cost tradeoff [$C(t)$] function can be called 'technology-push' innovations. Those made worthwhile because firms find themselves entering a period of especially high $v(t)$ values can be called 'demand-pull' innovations. On these two notions a more general theory of technological innovation can be built, although the task lies beyond the scope of the present paper.

After completing that paper, I turned to other lines of research and did not return to the problem as posed above until several years later.[5] A year after my 1967 paper was published, the *Review of Economics and Statistics* included an article by Yoram Barzel building upon my 'more general theory' suggestion, but with no citation to my prior work. Since Barzel attended the May 1966 conference at which I presented oral and written versions of the 1967 paper, he could scarcely have been unaware of my formulation. However, his model utilized a competitive equilibrium assumption I did not and would not have conceived. Those two contributions provide the foundation upon which I shall elaborate here.

The basic dynamic model
The basic dynamic model is illustrated in Figure 41.1 (reproduced with a slight error). On the supply side, suppose that carrying out in the current time period ($T=0$) the research and development cost (RD) required successfully to commercialize a new product or production process is RD_0, or, with the numerical assumptions of Figure 41.1, 2500. To keep matters simple, we assume with some violence to realism that the R&D project, once undertaken, is carried out instantaneously. As time goes on, exogenous advances in the knowledge base reduce the cost of performing the required R&D. These advances may come from the progress of relevant scientific and technological knowledge and/or through clues spilling over costlessly from

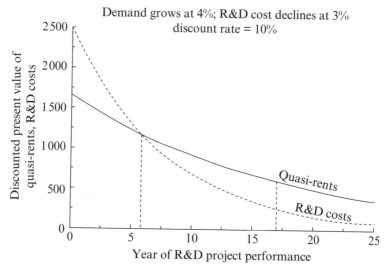

Figure 41.1 How changes in demand and technology induce innovation

successful solution of the technical problems confronting prior product or process development generations. The advances are assumed (somewhat implausibly) in Figure 41.1 to occur continuously and smoothly at the rate of (100) per cent per year, or, as the figure is drawn, at 3 per cent annually. Thus, from year zero's vantage point, the cost of performing the requisite R&D in year T is $RD_0\, e^{-.03\, T}$. But, from that vantage point, a dollar spent in year T must be discounted to present value at the interest rate r, assumed in the Figure 41.1 illustration to be 10 per cent per year. Thus, at year zero, the equation for the R&D cost curve shown by the dashed line in Figure 41.1 is $RD_0\, e^{-(a+r)T} = 2500\, e^{-.13T}$.

On the demand side, suppose the quasi-rents realized from having a successful new product or process amount to $v_0 = 100$ per year in year zero and grow (e.g., because of general demand expansion) at a rate of $100\, g = 4$ per cent per year thereafter.[6] Assuming for algebraic simplicity an infinite time horizon, the discounted present value of benefits expected from an R&D project completed in year T amount to

$$V(T) = \int_{T}^{\infty} v_0\, e^{(g-r)t}\, dt = 100\, \frac{e^{(g-r)T}}{(r-g)}. \tag{41.1}$$

The graph of this discounted quasi-rent function, again viewed from the perspective of time zero, is shown by the solid line in Figure 41.1.

At time zero, discounted R&D costs exceed the discounted present value of anticipated quasi-rents, and so the project is not profitable to a would-be

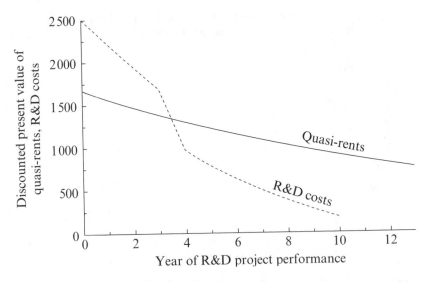

Figure 41.2   Technology-push innovation inducement

innovator. As the years advance, however, discounted quasi-rents fall less
rapidly than discounted R&D costs. In year 6, or more precisely, at $T = 5.8$,
discounted costs and quasi-rents are equal, and so the project becomes economically feasible.[7] The combination of technology-push (falling R&D
costs) and demand-pull (rising quasi-rents) provides the required economic
stimulus to innovation. If conduct of the R&D project can be delayed
beyond year 6, there is an increasing surplus of discounted anticipated
quasi-rents over R&D costs, so the project yields profits that, at least for
some time, are rising. On this, more later.

   With the assumptions of Figure 41.1, there is no unicausal inducement
mechanism. Figures 41.2 and 41.3 alter the picture. Figure 41.2 superim-
poses upon the numerical assumptions of Figure 41.1 a sudden knowledge
breakthrough during year 3 that sharply reduces R&D costs. Once the
implications of the breakthrough are recognized, a project that was previously considered unprofitable becomes profitable. This illustrates the pure
technology-push case. In Figure 41.3, discounted quasi-rents jump upward
because e.g. of a sudden change in current and expected energy costs, rendering an energy-saving innovation profitable that previously failed the
profitability test.[8] This is the pure demand-pull inducement scenario.

Market dynamics and market structure
We return now to Figure 41.1. As we saw, discounted quasi-rents first
exceed discounted R&D costs after year 6. But at that early date, there is

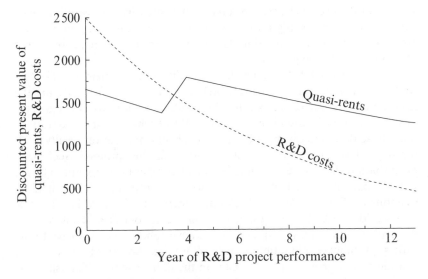

Figure 41.3   Demand-pull technology inducement

room in the market for only one firm carrying out the R&D project. If more firms conducted independent R&D projects, their combined discounted R&D costs would exceed discounted quasi-rents and the project would be unprofitable in the aggregate at, say, year 7. For reasons other than those advanced by Schumpeter, monopoly appears necessary to achieve the earliest possible technological progress. But if the firm conducting R&D were a monopolist unconcerned by threats of losing its would-be monopoly position to faster-acting rivals, the monopolist would not choose to innovate when the project first crosses the profitability threshold at year 6. Rather, seeing discounted R&D costs falling more rapidly than discounted quasi-rents, the monopolist would wait until it could achieve the maximum possible discounted difference between the two – given the numerical assumptions underlying Figure 41.1, at year 17, 11 years later than the time when the innovation first becomes profitable.[9]

Barzel's escape from this paradox is to assume that only one firm conducts the required R&D, after which it secures patent protection permitting it to monopolize the newly-developed product or process market. But it can only attain this favored position by pre-empting all would-be rivals with an early R&D date; indeed, if pre-innovation competition exhausts all supranormal profits, with the earliest possible (six-year) innovation timetable. Ex ante competition forces the pace of innovation toward completion in year 6, at which time either of two things must happen to validate the model's assumptions: rival firms whose presence forces the pace withdraw before significant R&D costs have been sunk, or they are forced to withdraw, e.g., because the government grants an exclusive franchise to carry out the necessary R&D to the firm offering the earliest innovation date in some kind of competitive bidding context.[10]

Needless to say, satisfaction of these conditions is problematic. The feasibility of awarding an exclusive R&D franchise to the firm offering the fastest innovation pace is especially doubtful, since entrants into a government choice process are likely to propose R&D schedules more ambitious than those they actually intend to pursue, or they may deliver results qualitatively inferior to (and less costly than) those they promise. Such optimistic bidding biases are a chronic feature of competitions organized by the U.S. Department of Defense in choosing contractors for individual weapons R&D programs. See Peck and Scherer (1962, pp. 411–20). Thus, in a world of steady but slow change in technological possibilities and demand stimuli, it may be difficult to achieve conditions conducive to the earliest profitable exploitation of new technological possibilities. At best, a considerable degree of indeterminacy in the inducement mechanism must be acknowledged.

The dilemma fades when demand or supply conditions change abruptly with scientific breakthroughs or demand-side shocks, as illustrated in Figures 41.2 and 41.3. Then, for a project that was unprofitable at one moment in time, a gap between quasi-rent and R&D cost functions suddenly opens up, perhaps to a magnitude allowing several firms to complete fast-paced competing R&D projects without exhausting the overall profit potential, or at least to permit several independent strands of low-cost preliminary research, after which most abandon the field for the more costly final development phases to the firms that have achieved the best early results.[11] This view is consistent with statistical evidence indicating systematically more intense R&D efforts in concentrated industries when advances in underlying scientific knowledge come gradually, but with a deterioration or even reversal of the relationship, i.e., with more intensive R&D in less tightly oligopolistic industries, when the science base is rapidly changing.[12] That a rapid pace of technological innovation can be sustained in fragmented or easily entered industries is also suggested by the predominant role of new and small firms in the US information technology and biotechnology industries during the last two decades of the 20th century.

Uncertainty and social welfare maximization
Figures 41.1 to 41.3 oversimplify reality in an important way, ignoring the pervasive role of uncertainty in technological innovation. Encountering unexpected technical problems is not uncommon in R&D projects, although research by Edwin Mansfield and colleagues (1977a) suggests that

a majority of projects do achieve their technical goals. Uncertainties in predicting whether a contemplated technical advance will satisfy the demands of the marketplace are without doubt much greater than uncertainties in determining whether a stated technical goal can be reached. This is shown, *inter alia*, by the experience of 110 US high-technology startup companies floating common stock offerings between 1983 and 1986 (Scherer *et al.*, 2000). By the time an initial public offering (IPO) was launched, the typical startup company had progressed sufficiently far in its R&D efforts to have surmounted most of the purely technical hurdles. But after public stock offerings were launched, 35 of the 110 companies failed altogether, usually because their products failed to gain substantial consumer acceptance. If initial $1000 investments had been made in the 52 1983–6 IPO companies whose securities continued to be traded to the end of 1995, the most successful five companies accounted for 70 per cent of the total December 1995 value of the 52 companies' stock market value. Analysis of month-by-month changes in individual companies' stock prices revealed a noisy random walk as the passage of time resolved market uncertainties.

Figure 41.4 adds the fog of uncertainty to the R&D cost and market payoff trajectories illustrated originally in Figure 41.1. The range of outcomes that might plausibly be foreseen ex ante is shown by clusters of points scattered about the expected cost and quasi-rent functions. With the addition of uncertainty, we see that benefits might be seen to exceed costs

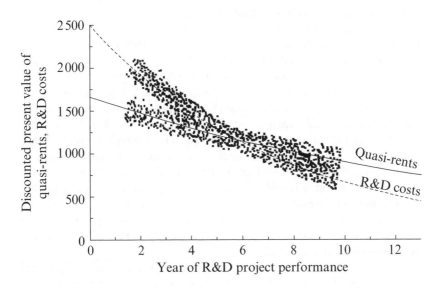

Figure 41.4   The impact of uncertainty

as early as year 3, but the anticipated break-even date might also come as late as year 10. If competition to be the first with the relevant new product or process is strong and a winner's curse prevails, the R&D project might be undertaken well in advance of the true break-even point at year 5.8.

This outcome might at first glance seem undesirable, since projects are undertaken whose costs exceed their benefits. But here a distinction must be made between private and social benefits. The anticipated payoffs that induce commercial innovation are those that the entity making an investment in R&D can expect to appropriate to its own benefit. These are called 'private' benefits. It is well-accepted that the benefits realized by all participants in the economy (including the innovator) from successful new products exceed, often by substantial ratios, the benefits appropriated by the innovator. If the new product is priced monopolistically, consumers realize a consumers' surplus from it (measured in the standard diagram by a triangular area) in addition to the profit or producer's surplus retained by the innovator. The more competition there is in pricing the new product, the larger will be the magnitude of the consumers' surplus relative to the producer's surplus. Also, the solution of technical problems in development and the identification of unmet consumer needs provide knowledge spillovers of value to other market participants. Mansfield and associates (1977b) found that, at the median for a sample of 17 innovations, discounted social (i.e., private plus external) benefits exceeded private benefits by a ratio of 2.25 to 1, with a range from 0.73 (for an innovation that cannibalized other products' surpluses) to 11.37.

To reflect the surplus of social over private benefits, one could add to Figure 41.1 (or similar diagrams) an additional function lying at most or all points above the discounted quasi-rents function. The simplest case is one in which the social benefits function exceeds the private quasi-rents function by a constant fraction k, with a slope for any given year steeper than that of the quasi-rents function. From this possibility emerge two new insights. First, social benefits normally begin to exceed R&D costs at an earlier date than the one (year 6 in Figure 41.1) at which break-even occurs in the relationship between private quasi-rents and R&D costs. Thus, 'premature' innovation because of uncertainty and the winner's curse need not be undesirable from a broader social perspective. Second, a social planner with complete information would seek not only to ensure that social benefits exceed R&D costs, but to choose an innovation date maximizing the surplus of discounted *social* (not private monopoly) benefits minus discounted private R&D costs.[13]

This welfare-maximizing innovation date will, under normal circumstances, occur later than the social break-even date. Whether it occurs before or after the date at which private quasi-rents first exceed R&D costs is ambiguous. For the case in which costs are declining and discounted benefits changing smoothly over time, it depends upon the year zero variable values, the rates at which costs and benefits are changing over time, and the size of the wedge between the social and private benefit curves. If the ratio of social benefits (including the innovator's producer surplus) to private benefits is k, the value of k at which the *socially* optimal R&D date coincides with the 'break-even' year at which discounted *private* quasi-rents equal discounted R&D costs, can be expressed by the formula:

$$k^* = (r + a)/(r - g), \tag{41.2}$$

where r is the relevant time discount rate (assumed to be the same for innovators and social welfare-maximizers), a as before is the rate at which R&D costs fall annually, and g is the rate at which private quasi-rents grow per year.[14] For the parameter values assumed in constructing Figure 41.1, $k^* = (0.10 + 0.03) / (0.10 - 0.04) = 2.167$, which is close to 2.25, the median social/private benefits ratio determined empirically by Mansfield *et al.* (1977b). Thus, for plausible parameter values, competition that leads to innovation dates sooner than those at which private break-even occurs can at least in principle be socially optimal. For given parameter constellations, the more the actual value of k exceeds k^*, the more desirable is an innovation pace faster than the private break-even pace. However, the more rapidly private benefits are growing and/or the more rapidly R&D costs are falling over time, the larger the wedge between private and social benefits must be to let the socially optimal innovation date precede the private break-even date.

Recognition of uncertainty leads to the identification of two additional general cases in which competitive 'duplication' of R&D projects leads to general welfare gains.

First, because R&D projects fail, especially when the correct technological path to a successful solution is difficult to identify ex ante, pursuing multiple, diverse R&D approaches in parallel is often desirable. In this instance, the quasi-rent function in Figure 41.1 might be reinterpreted as the expected value of the cost of the multiple R&D approaches required to achieve the desired end product. 'Required' here can be a misleading term, since the number of parallel approaches pursued affects both the probability of success and the speed at which a good solution emerges – variables which themselves are susceptible to strategic choice. See Nelson (1961) and Scherer (1966). In this additional sense, both the number of projects and the timing of their outcome are endogenous variables. The lower is the ex ante probability that a single R&D approach will be successful and the deeper the stream of anticipated benefits is from a successful solution, the larger the profit-maximizing number of parallel approaches will be.

Second, the approach pursued thus far has implicitly assumed that there is only one satisfactory solution to an innovative quest. But in fact, consumers have variegated tastes (and the purchasers of innovative producers' goods have variegated needs). Some specific innovative outcomes may satisfy few consumers, others many consumers. For such cases of what has been called 'horizontal product differentiation', diversity of consumer preferences combines with uncertainty as to which solutions best satisfy the wants of particular consumer clusters to make investing in R&D like throwing darts with imprecise aim at a dartboard, over which payoffs are distributed more or less randomly.

A dartboard experiment

To illustrate this second proposition, a Monte Carlo experiment was conducted. One hundred possible R&D outcomes were identified, with each of which a randomized discounted quasi-rent payoff was associated. Consistent with a considerable amount of empirical evidence, the distribution of payoffs was highly skewed, following a log normal distribution of the form $10^{normal\,(0,1)} \times 1000$. For the payoff matrix used in all iterations of the experiment, the mean payoff was \$5490, the median \$1310, and the maximum payoff \$91 700. The top ten payoffs accounted for 63.1 per cent of the total across all 100 payoffs. This degree of concentration in a relatively few 'winners' is typical of the outcome distributions resulting from investments in individual high-technology startup companies. See Scherer *et al.* (2000, p. 177).

If innovative projects could be aimed precisely at the most lucrative products or processes, innovators would in effect direct darts toward all prospects with expected quasi-rents exceeding R&D costs. Assuming a uniform R&D cost of \$5000 per project, the payoff distribution described in the previous paragraph would present 24 attractive targets. A precise single-shot 'hit' on each of these would yield summed quasi-rents of \$346 070, from which R&D costs of $24 \times 5000 = \$120\,000$ must be subtracted to yield a net profit of \$226 070.

If the R&D dart throwers are unable to aim with such perfect precision, but instead spray their shots randomly over the dart board's payoff space, a quite different outcome ensues. This process was simulated by assuming that each R&D project or dart throw landed at some random coordinate in the payoff space. The distribution of possible coordinate 'hits' was assumed to be uniformly random with replacement. The simulation was performed across an array of eight different sample sizes (i.e., number of dart throws) and, for each such sample, the procedure was replicated ten times with a fresh sample of randomly determined coordinate 'hit' locations. Multiple hits on a single coordinate location were assumed to add no quasi-rent value, e.g., as if the payoffs from a double hit were shared between two firms marketing a product with identical characteristics.

With R&D costs of $5000 per dart throw and assuming 24 throws, as in the perfect-aim case above, the average quasi-rent sum per iteration across ten 24-throw iterations was $137020. Subtracting from this average payoff total R&D costs of $24 \times 5000 = \$120000$, the average net profit per iteration was $17030. Thus, the innovative efforts yielded on average only slight supranormal profits, analogous to a single-shot innovation at approximately year 7 under the conditions graphed in Figure 41.1. However, as one expects in sampling from highly skewed potential payoff distributions, the results of the ten 24-shot iterations varied widely, with net profits after the deduction of R&D costs ranging from $14675 down to $-\$73010$.

The strategy pursued by dart-throwing R&D managers depends not only upon the distribution of potential payoffs but on the cost per R&D project (dart throw), which together determine the optimal number of throws. Figure 41.5 illustrates the dependency of net profits (i.e., summed quasi-rents less total R&D costs) upon the average cost per R&D project. With zero cost per R&D project (the top solid line in Figure 41.5), one continues throwing darts beyond 100 darts per iteration in the hope of hitting previously untouched payoff coordinates.[15] However, when each dart

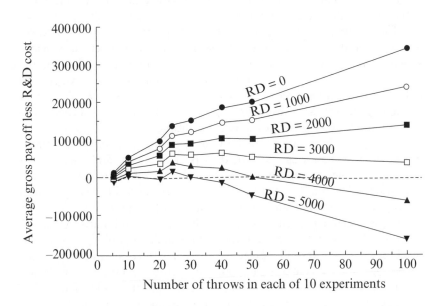

Figure 41.5   Net payoffs from dartboard experiment

throw entails cost, the attractiveness of large-number attacks eventually diminishes, the more so, the higher the cost per throw.

With R&D cost of $1000 per dart throw, an extension of the experiments recorded in Figure 41.5 shows, it is profitable to increase the number of throws per iteration to at least 200. A similar extension reveals that, with an R&D cost of $2000 per throw, the net income-maximizing number of throws is of the order of 100. With costs of $3000 per throw, the profit maximum lies in the range of 24 to 40 throws. (It is impossible to be more precise because, with such a highly skewed payoff distribution, considerable variability of outcomes remains even after the experiment is iterated ten times.) With even higher R&D costs per throw, the profit maxima lie in the range of 10 to 24 throws, although, again, the intrinsic variability of the results precludes greater precision. Quite generally, and completely consistent with the results of less richly specified models of optimal parallel paths strategies in research and development, the greater is the surplus of average payoffs over R&D costs for any given number of trials, the larger is the profit-maximizing number of trials.

When average payoffs are large relative to R&D costs, undertaking numerous trials (dart tosses) may be attractive not only because total payoffs rise by more than R&D costs, but also because proliferation of attacks on skew-distributed payoff targets reduces the relative variability of project outcomes. For the experiments described here, the coefficient of variation (i.e., the ratio of the standard deviation of payoffs to the average payoff) for repeated dart-tossing iterations ranged from 0.79 (for five tosses per iteration) down to 0.20 (for 100 tosses). This hedging benefit is clearly sought by the managers of high-technology venture fund portfolios in the United States. On average, the typical venture fund invests in roughly 40 individual start-up enterprises. Beyond this, the costs of overseeing and managing the diverse investment targets tend to increase disproportionately, discouraging further portfolio diversification.

Such a portfolio strategy can seldom be pursued by individual entrepreneurs who invest most or all of their personal assets and their time in innovation projects. But the innate variability of R&D project outcomes may in itself be an inducement to those entrepreneurs. I have argued previously, citing *inter alia* statistical evidence that horse race betters exhibit a skewness-loving propensity along with risk (i.e., standard deviation) aversion, that the entrepreneurs who initiate high-technology ventures in the United States respond positively to the known skewness of high-technology venture payoffs (assuming as before that *average* expected rewards exceed R&D costs).[16] If there is any truth in this hypothesis, we come full circle back to the speculations of Schumpeter (1942, p. 75) six decades ago:

Spectacular prizes much greater than would have been necessary to call forth the particular effort are thrown to a small minority of winners, thus propelling much more efficaciously than a more equal and more 'just' distribution would, the activity of that large majority of businessmen who receive in return very modest compensation or nothing or less than nothing, and yet do their utmost because they have the big prizes before their eyes and overrate their chances of doing equally well.

Conclusion

This analysis of the dart-throwing metaphor leaves unanswered a question raised earlier: why large gaps between R&D payoffs and costs open up to induce the exploration of multiple R&D paths by technological entrepreneurs. Competition among entrepreneurs pursuing parallel R&D projects can accelerate the pace at which innovative opportunities are exploited, but if it proceeds too far, squeezing to nothing the expected gap between minimal R&D costs and payoffs, it undermines the very logic of its existence.

The answer may lie in the existence of discontinuities, e.g., as scientific or applied research breakthroughs or abrupt changes in demand conditions create previously unavailable profit opportunities. Or it may result from uncertainty and the great difficulty of identifying the most lucrative targets for innovative investments. Until we know more about how opportunity-generating processes function, perplexities will remain in our microeconomic analyses of how innovation proceeds endogenously.

Notes

1. In four survey articles on 'New Growth Theory' in the *Journal of Economic Perspectives*, Winter, 1994, Paul Romer refers without a citation to his models as 'neo-Schumpeterian', and one other article cites Schumpeter (1934).
2. For a thorough literature review, see Thirtle and Ruttan (1987). For a brief but remarkably perceptive set of early insights, see Plant (1934), pp. 33–8.
3. For the most extensive confirming evidence, see Scherer (1982).
4. The other committee members were Alf Conrad, Zvi Griliches, Edwin Mansfield, Jesse Markham, Richard Nelson and M.J. Peck.
5. Notes written for 'job talks' I gave in Berkeley and Ann Arbor during January 1966 reveal that I presented a geometric version of the model. My first published extension was in Scherer (1970), pp. 426–32.
6. It is assumed throughout that monetary values are measured in units of constant purchasing power; i.e., compensating for whatever general inflation may be occurring.
7. As usual, the discount rate r implies that the firm making an investment is realizing a normal risk-adjusted rate of return.
8. See Popp (2002).
9. For an algebraic proof, see Scherer and Ross (1990), pp. 639–41. The delay with secure monopoly might be less if monopolists had lower R&D costs, e.g. because of scale economies or the ability to attract superior talent, or because of lower interest rates, than firms in more fragmented markets. These advantages were suggested in Schumpeter (1942, p. 101), but countervailing arguments can also be advanced.
10. This 'exclusive prospect' scenario was proposed as a practical policy model by Kitch (1977). It is also implicit in the theory of optimal patent life articulated by Nordhaus (1969).

11. On the characteristic low-early expenditure, high-final expenditure spending pattern in R&D projects, see Peck and Scherer (1962), p. 313.
12. See Scherer and Ross (1990), pp. 648–9.
13. For the relevant calculus in the zero quasi-rent growth case, see Scherer and Ross (1990), p. 641, note 71.
14. The proof is obtained by a simple extension of the methods used in Scherer and Ross (1990, p. 641, note 72), recognizing that the break-even equation is equation (2) in note 68.
15. There can be numerous multiple hits (ex post, duplicative R&D projects). With 100 trials or darts, the number of 'missed' payoff cells ranged from 35 to 40, implying at least that number of multiple hits.
    For the experiments with smaller samples, there was substantial outcome variability among the experiments. The initial result with samples of 20 was particularly low, kinking the lines in Figure 41.5 downward. Three additional runs of 10 experiments each were conducted for the $n = 20$ case, with the average result substituted in the version of Figure 41.5 presented here.
16. See Scherer (2001), citing Golec and Tamarkin (1998).

References

Barzel, Yoram (1968), 'Optimal timing of innovations', *Review of Economics and Statistics*, **50**, 348–55.
Fellner, William J. (1961), 'Two propositions in the theory of induced innovations', *Economic Journal*, **71**, 305–8.
Golec, Joseph and Maurry Tamarkin (1998), 'Bettors love skewness, not risk, at the horse track', *Journal of Political Economy*, **106**, 205–25.
Hicks, J.R. (1932), *The Theory of Wages*, London: Macmillan.
Kitch, Edmund W. (1977), 'The nature and function of the patent system', *Journal of Law & Economics*, **20**, 265–90.
Mansfield, Edwin, John Rapoport, Jerome Schnee, Sam Wagner and Michael Hamburger (1977a), *Research and Innovation in the Modern Corporation*, New York: Norton.
Mansfield, Edwin, John Rapoport, Jerome Schnee, Sam Wagner and Michael Hamburger (1977b), 'Social and private rates of return from industrial innovations', *Quarterly Journal of Economics*, **91**, 221–40.
Nelson, Richard R. (1959), 'The economics of invention: a survey of the literature', *Journal of Business*, **32**, 101–27.
Nelson, Richard R. (1961), 'Uncertainty, learning, and the economics of parallel research and development projects', *Review of Economics and Statistics*, **43**, 351–68.
Nordhaus, William D. (1969), *Invention, Growth, and Welfare: A Theoretical Treatment of Technological Change*, Cambridge: MIT Press.
Peck, Merton J. and F.M. Scherer (1962), *The Weapons Acquisition Process: An Economic Analysis*, Boston: Harvard Business School Division of Research.
Plant, Arnold (1934), 'The economic theory concerning patents for inventions', *Economica*, **1** n.s., 30–51.
Popp, David (2002), 'Induced innovation and energy prices', *American Economic Review*, **92**, 160–88.
Romer, Paul M. (1994), 'The origins of endogenous growth', *Journal of Economic Perspectives*, **8**, 3–22.
Scherer, F.M. (1966), 'Time–cost trade-offs in uncertain empirical research projects', *Naval Research Logistics Quarterly*, **13**, 71–82.
Scherer, F.M. (1967), 'Research and development resource allocation under rivalry', *Quarterly Journal of Economics*, **81**, 359–94.
Scherer, F.M. (1970), *Industrial Market Structure and Economic Performance*, Chicago: Rand McNally.
Scherer, F.M. (1982), 'Demand-pull and technological innovation: Schmookler revisited', *Journal of Industrial Economics*, **30**, 225–37.

Scherer, F.M. (2001), 'The innovation lottery', in Rochelle Dreyfuss, Harry First and Diane L. Zimmerman (eds), *Expanding the Boundaries of Intellectual Property*, New York: Oxford University Press, pp. 3–21.

Scherer, F.M. and David Ross (1990), *Industrial Market Structure and Economic Performance*, 3rd edn, Boston: Houghton-Mifflin.

Scherer, F.M. Dietmar Harhoff and Jörg Kukies (2000), 'Uncertainty and the size distribution of rewards from innovation', *Journal of Evolutionary Economics*, **10**, 175–200.

Schmookler, Jacob (1954), 'The level of inventive activity, *Review of Economics and Statistics*, **34**, 183–90.

Schmookler, Jacob (1966), *Invention and Economic Growth*, Cambridge: Harvard University Press.

Schumpeter, Joseph A. (1912), *Theorie der wirtschaftlichen Entwicklung*, Leipzig: Duncker & Humblot.

Schumpeter, Joseph A. (1934), *The Theory of Economic Development*, trans. Redvers Opie, Cambridge: Harvard University Press.

Schumpeter, Joseph A. (1942), *Capitalism, Socialism, and Democracy*, New York: Harper.

Thirtle, Colin G. and Vernon W. Ruttan (1987), *The Role of Demand and Supply in the Generation and Diffusion of Technical Change*, Chur: Harwood Academic Publishers.

42 New directions in Schumpeterian growth theory*
Elias Dinopoulos and Fuat Şener

1 Introduction

Schumpeterian growth is a particular type of economic growth which is based on the process of creative destruction.* The process of creative destruction was described in the writings of Joseph Schumpeter (1928, 1942) and refers to the endogenous introduction of new products and/or processes. For instance, in *Capitalism, Socialism and Democracy*, chapter 8, Schumpeter states:

> The essential point to grasp is that in dealing with capitalism we are dealing with an evolutionary process . . . The fundamental impulse that sets and keeps the capitalist engine in motion comes from the new consumer goods, the new methods of production, or transportation, the new forms of industrial organization that capitalist enterprise creates . . . In the case of retail trade the competition that matters arises not from additional shops of the same type, but from the department store, the chain store, the mail-order house and the super market, which are bound to destroy those pyramids sooner or later. Now a theoretical construction which neglects this essential element of the case neglects all that is most typically capitalist about it; even if correct in logic as well as in fact, it is like *Hamlet* without the Danish prince.

In other words, the essential feature of Schumpeterian growth models is the incorporation of technological progress which is generated by the endogenous introduction of product and/or process innovations. The term 'endogenous' refers to innovations that result from conscious actions undertaken by economic agents (firms or consumers) to maximize their objective function (profits or utility). Although Schumpeterian growth theory formalizes only a subset of Schumpeter's ideas, it is much closer to the concept of creative destruction than other existing economic growth theories.[1]

The birth of Schumpeterian growth theory came in the late 1980s and early 1990s with the publication of four articles and its rapid development has followed the general evolutionary process of creative destruction.[2] The merit and robustness of key assumptions of earlier models have been

*   Elias Dinopoulos would like to thank the Center for International Business Education and Research at the University of Florida for providing partial financial support. We would also like to thank Paul Segerstrom for very useful comments and suggestions.

questioned; certain implications have been tested and rejected; and state-of-the-art analytical techniques have resulted in new and more versatile models. Until the mid-1990s, growth theory witnessed a renaissance fueled by a rapidly expanding Schumpeterian growth literature under the label of 'endogenous' growth. Hundreds of articles and at least three textbooks analyzed various features of the 'new' growth theory, focusing on the effects of policies on long-run growth and welfare.[3]

By the mid-1990s, the development of the theory reached a blind intersection. In two influential articles, Jones (1995a, 1995b) argued that earlier Schumpeterian growth models incorporate a scale-effects property: the rate of technological progress is assumed to be proportional to the level of R&D investment services (which in turn are produced with a standard constant-returns-to-scale production function). For instance, if one doubles all R&D inputs, then the level of R&D investment doubles as well. This scale-related property implies that an economy's long-run per capita growth rate increases in its size, measured by the level of population. In the presence of positive population growth, the scale-effects property implies that per capita growth rate increases exponentially over time and it becomes infinite in the steady-state equilibrium. Jones argued that the scale-effects property is inconsistent with time-series evidence from several advanced countries. This evidence shows that resources devoted to R&D have been increasing exponentially, but the growth rates of total factor productivity and per capita output remain roughly constant over time.

The Jones critique raises the following fundamental questions: is the scale-effects property empirically relevant? Can one construct Schumpeterian growth models with positive population growth and bounded long-run growth? Can one develop scale-invariant Schumpeterian growth models which maintain the policy endogeneity of long-run growth? Affirmative answers to these questions are crucial for the evolution of Schumpeterian growth theory, for the following reasons. First, removal of the scale-effects property enhances the empirical relevance of the theory. Second, scale-invariant Schumpeterian growth models with endogenous technological change represent one more step towards a unified growth theory which would eventually combine the insights of neoclassical and Schumpeterian growth theories. Third, the development of scale-invariant long-run endogenous growth theory enhances their policy relevance and brings the theory closer to the spirit of Joseph Schumpeter (1937), who stated: 'There must be a purely economic theory of economic change which does not merely rely on external factors propelling the economic system from one equilibrium to another. It is such a theory . . . that I have tried to build . . . [and that] explains a number of phenomena, in particular the business cycle, more satisfactorily than it is possible to explain them by means of either the Walrasian or the Marshalian apparatus.'

This chapter intends to introduce the reader to the recent developments in Schumpeterian growth theory and to provide several useful insights on the scale-effects property. The rest of the chapter is organized as follows. Section 2 uses a simple analytical framework borrowed from Dinopoulos and Thompson (1999) and Jones (1999) to highlight the mathematics and economics of the scale-effects property and to illustrate three basic approaches to generating scale-invariant Schumpeterian growth. Section 3 offers an assessment of scale-invariant Schumpeterian growth models. Section 4 offers several concluding remarks and suggestions for further research.

2   An anatomy of scale effects

The scale-effects property in Schumpeterian growth models is related to two fundamental modeling building blocks: an economy's knowledge production function and its resource constraint. The former links the growth rate of knowledge (which is identical to the growth rate of technology) to R&D resources via a constant-returns-to-scale production function.[4] The latter requires that the sum of resources devoted to all activities must not exceed the available supply of these resources at each instant in time.

We can illustrate the role of the knowledge production function and the resource constraint by considering the simplest possible version of a Schumpeterian growth model. Consider an economy in which final output is produced by the following production function:

$$Y(t) = A(t)L_Y(t), \qquad (42.1)$$

where $Y(t)$ is the economy's final output at time t, $A(t)$ is the level of technology and $L_Y(t)$ is the amount of labor devoted to manufacturing of $Y(t)$. The following knowledge production function governs the evolution of technological progress:

$$g_A \equiv \frac{\dot{A}(t)}{A(t)} = \frac{L_A(t)}{X(t)}, \qquad (42.2)$$

where g_A denotes the growth rate of technology, $L_A(t)$ is the amount of aggregate resources devoted to R&D (i.e., the economy's scientists and engineers), and $X(t)$ is a measure of R&D difficulty. Higher values of $X(t)$ imply that the same amount of R&D resources generates a lower growth rate of technology.[5] In other words, the inverse of $X(t)$ is the total factor productivity in R&D. As will become clear below, assumptions that govern the evolution of $X(t)$ play a crucial role in regulating the scale-effects property and in conditioning the nature of long-run Schumpeterian growth.

For the time being, assume that labor is the only factor of production, and that the production of $X(t)$ does not require any economic resources. Under these two assumptions, the economy's resource constraint can be expressed by the following full-employment-of-labor condition:

$$L_Y(t) + L_A(t) = L(t), \tag{42.3}$$

where $L(t) = L_0 e^{tg_L}$ denotes the level of labor force (population) at time t, which is one measure of the economy's size; and $g_L > 0$ is the rate of population growth. The resource condition states that at each instant in time the amount of labor devoted to manufacturing plus the amount of labor devoted to R&D equals the economy's labor force.

Denote with $s(t) = L_Y(t)/L(t)$ the share of labor force employed in manufacturing. Equation (42.1) implies that the economy's per capita income is $y(t) = Y(t)/L(t) = A(t)s(t)$. Since $s(t)$ is bounded from above by one and from below by zero, it must be constant at the steady-state equilibrium (i.e., $s(t) = s$) and thus the long-run growth rate of output per capita is given by

$$g_y \equiv \frac{\dot{y}(t)}{y(t)} = \frac{\dot{A}(t)}{A(t)} = (1 - s)\frac{L(t)}{X(t)}, \tag{42.4}$$

where equations (42.2) and (42.3) along with $s(t) = L_Y(t)/L(t)$ were used to derive the right-hand-side of equation (42.4). Equation (42.4) states that the steady-state growth rate of output per capita equals the growth rate of technology. The latter is directly proportional to the economy's size, measured by the level of population $L(t)$, and inversely proportional to the level of R&D difficulty $X(t)$.

Dividing both sides of the resource condition (42.3) by the level of population and substituting $L_A(t) = g_A X(t)$, – see equation (42.2) – yields the following per capita resource condition:

$$s + g_A \frac{X(t)}{L(t)} = 1. \tag{42.5}$$

Equations (42.4) and (42.5) illustrate the basic building blocks of Schumpeterian growth models and hold at each instant in time independent of market structure considerations and independent of whether technological progress takes the form of variety accumulation or quality improvements. In the steady-state equilibrium, the share of labor devoted to manufacturing, s, and the growth rate of technological progress, g_A, must be constant over time. Consequently, the level of per capita R&D difficulty captured by the ratio $X(t)/L(t)$ must be constant in the long run.

2.1   Earlier Schumpeterian growth models

Earlier models of Schumpeterian growth generate endogenous long-run growth by adopting two basic assumptions. First, they assume that the labor force is constant over time, i.e., $g_L = 0$, and thus $L(t) = L_0$ in equations (42.4) and (42.5). Second, they typically assume that the R&D difficulty is a constant parameter, i.e., $X(t) = X_0$. These two assumptions imply that $X(t)/L(t) = X_0/L_0$ is constant over time and therefore equations (42.4) and (42.5) hold. In addition, it is obvious from equation (42.4) that long-run Schumpeterian growth is bounded and that any policy that alters the level of R&D resources, $L_A = (1 - s)L_0$, affects the rate of long-run growth g_A. Consequently, long-run Schumpeterian growth is endogenous in these models.

Romer (1990) developed such an endogenous Schumpeterian growth model based on horizontal product differentiation in which variety accumulation in intermediate capital goods drives the evolution of technological change. Segerstrom, Anant and Dinopoulos (1990), Aghion and Howitt (1992) and Grossman and Helpman (1991a, 1991b) set up the foundations for the development of the quality-ladders Schumpeterian growth model in which quality improvements based on stochastic and sequential R&D races constitute the source of endogenous growth. An extensive body of literature developed further the insights of these earlier Schumpeterian growth models.[6]

Jones (1995a) criticized the empirical relevance of this class of Schumpeterian growth models by focusing on the above-mentioned assumptions. He pointed out that various measures of per capita growth, such as the growth rate of total factor productivity, the flow of patents, and even the growth rate of income per capita, have remained roughly constant over time, whereas resources devoted to R&D, such as the number of scientists and engineers, have been increasing exponentially over time.

In the presence of positive population growth, i.e., $g_L > 0$, the right-hand side of (42.2) and (42.4) grows exponentially over time at the rate of population growth, but this leads to unbounded long-run growth of per capita output. In other words, under the assumption that $X(t) = X_0$, as the scale of the economy increases, so does the *rate* of long-run Schumpeterian growth. This unrealistic prediction is evident in the knowledge production function (42.4) and the resource condition (42.5), which represent two sides of the scale-effects–property coin. Following Jones's (1995a) critique, it became clear to growth theorists that there are strong theoretical and empirical arguments that call for the removal of scale effects from earlier Schumpeterian growth models.

2.2   Exogenous Schumpeterian growth models without scale effects

The first approach to the removal of scale effects employs the notion of *diminishing technological opportunities*. Jones (1995b) adopted this notion in a variety-expansion growth model à la Romer (1990), Segerstrom (1998) used the same approach in a quality-ladders Schumpeterian growth model, and Kortum (1997) provided theoretical foundations for the assumption of diminishing technological opportunities. The present framework can illustrate this approach by assuming that the level of R&D difficulty $X(t)$ increases over time as the level of technology $A(t)$ rises:

$$X(t) = A(t)^{1/\varphi}, \tag{42.6}$$

where $\varphi > 0$ is a constant parameter that captures the degree of diminishing technological opportunities. In Schumpeterian growth models of vertical product differentiation, the scale-effects property is removed by assuming that the level of R&D difficulty increases as R&D investment accumulates over time in each industry during an R&D race (Segerstrom, 1998) or when the R&D race ends and innovation occurs (Li, 2003). It is obvious from equations (42.4) and (42.5) that, since $X(t)/L(t)$ must be constant over time in the steady-state equilibrium, the growth rate of R&D difficulty must be equal to the exogenous growth rate of population, that is $\dot{X}(t)/X(t) = \dot{L}(t)/L(t) = g_L$. Equation (42.6) implies that the rate of growth of $X(t)$ is proportional to the rate of growth of technology: $\dot{X}(t)/X(t) = g_A/\varphi$. Combining these two expressions yields the basic result of this strand of literature:

$$g_A = \varphi g_L. \tag{42.7}$$

The growth rate of technology (and per capita income) is proportional to the exogenous population growth rate with the proportionality factor given by the parameter φ. The economic intuition associated with equation (42.7) is as follows: in the steady-state equilibrium because of diminishing returns to R&D efforts, individual researchers become less productive as the level of knowledge increases over time. To maintain a constant rate of innovation and growth, there must be an expansion in the employment of researchers. This is possible only if the economy's population is growing at a positive rate. If φ approaches zero, the level of R&D difficulty approaches infinity and economic growth stops. If φ approaches infinity, the level of R&D difficulty approaches unity and is time invariant. In this case, as the level of population increases exponentially, long-run Schumpeterian growth approaches infinity.

Since the population growth rate g_L and the parameter φ are not affected by policies by assumption, this class of models generates exogenous

Schumpeterian growth without scale effects. It should be emphasized, though, that, unlike the neoclassical model in which the rate of technological change is assumed to be constant in the short and long run, exogenous Schumpeterian growth models generate changes in the rate of technological change during the transition to the steady-state equilibrium. To see this, define per capita R&D difficulty as $x = X(t)/L(t)$, which implies that $\dot{x}/x = (g_A/\varphi) - g_L$. Notice that the resource condition defines the steady-state value of x as a function of the model's parameters. If a change in a policy-related parameter increases the steady-state value of x, then, during the transition to the new long-run equilibrium, $\dot{x} > 0$. This means that $g_A(t) > \varphi g_L$, that is, there must be a temporary acceleration in the rate of technological change.[7] In addition, these models are relatively simple to handle and generate interesting welfare results.

2.3 Endogenous scale-invariant Schumpeterian growth models

The second approach to the scale-effects problem employs a two-dimensional framework with horizontal and vertical product differentiation. Horizontal product differentiation takes the form of variety accumulation and removes the scale-effects property from these models in a way similar to the one used by exogenous Schumpeterian growth models. Vertical product differentiation takes the form of quality improvements or process innovations and generates endogenous long-run growth. This approach postulates a proportional relationship between (aggregate) R&D difficulty and the number of varieties. Under the right market structure assumptions the number of varieties, in turn, can be shown to be proportional to the size of population.

Consequently, a linear relationship emerges between R&D difficulty and the size of population which removes the scale-effects property and hence establishes the *variety-expansion* mechanism. The variety-expansion approach was suggested independently by Peretto (1998), where vertical product differentiation takes the form of process innovations, and Young (1998), where vertical product differentiation is modeled as quality improvements. Aghion and Howitt (1998, ch. 12), Dinopoulos and Thompson (1998) and Howitt (1999) have further developed this approach.

To illustrate the variety-expansion approach to the scale-effects problem, we need to introduce a bit of additional economic structure to the basic framework. Consider an economy consisting of $n(t)$ structurally-identical industries (firms) producing horizontally differentiated products (varieties). Assume that each industry's output is given by $z(t) = A_\iota(t)\ell_z$, where $z(t)$ is the industry-specific output, $A_\iota(t)$ is the industry-specific level of technology and ℓ_z is the number of manufacturing workers employed in a typical industry. The knowledge production function in a typical industry is

$$g_\iota \equiv \frac{\dot{A}_\iota(t)}{A_\iota(t)} = \ell_A, \tag{42.8}$$

where g_ι is the rate of industry-specific technological change, and ℓ_A is the number of R&D researchers employed in a typical industry. Equation (42.8) implies that the evolution of technological change *within* an industry exhibits scale effects: if the number of researchers ℓ_A doubles, then the growth rate of technology doubles as well.

The aggregate level of output in this economy is given by $Y(t) = z(t)n(t) = A_\iota(t)\ell_z n(t)$. Therefore, the growth rate of per capita output $y(t) = Y(t)/L(t)$ is given by

$$g_y \equiv \frac{\dot{y}(t)}{y(t)} = \frac{\dot{A}_\iota(t)}{A_\iota(t)} + \frac{\dot{n}(t)}{n(t)} - g_L = \ell_A + \frac{\dot{n}(t)}{n(t)} - g_L. \tag{42.9}$$

Observe that constant steady-state growth rate g_Y requires that both ℓ_A and $\dot{n}(t)/n(t)$ remain constant over time.

We follow Aghion and Howitt (1998, ch. 12) and propose a simple mechanism to determine the evolution of $n(t)$. Assume that the number of varieties $n(t)$ grows over time as a result of serendipitous imitation. Each imitation results in a new industry with the same technology level as the other industries. Each person in the economy has the same exogenous instantaneous probability of imitation ξdt, where ξ is the intensity of the Poisson process that governs the arrival of new varieties. This implies that $\dot{n}(t) = \xi L(t)$. For $\dot{n}(t)/n(t) = \xi L(t)/n(t)$ to be constant, $n(t)$ must grow at the rate of $L(t)$, which equals the population growth rate g_L. This implies that the per capita number of varieties $n(t)/L(t)$ converges to the constant ξ/g_L, which establishes

$$n(t) = [\xi/g_L]L(t) = \beta L(t), \tag{42.10}$$

where $\beta = \xi/g_L$ is used to simplify the expression. It is important to emphasize that the linear relationship between the number of varieties and the level of population is derived from a market-based mechanism with solid micro foundations. For instance, Young (1998, equation 17) generates a version of equation (42.10) under the standard assumptions of monopolistic competition and fixed-entry costs.[8]

Adopting the Aghion and Howitt (1998) mechanism, we can write the economy-wide resource constraint as $\ell_z n(t) + \ell_A n(t) = L(t)$, which states that at each instant in time manufacturing and R&D labor must be equal to the level of population. Substituting (42.10) in this expression yields the following per capita resource condition:

$$\ell_z + \ell_A = \frac{1}{\beta}.$$

(42.11)

In the steady-state equilibrium, the amount of labor devoted to manufacturing ℓ_Z and R&D ℓ_A activities within each industry must be constant over time. This implies that the increase in the level of population is absorbed by the proportional expansion of varieties (industries). Substituting $\dot{n}(t)/n(t) = g_L$ in (42.9) implies that the long-run growth rate of per capita output is:

$$g_y = \frac{\dot{A}_\iota(t)}{A_\iota(t)} = \ell_A.$$

(42.12)

Any policy that changes the allocation of labor between manufacturing and R&D within each industry affects long-run growth. In this sense, the removal of scale effects through the variety-expansion approach generates endogenous scale-invariant long-run Schumpeterian growth. If final output is given by a CES production function, say

$$Y = \left(\int_0^n z(i)^{1/\rho} di \right)^\rho$$

where $\rho > 1$, then substituting the corresponding expressions for $z(t)$, and using (42.12) yields the following expression for long-run Schumpeterian growth: $g_y = \ell_A + (\rho - 1)g_L$. In addition to the endogenous component of long-run growth, an exogenous component, proportional to the rate of population growth, is added to the long-run growth expression.

The relationship between the level of R&D difficulty $X(t)$ and the number of varieties $n(t)$ can be readily established if one assumes an aggregate knowledge production function as before:

$$g_A \equiv \frac{\dot{A}(t)}{A(t)} = \frac{L_A(t)}{X(t)} = \frac{\ell_A n(t)}{X(t)},$$

(42.13)

where $A(t)$ is the economy-wide level of technology and $L_A(t) = \ell_A n(t)$ is the economy-wide amount of labor devoted to R&D. If ℓ_A is constant, then bounded steady-state growth requires that the level of R&D difficulty grow at the rate of variety expansion, which in turn equals the rate of population growth; that is, $\dot{X}(t)/X(t) = \dot{n}(t)/n(t) = g_L$. This implies a linear relationship between the level of R&D difficulty and the size of population

$$X(t) = \kappa L(t),$$

(42.14)

where $\kappa > 0$ is an inconsequential positive parameter. It is clear from the above discussion that R&D is becoming more difficult as the number of varieties expands in such a way that the amount of resources per industry remains constant over time.

The third approach to the removal of scale effects employs the notion of Rent Protection Activities (RPAs). This novel approach has been proposed by Dinopoulos and Syropoulos (2006) in the context of a quality-ladders Schumpeterian-growth model developed by Grossman and Helpman (1991a). In quality-ladders models, there is a continuum of structurally identical industries covering the unit interval. In each industry the state-of-the-art quality product is produced by an incumbent monopolist who earns temporary economic profits (rents). Challengers raise claims to these rents by engaging in R&D investment to discover a higher-quality product and replace the incumbent monopolist. The latter has strong incentives to devote resources in various activities to protect her/his intellectual property and prolong the duration of temporary monopoly rents. Examples of RPAs include investments in trade secrecy, increasing the complexity of the product to reduce knowledge spillovers to potential challengers, expenditures to sustain legal teams to litigate patent infringement disputes and so on. In models that adopt the rent-protection approach to the removal of scale effects, the discovery of new products in each industry is governed by sequential stochastic innovation contests (as opposed to R&D races). Challengers choose the level of R&D investment and incumbents choose the level of RPAs. The level of R&D difficulty $X(t)$ is assumed to be directly proportional to the level of RPAs, and therefore it is endogenous.

We can illustrate the RPA approach to scale-invariant endogenous Schumpeterian growth by using our basic framework. Following Dinopoulos and Thompson (1999), one can model the level of technology in quality-ladders growth models as $A(t) = \lambda^{q(t)}$, where $\lambda > 1$ is a parameter measuring the size of each innovation and $q(t)$ is the expected number of innovations at time t in a typical industry. There is a continuum of independent, structurally-identical industries covering the unit interval. The expected flow of innovations per unit (instant) of time is governed by a Poisson process with intensity $I(t)$. Following Segerstrom (1998), we model the intensity of the Poisson process as $I(t) = L_A(t)/X(t)$, where $L_A(t)$ is the industry (and economy)-wide level of resources devoted to R&D, and $X(t)$ is the level of R&D difficulty. The assumption of a continuum of industries implies that aggregate growth is deterministic and the number of economy-wide innovations $q(t)$ obeys the differential equation $\dot{q}(t) = I(t)$. Taking logs and differentiating the level of technology $A(t)$ and substituting the above derived expressions yields an aggregate knowledge production function in quality-ladders Schumpeterian growth models:

$$g_A \equiv \frac{\dot{A}(t)}{A(t)} = [\log\lambda]I(t) = [\log\lambda]\frac{L_A(t)}{X(t)}. \tag{42.15}$$

Assume now that rent-protection services are produced using labor only that is specific to the production of these activities, say, lawyers. For simplicity of exposition, suppose that one unit of lawyer produces one unit of RPAs. The aggregate supply of lawyers $H(t)$ is an exogenous fraction of population; thus, $H(t) = \theta L(t)$, where $0 < \theta < 1$ is a parameter. The remaining fraction of the labor force $1 - \theta$ constitutes the supply of non-specialized labor which is allocated between manufacturing and R&D activities: $L_Y(t) + L_A(t) = (1 - \theta)L(t)$. Let $R(t)$ represent the level of industry-wide (and economy-wide) RPA. If one assumes that $X(t) = \beta R(t)$ with $\beta > 0$, which means that the level of R&D difficulty $X(t)$ is proportional to level of RPAs, then the full-employment condition for specialized labor is given by

$$X(t) = [\beta\theta]L(t). \tag{42.16}$$

Substituting equation (42.16) into (42.15) yields the main result of the RPA approach

$$g_A \equiv \frac{\dot{A}(t)}{A(t)} = \left[\frac{\log\lambda}{\beta\theta}\right]\left[\frac{L_A(t)}{L(t)}\right]. \tag{42.17}$$

Dividing both sides of the full-employment condition for non-specialized labor by the level of population and using (42.15) yields, with the exception of inconsequential constant parameters, equation (42.5). Equation (42.16) ensures that the per capita full-employment condition for non-specialized labor holds independently of whether or not there is positive population growth.

In the steady-state equilibrium, as the supply of labor increases exponentially, both the equilibrium number of R&D researchers employed by challengers and the number of lawyers employed by incumbents rise exponentially. The two effects cancel each other and the scale-effects property is removed. Notice that (42.17) does not depend on the population growth rate and holds even if the level of population is constant over time. The long-run growth rate of technology (and per capita utility) depends positively on the size of innovations, and on the share of labor devoted to R&D. Any policy that shifts resources from manufacturing to R&D activities increases the level of long-run Schumpeterian growth. In addition, changes in the effectiveness of RPAs (captured by β) or changes in the fraction of population engaged in RPAs (captured by θ) affect the rate of long-run growth.

3 An assessment

In this section we offer a few remarks which provide an admittedly subjective assessment of scale-invariant Schumpeterian growth models. The first remark has to do with a somewhat exaggerated criticism directed at the functional robustness of scale-invariant Schumpeterian growth models. Notice the striking similarity between equations (42.14) and (42.16). In both classes of endogenous Schumpeterian growth models, the level of R&D difficulty is a linear function of the level of population. This linear functional form has been characterized as a 'knife-edge' property that is unsatisfactory because it lacks functional robustness (see Jones, 1999, and especially Li, 2000, 2002).

We believe that the emphasis on functional robustness is rather misguided and it is largely based on a natural tendency to differentiate newly developed models from old ones. Even if one views (42.14) and (42.16) as knife-edge features, there are many examples of knife-edge properties and assumptions in economic theory. A case in point is the assumption of constant returns to scale, which requires that, if all inputs of production double, then output exactly doubles. This assumption has been used routinely to support perfectly competitive markets in a variety of contexts including neoclassical growth theory.[9] Another well accepted knife-edge property is the saddle-path stability condition as shown in the Cass–Koopmans–Ramsey version of the neoclassical growth model and in Segerstrom's (1998) scale-invariant growth model (among numerous others).

Finally, Temple (2003) points out that, in the steady-state equilibrium, the neoclassical growth model allows only labor-augmenting technological progress or the employment of a Cobb–Douglas aggregate production function.[10]

Another defense of the linear relationship between the level of R&D difficulty and the level of population is based on the following conjecture: *for any approach that generates scale-invariant endogenous Schumpeterian growth, there exists a market-based mechanism that determines endogenously the evolution of R&D difficulty.* In the variety-expansion approach, profit-maximization considerations coupled with market-driven free entry of monopolistically competitive firms establish the required linearity between $X(t)$ and the level of population $L(t)$. In the rent-protection approach, the optimal choice of RPAs by the typical monopolist to maximize expected discounted profits generates this linear relationship. In contrast, exogenous Schumpeterian growth models assume that the level of R&D difficulty is tied to the level of technology and, therefore, is not directly market-determined.

The following remark on the 'functional robustness' debate is borrowed from Temple (2003), who offers an excellent and insightful discussion on the long-run implications of growth theory. In the conclusion of his paper he states the following 'Five Obvious Rules for Thinking about Long-Run Growth':

> 1) Remember that the long-run is a theoretical abstraction that is sometimes of limited practical value. 2) Do not assume that a good model of growth has to yield a balanced growth path, or that long-run growth has to be endogenous. 3) Do not dismiss a model of growth because the long-run outcomes depend on knife-edge assumptions. 4) Remember that long-run predictions may be impossible to test. It will be extremely difficult to distinguish between models based on their predictions about long-run outcomes. 5) Do not undervalue level effects.

We fully agree with Temple's point of view that the knife-edge assumptions of endogenous growth models should be seen in a forgiving light and the emphasis should be placed on their comparative statics and especially the welfare properties of Schumpeterian growth models.

These remarks lead us to the following suggestion. Analyzing the steady-state equilibrium properties of Schumpeterian growth models is still very useful because it is simply easier to analyze the long-run equilibrium than transitional dynamics. We propose a shift from debating the robustness of particular assumptions in specific models to assessing the robustness of policy changes across various models, including those that carry the scale-effects property. For example, consider the current controversial issue of the dynamic effects of globalization on relative wage income inequality between advanced (North) and poor (South) countries. If one models globalization as an increase in the size of the South (motivated by China's entry into the world trading system), then the following three quality-ladders growth models of North–South product-cycle trade provide specific answers to this question. Grossman and Helpman (1991c), using an endogenous Schumpeterian growth model with scale effects, find that an increase in the size of the South does not affect the relative wage of Northern workers.[11] Şener (2002) uses a scale-invariant endogenous Schumpeterian growth model based on RPAs to establish that globalization increases the relative wage of Northern workers. Dinopoulos and Segerstrom (2006) employ a scale-invariant exogenous Schumpeterian growth model to establish that an increase in the size of the South reduces the relative wage of Northern workers. Could one trace these different predictions to knife-edge assumptions? We seriously doubt that this can be achieved without examining in more detail the structure of each model.

Our final remark has to do with the terminology employed in the present chapter compared to that used by other growth researchers. Following the path-breaking work of Romer (1990), earlier Schumpeterian growth models established what was called endogenous growth theory. This normative (policy-related) term quickly became popular because it accurately captured the property that in these earlier Schumpeterian growth models policy changes affected long-run per capita growth. In contrast, the neoclassical growth model predicts that per capita long-run growth is policy invariant. The development of scale-invariant growth models generated a class of growth models in which policy changes do not affect long-run growth, making the term 'endogenous' growth somewhat fuzzy and inaccurate. We believe that the policy-neutral term 'Schumpeterian growth' describes accurately and clearly all four classes of growth models and offers the well-deserved and long overdue credit to Joseph Schumpeter.

4 Conclusions

The present chapter provided an overview of recent developments in Schumpeterian growth theory, which envisions economic growth through the endogenous introduction of new products and/or processes. A simple theoretical framework was utilized to illustrate the scale-effects property of first-generation Schumpeterian growth models and to describe somewhat more formally the new directions of the theory. Three classes of Schumpeterian models generate scale-invariant long-run growth, depending on how the R&D difficulty is modeled. The diminishing technological opportunities approach generates exogenous long-run Schumpeterian growth, whereas the variety-expansion and the rent-protection approaches yield endogenous long-run growth. We offered our own conjecture on what we believe is the distinguishing feature of endogenous and exogenous scale-invariant Schumpeterian growth models: for any endogenous scale-invariant growth approach, there exists a market-based mechanism that directly determines the evolution of R&D difficulty endogenously. One interesting direction of future research is to establish formally the validity of this conjecture.

The development of scale-invariant Schumpeterian growth models draws legitimacy from three important considerations. First, the scale-effects property embodied in earlier models yields the counterfactual prediction that increasing R&D inputs generate higher long-run growth. This prediction is inconsistent with time-series evidence from several advanced countries. Second, in the presence of positive population growth, models with scale effects generate infinite per capita long-run growth. This is clearly unsatisfactory for researchers who are interested in analyzing the long-run properties of growth models. Third, scale-invariant growth models represent another important step towards a unified growth theory that combines the robustness and empirical relevance of the neoclassical growth model and the Schumpeterian mechanism of creative destruction. For instance, Jones (1995b) and Aghion and Howitt (1998, ch. 12) have already developed such integrated-growth models. More work in this exciting and important direction is needed.

We view first and second generation Schumpeterian growth models as horizontally differentiated approaches to Schumpeterian growth theory. Time and more research will tell which of these new directions will survive the process of creative destruction. This process has already started with the development of scale-invariant growth models that offer new insights in the fields of public policy, macroeconomics, international economics and economic development. Space limitations do not allow a survey of this rapidly expanding strand of growth literature, and therefore we have to classify this important task as a direction for future research in the field of Schumpeterian economics.

Notes

1. For instance, the neoclassical growth model assumes exogenous technological progress, the AK growth model focuses on the role of physical capital accumulation, and the Lucas (1988) model of growth emphasizes the importance of knowledge spillovers in the process of human-capital accumulation.
2. The four studies that developed the foundations of Schumpeterian growth theory are Romer (1990), Segerstrom, Anant and Dinopoulos (1990), Grossman and Helpman (1991a) and Aghion and Howitt (1992). Dinopoulos (1994) provides an overview of earlier Schumpeterian growth models, and Romer (1994) offers an excellent account on the origins of this theory.
3. A survey of this literature lies beyond the scope of this chapter. The interested reader is referred to Grossman and Helpman (1991b), Barro and Sala-i-Martin (1995) and especially Aghion and Howitt (1998) for more details.
4. The reason that the growth rate of technology (as opposed to just the change in the level of technology) enters on the left-hand-side of the knowledge production function can be traced to the non-rivalry of ideas. Romer (1990) provides an excellent discussion on this basic difference between the production of goods and the generation of ideas.
5. Segerstrom (1998) was the first to introduce variable $X(t)$ in the knowledge production function of a scale-invariant Schumpeterian growth model based on quality improvements.
6. Aghion and Howitt (1998) provide an excellent exposition of this body of literature.
7. Since policy changes have *temporary effects on growth*, Dinopoulos and Segerstrom (1999) christen this specification as the TEG specification of R&D difficulty. Segerstrom (1998) and Dinopoulos and Segerstrom (1999) provide more details on the implications of the TEG specification for transitional dynamics.
8. A similar result has been obtained by Kelly (2001) in a Schumpeterian growth model that distinguishes between innovating and non-innovating industries and allows for spillovers from innovating industries to neighboring industries. In this model, knowledge spillovers from innovating industries located on the border of the industry space results in the creation of a new industry. Kelly finds that scale effects are removed if and only if the growth rate in the number of industries equals the growth rate of population.
9. Incidentally, the argument that endogenous Schumpeterian growth models require knife-edge conditions can be equivalent to criticizing the constant returns to scale property of the knowledge production function. To see this, consider for instance the variety expansion model of section 2.3 and assume that $\dot{n}(t) = \xi[(L(t)]^\alpha$, with $\alpha \neq 1$. It is straightforward to show that the rate of per capita income growth would then be equal to

$$g_y \equiv \ell_A + \frac{\dot{n}(t)}{n} - g_L = \phi L(t)^{1-\alpha} + (\alpha - 1)g_L \, ;$$

hence, the scale-effects property would emerge. Thus, if $0 < \alpha < 1$, growth increases exponentially as t goes to infinity. If $\alpha = 1$, then $\ell_A = \phi$, and growth is endogenous so long as ϕ can be affected by policy (original case). Finally if $\alpha > 1$, then $g_Y = (\alpha - 1)g_L$ as t goes to infinity. These results are similar to the ones presented in Jones (1999, p. 142).
10. Jones (2003) provides an excellent discussion of this issue.
11. They actually consider two regimes: efficient and inefficient followers regimes. Each one has different wage implications. In the efficient followers regime (the more general case), an increase in the size of the South does not change the relative wage. In the inefficient followers regime, the relative wage of the North moves in an ambiguous direction as the size of the South expands.

References

Aghion, P. and Howitt, P. (1992), 'A model of growth through creative destruction', *Econometrica*, **60**, 323–51.

Aghion, P. and Howitt, P. (1998), *Endogenous Growth Theory*, MIT Press.

Barro, R. and Sala-i-Martin, X. (1995), *Economic Growth*, McGraw-Hill.

Dinopoulos, E. (1994), 'Schumpeterian growth theory: an overview', *Osaka City University Economic Review*, **21**, 1–21.

Dinopoulos, E. and Segerstrom, P. (1999), 'A Schumpeterian model of protection and relative wages', *American Economic Review*, **89**, 450–72.

Dinopoulos, E. and Segerstrom, P. (2006), 'North–South trade and economic growth', mimeo, Stockholm School of Economics (available at http://bear.cba.ufl.edu/dinopoulos/Research.html).

Dinopoulos, E. and Syropoulos, C. (2006), 'Rent protection as a barrier to innovation and growth', *Economic Theory*, forthcoming (available at http://bear.cba.ufl.edu/dinopoulos/Research.html).

Dinopoulos, E. and Thompson, P. (1998), 'Schumpeterian growth without scale effects', *Journal of Economic Growth*, **3**, 313–35.

Dinopoulos, E. and Thompson, P. (1999), 'Scale effects in Schumpeterian models of economic growth', *Journal of Evolutionary Economics*, **9**, 157–85.

Grossman, G. and Helpman, E. (1991a), 'Quality ladders in the theory of growth', *Review of Economic Studies*, **58**, 43–61.

Grossman, G. and Helpman, E. (1991b), *Innovation and Growth in the Global Economy*, MIT Press.

Grossman, G. and Helpman, E. (1991c), 'Quality ladders and product cycles', *Quarterly Journal of Economics*, **106**, 557–86.

Howitt, P. (1999), 'Steady endogenous growth with population and R&D inputs growing', *Journal of Political Economy*, **107**, 715–30.

Jones, C. (1995a), 'Time series tests of endogenous growth models', *Quarterly Journal of Economics*, **110**, 495–525.

Jones, C. (1995b), 'R&D-based models of economic growth', *Journal of Political Economy*, **103**, 759–84.

Jones, C. (1999), 'Growth: with or without scale effects?', *American Economic Review Papers and Proceedings*, **89**, 139–44.

Jones, C. (2003), 'Growth, capital shares, and a new perspective on production functions', mimeo, UC Berkeley.

Kelly, M. (2001), 'Linkages, thresholds, and development', *Journal of Economic Growth*, **6**, 39–53.

Kortum, S. (1997), 'Research, patenting and technological change', *Econometrica*, **65**, 1389–419.

Li, C. (2000), 'Endogenous vs semi-endogenous growth in a two-R&D-sector model', *Economic Journal*, **110**, C109–C122.

Li, C. (2002), 'Growth and scale effects: the role of knowledge spillovers', *Economics Letters*, **74**, 177–85.

Li, C. (2003), 'Endogenous growth without scale effects: a comment', *American Economic Review*, **93**(3), 1009–17.

Lucas, R. (1988), 'On the mechanics of economic development', *Journal of Monetary Economics*, **22**(1), 3–42.

Peretto, P. (1998), 'Technological change and population growth', *Journal of Economic Growth*, **3**(4), 283–311.

Romer, P. (1990), 'Endogenous technological change', *Journal of Political Economy*, **98**(5), S71–S102.

Romer, P. (1994), 'The origins of endogenous growth', *Journal of Economic Perspectives*, **8**, 3–22.

Schumpeter, J. (1928), 'The instability of capitalism', in R. Clemence (ed.), *Joseph A. Schumpeter: Essays on Entrepreneurs, Innovations, Business Cycles and the Evolution of Capitalism*; reprinted Transaction Publishers, 1989.

Schumpeter, J. (1937), 'Preface to the Japanese edition of 'Theorie Der Wirtschaftlichen Entwicklung', in R. Clemence (ed.), *Joseph A. Schumpeter: Essays on Entrepreneurs, Innovations, Business Cycles and the Evolution of Capitalism*; reprinted Transaction Publishers, 1989.

Schumpeter, J. (1942), *Capitalism, Socialism and Democracy*, Harper and Row.

Segerstrom, P. (1998), 'Endogenous growth without scale effects', *American Economic Review*, **88**, 1290–310.

Segerstrom, P., Anant, T.C.A. and Dinopoulos, E. (1990), 'A Schumpeterian model of the product life cycle', *American Economic Review*, **80**, 1077–92.

Şener, F. (2006), 'Intellectual property rights and rent protection in a North–South product-cycle model', mimeo, Union College (available at http://www1.union.edu/~senerm/).

Temple, J. (2003), 'The long-run implications of growth theories', *Journal of Economic Surveys* **17**(3), 497–510.

Young, A. (1998), 'Growth without scale effects', *Journal of Political Economy*, **106**, 41–63.

43 The dynamics of technology, growth and trade: a Schumpeterian perspective

Jan Fagerberg

Introduction

Why did some countries, such as, for instance, Japan and some other Asian economies in the second half of the twentieth century, grow much faster, and have much better trade performance, than most other countries? Is superior trade performance, what is often termed 'competitiveness', a condition for faster growth, or is it of only minor importance compared to other factors? Although long-run economic change, what he termed 'development', was Schumpeter's favourite topic, he did not enter into the discussion of why some countries succeed better in this respect than others, and how trade interacts with such outcomes. However, it might be argued that his perspective would be highly relevant for the analysis of this topic (Fagerberg, 2002, Introduction). In fact, as we shall see in the next section, Schumpeter's theory of innovation-based growth, with technological competition as its driving force, has been quite influential in shaping the research agenda in this area. But although many contributions in this area did, to some extent, embrace Schumpeter's dynamic outlook, applied work in this area has often failed to take innovation properly into account. The third section of the chapter outlines a synthetic framework, based on Schumpeterian logic, for analysing what shapes differences in growth and competitiveness, with particular emphasis on the role played by innovation and diffusion of technology. This framework is shown to encompass many of the points that have been raised in the applied literature.

Schumpeterian renaissance

The decades that followed Schumpeter's death in 1950 constituted a low tide for his ideas and evolutionary economics more generally (Fagerberg, 2003). Instead economists gradually adopted formal, mathematical equilibrium models of the type that Schumpeter admired but had found to be of little value for understanding long-run economic and social change. In spite of this, Schumpeterian ideas soon started to emerge in applied work. The reason for this was, as Schumpeter would have expected, that the formal equilibrium models had very little to say about many real world phenomena. Hence applied researchers were forced to look elsewhere for guidance in interpreting observed developments in, for instance, economic growth and international trade.

The starting point for many of these efforts was the finding by Leontief (1953) that actual patterns of trade seemed to deviate from what the equilibrium approach would predict.[1] As a response to this challenge several authors (Posner, 1961; Hirsch, 1965; Vernon, 1966) came up with the suggestion that the reason had to do with the fact that innovation constantly disrupts the equilibrium forces, so that the observed pattern of international trade reflects the interaction between innovation and diffusion of technology on a global scale, rather than a given distribution of natural and/or man-made assets across different countries or regions. A particularly clear and influential account of this dynamics was the one presented by Posner (1961). The essence of his reasoning can be captured by a two-country model, in which one country is more innovative than the other (and consequently has a technological lead), while the other (the technological laggard) relies more on imitation. New technologies emerge in the technologically leading country, which for a period has a temporary monopoly. However, in the course of time, the technological laggard will learn to cope with these technologies as well, and competition between producers from the two countries will arise. Generally, the level of income will be higher in the leading country, with the size of the income gap depending on the size of the technological gap. Just as increased innovation in the leading country would tend to increase the income gap, intensified technological catch-up (increased speed of imitation) by the laggard would contribute to its reduction. Krugman, one of the contributors in this area, put it well when he drew the following consequence of this logic: 'Like Alice and the Red Queen, the developed region has to keep running to stay in the same place' (1979, p. 262).

The spread of Schumpeterian ideas among applied researchers resulted in the decades that followed Posner's seminal contribution in a large number of empirical studies focusing on innovation diffusion, growth and trade in various sectors/industries. While a lot of the empirical literature that followed was quite eclectic, during the 1980s a number of contributions emerged based more explicitly on Schumpeterian arguments. Much of this work was initiated by the Science Policy Research Unit (SPRU) at the University of Sussex (UK). Researchers at SPRU attempted to expand and generalize the existing work in this area to a more fully-fledged theory of the dynamics of technology, growth and trade, and to back it up with solid empirical evidence based on extensive use of data on technological activities, particularly R&D and patent statistics (Pavitt and Soete, 1982; Dosi and Soete, 1983; Dosi *et al.*, 1990). In this literature innovation was assumed to be the primary factor behind long-run differences in specialization patterns, trade performance and economic growth. Other, more 'conventional' factors, while relevant, were relegated to a secondary position or assumed to be of a more short-term nature.

However, the 'SPRU approach' was not the only current that gained popularity as a result of the apparent failure of the standard neoclassical approach to cope with observed economic phenomena. For instance, the economic historian Gerschenkron (1962) had, on the basis of his studies of European catch-up processes, suggested that the technological gap between a frontier and a latecomer country represented 'a great promise' for the latter, since it provided the latecomer with the opportunity of imitating more advanced technology in use elsewhere. However, because of the stringent requirements for successful imitation of advanced technology, Gerschenkron argued, the fulfilment of this promise would require sustained efforts by the latecomers to be realized. This perspective, which arguably has a strong Schumpeterian flavour, was adopted by, among others Abramovitz (1979, 1986, 1994) in a series of analyses of differences in cross-country growth performance over the long run, emphasizing in particular the scope for catch-up and the various 'capabilities' that latecomers needed to generate in order to avoid 'falling behind'. A similar argument, emphasizing in particular the crucial role played by investment for technological catch-up, was made by Cornwall (1977), in an analysis that probably was the first attempt to present econometric tests of what has since been dubbed 'conditional convergence'.[2] These ideas were later taken up by Baumol *et al.* (1989), focusing on the catch-up in education, and since then there has been a plethora of empirical exercises of this type (see Fagerberg, 1994, 2000 for overviews). However, although many of the contributions discussed so far did place emphasis on technological change, their modelling approach and subsequent empirical testing did not explicitly take innovation (or R&D) into account. Hence, it might be argued that these contributions failed to take into account a vital aspect of the evolutionary dynamics (Fagerberg, 1987, 1988a). We discuss this in more detail in the next section.

Still another approach to 'why growth rates differ', more Keynesian in flavour (Thirlwall, 1979; Kaldor, 1981), put emphasis on the growth of world demand, and on the 'income elasticities of demand' for a country's exports and imports, in determining a country's growth performance.[3] This way of reasoning was based on the Keynesian view of export demand as an 'autonomous' force that propelled growth through various multipliers (Beckerman, 1962; Kaldor, 1970). However, as pointed out by Thirlwall, projections based on such an approach might lead to a growth path that would not be sustainable, for instance because it might imply an ever-increasing foreign debt. This, he suggested, could be remedied by introducing a restriction on the balance of trade, assuming, for instance, that governments would adjust fiscal and monetary policies towards this end (Thirlwall, 1979). In this model the growth of an open economy was shown to depend on growth of international trade, changes in relative prices (price competitiveness) and the ratio of the income elasticity of exports to that of imports. Thus, everything else assumed constant, the higher the income elasticity of exports relative to that of imports, the higher the rate of growth, and vice versa. However, as pointed out by Kaldor, these elasticities, allegedly reflecting the importance of so-called 'non-price factors', were themselves in need of explanation.[4] He argued, 'in a growing world economy the growth of exports is mainly to be explained by the income elasticity of foreign countries for a country's products; but it is a matter of the innovative ability and adaptive capacity of its manufacturers whether this income elasticity will tend to be large or small' (Kaldor, 1981, p. 603). Consistent with this argument, Fagerberg (1988b), in a contribution to be discussed in more detail in the next section, suggested including indicators of technological competitiveness (or innovative ability and adaptive capacity) directly in the equations for exports and imports.

As is evident from the above discussion, the Schumpeterian emphasis on innovation and diffusion as the source of growth (and technological competition as the mechanism through which this happens) came to have a strong influence on the research agenda in this area from the 1960s onwards, particularly among empirically oriented researchers. The influence on 'high theory' – the highly mathematized formal equilibrium models that Schumpeter admired but found of little use in his endeavours – came much later, around 1990, and although it had a big impact in that particular field, the resulting theoretical models have had surprisingly little impact on the applied agenda. For the sake of space we will not discuss the contribution from this modelling tradition in detail here, although we will visit it briefly later in the chapter.[5] What we will do in the following is present a synthetic framework for empirical analysis, based on earlier work by Fagerberg (1988a, 1988b), that encompasses a number of the points raised by the contributions discussed so far.

A synthetic framework
We will start by developing a very simple growth model based on Schumpeterian logic, which we will subsequently extend and refine. Assume that the GDP of a country (Y) is a multiplicative function of its technological knowledge (Q) and its capacity for exploiting the benefits of knowledge (C), and a constant (A_1):[6]

$$Y = A_1 Q^\alpha C^\beta \qquad (\alpha, \beta > 0). \qquad (43.1)$$

Its knowledge, in turn, is assumed to be a multiplicative function of knowledge diffused to the region from outside (D) and knowledge (or innovation) created in the region (N) and, again, a constant (A_2):

$$Q = A_2 D^\gamma N^\lambda \qquad (\gamma, \lambda > 0). \qquad (43.2)$$

Assume further, as is common in the literature, that the diffusion of external knowledge follows a logistic curve. This implies that the contribution of diffusion of externally available knowledge to economic growth is an increasing function of the distance between the level of knowledge appropriated in the country and that of the country on the technological frontier (for the frontier country, this contribution will be zero by definition). Let the total amount of knowledge, adjusted for differences in size of countries, in the frontier country and the country under consideration, be T_* and T, respectively:

$$d = \phi - \phi \frac{T}{T_*} \qquad (\phi > 0). \qquad (43.3)$$

By differentiating (43.2), using lower-case letters for growth-rates, and substituting (43.3) into it, we arrive at the following expression for the growth of a country's technological knowledge:

$$q = \gamma\phi - \gamma\phi \frac{T}{T_*} + \lambda n. \qquad (43.4)$$

By differentiating (43.1) and substituting (43.4) into it, we get the country's rate of growth:

$$y = \alpha\gamma\phi - \alpha\gamma\phi \frac{T}{T_*} + \alpha\lambda n + \beta c. \qquad (43.5)$$

Since our primary interest is in 'why growth rates differ', it may be useful to express the rate of growth of the country in relative terms (growth relative to the world average), y_{rel}:[7]

$$y_{rel} = y - w = -\alpha\gamma\phi \frac{T - T_w}{T_*} + \alpha\lambda(n - n_w) + \beta(c - c_w). \qquad (43.6)$$

Hence, following this perspective, the rate of growth of a country may be seen as the outcome of three sets of factors: (a) the potential for exploiting knowledge developed elsewhere, (b) creation of new knowledge in the country (innovation), and (c) complementary factors affecting the ability to exploit the potential entailed by knowledge (independently of where it is created).

The above model, simple as it is, encompasses many of the empirical models found in the literature. For instance, the empirical models used in the 'catching-up' literature (see, e.g., Baumol *et al.* 1989) can be seen as a version of (43.5)–(43.6) in which the innovation term is ignored. Fagerberg (1987, 1988a) applied this model to a sample of developed and medium-income countries, and showed that all three factors, innovation, diffusion and complementary capabilities, mattered for growth. It was shown that countries that caught up very fast also had very rapid growth of innovative activity. The analysis presented in Fagerberg (1988a) suggested that superior growth in innovative activity was the prime factor behind the huge difference in performance between Asian and Latin-American NIC countries in the 1970s and early 1980s. Fagerberg and Verspagen (2002) likewise found that the continuing rapid growth of the Asian NICs relative to other country groupings in the decade that followed was primarily caused by the rapid growth in its innovative performance, emphasizing the importance of including this factor in the empirical analysis.

Estimations of the model for different time periods (Fagerberg, 1987; Fagerberg and Verspagen, 2002) have shown that, while imitation has become more demanding over time (and hence more costly to undertake), innovation has become a more powerful factor in explaining observed differences in growth performance. This suggests that there may have been an important shift taking place in the returns to different types of strategies pursued by countries, and raises questions of what the explanations and the likely long-term consequences of this shift may be. The model has also been used to analyse the differences in growth performance across European regions, illustrating among other things the differences in technological dynamics across different parts of Europe (Cappelen *et al.*, 1999), and the growth-retarding character of some continuing structural and social challenges (Fagerberg and Verspagen, 1996; Fagerberg *et al.*, 1997). Arguably, the ability to identify such issues is one of the great advantages of this type of modelling, which by being flexible, open and close to the data-generating process (including an important element of inductive reasoning), attempts to avoid the fate, common for many formal contributions, of being trapped in a highly abstract, mathematized discourse based on far-reaching but highly dubious assumptions (that are usually not tested or even testable). Following Nelson and Winter (1982), who coined the concept 'appreciative theorizing' for such attempts to identify causal relationships, we may perhaps call the modelling strategy applied here 'appreciative modelling'.

The model discussed above opens up the analysis of international technology flows but abstracts from flows of goods and services. We will now introduce the latter. For simplicity we do this in a two-country framework, in which the other country is labelled 'world'. Define the share of a country's exports (X) in world demand (W) as $S_x = X / W$, and similarly the share of imports (M) in its own GDP (Y) as $S_m = M / Y$. For the sake of exposition we will assume that the market shares of a country are unaffected by the growth of the market, but we will relax this assumption later. Following the Schumpeterian logic outlined in the previous section, we will assume that, apart from a constant term, a country's market share for exports depends on three factors: its technological competitiveness (its knowledge assets relative to competitors), its capacity to exploit technology commercially (again relative to competitors) and its price (P) competitiveness (relative to prices on tradables in common currency).

$$S_x = A_3 \left(\frac{Q}{Q_W} \right)^\rho \left(\frac{C}{C_W} \right)^\mu \left(\frac{P}{P_W} \right)^{-\pi} \qquad (\rho, \mu, \pi > 0). \qquad (43.7)$$

Since, by definition, imports in this model are the 'world' 's exports, we may model the import share in the same way, using bars to distinguish the coefficients of the two equations:

$$S_M = A_4 \left(\frac{Q_W}{Q} \right)^{\bar\rho} \left(\frac{C_W}{C} \right)^{\bar\mu} \left(\frac{P_W}{P} \right)^{-\bar\pi} \qquad (\bar\rho, \bar\mu, \bar\pi > 0). \qquad (43.8)$$

By differentiating (43.7) and substituting (43.4) into it, and similarly for (43.8), we arrive at the dynamic expressions for the growth in market shares:

$$s_X = -\rho\gamma\phi \frac{T - T_W}{T_*} + \rho\lambda(n - n_W) + \mu(c - c_W) - \pi(p - p_W). \qquad (43.9)$$

$$s_M = -\bar\rho\gamma\phi \frac{T_W - T}{T_*} + \bar\rho\lambda(n_W - n) + \bar\mu(c_W - c) - \bar\pi(p_W - p). \qquad (43.10)$$

We see that the growth of the market share of a country depends on four factors:

- the potential for exploiting knowledge developed elsewhere, which depends on the country's level of technological development relative to the world average;
- creation of new knowledge in the country (innovation) relative to that of competitors;
- growth in the ability to exploit knowledge, independently of where it is created, relative to that of competitors;

- change in relative prices in common currency (price competitiveness).

Following Thirlwall (1979) and Fagerberg (1988b) we now introduce the requirement that trade in goods and services has to balance (if not in the short, then in the long run). Note that this requirement does not rule out the possibility that countries may have foreign debts (or assets). As is easily verified, we may multiply the left- or right-hand side of (43.11) with a scalar without any consequence for the subsequent deductions. Hence an alternative way to formulate the restriction might be that the surplus (deficit) used to service foreign debt (financed from assets abroad) should be a constant fraction of exports (or imports):

$$XP = MP_W. \tag{43.11}$$

By differentiating (43.11), substituting S_X and S_M into it and rearranging, we arrive at the dynamic form of the restriction:

$$y = (s_X - s_M) + (p - p_W) + w. \tag{43.12}$$

This assumption, it might be noted, has been extensively tested on data for developed economies, and found to hold good (Fagerberg, 1988b; Meliciani, 2001).

By substituting (43.9)–(43.10) into (43.12) and rearranging, we get the reduced form of the model:

$$y_{rel} = -(\rho + \bar{\rho})\gamma\phi\frac{T - T_W}{T_*} + (\rho + \bar{\rho})\lambda(n - n_W) + (\mu + \bar{\mu})(c - c_W)$$
$$+ [1 - (\pi + \bar{\pi})](p - p_W). \tag{43.13}$$

By comparing this with the similar reduced form of the growth model (43.6) we see that, apart from the last term on the right-hand side, the model has the same structure. The only difference is that the coefficients of the basic growth equation now are shown to be sums of coefficients for the similar variables in the market-share equations (for the domestic and world market). Hence, the sensitivity of the markets (or 'selection environments') for new technologies clearly matters for growth. The final term is the familiar Marshall–Lerner condition which states the sum of the price-elasticities for exports and imports (when measured in absolute value) has to be higher than one if deteriorating price-competitiveness is going to harm the external balance (and, in this case, the rate of growth of GDP).

We have modelled the market share equations on the assumption that, when not only price, but also technology and capacity, have been taken into account as competitive factors, demand may be assumed to have a unitary elasticity. This means, for instance, abstracting from other factors, that, if export demand grows by a certain percentage, exports will do the same, so that the market share remains unaffected. However, there are reasons to believe that this assumption, although appealing in its simplicity, does not necessarily apply in all cases. If a country has a pattern of specialization geared towards industries that are in high (low) demand internationally, the argument goes, its exports may grow faster (slower) than world demand, quite independently of what happens to other factors. Arguably this possibility might be expected to be of greatest relevance for small countries, since these are likely to be more specialized in their economic structure than large ones. To take this possibility into account, following Fagerberg (1988b), we introduce demand into the market shares equations:

$$S_x = A_3 \left(\frac{Q}{Q_w}\right)^\rho \left(\frac{C}{C_w}\right)^\mu \left(\frac{P}{P_w}\right)^{-\pi} W^{\tau-1}, \qquad (\tau > 0) \qquad (43.7')$$

$$S_m = A_4 \left(\frac{Q_w}{Q}\right)^{\bar\rho} \left(\frac{C_w}{C}\right)^{\bar\mu} \left(\frac{P_w}{P}\right)^{-\bar\pi} Y^{\bar\tau-1} \qquad (\bar\tau > 0). \qquad (43.8')$$

By, as previously, differentiating and substituting we arrive at the following expression for the reduced form:

$$y_{rel} = -\frac{(\rho + \bar\rho)}{\bar\tau}\gamma\phi\frac{T - T_W}{T_*} + \frac{(\rho + \bar\rho)}{\bar\tau}\lambda(n - n_W) + \frac{(\mu + \bar\mu)}{\bar\tau}(c - c_W)$$

$$+ \frac{1 - (\pi + \bar\pi)}{\bar\tau}(p - p_W) + \frac{\tau - \bar\tau}{\bar\tau}w. \qquad (43.13')$$

The first thing to note is that the higher the demand elasticity for imports, the lower the effect on growth of all other factors. This has to do with the requirement to keep external balance: the more import-intensive growth is, the harder it is to keep the balance in order. The second is that while, as before, the first three terms on the right-hand side resemble the basic growth model (43.6), the last two terms in (43.13') concur with the model suggested by Thirlwall (1979). Hence, both the basic model (43.6) and Thirlwall's model can be seen as special cases of a more general, open-economy model.[8]

The open-economy model, outlined above, has been applied to empirical data for developed economies by Fagerberg (1988b). The empirical results, based on data for 15 OECD countries from the early 1960s to the early 1980s, generally confirmed the importance of growth in technological and productive capacity for competitiveness. The impact of cost factors was found to be relatively marginal, consistent with the earlier findings by Kaldor (the so-called 'Kaldor paradox'; see Kaldor, 1978).[9] More recently, Meliciani (2001) has applied the model to a longer time series, including a more recent time period, with broadly similar results.[10]

Reflections
The framework developed here is purposively flexible. It has a hard core, based on Schumpeterian logic, to which other variables may be added to give a consistent picture and realistic, unbiased estimates of the impacts of the central variables. The framework may be developed in various ways, depending on the interests of the researcher. For instance, Verspagen (1991) has added a more complex modelling of the diffusion process that enhances the possibility for divergence in performance and 'lock-in' to inferior paths. There have also been attempts to endogenize the 'capacity' variable, by linking it to investment, taking into account the possible feedback on the latter from demand (GDP) growth (Fagerberg, 1988b). However, this is at best a very partial explanation of such differences in the capacity to exploit technological advance, and a broader framework, including differences in financial systems, support systems etc., would clearly be preferable. Similarly, one might wish to question the alleged exogenity of the price variable, noting, for instance, its relationships to costs, and the dependency of the latter variable on factors such as wages and labour productivity. Initially, one reason for not pursuing this further was the view that labour markets, and systems of wage determination, differ a lot across countries and hence might be difficult to fit into the framework of a general model. Moreover, going further in this direction would most likely require endogenization of labour productivity,[11] which arguably increases the complexity of the task (Verspagen, 1993). Despite these challenges this is certainly an issue that deserves serious attention.

We have left to the end what, in light of the most recent addition to the literature on growth, so-called 'new growth theory' (Romer, 1990; Grossman and Helpman, 1991; Aghion and Howitt, 1992), may be seen as the most burning issue, namely the possibility of endogenizing innovation. Basically, 'new growth theory' explains growth much in the same way as traditional (neoclassical) economic theory would explain any economic phenomenon, e.g., as the result of interaction between 'rational' actors, endowed with 'perfect information', and reacting to well known economic incentives in the accustomed way. The difference between this 'new growth theory' and its (neoclassical) predecessor(s) consists mainly of taking on board the facts that (a) IPRs (intellectual property rights) give some limited protection to innovators (and that markets for new technology therefore exist), and (b) that, in spite of IPRs, some of the benefits from innovation cannot be privately appropriated, but continue to spill over to other activities or agents and contribute to increased productivity/prof-itability (and hence growth) there. While, in this approach, the partial pro-tection offered by IPRs is important for explaining why innovations occur, it is the spillover part that ensures that growth does not cease (because of decreasing returns). However, these spillovers are (as in earlier vintages of neoclassical growth theory) basically seen as a 'public good', i.e., some-thing that is freely available for everybody (independent of location) and which consequently should have the same effects everywhere. Thus while, arguably, this approach correctly identifies some important features behind global growth, it does not provide us with much insight into why growth *differs* across contemporary developed economies and has, to the best of our knowledge, yet to generate any serious attempt to explain such differences. To do that one would probably have to dig much deeper into the way innovation and diffusion are embedded within national economies, i.e., in firms, networks, institution etc., and interact with other variables there. While a very profitable undertaking, and highly comple-mentary to the analysis presented in this chapter, it is not something that can be pursued further here.

Notes

1. We mention Leontief's contribution primarily because it influenced the subsequent lit-erature on growth and trade, not because we wish to discuss what shapes specialization patterns in international trade. For overviews that also covers the latter, see Fagerberg (1996) and Wakelin (1997, chs 2–3).
2. See Fagerberg and Verspagen (1999) for a discussion of Cornwall's approach (including its relevance for the global economy of today).
3. The income elasticity of exports is the growth in exports resulting from a 1 per cent increase in world demand, holding relative prices constant (and ignoring cyclical factors). Similarly for imports.
4. There are, of course, many factors that could be considered potentially relevant, and it is beyond the purpose of this chapter to discuss all of these in great detail. (See McCombie and Thirlwall, 1994, ch. 4.)
5. See, for instance, the discussion in Verspagen (1992) and Fagerberg (1994, 2000, 2002, Introduction).
6. Instead of seeing the model (43.1)–(43.6) as a model of GDP growth, one might con-sider it as a model of GDP per capita (worker) growth, in which case all variables would enter on a per capita (worker) basis. The first applications of the model was based on the former assumption, applied here, while later applications, for instance on regional growth, have generally assumed the latter. The relationship between the two versions of the model is straightforward. Note, however, that if the latter assumption was chosen, population (or labour force) growth would enter into the determination of GDP growth.
7. This is based on the assumption that the two countries face the same competitive con-ditions (elasticities) but vary in other respects.
8. If the demand elasticities are the same in both markets and the Marshall–Lerner condition is exactly satisfied (or relative prices do not change), the last two terms vanish, and we are back in a model that for all practical purposes is identical to (43.6). If, on the other hand,

the country's technological level is exactly average and both relative technology and relative capacity keep constant, the three first terms vanish, and only Thirlwall's model remains.

9.   Kaldor (1978) showed for a number of countries that, over the long term, market shares for exports and relative unit costs or prices tend to move together; i.e., that growing market shares and increasing relative costs or prices tend to go hand in hand. This was, of course, the opposite of what you would expect from the simplistic though at the time widely diffused approach focusing exclusively on the (assumedly negative) impact of increasing relative costs or prices on market shares, hence the term 'paradox'. Fagerberg (1996) has shown that this finding also applies to a more recent time period.

10. She also added a 'specialization' variable, reflecting the extent to which countries were specialized in technologically progressive sectors, to the market share equations, for which she found empirical support.

11. An easy way to endogenize labour productivity would be to let it depend on demand, through the incorporation into the model of the so-called 'Verdoorn's law', in the fashion suggested by Kaldor (1967). By doing so one might eliminate GDP growth and arrive at a reduced form with growth of labour productivity as the dependent variable. Such an equation would have a structure roughly similar to the growth equations presented above. However, as is probably obvious to the reader, this would imply that also employment growth would be determined by the model, and without any relationship whatsoever to factors such as labour supply and the working of labour markets. This would in the view of the present author be too simplistic. Hence, a broader framework appears necessary in order to deal with these challenges.

References

Abramovitz, M. (1979) 'Rapid growth potential and its realisation: the experience of capitalist economics in the postwar period', in E. Malinvaud (ed.), *Economic Growth and Resources: Vol. 1. The Major Issues*, London: Macmillan, pp. 1–30.

Abramovitz, M. (1986) Catching up, forging ahead, and falling behind, *Journal of Economic History*, **46**, 386–406.

Abramovitz, M. (1994) 'The origins of the postwar catch-up and convergence boom', in J. Fagerberg, B. Verspagen and N. von Tunzelmann (eds), *The Dynamics of Technology, Trade and Growth*, Aldershot, UK and Brookfield, USA: Edward Elgar, pp. 21–52.

Aghion, P. and P. Howitt (1992) A model of growth through creative destruction, *Econometrica*, **60**, 323–51.

Baumol, W.J., S.A. Batey Blackman and E.N. Wolff (1989) *Productivity and American Leadership: The Long View*, Cambridge, MA: MIT Press.

Beckerman, W. (1962) Projecting Europe's growth, *Economic Journal*, **72**, 912–25.

Cappelen, A., J. Fagerberg and B. Verspagen (1999) 'Lack of regional convergence', in J. Fagerberg, P. Guerrieri and B. Verspagen (eds), *The Economic Challenge for Europe: Adapting to Innovation-based Growth*, Cheltenham, UK and Northampton, MA, USA: Edward Elgar, ch. 6.

Cornwall, J. (1977) *Modern Capitalism: Its Growth and Transformation*, London: St. Martin's Press.

Dosi, G. and L. Soete (1983) Technology gaps and cost-based adjustment: some explorations of the determinants of international competitiveness, *Metroeconomica*, **35**, 357–82.

Dosi, G., K. Pavitt and L.G. Soete (1990) *The Economics of Technical Change and International Trade*, London: Harvester Wheatsheaf.

Fagerberg, J. (1987) A technology gap approach to why growth rates differ, *Research Policy*, **16**, 87–99; reprinted as chapter 1 in J. Fagerberg (2002) *Technology, Growth and Competitiveness: Selected Essays*, Cheltenham, UK and Northampton, MA, USA: Edward Elgar.

Fagerberg, J. (1988a) 'Why growth rates differ', in Giovanni Dosi *et al.* (eds), *Technical Change and Economic Theory*, London: Pinter, pp. 432–57.

Fagerberg, J. (1988b) International competitiveness, *Economic Journal*, **98**, 355–74; reprinted as chapter 12 in J. Fagerberg (2002) *Technology, Growth and Competitiveness: Selected Essays*, Cheltenham, UK and Northampton, MA, USA: Edward Elgar.

Fagerberg, J. (1994) Technology and international differences in growth rates, *Journal of Economic Literature*, **32**, 1147–75.

Fagerberg, J. (1996) Technology and competitiveness, *Oxford Review of Economic Policy*, **12**, 39–51; reprinted as chapter 16 in J. Fagerberg (2002) *Technology, Growth and Competitiveness: Selected Essays*, Cheltenham, UK and Northampton, MA, USA: Edward Elgar.

Fagerberg, J. (2000) 'Vision and fact: a critical essay on the growth literature', in J. Madrick (ed.), *Unconventional Wisdom, Alternative Perspectives on the New Economy*, New York: The Century Foundation, pp. 299–320; reprinted as chapter 6 in J. Fagerberg (2002) *Technology, Growth and Competitiveness: Selected Essays*, Cheltenham, UK and Northampton, MA, USA: Edward Elgar.

Fagerberg, J. (2002) *Technology, Growth and Competitiveness: Selected Essays*, Cheltenham, UK and Northampton, MA, USA: Edward Elgar.

Fagerberg, J. (2003) Schumpeter and the revival of evolutionary economics: an appraisal of the literature, *Journal of Evolutionary Economics*, **13**, 125–59.

Fagerberg, J. and B. Verspagen (1996), Heading for divergence? Regional growth in Europe reconsidered, *Journal of Common Market Studies*, **34**, 431–48; reprinted as chapter 4 in J. Fagerberg (2002) *Technology, Growth and Competitiveness: Selected Essays*, Cheltenham, UK and Northampton, MA, USA: Edward Elgar.

Fagerberg, J. and B. Verspagen (1999) 'Modern capitalism in the 1970s and 1980s', in Mark Setterfield (ed.), *Growth, Employment and Inflation*, London: Macmillan, pp. 113–26; reprinted as chapter 2 in J. Fagerberg (2002) *Technology, Growth and Competitiveness: Selected Essays*, Cheltenham, UK and Northampton, MA, USA: Edward Elgar.

Fagerberg, J., and B. Verspagen (2002) Technology gaps, innovation diffusion and transformation: an evolutionary interpretation, *Research Policy*, **31**, 1291–304.

Fagerberg, J., B. Verspagen and M. Caniëls (1997) Technology, growth and unemployment across European regions, *Regional Studies*, **31**, 457–66; reprinted as chapter 5 in J. Fagerberg (2002) *Technology, Growth and Competitiveness: Selected Essays*, Cheltenham, UK and Northampton, MA, USA: Edward Elgar.

Gerschenkron, A. (1962) *Economic Backwardness in Historical Perspective*, Cambridge, MA: The Belknap Press.

Grossman, G.M. and E. Helpman (1991) *Innovation and Growth in the Global Economy*, Cambridge, MA: The MIT Press.

Hirsch, S. (1965) The US electronics industry in international trade, *National Institute Economic Review*, **34**, 92–107.

Kaldor, N. (1967) *Strategic Factors in Economic Development*, Ithaca: Cornell University Press.

Kaldor, N. (1970) The case for regional policies, *Scottish Journal of Political Economy*, **17**, 337–48.

Kaldor, N. (1978) 'The effect of devaluations on trade in manufactures', in *Further Essays on Applied Economics*, London: Duckworth.

Kaldor, N. (1981) The role of increasing returns, technical progress and cumulative causation in the theory of international trade and economic growth, *Economie Appliquée* (ISMEA), **34**, 593–617.

Krugman, P. (1979) A model of innovation, technology transfer and the world distribution of income, *Journal of Political Economy*, **87**, 253–66.

Leontief, W. (1953) Domestic production and foreign trade: the American capital position reexamined, *Proceedings of the American Philosophical Society*, September, 332–49.

McCombie, J.S.L. and A.P. Thirlwall (1994) *Economic Growth and the Balance-of-Payments Constraint*, London: Macmillan.

Meliciani, V. (2001) *Technology, Trade and Growth in OECD Countries – Does Specialization Matter?*, London: Routledge.

Nelson, R.R. and S.G. Winter (1982) *An Evolutionary Theory of Economic Change*, Cambridge, MA: Harvard University Press.

Pavitt, K. and L. Soete (1982) 'International differences in economic growth and the international location of innovation', in H. Giersch (ed.), *Emerging Technologies: The Consequences for Economic Growth, Structural Change and Employment*, Tübingen: Mohr, pp. 105–33.

Posner, M.V. (1961) International trade and technical change, *Oxford Economic Papers*, **13**, 323–41.
Romer, P.M. (1990) Endogenous technological change, *Journal of Political Economy*, **98**, S71–S102.
Thirlwall, A.P. (1979) The balance of payments constraints as an explanation of international growth rate differences, *Banca Nazionale del Lavoro Quarterly Review*, **32**, 45–53.
Vernon, R. (1966) International investment and international trade in the product cycle, *Quarterly Journal of Economics*, **80**, 190–207.
Verspagen, B. (1991) A new empirical approach to catching up or falling behind, *Structural Change and Economic Dynamics*, **2**, 359–80.
Verspagen, B. (1992) Endogenous innovation in neo-classical models: a survey, *Journal of Macroeconomics*, **14**, 631–62.
Verspagen, B. (1993) 'Trade and knowledge spillovers in an evolutionary model of growth rate differentials', in A. Wagner (ed.), *Dezentrale Entscheidungsfindung bei Externen Effekten*, Tübingen: Franke Verlag, pp. 189–218.
Wakelin, K. (1997) *Trade and Innovation: Theory and Evidence*, Cheltenham, UK and Lyme, USA: Edward Elgar.

44 Innovation and employment
Marco Vivarelli

1 Introduction

The diffusion, in the last two decades, of a new 'technological paradigm' based on ICTs has implied a new emergence of the old debate about the possible employment consequences of innovation. Indeed, the fear of technological unemployment has always emerged in ages characterized by radical technological changes. For instance, the striking response of the English workers to the first industrial revolution was the destruction of machines under the charismatic lead of Ned Ludd in the industrial areas and of Captain Swing in the countryside (see Hobsbawm, 1968; Hobsbawm and Rudé, 1969). On the other hand, from its very beginning, the economic theory has pointed out the existence of economic forces which can compensate for the reduction in employment due to technological progress. Since the classical debate, two views have started to compete in dealing with the employment impact of technological progress: using Ricardo's words, the 'working class opinion' was characterized by the fear of being dismissed because of innovation (see Ricardo, 1951, p. 392), whilst the academic and political debate was mainly dominated by an ex ante confidence in the market compensation of dismissed workers.

Even nowadays, *mutatis mutandis*, the nature of the different long-term 'technological trajectories' can be of paramount importance in explaining national and regional differences in employment and unemployment trends. Obviously, this does not mean that short-term views focusing on prices (wages and interest rates) or on labour market regulation are not important, but they are probably insufficient in providing a complete interpretation of employment evolution.

In this chapter a classical framework will be provided (section 2), criticized (section 3) and used in giving an account of the empirical evidence (section 4). Main findings and conclusions will be discussed in the final section 5. While this chapter will be mainly devoted to a macroeconomic analysis, the reader interested in the microeconomic aspects of the relationship between innovation and employment can refer to Piva and Vivarelli (2003, 2004).

2 The classical 'compensation theory'

The economic discipline, since its foundation and as a part of the heroic attempt to render economics a proper 'science', has tried to dispel all concerns about the possible harmful effects of technological progress, on a basis of a rigorous, counterintuitive and 'scientific' theory. Indeed, in the first half of the 19th century, economists put forward a theory that Marx later called the 'compensation theory' (see Marx, 1961, vol. 1, ch. 13; 1969, ch. 18). This theory is made up of different market compensation mechanisms which are triggered by technological change itself and which can counterbalance the initial labour-saving impact of process innovation (for an extensive analysis, see also Vivarelli, 1995, chs 2 and 3; Petit, 1995; Vivarelli and Pianta, 2000, ch. 2; Pianta, 2004).

2.1   The compensation mechanism 'via new machines'
The same process innovations which displace workers in the user industries create new jobs in the capital sectors where the new machines are produced (see, for instance, Say, 1964, p. 87).

2.2   The compensation mechanism 'via decrease in prices'
On the one hand, process innovations involve the displacement of workers; on the other hand, these innovations themselves lead to a decrease in the unit costs of production and – in a competitive market – this effect is translated into decreasing prices; in turn, decreasing prices stimulate a new demand for products and so additional production and employment. This mechanism was singled out at the very beginning of the history of economic thought (Steuart, 1966, vol. II, p. 256).

This line of reasoning became the cornerstone of the compensation theory when Say's law became the focus of classical economic theory (see Say, 1964, p. 87). In a competitive world, the supply generates its own demand and technological change fully takes part in this self-adjusting process. The compensation mechanism 'via decrease in prices' has been re-proposed many times in the history of economic thought both by neoclassical economists (see Pigou, 1962, p. 672) and by modern theorists (see Neary, 1981; Stoneman, 1983, chs 11 and 12; Hall and Heffernan, 1985; Dobbs, Hill and Waterson, 1987; Nickell and Kong, 1989; Smolny, 1998).

2.3   The compensation mechanism 'via new investments'
In a world where the competitive convergence is not instantaneous, it is observed that during the gap between the decrease in costs – owing to technological progress – and the consequent fall in prices, extra profits may be accumulated by the innovative entrepreneurs. These profits are invested and so new productions and new jobs are created. Originally put forward by Ricardo (1951, vol. I, p. 396), this proposition has also been called forth by neoclassicals like Marshall (1961, p. 542) and by more recent dynamic models such as those by Hicks (1973), Stoneman (1983, pp. 177–81). The

role of lagged innovation in fostering employment evolution is also investigated in Van Reenen (1997) at a microeconomic level.

2.4 The compensation mechanism 'via decrease in wages'

As with other forms of unemployment, the direct effect of labour-saving technologies may be compensated within the labour market. In fact, in a neoclassical framework, with free competition and full substitutability between labour and capital, technological unemployment implies a decrease in wages and this should lead to a reverse shift back to more labour-intensive technologies. The first to apply this kind of argument was Wicksell (1961, p. 137), followed by Hicks (1932, p. 56) and Pigou (1933, p. 256).

In modern times, the wage adjustment is a component of partial equilibrium models such as those by Neary (1981) and Sinclair (1981) and general equilibrium analyses such as those by Layard and Nickell (1985), Venables (1985), Layard, Nickell and Jackman (1991), Davis (1998) and Addison and Teixeira (2001).

2.5 The compensation mechanism 'via increase in incomes'

Directly in contrast with the previous one, this compensation mechanism has been put forward by the Keynesian and Kaldorian tradition. In a Fordist mode of production, unions take part in the distribution of the fruits of technological progress. So it has to be taken into account that a portion of the cost savings due to innovation can be translated into higher income and hence higher consumption. This increase in demand leads to an increase in employment which may compensate the initial job losses due to process innovations (see Pasinetti, 1981; Boyer, 1988b, 1988c, 1990).

2.6 The compensation mechanism 'via new products'

Technological change is not only process innovation, but can imply the birth of entirely new economic branches where additional jobs can be created. Once again, the labour-intensive impact of product innovation was underlined by classical economists (Say, 1964, p. 88) and even the most severe critic of compensation theory admitted the positive employment benefits which can derive from this kind of technological progress (Marx, 1961, vol. I, p. 445).

In the current debate, various studies (Freeman, Clark and Soete, 1982; Freeman and Soete, 1987; Freeman and Soete, 1994; Vivarelli and Pianta, 2000; Edquist, Hommen and McKelvey, 2001) agree that product innovations have a positive impact on employment since they open the way to the development of either entire new goods or main differentiation of mature goods. The 'labour-friendly nature' of product innovation turns out to be particularly obvious at the microeconomic level (see, for instance, Entorf and Pohlmeier, 1990; and Brouwer, Kleinknecht and Reijnen, 1993).

3   A critique

On the one hand, technological change induces market forces which can potentially counterbalance the initial labour-saving effect of process innovation. In addition, a different form of technological progress, namely the diffusion of new products, can have a positive effect on employment trends. On the other hand, compensation mechanisms can be hindered by the existence of drawbacks which are often either neglected or misspecified by the neoclassical conventional wisdom. Using the same taxonomy which has been proposed above, the main criticisms of the compensation theory can be singled out as below.

3.1   With few exceptions (see Hicks, 1973), nowadays this compensation mechanism is not put forward any more. Indeed, Marx's critique of this mechanism was particularly sharp: 'the machine can only be employed profitably, if it . . . is the (annual) product of far fewer men than it replaces' (Marx, 1969, p. 552).

Moreover, labour-saving technologies spread around in the capital goods sector, as well; so this compensation is an endless story which can be only partial (Marx, 1969, p. 551). Finally, the new machines can be implemented either through additional investments (see subsection 3.3) or simply by substitution of the obsolete ones (scrapping). In the latter case, which is indeed the most frequent one, there is no compensation at all (see, for instance, Freeman, Clark and Soete, 1982).

3.2   As originally noted by Malthus (1964, vol. II, pp. 551–60; Sismondi, 1971, p. 284; and Mill, 1976, p. 97), the very first effect of a labour-saving technology is a decrease in the aggregate demand owing to the cancellation of the demand previously associated with the dismissed workers. So the mechanism 'via decrease in prices' deals with a decreased demand and has to more than counterbalance the initial decrease in the aggregate purchasing power.

In addition, this mechanism relies on Say's law and does not take into account that demand constraints might occur. Difficulties concerning the components of the 'effective demand' (in Keynes's terms) such as a low value of the 'marginal efficiency of capital' (see Keynes, 1973, ch. 11) can involve a delay in expenditure decisions and a lower demand elasticity. If such is the case, this compensation mechanism is hindered and technological unemployment ceases to be a temporary problem.

Finally, the effectiveness of the mechanism 'via decrease in prices' depends on the hypothesis of perfect competition. If an oligopolistic regime is dominant, the whole compensation is strongly weakened since cost savings are not necessarily and entirely translated into decreasing prices (see Sylos Labini, 1969, p. 160).

3.3   Also the compensation mechanism 'via new investments' relies on the Say's law assumption that the accumulated profits due to innovation are entirely and immediately translated into additional investments. Again, Marx's and Keynes's treatment of Say's law can be used to doubt the full effectiveness of this compensation mechanism. Moreover, the intrinsic nature of the new investments does matter; if these are capital-intensive, compensation can only be partial: 'The accumulation of capital, though originally appearing as its quantitative extension only, is effected, as we have seen, under a progressive qualitative change in its composition, under a constant increase of its constant, at the expense of its variable constituent' (Marx, 1961, vol. I, p. 628).

3.4   Also the mechanism 'via decrease in wages' contrasts with the Keynesian theory of effective demand. On the one hand, a decrease in wages can induce firms to hire additional workers, but, on the other hand, the decreased aggregate demand lowers employers' business expectations and so they tend to hire fewer workers.

A second criticism can be launched at this mechanism if the cumulative and irreversible nature of technological change is properly taken into account (see Rosenberg, 1976; Dosi, 1988). In this view, science and technology have their own rules: along a 'technological trajectory' a 'localized technological progress' occurs. If the cumulative and localized nature of innovation is taken into account, both the hypothesis of perfect substitutability between capital and labour assumed by neoclassical models and the possibility of a reverse in technological change appear to be quite unlikely.

3.5   During the 'golden age' of the 1950s and 1960s, the Fordist mode of production was based on a relevant change in the labour–wage nexus. Instead of leaving the wage to be regulated by a competitive labour market, workers were allowed to take possession of a relevant portion of productivity gains due to technological progress. In turn, the increased real wages involved mass consumption and this stimulated investments leading to further productivity gains through innovation and scale economies (Boyer, 1988a). Labour-saving technologies were introduced on a large scale, but the Kaldorian 'virtuous circle' allowed an important compensation 'via new incomes'.

Nowadays, the Fordist mode of production is over for many reasons that cannot be discussed here (see Boyer, 1988a, 1990). The distribution of income follows different rules (based more on Phillips's curve than on sharing the productivity gains) and labour markets have returned to being competitive and flexible. On the whole, this compensation mechanism has been strongly weakened in the new institutional contexts (see Appelbaum and Schettkat, 1995).

3.6 New products are still the more powerful way to counterbalance labour-saving process innovations, yet the 'welfare effect' (new branches of production) has to be compared with the 'substitution effect' (displacement of mature products; see Katsoulacos, 1986). Moreover, different 'techno-logical paradigms' are characterized by different clusters of new products which in turn have very different impacts on employment. So the introduc-tion of the automobile had a much higher labour-intensive effect than the diffusion of home computers. As a matter of fact, in different historical periods and different institutional frameworks, the relative balance between the labour-saving effect of process innovations and the labour-intensive impact of product ones can vary considerably.

A well-balanced conclusion about the compensation theory can be taken from Pasinetti (1981, p. 90):

> For the time being, we may draw the important conclusion that the structural dynamics of the economic system inevitably tend to generate what has rightly been called technological unemployment. At the same time, the very same structural dynamics produce counter-balancing movements which are capable of bringing macro-economic condition . . . towards fulfilment, but not automatically.

4 Empirical evidence

The 'classical taxonomy' discussed above can also be applied to the present forms of technological change and particularly to the introduction and diffusion of ICTs. Yet, taking into account the discussion in the previous sections, it is obvious that economic theory cannot provide a clear-cut answer about the employment effect of ICTs. Hence, attention should be turned to aggregate, sectoral and microeconomic empirical analyses which should take into account the different forms of innovation, their direct effects on labour, the various compensation mechanisms and the possible hindrances to these mechanisms.

Of course, this is not an easy task. While theoretical economists may develop clear models about the employment impact of process and product innovation, applied economists have to 'measure' technological change, the compensation mechanisms and the final employment impact of innova-tion; in this respect, at least three main problems arise.

First, technological change in general and ICT diffusion in particular are difficult to measure; traditional indicators such as R&D (input indicator), patents and crucial innovations (output indicators) are seldom fully available and are often inadequate to fully represent technological change (think, for instance, of the role of tacit knowledge and intangible investments in fostering ICT diffusion).

Second, as discussed in section 2, the final employment impact of innovation depends on institutional mechanisms which can be very different at the micro, sectoral and macro levels and can vary in different contexts, such as in different countries or different sectors within the same country.

Third, it is difficult to distinguish the final impact of innovation on employment, since the latter is influenced by many other factors: the macroeconomic and cyclical conditions, the labour market dynamics and regulations, the trends in working time and so on.

In addition to these general shortcomings, there are also problems which arise at each level of analysis. Starting from the microeconomic studies, the empirical analysis of the impact of ICTs at the firm's level is extremely useful in revealing the actual ways in which new products generate new jobs and labour-saving process innovation destroys old ones. Nevertheless, the main shortcoming of this kind of analysis consists in a 'positive bias' which tends to underline the positive employment consequences of innovation. In fact, once the empirical analysis is developed at the level of the single firms, innovative firms tend to be characterized by better employment performances since they gain market shares because of innovation. Even when the innovation is labour-saving, these analyses generally show a positive link between technology and employment since they do not take into account the important effect on the rivals, which are crowded out by the innovative firms (the so-called 'business stealing' effect: see Van Reenen, 1997; Piva and Vivarelli, 2003). For instance, Greenan and Guellec (2000), using data from French manufacturing sectors over the period 1986–90, found a positive relationship between innovation and employment at the firm's level (both product and process innovation). Yet, at the sectoral level, their results confirmed the idea that only product innovation creates additional jobs, while process innovation generates jobs within the innovative firm but at the expense of the competitors, leading to an overall negative effect at the sectoral level.

This bias can be corrected when the empirical analysis is carried out at the sectoral level: in this case, a researcher can take into account both the positive performance of innovative firms and the indirect effects on competitors and so he can investigate the final employment outcome. Yet sectoral analyses can also be affected by either a negative or a positive bias, according to the observation point of view (manufacturing versus services). For instance, Pianta (2000) and Antonucci and Pianta (2002) found an overall negative employment impact of technological change in manufacturing industries across five European countries, while Evangelista (2000) and Evangelista and Savona (2002) found a positive employment relationship in the most innovative and knowledge-intensive service sectors and a negative one in the case of finance-related sectors and most traditional services like trade and transport.

Finally, even at the sectoral level, the analysis cannot take into account all the direct and indirect effects of technological change. Only the aggregate macroeconomic studies can jointly assess (1) the labour displacement of process innovation in some economic sectors (mainly manufacturing); (2) the compensation effects which operate within those sectors (through decreasing prices and increasing investments) and in other sectors (through intersectoral flows of products and incomes); (3) the positive employment impact of product innovation in other sectors (mainly services). Yet aggregate empirical analyses are very difficult to put forward because of the three main general problems discussed above. Keeping these methodological remarks in mind, attention will now be focused on empirical contributions at the macroeconomic level, starting from input–output models.

Leontief and Duchin (1986) used input-output matrices to test the employment impact of automation assuming four different scenarios (characterized by different paces of technological change). The authors carried out their simulations taking future demand evolution as exogenous. While all four simulations led to an increasing employment trend, the study revealed a clear labour-saving bias of new technologies: in fact, more accelerated technological progress implied lower employment growth rates. Whitley and Wilson (1982, 1987) put forward a multisectoral dynamic model explicitly addressed to studying the employment impact of technological change using a compensation framework. In their first study, the authors forecast employment levels in 1990 for most sectors of the British economy and in their simulation compensation mechanisms were able to more than compensate initial job losses due to process innovation. Among the compensatory forces, the mechanism via decrease in prices proved the more effective, accounting for more than 50 per cent of compensation of the initial labour displacement. In their second study, the simulation scenario moved to the period 1985–95 and also took into account office automation and the public sector. In this case, compensation turned out to be only partial with an overall effect of new technologies equal to 288 000 job losses within the British economy. At any rate, compensation mechanisms proved effective in counterbalancing 280 000 initial job losses and most effective mechanisms appeared to be those 'via decrease in prices' and 'via new investments'. Very close in spirit to Whitley and Wilson's model is the framework proposed by Kalmbach and Kurz (1990). Their simulation of the impact of 'microelectronic-based best-practice techniques' on the West German economy showed compensation mechanisms at work, but unable to compensate fully for the initial labour displacement due to ICT diffusion.

Again concerning West Germany is the input–output study by Meyer-Krahmer (1992): using data referring to 51 sectors covering the entire economy in the 1980s, the author emulated the employment reaction of the German economy to innovation (in-house R&D spending and purchased R&D knowledge spillovers). His econometric results support the view that technological progress implies overall labour-saving effects, yet important sectoral differences emerge: while purchased R&D involves job losses in industries like textiles, clothing and electronic equipment, in-house R&D stimulates the demand for labour in sectors like chemicals and computer industries.

Departing from input–output models, two other streams of empirical literature can be singled out. On the one hand, some econometric studies within the 'compensation approach' (see section 2) tried to test the validity of (some) compensation mechanisms within a partial or general equilibrium framework. On the other hand, more recent studies turned their attention either to the direct relationship between growth and employment or to aggregate macroeconomic models.

Sinclair (1981), Layard and Nickell (1985) and Nickell and Kong (1989) belong to the first group of studies. In the first contribution, Sinclair put forward a macro IS/LM scheme and concluded that a positive employment compensation can occur if the demand elasticity and the elasticity of factor substitution are sufficiently high. Using estimates based on US data, the author found strong evidence supporting the mechanism via decrease in wages but not the mechanisms via decrease in prices. Layard and Nickell (1985) derived a demand for labour in a quasi-general equilibrium framework and stated that the crucial parameter was the elasticity of the demand for labour in response to a variation in the ratio between real wages and labour productivity; in fact, technological change increases labour productivity and, given adequate elasticity, proportionally the demand for labour and this can be enough to fully compensate initial job losses. Using data for the UK economy, the authors estimated an elasticity coefficient equal to 0.9 and this was sufficient (in the authors' opinion) to rule out innovation from the possible causes of British unemployment.

Finally, Nickell and Kong (1989) focused their attention on the operating of the compensation mechanism 'via decrease in prices' in nine UK two-digit industries. Putting forward a price equation where cost-saving effects of labour-saving technologies were fully transferred into decreasing prices, the authors found that in seven sectors out of nine a sufficiently high demand elasticity was able to imply an overall positive impact of techno-logical change on employment.

Turning our attention to the second stream of literature, according to the different nature of ICT diffusion (process versus product innovation) and to the different effectiveness of the compensation mechanisms, growth can be more or less labour-intensive. Boltho and Glyn (1995) elaborated data on OECD countries over sub-periods in 1960–93. Their main results from pooling estimates show that the employment/growth relationship is not so robust from a descriptive point of view, but it is confirmed by simple econo-metric estimates (univariate and contemporaneous). Interestingly enough, the positive correlation between GDP growth and employment growth is also confirmed over the period 1990–93 at odds with the notion of jobless growth as a result of ICT diffusion in the OECD economies.

Pini (1996) and Piacentini and Pini (2000) obtained less optimistic results. They carried out estimates of the employment elasticities, both in aggregate and by economic sectors, for the G-6 plus Sweden over the period 1960–97. In the 1990s, negative elasticities (jobless growth) were found in Italy, Germany, UK and Sweden, while all countries but Japan showed a decrease in such elasticities in comparison with the 1980s. Clear-cut find-ings emerged when attention was turned to the sectoral analysis: while all the countries showed negative elasticities for manufacturing, they also exhibited positive elasticities in services.

Padalino and Vivarelli (1997) put forward an empirical study on the G-7 economies over the period 1960–94. Their main conclusions were that (a) in the long run, a marked job creation in North America contrasts with mod-erate employment creation in Europe; (b) while in manufacturing post-Fordism and the diffusion of ICTs, technologies mean jobless growth and negative employment elasticities in all countries but Japan, no similar clear-cut evidence is detectable with regard to the whole economic system; (c) long-run evolution has to be distinguished from short-run correlation; while North America and Europe differ structurally in their job creation capacity in the long run, both of them continue to show a strong and statistically sig-nificant short-run correlation between growth and employment.

Of course, the relationship between growth and employment is only the final outcome of a complex interaction between technological change and employment which operates through many direct and indirect mechanisms, as described in sections 2 and 3. Vivarelli, 1995 (chs 7, 8 and 9) and Simonetti, Taylor and Vivarelli (2000) proposed a simultaneous equations macroeconomic model able jointly to take into account the direct labour-saving effect of process innovation, the different compensation mechanisms with their own hindrances and the job-creating impact of product inno-vation. Running three stages least squares regressions using American,

Italian, French and Japanese data over the period 1965–93, the authors showed that the more effective compensation mechanisms were those 'via decrease in prices' and 'via increase in incomes' (especially in European countries until the mid-1980s). The other mechanisms turned out to be less significant and conditional on the institutional structures of the different countries; for instance, the 'mechanism via decrease in wages' turned out to be relevant in the American flexible labour market. Finally, product innovation significantly revealed its labour-intensive potentiality only in the technological leader country in the period, namely the USA.

5   Conclusions

1   According to the 'compensation theory', market forces should assure a complete compensation of the initial labour-saving impact of process innovations. In section 3 a critique of this approach has been proposed, the general conclusion being that, although compensation is always working, the complete counterbalancing of dismissed workers cannot be assumed ex ante.

2   Given this theoretical indefiniteness, the risk is that the debate on the employment consequences of technological change may degenerate into a stalemate or into an ideological quarrel. One possible way out from this situation is to carry out empirical investigations which try to assess whether or not the demand for labour is affected by innovation.

3   As far as the available empirical evidence is concerned, contrasting results can emerge according to the different levels of analysis. While most microeconometric studies find a positive correlation between ICTs and employment, some doubts can be raised about the generalizability of such micro studies. Once attention is turned to the sectoral level, the distinction between product innovation (in labour-friendly growing sectors, such as new ICT-related services) and process innovation (in labour-saving restructuring sectors, mostly in manufacturing) becomes important. At the aggregate level, different input–output simulations can have opposite results according to the functioning of different 'within and between sectors' compensation mechanisms. Finally, contrasting empirical results – about the occurrence of jobless growth in different periods and different countries – are the outcome of different balances between product and process innovation and different degrees of effectiveness of compensation mechanisms.

4   On the whole, economists cannot propose a clear-cut diagnosis about the employment impact of innovation, either theoretically or empirically. A pragmatic approach should be put forward: the relationship between technological change and employment is a complex problem which cannot be entirely solved by partial equilibrium models or apodictical hypotheses

or unfounded empirical generalizations. Indeed, it is necessary to start from an 'open-minded' theoretical approach and from reliable data and then try patiently to discover, represent and estimate all the various direct and indirect effects of technological change.

References

Addison J. and Teixeira, P. 2001. Technology, employment and wages, *Labour*, **15**, 191–219.
Antonucci, T. and Pianta, M. 2002. Employment effects of product and process innovation in Europe, *International Review of Applied Economics*, **16**, 295–307.
Appelbaum, E. and Schettkat, R. 1995. Employment and productivity in industrialized economies, *International Labour Review*, **134**, 605–23.
Boltho, A. and Glyn, A. 1995. Can macroeconomic policies raise employment?, *International Labour Review*, **134**, 451–70.
Boyer, R. 1988a. 'Technical change and the theory of regulation', in G. Dosi, C. Freeman, R. Nelson, G. Silverberg and L. Soete (eds), *Technical Change and Economic Theory*, London: Pinter, pp. 67–94.
Boyer, R. 1988b. 'New technologies and employment in the 1980s: from science and technology to macroeconomic modelling', in J.A. Kregel, E. Matzner and A. Roncaglia (eds), *Barriers to Full Employment*, London: Macmillan, pp. 233–68.
Boyer, R. 1988c. Assessing the impact of R&D on employment: puzzle or consensus?, paper presented at the International Conference on New Technology: its Impacts on Labour Markets and the Employment System, December 5–7, Berlin.
Boyer, R. 1990. The capital labor relations in OECD countries: from the Fordist 'Golden Age' to contrasted national trajectories, working paper CEPREMAP, n.9020, Paris.
Brouwer, E., Kleinknecht, A. and Reijnen, J.O.N. 1993. Employment growth and innovation at the firm level: an empirical study, *Journal of Evolutionary Economics*, **3**, 153–9.
Davis, D.R. 1998. Technology, unemployment, and relative wages in a global economy, *European Economic Review*, **42**, 1613–33.
Dobbs, I.M., Hill, M.B. and Waterson, M. 1987. Industrial structure and the employment consequences of technical change, *Oxford Economic Papers*, **39**, 552–67.
Dosi, G. 1988. Source, procedure and microeconomic effects of innovation, *Journal of Economic Literature*, **26**, 1120–71.
Edquist, C., Hommen, L. and McKelvey, M. 2001. *Innovation and Employment: Product Versus Process Innovation*, Cheltenham, UK and Northampton, MA, USA: Edward Elgar.
Entorf, H. and Pohlmeier, W. 1990. 'Employment, innovation and export activities', in J.P. Florens (ed.), *Microeconometrics: Surveys and Applications*, London: Basil Blackwell.
Evangelista, R. 2000. 'Innovation and employment in services', in M. Vivarelli and M. Pianta (eds), *The Employment Impact of Innovation: Evidence and Policy*, London: Routledge, pp. 121–48.
Evangelista, R. and Savona, M. 2002. The impact of innovation on employment in services: evidence from Italy, *International Review of Applied Economics*, **16**, 309–18.
Freeman, C. and Soete, L. (eds). 1987. *Technical Change and Full Employment*, Oxford: Basil Blackwell.
Freeman, C. and Soete, L. 1994. *Work for All or Mass Unemployment? Computerised Technical Change into the Twenty-first Century*, London/New York: Pinter.
Freeman, C., Clark, J.B. and Soete, L. 1982. *Unemployment and Technical Innovation*, London: Pinter.
Greenan, N. and Guellec, D. 2000. Technological innovation and employment reallocation, *Labour*, **14**, 547–90.
Hall, P.H. and Heffernan, S.A. 1985. More on the employment effects of innovation, *Journal of Development Economics*, **17**, 151–62.
Hicks, J.R. 1932. *The Theory of Wages*, London: Macmillan.
Hicks, J.R. 1973. *Capital and Time*, Oxford: Oxford University Press.

Hobsbawm, E.J. 1968. *Industry and Empire: An Economic History of Britain since 1750*, Harmondsworth, Middlesex: Penguin Books.

Hobsbawm, E.J. and Rudé, G. 1969. *Captain Swing*, London: Penguin University Books.

Kalmbach, P. and Kurz, H.D. 1990. Micro-electronics and employment: a dynamic input–output study of the West German economy, *Structural Change and Economic Dynamics*, **1**, 371–86.

Katsoulacos, Y.S. 1986. *The Employment Effect of Technical Change*, Brighton: Wheatsheaf.

Keynes, J.M. 1973. *The General Theory of Employment, Interest and Money*, in *The Collected Writings of John Maynard Keynes*, London: Macmillan, first edn, 1936.

Layard, R. and Nickell, S. 1985. The causes of British unemployment, *National Institute Economic Review*, **111**, 62–85.

Layard, R., Nickell, S. and Jackman, R. 1991. *Unemployment: Macroeconomic Performance and the Labour Market*, Oxford: Oxford University Press.

Leontief, W. and Duchin, F. 1986. *The Future Impact of Automation on Workers*, Oxford: Oxford University Press.

Malthus, T.R. 1964. *Principles of Political Economy*, New York: M. Kelley, first edn, 1836.

Marshall, A. 1961. *Principles of Economics*, Cambridge: Macmillan, first edn, 1890.

Marx, K. 1961. *Capital*, Moscow: Foreign Languages Publishing House, first edn, 1867.

Marx, K. 1969. *Theories of Surplus Value*, London: Lawrence & Wishart, first edn, 1905–10.

Meyer-Krahmer, F. 1992, The effects of new technologies on employment, *Economics of Innovation and New Technology*, **2**, 131–49.

Mill, J.S. 1976. *Principles of Political Economy*, New York: M. Kelley, first edn, 1848.

Neary, J.P. 1981. On the short-run effects of technological progress, *Oxford Economic Papers*, **32**, 224–33.

Nickell, S. and Kong, P. 1989. Technical progress and jobs, Centre for Labour Economics, discussion paper n.366, London School of Economics, London.

Padalino, S. and Vivarelli, M. 1997. The employment intensity of economic growth in the G-7 countries, *International Labour Review*, **136**, 191–213.

Pasinetti, L. 1981. *Structural Change and Economic Growth*, Cambridge: Cambridge University Press.

Petit, P. 1995. 'Employment and technological change', in P. Stoneman (ed.), *Handbook of the Economics of Innovation and Technological Change*, Amsterdam: North-Holland, pp. 366–408.

Piacentini, P. and Pini, P. 2000. 'Growth and employment', in M. Vivarelli and M. Pianta (eds), *The Employment Impact of Innovation: Evidence and Policy*, London: Routledge, pp. 44–76.

Pianta, M. 2000. 'The employment impact of product and process innovations', in, M. Vivarelli and M. Pianta (eds), *The Employment Impact of Innovation: Evidence and Policy*, London: Routledge, pp. 77–95.

Pianta, M. 2004. 'Innovation and employment', in J. Fagerberg, D. Mowery and R. Nelson (eds), *The Oxford Handbook of Innovation*, Oxford: Oxford University Press, ch. 21.

Pigou, A. 1933. *The Theory of Unemployment*, London: Macmillan.

Pigou, A. 1962. *The Economics of Welfare*, London: Macmillan, first edn, 1920.

Pini, P. 1996, An integrated cumulative growth model: empirical evidence for nine OECD countries, 1960–1990, *Labour*, **10**, 93–150.

Piva, M. and Vivarelli, M. 2003. Innovation and employment: evidence from Italian micro-data, IZA Discussion Paper n. 730, Bonn.

Piva, M. and Vivarelli, M. 2004. Technological change and employment: some micro evidence from Italy, *Applied Economics Letters*, **11**, 373–6.

Ricardo, D. 1951. 'Principles of political economy', in P. Sraffa (ed.), *The Works and Correspondence of David Ricardo*, vol. 1, Cambridge: Cambridge University Press, third edn, 1821.

Rosenberg, N. 1976. *Perspectives on Technology*, Cambridge: Cambridge University Press.

Say, J.-B. 1964. *A Treatise on Political Economy or the Production, Distribution and Consumption of Wealth*, New York: M. Kelley, first edn, 1803.

Simonetti, R., Taylor, K. and Vivarelli, M. 2000. 'Modelling the employment impact of innovation', in, M. Vivarelli and M. Pianta (eds), *The Employment Impact of Innovation: Evidence and Policy*, London: Routledge, pp. 26–43.

Sinclair, P.J.N. 1981. When will technical progress destroy jobs?, *Oxford Economic Papers*, **31**, 1–18.

Sismondi, J.C.L. 1971. *Nouveaux Principes d'Economie Politique ou de la Richesse dans ses Rapports avec la Population*, Paris: Calmann-Levy, first edn, 1819.

Smolny, W. 1998. Innovations, prices and employment: a theoretical model and an empirical application for West German manufacturing firms, *Journal of Industrial Economics*, **46**, 359–81.

Steuart, J. 1966. *An Inquiry into the Principles of Political Economy*, Chicago, IL: Oliver and Boyd, first edn, 1767.

Stoneman, P. 1983. *The Economic Analysis of Technological Change*, Oxford: Oxford University Press.

Sylos Labini, P. 1969. *Oligopoly and Technical Progress*, Cambridge, MA: Harvard University Press, first edn, 1956.

Van Reenen, J. 1997. Employment and technological innovation: evidence from U.K. manufacturing firms, *Journal of Labour Economics*, **15**, 255–84.

Venables, A.J. 1985. The economic implications of a discrete technical change, *Oxford Economic Papers*, **37**, 230–48.

Vivarelli, M. 1995. *The Economics of Technology and Employment: Theory and Empirical Evidence*, Aldershot, UK and Brookfield, USA: Edward Elgar.

Vivarelli, M. and Pianta, M. (eds). 2000. *The Employment Impact of Innovation: Evidence and Policy*, London: Routledge.

Whitley, J.D. and Wilson, R.A. 1982. Quantifying the employment effects of micro-electronics, *Futures*, **14**, 486–95.

Whitley, J.D. and Wilson, R.A. 1987. Quantifying the impact of information technology on employment using a macroeconomic model of the United Kingdom economy, OECD, ICCP paper 12: Information Technology and Economic Prospects, OECD, Paris.

Wicksell, K. 1961. *Lectures on Political Economy*, London: Routledge & Kegan, first edn, 1901–6.

45 Macro-econometrics
John Foster

Introduction

Econometric modeling, using aggregated time series data, which we can label 'macro-econometrics', played a very important role in the development of macroeconomics in the postwar era. Reliable econometric models were sought to aid the design of macroeconomic policies and model-driven forecasts were required to implement them. Parallel attempts to use macroeconometrics in a scientific manner to verify and test economic hypotheses ran into difficulties quite quickly and, today, the main econometric methodology (vector error correction modeling (VECM)) is primarily directed at economic forecasting rather than hypothesis testing.

From an early stage, evolutionary and institutional economists argued that using regression analysis on aggregated time series data to construct linear, fixed-parameter econometric models, for either explanation or forecasting purposes, was doomed to failure because economic relationships are inherently nonlinear with parameters that shift because of the existence of pervasive structural and institutional change. It is for this reason that evolutionary economists have preferred to use simulation and calibration techniques that can deal with nonlinear relationships. Despite this, regression analysis has continued to be applied to model innovation diffusion processes at the level of industry and product classifications. So, although the notion that econometrics can be used at high levels of aggregation was rejected, its application in certain conditions was still seen as useful.

Innovation diffusion lies at the heart of neo-Schumpeterian evolutionary economics and the purpose here is to discuss how macro-econometrics can be employed, in the presence of appropriate time series data, to better understand how evolutionary economic processes operate. In so doing, it will be argued that it is possible to identify a neo-Schumpeterian econometric methodology that differs substantially from that embodied in VECM. This is an important matter because widespread acceptance of schools of thought in economics tends to hinge upon the validity of its empirical methodology. This was nowhere more clearly stated than by Joseph Schumpeter 70 years ago:

> The only way to a position in which our science might give positive advice on a large scale to politicians and business men, leads through quantitative work. For

as long as we are unable to put our arguments into figures, the voice of our science, although occasionally it may help to dispel gross errors, it will never be heard by practical men. They are, by instinct, econometricians all of them. (Schumpeter, 1933, p. 12)

Evolutionary macro-econometric modeling

Neo-Schumpeterian evolutionary economics has, in the main, been preoccupied with the operation of selection mechanisms. Variety in productive capabilities, stemming from the existence of novelty, is viewed as resulting in the differential growth of firms because of productivity and quality differences. If the link between profits and growth is sufficiently uniform across firms, those with the highest profits come to dominate. Thus, growth stems from non-average behaviors and the outcome that eventuates over time is not an average of these behaviors. At first sight, this process of 'replicator dynamics' seems to pose a difficulty in applying macro-econometrics because the latter is a method that deals with average associations between data series. However, this is something of a misunderstanding because non-average behavior in a regressed relationship is captured in an error term that is distributed over time whereas the non-average behavior relevant to the replicator dynamics relates to a distribution of behaviors at a point in historical time. Aggregation does, of course, mask cross-section differences but we can relate the non-stationarity that we observe in time series data to the phases that a replicator dynamic process goes through. Furthermore, it is likely that regression errors will exhibit certain distinct properties when the replicator dynamic process is in particular phases.

Average associations between variables over time occur because of the structural connections that, necessarily, exist in complex adaptive systems. These tend to persist over time but they vary in their magnitude and strength. However, this variation is not due to 'disequilibrium' precipitated by exogenous shocks to equilibrium states, as the VECM methodology would have it. Rather, it is what we might expect when self-organization and selection processes produce non-matching, non-equilibrium paths in variables that are systemically connected. Of course, exogenous shocks still have a part to play in inducing temporary deviations from non-equilibrium paths and, more importantly from an evolutionary economic perspective, in precipitating nonlinear discontinuities when homeostatic mechanisms fail to work.

What does the time path of a variable look like if it is determined by self-organization and selection processes? Consider, for example, the case of a set of firms in an industry applying different techniques to produce a good that is sold. Initially, sales will begin to grow thanks to the growth of synergetic connections that characterize self-organization. As sales tend towards market saturation, competitive selection will come to dominate and a few firms with the best techniques will survive because of their lower costs and/or higher-quality products. Once such firms have gained so much market power they are also likely to restrict output growth to raise prices and enjoy economic rents that are protected by barriers to entry. Thus, sales data for the product in question at the industry level are likely to trace out a logistic curve. This can be fitted as a simple historical relationship where the association between $X(t)$ and $X(t-1)$ exhibits a varying parameter that tends from zero to a maximum and then back to zero. The advantage of using the logistic curve to capture this parameter variation is that we can obtain a fixed parametric representation of such a nonlinear sigmoid growth path. However, as such, it is no more than a summary of the history of a growth indicator that reflects an underlying self-organization/selection process. As such, the curve does not depict this process directly but, rather, it traces out the path of an aggregate measure of the outputs of the process.

Many economists have viewed such logistic curves as tracing out disequilibrium dynamics (see Dixon, 1994, for a review) and/or learning trajectories (see Baba *et al.*, 1992, for an example) that conclude in equilibrium. Curve fitting can become quite sophisticated: a recent example is Bewley and Griffiths (1999) who introduce a Bayesian approach to modeling the logistic curve. The disequilibrium approach, of course, presupposes the existence of a limit that is a stable equilibrium position. This contrasts with the evolutionary perspective where an end stationary state is viewed as structurally unstable (see Allen, 2001). In this regard, Sarkar (1998) provides an insightful comparison of equilibrium and non-equilibrium approaches to the modeling of diffusion. However, given that the logistic equation is mathematically deterministic, the question arises as to whether it is valid to use it to capture non-equilibrium trajectories that are punctuated by structural discontinuities.

This issue is tackled in Foster and Wild (1999a, 1999b). They explain why the logistic diffusion equation can be viewed as an abstraction derived from an endogenous 'theory of historical process'. This theory views economic systems as 'dissipative structures' that use energy, materials and knowledge to fuel endogenous structural development, through parallel increases in order and complexity, towards a capacity limit. This leads, quite straightforwardly, to logistic trajectories that have to be augmented in various ways before they can be operationalized econometrically. Unlike traditional theories, such theories of historical processes are never separated from the historical domain of inquiry, they simply offer abstract representations of historical tendencies upon which deductive hypotheses can be added.

Foster and Wild (1999a) constructed an augmented logistic diffusion model (ALDM), that allows the diffusion rate and the capacity limit to be subject to exogenous and interactive effects. An ALDM can be based on several alternative logistic equations. The Mansfield variant, expressed in terms of a growth rate, was chosen because of its convenient properties:

$$ln X_t - ln X_{t-1} = b_1[1 - \{X_{t-1}/K(...)\} - a(...)]$$
$$+ b_2(...) + c\{ln X_t - ln X_{t-1}\}_{t-1} + e_t \qquad (45.1)$$

where b_1 is the underlying density dependent, or diffusion, coefficient (after allowing for deterioration rates, death rates, etc); $K(...)$ represents a carrying capacity which can vary because of exogenous external factors; $a(...)$ contains competitive factors due to the presence of other systems in the same 'niche', altering the effective capacity limit that can be attained; $b_2(...)$ contains exogenous influences which cause the net diffusion rate to vary. The lagged dependent variable, $\{ln X_t - ln X_{t-1}\}_{t-1}$, is included to capture 'momentum' effects, which cushion the impact of exogenous shocks.

Eq.(45.1) is an endogenous growth specification, which can be applied in historical episodes when structural development is taking place. As it stands, many might interpret it as the specification of a disequilibrium process, following a jump in a 'long-run equilibrium' K, given that ongoing structural change is homogenized into a growth measure. However, in the presence of structural change which is self-organizational/selectionist in character we cannot accept this interpretation because dissipative structures which structurally develop and, thus, grow towards a capacity limit are not in disequilibrium. If we rely upon evolutionary theory, we can predict that, as the growth of such systems tends towards zero, they do not approach a stable equilibrium but, rather, a state of structural instability.

In general, processes that involve endogenous structural change are not deterministic and cannot tend, asymptotically, to stable long-run equilibrium outcomes. However, this does not mean that the conventional notion of equilibration is inapplicable. A self-organizational/selectionist process can still be viewed as a moving temporary equilibrium, which tends, asymptotically, to K. Homoeostatic mechanisms of varying strength will operate to return such a trajectory to its logistic path when external shocks are experienced. If a growth process is perceived in this way, then structural instability relates to the extent to which the basin of attraction around such moving equilibria changes over time. If the logistic growth path is viewed as capturing the deterministic component of the process of structural development, then variation in the basin of attraction can be seen as reflecting its non-deterministic component. Synergetic theory suggests that there will be a tendency for the basin to narrow as the system in question moves up a logistic growth curve. The consequent fall in variance is associated with an increase in the likelihood that a given exogenous shock will induce a departure from the basin and structural discontinuity of some type.

Typically, students of technological diffusion draw families of logistic curves over time with gaps, or overlaps, between them stressing the uniqueness of each diffusion process with the gaps confirming the existence of structural discontinuities. Thus, there is implicit acceptance in such studies that a tendency towards saturation in a technological diffusion process is not a tendency towards a stable equilibrium. Foster and Wild (1999a) showed that the particular ALDM growth trajectory that they studied was not mean reverting, but neither was it a random walk, with or without drift. The level of the variable under investigation and the (moving) capacity limit were not linearly cointegrated. Thus, in the case considered, it was difficult to argue that the observed ALDM provided evidence in support of an equilibrium/disequilibrium process, from the standpoint either of deterministic or of stochastic trends in time series data. Foster and Wild (1999b) went on to show how spectral methods can be employed to detect the presence of self-organizational/selectionist change, as well as to test for the presence of a disequilibrium process of the traditional type.

If we think of fitting simple logistic curves as 'first level' econometrics in the presence of self-organizational/selectionist change and the Foster/Wild approach as a 'second level' approach which can capture the growth dynamics of developmental processes, well beyond simple cases of innovation diffusion, there remains a 'third level' where we are confronted with data that are aggregated across many products and sectors that are in a range of different evolutionary phases. It is this third level that is crucial in linking the principles of evolutionary economics to the aggregate contexts that are so familiar in mainstream econometric modeling. Let us now consider how such links can be forged.

Evolutionary macro-econometrics using highly aggregated data

Not only do the results in Foster and Wild (1999b) raise fundamental questions concerning the interpretation of evidence in VECM studies, but they also open up the possibility that we can apply evolutionary thinking in empirical contexts where the data do not involve a visible logistic diffusion path. As we aggregate data across firms and industries that are in a range of evolutionary phases, the data lose clear logistic patterns and become the 'stochastic trends' that are so familiar in macroeconomic data. Logistic trajectories can still be observed but only over very long periods, characterized by Kondratieff waves. As Schumpeter (1939) pointed out, these trajectories involve endogenous, nonequilibrium processes related to technological, organizational and energetic advances that are tractable even though formal connections with the behavior of firms and individuals are almost impossible to make.

Since Joseph Schumpeter wrote about these matters, notions of self-organization, inspired by advances in non-equilibrium thermodynamics, have augmented his vision of 'creative destruction'. If we think of any economic system as a dissipative structure that imports energy and materials and exports products and waste, this structure should become both more ordered and more complex as it develops. However, by necessity, structure involves orderings that exhibit a degree of irreversibility. This irreversibility places a boundary upon the extent to which a dissipative structure can develop. We can give expression to this tendency in quite a simple way if we translate everything into value terms. We have the following flow identity:

$$Y_t = Y_{t-1} + Z_t - W_t \qquad (45.2)$$

or

$$Y_t - Y_{t-1} = Z_t - W_t, \qquad (45.3)$$

where Y is the value flow of output characteristics of a system, W is the output value flow loss in a system due to wear and tear, breakdowns, etc, and Z is the output value flow increase due to new investments. Clearly, if Z exceeds W then there is growth and vica versa. Part of Z offsets W and part of it represents new value creation from the production of greater output of existing products or the output of new products. This is often thought of in terms of 'replacement' and 'net' components of investment expenditure but, as Scott (1989) stressed, this can be misleading because 'replacement' often involves the simultaneous upgrading of productive structure and output. Dissipative structure theory does not rely on such a distinction but, rather, predicts that growth will run out as Z becomes, increasingly, committed to dealing with W. In other words, Y will follow a logistic curve.

For example, a logistic curve can be derived from the following nonlinear relationships:

$$Z = z Y_{t-1} - m Y_{t-1}^2 + v, \qquad (45.4)$$

$$W = w Y_{t-1} + n Y_{t-1}^2 + u, \qquad (45.5)$$

where u and v represent non-deterministic factors. Therefore:

$$Y_t - Y_{t-1} = (z - w) Y_{t-1} - (m + n) Y_{t-1}^2 + u - v, \qquad (45.6)$$

if $K = (z-w)/(m+n)$ and $(z-w)) = b$.
Then

$$Y_t - Y_{t-1} = b Y_{t-1}[1 - (Y_{t-1}/K)] + (u - v). \qquad (45.7)$$

Thus the logistic curve can capture the growth of a dissipative structure as it engages in self-organizational development and is subject to selection mechanisms. Although the nonlinear form of eqs. (45.4) and (45.5) is quadratic, more complex logistic forms can be obtained by varying the exponent on the nonlinear Y_{t-1} term. For example, if we use a cubed Y_{t-1} instead of a squared one then the logistic limit relates to the square of Y_{t-1}. Any logistic form of this type is quite general in the sense that, even if m or n (but not both) is equal to zero, it will still exist. It is very likely that n will be positive since repair and maintenance requirements in dissipative structures cause W to rise non-linearly because of the irreversible character of parts of the productive structure. New output change, Z, is likely to have a density-dependent relation with output, generally discussed in terms of 'economies of scale' but, if there are learning effects that run out then m will be positive. In this regard, we must think of Z as being related both to all past investment and to learning effects. The non-deterministic elements, u and v are important because it is a u shock that starts a developmental process and a v shock that will induce a structural transition when growth has ceased. Also, these may be externally or internally generated and may or may not be random in character.

Because logistic curves have long been used in population ecology, K is commonly thought of as an environmental (or niche) delimiter. However, in economics it is more profitable to think of it as being endogenously determined by the irreversible nature of productive structure to a significant degree. This irreversibility results in a lack of adaptability in a process or in a product range, as development proceeds. Indeed, although we can think of an entrepreneur imagining a market niche for a new product, it is only in the process of pursuing this goal, through the organization of people and capital, that K becomes defined. Often, it is discovered that no niche exists, in the sense that no positive profits accrue, and the organization collapses.

The fact that Ks are the product of knowledge and imagination and are endogenously determined is what distinguishes economic development from its counterparts in biology and chemistry. Although much of K will be determined by 'founding structure' (Hannan and Freeman, 1989), there is always some scope for further endogenous shifts in it over time. So, in reality, the K limit can involve both exogenous 'environmental' limits and endogenously determined limits. In a sense, these are related because it is lack of adaptability that constrains the environmental range that a system can enter. The non-existent fully reversible system proposed in neoclassical economics can simply reconfigure itself to suit all environments but we know that this breaches some fundamental laws of systems (see Foster and Wild, 1996). Without a degree of irreversibility, i.e. order, there will be no dissipative structure.

If explanatory variables can be discovered that capture the role of exogenous factors in affecting b and K, then the underlying endogenous dynamics of the growth/development process can be observed. It is a remarkable fact that, particularly in innovation studies, we observe so many logistic paths that conform to eq. (45.7), even without such modeling exercises, suggesting that there is an inherent tendency for systems to exhibit behavior roughly coincident with eq. (45.4) and eq. (45.5). As we move from the traditional logistic equation set up to thinking in terms of logistic processes with endogenously determined K limits plus exogenous effects on b and K, we need not actually observe a logistic curve in the data.

Once we begin to think of logistic trajectories in these terms, we can see how we can deal with highly aggregated data. Conventional econometric modelers are seduced into thinking that macroeconomic time series data can be modeled using a linear, equilibrium/disequilibrium methodology, e.g. VECM, once non-stationarity has been eliminated from the data. However, if we view the whole economy as an interconnected dissipative structure, it will have its own aggregated eqs (45.4) and (45.5). Given the length of time involved in diffusion at this level, depicted in Kondratieff upswings, it is likely that the logistic form may not be discernable, even using two decades of data. This is even more likely if the diffusion rate and the capacity limit shift because of exogenous changes.

Growth in the economy arises from the fact that aggregate Z exceeds W, i.e., there is more creation than destruction going on in the economy. At the aggregate level, this means that Y must be progressing towards a K limit. However, this limit is not a summation of 'micro-Ks' since we can envisage an economy that is stationary in the aggregate but has many logistic processes going on, but growth is exactly offset by decline. For aggregate growth to occur, there must be an economy-wide developmental process of self-organization/selection going on that results in an excess of creation over destruction. This process is external to the firms and industries involved and has been expressed in the conventional literature in terms of economies of scale, spillovers, etc. In other words, 'non-stationarity' in aggregate time series, which is generally eliminated in VECM studies, in fact is central to any empirical investigation of economic growth. Yes, data aggregation blurs the differentiated nature of firms and other productive organizations and relates to very different evolutionary experiences, yet there remains a coherent story to tell about the economy employing macro-econometrics.

Conclusion

In this chapter, it has been argued that conventional econometric methodology – error correction models based on cointegrated variables and cast in VAR representations of data – are essentially forecasting strategies that contribute little to explanation. This methodology eliminates non-stationarity and, thus, any connection with the processes that drive economic growth. Consequently, this methodology is of little use to neo-Schumpeterian evolutionary economists who envisage economic growth in terms of self-organization, selection and creative destruction. This has led to a pessimistic view of econometric modeling, particularly using aggregated data. However, it has been argued that macro-econometrics is not, in itself, the problem. The problem lies with the timeless nature of conventional economic theory and the empirical methodology that is employed to connect such theory with historical data.

Macro-econometrics remains useful to evolutionary economists provided that economic systems are viewed as dissipative structures experiencing self-organization and selection. It is the diffusional nature of these processes that generates the continuity observed in data measuring growth and this provided the basis for econometric analysis. The Foster and Wild (1999a, 1999b) studies offer an operational econometric methodology that moves beyond the large literature of a logistic curve fitting into a general framework for modeling all time series.

What is suggested is an empirical agenda that has the capacity to highlight the relevance and importance of neo-Schumpeterian economics by applying it in contexts that are of strong contemporary interest, such as research on the drivers of economic growth. By interpreting existing evidence and respecifying models from such a perspective, it becomes possible to alter the theoretical frameworks that economists routinely apply. The consignment of economic history into the anonymity of the 'DGP' in the VECM approach can be reversed and the valid forces discussed in neoclassical economics can be returned to their proper Marshallian context, namely, as a body of price theory that helps us understand why historical tendencies move around in the short period.

References

Allen, P.M. (2001) 'Knowledge, ignorance and the evolution of complex systems', in J. Foster and J.S. Metcalfe (eds), *Frontiers of Evolutionary Economics: Competition, Self-Organization and Innovation Policy*, Cheltenham, UK and Northampton, MA, USA: Edward Elgar, pp. 313–50.

Baba, Y., Hendry, D.F. and Starr, R.M. (1992) The demand for M1 in the U.S.A., 1960–1988, *Review of Economic Studies*, **59**, 25–61.

Bewley, R. and Griffiths, W.E. (1999) A forecasting comparison of classical and Bayesian forecasting methods for modelling logistic diffusion, *UNE Working Papers in Econometrics and Applied Statistics*, no. 107, September.

Dixon, R. (1994) 'The logistic family of discrete dynamic models', in J. Creedy and V. Martin (eds), *Chaos and Non-Linear Models in Economics*, Aldershot, UK and Brookfield, USA: Edward Elgar.

Foster, J. and Wild, P. (1996) 'Economic evolution and the science of synergetics', *Journal of Evolutionary Economics*, **6**, 239–60.

Foster, J. and Wild, P. (1999a) Econometric modelling in the presence of evolutionary change, *Cambridge Journal of Economics*, **23**, 749–70.

Foster, J. and Wild, P. (1999b) Detecting self-organizational change in economic processes exhibiting logistic growth, *Journal of Evolutionary Economics*, **9**, 109–33; reprinted in U. Cantner, H. Hanusch and S. Klepper (eds), *Economic Evolution and Complexity*, New York: Physica-Verlag, 2000, pp. 159–84.

Hannan, M.T. and Freeman, J. (1989) *Organizational Ecology*, Cambridge, MA: Harvard University Press.

Sarkar, J. (1998) Technological diffusion: alternative theories and historical evidence, *Journal of Economic Surveys*, **12**(2), 131–76.

Schumpeter, J.A. (1933) The common sense of econometrics, *Econometrica*, **1**, 5–12.

Schumpeter, J.A. (1939) *Business Cycles Vol. I*, New York: McGraw-Hill.

Scott, M. (1989), *A New View of Economic Growth*, Oxford: Oxford University Press.

4.2
Development

46 The mechanisms of economic evolution: completing Schumpeter's theory
Richard H. Day

Introduction

Joseph Schumpeter introduced his famous theory of economic development with the description of an economy in a competitive, efficient, general equilibrium, or 'circular flow'. He then introduced entrepreneurs and banks. The former creates new combinations of the materials and forces of production while the latter creates purchasing power and places it in the hands of the former. Entrepreneurs can then attract the means of production from their current occupations by bidding up their prices, in this way bringing about a disequilibrium in product and factor markets. The temporary monopoly power of the entrepreneur enables profit to exist from which interest can be paid. This provides the source of livelihood for bankers and an incentive for additional entrepreneurial effort. The innovations occur in swarms, which leads to business cycles that are perpetuated in a more of less irregular fashion. The latter characteristic complicates economizing calculations, inducing the planning errors inherent in the uncertain trial of new combinations that begin an economic boom.

Schumpeter argued that, in the absence of entrepreneurs or bankers, ordinary people would not need 'to find their way towards the goal of greatest possible economic welfare by conscious and rational effort' (1934, p. 10), 'because each inherits an inventory of means and methods of production' (ibid., p. 6). Past influences have taught them 'what to do'. They are never conscious of all parts of the value system, 'do not pay attention to all the facts but only to certain indexes "ready at hand", they act in 'the ordinary daily round according to general custom or experience' (ibid., p. 40), resist change, and adapt slowly under pressure. Within the circular flow (ibid., p. 235) tradition or mere habit is enough to keep economic actors in line with their own best interests. Once in such a state, agents would stay there. It follows that new forces must be introduced to disrupt equilibrium once it is attained, ones that *do not function in the circular flow*, forces that break the circular flow and that internally generate and perpetuate fundamental change in the conditions and activities of economic life.[1]

For Schumpeter the disequilibrating forces are mediated by entrepreneurs and bankers who augment the pre-existing population of consumers and firms. Where do they come from and why do they emerge? To answer these questions, we have to ask a more fundamental one implied by the out-of-equilibrium conditions induced by innovation. The latter imply that the economy would no longer be perfectly coordinated. Can boundedly rational firms and households really bring such a state into existence, as Schumpeter assumed? A look at the current economy shows that they have not. A look at history shows they never have. But then how could economies get along as well as they have when they are evidently always somewhat out of whack?

The remainder of this chapter is devoted to answers to these questions and to the outline of a theory that follows from those answers. It is not so much a correction of Schumpeter but rather a completion of his theory that I have elsewhere referred to as 'the coevolution of market and state'.

Adaptive economizing out-of-equilibrium

To begin an explanation, let us take a closer look at economizing behavior out-of-equilibrium. So, in contrast to Schumpeter, assume the economy to begin with is in a disequilibrium situation. There is a population of individuals who are organized into a variety of households, firms, and government agencies. Production and consumption are determined by sequences of activities that include information gathering and processing. Current and past performance is considered. Current external conditions to some degree are taken into account. Plans of a more or less elaborate nature are drawn up. This takes time, especially in complex business firms. While this is going on, actions must take place in fact; resources must be allocated in fact; new capital must be constructed in fact; food must be produced and consumed in fact. Therefore, while actions may be influenced by existing plans, they have to be controlled by various mechanisms that are also determined by current operating conditions which themselves may not be accurately or correctly anticipated in existing plans or in the new plans being formed. This control system must operate in *real* time *and must be distinct from planning itself.*

Behavior is therefore determined by an Information–Planning–Control (IPC) system. Individuals and groups do not and cannot know what everyone is doing or what they will do in the future. They must construct an image of their environment and a record of the past that is of necessity simplified and imperfect. They must base plans on expectations that will not be fulfilled and data that may prove biased, wrong or misleading. They must construct controls that enable economic activity to continue when even the most carefully elaborated plans must be modified in the light of accumulating information or because they simply cannot be carried out.

The rational core of an IPC system is the plan. Its purpose is to identify actions that will further the agent's objectives. The function of economizing is to formulate plans that accomplish this purpose. The mathematical analog of economizing behavior is the optimizing algorithm that decomposes the planning problem into a sequence of simple calculations and binary comparisons that are applied iteratively. These iterative steps are usually nested within a sequence of approximations to the 'true' optimizing problem at hand. They converge to a true optimum only when the exact problem can be represented mathematically and then only for a relatively small class of problems that have very strong and often not very realistic regularity conditions.

It can be inferred categorically that most human plans are not and cannot be formulated exactly in mathematical terms. For that reason in real life economizing activity is focused on relatively simple, relatively stable choice situations that approximate and solve only a part of the problem of deciding what to do. Other behavioral rules must fill in the huge gap that is left between what needs to be done and what is planned by explicit economizing calculations. (In explaining how humans and organizations behave, it must always be remembered that rationality is a property of individual minds and is bounded. It is not a property of organizations or national economies.)

To summarize, economizing behavior is conditioned in several ways. First, it applies to only a part of the variables over which individuals and organizations have control. Second, it proceeds according to forms that are approximate, relatively simple, locally and iteratively applied. Because of these characteristics, models of economizing *behavior* are distinctly different than the sufficient existence conditions for individual optimality upon which general equilibrium theory builds.

Moreover, one cannot be sure that, when a planning procedure for solving a *perceived* problem converges, one has solved the real problem at hand. This suggests that optimum seeking behavior should not allow a succession of market punishments gradually to discourage search to the point where it disappears entirely. Rather, there should be continuing *unmotivated search* in an environment that may be 'irregular' or subject to drift or perturbation, or when local search in response to feedback can get 'stuck' in locally good but globally suboptimal decisions. Such search can be driven by curiosity, eccentricity, 'playfulness', or stubborn determination, but not economic calculation of the rational sort. *Evidently, the whole idea of optimality is fundamentally incompatible with wise behavior in an unfathomable world.* Certainly, it ought to be obvious that the optimum solution of a given planning problem is contingent on all the data, assumptions, estimates and predictions going into it. Many sorts of behavior, such as imitation or trial and error search may do just as well – or better.

A specific model of economizing behavior reflecting this point of view can be based on a frequently exploited practice of algorithm construction, the incorporation of more or less ad hoc rules that limit the distance succeeding steps take in a sequence of trial choices. This is the analog of the principle of local search that forms a part of the core of adaptive or behavioral economics. When explicitly represented in a mathematical model of economizing behavior it leads to a sequence of recursively connected simple, easily solvable optimization problems, each of whose constraints depends on solutions of programs earlier in the sequence and which define what I have called elsewhere 'zones of flexible response' within which local optimizing is exercised. The zone of flexible response is centered on past experience. It allows departures from the preceding choice to a greater or lesser extent that also depends on experience.

This representation of behavior might be called 'local optimizing' or 'cautious suboptimizing' with feedback or just 'adaptive economizing'. Its outcome is the formulation of a plan designed to identify most preferred actions. At this stage the control function takes over. Its responsibility is to carry out planned actions or to provide some contingent tactic to govern action until a new, more successful, plan can be thought through. In the subsequent discussion it will be sufficient to assume that agents will try to behave as close to their existing plan as possible given current conditions. If it is not feasible, they are faced with a survival problem pending identification of a new workable alternative.

Coordination
Transactions among agents are mutually interrelated actions involving the exchange of information and goods. How are transactions coordinated? Within Schumpeter's circular flow there is no problem. They occur according to competitive equilibrium prices that constitute information indexes upon which equilibrium plans can be based. But where do these equilibrium prices come from? General equilibrium theory by itself only determines conditions for their hypothetical existence. It does not specify who determines them or how they do it. It is usually implied that equilibrium prices are the outcome of a Bidding–Negotiation–Bargaining (BNB) process as in bond or fine art auctions or in real estate transactions.

Far more widely used, however, are Inventory–Order–Backlog–Price Adjustment (IOPA) procedures. Retail stores are inventories on display with order and price adjustment procedures that respond to the actual flow of sales but which, in the absence of outages, enable demand to be supplied without delay. Or, in the case of construction and expensive capital goods, orders are received and added to a 'backlog'. Product is then delivered from stock with minimal delay or after production takes place, the order backlog being adjusted accordingly. The specific character of the commodities involved, such as their storability, production time, or relative cost, determine the type of mechanism exploited.

The market mechanisms just described are often carried out within producing firms, usually in specialized sales or marketing departments. Independent agents also exist who mediate transactions. Separately owned and managed stores mediate transactions from producers or wholesalers through inventories on display. Stock brokers mediate, sell, and buy orders using their own stocks as stabilizing and coordinating inventories. Bank and other financial intermediaries govern the exchange of money and credit while informal or professional sales representatives, brokers, negotiators, arbitrators, lawyers, and courts mediate the bargaining processes. These fundamental mediating agents must be added to the households, firms, and 'auctioneers'.

They facilitate exchange when the flow of production equals demand. But their stocks or order backlogs take on special importance when production does not equal demand. Prices are adjusted periodically upwards if increasing order backlogs cause untimely delivery delays or if inventory decumulation threatens supply. Prices are adjusted downwards if excessive inventories build up or order backlogs fall below normal. Production need not equal demand but can be adjusted periodically in response to the market signals, that is, to changes in inventories and order backlogs. The impossible task of setting prices at equilibrium values need not hold up the functioning of the system indefinitely while their market clearing values are determined through interminable BNB procedures. In this way the economy can function out-of-equilibrium using IOPA mechanisms in response to what are real-time analogs of Walrasian tâtonnement.

To summarize: economies work viably because actions are governed by principles in addition to rationality. These principles include (1) the separation of information, planning, and control activities in economizing behavior that include contingent tactics to deal with surprises, and (2) the existence of explicit Inventory–Order–Price Adjustment mechanisms that mediate transactions compatible with feasible stock–flow relationships. Because equilibrium prices cannot govern behavior out-of-equilibrium, explicit price adjustment rules must emerge. They must be constructed in such a way that actions can take place more or less continuously even though current prices transmit more or less erroneous information and must themselves be adjusted according to unfolding information.

Our conclusion: economies can (in principle) work out-of-equilibrium.

Money, credit and entrepreneurship

Let us now consider the two elements that, in Schumpeter's theory, break the circular flow: money and entrepreneurship. The rudiments of money in the form of tokens backed by inventories of goods were introduced apparently in the earliest civilizations and, we may speculate, in the complex societies and perhaps even the hunting and food collecting cultures that preceded the development of formal arithmetic and language. In any case, it is clear that its origins are associated with records establishing ownership and control of goods that eventually became indirect instruments of exchange. Informal lending of labor or goods in exchange for later repayment in equivalent or enhanced terms became formalized in negotiable instruments of credit and debt. Their management eventually became elaborated in banking and other financial institutions. The use of debt instruments by governments to create money emerged, followed by the establishment of central banks for coordinating and stabilizing the associated markets for credits and debts throughout a national economy. One cannot imagine modern markets working effectively without these developments.

Indeed, it is clear that 'the various instruments and institutions making up the money and credit economy were human inventions that solved problems and created new opportunities. The fundamental problem that money solved was the elimination of lengthening strings of indirect exchanges among increasingly numerous and specialized individuals and organizations as economic growth proceeded. It established a double coincidence of wants in the first instance. The fundamental problem that credit solved was the coordination of production and consumption activities planned for different present and future periods of time by different agents. It opened up a vast arena for intertemporally coordinated exchange. The origin of banks, therefore, must be bound up with the innovations of money and credit.

The result is the vast hubbub in the modern world of production, borrowing, lending, exchange, and consumption among many millions of people who belong to millions of intersecting groups: families, households, private business firms, banks, government agencies, private clubs, political parties, and other organizations – all interacting through the many media of information flow, communication and exchange.

An economy that has evolved money and banks is pre-adapted for the entrepreneurial/credit expansion process. Entrepreneurs are the ones in the arena of human getting and spending that create new combinations from which the forms of economic activity and organization evolve. Even more, in a globally unstable economic world, *their* specific existence is a necessary condition for economic existence in general: out of the population of ideas they create are selected ones that lead to forms that prevent collapse, or that reshape a system so that it takes off on a new spiral of development.

The existence of entrepreneurs must no doubt be explained by the forces of biological and social evolution that explain human development generally. Certainly it is related to the emergence of creative intelligence, which should be distinguished from rationality. It has led to the origin, proliferation and growing sophistication of human culture. Once creative intelligence exists, the possibility of inventing economic structures exists: farms, firms, banks, and corporations.

Schumpeter taught us much of what we need to know about the nature of entrepreneurs but he did not explain why they intruded themselves on the circular flow. The explanation implied by the preceding argument is now clear. They do *not* intrude on the circular flow; they emerge in a disequilibrium, globally unstable economy with the fundamental function of *creating* the mechanisms that allow an economy to work out-of-equilibrium when its agents are boundedly rational, its transactions imperfectly coordinated, and its long-run behavior intrinsically and globally unstable.

Thus, they are both the result of evolution in its narrow biological sense and the mediator of evolution in its broader cultural sense. Once a part of human culture their activity does not switch on and off according to well-defined accounting messages or in response to carefully anticipated need. It functions more or less continuously, thereby imparting a continuous source of perturbation to the analytical structures that define routine production, consumption and managerial activity. The implication is that economies will evolve whether they need to or not. Economies are, therefore, intrinsically unstable and always have been.

The upshot of these observations is that economic development does not emerge out of an equilibrium state. Schumpeter's circular flow was a theoretical conceit, convenient for dramatizing the role of the entrepreneurial agents who introduced new things. But such persons are the result of the creative intelligence that all people have and always have had to some degree: a capacity to learn new things, to imagine future objectives, and find ways to bring them about. Some people, like Franklin, Madison, Ford, Edison, Marconi, or Steve Jobs, just have more than others. They create things that transform technology, government, management, and culture, things that induce new possibilities, enabling some to flourish, things that lead to the demise of old opportunities and occupations for others who are caught up in a struggle to accommodate themselves. Conflicts, therefore, inevitably arise as some are made better off and others worse off in the development process.

Institutions and development

From the very beginning of modern human life there have been unusually creative individuals who invented new things and new ways of producing them. Because of the disequilibrating consequences that followed, there have to have been equally creative individuals who could introduce new rules of social interaction that could reduce conflicts as they emerged. Out of these acts of entrepreneurship arose the elaborating rules of civil order that led to government structures as integral parts of the system of production, exchange, and consumption, especially in public goods and services, the mediation of conflict through legal procedure, and the management of external diseconomies through indirect transfer mechanisms.

It seems doubtful that this institution-creating entrepreneurial role can be described mathematically any more than can that of technological entrepreneurship. It is the task of political and economic historians to describe the innovations that seemed to have been responsible for upsetting current conditions or providing the means for maintaining viability in the face of existence threatening instabilities. They can also describe the antecedent conditions within which those innovations occurred and that favored their adoption. Certainly, a complete theory of economic development must take account of the evolution of both political and economic organizations and of culture generally; that is, after all, the conditioning context within which invention and innovation take place. What is crucial from the economic point of view is the fact that political and cultural changes modify the constraints and opportunities that condition individuals and that more generally foster the growth or decline of specific economic forms of organization. What is crucial from the political point of view is the fact that economic developments induce changes in governmental decision making and in the rules used by institutions making up the political order of society.

To illustrate the point, consider a recession accompanied by financial crises in which large numbers of firms and households experience insolvency. Serious downturns in past centuries led to the invention of bankruptcy proceedings by which resources under the control of an insolvent firm are expropriated and transferred to new owners by means of special institutions of the state. Severe recession, such as the Great Depression, led to still further innovations when a 'bank holiday' was declared and the entire private banking system reorganized under new laws and regulatory proceedings.

The point is also illustrated by the very long-run development of mankind in its passage from the hunting and food collecting band through village agriculture, the city-state, trading empires, the nation state, and into the present global information economy with its formation and dissolution of supra nation-state entities such as the Soviet Union, United Nations, NATO, the European Union and SEATO. Here the expansion in human numbers has been accompanied by improvements in productivity induced by countless innovations, large and small; first in the implements of hunting, clothing, shelter, and food processing, then in the various artifacts and organizational setups in agriculture, industry, and commerce. It was the success of innovations in hunting that led to human dominance over our mammalian competitors. It was the advance in their human numbers that induced an eventual switch to a settled agriculture, the process facilitated by innovation involving the planting, cultivating, and harvesting of plant foods. As the village agriculture flourished, human populations expanded more rapidly, resulting in crowding, competition, and conflict, eventually leading to a coalescing into cities. And so on.

I have described this coevolution of market and state in detail elsewhere.[2]

The point is, and perhaps it is an appropriate point on which to conclude this chapter, that it is the fundamental instability in human nature that is responsible for the instability of economic life. It is an instability induced by creative intelligence when new technologies and institutions are invented, innovated, and adopted. These in turn cause changes in the relative fortunes of society's members. These disparate fortunes induce organizational innovations that may, when effective, restore viability but which seem inevitably to lead eventually to new, unbalanced developments that invite further entrepreneurial activity.

So it is that capitalist development did not evolve because banks were invented and a new class of entrepreneurs suddenly came into being, as a naïve reading of Schumpeter's first book would suggest. Capitalist development is just a continuation of the unstable, unbalanced, development that has been the hallmark of human progress since Homo sapiens emerged.

Notes

1. The quotations are from Schumpeter (1934). For a more elaborate summary, see Day (1984).
2. See Day (2004), especially Chapters 10 and 12.

References

Day, Richard H., 1984, 'Disequilibrium economic dynamics: a post-Schumpeterian contribution', *Journal of Economic Behavior and Organization*, 5(1), 57–76.
Day, Richard H., 2004, *The Divergent Dynamics of Economic Growth: Studies in Adaptive Economizing, Technological Change and Economic Development*, New York: Cambridge University Press.
Schumpeter, Joseph, 1934, *Theory of Economic Development*, Cambridge, MA: Harvard University Press; trans. from the German 2nd edn of 1926 by Redvers Opie, Oxford, UK: Oxford University Press, 1961.

47 Innovation and demand
Esben Sloth Andersen

Introduction

Economic evolution is an immensely complex phenomenon, so there is an obvious need for simplifying the way we handle this phenomenon. Since Nelson and Winter's (1982) pioneering formalization of the Schumpeterian vision of innovation-driven evolution, the major simplification has been obtained by modelling the demand side of markets in the simplest possible way. This strategy has allowed a gradual increase in the sophistication of supply-side aspects of economic evolution, but the one-sided focus on supply is facing diminishing returns. Therefore, demand-side aspects of economic evolution have in recent years received increased attention. The present chapter argues that the new emphasis on demand-side factors is quite crucial for a deepened understanding of economic evolution. The major reasons are the following: first, demand represents the core force of selection that gives direction to the evolutionary process; second, firms' innovative activities relate, directly or indirectly, to the structure of expected and actual demand. Third, the demand side represents the most obvious way of turning to the much-needed analysis of macro-evolutionary change of the economic system.

Individual innovations and demand: the great debate

The distinction between invention, innovation and imitation/diffusion is often attributed to Schumpeter, but actually his approach put an overwhelming emphasis on innovation. For him the core characteristic of innovation is that it is a *difficult* change of some of the routines of the economic system. This conception has several consequences. First, since the function of innovative entrepreneurs is to perform the difficult implementation of 'new combinations', their efforts cannot be seen as simple applications of inventions or other kinds of relevant knowledge. Second, since the initial attempts at imitating a successful innovation is quite difficult, they should also be characterized as innovations. Thus, there is no clear-cut distinction between innovation and imitation/diffusion. Instead the innovative contents of a particular type of change become less and less significant until the change becomes a matter of routine. Third, there is no possibility that market demand can automatically bring about innovation. The demand side of the market is characterized by routine behaviour and limited foresight, so entrepreneurs become drivers of innovation even in the sense that they persuade buyers to change their preferences. Thus the Schumpeterian concept of innovation determines a specific view of the relationship between innovation and demand.

Although Schumpeter's concept of innovation became very influential, there were many economists and economic historians who upheld the classical and quite different concept of 'innovation'. According to this concept, incremental innovation is a normal aspect of economic life that is directly influenced by the 'technology push' by available inventions and the 'demand pull' created by increased incomes and changes in tastes. This classical view was renewed by Schmookler in studies of the relationship between the number of inventions and the level of demand in relation to different industries. He demonstrated that 'technology push' is not an independent variable. Instead changes in the number of inventions prove to be lagged reflections of changes in the level of demand. Thus it is really 'demand pull' that drives inventive activity and, presumably, innovative activity. This emphasis on demand-side factors was seen as a refutation of the supply-side orientation implied by the Schumpeterian concept of innovation. In retrospect, it is however obvious that Schumpeter and Schmookler were analysing different issues. First, Schumpeter excluded incremental and adaptive change from his concept of innovation while Schmookler emphasized these forms of change. Second, Schumpeter cut any automatic links between invention and innovation while Schmookler implicitly assumed such links. Third, Schumpeter argued about individual innovations while Schmookler dealt with aggregates of inventions and innovations. Thus the debate between Schumpeterian and Schmooklerian researchers during the 1960s and 1970s became quite confusing.

In a famous paper by Mowery and Rosenberg (1979) the results of the debate were evaluated. A series of empirical studies had tried to support the Schmooklerian view, but they had run into serious conceptual difficulties. Thus it was obvious that there is no automatic relation between inventions and innovations. But the most important problem was the confusion about the concept of demand. Schmookler's studies had upheld the standard definition of observed market demand, but the subsequent studies had included a much broader view that included expected demand as well as attention to basic wants of the buyers. Even Schumpeter would have admitted that considerations on the latter issues were crucial to any innovation, so the demand push theory seemed to have led to a dead end. This does not mean that the debate was without results (see e.g. Freeman, 1994). First, it drew attention to the fact that there are both radical and incremental innovations that may show different patterns of causation. Second, it emphasized the need for studying the role of user needs in innovative activities, for instance in terms of the innovative role of 'lead users' and 'user–producer interaction'. Third, it drove researchers to move from 'linear' models of innovation to the study of the complex interaction of the different determinants. Fourth, it pointed to the difficult process of 'market creation' with its standardization and networking processes among buyers as well as suppliers. Fifth, it became obvious that there was a need for studying innovation as an aggregate phenomenon instead of only focusing on individual innovations. Thus it seems somewhat misleading when McMeekin *et al.* (2002, p. 8) suggest that the debate has largely vanished. Instead it has branched into a number of sub-debates, and these debates have become more technically demanding because of the increased application of explicit models and econometric analysis. Thereby, much of the freshness (and naivety) of the original debate has disappeared, especially in relation to aggregate analysis. But this kind of study is not without fascinating research problems.

Accounting for the effects of selection and innovation
The great debate on the innovation–demand relationship took place at a time when the modern analysis of economic evolution had not yet been developed. This analysis may briefly be characterized as 'population thinking' (Metcalfe, 2001). According to this form of thinking, evolution takes place within heterogeneous populations whose average characteristics are changed by selection. In the case of a population of firms that produces a good for a particular market, selection is, directly or indirectly, performed through the buyers' choices based on prices and qualities. Thus the basic function of demand is to select between the varieties that are made available by innovation. But there are additional contributors to this selection, like the banks that to some extent determine the degree to which profits can be transformed into expansion.

To apply population thinking in an effective way, we need statistical analysis even to define basic evolutionary concepts like selection and innovation. We may measure the effectiveness of selection with respect to some quantitative characteristic (e.g. productivity) in terms of a regression coefficient ($\beta_{w,z}$). This coefficient measures how selection with respect to quantitative characteristics of individual firms (z_i) influences their expansion coefficients or 'fitnesses' (w_i). If the expansion coefficient is 1, then the capacity of the firm is unchanged, while a difference from unity means that the firm is in some sense being selected. Since we are mainly interested in relative change within the population, we also need to take into consideration the average expansion coefficient or average fitness ($\overline{w}$).

To produce any results, a selection mechanism of a given efficiency needs firms to vary with respect to the characteristic under study. The degree to which 'fuel' is available for the selection is depicted by the industry's variance with respect to the characteristic under study, and the relevant measure is the capacity-share weighted variance (Var(z)). Selection uses this fuel by expanding firms with above-average performance with respect to the characteristic. At the same time some of the fuel is used, so that, after selection has taken place, variance is smaller than before. Innovation largely serves to restore variance. But it also has an immediate effect that is comparable to that of selection. This is most obvious if we measure the change in the average level of the characteristic between two points of time ($\Delta\bar{z}$). Selection has an obvious effect on this change, but so does innovation. The size of the contribution of an innovation in any particular firm depends on the size of the change brought about by innovation, the capacity share of the firm and the degree to which this capacity share is changed thanks to super-normal growth during the period ($\Delta z_i(s_i w_i/\bar{w})$).

It is of great importance to bring together the contributions of the selection effect and the innovation effect to the change of an average characteristic like average productivity. This may be done in different ways, but recently evolutionary economists have become aware that evolutionary biologists have for quite some time had a very elegant and efficient way of doing so (Frank, 1998). This is George Price's formula for decomposing evolutionary change. In the present interpretation, this formula may be expressed as

$$\Delta\bar{z} = \text{Selection effect} + \text{Innovation effect} = \frac{\beta_{w,z}\text{Var}(z)}{\bar{w}} + \frac{E(w\Delta z)}{\bar{w}}.$$

The formula shows that short-term change of the average of a characteristic (say, productivity) is determined by two effects. The first is the selection effect that exploits the variance of the productivities (Var(z)). If this variance is large, then average productivity may increase quickly because firms with super-normal productivity are selected to obtain increased capacity shares. The effectiveness of this selection is influenced by the degree to which the relative expansion coefficients of firms reflect their productivities, and this degree is measured by regression of the expansion coefficients on the productivities ($\beta_{w,z}/\bar{w}$). Thus the efficiency of selection is an empirical question that we have to confront for each period in the analysis of economic evolution. The second term in the equation is the innovation effect (which may also include imitation). To see why this name is appropriate in the present context, we have to consider the meaning of the expected market-share weighted value of the firms' expansion coefficients times their productivity changes ($E(w\Delta z)$). If there is no change in the productivity of any of the individual firms ($\Delta z_i = 0$ for all i), then this value is zero. If some firms innovate or imitate ($\Delta z_i > 0$), then the expected aggregate effect is influenced by the capacity shares of these firms at the end of the period. Since innovative performance is to some extent determined by the size of firms, the innovation effect may be quite important.

As soon as we have grasped the logic of Price's decomposition of evolutionary change, we recognize that this formula may be used in a multi-level way. For instance, large firms are often composed of a set of plants that vary with respect to productivity. Therefore, we may also apply Price's formula to analyse the selection and innovation that take place within such firms. In this case we may consider the overall productivity change of a firm (Δz_i) as an aggregate that may be decomposed into a firm-level selection effect and a plant-level innovation effect. The firm-level selection effect changes the average productivity of the firm by promoting super-normal plants and demoting sub-normal plants. The size of the plant-level innovation effect depends both on the size of process innovations (and imitations) and on their spread across plants of different capacities.

The short-term accounting for evolutionary change must be complemented by considerations of long-term evolutionary outcomes. Here it is important to note that the selection effect may become zero for two reasons: either there is no productivity variance or the existing productivity variance has no effect on the change of capacity shares. The former situation is the long-term consequence of the selection effect in isolation: this effect simply increases average productivity by decreasing the productivity variance and increasing the concentration of the industry. However, in the Nelson–Winter model an increased monopoly power changes the regression of expansion rates on productivities. The reason is that a firm with a large capacity share increases profits by restraining output expansion. As a result, the industry may end up as a relatively stable oligopoly. An important question is what happens to the innovation effect in such an oligopoly. Although the Nelson–Winter model is not designed for a thorough answering of this question, it is obvious that the innovation effect comes to dominate over the selection effect. Oligopolistic firms are still motivated to increase their productivity, but their existence may also give raise to perverse selection effects, since the productivity leader may decrease its capacity.

Changing relationships between innovation and demand

Nelson and Winter's (1982, chs 12–14) evolutionary simulation model was designed to clarify the confusing Schumpeterian heritage. As was pointed out above, one of the controversial Schumpeter hypotheses concerns the relationship between innovation and demand. The confusion was partly due to the fact that Schumpeterians and Schmooklerians were treating the issue from different perspectives and at different levels of aggregation. Evolutionary economic analysis helps to clear up much of this confusion.

The simple Nelson–Winter model of process innovation provides some insights, but we shall soon need to move toward more complex models.

The two views of the innovation–demand relationship prove to be closely related to endogenous and exogenous changes in aggregate monetary demand (D) in the Nelson–Winter model. In the basic model the aggregate monetary demand for the output in the industry is fixed, so that price changes inversely with aggregate supply ($P = D/Q$). Let us instead assume that monetary demand is elastic to price in the sense that a lowering of the price in the present period increases monetary demand in the next period. In non-monopolistic situations both the selection effect and the innovation effect increase average productivity as well as output. This leads to a lower price in the present period and an increased aggregate demand in the next period. Thus we have the Schumpeterian pattern of process innovation preceding increasing demand. However, if aggregate demand changes for exogenous reasons, we see the Schmooklerian pattern of increased demand leading to invention and process innovation. Let us consider a situation of a relatively stable oligopoly and increase significantly the level of monetary demand. Then all firms experience increasing profits and start to expand their production. This expansion is most rapid for high-productivity firms, so the selection effect is restored by an increased regression of expansion on productivity. However, because of the routines for determining R&D efforts, an increase in employment also means an increase in innovative activities. This means that the chances of invention and innovation are increased, and the results show up in subsequent periods. If we allow for adaptation of the fraction of labour that is used for R&D, we see an increase in R&D intensity. The reason is that R&D productivity increases because the probabilistic cost of innovation can be spread over a larger output. There are thus several reasons why the Schmooklerian pattern emerges.

The way the Schumpeterian relationship between innovation and demand is produced in a simple Nelson–Winter model hardly reflects Schumpeter's original vision. This vision is much better handled by a model that includes product innovation. In their history-friendly model of the computer industry, Malerba *et al.* (1999) for instance include two types of computer users. The first type of users has a need for advanced performance rather than cheapness, while the needs of the second type of users cannot be fulfilled unless ease of use and cheapness is emphasized. Although the second type of users were always there, it is misleading to say that their demand drove the innovative efforts toward the huge market for small computers. As in the cases studied by Mowery and Rosenberg (1979), it is much more relevant to consider an innovation-driven evolution that ultimately brought forth an effective demand. In the case of the computer industry model, we may think in terms of two evolving characteristics of the industry: average performance and average cheapness. Before the industry started to produce personal computers, the efficiency of selection was large with respect to performance and small with respect to cheapness. But with the advent of personal computers, the computer industry was practically split into two sub-industries with different selection environments. As long as we study the industry as a whole, both regression coefficients are small. If, however, we study the evolution of two sub-industries separately, it becomes clear that the one is dominated by selection for performance while the second is dominated by selection for cheapness. By following the mature evolution of the personal computer industry, it also becomes clear that cheapness-oriented innovations dominate in core firms while performance innovations are more prominent in peripheral firms. This sub-industry seems to have entered a stage that to some extent may be analysed in Schmooklerian terms, but it should be emphasized that innovation is motivated by potential demand and that initially there was an extended Schumpeterian phase where only pioneering and very special users were able to give some guidance for innovative activities. Thus the Schumpeter–Schmookler controversy is resolved within the study of the industry life cycle (cf. e.g. Nelson and Winter, 2002).

Product innovation and endogenous preferences
Even in its extended versions, the Nelson–Winter model gives rather limited guidance to the debate on innovation and demand. Thus there is a need for a more radical rethinking of the model. This rethinking may start by applying a fundamentally modified version of the Lancaster approach to the demand theory (see, e.g., Saviotti, 1996). According to Lancaster, the utility of a good is evaluated by means of the utility effects of a small number of characteristics. In relation to a realistic theory of innovation, the problem is that there are a huge number of characteristics that are of potential relevance to any buyer of the good. For instance, the 'performance' of computers may be split up in a near-infinity of characteristics. Since buyers are boundedly rational, they have to focus on a few of these potentially relevant characteristics. Their bounded rationality also moves them to express their preferences for goods in terms of lexicographic orderings of the focal characteristics. Buyers thus select the variant of a good that is best with respect to the most preferred characteristic. If two variants are equal with respect to this characteristic, they base their choice on a secondary characteristic, and so on. In this way buyers economize their limited amount of attention on a few crucial characteristics. But this behaviour is based on large amounts of individual and social experience. This experience is necessary because the proper functioning of any good presupposes that a large number of characteristics have reached satisfactory quality levels, and these

levels cannot be checked in relation to particular choices. Instead they have to be taken for granted. But experience also singles out a few characteristics that buyers would like to change, and thereby they obtain a small and lexicographically ordered checklist. Since this checklist depends on their previous experience, it is obvious that they have endogenously changing preferences. But there are also other reasons for buyers to adapt their preferences to experience (Aversi *et al.*, 1999).

When buyers encounter a new innovation, they evaluate it according to their acquired preferences and not by any fixed and complete preferences. This evaluation defines a selection environment that can be used to discern between what may crudely be called Schmooklerian and Schumpeterian innovations. A Schmooklerian innovation is an innovation that takes place within the agenda defined by the established lexicographic preferences and standards. Thus it has to live up to the conventional requirements of the good as well as to improve it in one of the dimensions that buyers focus upon. In the simplest case, such an innovation represents what Lancaster calls 'vertical product differentiation', i.e. a product that is exactly like its competitor with respect to all characteristics, except that it is better with respect to a single characteristic. In contrast, a Schumpeterian innovation is an innovation that transcends the buyers' routine-based decision making. This transcendence has two aspects. First, the innovation is so radical that buyers are not automatically convinced that its many characteristics are such that it has an acceptable functioning. Second, the innovation has a superior performance with respect to characteristics that buyers are not accustomed to apply in their product selection. Such an innovation cannot in any meaningful sense be said to have been called forth by pre-existing demand, and the question is therefore how the innovation becomes selected. The standard Schumpeterian solution is to assume that the innovative entrepreneur persuades buyers to change their preferences (e.g. by marketing efforts). The adoption of the innovation may, however, also require a complex social process that largely takes place among different types of buyers. If we take this social process into account, several Schumpeterian innovations may to some extent prove to be reducible to Schmooklerian innovations. Such innovations may originally have been designed according to pre-existing preferences of sophisticated buyers in niche markets, but then a social process changes the preferences of ordinary buyers so that they adopt the innovation (see, e.g., Witt, 2002; McMeekin *et al.*, 2002).

The modelling of product innovation under the assumption of endogenous preferences can be done in many ways. At present, most insight seems to be gained from relatively simple models. If, for instance, we ignore the fact that the potentially relevant characteristics of a differentiated product is never fully known, then we may fairly quickly explore the important co-evolution between supply and demand. If we assume that buyers initially have different lexicographic orderings, then the innovations of the firms of a new industry will target different customer groups. The buyers will select different product variants, and occasionally consider whether to shift to other variants. If they have for an extended period of time adopted in a particular variant, then their preferences will become adopted in this variant. The evolution of the model of such a customer market shows many of the characteristics found in real markets, especially if we include directed innovative activity and marketing efforts. However, many issues of long-term evolution are missing. Standardization of individual quality characteristics may sometimes by explained by random drift, but it gains force by adding network effects in consumption, like the utility gain from a large user community of a particular computer system (Arthur, 1994). Furthermore, we may model the gradual expansion of the set of characteristics that have become standardized (Andersen, 1994). In such a model, the focus of attention of buyers shifts in a step-wise manner from one characteristic to the next. Thereby, the agenda for the routine-like innovative activities of the firms of the industry is also shifting.

Macro-evolutionary transformation and satiation of demand
Although modern evolutionary economics is much inspired by Schumpeter, most contributions have ignored the fact that he was largely confronting the macroscopic aspects of economic evolution. Thus the issue of the innovation–demand relationship has been treated at the level of individual innovations or individual industries rather than at the level of the aggregate economy. This discussion has instead been dominated by Keynesian or neoclassical economists. The reason is largely that the mechanisms through which selection and innovation interact with the macroeconomic state of the economy are immensely complex. At the moment we, therefore, need rather naïve models that relate innovation to the macroscopic level without abandoning too many of the Schumpeterian insights. Such models should as a minimum include a microeconomic level at which innovation takes place and a mesoeconomic level that allows us to handle the structural transformation of the economic system. The latter requirement implies that the extension of the Nelson–Winter model into a one-sector growth model is not sufficient. Some of the Schumpeter-inspired models within endogenous growth theory (see Aghion and Howitt, 1998) might be of relevance, but Pasinetti (1993) provides a more open-ended starting point. Although his abstract multisectoral model of structural economic dynamics in a pure labour economy is clearly of a post-Keynesian type, it is not without Schumpeterian inspirations, and it focuses attention on the innovation–demand relationship. In the present context, the main

problem with the Pasinetti model is that it operates at the level of aggregate sectors without any microfoundation. So the task is to reconstruct it in a way that gives it an evolutionary economic character (Verspagen, 1993, ch. 7; Andersen, 2001).

The basic intuition underlying the Pasinetti model is that consumers have hierarchically organized preferences. To simplify, we may say that any consumer wants to consume a satisfactory level of one good before consuming any of the next good in the hierarchy. If the list of goods and their prices and satiation levels are given, then it is clear how any consumer will distribute any given income among the goods. The demand starts from the bottom of the hierarchy and covers as many goods as possible up to their satiation levels. The quantity of last good that is chosen may, however, be only a fraction of its satiation level. Increasing incomes imply that consumers move their consumption frontiers, first by ensuring that the last good is consumed up to its satiation level, then by moving to the next good in the hierarchy. By assuming a uniform wage rate and uniform preferences, everyone in the economy has exactly the same consumption pattern. Against this background, it is not difficult to add an evolving supply side to the economy. The population of firms that produces a particular good competes by using labour-saving innovations, and the price of the good decreases. This means that part of the income of consumers can be spent for an expansion of the consumption frontier. However, this expansion is not without problems. First, although the next good in the hierarchy is defined in terms of basic consumer needs, its concrete form will be determined by innovations in firms that operate at the consumption frontier. Second, consumers have to learn about the characteristics and the ways of using new goods. If one of these two requirements is missing, then the consumption frontier cannot move, and consequently we see a satiation of aggregate demand. In that case the economy encounters what may be called 'technological unemployment'. The problem is that increasing productivity and fixed demand in the old sectors necessarily means a reduction in their demand for labour, and this part of the labour force is not absorbed in new sectors. To maintain long-term economic growth it is thus crucial to have firm innovation and consumer learning at the production and consumption frontier.

In the evolutionary version of the Pasinetti model, firms make two types of innovation. First, they engage in process innovation to increase productivity in the production of established goods. This form of innovation can become more or less systematized since there is a permanent pressure for cost reduction. Second, they engage in product innovation. Since this activity is only going on at the consumption frontier and since full-blown anticipatory behaviour is impossible in evolutionary models, this activity is quite sporadic and erratic. Thus it is unlikely that the new good will become available at the exact moment when demand for it begins to emerge. Furthermore, if we add initially heterogeneous preferences for the new good, further time is needed for establishing a standard version of the good and the appropriate set of consumer preferences. However, these problems are to a large extent the result of the assumption of a uniform wage rate in the whole economic system. If we allow for multiple levels of income, different consumers will meet the satiation constraint at different points of time. Some firms will serve the consumers that first meet the constraint, and their efforts will diminish or remove the constraint for consumers that later obtain an income that allows them to demand the good. This pattern demonstrates that the satiation problem is most radically met in a model where labour is totally homogeneous and where there are thus no income differences. There are, however, also problems at the other extreme with a very skewed income distribution, where a large range of goods are only demanded by a small minority.

The proposed multisectoral model of economic evolution is, of course, only a first and fairly naïve step toward an analysis of the interaction of innovation and demand in relation to aggregate economic transformation and growth. Many further ideas may be found in the neo-Schumpeterian analysis of cyclical economic evolution (including the Kondratieff wave literature). But even against the background of the present chapter it is obvious that the innovation–demand relationship is both interesting and complex. The complexity is a major reason why researchers tend to apply one-sided views. We need a further development of analytical tools to handle this complexity in a systematic manner and thus to overcome futile controversies over the innovation–demand relationship.

References

Aghion, P. and Howitt, P. (1998), *Endogenous Growth Theory*, Cambridge, MA and London: MIT Press.
Andersen, E.S. (1994), 'The evolution of economic complexity', in E. Helmstädter and M. Perlman (eds), *Behavioral Norms, Technological Progress and Economic Dynamics*, Ann Arbor, MI: Michigan University Press.
Andersen, E.S. (2001), Satiation in an evolutionary model of structural economic dynamics, *Journal of Evolutionary Economics*, **11**, 143–64.
Arthur, W. Brian (1994), *Increasing Returns and Path Dependence in the Economy*, Ann Arbor, MI: University of Michigan Press.
Aversi, R., Dosi, G., Fagiolo, G., Meccati, M. and Olivetti, C. (1999), Demand dynamics with socially evolving preferences, *Industrial and Corporate Change*, **8**, 353–408.
Frank, S.A. (1998), *Foundations of Social Evolution*, Princeton, NJ: Princeton University Press.
Freeman, C. (1994), The economics of technical change, *Cambridge Journal of Economics*, **18**, 463–514.
Malerba, F., Nelson, R.R., Orsenigo, L. and Winter, S.G. (1999), 'History-friendly' models of industry evolution: the computer industry, *Industrial and Corporate Change*, **8**, 1–36.

McMeekin, A., Green, K., Tomlinson, M. and Walsh, V. (eds) (2002), *Innovation by Demand: An Interdisciplinary Approach to the Study of Demand and its Role in Innovation*, Manchester and New York: Manchester University Press.

Metcalfe, J.S. (2001), 'Evolutionary approaches to population thinking and the problem of growth and development', in K. Dopfer (ed.), *Evolutionary Economics: Program and Scope*, Boston, MA: Kluwer.

Mowery, D. and Rosenberg, N. (1979), The influence of market demand upon innovation: a critical review of some recent empirical studies, *Research Policy*, **8**, 102–53.

Nelson, R.R. and Winter, S.G. (1982), *An Evolutionary Theory of Economic Change*, Cambridge, MA and London: Harvard University Press.

Nelson, R.R. and Winter, S.G. (2002), Evolutionary theorizing in economics, *Journal of Economic Perspectives*, **16**, 23–46.

Pasinetti, L.L. (1993), *Structural Economic Dynamics: A Theory of the Economic Consequences of Human Learning*, Cambridge: Cambridge University Press.

Saviotti, P.P. (1996), *Technological Evolution, Variety and the Economy*, Cheltenham, UK and Brookfield, USA: Edward Elgar.

Verspagen, Bart (1993), *Uneven Growth Between Interdependent Economies: An Evolutionary View on Technology Gaps, Trade and Growth*, Aldershot: Avebury.

Witt, U. (ed.) (2002), *Escaping Satiation: The Demand Side of Economic Growth*, Berlin: Springer.

48 Long waves, the pulsation of modern capitalism
Francisco Louçã

First suggested by the Russian economist Nikolai Kondratieff and then developed by Joseph Schumpeter and many other theoreticians and statisticians, the concept of 'long waves' of capitalist development was proposed in order to explain the long periods of dominance of expansion or depression. Since the crisis of 1973–4, and through the business cycles with the depressions of 1982, 1991–4 and from 2002, the deceleration of growth and accumulation, in spite of the immense possibilities offered by the ongoing technological revolution, highlights this form of pulsation of modern economies.

Yet, in order to justify the use of the concept of 'waves' or 'cycles', rather than simply 'stages' or 'periods' of historical evolution, it is necessary to distinguish *recurrent* phenomena in each period as well as the unique features of each technological revolution. Five of these recurrent features of the successive industrial revolutions are presented in this chapter. I should stress first of all that the theory and argument developed with Chris Freeman (Freeman and Louçã, 2001) is one which deals with developments within *industrial capitalist* economies. Our theory therefore has a relatively limited domain of application. It relates to the evolution of capitalist economics from the late eighteenth to the early twenty-first centuries. It postulates for this period the predominance within the leading economies of recognizably capitalist institutions and in particular of private ownership and of private wealth accumulation through profits. It is in this institutional context that the economic and technological evolution, which we examine, has occurred and, while other types of long cycle may well occur in other social systems, they are not my concern here. To criticize our theory as 'technological determinism' is therefore wide of the mark at first call. It is the very existence of certain social institutions which made possible the technological revolutions we have described. Moreover, these successive new technologies which we have analysed did not come from Mars and nor were they 'manna from heaven'; they were the outcome of human social activities and institutions. The following five characteristic processes illustrate the structure of recurrence out of which emerges the long wave pattern of modern economies.

The recurrence of exceptional super-profits of innovative entrepreneurship in successive long waves

Both some of the sternest critics of capitalism (for example, Karl Marx) and some of its most ardent admirers (for example, Friedrich von Hayek) have argued that one of the foremost characteristics of capitalism has been its capacity to generate and to diffuse a torrent of technical innovations. The exceptionally favourable confluence of cultural, political, economic, geographical, scientific and social circumstances in eighteenth-century Britain which gave rise to that upsurge of technical and organizational innovations known ever since as the 'Industrial Revolution'. Subsequently, other capitalist economies, and especially the United States, were not only able to achieve similar results but, as time went by, to outstrip Britain with new constellations of innovations.

Capitalist economies have been able to achieve these remarkable results, 'surpassing the wonders of the Ancient World', as Marx and Engels put it, by a combination of incentives and pressures affecting ultimately numerous firms and individuals. First of all, of course, a well-functioning capitalist economy offers the possibility, but by no means the certainty, of *profit* from successful innovation – and sometimes very large profit. This profit may be accompanied by other rewards: status, privilege, political advancement and fame. In our account we show that some of the most successful entrepreneurs in each technological revolution did indeed achieve extraordinarily large profits, although they did not necessarily seek the other advantages often sought by very wealthy individuals. Fame itself they could hardly avoid and indeed this was a very important social mechanism for the diffusion of their innovations and for efforts to surpass them. Arkwright, Wedgwood, Hudson, Brunel, the Vanderbilts, Carnegie, Krupp, Rockefeller, Rathenau, Siemens, Diesel, Ford, Gates and Murdoch are all examples of entrepreneurs and inventors, who achieved both fame and fortune through their innovations, whether technical, organizational or both.

A number of long wave theorists have constructed models of the behaviour of the economic system based mainly on long-term fluctuations in the *aggregate* rate of profit. That was the case, for instance, of Ernest Mandel. He argued quite plausibly that a fall in the rate of profit tends to occur after a long period of prosperity and expansion, partly because of the Schumpeterian processes of erosion of innovators' profits during diffusion and partly through wider pressures from rising costs of inputs. These tendencies for the rate of profit to fall at the peak of a long boom are among the main reasons explaining the upper turning point in the long wave and the onset of a prolonged downswing in which generally lower rates of profit prevail. The statistics are very difficult to assemble, especially for the nineteenth century but, such as they are, they do provide some support for this interpretation. I certainly do not wish to deny the plausibility of these models, but since my current emphasis is mainly on *structural* change and on divergent *sectoral* phenomena, the exceptionally large 'super-profits' which may be realized through the exploitation of major radical innovations are stressed. These profits appear all the more remarkable if they are made during a period of general decline in the rate of profit in the 'down-swing' phase of the long wave. Although he disagrees with Mandel and other long wave theorists on the *aggregate* rate of profit, Tylecote (1992) also points to the extraordinary importance of the demonstration effect for key innovations in each long wave.

With Freeman, I have argued that this demonstration effect is not only one of clear-cut technical efficiency but also one of great profitability and great potential for widespread application. This effect was so powerful in the case of Arkwright's water-frame that it led some of his rivals and competitors to attempt the physical destruction of his equipment. Despite this hostility, the successful and highly profitable operations of Cromford mill and his other factories stimulated numerous imitators to invest in cotton mills, especially after the expiry of his disputed patents. Some of the early canal investments, such as the Worsley–Manchester Canal, made very good profits. On a far greater scale, the Rainhill Trials of various steam loco-motives followed by the successful and profitable operation of the Liverpool–Manchester Railway led to an enormous boom in railway investment and indeed to a huge financial bubble based on the excitement caused by often exaggerated estimates of the potential profits to be made. Railway promoters, such as George Hudson in Britain and the Vanderbilts in the United States, made huge profits from speculation and financial manipulation, rather than technical innovation, even though Hudson lost his fortune in the end. The profits of Carnegie, Krupp and Ford provided examples of the vast amounts that could be accumulated by successful innovative entrepreneurship. The profits of IBM were not so much the result of *individual* entrepreneurship as of *company* performance. They were nevertheless hugely impressive and IBM was on some measures the most profitable firm in the world before it suffered setbacks in the 1980s, and its place as the most profitable player in ICT was usurped by Microsoft.

The first distinguishing recurrent characteristic, therefore, of the long waves which we have analysed is that in each case, although the individual innovations were unique and very different, a cluster of innovations emerged which offered the clear-cut potential for immense profits, based on proven technical superiority to previous modes of production. Minor incremental improvements were, of course, occurring all the time but the innovations, which were at the heart of each wave we have analysed, offered quite dramatic changes in productivity and profitability. However, these highly profitable innovations were not isolated events but part of a constellation of interrelated product, process and organizational innovations. Numerous other firms jumped on the band-wagon, as Schumpeter had suggested, including many small new firms. Sometimes it was a new *process* which generated the main super-profits, sometimes it was an array of new products, sometimes it was mainly organizational changes, as in the case of Ford's assembly line or the Internet, but in all cases there were interdependent developments, both technically and economically. The dramatic demonstration effects did not just make a fortune for individual entrepreneurs, but served to propel an entire technological system and to accelerate its diffusion world-wide. The first recurrent characteristic of long wave behaviour therefore is directly connected to the second: the potential for very widespread application.

The recurrence of pervasive constellations of technical and organizational innovations

Each wave is characterized not just by one or two big innovations, nor yet by a cluster of quite discrete individual innovations, but by a constellation of interdependent and mutually supportive technical and organizational innovations. Each of these constellations or paradigms has certain characteristics, which are common to them all. They all have identifiable and obvious *core inputs*, which have falling prices relative to other commodities during the critical transition period between one paradigm and the next. The principal producers and users of these inputs became the leading sectors (motive and carrier branches) in the upsurge of the economy. The demonstration effects occur relatively early in the diffusion of each new technological revolution and, whether they occur most conspicuously in firms making core inputs, in other leading sectors, or in associated infrastructures, they help to propel the diffusion of the whole constellation and not only one part of it.

It is not just the excitement generated by the first demonstration effects, important though these undoubtedly are, but the long-term potential which has become visible and which has reverberations throughout the system as more and more applications of the new paradigm appear on the horizon. A second recurrent feature of the long waves, in our view, is therefore that each one is characterized by the emergence and experimental testing of a new combination of interrelated innovations, which demonstrate remarkable gains in productivity and profitability at first in a few applications, but with the clear potential for very pervasive diffusion. Ultimately, this full potential is realized in a period of prolonged prosperity but only after a structural crisis of adjustment. Numerous examples of the pervasiveness of new technology systems in each new wave, are, for example, the applications of steel and of electricity, of iron and steam power, of oil and internal combustion, and computers.

The recurrence of waves of organizational and management changes in enterprises

A third recurrent feature of each revolution is that organizational and managerial changes introduced in the new leading sectors are widely imitated elsewhere. A new management style becomes fashionable and in the later waves in the twentieth century is diffused by management consultants as well as through the media and by word of mouth. The very success of the leading firms is sufficient in itself to stimulate imitative efforts in relation to their new management style but, of course, the technical innovations which they introduce are often also directly conducive to organizational changes in those firms which adopt them. Computers and mobile phones are two obvious contemporary examples but some organizational styles are not so directly dependent on technical innovations and have a momentum of their own. The sheer growth in the *size* of leading firms was itself an important factor in organizational and managerial changes in the nineteenth and twentieth centuries. The trends in organizational change are more complex than the narrowly technical changes but we would nevertheless claim that there is an identifiable recurrence of a new management style in each Kondratieff wave, which influences many firms, although in diverse ways, throughout the economy.

This does not mean of course that *every* firm in *every* industry adopts a similar management style or organizational structure. The idea of a *representative* firm characterizing all firms is one, which has been widely influential in economic theory, but it is not one which we embrace. On the contrary, I maintain that with each technological revolution, the effects are very varied. With the mass production style, for example, firms in some industries were capable of introducing standardized products and using an assembly line resembling the Fordist line in the automobile industry. Many others continued to produce unique customized or small batch products. Still others modified some features of the Fordist management style so that there were actually many varieties of Fordism, even within the automobile industry itself. Only a minority of firms became recognizably 'Fordist'. Nevertheless, in industries as diverse as tourism, fast food, retail distribution and clothing, the influence of Fordist management philosophy and organizational change is clearly evident. Similarly with electrification, this led on the one hand to the growth of some giant electrical firms with specialized departmental management structures. On the other hand, it facilitated the decentralized success of many small firms taking advantage of the new flexibility permitted by electric machinery.

Recurrent crises of structural adjustment

These examples show that there is some danger of making too schematic a model of the successive technological revolutions, which would do violence to their individual variety. This is especially the case because each one of them not only embodies a unique combination of products and processes but also affects other parts of the economy very unevenly, requiring different types of machinery, of materials and components, of distribution and of supporting services. Some entirely new branches of the economy are called into existence while other branches experience only marginal changes. Moreover, sometimes they affect particular *occupations* within industries and services which are otherwise little affected. The process of diffusion is therefore unpredictable and extremely uneven as new applications are explored, tested, expanded, modified or rejected. Nevertheless, a clearly observable and recurrent characteristic of each new technological revolution is its *pervasive* effect on the structure of the economic system. Although the *induced* branches of the economy are different, they are very significant in every case, and so too are the induced changes in skill requirements and hence in the education and training systems.

The fourth recurrent characteristic of each long wave is therefore a *crisis of structural adjustment* as the skills and distribution of the labour force and of firms adapt to the new paradigm.

Recurrent high levels of structural unemployment are an important manifestation of these adjustment crises in each long wave. The statistics for the nineteenth century are very poor, but there is strong evidence of very serious unemployment in the 1830s and 1840s in Britain, while David Wells commented on the widespread unemployment in most industrial countries in the 1880s and especially in those which were most advanced in the use of machinery. There is, of course, abundant statistical evidence of the heavy structural unemployment in the 1920s and 1930s and again in the 1980s and 1990s. Even in the 1920s boom in the United States, as the NBER pointed out, there were sectors experiencing severe adjustment problems, such as coal, railways and ship-building. In Germany and Britain, heavy industry generally, but especially the steel industry and the ship-building industry, experienced prolonged problems of structural adjustment. In the 1980s, the automobile industry, the oil industry, the synthetic materials industry and again the steel industry were among the many industries which experienced severe adjustment problems.

Recurrent changes in the regulatory regime

Finally, a recurrent feature of the qualitative changes engendered by the long wave is a periodic reconfiguration of the *regime of regulation* of technology and of the economy more generally. It is quite obvious that such extensive changes as mechanization, electrification, motorization and computerization raise entirely new requirements for education and training, which have led with each successive crisis of structural adjustment to a variety of movements for education reform. It is also obvious that each major new technology entails new requirements for safety and protection, whether of operatives in industry, consumers or people in certain exposed areas. However, the recurrent changes in regulatory regime go well beyond these immediate and obvious induced effects. Even at this elementary level regulatory requirements can raise some fundamental *political* issues such as 'self-regulation' of industries versus state regulation, national versus international regulation or local versus national. They also raise questions of *standards* which tend also to become an area of conflicts and dispute, both between competing groups, seeking to promote their own version of the new technology, and between nations seeking to protect their own interests. Especially in the case of new infrastructural investment, questions of *ownership* and control also arise. If private ownership is the solution which is adopted in any particular case, this again immediately gives rise to questions of monopoly, competition and price regulation. Equally problematic are the questions of trade and protection, whether of new or of older industries. Typically, the leaders in a new wave of technology, such as Britain in the nineteenth century or the United States in the twentieth century, will tend to advocate the opening up of world markets to the new products and services in which they excel, while catching-up countries will often deploy 'infant industry' arguments to justify various forms of protection. The leading countries will seek to advocate and, if they have the strength, to impose an international regulatory regime with institutions which promote the interests of their leading industries. Thus, what is at stake in each structural crisis is a reconstitution of the entire institutional and social framework because there is a mismatch between the regulatory framework, developed and consolidated for a previous generation for older technologies and industries, and the needs of the newly emerging constellation and the interests of the new technological leaders.

Once a new technological and regulatory regime has become dominant and firmly established, the phenomenon of 'lock in' to the new regime becomes widely apparent. This is the case not only with lock in to dominant designs, technical standards, components and so forth but also to all kinds of social standards and institutions, variable though these may be between different countries in response to the changing balance of social and political forces in each country and on the international stage.

Social, political and cultural changes in the long wave

These five features indicate a social and economic structural process and its difficulties. But, indeed, the impact of these tempests of change is not limited to the domain of economic relations: this discussion of recurrent changes characteristic of each long wave has already gone beyond purely economic and technological phenomena. Especially the crisis of structural adjustment and the periodic changes in the regulatory regime raise fundamental questions of the relationship between technical change, political change and cultural change. A very good example of this was the attempt to negotiate a new 'Round' of reductions in barriers to trade at the Seattle meeting of the World Trade Organization in December 1999. The United States representatives, supported by some of their allies, were anxious to use this meeting to promote easier access for the new products and services in which United States firms are dominant, such as E-commerce and GM Foods, but as an American commentator pointed out, the arguments in support of their objectives went far beyond the simple reductions in tariffs which were the staple diet of many previous successful trade negotiations over the last few decades. So-called 'non-tariff barriers' had become steadily more important in the successive 'Rounds' of trade negotiations and the conflicts both inside and outside the Conference Hall at Seattle showed the deep apprehension aroused by this trend. In fact, some time before the WTO Seattle meeting began, the OECD had organized discussions on an international treaty on foreign investment, whose intention was to do away with those national laws and business procedures which restricted practices allowed in one country, but not another. Each country would be obliged to grant corporations all the privileges allowed by any other country. Clearly, this would seriously undermine legislation in any country designed to protect the environment or labour and welfare legislation. The conflicts at Seattle were in part provoked by fears of this interpretation of 'globalization' has well as by other more enduring trade conflicts between the developing countries and the rich countries, as in the case of agriculture. Paul Krugman introduced 'Seattle Man' and 'Davos Man' to symbolize the conflict of ideas at the time of the 'World Economic Forum' of top business people at Davos in January 2000. And the opposition between the 'Davos' and the 'Seattle man' has developed ever since.

This example is sufficient to show that changes in the regulatory regime, whether at national level or international level, can raise the most fundamental political and ideological conflicts within and between nations. Lloyd-Jones and Lewis (1998) have made a particularly valuable study of the conflicts over the Corn Laws in the 1830s and 1840s in Britain and the later conflict on Tariff Reform in Britain in the late nineteenth and early twentieth centuries. Both of these conflicts split the ruling Tory Party from top to bottom and led to major re-alignments in British politics and each was associated with a long wave structural crisis. The problems of tariff protection also had profound effects in the United States, Germany and Japan as they were industrializing and catching up in technology. However, the political dimensions of free trade and tariff reform clearly go far beyond just the question of regulating some new products and services, or protecting older industries, even though these problems may trigger the conflicts. Fundamental national interests, as well as those of particular industries, are often felt to be at stake and friction over trade issues can be a major source of friction in international relations more generally, as illustrated in the Anglo-German naval armaments race before 1914.

The depth of the social conflicts, which may be exacerbated during a structural crisis, is illustrated no less clearly by the labour conflicts which are engendered. The widespread social unrest as well as the outbreaks of 'Luddism' associated with the destruction of old crafts and occupations, such as those of the hand-loom weavers, illustrate this point. Some historians have argued that Luddism, especially in the hosiery industry in Nottinghamshire, was inspired mainly by the desire to protect British quality standards in foreign trade. The workers supposedly feared more the loss of jobs through the erosion of British sales in foreign markets than that simply from mechanization. Whatever the interpretation may be, it is fairly obvious that the destruction of the livelihood of hundreds of thousands of people is bound to be a cause of acute social unrest and this has indeed been the case in every crisis of structural adjustment. There are also bound to be conflicts within the expanding industries and technologies over pay, status and working conditions for various groups of managers and workers. The scale of the organizational and managerial changes in each technological revolution means that these are likely to be non-trivial.

References

Freeman, C. and F. Louçã (2001), *As Time Goes By: From the Industrial Revolutions to the Information Revolution*, Oxford: Oxford University Press.
Lloyd-Jones, R. and M.J. Lewis (1998), *British Industrial Capitalism since the Industrial Revolution*, London: UCL Press.
Tylecote, A. (1992), *The Long Wave in the World Economy: The Present Crisis in Historical Perspective*, London: Routledge.

49 Finance and technical change: a long-term view

Carlota Perez

Ever since Kuznets published his review[1] of *Business Cycles* questioning the sudden clustering of entrepreneurial talent that was supposed to accompany each technological revolution,[2] Schumpeter's followers have felt uneasy about this unexplained feature of his model. Yet apparently no one has stopped to question Schumpeter's treatment of the clustering of 'wildcat or reckless banking', dismissing it as a random and unnecessary phenomenon to be excluded from his model, together with speculative manias.[3]

Keeping Schumpeter's basic assumptions about innovations based on credit creation as the force behind capitalist dynamics, this chapter will present an alternative model of the process of propagation of technological revolutions. On that basis it will propose (a) an explanation of the clustering and the spacing of technical change in successive revolutions; (b) an argument for the recurrence of clusters of bold financiers together with clusters of production entrepreneurs, and (c) an interpretation of major financial bubbles as massive episodes of credit creation, associated with the process of assimilation of each technological revolution.

The model is a stylized narrative, based on a historically recurring sequence of phases in the diffusion of each technological revolution, from its visible irruption after a long period of gestation, through its assimilation by the economic and social system to the exhaustion of its innovation potential at maturity. But it is not merely descriptive. It is constructed through the identification of possible causal chains between agents and spheres in capitalist society. What the model attempts to do is identify the repetition of certain underlying patterns and to propose plausible explanations.

The reader is asked to keep this purpose in mind, together with the additional caveat that neither the evidence nor much subtlety can be included in the limited space of a chapter.[4] Suffice it to say that this model is not a straitjacket to be forced upon history. Rather than ignore the immense richness of historical evolution, it emphasizes the uniqueness of each occurrence and recognizes the many irregularities and overlaps that cannot be captured by abstraction. Its only claim is to serve as a useful heuristic tool for historical exploration and as a framework for theoretical analysis.

1   The entrepreneur and the banker

In Schumpeter's basic definition of capitalism as 'that form of private property economy in which innovations are carried out by means of borrowed money',[5] we find his characteristic separation of borrower and lender, entrepreneur and banker, as the two faces of the innovation coin. This is not, however, how his legacy has been interpreted and enriched by the great majority of neo-Schumpeterians. The accent has almost invariably been on the entrepreneur to the neglect of the financial agent, no matter how obviously indispensable this agent may be to innovation.

Ironically, this bias can be traced back to Schumpeter himself. In many passages he defines the entrepreneur as the dynamic force driving innovations, he hails him as the leader, the real hero of development, the agent of profit creation,[6] whereas the banker is merely a 'bridge', a facilitator, the one that provides the means for the entrepreneur to exercise his creative will.[7]

Furthermore, whereas Schumpeter makes a clear contrast between the bold entrepreneur, breaking all routines, and the manager who simply conducts the daily business of the firm, he makes no equivalent distinction among financiers or bankers. These perform both the routine functions of intermediation and the selection of entrepreneurial projects for credit creation. In this latter function they are expected to be highly independent, experienced and serious.[8] Yet, as will be further discussed below, there is every reason to suspect that those radical innovative breaks also require bold and risk-loving bankers, because the 'serious' ones would share the same mental routines as the heads or managers of the established firms. In fact, the historical recurrence of bursts of 'wildcat or reckless' finance in the periods of intense investment in technological revolutions, suggests that these phenomena may be causally connected.

Essentially, then, although Schumpeter emphasized the double agency in the process of capitalist development, he concentrated attention on the production entrepreneur and neglected the innovative side of the financier. This has shaped his intellectual legacy and influenced the work of his successors.

2   The double character of routines as obstacles and guides for innovation

Schumpeter's innovator needs extraordinary will power not only because he is doing something truly new but also – and especially – because he must overcome the inertial force of established routines. Undoubtedly, radical innovations confront the stubborn resistance of routines on all fronts, yet routines have also been found to guide successive innovations. There is a wide body of neo-Schumpeterian literature analyzing the role of natural trajectories as sets of criteria steering the direction of (and stimulating the search for) incremental innovations.[9]

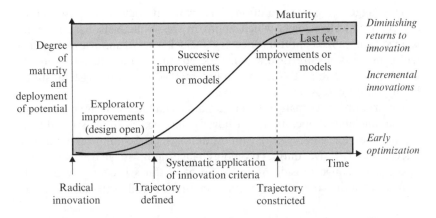

Source: Based on Nelson and Winter, Dosi, Wolf, Abernathy and Utterback, Arthur and others.

Figure 49.1   Technological trajectories as routines for innovation

Chris Freeman questioned the validity of Schumpeter's dismissive treatment of incremental innovations[10] as part of the routine of continuous flow.[11] Indeed, anyone who witnessed, in the 1980s and 1990s, the 'creative destruction' processes in the microcomputer industry, during the ferocious competition for both the dominant design and the operating system, would find it difficult to range such incremental changes in Schumpeter's non-entrepreneurial routine operations.

In fact, what researchers have found is not only that continuous incremental change is guided by shared heuristic routines but also that many radical innovations emerge as a response to the critical conditions (or decreasing returns to investment in technical improvement) faced by the firm or the industry, when innovation along a technological trajectory reaches maturity (see Figure 49.1).[12]

Even radical innovations, however, are not usually isolated events, nor are they mainly the replacement of obsolete products or processes. As Schumpeter often insisted, radical innovations come in clusters. But, such clusters are not disconnected random agglomerations of new things. Following upon Keirstead's notion of *constellations*,[13] Chris Freeman proposed the term 'new technology systems'[14] to emphasize the strong inter-relations and inter-dependences among the innovations within a Schumpeterian cluster. Such interconnected innovations in products and processes, in equipment and organization, technical and managerial, form a coherent and mutually enhancing set of technologies and industries, capable of carrying a wave of growth in the economy.

This suggests that the evolution of a new technology system also follows a certain collective logic, which approximates what Nelson and Winter termed 'generalized natural trajectory'.[15] Such a set of innovative routines will constantly inspire further scientific advances and interacting innovations that contribute to the growth potential of the whole system, stimulating change across several industries.

Thus routines play many roles in relation to change. There are routines for normal unchanged operation, which was Schumpeter's emphasis, and there are routines for guiding serial innovation, which Schumpeter tended to underestimate.[16] Live routines promote change along known trajectories and discourage change outside of them. Spent routines become obstacles to change but at the same time create the conditions to call forth radical change.

3   Techno-economic paradigms as the meta-routines for a long period

Technological revolutions are a special type of cluster. Each one is, in fact, a cluster of clusters or a system of technology systems. The present author has suggested that what distinguishes a technological revolution from an individual technology system, however radically new, is its all-pervasive character, its capacity to go beyond the industries it creates and to provide generic technologies that modernize the whole economic structure. This overarching process of transformation takes place thanks to the gradual construction of a new *techno-economic paradigm*, a shared commonsense model of best technical and organizational practice for the use of that set of pervasive technologies which provides a generalized quantum jump in productivity and quality.[17]

The techno-economic paradigm of each technological revolution defines the meta-routines for the whole economy. It provides the application models for the spread of the new generic technologies throughout the production landscape as well as the general principles guiding operations and even the search for new solutions, be they to fuel growth or to introduce incremental or radical innovation, be they for modernizing the established products, processes or industries or for creating novel ones. Each paradigm constitutes a new and universally applicable organizational logic for taking best advantage of the wealth-creating and modernizing potential that drives the whole Schumpeterian 'gale of creative destruction'.

Thus one could see successive technological revolutions involving an interrelated set of new technologies, industries and infrastructures, establishing a set of innovative routines in the form of a techno-economic paradigm and lasting about half a century (see Table 49.1). Each set, however, can only become the standard after overcoming the resistance of those who had adopted and practiced the previous paradigm, who will fiercely hold on to it, even if it is no longer effective.

Table 49.1 The industries, infrastructures and paradigms of each technological revolution

Technological revolution (core country)	New technologies and new or redefined industries	New or redefined infrastructures	Techno-economic paradigm 'Commonsense' innovation principles
FIRST: From 1771 **The 'Industrial Revolution'** (Britain)	Mechanized cotton industry Wrought iron Machinery	Canals Waterways Turnpike roads Water power (highly improved water wheels)	Factory production Mechanization Productivity/time keeping and time saving Fluidity of movement (as ideal for machines with water power and for transport through canals and other waterways) Local networks
SECOND: From 1829 **Age of Steam and Railways** (In Britain and spreading to Continent and USA)	Steam engines and machinery (made in iron; fuelled by coal) Iron and coal mining (now playing a central role in growth)* Railway construction Rolling stock production Steam power for many industries (including textiles)	Railways (use of steam engine) Universal postal service Telegraph (mainly nationally along railway lines) Great ports, great depots and worldwide sailing ships City gas	Economies of agglomeration/ industrial cities/national markets Power centres with national networks Scale as progress Standard parts/machine-made machines Energy where needed (steam) Interdependent movement (of machines and of means of transport)

Table 49.1 (continued)

Technological revolution (core country)	New technologies and new or redefined industries	New or redefined infrastructures	Techno-economic paradigm 'Commonsense' innovation principles
THIRD: From 1875 **Age of Steel, Electricity and Heavy Engineering** (USA and Germany overtaking Britain)	Cheap steel (especially Bessemer) Full development of steam engine for steel ships Heavy chemistry and civil engineering Electrical equipment industry Copper and cables Canned and bottled food Paper and packaging	Worldwide shipping in rapid steel steamships (use of Suez Canal) Worldwide railways (use of cheap steel rails and bolts in standard sizes). Great bridges and tunnels Worldwide telegraph Telephone (mainly nationally) Electrical networks (for illumination and industrial use)	Giant structures (steel) Economies of scale of plant/vertical integration Distributed power for industry (electricity) Science as a productive force Worldwide networks and empires (including cartels) Universal standardization Cost accounting for control and efficiency Great scale for world market power/ 'small' is successful, if local
FOURTH: From 1908 **Age of Oil, the Automobile and Mass Production** (In USA and spreading to Europe)	Mass-produced automobiles Cheap oil and oil fuels Petrochemicals (synthetics) Internal combustion engine for automobiles, transport, tractors, airplanes, war tanks and electricity	Networks of roads, highways, ports and airports Networks of oil ducts Universal electricity (industry and homes) Worldwide analog	Mass production/mass markets Economies of scale (product and market volume)/horizontal integration Standardization of products Energy intensity (oil-based) Synthetic materials

	Home electrical appliances Refrigerated and frozen foods	telecommunications (telephone, telex and cablegram) wire and wireless	Functional specialization/hierarchical pyramids Centralization/metropolitan centres, suburbanization National powers, world agreements and confrontations
FIFTH: From 1971 **Age of Information and Telecommunications** (In USA, spreading to Europe and Asia)	The information revolution: Cheap microelectronics Computers, software Telecommunications Control instruments Computer-aided biotechnology and new materials	World digital telecommunications (cable, fibre optics, radio and satellite) Internet/electronic mail and other e-services Multiple source, flexible use, electricity networks High-speed physical transport links (by land, air and water)	Information intensity (microelectronics-based ICT) Decentralized integration/network structures Knowledge as capital/intangible value added Heterogeneity, diversity, adaptability Segmentation of markets/proliferation of niches Economies of scope and specialization combined with scale Globalization/interaction between the global and the local Inward and outward co-operation/clusters Instant contact and action/instant global communications

Note: * These traditional industries acquire a new role and a new dynamism when serving as the material and the fuel of the world of railways and machinery.

Source: Perez (2002), Tables 2.2 and 2.3, pp. 14 and 18.

It is when these trajectories or meta-routines approach the exhaustion of their innovative possibilities that a paradigm shift is necessary. Radically breaking with the exhausted paradigm and opening whole new trajectories is the role of revolutionary innovators. It is in those cases that the Schumpeterian view of routines as obstacles to change is fully valid, yet those are precisely the situations when, to fulfill their role, the entrepreneurs will require the support of bold and innovative bankers, probably even 'reckless' ones.

4   Production and financial capital: different and complementary agents

Finance, in one form or another, accompanies most innovations, be they incremental or radical. Decisions to provide funds for innovations are only taken by the entrepreneurs themselves in those cases when they (or their firms) possess enough wealth to be self-sufficient. In most situations, the actual funding decision is taken by an investor or a bank manager, a stock-broker, a financial manager inside a big firm[18] or some other financial agent. The question is: by what criteria are those decisions guided? What gives the financial decision maker the 'feeling' that a particular project is likely to succeed? The answer proposed in this chapter is that the financial side follows similar criteria to those followed by innovation on the production side. It is the techno-economic paradigm of each technological revolution that influences the entrepreneurs and the financiers, the managers and the innovators, the investors and the consumers, both in their individual decisions and in their interactions.[19] In other words, the paradigm constitutes the common thought model of all the economic agents, their shared 'common sense', for the whole period of propagation of that set of technologies.

Nevertheless, there is a fundamental difference between the agents of production capital and those of financial capital. They will share the same paradigm and act in unison to fund growth and innovation, as long as it is successful in practice and profitable. However, once signs of exhaustion appear, the different depth of commitment to a particular paradigm becomes evident. For the production enterprise, the exhausted trajectory is profoundly embedded in existing investment in equipment, in structures, in knowledge and experience, in the organization and the personnel and in the external networks of suppliers, distributors and clients.[20] For financial capital the paradigm is mainly a set of criteria for judging what is likely to be successful, basically a thought model, relatively easy to abandon when it fails, no matter how strongly rooted it may be in ideas and in decision-making practice.

Production capital is the agent for the accumulation of wealth-making capacity; its natural horizon is long-term and it remains tied to its expertise.

Financial capital is the agent for reallocating wealth in order to constantly maximize short-term returns. Production capital is therefore path-dependent while financial capital is fundamentally footloose and flexible.[21]

This distinction in nature, function and motives, between production capital and financial capital, will underlie the explanation provided below of the clustering of bold financiers in support of the swarms of entrepreneurs in the early diffusion decades of a technological revolution.

5   Technological revolutions and great surges of development

As indicated in Table 49.1 above, the world has witnessed five technological upheavals since the Industrial Revolution in England (although in Schumpeter's lifetime only three and a half were available for study). They are the creative gales of destruction that Schumpeter called 'technological revolutions'. In his view of the multicyclical nature of capitalism such massive changes underlay the longest of these cycles: the *long waves of economic growth*, lasting around half a century.[22]

Focusing on the propagation of these technological revolutions and their assimilation by the economic and social system, the present author has proposed the concept of 'great surges of development',[23] departing from Schumpeter's notion of long waves in some fundamental aspects. Long waves, in Schumpeter's version, are measured by major fluctuations of GNP around the long-term dynamic equilibrium growth trend. They are the manifestation of a technological revolution in the economic sphere and are a consequence of the operation of the market mechanism. In conformity with this notion, Schumpeter sees no role for government policy or social intervention, except in very critical circumstances. Long waves are therefore to be understood as major *economic cycles*.[24]

Great surges of development, by contrast, represent the gradual integral transformation of both the techno-economic and the socio-institutional spheres of the social system, through the assimilation of each major cluster of technical change. A great surge is thus defined as the process by which a technological revolution and its techno-economic paradigm propagate across the economy, leading to structural changes in production, distribution, communication and consumption, as well as to profound and qualitative social changes. Society, in turn, influences the path taken by the revolution. In other words, the concept stretches far beyond the economy, to encompass societal – even cultural – change.[25]

This significant shift in emphasis and in scope leads to very different dating and to another way of conceptualizing the relationship between technological, economic and social changes as well as between financial and production capital. The change in the term, from waves to surges, formalizes this break.[26]

6   The sequence of diffusion of each technological revolution

Each great surge is initiated with a *big-bang*, a publicly recognized innovative breakthrough that inflames the imagination of entrepreneurs and launches the entrepreneurial swarming in restricted sectors and geographic regions, so much so that it is likely to go unnoticed in economic statistics. It is the microprocessor for the fifth, the Model-T for the fourth and so on back to Arkwright's Cromford mill for the first. From the big-bang on, there is an ever more intense process of diffusion and assimilation that in a few decades ends up encompassing the bulk of activities in the core country or countries. Each revolution sets a higher potential level of productivity and quality across the board so that each surge is the movement onto that higher productivity plateau of the whole group of core economies involved.[27]

As shown in Figure 49.2, the process of diffusion involved in each surge can be seen as divided into two periods, *Installation* and *Deployment*, each lasting around 20 to 30 years. The installation period begins with the big-bang of the technological revolution and represents the battle of the new entrepreneurs to overcome the resistance of the old paradigm, which is deeply embedded in the minds and the practices, in the equipment and the

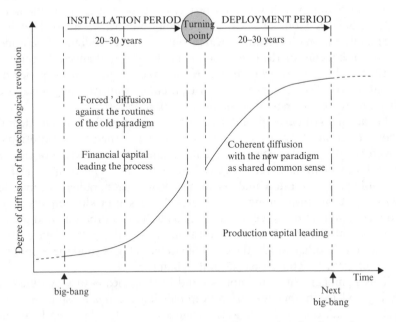

Figure 49.2   Two different periods in the diffusion of technological revolutions

experience, in the norms and the law, as well as in the power structures of the economy and society. The leadership of the process in that period moves increasingly to the hands of financial capital, which can break free from the power of incumbent production capital, now becoming conservative, and back the new entrepreneurs in the process of establishing the emerging paradigm. A financial bubble usually characterizes the final phase of installation. 'Canal mania' in the 1790s, 'railway mania' in the 1840s, the 'roaring 1920s' and the bubble of the 1990s are examples of such frenzy phases.[28] Thus the installation period ends with a financial collapse, having accomplished its task, including the replacement of the industries (and firms) that act as the engines of growth of the economy, the installation of the new infrastructure providing externalities for everybody and the general acceptance of the 'common sense' criterion for best practice of the new paradigm.

Between the two periods, installation and deployment, there would usually be a recession of uncertain duration, when all the negative social and economic consequences of the bubble come to the fore and gather intense pressure for radical policy changes. These new policies generally tend to regulate financial practices and to contribute to the expansion of markets through public demand or income redistribution. In essence, at this turning point, the conditions are there for the socio-institutional framework to be modified in ways that would make it possible for the new production capital, incarnate in the already powerful new firms and industries, to take the helm of the economy away from financial capital.[29]

The deployment period that follows is the reign of the recently established paradigm and involves its growing embeddedness in all spheres of society. The economic process is now increasingly in the hands of the leaders of production capital, mainly the new but also the old giants already modernized. The meta-routines of the paradigm are now effective both for operation and growth and for continuous innovation, incremental and radical, product and process, organizational and technical. Major externalities, from low-cost access to the new infrastructure to adequate distribution channels and the education of workers and consumers, facilitate innovations compatible with the now established paradigm. This shared logic based on shared advantages leads to the weaving of a strong mesh of economic inter-relations that tends to mold, exclude or marginalize innovations that are not directly compatible with it. This period ends when the potential of that revolution and its paradigm approach exhaustion and there is a constriction in the growth of markets, productivity and profits along the established trajectories.

However, no technological revolution grows in a 'green field site'. Before its big-bang, the intervening technologies had gone through a long process of gestation in the midst of the deployment period of the previous paradigm, being shaped by its requirements. Neither do the industries and technology systems of a revolution disappear meekly at maturity. They remain stubbornly struggling for survival, during the installation of the next, and only gradually modernize, adopting the new principles when they are forced by the market superiority of the new paradigm. These two long overlaps between the life cycles of successive paradigms (see Figure 49.3) are essential to the argument being presented here, because they are the scene of the battles between the forces of inertia and the forces of change, and it is the context and the nature of these battles that will determine the quality and the quantity of technological and financial opportunities at each phase.

7   Why technical change occurs by revolutions

For Schumpeter technological opportunities 'are always present, abundantly accumulated by all sorts of people'.[31] It is the entrepreneurs who decide when to turn those possibilities into innovations by exercising their leadership (if they find, of course, bankers willing to finance them). There is even a very strong statement in his *Theory of Economic Development*, warning that the excessive emphasis on invention may be 'downright misleading'.[32]

While agreeing that the relative independence of scientific and technological research constantly provides a vast untapped pool of potential innovations,[33] this still leaves some big open questions. If opportunities, entrepreneurs and supportive bankers are always equally available, why does technical change occur by revolutions? Why do actual innovations cluster and why do such clusters occur about every half a century? Some powerful process must be at work, providing an exclusion–inclusion mechanism.[34]

This chapter holds that the opportunities for entrepreneurs to profitably tap into the pool of usable science and technology change strongly over time and are very much shaped by the phases of each surge of development.[35]

Specifically, as Kuznets originally suggested,[36] the radical innovations conforming each successive technological revolution tend to come together into a powerful cluster only when the deployment of the previous revolution approaches exhaustion and maturity. This notion was also at the core of Gerhard Mensch's *Stalemate in Technology* as an explanation of the clustering of innovations.[37]

7.1   Embedded paradigms as inclusion–exclusion mechanisms

The mechanism at work is the social embeddedness of the techno-economic paradigm and its role as provider of externalities. During deployment, the

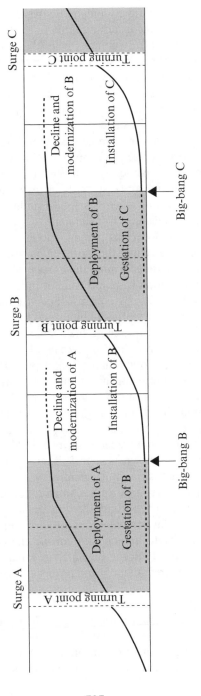

Figure 49.3   The overlaps in the gestation, diffusion and decline of successive surges[30]

principles of the paradigm are not only present as common sense in production, investment, trade and consumption; they are also embedded in the territory in terms of cheap infrastructures, available suppliers and distribution channels, adequately trained personnel and established regulations, as well as entrenched in the habits of a way of life. These massive externalities work as a strong *inclusion mechanism* to favor product innovations that are compatible with the paradigm and follow its expected trajectories. Such products are readily accepted and easily woven into the mesh of the growing economic system. In the fourth surge, for example, once most homes had electricity and learned to use the first few electrical appliances, such as refrigerators, radios and vacuum cleaners, a whole series of radical innovations were easily incorporated into the production and distribution streams and into the way of life of consumers, from washing machines, food-blenders and record players to dish washers, freezers and color-TV. The same happened with the long series of important radical innovations in synthetic materials and fibers, which were gradually incorporated into the textile, engineering, packaging and consumer goods industries, transforming the input profile of the economy and the machinery required for a wide spectrum of processes.

Non-compatible products, by contrast, find it difficult to penetrate the established patterns and tend either to be shaped to adapt or to be marginalized and even excluded. In those cases, the reigning paradigm and its embedded externalities act as an *exclusion mechanism*. Semiconductors in their initial phase, for instance, found an ideal mass production niche by serving to stretch the life of mature consumer audio-equipment, through making them portable and rejuvenating their markets. The first integrated circuits, however, were marginalized in hearing aids or special military applications. Far back in history, during the first great surge, the early steam engines were used to drain water out of mines, before anyone could imagine the major role they would play in transport years later. It is out of those technologies that are 'waiting in the wings', going through a sort of gestation period, that the next revolution is likely to come together, when conditions become favorable.

During deployment, then, both production and financial capital are satisfied with the successive investment and innovation opportunities associated with the successive new technology systems of the current technological revolution. New products appear regularly in expanding markets, strong companies are further strengthened, and profits are good . . . until maturity sets in.

7.2   Exhaustion of opportunity trajectories leading idle money to search elsewhere

Once there is paradigm constriction, once the innovation trajectories of successive products, industries and technology systems start drying up, there are fewer and fewer profitable uses for the mass of profits still being produced. Such idle money ends up piling up in the hands of financial capital, which is ready to experiment. It will accompany production capital in its search for faraway markets and/or lower cost production sites and it might 'innovate' in speculative schemes or in ways of making doubtfully legitimate profit.[38]

Financial capital is also likely to find and fund two types of eager creditors with important consequences. On the one hand, there is the opportunity of making easy loans abroad. From the canal building credit given by the British to various states in the USA during the maturity and decline of the first surge (1820s–30s), to the diverse forms of development funding given to the Third World in those of the fourth (1960s–70s), each wave of such loans has later led to a debt crisis.[39]

On the other hand, the dearth of innovative opportunities in the old paradigm opens the eyes of the financiers to truly path-breaking possibilities. The new entrepreneurs, the potential bearers of the next technological revolution, can be noticed and can get the funds they might not have secured a few years earlier. It is their obvious initial success that will, in Schumpeterian fashion, launch the swarm of imitators. Both the entrepreneurs and the financiers will concentrate their efforts and resources on furthering, expanding and multiplying the products and industries of the new technology systems of the revolution.[40]

7.3 The role of finance in fostering the new paradigm

As Schumpeter expected, the new combinations will usually be made by new firms.[41] The entrepreneurs pushing the technological revolution are likely to be inexperienced in business and will also often be young. They will, therefore, need the help of bankers or financiers in more ways than just funding.

Yet it is not evident that the truly experienced financiers will be capable of understanding the essence of the new technologies or of visualizing the implicit change in direction. Their expertise is deeply rooted in the waning paradigm. J.P. Morgan, at the height of his power and having been the financial brain propelling the third surge, rebuffed Henry Ford, considering automobiles as rich men's toys.[42] Paradigm blindness is a natural phenomenon associated with the 'over-adaptation' experienced by society as it engages in the full deployment of a particular technological revolution. J. Watson Sr the first head of IBM, less than two decades away from the information revolution, thought that a few computers would fulfill all of the world's needs.

Hence, not only do the new entrepreneurs need to be imbued with the logic of the emerging technologies, their financial counterparts need to share that understanding. This is why the early financiers of each techno-logical revolution tend to be family, friends and, gradually, venture capi-talists, who believe in the technologies and are willing to take the risks that the big traditional ones will not assume. A much younger J.P. Morgan, in 1878, did take big risks with new ideas. He funded Edison at the very begin-ning of electricity. In a sense, the early financiers backing the revolutionary products are true risk takers and often participate actively in the business management of the innovation process itself. In this sense, they could be seen as *financial entrepreneurs*.[43]

7.4   An endogenous process with a specific rhythm

The gradual exhaustion of the innovation potential within the trajectories of the prevailing paradigm puts more and more idle money in the hands of financial capital, inducing it to break loose and to go looking for whatever opportunities may be available outside the well-trodden paths. The search will include supporting entrepreneurs that are tapping the vast pool of pos-sibilities underestimated by the prevailing paradigm. This creates the conditions favorable for the coming together of the next technological rev-olution, which appears to both potential entrepreneurs and potential financiers as an opportunity explosion in what was becoming a barren innovation landscape. The extraordinary profits and the extraordinary growth rates that characterize the early innovations will be the force unleashing the clusters of entrepreneurs and bold financiers.

Thus, the clustering of innovative entrepreneurs – and of bold financiers – is not a random phenomenon, even though such audacious potential agents of change may be randomly distributed in the population at any point in time. The conditions for the double clustering are endoge-nously generated by the techno-economic system. It is the exhaustion of the current potential that lifts the exclusion mechanisms and opens the door for the aspiring entrepreneurs and the bold financiers to come together and bring forth new solutions.

The major advantages provided to the participants in the deployment of a paradigm also explain the spacing between successive revolutions, allow-ing enough time for each one to run its course. The amounts of investment involved in the growth of the new industries, and in the expansion of each infrastructure, the need to unlearn massively the old paradigm and adopt the new, the significant changes that must be induced on the territory, in the institutions and in the minds of people and society, will all contribute to exclude any new revolution from irrupting before most of the wealth-creating potential of the current one has been exploited. That same energy of contention and exclusion will turn into a powerful force to invite change, once the established investment and profit opportunities dwindle.

8 Financial bubbles as massive processes of credit creation

The irruption of a technological revolution finds an environment that is inevitably unfavorable and even hostile. It is, by definition, a breakthrough; it is the abandonment of the accepted trajectories and practice; it means the introduction of a novel way of doing things and a set of new products, industries and infrastructures that threaten the existing ones in one way or another. It is Schumpeterian *creative destruction* at its most visible. It will therefore elicit ferocious resistance both from those that are really set for losing and from those that have not yet discovered they might benefit from it.[44]

While the powerful firms from the previous surge may be willing to use some of the new technologies to stretch their stagnant productivity or solve some of their problems, they are unlikely to be the champions of the emerging constellation. They might, on the contrary, be particularly conservative, especially if direct threats to their products are apparent.

8.1 The power of finance backing the paradigm shift

The new firms are too small, too weak or too inexperienced to confront the resistance of the establishment by themselves. The difference between weight and rate marks the early diffusion of each technological revolution. The heavyweights that still make up the bulk of the economy grow slowly or decline while those with the fast growth rates are still too lightweight to make a major difference. Only with the increasing power of financial capital on their side can they successfully wage the battles to change the socio-institutional routines, to generate the adequate manpower, to establish the new norms and other favorable conditions and to remove the many obstacles inherited from the old paradigm. This is increasingly important for financial capital, as it gets more and more involved with the new technologies and the new industries. As Schumpeter insisted, it is the capitalist that faces the risk: 'the entrepreneur never bears the risk'.[45]

So the early venture capitalists are true adventurers and not mere bridges for innovation. They are in the front line of the battle against the old routines and the obstacles and in favor of the construction of an enabling environment to facilitate the diffusion of the emerging paradigm. Historically, they have tended to do this through the unmitigated defence of free markets and *laissez faire,* turning the installation periods into the hardest and most individualistic form of capitalism. Hence, in terms of institutions, the creative destruction process in this period tends to have an overdose of destruction.[46]

In the early (or irruption) phase of the installation period, both the entrepreneurs and their financiers are engaged in an intense exploration process, trying to understand what is successful from the new range of the possible and under what conditions. This trial and error process involves high risks and can yield high stakes. The higher the prizes obtained, the more intense the swarms of imitators will be; the more consistent the key features of success, the more clearly the general trajectories of the techno-economic paradigm will become visible, facilitating further innovation on a wider and wider spectrum.

The Model-T gave high visibility to the principles for mass production, which soon fuelled swarms of imitators not only in automobiles and their components but also in other mechanical and electrical manufactures.[47] The full spread of the paradigm as such will come later, when completely unrelated industries such as food, packaging or even tourism make leaps in productivity and quality by applying the same principles.

8.2 The making of the bubble

In essence, the techno-economic paradigm, once it is fully articulated and has spread enough, turns into a *risk-reduction mechanism*, partly real, partly illusory. Gradually, certain ready-made formulas become paths to ready-made profits and the new financiers entering the game no longer need to be so knowledgeable, only audacious. In the first surge, making a canal from any river to any other looked naturally profitable. Decades later, in the 1840s, a railway uniting any two cities was perceived as an obviously winning bet, just as in the late 1990s the dot.com craze was seen as the quick path to becoming a millionaire. Whether such expectations are warranted or not is irrelevant. The phenomenon has occurred with every surge a decade or two after the big-bang and, in every case, the faith in the profit-making power of the industries and infrastructures of the revolution spreads widely and attracts all available money into the financial whirlpool. It is the making of the financial bubble, the collapse of which will end the installation period.

Opportunities grow explosively. Innumerable entrepreneurs will offer their projects to the also growing number of financiers. If they seem to follow the new paradigm, all projects, good and bad, honest and crooked, are likely to have access to the required funds. In particular, the infrastructure of the revolution will be able to spread very far and will most likely over-invest, if judged by its overall profitability and by the capacity of the economy to use it at the time. Existing firms will also be funded when they propose to modernize by applying the new paradigm.

But, again, the weight-rate factors come into play. Even growing at an amazingly frantic pace, the new or modernizing industries cannot absorb the growing amounts of investment money brought to the stock market[48] in pursuit of the extraordinary profits now expected by all. However, financial capital will not be deterred. It will now innovate in ways that turn the stock market into a casino, decoupling from the real economy and building extraordinary paper mountains. It will speculate with whatever is at hand, from gold to real estate, and will also invent all sorts of bonds and derivatives, inverted pyramids and even less legitimate schemes.[49] High profit expectations will be kept alive by the financial wizards in a growing atmosphere of 'irrational exuberance'[50] and, for a while, people will actually receive them, at least in the form of capital gains, even if in the real economy only a very few firms are generating levels of profit to warrant such excess confidence (though some fraudulently simulate having them).

Thus, the bold and entrepreneurial financial capital of early installation becomes the reckless capital of the late – or frenzy – phase of that period. In its search for newer and newer ways of guaranteeing a high return on all investment, be it related to the technological revolution or not, it systematically contributes to the hyperinflation of assets that underlies the bubble. As paper profits are further reinvested in the same casino, they intensify the phenomenon even further and attract ever more investors, including those who had never put their money anywhere beyond the family coffer or the corner savings bank.

8.3   *When the job is done, it is time for the changeover in leadership*
In this way, financial capital unwittingly guarantees that the industries and infrastructures of the technological revolution will become large enough to influence the economy and the firms involved powerful enough to serve as the leaders and engines of growth for the next deployment period. The bubble at the end of installation can be understood as a gigantic process of collective credit creation, orchestrated by the financial world in the stock market.[51]

The collapse of the bubble will inevitably come and much of the illusory paper wealth will disappear. But the installation of the paradigm in the minds and in the territory, as principles, as industries and as fully-fledged infrastructures, will have been achieved.

After the ensuing recession reveals the ills of the bubble and the tensions behind it, there will be the need to swing the pendulum back in terms both of greater attention to social interests, as opposed to the greedy individualism fueled by the financial frenzy, and of limiting the powers of financial capital, handing the guidance of the economy over to production capital, now represented by the new engines of growth, which are ready to develop long-term expansion strategies. Disappointment with the stock market as a source of quick and easy wealth reintroduces rationality in investment decisions;[52] regulation and other conditioning factors will bring financial capital back into a complementary role, until the end of the surge calls it out again for the next transformation. But the passage from installation to deployment can be a very difficult political process, full of tensions, economic instability and uncertainty; it can be short or quite long (the turning point of the fourth surge lasted from 1929 until the Bretton Woods agreements of 1943, almost at the end of WWII).[53]

9   Summary and conclusion

This chapter has argued that financial capital has a fundamental role in the articulation and propagation of technological revolutions. It also proposes an inclusion–exclusion mechanism that would explain why technical change occurs by successive revolutions with several decades between them. In doing so, it reaffirmed Schumpeter's view of the clustering of entrepreneurship in certain periods. But, in contrast with Schumpeter, it held that the bunching of intense radical change also brings forth clusters of bold – sometimes reckless – financiers in support of the production entrepreneurs. Major financial bubbles were interpreted as massive processes of credit creation to install each technological revolution. The arguments are rooted in a stylized model of the diffusion and assimilation of technological revolutions based on historical recurrence, the main purpose of which is to serve as a heuristic device.

9.1   Finance and paradigm shifts

A central element in the model presented is the concept of *techno-economic paradigm* as the set of generic technologies and organizational principles that emerge with each technological revolution and guide its diffusion, through being adopted as shared best-practice common sense by all the economic agents. It is this aspect of each technological revolution that provides the potential for modernizing the whole economy, which gradually reaches a higher productivity level. This process, designated as a *great surge of development*, would take about half a century to unfold in a very uneven manner, sometimes turbulent, sometimes more harmonious.

Each paradigm becomes so embedded in the techno-economic and the socio-institutional spheres of society that compatible innovations benefit from massive externalities and their success and profitability are greatly facilitated. What is suggested is that, through the agency of the embedded paradigm, each surge establishes an inclusion–exclusion mechanism that rewards innovations following the meta-routines of the paradigm and discourages, reshapes or marginalizes non-compatible innovations, which would be much more difficult and less profitable.

Only when the potential of that revolution is exhausted can the conditions become favorable for the next revolution to come together, but at that stage the new paradigm will confront enormous resistance. Incumbent producers are likely to be among the main inertial forces. By its very nature, production capital is tied to its previous history of investment, knowledge, experience, personnel and external networks. Financial capital, by contrast, is fundamentally mobile. It can therefore break loose from the mature sectors of the economy and reallocate funds to any emerging technologies outside the well-trodden paths. In this manner, it contributes to the articulation of the next technological revolution and the diffusion of its paradigm. In searching its own enrichment through sharing in the extraordinary profits of the new products and industries, it also helps remove institutional obstacles and strengthens the successful entrepreneurial firms, which will gradually become strong enough to replace the engines of growth of the previous paradigm and to take control over from financial capital.

The model thus proposes a causal chain with a mechanism for the spacing of technological revolutions, giving a role to financial capital in their articulation and in facilitating the replacement of the leading firms of each surge. It is based on the notion of techno-economic paradigms as meta-routines for innovation and on the functional separation of production and financial capital. Both aspects would be essential to the dynamic character of capitalism.

9.2   Clusters of bold financiers and the invisible hand for credit creation

The bunching of innovation opportunities with the irruption of each technological revolution would be the cause behind the periodic clustering of audacious entrepreneurs. It would also explain the subsequent clustering of bold even reckless financiers accompanying and fostering the paradigm shift and gradually leading to a major financial bubble.

These recurring episodes of reckless banking or stock market manias, rather than being anomalies, would work as an invisible hand for massive credit creation, facilitating the full installation of each technological revolution and its paradigm.

The hyperinflation of assets provides enough funds for experimenting widely with the new technological possibilities of the revolution, for modernizing much of the existing firms and plants, for over-investing in the new infrastructure and also for setting up innumerable forms of casino-like speculative schemes.

Assigning a role to financial bubbles in the diffusion of technological revolutions would assign a role to reckless finance in the dynamics of capitalist growth, ranging the phenomenon among the 'natural' features of capitalism, in stark contrast to Schumpeter's view on the matter.

9.3   The research ahead

Much research is still required to test further the validity of the model presented and to achieve a deeper understanding of the difference between the recurrent phenomena and their unique manifestations.

If the interpretation presented here is accepted as plausible, it begs the question of the inevitability of the bubble. Would this be the only way in which capitalism can install a paradigm and lure enough capital into investing in its particular infrastructure to make it into an all-pervasive externality? Does understanding the phenomenon open the way for the construction of a solution that is less socially painful?

In any case, further research will contribute to deepening the understanding of the relationship between finance and innovation as well as of the impact of technological innovation on financial practice. This could correct the imbalance that has heretofore prevailed among neo-Schumpeterians and, not heeding Schumpeter's warnings against them, would enhance the capacity to provide policy recommendations.

Notes

1. Kuznets (1940), pp. 261–2.
2. Schumpeter (1939: 1982), p. 223.
3. Schumpeter (1939: 1982), pp. 792, 877.
4. For a more complete presentation of the model, see Perez (2002).
5. Schumpeter (1939: 1982), p. 179.
6. Schumpeter (1911: 1961), pp. 92–94 and (1939, 1982), pp. 405–6.
7. Schumpeter (1911: 1961), pp. 74, 107, 117.
8. Schumpeter (1939: 1982), pp. 116–17.
9. Nelson and Winter (1982), pp. 128–36; Dosi (1982); Rosenberg (1969); Sahal (1985) and others. See Freeman (1990).
10. Freeman (1992), pp. 75–81.
11. Freeman and Louçã (2001), ch. 2
12. This pattern of radical change–systemic increments–crisis–radical change is what led Giovanni Dosi to use the term 'technological paradigms', by analogy with Thomas Kuhn's (1962) description of a similar process in scientific practice.
13. Keirstead (1948).
14. Freeman *et al.* (1982), ch. 4.
15. Nelson and Winter (1977). See also Freeman *et al.* (1982), p. 74.
16. See Nelson and Winter (1982) about 'routines as genes', pp. 134–6.
17. Perez (1985), pp. 441–2.
18. In modern times, most major corporations fund much of their innovation investment from retained earnings. Thus the complexity of the decision-making process is internalized. Their organizations usually establish explicit mechanisms for decision making, whereby financial managers and 'intrapreneurs' (production, R&D or marketing managers) discuss and assess innovation projects from points of view that reflect their respective roles.
19. Perez (2002), p. 9.
20. Perez and Soete (1988).
21. Perez (2002), pp. 71–3.
22. Schumpeter (1939: 1982), pp. 164–74.
23. Perez (2002), ch. 2 and pp. 22–3.
24. Schumpeter (1939: 1982), pp. 695–700, after considering the wider sociopolitical implications, insists on keeping all non-economic effects of technical change out of his model, as 'external factors'.
25. Perez (2002), p. 20 and ch. 3.
26. Since 1983, in the author's work and in her collaboration with Chris Freeman (see Freeman and Perez, 1988) both the term 'long waves' and the dating were kept as close

to Schumpeter's as the need for differentiation allowed. It was in 2000–2002, in the process of developing the whole model, including the role of finance, that the break became indispensable.

27. For dates of big bangs and indication of core countries, see the first column of Table 49.1 above. For further discussion and dating see Perez (2002), p. 20 and ch. 5, especially pp. 56–9.

28. The third surge, from the 1870s, is a peculiar case partly because it constitutes the first process of globalization and the first confrontation for the role of core country in the world economy, through the forging ahead of the USA and Germany as challengers and the decline of British power. For a brief discussion, see Perez (2002), p. 58.

29. Perez (2002), ch. 11.

30. The figure evokes Mensch's (1975, 1979) metamorphosis model of cycles of structural change.

31. Schumpeter (1911: 1961), pp. 88, 197.

32. Schumpeter (1911: 1961), p. 89.

33. From the 1980s, a strong tendency has become prevalent towards forcing publicly funded research to be of immediate relevance to existing industry and towards concentrating support on the few already successful centers of excellence. One could ponder about the medium and long-term consequences of this for radical innovation potential.

34. This was one of the main challenges made by Rosenberg and Frischtak (1984) to long wave proponents.

35. Perez (2002), ch. 3, pp. 27–35.

36. Kuznets (1953), p. 113.

37. Mensch (1975: 1979).

38. For the behavior of financial capital when the fourth surge reached maturity, from the 1960s onwards, see Strange (1986).

39. Perez (2002), ch. 8.

40. Every one of these processes takes a uniquely different form, depending on the peculiar features of the particular revolution. There is a huge difference between designing and making minicomputers in a garage and designing and making steam engines, Bessemer steel converters or electrical generators.

41. Schumpeter (1911: 1961), pp. 66, 75, 137, 156.

42. Chernow (1990), p. 221.

43. Janeway (1986) suggests that venture capital plays a double role as banker and entrepreneur.

44. Schumpeter (1911: 1961), pp. 86–7.

45. Schumpeter (1911: 1961), pp. 75, 137 and (1939: 1982), p. 104.

46. It should be noted that in many cases the technologies at the center of the revolution are based on a previous accumulation of a common pool of scientific and technical knowledge, often funded by public institutions, during the gestation period and even earlier. But once they make the market breakthroughs and become the source of extraordinary profits, there is enough attraction for private funds to take over, even for a substantial part of the required scientific research.

47. The growth of the core industries of each technological revolution is at the heart of the rise and collapse of the stock market boom. The striking similarities in the behavior of the PC industry (in the fifth surge) and the automobile industry (in the fourth), in terms of stock market price volatility, number of firms and sales volumes, are shown in Mazzucato (2002).

48. The attraction becomes so powerful that after the funds that would normally be tagged for investment have moved towards an equity preference, potential investors turn to bank loans to enter the stock market (For the case in the 1920s, see Hoover, 1929, p. xii). This aspect approximates the present interpretation to those that explain bubbles as overextended credit booms. A particularly interesting analysis of the 1929 crash and its aftermath along these lines is found in Eichengreen and Mitchener (2003).

49. Perez (2002), ch. 10 and 13.

50. Shiller (2000: 2001).

51. In the first two surges, the stock market was not fully developed and the bubbles were inflated by bold ambitious characters such as Hudson in the British railway boom of the 1840s. But the basic social nature of the money whirlpool phenomenon is the same.
52. In the introduction to the 2001 edition of his *Irrational Exuberance*, Shiller (2000: 2001, pp. xii–xiv) reports that he repeated his pre-NASDAQ collapse surveys and found to his dismay that the excess confidence in equity investment had hardly been dented by the crash. This has not been typical of previous surges, which would suggest an interesting peculiarity of the present case, in the sense of not providing enough social pressures towards regulatory intervention to curb financial capital.
53. Perez (2002), pp. 125–6.

Bibliography

Arhur, W. Brian (1988), 'Competing technologies: an overview', in Dosi *et al.* (eds), pp. 590–607.
Chernow, Ron (1990), *The House of Morgan*, New York, London, Toronto, Sydney, Tokyo, Singapore: Simon & Schuster.
Dosi, Giovanni (1982), 'Technical paradigms and technological trajectories: a suggested interpretation of the determinants of technical change', *Research Policy*, **2**(3), 147–62.
Dosi, Giovanni, Freeman, Chris, Nelson, Richard, Silverberg, Gerald and Soete, Luc (eds) (1988), *Technical Change and Economic Theory*, London and New York: Columbia University Press and Pinter.
Eichengreen, Barry and Mitchener, Kris (2004), 'The Great Depression as a credit boom gone wrong', *Research in Economic History*, **22**, 183–237.
Freeman, Chris (ed.) (1990), *The Economics of Innovation: An Elgar Reference Collection*, Aldershot, UK and Brookfield, USA: Edward Elgar.
Freeman, Chris (1992), *The Economics of Hope*, London and New York: Pinter.
Freeman, Chris and Louçã, Francisco (2001), *As Time Goes By: From the Industrial Revolution to the Information Revolution*, Oxford: Oxford University Press.
Freeman, Chris and Perez, Carlota (1988), 'Structural crises of adjustment: business cycles and investment behavior', in Dosi *et al.* (eds), pp. 38–66.
Freeman, Chris, Clark, John and Soete, Luc (1982), *Unemployment and Technical Innovation: A Study of Long Waves and Economic Development*, London: Frances Pinter.
Galbraith, John Kenneth (1990: 1993), *A Short History of Financial Euphoria*, New York: Whittle-Penguin.
Hoover, Herbert, Chairman (1929), *Recent Changes in the United States, Report of the Committee on Recent Economic Changes of the President's Conference on Unemployment*, New York, London: McGraw-Hill.
Janeway, William H. (1986), 'Doing capitalism: notes on the practice of venture capitalism', *Journal of Economic Issues*, **XX**(2), June, 431–41.
Keirstead, Burton Seely (1948), *The Theory of Economic Change*, Toronto: Macmillan.
Kuhn, Thomas (1962, 1970), *The Structure of Scientific Revolutions*, 2nd edn, enlarged, Chicago, IL: University of Chicago Press.
Kuznets, Simon (1940), 'Schumpeter's Business Cycles', *American Economic Review*, **30**, 257–71.
Kuznets, Simon (1953), *Economic Change*, New York: W.W. Norton.
Mazzucato, Mariana (2002), 'The PC industry: new economy or early life-cycle?', *Review of Economic Dynamics*, **5**, 318–45.
Mensch, Gerhard (1975, 1979), *Stalemate in Technology*, Cambridge, MA: Ballinger.
Nelson, Richard and Winter, Sidney G, (1977), 'In search of a useful theory of innovation', *Research Policy*, **6**(1), 36–76.
Nelson, Richard and Winter, Sidney G, (1982), *An Evolutionary Theory of Economic Change*, Cambridge, MA and London: Harvard University Press.
Perez, Carlota (1985), 'Microelectronics, long waves and world structural change: new perspectives for developing countries', *World Development*, **13**(3), 441–63.
Perez, Carlota (2002), *Technological Revolutions and Financial Capital: The Dynamics of Bubbles and Golden Ages*, Cheltenham, UK and Northampton, MA, USA: Edward Elgar.

Perez, Carlota and Soete, Luc (1988), 'Catching up in technology: entry barriers and windows of opportunity', in Dosi *et al.* (eds), pp. 458–79.

Rosenberg, Nathan (1969), 'The direction of technical change: inducement mechanisms and focusing devices', *Economic Development and Cultural Change*, **19**, 1–24.

Rosenberg, Nathan and Frischtak, Claudio (1984), Technological innovation and long waves, *Cambridge Journal of Economics*, **8**, 7–24.

Sahal, Devendra (1985), 'Technological guideposts and innovation avenues', *Research Policy*, **14**(2), 441–63 (reproduced in Freeman (ed.), 1990).

Schumpeter, Joseph A. (1911: 1961), *The Theory of Economic Development*, New York: Oxford University Press.

Schumpeter, Joseph A. (1939: 1982), *Business Cycles,* 2 vols, Philadelphia: Porcupine Press.

Shiller, Robert, J. (2000: 2001), *Irrational Exuberance*, Princeton, NJ and Oxford, Princeton University Press.

Strange, Susan (1986), *Casino Capitalism*, Oxford: Blackwell.

Utterback and Abernathy (1975), 'A dynamic model of process and product innovation', *Omega*, **3**(6), 639–56 (reproduced in Freeman (ed.), 1990).

Wolf, Julius (1912), *Die Volkswirtschaft der Gegenwart und Zukunft* (A. Deichertsche Verlagsbuchandlung), Leipzig: Deichert.

50 Long waves: conceptual, empirical and modelling issues

Gerald Silverberg

1 Introduction

The theory of long waves is exceptionally fortunate in that, while there is no general consensus that they exist or, assuming that they do, what an appropriate theory should be, thanks to the unstinting efforts of several researchers, we have encyclopaedic compendia of the literature (Freeman, 1996; Reijnders and Louçã, 1999) and a recent valiant attempt to write modern economic history from a long-wave perspective (Freeman and Louçã, 2001). The purpose of this entry is to review succinctly the controversy about what long waves might mean as a phenomenon, how they might be measured and modelled, and where they might fit into an overarching theory of economic dynamics and evolution. The seminal work of Kondratieff (1925/1979) and Schumpeter (1939) of course will play a central role, but I will also draw on recent work in complex modelling, nonlinear dynamics and time-series econometrics to put the debate into a more contemporary perspective. As was frequently Schumpeter's fate, however, his name has become associated in the subsequent literature with various hypotheses that he never made in the form they were later expressed, and, to judge by what he did write, to which he almost certainly did not subscribe.

Nevertheless, Schumpeter's basic ideas about the central importance of the innovation process and its disequilibrim character, the role of the entrepreneur or the large, bureaucratic R&D-based firm, creative destruction as the driving force behind structural change, and aggregate fluctuations at different time scales as inseparable features of the capitalist process of development, have all become basic tenets of the neo-Schumpeterian research paradigm in economics.

The most agnostic approach to long waves is simply to regard them as a discernable but otherwise inexplicable pattern in aggregate time series of real and price variables. By the end of the nineteenth and beginning of the twentieth centuries it was apparent, even given the inadequacy of the available data, that in addition to the long-surmised trade (Juglar) and inventory cycles (Kitchen) of a two-to-ten-year period, economies developed irregularly on even longer time scales (it was, prior to Kondratieff, particularly Marxists such as Parvus, de Wolff and van Gelderen who were especially awake to such possibilities). It is probably only natural that observers would attempt to interpret this irregularity in terms of periodic or regular cycles, just as gamblers will attempt to read all sorts of regularities, including cyclical patterns, into the spin of a roulette wheel (which is not to deny that even roulette wheels may display subtle and exploitable regularities). Pattern, predictability and causality, however, are very different things. A pattern in the past need never repeat itself in the future and need not imply that any specific mechanism is responsible for its occurrence and can be used for forecasting (think of a run of ten red 17s during an evening of roulette). Yet humans do seem to have a natural proclivity to attach deeper significance to perceived (or even) imagined patterns, a proclivity we can dignify with the name 'induction' and perhaps even elevate to the basic urge underlying all scientific discovery. Nevertheless we must always be wary not to fall victim to a gambler's equally strong propensity for self-delusion, superstition, and even desire for metaphysical revelation. Only the control of statistical methodology, as inadequate as it often is, and critical reasoning can limit the excesses of this tendency. By the same token no hypothesis should be simply rejected out of hand just because it appears too neat and all-encompassing (think of the early opposition to Wegener's theory of continental drift, based as it was on the often remarked, all too neat fit of the east coast of South America into the west coast of Africa, or Kepler's theory of the Platonic solids as an explanation of the spacing of the planetary orbits). Such hypotheses, even when they prove mistaken, can often be fruitful inspirations for empirical and theoretical research. It is in this spirit that I will treat the long-wave hypothesis as a source of a number of useful conjectures and, even if untenable or untestable in its original formulation, as amenable to a modern interpretation with important empirical implications.

Kondratieff was the first modern econometrician to attempt to identify long waves from the data. Kondratieff, however, did not content himself with just this numerical exercise, as pathbreaking as it was, but went on to outline a general cyclical theory that is especially impressive for the range of phenomena it attempts to endogenize. These include gold discoveries, inventions, wars and, particularly, investment cycles in infrastructure. Phenomena that conventionally had been assumed exogenous to the economic system, he argued, were actually components of a larger feedback process, a process in some respect even more cogent and encompassing than the one Marx had sketched.[1]

This tendency to imbue the at first sight purely numerical observation of long-term fluctuations in some time series with systemic significance is characteristic, on the one hand, in a more limited domain, of Schumpeter's conceptual scheme (singling out innovations for pride of place in a more strictly economic context) and, on the other, of a number of scholars coming from a political science background. The latter have attempted to wed political and economic considerations into a world systems-level theory of hegemonic or leadership cycles (Modelski, 1987; Goldstein, 1988; Modelski and Thompson, 1996) in which warfare and patterns of international trade and capital flows play the crucial role,[2] or have focused on long-term changes in the distribution of income and the nature of collective bargaining in a theory of the 'social structures of accumulation' or 'regulation' (Gordon, 1989; Boyer, 1988). While these 'non-Schumpeterian' long-wave theories will not be examined further here, they do highlight the need to embed purely economic considerations into a wider social, political and even cultural context. This is one of the themes of Freeman and Louçã (2001), drawing on the work of Perez (1983) and Freeman and Perez (1988), who argue that the diffusion of new technologies is conditioned on a proper match between the new techno-economic system and appropriate institutions, legal frameworks, labour relations and cultural attitudes, and that these might only adapt with considerable delay and in a somewhat discontinuous manner.[3] Nevertheless one has the impression that this interplay between the social and the techno-economic is almost always decided in favour of the latter, with the social merely serving as a passive retarding factor which periodically breaks down in the face of the technological onslaught and ultimately adjusts to the inevitable.

Freeman and Louçã find the evidence for their vision of long waves in both the econometric and the modelling literature unsatisfactory and resort to a version of long waves somewhat between a mere dating scheme (comparable to the anthropologist's classification of human cultural evolution based on old and new stone ages, bronze age, iron age, etc.) and that of Angus Maddison (1991), a pronounced sceptic on the subject of long waves, with its individual reading of phases of capitalist development in terms of historical factors unique to each phase. They differ from Maddison in their emphasis on the recurrent character of these phases (thus attributing to them the property of cycles or waves) based on the same underlying mechanism, even if the phases are by no means strictly regular or periodic (or at least cannot be shown to be so given the current state of the art).[4] While their attempt to integrate the Perez mismatch theory is original, in other respects their narrative of capitalist economic history, aside from being brought up to date, does not differ significantly from that of Schumpeter (in fact, the latter is in many respects much more detailed). What stands out, however, in the Schumpeterian tradition is the endeavour to provide a fully causal explanation of long-term economic fluctuations that synthesizes historically significant stochastic elements (datable Schumpeterian innovations, as opposed to the unidentified random 'innovations' of conventional econometric modelling) with deterministic ones, in a nontrivial way.

2   The identification of long waves: theory-free econometrics?

The question of our ability to discern long-run patterns in the record of aggregate economic time series turns out to be more fraught with technical difficulties than one would at first imagine. This line of research was initiated by Kondratieff (1925/1935/1979), who was one of the first to apply modern methods of trend elimination and residual analysis to a large number of price and output series. As we shall see, even with the enormous advance of econometric methods since his day, this problem still cannot be satisfactorily resolved, quite aside from the question of the quality of the data and the shortness of the series.

The main reason for the difficulty is the fact that most long-period time series, such as for GDP, GDP per capita, and even for prices, are not stationary, as is obviously the case for any growth process. An alternative would be to use series that do not a priori contain a trend, such as unemployment rates, income shares, and possibly profit rates (although the Marxist prior on the latter is for a falling trend). Unfortunately, it is even more difficult to define and compile these variables consistently over so much longer periods than the usual ones, so very little serious work has been done with them. Trend variables must first have the trend removed in the Kondratieff approach before looking for cyclical patterns in the residuals. But without a convincing argument for a particular trend form, one can produce almost any long-period cycle one wishes by using, e.g., higher-order polynomial trends. This critique was already levelled at Kondratieff by Frickey (1942) among others.

Periodogram or spectral analysis, whose application in economics dates back to at least Beveridge (1922) and with which Schumpeter was thoroughly familiar and not even unsympathetic despite negative results,[5] unfortunately did not belong to Kondratieff's toolbox. But it is the main tool for detecting cycles in time-series statistics. Unfortunately it is only really defined for stationary series.[6] When applied to nonstationary series, the trend will show up in the low-frequency region and be inseparable from any low-frequency (i.e., long-period) cycles. Thus one is again forced to use a detrending or other procedure to make the series stationary. One method intrinsically related to spectral analysis is to use a linear filter (see Metz, 1987, 1992) to eliminate frequencies below those of interest without distorting the rest of the spectral signature. While this method finesses the question of defining a trend, the trend, however defined, may also induce spectral energy in the relevant range and thus contaminate the result. And in fact the method has not proved robust to changes in the range of the data used or to the setting of the cutoffs.

Another standard method for making economic series stationary is to take first differences (usually of the log of the series, thus approximating the growth rate). What was originally a completely 'agnostic' numerical method to make a series stationary has acquired an exaggerated statistical meaning since the so-called 'unit root debate' arose about the fundamental distinction between trend and difference stationarity (Nelson and Plosser, 1982) as fundamentally different macroeconomic paradigms in (mostly short-period) business cycle econometrics. While the knife-edge sharpness of this distinction has proved to be less clear-cut in finite data sets than originally thought, first differencing sidesteps the spurious cycle problem of trend-elimination exercises and has become standard in time-series econometrics.

Modern spectral studies of long waves include Ewijk (1982), Haustein and Neuwirth (1982), Metz (1987, 1992) and Reijnders (1990), but, as noted above, the technique was already current in Schumpeter's day. An alternative method has recently been proposed by Goldstein (1999), who has applied structural time series modelling to combine deterministic and stochastic trends and, much like Schumpeter, cycles of three different periods, to a multi-country panel, to argue for the existence and synchrony of long waves. Whether this methodology will stand the test of time remains to be seen.

However, spectral analysis has not provided very convincing evidence of long waves (or any other distinctive cyclical period for that matter) until now. Partly, of course, this is due to the fact that the data must span at least one complete cycle, or better several, so that the identification of 50-year cycles requires at least 100–200 years of annual data. But partly this may be the result of a phenomenon already noted by Granger (1966): the spectra of economic time series display a typical more or less smooth shape, declining from low to high frequencies without any pronounced peaks. Spectra with this distributed shape without evidence of individual characteristic frequencies imply that the time series display cycles of all periods and cannot be thought of as strictly periodic or the sum of a small number of individual frequencies.[7] Finite time series of this type subject to random noise will display some individual peaks around the distributed envelope, but these may simply be random epiphenomenon not reproducible from other data and not due to any robust underlying mechanism. Only peaks standing out by an order of magnitude or more, and invariant to standard methods of detrending (such as removal of an exponential trend or first differencing) can really be taken seriously as indications of periodic components. One can conjecture that reported confirmations of Kondratieff and Kuznets cycles have only been overinterpretations of the noise component of continuously distributed spectra. Thus the project of classical time-series analysis may fail in this case, but the door opens to a much wider class of interesting mechanisms which has formed the object of attention since the 1960s, such as long memory, fractional Brownian motion, chaos, Levy walks and the like.[8] The key difference between these time-series models and classical ones is the existence of long fluctuations at any scale, with no privileged time unit. It may be that only the limits of our data impose a long wave model of a 50-year or any other length. Presumably, if we had significantly longer data series (on the assumption that the underlying mechanism remained unchanged for such long periods of time) we would find long waves of arbitrarily long period, or at least longer than 50 years, the upper limit of our current resolving power. The hegemony cycle literature even posits a 150-year cycle. Thus the historical obsession with finding a 50-year cycle may be blinding researchers to a much richer range of phenomena of equal or even superior theoretical interest.

3 Schumpeter's conceptual framework: clustering of innovations
It will not be necessary to recapitulate Schumpeter's model of economic development in any detail here except to identify those features that have stimulated an active programme of research since the publication of his seminal works (Schumpeter, 1919, 1939, 1947). As is the case with many other 'classical' authors, debates have been sparked by conjectures attributed to Schumpeter that cannot really be found in his writings and to which it is even highly unlikely he would have subscribed. Such is the case with the 'clustering of innovations' hypothesis, which claims something like the statement that major innovations occur in clusters with an approximate 50-year spacing (see Silverberg and Verspagen, 2003a for a number of alternative formulations of this hypothesis that are amenable to statistical testing). Schumpeter distinguishes between radical and incremental innovations (without by any means downgrading the importance of the latter: see e.g. his discussion of the motorcar industry). Radical innovations in particular may open up new industrial sectors and lead to a rapid expansion of new demand. While a radical innovation may trigger a swarm of imitators (as well as improvements and 'collateral' innovations) in the Schumpeterian framework, this is by no means equivalent to the statement that unrelated radical innovations tend to cluster in time, the hypothesis that has actually been tested in the literature. And for a radical innovation to trigger a long wave of economic activity (in whatever sense of the term we choose to formalize this), Schumpeter nowhere insists that it be part of a cluster of such innovations, only that it be radical enough in itself. That no innovation stands alone and in isolation historically from a web of others is a truism, but this is a different hypothesis than the clustering one. Perhaps a better formulation is that of Perez (1983), who speaks of interrelated technological systems rather than isolated innovations, as the technological substrate of long waves (e.g. the complex of AC and DC electrical

innovations between the 1870s and 1900, or the electronic revolution of the late 1930s to the 1970s based on valves, transistors, and integrated circuits). Thus it is a curious fact of the sociology of science that one of the principal consequences of Schumpeter's work is that a not insubstantial literature arose concerned with the questions of clustering per se.[9]

This body of research is generally thought to have been initiated by Mensch (1975, English translation 1979), but a largely overlooked paper by Sahal (1974) both predates it and is methodologically superior to most of the work that followed (although it employed rather short time series and thus is not of much relevance to the long-wave debate). Aside from deciding what the correct hypothesis to be tested is, there are two main stumbling blocks in this literature. First, it is not as simple a matter as it seems to assemble a list of radical innovations with their dates, and the associated time series to represent the 'intensity' of innovative activity. There is no obvious objective way of identifying the innovations (expert opinion was mostly used), and dating is often highly controversial and ambiguous. And simply counting them on an annual basis is also not clearly the right way to weigh them. Thus Clark, Freeman and Soete (1981) and Freeman, Clark and Soete (1982) take Mensch seriously to task for relying (and then somewhat arbitrarily) on the data from Jewkes, Sawers and Stillerman (1958), which was neither meant to be a representative sample nor focuses so much on innovation as invention. Kleinknecht (1990a, 1990b) combines several data sets with multicounting of innovations found in several sources as an implicit but rather arbitrary weighting scheme, while Silverberg and Verspagen (2003a) only count these innovations once in their combined sample and consistently use the earliest dating.

What many authors (with the exception of Sahal) did not explicitly realize is that the null hypothesis of a stochastic count process with no clustering is a (time-homogeneous or inhomogeneous) Poisson process. This does not mar Mensch's work since he used a runs test of identical and independent distribution, but it is fatal to the methodology of Kleinknecht and that of Solomou (1986), who used t- and z-tests of normality. Moreover, the very apparent time trend must also be taken into account, which will seriously affect all of the longer data series. Finally, the procedure of decomposing the time series into subperiods (usually based on some dating of long waves with a lag) also employed by Kleinknecht and Solomou further invalidates their work since it may implicitly be selecting for random periods of above and below-average activity, as Silverberg and Lehnert (1993) argue. An alternative is represented by the nonparametric Poisson tests proposed by the latter authors, who show that an exponential time trend of the Poisson arrival rate is highly significant, with a growth rate of between one-half and 1 per cent p.a., depending on the series. But even after conditioning on the

trend with an appropriate detrending method, the series are still characterized by significant if much lower overdispersion (variance higher than the
mean), indicating some form of residual clustering.

To investigate this issue further, Silverberg and Verspagen (2003a)
employ Poisson regression techniques, which allow both the fitting of more
complicated deterministic trends and accounting for the overdispersion by
making use of a negative binomial model. This model allows for clustering,
but owing to a purely random mechanism superimposed on the original
Poisson model. They show that a second-order polynomial, negative binomial model is significantly preferred to a pure Poisson model of the same
or higher order, indicating both that the trend is more complex and that real
clustering occurs. Further tests of periodicity of the clustering and clustering persistence were all negative, indicating that, while clustering certainly
occurs, it seems to be purely random and not explicable in terms of a predictable time dependence or due to 'knock-on' effects. This is quite a
different interpretation of the 'Schumpeterian' clustering hypothesis that
does not conform to any of the naïve views (to the extent that they can be
formalized) of how clustering occurs. Nevertheless it may be consistent
with a much more 'complex-systems' understanding of the long-wave phenomenon, and with the empirical record, once we give up an obsession with
discovering periodicities.

One interpretation of clustering in terms of purely economic considerations is Mensch's (1975/1979) 'depression-trigger' hypothesis. Mensch
shows that inventions are more randomly distributed than innovations, and
argues that the latter are deliberately neglected in good times when entrepreneurs can continue to exploit existing technologies profitably and are
only, and then perhaps even reluctantly, further developed to operational
levels and adopted in bad times when falling profit rates leave them with no
alternative. This would seem to fly in the face of Schmookler's (1966)
hypothesis that innovative activity seems to follow demand growth. This
contradiction may perhaps be reconciled by observing that Mensch is
dealing with radical innovations while Schmookler, relying on patent data,
is clearly concerned with incremental ones.

The complex relationship between economic activity and innovation
again came to the fore in the 1970s and 1980s in the 'productivity slowdown' controversy initiated by Solow, who observed that the purported
microelectronics and computer revolutions coincided in time with a pronounced long-term decline in productivity growth. Quite aside from such
specific factors as the oil crisis, Silverberg and Lehnert (1993) show that the
contemporaneous cross-correlation between a (trailing) measure of innovative activity and aggregate productivity growth is essentially zero, even
though the former is an excellent predictor of the latter, but only after a

time interval of 20–30 years. And causality, at least in their model, is exclusively from innovation to macroeconomics, and not vice versa. This lag should not be surprising, since innovations only impact on the economy once they have really begun to diffuse (in fact, their maximum impact is when diffusion has gone precisely halfway for a logistic process), and this can take a considerable amount of time, as diffusion research has confirmed time and again. Models that do not take diffusion realistically into account and posit a near instantaneous relationship will always miss this point. Appealing to an analogy with the economic history of electrification, David (1991) also argues that the productivity implications of computers will not show up in aggregate statistics for many years. The productivity growth revival of the 1990s has perhaps already borne this out.

One way of modelling the innovation process that seems to generate exactly this kind of result has been proposed by Silverberg (2002) and explored theoretically and empirically by Silverberg and Verspagen (2003b, 2005). Invoking percolation theory to represent a multidimensional technology space, this model shows how clustering can occur naturally both in the temporal and 'technospatial' domains without any explicit recourse to a long-wave argument. Clustering is shown to increase with the 'radicality' of the innovation measure, consistent with the relative smoothness of patent indicators and the extreme jumpiness and lumpiness of radical innovation time series. It also produces the highly skewed and possibly scale-free distributions of innovation sizes and returns that can be found in the data (see, e.g., Scherer, Harhoff and Kukies, 2000), as well as 'technological trajectories' (Dosi, 1982). Thus we are now intellectually in a position to begin to transcend the dichotomy between radical and incremental innovations and realize that innovations come in a (possibly fractal) continuum of sizes and are interdependent in complex ways. A simple growth model that directly translates this Paretian distribution of innovation sizes into fluctuating growth rates is Sornette and Zajdenweber (1999).

4   Schumpeter's conceptual framework: leading sectors and creative destruction

Schumpeter's evolutionary model is multisectoral, driven by profit disequilibria, and associated with new technology diffusion. Very few studies, either empirical or theoretical, have managed to combine all three elements. True multisectoral models have relied on input–output analysis, but it is very difficult to do so outside of an equilibrium setting either in the structural (balanced growth) or the macroeconomic (market clearing) senses. Thus Pasinetti (1981) analyses sectoral structural change (the weights of different sectors in the economy change systematically over time owing to both demand and supply factors), but in such a way that full employment is always maintained and no technology diffusion or creative destruction is evident.[10] Nelson and Winter (1982) analyse a disequilibrium evolutionary model with multiple distinct (but disembodied) technologies and goods/labour market clearing, but only one final goods sector. Technologies diffuse through higher relative growth rates (owing to profit rate disparities) and imitation, but nothing like aggregate long waves has been shown to emerge.

The technology diffusion literature has uncovered evidence of long-wave behaviour, particularly in the framework of the multiple replacement model (Nakicenovic, 1987; Grübler, 1990). Inspired by the original work of Fisher and Pry (1971), one can look at technology diffusion as a niche-filling exercise with successive technologies filling the (fixed) basic needs of the 'econosphere'. By fitting logistic curves to the diffusion in market shares (or percentage of saturation level attained), diffusion times and midpoints of the process for major technologies (particularly infrastructures such as transport and energy systems) can be calculated. These diffusion times are often of the order of 50 years, but particularly remarkable is the fact that the spacing between the diffusion curves is surprisingly regular and also around 50 years. This is especially true for infrastructures, while other technologies display much faster diffusion times and more irregular spacing between successive waves or generations.

Aside from the plausibility of these empirical regularities (which are reminiscent of Kondratieff's own emphasis on waves of infrastructure investment, although Kondratieff did not emphasize the technological replacement aspect), this work highlights the role of investment in fixed capital and infrastructure and the corresponding creative destruction of old installed capacity in the generation of long waves. Thus in compiling a diffusion-based time series of innovation activity, Nakicenovic computes the first derivative of the diffusion curves (representing the rate of growth and replacement) rather than the date of introduction of the innovation to proxy its impact on the economy. This addresses the objection Kuznets (1940) raised to Schumpeter's model that the stochastic nature of innovations and the widely varying rates of diffusion would obscure any long-wave pattern rather than reinforce it.[11] If some innovations, such as those related to infrastructures (railroads, telephone networks, the Internet, oil and the internal combustion engine) are very widespread and pervasive, they can generate investment waves of such magnitude as to swamp the fluctuations due to other investment activity in the economy. In fact, they may even entrain synchronized waves of investment in other sectors (the motel/fast food/shopping centre/suburban tract housing complex with respect to cars, for example), a fact Schumpeter had also observed (1939, pp. 166–7). But why these infrastructure replacement cycles should be characterized by 50-year periods is still a mystery.

For innovations to induce investment waves they need to be embodied in capital goods. While this observation seems self-evident, very few economic models have taken this seriously since a flirtation with vintage models in the 1960s (and then mostly in a steady-state growth framework). Exceptions with a disequilibrium, Schumpeterian flavour are Iwai (1984a, 1984b, 2000), Nelson (1968), Silverberg (1984), Silverberg and Lehnert (1993, 1996), Silverberg and Verspagen (1994, 1996), Soete and Turner (1984), Henkin and Polterovich (1991) and Franke (2001). The basic assumption of all of these models is that the rate of investment in a capital-embodied technology will be proportional to its profit rate, and thus its share in the total capital stock will obey replicator dynamics, a form of dynamical Darwinism and a natural representation of creative destruction. Additionally, when embedded in a macroeconomic framework, the induced investment effects derived from technological competition can have important multiplier effects that will influence the level of effective demand. Whether and what kinds of fluctuating aggregate patterns such mechanisms can produce is treated in the next section.

The neoclassical endogenous growth literature has also taken up the theme of creative destruction (Aghion and Howitt, 1992; Cheng and Dinopoulos, 1992; Dinopoulos and Cheng, 1996) in a somewhat different stylized fashion. Technologies are regarded as intermediate goods instead of capital goods, and using patent race-like arguments, a rational expectations intertemporal equilibrium can be derived for the level of R&D investment and the (stochastic) rate of economic growth. Thus even though individual innovators attain temporary monopolistic positions and earn the associated quasi-rents, the model is as hyperrational and general equilibrium as one might desire. Whether such an approach can really be regarded as a faithful formalization of the Schumpeterian vision can be debated, to say the least. But from a neoclassical perspective this has been a very fruitful leap of paradigm.

The neoclassical embrace of a distinct category of radical innovation has taken the form of the concept of 'general-purposed technologies' (GPT) (Bresnahan and Trajtenberg, 1995; Helpman, 1998), albeit without specific reference to Schumpeter or the theory of long waves. Nevertheless, it has been invoked to explain the same class of phenomena, even if the models make rather ad hoc modifications to make room for it: long-term fluctuations in productivity growth correlated across sectors, temporary declines in productivity due to initial learning effects, leading sectors and intersectoral spillovers. On the latter issue Carlaw and Lipsey (2002) argue that new GPTs create technological externalities that cannot be captured with conventional total factor productivity indicators. Cheng and Dinopoulos (1992; Dinopoulos and Cheng, 1996) also distinguish between breakthrough and improvement innovations in their general-equilibrium model of Schumpeterian fluctuations.

From the perspective of economic history, W.W. Rostow's (1960) work has most strongly emphasized the essential role of leading sectors in economic development. Thompson (1990) has attempted to quantify the role of leading sectors in a time-series analysis. What is still missing in the historical approaches is an objective method to identify the leading sectors at various times and to measure dynamically their overall effects on the economy due to input–output linkages, technological spillovers, investment multipliers and the like.

5 Schumpeter's conceptual framework: macroeconomics and aggregate fluctuations

A number of long-wave models exist that are both purely aggregate in character and not really Schumpeterian, particularly in the sense of not admitting distinct technological innovations. Nevertheless I include them here because they elucidate mechanisms that could play a role in more properly Schumpeterian approaches. The first class derives from Jay Forrester's National Model of the 1970s, best elucidated in Sterman (1985). These are nonlinear multiplier–accelerator models that lead to robust limit cycle attractors based on what they call the 'capital self-ordering principle': the central capital-goods sector must order equipment from itself to build up the necessary capacity to satisfy final demand, but since it cannot distinguish between this 'bootstrapped' demand and optimal investment except in a centrally planned economy (and even there, with the nonlinear capacity constraint, it is not a trivial optimization problem to solve), it can enter into an unstable autocatalytic loop. While this observation is certainly true and important, the specific simplifying assumptions of the model probably exaggerate the magnitude of the effect, which would undoubtedly be radically changed anyway by the admission of true innovations. And the time-series distinctness of their limit cycle, in terms of both amplitude and frequency, would mean that, were such a mechanism really at work, econometricians could not help but be overwhelmed by it in the data, regardless of their methodology (ergo it cannot be present in this form). A modification of the model in Sterman and Mosekilde (1994) shows that entrainment between short and long-period business cycle mechanisms leads to a more complex cyclical pattern. Goodwin (1987, 1990) also develops an aggregate nonlinear dynamic model based on a 'Roman fountain' formulation of the investment accelerator function that generates chaotic dynamics instead of strictly periodic behaviour. And chaos, it should be noted, will usually also have a distributed rather than a discrete spectrum, even if it has not been detected (as difficult as that is on short data sets) in empirical data on growth until now.

The neoclassical, general equilibrium models of creative destruction have aggregate cyclical properties that have not been studied in detail. In an R&D steady state, the Aghion and Howitt (1992) model produces a Poisson jumping process for aggregate productivity, certainly nothing anyone would seriously look for in the empirical record. Under certain circumstances they show that the R&D rate can converge to a two-period cycle (each phase of which is of stochastically determined length). These results, while intriguing, are artefacts of their assumptions that at any one time only one technology is employed in the entire economy (perhaps an over-interpretation of general purposeness) and that the transition between technologies is instantaneous. Nor do innovations have any investment repercussions, since they are considered to be mere intermediate goods that can always be produced with existing productive capacity once their 'blueprints' have been discovered by R&D firms.

Cheng and Dinopoulos (1992; Dinopoulos and Cheng, 1996) also derive fluctuating aggregate behaviour from their rather similar model of Schumpeterian innovative activity, due to the interacting effects of radical and improving innovations. Li (2001) is somewhat parallel in structure but identifies a different underlying mechanism: paradigm shifts due to scientific discoveries, with subsequent technological innovations within any such scientific paradigm subject to diminishing returns. The alternation between the two produces long-wave fluctuations, but of an as yet unspecified character.

Silverberg and Lehnert (1993, 1996) investigate in more detail the time-series properties of their model under the assumption that the innovation rate is constant.[12] Since innovations are then generated by a time-homogeneous Poisson process, they arrive unevenly but, in a strict statistic sense, do not cluster. Nevertheless the model robustly generates significant spectral density in the 'Kondratieff' range of 40–60 years without being in any sense strictly periodic. These authors then investigate whether a classical ARMA-type stochastic model or a nonlinear model provides a better explanation of the artificially generated time series. They produce quite convincing evidence in favour of the latter, based on such modern methods as false nearest neighbours, the correlation dimension, Lyapunov exponents and nonlinear predictability. In fact, the high-dimensional dynamic system that generates the data can be shown to be reducible to an underlying dynamic involving only two to four principal variables. These results are robust with respect to changes in parameters and some modifications of model structure, such as allowing the innovation rate to react to changes in profits.

Silverberg and Verspagen (1994, 1996) take this model one step further by allowing the R&D rate to be determined endogenously as the result of

an evolutionary learning mechanism. Individual firms use boundedly rational investment rules to determine the share of R&D in their investment
portfolios and can experiment with small changes and imitate each other.
The competitive dynamics leads to a convergence over the long term to an
evolutionary growth 'steady state', but only after passing through a succession of R&D and industrial structure stages. While long waves are not
the focus of these studies, they are still present just as in the original
Silverberg and Lehnert studies even under these much more dynamic conditions. Thus long waves seem to be a very robust feature of this modelling
approach, which one may consider to be a much more faithful formulation
of Schumpeter's original vision even if still highly stylized. Franke (2001),
by combining features of the Silverberg and Lehnert model with Iwai's very
similar approach, shows in numerical experiments that the length of the
cycles is related to the lifetimes of the capital stocks associated with each
innovation.

6 Moral and conclusions

There can be no doubt that long-period fluctuations take place in the world
economy and it is not surprising that scholars have been attempting to make
sense of them for almost a century. It is also not surprising that a cyclical
hypothesis was the first to be seized upon. The idea that human fate is solely
the plaything of purely random forces is probably too disturbing for most
to stomach, and probably also not entirely true. Furthermore, the attempt
to connect such long-period fluctuations with underlying mechanisms
implicated in other aspects of economic life, such as innovation, technology
diffusion, financial conditions and the competitive role of entrepreneurship,
has fruitfully stimulated research into understanding the economy as a systemic whole governed by complicated feedback relationships.

Nevertheless, the search for Kondratieff waves has sometimes taken on
the character of a religious quest or a search for a holy grail, as if the existence of such waves had crucial implications for human salvation (quite
aside from its erstwhile perceived challenge to a Marxist theory of crisis).
A more sober perspective has also led to the other extreme – not only a
rejection of the hypothesis on hard-nosed econometric grounds, but an
abhorrence of research in this area as if it were somehow tainted with a
New Age or astrological cachet. Neither of these positions is justified, and
neither is fruitful. In fact, both may have obscured a very rich terrain of
research in which we do not merely prove or refute things we have always
yearned for or abhorred, but we actually discover relationships we neither
had any vested interests in nor at first could even conceive.

My personal position is that Schumpeter's model is basically correct:
there is an important, perhaps even dominant, relationship between

innovation, disequilibrium forms of competition, imitation, technology diffusion, the operation of financial markets, structural change, investment multipliers, and aggregate activity. Existing models have begun to connect these pieces of the puzzle together in a dynamic way, and they indicate that we may truly be dealing with what complex systems modellers call 'emergent phenomena'. However, these models are still in a very primitive state and our empirical knowledge is also woefully inadequate. Nevertheless, it is essential that we continue to seek the connection between such models and their expression at the level of statistically testable aggregate time series effects, the original thrust of Kondratieff's work. It is not enough to say that there are no discernable patterns in the data and thus they are no longer worth studying, or that the statistical analysis is irrelevant to the question. It certainly was the case that Kondratieff, Schumpeter and other proponents of long-wave theory believed that waves could be detected in the data with appropriate techniques that would also stand up to technical criticism. To turn one's back on this issue is to retreat into metaphysics or relegate long-wave analysis to a sophistic form of the very legitimate kind of historical analysis practised by Rostow, Kindleberger, Maddison and Landes.

But it would also be tantamount to closing one's eyes to important scientific alternatives, such as that long waves are not to be found in strict periodicity but rather in complex distributed spectra that are often the hallmarks of interesting but nontrivial complex systems. Innovations may indeed cluster, but not in any deterministic sense, and their pattern may shed light on a unified mechanism explaining a range of their properties. Aggregate economic activity, simultaneously with certain patterns of structural change, may obey certain laws that dialectically intertwine chance and necessity and produce robust patterns, but ones that do not lend themselves to any very simple forecasting. It is on this note that I hope long waves will long be with us as a field of scientific research.

Notes

1. Kondratieff himself was not a Marxist and confronted intense criticism from Trotsky and Oparin for what they took to be a fatal ideological challenge to Marx's theory of the inevitable final crisis of capitalism. His incarceration and execution under Stalin, it is now believed, is due less to his theory of long waves than to his advocacy of the priority of agriculture and a market framework in Soviet economic planning.
2. But see Kindleberger (1999) for a more sceptical view of the plausibility of these theories, despite the impressive array of disparate phenomena these authors have combined in their arguments.
3. In some sense Perez's theory of social mismatch is reminiscent in the small of Marx's opposition of material substructure (residing primarily in technology) and sociopolitical superstructure, requiring revolution to reconcile the two at a higher historical stage of development. Having long waves accomplish this rematching makes the process both less revolutionary and more frequent.

4. In this they accord with other modern works in the Kondratieff revival, such as van Duijn (1983), Berry (1991) and Tylecote (1992, 1994). While Berry falls victim to the moving average's well-known ability to generate cycles of arbitrary period by repeated application (the Slutzky effect), Tylecote displays extreme virtuosity in explaining departures from the a priori scheme with ad hoc reasoning.

5. Schumpeter (1939, p. 166fn) on periodograms: 'The result of the experiment [Wilson, 1934] was . . . negative and presents many discouraging features . . . for instance, considerable differences between the shapes of the periodogram for various subperiods and between each of them and the periodogram for the entire period. . . . It might, therefore, be asked why the writer, thinking thus and, moreover, entirely unwilling to abide by the results the analysis gives, nevertheless attaches importance to periodograms. The answer is simply that they render service in exploring the material, even if results are negative or untrustworthy: some of our problems might be stated in terms of the periodograms we get.'

6. See Brockwell and Davis (1987). For a discussion of the problem of differentiating spurious from real cycles in stationary time series, see Beck (1991) and Goldstein (1991).

7. Perhaps surprisingly, this does not at all contradict Schumpeter's own expectations, despite the received interpretation of his work. Thus: 'there is nothing in the working of our model to point to periodicity in the cyclical process of economic evolution if that term is taken to mean a constant period . . . All we can thus far say about the duration of the units of that process and of each of their two phases [prosperity and depression] is that it will depend on the nature of the particular innovation that carries a given cycle, the actual structure of the industrial organism that responds to them, and the financial conditions and habits prevailing in the business community in each case. But that is enough and it seems entirely unjustified to deny the existence of a phenomenon because it fails to conform to certain arbitrary standards of regularity' (p. 143). And 'there is a theoretically indefinite number of fluctuations present in our material at any time, the word *present* meaning that there are real factors at work to produce them and *not merely that the material may be decomposed into them by formal methods*' (1939, p. 168). Further: 'it cannot be emphasized too strongly that the three-cycle schema does not follow from our model – although multiplicity of cycles does' (p. 169). While this agnosticism appears to make Schumpeter a much more modern thinker than his epigones were prepared to give him credit for, it remains unclear what Schumpeter was then concretely predicting as evidence of his model, thereby making himself possibly unfalsifiable in the Popperian sense. In practice he merrily proceeded to apply the three-cycle model without compunction in the rest of his *Business Cycles* despite these disclaimers about its intrinsic irrelevance.

   Mandelbrot (1997, pp. 55ff.) facetiously remarks that 'Statisticians and historians find it convenient to describe price records as involving random fluctuations that add to trends and a diversity of "cycles" of short, medium and long duration. Most economists view those cycles as significant, but Keynes asserted in jest that their main utility is to help long treatises on economic history be broken into manageable smaller volumes.' In a somewhat more serious vein he adds (p. 57), 'Surprisingly, ex post examination of samples from this process [fractional Brownian motion] revealed that *every* sample seems to exhibit three cycles. This striking "rule of three" is true for all sample durations, because it is an aspect of self-affinity . . . Could it be a simple coincidence that the "long cycles" Kondratiev observed in a sample of a hundred-odd years consisted in three oscillations? Similar cycles are claimed to exist in weather and hydrological records, and it is in their context that I pioneered an indirect approach to long-run dependence that throws deep doubt on the "reality" of long cycles.'

8. I cannot go into any detail on this question here. Suffice it to refer to Diebolt (2005), Silverberg and Lehnert (1996), Michelacci and Zaffaroni (2000) and Silverberg and Verspagen (2003c) for some examples.

9. This is quite parallel to that other great 'Schumpeterian' conjecture concerning the supposed positive relationship between concentration, size and R&D intensity implied in Schumpeter (1947). See Cohen and Levin (1989).

10. But see Reati (1998) for an attempt to integrate major technological revolutions into the Pasinetti framework.
11. Again, this is an objective Schumpeter seems to have anticipated without really refuting: 'First, if innovations are at the root of cyclical fluctuations, these cannot be expected to form a single wavelike movement, because the periods of gestation and of absorption of effects by the economic system will not, in general, be equal for all innovations that are undertaken at any time. There will be innovations of relatively long span, and along with them others will be undertaken which run their course, on the back of the wave created by the former, in shorter periods. This at once suggests both multiplicity of fluctuations and the kind of interference between them which we are to expect' (1939, pp. 166–7).
12. Recall that this model assumes that innovations are capital-embodied and that the relative rates of growth of their associated capital 'vintages' is proportional to their profit rates. A Philips-curve like wage mechanism ensures that, even without assuming labour market clearing, in the long run real wages track productivity growth even though they may fluctuate, as does employment, at different time scales.

References

Aghion, P. and Howitt, P., 1992, A model of growth through creative destruction, *Econometrica*, **60**, 323–51.
Beck, N. 1991, The illusion of cycles in international relations, *International Studies Quarterly*, **35**, 455–76.
Berry, B.J.L., 1991, *Long-Wave Rhythms in Economic Development and Political Behavior*, Baltimore, MD: Johns Hopkins University Press.
Beveridge, S.W., 1922, Wheat prices and rainfall in Western Europe, *Journal of the Royal Statistical Society*, **85**, 412–59.
Boyer, R., 1988, 'Formalizing growth regimes', in G. Dosi, C. Freeman, R. Nelson, G. Silverberg and L. Soete (eds), *Technical Change and Economic Theory*, London and New York: Pinter.
Bresnahan, T.F. and Trajtenberg, M., 1995, General purpose technologies: engines of Growth?, *Journal of Econometrics*, **65**(1), 83–108.
Brockwell, P.J. and Davis, R.A., 1987, *Time Series: Theory and Methods*, New York: Springer-Verlag.
Carlaw, K.I. and Lipsey, R.G., 2002, Externalities, technological complementarities and sustained economic growth, *Research Policy*, **31**(8–9), 1305–15.
Cheng, L.K. and Dinopoulos, E., 1992, 'A Schumpeterian model of economic growth and fluctuations', Department of Economics, University of Florida.
Clark, J.B., Freeman, C. and Soete, L., 1981, Long waves, inventions, and innovations, *Futures*, **13**, 308–22.
Cohen, W.M. and Levin, R., 1989, 'Empirical studies of innovation and market structure', in R. Schmalensee and R. Willig (eds), *The Handbook of Industrial Organization*, Amsterdam: North-Holland.
David, P., 1991, 'Computer and dynamo: the modern productivity paradox in a not-too-distant mirror', *Technology and Productivity: The Challenge for Economic Policy*, Paris: OECD.
Diebolt, C., 2005, Long cycles revisited. An essay in econometric history, *Économies et Sociétés*, **1**, 23–47.
Dinopoulos, E. and Cheng, L.K., 1996, A multisectoral general equilibrium model of Schumpeterian growth and fluctuations, *Journal of Economic Dynamics and Control*, **20**(5), 905–23.
Dosi, G., 1982, Technological paradigms and technological trajectories, *Research Policy*, **11**, 147–62.
Ewijk, C.v., 1982, A spectral analysis of the Kondratieff cycle, *Kyklos*, **35**, 324–72.
Fisher, J.C. and Pry, R.H., 1971, A simple substitution model of technological change, *Technological Forecasting and Social Change,* **3**, 75–88.
Franke, R., 2001, Wave trains, innovation noise, and long waves, *Journal of Economic Behavior and Organization*, **45**, 49–68.

Freeman, C., (ed.), 1996, *Long Wave Theory*, Cheltenham, UK and Brookfield, USA: Edward Elgar.

Freeman, C. and Louçã, F., 2001, *As Time Goes By: From the Industrial Revolutions to the Information Revolution*, Oxford: Oxford University Press.

Freeman, C. and Perez, C., 1988, 'Structural crises of adjustment, business cycles and investment behavior', in G. Dosi, C. Freeman, R. Nelson, G. Silverberg and L. Soete (eds), *Technical Change and Economic Theory*, London and New York: Pinter.

Freeman, C., Clark, J. and Soete, L., 1982, *Unemployment and Technical Innovation: A Study of Long Waves in Economic Development*, London: Pinter.

Frickey, E., 1942, *Economic Fluctuations in the United States: A Systematic Analysis of Long Run Trends and Business Cycles 1866–1914*, Cambridge, MA: Harvard University Press.

Goldstein, J.S., 1988, *Long Cycles. Prosperity and War in the Modern Age*, New Haven and London: Yale University Press.

Goldstein, J.S., 1991, The possibility of cycles in international relations, *International Studies Quarterly*, **35**, 477–80.

Goldstein, J.P., 1999, The existence, endogeneity, and synchronization of long waves: structural time series model estimates, *Review of Radical Political Economics*, **31**, 61–101.

Goodwin, R.M., 1987, 'The economy as an evolutionary pulsator', in T. Vasko (ed.), *The Long-Wave Debate*, Berlin: Springer-Verlag.

Goodwin, R.M., 1990, *Chaotic Economic Dynamics*, Oxford: Clarendon Press.

Gordon, D.M., 1989, 'What makes epochs? A comparative analysis of technological and social explanations of long economic swings', in M. Di Matteo, R.M. Goodwin and A. Vercelli (eds), *Technological and Social Factors in Long Term Fluctuations*, Berlin: Springer-Verlag.

Granger, C.W.J., 1966, The typical spectral shape of an economic variable, *Econometrica*, **34**(1), 150–61.

Grübler, A., 1990, *The Rise and Decline of Infrastructures. Dynamics of Evolution and Technological Change in Transport*, Heidelberg: Physica-Verlag.

Haustein, H.D. and Neuwirth, E., 1982, Long waves in world industrial production, energy consumption, innovations, inventions, and patents and their identification by spectral analysis, *Technological Forecasting and Social Change*, **22**, 53–89.

Helpman, E., (ed.), 1998, *General Purpose Technologies*, Cambridge, MA: MIT.

Henkin, G.M. and Polterovich, V.M., 1991, Schumpeterian dynamics as a non-linear wave theory, *Journal of Mathematical Economics*, **20**, 551–90.

Iwai, K., 1984a, Schumpeterian dynamics. I: an evolutionary model of innovation and imitation, *Journal of Economic Behavior and Organization*, **5**, 159–90.

Iwai, K., 1984b, Schumpeterian dynamics. II: technological progress, firm growth and 'economic selection', *Journal of Economic Behavior and Organization*, **5**, 321–51.

Iwai, K., 2000, A contribution to the evolutionary theory of innovation, imitation and growth, *Journal of Economic Behavior and Organization*, **43**(2), 167–98.

Jewkes, J., Sawers, D. and Stillerman, R., 1958, *The Sources of Invention*, London: Macmillan.

Kindleberger, C.P., 1999, 'Long waves in economics and politics: a review article', *Essays in History: Financial, Economic, Personal*, Ann Arbor, MI: University of Michigan Press.

Kleinknecht, A., 1990a, Are there Schumpeterian waves of innovations?, *Cambridge Journal of Economics*, **14**, 81–92.

Kleinknecht, A., 1990b, 'Schumpeterian waves of innovation? Summarizing the evidence', in T. Vasko, R. Ayres and L. Fontvieille (eds), *Life Cycles and Long Waves*, Berlin: Springer-Verlag.

Kondratieff, N.D., 1979, The long waves in economic life, *Review*, **2**, 519–62.

Kuznets, S., 1940, Schumpeter's business cycles, *American Economic Review*, **30**, 257–71.

Li, C.W., 2001, Science, diminishing returns and long waves, *The Manchester School*, **69**(5), 553–73.

Maddison, A., 1991, *Dynamic Forces in Capitalist Development*, Oxford: Oxford University Press.

Mandelbrot, B.B., 1997, *Fractals and Scaling in Finance: Discontinuity, Concentration, Risk*, New York: Springer-Verlag.

Mensch, G.O., 1975, *Das technologische Patt*, Frankfurt: Umschau (English translation, *Stalemate in Technology: Innovations Overcome the Depression*, New York: Harper, 1979).

Metz, R., 1987, 'Kondratieff and the theory of linear filters', in T. Vasko (ed.), *The Long Wave Debate: Selected Papers*, Berlin: Springer-Verlag.

Metz, R., 1992, 'A re-examination of long waves in aggregate production Series', in A. Kleinknecht, E. Mendel and I. Wallerstein (eds), *New Findings in Long-Wave Research*, London: Macmillan.

Michelacci, C. and Zaffaroni, P., 2000, (Fractional) beta convergence, *Journal of Monetary Economics*, **45**, 129–53.

Modelski, G., 1987, *Long Cycles in World Politics*, London: Macmillan.

Modelski, G. and Thompson, W.R., 1996, *Leading Sectors and World Powers: The Coevolution of Global Politics and Economics*, Columbia, SC: University of South Carolina Press.

Nakicenovic, N., 1987, 'Technological substitution and long waves in the USA', in T. Vasko (ed.), *The Long-Wave Debate*, Berlin: Springer-Verlag.

Nelson, R., 1968, A diffusion model of international productivity differences in manufacturing industry, *American Economic Review*, **58**, 1218–48.

Nelson, R. and Plosser, C.I., 1982, Trends and random walks in macroeconomic time series: some evidence and implications, *Journal of Monetary Economics*, **10**, 139–62.

Nelson, R.R. and Winter, S.G., 1982, *An Evolutionary Theory of Economic Change*, Cambridge, MA: The Belknap Press of Harvard University Press.

Pasinetti, L.L., 1981, *Structural Change and Economic Growth. A Theoretical Essay on the Dynamics of the Wealth of Nations*, Cambridge: Cambridge University Press.

Perez, C., 1983, Structural change and the assimilation of new technologies in the economic and social system, *Futures*, **15**, 357–75.

Reati, A., 1998, A long-wave pattern for output and employment in Pasinetti's model of structural change, *Economie Appliquée*, **51**(2), 29–77.

Reijnders, J., 1990, *Long Waves in Economic Development. Kondratieff, Schumpeter and the Enigma of Long Waves*, Aldershot, UK and Brookfield, USA: Edward Elgar.

Reijnders, J. and Louçã, F. (eds) 1999, *The Foundations of Long Wave Theory: Models and Methodology*, Cheltenham, UK and Northampton, MA, USA: Edward Elgar.

Rostow, W.W., 1960, *The Stages of Economic Growth: A Non-Communist Manifesto*, Cambridge, MA: Cambridge University Press.

Sahal, D., 1974, Generalized Poisson and related models of technological innovation, *Technological Forecasting and Social Change*, **6**, 403–36.

Scherer, F.M., Harhoff, D. and Kukies, J., 2000, Uncertainty and the size distribution of rewards from innovation, *Journal of Evolutionary Economics*, **10**, 175–200.

Schmookler, J., 1966, *Invention and Economic Growth*, Cambridge, MA: Harvard University Press.

Schumpeter, J., 1919, *Theorie der wirtschaftlichen Entwicklung* (English translation: *The Theory of Economic Development*, Cambridge, MA: Harvard University Press, 1934).

Schumpeter, J.A., 1939, *Business Cycles: A Theoretical, Historical and Statistical Analysis of the Capitalist Process*, New York: McGraw-Hill.

Schumpeter, J., 1947, *Capitalism, Socialism, and Democracy*, New York: Harper.

Silverberg, G., 1984, 'Embodied technical progress in a dynamic economic model: the self-organization paradigm', in R. Goodwin, M. Krüger and A. Vercelli (eds), *Nonlinear Models of Fluctuating Growth*, Berlin-Heidelberg-New York: Springer-Verlag.

Silverberg, G., 2002, The discrete charm of the bourgeoisie: quantum and continuous perspectives on innovation and growth, *Research Policy*, **31**, 1275–89.

Silverberg, G. and Lehnert, D., 1993, Long waves and evolutionary chaos in a simple Schumpeterian model of embodied technical change, *Structural Change and Economic Dynamics*, **4**, 9–37.

Silverberg, G. and Lehnert, D., 1996, 'Evolutionary chaos: growth fluctuations in a Schumpeterian model of creative destruction, in W.A. Barnett, A. Kirman and M. Salmon (eds), *Nonlinear Dynamics in Economics*, Cambridge: Cambridge University Press.

Silverberg, G. and Verspagen, B., 1994, Collective learning, innovation and growth in a boundedly rational, evolutionary world, *Journal of Evolutionary Economics*, **4**, 207–26.

Silverberg, G. and Verspagen, B., 1996, 'From the artificial to the endogenous: modelling evolutionary adaptation and economic growth', in E. Helmstädter and M. Perlman (eds), *Behavorial Norms, Technological Progress and Economic Dynamics: Studies in Schumpeterian Economics*, Ann Arbor, MI: University of Michigan Press.

Silverberg, G. and Verspagen, B., 2003a, Breaking the waves: a Poisson regression approach to Schumpeterian clustering of basic innovations, *Cambridge Journal of Economics*, **27**, 671–93.

Silverberg, G. and Verspagen, B., 2003b, Brewing the future: stylized facts about innovation and their confrontation with a percolation model, Eindhoven: ECIS Working Paper (www.tm.tue.nl/ecis/Working%20Papers/eciswp 80.pdf).

Silverberg, G. and Verspagen, B., 2003c, 'Long memory and economic growth in the world economy since the 19th century', in G. Rangarajan and M. Ding (eds), *Processes with Long Range Correlations: Theory and Applications*, Berlin: Springer.

Silverberg, G. and Verspagen, B., 2005, A percolation model of innovation in complex technology spaces, *Journal of Economic Dynamics and Control*, **29**, 225–44.

Soete, L. and Turner, R., 1984, Technology diffusion and the rate of technical change, *Economic Journal*, **94**, 612–23.

Solomou, S., 1986, Innovation clusters and Kondratieff long waves in economic growth, *Cambridge Journal of Economics*, **10**, 101–12.

Sornette, D. and Zajdenweber, D., 1999, The economic return of research: the Pareto law and its implications, *European Physical Journal B*, **8**(4), 653–64.

Sterman, J., 1985, A behavioral model of the economic long wave, *Journal of Economic Behavior and Organization*, **6**, 17–53.

Sterman, J.D. and Mosekilde, E., 1994, 'Business cycles and long waves: a behavioral disequilibrium perspective', in W. Semmler (ed.), *Business Cycles: Theory and Empirical Methods*, Dordrecht: Kluwer.

Thompson, W.R., 1990, Long waves, technological innovation, and relative decline, *International Organization*, **44**(2), 201–33.

Tylecote, A., 1992, *The Long Wave in the World Economy*, London: Routledge & Kegan Paul.

Tylecote, A., 1994, Long waves, long cycles, and long swings, *Journal of Economic Issues*, **28**(2), 477–88.

van Duijn, J.J., 1983, *The Long Wave in Economic Life*, Boston, MA: Allen and Unwin.

Wilson, E.B., 1934, The periodogram of American business activity, *Quarterly Journal of Economics*, **48**, 375–417.

51 Qualitative change and economic development
P.P. Saviotti

1 Introduction

Qualitatively different entities, such as an apple and a typing machine, are non-commensurable or comparable. They cannot be added up in the same category. Thus, if we were to calculate how many apples and typing machines our economic system contains at a given time, we would have to give the results of two separate sums, one for each of these two entities. Non-commensurability creates considerable difficulties for economics, as it does for other disciplines. For example, if we are interested in the role played by capital goods in economic development, we have to express the amount of capital goods used in particular activities in terms of their values. Capital goods that are qualitatively different, and therefore cannot be compared directly in terms of their physical characteristics, become comparable when measured in terms of their price. While this might seem a solution to the problem of qualitative change, it is only a partial solution. If capital intensity in a given economy were to increase very rapidly, but if in the meantime the efficiency with which capital goods are provided were to increase even faster, the total value of capital goods could fall while the quantity used in the economy increased. Furthermore, the nature of capital goods could change during the process considered above. In this case the effect of the same quantity of capital goods could increase even if their price were to fall in the meantime. Computers have provided recently quite a spectacular example of this situation. Summarizing these considerations, we could say that qualitatively different entities can sometimes be measured by means of a common unit when these entities affect a common variable. In other words, we can never compare the *direct* properties of two qualitatively different entities, but we can sometimes compare the effects of these entities when they affect a common variable (e.g. two different types of capital goods affecting the productivity of a firm).

Technological innovation, especially when it is radical, creates qualitatively new entities. It is precisely this ability that gives it the role hypothesized by Schumpeter in economic development. According to Fagerberg (2003, p. 127), Schumpeter (1934) considered capitalist evolution an open process of development driven by innovation, a view which is shared, although implicitly, by most neo-Schumpeterian economists. The presence and the central role of qualitative change in economic development is probably responsible for the difficulties encountered in modelling Schumpeterian economic evolution.

In spite of the central importance played by qualitative change in Schumpeter's work, the term 'qualitative change' is virtually absent in the economics literature. In what follows of this chapter it will be argued that several concepts widely used by economists are intrinsically connected to qualitative change. Thus, qualitative change has been far more present in the economics literature, and in particular in the work of neo-Schumpeterian economists, than the results of a search for the term itself would indicate. Furthermore, there is a rich literature dealing with the closely related though non-identical problem of quality change. This literature focused on a much lower level of aggregation, that of a product group, with respect to Schumpeter's analysis of economic development. Nevertheless, some results of the analysis of quality change are useful in a generalized analysis of qualitative change.

To stress the importance of qualitative change does not mean that quantitative change is unimportant. In fact, the boundaries between qualitative and quantitative change are sometimes both fuzzy and shifting. A new product created by a radical innovation usually undergoes a number of incremental innovations that improve its performance without transforming its nature, as is found for example in product and industry life cycles (Klepper, 1996; Jovanovic and MacDonald, 1994). Moreover, there are ways to reduce qualitatively different entities to combinations of common components. This procedure, often used in different disciplines, allows us to perform measurements of the relative properties of qualitatively different entities. Examples of this procedure are the reduction of complex objects, such as biological cells, physical objects or goods to combinations of entities at a lower level of aggregation, such as atoms, molecules or characteristics.

Qualitative change will be seen in this chapter (a) to have important economic implications and (b) to require analytical instruments and approaches different from those adapted to quantitative change.

2 Conceptual background

2.1 Related concepts

We have seen in the previous section that the term 'qualitative change' is rarely used by neo-Schumpeterian economists, although it plays a fundamental role in Schumpeter's work (Fagerberg, 2003). However, a large number of concepts widely used by neo-Schumpeterian economists and by scholars of innovation are closely related to the distinction between qualitative and quantitative change. Amongst the earliest contributions of scholars of inovation there was the distinction between radical and incremental innovation (Freeman, 1982; Freeman and Soete, 1997). A radical innovation is so completely different from an incremental one as to be considered a form of qualitative change. A radical innovation represents a discontinuity in the evolution of a technology while an incremental innovation represents only a continuous, quantitative improvement in an existing technology. Furthermore, a radical innovation can be considered a revolution, and it is radical innovations which give rise to new technological paradigms (Dosi, 1982). In a similar way concepts like technological guideposts (Sahal, 1985), dominant designs (Abernathy and Utterback, 1975) and technological regimes (Nelson and Winter, 1977, 1982) involve the existence of qualitative change during certain stages of their economic development. The emergence of a new, later to become dominant, design or of a technological regime creates a discontinuity in technological, and possibly in economic, development, although the subsequent trajectories of improvement are likely to be based mostly on incremental innovations.

The existence of qualitative change has both taxonomic and dynamic implications. Essentially, the taxonomic implications involve the ability to distinguish radical from incremental innovation. On the other hand, dynamic implications are related to the ways in which qualitative change affects economic development. In other words, in general we can expect radical innovations to have a different impact on economic development with respect to incremental innovations. The dynamic component was very central to Schumpeter's work, while the taxonomic component was virtually absent. Important changes in economic development, such as the recovery of an economy from a recession or a depression, could only be due to clusters of radical innovations.

An immediate consequence of the existence of qualitative change and of its emergence at given times is the change it entails in the composition of the economic system. The term 'composition' is here to be understood as the list of all the activities, objects and actors required to give a complete description of the economic system at a given time. Objects are goods and services, which are produced by certain processes (activities) carried out by institutional actors (firms and other types of institutions). Qualitatively different entities have to be classified in separate categories. Thus, the emergence of qualitatively different entities created by radical innovations requires the creation of new classes into which these entities are going to be placed. As a consequence, qualitative change as created by radical innovations changes the composition of the economic system. The literature on structural change bears a close relationship to the neo-Schumpeterian analysis of innovation because it is concerned with the emergence of new sectors, the changing weights of surviving sectors and the disappearance of old ones. To the extent that the composition of an economic system can be equated to the list of existing industrial sectors and of their relative weights, then the literature on structural change is almost identical to the neo-Schumpeterian literature on innovation. Important examples of this literature are Salter (1960), Cornwall (1977), Pasinetti (1981, 1993), Fagerberg (2000), Fagerberg and Verspagen (1999), Verspagen (1993, 2002). To this extent structural change is equal to qualitative change. However, the composition of the economic system is not fully described by the list of industrial sectors it contains and by their relative weights. Each industrial sector is still highly heterogeneous and the nature of the entities that it contains changes in the course of time. For example, cars, computers, telephones etc. changed enormously during their evolution. A full description of the relevant industrial sectors would have to include a complete specification of all the objects, cars, computers, telephones etc. Such a description of the composition of the economic system would have very high information costs and it would be very impractical. In general, rather than using a complete description of the composition of the economic system, simplified descriptions are used for specific purposes. For example, a description of the output of industrial sectors is useful to provide a broad and still somewhat aggregate view of the evolution of the economy, but it would clearly not be sufficient for a firm trying to plan its future development. Thus, structural change is a subset of qualitative change.

Let us finally take into account that qualitative change in an economy involves the existence of boundaries separating different sets of objects and that these boundaries need to be created during the emergence phase of new objects. A further concept related to qualitative change is that of structure. The structure of a system can be considered as given by the components of the system and by their patterns of interaction. A system's structure is thus related to its composition. When the composition of a system is changed by the introduction of new sectors and the disappearance of old ones, old interactions are destroyed and new ones created.

Summarizing this section, we could say that, although the concept of qualitative change is used very rarely in neo-Schumpeterian economics, a large number of concepts, some of which are currently used by these economists, bear a very close relationship to the distinction between qualitative and quantitative change. Qualitative change can be considered a unifying concept, bringing unity to distinctions such as the one between radical and incremental innovation, continuous and discontinuous development, and to concepts such as technological paradigms, dominant designs, technological regimes, technological guideposts etc.

2.2   *Quality change*

The existence of quality differences amongst products has been perceived since the beginning of modern economics. Adam Smith realized that labour could be of variable quality (Wadman, 2000, p. 7). Likewise, Marshall and Wicksell were aware of quality differences amongst different goods (ibid., pp. 8–10). However, the explicit separation of quality from quantity took a long time to emerge in economics. At the beginning quality was always defined by its ability to provide satisfaction or utility, or to command a higher price (Wadman, 2000). While the correspondence of higher quality with higher price or with greater utility is perfectly logical, this approach neglected the need for an independent and objective measure of quality by means of which the correspondence between quality and price or between quality and utility could be tested. In fact, several economists concerned with the problem of quality doubted that quality could be measured at all. For example, for Wicksell, quality was an essentially subjective concept (Wadman, 2000, p. 9), while Chamberlin thought quality to be immeasurable (ibid., p. 13).

Thus, the explicit separation of quality from quantity was slow to emerge. Theil (1951–2), Houthakker (1951–2) and Hirshleifer (1955) were important precursors. Hirshleifer developed an approach in which consumers' choices were defined by means of cost and utility in a quantity/quality space. Houthakker had independent indices for the quality and quantity of a given product. In spite of the importance of the problem their work was not widely adopted by other economists. The decisive step in the separation of quality from quantity came with the introduction of a characteristics approach (Lancaster, 1966, 1971; Ironmonger, 1972) and of the hedonic price method (e.g. Griliches, 1964, 1967, 1971). Although there were some differences between Ironmonger and Lancaster, and although the hedonic price method lacked solid theoretical foundations, all these approaches have a common core, in which the quality of each product variant is decomposed into a number of components, some of which may be common to different products. In other words, they share a characteristics approach.

It is worth pointing out here that within a characteristics approach quality increases whenever new characteristics are added and when the quantities or levels of existing characteristics increase. Thus, the boundary between quantity and quality is never completely sharp.

The work about quality described above has very close links with the literature on product differentiation. Distinguishable varieties of the same product can give their sellers a degree of monopoly if their buyers can be persuaded to pay a monopolistic price for the greater utility that they can derive from them. In other words, the existence of quality gives rise to product differentiation and to monopolistic competition (Chamberlin, 1933). It is to be pointed out here that in this chapter the term 'variety' is used both as the variable measuring the differentiation of a given system and as any instance of a distinguishable entity (e.g. a product model) which can raise overall variety. This ambiguity is quite frequent in the literature and no attempt will be made to correct it here.

The implications of qualitative change for competition will be discussed later (see section 3.5), but we need to mention here the problem of groups. The different products in an economy need to be classified in different groups based on their similarity, because the interactions of different products and their patterns of interaction are not necessarily identical. In particular, competition occurs between similar products. However, the possibility to establish clearly defined boundaries between different product classes becomes more uncertain as the extent of product differentiation in an economy increases, and as correspondingly qualitative change plays a greater role. If we vary gradually the levels of the existing characteristics of a given product or add new characteristics to it, when does the product cease to be a member of its previous group and when does it need to be placed in a new group? In other words, product groups can have fuzzy and shifting boundaries. Furthermore, as completely new products emerge, new groups need to be created accordingly. We can understand here that classifications of markets and of industrial sectors are not as easy to create or to maintain as economists would like to believe, and that the composition of the economic system needs to change in the course of economic development by means of changes both internal and external to particular sectors.

An important extension of this literature used the concept of variety as a measure of the differentiation of a given product group. Two traditions of thought, linked to the work of Chamberlin (1933) and of Hotelling (1929) have given rise to this literature. The former stressed the differentiation and limited substitutability of products within an industry/product group, and the effects it would have on competition, by giving each firm a degree of monopoly. The latter examined the problem of where different sellers of a given commodity would locate in a one-dimensional space (e.g. a street). In this case the growing dispersion of sellers would imply a greater product differentiation or variety. According to Chamberlin, monopolistic competition would lead to an excessive variety, while for Hotelling the minimum possible differentiation would take place. Neither of these conclusions is particularly robust. Several neo-Chamberlin models (Dixit and Stiglitz, 1977) and neo-Hotelling (Salop, 1979; Eaton and Lipsey, 1975; Lancaster, 1975, 1979) arrive at different results. An important development in this area was represented by the utilization of a characteristics approach to replace geographic space by a virtual space of goods, or of their characteristics, in locational analogue models (Lancaster, 1979, 1990). These papers constituted an important development in the study of product differentiation and of its impact on consumer welfare. Although very often their results differed according to their assumptions, they all led to some common conclusions, such as that the resultant variety is likely to increase the lower are scale economies or the lower is the substitutability of products in different groups (Saviotti, 1996, p. 101).

The papers about quality change described above were clearly disconnected from the work of Schumpeter. These papers were focused on the level of aggregation of a product group and concerned with the very short term, that is, with an essentially static analysis. Schumpeter, on the contrary, was concerned with long-run processes of economic development and with the level of aggregation of the whole economic system, although his approach was not exclusively macro-economic. In spite of this evident lack of connection with the work of Schumpeter, the literature on quality change provided both analytical tools that could be usefully adapted to the study of innovation and some micro-economic foundations for the study of qualitative change.

3   Analytical and modelling implications

3.1   A representation of product technology
Qualitative change occurs when completely new entities, qualitatively different from those that existed before, emerge within the economic system. The main components of the system can be considered actors (individual and institutional), activities (transformation processes) and objects (goods and services). Thus, qualitative change can be expected to lead to the appearance of new actors, new activities and new objects. Any representation of these new entities must be based on new variables. In what follows we will concentrate on product technology. Although this amounts to neglecting a large part of the composition of the economic system, some of the considerations developed here are useful for a more general analysis of qualitative change. Of course, this implies that the present chapter is not a definitive statement about qualitative change but that it only sets the ground for the exploration of this topic.

Any product is the result of a technology that was first created by an innovation at a given time and that underwent subsequent improvements during its life cycle. Most products are today complex and multidimensional and they need to be represented by several characteristics. The considerations that follow can be considered an extension of Lancaster's (1966, 1971) approach. However, a crucial difference with respect to Lancaster's approach consists of the distinction between the internal structure of a product technology and the services that it provides for its users. A number of reasons can be quoted for introducing this distinction.

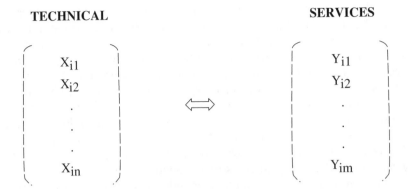

*Figure 51.1   The twin characteristics representation of technology i: the
double arrow between technical and service characteristics
indicates the correspondence between the two sets*

1. Services are not produced *directly*. They are so to say embodied in a
    physical product which supplies these services.
2. Consumer and user demand is affected uniquely by services.
3. Different products, that is having different internal structures, can
    supply similar services. Relevant examples are piston, turboprop and
    jet aero-engines, mechanical and digital watches, numeric and tradi-
    tional photographic cameras etc.

A product technology is then represented by two sets of characteristics, one
corresponding to the internal structure (technical characteristics) and the
other to the services supplied (service characteristics): see Figure 51.1.

   The arrow linking the two sets of characteristics implies that they cannot
vary in a random way, but that technical characteristics are the cause, or
determinant, of services. Producers modify technical characteristics in
order to provide the desired level of services (Saviotti and Metcalfe, 1984).
If we were to extend this representation to actors and activities we should
use for each of them at least *one* separate set of characteristics. Within this
framework there would be a correspondence between process characteristics and product technical characteristics and a second correspondence
between technical and service characteristics. This approach can in principle be extended to the provision of services by suppressing technical
characteristics. Thus a set of services would be directly produced by means
of a process technology without the intermediate embodiment in technical characteristics (for a similar approach to services, see Gallouj and
Weinstein, 1997).

Further support for the adoption of the twin characteristics approach comes from Simon's (1969, in particular 'Understanding the natural and the artificial world', pp. 2–29) distinction between the internal structure of a system, its external environment and the interface separating them. Technical characteristics represent the internal structure and service characteristics of the interface between the system and its external environment. Adaptation of a system occurs by means of an ever-closer correspondence between service characteristics and the external environment. Based on the N-K model and on its extension by Altenberg (1997) to biological systems, Frenken (2001) showed that technical characteristics can be compared to genotypes and service characteristics to phenotypes.

The twin characteristics approach provides us with an important taxonomic tool. For example, two product technologies can be considered different if they contain different technical characteristics. Thus, a jet and a piston and propeller aero engine are two different technologies. A radical innovation involves a new set of either technical or of technical and service characteristics. A dominant design (Abernathy and Utterback, 1975) or a technological paradigm (Dosi, 1982) are centred on a new set of technical characteristics, although they also include the complementary knowledge and institutions required to support the new product technology (Saviotti, 1996).

The taxonomic applications of the twin characteristics approach are not limited to single products but extend to the interaction of different products. Thus, two products supplying the same types of services are perfect substitutes, while their substitutability becomes imperfect or partial when some of the service characteristics are different. Dynamically, what was initially one product can specialize by separating into two sets of service characteristics with limited or no overlap (Saviotti, 1996). It is worth noting here that, while the twin characteristics representation provides a powerful means to describe qualitative change, it does so by decomposing qualitatively different entities into lower-level components (characteristics). In a sense the boundary between qualitative and quantitative change becomes fuzzy. If we start with a given product defined by a set of technical and service characteristics, and if we gradually add new technical characteristics to the product, when does it cease to be what it was and become a new product? However, this difficulty provides us with important insights, as will be seen later in a discussion of competition.

3.2   Aggregation

The previous representation of product technology was obviously focused on a micro-economic level of aggregation. In what follows it will be pointed out that the role of qualitative change in economic development can only be adequately studied by taking into account the composition of the system itself. An exclusively macro-economic approach, that is an approach that concentrates on finding the relationships between variables conceived and measured at a macro-economic level, cannot suffice. An exclusively macro-economic approach inevitably hides the role of qualitative change and of composition. When we concentrate on the time path of an aggregate variable we do not know if the change in its value is due to the changing performance of existing agents or to the emergence of new agents. On the other hand, if the aggregate variable is calculated by adding up or combining the contributions of individual agents, we can in principle understand the role of qualitative change.

Starting from the previous representation of an individual product, we can define an industrial sector as the collection of firms producing a unique but differentiated product. We will then be able to represent the sector in service characteristics space as the collection of points corresponding to the product models produced by its firms. Firms producing products with different technical characteristics but providing the same types of services will be included in the same sector. The population of product models is a cloud, whose density depends on the extent of differentiation of the sector: the more differentiated the sector, the more diffuse the population of product models will be (Figure 51.2). In time the cloud representing the sector can move away from the origin, as a consequence of growing product performance, or separate into several populations, corresponding to the specialization of an industrial sector (Saviotti, 1996; Saviotti and Pyka, 2004).

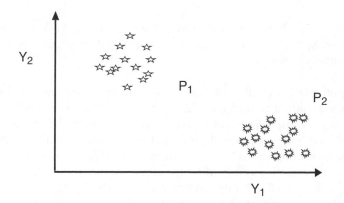

Figure 51.2   Examples of two technological/product populations in the same dimensions, Y_1 and Y_2, of characteristics space

3.3   Variety

To treat analytically the role of qualitative change in economic development we need to find a representation of the composition of the economic system. Such a representation is provided by variety, defined as the number of actors, activities and objects required to describe the economic system. According to Stirling (1998), *diversity* is the concept that expresses more completely the differentiation of a system, and variety is only one of the three possible measures of diversity, the other ones being *balance* and *disparity*. While the value of this distinction is not denied here, the remaining part of this chapter is based exclusively on variety. A full discussion of the concept of diversity and of its measures would certainly contribute to the refinement of the analysis of qualitative change, but it is incompatible with the space constraints of this chapter. Furthermore, one of the measures of variety used by the author of this chapter and by his collaborators, Shannon and Weaver's informational entropy function, takes into account both variety and balance.

In this chapter variety is used at a higher level of aggregation than the one traditionally used in the economic literature on quality change or on monopolistic competition. While traditionally variety measured the degree of differentiation of a product group, in the present chapter it is used to measure the degree of differentiation of economic systems at different levels of aggregation, starting from a firm or an individual product and ending with the world economy. In this chapter, then, variety is a measure of the extent of differentiation of the economic system. Two hypotheses link variety to economic development:

Hypothesis 1:   The growth in variety is a necessary requirement for long-term economic development.

Hypothesis 2:   Variety growth, leading to new sectors, and efficiency growth in pre-existing sectors, are complementary and not independent aspects of economic development.

Hypothesis 2 can also be interpreted as expressing the relationship between quantitative and qualitative change in economic development. Efficiency growth in pre-existing sectors measures only the change in the quantities of output produced per unit of input. Thus, quantitative change in existing routines creates the conditions required for the new activities. A somewhat similar approach, although expressed in formally very different terms, has been adopted by Andersen (1994). He developed a model in which the development of the economy is due to the joint action of two operators, an α operator creating novelty and a β operator taking care of existing routines.

The previous two hypotheses can be justified by the imbalance between productivity growth and demand growth (Pasinetti, 1981, 1993). The imbalance arising from continuous productivity growth in the presence of saturating demand for existing goods and services can be compensated by the emergence of new goods and services. Compensation would occur by the re-employment of resources, including labour, that would be potentially displaced by the growing productivity of pre-existing sectors. Yet this growing productivity would be required to provide the resources needed for the creation of new sectors in a way similar to what happened during the process of industrialization. Then productivity growth in agriculture created the resources required for industrialization (Kuznets, 1965). Similarly productivity growth in pre-existing sectors creates the resources required for search activities and thus for the generation of new products and services. In a Schumpeterian fashion, the growing productivity of the routines constituting the circular flow creates the resources required for innovation, without which economic development would come to a halt.

To the extent that the previous hypotheses are valid, the concept of creative destruction needs to be slightly reformulated. As it was expressed by Schumpeter (1943) it could have meant that an innovation *always* leads to a new activity that replaces an existing routine. If this were the case then the variety of the economic system would remain constant during economic development. If, on the contrary, variety increases during economic development it means that the number of new activities created by innovation is greater than the number of routines that become extinguished. In other words, there is more creation than destruction. However, older routines tend to be compressed within the economic system by means of their efficiency growth. For this reason we will identify two important forces in economic development, creativity and efficiency. The previous two hypotheses could then be reformulated by saying that there is no development without creativity and that creativity and efficiency are two complementary forces.

To conclude this section, we have to point out that the concept of variety has been used with very different meanings also by evolutionary economists. For example, Metcalfe (1994, 1998), while discussing the applications to economics of Fisher's fundamental theorem of natural selection, states (1998, p. 61), 'selection improves the average fitness of the population, and that the rate of improvement in average fitness is equal to the variance of fitness'. Clearly, this is the variance of a homogeneous variable, while variety as used in this chapter is the number of (or a function of) distinguishable elements in the system. These two uses are not only different but in fact complementary. To the extent that we consider firm efficiency as an indicator of fitness, falling efficiency variance within an established activity leads to average efficiency growth in the same activity, thus leading (hypothesis 2) to the creation of new activities elsewhere in the economy.

3.4   *Measures of variety*

Measures of variety can be developed based on the twin characteristics approach. Amongst the wide range of functions available (Stirling, 1998) developed by biologists, physicists, ecologists etc. the present author and his collaborators used Shannon and Weaver's entropy function (1949) (see also the chapter by Frenken in this volume) and Weitzman's function (1992). Variety was found to grow for those technologies that, during the course of their evolution, can generate a growing range of usable services. For example, the range of speeds, payloads, etc. grew substantially for aircraft technology during its life cycle (Frenken *et al.*, 1999). This growth allowed aircraft to become increasingly specialized as light business planes, military fighters, large passenger or cargo planes etc. As the range of services expands a growing number of niches can be created within it. On the contrary, helicopter technology supplies an almost constant range of services and its variety falls slightly during its life cycle. It must be stressed that it is the range of *usable* and not of *total* services that can act as a determinant of variety. Thus, the variety of microcomputers falls slightly from the 1980s to the end of the 1990s although the range of services included between the earliest and the latest models of this period is very wide. However, computer models produced in the early 1980s would have been completely unusable by the end of the 1990s, even if they had been sold at an extremely low price. The growing sophistication of available software and the complementarity of hardware and software made the early models of computers completely obsolete.

Petroleum refining constitutes the only example of process technology of which variety was measured (Nguyen *et al.*, 2003). Here variety was found to fall when the technology was adapting to changing and expanding demand by means of incremental innovation (1932–77), to grow when the technology was subjected to the shock constituted by the 1970s oil crisis (1978–86), and to fall again as oil prices fell back to reasonable values from the mid-1980s.

The measures of variety carried out so far are still too limited. Further work is required for a complete test of hypothesis 1 or to confirm the explanations proposed for the relative growth of variety of different technologies.

3.5   *Competition*

As for many other fields of economics a theory of competition needs to be modified to take into account qualitative change. In a general sense competition implies similarity. Thus, firms producing identical products compete while firms producing completely different products do not compete. The intensity of competition depends on the degree of substitutability of different firms' outputs. As early students of monopolistic competition have realized, product differentiation can provide firms with a degree of local monopoly, the 'local' referring to the characteristics space where the outputs of the firms are represented. The degree of local monopoly is inversely proportional to the substitutability, or similarity, of the firms' products. In characteristics space competition is expected to be proportional to the density of product models (Saviotti and Pyka, 2004; Saviotti and Krafft, 2003). In this representation the intensity of competition can be made to vary between a maximum value, corresponding to the multidimensional analogue of perfect competition, and continuously decreasing values obtained when the extent of product differentiation is increased gradually. Competition can also occur between different sectors (ibid.). The most common example of this situation is provided by different product technologies supplying some common services (e.g. transport, telecommunications, time measurement, photography). However, the possibility of inter-sector competition is more general than in the previous examples. For instance, different leisure activities (e.g. theatre, football, photography) can compete for consumers' time and resources. Thus, inter-sector competition is quite a general phenomenon and it is an important component of market contestability (Baumol *et al.*, 1982).

3.6 Demand

The emergence of qualitatively new goods and services raises the problem of demand formation. Unless we assume that consumers have preferences for objects of which they know neither the properties nor the contribution these objects can make to their utility, we have to admit that preferences need to be formed before the consumption of a new good or service can begin to develop. Schumpeter was aware that producers have to 'educate' consumers to teach them how to use the new goods and services. However, we cannot assume that even producers have a perfect knowledge of the properties of their own goods and services, and above all of how they can suit consumers' requirements, at the beginning of the goods' or services' life cycles. This is particularly true the more radical the novelty of goods and services is with respect to their predecessors. Thus, we can expect producers to introduce new goods and services in the expectation that a potential demand for them will exist. Of course, this demand will be very broadly defined and subject to a high uncertainty in the early phases of the new goods or services life cycle. New goods and services do not remain constant after their introduction, but are subject to post-innovation improvement (Georghiou *et al.*, 1984), a process which can greatly enhance their performance and reduce their cost, thereby increasing the size of the corresponding markets. In this process consumers gradually learn how to use new goods and services, and thus form their preferences, while producers learn how to detect these increasingly refined preferences (Saviotti, 2001). This process of mutual learning is a co-evolution of supply and demand. The usual assumption that preferences are given can only hold for the static or short-range analysis of goods and services already in the mature phase of their life cycle. Preference and demand creation becomes a legitimate concern for economists studying phenomena involving qualitative change and occurring over a very long range of time.

3.7   Models of economic growth and development

The composition of the economic system has been excluded by growth models until they were purely macro-economic. Such models were uniquely concerned with relationships between aggregate variables measured independently of the composition of the economic system. The most important example of this vintage of models is Solow (1956). Starting from the late 1980s a series of growth models attempting to take into account either the emergence of new goods and services or the endogenous character of technological change were developed. Notable examples of the first type are Grossman and Helpman (1991a, 1991b), Stokey (1988, 1991), Young (1991) and Lucas (1988, 1993). In these models new goods are hierarchically classified, with either the newer or the better ones occupying higher positions in the classifications. Examples of the second type are Romer (1987, 1990) and Aghion and Howitt (1998). In both models the R&D activity leads to the creation of new capital goods which can either be added to the pre-existing ones (Romer, 1987, 1990) or replace them (Aghion and Howitt, 1998). However, in none of these cases is the composition of the economic system is endogenously generated.

The composition of the economic system has for a long time been taken into account in the literature on structural change. Important examples of this research are the work by Salter (1960), by Cornwall (1977) and more recently by Verspagen (1993, 2002), Fagerberg (2000) and by Fagerberg and Verspagen (1999). Perhaps the most important attempt to formulate a theoretical model linking structural change and economic growth was made by Pasinetti (1981, 1993). However, this past work on structural change still leads to a number of problems. First, the definition of structural change used by the previously quoted authors refers to the emergence of new sectors, to the disappearance of older ones and to their changing weights in the economic system. Aspects of qualitative change taking place at a lower level of aggregation, although having impacts at the sectoral level, are not taken into account. In this chapter the term 'qualitative change' refers to a wider range of changes in the composition of the economic system. Second, the possibility to detect structural change and to study its effects depends heavily on the availability of statistical data about production and above all on the definition of industrial sectors used. Statistical classifications of production are changed infrequently and in ways that do not necessarily reflect the real changes taking place in the economy. Thus, as emerges clearly from the work of Fagerberg and Verspagen (1999, 2002), the industrial classification that they have to use in order to compare a large number of countries hides some types of structural change. Third, these studies on structural change have remained somewhat separate with respect to the macro-economic growth models. Fourth, even the most sophisticated model linking structural change and economic growth, that of Pasinetti, has very limited dynamic features: it tells us that the continued development of the economic system can be assured only by the existence of inducements to the creation of new sectors, but the nature of these inducements and the dynamics by means of which they give rise to innovations and to new activities is not analysed.

Saviotti and Pyka (2004) developed a model of economic development that includes qualitative change amongst its main determinants and in which changes in the composition of the economic system are endogenously generated and behave as determinants of future economic growth. Furthermore, this model helps to bridge the gap between macro-economic growth models and structural change studies. A new sector is created here by a pervasive innovation, which gives rise to an *adjustment gap*. The adjustment gap is the size of the potential market created by the innovation. The market is potential because neither production capacity nor demand exist in the normal sense of the term. Both are only created gradually as the new sector develops. As the innovation becomes available entrepreneurs create new firms induced by the expectation of a temporary monopoly. The dynamics of the sector depends on the balance between the entry and exit of firms. The rate of entry is determined jointly by the size of the potential market and by financial availability, the latter being not just the quantity of money existing in an economic system, but the fraction of that money that economic agents are willing to allocate to the new sector. Exit is determined by the intensity of competition and by mergers and acquisitions. Following the creation of the sector the adjustment gap is gradually closed, leading to demand saturation. Falling entry combined with mergers and acquisitions gradually reduces the number of firms while increasing their average size. In this process the sector changes from an innovative to a mature one, or it becomes one more routine of the economic system.

A sectoral dynamics of the type described in the previous paragraph provides the inducement to the creation of new sectors. Once older sectors are saturated entrepreneurs are once more induced by the expectation of a temporary monopoly to create new niches, based on emerging innovations. While some of these niches might create substitutes for existing sectors, most of them will lead to radically new products and services. In this case the net variety of the economic system will grow. Growing variety allows aggregate output and employment to keep growing even when sectoral output and employment start falling. In its present form this model is still very simplified, but it contains the seeds of a more general treatment of the role of qualitative change in economic development.

4   Underlying theoretical foundations

Qualitative change, the central subject of this chapter, emerges when new entities, distinguishable from the pre-existing ones, are created by the process of economic development. The presence of qualitative change within economic systems is a very important challenge for economics but it raises considerable problems. A theory of the development of these systems should be able to predict the conditions of emergence and the nature of new entities. Although the exact prediction of the nature of radical innovations is in principle impossible, otherwise they would not be radical innovations, we can expect a theory to be able to predict some general stylized facts that we observe about the emergence of qualitative change. For example, both economic and biological development give rise to new 'species', although over a very different time scale. These development processes create increasing order and structure within the corresponding systems. Both higher animal species and more recent societies are more complex than their predecessors. Furthermore, the transitions occurring within these systems are generally irreversible and path-dependent. Finally, the diversity of economic systems seems to be increasing in the course of their evolution.

A number of theories have been developed recently to deal with the properties and the dynamics of complex systems. These theories were created within different disciplines and are not necessarily perfectly coherent. However, they have some features that make them in principle more suitable for the analysis of qualitative change than the more established economic theories, which are more appropriate for processes involving mainly quantitative change. For example, out of equilibrium thermodynamics predicts that dissipative systems can give rise to order and structure as they move away from equilibrium, even if they start from a disordered or structureless system (Nicolis and Prigogine, 1989). Furthermore, the same systems, when they move sufficiently far away from equilibrium, can give rise to bifurcations, thus increasing the number of possible states of the system (ibid., ch. 3). Also, the transitions of dissipative systems are characterized by irreversibility and path dependence, two features of economic evolution recently highlighted by economists (Arthur, 1989; David, 1985). Other theories of complexity deal with the formation and properties of networks (Barabasi *et al.*, 1999, 2002; Reka *et al.*, 2000; Reka and Basabasi, 2002). Networks can be considered a generalized representation of the structure of socio-economic systems. The emergence of new technologies is generally accompanied by the creation of new networks linking together either the actors creating, using and regulating the new technologies, or the conceptual structures constituting the knowledge related to the new technologies. The examples given so far are not intended to provide a survey of theories of complexity, but only to point out that such theories are in principle more suitable for the treatment of qualitative change than more established economic theories. We can expect theories of complexity to help us in what is one of the most important challenges for economics, the analysis of qualitative change.

References

Abernathy, W.J. and Utterback, J.M. (1975), A dynamic model of process and product innovation, *Omega*, **3**, 639–56.

Aghion P. and Howitt P. (1998), *Endogenous Growth Theory*, Cambridge, MA: The MIT Press.

Altenberg L. (1997), 'N-K fitness landscapes', in T. Back, D. Fogel and Z. Michalewicz (eds), *The Handbook of Evolutionary Computation*, Oxford: Oxford University Press.

Andersen, E.S. (1994), *Evolutionary Economics: Post Schumpeterian Contributions*, London: Pinter.

Arthur, W.B. (1989) Competing technologies, increasing returns, and lock-in by historical events, *The Economic Journal*, **99**, 116–31.

Barabasi A., Reka A. and Jeong H. (1999), Mean field theory for scale free random networks, *Physica*, A 272, 173–87.

Barabasi, Albert-Laszlo (2002), *Linked: the New Science of Networks*, New York: Perseus Publishing.

Baumol, W.J., Panzar J.C. and Willig R.D. (1982), *Contestable Markets and the Theory of Industry Structure*, San Diego, CA: Harcourt Brace Jovanovich.

Chamberlin, E. (1933), *The Theory of Monopolistic Competition*, Cambridge, MA: Harvard University Press.

Cornwall, J. (1977), *Modern Capitalism: its Growth and Transformation*, London: Martin Robertson.

David, P.A. (1985), Clio and the economics of QWERTY, *American Economic Review*, **75**, 332–7.

Dixit, A.K. and Stiglitz, J.E. (1977), Monopolistic competition and optimum product diversity, *American Economic Review*, **67**, 297–308.

Dosi, G. (1982), Technological paradigms and technological trajectories: a suggested interpretation of the determinants and directions of technical change, *Research Policy*, **11**, 147–62.

Eaton, B.C. and Lipsey, R.G. (1975), The principle of minimum differentiation reconsidered: some new developments in the theory of spatial competition, *Review of Economic Studies*, **42**, 27–49.

Fagerberg J. (2000), Technological progress, structural change and productivity growth: a comparative study, working paper no. 5/2000, Centre for Technology, Innovation and Culture, University of Oslo.

Fagerberg, J. (2003), Schumpeter and the revival of evolutionary economics, *Journal of Evolutionary Economics*, **13**, 125–59.

Fagerberg, J. and Verspagen, B. (1999), Productivity, R&D spillovers and trade, working paper no. 3/1999, Centre for Technology, Innovation and Culture, University of Oslo.

Fagerberg, J. and Verspagen, B. (2002), Technology-gaps, innovation diffusion and transformation: an evolutionary interpretation, *Research Policy*, **31**, 1291–304.

Freeman, C. (1982), *The Economics of Industrial Innovation*, London: Pinter.

Freeman, C. and Soete, L. (1997), *The Economics of Industrial Innovation*, London: Pinter.

Frenken, K. (2001), Understanding product innovation using complex systems theory, PhD. thesis, University of Amsterdam.

Frenken, K., Saviotti, P.P. and Trommetter, M. (1999), Variety and niche creation in aircraft, helicopters, motorcycles and microcomputers, *Research Policy*, **28**, 469–88.

Gallouj, F. and Weinstein, O. (1997), Innovation in services, *Research Policy*, **26**, 537–56.

Georghiou, L., Metcalfe, J.S., Evans, J., Ray, T. and Gibbons, M. (1984), *Post-Innovation Performance*, London: Macmillan.

Griliches, Z. (1964), 'Notes on the measurement of price and quality changes', *Models of Income Determination. Studies in Income and Wealth*, **28**, Princeton, NJ: NBER, pp. 301–404.

Griliches, Z. (1967), 'Hedonic price indexes revisited: some notes on the state of the art', *Proceedings of the Business and Economics Statistics Section*, American Statistical Association, pp. 324–32.

Griliches, Z. (1971), 'Hedonic price indexes for automobiles: an econometric analysis of quality change', in Z. Griliches (ed.), *Price Indexes and Quality Change*, Cambridge, MA: Harvard University Press.

Grossman, G.M. and Helpman, E. (1991a), Quality ladder and product cycles, *Quarterly Journal of Economics*, **106**, 557–86.

Grossman, G.M. and Helpman, E. (1991b), *Innovation and Growth in the Global Economy*, Cambridge, MA: MIT Press.

Hirshleifer, J. (1955), The exchange between quantity and quality, *Quarterly Journal of Economics*, **69**, 596–606.

Hotelling, H. (1929), Stability in competition, *Economic Journal*, **39**, 41–57.

Houthakker, H. (1951–2), Compensated changes in quantities and qualities consumed, *Review of Economic Studies*, **19**(3), 155–64.

Ironmonger, D.S. (1972), *New Commodities and Consumer Behaviour*, Cambridge: Cambridge University Press.

Jovanovic, B. and MacDonald, G.M. (1994), The life cycle of a competitive industry, *Journal of Political Economy*, **102**, 322–47.

Klepper, S. (1996), Entry, exit growth and innovation over the product life cycle, *American Economic Review*, **86**, 562–83.

Kuznets, S. (1965), *Economic Growth and Structure*, New York: Norton.

Lancaster, K.J. (1966), A new approach to consumer theory, *Journal of Political Economy*, **14**, 133–56.

Lancaster, K.J. (1971), *Consumer Demand: a New Approach*, New York: Columbia University Press.

Lancaster, K.J. (1975), Socially optimal product differentiation, *American Economic Review*, 567–85.

Lancaster, K.J. (1979), *Variety, Equity and Efficiency*, New York: Columbia University Press.

Lancaster, K.J. (1990), The economics of product variety: a survey, *Marketing Science*, **9**, 189–206.

Lucas, R.E. (1988), On the mechanics of economic development, *Journal of Monetary Economics*, **22**, 3–42.

Lucas, R.E. (1993), Making a miracle, *Econometrica*, **61**, 251–72.

Metcalfe, J.S. (1994), Competition, Fisher's principle and increasing returns in the selection process, *Journal of Evolutionary Economics*, **4**, 327–46.

Metcalfe, J.S. (1998), *Evolutionary Economics and Creative Destruction*, London: Routledge.

Nelson, R. and Winter, S. (1977), In search of a useful theory of innovation, *Research Policy*, **6**, 36–76.

Nelson, R.R. and Winter, S.G. (1982), *An Evolutionary Theory of Economic Change*, Cambridge, MA: Harvard University Press.

Nguyen, P., Saviotti, P.P., Trommetter, M. and Bourgeois, B. (2003),Variety and the evolution of refinery processing, Université Pierre Mendès-France, Grenoble.

Nicolis, G. and Prigogine, I. (1989), *Exploring Complexity*, New York: Freeman.

Pasinetti, L.L. (1981), *Structural Change and Economic Growth*, Cambridge: Cambridge University Press.

Pasinetti, L.L. (1993), *Structural Economic Dynamics*, Cambridge: Cambridge University Press.

Reka, A. and Barabasi, A. (2002), Statistical mechanics of complex networks, *Reviews of Modern Physics*, **74**, 47–97.

Reka, A., Jeong, H. and Barabasi, A. (2000), Error and attack tolerance of complex networks, *Nature*, **406**, 378–82.

Romer, P. (1987), Growth based on increasing returns due to specialization, *American Economic Review*, **77**, 56–62.

Romer, P. (1990), Endogenous technical progress, *Journal of Political Economy*, **98**, 71–102.

Sahal, D. (1985), Technology guide posts and innovation avenues, *Research Policy*, **14**(2), 61–82.

Salop, S.C. (1979), Monopolistic competition with outside goods, *Bell Journal of Economics*, **10**, 141–56.

Salter, W.E.G. (1960), *Productivity and Technical Change*, Cambridge: Cambridge University Press.

Saviotti, P.P. (1996), *Technological Evolution, Variety and the Economy*, Cheltenham, UK and Brookfield, USA: Edward Elgar.

Saviotti, P.P. (2001), Variety, growth and demand, *Journal of Evolutionary economics*, **11**, 119–42.

Saviotti, P.P. and Krafft J. (2003), Towards a generalized definition of competition, mimeo, IDEFI, Sophia Antipolis, July.

Saviotti, P.P. and Metcalfe, J.S. (1984), A theoretical approach to the construction of technological output indicators, *Research Policy*, **13**, 141–51.

Saviotti, P.P. and Pyka, A. (2004), Economic development by the creation of new sectors, *Journal of Evolutionary Economics*, **14**(1), 1–36.

Schumpeter, J. ([1912] 1934), *The Theory of Economic Development*, Cambridge, MA: Harvard University Press.

Schumpeter, J. ([1943] 1976), *Capitalism, Socialism and Democracy*, London: George Allen and Unwin.

Shannon, C.E. and Weaver, W. (1949), *The Mathematical Theory of Communication*, Urbana, IL: University of Illinois Press.

Simon, H.A. (1969), *The Sciences of the Artificial*, Cambridge, MA and London: MIT Press.

Solow, R.M. (1956), A contribution to the theory of economic growth, *Quarterly Journal of Economics*, **70**, 65–94.

Stirling, A. (1998), On the economics and analysis of diversity, SPRU electronic working papers series (available at http://www.sussex.ac.uk/spru/docs/sewps/index.html).

Stokey, N.L. (1988), Learning by doing and the introduction of new goods, *Journal of Political Economy*, **96**, 701–17.

Stokey, N.L. (1991), Human capital, product quality and growth, *Quarterly Journal of Economics*, **106**, 587–616.

Theil, H. (1951–2), Qualities prices and budget enquiries, *Review of Economic Studies*, **19**(3), 129–47.

Verspagen, B. (1993), *Uneven Growth between Interdependent Economies*, Aldershot: Avebury.

Verspagen, B. (2002), Structural change and technology, a long view, paper presented at the 2002 DRUID Conference.

Wadman, W.M. (2000), *Variable Quality in Consumer Theory, Toward a Dynamic Microeconomic Theory of the Consumer*, New York: Sharpe.

Weitzman, M.L. (1992), On diversity, *Quarterly Journal of Economics*, **107**, 363–406.

Young, A. (1991), Learning by doing and the dynamic effects of international trade, *Quarterly Journal of Economics*, **106**, 369–406.

52 Understanding economic growth as the central task of economic analysis
Richard R. Nelson

This chapter has three sections.[1] I begin by endorsing Schumpeter's argument that understanding economic growth ought to be the central focus of economic analysis, and proposing that modern evolutionary economic theory has its central focus just there. In section 2, I turn to the origins of modern evolutionary economic theory as an endeavor inspired by Schumpeter, and the progress in understanding growth that an evolutionary theory has made possible. However, I propose that, while significant progress has been made proceeding along established paths, the endeavor now is running into diminishing returns. Section 3 offers my thoughts on new directions I think highly valuable to pursue, in order to develop a truly illuminating theory of economic growth.

1 Economic growth as the appropriate central focus of economic analysis

The cumulatively vast increases in living standards and productivity experienced by a significant part of the world's population clearly is the most dramatic and beneficial achievement of the market-oriented economies that began to emerge in the late 18th and early 19th centuries. Surely the primary task of economic theory should be to illuminate how this miracle was accomplished, and the determinants of economic growth in the future.

This is not simply my point of view. It certainly was Schumpeter's. And Schumpeter's position on this was not radical. Indeed, it reflected the writings of many of the great classical economists whose work preceded his. Thus reflect on Adam Smith's *The Wealth of Nations* (first published 1776). This book is basically an analysis of the factors driving the economic growth that was occurring in the UK in the late 18th century, along with a diagnosis as to why it was not occurring so effectively elsewhere. The treatise starts out with the famous discussion of the dynamics that Smith believed had so dramatically improved productivity in pin making. This central orientation to the phenomena of economic growth is present in many of the works of the 19th-century classical economists. Analysis of the determinants of prices and wages also was an important issue in the classical economics writings, but, as in Smith, tended to be treated after the sources of economic growth had been laid out.

However, this certainly is not the orientation of contemporary neoclassical economics, at least as the subject is laid out in general textbooks. There the heart of modern economic science is presented as being the neoclassical theory of the determinants of the pattern of inputs, outputs, and prices, under conditions of a hypothetical equilibrium. The orientation is partly positive, and partly normative, with the normative apparatus linked to the concept of Pareto optimality, and analysis of the conditions under which market equilibria meet, or deviate from, the necessary conditions.

This is not to say that economic growth is ignored in introductory texts. In many of them, analysis of economic growth is given high priority. However, generally economic growth is brought up as a subject of analysis only after the students are assumed to have standard microeconomic theory under control. And the tools of analysis of economic growth that are used are basically those of equilibrium microeconomics, augmented to take aboard the possibility of continuing technological advance. This is so not only in introductory treatments, but also in more advanced neoclassical treatises on growth. Solow's pioneering theoretical and empirical writings on growth (1956, 1957) were based exactly on neoclassical simple microeconomic theory, principally the theory of the firm in market equilibrium, that was the standard then and is now, augmented to include the possibility of technological advance over time. It is fair to say that the new neoclassical growth theory has stayed very much like the old, in these respects. (For a discussion, see Nelson, 1998.)

Put more generally, contemporary neoclassical economics is basically about conditions of general equilibrium. Analysis of economic growth is largely a graft on that subject.

The shift in the orientation of the main line of economics away from a central focus on long-run economic growth, and towards a focus on conditions of economic equilibrium, comes with the rise of neoclassical economic theory. Marshall's reflections on this are interesting. In the preface to his *Principles* (1948, 8th edn, first published 1907) he says, in effect, that the important questions for economics lie in the dynamics, and that biological conceptions seemed the appropriate route into economic dynamics. But then he goes on to say that the tools for analyzing equilibrium conditions were better honed, and so this is what his book would largely be about. Marshall never got around to writing that second volume on economic dynamics that implicitly he had promised.

Schumpeter's views here are very clear. In his writings from *The Theory of Economic Development* (1934) through his *Capitalism, Socialism, and Democracy* (1942) he is arguing against the prevailing trend among economists to define the core of the discipline as about firm and household behavior, prices and quantities, under conditions of equilibrium, whereas it was clear (to Schumpeter) that the main thing about capitalism was that it was an engine of progress.

This certainly does not mean a lack of interest in the question of what lies behind the allocation of resources in an economy at any time, or the pattern of output and prices, but Schumpeter's view on these matters was dynamic, not static. He argued that one could not understand the processes driving economic growth without consideration of what was going on in different economic sectors, which was leading to a changing pattern of prices and allocation of resources. That is, Schumpeter's theory of the mix of outputs and inputs among industries, and product and factor prices, was part of his theory of economic growth.

Nor does a central focus on economic growth play down the role of market organization of economic activity, the activities of for-profit firms, and competition, as key elements behind the successful performance of capitalism. Rather, it views successful performance in a different light, and sees the role of competition in a different way.

In any case, the central reason I am an evolutionary economist is that evolutionary theory is, at its core, a theory of economic growth. It is indeed concerned with illuminating the factors behind prevailing patterns of outputs, inputs, and prices, but sees these as in a dynamic context.

2   The development of evolutionary growth theory and diminishing returns

When Sidney Winter and I set out to write *An Evolutionary Theory of Economic Change*, much of our inspiration came from Schumpeter. It may be somewhat ironic that I discovered Schumpeter, or rather came to understand what he was arguing and the importance of that argument, in research motivated by Solow's neoclassical theory of economic growth. Motivated by Solow's arguments and other empirical studies documenting the importance of technological advance, I and other young scholars set out to study the process empirically. A number of us came to realize that the phenomena we were finding were completely incompatible with those basic premises. While Schumpeter had made the argument long before, the economists studying technological advance, pointed in that direction by Solow, came on their own to see that innovation, technological or otherwise, could not be understood within the confines of a theory that assumed continuing equilibrium. Rather, one needed a theory that saw technology, and other aspects of the economic system, as undergoing continuing evolution.

The proposal that one should model technology as evolving, and that economic growth more broadly should be understood as proceeding through an evolutionary process, were scarcely new ideas. Thus in the early 18th century Mandeville (1924, first published 1714) argued that the basic design of the sophisticated naval fighting ships of his day, which he regarded as the pinnacle of technological accomplishment then, was the result of a multitude of cumulative advances made over a long period of time by many people, rather than something that was the result of a coherent, worked out plan. Adam Smith's discussion of the coevolution of advances in the technology of pin making and the increasing division of labor in the operations, both driven by and interacting with a growing extent of the market, has a similar evolutionary flavor. These early accounts, put forth well prior to Darwin, did not articulate a crisp theory of variation and selection as the cumulative mechanism at work, of the sort introduced in the new evolutionary growth theory. But something like that was implicit.

I confess that, when Sidney Winter and I were developing *An Evolutionary Theory of Economic Change* (1982), while we clearly recognized the intellectual base of our work in Schumpeter, I did not realize the extent to which what we were developing had been foreshadowed by an earlier pre-modern neoclassical tradition in economics. Of course we had available to us a large body of technique and pieces of theory that were not there at the times of the earlier writings, like the theorizing of the Carnegie Tech crew–Simon, March, and Cyert – on bounded rationality, and their articulation of *A Behavioral Theory of the Firm* (Cyert and March, 1963). However, increasingly I am of the belief that modern economic evolutionary theory can be thought of as a renaissance of an older tradition in economics that got sandbagged.

What Winter and I did, of course, was to marry an evolutionary theory of technological change with a behavioral theory of the firm, augmented to include innovation as a central firm activity, and placed in a context of Schumpeterian competition. To attack the phenomena addressed by neoclassical growth theory, we treated technologies as activities that used labor and capital to produce output, and built in mechanisms regulating the change over time in supplies of labor and capital.

This formulation obviously struck a responsive chord. It has spawned a major research tradition. I want to express my particular enthusiasm for the fine mix of, and overlap between, empirical and theoretical research that has marked our research enterprise. The interaction between appreciative and formal theory has been strong, and I think very fruitful.

However, in my view much, too much, of the research within this tradition has stayed too close to certain features of the early work, which I think is causing the endeavor to run into sharply diminishing returns. Here I want to highlight three aspects of my early modeling with Winter that probably now are obstacles to further progress, and need to be got out of the way.

First, perhaps because we were so focused on showing that sophisticated effective practice could be explained without assuming that the individuals and organizations engaging in such practice had devised and chosen what they were doing from a large range of perceived alternatives, we played down the role of cognition, understanding and conscious problem solving, in the evolution of practice. In so doing in effect we were playing down the importance of human knowledge in the advance of know-how, and in particular were repressing the important roles that the advance of science had played in the evolution of practice in a number of areas. It is time, I believe, to build more closely into economic evolutionary models the nature and evolution of the knowledge that guides attempts to improve practice.

Second, the model Winter and I developed to try to explain experienced economic growth focused on technologies as the body of practice that had experienced the most rapid evolution. While we stated that other aspects of business practice also went through evolutionary change, we did not do much with that proposition. A major reason, or at least my reason, was conviction that it was the rapid and continuing evolution of technologies that was the basic driving force behind the growth that had been experienced.

I think the tack we took was the right one, then. But I think evolutionary growth theorizing has, until recently at least, neglected the evolution of business practice, organizational forms, and institutions more generally. Bhaven Sampat and I (2001) have proposed that these kinds of variables can be regarded as social technologies, as contrasted with physical technologies, and that the evolution of social technologies is an important, and usually neglected, part of the economic growth story. In many cases social technologies have had to change in order that society is able to take advantage of the new physical technologies. At the same time the evolution of social technologies seems to be more sticky and less well oriented than the evolution of physical technologies. Getting a better grip on this set of issues ought to be high on the research agenda.

Third, we followed Solow and other neoclassical growth theorists in seeing economic growth as a macroeconomic phenomenon. Solow's (1957) empirical article, while linked to his 1956 theoretical piece, also was in a tradition of empirical analysis of the factors behind economic growth that was being conducted by scholars at the NBER, that made use of the newly available time series of GNP. The GNP series provided an aggregate measure of the total production and growth over time of an economy's output, which could be compared with aggregate measures of an economy's labor inputs and its capital stock and the changes in these over time. The evidence that aggregate output had increased at a significantly faster rate than had total inputs was reported in several publications prior to Solow's famous paper, and these earlier publications also put forth the proposition that the greater increase of output than inputs was evidence of the importance of technological advance.

I believe that it is highly useful to have an aggregate measure of economic production, and of the rate of economic growth. However, a long time ago, particularly in his *Business Cycles*, Schumpeter insisted that viewing growth as a macroeconomic phenomenon blinded the analyst to the fact that the real economy consists of many different economic sectors, and that economic growth involved in an essential way the rise of new industries and sectors and the decline of old ones. As Stanley Metcalfe has argued in several recent essays (2002, 2003), creative destruction is not simply about firms, but about industries. The current generation of evolutionary growth models has not recognized this adequately. I consider it an open question whether Schumpeter's long wave theory, the heart of which is the proposition that the driving force of growth at any time lies in the rapid advance of a small number of critical technologies, is basically correct or not. But I think it important that evolutionary growth theory be able to address that debate.

I believe that our common efforts to date on developing an evolutionary theory of economic growth have been very successful. But there are clear diminishing returns in continuing down the old paths. It is time, I would like to argue, for setting out in new directions.

3 Promising new directions

I focus here on the three limitations of the earlier evolutionary growth theory that I have identified above, and give my thoughts as to promising new directions to take.

As I noted, the early versions of evolutionary economic theory perhaps leaned backwards too far in trying to demonstrate that the often very sophisticated and powerful human practices that were involved in economic activity could be, and should be, understood not as the result of human omniscience and global deliberation, but as the long-term achievements of an evolutionary process in which individual action and choice in any instance generally involved no more than ordinary sophistication and skill. The human and organizational rationality in evolutionary theories clearly is a bounded rationality. The amazing progress achieved in many areas over the long run is the result of the power of the evolutionary processes at work.

While I am sure the basic perspective here is absolutely correct, it tends to repress the fact that, at least in modern times, the strength of human knowledge that is brought to search and problem solving in a number of areas is extremely impressive. And while that knowledge itself needs to be understood as having been the result of an evolutionary process, the character and strength of knowledge at any time profoundly affects how the evolutionary processes at work at that time proceed. Joel Mokyr (2002, 2004) has argued that the development of strong scientific knowledge relevant to advancing technologies, which occurred during the 19th century, was the key factor enabling technological development to become a sustained phenomenon, rather than proceeding in fits and starts.

Economic evolution, human cultural evolution more generally, clearly differs from biological evolution in that the human and organizational actors are purposeful, they often make conscious efforts to find better ways of doing things, and their efforts to innovate are far from completely blind. I propose that, when the knowledge that can be used to guide search (and problem solving within search) is strong, it lends power to the effort in four different ways. (The following discussion follows on that of Nelson, 2000.)

First, it enables the searcher to focus effectively; knowledge identifies certain potential pathways as likely dead-ends, and identifies others as promising to pursue. Second, strong knowledge highlights markers that one can see if one goes down a particular path, that indicate whether that path is going in a plausible broad direction or not, and also the kinds of changes in direction that seem appropriate. Third, after a new practice is developed and actually employed, the strength of knowledge affects the ability to evaluate that practice accurately in a timely fashion.

Fourth, a strong knowledge base often permits a good deal of the searching and problem solving to proceed offline. In so doing, it changes the nature of the exploitation versus exploration conflict that Jim March and others have highlighted, by permitting much of the latter to proceed offline, until strong evidence is accumulated that the practice being explored should be adopted. If one reflects on it, this is exactly what Research and Development is all about – offline exploration through doing theoretical calculations, constructing and testing models – and working with pilot plants or test vehicles to learn more about their properties, without a commitment to actually put the new design or practice into operation until it is well tested.

From this perspective, evolutionary processes are very much learning processes. A certain portion of the writing in evolutionary economics recognizes this, implicitly or explicitly. Of course, from a certain point of view, biological evolutionary processes can be interpreted as learning processes in which a species learns how better to survive and prosper. But what is going on in human cultural evolution is that knowledge is accumulating in the heads of human beings. Individuals, and individual organizations, are learning to do things better, and the society as a whole is learning.

A central part of that learning is simply learning about ways of doing things that had not been thought of before, or at least not seriously explored, and about the performance of these ways of doing things. However, it is clear that, in the process of learning about and how to implement new practices, like Mandeville's ship designs, what is learned transcends the details of particular practices, techniques, and designs, and a broad body of understanding thus evolves along with a body of practice. Mandeville's ship designers improve their general understanding of the principles of good ship design as they go about modifying their old designs, in most cases for the better, but occasionally for the worse.

However, while important parts of the knowledge base for search and problem solving in a field develop almost as a byproduct of actual experience, particularly over the last two centuries, a large number of fields of applications-oriented science have been institutionalized. Today, virtually every field of human practice, from ship designing, to the design of computers, to medical practice, to the practice of business management, has associated with it an applications-oriented field of research and training, like the engineering disciplines, or fields like pathology and bacteriology, managerial economics, and organization theory. But it is clear that some of these applications-oriented sciences are much more powerful than others.

More generally, the strength of the knowledge base to guide search and problem solving, that has been achieved both through drawing on the lessons of experience, and through the development of the background applications-oriented sciences, differs enormously across fields of human practice. In some areas, efforts at design and problem solving work from a strong enough base of understanding that theoretical and empirical calculation can relatively sharply identify highly promising directions, and evidence gained through offline experimentation and testing can provide quite reliable estimates of how a particular new design, or practice, will actually work. This powerful background knowledge does not eliminate the need for learning through actual doing and using, but it enables an enormous amount to be learned before the innovator actually has to go online with the major commitments that that usually entails.

In other cases the knowledge base may be quite weak. Calculation and analysis of perceived alternatives may not take the venture very far, and the ability to learn through offline experimentation and testing may be highly limited. In this latter situation, about the only way to move forward is through actual trying, and learning through doing and using, and even that learning may be relatively unreliable and slow in coming. I propose that the rate of progress in the latter cases is going to be much slower than the rate of progress in the former.

I want to set this line of analysis aside for a moment and get into my second line of discussion, about the high priority of bringing organizational practice, organization form, laws and public policies, and institutions more broadly, explicitly into an evolutionary theory of economic growth. However, the connections I will draw shortly between theme 1 and theme 2 might already be obvious.

The evidence is overwhelming that it is the advance of technology that has been the basic driving force behind the increase in productivity and living standards that has been achieved over the past two centuries. But changes in organizational practice and form, and institutional structures more broadly, also are an important part of the story. Adam Smith recognized this, in his discussion of pin making. There he highlighted both the invention of many different kinds of machinery and the increasing division of labor, associated with the dramatic increases in mechanization both as cause and effect.

Albert Chandler's great studies (particularly *Scale and Scope*, 1990) were focused on the changes in the structure of business firms, and business practice, that were needed to take full advantage of the development toward the middle of the 19th century of railroad and telegraph technologies, that opened the potentiality for firms to buy inputs and sell outputs over a much wider range of space than had been customary before, and the complementary advances in capital goods technologies, which together opened up the possibilities of great economies of scale and scope. Chandler notes that these much larger firms required a larger and more sophisticated managerial team than could be recruited through tapping family and friends, which had been the custom when companies were small. The concept of professional management came into existence, and shortly thereafter business schools arose to train professional managers. The very large financial requirements of the modern corporation led to changes in the organization of banking, and gradually to the emergence of the modern stock market. A wide range of new law was needed to support, and control, these developments.

John Joseph Beer (1959) and Peter Murmann (2003) have told a parallel story regarding the rise of the modern dyestuff industry during the last half of the 19th century. As with the Chandler story, advances in physical technology, in this particular case enabled by significant improvements in understanding and technique in organic chemistry, started the cascade of developments. The industrial research laboratory emerged as a structure enabling firms to hire and effectively employ inventors with advanced training in the relevant fields of science. The rapidly growing dyestuffs industry was the source of a large and rapidly growing demand for highly trained chemists. The German university system adapted to meet these demands, helped by significant funding coming from governments.

Or consider developments in medical care over the last century. Again, the driving force has been significant improvements in scientific knowledge bearing on medicine, and the development of a wide range of chemical substances, physical devices and artifacts, and medical practice, that are effective across a wide range of diseases. These advances greatly increased the skill requirements of physicians, and led to the development of the modern medical school. Hospitals changed their nature from places where the sick and dying were, in effect, simply kept, to places where sophisticated medicine was practiced. The new medicine was also very expensive and the institution of medical insurance began to arise. A wide variety of new government policies came into place, both to provide financial support for the practice of medicine, and also for medical research. The modern research-based pharmaceutical company, drawing on scientific understanding and trained people from the universities, and selling its products on a market dominated by third-party payment, is largely a post-World War II phenomenon. And so are various forms of pharmaceuticals regulation.

In each of the cases above, while the advance of physical technologies was central in the story, development also involved new modes of organization and organizational practice, and new institutions more broadly. I have told these different stories in a certain amount of detail to make persuasive my argument that economic growth needs to be understood as a process driven by the coevolution of physical and social technologies, to use the terms Sampat and I proposed. It is fair to say that neither neoclassical nor evolutionary growth theory has taken the social technologies part of that story as seriously as it should.

Let me now link the discussion back to my earlier proposition about the significance of differences across areas of human practice in the extent to which the knowledge base permits sharp focus on promising pathways for improvement, ability to learn a lot by relatively low-cost offline experimentation, and quick reliable feedback of the efficacy of a new practice once it is put in place. Without denying significant intra-class variability, the apparent differences on average in these respects between efforts to advance physical technologies, and social technologies, are striking. Virtually all stories that I know about of significant physical invention in the 20th century describe the calculation, the offline experimentation, the deliberate and usually reliable testing, that were involved in the efforts. In contrast, these aspects are strikingly missing from the accounts that I know about of efforts to advance social technologies, to implement a new business practice, or put in place a new public policy. Institutional learning seems to be just much more difficult than learning regarding physical technologies.

I want to turn now to the third area that I flagged. I think evolutionary growth theory needs to recognize more explicitly the multi-sector nature of economic activity. This would involve, first, recognizing and incorporating inter-industry differences in the pattern of growth being experienced at any time, and second, coming to grips with inter-industry coordination mechanisms. There are two building blocks I want to highlight here: the growing literature on industrial dynamics, and the new writings on Schumpeter's theory of long waves.

I do not know if the scholars who have been contributing to the advance ot empirical and theoretical understanding of 'industrial dynamics' (for example, Malerba and Orsenigo, 1997; Malerba, 2002) would consider their work to be part of growth theory. But I would. A key characteristic of this work is that it recognizes, and attempts to explain, differences across industries. These differences have included the size of the firms who are most active in innovation, whether innovation is coming from firms in the industry or from upstream firms, or both, and the links of technological advance in the industry with science. As the result of this work, we are now able to see significant differences across industries in these regards.

Also, technologies and industries change over time. Many (not all) seem to experience a more or less systematic product or technology cycle from infancy to maturity. To some extent, cross-industry variation at any time is associated with the different levels of maturity of different industries (see for example, Klepper, 1996). A problem with the industry life cycle literature, at least in its early form, was that implicitly it saw industries as having a single cycle. However, as empirical research in this area has proceeded, it has become clear that many industries experience a succession of cycles, with a particular cycle being associated with the emergence of a promising technology, and then its maturation, followed by a renaissance of activity in the industry as a new technology emerges and replaces the older one, etc. (See, for example, Mowery and Nelson, 1999.)

My own contribution to research in this area has been to propose that an industry or technology life cycle needs to be understood as involving the evolution of social technologies, as well as physical technologies, or rather the coevolution of both. Thus, organizational forms and practice, and the supporting institutional structures, change over the course of a technology or an industry life cycle. An extremely interesting question is whether the social technologies that are fruitful in one technological era also are the ones needed to be fruitful when a new technology succeeds the old. The considerable business school literature on competence-enhancing and competence-destroying technological advance is basically about this question. (For a survey and a collection of good studies, see Dosi, Nelson and Winter, 2000.)

While there is little cross-referencing, the literature on technology life cycles, and the rapidly growing literature on long waves of economic activity have a lot in common. The latter literature is, of course, motivated by Schumpeter's theory put forth in his *Business Cycles* (1939). Schumpeter's basic proposal was that economic growth in Europe and the United States had gone through a number of eras, with economic growth in each era largely driven by technological advance in a few key industries, whose effects fanned out to influence the economy as a whole. The wave aspect of the theory was very similar to the life cycle properties in the literature I have just discussed. In Schumpeter's case, a new cluster of technologies emerge, then advance rapidly, then slow down as they mature. The successive cycles phenomenon in particular industries that I have described is very similar to Schumpeter's theory that growth more broadly proceeds in successive waves.

After a brief flurry of attention shortly after he put it forth, Schumpeter's long wave theory received little continuing attention, perhaps because it seemed to have nothing to do with the neoclassical growth theory that soon emerged. Nor until recently have evolutionary theorists paid much attention to it. However, largely through the work of Carlota Perez (1983) and Christopher Freeman (particularly in Freeman and Louçã, 2001), in recent years there has been a surge of writing on growth oriented by that theory, but with a new twist.

What Perez and Freeman have done is to bring institutions and institutional evolution into the picture. The argument is that the forms of business organization and practice, legal structures, government policies and institutions more generally, that facilitate progress in one era often are not the same as those that facilitated in the preceding era. And institutional innovation, or change more generally, is difficult. Thus, the countries that led the world in one era often tend to fall back in the following era, where different countries are fortunate enough to have in place the bases for the institutions that have become appropriate, or somehow are able to create the right ones.

I find the broad outlines of this theory convincing. Thus far its development has been exclusively through the vehicle of what Winter and I have called 'appreciative theorizing'. But the time may be coming when some more formal theorizing can help sharpen and advance conceptualization.

It should be apparent that the basic theoretical ingredients needed to model industry product cycles also are needed to model broader economic development over a long wave, or a sequence of them. There is a need to explore the sources of diminishing returns to efforts to advance technology in a field, and the factors that renew opportunities. The effects of the pace and pattern of technological change on firm and industry structure need to be modeled. There is need to incorporate social technologies in a model, in a way that captures the ways in which social technologies and their evolution both mold and reflect developments in physical technologies.

But there also is a need to deal explicitly with the multisectoral nature of economic activity. Under long wave theory economic growth in any era is driven by rapid technological advance in a small number of industries. However, these rapidly advancing technologies are affecting a large number of industries, partly through providing new inputs, partly because some industries are complements and others substitutes for the sectors where technological advance is most rapid. We need to learn to model these interactions, and their effects on relative prices, and in turn how changes in relative prices affect the allocation of resources across different industries.

I propose that we already have built into evolutionary economic theory the heart of an analysis of the factors causing changes in relative prices over time. To a first approximation, prices move with unit costs, although perhaps with a lag. Relative prices decline in industries experiencing the most rapid productivity growth, rise in those experiencing little progress.

To proceed further down this path, of course, requires that we develop a more explicit theory of how demand is influenced by prices than that contained in contemporary evolutionary models. Such a formulation would include specification within an evolutionary theory of concepts analogous to substitutes and complements in final consumption as well as in production. I suggest that this would involve both opening up the routine concept to incorporate variations tied to prices, and more elaborate treatment of how prices influence the direction of search, along the lines Winter and I sketched in chapter 7 of our 1982 book. These adaptations, together with more detailed treatment of the response of investments to differences in profits from pursuing different paths of expansion, would take evolutionary theory a long way forward.

I want to conclude this chapter by observing that a successful development of evolutionary growth theory along these lines would do much more than simply improve its ability to illuminate economic growth as we have experienced it. It would enable evolutionary theory to encompass much of the subject matter treated in neoclassical economics as aspects of 'general equilibrium' theory. But it would treat the prevailing pattern of inputs, outputs, and product and factor prices as a frame in the moving picture defined by the evolutionary processes driving economic growth. In my view, this would be an enormous accomplishment.

Note

1.   The gist of this essay was presented as a keynote address at the Schumpeter Society meetings in Milan, 9–11 June 2004.

References

Beer, J.J. (1959), *The Emergence of the German Dye Industry*, Urbana, IL: University of Illinois Press.

Chandler, A.D. (1990), *Scale and Scope*, Cambridge, MA: Harvard University Press.

Cyert, R. and March, J. (1963), *A Behavioral Theory of the Firm*, Englewood Cliffs, NJ: Prentice-Hall.

Dosi, G., Nelson, R. and Winter, S. (2000), *The Nature and Dynamics of Organizational Capabilities*, Oxford: Oxford University Press.

Freeman, C. and Louçã, F. (2001), *As Time Goes By*, New York: Oxford University Press.

Klepper, S. (1996), Entry, exit, growth, and innovation over the product cycle, *American Economic Review*, **86**(30), 562–83.

Malerba, F. (2002), Sectoral systems of innovation and production, *Research Policy*, **31**(2), 247–64.

Malerba, F. and Orsenigo, L. (1997), Technological regimes and sectoral patterns of innovative activities, *Industrial and Corporate Change*, **6**(1), 83–117.

Mandeville, B. (1924, originally published 1714), *The Fable of the Bees*, vol. 2, Oxford: Oxford University Press, pp. 141–2.

Marshall, A. (1948, first published 1907), *Principles of Economics*, 8th edn, London: Macmillan.

Metcalfe, S. (2002), Knowledge of growth and the growth of knowledge, *Journal of Evolutionary Economics*, **12**, 3–15.

Metcalfe, S. (2003), Industrial growth and the theory of retardation; precursors of an adaptive evolutionary theory of economic change, *Revue Economique*, **54**, 407–31.

Mokyr, J. (2002), *The Gift of Athena: Historical Origins of the Knowledge Economy*, Princeton, NJ: Princeton University Press.

Mokyr, J. (2004), 'Useful knowledge as an evolving system: a view from economic history', paper presented at the Jena Workshop on Evolutionary Concepts in Economics and Biology, 2–4 Dec.

Mowery, D. and Nelson, R. (1999), *The Sources of Economic Growth*, Cambridge: Cambridge University Press.

Murmann, P. (2003), *Knowledge and Competitive Advantage*, Cambridge: Cambridge University Press.

Nelson, R.R. (1998), The agenda for growth theory: a different point of view, *Cambridge Journal of Economics*, **22**(4), 497–520.

Nelson, R.R. (2000), Selection criteria and selection processes in cultural evolution theories, in J. Ziman (ed.), *Technological Innovation as an Evolutionary Process*, Cambridge: Cambridge University Press, pp. 66–74.

Nelson, R.R. and Sampat, B. (2001), Making sense of institutions as a factor shaping economic performance, *Journal of Economic Behavior and Organization*, **44**(1), 31–54.

Nelson, R. and Winter, S. (1982), *An Evolutionary Theory of Economic Change*, Cambridge, MA: Harvard University Press.

Perez, C. (1983), Structural change and the assimilation of new technology in the economic and social system, *Futures*, **15**(4), October, 357–75.

Schumpeter, J. (1934), *The Theory of Economic Development*, Cambridge, MA: Harvard University Press.

Schumpeter, J. (1939), *Business Cycles*, New York: Prentice-Hall.

Schumpeter, J. (1942), *Capitalism, Socialism, and Democracy*, New York: Harper and Row.

Smith, A. (1937, first published 1776), *The Wealth of Nations*, London: Henry G. Bohn.

Solow, R. (1956), A contribution to the theory of economic growth, *Quarterly Journal of Economics*, **70**(1), 65–94.

Solow, R. (1957), Technical change and the aggregate production function, *Review of Economics and Statistics*, **39**(3), 312–20.

PART 5

NEO-SCHUMPETERIAN ECONOMICS AND THE SYSTEMIC VIEW

53 Innovation systems: a survey of the literature from a Schumpeterian perspective
Bo Carlsson

Introduction

The concepts of innovation and entrepreneurship are probably Schumpeter's most distinctive contributions to economics.* One of the recurring themes in the writings of Schumpeter is the role of innovation ('new combinations') and entrepreneurship in economic growth. But his views on this topic changed over time. In his earlier view (articulated in *The Theory of Economic Development*, originally published in 1912), Schumpeter emphasized the function of entrepreneurs as that of carrying out new combinations; he viewed the occurrence of discontinuous and 'revolutionary' change as the essence of 'economic development' which breaks the economy out of its static ('circular flow') mode and sets it on a dynamic path of fits and starts. Three decades later, in his *Capitalism, Socialism, and Democracy* (1942), Schumpeter took the view that dynamic capitalism was doomed to fail because the very efficiency of capitalist enterprise would lead to monopolistic structures and the disappearance of the entrepreneur.

Schumpeter distinguished clearly, particularly in his early work, between the circular flow view of 'economic life', 'the economic system's tendency towards an equilibrium position' (Schumpeter, 1912, quoted in Schumpeter, 1949, p. 62), and the 'economic development' view in which 'changes in economic life are not forced upon it from without but arise by its own initiative, from within' (ibid., p. 63). Thus, the idea of studying innovation occurring within an economic system is certainly consistent with Schumpeter's emphasis on the need to understand not only innovation as a source of growth but also how it arises within the economic system, how it is implemented, as well as what its effects are on the economy and society. Yet, as Freeman has pointed out, in spite of Schumpeter's emphasis on the entrepreneurial function, his focus on the individual entrepreneur is the reason for the absence in his theory of 'multiple sources of information inputs from within and from outside the innovating organization and

* Financial support for this study from the Swedish Agency for Innovation Systems (VINNOVA) is gratefully acknowledged. I would also like to thank Xiaoling Yu for able research assistance.

857

the importance of a "national system of innovation" – the supporting network of scientific and technical institutions, the infrastructure, and the social environment' (Freeman, 1990, p. 26).

For reasons too complex to discuss here, most 'Schumpeterian' analysis has come to be based on *Capitalism, Socialism, and Democracy* rather than on *The Theory of Economic Development*. This is certainly true of the innovation systems literature, as will become apparent below.

The purpose of this chapter is to survey the literature on innovation systems that has emerged over the last two decades and to provide a broad overview of its contents: the types of innovation systems studied, the main questions analyzed and the main lessons learned. The chapter is organized as follows. We begin with a discussion of the theoretical motivation for the study of innovation systems. Next, an overview of the literature is provided, organized according to the types of systems studied: national, regional, sectoral and technological innovation systems. This is followed by a review of some of the important features and contributions of the literature. The chapter concludes with a discussion of lessons learned and future avenues of research.

Why study innovation systems?

The basic motivation for the study of innovation was provided by Schumpeter: the need to understand the nature and sources of economic growth. 'There is no disagreement with [Schumpeter's] insistence that innovation incessantly revolutionizes the economic structure and that this process of creative destruction is the essential fact about capitalism (Freeman, 1990, p. 22, quoting Schumpeter, 1942, p. 83). In this regard the study of innovation systems is similar to endogenous ('new') growth theory. Indeed, it is interesting to note that the study of innovation systems began in the late 1980s, at about the same time as the first publications on endogenous growth theory appeared (Romer, 1986, 1990; Lucas, 1988). But it differs fundamentally from endogenous growth theory. Whereas the latter focuses on the role of knowledge in macroeconomic growth, it leaves 'knowledge' in a black box in the aggregate production function. Innovation systems, on the other hand, refer to the microeconomic contents of the black box. In particular, innovation systems emphasize and analyze the role of institutions; as a result, both the analysis itself and the policy discussion to which it gives rise are much richer empirically and more qualitatively oriented. Also, the analysis is much less formal in nature. However, as this survey will show, there is still a gap in our understanding of the mechanisms that link knowledge and knowledge formation to economic growth.

Thus, the importance of innovation for economic growth may be taken for granted. But why study innovation *systems*? Innovation is closely related to knowledge: 'new combinations' give rise to new knowledge. Given a vast opportunity set and bounded rationality, actors in the economy gain knowledge both through their own efforts and (if they have sufficient absorptive capacity) through spillovers from other actors. Thus, internal R&D is necessary but not sufficient for economic growth. The very term 'spillover' suggests the unintended nature of the knowledge flow from the point of view of the individual actor undertaking research. It also suggests that the transfer of knowledge frequently takes the form of non-market interaction.[1] In fact, the more knowledge-intensive an activity is, the more it depends on non-market interaction. As a result, clustering of activity, both geographically and in terms of inter-industry linkages, is common in many industries, particularly in high-tech sectors such as biotechnology, electronics and computers, and software. Clustering facilitates the sharing and transfer of knowledge, competence, and skills.

Innovation systems can be viewed as institutional arrangements to facilitate spillovers (provide connectivity) among economic actors. Put differently, the systems concept is necessary in analyzing the economic impact of innovation when non-market synergies are important.

A systems framework brings out three things. First, *it makes it necessary to specify the components (and therefore the boundaries) of the system.* In some cases the boundaries of the system may be exogenous or easily defined by geography or administrative units, while in others the determination of boundaries is an inherent part of the analysis. Similarly, the components to be included, e.g., the various actors (individuals and firms, buyers and sellers) that normally interact in markets, as well as academic units, research institutes, government agencies, trade associations, and other units making up the institutional infrastructure, are sometimes easily defined, sometimes not.

Second, *the relationships among the various components in the system need to be analyzed,* especially the non-market-mediated interaction in the form of knowledge spillovers. In the areas of economic activity that are the most dynamic in terms of innovative activity, such spillovers are often pervasive, not rare exceptions. Therefore, they need to be included in the analysis, i.e., they are part of the system.

Third, *the attributes or characteristics of the components need to be specified.* These include the competencies and functions of the components that determine the system's performance (Carlsson, 1998, p. 158).

Statistical survey of innovation system studies, 1987–2002

The study of innovation systems began in the late 1980s, the first published reference being Freeman (1987). There were several precursors (Bowers *et al.*, 1981; Krupp, 1984; Saviotti, 1986) based on the engineering concept of 'technological systems' referring to complex systems of physical artifacts such as large electrical systems (Hughes, 1983; Bijker *et al.*, 1987; Mayntz and Hughes, 1988). This literature is not included in this survey.[2]

The most common definitions of innovation systems refer to national, regional, sectoral, and technological innovation systems. In addition, recently there has emerged literature on other innovation systems, particularly at the firm level. As suggested by their names, national and regional innovation systems refer to innovative activities within national and regional boundaries, respectively. Sectoral innovation systems refer to individual sectors or industries, while technological innovation systems are defined by a particular technology or set of technologies rather than by a geographic region or industry. To avoid confusion with the engineering concept of 'technological system', the term 'technological *innovation system*' will be used here.

The notion of innovation systems has generated a lot of interest among economists and other social scientists, as well as engineers. As a result, a large literature now exists. By the end of 2002, more than a thousand studies of innovation systems had been published. Collecting all these into a database proved to be a daunting and time-consuming task. After eliminating newspaper articles, book reviews, double counting of entries, as well as references to 'technological systems' in the engineering sense, we are left with about 750 entries. Half of this literature refers to national innovation systems (NIS). The other half is equally distributed between studies of regional innovation systems (RIS) and studies of sectoral/technological systems. Of these studies, 309 (41 per cent) were published in journals, the rest in books (42 monographs, 37 edited volumes and 364 chapters in books). The fact that most studies are published in books complicates the task of surveying and classifying this literature, since abstracts are available only for journal articles. Therefore, it has not been possible to review this whole literature in detail. Beyond the statistical summary and classification presented here, there are many topics to explore in further research; some of these are indicated in the analysis that follows. But the analysis of the more specific content of the literature remains somewhat impressionistic and superficial at this time; much more could be done.

National innovation systems (NIS)
Of the 381 publications classified as NIS studies, 147 (38 per cent) are focused on individual countries, of which 55 study European countries, 47 Asian countries, 22 Latin America, 14 North America, and nine the rest of the world. Japan is the most frequently studied country (17 studies), followed by China (11), Finland and Germany (nine each). The most

common orientation of these studies is toward policy discussion (66), general description of national innovation systems (21), and focus on a particular sector or industry (19). About one-third of these studies deal with developing or transition economies.

A total of 51 NIS studies are comparative in nature (comparing one country or set of countries with another); 164 (43 per cent of NIS studies) are not focused on any particular country or group of countries but discuss concepts/theory (56), policy (43), issues having to do with globalization (42), or other issues without reference to country. These could also be classified as general innovation system studies.

Regional innovation systems (RIS)

There are 201 studies focused on regional innovation systems (RIS). Slightly more than half (103 studies) are empirically oriented, focusing mostly on a particular region (62) or on multiple regions (24). More than half of these studies deal with regions within Europe. The other empirical studies are case studies of various sorts involving innovation surveys, patent analyses, globalization issues, or innovation policy. Of the 93 non-empirical RIS studies, 70 are conceptual in nature and 11 are policy-oriented.

Sectoral innovation systems (SIS)

There are 49 published studies of sectoral innovation systems (SIS), 30 of which focus on individual sectors or industries (the service sectors and the biomedical/pharmaceutical industry being most heavily represented); nine studies are conceptual, three are comparative, four are policy-oriented. The remaining three fall into a miscellaneous category.

Technological innovation systems (TIS)

The technological innovation system studies differ from others not only in that they are more narrowly focused (being defined by a particular technology or set of technologies rather than a geographic region or industry) but also in that they are more conceptual/theoretical in nature. This is largely a result of the need to establish both the core and the boundaries of the systems before the analysis can take place. These issues are much less problematic in other approaches. Also, technological innovation systems have three dimensions (cognitive, institutional/organizational, and economic: see Carlsson, 2002), while other approaches focus primarily on institutions. Thus, of the 149 studies of technological innovation systems, more than one-third (57) are conceptual in nature. The remaining two-thirds are either case studies of various sorts or otherwise classified. The biotech/biomedical/pharmaceutical sector is the most frequently studied

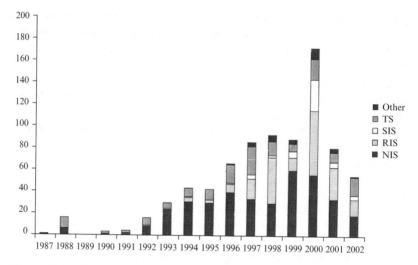

Figure 53.1   Innovation studies, 1987–2002

(17 studies), followed by agriculture (8), factory automation (6), and information technology (5).

Other innovation systems

The 'Other innovation systems' category contains 30 publications, 19 of which are conceptual in nature without specific reference to any of the types of innovation systems previously mentioned, or refer to innovation systems in general; 11 focus on corporate innovation systems and related management issues.

As shown in Figure 53.1, the number and focus of innovation studies have varied over time. After the first few studies on NIS (Freeman, 1987; Lundvall, 1992; Nelson and Rosenberg, 1993) and technological innovation systems (particularly focused on agriculture) in the late 1980s, the numbers increased dramatically in the early 1990s, peaking at 175 in 2000, and then declined sharply. Regional and sectoral innovation system studies began to appear in the late 1990s. The large number of studies published in 2000 appears to be a coincidental result of several books being published in the same year. The number of publications of RIS and SIS studies was particularly large that year compared with other years. Several books on RIS were published by Dunning, Holbrook, Boekema and others. Similarly, half of the SIS studies published in 2000 are chapters in books on the service sector (edited by Metcalfe and Miles, Boden and Miles and Andersen *et al.*, respectively).

Overview of topics and themes

Of all the innovation systems publications, 206 (27 per cent) are conceptual/theoretical in nature. As indicated already, the definition of boundaries and core activities is more problematic in regional and technological innovation systems than in others. This is reflected in the fact that a larger share of the regional (36 per cent) and technological (34 per cent) innovation system studies are conceptual than is the case for other systems. The corresponding numbers for SIS and NIS are 21 per cent and 16 per cent, respectively.

Of all the innovation system publications, 11 per cent have a sector focus. As one would expect, the SIS studies are the most sector-oriented: 58 per cent. (Other SIS studies are primarily conceptual in nature.) It is perhaps more surprising that as many as 9 per cent of both NIS and TIS studies and only 4 per cent of regional studies are focused on a particular sector or industry. To some extent this reflects difficulties of appropriate labeling. For example, studies of the role of particular sectors in a national innovation system are generally classified as both NIS and SIS. They are often parts of edited volumes focusing on a particular national innovation system and its components. In other cases the terminology used in the studies refers to national innovation systems, even though a sectoral designation would be more appropriate. Similarly, some TIS studies use the term 'technological' when 'sectoral' would be more appropriate. These difficulties are an unavoidable result of the procedure used to identify entries in the database. It is interesting to note, however, that the sector focus has shifted markedly over time. All innovation system studies have become much more sector-oriented (18 per cent in 2000–2002, compared with only 11 per cent in 1987–99). The shift has been particularly dramatic in NIS studies: from 6 per cent in 1987–99 to 16 per cent in 2000–2002. This suggests that, as more has been learned about innovation systems at all levels (and especially at the national level), there is a greater need for more detailed, micro-based studies.

Only a small subset (about 60 studies) can be considered 'dynamic' in the sense that they focus on a historical process or development over time rather than on a snapshot of a system in a particular time period. There are even fewer studies dealing with new system formation, leaving an as yet wide-open area for future research. It is tempting to conclude that Schumpeter's vision of the dynamics of what he called the 'economic system' is not yet fully developed: most studies still adhere to a static view of the world.

Schumpeter distinguished sharply between invention (the original idea for a new product or process), innovation (its conversion into a commercializable product) and the diffusion of innovations. The innovation systems literature is heavily oriented to the earlier (invention) stage and, to some extent, diffusion, with relatively little emphasis on the innovative (entrepreneurial) stage. This is somewhat surprising, given the prominence of entrepreneurship in Schumpeter's work, and the Schumpeterian origin of innovation system studies. Only about 20 studies address entrepreneurial issues. Thus, it appears that innovation systems are more deeply rooted in Schumpeter's later work (*Capitalism, Socialism, and Democracy*) than in his earlier work (*The Theory of Economic Development*) that features the individual entrepreneur more prominently. It also appears that, to the extent that entrepreneurial activity is necessary to convert innovation into economic growth, there is a missing link in the innovation systems literature.

This is reflected also in the discussion and analysis of public policy in the literature. Of all the publications, 190 (25 per cent) deal with policy issues. The NIS studies tend to be the most policy-oriented (34 per cent), while 24 per cent of RIS and 13 and 12 per cent of sectoral and technological innovation system studies, respectively, have a policy focus. Again, this state of affairs is no surprise. To a large extent it reflects the fact that it is easier to identify the relevant policy makers with respect to nations and regions than in sectoral and technological systems. It is also easier to identify policy measures at the national level than at other levels.

As one would expect, the policy discussion in the NIS studies tends to focus on national policies with respect to the technology infrastructure: promotion of R&D, intellectual property rights (especially, patent laws), the role of public and private research and technology institutes (particularly university–industry collaboration, technology transfer, and the role of science parks), as well as trade policy and the role of foreign direct investment. This reflects the fact that public policies in all these areas form an important part of the infrastructure for all innovation systems within nations (including regional, sectoral, and technological innovation systems). The lower the level of aggregation, the more qualitative and specific the policy analysis becomes, focusing more on interaction among actors and on institution building. It is therefore difficult to summarize briefly. However, it can safely be said that, throughout the innovation systems literature, the primary policy concern is to improve the technology infrastructure and therefore increase the supply (and to some extent improve the diffusion) of innovations rather than stimulating entrepreneurship.

Even though institutions are deeply imbedded in innovation systems and are the primary focus in many studies, it should be noted that the definition of 'institutions' varies among studies and that, as a result, there is considerable confusion about what institutions are and what role they play. Some authors, (e.g., Freeman, 1987; Nelson and Rosenberg, 1993) refer to institutions as networks or organizations supporting technical innovation, while Lundvall (1992) stresses the 'institutional set-up' in the sense of rules or regimes that determine behavior. Carlsson and Stankiewicz (1991) refer to the set of institutional arrangements in the form of both regimes and organizations.[3] What is clear is that most innovation system studies use the notion of supporting organizations and that there is not much analysis or discussion of the specific mechanisms through which institutions work.

One consequence of this lack of in-depth analysis of institutional arrangements is a relative neglect of the role of financial institutions, mechanisms, and arrangements. Only five studies have finance as their primary focus. This is in sharp contrast to Schumpeter's thinking. As Freeman has observed, Schumpeter devoted far more attention to the financial side of business cycles (in his *Business Cycles*, published in 1939) than to inventions and innovations. 'More important was his preoccupation with the individual entrepreneur and the individual innovation, and his reluctance to conceptualize invention, innovation, and technology accumulation as a social process. This is related to his theory of diffusion with its sharp distinction between truly original entrepreneurs and routine managers and imitators' (Freeman, 1990, p. 24). Of course, another reason for the relative lack of emphasis on the finance of entrepreneurial enterprise is the limited attention given to entrepreneurial activities in innovation systems.

More or less in parallel with innovation system studies there has emerged another branch of economic analysis that has many similar features, namely the study of industry clusters. A lot of this work has been inspired by Porter (1990) and colleagues. What is the difference between a cluster and an innovation system? If a cluster is defined as a set of closely related business activities in a certain geographic region, the difference would be that an innovation system differs from a cluster in that it takes into consideration the whole set of factors (especially institutional ones) that are conducive to the formation of a cluster. Most cluster definitions in the literature thus far ignore institutions (Porter being a notable exception). Probably mostly for this reason there is surprisingly little overlap between 'cluster-focused' and innovation system-focused publications: only 63 out of 752 innovation system publications reviewed here mention clusters. But the overlap between the two strands of literature has increased over time, most of it involving publications in 1996 and later.

As mentioned earlier, about 50 NIS studies are focused on individual developing or transition countries. Many of these are cross-referenced as SIS or TIS studies also. Beyond these, there is an additional handful (about ten) publications dealing with innovation systems in developing/transition economies but not focusing on any particular country. It seems fair to say that this is a relatively undeveloped part of the innovation systems literature.

But there seems to be increasing interest in innovation systems in developing or transition economies; the vast majority of publications in this area have appeared in 1999 or later. Many of these studies deal with the problem of catching up with more advanced countries and importing technology, knowledge, and ideas, particularly via direct foreign investment and repatriation of nationals educated abroad.

Another area that has not received much attention in the innovation systems literature is the performance of various systems. Only about 20 studies are aimed at assessing the performance of innovation systems. There may be several reasons for this. One is certainly the difficulty of measuring performance: what indicators should be used? (Only 11 studies discuss measurement issues specifically.) What indicates high or low performance; i.e., what should be the standard? Relative to a different time period? This requires historical data that are difficult to obtain. Comparisons with other systems? Given the detailed and complex data requirements, such analyses are also extremely difficult.

One consequence of the lack of performance data and analyses is that there is still no connection between innovation and economic growth. Through the study of innovation systems we have learned a lot about the contents of the 'black box' that converts innovation into economic growth, but there are still missing links. As already indicated, the role of entrepreneurship connecting invention via innovation to successful commercial application and diffusion is poorly understood. While there has been a lot of recent work on entrepreneurship, it has not generally been integrated with innovation systems. Also, there has not been much theoretical work explicitly connecting innovation systems to economic growth. As a result, there is little formal modeling in the innovation systems literature. Only ten studies involve modeling; six of these pertain to technological innovation systems. Beyond a few simulation studies there is no empirical testing of hypotheses. Thus, in spite of hundreds of innovation system studies, we have not really advanced much (yet) beyond the endogenous growth model. We still lack understanding of how to measure success and what makes innovation systems successful. There is still much to be done.

What have we learned, and what difference does research on innovation systems make?

Perhaps the most important insight gained from the study of innovation systems is a better understanding of how complex innovation systems are, and how complex the growth process is. There is much more to innovation – and to economic growth – than an aggregate production function captures. Even though there are still missing elements in our understanding of the links between innovation and economic growth, the study of innovation systems has already resulted in a deeper and more comprehensive view of economic growth. This is certainly consistent with Schumpeter's ideas about growth originating within the system and about the role of history and institutions. The new insights are limited but they are still useful in that (1) they help economists better understand how to think about innovation and its role in economic growth, and (2) they put industrial/technology policy in a broader framework than was the case previously. The questions raised are different and more qualitatively oriented, with attention given not only to the end results but also to the mechanisms involved. Even though the policy recommendations may differ, there is certainly consensus that more attention than in the past needs to be given to institutions and institution building. Policy makers have responded at all levels, from international organizations such as the OECD and national governments (by reorganizing their technology policies and agencies to focus on innovation *systems* as distinct from more piecemeal policies) to regional and sectoral agencies. The various systems approaches are complements, not substitutes, each focusing on a particular domain with its own issues, problems and opportunities. The policy recommendations vary among the various systems approaches, but they are not necessarily inconsistent. They basically reflect the fact that different systems address different questions.

Though the study of innovation systems has charted a new course in economic analysis, it is not a smooth and easy one. There are many obstacles and bumps in the road ahead: how to formalize the theoretical insights that have already been gained; how to link microeconomic phenomena to macroeconomic outcomes; and how to measure correctly both inputs and outputs are just a few. There seems to be no escaping building the micro foundations (i.e., micro dynamics) for understanding macroeconomic growth. Innovation system studies represent an important step in the right direction.

Notes

1. While knowledge may be transferred through market transactions (contracts), it seems inappropriate to refer to such knowledge transfers as 'spillovers'.
2. For a description of the methodology used in this study, see the Appendix.
3. For further discussion of these definitions, see Edquist and Johnson (1997).

Appendix
Data sources
Data for the present study have been obtained from a variety of sources, mostly on-line. The Social Science Citation Index as well as ABI Inform and EconLit were used to obtain references and abstracts for journal articles. In some cases data had to be entered separately for journals not covered in these indices. For books the main sources were EconLit and

library catalogs, particularly OhioLink, a joint catalog of the university libraries in Ohio. In a few cases data were entered separately, based on the author's own research.

Methodology

The above-mentioned databases were searched for references using various combinations of the keywords: Innovation System or Systems, National Innovation System(s), Regional Innovation System(s), Sectoral Innovation System(s), and Technological System(s). This search yielded over 600 references that were then entered into a database using the EndNote program. Each entry was given an initial classification depending on what keyword combination had been used to identify the publication. Multiple entries of the same publication were eliminated, but only after all the appropriate classifications had been recorded. (Thus, for example, entries found under the keywords 'National Innovation System' and also under 'Regional System of Innovation' were classified with both an NIS and an RIS code.) Newspaper articles and book reviews were eliminated. Publications pertaining to the engineering definition of 'Technological System' were also eliminated. Through this process, about 100 entries were removed.

A classification system for each type of innovation system was devised as follows:

NIS studies were classified according to the following categories:
  Individual country focus
  Comparative studies
  Non-country focus
  Conceptual
  Sector or industry focus
  Policy-oriented
  Performance assessment-oriented
  Developing/transition economy focus
  Concern with globalization (incl. multinational firms and direct foreign
    investment)
  General description of NIS
  Management/business behavior-oriented
  Miscellaneous
RIS studies were classified as follows:
  Empirical
    Focus on a particular region
      Europe
      Outside Europe
        Canada

                    Other
                Multiple regions
                    Europe
                    Outside Europe
            Non-empirical
                Conceptual
                Other
                    Policy
                    Globalization
                    Miscellaneous
SIS studies were classified as follows:
    Conceptual
    Sector or industry focus
        Service sector
        Biomedical/pharmaceutical
        Other sectors/industries
    Comparative
    Policy-oriented
    Miscellaneous
TIS studies were classified as follows:
    Case studies
        Historical/evolutionary
            Biotechnology/Biomedicine/Pharmaceutical
            Agriculture
            Factory Automation
            Information Technology
            Other industries
        Other case studies
            Comparative
            Policy-oriented
            Miscellaneous
    Conceptual
        Modeling
        Policy-oriented
        Other
    Miscellaneous

Each entry in the database was coded (manually) with the appropriate labels. Most entries were found to fit in several categories and thus received several labels. For journal articles, titles, abstracts and keywords were used to classify items. For many books (including most edited volumes), a table of contents was available on-line, but no abstract or keyword. In some cases a table of contents was not available on-line but was entered separately from other sources. In the remaining cases (mostly monographs) only the title was available. For edited volumes with table of contents, each relevant chapter was entered separately under its author's name. Thus, an edited volume with 12 chapters might be represented by 13 entries in the database (one entry for each chapter and one for the volume as a whole). In cases where only one or two chapters could be classified, only the chapters were entered into the database and the book entry was removed.

Through this process several hundred entries were added to the database. After further checking, the final database for this study included 752 items.

References

Andersen, B., J. Howells, R. Hull, I. Miles and J. Roberts (eds) (2000). *Knowledge and Innovation in the New Service Economy*, PREST/CRIC studies in science, technology, and innovation, Cheltenham, UK and Northampton, MA: Edward Elgar.

Bijker, W.E., T.P. Hughes and T. Pinch (eds) (1987). *The Social Construction of Technological Systems: New Directions in the Sociology and History of Technology*, Cambridge, MA: MIT Press.

Boden, M. and I. Miles (eds) (2000). *Services and the Knowledge-Based Economy*, London: Continuum.

Bowers, D.A., C.R. Mitchell and K. Webb (1981). Modelling bicommunal conflict: structuring the model, *Futures*, **13**(1), 31.

Carlsson, B. (1998). 'Innovation and knowledge spillovers: a systems cum evolutionary perspective', in G. Eliasson and C. Green (eds), *Microfoundations of Economic Growth: A Schumpeterian Perspective*, Ann Arbor, MI: The University of Michigan Press, pp. 156–68.

Carlsson, B. (ed.) (2002). *Technological Systems in the Bio Industries: An International Study*, Boston, MA: Kluwer Academic Publishers.

Carlsson, B. and R. Stankiewicz (1991). On the nature, function and composition of technological systems, *Journal of Evolutionary Economics*, **1**(2), 93–118.

Edquist, C. and B. Johnson (1997). 'Institutions and organizations in systems of innovation', in C. Edquist (ed.), *Systems of Innovation: Technologies, Institutions and Organizations*, London and Washington: Pinter, pp. 41–63.

Freeman, C. (1987). *Technology Policy and Economic Performance: Lessons from Japan*, London: Pinter.

Freeman, C. (1990). 'Schumpeter's business cycles revisited', in A. Heertje and M. Perlman (eds), *Evolving Technology and Market Structure: Studies in Schumpeterian Economics*, Ann Arbor, MI: The University of Michigan Press, pp. 17–38.

Hughes, T.P. (1983). *Networks of Power: Electrification in Western Society, 1880–1930*, Baltimore, MD: Johns Hopkins University Press.

Krupp, H. (1984). 'Overview of policy issues: panel report on the functions of non-university research institutes in national R&D and innovation systems and the contributions of universities', in H.I. Fusfeld and C.S. Haklisch (eds), *University–Industry Research Interactions*, New York: Pergamon, pp. 95–100.

Lucas, R.E., Jr (1988). On the mechanics of economic development, *Journal of Monetary Economics*, **22**, 3–42.

Lundvall, B.-Å. (ed.) (1992). *National Systems of Innovation : Towards a Theory of Innovation and Interactive Learning*, London and New York: Pinter Publishers.

Mayntz, R. and T.P. Hughes (eds) (1988). *The Development of Large Technical Systems*, Boulder, CO: Westview Press.

Metcalfe, J.S. and I. Miles (eds) (2000). *Innovation Systems in the Service Economy: Measurement and Case Study Analysis*, Boston, MA: Kluwer Academic Publishers.

Nelson, R.R. and N. Rosenberg (1993). 'Technical innovation and national systems', in R.R. Nelson (ed.), *National Innovation Systems: A Comparative Analysis*, New York: Oxford University Press.

Porter, M.E. (1990). *The Competitive Advantage of Nations*, New York: The Free Press.

Romer, P. (1986). Increasing returns and long-run growth, *Journal of Political Economy*, **94**(5), 1002–37.

Romer, P. (1990). Endogenous technological change, *Journal of Political Economy*, **98**(5, pt 2), S71–S102.

Saviotti, P.P. (1986). Systems theory and technological change, *Futures*, **18**(6), 773.

Schumpeter, J.A. (1912). *Theorie der Wirtschaftlichen Entwicklung* (English translation, 1934: *The Theory of Economic Development*, Cambridge, MA: Harvard University Press), Leipzig: Duncker and Humblot.

Schumpeter, J.A. (1939). *Business Cycles: A Theoretical, Historical, and Statistical Analysis*, New York: McGraw-Hill.

Schumpeter, J.A. (1942). *Capitalism, Socialism, and Democracy*, London: Allen and Unwin.

Schumpeter, J.A. (1949). *The Theory of Economic Development* (German original 1912), Cambridge, MA: Harvard University Press.

54 National innovation systems: from List to Freeman

Bengt-Åke Lundvall

Introduction

Today it is possible to follow the diffusion of new concepts in time and space by using search machines on the Internet. Giving 'Google' the formula 'national innovation system' you end up with a total of more than 200,000 references. Going through the references you will find that most of them are recent and that many of them are related to innovation policy efforts at the national level while others are references to new contributions to social science.

Looking more closely at the specific references shows that the concept informs policy makers all over the world, including the biggest countries in the world such as the USA, Japan, Russia, Brazil, South Africa, China and India, but also many small countries at very different stages of economic development.[1] This rate of diffusion is quite impressive taking into account that 15 years ago only a handful of scholars had heard about the concept. The concept has been taken on as a tool by policy makers at the national level as well as by experts in international organizations for economic co-operation such as OECD, UNCTAD, the World Bank and the EU Commission.

It has also inspired analytical efforts related to different disciplines within social science. Economists, business economists, economic historians, sociologists and, not least, economic geographers have utilized the concept in their attempts to explain and understand phenomena related to innovation and competence building. Directly and indirectly the concept has affected the direction of analytical efforts in different disciplines. One example is the growing analytical efforts to understand the formation and importance of industrial clusters and other vertically interconnected meso-units, as opposed to the traditional focus on the 'industry' as an analytical unit in industrial economics. The growing number of studies of industrial districts understood as regional knowledge-based networks of firms and institutions has changed the way geographical location and agglomeration is explained in economic geography. In both cases recent progress has been inspired by the systemic approach to innovation processes.

It may be worthwhile to reflect upon how and why the concept has spread so rapidly among scholars and policy makers. In this chapter we try to see how the concept originated and developed. Actually, this story has some parallels with the way major innovations such as the computer occurred and developed. Put briefly, Friedrich List may be seen as the Babbage and Christopher Freeman as the Shockley of the NSI concept. The parallel efforts to develop the modern computer and the co-existence of alternative configurations (interpretations) may be found also in the development of the NSI concept.

A concept with roots far back in history: from List to Freeman

Some of the basic ideas behind the concept 'national systems of innovation' go back to Friedrich List (List, 1841). His concept 'national systems of production' took into account a wide set of national institutions including those engaged in education and training as well as infrastructures such as networks for transportation of people and commodities (Freeman, 1995). He focused on the development of productive forces rather than on allocation issues. He was critical and polemic regarding the 'cosmopolitan' approach of Adam Smith, where free trade was assumed to be to the advantage of the weak as well as the strong national economies. Referring to the 'national production system', List pointed to the need to build national infrastructure and institutions in order to promote the accumulation of 'mental capital' and use it to spur economic development rather than just to sit back and trust 'the invisible hand' to solve all problems.

The first written contribution that used the concept 'national system of innovation' is, to the best of my knowledge, an unpublished paper by Christopher Freeman from 1982 that he worked out for the OECD expert group on Science, Technology and Competitiveness (Freeman, 1981, p. 18). The paper, titled 'Technological infrastructure and international competitiveness', was written very much in the spirit of Friedrich List, pointing out the importance of an active role for government in promoting technological infrastructure.

It pointed to the limited relevance of short-term strategies such as manipulating national wage and currency rates when it comes to strengthening the international competitiveness of an economy. One of the major points in the paper is that, in order to explain why and how world economic supremacy moves from one country to another, we need to consider how new technological systems come forward and how they match or mismatch the existing national patterns of institutions. Countries thriving in an era where one technological system is dominant may become victims of their own success since they will have great difficulties in adapting their institutional set-up to the new technological system.[2]

Parallel efforts to develop the innovation system concept

At the beginning of the 1980s the idea of a national system of innovation was immanent in the work of several economists working on innovation research. Dick Nelson and other US scholars worked on comparing the role of US universities in relation to innovation in firms with such patterns in Japan and Europe. SPRU at Sussex University pursued several studies comparing industrial development in Germany and the UK, covering for instance differences in the management of innovation, work practices and engineering education. More often than not the analysis concluded that there were serious weaknesses in the British system.

The idea of a national system of innovation was immanent also in the research program pursued by the IKE group at Aalborg University.[3] The program was inspired both by French structuralist economists, who used the concept 'national system of production' as an analytical tool in explaining economic growth, and by the SPRU tradition with its focus on international comparative studies of innovation. In the early 1980s we were struggling toward establishing 'a new combination' based on these two elements and building upon our own empirical work, and in several working papers and publications from this period we referred to 'the innovative capability of the national system of production'. The first time the more handy 'innovation system' appears in an Aalborg publication is in Lundvall (1985), but then without the adjective 'national'. In this booklet on user–producer interaction and product innovation the concept was used to analyze innovation processes involving firms and knowledge institutions in interaction. A general assumption behind the analysis, that remains central in more recent work on innovation systems, was that innovation and learning are context-dependent, interactive processes, rooted in the production structure.

Again, it was Chris Freeman who brought the modern version of the full concept 'national innovation system' into the literature. He did so in 1987 in his book on innovation in Japan (Freeman, 1987). Here the analysis was quite inclusive, taking into account the intraorganizational as well as interorganizational characteristics of firms, corporate governance, the education system and, not least, the role of government. When Freeman collaborated with Nelson and others in the major project on technical change and economic theory the outcome was a section on 'national systems of innovation' (Freeman, 1988; Lundvall, 1988; Nelson, 1988). There followed three major edited volumes on the subject (Lundvall, 1992; Nelson, 1993; Edquist, 1997). While the book edited by Nelson brings together a number of case studies, the books edited by Lundvall and Edquist were organized according to different dimensions of or perspectives on innovation systems.

The contribution by Michael Porter on the competitive advantage of nations should also be mentioned here. He does not explicitly use the innovation system concept but there is substantial overlap between his approach and the literature referred to above (Porter, 1990). Especially worth noting is his emphasis on feedback mechanisms from and interaction with domestic suppliers and users as a factor that gives competitive advantage. By bringing in these considerations he opens up a debate on the potentialities of structural industrial policy.

Another strand of analysis goes under the heading of 'social systems of innovation' (Amable *et al.*, 1997). Here the focus is on socio-economic institutions and on nation-specific regularities related to labor markets, financial markets and industrial relations. It combines important elements from the 'school of regulation' with an analysis of innovative outcomes.

In the early 1990s, Whitley and others developed the parallel idea of 'national business systems' (Whitley, 1994; see Lundvall, 1999, for a comparison with the NSI concept). The national business system approach is going further toward linking the management styles, such as the degree of centralization in decision making to the national framework in terms of state intervention and workings of markets for labor and finance. It is less oriented toward innovation and change.

Common characteristics of innovation system approaches
As will be demonstrated below there are competing conceptions regarding what constitutes the core elements of an innovation system and there is also some disagreement on where to draw the borderlines of the system. Still it might be useful to see what the different definitions have in common. This it is my own interpretation and it might not be shared by everybody working in the field.

A first common characteristic is the assumption that national systems differ in terms of their specialization in production, trade and knowledge (Archibugi and Pianta, 1992). This is not a controversial assumption – for instance neo-classical trade theory would lead us to a similar assumption. One important difference is that among NSI analysts it is assumed that there is a dynamic coupling between what countries do and what people and firms in these countries know how to do. These couplings imply, first, that both the production structure and the knowledge structure will change only slowly and, second, that such change must involve learning as well as industrial change.

A second assumption behind the idea of innovation systems is that elements of knowledge important for economic performance are localized and not easily moved from one place to another. It is obvious that in a fictive neo-classical world where knowledge equalled information and where society was populated by perfectly rational agents, each with unlimited access to information, national innovation systems would be a completely unnecessary construct. A common assumption behind the innovation system perspective is that knowledge is something more than information and that it includes tacit elements.

A third assumption that makes it understandable why knowledge is localized is that important elements of knowledge are embodied in the minds and bodies of agents, in routines of firms and not least in relationships between people and organizations (Dosi, 1999).

A fourth assumption central to the idea of innovation systems is the focus on *interaction* and *relationships*. The relationships may be seen as carriers of knowledge and the interaction as processes where new knowledge is produced. This assumption reflects the stylized fact that firms, knowledge institutions and people do not innovate alone. This implies that the system needs to be characterized *simultaneously* through its elements and through the relationships between those elements. It is necessary to take into account the relationships when explaining how the elements change and – the other way around – what goes on inside the elements shapes and reshapes the relationships between them. Perhaps the most basic characteristic of the innovation system approach is that it is 'interactionist'.[4]

Sometimes characteristics of interaction and relationships have been named 'institutions', referring to the way this concept is used in its sociological sense: as informal and formal norms and rules regulating how people interact (Johnson, 1992). An alternative terminology emanating from evolutionary economics and the management literature is to refer to 'routines' as more or less standardized procedures followed by economic agents and organizations when they act and when they interact with each other (Dosi, 1999).

This is the other major dimension in which national systems tend to differ from each other. While neo-classical theory imposes one general rule of behavior (utility and profit maximization) on all agents, independently of time and space, the institutional approach recognizes that the history and context make a difference. The transaction cost approach, where the assumption of 'opportunistic behavior' takes us one step further in terms of unhampered instrumental and strategic behavior, has actually been helpful in demonstrating that the idea of one single rule of behavior is unacceptable (Lundvall, 1992). Recent attempts to measure social capital in different national contexts, primitive as they are, tend to show very dramatic differences between national systems regarding the preparedness to collaborate and trust individuals outside the primary group of the family (OECD, 2001).

Concepts such as institutions and routines are useful in a theoretical context but they are somewhat elusive when it comes to empirical (and especially when it comes to historical) studies. The development of formal and tangible elements of the technological infrastructure is more simple to describe and analyze. It is easier to track the history of the R&D department, universities and professional training of engineers than it is to capture changes in how people interact and communicate. And how such formal institutions and organizations function and interact with other parts of the system is certainly highly relevant for the understanding of the system as a whole. But the aim of a full-blown analysis of innovation systems remains in order to understand how international differences in both the tangible technological infrastructure and in behavior affect innovation outcomes.

A specific issue of theoretical interest is that the most advanced attempts to explain growth in standard economics – the new growth theory – tends to come up with conclusions where small innovation systems should be handicapped as compared to big ones (Romer, 1990; Fagerberg, 1995). Here the further analysis of 'social capital' as a factor promoting growth through its impact on learning capabilities may be one way to solve the paradox that small countries in the west and north of Europe have been more successful in mobilizing new technologies in promoting economic growth than most of the bigger and less homogeneous European national systems.[5]

Different definitions of the 'national innovation system'
It is obvious that different authors mean different things when referring to a national system of innovation. Some major differences have to do with the focus of the analysis and with how broad the definition is in relation to institutions and markets.

Authors from the USA with a background in studying science and technology policy, tend to focus the analysis on 'the innovation system in the narrow sense'. They regard the NSI concept as a follow-up and broadening of earlier analyses of national science systems and national technology policies (see, for instance, the definition given in Mowery and Oxley, 1995, p. 80). The focus is upon the systemic relationships between R&D efforts in firms, S&T organizations, including universities, and public policy. The analysis may include markets for knowledge (intellectual property rights) and the venture capital aspects of financial markets, but seldom the broader set of institutions shaping competence building in the economy, such as education of ordinary workers, industrial relations and labor market dynamics. The interaction and relationships at the center of the analysis is the one between knowledge institutions and firms.

The Freeman version and the 'Aalborg version' of the national innovation system approach (Freeman, 1987; Freeman and Lundvall, 1988) aims at understanding 'the innovation system in the broad sense'. First the definition of 'innovation' is broader. Innovation is defined as a continuous cumulative process involving not only radical and incremental innovation but also the diffusion, absorption and use of innovation. Second, a wider set of sources of innovation are taken into account. Innovation is seen as reflecting, besides science and R&D, interactive learning taking place in connection with ongoing activities in production and sales. Therefore the analysis takes its starting point in the process of production and product development, assuming, for instance, that the interaction with users is fundamental for product innovation.

To a certain degree, these differences in focus reflect the national origin of the analysts. In small countries such as Denmark, as in developing countries (a major concern for Christopher Freeman) it is obvious that the competence base most critical for innovation in the economy as a whole is not scientific knowledge. Incremental innovation, 'absorptive capacity' and economic performance will typically reflect the skills and motivation of employees as well as interorganizational and intraorganizational relationships and characteristics. Science-based sectors may be rapidly growing but their shares of total employment and exports remain relatively small.

In the USA, aggregate economic growth is more directly connected with the expansion of science-based sectors. In these sectors big US firms have an international lead and they introduce radical innovation in areas where the interaction with science is crucial for success. Even so, it may be argued that the broader approach could be useful also in the USA since some of the weaknesses of the US system may reflect the limited mobilization of employees in processes of technical and organizational change and a general weakness when it comes to establish cooperation among people and among firms. This was actually one of the major conclusions from the 'Made in America' MIT study (Dertoutzos *et al.*, 1989).

Other systems concepts
The basic idea of the innovation system may be seen as a generic concept that has found its application in several contexts other than the national. Over the last decade there have been several new concepts emphasizing the systemic characteristics of innovation but with focus on other levels of the economy than the nation state. The literature on 'regional systems of innovation' has grown rapidly (Maskell and Malmberg, 1997). Bo Carlsson, with colleagues from Sweden, had already introduced the concept 'technological system' in the early 1990s (Carlsson and Jacobsson, 1997) while Franco Malerba and his colleagues in Italy developed the concept of sectoral systems of innovation (Breschi and Malerba, 1997).

The regional, technological and sectoral systems have much in common with the basic characteristics of the national innovation system approach.

They focus on the interaction and interdependency between actors and organizations and upon the impact on innovation performance. But again they differ in their delimitation of the system. The regional system approach operates with a delimitation of the system corresponding to the 'innovation system in a broad sense', taking into account many different dimensions including the skill formation among workers. There is a tendency for the technological system approach to be more in line with the US 'narrow sense' focus on the science–technology nexus and on the interaction between knowledge institutions and firms.

The sectoral system of innovation is in a sense less systemic than the others since it is less focused on interaction and vertical relationships. At its core is an attempt to develop a taxonomy of industries based on a 'technological regime'. With reference to Schumpeter, sectors are, for instance, characterized as dominated by respectively Mark I or Mark II firms. This taxonomy is applied to the respective 'technological regime' with the mode of competition and other characteristics of sectors central in evolutionary industrial economics. The approach is interesting also because, when linked to international specialization, it offers an opportunity to analyze the co-evolution of sector specialization and institutional characteristics and how this co-evolution shapes and reshapes national systems of innovation in both these dimensions.

Schumpeter's theoretical testament and national innovation systems
Andersen (1996, pp. 1–8) shows how it is possible to find support for rather different methodological positions in Schumpeter's works. Schumpeter certainly felt a strong attraction to and was a great admirer of the new more formalized economics, including its use of mathematics and statistics, but he made it clear that he based his own work on 'the combination of personal observation, historical studies and economic theory'. He pointed out that 'there is nothing in my structures that has not a living piece of reality living behind it'. In his practice he certainly was a representative for what in modern sociology is known as 'grounded theory'.

Never was he so provocative in pointing in this direction as in his very last paper, presented two months before his death and addressed to an NBER conference on business cycles, gathering the elite among mathematical and model-building US economists. He was well aware of the degree of provocation, saying that now he would 'let the murder out':

> To let the murder out and to start my final thesis, what is really required is a large number collection of industrial and locational monographs all drawn up according to the same plan and giving proper attention on the one hand to the incessant historical change in production and consumption functions and on the other hand to the quality and behavior of the leading personnel. (Schumpeter, 1951, p. 314, here quoted from Andersen, 1996, p. 3)

He goes on to argue that the understanding of macro phenomena such as business cycles have to build upon insight into what happens with specific firms and industries. It is clear that Schumpeter at the end of his career endorsed theory building based upon comparative case studies. His proposals sound very much like a program for building theory through studying and comparing systems of innovation at different levels.

Notes

1. As far as I know, the Prime Minister of Finland was the first highly placed politician using the concept in referring to the need to strengthen the Finnish innovation system; he did so as early as the beginning of the 1990s. Some ten years later, the President of China, in a speech to the Chinese Engineering Academy, made a similar remark referring to the Chinese innovation system.
2. It is not surprising that Freeman's paper was never made public by the OECD since its message was not in tune with the neo-liberal ideas that were even more dominating the organization at that time. Actually, the publication of the report from the expert group, where R. Ingram was chairman, Francois Chesnais the academic secretary and I representing the Danish government, was delayed by several years because 'there were problems with the printing capacity of the OECD-secretariat'.
3. It should be mentioned that we had the privilege to interact with Christopher Freeman in several projects in this period and that many of our ideas were shaped in a dialogue with him (see, for instance, Freeman, 1981).
4. Actually the NSI approach has much in common with the methodological perspectives of the social psychological pragmatist school of Chicago and not least with the ideas of George Herbert Mead.
5. The idea that there might be a small country advantage rooted in the density of social interaction is not new. Svennilson (1960) and Kuznets (1960) both point in this direction when analyzing the importance of nation states in the context of economic growth.

References

Amable, B., Boyer, R. and Barré, R. (1997), *Les systèmes d'innovation a l'ère de la globalization*, Paris: Economica.
Andersen, E.S. (1996), *Evolutionary Economics: Post-Schumpeterian Contributions*, London: Pinter Publishers.
Archibugi, D. and Pianta, M. (1992), *The Technological Specialization of Advanced Countries*, Dordrecht: Kluwer Academic Publishers.
Breschi, S. and Malerba, F. (1997), 'Sectoral innovation systems', in C. Edquist (ed.), *Systems of Innovation: Technologies, Institutions and Organizations*, London: Pinter Publishers.
Carlsson, B. and Jacobsson, S. (1997), 'Diversity creation and technological systems: a technology policy perspective', in C. Edquist (ed.), *Systems of Innovation: Technologies, Institutions and Organizations*, London: Pinter Publishers.
Dertoutzos, M.L., Lester, R.K. and Solow, R.M. (1989), *Made in America*, Cambridge, MA: MIT Press.
Dosi, G. (1999), 'Some notes on national systems of innovation and production and their implication for economic analysis', in D. Archibugi, J. Howells and J. Michie (eds), *Innovation Policy in a Global Economy*, Cambridge: Cambridge University Press.
Edquist, C. (ed.) (1997), *Systems of Innovation: Technologies, Institutions and Organizations*, London: Pinter Publishers.
Fagerberg, J. (1995), User–producer interaction, learning and comparative advantage, *Cambridge Journal of Economics*, **19**, 243–56.

Freeman, C. (1981), 'Technological infrastructure and international competitiveness', draft paper submitted to the OECD ad hoc-group on science, technology and competitiveness, August, mimeo.

Freeman, C. (1987), *Technology Policy and Economic Performance: Lessons from Japan*, London: Pinter Publishers.

Freeman, C. (1988), 'Japan: a new national innovation system?', in G. Dosi, C. Freeman, R.R. Nelson, G. Silverberg and L. Soete (eds), *Technical Change and Economic Theory*, London: Pinter Publishers.

Freeman, C. (1995), The national innovation systems in historical perspective, *Cambridge Journal of Economics*, **19**(1).

Freeman, C. and Lundvall, B.-Å. (eds) (1988), *Small Countries Facing the Technological Revolution*, London: Pinter Publishers.

Johnson, B. (1992), 'Institutional learning', in B.-Å. Lundvall (ed.), *National Innovation Systems: Towards a Theory of Innovation and Interactive Learning*, London: Pinter Publishers.

Kuznets, S. (1960), 'Economic growth of small nations', in E.A.G. Robinson (ed.), *Economic Consequences of the Size of Nations*, proceedings of a conference held by the International Economic Association, London: Macmillan.

List, F. (1841), *Das Nationale System der Politischen Ökonomie*, Basle: Kyklos (translated and published under the title 'The National System of Political Economy', London: Longmans, Green and Co., 1841).

Lundvall, B.-Å. (1985), *Product Innovation and User–Producer Interaction*, Aalborg: Aalborg University Press.

Lundvall, B.-Å. (1988), 'Innovation as an interactive process: from user–producer interaction to the National Innovation Systems', in G. Dosi, C. Freeman, R.R. Nelson, G. Silverberg and L. Soete (eds), *Technical Change and Economic Theory*, London: Pinter Publishers.

Lundvall, B.-Å. (ed.) (1992), *National Innovation Systems: Towards a Theory of Innovation and Interactive Learning*, London: Pinter Publishers.

Lundvall, B.-Å. (1999), National business systems and national systems of innovation, *International Studies of Management and Organization*, **2**, 60–77.

Maskell, P. and Malmberg, A. (1997), Towards an explanation of regional specialization and industry agglomeration, *European Planning Studies*, **5**(1), 25–41.

Mowery, D.C. and Oxley, J.E. (1995), Inward technology transfer and competitiveness: the role of National Innovation Systems, *Cambridge Journal of Economics*, **19**(1).

Nelson, R.R. (1988), 'Institutions supporting technical change in the United States', in G. Dosi, C. Freeman, R.R. Nelson, G. Silverberg and L. Soete (eds), *Technical Change and Economic Theory*, London: Pinter Publishers.

Nelson, R.R. (ed.) (1993), *National Innovation Systems: A Comparative Analysis*, Oxford: Oxford University Press.

OECD (2001), *OECD Science, Technology and Industry Scoreboard 2001 – Towards a Knowledge-based Economy*, Paris: OECD.

Porter, M. (1990), *The Competitive Advantage of Nations*, London: Macmillan.

Romer, P. (1990), Endogenous technical change, *Journal of Political Economy*, **98**, 71–102.

Schumpeter, J.A. (1951), *Essays on Economic Topics*, edited by R.V. Clemence, Port Washington, NY: Kennikat Press.

Svennilson, I. (1960), 'The concept of the nation and its relevance to economic' in E.A.G. Robinson (ed.), *Economic Consequences of the Size of Nations*, proceedings of a conference held by the International Economic Association, London: Macmillan.

Whitley, R. (ed.) (1994), *European Business Systems*, London: Sage Publications.

55 Catching a glimpse of national systems of innovation: the input–output approach
Hermann Schnabl

1 Introduction

Long after Schumpeter pioneered the idea that innovations are at the heart of the economic growth process and a main source of economic evolution, this is the standard even in orthodox economic theory. We must, therefore, not be astonished that there are many different approaches to the analysis of possible pathways of 'transformation' of innovations into changing economic structures and performance. The achievements, from Solow (1957) to Romer (1986) or Grossman and Helpman (1991) in the area of orthodox economics, or Nelson and Winter (1982), Freeman (1987) or Patel and Pavitt (1994), as examples of the evolutionary neo-Schumpeterian type of economics, mark milestones of bringing 'innovation' into the center of economic thinking. This process could be subsumed under the general heading 'Analysis of systems of innovation' (Los and Verspagen, 2002), which is a very broad concept for getting a hold on the innovation phenomenon which, besides the core activity of 'innovating', encompasses different styles of innovation, informal institutions of learning and national (Lundvall, 1998, p. 409), sectoral (Breschi and Malerba, 1997) or regional (DeBresson, 1996) blends of approaches to 'time horizons', 'trust' or the way 'authorities' act with respect to innovation activities.

Empirical approaches to the analysis of this phenomenon are as widespread as the topic itself. This chapter focuses on the sectoral input–output approach, which rests on the basic recognition that technical change is based on the innovation activities of firms and the diffusion of knowledge incorporated in 'new' products, which are due to generic or incremental innovations in those firms. However, the single firm is not the focus of the analysis here, but rather whole branches or 'sectors' which are already, according to input–output traditions, sorted along prominent technological features. This might not always be an optimum approach to catch the current profile of technological advances in a national economy but the empirical researcher has always to compromise between the availability and the given quality of data and a certain goal of analysis, e.g. to catch certain aspects of a national innovation system. Thus, we must state that the empirical analyses of systems of innovation are always focused on 'proxies' because the definition of the phenomenon itself is rather 'soft'.

There are several indicators to the innovation process, which together describe the phenomena of innovation, such as R&D expenditures, the numbers of patents, the use of licences, marketing activities for 'new' products, patent literature citations etc. and one could fill libraries with the analyses of all the different indicators. It may, however, seem surprising that, if one applies different indicators to the same innovation system, the different analyses tend to produce a homogenous picture of the whole system; i.e. we have good reason to assume a *holographic metaphor* for innovation analyses. Despite the fact that an innovation analysis is restricted to only catching certain very limited aspects of the innovation system, it reveals more or less the whole picture of the system, which – staying with the metaphor – is somewhat faint or blurred, as would be a real hologram if you cut off larger portions of its projection basis. One may ameliorate this picture by adding more 'proxy' indicators to the analysis, which usually confirm and shape the picture already developed (Marengo and Sterlacchini, 1989; Schnabl, 2000).

According to the input–output perspective, where the products of one sector are the inputs of other sectors and thus 'transport' technological knowledge incorporated in those products downstream, a given sector also profits from the technological spillovers that travel with its inputs. Thus, the innovation effects do not only consist of the innovative activities created by the sector itself, but also of innovations that are 'imported' from other sectors via intermediary products or investment goods (including the use of patents/licences, cf. also Wolff, 1997; Verspagen, 1997).

To answer the question as to how much spillover a sector receives from the innovation efforts of other sectors included in intermediate goods, a so-called 'subsystem approach' is chosen here. As an indicator (= proxy) of the innovation activities of a sector, the R&D expenditures of that sector may be used as well as other possible indicators such as innovation expenditures (broader definition), R&D capital, R&D personnel or even patent numbers (cf., e.g., Keller, 1997). Each of these could, in principle, be suitable for signalling the innovation activities within the whole system of innovation. The formal advantage of the suggested approach is that we can combine quite different innovation indicators with the 'given' input–output data of the production system. Moreover, we are able to integrate the methodology of the so-called 'subsystem minimal-flow analysis' (SMFA). This tool, developed by the author (Schnabl, 1995a), more or less automatically identifies important technology delivery and technology user sectors, as well as their mutual connections. The result is finally a 'molecule' picture or 'system-of-innovation-compound' (see Figures 55.1 and 55.2) of the inter-industry technology flows under analysis, which mirrors the current core structure of the innovation system under investigation.

The following paragraphs describe the mentioned technique in more detail and show an empirical example of the 'innovation compound' of Germany in 1986 and 1995.

2   The subsystem approach

It is necessary to understand the basics of the subsystem approach. The concept of subsystems began with Sraffa (Sraffa, 1976) and Pasinetti (Pasinetti, 1973) and soon became an interesting component of input–output analysis. According to the simple Leontief input–output model given in eq. (55.1)

$$\mathbf{x} = (I - A)^{-1}\, \mathbf{y} = L\, \mathbf{y}, \qquad (55.1)$$

where $\mathbf{x}$ is a vector of dimension n, ($n =$ number of sectors), $\mathbf{y}$ the vector of final demand and A the so-called 'input-coefficient matrix' of dimension $n \times n$; a single element l_{ij} of the Leontief inverse L may be interpreted as the *multisector multiplier*. Therefore, a certain column of those elements within the Leontief inverse, let us say l_j,

$$l_j = (l_{1,j}, l_{2,j} \dots, l_{n,j}) \qquad (55.2)$$

is called the *subsystem* of sector j because the column of those multisector multipliers tells how much each of the n sectors j, $j = 1, 2, \dots, n$, has to produce directly (first round of stimulated production) and/or indirectly (all further 'echos' of this first round production through other sectors) in order to enable an increase in the final demand of sector j by *one* unit (i.e. 1€ or 1 billion €). Thus, in the input–output context, each sector is part of a subsystem of another sector. Thus the subsystem defines the total of necessary inputs sector j has to have in order to produce its own product.

The subsystem has a kind of twin, which is not as famous: we may call it the *distribution system*. While we extract the subsystem of sector j by extracting the jth *column* of the Leontief inverse, a glance at the *rows* shows something similar, but with respect to the *output* direction: the distribution of the products of sector i to all the other sectors. There is, however, a lack of symmetry here. While the input view which leads to the subsystem is based on the property of production necessities due to a sectoral production function, the 'distribution' has no such direct foundation in production theory. However, in the empirical reality, we find rather stable sectoral distribution coefficients which could be caused indirectly by technological relations or just by human ways of sticking to good business relations.

We are only one step ahead of the whole concept of the subsystem approach: the distribution of 'something' along the distribution system which is more or less incorporated in the goods produced and then comes with the delivery of this good. If we think of technology, we may take any reasonable indicator reflecting innovation activities and 'distribute' it along with the observable distribution of output goods of each sector i to all the other[1] sectors $j = 1,2,\ldots,n$. If we take, as an example, R&D expenditures in value terms, call it the R&D vector, then we can formulate the model as given in eq. (55.3) (cf. also Schnabl, 1995a, 1995b).

$$X_{R\&D} = <R\&D> <x>^{-1} (I - A)^{-1} <y>, \qquad (55.3)$$

where $<R\&D>$ now is the diagonalized vector of sectoral R&D expenditures. The matrix $X_{R\&D}$ is called the *R&D flow matrix* or matrix of intermediary technology flows (Schnabl, 1995a). In a row perspective, it reflects an 'imputation' of spillovers of the R&D expenditures of the sectors i, ($i = 1,\ldots,n$) to the n subsystems. As we already know, this shows how each sector i 'dedicates' its own R&D expenditures to the production of its own as well as the other final demand goods j, ($j = 1,\ldots,n$).

In summary, the *rows* of the R&D flow matrix show to what extent a single row sector i will be a technology deliverer to the production of the other final demand goods, while the *columns* show the contribution of the R&D efforts of other sectors to the final demand category of that subsystem. This in turn signifies to what extent the producer sector of the corresponding good j is a technology user. Thus the R&D flow matrix $X_{R\&D}$ mirrors the imputed inter-industry technology flows.

3   The subsystem MFA

The final step is then to visualize the flows by the use of the so-called 'subsystem MFA' (SMFA), which works *analogously* to the already known MFA (MFA = *M*inimal *F*low *A*nalysis, a tool for the elaboration of the so-called 'characteristic structure' of a production system; Schnabl, 1994) which, however, is not identical to the original MFA.

Similarly, as in the MFA, the Matrix $X_{R\&D}$ will be split into hierarchical layers which are defined according to the Eulerian power series of the Leontief inverse. These layers are the basis for deducing the R&D flows, as outlined in more detail in Schnabl (1995a, 1995b) and as briefly shown in the following equations. If we start with the well-known extension of the Leontief inverse and substitute $(I - A)^{-1}$ in eq. (55.3) accordingly,

$$L = (I - A)^{-1} = I + A + A^2 + A^3\ldots \qquad (55.4)$$

we can then separate the single terms into the mentioned 'layers' as given in eq. (55.5) to (55.7):

$$X_1 = <\mathbf{R\&D}><x>^{-1}A^1<y> \tag{55.5}$$

$$X_2 = <\mathbf{R\&D}><x>^{-1}A^2<y> \tag{55.6}$$

$$X_3 = <\mathbf{R\&D}><x>^{-1}A^3<y> \qquad \text{etc.} \tag{55.7}$$

The layers X_1, X_2, X_3,. . . etc. obtained in this process reflect the intersectoral technology flows as imputed to be exchanged between the sectors in the first round (X_1), the second round (X_2), etc. Of course, this approach of 'imputed' technology flows, heavily based on the assumption of underlying linear production functions, is quite debatable. But besides the fact that we have a kind of accepted convention here (which, in the end, is not a scientific proof at all), it is a proxy model which already has proven its workability, and (more importantly) is used here only in the sense of a 'consistent', i.e. tautological derivation, since, in contrast to standard input–output projection models using different time indices, we implicitly use the *same* time index; i.e. all the matrices and vectors used in eq. (55.3) refer to the same year in an empirical investigation. Thus, the approach to deriving a characteristic structure of the intersectoral technology flows of a country ends up in a graph for the year under investigation only. Therefore, the only way to get a glimpse of 'development' is to make a comparison of the structures of different years (cf. Figures 55.1 and 55.2).

In deriving this characteristic structure, we must decide which technology flow is 'important' and which is not. This is done by an endogenized procedure of MFA for finding a filter F which provides this distinction (for more detail, see Schnabl, 1994), using principles of information theory in order to 'catch' a kind of maximum informative structure (for other approaches, see also Gosh and Roy, 1998; Gregori and Schachter, 1999).

The next step of analysis is the *binarization* of technology flows. The flows will be checked in each of the k layers X_k with $k = 1,2,...,n-1$ for their importance. Thus all the technology flow layers X_1, X_2, X_3,. . . are compared, entry by entry to the filter F and then translated into the corresponding adjacency matrices W_1, W_2, W_3,. . . etc. That is, if the entry ij of a layer X_k of the given innovation flow matrix is $x_{ij}^k \geq F$, then the entry $w_{ij}{}^k$ of the corresponding adjacency matrix $\mathbf{W_k}$ constructed in parallel, contains the value 1, otherwise zero. Therefore the adjacency matrix $\mathbf{W_k}$ consists only of zeros or ones. It must be emphasized here that the filter F, once chosen, does not only remain the same critical threshold within *one* layer X_k but is

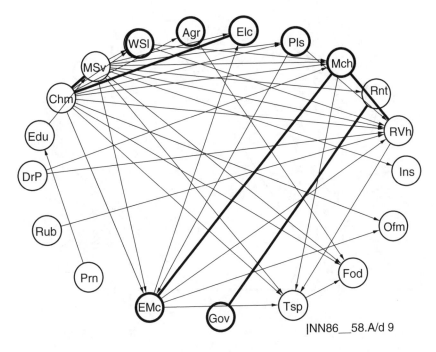

|NN86__58.A/d 9

Figure 55.1   The characteristic technology-flow structure for Germany,
1986[2]

fixed for *all* the layers X_k, $k = 1,2,\ldots, n\text{-}1$. It is clear that, if we step into 'deeper' intermediary flows as given in X_3 or X_4 etc. according to the vanishing powers of A in eqs (55.6) and (55.7), we will be finished very quickly if we have a filter F chosen relatively high as compared with the average value X^k_{ij}. Therefore, a high filter F brings a good structure, already in the early phase of the graph-theoretical mapping, whereas a low filter value allows for a deep-reaching structure but does not differentiate very well. Therefore the optimum filter will be somewhere between the extremes of possible F values.

Thus the $\mathbf{W}_k$ matrices for a *given* value of F, consist of only the 'economically significant' links reflected by the decrease of 1-entries with rising k. Each $\mathbf{W}_k$ matrix tells how many flows $\geq F$ exist *at* the respective intermediary level k, but they do not reflect links of greater distance (i.e. in between these levels). We are, of course, interested in these as well. In order to get the whole picture, we must use simple graph theory (cf. Harary, Norman and Cartwright, 1965). The way to do this is by linking the $\mathbf{W}_k$s according to eq. (55.8) or, in recursive form, eq. (55.9):

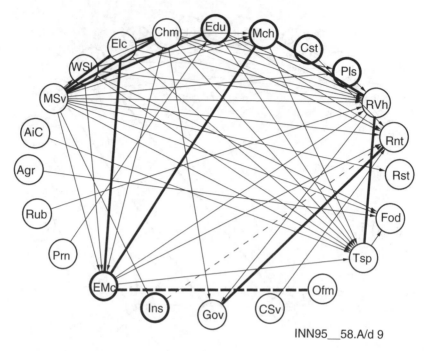

INN95__58.A/d 9

Figure 55.2   The characteristic technology-flow structure for Germany,
1995

$$W^{(1)} = W_1 * W^{(0)} = W_1 * I = W_1 \qquad (55.8)$$

and in generalized notation

$$W^{(k)} = W_{k-1} W^{(k-1)} \qquad (55.9)$$

for $k > 2$. Equation (55.9) determines the links between the layers, where the matrix multiplication is done in a Boolean way, i.e., the condensation of the product matrices $W^{(k)}$ into a so-called dependence matrix **D** is achieved by using Boole's addition (i.e. $1 + \#1 = 1$, signified by #):

$$D = {}_\#(W^{(1)} + W^{(2)} + W^{(3)} + \ldots) \qquad (55.10)$$

An entry d_{ij} is only 1 if there exists at least one (direct or indirect) technology flow from sector i to sector j satisfying the filter condition. The dependence matrix **D** is necessary to develop the so-called 'connexity matrix' **H**, which is given by eq. (55.11):

$$h_{ij} = d_{ij} + d_{ji}. \tag{55.11}$$

Thus, the connexity matrix **H** *qualifies* all connections by three indices, i.e., 0, 1, 2. As with the procedure of eq. (55.9) this is an efficient standard graph-theoretical technique in order to label automatically each sector with respect to its *degree* of connectivity. The individual values of h_{ij} then denote different types of connection:

$h_{ij} =$
   0 sectors i and j are isolated;
   1 a unidirectional flow exists from sector i to j;
   2 a bilateral relationship between sector i and j exists. The flows between sector i and j have at least the defined minimum.

All steps described above for a given filter value F are done 50 times by scanning through the range of sensible F values in equidistant steps, from $F = 0$ to a final filter value which would destroy the 'last' bilateral link. This scanning procedure produces 50 different 'structures' of the input–output table under investigation. The further steps of the SMFA – especially the extraction of the optimal filter F (= *endogenized Filter* F_{end}) from all 50 applied filter levels using an entropy concept to determine a structure with maximum information content – are the same as described in Schnabl (1994) for the MFA. We now present an empirical example that shows the potential of the described methodology.

4 An empirical example: Germany's system of innovation

4.1 Presentation of the results

Before we go into the details of empirical results, it seems necessary to make some remarks on their representation. The SMFA results are displayed in an ellipse graph (cf. Figures 55.1 and 55.2). Sectors not shown are, according to the endogenous filter used, interpreted to be not important for the technology flow system (with respect to the other imputed R&D flows in the matrix $X_{R\&D}$). The represented (= important) sectors may be identified by their location, which is given by a so-called 'centrality coefficient' as well as according to their links, depicted by different kinds of lines or arrows.

To obtain the position of an individual sector within the ellipse, a centrality coefficient c is used (for more details, see Schnabl, 1994). This coefficient, which is roughly defined as the ratio of input and output flows, maps into the interval [0; 2] and allows for a differentiation into source, center and sink sectors. Center sectors are emphasized by a bold circle and have roughly as many input relations as output relations. The ratio is about

$c = 1$. Thus sectors with $c \in [0.7, 1.3]$ were marked as center sectors (bold circles). The source sectors with a centrality coefficient below 0.7 are so-called 'technology deliverers' within the R&D flow system; their innovation output is higher than their innovation input, whereas the sink sectors ($c > 1.3$) are the main 'technology users' within the system – and have a higher innovation input than output.

We may recognize intertemporal changes of sectors between the three groups and start further investigations if necessary. While a normal innovation flow is represented by a simple arrow, a bold line (without arrow) denotes bilateral flow connections. Moreover, broken lines – fat or simple arrows – denote connections given at one filter level below the endogenous filter level. Thus broken lines hint at a possible 'death' or 'birth' of the corresponding link when analyzed in an intertemporal context. Which interpretation is correct may be decided by comparing successive graphs (Schnabl, 1995a). This opens up the possibility to realize basic features of structural development and to grasp hints for potential future development patterns.

4.2   The German inter-industry innovation system

Figures 55.1 and 55.2 show the structure of the German inter-industry technology flow system for the years 1986 and 1995. For this empirical example, we used the data of the German input–output table for 1986 and 1995 (Federal Statistical Office, 2000) and, as the necessary innovation–indicator, the vector of so-called 'innovation expenditures' calculated by the Ifo-Institute, Munich[3] for the same years. This indicator is a special type of R&D indicator, since it does not only contain pure R&D expenditures but also incorporates marketing costs included in the activities to promote certain innovations of the firms. Thus a disadvantage of the 'pure' R&D indicator is at least partially compensated for: since the success rate of R&D expenditures cannot be forecast adequately, this loosens the correlation between the innovation (in a final sense) and the efforts taken to achieve them, which indicates that the R&D expenditures are a pure input indicator. Adding the innovation-specific marketing costs shifts the relevance of this indicator more towards the features of an output indicator and thus we expect a closer correlation with the 'success rate' of the imputed technology flows. In other words, this type of indicator should make the 'indication' for a sectoral technology flow less 'proxy'.

Table 55.1 shows the distribution of the R&D sectors for Germany qualified as important by the SMFA according to the three categories of source sectors centre and sink sectors.

A comparison of Figures 55.1 and 55.2 as well as of both rows of Table 55.1 shows that there are typical locations for some sectors (put in a

Table 55.1   Grouping of relevant sectors for Germany, 1986,1995

Year	Source sectors		Centre		Sink sectors	
G1986	Chm,MSv,Rub,Prn,Edu		WSl,Agr,Elc,Pls,		Ins,Rnt,RVh,Ofm,Fod,Tsp	
		DrP	Mch,Emc,Gov			
G1995	Chm,MSv,Rub,Prn		Pls,Mch,Emc		Rnt,RVh,Ofm,Fod,Tsp	
	AiC	Sl,Agr,Elc	Edu	Ins	Gov	*Csv*

'column' display). The sectors *Chm* (Chemical products), *MSv* (Market Services), *Rub* (Rubber products) and *Prn* (Printing) belong to the group of source sectors (1986 as well as 1995) and are therefore the typical technology deliverers (TD) of the innovation system, while *Rnt* (Renting), *RVh* (Road Vehicles), *Ofm* (Office machines), *Fod* (Food) and *Tsp* (Transport) are members of the group of sink sectors (for the list of sectors and sector specifications, see Appendix A) and therefore are technology users (TU).

There are, however, several sectors which show some changing behavior between the two years. The sectors *Edu* (Education/Research), TD in 1986 and *Ins* (Insurance) become center sectors in 1995; the *Gov* (Government services), a center sector in 1986, turns into a TU in 1995. Besides those changes of 'position' in-between groups there is another source of 'change' due to the fact that new sectors emerge, such as *AiC* (Aircraft industries), a TD in 1995 which was not 'important' in 1986, and similarly *Csv* (Construction services), a TU for the same year, characterized by italic letters. The opposite move, a 'death' of importance, also occurs: *DrP* (Drawing Plants) vanishes from the list of important sectors after 1986.

The stable center sectors are given by *Pls* (Plastic products), *Mch* (Machinery) and *Emc* (Electrical machinery), while the sectors *WSl* (Wholesale), *Agr* (Agricultural Products) and *Elc* (Electrical Power) change from center to source in 1995 and become TD. Owing to limitations of space, this contribution is restricted to only showing the structural pattern and not extending the analysis to include possible reasons for those changes.

Another perspective is to look for bilateral linkages. This type of link between sectors may be interpreted as a potential feedback of interchanged innovations which could then be the source of incubation of further innovations: this depends on which of the following factors contributed to the 'strong' link of a bilateral connection: higher than average R&D expenditures, input coefficients a_{ij}/a_{ji} or sectoral final demand y_i (cf. eqs (55.5) to (55.7)). Which one applies, may be found by closer inspection.

For 1986, we have three bilateral chains: (*MSv*=*Chm*=*Elc*), (i.e. Market services, Chemistry, Electrical power), (*Emc*=*Mch*=*RVh*) (i.e. Electrical machinery, Machinery, Road Vehicles) and $(Gov=Rnt)$, (Government, Renting), where the sign '=' stands for 'bilateral connection'.

In 1995, this pattern is extended to a kind of 'spider-superstructure' $(ELC=MSv=Chm)=Emc=Mch=RVh=Tsp$, where $(Elc=MSv=Chm)$ form a bilateral triangle, a structure even more strongly interconnected because each of the three sectors stimulates other sectors and is stimulated by them at the same time, while the rest form a chain or a tail with the triangle as 'head' of the structure. As a future perspective, *Emc* could turn into a 'sub-spider-position' if we take the bilateral connection $Emc=Ofm$ (broken bold line in Figure 55.2) into account, which is classified as 'weaker' compared to the other bold lines. These superstructures of the German system of innovation may be viewed as its structural core, which can, as the example shows, be sketched like the structure of a chemical compound. The metaphor can be extended even further: as a comparison of Figures 55.1 and 55.2 shows, some of the bilateral links developed from simple arrows. Moreover, it may be expected that 'weak' bilateral links (broken bold lines) tend to turn into a standard bilateral link and bilateral chains tend to 'close' at certain positions into a bilateral triangle or even a higher superstructure. These are only tendencies which, however, form a certain basis for 'expectations' which may stimulate further detailed investigations. The main resources of these 'expected developments' are, besides a more or less autonomous development of technology itself, the differing elasticities of sectoral final demand as well as the elasticities of input coefficients (see the so-called 'Elasticity coefficient analysis', Schnabl, 2003; Schnabl, 1994, for the findings of a vanishing 'food-backbone' in the German production structure, as an example of the effects of decreasing income elasticities).

5   Summary
Our result is not surprising to somebody already familiar with investigations in systems of innovation. From 1986 to 1995, the sectors *Chm* (source sector) *Emc*, *Mch* (stable centre sector) and *RVh*, *Rnt*, *Fod* and *Tsp* (stable sink sectors) form the characteristic 'R&D flow system'. Four of them, Chemistry, Electrical machinery, Machinery and Road Vehicles, accompanied by Office machines, show up as important in almost every known empirical analysis of innovation systems (cf. Marengo and Sterlacchini, 1989; Schnabl, 2000, p. 175).

However, the methodology introduced here has additional potential insofar as it may not only tell *which* sectors are important but, moreover, *how* they are linked together and – as the chemical compound metaphor tells – which of them have a higher propensity to even closer links in the future. This, however, should not be mistaken as a kind of economic law but only be seen as a tentative approach to make well-founded guesses of future potentials based on a history better understood by tools such as the SMFA.

Notes

1. It must be mentioned that, in the distribution system, sector i also delivers to itself and in the subsystem sector j also gets inputs from itself. These so-called 'intrasectoral' deliveries appear on the main diagonal of the Leontief inverse and do not reflect sectoral interconnectivity, which is one of the basic issues here.
2. The lower right-hand signature of each graph tells to which table the graph belongs (in order to avoid a mix-up of graphs, once printed on paper. The coding is as follows: INN86: innovation expenditures for the year 1986; 58: dimension of IO-table used, this is the standard number of sectors in the official German IO-table; A/d9: 'A' stands for the German word 'Aktuell' which means that the *current* y vector of the year 1986 was used for the calculation (instead of a standardized y vector $\mathbf{y} = (1,1,1,...)$; finally the 'd9' code tells us that the filter used for plotting the graph was level 9 of the 50 possible. This ninth filter corresponds precisely to a certain amount of F (in money units) which could be looked up, but which would be, owing to inflationary effects, much less informative than its relative position within these 50 filter levels.
3. We wish to thank the Ifo-Institute for their generosity in making the two vectors for 1986 and 1995 available for this research.

References

Breschi, S. and Malerba, F. (1997), 'Sectoral innovation systems: technological regimes, Schumpeterian dynamics and spatial boundaries', in C. Edquist (ed.), *Systems of Innovation: Technologies, Institutions and Organisations*, London: Pinter, pp. 130–56.

DeBresson, C. (1996), *Economic Interdependence and Innovative Activity*, Cheltenham, UK and Brookfield, USA: Edward Elgar.

Federal Statistical Office (2000), Fachserie 18, Reihe 2, 'Input–Output-Rechnung 1995', Wiesbaden.

Freeman, C. (1987), *Technology Policy and Economic Performance: Lessons from Japan*, London: Pinter.

Gosh, S. and Roy, J. (1998), Qualitative input–output analysis of the Indian economic structure, *Economic Systems Research*, **10**(3), 263–73.

Gregori, T. and Schachter, G. (1999), Assessing aggregate structural change, *Economic Systems Research*, **11**(1), 67–81.

Grossman, G.M. and Helpman, E. (1991), *Innovation and Growth in the Global Economy*, Cambridge, MA: MIT Press.

Harary, F., Norman, R.Z. and Cartwright, D. (1965), *Structural Models: An Introduction to the Theory of Directed Graphs*, New York: Macmillan.

Keller, W. (1997), Technology flows between industries: identification and productivity effects, *Economic Systems Research*, **9**(2), 213–20 (Special Issue: Invention Input–Output Analysis).

Los, B. and Verspagen, B. (2002), An introduction to the analysis of systems of innovation: scientific and technological interdependencies, *Economic Systems Research*, **14**, 315–22.

Lundvall, B.-Å. (1998), Why study national systems and national styles of innovation? *Technology, Analysis and Strategic Management*, **10**, 407–21.

Marengo, L. and Sterlacchini, A. (1989), Intersectoral technology flows – methodological aspects and empirical applications, paper presented at the 9th International Conference on Input–Output Techniques, Kezthely, Ungarn.

Nelson, R.R. and Winter, S.G. (1982), *An Evolutionary Theory of Economic Change*, Cambridge, MA: Harvard University Press.

Pasinetti, L. (1973), The notion of vertical integration in economic analysis, *Metroeconomica*, **25**, 1–25.

Patel, P. and Pavitt, K. (1994), National innovation systems: why they are important and how they might be measured and compared, *Economics of Innovation and New Technology*, **3**, 77–95.

Romer, P. (1986), Increasing returns and long-run growth, *Journal of Political Economy*, **94**, 1002–37.

Schnabl, H. (1994), The evolution of production structures – analysed by a multilayer procedure, *Economic Systems Research*, **6**, 51–68.

Schnabl, H. (1995a), The subsystem-MFA: a qualitative method for analysing national innovation systems: the case of Germany, *Economic Systems Research*, **7**(4), 383–96.

Schnabl, H. (1995b), 'Technologieverflechtung in der Bundesrepublik Deutschland – ein Subsystemansatz', in H. Schnabl (ed.), *Technologieverflechtung und Strukturwandel*, Tübingen: J.C.B. Mohr.

Schnabl, H. (2000), *Struktur-Evolution. Innovation, Technologieverflechtung und sektoraler Strukturwandel*, Munich, Vienna: Oldenbourg Verlag.

Schnabl, H. (2003), The ECA-method for identifying sensitive reactions within an IO-context, *Economic Systems Research*, **15**(4), 495–504.

Solow, R.M. (1957), Technical change and the aggregate production function, *Review of Economics and Statistics*, **39**, 312–20.

Sraffa, P. (1976), *Warenproduktion mittels Waren*, Frankfurt a.M.: Suhrkamp.

Verspagen, B. (1997), Measuring intersectoral technology spillovers: estimates from the European and US patent office databases, *Economic Systems Research*, **9**(1), 47–66.

Wolff, E.N. (1997), Spillovers, linkages and technical change, *Economic Systems Research*, **9**(1), 9–24 (Special Issue, Intersectoral R&D Spillovers).

Appendix A   list of symbols and sector names

1	Agr	Agriculture
2	Fis	Fishery, etc.
3	Elc	Electric Power
4	Gas	Gas
5	Wat	Water
6	CoM	Coal Mining
7	Mng	Mining
8	Oil	Crude Oil
9	Chm	Chemical Products
10	MOi	Mineral Oil
11	Pls	Plastic Products
12	Rub	Rubber Products
13	Stn	Stones/Clays
14	Cer	Ceramics
15	Gls	Glass Products
16	ISt	Iron/Steel
17	NfM	Non-ferrous Metals
18	Cir	Casting Iron
19	DrP	Drawing Plants
20	StM	Structural Metal
21	Mch	Machinery

22	OfM	Office Machines
23	RVh	Road Vehicles
24	WaV	Water Vehicles
25	AiC	Aircraft/Spacecraft
26	EMc	Electrical Machinery
27	FMc	Fine mechanics
28	IMt	Iron/Metal Products
29	MuI	Musical Instruments
30	Wod	Wood
31	WMn	Wooden Manufacture
32	PPp	Pulp and Paper
33	PPr	Paper Products
34	Prn	Printing
35	Lea	Leather
36	Txt	Textiles
37	Cth	Clothing
38	Fod	Food
39	Bev	Beverages
40	Tbc	Tobacco
41	Cst	Construction
42	CSv	Construction Services
43	WSl	Wholesale Trade
44	Trd	Trade
45	RWy	Railway Services
46	Shp	Ship Transport
47	PTT	Post, Telecom
48	Tsp	Transport (other)
49	Bnk	Banking Services
50	Ins	Insurance
51	Rnt	Renting
52	Rst	Restaurants
53	Edu	Education/Research
54	Hea	Health Services
55	MSv	Market Services
56	Gov	Government Services
57	SIn	Social Insurance
58	PrO	Private Organizations

56 Schumpeter and varieties of innovation: lessons from the rise of regional innovation systems research
Philip Cooke and Nicole Schall

1 Introduction

In Cooke *et al.* (2000), we gave an extended account of the first systematic comparative analysis of Regional Innovation Systems (RIS) using identical methodology across 11 European regions. Region is defined, at least in terms of innovation co-ordination, as the meso-level of governance, between national and local. Thus our regions are places like Wallonia, the Basque Country, Baden-Württemberg, Friuli-Venezia-Giulia and Wales, each having its own Parliament with responsibilities to make policies, including innovation policies. It is crucial to stress that RIS are not like stove pipes or silos, but rather like leaky buckets used for shooting practice and with holes also in the bottom. Thus interactions towards the RIS come from the outside in all directions and similarly in a *transceiver* manner they are also directed outwards. It is important to stress this 'open systems' setting for any candidate RIS as many economic geographers, although fewer economists, political scientists or sociologists of innovation, have trouble comprehending this fundamental geographic notion of open systems regional governance as a noteworthy arena of debate, action, policy and evaluation of outcomes, especially in this context, which refers mainly to innovation.

A complexity, which political science has little difficulty in managing intellectually, is that the organizing and interlinking of power and influence occurs at multiple levels of governance. A useful framework for analysing policy from such a perspective is to postulate the idea of 'multi-level governance' (MLG) and analyse action and processes accordingly, noticing relevant coalescences and divergences among policies at key points in the MLG system. In Cooke *et al.* (2000) we did this and found explanations for the failure of policy proposals for certain regions where the nation state was over-intrusive with redundant perceptions of appropriate innovation categories. This met rejection from the supranational innovation funding and policy body in question, the EU. By contrast, where MLG was practised and even the lowest, municipal level was included in the innovation policy formation process, a more satisfactory outcome occurred. Thus, despite what some economic geographers say, with their abstraction to 'scale' to capture such effects, further complexified by tackling arrays of scales simultaneously so that globalization and (Schumpeterian) welfare notions get mixed up with economics, there is a regional *purchase*, as defined, on innovation policy in many countries. 'Purchase' means 'being a player' or 'being of consequence', not always or even the most important player, but a player capable of evolving distinctive variants on themes operating at different MLG levels that are relevant to the matter in hand. Thus we profoundly disagree with the likes of Bathelt (2003) who says regions do not exist, the only systems relevant to innovation being national, and they are such because they are *closed* systems. This is the 'fallacy of composition' taken to an absurd degree. Equally, we reject the confusion in 'scale' critiques like Mackinnon *et al.* (2002) who argue it is mistaken to invest 'region' with any influential role, but equally mistaken to deny 'region' with specificity. This seems to be wanting to have it both ways while denying policy specificity as a case in point.

In what follows we will report on the way we found, by direct inspection, how firms innovate and whether that equates to academic definitions of innovation, notably that promoted by the neo-Schumpeterian school as 'commercialization of new knowledge' to put it at its simplest. These results arose in examining the extent to which an RIS was identifiable in Wales, one of the 11 regions studied in the aforementioned research project. On balance we concluded there were characteristics of RIS such as sub-systems of knowledge *exploration* and *generation*, connecting firms to local and non- local universities and sub-systems of knowledge *exploitation* and *commercialization*, where, for example, new knowledge arising from such interactions was successfully sold at market. But much of this was orchestrated by the economic development machinery of government and its economic development agencies. Wales is thus an Institutional RIS (IRIS) compared to somewhere like Massachusetts, where entrepreneurship drives the RIS (ERIS). Having made this distinction (in 2003), a smart colleague asked if I (lead author) remembered Sidney Winter's (1984) article on institutional and entrepreneurial technological regimes, as it sounded similar. Of course, I had to admit I had never heard of it. In the next section we describe our methodological approach. Then we discuss the details of the results of intensive face-to-face interviews with firms. We reflect on the meaning of the results for policy before concluding.

2 Methodological approach

Our initial postal survey in the RIS research project (project acronym REGIS) enabled us to collect questionnaire information about 103 firms in automotive, electronics and healthcare industries. The assembled information enabled us to profile businesses in terms of performance, innovativeness, inter-firm and firm–organization co-operation patterns. However this survey gave us little information about the factors and processes of importance to more qualitative questions concerning competitiveness, co-operation and innovation. Thus face-to-face interviews were conducted with 15 companies to illuminate the innovation mechanisms of firms in the wider context of the organizational innovation support infrastructure in the region. We sought the nature and sources of their innovative activities, as well as their motivation for pursuing them. These are analysed in relation to the industry structure and the nature of supplier–buyer and plant–headquarters relationships. Innovation opportunities and barriers are then further examined in the RIS perspective in order to point out strengths and weaknesses of firms, organizations and their interface.

The 15 firms were selected, out of a total of 103 that responded to our mailed survey, because of their sectoral and innovation representativeness regarding the larger sample. Five companies were from the automotive industry, six were from electronics and four from healthcare. Why these industries? Because they are those having the strongest profile as 'clusters' with strong vertical and/or horizontal linkages and relations with knowledge and policy institutions. This region is an IRIS with some ERIS features in the SME population. Representativeness was pinned down by matching the sample to the industrial structure of these clusters in Wales, selecting a majority of small and middle-sized companies as well as a mix of single and multi-plant firms.[1]

In order to understand non-innovative behaviour and innovation barriers in the studied clusters, non-innovative firms were included in the sample. These companies would still modify their products according to fashion or customer demand, but cannot be considered as having introduced a 'new' product to the market.

The sample is slightly biased towards more innovative firms in order to find out about the processes and relationships underlying innovative activity in Wales. Nevertheless, the product and process innovations reported by firms are sometimes minor, and the question of whether or not the new product is actually an innovation arises. Table 56.1 provides an overview of the 15 face-to-face interviewed firms on these issues, representative of the sample of 103 companies that responded to the mailed survey.

3   Innovation: nature, sources and co-operation patterns

According to OECD, 'scientific and technological innovation may be considered as the transformation of an idea into a new or improved product introduced on the market, into a new or improved operational process used in industry and commerce, or into a new approach to a social service' (OECD, 1993). *Scientific* innovation refers to general, fundamental and abstract forms of knowledge, whereas *technological* innovation is specific

Table 56.1   Firm sample by size, cluster and employment (in brackets)

Size	Automotive	Electronics	Healthcare
1–49	Avonride (43)	**Gwent Cables (8)** S-W Cables (14) IndElectAuto (40) **Radun (41)**	Bioanalysis (8) Magstim (26)
50–199	**R-Tek (94)**	Stilexo (74)	**Simbec Research (85)** **Perkin-Elmer (189)**
200+	**Seal Techno (290)** **Borg Warner (260)** **Standard Products (320)**	**Matsushita (250)**	

Note: Firms in **bold** are multi-plant firms.

and practical, and results in new products and processes and significant technological change in products and processes. Scientific innovation nearly always occurs in university or public research laboratories; firms are mainly active in the application of new knowledge to various fields.

According to the REGIS mailed survey in Wales, 63 per cent of surveyed firms were engaged in product innovation (45 per cent of them had introduced a new product to the market in the three years 1993–6) and 52 per cent in process innovation (20 per cent of them had introduced a new process to the market during 1993–6). These numbers are considerable and thus, in order to verify the answer given in our questionnaire, one of the first questions in our face-to-face interview was on the nature of the product and innovative activity carried out within the company.

One company (Bioanalysis) conducts in-house basic research, but none of our interviewed companies has implemented a scientific innovation. However, a large majority of firms that had stated that they had implemented a technological innovation by introducing a new product in the three years 1993–6 had indeed done so. However, the new product offered by three out of the 15 companies only involved some modifications and not 'significant technological change'. These distinctions will be discussed in more detail below.

On the other hand, there is one healthcare company (Perkin-Elmer) that stated that it had not introduced any new products between 1993 and 1996; their research and development function is carried out at their headquarters laboratories. However, most of their products (e.g. sampling and sequencing analysis instruments) are customized and respond to specific needs expressed by customers from different fields (environmental, biochemistry etc.). Therefore, each of the resulting products can be considered as a distinct technological innovation.

Table 56.2   The sample by cluster, size and main product

	Firm	Main product or product range	
Automotive	Avonride (43)	Axle manufacture, wheels and tyres	
	R-Tek (94)	Moulded indoor car panels	
	Seal Techno (290)	Seals, valves and polymer gaskets	
	Borg Warner (260)	4-wheel drive transfer cases	
	Standard products (320)	Rubber seals for car windows	
Electronics	**Gwent Cables (8)**	Cable connections	
	S-W Cables (14)	Retail of specialized cables	
	IndElect. Auto (40)	System integration (i.e., automated process control)	
	Radun (41)	Wheel speed measuring sensors, 'sentinel' registration system, electronics assembler	
	Stilexo (74)	TV stands and consoles	
	Matsushita (250)	Printed circuit systems	
Healthcare	Bioanalysis (8)	Chemiluminescent analytical systems	+
	Magstim (26)	Magnetic nerves stimulator	+
	Simbec Research (85)	Drug testing	+
	Perkin-Elmer (189)	Scientific instruments (automated sample analysis)	+

Notes: Companies in **bold** are UK (not Wales) or foreign-owned multi-plants;
+ = implementation of and product or process innovation, respectively.

The distinction between *product* and *process* innovation has been particularly difficult for the innovation–intense healthcare sector. For these companies, the application of a technology generates products and processes that are intertwined in nature (e.g. drugs in pharmaceuticals) and are difficult to distinguish. Given the peculiarities of the healthcare sector, we have considered these companies as *product* innovators rather then (production) *process* innovators. For most companies in automotive or electronics, especially manufacturing companies, this distinction did not cause any difficulties.

Thus in Table 56.2, we present the main innovations by *products* or range of products produced by the company, indicating the adoption of new or significantly improved production methods (*process* innovation).

A high proportion of interviewed companies were relatively specialized, with two products produced on average and mostly using the same technology for both. The exception was Radun Control which, despite its small size, was very diversified in both number and nature of activities. The company provides a subcontract assembly service to all of the television manufacturers in South Wales, designs and develops speed-measuring sensors and associated instrumentation, hardware and software, and designs and manufactures magnetic recording heads and equipment. Furthermore, the company had heavily invested in the development of the 'Sentinel' registration system based on magnetic swipe cards. This was a radically new product on which the general manager aimed to base the future of his company. Selling at €40 000 (per item), the product was successfully marketed to the healthcare industry. Thus, Radun Control is the exception of our sample in which the tendency for small single companies is to specialize in niche markets and focus on one or two products within this niche.

Most firms implemented some kind of innovation, as indicated in Table 56.3. Automotive and electronics manufacturing companies pointed out the correspondence between *product* and *process* innovation. Product innovation usually involves process innovation as a necessity for production processes to be updated to enable implementation of production. Companies indicating a product innovation but not a process innovation are small firms focusing on research and development and outsourcing production or outlicensing their technology.

The distinction between scientific and technological innovation is useful in that it is defined in relation to the nature of *knowledge*, but it tells us little about the 'new' or 'improved' *product*. Thus, in order to reflect on the nature of these innovations in the latter sense, we suggest a distinction between a major product innovation and an incremental product innovation (see Table 56.1):

A *major product innovation* describes a product whose intended use, performance characteristics, attributes, design properties or use of materials and components differ significantly compared with previously manufactured products. Such innovation can involve radically new technologies [in which case it is a *radical innovation*][2] or can be based on combining existing technologies in new uses [in which case it is a *recombination innovation*]. (OECD, 1993)

An *incremental product innovation* concerns an existing product whose performance has been significantly enhanced or upgraded. This again can take two forms (in terms of improved *performance* or *lower cost*) through use of higher performance components or materials, or a complex product which consists of a number of integrated technical sub-systems may be improved by partial changes to one of the subsystems. (OECD, 1993)

Bioanalysis and the Magstim company both developed from academic research departments of universities. Within their previous position in

Table 56.3   Classification of interviewed firms by type of product innovation

Major product innovation		Incremental product innovation		
Radical	Recombination	Higher performance	Lower costs	Modification
Bioanalysis	IndElect Auto	Seal Technology		**Standard Products**
Magstim	**Perkin-Elmer**	Avonride	**Stilexo**	**Borg Warner**
	Radun Control	**Simbec Research**		**R-Tek**
				Matsushita
				Gwent Cables
				S-W Cables

NB: Companies in **bold** are externally (rest of UK or foreign)-owned multi-plants.

academia, both company owners researched and applied a radically new technology which today is at the core of the company: chemiluminescence and magnetic nerve stimulation, respectively. The technology currently used by Bioanalysis was patented in the early 1980s. The process of organizing the exploitation of this patent through the translation into the first marketable products took nearly 15 years.

Chemiluminescence is the emission of light from certain high-energy chemical reactions. Bioanalysis' proprietary technology involves linking chemiluminescent substances, reproduced in the laboratory, to binding reagents for use in analytical methods. This technology enabled the analysis of a large variety of substances, from small organic chemicals to viruses and bacteria in the bloodstream. Bioanalysis's more recent developments include diagnostic screening methods (i.e. detection and measurement of anti-HIV, Hepatitis B, insulin and proinsulin), environmental and food testing. Bioanalysis has successfully licensed and transferred the chemiluminescence technology to major diagnostics companies in the area of human clinical testing. The Magstim Company is active in the field of nerve stimulation and monitoring. It develops, manufactures and markets equipment for medical organizations, enabling them to assess, protect and stimulate the functioning of the nervous system in various applications (i.e. diagnostics for nervous disorders, locating and monitoring motor nerves during surgery).

As noted, Radun Control developed a new product, 'Sentinel', an electronic attendance register based on the use of magnetic strip 'swipe' cards. The product was an application of microelectronics technology to education and registration in general. It successfully launched as a patient monitoring system first sold to hospitals in the UK in the year 2000. Industrial

Electronics Automation and Perkin-Elmer are the other two 'recombination' innovators. Both had associated knowledge in testing and sample analysis with information technology (industrial automation, software). This has resulted in new products with new characteristics and functions that go beyond the possibilities offered by similar instruments used in the field. Smart card and scanning electron microscopy applications were areas in which customized recombinations had been conducted and successfully marketed. In the former case the innovation was made in the region and sold successfully outside it, including to a Japanese firm, Takiron, producer of vehicle batteries, UK firm Fyffes, the fruit shipper operating in the West Indies, and London's water company, Thames Water amongst others. The versatility of the recombinations is evident from this group of customers. Perkin-Elmer's innovation was customized for a regional (university) user with innovation interactions between the project management office near Cardiff and R&D support brought in from California, where the firm is headquartered.

Innovation activity of 'incremental innovators' aims at shifting the frontiers of the performance offered by this product on a vertical function (i.e. precision, durability, security). Thus Seal Technology R&D concentrates on material development, design improvement, performance enhancement and increased longevity in automotive sealing connections. Avonride focuses on developing and manufacturing axles used in vehicle trailers. The product is patented and innovative in two respects: firstly it is more user-friendly and enables the opening of the car boot while the car is linked to the caravan, and secondly it offers higher resistance than conventional axles. The speed, accuracy and capacity of the clinical and bioanalytical tests delivered by Simbec Research are regularly upgraded.

Incremental innovation also includes improvements in terms of the combined criteria of equal or increased performance at *lower costs*. Stilexo regularly improves its product by using cheaper materials in order to reduce the production costs of its TV consoles, but offering at the same time equivalent or increased resistance to corrosion. South-Wales Cables is an assembler of specialized electrical cables and connectors for large industrial users. Each order is customized to respond to customer needs. Gwent Cables is a similar firm operating in the PC and telecom markets. Borg Warner, Standard Products, Matsushita and R-Tek are companies that can be considered as *product* non-innovators or *product* 'modifiers' in their Wales plants. The Welsh Borg Warner and Standard Products plants, for instance, are typical manufacturing plants, that modify their product range according to changes in the car industry and to orders through headquarters. The Welsh plants do not have any in-house R&D capability and all innovation activities, independent of production, are carried out within the respective headquarters. Similarly R-Tek and Matsushita are Japanese-owned companies within which the main activity of the Wales R-Tek is to manufacture moulded indoor panels, the design of which is provided by the company headquarters in Japan.

Nevertheless, all three companies implement locally *process* innovation. In the case of US-owned Borg Warner, their German research laboratory designs the new product but the Welsh plant searches for 'process solutions' (mostly bought from Swiss machine tool companies) in order to produce large quantities of the new product. It was within this activity of setting up the production processes that Borg-Warner Wales managed to develop a machine-tool that is now patented and commercialized as a new company product. Its requirement was said to be 'impossible' by its Swiss machine supplier (stamping rather than milling steering gear junction parts). Interestingly, once the company realized the commercial potential of the process innovation it had produced, it actually abandoned the idea of producing the product that the machine was supposed to deliver (the time lag would have been too long), and concentrated fully on the development of the process.

Process innovation conducted by R-Tek at its Welsh plant was much involved in *testing*, an underresearched aspect in innovation research, in order to improve the glues (from an efficiency, resistance and ecological point of view) used for the assembly of the door panel parts. The new water-based (as opposed to silicon-based) glue met new environmental standards and would also enable the production process to raise effectiveness in terms of costs, as a result of the reduction of the time and equipment needed for the task. The objective of the company was to demonstrate innovative capacities to the Japanese headquarters and convince it to adopt the new process in all production plants. Both examples show that regional manufacturing plants are capable of developing their R&D activities by dedicating spare capacity to process innovation and exploiting the narrow innovative margin allowed by headquarters. Accordingly these companies expected to become more involved in innovative activity in future.

The frequency of innovation in the interviewed firms is variable. For radical innovators, applications and refinements of the technology occur frequently and result in patented knowledge. However the actual translation into a product innovation takes much longer. For the other categories, the frequency of introduction of a new product depends mainly on the product life cycle of the preceding product and on customer demand. However a number of companies (especially those with major product innovations) tend to find new applications and introduce a new product long before the slope of the product life cycle curve decreases. In our sample, frequency of innovation is mostly influenced by customer demand for both incremental innovators and producers/suppliers of modified products.

4   Motivation for innovating and inter-firm co-operation patterns

In the preceding section were described typical instances of innovative activity in the sampled firms. This section aims to explain the factors that influence innovative activity and behaviour towards innovation amongst the sampled firms. Firstly, what are the reasons for our 15 firms to pursue innovation? We observed a high degree of convergence in firm's responses, and most companies gave a combination of reasons:

- Cut costs of product,
- Improve quality of product,
- Take cost out of production,
- Meet customer demand (i.e. customization, performance),
- Strengthen position in a niche market (i.e. SMEs),
- Meet requirements of large global customers (e.g. Japanese), especially with regard to management techniques, to improve their position in supplier competition.

When we look more closely at the responses and try to determine patterns in companies' opinions, there are variations both *within* and *across* industries.

Firstly, variations of innovative behaviour *within industries* can mainly be related to the status of the company. Thus, the function of the Welsh plant within the overall company and the degree of decentralization of decision making in the company are crucial. As mentioned earlier, the Borg Warner plant in Wales is a typical manufacturing plant with no plant R&D laboratory. Even if the plant hoped to start R&D activity officially at some point in the future, company R&D remains based in the US headquarters and German laboratory facilities. Similarly, R-Tek is a Japanese-owned manufacturing plant that, apart from some testing, does not carry out R&D activity in Wales. The design of the product, as well as a list of preferred suppliers, is arranged by the Japanese headquarters. On the other hand Stilexo (Swedish-owned) is given some possibilities by their headquarters to innovate, especially in the form of customization and incremental innovation in order to reduce costs. For instance, Stilexo meets its customers (mainly Japanese transplants in the South Wales electronics cluster) and discusses the final details of product specifications that are initially broadly given by the Swedish headquarters. At the other end of the scale is Seal Technology, with headquarters in Cardiff. The company is equipped with an R&D laboratory and is active in designing, prototyping and testing new products before introducing them to the market. It interacts permanently with Cardiff University engineers through the Teaching Company Scheme.[3] The logic for a manufacturing plant is typically to perform as well as possible from the low-cost–high-quality perspective. Thus in our sample the motivations for these companies to innovate are mostly cost and quality-related, with a stronger incentive to introduce process innovation. The single firm is closer to the headquarters' situation in this respect: it is able to make decisions on all aspects of the company and its activity.

The interviews have suggested a second major determinant for innovative behaviour in our companies: the degree of innovation depends on the nature of the company's product and co-operative relationships within the supply chain entailed by the nature of the product. In order to develop this idea, we first have to note that the degree of vertical disintegration of labour, or the specialization of supplier firms, occurs to different degrees in each industry. Thus the automotive and electronics industries are well known for their complex subcontract production systems where assemblers, suppliers and distributors are linked in subcontracting and alliances. Funk (1992) has termed these industries 'discrete parts industries' as opposed to the 'non-discrete parts industries' based around processes (i.e. chemicals, pharmaceuticals, biotechnology industries) and using mainly raw materials. The supply chain is an important framework for the analysis in the first type of industries, whereas it is much less significant for the 'non-discrete parts industries'.

4.1   The case of the automotive and electronics industries

The 'discrete parts industries' lend themselves to the development of a sub-contracting system with multiple layers, in which the supplier has a variable degree of involvement according to whether he is a supplier of standardized products/simple operations (e.g. assembly) or a supplier of strategically sensitive parts or instruments. Such parts (e.g. engines, gearbox) have high innovative potential and are considered to be a determinant of the competitiveness of the end product (e.g. the car in the case of the automotive industry).

Our research confirms the existence of a link between the nature of the product, the extent to which suppliers are asked to be involved in the design and development of products, and their scope of innovative activity. In our sample, we have a variety of situations, including both extremes. Indeed, automotive and electronics companies who are involved in supply chains but supply standardized products that are occasionally improved or modified, are amongst the least innovative of our sample (e.g. Stilexo, Standard Products, Matsushita, R-Tek). For these companies the buyer (i.e. Sony, Ford or GM), supplies the specifications of the product corresponding to the new model. The role of the company is then to produce these products according to the low-cost–high-quality criterion.

At the other end, companies that are part of a supply chain, but are suppliers of strategically important systems or whole products (Industrial Electronics Automation) have closer relationships with their buyer and

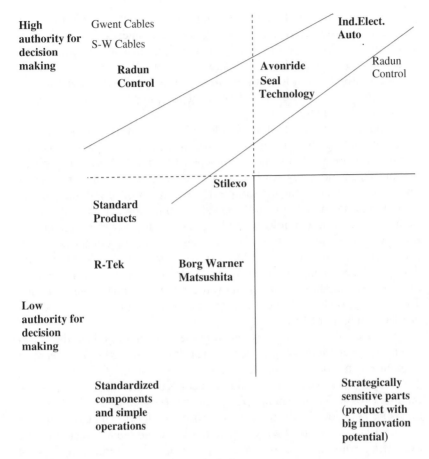

NB: Companies in **bold** belong to a supply chain.

Figure 56.1   *Interviewed companies in automotive and electronics industries: degree of authority for decision making and nature of product*

significant in-house R&D activity. The company works closely with Jaguar engineers, for instance, in order to develop a fully automated load/deflection test rig which will accurately reproduce driver input to operate the vehicles' automatic gear change, brake pedal and throttle pedal controls. This is crucial equipment for Jaguar as it will enable the car company to evaluate the vehicle's control system and remain 'best in class'.

To summarize the two main dimensions suggested for the explanation of innovative activity and motivation we use Figure 56.1. The interviewed firms are placed according to the combination of their status and nature of product. Companies in **bold** belong to a supply chain, either in the automotive or in the electronics industry. For example, 'Radun Control', according to which specific activity among the diversity is carried out, would belong to two different places in this figure. It can be considered as part of a supply chain for its assembly services (e.g. assembly of remote controls for Sony), and as an independent company for its major product innovation, 'Sentinel'.

By comparing Figure 56.1 and Table 56.3 on the nature of product innovation, we indeed observe that companies located in the upper right corner of the figure are most innovative. They benefit from the power of decision making and conducting R&D and are active in a field of 'strategically important' products. In our sample these firms all appear to be either 'recombination' or 'incremental' innovators. In the lower part of the figure we have plants whose innovative activity is restricted by centralized corporate decision making and R&D laboratories in other parts of the company. The closer we move to the left-hand side of the diagram, the more standardized the company's product or service and the higher the price competition, restricting the company's innovate activity. We can further note that, according to Table 56.3, these companies mainly belong to the 'modified product' category of firms.

The results of our interviews illustrate the two main trends in the literature on supplier relationships. The first regards subcontracting as a means to overcome temporaily the internal capacity constraints of the firm or to produce at lower cost than could be achieved internally, by exploiting economies of scale, for instance (Atkinson and Meager, 1986). The design is most often provided by the buyer and the criterion for the choice of supplier is primarily price. This often results in low trust and volatile relationships. Suppliers are not inclined to have a high degree of involvement, to allocate resources or to take the risks that innovation requires. Secondly, outsourcing can be decided for strategically important components, in which case the supplier is regarded as a crucial co-operation partner in innovation. This type of relationship requires efficient communication channels between the parties and a high level of trust. However, buyers are able to bargain harder if they do not enter this type of close and long-run co-operation. Therefore price competition can prevent the formation of close partnership and thus hinder the diffusion of knowledge and innovation along the supply chain. This, in turn, would prevent suppliers developing and making use of their innovative potential, other than innovating in order to cut costs.

This is confirmed by our research: suppliers of standardized products typically have the price-competition type of relationship with their buyers whereas suppliers of strategically sensitive parts are more likely to build an interactive partnership.

However, we found that in some cases hybrid forms of co-operation, where suppliers of standardized products would still have an incentive to innovate, were possible, especially in process or organizational innovation. In particular, Japanese companies located in Wales have been progressive in introducing a number of mechanisms that stimulate innovation by rewarding the supplier in the form of higher product unit profit or increased order of product. Thus Stilexo, R-Tek and Standard Products, who supply Hitachi, Honda and Ford, are given fixed price reduction targets over a number of years by their buyer (5 per cent decrease in the price each year). This target is the condition for the contract between the two parties to hold. Thus, if the company manages to increase its efficiency to a level above that fixed target, its profit increases by the whole of that amount. This results for these suppliers in an incentive to introduce *process* and *organizational* innovation in order to cut costs more effectively.

Another mechanism is that the buyer ranks suppliers according to their performance in quality, delivery and other aspects and selects the better performing firms for higher orders. Thus the Welsh Stilexo plant is a preferred supplier to Hitachi, Sony and Panasonic operations in Wales, whereas R-Tek received Honda's prestigious 'Best Supplier Award In Overall Performance' as well as 'Best Quality Performance Award' and 'Best Delivery Performance Award' in 1994. Companies highly value these awards as crucial references for the development of the company customer base: as important as the achievement of official quality standards. In order to achieve this level of quality and management (i.e. adoption of Just in Time [JIT] or Total Quality Control [TQC]), Japanese companies assist their suppliers in making incremental improvements in the production processes and quality of their products. This enables the diffusion and exploitation of management techniques developed in these leading Japanese companies at the regional level, as well as innovative behaviour.

Finally, companies within our sample that do not belong to a supply chain are independent, mostly small, companies that operate in niche markets. They innovate in order to strengthen their position within that market, and acquire sufficient expertise and the vision that will enable them to move out of that niche if competition hardens. Among them are our four healthcare companies.

4.2   The case of the healthcare industry
Healthcare is clearly one of the 'non-discrete parts industries'. Unlike the automotive and electronics industry, the healthcare industry is not characterized by a developed network of subcontracting relationships. In particular, pharmaceuticals and 'biomedicine' are known as science-based industries where upstream linkages with academia (and entrepreneurial

firms) are predominant. Things are slightly different in the field of medical devices where the interaction with the customer can guide R&D efforts and help secure commercial success. Innovation is at the heart of our two radical innovators. Both Bioanalysis and the Magstim Company are independent Welsh SMEs that originated in academia, and were established in order to exploit the possibilities of scientific innovation, patented by business owners in the early 1980s.

Thus both companies' success relies entirely on their innovative activity in highly specialized market segments. Only one other (US) company is currently using Bioanalysis technology (a licensee), whereas the world market segment of magnetic nerves stimulation is shared among three companies: a Danish, a US and the Magstim Company. In both cases the technology contains very high potential for further applications and, in 2000, three further companies were spun out of Magstim to specialize in particular applications, which are further technological niches. These companies deal mainly with R&D and could not meet the needs of large markets. Even if there is a large scope for manufacturing the technology developed, none of the companies intends to go into manufacturing. Both companies are aware that the exploitation of new 'mass-market' innovations requires complementary assets in marketing, distribution, finance and production facilities as well as a corresponding company culture, which the company does not have at the moment. Their business strategy is to focus on these higher added value and intellectually stimulating activities, through which they would retain their initial core competence acquired in academia. They say that the market place is less competitive (especially with regard to price competition) in these niche markets, but followers can catch up quickly. Thus their business strategy consists in strengthening their position in the niche market and being prepared eventually to move on from it as competition catches up. Basic and applied research in a diversified range of areas enables the company to do that.

The situation is different for Simbec research and Perkin Elmer, who are active in the field of testing and manufacturing of sample analysis instruments. Innovation here is motivated by high customer expectations in the form of customization of instruments or performance of testing services.

5   Sources of innovation and co-operation patterns

When asked about the origin of their innovative ideas, the interviewed firms indicated five main sources and often a combination of these sources: customers and users, employees within the company, informal conversation with colleagues/network persons, university/academia, and specialized literature. We notice here that the important sources of ideas for innovation mentioned, especially by indigenous firms, are both internal and external to the company.

The source *customer and users* is by far the most popular; it was mentioned by nearly all firms. The user–producer relationship was less important for Bioanalysis which organizes its activities along a number of research themes, from which products develop. This is slightly different in the field of medical devices (i.e. Magstim Co.) where the interaction with the customer can guide R&D efforts and help secure commercial success.

For all manufacturers, on the other hand, communicating with the customer is crucial; especially for those who benefit from their single-firm status or from a high degree of autonomy for innovation activities. The strongest interactive link between customers and users appears to be for 'recombination' innovations, which in essence embody two fields of activity or technology. The interactive relationship takes place most often in the process of applying the firm's core technology to a new field (the field of the customer) or by customizing an existing innovation to specific needs of a customer.

For Industrial Electronic Automation, for instance, the customer as a source of innovation is of vital importance. The company pursues some independent R&D activities, but the biggest proportion of activity is initiated by a specific requirement of a customer. The initiation phase and development of the customization of a product are similar in many interviewed companies. First, the customer approaches the company with a specific need, the company then estimates whether the current state of technology in the company could respond to that need and what the R&D investment for the implementation of the requirement would be. In some cases the requirement can be fulfilled by using the current expertise available in the company. Both parties then engage in a contract and the producer delivers the product. If this is not possible, the company considers whether the need reflects a wider demand for that particular product in the sector.

Indeed, customization can be a one-off product or innovation, but in some cases it can reflect a wider need of that particular sector. These customers could be qualified as 'lead users' (Von Hippel, 1988) as they seem to face needs that will be general in a market place some months or years before the bulk of that market place encounters them, and that the solution to their needs generates a substantial benefit. The role of these 'lead users' could be even more important to the manufacturer's innovative output from the moment they introduce him to a whole new range of needs to which he can respond with new products and processes.

Thus, the interest of a company to invest in the development of one particular customized product depends on the expected market demand of this or related products. This is the point where some of our companies encounter problems: such a business strategy sometimes requires heavy market research and small companies do not always have the resources to fully investigate the market. Another aspect of this issue is that all companies that we have interviewed said that they know the market place well. However, the question is whether they know the future prospects of this market well enough in order to place their innovative activities in its dynamics.

The user can even have a stronger role in sectors where science appears predominantly in the user's environment. This is the case of the medical device industry where scientists sometimes have very clear ideas about devices needed and knowledge available in order to develop the corresponding products. This is the case for the Magstim Company, which closely co-operates with non-regional neurologists, neurophysiologists and neurosurgeons from various medical bodies (such as the Dental School of Guy's & St. Thomas' Hospital, London) as well as researchers in the field. These customers or researchers have a high input for product design at both professional (e.g. product function) and technological level. For this firm, the involvement of the customer in the innovation process and the maintenance of a good relationship has engendered customer-initiated improvements.

The second main source of innovative ideas mentioned is *employees within the company*. This source of innovation has been mentioned by many product innovators and systematically by all firms who have implemented a process innovation. This confirms the importance of company human capital for the exploitation of innovation potential rooted in manufacturing routines, the generation or integration of knowledge available within the company or in its environment.

As we will see in a later section, human resources is a crucial issue for innovation, especially so because it seems to operate as a barrier to innovation. Employers find it difficult to recruit the right staff at both shop-floor and engineer level. Interestingly, this is more so for the electronics and automotive sector, but does not seem to be such a problem in the younger and smaller healthcare sector. On the other hand, the healthcare sector seems to tap more into UK-wide potential, and manages to attract highly specialized staff to Wales. This seems to be more difficult to achieve in the other two sectors, because of the tendency of firms to advertise regionally.

Informal conversations with colleagues from other companies or friends is an important mechanism for the exchange of ideas. Several companies have mentioned the pub or 'meetings after the official meeting' as an important place where you can approach people more personally. This is especially important for customer–user relationships, where a general conversation about the industry can sometimes point to specific needs of the sector. The company manager can then identify where his company and strategy can fit with these needs.

It is important to note that firms who tend to use such informal networking in Wales are the most innovative indigenous firms who co-operate with the regional innovation infrastructure (IEA, Magstim Co, Radun Control). This suggests that the social network of company managers and their communication and networking skills within the region are crucial for innovation in the company. Hence, regional *proximity* matters in innovation as *knowledge spillovers* may lead to contracts, as hinted at in the relevant literature (Cooke, 2002; Malmberg and Maskell, 2002; for *pecuniary* spillovers, see Breschi and Lissoni, 2001). This could constitute a substantial advantage for indigenous Welsh companies over larger foreign innovators. The challenge is to make these companies aware of the importance of informal networking and maybe to increase the readiness of regional organizations or firms to interact in networking with regional companies, and find the right balance between the provision of this type of support services and work with inward investors.

University/academia was mentioned by a majority of interviewed firms as a major partner in technology-related aspects of innovation. It is only for a minority of firms (i.e. radical innovators/spinoff companies) that the university is considered as a source of innovative ideas. More generally, it is regarded as a source of knowledge, competences and labour to which the company can have recourse when it encounters technology-related problems, especially when highly specialized and expensive equipment (testing) is required. A large number of sampled firms (seven of them) have established long-term partnerships with university departments which take the form of PhD and basic research funding, exclusive licensing and subcontracting (testing).

For both our radical innovators, however, university departments are considered as the major source for the original idea that enabled the establishment of the company and the sustainability of its leadership and competitive advantage over the following years: Bioanalysis spun off locally from Cardiff University Medical School, whereas the Magstim Co. holds an exclusive licence from the University of Sheffield.

These radical innovators in science-based industry also mentioned the *specialized literature* as one of the most important sources of insights for innovation. This has been cited by other innovators, but to a much lesser extent. IEA, which can be considered as one of the most innovative companies of our sample (i.e. recombinator), although in electronics, regularly refers to the literature to keep up with the latest technological developments; this gives the company further insights for R&D activities.

The following Table 56.4 summarizes the nature of innovation and the process of innovating.

Table 56.4   The nature of innovation and the process of innovating

Type of innovator:	Radical	Recombination	Incremental	Modification
Why do firms innovate?	keep first in market niche	diversify, address new markets with current technology	improve performance and lower costs	satisfy customer demand
Source of innovation	internal and university expertise	customer and internal expertise	customer and internal expertise	customer
Implementation of innovation	internal and university expertise	internal	internal	internal
Relationship with customers	co-operative (based on innovativeness)	joint project specification, contractual	based on cost	based on cost
Position in supply chain (type of firm)	mostly small independent firms	suppliers of systems specified with customer	system suppliers	suppliers of standardized parts
Interactions within the *regional innovation system* & firm 'cluster'	limited (independent firms)	moderate in the region (also outside)	high regional linkages	very high (systematic interaction)

6   Barriers to innovation

Opinions on barriers to innovation mentioned by Welsh firms are very convergent. They relate to five main points, that we present below in order of importance: human resources, financial resources both for R&D and for market research, function of the Welsh plant in large firms and centralized decision making, company culture, and property rights.

The issue of *human resources* for innovation is manifest and manifold. First, the actual needs for skilled workers are at different levels: graduates in manufacturing (especially production engineers), shopfloor workers with IT skills, and R&D engineers. This situation is exacerbated by the increasing need for skilled workers at all levels of manufacturing activity thanks to technological change in production methods (diffusion of computerized and automated equipment) on the one hand, and on the other, the external growth in need for skilled workers from foreign investors into Wales. Therefore firms not only faced the problems common to all manufacturing regions of 'reprocessing' the workforce and adapting it to modern technology-based production methods. Firms had also to address the question of large supplies of skilled labour required by the growth of the sector through the establishment of large foreign firms. This resulted in competition for local workers, to the cost of some indigenous firms who could not afford to retain their workers by increasing their wages.

This in turn affected the level of resources that the company was willing to spend on training. Indeed, workers who had acquired some training and experience in a small company were valuable on the labour market, and these innovative SMEs regularly reported such workers being poached by large foreign investors. Several interviewed companies reported that some good elements of their staff had already handed in their 'leaving letter' as a result of semiconductor multinational LG opening its 6000 workers plant in Newport in 1998. This firm only reached 1800 employment and effectively closed in 2003, transferring production to China, an indicator of the hypermobility of such capital in recent years. The mechanism described by companies is that of a vertical shift of the inter-firm employment structure: LG, for instance, poached highly skilled workers from dynamic smaller firms, who tried to attract workers with a level of qualification slightly lower from lesser firms, and the latter sought a workforce further down the ladder. The question is then: who are the firms that are at the very end? They are mainly small indigenous firms with limited resources, and for which human resources are a crucial (conscious or unconscious) barrier for innovation activity.

A solution to the human resources barriers to innovation would be to set up more courses in manufacturing-related disciplines. This is where a functioning RIS operates to overcome barriers where the real difficulty for public policy appears: these curricula do not attract the number of school leavers required to bridge the skills gap in the economy. There is a cultural apprehensiveness of young people against choosing the manufacturing route as it is not given prestige by society or the educational system.

The second major barrier to innovation for innovative businesses is *financial*. Middle sized firms in the range of 25–100 employees find it particularly difficult to raise funding for their innovative activities and expanding their company. They are too large to apply for grants directed to start-up companies, and too small to generate projects that would be large enough to satisfy job creation criteria for discretionary assistance, possibly including 'state aids' problems. Thus, for example, Avonride had attempted to access finance on several occasions over the five years prior to our interviews. The projects presented would have involved an increase in employment of three to five people. This was too low to satisfy the employment criteria requested by the scheme, even if in relative terms this meant a 10 per cent increase in company employment.

More specifically firms commented on their difficulties in the early stages of the innovation process, up to the prototype stage, when investment is substantial and risks are high. At that early stage the company faces the technological and feasibility problems of the development of the new product, and simultaneously the market research needed to assess the market potential for that product. Some grants and loans (e.g. SMART[4]) that are available from regional or national programmes are aimed at this early stage, but only a few companies qualify for such grants. On the other hand, potential applicants who have started some preliminary development and seek finance following this exploratory phase do not qualify for such grants (e.g. SMART, Regional Innovation Grants): 'grants cannot be paid towards projects which have already started prior to approval'.

Radun Control, for instance, is a company that managed to overcome the technological problems of developing a new product, 'Sentinel', but overlooked the importance of initial market research. The company later sought to find a *market* for the product originally directed to meet registration needs in the educational sector. Low public investment in Britain in education made this registration system a luxury that state schools could not afford. The company manager first turned to the Far East, with the hope of finding a suitable market there, before changing market focus and finding a major customer in the UK National Health Service.

Avonride, producer of axles, adopted an innovative solution to its marketing problems. The company identified a market niche for its product in Germany, but found it difficult to manage the distance in order both to sell the product and to develop close collaboration with German customers. The company therefore employed a German marketing manager who set up a small office at his home from where he visits potential customers all over the country. The operation proved successful after six months, when the first orders from German companies came in. This innovative option is a wise one for small companies; it saves travel costs and companies gain from reducing the cultural gap with their suppliers. Small suppliers serving a similar market with complementary products could obviously in principle *share* such a marketing manager.

For some companies, finance is also a problem for the purchase of equipment in order to improve processes. This would enable some small companies to increase their productivity substantially and to address needs of higher-profile customers. This type of investment primarily affects the company's turnover in the short term. The question is whether it would also contribute to the enhancement of the company technology base and an increased scope for innovation activity in the long run.

As pointed out in a preceding section, the *function of the Welsh plant in large firms* and more specifically its degree of authority regarding innovation activities determine the scope of innovation carried out in Wales. Some Welsh plants expressed their interest in getting more involved in R&D. A number of manufacturing plants are already involved in process innovation. They hope that in future headquarters will give them more freedom to concentrate upon product innovation, and develop a long-term strategic plan for the plant.

The development of R&D functions must however be accompanied by a change in *company culture*. A few Welsh plants have explicitly declared that such changes are needed in their branch plant in order to develop innovative activity successfully. Stilexo, manufacturer of TV consoles and chairs, is a Swedish family-owned company that has identified a market niche in South Wales for their product and subsequently set up a manufacturing plant in the area. The company culture has a conservative character and innovation has only been considered as an issue in recent years. Similarly the company only realized recently that skilled workers in the Welsh plant can contribute to incremental innovation activity and the general dynamic of the plant. Thus, the Welsh plant now engages in a 'modernization' process, including the promotion of an innovation culture, with, for instance, the recruitment of an industrial designer. This, however, could be to the detriment of lifelong but unskilled workers, who see their role in the company weakened and maybe made redundant.

Other branch plants are aware of cultural changes and skills upgrading that are needed for the plant to develop appropriate learning mechanisms and carry out effective innovation activity. This is especially the case for manufacturing areas of plants with long-established workers who are reluctant to change. Two further aspects have been pointed out by our sampled firms: changing the inward-looking character of the plant as well as changing the organization of overstressed companies, who focus on productivity rather than innovation to sustain their competitive advantage.

Cultural factors, however, also affect single indigenous, especially small, firms. Some of these companies (such as Gwent Cables) lack the ambition or maybe 'entrepreneurial spirit' that is needed for the development of a business strategy. This reflects aspects of the Welsh culture, still marked by the historical dependence on coal and steel industries and maybe a higher degree of aversion to risk or relative lack of ambition.

The question of *industrial property* rights can sometimes be very time and energy-consuming, time and energy which otherwise could be devoted to further innovation. This is especially true for Welsh firms who have not accorded enough importance to the protection of their innovations in the first place. Generally, firms regarded it as a vital issue; especially those who operate in highly specialized market niches. Confidentiality is a major driver for the formation of alliances with customers: a formal agreement on confidentiality enables them to exchange information more freely and enter more details of the product or technology specification. The level of trust required in non-contractual relationships is too high and can in many cases not be achieved.

7   What do firms tell us about the 'regional innovation system'?

Firm opinions about the regional innovation infrastructure were mixed. There are some undeniable success stories where regional programmes and services offered by organizations had a crucial impact upon innovation and performance of Welsh businesses. On the other hand, there are opinions that are more mitigated or variable according to the organization with which the company has co-operated.

In the following we will present the results of the interviews on firm–organization co-operation experience and perception by Welsh businesses of the regional innovation infrastructure. We will mainly address the following questions. Who do regional firms co-operate with and perceive as important for innovative activities? How is this co-operation achieved? The reality of firm–organisation co-operation involves elements of the support infrastructure used by sampled firms. Organizations used by our sampled firms and the nature of the service provided are as shown in Table 56.5.

From our interviews, we found that nearly all companies used one or another support service provided by regional organizations. These companies identified and used elements in the Welsh support infrastructure that are relevant to them, even if the downside of it seems to be the time and energy necessary to access these services. But as one company who has benefited from a number of these support services put it: '*We know that the support infrastructure is a maze, but we see an advantage in bothering with it.*' This quotation reflects well the general feeling that we have gathered during our company visits.

Among firms who make the least use of the services offered are companies with a low degree of autonomy and who mainly concentrate on manufacturing activities in their Wales plant. However these companies are increasingly aware of their need for skilled staff, as production methods change and computerized manufacturing, for instance, becomes much more widespread. The Training Agencies (formerly TECs), and to a lesser extent the Further Education Colleges, are the main partners of these companies in the upgrading of their current worker skills. The work of TECs

Table 56.5   Organizations used by sampled firms and nature of co-operation/service provided, 1993–6

Organization used by sampled firms	Nature of the co-operation or service provided
Training and Enterprise Councils Since 1999, ELWa (the National Training Agency for Wales) (closed in 2006)	Specific training at intermediate level Investors in people Modern apprenticeship, National Vocational Qualification FE colleges Language training
Welsh Development Agency (closed in 2006)	Informal contacts Supplier group (i.e. automotive) Industrial sites Technology project Source Wales 'Stratagem', time to market initiative Welsh Relay Centre (i.e. EU-FUSE grants) Session with consultants Small Firm Loan Guarantee Scheme SMART (since 2002)
University Departments	Graduate placement PhD funding Testing Research Purchase of exclusive licence
Teaching Company Scheme	Graduate in a firm
Welsh Office (Department of Trade and Industry) Since 1999, National Assembly for Wales	Regional Selective Assistance Grants SMART SPUR
Welsh Quality Centre	Seminars on quality, standards etc.
Lean Enterprise Research Centre (Cardiff University Business School)	Informal contacts
Venture Capital Companies (i.e. 3i)	Venture capital loans

was well understood but only a few firms commented on their experience. Nevertheless, some firms have specific needs, and it is not possible for public training organizations to respond to very small-scale requirements. Most of the sampled companies organized training internally, but some took the opportunity for their staff to join training classes organized for larger firms. This suggested some horizontal networking between firms in the field of training as a solution to requirements. The TECs used to play a co-ordinating role by bringing firms together for training purposes. This is something needing greater emphasis in future.

More innovative firms successfully used graduate placements and the University Teaching Company Scheme to upgrade their skills base and to strengthen their links with university expertise. Thus two companies mentioned their use of the 'Teaching Company Scheme', three companies had experienced one-year student 'sandwich placements' and three companies funded a PhD student at university. The firms' opinions on these experiences were very positive. Most companies repeated the operation for subsequent years. The company benefits from university graduate staff with little additional costs for the adaptation periods of their skills to the companies' needs. But, by using these placement opportunities, firms are equally interested in developing their links with university departments and benefiting from equipment and facilities available in academia, that smaller firms or firms at an early stage of developing their R&D activities could not afford.

Co-operation with universities, for the purpose of skills recruitment or R&D activities, is fully institutionalized, with over half of our firms having relationships with university departments. All major product innovators, for instance, had strong co-operative links with universities, most often in the form of research or PhD funding, with a view to gaining a student researching the company's specific field of technology for future R&D activity. Incremental innovators were most interested in using the university equipment via student placements or subcontracting of testing of improved products. The perception of universities by Welsh firms was positive. Even companies who were in the 'modification' category, carrying out very limited R&D, with the hope of increasing it in future, took the opportunity of our visit to ask us more about relevant university departments. University–firm co-operation is therefore widely perceived as complementary to in-house R&D activity.

At present it is reasonable to say that university–firm relationships in Wales are primarily seen as a response to firms' difficulties in recruiting qualified staff, and in the second place as an opportunity to access university equipment. The accessing of knowledge from universities follows from these initial incentives, and is highly valued by firms who have experienced it. The extension of knowledge exchanges was a next step in the process of strengthening university–firm co-operative relationships.

Nearly all firms had contacts with the Welsh Development Agency (WDA). In many cases, the WDA provided the industrial site, built the manufacturing plant and helped firms move or extend their site. But firms also mentioned the WDA business and innovation support programmes. In particular, the 'Sources Wales Database' and 'Supplier Groups' were support services provided by Source Wales, a WDA supplier development programme. The objective of 'Source Wales' was to locate and secure worldwide opportunities for the sale of products from Welsh companies. The team also provided advice on benchmarking, production methods, strategies and management of the product development process.

Thus, three firms were part of the Automotive Supplier Group and found the opportunity to meet other suppliers and sharing information and experience with them very important. These firms' feeling was that this type of initiative was important for the firm to learn more about the industry, but also essentially for breaking the daily routine in order to start thinking about their company product and strategy in a more objective way. Thus Standard Products, a manufacturer of rubber window seals, joined the Supplier Group, and learnt important facts about components that were directly connected with seals in the end product (i.e. glass, automatic window-closing system).

Discussion between these three manufacturers helped to solve problems for Standard Products and for the producer of the closing system. The problem for the closing system was that the motor needed to be very powerful actually to push the window into the upper part of the seal. This could be solved by Standard Products by using looser rubber sealings. Standard Products, on the other hand, had difficulties in accuracy of the seals owing to only an approximate knowledge of the glass industry. Conversations within the supplier group enabled understanding of where the limitations of the glass material lies and subsequently enabled improvement in the accuracy of the seals.

The success story with Source Wales, besides the firm's excellent rating of services provided, was the fact that the programme helped another sampled indigenous innovative company to win a £1 million order. This had the effect of doubling the company's turnover. This was achieved through the Source Wales Database, that the unit diffused at trade fairs or to large assembly customers in order to promote the interests of Welsh suppliers within and outside the region. It was interesting to learn that this company interacted very closely and frequently with Source Wales (on a daily basis, according to the business manager), either during office hours or more informally in social events or after-work meetings in a pub. In both cases, Source Wales achieved its objectives, and despite the fact that some of the firms that we interviewed were not aware of its existence, the programme was very popular among the South Wales suppliers of automotive and electronics components.

This made other WDA initiatives aimed at firms from other sectors or independent SMEs look rather weak. There is a general feeling among these firms that, to benefit from WDA support services, '*you need to either have a high profile product or be Japanese*'. Especially the latter point of WDA initiatives focusing too much on inward investors has been mentioned by three independent Welsh firms. One of them is amongst our 'radical innovators'. These firms believe that the WDA is not concerned about small companies that do not belong to one of these strong sectoral supply chains in Wales. Nevertheless, two of these firms had approached the WDA, and organized a meeting with people from the 'Technology Transfer Unit', but there was not enough feedback from the Agency and firms were left with having to approach the Agency again, which they did not do.

This suggests that the Welsh Development Agency, consciously or unconsciously, has in some cases a preconceived idea about certain firms. The Welsh manufacturing base is strong and the co-ordination mechanisms introduced by the WDA and other regional organizations have no doubt extended and strengthened it. However, the interviews suggest that independent indigenous firms (e.g. not part of a supply chain) need suitable initiatives to support them too.

Co-operation with the Welsh Office (now Welsh Assembly Government) is mainly in the field of *finance*. Indeed, regional venture capital is rather scarce in Wales; the main sources in the 1990s were from the national government and distributed to regions via regional ministries. Four interviewed companies have benefited from six grants and innovation awards (SMART, SPUR). Other companies tried to apply for such grants or awards, but their product would not qualify. The four companies who benefited from the Welsh Office services in this field were satisfied with the support that they received in their preparation of the application and complaints about bureaucracy were not exaggerated.

One of these companies has also benefited from an EU–FUSE grant delivered by the Welsh Relay Centre based in the WDA. Apart from the WDA Technology Growth Fund, venture capital company 3i was the main private venture funding opportunity for innovation in Wales. Two firms obtained loans from 3i but this money is expensive and the organization was said to be relatively risk-averse. Nevertheless, this leaves us with one company (Magstim Company) which has benefited from three grants and three loans in the past, which amounts to over half of the venture capital facilities accessed by sampled firms.

The Regional Selective Assistance and Regional Enterprise grants, that are aimed at manufacturing firms investing in projects which create or safeguard jobs in an Assisted Area in Wales, have had a particularly important impact on firms. The capital investment involved by such projects has both impacted firm performance and enabled developments which would otherwise not have been possible to carry out. Thus firms that did not qualify for the high-profile SMART or SPUR awards could benefit from RSA or Regional Enterprise grants to boost their activity, even if at a much lower innovation level. This suggests that venture capital is scarce in Wales and furthermore that it is absorbed by a small number of firms. It may be necessary to question the criteria and cumulative nature of these grants which at present seem to favour (maybe rightly?) particular firms.

8 Conclusions

The principal conclusions of this research are the following. First, there is a considerable amount of variation in the innovation conducted in a regional economy. Some of it (a minority), in the studied Regional Innovation System is world-level leading edge, especially in biomedicine, closely related to university medical research. Here, radical innovation can be found. Less novel but still creative is innovation we refer to as involving recombination of core technologies to meet new, customized, market demand, often in a variety of industry sectors. Last, the majority of innovation conducted in Welsh industry is incremental. This is to meet customer demand in the supply chain. It can involve high-grade process innovation to meet apparently mundane product innovation requirements. Of central importance to our opening remarks is that the scale question involves a kind of scale involution (from the firm's perspective) not, importantly from the *deus ex machina* of the academic ivory tower. Thus what is needed for innovation is brought in locally or globally to the firm in its local setting. The firm is structurally and relationally *embedded*, but not imprisoned in its Regional Innovation System (Cooke, 2002).

Parts of the Welsh economy, particularly those associated with automotive and electronic engineering, operate in a reasonably systemic fashion. There is fierce local rivalry among Japanese and, temporarily, Korean electronic firms, though perhaps more complementarities among automotive components suppliers. Some suppliers serve both sectors, many receive soft enterprise support from enterprise support organizations, and there is growing evidence of linkage by some firms to knowledge centres such as universities for research, but more likely consultancy, testing and equipment use. But innovation involves substantial intra-regional and extra regional interaction, vertically and horizontally. In discussion with firms it was necessary to have recourse to original Schumpeterian thinking to capture an important category we found and Schumpeter theorized. This was *recombination* innovation, which as we showed was not an insignificant category of innovation in the system studied.

Finally, policy can usefully integrate different strands of enterprise support to enhance the 'knowledge system culture' which has evolved to develop and help such innovator firms escape from a debilitating competition with low-wage producers in other countries, which cannot be won. Markets are by no means perfect mechanisms for achieving initiation of this process, but are powerful drivers once the co-evolution of a vision of the firm's specific innovation trajectory is identified. European and other advanced economy firms must move into higher value-added, higher-skill, more innovation-intensive production. This requires integrated policy support, linking access to university research, skills, marketing and business intelligence competencies with the funding to help pay for it. The Regional Innovation System is clearly the key means for helping ensure this upgrading process in generic terms.

Notes

1. In the REGIS project small was defined as 10–49, medium as 50–99, and large as firms with 200+ employees. This is due to the structure of the economy in Wales; most firms fall in the first two categories (see Cooke and Schall, REGIS working paper no. 2, March 1997).
2. This arises from Schumpeter's reference to innovation from new combinations (Schumpeter, 1939).
3. This is a PhD fellowship funded by government, company and university.
4. SMART (Small Firms Merit Award for Research and Technology) awards are UK Government grants, given by regional administrations or agencies (e.g. in Wales by the Welsh Development Agency) to establish the feasibility of innovations and inventions and to help the development of products through to the pre-production state.

Acknowledgements

This paper arose from a European Union DG XII Targeted Socio-Economic Research Programme project entitled 'Regional Innovation Systems: Designing for the Future'. We are grateful to the funding body and to our project collegues, P.Boekholt (Netherlands), G.Bechtle (Germany), E. de Castro (Portugal), G. Etxebarria (Spain), M. Quevit (Belgium), M. Schenkel (Italy), G. Schienstock (Finland) and F. Toedtling (Austria). We are also grateful for the opportunity to publish this original account at the invitation of Andreas Pyka. The usual disclaimer applies.

Bibliography

Atkinson, J. and Meager, N. (1986) *Changing Working Patterns: How Companies Achieve Flexibility to Meet New Needs*, London: NEDO.
Bathelt, H. (2003) Growth regimes in spatial perspective 1: innovation, institutions and social systems, *Progress in Human Geography*, **27**, 789–804.
Breschi, S. and Lissoni, F. (2001) Knowledge spillovers and local innovation systems: a critical survey, *Industrial & Corporate Change*, **10**, 975–1005.
Cooke, P. (2002) *Knowledge Economies*, London: Routledge.
Cooke, P. and Schall, N. (1997a) Regional innovation for competitive advantage: the case of Wales, *REGIS working paper no.2*, Cardiff University, Wales.
Cooke, P. and Schall, N. (1997b) The promotion of systemic regional innovation in Wales, *RIR working paper no.26*, Cardiff, CASS-UWCC.
Cooke, P., Boekholt, P. and Tödtling, F. (2000) *The Governance of Innovation in Europe*, London: Pinter.

Funk, J. (1992) *The Teamwork Advantage: An Inside Look at Japanese Product and Technology Development*, Cambridge, MA: Productivity Press.

Mackinnon, D., Cumbers, A. and Chapman, K. (2002) Learning, innovation and regional development: a critical appraisal of recent debates, *Progress in Human Geography*, **26**, 293–311.

Malmberg, A. and Maskell, P. (2002) The elusive concept of localisation economies: towards a knowledge-based theory of spatial clustering, *Environment & Planning A*, **34**, 429–49.

OECD (1993) *Proposed Standard Practice for Surveys of Research and Experimental Development ('Frascati Manual')*, Paris: OECD.

Schumpeter, J. (1939) *Business Cycles*, New York: McGraw-Hill.

Von Hippel, E. (1988) *The Sources of Innovation*, Oxford: Oxford University Press.

Winter, S. (1984) Schumpeterian competition in alternative technological regimes, *Journal of Economic Behaviour & Organisation*, **5**, 287–320.

57 Fundamentals of the concept of national innovation systems
Markus Balzat and Horst Hanusch

1 Abstract

This part of the present companion deals with the concept of national innovation systems (NIS concept). Mainly because of its theoretical under-pinning, leading to a strong empirical orientation and high innovation policy relevance, this approach has in recent years become increasingly significant. It now constitutes a powerful and widely applied framework for the economic analysis of nation-specific innovation patterns as well as for practical policymaking in industrialized countries. Against this background, the basic purpose of this chapter is of a rather fundamental nature because it addresses basic conceptual issues related to this research branch. In addition, the present chapter aims to provide a brief overview of key features and main development lines of the concept of national innovation systems.

2 Introductory remarks

Innovation processes have long been treated in economics as black boxes. By giving them a purely exogenous character and by defining rigorous assumptions about innovating actors, it has become possible to integrate these processes into formal (equilibrium) models. Thereby, however, the characteristics and the actual organization of innovative activities[1] as well as their main patterns have been largely neglected.

Starting from this essential caveat of standard economic theory, modern innovation theory – including predominantly neo-Schumpeterian concepts and evolutionary economic theory – principally aims to contribute to a better understanding of innovation processes as they take place in reality. In doing so, it is sought to identify and analyze the structures, determinants and outcomes of innovative activities in different locations, institutional settings, and industrial sectors as well as in different time periods.

If the real attributes of innovation processes are considered, these are – at least implicitly – viewed as complex systems. The complexity and systemic attributes of innovation processes in reality already spring from their main features: rather than being isolated efforts, they normally entail many different actors or organizations with heterogeneous (technological)

926

capabilities, differing information about market conditions and technological opportunities, varying aims and dissimilar financial means. Furthermore, and given that these heterogeneously endowed actors are able to learn, innovation processes obtain a dynamic, evolutionary dimension. The outcomes of innovation processes are therefore strongly determined by interdependent relations between heterogeneous and learning actors. The context-specific patterns in these relations largely depend on the willingness and ability of involved (or potential) actors to cooperate, their technological knowledge and their institutional surrounding conditions. The present shape of these framework conditions in turn is the result of their historical development, just as the knowledge of innovating actors results from long-term and cumulative processes. As a consequence, the observable results of innovative activities strongly depend on historical developments as well. Taken together, innovative activities are shaped by applied economic and institutional routines, specifics of local demand, entrepreneurial spirit, learning processes and, last but not least, a good portion of chance.

Given all these typical features of real innovation processes, the economic analysis of innovations is in fact a highly challenging task. At the same time, and certainly owing to their high economic impact, the empirical analysis and theoretical corroboration of innovation processes have become increasingly important in recent years, so that the economics of innovation as such has become an important and rapidly growing field in economics within the last two decades.

3 Key features of the concept of national innovation systems

The just described fundamental properties of real innovation processes inevitably give rise to a systemic perspective, and the concept of national innovation systems exemplifies such an analytical perspective. Accordingly, and just like other kinds of (non-economic) systems, national innovation systems are presumed to be made up of several components, linkages between them and a system environment. More specifically, the NIS approach presupposes that the interplay between national actors (i.e. different kinds of organizations and entrepreneurs) and nation-specific institutional framework conditions (including economic and non-economic aspects) characterizes innovative activities in a country.

Despite its focus on national actors and nation-specific institutional settings, the concept does not consider national systems of innovation as closed systems. Already, since the introduction of the NIS approach, and not as a consequence of the alleged 'globalization' of economic activities in general and of innovative action in particular, national systems of innovation have been viewed as open systems. Correspondingly, international links in innovative action – entailing, most importantly, collaborative research and development efforts – have ever since been viewed as important determinants of innovative activities. At the same time, though, the research on national innovation systems concentrates on the analysis of national peculiarities in the organization of innovative activities.

In consistency with systems theory, it is also possible to define the objectives of national innovation systems. These comprise the generation, absorption and dissemination of innovations. These central objectives of national innovation systems are also made explicit by Whitley (2001: 10305) who defines national innovation systems as 'nationally distinct configurations of institutions and organizations that structure the development, diffusion, and use of new technologies, products, and processes in different ways'.[2] In summary, national innovation systems can be defined as including 'all important economic, social, political, organizational, institutional, and other factors that influence the development, diffusion and use of innovations' (Edquist, 2005: 182) on the country level. It follows from this terminological delineation that, by using the NIS approach, innovative activity is analyzed in a rather broad sense. Instead of concentrating exclusively on single aspects of innovation processes, such as, for instance, the number of introduced product and process innovations in a country, a holistic perspective of innovative activities on the country level is principally inherent of the NIS concept. Likewise, the present structure, the development and the (however defined) performance of a national innovation system are determined by various coevolutionary processes of economic, social, political, technological and institutional factors.

Yet the accurate differentiation between institutions and organizations is not made in all applications of the NIS concept. These and similar terminological inconsistencies in the NIS literature illustrate a further key characteristic of the NIS approach, namely the attribute of conceptual diversity. Without doubt, the conceptual diversity stems from the fact that the national systems of innovation approach is a rather young academic discipline that still leaves room for different interpretations of fundamental terms and assumptions as well as for different directions in applied research. The existing conceptual pluralism of the NIS approach – including its underlying theoretical and conceptual constructs and its diversity in methodologies employed in empirical applications – will also become manifest in the outline of the development lines of this concept, which will be provided in the subsequent section.

However, and in accordance with the so-called 'Aalborg version of the NIS approach',[3] the distinction between the technical terms 'institutions' and 'organizations' shall be made here as well for reasons of terminological and conceptual clarity.[4] Illustratively, institutions can be described as 'the rules of the game in a society' (North, 1990: 3). Institutions can accordingly be defined as 'systems of established and prevalent social rules that structure social interaction' (Hodgson, 2006: 2). These surrounding conditions of a national innovation system are mainly constituted by formal and informal rules, including laws, norms, rules of conduct, business routines, language etc. Related to the thematic orientation of the NIS concept, institutions can be assumed (i) to have distinctive national configurations and (ii) to both enable and impair novelty-generating efforts by national organizations. According to Hodgson (2006), these can be defined as exemplifying a particular subset of institutions with additional features, namely 'criteria to establish their boundaries and to distinguish their members from non-members, [. . .] principles of sovereignty concerning who is in charge and [. . .] chains of command delineating responsibilities within the organization'.

Apart from existing dissimilarities in the definition of technical terms in the NIS literature, some further and commonly accepted fundamentals of the NIS approach can be identified. Already in earlier contributions to the NIS literature, these characteristics of the NIS concept have been elucidated, especially in Edquist (1997a). Based on the corresponding list of basic attributes of the NIS concept, one of its most important assumptions is the rejection of the notion of system optimality. That is because any theoretically derived national innovation system with an abstract, optimal structure clearly contradicts the realistic, evidence-based and historical analysis carried out within the NIS concept. Hence, rather than attempting to find or theoretically derive an optimal system, real systems and the existing differences between them are at the centre of attention in the research on national innovation systems. This also has consequences for the design of innovation policy,[5] because, given the complexity and heterogeneity of national innovation systems in reality, it is obviously impossible to copy certain elements of a successful system and implement these in another, less successful system.

The rejection of system optimality is closely linked with two further basic theoretical constructs that form the NIS concept. These are the notions of path dependence and historical uniqueness. These concepts imply that innovation processes are irreversible, cumulative and open processes. If innovation processes are (as depicted above) viewed as institutionally embedded activities, the presumptions of historical uniqueness and path dependence also apply to the evolution of institutional framework conditions. If historical circumstances are supposed to have nuanced country-level features, innovation and learning activities will consequently possess deep and at the same time historically grown national specifics as well. This also implies that the amount, the direction and also the outcomes of innovative activities are decisively shaped by nation-specific institutional framework conditions. It follows furthermore from this assumption that not only the composition of innovation systems but also the interaction patterns therein vary significantly from one country to another. Together with the notion of path dependence and, as a consequence, the assumed sluggish adjustment of institutional settings, cross-national differences in the set-up of innovation systems obtain a long-term character.

The combination of these main assumptions implies that a national innovation system can also be defined as a historically developed subsystem of a national economy in which there are strong interdependencies in the carrying out of innovative activity between different kinds of organizations and institutions.

These basic presumptions and their direct effect on the research programme of the NIS concept pave the way for a more direct linkage of the NIS literature with a recently elaborated concept in economics, the varieties of capitalism concept as introduced by Hall and Soskice (2001). This branch of literature seeks to identify and classify different forms of capitalistic market organization. Like the NIS approach, the varieties of capitalism approach thereby focuses on the identification and analysis of nation-specific institutional framework conditions and on resulting international differences in economic performance and industrial structures. Recently, Amable and Petit (2001) and Amable (2003) have expanded the empirical treatment of the varieties of capitalism concept by generating an empirically derived country-level taxonomy of capitalism in its various forms of appearance in highly industrialized economies.

In view of these fundamentals of the NIS concept, this young but rapidly disseminating approach (see the contribution of Bo Carlsson to the present volume) clearly exemplifies an interdisciplinary reference framework for the economic analysis of innovations. Above all, it comprises an application of basic principles and insights of general systems theory and complexity science on the one hand, evolutionary as well as neo-Schumpeterian economic theory on the other. The qualitative and quantitative analysis of complex systems, though, has already, prior to the development of the approach of national innovation systems, become a main research topic in non-economic disciplines, especially in natural sciences and information technology. Therefore the creation and elaboration of linkages and, as a consequence, the realization of mutually important cross-fertilization effects between these latter research fields and the systems of innovation approach are natural and required alike. From an economic perspective, and regarding the elaboration of the concept of innovation systems more generally, the careful examination and theoretical underpinning of innovative activities can thus be expected to be significantly advanced by the creation and intensification of cross-disciplinary links to scientific fields that also deal with complex systems and likewise with comparable phenomena that take place in nature or society.

4 A brief overview of the development lines of the NIS concept[6]

Based on the description of these characteristics of the NIS approach, its main development lines will now be presented. The origins of the NIS concept have been laid with theoretical contributions dealing with the organization of modern innovation processes and leading to the crowding out of the linear, strictly sequential mode of innovation processes. Deviating from the formerly prevailing procedural perception of innovative activities, non-linear and context-specific attributes of innovation processes have been identified and explicated (see, e.g., Kline and Rosenberg, 1986). In these and related works, special attention has also been given to different forms of interaction between sellers and buyers and the influence of location-typical institutional settings on these interdependencies (see Lundvall, 1985, 1988). At the same time, first descriptive case studies of nationally distinctive innovation and policy patterns have appeared. These highlighted the very existence, the historical emergence and the current form of pronounced nation-specific aspects of innovative activities and their institutional determinants (see Freeman, 1987). Further influential contributions to the national systems of innovation approach have been made in the late 1980s (see Part V in Dosi *et al.*, 1988).

In the early 1990s, the NIS approach was elaborated significantly in theoretical as well as in empirical respects. In 1992, Lundvall edited a volume that entailed important contributions to the theoretical foundations of the concept, emphasizing its deep roots in evolutionary and neo-Schumpeterian economics. To a lesser extent, empirical issues have also been addressed in this volume which should later become a standard reference in the NIS literature.

Only one year later, in 1993, the NIS concept had been decisively extended in empirical terms by a rich collection of empirical case studies, most of these being single-country studies. This collection of studies was edited by Richard Nelson. For the most part, the analyzed countries in the Nelson (1993) volume are highly industrialized nations, while a smaller fraction of countries belong to the groups of low- and middle-income nations. Both the design and the focus of the empirical NIS studies in the corresponding book are good representations of early contributions to the NIS literature. A first common feature of these is the analysis of one country at a time. A second common characteristic is the explicit consideration of historical developments. Finally, a third specific feature of these early NIS studies is a purely descriptive procedure. Perhaps a main reason for the typical set-up of these studies is that initially the NIS concept was utilized as a means to reveal the central structural elements, the most important private and public actors, the most decisive institutional framework conditions and the direction of innovative activities in different countries.

The outcomes of these and related studies not only extended the scientific content of this body of research but they also had high policy relevance. As a result of this, the NIS concept has been increasingly used by large international organizations such as the EU, the OECD and the UN as an analytical framework for the study of innovation processes at the country level. At the same time, the concept has also attracted growing interest from policymakers around the globe. This led to the conduct of publicly funded, mission-oriented research, aiming to derive new or modify existing innovation policy measures in order to bring about improvements of the functioning of national systems of innovation.

Thanks to the rapid dissemination of the NIS concept in academia as well as in the political sphere, its applications and analytical methods have of course become broader and more diversified. In this process, and deviating from the just described early case studies of national innovation systems, international comparisons and performance evaluations within the NIS framework have gradually moved into the focus of academic research. Likewise, relatively less importance has been given in more recently conducted comparative NIS studies to the explanation and consideration of historically grown institutional structures of the analyzed national systems of innovation.

These latest extensions of the NIS literature have certainly brought about a convergence of two intuitively conflicting streams. One of these is related to the origins of the NIS approach and puts strong emphasis on nation-typical systemic structures and on descriptions of the main actors involved in innovation processes. The second stream, which seeks to pave the way for NIS comparisons, concentrates on the outcomes or the functioning of different systems. It is oriented towards performance and efficiency comparisons, making it at the same time necessary to partially abstract from the sheer complexity of real national innovation systems. These abstractions are required in order to make the systems comparable by means of analytical methods or models. The basic rationale behind these types of studies lies in the detection of structural strengths and weaknesses of different systems and – on these grounds – in the initiation of mutual learning processes that may lead to performance improvements of the studied systems.

A look at the existing literature shows that there have been several attempts made to formalize the NIS concept in empirical applications.[7] In some cases, these vital extensions and elaborations of the NIS literature have involved the creation of intradisciplinary linkages or the amplification of thus far merely implicit associations of the NIS framework with other streams of literature. The introduction of the so-called concept of 'national innovation capacity' by Furman *et al.* (2002), for instance, has entailed a combination of the NIS concept with elements of endogenous growth theory and also with basic principles of the concept of industrial clusters. By creating an explicit linkage between the above-mentioned varieties of capitalism concept and the NIS approach, Balzat and Pyka (2006) have only recently employed clustering techniques in order to develop a classification of 18 national innovation systems in the OECD according to a delineation of key components of these systems in highly industrialized countries.[8] Future empirical work within the conceptual frame of national innovation systems, especially if it aims to investigate in a formalized way the complex interdependencies in national innovative activities as they exist in reality, may well lead to the creation of further and interdisciplinary links.

Beyond the carrying out of these formalized comparative studies, aiming to provide new alternatives for the structured and quantitative comparison (or performance evaluation) of national innovation systems, another observable stream in the NIS literature regards the analysis of countries beyond the group of highly industrialized economies. In terms of the geographical dimension, these NIS studies mainly deal with countries in Eastern Europe, Latin America, and East Asia.[9] The level of economic development of the analyzed countries thereby ranges from developing nations to middle-income countries. Obviously, questions concerning the applicability of the NIS concept, the very existence and the development stage of national systems of innovation in the corresponding countries are often central research issues in these kinds of contributions to the NIS literature. However, international performance comparisons, mostly on the basis of several structural indicators of innovative efforts and outcomes, are carried out as well in a few of these NIS studies. In this way, this line of research, which extends the scope and the applicability of the NIS approach to less industrialized economies, is closely related to the aforementioned development line of formalized performance comparisons across national innovation systems in high-income countries.

Beyond these main development lines of the NIS approach as such, the development of this approach may also be viewed more broadly in the sense that its scientific impact on the systemic analysis of innovations in economics is considered. In doing so, the influence of the national systems of innovation framework on the introduction and empirical verification of otherwise delineated systems of innovation need to be mentioned. That is because, starting from the identification of profound cross-national differences in the structure and organization of innovative activities within the NIS framework in the 1980s, alternative configurations of innovation systems have been defined in the years thereafter. Likewise, the systemic perception of innovative activities in the economics of innovation literature meanwhile consists of various subbranches. In geographical respect, innovation systems are also delineated and analyzed on the regional level (see, e.g., Cooke *et al.*, 1997; Cooke, 2001). In addition to these two geographically defined subapproaches of national and regional innovation systems, the conceptual frameworks of sectoral (e.g. Malerba, 2002, 2004) innovation systems and technological systems (e.g. Carlsson and Stankiewicz, 1991) provide two alternatives for the meso-economic analysis of innovative activities. For the microeconomic analysis of innovation patterns, there currently exist the concepts of corporate (e.g. Janne, 2002; Cantwell *et al.*, 2002) or business (e.g. Whitley, 1999, 2000) innovation systems.

Although the various subconcepts of the innovation systems approach are complementary to each other, the precise definition and demarcation of innovation or technological systems needs to be well-founded in corresponding analyses. In the existing literature, the definition and relevance of distinctive boundaries of innovation systems have always constituted – and will presumably continue to constitute – important and controversially discussed issues. By clearly motivating the application of the employed subconcept or the utilized combination of several subconcepts within the more general approach of innovation systems, much can be done to improve the theoretical underpinning and the acceptance of the systems of innovation perspective in economics.[10] On the contrary, if these aspects fail to be explained, the systems of innovation approach degenerates to a mere label rather than fulfilling standard scientific requirements.[11]

5 Summary

This chapter has focused on the approach of national innovation systems and has outlined some of its basic characteristics as well as its main development lines. While Bengt-Åke Lundvall, known as one of the founding fathers of the NIS concept, describes in his contribution to this volume the historical roots and the early development stages of this approach and its relations to the work by Friedrich List, Hermann Schnabl addresses empirical issues related to the NIS concept and presents a model for the quantitative analysis of the various input–output relations as they prevail in national innovation systems. Related to these two contributions to the present volume, this chapter has been of a more general nature, aiming to provide a brief overview of the NIS concept.

Being grounded on a variety of theories, including systems theory, complexity science and – most importantly – basic principles of evolutionary and neo-Schumpeterian economic theory, the NIS approach exemplifies an interdisciplinary branch of research in modern innovation theory. In essence, national innovation systems consist of public and private organizations in a country, national institutional framework, and interdependencies between them. The conceptual frame of national innovation systems basically views innovative activities as interactive and collective processes that possess distinctive and relatively stable nation-typical features. Thus, innovative activities within a country are supposed to be driven by nation-typical institutional settings, organizational structures and routines. The existence as well as the persistence of these country-level differences, leading to profound international variations in innovation patterns (and possibly in real economic performance disparities on the country level), is supposed to stem primarily from historical developments.

A key research field within the NIS framework regards the analysis of how these structural variations between nations translate into divergent patterns in technological outcomes and performance as well as in varying industrial structures that in turn give rise to country-level differences in innovative activities. Hence, the concept of national innovation systems has been developed as a reference framework for the analysis of these national attributes of innovation-related activities, entailing – above all – the identification of nation-specific organizational structures, institutional surrounding conditions, innovation policy programmes and measurable outcomes of innovation processes. Since economic growth and international competitiveness are largely innovation-based, the NIS literature also contributes to the explanation of disparities across capitalist countries in these real economic aspects.

A typical feature of the NIS concept is that it is a rather broad and qualitatively corroborated approach that accounts for a broad range of economic and non-economic determinants of innovation processes. As a consequence of this characteristic, interpretations of the NIS concept and addressed research questions vary significantly in their scientific applications. Because of its underlying theoretical constructs and its fundamental presumptions of the organization of innovative activities in capitalist economies, the NIS approach allows for an evidence-based and empirically oriented study of innovation patterns in highly industrialized and emerging countries. Having been introduced in the 1980s, this concept can indeed be denoted as a rather young research stream in economics. Owing to its thematic orientation and its rapid dissemination in recent years, the concept meanwhile constitutes a powerful scientific framework in the economics of innovation literature. Beyond its increasing scientific meaning, single-country studies as well as comparative studies on the basis of the NIS approach have meanwhile gained high policy relevance. That is mainly because, grounded on the exposure of distinctive national innovation patterns together with the targeted identification of relative strengths and weaknesses of national systems of innovation, important conclusions can be drawn for innovation policy.[12]

With regard to the further scientific development and possible empirical expansions of the NIS concept, individual country studies will continue to constitute important contributions to this research branch because these may in a very detailed way identify and explain existing innovative structures and institutional surrounding conditions in a certain country. In doing so, these single-country studies can illuminate current structures and determinants of innovative activities from a historical perspective. These kinds of typically qualitative case studies, though, need to be complemented by international comparisons of national innovation systems. These comparative studies may focus on the systemic strengths and weaknesses of various national innovation systems, but also on their basic similarities and their performance. In this way, these cross-national analyses are vital contributions to the existing literature. The conduct of international comparisons within the framework of national innovation systems naturally springs from its theoretical and conceptual origins and in particular from its rejection of system optimality (which is, of course, inherent in any of the various subapproaches within the systems of innovation approach). As a result of the denial of a theoretically derived optimal national innovation system, mutual learning processes on the basis of detailed empirical comparisons of national innovation systems have a great potential for paving the way for targeted system improvements in the studied countries but also for more effective international coordination of innovation policy measures.

Notes

1. In this chapter the terms 'innovation processes' and 'innovative activities' are used as synonymous expressions. Hence, the expression 'innovation process' in this contribution does not imply that the novelty-generating activities proceed in a linear, strictly sequential manner. Instead, these activities are assumed to have a systemic dimension, including feedbacks and interdependencies of various kinds.
2. Likewise, Galli and Teubal (1997: 345) define national systems of innovation as 'the set of organizations, institutions, and linkages for the generation, diffusion, and application of scientific and technological knowledge in a specific country'. A more detailed list of the main functions of national systems of innovation can also be found in Galli and Teubal (1997: 347).
3. The so-called 'Aalborg version' of the national systems of innovation approach signifies the delineation and thematic orientation of this concept as elucidated in Lundvall (1992) or in Edquist (1997b). For a detailed comparison and critical discussion of different versions and interpretations of the NIS approach, see McKelvey (1991).
4. See also Edquist and Johnson (1997) for helpful clarifications of these terminological issues.
5. Innovation policy is in this chapter understood as defined earlier by Edquist *et al.* (2001: 130).
6. For a more extensive overview of the main development lines of the NIS concept, see Balzat and Hanusch (2004).
7. See, for instance, Nasierowski and Arcelus (2003). A further alternative for the formalization of the NIS concept in empirical applications is provided by Balzat (2006), who

evaluates the performance of, in total, 18 national innovation systems in the OECD area, including 16 European countries, the USA and Japan.

8. While comparative NIS studies have thus far typically been confined to the identification of cross-national dissimilarities, a particular focus in this study is on the detection of nation-spanning similarities in the structure of national innovation systems. Correspondingly, a central outcome of the study by Balzat and Pyka (2006) is a categorization of national systems of innovation into different clusters, while each of the identified clusters represents distinctive cross-national structural similarities.

9. See, for instance, Alcorta and Peres (1998) or Arocena and Stutz (2000) for comparative studies of several national innovation systems in Latin American and Caribbean countries. Cassiolato and Lastres (2000) reveal nation-typical structures of innovative activities in the Mercosur countries, while Chung (2001) provides a comparison of the North and South Korean national innovation systems. For studies of NIS in Eastern European countries, see e.g. Radosevic (1999) or Högselius (2005). Intarakumnerd *et al.* (2002) apply the NIS framework to Thailand in order to analyze the technological catch-up of this country.

10. In empirical applications, the proved existence of characteristic features of the utilized systemic subapproach, theoretical insights into the organization of innovation processes and, of course, the addressed research questions need to be taken into account in the selection of the systemic boundary.

11. See Edquist (2005: 192) who claims that the NIS approach has been employed as a buzzword or 'label' rather than as an analytical concept in several of the OECD publications on national innovation systems in the previous years.

12. Especially in the European Union, there can be expected a strong demand for detailed studies of national systems of innovation, which is to a large extent induced by the Union's strategic goals as defined in the Lisbon Agenda in the year 2000. Its realization ultimately rests upon the stimulation of innovation-based growth and a reduction of unemployment in the member states of the EU.

References

Alcorta, L. and Peres, W. (1998), Innovation systems and technological specialization in Latin America and the Caribbean, *Research Policy*, **26** (7–8), 857–81.

Amable, B. (2003), *The Diversity of Modern Capitalism*, Oxford, UK: Oxford University Press.

Amable, B. and Petit, P. (2001), The Diversity of Social Systems of Innovation and Production during the 1990s, CEPREMAP working paper series, no. 0115, Paris.

Arocena, R. and Stutz, J. (2000), Looking at national systems of innovation from the South, *Industry and Innovation*, **7** (1), 55–75.

Balzat, M. (2006), *An Economic Analysis of Innovation: Extending the Concept of National Innovation Systems*, Cheltenham, UK and Northampton, MA, USA: Edward Elgar Publishing.

Balzat, M. and Hanusch, H. (2004), Recent trends in the research on national innovation systems, *Journal of Evolutionary Economics*, **14** (2), 197–210.

Balzat, M. and Pyka, A. (2006), 'Mapping national innovation systems in the OECD area', *International Journal of Technology and Globalisation*, **2** (1–2), 158–76.

Cantwell, J., Dunning, J.H. and Janne, O.E. (2002), Evolution of multinational corporate technological systems in the UK and US, *Journal of Interdisciplinary Economics*, **13** (1–2), 135–63.

Carlsson, B. and Stankiewicz, R. (1991), On the nature, function, and composition of technological systems, *Journal of Evolutionary Economics*, **1** (2), 93–118.

Cassiolato, J.E. and Lastres, H.M. (2000), Local systems of innovation in Mercosur countries, *Industry and Innovation*, **7** (1), 33–55.

Chung, S. (2001), Unification of South and North Korean innovation systems, *Technovation*, **21** (2), 99–107.

Cooke, P. (2001), Regional innovation systems, clusters, and the knowledge economy, *Industrial and Corporate Change*, **10** (4), 945–74.

Cooke, P., Uranga, M. and Etxebarria, G. (1997), Regional innovation systems: institutional and organizational dimensions, *Research Policy*, **26** (4), 475–91.

Dosi, G., Freeman, C., Nelson, R., Silverberg, G. and Soete, L. (eds) (1988), *Technical Change and Economic Theory*, London: Pinter.

Edquist, C. (1997a), 'Systems of innovation approaches – their emergence and characteristics', in C. Edquist (ed.), *Systems of Innovation: Technologies, Organisations and Institutions*, London: Pinter, pp. 1–35.

Edquist, C. (ed.) (1997b), *Systems of Innovation: Technologies, Organisations and Institutions*, London: Pinter.

Edquist, C. (2005), 'Systems of innovation: perspectives and challenges', in J. Fagerberg, D. Mowery and R.R. Nelson (eds), *The Oxford Handbook of Innovation*, Oxford, UK: Oxford University Press, pp. 181–208.

Edquist, C. and Johnson, B. (1997), 'Institutions and organizations in systems of innovation', in C. Edquist (ed.), *Systems of Innovation: Technologies, Institutions and Organizations*, London: Pinter, pp. 41–63.

Edquist, C., Hommen, L. and McKelvey, M. (2001), *Innovation and Employment: Process versus Product Innovation*, Cheltenham, UK and Northampton, MA, USA: Edward Elgar.

Freeman, C. (1987), *Technology and Economic Performance: Lessons from Japan*, London: Pinter.

Freeman, C. (1988), 'Japan: a new national system of innovation?', in G. Dosi, C. Freeman, R. Nelson, G. Silverberg and L. Soete (eds), *Technical Change and Economic Theory*, London: Pinter, pp. 330–48.

Furman, J.L., Porter, M.E. and Stern, S. (2002), 'The determinants of national innovative capacity', *Research Policy*, **31** (6), 899–933.

Galli, R. and Teubal, M. (1997), 'Paradigmatic shifts in national innovation systems', in C. Edquist (ed.), *Systems of Innovation: Technologies, Organisations and Institutions*, London: Pinter, pp. 342–70.

Hall, P. and Soskice, D. (eds) (2001), *Varieties of Capitalism: The Institutional Foundations of Comparative Advantage*, Oxford, UK: Oxford University Press.

Hodgson, G.M. (2006), 'What are institutions?', *Journal of Economic Issues*, March.

Högselius, P. (2005), *The Dynamics of Innovation in Eastern Europe: Lessons from Estonia*, Cheltenham, UK and Northampton, MA, USA: Edward Elgar Publishing.

Intarakumnerd, P., Chairatana, P. and Tangchitpiboon, T. (2002), National innovation systems in less successful developing countries: the case of Thailand, *Research Policy*, **31** (8–9), 1445–57.

Janne, O.E.M. (2002), The emergence of corporate integrated innovation systems across regions. The case of the chemical and pharmaceutical industry in Germany, the UK and Belgium, *Journal of International Management*, **8**, 1–23.

Kline, J. and Rosenberg, N. (1986), 'An overview of innovation', in R. Landau and N. Rosenberg (eds), *The Positive Sum Strategy: Harnessing Technology for Economic Growth*, Washington, DC: National Academy Press, pp. 275–305.

Lundvall, B.-Å. (1985), *Product Innovation and User–Producer Interaction*, Aalborg, Denmark: Aalborg University Press.

Lundvall, B.-Å. (1988), 'Innovation an interactive process – from user–producer interaction to the national system of innovation', in G. Dosi, C. Freeman, R. Nelson, G. Silverberg and L. Soete (eds), *Technical Change and Economic Theory*, London: Pinter, pp. 349–69.

Lundvall, B.-Å. (ed.) (1992), *National Systems of Innovation: Towards a Theory of Innovation and Interactive Learning*, London: Pinter.

Malerba, F. (2002), Sectoral systems of innovation and production, *Research Policy*, **31** (2), 247–64.

Malerba, F. (2004), 'Sectoral systems: basic concepts', in F. Malerba (ed.), *Sectoral Systems of Innovation: Concepts, Issues and Analyses of Six Major Sectors in Europe*, Cambridge, MA: Cambridge University Press, pp. 9–41.

McKelvey, M. (1991), 'How do national systems of innovation differ? A critical analysis of Porter, Freeman, Lundvall and Nelson', in G.M. Hodgson and E. Screpanti (eds),

Rethinking Economics: Markets, Technology and Economic Evolution, Aldershot, UK and Brookfield, USA: Edward Elgar Publishing, pp. 117–37.

Nasierowski, W. and Arcelus, F.J. (2003), On the efficiency of national innovation systems, *Socio-Economic Planning Sciences*, **37** (3), 215–34.

Nelson, R.R. (ed.) (1993), *National Innovation Systems: A Comparative Analysis*, Oxford: Oxford University Press.

North, D.C. (1990), *Institutions, Institutional Change and Economic Performance*, Cambridge, MA: Cambridge University Press.

Radosevic, S. (1999), Transformation of science and technology systems into systems of innovation in central and eastern Europe: the emerging patterns and determinants, *Structural Change and Economic Dynamics*, **10** (3–4), 277–320.

Whitley, R. (1999), *Divergent Capitalisms: The Social Structuring and Change of Business Systems*, Oxford, UK: Oxford University Press.

Whitley, R. (2000), The institutional structuring of innovation strategies: business systems, firm types and patterns of technical change in different market economies, *Organization Studies*, **21**, 855–86.

Whitley, R.D. (2001), 'National innovation systems', in N.J. Smelser and P.B. Baltes (eds), *International Encyclopedia of the Social & Behavioral Sciences*, Oxford, UK: Elsevier, pp. 10305–11.

PART 6

RESEARCH AND TECHNOLOGY POLICY

58 Policy for innovation
J. Stanley Metcalfe

Introduction

The topic of this chapter is the rationale for innovation policy in advanced market economies. Since innovation and its correlates, invention and the diffusion of innovation, play such a central role in the performance of modern economies, indeed they constitute a defining element in the claim that they are knowledge-based, it is hardly surprising that this rationale should be an indispensable part of economic policy more generally. The Barcelona Accord on R&D spending[1] suggests how important this issue is for European governments, and raises a question as to whether policy frameworks and instruments exist to reach the objectives of this accord. In particular, will it be possible to protect any sustained increase in innovation expenditures from the effects of diminishing marginal returns in the short run and in the long run?[2] We will suggest that the traditional rationale for innovation policy, market failure, is flawed in its understanding of the innovation process and, more fundamentally, flawed in its understanding of the wider process of innovation and competition in the modern world. Furthermore, processes of innovation depend on the emergence of innovation systems connecting the many actors engaged in the innovation process, and that these systems are essentially self-organizing and self-transforming. Innovation systems do not exist naturally but have to be constructed, instituted for a purpose, usually but not uniquely to facilitate the pursuit of innovation in search of competitive advantages by firms. To anticipate the conclusion, innovation policy should be about facilitating the self-organization of innovation systems across the entire economy, not only in 'new' sectors.

In sustaining this claim, we shall argue that innovation is one element, perhaps the most important, of the general class of investment activities in an economy, that it is complementary with other classes of investment undertaken by firms and other organizations, and that it requires much more than expenditure on science and technology for its realization. A functioning S&T policy is in the first instance a stimulus to knowledge and invention; in the process it facilitates innovation but the connection between the two is essentially a matter of investment, of present commitment in anticipation of future return, and it is equally important that policy promote the general process of investment if innovation is to flourish. Thus

943

R&D may be a necessary underpinning for innovation but it is certainly not sufficient: other complementary investments in skills, productive capacity and markets are also required. As an innovation policy lever on its own, S&T policy leaves much to be desired. Moreover, all investment is uncertain in its consequences but investment in innovation is particularly prone to the unexpected and the unintended consequences of action, precisely because innovation is a major source of business uncertainty. In exploring the limits of the market failure doctrine we also draw attention to the general limitations of an equilibrium approach to the analysis of innovation and competition and suggest that an adaptive evolutionary process view is a far sounder framework for understanding and policy guidance. Innovation involves the growth of multiple kinds of knowledge, including knowledge of how to organize and knowledge of the market opportunities and these different kinds of knowledge, complementary to scientific and technological knowledge, are generated within the competitive market process. Innovation is a route to competitive advantage but the converse is true also, that competition shapes the innovation process; the two phenomena are inseparable. In developing the argument, we will amplify the idea of innovation systems but not only from a national perspective. Rather we emphasize the local character of innovation systems and the need for policy to deal with the issues surrounding their birth, growth, stabilization and, if necessary, decline. National arrangements influence the ecology of organizations and the institutional rules of the game that enable innovation systems to be formed but innovation systems are not intrinsically national. Indeed a central implication of the unification of the European market is that 'local innovation systems' will cross national boundaries, with the prospect that national policies develop inconsistencies that are inimical to innovation performance.

Attributes of the innovation process
We begin with a brief statement of the relevant attributes of the innovation process. Innovation is, first and foremost, a matter of business experimentation, the economic trial of ideas that are intended to increase the profit, or improve the market strength, of a firm. Innovation, in this regard, is the principal way that a firm can acquire a competitive advantage relative to its business rivals. As a process of experimentation, a discovery process, the outcomes are necessarily uncertain; no firm can foresee if rivals will produce better innovations nor can it know in advance, even when all technical problems are solved, that consumers will pay a price and purchase a quantity that justifies the outlay of resources to generate a new or improved product or manufacturing process. This is not a matter of calculable risk, for probabilities cannot be formed in respect of unique events, or events

that change the conditions under which future events occur. There is an inevitable penumbra of doubt that makes all innovations blind variations in practice, and the more the innovation deviates from established practice the greater the fog of irresolution. Perhaps the fundamental point is that innovations are surprises, novelties, truly unexpected consequences of a particular kind of knowledge-based capitalism. This does not mean that innovation is irrational behaviour: firms are presumed to innovate in ways to make the most of the opportunities and resources at their disposal; however, neither the opportunities nor the resources available can be specified with precision in advance. Innovation is a question of dealing with the bounds on human decision making; it is to a substantial degree a matter of judgment, imagination and guesswork, and the optimistic conjecturing of future possible economic worlds. Consequently, policy instruments must be subject to the same penumbra of doubt in terms of their effects on the innovation process; there will be unanticipated consequences of innovation policy and great difficulty in tracing cause–effect relationships in the evaluation of policy.

The second attribute of the innovation process is the necessity of new beliefs and knowledge to emerge before innovation is possible. Moreover, innovation requires the drawing together of many different kinds of information, on the properties of a device or method, on the way to organize production and the perceived needs of the market. It is the combination of these elements that matters and the principal locus of combination in capitalism is the firm.[3] Thus, while many agencies may provide information valuable to the innovation in question, only the innovating firm can combine them into a plan for innovation and execute that plan. Neither universities, nor government laboratories, nor knowledge consultancies, which play an increasingly important role, have this final combinatorial responsibility; in this, the for-profit firm is unique. The corollary of this is that multiple kinds of knowledge are typically required to innovate and many of the sources of this knowledge will lie outside the firm, which has to extract the necessary information and integrate it into its own knowledge (Gibbons *et al.*, 1994). Consequently, the external organization of the firm and the management of its internal processes are essential elements in the innovation process and this insight is the foundation of the innovation systems perspective.

The third attribute of innovative activity is that it is embedded in the market process. Not only do firms innovate to generate market advantages relative to their perceived rivals, so that the functioning of markets shapes the return to innovation, but market processes influence the outcomes of innovation and the ability to innovate. The way users respond to an innovation and the ability of a firm to raise capital and acquire skilled labour and components necessary to an innovation are essential market process determinants of innovation activity. The fundamental test for successful innovation is not that it works but that it is profitable ex post, and this is a matter of market process. If markets are inefficient and distorted, this can only harm the innovation process and when incumbents and conservative users unduly control the relevant markets, the effect will be similar. It follows that competition policy and an efficient markets policy, more generally, are necessary elements in innovation policy. Conversely, a pro-innovation policy is perhaps the most effective contribution to a strong competition policy.

Since innovation entails the acquisition of new knowledge, we need to be clear what is meant by knowledge, and the processes by which it is generated and diffused. Knowledge has a unique property, it always and only ever exists in the minds of individuals and it is only in individual minds that new innovative concepts and thoughts can emerge. This is fundamental, it is why we recognize the entrepreneur and the prize-winning scientist – they are different as individuals – and from it follows the fact that knowledge is always tacit; it is never codified as knowledge. What is articulated and codified is information but information is only ever a public representation of individual knowledge, sometimes virtually a perfect representation but in many significant cases not. As Michael Polanyi expressed it, we know more than we can say and can say more than we can write. Since economic activity in firms and beyond depends on the ability of teams of individuals to co-ordinate their actions, it follows that processes must exist for correlating the knowledge of the individual members so that they understand and act in common. In regard to innovation, the internal organization and business plan of the firm are the primary means of co-ordinating information flow and turning individual knowledge into the necessary hierarchy of understanding and actions. It may be helpful to conceive of the organization of a firm as an operator, a local network of interaction through which what the individual members of the firm know is combined to collective effect and joint understanding. The spread of understanding in correlated minds is essentially a social process of human interaction; however, a chief consequence of information technology is that information can be communicated at a distance and this makes possible the inclusion of a firm in wider, less personal networks, including the scientific and technological networks that communicate almost exclusively in written form. To call these 'knowledge networks' may be understandable, but it is a mistake. The relevant networks are information networks, perhaps better expressed as networks of understanding, and their significance is in shaping what individuals in firms, and other organizations, transmit and receive as information. It is not that information is transmitted with error, it may be; rather, what matters is that information may legitimately be 'read' by recipient and transmitter in different ways. The interpretation of the message is not in the message but in the different minds of the parties concerned (Arthur, 2000). Indeed the growth of knowledge depends on this possibility of divergent interpretation of the information flux. All innovations, like scientific break-throughs, are based on disagreement, on a different reading of information, much of which is currently available in the public domain. Thus, the prior knowledge state influences what is 'read' and what is 'expressed' and, as Rosenberg (1990), made clear, firms have to invest in their own under-standing if they are to participate effectively in innovation information net-works and this is why it is necessary for them to conduct their own R&D.[4] Thus, while information is a public good, in the sense of being useable indefinitely, it is not a free good; scarce mental capacity must always be engaged to convert it to and from private knowledge (Cohendet and Meyer-Krahmer, 2001). Here we find one of the principal sources of variation in the innovation process: innovations are conceived in individual minds and these minds differ. It only needs a moment's reflection to recognize that if all individuals held the same beliefs there could be no growth of knowledge and no innovation and thus the beliefs in question could not have emerged in the first place. Idiosyncrasy, individuality, imagination are the indis-pensable elements in the innovation process and the way innovation policy is framed must recognize this fact; indeed, without them entrepreneurship would not be recognizable. The obvious corollary for the policy process is that innovation cannot be planned from on high; it emerges from below.

Scholars interested in innovation have for many years drawn upon the useful Polanyian (1958) distinction between tacit and codified knowledge, the former embodied in human skill and practice, the latter in material form. Tacitness is presented as a reason why information does not flow freely, while codification is a process to make information public. Thus, Callon (1994) is quite right to point out that the limits to excludability depend upon the way in which information is embodied in different com-munication media, and that access to any particular knowledge depends upon complementary assets being accumulated to give the capability to maintain and use knowledge-based statements. However, it is important to recognize the point that the division of knowledge into mutually exclusive categories, codified and tacit, does not uniquely reflect properties of the knowledge itself. Rather, it is in part an economic decision dependent on the scale on which the information is to be used and the costs of codifica-tion. It is thus inextricably linked with the division of labour in the economy more widely (Cowen *et al.*, 2000).

The fourth implication for the innovation process is that the systemic, emergent nature of group understanding leads directly to the basis of inno-vation systems. There is an increasingly elaborate division of labour in the generation of knowledge; to use an old economic concept, the division of knowledge labour is becoming increasingly 'roundabout' in nature. Since Adam Smith, scholars have recognized that the knowledge contained in any economy or organization is based on a division of mental specialism. It is not simply that the division of labour raises the productivity of the pin maker, it also raises the productivity of the 'philosopher and man of speculation' and greatly augments the ability to generate knowledge in the process. When this division of labour is not contained within the firm we have the conditions for an innovation system to emerge and the necessity of the co-ordination of the divers minds within that system. Innovation systems are the necessary consequence of this division of knowledge; and these systems do not arise naturally, they have to be organized and are not to be taken for granted. This self-organization process is a central concern of innovation policy from a systems failure perspective. Innovation systems are, in Hayekian terms, a form of spontaneous order, that is to say they are self-organizing. Perhaps the most obvious characteristic of modern economies is the distributed nature of knowledge generation and the consequent distributedness of the resultant innovation processes across multiple organizations, multiple minds and multiple kinds of knowledge (Coombs *et al.*, 2003). As a system, what matters are the natures of the component parts, the patterns of interconnection and the drawing of the relevant boundaries and each of these aspects forms a dimension of innovation policy, as we explore below.

Fifthly, and finally, it is helpful to group the factors that influence the ability to innovate into four broad categories, perceived opportunities, available resources, incentives and the capabilities to manage the process. In principle, we could imagine policy levers for each of these elements but what matters is that all four need to be addressed if policy is to be effective. Thus increasing the resources devoted to innovation is likely to run into rapidly diminishing returns if new opportunities are not perceived or if the management of innovation is weak and poorly connected with other activities in the firm. It is this point primarily that the systems innovation perspective addresses (Carter and Williams, 1958).

The limits to market failure
The development of an economics of information and knowledge in the 1960s led scholars to the realization that knowledge and information are not normal economic commodities but possess attributes that do not make them natural candidates for market exchange (Nelson, 1959; Arrow, 1962). The market failure doctrine and the rationale it provides for innovation policy has followed from these insights. Central to it is the idea that markets in relation to knowledge and information have an inherent tendency to

produce socially inefficient outcomes, inefficiencies, which provide the justification for failure-correcting, public policies. The private hand is not guided to produce and use the socially optimal amount of knowledge, and the optimizing policy maker is justified in corrective intervention through the joint provision of resources and incentives at the margin. This has proved to be a powerful set of ideas for shaping policy debate, particularly concerning the public support of university-based science and technology that are far from market application; it has been a far less useful means of designing specific innovation policies in relation to private firms. The reason is clear; the idea of a perfectly competitive allocation of resources (the doctrine of Pareto optimality) on which the idea of market failure is premised is a distorting mirror in which to reflect the operation of a restless, innovation-guided capitalism. This doctrine seriously misreads the nature and role of competition in modern societies through its failure to realize that capitalism and equilibrium are incompatible concepts, that innovation and enterprise preclude equilibrium and perfect competition.

Why does the market failure doctrine fail in respect of innovation? The reasons are hidden within the properties of a perfectly competitive economy. In such a world, not only must all agents be denied the power to influence prices of products and productive factors, there must also be a complete set of markets that values all consequences of all economic action in the present and in the indefinite future. In practice, the set of possible markets is incomplete, and those markets that do exist do not price all the consequences of action.

Consequences of action that are not priced accurately in the markets that operate are called externalities and, from an innovation perspective, the most significant externalities relate to imperfect property rights in the exploitation of knowledge. If the works of the inventor can be copied without cost, others may turn invention into innovation, and erode the incentives to invest in invention. This has long been recognized as a justification for patent and copyright systems and rightly so. Nonetheless, the practical implications of intellectual property protection are less straightforward. The problems are twofold. It is not information spillovers per se that damage the incentive to invest in knowledge production, but a presumption of instantaneous and complete spillover, an unlikely state of affairs for reasons which become clear below.[5] Absent this, and recognizing existence of many practical ways that firms have developed for protecting knowledge acquired privately, it becomes clear that inventors and innovators may still gain an adequate return from their investments without patent protection. Secrecy, or a short product life cycle, are familiar examples and help explain why patent protection is only considered significant in a small number of industries, those with high invention costs and long lead times to market. Secondly, this doctrine is far too negative: not all information spillovers are between direct competitors or diminish innovation opportunities. The difficulty arises from thinking that all firms are the same, losing sight of the fact that they read the information flow with different 'minds'. Spillovers can, and generally will, have positive benefits in stimulating the differential creation of new knowledge, which should not be underestimated; indeed, this is why patents are designed to put inventive ideas in the public domain. There is no reason why an alert firm should not gain more than it loses from the unplanned flow of information and so enrich its innovative capacity. In this regard, information spillovers are to be encouraged and one might expect firms to try to manage this process through links with other knowledge-generating institutions, which is precisely what we observe in practice.[6] What is interesting about the idea of property rights in commercially valuable knowledge is that they sit side by side with very imperfect property rights in economic activities more generally.[7] Copy my invention and I can pursue you in the courts. Make a better but unrelated equivalent and there is nothing we can do except compete. Indeed, if it were otherwise, it is difficult to see how capitalism could have been the source of so much economic change and development. This means of course that competition is an uncertain process. Investors, whether their assets are in paper titles or human skills, are ever open to the erosion of their worth by innovations made by others; this is why innovation-driven capitalism is, from a welfare point of view, an uncomfortable restless system. The fact that, on average, innovation enhances the standard of living should not blind us to this fact and to the inherently uncertain, potentially painful nature of innovation-related economic processes. From a policy viewpoint, one immediate implication is that the scope of patents should not be drawn too broadly, for this simply limits the ability of others to explore creatively the design space which any patented invention has placed in the public domain. A world with no spillovers simply restricts, perhaps makes impossible, the wider and deeper growth of knowledge. Thus, broad patents have the potential to damage the creativity of the capitalist model (Merges and Nelson, 1990).

   Externalities do not exhaust the idea of defective markets. Perhaps more important is the absence in general of futures markets to guide investment decisions. All innovations are investments, activities that require current outlay in advance of the economic return. Yet the markets to trade these future outputs, by establishing the price today for an activity to be sold, say, a year hence, exist only for a narrow range of standardized commodities that are broadly speaking unaffected by the prospect of innovation. In the absence of known prices, the only recourse is to substitute the judgment of entrepreneurs. As Shackle (1972) has so carefully expressed the point, enterprise cannot be based on knowledge only in the belief that success will follow the commitment to action. This uncertainty is intrinsic to the market process, for the most significant sources of uncertainty relate not to whether it will rain a year from today but whether others will have developed superior innovations by that date. It is not the game against nature that matters but the capitalist game of innovation, of rival against rival. In modern capitalism, genuine uncertainty is 'built in', as it were, and its consequences for the willingness to invest in innovation are far more difficult to cope with, for innovations, like all discoveries, are unique events for which the probability calculus is an inappropriate tool of analysis. Much decision making about knowledge creation is at root an act of faith; it is a matter of the conjecture of imagined future worlds with necessarily unpredictable time delays between knowledge creation, application and market testing (Loasby, 1999). Keynes's much ignored notion of animal spirits is certainly appropriate as a route to understanding innovation in capitalism. Moreover, it is not at all obvious that the process of accumulation of scientific or technological knowledge is any less hazardous than the accumulation of market knowledge (Callon, 1994). A central implication of this theme is that investment becomes impossibly difficult in perfectly competitive markets, as pointed out by Richardson (1961). Current market prices do not convey the information required to invest since they do not convey information about the investment plans of rivals. Consequently, firms seek other ways to co-ordinate tacitly or explicitly their activities, whether complementary or competitive, and these necessitate deviations from the atomistic competitive ideal. Although Richardson directed his analysis at investment in productive capacity, it applies equally well to investment in innovation, and one would predict a need for market imperfections if such investment is to be stimulated. One consequence of all this is that innovation processes are mediated by a range of non-market methods, primarily involving information networks and other forms of arrangement between organizations and individuals, procedures which build confidence and trust and work to limit the damaging consequences of uncertain, asymmetric information. These arrangements are precisely contrary to the idea of competition between isolated, atomistic, independent firms. Without market power, to a degree, innovation becomes an unlikely occurrence, and collaborative R&D arrangements, for example, are one way of dealing with the implied co-ordination failures.

Thus it is the innovative nature of capitalism that prevents the emergence of a full complement of future markets that gives the price mechanism a constitutional weakness. As economists know too well, only in a stationary state could we expect this difficulty to be resolved by tradition and habit if not by rational calculation, and 'stationary' is not an adjective to apply to capitalism at any stage of history. Thus, it is not at all obvious from a wider view that the missing markets constitute market failures in the broader context. Uncertainty and asymmetries in knowledge are direct consequences of a market process in which innovation is the driving force for competition. It is surely perverse to label as market failures phenomena which are integral to the competitive market process and which give modern capitalism its unique dynamic properties. Nor is there any obvious way that policy could 'correct' for lack of futures markets; they are simply intrinsic to the process of innovation and economic change. The fundamental fact is that profits follow from the deployment of ideas that others do not have, with the consequence that the whole system dynamic depends upon the generation of unquantifiable uncertainty and asymmetries in information. One cannot sensibly argue that the economy would perform better if innovation-related uncertainties were reduced, for the only way to reduce these uncertainties is to reduce the incidence of innovation and thus to undermine the mainspring of economic progress. This does not deny that radical uncertainty can be a justification for policy intervention. Indeed the rationale for the public support of fundamental research in science and technology lies in the fact that the links between these general categories of knowledge and market exploitation of specific innovations is often so tenuous that private firms would, quite legitimately, find no justification for investing in these kinds of knowledge. Yet even here, the matter is not clear-cut. For by no means all university research in fundamental science and technology is funded by government, and of that which is, a proportion is directed at meeting the mission objectives of government agencies in such areas as defence or health. Similarly, non-academic organizations carry out a substantial volume of work on fundamental science and technology; indeed, large private firms, usually multinational firms, can often boast far more advanced research facilities than can many universities.[8]

Having dealt with the problem of missing markets, consider next the idea that perfect competition requires an absence of market power, in particular that each firm be small relative to the scale of market to make this possible. Yet, fundamental to the economics of knowledge production and dissemination, is the fact that the exploitation of all knowledge is subject to increasing returns: the fixed cost of producing an item of knowledge can be spread over a greater volume of output, as it is used more widely and more intensively in the production process. Since one cannot innovate on the basis of a fraction of a technology or a quarter of a scientific fact, there is necessarily an indivisible cost of creating the complete set of knowledge behind an innovation. Consequently, the costs of exploiting an innovation fall with the scale of exploitation, precisely the condition which removes the possibility of perfect competition. Furthermore, every investment in innovation now requires its own expected minimum scale of exploitation if an adequate return is to follow. The result of these considerations is the complete inability of the perfectly competitive model to provide guiding innovation policy principles in a world where firms are required to innovate in order to compete (Stiglitz, 1994). The overhead innovation costs, which firms must incur unavoidably, mean that their behaviour will at best be imperfectly competitive and that there will be systematic and uneven deviations between prices and marginal production costs across the economy. The only way the fixed costs of knowledge production could be recovered, independently of prices and outputs, would be for public laboratories to develop that knowledge or for all private research and development expenses to be fully subsidized from the public purse. This is not a model for innovation likely to commend itself outside of very special cases such as metrology and public technical standards (Tassey, 1992).

Nor do missing markets and market power exhaust the difficulties in using perfect competition to reflect modern capitalism. There is also the so-called 'public good problem'. All knowledge and information has the intriguing property that it is used but not consumed in its using and that, once discovered, it is in principle useable by any individual on any number of occasions to any degree. In the terminology of economics, there is non-rivalry and non-excludability of knowledge. This terminology is not well chosen in relation to knowledge and information. We argued in the previous section that knowledge is only ever private and is certainly excludable by choice of the knowing individual. It is a representation of that knowledge, information, that is placed in the public domain but this is only accessible to everyone in principle. In practice, and as a direct consequence of the division of knowledge labour, to gain knowledge from information requires prior background knowledge to read that information and this knowledge has not been acquired without opportunity cost. There is much more to the transfer of knowledge than the costs of communication in the narrow sense. In many cases the interchange of knowledge requires communication between correlated 'like minds' only open to those who have acquired comparable abilities to understand the significance of new scientific and technological information. Self-exclusion follows from an inability to make the necessary background investments; information may be 'free' but the ability to extract knowledge from it is not, and it is the knowledge that matters for innovation (Mowery and Rosenberg, 1989; Rosenberg, 1990; Hicks, 1995; Veugelers, 1997).

To a degree, these different dimensions of market failure are interrelated. The public good aspect of information links directly to information spillovers and the externality problem. The fact that knowledge can be used repeatedly connects to the increasing returns dimension of the exploitation of information, whether in producing goods or, more significantly, in the further production of knowledge. In each case, we are led to deviations from the perfectly competitive market ideal but it is not at all obvious that affairs can be arranged otherwise. All economies are knowledge-based and the problems of the economics of knowledge and information are not an optional extra, they are intrinsic to the nature of a capitalist, market economy. When we turn to innovation policy, it is apparent that we are in difficulty, basing the rationale on a model of perfect competition. Leaving aside the well-recognized imperfections which governments can be subject to when they intervene, backing the wrong horse too quickly or maintaining programmes long after the evidence against continuation is conclusive (Walker, 2000), it is clear that market failure as a policy framework leaves much to be desired (Metcalfe, 1995a, 1995b). Market failure is a general rubric, not a recipe for stimulating individual innovations. The market failure framework, despite its formal elegance, is an empty box. In the presence of the apparent market distortions in relation to knowledge and information, there is no warrant for the idea that piecemeal policy can improve economic welfare; the world is simply too complicated to avoid these problems of the second best. Perhaps the problem is deeper, in that the issues of uncertainty, spillovers, increasing returns and public goods are not failures at all but vital elements in the evolutionary process that is capitalism. This thought takes us to the nature of competition and the idea of innovation systems and their failure as the basis for policy.

Innovation systems and the competitive process
The foundation stone of an alternative approach is the idea of competition as an evolutionary process, not as a state of equilibrium. In this perspective innovation plays the central role as the source of the differences in firm behaviours that give rise to competitive advantages. Rivalry depends on differential behaviour and these differences are resolved into differences in profitability and the consequential differences in the relative growth of rival producers. If markets are working well from an evolutionary perspective, firms with superior competitive knowledge and practice are able to grow at the expense of less competitive rivals. This is the central dynamic of evolutionary competition as a dynamic discovery process. All competition requires is rivalry, and two firms can be as competitive as many. In such a view, the roles of markets is to co-ordinate and evaluate rival business conjectures and so guide the economic change we (partially) measure in raising standards of living. This involves adaptation to new opportunities, new needs and new resources and market institutions are to be judged, not by the canon of Pareto optimality, but by their openness in stimulating innovation and adapting to change (Metcalfe and Georghiou, 1998).

Thus, the central weakness of the market failure approach to innovation policy is not its lack of precision but its attempt to establish a policy perspective within the confines of the static equilibrium theory of markets and industry. The market failure arguments identify significant features of the production and use of knowledge but these features have their full impact only in relation to the dynamic nature of the competitive process. Economic progress depends on the ongoing creation of private, asymmetric knowledge, knowledge which is sufficiently reliable and defendable to justify the original investment, yet has prospective returns that are not only uncertain to the investor but create uncertainty in complementary and competitive fashion to other investors. The imperfections identified in the market failure approach are to be viewed now in a different perspective, as integral and necessary aspects of the production and dissemination of knowledge in a market economy. From this perspective, it is surely perverse to call them imperfections or market failures. This is, of course, not a new point: for those who have studied Schumpeter, they are the natural features of an economic process driven by creative destruction. Another way of putting this is to say that, without asymmetries of knowledge and the correlated uncertainties and indivisibilities, the competitive process has nothing with which to work. The quasi-public good nature of knowledge, indivisibility and increasing returns, the inherent uncertainties of creative, trial and error processes and the imperfect nature of property rights in knowledge, are essential if market capitalism is to function. They are not imperfections to be corrected by policy.

Several important themes now fit into place in a way that is impossible with the market failure doctrine. First and foremost among them is entrepreneurship, a phenomenon which has no meaning in economic equilibria of any kind. Entrepreneurs introduce novelty into the economy, they disrupt established patterns of market activity, they create uncertainty, and they provide the fuel that fires the process of economic evolution. The fact that the framework of perfect competition cannot incorporate the entrepreneur is a telling statement of its inapplicability to an innovation driven economy. Secondly, the reward to entrepreneurship is the differential economic reward, which comes from introducing economic improvements relative to existing practice. Such abnormal rewards are not the consequence of market imperfections, they do not necessarily reflect the undesirable use of market power; they are instead the rewards to superior performance and are to be judged as such. It is a view that abnormal profits are the socially undesirable consequences of market concentration that is the real Achilles heel of the market failure approach, and, which denies it anything useful to say in the appraisal of knowledge-based, innovative economies (Littlechild, 1981). Thirdly, this perspective of competition and innovation as a coupled dynamic process provides us with a framework to formulate innovation policy. Innovations create the differences in behaviour, which we identify as competitive advantages, and the possibility of competition provides the route and the incentives to challenge established market positions. Moreover, to the extent that market institutions function properly, firms with superior innovations will command an increasing share of the available scarce productive resources, the process that is the link between innovations in particular and economic growth in general.[9] This suggests that the innovation policy and competition policy are complementary, indeed that a pro-innovation policy may be the surest form of competition policy, and that its broad purpose is to ensure that conditions remain in place for the continued creation and exploitation of asymmetries of knowledge.

In truly competitive markets, all established positions are open to challenge and it is this link between innovation and competition which has proved to be the reservoir of economic growth. Thus, capitalism is necessarily restless, occasionally kaleidoscopic, and competition is at root a process for diffusing diverse discoveries, the utility of which cannot readily be predicted in advance. The market mechanism is a framework within which to conduct innovative experiments and a framework for facilitating economic adaptation to those experiments.[10] The key issue, therefore, is how this competitive process interacts with the conditions that promote innovation.

Increasing returns, 'roundabout' knowledge production and innovation systems

We have referred already to the inevitable presence of increasing returns in a knowledge-based economy, the fact that the returns to investments in innovation increase with the scale of their exploitation. This rules out a perfectly competitive allocation of resources but there is much more to the phenomenon than is suggested by this perspective. As Adam Smith understood so clearly, increasing returns applies to the generation of knowledge as well as to its exploitation precisely because of the increasing specialization of bodies of knowledge and knowledge-generating institutions. What we are observing in modern innovation systems is the increasingly roundabout nature of production, not of material artefacts but of knowledge in general and innovation-related knowledge in particular (Young, 1928). Two features shape the modern innovation process, namely, increasing complementarities of different kinds of knowledge together with increasing dissimilarity of these bodies of knowledge, a reflection of an increasingly fine division of labour in knowledge production (Richardson, 1972). Innovating firms need to draw on and integrate multiple bodies of knowledge, whether scientific, technological or market-based, produced in an increasing range of increasingly specialized contexts.[11] At the same time to understand the significance of and contribute to advances in these various kinds of knowledge is increasingly beyond the internal capabilities of the individual firm. Consequently, firms must increasingly complement their own R&D efforts by gaining access to externally generated knowledge and learn how to manage a wide spectrum of collaborative arrangements for knowledge generation (Coombs and Metcalfe, 2000). The consequence is that innovations take place increasingly in a systemic context with respect to the use of new technologies and their generation. How they do so is a question of the co-ordination of the division of labour in innovation systems. This is a central difference from the market failure approach, which views innovation as a problem internal to the firm. Instead, we have to enquire how groups of different kinds of organizations are co-ordinated to give innovation processes a systemic dimension.

The essential point is the distinction made above between private knowledge and public understanding. All new knowledge arises only in the minds of individuals and if it is to have wider effect it must not only be communicated to other minds, these minds must absorb it and reach similar understanding of the phenomena in focus. In short, knowledge must be correlated across individuals. This is essential for any joint action and it is essential to the further growth of knowledge, as enquiring minds respond to the information that constitutes the testimony of others. The consequence of this is that what is understood is systemic, covering multiple individuals, it is combinatorial and it is emergent. Not only is understanding complicated, in the sense of the multiplicity of minds involved, it is also dynamically complex, in the sense that its development generates novelty in unpredictable and unintended ways; this is one foundation for the uncertainty that underlies innovation-led capitalism. Capitalism is a restless, evolving system precisely because its knowledge foundations are restless and adaptive too. The process of correlation of knowledge is complicated further by the fact that individuals typically express and communicate their knowledge in the context of the organizations of which they are members, and the rules and routines of these organizations shape the interplay of information both within and without that organization. Thus, all knowledge systems are constructed around multiple minds in multiple organizational contexts and here we should distinguish invention systems from innovation systems proper. The science and technology systems composed of universities, and public and private research laboratories, are primarily invention systems, and, as Schumpeter insisted, invention is conceptually distinct from innovation. Innovation systems depend on additional sets of actors in relation to the availability of productive inputs, the design of organization and the engagement with customers and they depend on the unique role of the firm to combine the knowledge of these elements to achieve innovation. The knowledge and ability to organize a productive activity, to identify markets and to mobilize resources, are essential elements in the innovation process; for innovations involve not only the generation of knowledge but the economic application of knowledge. Thus, innovation systems are embedded in the market process, with customers, suppliers and even rivals on occasions acting as important system components (Lundvall, 1986, 1992). Markets are the context in which resource problems in relation to innovation are solved and in which innovation opportunities are identified.

However, systems are not defined only in terms of their components, in this case knowledgeable individuals in organizations; the nature of the system also depends on how these individuals are connected by flows of information and the purpose that lies below the flow of information. The correlation of knowledge requires communication of information and indicates the importance of the connections in the innovation system and the need for these connections to change as the innovation problems change. In many important cases, communication requires personal interaction and its correlates of trust and empathy between the individuals. In other cases, particularly in regard to science and technology, communication can rely on communication technology so that much of the information considered reliable comes from minds that are distant and anonymous. Indeed, it is these non-social forms of communication, information technology broadly defined, that have transformed knowledge generation. By permitting connection between a far greater number of minds than is possible through personal interaction alone, information technology has been of vital importance not only to correlate knowledge more widely but to stimulate the further growth of private knowledge within innovation systems.

Yet science and technology systems are not innovation systems, the latter are far more limited in scope and directed to specific business objectives; that is to say, they are focused on local problem sequences reflecting the proprietorial concerns of the innovating firm. The most appropriate way to conceive of these systems is that they self-organize and that private firms take the lead in stimulating the self-organization of the knowledgable minds in the system. This means that innovation systems are locally dynamic entities, they are born, grow, stabilize and ultimately decline and fail and that the basis for the dynamic of self-organization is the evolution of the particular innovation problem sequence. Part of the dynamic of system change is that the growth of knowledge depends on disagreement across individuals and the fact that the solution to one problem typically opens up new problems that may require different kinds of knowledge in their solution. As Cohendet and Meyer-Krahmer (2001) point out, innovation systems operate as recursive trial and error processes for stimulating the growth of knowledge in relation to specific problems. The consequence of this is that, as the problem sequence evolves, so too do the components and connections defining the particular innovation system. Thus, there seems great merit in seeing innovation systems as a form of self-transforming, spontaneous order that interacts with the process of market competition outlined above. Perhaps the key point to note is that innovation systems are the bridge between invention systems and market systems.

What is at stake here is the development of the innovation infrastructure in the economy, an information infrastructure that facilitates the intercommunication of existing knowledge to shape mutually the future agendas and dispositions of resources of different organizations around innovation problem sequences. It is an infrastructure to correlate knowledge through communication and to co-ordinate access to complementary kinds of knowledge required to innovate (Edquist, 1997; Carlsson, 1997; Nelson, 1993). Many organizations are involved: private firms operating in market contexts, universities and other educational bodies, professional societies and government laboratories, private consultancies and industrial research associations, but only the first of these is in the unique position to combine the multiple kinds of knowledge to innovative effect. Between them there is a strong division of labour and, because of the economic peculiarities of information noted above, a predominance of co-ordination by networks, public committee structures and other non-market mediated methods (Tassey, 1992; Teubal, 1996). The division of labour is of considerable significance for the degree to which the different elements of the system are connected. Different organizations typically have different cultures, use different 'languages', explore different missions, operate to different timescales and espouse different ultimate objectives. Consequently, information is 'sticky', it is partially unintelligible, it does not flow easily between different institutions or disciplines and thus it is difficult to correlate knowledge to the desired degree. Thus, there is a major problem to be addressed in seeking to achieve greater connectivity of information flow processes.[12]

One influential strand of thinking in this area has been to emphasize the national domain of the science and technology infrastructure, and rightly so (Freeman, 1987, 1994; Lundvall, 1986, 1992; Nelson, 1993). Policy formulation and implementation is essentially a national process, reflected in language, law and the nature of national institutions and conventions. However, there are good reasons to elaborate the national perspective both downwards and outwards. It is important to recognize that different activities have different supporting knowledge infrastructures so that a sectoral innovation system perspective becomes essential.[13] This is simply one way of recognizing the specificity of the broad innovation opportunities facing firms (Carlsson, 1995; Malerba *et al.*, 2004). On the other hand, it is clear that the sectoral infrastructures frequently transcend national boundaries; a firm may draw on several national ecologies in its pursuit of innovation, depending on where the knowledgable individuals are located. Gibbons and colleagues (1994), draw attention to the emerging characteristics of knowledge production, a view which fits exactly with the view that innovation requires many kinds of knowledge for its successful prosecution. What they term 'mode-2' knowledge is produced in the context of application, seeks solutions to problems on a transdisciplinary basis, is tested by its workability, not its truthfulness, and involves a multiplicity of organizational actors, locations and skills. Together this entails a distributed system for innovation with no one-to-one correspondence with traditional national or sector boundaries.

While nations and sectors contain the ecologies of knowledgable individuals usually working within organizations, these ecologies do not constitute innovation systems. Systems require connections as well as components, and it is the formation of the connections which is the necessary step in the creation of any innovation system. Innovation systems do not occur naturally, they self-organize to bring together new knowledge and the resources to exploit that knowledge, and the template they self-organize around is the problem sequence that defines the innovation opportunity. Hence, innovation systems are emergent phenomena, created for a purpose; they will change in content and pattern of connection as the problem sequence evolves, and they are constructed at a micro scale. Within these networks, firms, the unique organizations that combine the multiple kinds of knowledge to innovative effect, play the key role in the self-organization process. Science and technology systems, networks and communities of practice, are necessary parts of the innovation networks but they are not sufficient.

Policy for innovation systems failure

Reflection on the above leads to a new rationale for innovation policy, which subsumes science and technology policy within its remit; this is the rationale based on a system failure perspective. Here the primary role of the state is to facilitate the emergence of innovation systems. In so doing 'government' takes responsibility for the ecology of organizations and institutions that facilitates business experimentation but recognizes that without the necessary interconnections the ecology is not a system. Since competition depends on innovation and innovation depends on the emergence of distributed innovation systems, it is clear that this provides an interesting alternative to the market failure perspective on innovation policy.[14] The state is not promoting individual innovation events in this view, rather it is setting the framework conditions in which innovation systems can better self-organize across the range of activities in an economy. Because systems are defined by components interacting within boundaries, it follows that a system failure policy seeks to address missing components, missing connections and misplaced boundaries. Each of these is a problem associated with the division of knowledge labour and the increasingly roundabout knowledge production processes and the location of relevant knowledge in specialized organizations.

The availability of components is none other than the availability of knowledgable individuals that can be allocated to an innovation process either in a firm or in some other knowledge organization. The supply of knowledgable minds to which innovating firms have access is perhaps the most crucial aspect of the innovation systems approach and of innovation policy, for it is individuals within organizations who are the elemental components of innovation systems. Their availability is, in part, a general question about the wider education process but, more specifically, it concerns the quality of the science and technology system in a country. 'Are there sufficient knowledgable individuals in relation to multiple branches of knowledge, in place or in training, on which firms can draw to solve innovation problems?' is the question that governments need to answer. Capabilities may be weak in some areas and non-existent in others, and government has a role to ensure that a sufficiently rich knowledge ecology is available from which innovation systems can be assembled.

The availability of knowledgable individuals is a necessary but not sufficient condition for the emergence of an innovation system; the requirement is for these individuals to be co-ordinated around the solution of innovation problem sequences. When the individuals are not employed by the innovating firm, then only an external transfer arrangement can communicate what they know to the firm, and here there is a wide spectrum of possibilities, not only in relation to the external organization of the firm but also in relation to the external organization of other knowledge-holding organizations. All organizations in a systemic context must be consciously outward-oriented if system failure is not to occur. Self-organization can fail because the different individuals are within organizations whose agendas and practices are misaligned in respect of a particular innovation problem sequence. The rules that shape each knowledge organization are often effective barriers to communication with other organizations, a natural consequence of the different purposes of each organization and the primary need to focus on internal procedures. In many cases, the information has to be elicited in some form of implicit or explicit contractual arrangement through a direct process of personal interaction. This is the social network basis for innovation systems. In all cases, the knowledge of the existing members of the firm is crucial to the ability to identify and absorb external information (Cohen and Levinthal, 1990). Thus, for example, firms and universities are remarkably different kinds of knowledge organization, they reflect a natural division of specialization and each is to be presumed appropriate to task; consequently, it would be as foolish to make universities operate like firms as it would be to attempt the converse. Yet their differences are a potent source of innovation system failures, and the systems failure policy response to this problem is the design of effective bridging arrangements, notionally between different organizations but ultimately between individuals.

Increasingly, in the past two decades, policy makers in the USA and Europe have followed a systems failure approach without perhaps realizing its systemic foundations. The current emphasis on collaborative research programmes containing firms, customers, suppliers and universities, the incentives to set up science parks or university incubators, the emphasis on cluster development programmes, the establishment of technology transfer offices in universities, the funding of major industrial R&D programmes within university laboratories, and the intensive national efforts at foresight activity are important examples of bridging mechanisms. Each of these is a device, whether conscious or not, to deal with a systemic failure in the innovation process, a failure in the self-organization of connection and interaction. Bridging processes are not designed to generate passive flows of information but to engage all the parties in an alignment of knowledge-generating and information-sharing processes, that is, to create a distributed innovation system (Coombs *et al.*, 2003). Distributed innovation processes are partnerships with reciprocal obligations as well as collaborations in pursuit of shared objectives. Since firms are likely to be the lead partners in defining the innovation problem sequences, it is vital that they have the internal capabilities to interact with other knowledge agencies. There is consequently little point in governments supporting S&T in universities and public laboratories in the hope that it will lead to greater wealth creation unless private firms throughout the economy have the R&D capacity to ask the right questions of external individuals. This is one reason why tax credits for R&D, for example, may be a useful complement to an innovation systems policy.

However, the fact that problem sequences evolve implies that the related innovation systems need to evolve also. Policy can only facilitate, it cannot design because design is always emergent. The members of a system and their connections will change over time and eventually any system becomes redundant as its underlying innovation opportunities are exhausted. It is important, therefore, that innovation systems are seen as transient, that they have useful lives, and that they need to be dissolved when their purpose is fulfilled. In innovation policy as elsewhere, there is an ever-present danger of preserving arrangements designed and instituted for yesterday's problems, not the problems of the future (Walker, 2000).

Conclusion

In this chapter, I have reviewed recent developments in innovation policy and attempted to view them through the lens of new developments in thinking about innovation systems and the processes that form them. Here the fundamental insight is the experimental, evolutionary nature of a market and network economy. As Schumpeter aptly observed, capitalism works by means of creative destruction, a process that is played out on a global scale. Patterns of international competition are ever-changing and an advanced country must be ever aware of new opportunities and threats if its standard of living is to be sustained. Central to a response must be its rate of innovative experimentation and a consistent thread to policy has emerged in the past 20 years based on a distributed innovation perspective and innovation-led competition. In this new approach, it is the transient, institutionalized basis of innovation that is the focus of attention, rather than expenditure on research and development. I have called this the 'system failure perspective'. From a political point of view this raises an interesting problem. Experimental economies experience many failures as well as successes; blind variation means that a great deal of effort is wasted, but this is a necessary part of the process of knowledge accumulation. As a general rule, concerns for public accountability within the political process do not easily accommodate the notion of misdirected effort, which often appears so clearly with the benefit of sufficient hindsight. Governments must learn to be experimental and adaptive too, just like the firms and other organizations whose innovative efforts they seek to jointly stimulate. In this way they can expect to facilitate the self-organization of innovation systems and underpin the future self-transformations of the economy on which standards of living will depend.

Notes

1. To raise European R&D to 3 per cent of GDP by 2010 with at least two-thirds of this contributed by industry.
2. Diminishing returns to the economic payoff, not diminishing returns to the growth of scientific and technical knowledge.
3. Broadly defined to include not-for-profit organizations that produce goods and services, such as hospitals, as well as the traditional for-profit business organization.
4. It is said that the British system of Industrial, Co-operative Research Associations, set up primarily in fragmented industries, failed to raise innovation performance, precisely because their target firms did not invest in acquiring their own capacity to understand the research and development carried out on their behalf.
5. I note in passing that what is spilt is information (messages) not knowledge. The knowledge content of any information flow is, of course, notoriously unpredictable as any

university examiner knows only too well. That this is so is essential to the emergence of novelty.

6. Hence the increasing volume of work which points to the role of knowledge spillovers in productivity growth. Cf. Griliches (1998) for an authoritative treatment.

7. It is worth noting that competition authorities in the UK have taken a dim view of firms which refuse to grant licences to exploit their patents and of attempts to use licences to distort the competitive process.

8. Narin *et al.* (1997) find that, of the US scientific papers cited by US industrial patents, only 50 per cent came from academic sources, while 32 per cent came from scientists working in industry.

9. As an aside here, we note that competition is not to be judged by market structure. The way to judge the efficacy of competitive arrangements is to consider the degree to which rivals can gain market share at the expense of each other and the degree to which they are innovating in the pursuit of competitive advantage.

10. This theme of the experimental economy has been particularly important in the work of Eliasson (1998). It has an inevitable Austrian hue, that markets are devices to make the best of our limited knowledge (Rosenberg, 1990).

11. Cf. Granstrand *et al.* (1997) for evidence that large corporations are increasingly diversified in the technological fields which they employ, and more diversified relative to their product fields. See also Kodama's work on technology fusion (1995).

12. Cf. Andersen *et al.* (1998) and Green *et al.* (1998) for further elaboration of the systems perspective. Also see Edquist (1997), for a quite excellent overview of the current state of the art.

13. There is a growing literature on regional innovation linkages in which an attempt is made to correlate innovation clusters with the processes of university-based scientific activity. See Varga (1998) for a review and empirical study of linkages in the USA. The paper by Malerba *et al.* (2004) is a comprehensive summary of these sectoral perspectives.

14. Cohendet and Meyer-Krahmer (2001) use the phrase 'knowledge-oriented policies' to capture much of what is meant here.

References

Andersen, B., Metcalfe, J.S. and Tether, B., 1998, 'Innovation systems as instituted economic processes', in J.S. Metcalfe and I. Miles (eds), *Innovation Systems in the Service Economy: Measurement and Case Study Analysis*, Dordrecht: Kluwer Academic Publishers.

Arrow, K., 1962, 'Economic welfare and the allocation of resources to invention', in R.R. Nelson (ed.), *The Rate and Direction of Inventive Activity: Economic and Social Factors*, New York: NBER.

Arthur, W.B. 2000, 'Cognition: the black box of economics', in D. Colander (ed.), *The Complexity Vision and the Teaching of Economics*, Cheltenham, UK and Northampton, MA, USA: Edward Elgar.

Callon, M., 1994, Is science a public good?, *Science, Technology and Human Values*, **19**, 395–424.

Carlsson, B. (ed.), 1995, *Technological Systems and Economic Performance: The Case of Factory Automation*, Dordrecht: Kluwer Academic Publishers.

Carlsson, B. (ed.), 1997, *Technological Systems and Industrial Dynamics*, Dordrecht: Kluwer.

Carter, C. and Williams, B.R., 1958, *Industry and Technical Progress*, Oxford: Oxford University Press.

Cohen, W.M. and Levinthal, D., 1990, Absorptive capacity: a new perspective on learning and innovation, *Administrative Science Quarterly*, **35**, 128–52.

Cohendet, P. and Meyer-Krahmer, F., 2001, The theoretical and policy implications of knowledge codification, *Research Policy*, **30**, 1563–91.

Coombs, R. and Metcalfe, J.S., 2000, 'Organizing for innovation: co-ordinating distributed innovation capabilities', in N. Foss and V. Mahnke, (eds), *Competence, Governance and Entrepreneurship: Advances in Economic Strategy Research*, Oxford: Oxford University Press.

Coombs, R., Harvey, M. and Tether, B., 2003, Analysing distributed innovation processes, *Industrial and Corporate Change*, **12**, 1125–55.

Cowen, R.P., David, P. and Foray, D., 2000, The explicit economics of knowledge codification and tacitness, *Industrial and Corporate Change*, **9**, 211–53.

Edquist, C. (ed.), 1997, *Systems of Innovation: Technologies, Institutions and Organizations*, London: Pinter.

Eliasson, G., 1998, 'On the micro foundations of economic growth', in J. Lesourne and A. Orléan (eds), *Advances in Self-Organization and Evolutionary Economics*, London: Economica.

Freeman, C., 1987, *Technology Policy and Economic Performance*, London: Pinter.

Freeman, C., 1994, The economics of technical change, *Cambridge Journal of Economics*, **18**, 463–515.

Gibbons, M., Limoges, C., Nowotny, H., Schwartzman, S., Scott, P. and Trow, M., 1994, *The New Production of Knowledge*, London: Sage.

Granstrand, O., Patel, P. and Pavitt, K., 1997, Multi-technology corporations: why they have 'distributed' rather than 'core' competences, *California Management Review*, **39**, 8–25.

Green, K., Hull, R., Walsh, V. and McMeekin, A., 1998, 'The construction of the techno-economic: networks vs paradigms', *CRIC Discussion Paper*, no. 17, University of Manchester.

Griliches, Z., 1998, *R&D and Productivity: The Econometric Evidence*, Chicago: University of Chicago Press.

Hicks, D., 1995, Published papers, tacit competencies and corporate management of the public/private character of knowledge, *Industrial and Corporate Change*, **4**, 401–24.

Kodama, F., 1995, *Emerging Patterns of Innovation*, Cambridge, MA: Harvard Business School Press.

Littlechild, S., 1981, Misleading calculations of the social cost of monopoly power, *Economic Journal*, **91**, 348–63.

Loasby, B., 1999, *Knowledge, Institutions and Evolution in Economics*, London: Routledge.

Lundvall, B.-Å., 1986, *Production Innovation and User-Producer Interaction*, Denmark: Aalborg University Press.

Lundvall, B.-Å. (ed.), 1992, *National Systems of Innovation: Towards A Theory of Innovation and Interactive Learning*, London: Pinter.

Malerba, F., Edquist, C. and Steinmueller, E. (eds), 2004, *Sectoral Systems of Innovation*, Cambridge: Cambridge University Press.

Merges, R.P. and Nelson, R., 1990, On the complex economics of patent scope, *The Columbia Law Review*, **90**, 839–916.

Metcalfe, J.S., 1995a, 'The economic foundations of technological policy: equilibrium and evolutionary perspectives', in P. Stoneman (ed.), *Handbook of the Economics of Innovation and Technological Change*, Oxford: Blackwell.

Metcalfe, J.S., 1995b, Technology systems and technology policy in an evolutionary framework, *Cambridge Journal of Economics*, **19**, 25–46.

Metcalfe, J.S. and Georghiou, L., 1998, Equilibrium and evolutionary foundations of technology policy, *Science, Technology Industry Review*, OECD, **22**, 75–100.

Mowery, D.C. and Rosenberg, N., 1989, *Technology and the Pursuit of Economic Growth*, Cambridge: Cambridge University Press.

Narin, F., Hamilton, K.S. and Olivastro, D., 1997, The increasing linkage between US technology and public science, *Research Policy*, **26**, 317–30.

Nelson, R.R., 1959, The simple economics of basic scientific research, *Journal of Political Economy*, **67**, 297–306.

Nelson, R., 1993, *National Innovation Systems*, New York: Oxford University Press.

Polanyi, M., 1958, *Personal Knowledge*, London: Routledge.

Richardson, G.B., 1961, *Information and Investment*, Oxford: Oxford University Press.

Richardson, G.B., 1972, The organisation of industry, *Economic Journal*, **82**, 883–96.

Rosenberg, N., 1990, Why do firms do basic research (with their own money)?, *Research Policy*, **19**, 165–74.

Shackle, G.L.S., 1972, *Epistemics and Economics*, Cambridge: Cambridge University Press.

Smith, A., 1776, *An Enquiry into the Nature and Causes of the Wealth of Nations* (Cannan edition 1904), New York: The Modern Library.

Stiglitz, J.E., 1994, *Whither Socialism?*, Oxford: Oxford University Press.

Tassey, G., 1992, *Technology Infrastructure and Competitive Position*, Dordrecht: Kluwer.

Teubal, M., 1996, R&D and technology policy in NICs as learning processes, *World Development*, **24**, 449–60.

Varga, A., 1998, *University Research and Regional Innovation*, London: Kluwer Academic.

Veugelers, R., 1997, Internal R&D expenditures and external technology sourcing, *Research Policy*, **26**, 303–15.

Walker, W., 2000, Entrapment in large technology systems: institutional commitment and power relations, *Research Policy*, **29**(7–8), 833–46.

Young, A., 1928, Increasing returns and economic progress, *Economic Journal*, **38**, 527–42.

59 Growth policy
Horst Siebert

A high GDP growth rate traditionally is one of the main targets of economic policy. In achieving higher growth, a country can improve the well-being of its citizens, reduce unemployment, alleviate the strains of structural change and generate funds for public and merit goods.

In order to answer the question how a high growth path can be realized, we have to look for the variables strategic for economic growth. Ideally, we would start from an econometrically tested model of economic growth that would specify the exact relevance of each growth determinant. Then, for each growth factor, we would be aware of its exact contribution to the growth rate in a given period. For instance, we would know the production elasticities of all the factors of production, i.e. of labor, physical and human capital, technology and institutional arrangements.[1] I will here follow a less ambitious approach in discussing factors that, when positively influenced by economic policy, can reasonably be expected to contribute to economic growth.

Increasing the labor supply

Starting from a macroeconomic production function, a first approach of growth policy is to increase the labor supply since labor contributes positively to output with a production elasticity of about 0.3. In this context, the reproductive behavior is normally not seen as a target variable of government activity, and rightly so because it is an individual decision. Nevertheless, government can influence conditions that may have an indirect impact on the reproductive behavior in a society. But a pure increase in the size of the population, though positively stimulating the GDP growth rate when the newly born eventually enter the workforce, does not augment GDP per capita which must be seen as the relevant measure of well-being. Therefore, this attempt to influence population dynamics is hardly an instrument of growth policy. This also holds for immigration policy if immigrants are an exact replica of the existing population. If, however, a country succeeds in attracting immigrants with a high qualification, this can be a most relevant instrument of growth policy. Such an immigration policy is selective in the sense that a country aims for people with a high qualification who can be complementary to capital or to less qualified labor. Very often, immigrants exhibit more determination for achievement than the people in place, which can have positive long-run productivity effects. They also may be prepared to move into bottlenecks for which the domestic labor force is not available, for instance in agglomerations. An explicit immigration policy can also be a policy approach when the existing capital stock cannot be adequately equipped with domestic workers (an oversupply of capital as in West Germany in the 1960s) or if open spaces exist, as in North America in the 19th century.

Other avenues of population policy are to raise the participation rate of women or to increase the working span in the life cycle. Finally, an important aspect is not to leave labor idle. High unemployment means that the active labor force is unnecessarily curtailed, that production could be higher and that fewer governmental funds would have to be spent for unemployment benefits (see below). Whether the potential labor force can be fully utilized depends, among other things, on the wage level and on the wage structure, i.e. on the institutional conditions that are relevant for the labor market.

With the expected ageing of population in some major countries of the world, especially in Europe, labor as a growth determinant is likely to have a negative impact on the GDP growth rate under *ceteris paribus* conditions. Other determinants will have to make up for it if a high growth path is to be reached (Siebert, 2002b).

Capital accumulation
Since output depends on the capital stock with its production elasticity traditionally estimated at 0.7 under the assumption of a given technology, investment is another line of attack of growth policy. Countries with a high share of investment in GDP tend to have a high growth rate. The role of capital is especially relevant in the context of convergence, an approach that explains why countries are catching up. With an increase in the capital stock, a country moves down its marginal productivity curve of capital, the return to capital falls and capital's contribution to the growth rate declines unless the marginal productivity of capital curve shifts upward thanks to technological progress.

An important aspect is the institutional arrangement of the capital market that allocates savings to the competing uses in investment. A more efficient allocation of savings helps economic growth. Thus, the tax system and institutional features should be neutral in the allocation of savings between competing uses, be these different legal types of firms, large or small firms or incumbents or new firms. Retained earnings should not receive preferential treatment, so that existing firms or the status quo have an artificial competitive edge over newcomers; nor should larger firms be preferred.

The tax system should not discriminate against investment spending. On the contrary, there are good reasons to exclude investment spending from expenditure taxes and other forms of indirect taxation and to put more weight on consumption taxes in order to foster capital accumulation. Income from capital may be taxed, but there are limits with capital becoming more mobile internationally and thus having an outside option.

A country can accumulate more capital than it saves and thus temporarily increase its growth rate with capital imports. The benefit of a high GDP today, however, requires interest to be paid tomorrow, so that the condition $F_K > r$ must be satisfied, i.e. the marginal productivity of capital must be higher than the interest rate of credits. If this condition is violated, servicing foreign debt will be a burden that causes a wedge between consumption per head and GDP per capita.

Conducive conditions for innovation

Technological progress, that is new products, new production processes and new organizational methods, represents a major driving force in economic growth. They shift the production possibility frontier outward, new products by enlarging the product set and new processes by requiring fewer inputs for a given output.

Innovation is to be understood as an endogenous process that is driven by competition between firms, that is, as a technological race for a higher market share, where the new product or the new technology grants a (temporary) monopolistic position. An important element of innovation is the entrepreneur, the Schumpeterian entrepreneur (Schumpeter, 1911), who takes over risk and implements new combinations of factors of production in a process of 'creative destruction'. For growth you need the entrepreneur. The Schumpeterian entrepreneur is different from the imitator who only mimicks a new product or a new technology and from the administrative manager who runs a business along established lines. It is essential that the role of the entrepreneur be accepted in society. Growth policy therefore has the task to promote the recognition of the entrepreneur in society; it is negative for growth if policy takes a line that continuously meets the opposition of the entrepreneur.

Growth policy has to create an economic environment in which inventions, innovation and investment flourish. It has to enhance technological change as a process endogenous to an economy. Ease of market entry is a key prerequisite for economic dynamics, both in newly emerging and in traditional industries. Most relevant is market entry regulation in the new technological areas of biotechnology, pharmaceuticals, communication and information. Regulations to obtain a business permit, to build a factory or construct a new building, and to license a new product define market entry. Analogous to the theory of effective protection, protected areas are equivalent to a tax on downstream industries and activities. Market exit regulations affect market entry as well. Product markets should be opened up to competition where regulation is no longer justified. Here the preparedness of society to take on new technological risk is a factor influencing economic growth. For a strong endogenous process of technological change, a tax system is required that induces firms to build capital and to innovate, and that does not slow down and restrict entrepreneurial effort.

The institutional set-up of corporate governance has an impact on innovation and capital accumulation. Bank-oriented systems of corporate governance such as the German *Hausbanken* tend to favor credits, in contrast to equity, where risks are limited by assets or by information based on personal relationships. Then, innovation naturally involving high risks ends up being financed from retained earnings. This, however, means that technological progress often only represents a marginal improvement of a given technology, that technological leapfrogging does not take place and that incumbents play a larger role in innovation. Market-based systems of corporate governance are more open to new technologies. In any case, a prerequisite for innovation is access to capital in the venture capital market, bypassing the traditional ties to banks as the only financial intermediaries.

A continuous flow of inventions and innovations cannot be generated by governments. Starting from a Hayekian view of technological progress, the flow of new technologies must come from a decentralized process. The role of governments is to take care of basic research and to ease the diffusion of new technical knowledge. The state should refrain from attempting to 'make' the strategic sectors. In any case, it should be recognized that the economies in most countries are not industry-based any more, but service-based and knowledge-based, and that the innovative dynamics no longer is solely determined by efforts in industrial R&D. Successful innovation in new technology fields, such as e-business or biotechnology, depends much more on open markets and favorable conditions for technology-intensive start-ups than on conventional R&D subsidies. Innovation policy should therefore be less concerned with distributing public funds and more with removing market barriers for innovative activities.

Human capital

The underlying paradigm of traditional growth theory has been that economic growth is driven by labor, capital and technology. This approach, relevant for the industrial society and also the service economy, no longer holds for the information and knowledge society where human capital becomes the major determinant of growth and where traditional labor (excluding human capital) may only have a production elasticity between 0.3 and 0.4, whereas human capital, together with physical capital, may reach an elasticity between 0.6 and 0.7 (Minkiw, Romer and Weil 1992).[2] In any case, even in the traditional approach of economic growth, the quality of labor is a decisive factor.

With human capital being a major determinant of economic growth, the tax system should not disfavor human capital accumulation relative to the accumulation of physical capital. This also applies to contributions to the social security systems that are based on labor income and imply high (average and marginal) tax and contribution rates. For instance, they are running up to 20 per cent of GDP in the continental countries, whereas they account for 7 per cent in the USA and 6 per cent in the UK. This means a high tax wedge and a disincentive for human capital formation as well as for effort. A reform of social insurance is therefore mandatory from the point of view of growth policy distinguishing between large risks that people cannot cover themselves and small risks on whose coverage they decide themselves.

Another important element in a strategy for growth is the organizational conditions for human capital formation. Thus, one should make sure that the primary and secondary school system is efficient. Vocational training systems combining formal schooling and training on the job for the young, such as in Germany, represent a promising approach, but they must be more innovative with respect to the new job opportunities, for instance in the information and communication industry. In major European countries the university system is inflexible and rigid, being steered by administrative procedures, somewhat similar to central planning. This system should be opened to competition. Universities should compete for the best researchers and students and students should compete for the best universities. One should make sure that all the talents available in a society are used. Where labor market laws and the practice of governance stand in the way of competition, the institutional set-up should be redone. This also applies to the large research institutes.

Stability of the institutional conditions and doing away with the impediments to growth

As has already become apparent under the different headings, institutional conditions play an important role in growth. The stability of institutional arrangements, if they are positive for growth, is paramount. It allows the private sector to have a stable frame of reference in a longer time horizon. This is relevant for all intertemporal decisions relating to savings and consumption, investment in physical and human capital, migration and the location of firms. Moreover, one has to make sure that institutional conditions do not make an economy vulnerable to shocks, as they apparently do in some continental countries of Europe, for instance in Germany. Finally, in order to set free the propellants of growth, impediments of growth have to be abolished, that is inefficiencies in the institutional arrangements that reduce the production potential. This relates to the regulation of the product market, labor market and capital market. Most prominent is the inflexibility of the labor markets in the major continental countries.

In the product market, regulation typically restrains market entry and exit or restrains parameters of the firm. Regulation has to be scrutinized continuously as to whether it is still justified, whether its benefits outweigh its costs and whether the objectives motivating it can be achieved more efficiently. In quite a few cases, regulations favor vested interests and traditional sectors. Competition policy with the goal of keeping markets open is another important element of the institutional framework from the point of view of growth policy.

In the labor market, regulation in many countries is at the root of the unemployment problem, especially in continental Europe. Here the rigidity of the labor market is one of the most important impediments to growth. Unemployment is ratcheting upwards in each recession; hysteresis follows. External shocks hit the European workers for a longer duration and consequently harder than workers in other regions of the world. This requires refashioning the institutional set-up of the labor market.

Here are some of the avenues which have to be followed in the continental systems. All legal rules that are to the disfavor of the jobless are to be changed. Market entry barriers for the jobless should be abolished. The incumbents, i.e. the jobholders, should not be protected when this implies that the outsiders remain unemployed. Deviations from negotiated wages should be allowed when this creates jobs or saves jobs. Rules should be changed in such a way that wage formation moves (a little bit) closer to the market process. This would imply that annual wage increases get more in line with productivity growth without needing unemployment. It would also mean a higher degree of wage differentiation, necessary because of different qualifications, different regional situations and different conditions in the firms.

Within the institutional set-up of continental countries, efficient labor contracts represent a promising instrument. They comprise working time, wages and employment guarantees. Such contracts are Pareto-efficient, and both the firm and the worker can benefit from them. Therefore, such contracts should be made possible. Since employment guarantees cannot be given by centralized employers' associations, these contracts have to done in a decentralized way, that is in the firms. We therefore have to look for institutional forms which allow these decentralized contracts, which means a two-tier wage bargaining system where important aspects of the wage contract, such as job security, are dealt with at the firm level.

Employment guarantees in efficient labor contracts give some flexibility because they allow a trade-off between the other variables of the wage contract, wages and working time. Other forms of flexibility should be applied as well. A first approach is to adjust individual working time with a slow-down of economic activity (and to adjust labor income downward in a downturn, though possibly not proportionally). This secures jobs and allows working time to 'breathe' with the level of activity. A second approach is to make working time more flexible in a general fashion. An example is the approaches in Germany, for instance an annual budget of working hours per year for each worker, or even life-long budgets of working hours. This approach gives more flexibility than a 35-hour working week. It allows productivity gains that can be shared between workers (for their income) and firms (for their competitiveness). A third approach is a bonus system with a fixed and a flexible part of salaries so that some risk sharing takes place.

In order to prevent the lower segment of the labor market from drying up, wages should not be declared mandatory. In countries with a minimum wage, the concept of the minimum wage should be given up because, if minimum wages are binding (for instance, in low-income regions, for the young), they destroy jobs. Minimum wages are at the root of youth unemployment. In countries where the reservation wage plays a similar role to the minimum wage, the reservation wage that is determined by the benefits of the social security system should be redefined.

In the capital market, countries should choose the system that is most adequate for economic growth. The bank-based system seems to have some disadvantages if one wants to finance new technologies that are on a completely different trajectory from the technological set-up of the existing firms. Countries also must make a choice with respect to the institutional set-up of their corporate governance as regards codetermination. As with the bank-oriented system of the capital market, codetermination seems to favor the existing technology and its marginal improvement.

The role of government
Besides defining the frame of reference for the private sector in the institutional set-up and besides specifying taxes, the government influences the growth performance of the economy by the size and by the type of its expenditures. It can be argued that the growth rate is a function of the size of government in the economy, i.e. of its share in GDP. Under *ceteris paribus* conditions, we can expect an inverted U-shaped curve where a threshold on the growth rate of a country (on the vertical axis) declines with

an increasing share of government in GDP (on the horizontal axis). Growth policy therefore has to evaluate continuously the role of government and to question whether a share of government activities of 50 per cent of GDP, as in the continental countries, is justified. In some sectors, government activities can be privatized, as in telecommunications, and more efficiency can be obtained. Public monopolies can be dismantled by defining new property rights. When the social security system has lost financial solidity and when social absorption has reached a level such that it has a negative impact on the economic base of a country, it has to be restructured.

Consumptive governmental expenditures, although having a positive effect on the demand side, withdraw resources from the private sector. This withdrawal effect reduces the rate of growth unless resources in the government sector are used for productive purposes and unless their productivity is higher than that of the resources withdrawn from the private sector.

Subsidies require sizable financial resources[3] and imply distortions and efficiency losses. They tend to protect and favor old sectors and they impede structural change. Subsidies should be done away with.

Long-run constraints
Growth policy needs a long time horizon, therefore a decisive element is to integrate the long-run opportunity costs of economic decisions that are taken today. In growth policy as in any other policy area, quick benefits should not be sought at the price of long-run costs. This demand contrasts with the inherent tendency of politics to look for short-run fixes and to buy time. This conflict is relevant for budget policy, the social security system, the use of the environment and many other areas.

The government running a budget deficit generates a higher interest load in the future and thus reduces its future manoeuvering space. It puts a burden on future generations. When market participants anticipate the future burden in the form of expected higher taxation, confidence is lost and the positive demand effect of higher government spending vanishes. Additional debt then has a negative growth effect. It is for this reason that institutional constraints are needed to restrain the behavior of politicians. These may be national constitutional constraints in each country, for instance on the permissible level of new public debt, or international rules such as in the Stability and Growth Pact.

The social security systems have to respect an intertemporal budget restraint; the present value of expenditures should not surpass the present value of revenue, assuming a period of three to five decades. If this condition is not satisfied, we have a similar loss of confidence to that in the case of government debt.

In principle, these considerations apply to other restraints as well, for instance to the balance of payment. A country should take care not to take a position in which it becomes vulnerable because it finances its current account deficit with short-term capital inflows that can reverse themselves instantaneously.

The use of natural resources and of the environment deserve analogous arguments. A high growth rate may be obtained at the cost of environmental degradation, and more specifically at the cost of long-run damages that may be hard or impossible to repair (Siebert, 1998). Here, growth policy has to integrate the user costs of its current decisions for future generations.

Demand policy
Since aggregate demand can restrain the extent to which the production potential of the economy is idle, demand conditions can be an element of growth theory. One has to make sure that demand is sufficient, so that the production capacity is fully utilized. A related view is to keep the economy running, for instance through a deliberate undervaluation of the domestic currency. This short-run approach to growth policy is liked very much by politicians because it buys time, especially prior to an election, when the politicians' time preference rate is up at the two-digit level. In these considerations, the stimulation of demand should not ignore the long-run costs, for instance of budget deficits if government expenditures are used to stimulate aggregate demand. This also holds for the long-run costs of a high inflation rate that has to be brought down or for a realignment of the distorted exchange rate becoming necessary at a later point in time.

Monetary and financial stability
Avoiding monetary and financial disturbance is an important prerequisite for growth. Monetary policy can best serve a growth strategy by providing a stable money in the long run. At the same time it has to provide sufficient liquidity such that the demand side is not restricted and can go along with the increase in the production potential. Monetary policy must be aware of the time-lag involved between the actual money supply and the price level, eight to ten quarters down the road, at least in quite a few economies.

A more traditional failure of monetary policy that is negative for growth is that short-run stimulation and excessive liquidity require a stabilization recession at some time in the future because otherwise price-level stability cannot be obtained (as in the USA in 1981). Another traditional problem is hyperinflation of the Latin American type. These failures can be prevented by the independence of the central bank. A more recent and a somewhat forgotten form of monetary failure is excessive liquidity creating a bubble without affecting price-level stability. The example of the burst Japanese bubble and its aftermaths in the 1990s show this new risk of failure for monetary policy and the severe negative implications for growth that can follow from excessive liquidity (Siebert, 2002a). Currency crises of the Latin American type with an excessive expansion of the money supply and an insufficient crawling peg are a target of monetary policy, whereas the Asian-type currency crises seem to have a different cause, the main one lying in the insufficient regulatory system.

Monetary policy also seeks to prevent a deflation, i.e. a spiraling downward of the price level; this would represent a major disturbance of the growth process in that market participants can sit and wait with their spending for consumption and investment until prices have fallen further.

Taking a long-run view on the conflict between equity and efficiency

High growth rates can be in conflict with equity, as illustrated by an inverted U-curve where a threshold on the growth rate (on the vertical axis) declines with an increase in equity (on the horizontal axis). This corresponds to the inverted U-curve between growth and the share of government in GDP. Here society has to make a choice on how much equity it wants and which growth rate it is prepared to forgo in order to have more growth.

Care should be taken on how equity is defined. Equity should not mean equity predominantly in a static context for those of today. We should interpret distribution and social equity in an intertemporal sense. We should look at the question whether income per capita will improve in the medium run and we should study vertical mobility in the income distribution over five or more years. According to empirical analyses, vertical income mobility is a relevant fact.[4] Equity can also not mean equity for those employed at the cost of discrimination against the unemployed. This would mean social exclusion.

Relying on competition

Growth policy should rely on competition to find new solutions and overcome the status quo. Competition is a decentralized process in which an efficient allocation is obtained more or less automatically and where change occurs also in a decentralized way from below and also automatically. The alternative approach would consist in corporatist round tables and other related procedures where the groups involved determine the change to be made. Then, if traditional sectors tend to be protected, structural rigidities will not be overcome.

The governance system of an economy should make use of competition, i.e. it should be market-based. This is an issue for countries with a bank-based allocation of capital instead of a market-based one, for countries with an administratively steered governmental university system instead of one being competition-oriented and reliance on procedures finding a consensus on all layers such as in distributive federalism and in codetermination.

Locational and institutional competition is an important vehicle to force firms and other market participants to use their imagination to cut costs and to find new products. It can also induce the government to improve its way of operating. Competition will prove to be a discovery process that reveals more efficient solutions. It will make an economy strong and robust in the long run.

An important aspect is the openness of the economy. Openness means gains from trade, i.e. additional benefits not possible in a closed economy. But openness also means a higher intensity of competition. Protectionism is not a viable alternative, it implies less growth and lower welfare for the countries of the world.

Notes

1. For such an approach compare, German Council of Economic Advisers, Annual Report 2002, p. 205.
2. 0.37 for the OECD countries, 0.28 worldwide.
3. In Germany, 7.5 per cent of GDP, if a broad concept of subsidies is applied.
4. For instance, in Germany, 73.7 per cent of those below 50 per cent of median income in West Germany in 1995, were in a higher relative income position after four years. See German Council of Economic Advisers (2000), Table 69.

Bibliography

German Council of Economic Advisers (2002), *Annual Report 2002*, Wiesbaden: German Council of Economic Advisers.

Higgins, B. (1959), *Economic Development: Principles, Problems and Policies*, New York: Norton & Co.

Maddison, A. (1991), *Dynamic Forces in Capitalist Development*, Oxford: Oxford University Press.

Mankiw, N.G., Romer, D. and Weil, D.N. (1992), A contribution to the empirics of economic growth, *Quarterly Journal of Economics*, **107**, 407–37.

North, D. (1990), *Institutions, Institutional Change and Economic Performance*, Cambridge: Cambridge University Press.

OECD (2003), *The Sources of Economic Growth in OECD Countries*, Paris: OECD.

Olson, M. (1982), *The Rise and Decline of Nations: Economic Growth, Stagflation and Social Rigidities*, New Haven: Yale University Press.

Schumpeter, J. (1911), *Theorie der wirtschaftlichen Entwicklung*, Leipzig: Duncker & Humblot, English edn (1934), *The Theory of Economic Development*, Cambridge: Harvard University Press.

Siebert, H. (1998), *Economics of the Environment. Theory and Policy*, 5th edn, New York: Springer.

Siebert, H. (2001), How the EU can move to a higher growth path: some considerations, *Kiel Discussion Paper*, **383**, Kiel.

Siebert, H. (2002a), *The World Economy*, 2nd edn, London: Routledge.

Siebert, H. (ed.) (2002b), *Economic Policy for Aging Societies*, Berlin: Springer.

Siebert, H. and Stolpe, M. (2002), 'Germany', in B. Steil *et al.* (eds), *Technological Innovation and Economic Performance*, Princeton and Oxford: Princeton University Press, pp. 112–47.

60 Time strategies in innovation policy
Georg Erdmann, Jan Nill, Christian Sartorius and Stefan Zundel

Introduction

While business leaders and business economists are well aware that the success story of decisions concerning the market introduction of innovative products, processes, financing and marketing strategies strongly depends on the right timing of the measures undertaken, mainstream macroeconomics almost completely disregards this aspect. While business cycle theory has proposed strategies towards time strategies in monetary and fiscal policy, proposals towards developing time strategies in innovation policy are of minor concern in mainstream economics.

Our motivation to think about time strategies in innovation policy is based on the assumption that the socially most acceptable way for achieving a more sustainable development will be the effective implementation of innovations, i.e. novel technical or institutional solutions allowing the solving of a given sustainability problem with lesser effort and costs. The approach of this chapter is inspired by the idea that the timing of political measures in favor of innovations is an important condition for its success or failure: if political impulses are set at the wrong time, they risk failure in the sense that effects come out that are not worth mentioning or that the effects are rather costly with respect to the benefits created. If, however, these impulses are initiated at the right point in time, they can significantly influence the further development even when limited in scale and time.

This chapter elaborates the concept of time strategies by using the concept of inhomogeneity in time that belongs to the major theoretical approaches in evolutionary economics. Phases of relative stability – in the vernacular of mainstream economics, a dynamic equilibrium – alternate with relatively short phases of instability during which major changes, basic innovations, are more likely to occur and, thus, change the trajectory of the system under consideration. This chapter distinguishes the techno-economic and the political system in order to analyze mutual impulses on the course of stability and instability phases.

Instability phases represent so-called 'windows of opportunity' for innovation policy as innovations favoring the sustainable development are more likely to get their way than during phases of relative stability. The value of this approach crucially depends on whether or not decision makers are able to anticipate approaching phases of instability. The chapter addresses this concept in more detail and presents ideas about key variables that may allow the anticipation of windows of opportunity by political decision makers.

Systems analysis in terms of non-homogeneous time

The behavior of systems in time, the system dynamics, can be described with the help of non-linear differential equations of the following type:

$$\frac{dX}{dt} = F(X,Y,t), \tag{60.1}$$

where $X(t)$ is a vector of endogenous variables, $Y(t)$ is a vector of exogenous variables, and t is time.

For such a differential equation, a potential function exists. It is defined as the integral of the differential equation and describes the forces which act on the system depending on its endogenous state, X. Erdmann (1993) illustrates this by means of a simple example:

$$\frac{dx}{dt} = -2ax - 4bx^3, \tag{60.2}$$

where x is the internal state of the system and a, b are system parameters.

The corresponding potential function holds:

$$V(x) = -\int \frac{dx}{dt} dx = ax^2 + bx^4. \tag{60.3}$$

Figure 60.1 shows the potential function for two specifications of the parameters a and b. On the right-hand side, the system has a single stable equilibrium in state x_0. In the case where the state of the system were eventually to move away from this equilibrium, it would tend to return to this state. If political decision makers were trying to stabilize the system outside this state, they would have to execute a continuous force. This figure is somehow equivalent to the mainstream economic view about market failures according to which government, aiming at correcting for these failures, must execute a continuous force. Thereby, the equilibrium in x_0 is moved gradually into the direction of the political impulse whereby the impact of the instrument increases with its strength.

The right-hand side of Figure 60.1 shows two stable equilibria in x_1 and x_2, whereas the state x_0 represents an unstable equilibrium. This configuration emerges from the situation on the left-hand side with only one stable equilibrium by changing system parameters a and b. Following this change, the system will no longer be stabilized in the initial state x_0 but will tend to

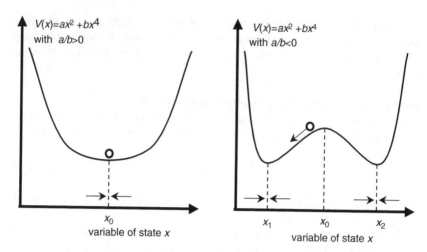

Figure 60.1   Potential functions

shift towards one of the new equilibria. Before this happens, the system is *instable* in the sense that weak impulses are sufficient to determine the future trajectory of the system. If the direction of the system is changed through an innovative activity, its major impact justifies labelling it a *basic innovation*. The weak impulses may be due to actions from political decision makers. The applied instrument can exert its influence even if it is applied only during a certain period of time while the system has not yet approached the new equilibrium. In spite of the temporal intervention, its long-term impact would be important and sustainable compared to the impact of the continuous government intervention outside a window of opportunity.

Initial small and temporary political impulses have the potential to change almost irreversibly the system in one or the other direction. The later dynamics of the system depends on the selection during this instability phase. It is *path-dependent*. Dosi (1988) introduced the term 'technological paradigm'. Accordingly, 'a technological paradigm can be defined as a "pattern" for solution of selected techno-economic problems based on highly selected principles derived from the natural sciences' (ibid., 224). If a certain market is dominated by one technological paradigm, the development of other technologies in this market is limited, but as the involved actors are specialized in their technological activities, economies of scale, learning effects and positive network externalities can be exploited. The series of incremental follow-up innovations within a technological paradigm is called 'a technological trajectory'.

Empirical evidence shows that the technology selection is not fully irreversible. There are many factors which can destabilize a given equilibrium.

Some examples are changing preferences, new scientific insights, and economic and environmental problems associated with the dominating technological paradigm. These and many other factors (see below) establish continuously changing conditions for innovations. Translated into the systems dynamics model, the parameters of the system may vary over time. But only during rather limited periods of time (i.e. phases of instability) can a stable equilibrium become sufficiently unstable, offering the chance to leave the present technological trajectory.

In addition the change of a given technological trajectory – or the move to another equilibrium – may result from successful innovative attempts of particular market players or political decision makers. In terms of the systems dynamics model, these attempts represent stochastic fluctuations. If the potential barrier between two stable equilibria is low, these fluctuations may be large enough to overcome the barrier between two equilibria and lead to the selection of a different technological trajectory. If, however, the potential barrier is high, these impulses may not have the capacity to overcome the lock-in of the system in the given equilibrium.

Fluctuations in social and economic systems are the result of a special type of actor. Entrepreneurs – or change agents – are able and willing to bear the risk of trying innovative attempts. The presence of change agents and their behavior in specific circumstances cannot be anticipated in general. Therefore, this is reflected in systems dynamics models by (seemingly stochastic) fluctuations that are beyond predictability. However, the evolution of the general conditions that may present the chance for those fluctuations to become influential in changing a technological trajectory can be analyzed and to some extent anticipated. Accordingly, our analysis is, in principle, restricted to the anticipation of opportunities, not of actions. In addition, case studies may help us gain occasional knowledge about the existence and impacts of possible change agents.

Innovation strategies in inhomogeneous time
Obviously, the succession of stable and unstable system states offers an approach to describing the management of time strategies in techno-economic, political and social systems. Unlike what happens in periods of instability, if impulses are executed during a stable period a strong force is needed to establish a basic innovation. Unstable periods in this sense may be viewed as windows of opportunity for innovation policy. Before discussing this aspect in more detail, a word of caution is in order: we have to distinguish between the prediction of an unstable state of a given system and the forecast of a new equilibrium. When an unstable situation is approaching, a predictive statement about the future trajectory is possible if the equilibrium structure is characterized by only one stable state. But

normally the number of equilibrium states is larger than one. Then, during windows of opportunity, it may be possible to determine the probability with which the current equilibrium will be left, but no prediction can be made as to which new equilibrium may, potentially, be reached.

Uncertainty is thus an important feature of innovation policy. It is well known that, particularly in the early stages of basic innovations, the economic and ecological properties of the new equilibrium can hardly be predicted. The economic and ecological superiority of a technology is, to some extent, the result of a self-enforcing process, learning curves, network externalities etc.

This does not mean that no scientifically based advice can be given to political decision makers for developing strategies and timing of measures and instruments aimed at strengthening the development and the introduction of innovations towards a sustainable development. Advice to political decision makers is based on the idea that temporarily limited measures can quite successfully trigger the introduction of innovations. A condition is that measures be applied in situations where a window of opportunity has opened. Political decision makers should carefully observe the approach of these window situations and stimulate – if such a situation has been identified – an irreversible selection of a seemingly favorable technological trajectory through determined and powerful but temporary measures. The discussion of criteria for the appropriate determination of the time periods for the measures is reserved for a later paper.

The proposal does not mean that no continuous policy impulses should be applied. Instead, instruments such as Pigou taxes are justified and can be applied apart from additional temporal measures. If the innovation policy would apply temporal instruments, then, after the removal of the measure, one of the following consequences will be observed.

First, it may turn out that, in terms of competitiveness, the new technological trajectory will fall behind the old technology. Accordingly, the decision makers have to recognize ex post that the new technology was not yet ready for commercialization in the mass market and that the assumed window of opportunity did not really exist. An actual example is the present political support for wind power plants in Germany. In spite of the technical progress in recent years, it is quite unlikely that the wind power industry will presently survive in Germany without any further support. However, in other countries and locations with better wind conditions, this technology is close to competitive. Taking a broader point of view, the German wind power policy is close to being successful.

Second, it may turn out that the new technological paradigm is successfully introduced but less favorable for achieving the sustainability targets than originally expected. Accordingly, the political decision makers have to recognize ex post that the stimulated selection during a window of opportunity situation had been wrong. In this case, political abstention would have been better. Unfortunately the techno-economic system is now locked into the inferior technological trajectory, implying a setback in achieving sustainable development. An example is the political support of nuclear power production in many industrial countries during the second half of the 20th century. But it is questionable whether the possibility of such an outcome should motivate political decision makers generally to abstain from any innovation stimuli once an opportunity has been identified. Rather, we should recognize that it is not possible to act without ever making errors. Innovative progress is usually the result of trial and error. What is crucial is the capacity to learn from errors, for example through technology assessment activities.

Third, it may turn out that the new technological paradigm is successfully introduced and favorable for achieving the sustainability targets. This, of course, is the desired outcome of innovation policy. The applied instruments may be withdrawn without any disadvantage to the sustainable development trajectory which leads to a deregulation and liberalization effect and creates the scope for innovation policy to address new problems and challenges.

The above discussion refers to situations in which political decision makers assume instability situations. If decision makers perceive stable situations in which no window of opportunity is open, then another strategy should be applied. The key idea is that it would be preferable to have a choice between alternative technology trajectories once a window of opportunity becomes open. In periods of stability, the classical instrumentation for supporting the innovativeness in the society applies: investing in human capital, research and development (R&D), education, university research, patent law, public research budgets etc. A trade-off between the multiple technological research directions on the one hand, and on the other, economies of scale in R&D along a single technological paradigm has to be accepted, but it seems wise to allow for diversity in research and development.

Technology selection takes place several times during the innovation process, which reaches from the establishment of a promising idea via the proof of technical feasibility, the construction of small demonstration and industrial scale plants, to the development of first market niches and the diffusion of the new technology. At each stage, stop-or-go decisions are made in order to limit innovation costs and risks depending on the costs and time needed. In the case of high R&D costs, decisions taken during pre-market periods are irreversible to some extent. The selection environment is determined by technical and economic factors such as scientific knowledge, expected technical potentials, costs, returns, risks and competition, but it also includes scientific, social, cultural and administrative components and factors (such as social acceptance and demand). As far as the analysis of sustainability problems and proposed solutions can assess the appropriate selection during early stages of the innovation process, the public R&D budget may be used to bias it. Otherwise, a diverse portfolio of innovative approaches is preferable. Multinational cooperation and coordination may be used to limit the public expenditures.

One may object to this proposal that the government should leave the selection process to market forces and restrict its intervention to framework policies such as eco-taxes and other instruments for internalizing external effects. The first reply to this objection is that our approach does not reject the idea of applying instruments correcting for market distortions on a continuous scale – as long as the market distortions and externalities are not yet overcome through successful innovations. The second reply is the observation that political decision makers cannot abstain from interventions and regulations. As this is the empirical reality, it would be better to rely on temporal regulations that are automatically withdrawn after some time than to be kept in a process of cumulative regulation. But a deeper discussion of this normative question is beyond the scope of this chapter.

Identification and anticipation of instability situations

The proposed innovation strategies are feasible if situations of instability (windows of opportunity for the implementation and diffusion of new technological paradigms) can be empirically identified and possibly anticipated. There are examples in economic history showing that business experts and political decision makers have been able to achieve such results. Likewise, other examples show the contrary. A more systematic analysis of this issue would be helpful as it would reduce errors and improve the success of time strategies

The scientific analysis of this question has to start with a deeper understanding of the genesis of instability situations and must identify relevant variables which can be observed empirically. For this purpose, we distinguish three subsystems.

First, there is the social–cultural system, which includes social entrepreneurs (non-governmental organizations), journalists, priests, artists, scientists etc. and is determined by interactions between these entrepreneurs, values, life styles, social problem perceptions and social movements. Prominent examples for instability situations are revolutionary events such as the student protests of 1968 or the breaking of the Iron Curtain in Europe in 1989. Instabilities related to environmental problems are due to major accidents (Bophal, Chernobyl) or scientific discoveries of serious environmental problems which are taken up by social entrepreneurs, media etc. Such accidents, scientific discoveries (ozone layer) and the reactions of social entrepreneurs (Brent Spar) cannot be anticipated, but the inclination of the social–cultural system towards instability is influenced by slow and predictable variables such as growing societal tensions or an increased discrepancy between political proclamations and political actions.

Second, there is the political system, which includes decision makers in parliaments, governments, administration bodies and lobbyists from interest groups and trade unions; is determined by the institutional framework, election rules, formal norms and their implementation. Prominent examples of instability situations are the change of the ruling party, the replacement of a leading government member, or a major political–economic crisis. Also changes on the political agenda or discontinuities in mental models, for example due to certain decisions of the Constitution Court or – in EU-member states – the European Court or the occurrence of new interest groups, may be regarded as instabilities and windows of opportunity within the political system.

Third, there is the techno-economic system, which includes decision makers in companies and is determined by markets, investments, productivity developments, competition and government regulation. Instability situations are characterized by abrupt market changes such as the sudden disappearance of major players (Enron), a sudden shortage and price increase of oil products, a sharp increase/decline in stock prices or the capacity of the financial sector to finance investments (new economy bubble) and the introduction of a new regulation. An important factor is the progress and market readiness of one of several promising new technologies which challenges the incumbent market players.

Obviously, the stability and instability phases of the three subsystems are mutually related. In each subsystem, instability phases may be due to internal factors, but instabilities may also arise through influences from the other subsystems. One possible interaction is shown in Figure 60.2 and may run as follows: the starting point is a social or environmental problem coming from the economic system. This problem may affect the social–cultural system through the influence of political entrepreneurs and media, according to which the pressure on the political system to do something increases. Whether or not the political system will react to this pressure depends on the pressure from the socio-cultural system, the existence of realizable (technical) solutions and the strength of the opposition from incumbent actors.[1] If a new political regulation comes into force, this may finally destabilize the present technological trajectory and open the field for the successful market introduction of innovations. This, in environmental policy, quite common interaction pattern suggests that the politi-

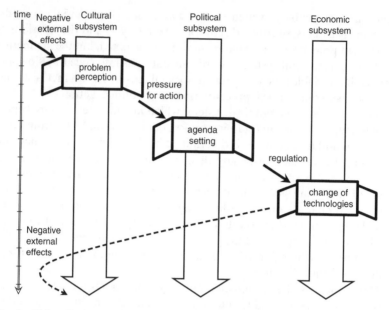

Figure 60.2   Sequence of windows of opportunity

cal decision makers do not give enough time to the economic system for developing basic innovations. As a consequence, the economic actors turn to end-of-pipe technologies instead of new integrated technological solutions. An example is the missed replacement of the amalgam technology for chlorine production process by the membrane technology in Europe in the 1980s.

According to another interaction pattern, the series of events starts with an endogenous innovation process in the economic system, which is picked up by the political system once it realizes the potential of the technological trajectory to contribute to the solution of a relevant problem. In this case the socio-cultural system plays a minor role. The advance towards sustainable development is an unintended consequence of the original innovation process motivated by other reasons. An example from the power industry is the development of the combined-cycle gas turbine in the 1980s. Governments could have introduced regulations favoring this technology that contributes through its high fuel efficiency to the reduction of greenhouse gases. It is well known, however, that this potential has not yet been exploited in many countries, including, for example in Germany, with its strong traditions in the coal industry. It will be interesting to observe whether the introduction of a CO_2 certificate system in Europe, planned for 2005, will be able to change that.

A slightly different interaction pattern has a poorly developed new technology at its origin which is, however, assumed to be able to solve an environmental problem some time in the future. If this is regarded by the political system as a chance of sustainable development, anticipated regulation or pressure from the socio-cultural system may then lead the industry to intensify R&D without an immediate explicit impulse from the political system. An example of this interaction is the present effort of the vehicle industry towards alternative fuels such as hydrogen or bio fuel.

These examples highlight the complexity of the system dynamics that determines the evolution of stable and instable constellations and the emergence of windows of opportunity. Accordingly, a large number of factors and variables and the relations between them have to be taken into consideration in order to identify and anticipate an approaching window of opportunity. We have to distinguish fast and slow variables. Fast variables are sudden events such as an important accident with catastrophic consequences for the environment, or the health of people or the economy. These cannot be predicted. Slow variables may stem from cumulative processes that steadily increase the tension within socio-cultural, political and technico-economic systems. For most of the slow-moving variables, empirical data can be collected. Others require the definition of appropriate indicators.

Typical slow variables in social and political systems are value changes, a steadily increasing contradictory policy, or a growing dissatisfaction within the population (measurable through opinion polls). These factors can release, through their dynamic interactions, political crises that play an important role in overcoming institutional path dependencies and/or changes in the strength and weight of interest groups and networks (for example, Sabatier, 1993). Institutional political cycles such as election periods, programme evaluations or annual budget negotiations are associated with opportunities for changing the political agenda (Howlett, 1998).

Slow economic variables indicating a possibly approaching instability are a growing and sustainable unemployment, a growing government debt combined with high tax rates, a business cycle depression, a change in relative costs between different technologies, declining phase in the life cycle of a technology or the decline of sunk costs associated with the introduction of a new technology (Schumpeter's *creative destruction*). The later variables are particularly relevant for the identification of approaching instabilities in technological trajectories.

Conclusion

The above discussion shows that the practical application of time strategies should be a feasible task for political decision makers. With a careful and unprejudiced analysis of the system under consideration, it should, in many cases, be possible to identify approaching situations of instability, through the observation of the evolution of slow-moving social–cultural, political and techno-economic variables. If significant differences between the expected properties of available technological trajectories are obvious, then political decision makers are well advised to use the (observed or assumed) instability as a window of opportunity for determined and powerful but temporary measures towards biasing the market selection into the most promising direction. As far as the socially most favorable approach towards achieving targets such as sustainable development consists of innovations, particularly technological innovations, this would be, as far as our analysis as well as a large number of case studies show, the most efficient strategy. We understand the proposed temporal application of measures towards bringing innovative technologies onto the market, not as an alternative but as a supplement to the application of continuous policy impulses such as Pigouvian taxes correcting for externalities.

The approach developed here thus far is subject to further research questions. For example, the determination of time periods over which temporal instruments should be applied is missing. The interaction between the social–cultural, the political and the techno-economic system needs more attention. The quantitative relations between slow variables and the likelihood of instability situations is an open empirical question. Case studies may help to develop the concept further.

But, still in its present form, the concept of time strategies proves that evolutionary and neo-Schumpeterian theories have a significant potential to improve policy decision making.

Note

1. An economic variable reflecting the expected opposition to new regulations depends on the amount of sunk costs that may arise with the replacement of the present technology by a new technology.

Bibliography

Arthur, W.B. (1988) 'Self-reinforcing mechanisms in economics', in P.W. Anderson, K.J. Arrow and D. Pines (eds), *The Economy as an Evolving Complex System*, Redwood City: Addison-Wesley, pp. 9–31.
Dosi, G. (1988) 'The nature of the innovative process', in G. Dosi, C. Freeman, R. Nelson, G. Silverberg and L. Soete (eds), *Technical Change and Economic Theory*, London, New York: Pinter, pp. 221–38.
Erdmann, G. (1993) *Elemente einer evolutorischen Innovationstheorie*, Tübingen: Mohr (Paul Siebeck).
Erdmann, G. (1999) 'GHG policies and the role of innovations', in B. Eliasson, P. Riemer and A. Wokaun (eds), *Greenhouse Gas Control Technologies*, Proceedings of the 4th International Conference on Greenhouse Gas Control Technologies, Amsterdam: Pergamon, pp. 447–56.
Howlett, M. (1997) Issue-attention and punctuated equilibria models reconsidered: an empirical examination of the dynamics of agenda setting in Canada, *Canadian Journal of Political Science*, **30**, 3–29.

Howlett, M. (1998) Predictable and unpredictable policy windows: institutional and exogenous correlates of Canadian federal agenda setting, *Canadian Journal of Political Science*, **31**, 495–524.

Kemp, R. (2000) 'Technology and environmental policy: innovation effects of past policies and suggestions for improvement', in OECD (ed.), *Innovation and the Environment*, Paris: OECD, pp. 35–61.

Sabatier, P. (1993) 'Advocacy-Koalitionen, Policy-Wandel und Policy-Lernen: Eine Alternative zur Phasenheuristik', in A. Héritier (ed.), *Policy-Analyse, Kritik und Neuorientierung*, PVS Sonderheft 24/1993, Opladen: Westdeutscher Verlag, pp. 116–48.

Sartorius, C. (2003) 'Indicators for a sustainable technology development – a dynamic perspective', in J. Horbach (ed.), *Indicator Systems for Sustainable Innovation*, Heidelberg, New York: Physica, pp. 43–70.

Sartorius, C. and Zundel, S. (eds) (2005) *Time Strategies, Innovation and Environmental Policy*, Cheltenham, UK and Northampton, MA, USA: Edward Elgar.

61 Macroeconomic policy
Hardy Hanappi

The first part of this contribution discusses the emergence of the term 'macroeconomic policy', both historically and conceptionally. In the second part a more technical account of models for macroeconomic policy from the perspective of evolutionary economics is provided. As conclusion a brief outlook is presented.

Emergence of the concept

There is a striking paradox in the history of evolutionary economic theory: while most of its proponents held very explicit, and often heretical views on macroeconomic policy, a theoretical treatment of these issues is almost completely missing in their theoretical works.[1]

To a certain degree this contradiction can be explained by adding some background information to the concept 'macroeconomics'. Indeed for the majority of modern economists macroeconomics as an independent field of economics was born with John Maynard Keynes's *General Theory of Employment, Interest and Money* in 1936. Keynes's major methodological innovation clearly consisted of a twofold shift of focus of economic theory:

1. Economics has to concentrate on the short-run ('in the long-run we are all dead') rather than looking for eternal laws governing the long-run.
2. Economics should consider measured, aggregate variables – including those describing actions of institutions (e.g. the state, unions) – rather than constructing variables describing innate properties of economic micro-units (individuals and firms).

This conceptualization of what macroeconomics is dealing with, i.e. aggregate short-run behavior of nation states, of course limits the meaning of 'macroeconomic policy'. In the sequel Keynesians further categorized such policy measures into two groups of state interventions (fiscal and monetary policy) thus further narrowing the scope for evolutionary considerations within this framework.

This already very limited meaning of the concept 'macroeconomic policy' was even further restricted by Keynes's most influential innovation with respect to the dynamics of the object of economic investigations: economies are driven by effective demand. Even today most macroeconomic models still stick to the assumption that in developed economies growth is subject to the limits set by a slowly expanding aggregate demand rather than by restrictions on the supply-side. The neglect of supply-side dynamics evidently implies a neglect of supply-side macroeconomic policies.

It is therefore not at all surprising that those economists after Keynes, who considered themselves as part of the still heterogeneous camp of evolutionary economics, usually were not inclined to contribute to a subject that in its Keynesian mainstream definition looked strange to them: excluding the interplay between short-run and long-run, between entities (institutions and agents) of different power and size, between production and demand. So this solves one part of the above-mentioned paradox.

Dropping the narrow Keynesian definition of macroeconomic policy it remains open to explain why evolutionary economists by their very focus are driven to draw conclusions, often strong conclusions, for economic policy. For this purpose it is instructive to take a look at two representatives of classical evolutionary economics, two economists representing the two opposite poles of the political spectrum: Thomas Malthus and Karl Marx. The common basis that makes them comparable is that both consider the evolution of human society as the final outcome of an ultra long-run evolution of life on earth, thus following some 'natural' trajectories to be discovered and described. The difference in their views on intervention in this process stems from the different dynamics they claim to have discovered. Malthus sees more and stronger 'natural' forces governing the process than the policy measures of his times (partly based on Rousseau's visions) pretended to overcome. As a consequence his policy conclusions are defensive, i.e. proposed interventions are useless, they should be abandoned. Note that this is a strong – and nowadays very familiar – policy recommendation. Marx, building on Hegelian dialectics, views social evolution as *less* 'natural' in the sense that self-organizing revolutions lead to ever-new emergence of forms. In this framework more or less aggressive intervention of social entities at all levels are the prime motor for emergence rather than being a disturbance of a 'natural' process. Again this is (and always was conceived as) a strong policy recommendation. Both political poles refer to a long-run dynamics that includes important, intervention-inducing short-run developments – conceived either as disturbances or as constituent elements. Macroeconomic policy thus for both consists of a mix between long-run and short-run measures. For Malthus-type trajectories, the short-run prescription is hands-off and the long-run policy consists of the installation of an institutional framework that promises to further the stabilizing processes of the hypothesized 'natural' state best. Inverting this mix, Marx-type trajectories call for short-run and medium-run interventions of social entities driving the system towards something called 'progress', which is a long-run development that only can be understood in retrospect, and therefore escapes any long-run intervention.

Viewed against this background, Keynes's position indeed is a strange one. Insisting on short-run intervention reminds us of a Marx-type background, but there is a trajectory aimed at, and it surely looks rather like a Malthus-type path. Upsetting this mix, Keynes's antipode, Schumpeter, was closer to Malthus's short-run laisser-faire but saw no long-run perspective for capitalism. And Schumpeter carefully avoided the label 'evolutionary' for his contributions. From this perspective the well-known *bon mot* makes sense: 'While Keynes thought that capitalism is economically unstable but politically stable, Schumpeter thought that it is economically stable but politically unstable'; just insert 'in the short-run' for 'economically' and 'in the long-run' for 'politically'.

So, while the Keynes–Schumpeter generation of economists were rather reluctant to consider themselves evolutionary economists – the glamour of Darwin's evolutionary theory was 'last century' and 'revolution' seemed to be the more acute term of the time – the last great ancestor of evolutionary economics in the 19th century, Thorstein Veblen, had judged macroeconomic policy issues as follows:

> The outcome of the method [marginalist economic analysis, H.H.], at its best, is a body of logically consistent propositions concerning the normal relations of things – a system of economic taxonomy. At its worst, it is a body of maxims for the conduct of business and a polemical discussion of disputed points of policy. (Veblen, 1898)

In other words, Veblen had identified the hidden policy agenda of the marginalist revolution of Menger, Jevons and Walras, and denounced it. At the same time he was well aware that their logical consistency was clearly an advance, in particular as compared to the 'naturalistic' type of economics of his time: an approach that much too often referred to presupposed 'normal' circumstances to which economic systems always should return. This latter attitude was the very reason why he thought that 'economics is not an evolutionary science' yet.

Taking a great leap forward in time to consider the positions of contemporary evolutionary economists towards macroeconomic policy it is striking to see how little the broad spectrum of basic attitudes – from Malthus to Marx – has changed. Despite the enormous advances in formal tools used to express these policy views, their broad diversity even became a characteristic of contemporary evolutionary economics. But at the same time it is precisely this advance in analytical and in simulation tools that makes a difference in the intellectual intercourse between the diverging streams within evolutionary economics. Taking all those aspects that were excluded by Keynes's definition on board (i.e. all three above-mentioned interplays), the new language elements help to construct an evolving macroeconomic policy.

It is evident that, under such circumstances, a certain division of intellectual labor appears. Some contributors, who are more strongly rooted in the Keynesian tradition (e.g. J. Foster, 1987), try to augment Keynesian macro-models by adding evolutionary features.[2] In particular, the availability of macroeconomic data collected by statistical offices which often were a byproduct of Keynesian economics is surely an incentive to produce evolutionary models along these lines. Others (e.g. G. Hodgson, 1988; H. Hanappi, 2002) try to include emergence and exit of institutions in such macro-models as well. For a large group of evolutionary economists the emphasis on technology policy (e.g. G. Mensch, 1979) as the most important part of macroeconomic policy has become their central concern. Another group is taking up the old Malthusian questions of linking demographic developments to economic aggregates (e.g. R. Day, 1999, pp. 157–360), a burning macroeconomic policy topic if one considers current debates on social security funds and pensions.

Today evolutionary economics considers macroeconomic policy to be a wide field. It still includes fiscal and monetary policy,[3] but it adds long-run dynamics. It still includes aggregate variables, but it adds micro-political interventions by influencing the expectations of smaller social entities. It adds other policy fields: technology, exchange rates, immigration, demography. . . . It can do all this – and even study non-linear disequilibrium scenarios of them – by using the new simulation tools available.

Evolutionary modeling strategies for macroeconomic policy

More to the technical detail, an evolutionary macroeconomic policy model consists of four sets of variables linked to each other by relations, which usually are formulated as computer programs, equation systems or (in a preliminary stage) as text.

The *first set* are the *goal variables*, those aggregates that enter what is usually called a social welfare function. Standard macroeconomic theory typically considered five such aggregates: real GDP growth rate, unemployment rate, inflation rate, net export share in GDP and budget deficit as share of GDP. Even for short-term considerations the combination of these variables into a single welfare measure is far from trivial; they usually are strongly interdependent, often in a non-linear way, and even the sign of several relations is still open to debate. For some aggregates the optimal level seems to be obvious – no unemployment, zero inflation rate – but even that might not be true. Structural unemployment might increase welfare by enhancing technical progress, some small inflation rate might induce money owners to carry their money to the bank to get at least a small interest rate, thus increasing available funds for new investment. Other variables do not have evident optimal levels at all, not to speak of the asymmetric dynamics around these levels. Evolutionary economics adds further problems. We may mention just the more important ones. Including the long-run time horizons implies taking care of *J*-curve effects, i.e. there is a dynamic trade-off that can make short-term utility losses smaller than long-run utility gains of vectors of goal variables.

In particular, time horizons can be long enough to allow for emergence and disappearance of goal variables.[4] Indeed, this is one of the core topics of evolutionary theory. Furthermore, it has to be considered from a microeconomic as well as from a macroeconomic point of view. What appears as a new goal of microeconomic agents might well be invisible for macroeconomics, whereas a macroeconomic objective often can look irrelevant for micro units. Probably one of the more interesting types of evolutionary economic models deals exactly with simulation of the policy processes that make goals visible or invisible.

The new areas of possible goal variables, technology policy, environmental policy (more general: endogenous utilities), information policy (taking account of sustained expectation disequilibria, and all types of game-theoretic lock-ins) and the recently booming renaissance of directly coercive policy measures (i.e. cold economic war and constrained hot war) really open up a broad spectrum of possible goals.

The choice of the set of goal variables for macroeconomic policy, including a welfare-measuring procedure that combines them, is not just a matter of setting a standard. For evolutionary economists it necessarily is rather an art that the model-builder has to bring into the picture, choosing with care and intuition.

The *second set* of variables consists of *exogenous variables not controlled by the entities modeled*. In mainstream macroeconomic theory these variables are often considered to be of minor importance, since they influence goals only by their assumed, exogenous values. In the Keynesian macroeconomic policy concept they typically represent slowly changing, though important, influences. Since in this concept only the short-run is modeled, their role is very limited. The essentially richer approach of evolutionary economics assigns a much more important role to this set of variables. In a sense they designate the borderline between what is modeled and what is not modeled. Since evolutionary views do have the tendency to include more and more neighboring problem areas, often crossing borderlines between traditionally separated economic fields, the choice of where to stop is far less trivial. Since a longer time-period is involved, these borders eventually can shift; their specification really is as important as any other part of the modeling work. Not only is the case that uncontrolled exogenous variables might become endogenous goals (e.g. carbon dioxide emissions) rather common, sometimes important endogenous variables suddenly vanish (e.g. exchange rates between European currencies after the introduction of the Euro).

This also sheds some light on the *methods* preferred by evolutionary macroeconomic policy: while the Keynesian tradition typically was based on comparative statics, i.e. two static equilibria with different sets of exogenous variables were compared, evolutionary economists compare different sets of dynamic trajectories with possibly changing roles of variables and with no special emphasis on equilibrium paths. Moreover, since sudden changes in relationships might occur owing to a sudden change in the status of a variable at certain points in time, these changes are rather inconvenient to model by use of the standard mathematical apparatus (difference-differential equation systems), but they almost naturally lend themselves to algorithmic formulations in computer simulations. So, instead of distinguishing cases where different functional relationships are valid, the algorithmic formulation simply contains a jump to a new sub-program that is conditioned by the variables hitting thresholds. The switch from the continuous developments in one regime to a sudden break towards a new regime (from quantity to quality, as the older methodological discourse would call it) thus looks quite plausible if algorithmic formulations are used.

We now turn to the *third set* of variables, the *exogenous variables controlled by social entities*, those variables that often are referred to as *instruments* of macroeconomic policy. Again the evolutionary approach dramatically increases the number as well as the specification details of these variables, in particular if compared to the Keynesian framework. The latter typically starts with just two variables in this set, government expenditure and money supply, and then proceeds mainly to include a few refinements. Tax rates, instruments influencing repercussions in open economies, and instruments that enter behavioral equations of wage and price setting are typical candidates for such refinements. As mainstream Keynesian economists try to include more and more of these improvements to provide a better picture of what happens in real economic policy, they more and more are doing what evolutionary economists do. If they finally drop the technical trick of introducing equilibrium conditions to get rid of hard to describe dynamics, then this asymptotic methodological convergence comes close to its qualitative jump towards evolutionary macroeconomics. But there still is something missing.

One element that is missing is the micro–macro relation referred to earlier.[5] Indeed, the conservative reaction to Keynesian macroeconomic policy that surfaced in the 1980s as the theoretical arm of Reagenomics, the so-called 'new classical macroeconomics', pointed at exactly that problem: if micro-units anticipate the actions of macro-units (the setting of instruments), then the standard results of Keynesian macroeconomic policy can easily be reversed. This is the economic content that the so-called 'rational expectations school' (e.g. Thomas Sargent, 1986), emphasized. The merit of this school doubtless was to highlight the importance of the expectation processes of economic micro-units, a task that it shares with evolutionary economics. But as one of the most innovative scholars of the social sciences, Herbert Simon, realized long before, anticipation of real-life micro-units takes place with rather limited information-processing capacities of the latter. The overriding economic policy objective of the rational expectations school, namely to prove that an increase in government expenditure will not increase real GDP but will only lead to more inflation,[6] seduced the proponents of this school to sacrifice realism, to assume a counterfactual world where knowledge is complete and all micro-units are hyperrational and unconstrained in their problem-solving capacities. Of course, in such a world there is no room for Keynesian politics, and there is no room for evolution. So with respect to the content of the anticipation models that are suggested to describe micro- and macroeconomic entities there is a sharp contrast between the rational expectations school and evolutionary economics. The latter insist on models that are adequate to the actual, heterogeneous information processing possibilities of economic actors.

In fact, this view, held by evolutionary economists, opens up an extremely important new area of instrument variables. Since models used by entities can evolve and are learned, there exist two major sources from where they come. They are either developed in direct interaction with the non-human environment, or they are learned from other social entities.[7] To teach others, or, in a less friendly language, to manipulate their models, is only a straightforward extension of the concept of coercive power. By making perception and communication processes as well as their capacity constraints explicit, evolutionary economics is in principle prepared to grasp the peculiarities of the current global information and communication technology (ICT) revolution, something totally out of reach for the new classical macroeconomics.

This latter aspect, manipulating models and using models manipulated by others, evidently calls for game-theoretic considerations. Much of the work done in the area of macroeconomic game theory started with simple extensions of the usual comparative statics approach to comparisons of Nash equilibria (e.g. in games played by central banks, ministry of finance, unions and so on). More recently, the new interpretation of Nash equilibria as evolutionary stable strategies has given these extensions an evolutionary twist. Nevertheless, the further development hinted at above, the inclusion of dynamic strategic manipulation of models from macro-agents to micro-agents and the counter-running political feedback process, are still only rarely touched upon by recent research papers. The potential of such work for actual macroeconomic policy, of course, is tremendous. In a sense, one precondition is to develop applied game theory in an appropriate direction, that is taking information process characteristics seriously, shaping formal tools according to the needs of the content of our discipline rather than vice versa. Another precondition surely consists of extensive empirical work concerning the actual model-building and decision-making process of social entities. If manipulation (teaching) enters the scene as an instrument variable, then its effects (as perceived, communicated or even actually exist-ing) have to be empirically disentangled to allow for a first set of model hypotheses. After more than 200 years, the French Enlightenment thus be could re-interpreted as evolutionary macroeconomic policy.

The fourth and final set of variables to be considered has the seemingly uninteresting label of *auxiliary variables*. For many economists the intro-duction of these variables is just a matter of notational convenience: they are names for results of simple, repeatedly occurring sequences of compu-tations (disposable income), or names used to simplify the understanding researchers working in competing theories (e.g. primary deficit), or names invented and used by those providing empirical data (in particular, central statistical offices). From an evolutionary perspective these variables are far less arbitrary than is usually assumed. First, several important concepts that finally lead to measurable essential variables made their first appear-ance as some vague auxiliary influence (the best known example comes from physics: the concept of heat). Second, auxiliary variables, though easily replaceable by a sequence of calculations involving other variables, might bear an important meaning for a social entity using it, a meaning which could explain actual actions taken better than anything else (e.g. budget deficit quota).

These considerations suggest that evolutionary macroeconomic policy should look at the set of auxiliary variables as a kind of pool for potentially important variables. Certainly, they are just of latent importance in the model at hand, but there is a reason why they are in this pool, and there is every reason to handle entry and exit from this pool very consciously. Building evolutionary macroeconomic models is itself an evolutionary process. Once a model is set up, it is continuously further adapted to advance the on-going policy process. It is never designed to work on the basis of eternal economic laws, it necessarily has to change with changing views of modeled entities, entry and exit of variables and agents in the course of dis-equilibrium processes that hit thresholds. In this endlessly pulsating flux, the pool of auxiliary variables serves as a buffer, keeping vanishing variables for some time before they finally are discarded or experience a renaissance, or storing new ones for testing their importance. In short, the pool of auxiliary variables enhances the flexibility of evolutionary macroeconomic modeling.

All four sets of variables are connected by relations that link them over time. Since any reaction in the real world takes time – not only in physics is the notion of contemporaneity fictitious – a large part of a macroeconomic policy model will be dynamic.[8] Using the model for the study of comparative dynamics then involves assumptions about starting values to derive more qualitative general results, or additional macroeconometric estimations to arrive at some quantitative issues. In the latter case it nevertheless should be kept in mind that that the purpose of an evolutionary macroeconometric model always is the *exploration of possible futures*, of implications of diverging and converging processes, bottlenecks, quantitative and qualitative change and breaks. Since the foundation of the approach is not the discovery of the one and only correct model that governs actual system behavior, it would be misleading to judge models only by forecasting accuracy. Though prognostic quality surely still is a virtue, it is just one ingredient. What is of central importance for evolutionary macroeconomic policy is their usefulness with respect to welfare increase. They can throw some light on possible future states of the world and show some trajectories that without the use of the model would not have been noticed. They also help to assess quantitative magnitudes involved in the dynamics, something often ignored even by the specialists in the field. But, once used, these models can easily change the course of events they forecast; they can be self-destroying prophecies. While this does terrible damage to their forecasting accuracy it often can be welfare increasing, so the latter is the only ultimate measure for an evolutionary macroeconomic policy model.

Outlook

Of course, such detailed and multifaceted work does not result in an overall general policy prescription. What it actually does, is to transform ill-posed and often too general questions into operational and clearer options from which to choose. For example, the question of more market processes or fewer market processes in a policy field leads to an algorithmic specification of possible market mechanisms to be combined with several types of non-market mechanisms. Properties of simulated combinations of these can be compared in their short- and long-run implications, and instead of a grand ideological decision, down-to-earth options become visible.

Indeed, this property of being specific, close to the disequilibrated, nonlinear world we are living in, is the great advantage of evolutionary macroeconomic policy. This is exactly what makes it attractive for political decision makers – at least those interested in rational decisions. It is, or at least tries to be, the opposite of a religious economics, a system of faith in general principles that are fitted to every newly appearing situation.

Despite its most promising future, evolutionary macroeconomic policy must be said to be still in its infancy. The tasks and methods of evolutionary macroeconomic policy described so far certainly bypass Keynesian macroeconomic policy, not to speak of (the avoidance of) policies implied by the new classical macroeconomics. They are what postmodern chattering classes would denounce as 'a grand story'. And a grand story will need a grand community of researchers for its evolution.

Notes

1. In a recent contribution, Ulrich Witt comes to a similar conclusion: 'However, what has so far only rarely been addressed as an own object of theoretical reflections in evolutionary economics is the theory of economic policy making' (U. Witt, 2003, p. 77).
2. Some recent contributions in disequilibrium macroeconomics that combine the Keynesian approach (e.g. Flaschel *et al.*, 1997) with Goodwin, Schumpeter and Marx traditions (e.g. Foley and Michl, 1999) are important for evolutionary macroeconomic policy too – even if the authors do not consider themselves as evolutionary economists.
3. An impressive case for the enduring importance of fiscal policy was recently made by Philip Arestis and Malcolm Sawyer (2003).
4. The introduction of endogenous preferences, in particular in evolutionary economics, has been the topic of volume 97 of the *Journal of Economic Theory* (L. Samuelson, 2001a; see also L. Samuelson, 2001b).
5. A similar consideration can be found in J. Foster (1987, p. 204), where the notion of *micro–macro consciousness* is introduced.
6. Conservative economic policy was directed mainly against Keynes's idea to increase effective demand by increasing government expenditure. In particular, the higher propensity to consume of poorer parts of the population would have implied direct additional expenditure for these social strata. Ironically enough, Ronald Reagan initiated an enormous increase in government expenditure in 1980 – though not by increasing social transfers but by military expenditure on the *Star Wars Initiative* – making him an extraordinary Keynesian.
7. The overwhelming majority of economically relevant human behavior stems from this second type of learning process.
8. Only some definitions of variables can be static.

References

Arestis, P. and Sawyer, M., 2003, Reinventing Fiscal Policy, working paper no. 381, The Levy Economics Institute of Bard College, New York.

Day, R., 1999, *Complex Economic Dynamics (vol. II), An Introduction to Macroeconomic Dynamics*, Cambridge, MA: MIT Press.

Flaschel, P., Franke, R. and Semmler, W., 1997, *Dynamic Macroeconomics*, Cambridge, MA: MIT Press.

Foley, D.K. and Michl, T., 1999, *Growth and Distribution*, Cambridge, MA: Harvard University Press.

Foster, J., 1987, *Evolutionary Macroeconomics*, London: Unwin Hyman.

Hanappi, H., 2002, 'Endogenisierung von Institutionen', in M. Lehmann-Waffenschmidt, pp. 113–31.

Hodgson, G., 1988, *Economics and Institutions*, Cambridge: Policy Press.

Keynes, J.M., 1936, *The General Theory of Employment, Interest and Money*, London: Macmillan.

Lehmann-Waffenschmidt, M., 2002, *Studien zur Evolutorischen Ökonomik V*, Berlin: Duncker & Humblot.

Malthus, T., 1820, *Principles of Political Economy*, London: John Murray.

Marx, K., 1967, *Capital*, New York: International Publishers.

Mensch, G., 1979, *Stalemate in Technology: Innovations overcome Depression*, New York: Ballinger.

Samuelson, L., 2001a, Introduction to the evolution of preferences, *Journal of Economic Theory*, **97**, 225–30.

Samuelson, L., 2001b, Analogies, adaptation, and anomalies, *Journal of Economic Theory*, **97**, 320–66.

Sargent, T.J., 1986, *Rational Expectations and Inflation*, New York: Harper & Row.

Veblen, T., 1898, Why is economics not an evolutionary science?, *The Quarterly Journal of Economics*, **12**.

Witt, U., 2003, Economic policy making in evolutionary perspective, *Journal of Evolutionary Economics*, **13**, 77–94.

PART 7

THE IMPACT OF NEO-SCHUMPETERIAN THINKING ON DIFFERENT FIELDS

62 Schumpeter's influence on game theory
Jacques Lesourne

1. Introduction

Great creators' innovations, especially in social sciences, often contain terms, the existence of which is discovered only after new developments have matured. It is true in particular in the case of Joseph Schumpeter who, by insisting on the role of innovating and risk-taking entrepreneurs, introduced in economic thinking a crack which has progressively broadened and of which we now perceive all the consequences.

The entrepreneur is indeed quite different from the cost-reducer of perfect competition who, constrained on prices and on the nature of the product, smashes expenditures and adapts production. The first is a creator. The second is passive. But, as a consequence of his introduction of discontinuities, the entrepreneur must expect reactions from his competitors, his buyers or his employees. Therefore, sooner or later, Schumpeterian economy and theory of games had to come across. Nevertheless, the convergence has been slow and is not yet completed.

As for the theory of games, the turning point is well known: 1944, the date of the publication of *Theory of Games and Economic Behaviour* by von Neumann and Morgenstern, only two years after *Capitalism, Socialism and Democracy* (1942). However, before this fundamental work, there was the long preamble of duopoly theory, from Cournot to Bertrand and Stackelberg. It deserves more than a mention, since in Cournot's model, where each firm adapts its production assuming given the other's production, appear the roots of the concept of Nash equilibrium, but it is still difficult to conceive the duopolists whose behaviour is rather passive as potential entrepreneurs.

In the 1940s, the Schumpeter entrepreneur and the von Neumann player remained foreign to each other and with not much to interchange. Let us forget for a while the first of the two to sketch the history of the second, a few paragraphs of story, at the end of which will emerge the entrepreneur's figure.

2. The von Neumann player

The 1944 book has truly founded the theory through its introduction of notions, such as a game, a player, a strategy, an outcome. It has separated cooperative and non-cooperative games, distinguished pure and mixed strategies and proved an important theorem about the existence, in zero-sum games, of mixed strategies equilibria.

However, simultaneously, this construction founds the basis of a specific discipline without any privileged link with any social science, be it economics, political science or various branches of sociology. And, for years, theory of games will develop, introducing the steps of a game, the diverse information situations, several notions of equilibrium, repeated games, and will start to discover the nice subtleties of the prisoner's dilemma. As for the economists, they remained hungry, conscious that, in this kitchen, the cooking could be essential for their science, but disappointed that the elements liable to be introduced in competition theory were so thin.

The introduction of the *Nash equilibrium* started a phase the meaning of which we understand better retrospectively. Superficially, a Nash equilibrium in a two players' game is only a generalization of the old Cournot equilibrium in a duopoly. But what is important is the awareness it brings that the players' reasonings and computations are done before any effective move. Hence there is a deep connection between the Walras auctioneer and the Nash equilibrium. First, the auctioneer tests prices, registers demands and supplies, notes disequilbria and adjusts his proposals until demands and supplies are equal, then blows his whistle, announces prices and gives the agents the freedom to contract. The essential has happened before the exchanges.

Second, the players in Nash equilibrium elaborate separately an individual strategy, then compute the other's answers, revise their choice until (assuming the existence of only one equilibrium) they have determined a pair of strategies, each of the two being a best answer to the other. They then exchange a signal and play simultaneously. Everything was conceived in their hand before any action. Nevertheless, at this stage, the economist is still compelled to realize that game theory does not bring elements to microeconomics.

3.   Oligopoly theory

However, a break will be made with the introduction by R. Selten of the *sub-game perfect equilibria*. In this concept, each player's reasoning results from *backward induction*, the player choosing at every step the optimal action, taking into account the future optimal actions of the others. This assumption enables us to understand the stability of an already established equilibrium, but it does not explain the equilibrium formation. It is still necessary to suppose either that the players, having a common knowledge of the game, develop separate reasonings which lead them to discover simultaneously the equilibrium, or that there exists a role devoted to a fictive entity, a Nashian regulator, counterpart in game theory of the Walrasian auctioneer.

In spite of these difficulties, the concept of sub-game perfect equilibria has enabled an important development of the theory of duopoly and oligopoly (Fudenberg and Tirole, 1986). In the case of a duopoly, each competitor moves successively, choosing for instance the level of investment, taking into account the past decisions and the postulated future behaviour of his competitor. An old economic problem is therefore solved, the problem of a first period behaviour of a monopolist who may be confronted in a second period with the entry of a competitor on the market.

Nevertheless, if, at this stage, theory of games influences microeconomic theory, this influence is still pretty far from Schumpeter's considerations. The emergence of evolutionary games will change the picture.

4. Evolutionary game theory

Created 20 years ago (Maynard Smith, 1982), the theory of evolutionary games is in full development (Weibull, 1995; Young, 1998). It tries to introduce less demanding assumptions with respect to agents' adaptations through their dynamic interactions:

> Players have very limited information about their adversaries' characteristics as well as bounded and spatially local information on the game process. They are only endowed with a limited rationality, their beliefs consisting only in possible extrapolating expectations and their actions trying to improve the fulfilment of their objectives. They are however engaged in sequential meetings so that the effect of repetitions replaces the Walrasian auctioneer or the role of crossed expectations. (Lesourne, Orléan and Walliser, 2002)

The evolutionary games may be divided into three families:

In a first family, the players adopt an *epistemic learning*, revise progressively their beliefs, taking into account observations, and using these beliefs to define their moves. Each player is endowed with a weakened cognitive rationality which leads him to revise through various heuristic rules his beliefs regarding his adversary and enables him to anticipate, at least in a probabilistic way, the future move of the latter. He always maximizes his utility function, taking into account his expectation about the others, but his first best answer concerns only the present period and not the following ones.

In a second family, players exhibit *behavioural learning*, during which they reinforce actions having obtained good results in the past and restrain those leading to poor results. In other words, they select randomly an action, without any elimination, with a probability being an increasing function of the utility index.

In a third family, players follow an *evolutionary process* through which they reproduce themselves according to the results obtained during their random and local interactions. Any player adopts a fixed strategy, with a cognitive as well as an instrumental rationality practically inexistent. It represents in fact the population of agents adopting the same strategy, this population being characterized by its proportion within the set of players' strategies. The rate of reproduction of an agent is a function of the utility obtained during a random interaction. In addition, there is a possibility of a mutation of the agent towards another strategy according to an exogenous random rule.

Two remarks on this grouping:

- The models of behavioural learning are isomorphic to the models with an evolutionary process, the probability of use of a strategy by a player replacing the proportion of players using this strategy. Therefore, an economist is essentially interested in the first two families.
- The models of these two families may naturally be combined to give rise to hybrid models.

5.   Evolutionary games and evolutionary microeconomics

What is the contribution of evolutionary games to evolutionary microeconomics? The latter has liberated itself from the Walras auctioneer, showing (Lesourne, 1991) that adaptive agents may, through random exploration of the solutions and an evolution of their minimal demands, build collectively, though without any conscience of it, a unique price system and a separation between the supplies and demands which are fulfilled and those which are not. In other words, there exists a market self-organizing process which operates without the intervention of an external regulator. A necessary condition: any solution must have a non-zero probability to be discovered by an agent and there are no irreversibility costs at all.

The symmetrical problem in games is the following: as regards agents who are periodically opposed and undergo epistemic or behavioural learning, are they going to reach a stable equilibrium in strategies corresponding, for instance, to a Nash equilibrium in pure strategies? When this is so, their search enables them to be free either from the information and the computations of the classical game theory, or from the Nashian regulator.

Unfortunately, the answers to such questions are complex, because the theory of evolutionary games is very sensitive to model details and has to be studied for particular classes of games in normal forms, with a range of processes from very simple to those combining ideas from diverse origins (aspiration threshold, imitation mechanism, reinforcement effect).

As written in Lesourne, Orlean and Walliser in 2002, the issues now seem to be the following:

From a formal point of view, the most robust result states the elimination of the strategies strictly dominated during any process improving utility, a condition usually satisfied. In fact, if a process reinforces the pure strategies generating a utility above the average, it progressively leads to the disappearance of the dominated strategy under the condition that the dominating strategy is effectively present. An almost as robust result asserts that a Nash equilibrium is always a rest-state (a state in which the process remains when it is in it) for any deterministic process (without random perturbations).

A less robust asymptotic result ascertains that Nash strict equilibria in pure strategies are attractors for many usual processes, contrary to Nash equilibria in mixed strategies, because a deviation of a player from a Nash strict equilibrium in any direction leads to a strict loss in utility which induces all the players to come back towards the initial situation. Finally, a complementary result states that, for a process including a permanent random element, the system remains for some time in a Nash equilibrium but may abruptly jump towards another Nash equilibrium. Indeed, if random shocks sufficiently dispersed maintain the system around the equilibrium, polarized random shocks may push the system out of its attraction basin to join another equilibrium.

From a more qualitative point of view, the existence of random shocks considerably modifies the asymptotic and transitory properties of a system by comparison with a deterministic process. These shocks have different impacts according to their origin, whether they bear on the occurence of interactions between players, or the statistical observation conditions of the players or on exploration behaviours in the selection of actions.

Well studied for games in normal form, the asymptotic properties of evolutionary systems have to be examined for games in developed form. The question is to know whether the perfect equilibrium may be obtained as a limit for a learning process. Various processes have already been studied. For instance, a player may attribute a utility to any branch of the tree, a utility related to the result obtained when this arrow is used and apply a probabilistic choice model for all the arrows.

In addition, if the asymptotic process properties begin to be well explored, the situation is different for the transitory properties which are also interesting.

6. The future potentials

This summary of the present state of the research on evolutionary games shows that this field is in full development, but that the possible results are promising and raise highly interesting questions.

First, individuals may discover an equilibrium in a game situation, either out of information treatment and intelligent reasoning, or through adaptation. In the second case, they construct a solution through the evolution of their respective behaviours.

One discovers here the major subjects with which economic science begins to be confronted: the human being has at his disposal a range of behaviours, at one extreme very sophisticated intellectual behaviours, such as those utilized to prove theorems in mathematics; at the other extreme very elementary behaviours of trials and errors in which the succession of tests leads to a solution. We do not know yet how an individual, in a given practical situation, makes his choice in the range or jumps from one range to another.

Second, when a reasonable process leads to a final situation which is not an equilibrium in the usual sense of the theory of games, the result must not be looked at as a failure in the search for a convergent mechanism. On the contrary, one should ask whether, in reality, such situations do not occur because the individuals enter traps as a consequence of a process which seemed to them acceptable.

Evolutionary games therefore still have a lot to tell us about conflicts and cooperation between agents.

7. Conclusions

Apparently, we are not yet back to Joseph Schumpeter and his entrepreneur. In reality, we are very close. We have just to differentiate the adaptative processes selected by the different players to introduce in the dynamics more or less creative agents. It will allow for the description of the conditions of emergence of a dichotomy already visible in evolutionary microeconomic models:

- In a first category of models (including the model of a market without irreversibility costs and with a non-zero probability of access to any possibility by all the agents), the existence of a 'creative agent' confers on him only transitory advantages and does not modify to his profit the stable equilibrium to which the system converges.
- In a single category of models (for instance the model of a market on which retailers select with a limited rationality the selling price offered and the quantity they put on sale (Lesourne, 1991), the agents' routines have an influence on the nature of the stable state. The presence of 'active' agents, if they are not too numerous, has an impact on the equilibrium price structure, the 'active' agents being assured of having a situation better than that of the others. At this stage, the dynamic processes suggested by the evolutionary games lead to a vision of creative competitors very close to that of Schumpeter.

References

Fudenberg, D. and J. Tirole, *Dynamic Models of Oligopoly*, Harwood, 1986.

Lesourne, J., Economie de l'ordre et du désordre, *Economica*, 1991.

Lesourne J., A. Orléan and B. Walliser, *Leçons de microéconomie évolutionniste*, O. Jacob, 2002.

Schumpeter, J.A., *Capitalism, Socialism and Democracy*, Harper & Brothers, 1942.

Smith, J.M., *Evolution and the Theory of Games*, Cambridge University Press, 1982.

von Neumann, J. and O. Morgenstern, *Theory of Games and Economic Behavior*, Princeton University Press, 1944.

Weibull, J., *Evolutionary Game Theory*, MIT Press, 1995.

Young, H.P., *Individual Strategy and Social Structure, an Evolutionary Theory of Institutions*, Princeton University Press, 1998.

63 Transaction costs, innovation and learning
Bart Nooteboom

Introduction

This chapter discusses interorganizational relationships (IORs) from the perspective of innovation and learning. In such relations, transaction costs play an important role, but they need to be reconsidered from the perspective of learning.[1]

IORs are not new. They go back at least as far as Adam Smith's argument for division of labour between firms, for the sake of productive efficiencies of specialization. Such specialization in firms by definition entails relations between firms, in outsourcing and collaboration. Renewed interest in IORs is due to recent developments in technology and markets. In technology, there is fast development and proliferation of novel opportunities, e.g. in information and communication technology (ICT), micro-mechanics, optics, sensors, their combination in robotization, biotechnology, new materials and surface technologies. In markets, there is renewed globalization,[2] partly as a result of new opportunities offered by ICT, for market entry and for coordinating activities across markets and organizations. As noted by Adam Smith, the extent of specialization and economy of scale is limited by the size of the market. Market extension by globalization thus furthers specialization and its consequent relations between firms. Furthermore, as a result of emerging complexity and rapid change of markets and technology, competition has increasingly become a 'race to the market' with new or improved products. To have any chance of winning such races, one needs to shed activities, as much as strategically possible, that are not part of the 'core competencies' (Prahalad and Hamel, 1990) that constitute competitive advantage. Other, complementary, competencies must then be sought from outside partners. Such outside sourcing also maximizes the flexibility in configurations of activities that is needed under rapid change. For example, in order to reduce development times of new products and to reduce risks of maladjustment to customer needs, suppliers should be brought in as a partner in developing and launching a new product.

The sourcing decision – what to make and what to buy – is a special case of the more general decision of what to do inside one's own organization, and what to do outside, in collaboration with other organizations. Sourcing entails vertical collaboration, in the supply chain, including marketing and distribution. Relations may also be horizontal, with competitors, or lateral, with firms in other industries. Next to the question *what* to do inside or outside, and *why*, there are the questions *with whom* to collaborate, and *how*: in what *forms of organization*, in *what networks*, with what *instruments for governance*, and in what kind of *process*.

In this chapter, it is not possible to address all these questions, and there is no need to duplicate the large literature on the subject of IORs (for a recent, integrated account, see Nooteboom, 2004b). This chapter focuses on one aspect that is still ill-developed in the literature: the combination of innovation and transaction costs. It discusses the theoretical consequences of including innovation and learning, and implications for the boundaries of the firm, in particular for the choice between integration in a firm and alliances between firms, and for instruments for governing relational risk.

Transaction cost economics (TCE) needs to be modified and extended, since it offers at best comparative statics, and by its own admission (Williamson, 1985: 143; 1999: 1103) does not, in its established form, incorporate innovation and learning. This chapter combines a perspective of dynamic competencies, in learning and innovation, and a governance perspective, in the management of relational risk. While TCE neglects the competence side, studies of competence often neglect the governance side. For that, TCE still offers important insights into some causes and effects of relational risk (i.e. 'hold-up risk') and instruments for their governance.

The competence perspective goes back to the work of Edith Penrose (1959). It emphasizes differences of competence between organizations. Competition is seen not only, and not even primarily, as competing on the price of a homogenous product, i.e. a product that can be closely substituted by users between different suppliers, but also, and primarily, as an attempt to maintain competencies that are scarce and difficult to imitate by potential competitors (Lippman and Rumelt, 1982), to achieve higher profit. Such variety among firms is also a crucial feature of evolutionary economics, with its explanatory triad of variety, selection and transmission. Variety among firms makes nonsense of analysing an industry on the basis of a 'representative firm'.

This chapter begins with a summary of standard TCE, followed by criticism, from the perspective of innovation and learning. For a transformation and extension of the theory, the chapter proceeds with the summary of a theory of knowledge and learning, derived from Nooteboom (2000a). According to this theory, knowledge is constructed on the basis of mental categories that are formed in interaction with the environment. This develops into the notion of an organization as a 'focusing device', which yields an additional view on the boundaries of the firm, next to other views, including TCE. It also provides a cognitive argument for interorganizational relations, next to the customary arguments that will be summarized later. Such relations serve to compensate for the organizational myopia that results from organizational focus. This perspective of learning has implications for the choice of the form of collaboration, and for the selection of instruments for the governance of relational risk, which deviate from TCE.

Transaction cost economics

Chiles and McMackin (1996) distinguished two perspectives in TCE. The first is a long-term evolutionary perspective, where objective transaction costs determine the survival of the fittest governance forms. The second is a short-term managerial choice perspective, where managers act on subjective costs that are based on a variety of perceptions and evaluations of risk. The latter explains why firms in similar circumstances may make different make-or-buy trade-offs. This chapter takes the latter perspective.

The behavioural assumptions of TCE are that rationality is bounded and that people may be opportunistic. While people aim to be rational, their capacity to do so is limited, owing to two types of uncertainty: behavioural uncertainty concerning the intentions and competencies of transaction partners and environmental uncertainty concerning conditions that may affect the execution of agreements and the outcomes of cooperation. As a result, closed contracts that foresee and regulate all possible eventualities are impossible. Not everybody is equally opportunistic, but the possibility of opportunism exists, and prior to a relation one does not know to what extent it may arise. Opportunism is defined as 'interest seeking with guile'. This includes actions against the interest of a partner, and against the letter or intent of an agreement, when the occasion presents itself, where necessary with the aid of lies or concealment of the truth. The opportunity for this follows from unpredictability of conditions and asymmetric information.

Williamson (1985: 1) defined a transaction as 'transfer across a technologically separable interface'. This includes transfers within an organization. A transaction is an event that takes place during a process of exchange, in which the transaction has a past and a future. Here, I prefer to define the transaction as the moment at which agreement is established and ownership rights are transferred. Such rights include either claims to profit or decision rights, or both. When it is restricted to decision rights it can still apply within organizations.

In the process of exchange one can distinguish three stages, of what I call 'Contact', 'Contract' and 'Control' (Nooteboom, 1999a). Before the arrangement of a contract or other agreement arises one must find a transaction partner (Contact). This entails search costs on the part of the user and marketing costs on the part of the supplier. Search costs are associated with becoming aware of a need, and possibilities for fulfilling it, searching for fitting solutions and alternatives and their evaluation. Marketing costs form the mirror image of this: the research of latent or manifest needs among potential customers, possibilities to satisfy them, development of specifications, tests and search for entry to customers. In the stage of Contract there are costs of preparing and concluding a contract or other type of agreement, as much as possible in anticipation of possible problems that might occur after transaction, in the stage of control. In the stage of Control there are costs of monitoring of the execution of the agreement, 'haggling' about it, problem solving, renegotiation and adjustment of the agreement, enforcement, and application of sanctions, litigation and possible loss of 'specific investments' and 'hostages' if the relation breaks.

Costs of contract and control arise especially when parties become dependent upon each other owing to costs of switching to a different partner. In particular, these obtain when the transaction entails 'specific investments' that are worth less or nothing outside the alliance (Williamson, 1975), so that they would need to be made anew with a different partner.

> A classic example of a specific investment is the die in which a part of a car (door, hood) is stamped into shape. It has the shape of the part and is therefore as 'specific' as anything can get. It is also expensive because it is large and made of hard, durable material, to survive the force of stamping and maintain a constant shape. The investment in the die is not recouped until a large number of items has been stamped, and that requires a minimal volume or duration of production. If production is stopped, the die has no more than scrap value.

Transaction-specific investments can occur at both buyer and supplier. There are three kinds of transaction-specific investments: 'site specificity', 'physical asset specificity' and 'human asset specificity'. Williamson further recognized the category of 'dedicated assets': expansion of capacity only to serve a given partner.

> Some examples of site specificity are infrastructural facilities (roads, pipes and ducts, homes, shops) for labourers of a remote mining facility; supply of heat from cooling water from a factory for heating of adjacent homes (due to rapid loss of heat in transport); a warehouse or production facility 'at the doorstep' of a customer, to provide 'just in time' supply. An example of human asset specificity is training dedicated to specific demands of the partner.

Transaction costs due to specific investments yield a reason for integrating activities within a single firm, which offers better control of opportunism and uncertainty (Williamson, 1975), because of administrative fiat in obtaining information to judge actions and in imposing solutions, which goes far beyond what one could achieve in a court of law on the basis of a contract with an outside, independent partner. TCE predicts that there should and will be more integration to the extent that there are more specific investments and uncertainty is greater. Integration can be achieved through sales of assets, a merger or acquisition, or an equity joint venture (in the following, 'joint venture' refers to 'equity joint venture'). But a non-integrative, contractual alliance between different firms has advantages over integration: more 'high-powered incentives' in separate firms that are responsible for their own survival, economies of scale in production by specialized firms (Williamson, 1975), and greater flexibility in the configuration of complementary competencies or assets. However, such alliances raise complicated issues of 'governance', in 'hybrid' forms of organization 'between market and hierarchy' (Williamson, 1991), to deal with the fiduciary risks of dependence and corresponding problems of coordination.

An important issue is the extent to which dependence due to specific investments is symmetric between partners. When a supplier engages in specific investments, this does not only make him dependent, but also his buyer, because, when a break in supply occurs, the buyer will not have an immediate substitute of equal quality and cost. It will take an alternative supplier time to set up specific investments, and meanwhile the buyer will either face a discontinuity of supply or he will have to accept temporarily a product that does not fit his requirements, i.e. has lower quality. Also, apart from physical assets, a buyer will need to make adjustments in procedures, organization, knowledge to adapt to the specialized product, assets or competencies of the supplier, and these also constitute specific investments. At least he will have to invest in specific knowledge of the supplier's procedures, people involved, etc. However, there is no guarantee that dependence due to specific investments is symmetric. Generally, the weight of specific investments, in a variety of resources, including both physical and human resource assets, tends to be higher on the supplier's side.

In IORs, there are several means to reduce the risk of one-sided dependence due to specific investments. One is to restrict opportunities for opportunism by contract, e.g. by forcing the partner to continue transactions until the cost of investment has been recouped. Another is to have the partner participate in the ownership of the investment. But, to do this, the partner may in turn demand guarantees against the misuse of such guarantees, e.g. that the investment is indeed specific and is not used for transactions with others. There may also be an exchange of 'hostages', defined as things that are of value only to the giver and not to the keeper, so that the latter will not hesitate to destroy the hostage when the hostage giver reneges on his commitment. Often, a hostage takes the form of sensitive information from or about a partner that would cause damage when destroyed or leaked to the partner's competitors. Another instrument is to reduce the partner's incentives or inclination to utilize opportunities for opportunism. These can impinge on the partner's self-interest, or on his sense of loyalty. This may include reputation effects: if the partner gets known to be unreliable, it will jeopardize future transactions.

Generally, the cost and delay of setting up and maintaining elaborate schemes of governance between two partners ('bilateral governance') are substantial. When the transaction involved is small or infrequent, the benefit is not worth the cost, and one will prefer to keep contracts simple and engage a trusted third party to act as an arbitrator ('trilateral governance'). The classic example is an architect who arbitrates in transactions between a builder and a supplier of building materials.

A relatively minor point of criticism of TCE is that the theory would be more consistent in taking the relation rather than the transaction as the unit of analysis. The essential notion of the 'fundamental transformation' from 'large to small numbers bargaining', as a result of specific investments, requires it. The issue is, precisely, that an investment, made to conduct any transaction at all, is tied to a transaction partner, and thereby requires ongoing transactions in that particular relationship.

Another relatively minor point of criticism of TCE is that it suggests that specific products require specific investments: that when one tailors a product to special needs one needs to make investments that can cater only to those specialized needs. However, to the extent that technology is flexible, an investment can, by definition, be used to produce a range of differentiated products (Nooteboom, 1993a). For example, a programmable workbench for machining metal can yield parts of a variety of shapes and functions, without the operator needing to adapt his skill. Software for designing and testing virtual prototypes of machines, cars or airplanes by means of computer simulation yields much greater flexibility for a range of different designs than old-fashioned physical prototypes subjected to 'real' testing (such as testing the aerodynamic properties of a car in a wind tunnel).

A more fundamental point of criticism is that TCE neglects effects of the embeddedness of relations in wider networks, as studied in sociology. However, that goes beyond the scope of this chapter. Two other fundamental points of criticism concern the lack of innovation and learning in TCE, and its neglect of trust. These are of particular interest from a neo-Schumpeterian view, and are discussed below.

Innovation and learning
As Williamson (1985: 143) himself admitted: 'the study of economic organisation in a regime of rapid innovation poses much more difficult issues than those addressed here'. Williamson (1999) claimed that he fully accepts

bounded rationality: there is fundamental uncertainty concerning future contingencies. However, he claims, there is foresight: one can take such uncertainty into account, infer the hazards that follow from it and conduct governance accordingly (in a 'discriminating alignment') and 'efficiently', i.e. in an optimal fashion (to yield an 'economizing result'). We are not myopic, Williamson claims: we are not so stupid as not to take uncertainties into account when we design governance. And indeed, we can to some extent take risks and uncertainty into account. Firms can spread risks by participating in different markets, in the same way that investors can spread risks in a portfolio of investments. Beyond that, to deal with real or radical uncertainty, we can construct scenarios of possible futures, prepare contingency plans for them, and identify the robustness of strategies across different scenarios. Shell Oil Company, for example, developed this in the 1970s, in anticipation of oil crises.

Scholars in the competence perspective do not assume myopia, as Williamson accuses them of doing. However, they ask, as TCE does not, what the implications of bounded rationality are for the correct identification of relevant hazards. Bounded rationality implies that we might be mistaken about them. Williamson (1999: 1103) admits that TCE 'makes only limited contact with the subject of learning', and indicates that we may be mistaken about hazards and may learn about them as events unfold (ibid.: 1104). And apart from hazards there are new options. In spite of great imagination and ingenuity, the scenarios we invented may not include what actually arises. Also, preferences may shift. That is part of learning. And if new insights in hazards arise, new scenarios, or new options or goals, are we then able to shift from the governance structure engaged upon to an adapted, optimal form? That would always be possible only if there is no path-dependence or lock-in in governance, and that is a strong claim to make.

This is related to the issue of 'efficient', optimal outcomes. Williamson's argument is that 'dysfunctional consequences and other long run propensities will not be mindlessly repeated or ignored' (ibid.: 1105). But the argument begs a number of questions. It implies that dysfunctionality and long-run propensities are stable, so that experience in the past is indicative of the future. There is no guarantee that this is the case. Indeed, in innovation and learning it is not, almost by definition. And if we could correctly adapt our foresight, how can we be sure that the firm survives to implement the lesson in time? TCE seems to fall back on the notion of selection: inefficient forms of organization will be weeded out by 'the market'. That is the usual assumption behind the economist's assumption of efficient outcomes, going back to Alchian (1950). But if that is Williamson's argument, he is deviating from the perspective of the firm strategist, who is talking about the survival of the firm (Chiles and McMackin, 1996). Furthermore, the selection argument was already shown to be weak by Winter (1964). In selection it is not the best possible but the best available in the population that survives. In the presence of economy of scale, inefficient large firms may push out efficient small firms, and thus inefficiency may survive. Furthermore, efficient selection cannot be taken for granted in view of possible monopolies, entry barriers and transaction costs.

Williamson claims that his theory is intertemporal, incorporating the passage of time, and indeed he claims that this is *central to* TCE (1999: 1101). And indeed, up to a point it does incorporate intertemporality. It makes a distinction between ex ante considerations, before commitment of transaction-specific investments, and ex post considerations, after their commitment. This yields the 'fundamental transformation' from multiple to 'small numbers' of options. The theory also is intertemporal in the sense of taking uncertainty concerning future contingencies into account, as discussed in the previous section. However, TCE does not go far enough and, again, is not consistent in this. Williamson (ibid.) does claim that 'governance structures are predominantly instruments for adaptation, it being the case that adaptation . . . is the central problem of economic organisation; organisation has an intertemporal life of its own'. He admits, however, that this 'is not to say that it [TCE] has worked all of these out in a satisfactory way. I entirely agree that transaction cost economics stands to benefit from more fully dynamic constructions. But whereas saying dynamics is easy, doing dynamics is hard'. This is in line with Williamson's other admission, quoted above, that learning is not well developed in TCE. Nowadays innovation and learning are crucial, and should be at the core of theory.

TCE appears to adhere to a naïve theory of knowledge and competence, with the assumption that technology is accessible more or less 'from the shelf', to anyone who pays its price. However, firms may need to contract some good or service from outside simply because it is not itself capable of providing it, or may need to produce it itself because no one else has the resources needed. Furthermore, to understand what other firms supply, to evaluate it and to incorporate it in internal activities, requires appropriate 'absorptive capacity' (Cohen and Levinthal, 1990). A deeper, cognitive issue arises from the theory of knowledge employed in this chapter, which will be outlined in the next section.

Cognitive distance and organizational focus
After criticism of TCE, attention now turns to ways to mend its shortcomings. Here, attention is paid to innovation and learning. Diversity is a crucial condition for learning and innovation, to produce Schumpeterian 'novel combinations', as demonstrated in evolutionary economics (Nelson

and Winter, 1982). Diversity is associated with the number of agents (people, firms) with different knowledge and/or skills, who are involved in a process of learning or innovation by interaction. However, next to the number of agents involved, a second dimension of diversity is the degree to which their knowledge or skills are different. This yields the notion of 'cognitive distance', based on a constructivist, interactionist view of knowledge (Mead, 1934; Berger and Luckmann, 1967; Weick, 1979, 1995; Nooteboom, 2000a). According to this view, people perceive, interpret, understand and evaluate the world according to mental categories (or cognitive frames, or models; cf. Johnson-Laird, 1983), which they have developed in interaction with their physical and social environment. As a result, people see and know the world differently to the extent that their cognition has developed in different conditions (national, regional and organizational culture, customs/habits, social norms/values, education, technologies, markets). This yields the notion of cognitive distance, and the notion of a firm as a 'focusing device', as part of a 'cognitive theory of the firm', proposed by Nooteboom (2000a). This view can be seen as harking back to Austrian perspectives of the firm (Menger, von Mises, von Hayek), with attention to problems of learning, localized knowledge, and the market as a 'discovery process'. The key features of the theory are summarized below.

Here, cognition is to be seen in a broad sense, including not only rational evaluation but also emotion-laden value judgements, and heuristics of attribution, inference and decision making that we know from social psychology (Bazerman, 1998; Tversky and Kahneman, 1983). In a firm, people need to achieve a common purpose, and for this they need some more or less tacit shared ways of seeing and interpreting the world. In view of incentive problems, in monitoring and control, especially in contemporary organizations of more or less autonomous professionals, and the desire for intrinsic next to extrinsic motives (Frey, 2002), people in organizations also need to share more or less tacit values and norms, to align objectives, govern relational risk and to provide a basis for conflict resolution. Owing to uncertainty concerning contingencies of collaboration, and limited opportunities for monitoring, ex ante measures of governance are seldom complete, and need to be supplemented with ex post adaptation. Organizational focus, provided by organizational culture, yields an epistemological and normative 'substrate' to achieve this, as a basis for shared processes of attribution, mutual adaptation and decision making. In other words, cognitive distance needs to be restricted for the sake of coordination. Organizational culture incorporates fundamental views and intuitions regarding the relation between the firm and its environment, attitude to risk, the nature of knowledge, the nature of man and of relations between people, which inform content and process of strategy, organizational structure, and styles of decision making and coordination (Schein, 1985). One aspect of entrepreneurship, which links with Schumpeter's notion of the entrepreneur as a charismatic figure, is that it is his central task to achieve this: to align perceptions, understandings, goals and motives.[3]

Note that the notion of focus does not entail the need for people to agree on everything, or see everything the same way. Indeed, such lack of diversity would prevent both division of labour and innovation within the firm. However, there are some things they may have to agree on, and some views they need to share, on goals, norms, values and ways of doing things. Organizational focus needs to be tight, in the sense of allowing for little ambiguity and variety of meanings and standards, if the productive system of a firm, for the sake of exploitation, is 'systemic', as opposed to 'stand–alone' (Langlois and Robertson, 1995). Exploitation is systemic when there is a complex division of labour, with many elements and a dense structure of relations between them, with tight constraints on their interfaces. An example is an oil refinery. In more stand-alone systems, elements of the system are connected with few other elements, and connections are loose, allowing for some ambiguity and deviation from standards on interfaces. An example is a consultancy firm. An intermediate system, between systemic and stand-alone, is a modular system. Here, there are also multiple, connected elements, as in the systemic case, but the standards on interfaces allow for variety, where different modules can be plugged into the system.

Organizational focus yields a risk of myopia (in 'group think'): relevant opportunities and threats to the firm are not seen. To compensate for this, firms need outside contacts for 'external economy of cognitive scope' (Nooteboom, 1992). On the basis of different experiences, with different technologies and different markets, and different organizational histories, in other words at some cognitive distance, outside firms perceive, interpret and understand phenomena differently, and this may compensate for organizational myopia. This yields a new purpose for interorganizational alliances, next to the usual considerations, known from the alliance literature, such as economies of scale and scope, risk spreading, complementarity of competence, flexibility, setting market standards, and speed and efficiency of market entry.

The different foci of firms entail cognitive distance between firms. In processes of learning and innovation, in interaction between firms, this yields both an opportunity and a problem. The opportunity lies in diversity: the novelty value of a relation increases with cognitive distance. However, mutual understanding decreases with cognitive distance. If effectiveness of learning by interaction is the mathematical product of novelty value and understandability, the result is an inverse-U shaped relation with cognitive distance. Optimal cognitive distance lies at the maximum of the curve. This

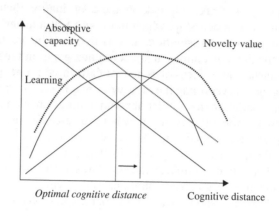

Source: Nooteboom (1999).

Figure 63.1 Optimal cognitive distance

is illustrated in Figure 63.1. Here the downward-sloping line represents understandability, on the basis of 'absorptive capacity'. The upward sloping line represents the novelty value of a relation. The optimal level of cognitive distance from a learning perspective lies in-between very low and very high levels of cognitive distance. Absorptive capacity is not fixed. It may be raised, and then, as illustrated in the figure, optimal cognitive distance increases, together with the innovative output of collaboration. For more codified knowledge, absorptive capacity may be raised by R&D, and for more tacit knowledge it may be raised by cumulative experience in communication with people who think differently. Note that, owing to the integration, in cognition, of both rationality and emotion-laden value judgements, cognitive distance also includes differences in goals and in attitudes towards organization, fair dealing, and the like.

Wuyts *et al.* (2005) put the hypothesis of optimal cognitive distance to two empirical tests. The first test was conducted on a combination of the basic hypothesis of optimal cognitive distance with the second hypothesis that cognitive distance decreases with increased frequency and duration of interaction. This yields the hypothesis of an inverted U-shaped relation between radical technological innovation and the extent to which firms ally with the same partners over time. That hypothesis was tested on data on vertical alliances between biotech and pharma companies, and was supported. The second test was conducted on a combination of the basic hypothesis of optimal cognitive distance with a second hypothesis that the likelihood of a collaborative alliance increases with the expected performance of collaborative innovation. This yielded the derived hypothesis that the likelihood of an alliance for innovation has an inverted U-shaped relation with cognitive distance. That hypothesis was tested on data on horizontal alliances in ICT industries. Partial support was found. Technology-related measures of cognitive distance were not found to have any significant effect, but several indicators of differences in firms' organizational characteristics proved to have the expected inverted U-shaped effect. Three considerations were offered to explain why organizational aspects turned out to be more important than technological ones in ICT industries. First, as indicated in the earlier theoretical discussion, when a technology is systemic, as is the case in ICT, then, almost by definition, organizational issues are more important than in the case of stand-alone technology, as in biotechnology. Second, in the ICT case the alliances are horizontal, and there the threat of mutual competition between alliance partners is higher than in vertical alliances, as in the pharma-biotech case. That requires more attention to issues of governance and organization. Third, according to innovation theory there is a cycle of innovation where, after a stage of volatility, technology converges on a 'dominant design'. Then demand and competition increase, and attention shifts to organization for commercialization (market entry, access to distribution channels) and efficient production, which may in turn lead to a dominant design in organization (Abernathy, 1978; Abernathy and Clark, 1985; Abernathy and Utterback, 1978). ICT industries are largely in that stage of shifting innovation from technology to organization.

Trust
TCE has been ambiguous about trust. In his 1975 book, Williamson employed the notion of 'atmosphere', which comes close, it appears, to trust. In his 1985 book, trust is not dealt with. Later, Williamson (1993) faced the issue squarely and asked a very good, challenging question: does trust go beyond calculative self-interest? If it does not, it adds nothing to existing economic analysis. If it does, it entails blind trust and that is inadvisable in market relations, outside relations of family or friendship. In markets it will not survive. Thus, Williamson argued, whichever way you look at it, trust can be discarded. In his 1999 article, Williamson suggests that scholars in the competence perspective 'presume the absence of opportunism . . . [and thereby] . . . enter the world of utopian fantasies'. Of course, those scholars are not that naïve. They accept the possibility of opportunism but they reject Williamson's neglect of trust.

TCE does not assume that everyone is equally opportunistic, but that prior to a transaction one can have no reliable information about one's partner's degree of opportunism, and therefore one has to *assume* opportunism, as a basis for governance, to avoid the hazard involved. Williamson

(1985: 59) argued as follows: 'inasmuch as a great deal of the relevant information about trustworthiness or its absence that is generated during the course of bilateral trading is essentially private information – in that it cannot be fully communicated to and shared with others – knowledge about behavioural uncertainties is very uneven'. This may be so. But it yields insufficient argument to ignore trust. Why should it be easy to incorporate trust? Even if it is difficult, disregarding it may be worse. When Williamson argues for the *assumption* of opportunism, he does not seem to be aware of the price one pays for that. It leads one to possibly costly contracting. Because of economies of scale in transaction costs it is especially costly for or with regard to small firms (Nooteboom, 1993b). What is worse, such a contract might seriously constrain the freedom and open-endedness of action that is crucial especially when the collaboration is aimed at innovation and the development of new competencies. Even worse than that, the expression of distrust, based on the assumption of opportunism, is likely to destroy the basis for building up trust as the relation unfolds. There is much evidence in the trust literature that distrust breeds distrust and may even elicit opportunism. Then the assumption of opportunism may become self-fulfilling, with considerable costs of contracting and loss of perspective for a fruitful relationship.

At some level trust is inevitable. Markets could not work without non-calculative trust. Complete lack of trust beyond calculative self-interest would prevent one from entering any relation and would thereby deprive one from evidence that may contradict mistrust. Absence of trust would yield an infinite regress of seeking safeguards for the hazards involved in ambiguity concerning the terms of safeguards. Such ambiguity is inevitable: even legal language does not yield complete lack of ambiguity. No language can. It has been recognized by others that, even if all relevant contingencies were known, there would still be incompleteness of contracts because of 'bounded writing and communication skills' (Hart, 1990: 699) and the fact that 'language would not be rich and precise enough to describe all the eventualities' (Milgrom and Roberts, 1992: 129). On the other hand, too much trust will be corrected by experience that invalidates it. The question now is what the basis for 'genuine' trust might be. There is a vast literature on trust that cannot fully be discussed here (for a survey, see Nooteboom, 2002). There is a widespread view that trust, in a wide sense, includes elements of control or 'deterrence', including both legal coercion and control by incentives and dependence, as well as elements that go beyond control, as a basis for 'goodwill' or 'benevolence' (see e.g. the special issue of *Organization Studies* on 'Trust and control in organizational relations', **22**(2), 2001). As noted by Maguire *et al.* (2001: 286), if we do not include the latter, we conflate trust and power. The first (control or deterrence) is part of calculative self-interest, but the latter (benevolence) is not. Many authors feel that control is foreign to the notion of trust, and that 'genuine' trust is based on other, more social and personal foundations of trustworthiness. This is in accordance with Williamson's view that the notion of trust is meaningful (in what we called 'genuine trust') only if it goes beyond calculative self-interest. Therefore, trust has been defined as the expectation that a partner will not engage in opportunistic behaviour, even in the face of countervailing short-term opportunities and incentives (Bradach and Eccles, 1989; Chiles and McMackin, 1996; Nooteboom, 1996).

There are several foundations of trust beyond calculative self-interest. One lies in norms and values concerning decent behaviour, or ethics, which constrain opportunism. Within firms, this is part of the culture of a firm, as part of its focus, as indicated before. In several writings, Williamson seemed to acknowledge, often implicitly, that norms of behaviour are part of the institutional environment, or of the institutional arrangements of firms. But how does this square with his 1993 rejection of trust that goes beyond calculative self-interest? If norms of behaviour are conducive to trust, are they then part of calculative self-interest? Norms of behaviour are not calculative, selected rationally, but are socially inculcated, and form part of tacit, unreflective principles of behaviour. They go beyond utility.

Williamson (1993) explicitly rejected other foundations of genuine trust, such as loyalty based on empathy, identification, friendship, and reciprocity. Those, he claimed, should be reserved for friends and family only. But, inevitably, such social–psychological phenomena also play a role in business relations. Furthermore, one can learn to trust and be trustworthy, in a way that is not blind or irrational. Here, the lack of learning in TCE connects with its lack of trust. As a transaction relation unfolds in time, one can accumulate more or less reliable information about trustworthiness. And such experience can be communicated in reputation mechanisms. The sociological literature gives extensive instructions on how to infer intentional trustworthiness from observed behaviour (Deutsch, 1973). Did the partner act not only according to the letter but also to the spirit of the agreement? Did he give timely warnings about unforeseen changes or problems? Was he open about relevant contingencies, and truthful about his dealings with others who might constitute a threat to oneself? Did he defect to more attractive alternatives at the earliest opportunity? Or to use Hirschman's (1970) notions of 'voice' and 'exit': how much voice rather than exit did he exhibit? Furthermore, the literature on trust indicates the possibility that in interaction partners may get to understand each other better, which enables a better judgement of trustworthiness, in 'knowledge based trust'. In ongoing interaction they may first develop insight in each other's cognitive frames, in empathy. This does not entail that they always agree. There may be sharp disagreements, but those are combined with a willingness to express and discuss them more or less openly, in 'voice', extending mutual benefit of the doubt. As a result, conflicts may deepen the relationship rather than breaking it. Next, partners may develop shared cognitive frames, by which they may identify with each other's goals, in 'identification-based trust', with understanding or even sympathy for weaknesses and mistakes (McAllister, 1995; Lewicki and Bunker, 1996).

Another, though related, basis for trusting behaviour lies in routinization (Nooteboom, 1996; Nooteboom *et al.*, 1997). Herbert Simon a long time ago showed that routines have survival value because they reserve our scarce capacity of 'focal awareness' in rational, calculative thought, for conditions that are new and demand priority. When things go well for a while in a relationship, one tends to take at least some of it for granted. One may no longer think of opportunities for opportunism open to a partner, or to oneself. And it seems rather odd to call routines 'calculative'. How can something that is subconscious be calculative? I proposed (Nooteboom, 2002) that, on the basis of experience in relations, trustworthiness is assumed until evidence to the contrary emerges. In other words, trust is a 'default'. The possibility of opportunism is relegated to 'subsidiary awareness' (Polanyi, 1962).

In spite of all this, surely Williamson was right in his warning of the dangers of trust that becomes blind. However, he went overboard when stating that authors in the competence perspective 'presume the absence of opportunism . . . [and thereby] . . . enter the world of utopian fantasies' (Williamson, 1999). Most authors in the competence perspective do not wish to suggest either that there is no threat of opportunism or that self-interest or control are absent, or that altruism and goodwill operate independently from it. The relation between the two is a subject for extensive debate. As noted by Bachmann (in Lane and Bachmann, 2000: 303), trust is a hybrid phenomenon, including both calculation and goodwill. Trust can work without becoming unconditional, which would indeed be unwise, as Williamson suggests. While trust is not always calculative, it is constrained by possibilities of opportunism (Pettit, 1995).

One way to model trustworthiness is in terms of a limited resistance to temptation towards opportunism. This may be modelled as a threshold for defection: one does not opportunistically defect until the advantage one can gain with it exceeds the threshold.[4] This threshold depends on the wider cultural environment, the narrower cultural environment of a firm one works for, personal upbringing, and personal relations. It is likely to adapt as a function of experience. It also depends on pressures of competition and survival. In competitive markets trustworthiness will be less than in more protected ones. Trust may then be modelled as based on an assumption, perception or inference of such a (limited) resistance to temptation of opportunism. Within that limit, one can economize on contracting. When temptation becomes too great, trust is likely to make way for calculation. So, even though trust is and should be limited, since indeed unconditional trust is unwise, within the margin of perceived or assumed trustworthiness it can save on contracting.

Routines are not unconditional, unless they have sunk so deeply into our nature that they have become instincts. Generally, when something out of the ordinary occurs, our awareness shifts from subsidiary to 'focal' and we look critically at what is going on. As Simon (1983) pointed out, we need emotions of danger and excitement to catapult us into focal awareness. In relations of voice, we must next control emotions to give the partner the benefit of the doubt, rather than immediately assume the worst. Thus, routine behaviour is not necessarily blind, or more accurately, it is not unconditional. Does this triggering back into focal awareness, then, make routines calculative? Again, can subsidiary awareness be called calculative? And can emotional triggering be called calculative?

Nooteboom *et al.* (1997) conducted an empirical test of explanations of perceived relational risk of suppliers, on the basis of TCE variables and variables relating to non-calculative trust. Both explanations were confirmed, showing that TCE and non-TCE variables can be complementary. The TCE variables were specific investments, mutual dependence, legal and private ordering. The trust variables, beyond TCE, were the development of joint norms of behaviour and routinization. The test was conducted on data from ten customer relations for each of ten producers of electrical/electronic components.

Further extensions
The inclusion of learning and trust leads on to further extensions of TCE. One extension is effects of scale in transaction costs. Transaction costs differ between large and small firms. There are effects of scale on both sides of a transaction relation: a small firm as supplier and as a customer (Nooteboom, 1993b). Transaction costs, in all stages of contact, contract and control, are higher for a small firm owing to a lack of staff support in marketing, legal matters, personnel, finance and accounting. The set-up costs of governance are high relative to the size of the transaction. Therefore, in relations with small firms, use will more often be made of an outside arbitrator or mediator to settle conflicts, instead of detailed contracts and formal procedural agreements ('trilateral governance'). Costs of monitoring and control are higher because of a greater tacitness of knowledge: there are fewer formal, documented sources of information, which

makes small firms more inscrutable. One needs to extract the required information from the minds of people, or deduce it from their actions. That is also why small firms are often unattractive customers for consultants. This problem is exacerbated by the fact that small firms are more diverse than large ones (Nooteboom, 1994).[5] The inscrutability and diversity of small firms yield problems in the stages of contract and control. There is less formal documentation as a basis for contracts or other agreements and for monitoring compliance with them. Note that here there is a double effect. First, there is an effect of scale in setting up a contract and a monitoring system. Second, there is less documented information available for it. Given a certain volume per transaction, a smaller firm has fewer transaction partners, and therefore less spread of relational risk. One can try to improve this by taking a larger number of partners, with a smaller transaction per partner, but that is often not attractive owing to effects of scale in transactions, because of minimum set-up costs of contact, contract and control, as indicated above. A small firm may also burden its partner with a greater risk of discontinuity due to default, because, owing to a smaller spread of commercial risk across multiple products and markets, default risk is higher for smaller firms. Small firms may also raise the suspicion that they are opportunistically engaging in 'hit and run' – going for a fast profit with an unreliable or bad quality product, or a product without future support – and leave the market when the damage becomes evident.[6]

In an extended theory of transactions, there are also two extensions of the notion of specific investments. One is the investment in mutual understanding, needed to cross cognitive distance, in the building of mutual empathy, i.e. understanding of a partner's cognition. This may to a large extent be relation-specific. Related to this, the second extension is the building of relation-specific trust, by mutual understanding, which helps to identify limits of trustworthiness, in different respects (competence, benevolence), under different conditions. As discussed, an issue concerning trust is the relation between personal and organizational trust. In IORs, one needs to trust both the organization, in both its competence and intentions to support and guide the conduct of its people, and the competence and intentions of the people one deals with. The two are connected by the roles that people have in organizations.[7] It takes time and effort to get to know all this, and to develop coherent individual and organizational trust. Especially for small suppliers to large firms, this may entail a very high and highly relation-specific investment, relative to the volume of trade involved.

Another extension is the inclusion of spillover risk next to the hold-up risk analysed by TCE. Spillover risk is the risk that knowledge that forms part of competitive advantage is absorbed and used for competition by partners, in direct or indirect relationships. For an assessment of this risk one should, first of all, take into account that the questions should not be only how much knowledge spills over outwards but also how much spills over inwards, and what the net advantage is. Spillover risk further depends on a number of contingencies (Nooteboom, 1999a). Tacit knowledge spills over less easily than codified knowledge. Whether spillover matters for competition depends on the absorptive capacity of potential competitors, i.e. their ability to understand what they see (taking into account 'causal ambiguity') and, after that, to implement knowledge for effective competition, given organizational focus. Finally, if by the time all that has happened the knowledge involved has changed, one would not care. These considerations are of great importance for the structure and governance of IORs, as will be shown later.

Boundaries of the firm
From the beginning of TCE (Coase, 1937), a core question concerned the purpose and the boundaries of the firm. Different answers are reviewed here. They are not necessarily substitutes, and can well complement each other. For example, cognitive and transaction cost arguments may be combined. To answer such questions, let us first consider some key features of organization.

The basic features of an organization include a *structure of elements* (subsidiaries, divisions, teams, individual people) that have resources and *repertoires of action* (competencies), with *decision rules* that govern *choice* from those repertoires, to achieve *goals*, in *coordination* (which includes governance) between those elements. Coordination is needed to the extent that elements are connected; i.e. their actions, in both their selection and performance, depend on each other. The position that an element has in a structure (its pattern of ties with other elements) constitutes its *role* in the organization (Nooteboom and Bogenrieder, 2002). Note that there may be different levels of repertoires, including those for the development of repertoires (learning). In organizations, many actions and decision rules or heuristics are routinized, and may have a large tacit component. In other words, they constitute organizational routines (Nelson and Winter, 1982). Decision rules may or may not be rationally designed, and they incorporate decision heuristics from social psychology. Goals also may be largely tacit. Different elements in the organization may or may not know or understand some or all of each other's actions and repertoires, and may or may not agree on each other's goals. In other words, there may be differences in semantics and values, and some of those may even be irreconcilable. However that may be, it was argued above that an organization requires a certain 'focus', of some shared views of the world, goals and ways of doing things, in order to function and survive as a collective. This focus may be wide, allowing for much diversity, or narrow, depending on a variety of conditions. In other words, an organization puts limits, somewhere, on cognitive diversity.

There are a number of familiar arguments for the existence of organizations. A legal argument for organization derives from the need for a legal identity of a group of people working together, to regulate ownership of assets, conditions of employment, liability and accountability. In the literature on IORs, there are claims that boundaries of firms are blurring, in forms of organization 'between market and hierarchy'. This is correct in the sense that, in IORs, forms of governance extend across boundaries of the firm, in forms of semi-integration. In the legal sense, however, boundaries remain clear (Hodgson, 2002). In other words, boundaries of organizations as forms of co-ordination do indeed blur, but boundaries of organizations as legal entities do not. The legal argument does not, however, specify what activities have to be combined in an organization, and why.

Economics has given a variety of arguments for integrating different activities in an organization. One is technical: when complementary activities are technically inseparable, they need to be integrated by definition. A second type of economic theory derives from the need to align incentives in complementary activities, in the face of possible problems of monitoring, due to asymmetric information. One branch of that theory is 'principal–agent' theory. That will not be used in this chapter, because it puts the analysis of collaboration on the wrong foot, with its assumption that there is a clear, independent principal ('boss') on one side, and a dependent agent on the other side, who is driven to satisfy the demands of the principal. In IORs, dependence and power are often not balanced, but nevertheless, in collaboration agents are to be seen as each other's principals and agents at the same time. One of the main obstacles in collaboration is that people tend to take a one-sided principal–agent view.[8]

Another branch of this type of economic theory is transaction cost economics, as discussed above. According to this theory, boundaries of the firm arise from a trade-off between, on the one hand, costs of contact, contract and control, which are higher outside than inside a firm, and, on the other, advantages of scale and motivation in outside, independent, specialized production. In this chapter, a new, cognitive, argument is offered, as discussed above. Organizations need a cognitive focus, which entails a danger of myopia, which is to be mended by access to complementary cognition from outside partners, at optimal cognitive distance ('external economy of cognitive scope'). Organizational boundaries are determined by the tightness of organizational focus, which depends on several conditions (Nooteboom, 2000a). One condition is the relation between exploitation and exploration, and the position in this that is chosen by the firm.

Exploration requires a wider focus, and exploitation a narrower one. How difficult it is to combine the two in one organization depends on how systemic v. stand-alone exploitation is. Highly systemic exploitation yields problems in allowing for the wider scope needed for exploration. One may specialize in either exploitation or exploration, and 'outsource' the other in IORs. The notion of focus is related to the notion of 'core competence' from the business literature (Prahalad and Hamel, 1990). That notion refers to competencies in which a firm can distinguish itself from competitors, to make profit from specialities that cannot easily be imitated. It is meant to go beyond existing capabilities, to include the ability to develop new ones. The notion also seems similar to that of organizational routines, on different levels, indicated above.

In much of the business literature on IORs, opinion seems to have settled on a rather extreme view in favour of outsourcing everything that is not part of 'core competencies'. However, that may go too far.[9] The question of course is what, exactly, is to be seen as part of core competence, and what is meant by the qualification, given above, that one should outsource as much as 'strategically possible'. When is something not to be outsourced even if it is not part of core competence?

Philips Company is a user of chips (semiconductors) as components in many kinds of consumer electronics. A compact disc player, for example, requires a combination of mechanics, laser technology, electro-technology, control technology and informatics. Should Philips make its own chips, or contract them from specialist producers? The production of chips entails high tech surface technology, to affect, at a microscopic level, the conducting properties of a silicon disc by means of sophisticated physical and chemical processes. That does not seem to fit with Philips' core competencies. So, according to the maxim of sticking to core competencies, it seems reasonable to have it contracted out. But there are strategic complications. The first is that the world-class producers of chips are the same Japanese companies that compete with Philips in the market for consumer electronics. Should one become dependent for supply on one's main competitors? The second complication is that the development of technology and markets is very rapid, and new products often arise from novel combinations of existing technologies, and often one needs to react fast to novel opportunities. The 'window of opportunity' is narrow and passes fast. For this reason one may need to maintain competence in an area that in a static situation one should surrender. The production of semiconductors requires sophisticated (miniaturized, uncontaminated and perfectly accurate) technology, with physical and chemical processes for etching micro patterns on the surface of silicon slices, and modifying conductive properties in those patterns. Similar technology can also be used for the deposition of thin layers on surfaces for other purposes, such as hardening materials, coating photovoltaic cells or the production of sensors. Thus, the technology of chips production is a 'platform' technology, which contributes to other products than chips, which might fit well in Philips product portfolio. To keep such future options open, chips production may have to be seen as part of core competence.

The hypothesis concerning 'external economy of cognitive scope' entails that greater uncertainty in an industry, in terms of the volatility of technology and markets, yields a greater need to engage in outside relations with other organizations, to correct for the myopia of organizational focus. Thus, the hypothesis entails that in such industries there will be more outside relations, in inter-firm alliances for innovation and technical development. This is contrary to the hypothesis from transaction cost economics (TCE) that, in the presence of transaction-specific investments, increased uncertainty yields an incentive to integrate activities under a single 'hierarchy' (Williamson, 1975, 1985). The argument from TCE is that the dependence resulting from specific investments yields a risk of 'hold-up', which is difficult to control between firms under conditions of uncertainty concerning contingencies of contract execution, and easier to control under conditions of managerial fiat, in a hierarchy, which yields more scope for demanding information for monitoring, and for resolving conflicts of hold-up. I do not deny that argument. However, I propose that, from the theory of learning used here, there may be an overriding argument in favour of outside relations, for the sake of external economy of cognitive scope. The problem of hold-up that may arise from specific investments then has to be resolved by relational governance, which reconnects our theory with TCE.

The hypothesis of an increased need for alliances under conditions of volatility has been confirmed by Colombo and Garrone (1998). They analysed the strategies of telecommunication carriers in the early 1990s and found that, in Internet services and content, where technology and demand uncertainty were especially high, the relative rate of alliance formation was higher than in other communication industries characterized by absence of such extreme uncertainty. In addition, in the former industries a large share of the alliances established by telecommunication carriers had an intersectoral nature, linking them with firms from a variety of industries; this suggests that external economies of cognitive scope may have played a key role in alliance formation.

Mergers/acquisitions or alliances?
There are many forms of IORs, which vary along a number of dimensions: number of participants, network structure, and type and strength of ties, including ownership and control. Here, the literature benefits from extensive network analysis in sociology. Network structure includes features such as density, centrality and structural holes. Ties may have wide or narrow scope, depending on the range of activities included in them. Strength of ties has a number of dimensions: frequency of contact, duration, size of investments, specificity of investments, and openness of communication.

Table 63.1   Reasons for an MA or alliance

	MA (integration)	Alliance (keeping distance)
Efficiency	inseparable economy of scale in core activities inseparable economy of scope	economy of scale in non-core activities motivating force of independence lower costs and risks of integration
Competence	maintain appropriability, options for future competence, spillover control rejuvenation provide management for a growing firm	maintain focus on core competence maintain diversity, cognitive distance maintain entrepreneurial drive
Positional advantage	control hold-up risk control quality brand name protect other partners from spillover ensure against takeover, keep out competition	maintain flexibility maintain local identity/brand of partner
By default	partner only available in MA difficulty of evaluating a takeover candidate collusion forbidden by competition authorities	partner only available in alliance interest only in part of a partner MA forbidden by competition authorities
Rule of thumb	*in case of same core competencies same markets*	*in case of complementary competencies markets*

For a systematic discussion, see Nooteboom (2004b). Here, only a key question is discussed, related to the boundaries of the firm: when do firms engage in integration, in merger or acquisition (MA), and when do they keep a distance, in alliances between formally independent organizations? This section analyses this choice both normatively, i.e. in terms of what is good for the firm, depending on conditions, and descriptively, i.e. according to what choices are actually made, and why.

Note that an MA entails integration in the legal entity of one organization. Within that organization, it might allow for high degrees of decentralization. Table 63.1 summarizes the argument for the alternatives of an MA and an alliance.

Overall, the argument for integration, in an MA, is that it yields more control, in particular of hold-up and spillover risk, and of present and future core competencies. For hold-up, the argument comes from TCE. Within a firm, under the grasp of 'administrative fiat', in an employment relation, one can demand more information for control and one can impose more decisions than one could in respect of an independent partner. A similar argument applies to spillover risk: one can monitor and control better what happens to information. Of course, even within organizations this may not be easy, as a result of asymmetric information, tacit knowledge, and misaligned incentives and motivations. However, under the legal umbrella of a firm, one has more opportunities than one has between different firms.

As discussed earlier, an argument for integration may also be that one needs to maintain control of activities or resources that are complementary to core competencies, i.e. are needed to utilize them or to appropriate their advantages, or that are needed to retain options for future core competencies. The example was given of the chips division of Philips Company. Philips might have to hold on to it since it appears to be a platform technology for a range of potential future markets. Another possible argument is that one may need to retain a certain capability in an outsourced activity to be able to judge its quality, for the selection and governance of outside relationships. However, there may be ample opportunities to maintain options for future core competencies in alliances. And capability of judging supplier quality may be derived from a joint benchmarking service, in the industry.

The takeover of a young, dynamic, innovative firm may serve to rejuvenate an old firm (Vermeulen and Barkema, 2001). In a growing new firm, the entrepreneur often has to turn himself around to the role of an administrator, or hire one, to delegate work and institute formal structures and procedures for the coordination of more specialized activities in large-scale production and distribution. He may not be able or willing to do that, and it may be to the benefit of the firm when it is taken over by a firm with a better managerial capability. However, it may be more likely that the entrepreneurial dynamic of the small firm is stifled in the bureaucracy of the acquirer, in which case it should stay separate.

Overall, the argument for an alliance is that it allows partners to maintain more focus of core competence, more flexibility of configuration and more variety of competence for the sake of innovation and learning. The flexibility argument derives from rigidities in re-arrangement of activities within organizations. This varies across business systems: it is less in the USA than in continental Europe and Japan. Hence, network structures of firms are needed more in the latter regions (Nooteboom, 1999c).

Also, as recognized in TCE, an independent firm that is responsible for its own survival will be more motivated to perform than an internal department that is assured of its custom. Another great advantage of an alliance is that it entails fewer problems of clashes between different cultures, structures and procedures, in management, decision making, remuneration, labour conditions, reporting procedures and norms of conflict resolution, which often turn out to be the biggest obstacles for a successful MA. Of course, such clashes can also occur in alliances, but less integration still entails fewer problems of integration.

There is an argument of scale for both forms. In production, many economies of scale have been reduced, e.g. in computing. However, there is still economy of scale in, for instance, distribution channels, communication networks, network externalities and brand name. For integration, the argument of scale is that one pools volume in activities in which one specializes. For outsourcing, the argument is that for activities that one does not specialize in, an outside, specialized producer can collect more volume, producing for multiple users. That may also offer more opportunities for professional development and career to staff that are specialized in that activity. Note the argument from TCE that, if assets are so dedicated that a supplier can produce only for the one user, the scale argument for outsourcing disappears. There is an argument of economies of scale or scope for integration only if they are inseparable (Williamson, 1975). It depends how systemic rather than stand-alone activities are (Langlois and Robertson, 1995).

> One form of economy of scope is that different activities share the same underlying fixed cost, for example of R&D, management and administration, communication network or brand name. When one of the activities is dropped, the utilization of fixed costs may drop. However, this is not necessarily so. It may be possible to share such overhead with others, as happens, for example, in 'incubators' for small firms, or collaboration in an R&D consortium.

From the perspective of brand image, there are arguments for both integration and separation. In an alliance there may be too great a risk that the image or quality of a brand allotted to partners will not be maintained sufficiently scrupulously. On the other hand, it may be better to maintain an independent, outside brand, to preserve its local identity.

> The Dutch RABO bank years ago wanted to move into consumer credit, but felt that it would detract from its brand identity, which was associated with savings accounts, and therefore consumer credit was offered by a separate subsidiary with a different name ('Lage Landen'). However, years later consumer credit had become a normal product, required in the product range of any bank, and RABO incorporated the 'Lage Landen' under its own name.
> Staying with the RABO bank, an illustration of reinforcing one's product range by pooling complementary products is the cooperation between RABO,

who offered a personal securities investment service through its advisors, and ROBECO, who offered a security investment fund to which consumers could subscribe by phone, without intermediaries. The two were pooled to yield a full line of service.

Finally, there are reasons of default. One is that one would like to take one form but it is not available, because a partner is only available for the other form, or because it is forbidden by competition authorities.

In the airline business, for example, MA are problematic for reasons of national pride and interest, perhaps strategic military reasons, and the fact that landing rights are nationally allocated.

Another default is that one would like to take over only part of a larger firm, but it is not separately available for takeover, without the rest, in which one is not interested because it would dilute core competence. Another is that one cannot judge the value of a takeover candidate and needs some period of collaboration in an alliance to find out. Previously, value could more easily be judged by adding up values of material assets than now, when intangibles such as brand name, reputation, skills and knowledge are often more important, and difficult to value.

Clearly, the choice between MA and alliance is quite complex. If one wants a simpler, general rule of thumb, it is as follows: consider full integration, in an MA, only if the partner engages in the same core activities in the same markets. In all other cases, i.e. when activities and/or markets are different, the rule of thumb suggests an alliance. According to this rule, what one would expect, on the whole, is vertical disintegration and horizontal integration.

In banking, increase of efficiency in an MA can, for example, be achieved by eliminating one of two branch offices (or automatic teller machines) in locations where both banks are represented. Threshold costs in specialized knowledge of specific industries and in setting up ICT networks and databases can be shared. Reserves to cover risks of defaulting customers can be shared and spread. In an MA between banking and insurance there are economies of scope in the utilization of branch offices, ICT networks, advertising, customer relations. Such economy is further enhanced by adding travel bookings. In MAs in banking, insurance and accounting an important motive also is the building of a worldwide network of offices from different companies pooling their offices in different continents, in order to yield global service to global customers. However, here one could ask whether the same objectives could not be achieved in an alliance, with the added advantages associated with that.

There are four theoretical arguments for the rule of thumb. First, in horizontal collaboration, with the same activities in the same markets, partners are direct competitors, and it is most difficult to control conflict without integration. The game is more likely to be zero-sum. The temptation to exploit dependence is greatest. There is a threat of direct rather than indirect spillover. Second, in horizontal collaboration core competence is more similar, so that integration does not dilute it too much. Third, here the cognitive advantages of alliances are less: the diversity in knowledge is already minimal, with small cognitive distance, and thus there is less need to preserve it by staying apart. Fourth, with the same products, technology and markets, differences in culture, structure and procedures are likely to be minimal. Of course, they can still be significant.

> The Dutch steel corporation ['Hoogovens'] a long time ago undertook a merger with a German colleague. After ten years of struggle it was broken up again, because attempts to integrate the two companies remained unsuccessful. Ten years after that, in Hoogovens there were still two rival camps, those who had supported the merger, and were held responsible for its failure, and the opponents, who were blamed by the proponents for having sabotaged the merger. Ten years after that, Hoogovens merged with British Steel, in CORUS. At present (March, 2003), that merger is about to collapse, owing to a conflict of interest. The British side has suffered from a more senescent technological outfit and a high exchange rate for the pound. To generate funds for restructuring, the British leadership of CORUS wanted to sell off a Dutch aluminium subsidiary, but this was blocked by the supervisory board of the Dutch branch, which was challenged by the British, in front of a Dutch court, which ruled that the Dutch action was legal. This reflects, among other things, a different view of corporate governance.

One important qualification of the rule of thumb is the following. The overlap of activities and markets, which would favour integration, does not concern the situation prior to collaboration, but afterwards. In other words, if collaboration would lead to such overlap, integration may be needed before that overlap arises. In other words, one should look, not at current, but at intended, core competencies.

The argument for the rule of thumb is not only theoretical. Bleeke and Ernst (1991) showed empirically that, when this rule is applied, the success rate of both MA and alliances rises substantially. If for a given method of measurement the success rate is less than 50 per cent without the rule, success rises to 75 per cent with the rule, for both MA and alliances. However, the rule given above is only a rule of thumb, to which there are exceptions. For more detailed analysis one can use Table 63.1, with the corresponding logic set out above.

Next to good reasons for MA, alliances and outsourcing, there are also reasons that are bad, in the sense that they are not in the interests of the firms involved. One such reason is the bandwagon effect: one engages in a practice because it is the fashion to do so. When a practice becomes established, the drive for legitimation may yield pressure to adopt it without much critical evaluation. Another reason is a prisoner's dilemma that applies especially to MA: if one does not take over one may be taken over, which may yield a loss of managerial position, so one tries to be the first to take over, even though it would be best for all to stay apart. Another reason is managerial *hubris*: managers want to make a mark and appear decisive or macho. This also applies especially to MAs: these are quicker, more visible and dramatic than collaboration between independent firms. There is also the often illusory presumption that a takeover is easier than an alliance. Subsequently, however, the MA often fails owing to problems of integration and has to be disentangled again. Even speed is a dubious argument. It may on the surface seem that an MA is in place faster than an alliance, for which one must negotiate longer and set up an elaborate system of 'bilateral governance'. However, the speed of an MA is misleading: the decision may be made quickly, but the subsequent process of integration is often much slower and more problematic than assumed. An alliance is often better even if in the longer run a takeover is the best option, to allow for the process of trust development, discussed before. Also, it yields the option to retract when failure emerges, without too much loss of investment.

Bad reasons of bandwagon effects, managerial hubris or macho behaviour, and career profile may also thwart alliances. However, here the damage is more limited, and it is easier to retrench when failure emerges.

Governance

The earlier analysis shows that, in addition to the usual instruments to govern risk of opportunism, taken from TCE, there are also sources of trust that go beyond them. The first include hierarchical and legal control, mutual dependence, hostages, and reputation. The latter include ethical norms and values in the institutional environment, and the building of relation-specific norms, empathy, identification and routinization. Table 63.2 gives a survey of instruments, which includes instruments for the governance of both hold-up and spillover risk. Every instrument also has its drawbacks, which are also specified in the table.

The first instrument entails a cop-out. In view of relational risk, hold-up is avoided by not engaging in dedicated investments, and spillover is avoided by not giving away any sensitive knowledge. The opportunity cost of this is that one may miss opportunities to achieve high added value in the production of specialities by investing in collaboration and learning with partners. The second instrument is integration in a merger or acquisition (MA), with the advantages and drawbacks discussed in the previous section.

Below the thin rule in Table 63.2, there are instruments for alliances between formally autonomous organizations, where one accepts risks of

Table 63.2   Instruments of governance and their drawbacks

Instrument	Drawback
Risk avoidance no specific investments, no knowledge transfer	lower added value, with less product differentiation (in case of dedicated technology), no learning
Integration MA	less flexibity, variety, motivation, problems of integration (see Chapter 3)
Number of partners maintain alternatives demand exclusiveness	mutiple set-up costs, spillover risk for partners limitation of variety learning
Contracts	problematic under uncertainty, can be expensive strait-jacket in innovation, can generate distrust
Self-interest mutual dependence hostages, reputation	opportunistic: requires monitoring and is sensitive to change of capabilities, conditions and entry of new players
Trust	needs building up if not already present, has limits: how reliable? Relation between individual and organization
Go-betweens	may not be available; how reliable?
Network position	needs time to build, side-effects

dependence due to specific investments and of spillover, and seeks to control them by other means than full integration in one organization. One option is to maintain multiple partners, in order not to become dependent on any one of them, and to demand exclusiveness from any partner, to prevent spillover. However, maintaining relations with alternative partners entails a multiplication of costs in dedicated investments and the governance needed to control the risks involved. Exclusiveness entails, in the specific activity involved, one's forbidding the partner to engage in relations with one's competitors. The first problem with this is that the demand of exclusiveness forbids the partner what one allows oneself: partnerships with the partner's competitors. By having those relations one increases the spillover risk for partners. As a result, none of them may be willing to give sensitive information, which degrades their value as sources of complementary competence and learning. Furthermore, the demand for exclusiveness blocks the variety of the partner's sources of learning, which reduces his value as a partner in learning, at a cognitive distance that is maintained by his interaction with outside contacts. Hence one should consider whether spillover is really a significant risk, as discussed before. If it is not, all parties can gain from maintaining multiple partners, perhaps for maintaining bargaining position, but especially for maintaining variety of sources of learning and flexibility of configurations.

A second instrument is a contract, in an attempt to close off 'opportunities for opportunism', by contracts. The problem with this instrument is fourfold. First, it can be expensive to set up. Second, it can be ineffective for lack of possibilities to monitor compliance, owing to asymmetric information. Even if one can properly assess the execution of agreements, especially small principals may not be in a position to threaten litigation credibly, because of the economies of scale involved. A scale effect arises when the risk, effort and cost of litigation are large relative to the damage involved. Third, contracts have limited feasibility because of uncertainty concerning future contingencies that affect contract execution. This applies especially when the purpose of collaboration is innovation. Finally, detailed contracts for the purpose of closing off opportunities for opportunism express distrust, which can raise reciprocal suspicion and distrust, with the risk of ending up in a vicious circle of regulation and distrust that limits the scope for exploration of novelty and obstructs the build-up of trust as an alternative approach to governance.

Another approach is to aim at the self-interest of the partner and limit incentives to utilize any opportunities for opportunism left by incomplete contracts. These instruments have been mostly developed in TCE. Self-interest may arise from mutual dependence, in several ways. One is that the partner participates more or less equally in the ownership and hence the risk of dedicated assets. A second approach to self-interest is to use one's own dedicated investments to build and offer a unique, valuable competence to the partner. Thus, the effect of dedicated investments can go in different directions: it makes one dependent, owing to switching costs, but it can also make the partner dependent by offering him high and unique value. This instrument can yield an upward spiral of value, where partners engage in a competition to be of unique value for each other.

Dependence also arises from a hostage, as also suggested by TCE. One form of hostage is minority participation, where one can sell one's shares to someone who is eager to undertake a hostile takeover of the partner. A more prevalent form is sensitive information. Here, the notion of hostage connects with the notion of spillover. One may threaten to pass on sensitive knowledge to a partner's competitor. Reputation also is a matter of self-interest: one behaves well in order not to sacrifice potentially profitable relations with others in the future.

The limitation of instruments aimed at self-interest is that they are not based on intrinsic motivation, and require monitoring, which may be difficult, especially in innovation. Furthermore, balance of mutual dependence is sensitive to technological change and to the entry of new players that might offer more attractive partnerships. Hostages may die or may not be returned in spite of compliance to the agreement. Reputation mechanisms may not be in place, or may work imperfectly (Hill, 1990; Lazaric and Lorenz, 1998). They require that a defector cannot escape or dodge a breakdown of reputation, e.g. by selling the business or switching to another industry or another country. Complaints of bad behaviour have to be checked for their truth and be communicated to potential future partners of the culprit. Beyond self-interest, one may also appeal to more intrinsic motives that determine 'inclinations towards opportunism'. This yields the role of trust, discussed above. Another possibility is to employ the services of a third party or 'go-between', which will not be specified here.

One will generally select some combination of mutually compatible and supporting instruments from the toolbox of governance, and the use of a single instrument will be rare. There is no single and universal best recipe for governing IORs. The choice and effectiveness of instruments depend on conditions: the goals of collaboration, characteristics of the participants, technology, markets and the institutional environment.

For example, there is no sense in contracts when the appropriate legal institutions are not in place (lack of appropriate laws), or are not effective (police or judiciary are corrupt), or when compliance cannot be monitored (for lack of accounting procedures). When technology is flexible, so that one can produce a range of different specific products with one set-up, the specificity of investments and hence the problem of hold-up is limited. Possibilities of spillover are constrained when knowledge is tacit, and do not matter when technology changes fast. Reputation mechanisms do not work when there are ample exit opportunities for defectors. Trust is difficult in a distrustful environment, where cheating rather than loyalty is the norm.

Innovation has its special conditions. Exchange of knowledge is crucial, with corresponding risks of spillover. Especially in innovation, the competencies and intentions of strangers are difficult to judge. Relevant reputation has not yet been built up. Uncertainty is great, limiting the possibility of specifying the contingencies of a contract. Specific investments are needed to set up mutual understanding. There is significant hold-up risk. Detailed contracts would limit the variety and scope for the unpredictable actions and initiatives that innovation requires. Under these conditions, trust is most needed to limit relational risk. An additional problem with contracts is that they may obstruct the building of trust. This does not mean that there are or should be no contracts at all. Indeed, there will almost always be some form of contract. However, they should then not be too detailed with the purpose of controlling hold-up risk.

Especially in innovation, a productive combination of instruments is mutual dependence complemented by trust, on the basis of an emerging experience in competent and loyal collaboration. Trust is needed besides mutual dependence, because the latter is sensitive to changing conditions. Trust is more difficult under asymmetric dependence because the more dependent side may be overly suspicious (Klein Woolthuis, 1999), in the so-called 'Calimero syndrome'. In all this, go-betweens can help. Without them the building of trust may be too slow.

In the literature, contracts and trust are primarily seen as substitutes. Less trust requires more contracts, and detailed contracts can obstruct the building of trust. However, this view is too simplistic. Trust and control can also be complements (Das and Teng, 1998, 2001; Klein Woolthuis, 1999; Klein Woolthuis *et al.*, 2006). First of all, as discussed above, trust has its limits, and where trusts ends contracts begin. Second, there may be a need for an extensive contract, not so much to foreclose opportunities for opportunism, but to serve as a record of agreements in a situation where co-ordination is technically complex. Third, a simple contract may provide the basis for building trust, rather than being a substitute for it. Fourth, one may need to build up trust before engaging in the costs and risks of setting up an extensive contract. This risk may include a spillover risk: in the course of negotiation much information is divulged for partners to assess each other. Finally, a contract may be psychological and serve to flag trust, and signing a contract may constitute a ritual of agreement.

Perhaps the most important point is that relationships should be seen as processes rather than entities that are instituted and left to themselves. Conditions may change. A frequent problem is that a relationship starts with a balance of dependence, but in time the attractiveness of one of the partners slips, owing to slower learning, appropriation of his knowledge by the other partner or institutional, technological or commercial change.

Choice of instruments for governance may be constrained. Options depend on the structure of the networks one is in, and on one's position in them. Coleman (1988) proposed that a dense structure with strong ties enables the build-up of reputation, the formation of coalitions, and social capital, in the form of trust and social norms. This helps governance, but also constrains actions.

Strong ties, in the sense of high frequency and intensity, and long duration, yield shared experience, which reduce cognitive distance, and enable the development of empathy and identification.[10] These help governance, but can weaken competence building, in the elimination of cognitive distance needed for learning. Dense networks with strong ties can also yield inefficiencies due to redundant ties, and rigidities due to lock-in into the network, with exit prevented by coalitions of network members. Thus, IORs may yield rigidity. As a result, ending a relationship may be as important, and arguably more difficult, than beginning one. A more detailed analysis of the process of relationship development is beyond the scope of this chapter (see Nooteboom, 2004b).

Notes

1. Parts of the text of this chapter were taken from Nooteboom (1999a, 2004a, 2004b).
2. Renewed, i.e., after the globalization that occurred in pre-WW1 imperialism.
3. Related to this, perhaps, Adam Smith recognized 'authority' next to utility, in politics and organization, to establish allegiance to joint goals, as discussed by Khalil (2002).
4. This feature has been included in an agent-based computational model of the build-up and breakdown of trust in buyer–supplier relations (Klos and Nooteboom, 2001).
5. First, as a motivational or 'final' cause, they have more diverse goals of entrepreneurship: not necessarily maximum profit or growth, but also independence, going their own way, maintenance of a traditional life or way of doing things, staying small and informal or wanting to try out things which are rejected in large firms. Second, as a conditional cause which makes this possible, small firms exist more on private capital and are therefore less subject to the rigours and criteria of success imposed by capital markets. Connected with this, they are not subjected to an outside supervisory board. These factors leave more room for idiosyncratic goals and ways of doing things.
6. This is more probable for small than for large firms, who have invested more in reputation, face wider consequences of reputational damage, across products and markets, in a larger portfolio, and find it more difficult to hide after they run. In other words: small firms may lack the discipline of reputation. To eliminate suspicion, the small firm may need to demonstrate that it is committed to the longer term, vulnerable to reputational loss, and it may need to point to the existence of exacting partners who can be expected to be critical and competent in judging the reliability of the small firm.
7. This is connected, for example, with the notion of the 'buy group' in industrial (B to B) marketing: the different people involved in a buy decision, and their distribution of power and competence.
8. Such a perspective is usually taken, also, in theories of corporate governance, with shareholders in the seat of the principal. Taking that approach, one fixes shareholder value as the basic value of firms from the start. One can also take a more balanced view of different 'stakeholders', in a balancing of their interests (Nooteboom, 1999b).
9. Teece (1986), Bettis *et al.* (1992), Chesbrough and Teece (1996).
10. McAllister (1995), Lewicki and Bunker (1996).

References

Abernathy, W.J. (1978). *The Productivity Dilemma: Roadblock to Innovation in the Automobile Industry*, Baltimore: Johns Hopkins University Press.
—— and K.B. Clark (1985). Innovation: mapping the winds of creative destruction, *Research Policy*, **14**, 3–22.
—— and J.M. Utterback (1978). Patterns of industrial innovation, *Technology Review*, **81**, June/July, 41–7.
Alchian, A. (1950). Uncertainty, evolution and economic theory, *The Journal of Political Economy*, **43**, February (1), 211–21.
Bazerman, M. (1998). *Judgement in Managerial Decision Making*, New York: Wiley.
Berger, P. and T. Luckmann (1967). *The Social Construction of Reality*, New York: Doubleday.
Bettis, R., S. Bradley and G. Hamel (1992). Outsourcing and industrial decline, *Academy of Management Executive*, **6**(1), 7–16.

Bleeke, J. and D. Ernst (1991). The way to win in cross-border alliances, *Harvard Business Review*, November/December, 127–35.

Bradach, J.L. and R.G. Eccles (1989). Markets versus hierarchies: from ideal types to plural forms, *Annual Review of Sociology*, **15**, 97–118.

Chesbrough, H.W. and D.J. Teece (1996). When is virtual virtuous? Organizing for innovation, *Harvard Business Review*, Jan.–Feb., 65–73.

Chiles, T.H. and J.F. McMackin (1996). Integrating variable risk preferences, trust, and transaction cost economics, *Academy of Management Review*, **21**(7), 73–99.

Coase, R. (1937). The nature of the firm, *Economica N.S.*, **4**, 386–405.

Cohen, M.D. and D.A. Levinthal (1990). Absorptive capacity: a new perspective on learning innovation, *Administrative Science Quarterly*, **35**, 128–52.

Coleman, J.S. (1988). Social capital in the creation of human capital, *American Journal of Sociology*, **94** (special supplement), 95–120.

Colombo, M.G. and P. Garrone (1998). Common carriers' entry into multimedia services, *Information Economics and Policy*, **10**, 77–105.

Das, T.K. and B.S. Teng (1998). Between trust and control: developing confidence in partner cooperation in alliances, *Academy of Management Review*, **23**(3), 491–512.

—— (2001). Trust, control and risk in strategic alliances: an integrated framework, *Organization Studies*, **22**(2), 251–84.

Deutsch, M. (1973). *The Resolution of Conflict: Constructive and Destructive Processes*, New Haven: Yale University Press.

Frey, B.S. (2002). What can economists learn from happiness research?, *Journal of Economic Literature*, **40**(2), 402–35.

Hart, O. (1990). Is bounded rationality an important element of a theory of institutions?, *Journal of Institutional and Theoretical Economics*, **146**, 696–702.

Hill, C.W.L. (1990). Cooperation, opportunism and the invisible hand: implications for transaction cost theory, *Academy of Management Review*, **15**(3), 500–513.

Hirschman, A.O. (1970). *Exit, Voice and Loyalty: Responses to Decline in Firms, Organizations and States*, Cambridge, MA: Harvard University Press.

Hodgson, G.M. (2002). The legal nature of the firm and the myth of the firm–market hybrid, *International Journal of the Economics of Business*, **9**(1)(February), 37–60.

Johnson-Laird, P.N. (1983). *Mental Models*, Cambridge: Cambridge University Press.

Khalil, E.L. (2002). Is Adam Smith liberal?, *Journal of Institutional and Theoretical Economics*, **158**, 664–94.

Klein Woolthuis, R. (1999). Sleeping with the enemy: trust, dependence and contracts in interorganisational relationships, doctoral dissertation, Twente University, Enschede, the Netherlands.

——, B. Hillebrand and B. Nooteboom (2006). Trust, contract and relationship development, *Organization Studies*, **26**(6), 813–40.

Klos, T. and B. Nooteboom (2001). Agent-based computational transaction cost economics, *Journal of Economic Dynamics and Control*, **25**, 503–26.

Lane, C. and R. Bachmann (2000 paperback edn, 1st edn 1998). *Trust Within and Between Organizations*, Oxford: Oxford University Press.

Langlois, R.N. and P.L. Robertson (1995). *Firms, Markets Economic Change*, London: Routledge.

Lazaric, N. and E. Lorenz (1998). 'The learning dynamics of trust, reputation confidence', in N. Lazaric and E. Lorenz (eds), *Trust and Economic Learning*, Cheltenham, UK and Lyme, USA: Edward Elgar, pp. 1–22.

Lewicki, R.J. and B.B. Bunker (1996). 'Developing and maintaining trust in work relationships', in R.M. Kramer and T.R. Tyler (eds), *Trust in Organizations: Frontiers of Theory Research*, Thousand Oaks: Sage Publications, pp. 114–39.

Lippman, S. and R.P. Rumelt (1982). Uncertain imitability: an analysis of interfirm differences in efficiency under competition, *Bell Journal of Economics*, **13**, 418–38.

Maguire, S., N. Philips and C. Hardy (2001). When 'silence=death', keep talking: trust, control and the discursive construction of identity in the Canadian HIV/AIDS treatment domain', *Organization Studies*, **22**(2), 285–310.

McAllister, D.J. (1995). Affect- and cognition based trust as foundations for interpersonal cooperation in organizations, *Academy of Management Journal*, **38**(1), 24–59.

Mead, G.H. (1934). *Mind, Self and Society: From the Standpoint of a Social Behaviorist*, Chicago: University of Chicago Press.

Milgrom, P. and J. Roberts (1992). *Economics, Organization and Management*, Englewood Cliffs: Prentice-Hall.

Nelson, R.R. and S. Winter (1982). *An Evolutionary Theory of Economic Change*, Cambridge: Cambridge University Press.

Nooteboom, B. (1992). Towards a dynamic theory of transactions, *Journal of Evolutionary Economics*, **2**, 281–99.

—— (1993a). An analysis of specificity in transaction cost economics, *Organization Studies*, **14**(3), 443–51.

—— (1993b). Firm size effects on transaction costs, *Small Business Economics*, **5**, 283–95.

—— (1994). Innovation and diffusion in small business: theory and empirical evidence, *Small Business Economics*, **6**, 327–47.

—— (1996). Trust, opportunism and governance: a process and control model, *Organization Studies*, **17**(6), 985–1010.

—— (1999a). *Inter-firm Alliances: Analysis and Design*, London: Routledge.

—— (1999b). Exit and voiced based systems of corporate control, *Journal of Economic Issues*, **33**(4), 845–60.

—— (1999c). Innovation and inter-firm linkages: new implications for policy, *Research Policy*, **28**, 793–805.

—— (2000a). *Learning and Innovation in Organizations and Economies*, Oxford: Oxford University Press.

—— (2000b). Institutions and forms of coordination in innovation systems, *Organization Studies*, **21**(5), 915–39.

—— (2002). *Trust: Forms, Foundations, Functions, Failures and Figures*, Cheltenham, UK and Northampton, MA, USA: Edward Elgar.

—— (2004a). Governance and competence, how can they be combined? *Cambridge Journal of Economics*, **28**(4), 505–26.

—— (2004b). *Inter-firm Collaboration, Learning and Networks: an Integrated Approach*, London: Routledge.

—— and I. Bogenrieder (2002). Change of routines: a multi-level analysis, ERIM research report, Rotterdam School of Management, Erasmus University Rotterdam.

—— J. Berger and N.G. Noorderhaven (1997). Effects of trust and governance on relational risk, *Academy of Management Journal*, **40**(2), 308–38.

Penrose, E. (1959). *The Theory of the Growth of the Firm*, New York: Wiley.

Pettit, P. (1995). The virtual reality of homo economicus, *The Monist*, **78**(3), 308–29.

Polanyi, M. (1962). *Personal Knowledge*, London: Routledge.

Prahalad, C. and G. Hamel (1990). The core competences of the corporation, *Harvard Business Review*, May–June.

Schein, E.H. (1985). *Organizational Culture and Leadership*, San Francisco: Jossey-Bass.

Simon, H.A. (1983). *Reason in Human Affairs*, Oxford: Basil Blackwell.

Teece, D.J. (1986). Profiting from technological innovation: implications for integration, collaboration, licensing and public policy, *Research Policy*, **15**, 285–305.

Tversky, A. and D. Kahneman (1983). Probability, representativeness, and the conjunction fallacy, *Psychological Review*, **90**(4), 293–315.

Vermeulen, F. and H. Barkema (2001). Learning through acquisitions, *Academy of Management Journal*, **44**(3), 457–76.

Weick, K.F. (1979). *The Social Psychology of Organizing*, Reading, MA: Addison-Wesley.

—— (1995). *Sensemaking in Organizations*, Thousand Oaks, CA: Sage.

Williamson, O.E. (1975). *Markets and Hierarchies*, New York: Free Press.

—— (1985). *The Economic Institutions of Capitalism; Firms' Markets, Relational Contracting*, New York: Free Press.

—— (1991). Comparative economic organization: the analysis of discrete structural alternatives, *Administrative Science Quarterly*, **36**, 269–96.

Williamson, O.E. (1993). Calculativeness, trust, and economic organization, *Journal of Law and Economics*, **36**, 453–86.

—— (1999). Strategy research: governance and competence perspectives, *Strategic Management Journal*, **20**, 1087–1108.

Winter, S.G. (1964). Economic 'natural selection' and the theory of the firm, *Yale Economic Essays*, **4** (spring), 225–72.

Wuyts, S., M.G. Colombo, S. Dutta and B. Nooteboom (2005). Empirical tests of optimal cognitive distance, *Journal of Economic Behaviour and Organization*, **58**(2), 277–302.

64 Austrian economics and innovation
Jean-Luc Gaffard

1 Introduction

Technology, usually defined as a given combination of production factors involving a given economic performance, is not a precondition of an innovation process, but rather is the uncertain result of this process. Productivity gains or an increasing variety of goods, which motivate innovative investments, are not necessarily obtained once the innovative choice has been made. The capture of productivity gains depends on economic conditions in which the innovation process takes place step-by-step. This is the actual contribution of Austrian economics to the analysis of innovation both because it considers that production takes time and that competition is also a process in time dedicated to acquiring information and knowledge.

The Austrian school (Böhm-Bawerk and Menger, later on Hayek and Schumpeter) was concerned about the relations of capital and time. In its perspective, 'the characterization form of production is a sequence in which inputs are followed by outputs. Production has a time structure, so capital has a time structure' (Hicks, 1983, p. 100). This implicitly leads to a focus on the existence of disequilibrium phenomena that are derived from any innovative choice. The latter results in a breaking-up of the structure of the productive capacity (in its time structure), which is the dominant aspect of the gale of destructive creation evoked by Schumpeter (1943). This breaking-up itself results in the appearance of co-ordination problems both at the firm level and at the level of the economy as a whole: costs and proceeds are no longer synchronized, and supply and demand are no longer equal at each moment of time and over time (Amendola and Gaffard, 1988, 1998). Thus, competition as a process becomes essential. This is the way in which co-ordination problems are dealt with, which determines the performance of the firm and/or the economy. In order to illustrate this approach of economic change, two standard analytical problems will be addressed: the problem of productivity (or performance) slowdown and the problem of sustainability of competition in a context marked by frequent and strong innovations.

2 Innovation as a process in time

On the so-called 'neo-classical' side, we have what we might by now consider to be the 'traditional' or materialist approach, stemming from the theory of technical progress as it has been developed within the context of the dominant production theory. The focus, in this approach, is on the configuration of the productive capacity of the economy (of the firm or of the industry) that results from the adoption of a given technological advance and is uniquely determined by the characteristics of the latter. The analysis consists in deducing the effects of the change on the relevant magnitudes of the economy (productivity, employment etc.) from a comparison of the features of its productive structure before and after the change. The relevant aspect of the *productive* problem is regarded as (the utilization of) the given equipment, while the relevant aspect of the *technological* problem is regarded as the embodiment of the idea, or of the improvement, in the equipment itself. Different techniques can then be classified and compared on the basis of given criteria, and the problem of the choice of technique can be structured as a typical maximization problem in a context in which the choice set is given and the outcomes of the choices are known. The solution is obvious: once a technique has been defined as superior according to some criterion (e.g. a higher profit rate for a given wage rate) it should be selected from a welfare viewpoint, and the only problem for the economy is then to have good incentives (that is, the good structures) and to adjust its productive capacity to this technique. The process of innovation, in this context, is identified with the diffusion of innovation, that is, with the extent and the speed at which the economy proceeds to adopt a superior technique.

On the Austrian side, the process of change is at the same time one of development of the technology and of transformation of the productive structure (or the capital structure) of the economy (Menger, 1871; Hicks, 1973; Lachmannn, 1977; Amendola and Gaffard, 1988, 1998). An innovative choice implies the breaking-up of the existing industrial structure and a modification of market conditions, followed by a gradual reshaping which reflects the changes in cost conditions, in profitability and in relative prices, the modification of the consumers' preference system, and all the other events that represent the specific episodes that mark the actual profile of the process of innovation. The latter appears as a process of research and learning, which results in the appearance of new productive options which bring about a modification of the environment itself. Technology is the result of the process of innovation, and not a precondition of it. The process of innovation is a process of 'creation of technology' which, when successfully brought about, makes it possible to obtain increasing returns.

The problem of technological change thus consists not so much in the choice between given alternatives as in a search for co-ordinating as well as possible the innovation process. Accordingly, the economic aspect of this problem is no longer represented by the 'rationality' of the choice between known alternatives, but by the 'viability' of the process through which a different alternative is brought about: a viability that depends in turn on how co-ordination problems are dealt with step-by-step, that is, on how the process of competition takes place.

The change in productive capacity required by innovative choices cannot be reduced to the instantaneous substitution of more machines or equipment for less labor, or to the substitution of more knowledge for less physical equipment. Capital goods as well as capital and labor are complementary. New machines and new labor skills are used instead of the old ones. Substitution concerns processes and not factors of one particular process (Georgescu-Roegen, 1971). It takes time and requires co-ordination.

3   Co-ordination issues

All capital goods fit into a structure determined by production plans that are generally inconsistent with each other and have to be reconsidered systematically. The existing capital structure does not form the constant backbone of production plans. Uncertainty and inconsistency result in maladjustments of this structure that are a feature of industrial fluctuations (Lachmann, 1977). However, co-ordination among firms, when it is successfully brought about, allows the structure of capital to be more or less consistent with economic progress at the industry (and economy) level. In this analysis, investment is not an addition to a homogenous stock of capital and, hence, given the fact that the accumulation of capital implies a qualitative change, there are no diminishing returns to capital. But, on the other hand, economic progress cannot be assimilated with the accumulation of capital. Instead of assuming that acts of many people are consistent with one another, intertemporal inconsistency is taken for granted and the conditions for re-establishing it, which determine the actual return of capital, are to be considered.

As should be well known, the profitability of any investment project depends on the setting up of a satisfactory amount of both complementary and competitive investments along the way (Richardson, [1960] 1990). The volume of competitive investment must not exceed a critical limit set by the demand available, and the volume of complementary investment has to go beyond a minimal threshold for the investment project to be considered feasible. A specific co-ordination problem is then involved, which arises at the junction of two lags: the delay of construction of productive capacity – which entails sunk costs – and the delay of transmission of market information, which implies uncertainty. Both lags must be taken into account in the analysis, because cancelling one of them also cancels the co-ordination problem. Thus the absence of the latter lag guarantees the equilibrium between supply and demand in each period of the sequence through which a superior technique is adopted by the economy. The overlooking of the lag represented by the construction phase, even in the presence of incomplete information leading to mistakes in investment, allows not only for a revision of plans, but also has to be instantaneous, so as to cancel imbalances at the very moment of their appearance.

As a matter of fact, any technological change results in a change in the balance of production processes between construction and utilization, which, given the existence of both production and decision lags, induces discrepancies between costs and proceeds. Costs depend not only on the current output, but also on the total *volume* of output, the moment at which the first unit of output is to be completed, and the length of the interval over which the output is made available (Alchian, 1959, p. 24). Sunk costs are the expression not only of the existence of investment costs, but also of the divorce between costs and proceeds at each step of an evolutionary process triggered by the breaking of the intertemporal complementarity of the production process as the result of the attempt to carry out an innovation. The characteristic of sunk costs is that they will only be recovered when (and if) the process itself is actually established. This means we must not only take into account the whole period of construction of the new productive capacity, but go further until the stream of receipts from the new output has reached a certain size and the change has thus proved viable. In a context of gradual reshaping, costs depend not only on the current production but also on the length of construction of the new productive capacity, on the length of utilization of this capacity, and on the total volume of output produced over the successive periods. These are not data but results of the process itself.

Here, competition comes to the fore: 'Competitive market forces will cause dis-co-ordination as well as co-ordination of agents' plans. In fact, they cannot do the latter without doing the former' (Lachmann, 1985, p. 5). Moreover, firms do not know ex ante whether it pays to innovate. 'Indeed the answer to this question for any single firm depends on the choices made by other firms, and reality does not contain any provisions for firms to test their policies before adopting them. Thus there is little reason to expect equilibrium policy configurations to arise. Only the course of events over time will determine and reveal what strategies are the better ones' (Nelson and Winter, 1982, p. 286).

4 The productivity slowdown

The introduction of a new and superior technique does not necessarily result in better performance. Firms may be confronted with a maladapted productive capacity that prevents an instantaneous capture of the productivity gains (or the immediate production of the new variety of final goods).

A neo-Schumpeterian approach provides some theoretical benchmarks that serve the purpose of explaining in which way some properties of an innovation-driven growth process generate output and productivity fluctuations. Productivity slowdown would be a temporary phenomenon in an evolution driven by radical innovations. The need for learning, the building up of new intermediate goods and hence the existence of diffusion lags in the first phase of development of new 'general purpose technology', make the innovative activity costly and time-consuming (Helpman and Trajtenberg, 1998; Aghion and Howitt, 1998). Compatibility problems associated with the emergence of a new technology come to the fore and the starting value for experience declines, generating a fall in performances. Adoption and diffusion are delayed because firms may not be aware that a new technology exists, that it is suitable, and where to acquire the complementary assets, and hence have to bear search costs. Never is the existence of out-of-equilibrium co-ordination issues considered.

A neo-Austrian representation of the production process (Hicks, 1973) is suited to dealing with the out-of-equilibrium time articulation of events. It descended from the Austrian theory of capital, which introduced the distinction between goods of different orders and the concept of complementarity between these goods (Menger, 1871), and celebrated the technical structure of production (Böhm-Bawerk, 1889; Wieser, 1914) before being further elaborated by Wicksell (1901) and Hayek (1941). Production appears as a scheme for transforming in time a sequence of primary labor inputs into a sequence of final output. The production process is fully vertically integrated: this makes it possible both to exhibit explicitly the phase of construction of productive capacity by bringing it inside the production process and to stress that it must necessarily come before the phase of utilization of the same capacity. This representation of the production process must be coupled with a representation of the competition process that focuses on its sequential character, that is, on the fact that it is essentially based on trial and error algorithms, where prices and quantities partially reflect reaction to market disequilibria (Amendola and Gaffard, 1988, 1998). Within this framework, the productivity slowdown is no longer the result of the specificity of the learning process which would reveal the properties of new technologies. It will be presented as the result of the economic conditions in which the out-of-equilibrium process stirred by technological shocks takes place. Thus, a productivity slowdown, when occurring, reveals co-ordination failures that result in an unsustainable growth process.

Technological shocks imply, for example, a modification of the structure of the demand for labor so as to make it no longer consistent with the existing structure of supply, and hence the appearance of a human resource constraint. Furthermore, the adoption of a new technique is associated with a learning process resulting in a more or less complete adaptation of the structure of labor supply to the prevailing structure of labor demand. This process is not only the source of a greater productivity but also the means to re-absorb the disequilibrium on the labor market, and that on the market for final output associated with it, resulting from the original technological shock. However, the unemployment and productivity gradually taken care of by the learning process originally arises from the mismatch between the demand and supply of skills resulting from the technological shock. This determines, in turn, a reduction of the demand for final output and unemployment of a Keynesian type. Furthermore, a shortage of capital (the supply of money acts here as a brake to investment in productive capacity) determines an unemployment of a Ricardian type. Without any additional finance, labor productivity falls dramatically. A scrapping of production processes in the phase of utilization and a bias towards construction processes characterizes the distortion of productive capacity. Despite the existence of a technical matching process between supply of and demand for labor, benefits of the new technology will not be captured. With additional finance, firms converge to a new quasi-dynamic equilibrium characterized by a higher level of productivity, and also by higher real wages. Appropriate finance constraints help to capture the gains associated with the new technology by making the learning effective.

5   The sustainability of competition

From the Austrian perspective, the process of competition appears as a complex process which is a blend of market and organizational forces. Market forces (price mechanisms) have an impact on technical and organizational changes within firms. Organizational and technical choices influence in turn market conditions.

On the neo-classical side, competition is the force that equates supplies and demands within a given industrial structure and a given technology. It is a descriptive term that defines a given state of affairs corresponding to given costs conditions and given perfect or imperfect information structures. In particular, models of oligopoly competition deal with the intensity of competition and the characteristics of industrial structures as determined by given information and cost conditions, i.e., with given states of affairs as expressed by given market structures. On the Austrian side, oligopoly competition is concerned with a dynamic process of rivalry that may be destructive or creative. It can result in a waste of productive resources and no real advantage for the customers or, alternatively, may allow firms (and customers) to benefit from increasing returns.

The idea of competition as an ordering force, which dominates both classical and Austrian economics, is a disequilibrium concept of market activity. Hayek (1937, 1948) pointed out that the superiority of the 'competitive market mechanism' over 'socialist planning' depends, not on the properties of an equilibrium position, which could never be reached, but rather on the working of the market economy out of equilibrium. Competition is a process of discovery of the relevant market information, that is, the information that comes from the interaction in time between economic agents and makes co-ordination possible. It is the concept of competition best suited to an innovation process portrayed as a qualitative change, that is, with a change which takes place through distortions of productive capacity, and implies the appearance of problems of co-ordination between supply and demand. On the other hand, an orderly competition should be an equilibrating process in the sense that it makes innovative choices viable. Competition is really successful when price and quantity adjustments are carried out which make it possible to obtain normal profits; that is, when these adjustments do not result in a waste of productive resources. Thus viewed, competition not only co-exists with increasing returns, but helps firms to capture them (Richardson, [1975] 1998).

When competition operates as an ordering force, competing firms are not making similar products in given and unchanged cost conditions. They undertake innovative activities. But, at any given moment, the productive capacity of a firm cannot be chosen. It is inherited from past decisions, so that the problem which it actually faces is how to make the best use of this capacity and not 'what it should do if it were given unlimited time to adjust itself to constant conditions' (Hayek, 1948, p. 102). Out-of-equilibrium, in a context without complete information where bounded behaviors are relevant, constraints emerge at each successive step. A sequential strategy, by establishing new and changing relations with other subjects in order to deal with these constraints, appears as a tool for acquiring information and knowledge on the way. The relevant constraints, not only financial and human constraints, but also established relations (such as, for example, collusive behaviors) are inherited from the past, as brought about by the evolution of the economy shaped by technology and the prevailing forms of organization. Thus, the time dimension of production, together with the time dimension of decision processes, is the main problem concerning a firm which decides to set up a new productive capacity. During the period of construction of an entirely new productive capacity, the innovative firm has to bear sunk costs that result in a temporary competitive disadvantage, because the price charged does not cover the current cost or, on the contrary, because the price is temporarily higher so as to cover this cost. At the end of the phase of construction, there will be a period during which the first mover will take advantage of its innovative choice, as he will be alone in possession of the new superior productive capacity. This will last until a competitor will have had time to get the superior capacity operative. The existence and the interaction of these different periods and of the lags associated with them, which are the expression of the time dimension of the production process and of the decision process, are the main aspect of the process of change. In this process the end of the road is never reached, the market is never in 'perfect competition', but strong competition may obtain that results in increasing returns and welfare gains.

Within a neo-Austrian framework, two or more firms compete with one another by innovating (Amendola, Gaffard and Musso, 2000, 2003, 2004). Each successive innovation consists in introducing a new and superior technology characterized by increased construction costs more than compensated by lower utilization costs. What happens to the firms involved in an innovation process – what happens to their cost performances and market shares, and hence what happens to the market structure – then results from the deformation of the structure of productive capacity of the different firms involved, which will be amplified or dampened according to the nature of the co-ordination mechanisms that prevail along the way. The possibility of taking advantage of innovations essentially depends on the ability of each firm to maintain a structure of the productive capacity that sustains a quasi-steady state. This depends, in turn, on the working of the market co-ordination mechanism. The availability of productive resources, the constraints that these may impose on production processes, and the equilibrating (or disequilibrating) role performed by price and wage regimes, are the essential elements of the co-ordination mechanism at work. It follows that the success (or failure) of the introduction of new technologies and the emergence and evolution of given market structures does not depend on the properties of technology, but on the capacity to co-ordinate the activity of the different firms participating in the restructuring process involved, which results in a certain degree of stability of the market structures. Thus, technological advances do not determine the dynamics of the number of firms. On the contrary, this is actually identified only once a stabilization of the market structure signals that viability conditions have been fulfilled.

As a matter of fact, industry may converge to a dynamic equilibrium state characterized by a stable and balanced distribution of market shares. Technical increasing returns may be fully exploited by all existing firms, benefiting not only the firms themselves through increasing profits, but also the consumers through falling prices and the workers through rising wages. On the one hand, a strong enough external financial constraint helps the firms to be better co-ordinated with one another, by not allowing over-investment at the level of the industry (an excessive 'capacity competition'). On the other hand, price (and wage) rigidity avoids the problem of too-strong variations in reaction to market disequilibria not transmitting the appropriate signals, which may result in inconsistent changes in the production structure. These constraints, in a sequential process of change, are not only limits on the activity carried out but can also help in keeping the economy within the boundaries of a stability corridor. Indeed, imperfect competition appears as a means for firms and industry to be viable and really exploit the returns of technology.

Finally, understanding the competitive process consists in giving more consistency to the notion of price competition in relation to the other means of competition. Prices are regulated by production costs and competition must be related to a search for cost reductions. So, the question relates to a knowledge of the regulator of costs, and the answer is not provided in the standard economic theory which merely assumes the minimization of costs (that corresponds to the efficiency axiom of standard production theory). The role of prices is not to send instantaneous signals, but to contribute to creating the conditions that prevent cumulative processes from leading to excessive market imbalances and hence resulting in a threat to the viability of the economy. In this sense of not reacting immediately to instantaneous cost changes or market imbalances, a price viscosity is required. Full and instantaneous adjustments, taking into account that price changes react on costs, would in fact exacerbate rather than smooth distortions of productive capacity and market imbalances.

References

Aghion, P. and P. Howitt (1998): *Endogenous Growth Theory*, Cambridge, MA: MIT Press.

Alchian, A. (1959): 'Costs and outputs', in M. Abramovitz et al. (eds), *The Allocation of Economic Resources*, Stanford: Stanford University Press.

Amendola, M. and J-L. Gaffard (1988): *The Innovative Choice: an Economic Analysis of the Dynamics of Technology*, Oxford: Basil Blackwell.

Amendola, M. and Gaffard, J-L. (1998): *Out of Equilibrium*, Oxford: Clarendon Press.

Amendola, M., J-L. Gaffard and P. Musso (2000): Competition, innovation and increasing returns, *Economics of Innovation and New Technology*, **9**, 149–81.

Amendola, M., J-L. Gaffard and P. Musso (2003): Co-ordinating the process of competition: the role of finance constraints, *Review of Austrian Economics*, **16**(2–3), 183–204.

Amendola, M., J-L. Gaffard and P. Musso (2004): 'Viability of innovation processes, emergence and stability of market structures', in M. Gallegati, A. Kirman and M. Marsili (eds), *Complex Dynamics of Economic Interaction*, Berlin: Springer Verlag, pp. 49–78.

Böhm-Bawerk, E. (1889): *Positive Theorie des Kapitales*, English translation, 1891, *The Positive Theory of Capital*, reprinted 1923, New York.

Georgescu-Roegen, N. (1971): *The Entropy Law and the Economic Process*, Cambridge, MA: Harvard University Press.

Hayek, F.A. (1937): Economics and knowledge, *Economica*, N.S, **4**, reprinted in F.A. Hayek (1948).

Hayek, F.A. (1941): *The Pure Theory of Capital*, London: Routledge and Kegan Paul.

Hayek, F.A. (1948), *Individualism and Economic Order*, Chicago: University of Chicago Press.

Helpman, E. and M. Trajtenberg (1998): 'A time to sow and a time to reap', in E. Helpman (ed.), *General Purpose Technologies and Economic Growth*, Cambridge, MA: MIT Press.

Hicks, J.R. (1973): *Capital and Time*, Oxford: Clarendon Press.

Hicks, J.R. (1983): 'The Austrian theory of capital and its rebirth in modern economics', in *Classics and Moderns*, collected essays on economic theory III, Oxford: Blackwell.

Lachmann, L. (1977): *Capital and its Structure*, Kansas City: Sheed Andrews and McMeel.

Lachmann, L. (1985): *The Market as an Economic Process*, Oxford: Blackwell.

Menger, C. (1871): *Grundsätze der Volkswirtschaftslehre*, English translation, *Principles of Economics*, reprinted New York: New York University Press.

Nelson, R. and S. Winter (1982): *An Evolutionary Theory of Economic Change*, Cambridge, MA: The Belknap Press of Harvard University Press.

Richardson, G.B. (1960): *Information and Investment: A Study in the Working of the Competitive Economy*, Oxford: Clarendon Press (second edition, 1990).

Richardson, G.B. (1975): 'Adam Smith on competition and increasing returns', in A. Skinner and T. Wilson (eds), *Essays on Adam Smith*, Oxford: Oxford University Press, reprinted in G.B. Richardson (1998): *The Economics of Imperfect Knowledge*, Cheltenham, UK and Lyme, USA: Edward Elgar.

Schumpeter, J.A. (1943): *Capitalism, Socialism and Democracy*, London: Allen and Unwin.

von Wieser, F. (1914): *Social Economics*, New York: Adelphi Co., 1927, English translation, *Theorie der gesellschaftlichen Wirtschaft, Grundriß der Sozialökonomik I. Abteilung Wirtschaft und Wirtschaftswissenschaft*, Tübingen: J.C.B. Mohr.

Wicksell, K. (1901): *Lectures on Political Economy*, vol. I, English translation (1934), London: George Routledge and Sons; reprinted 1977, Augustus M. Kelley.

65 On Austrian-Schumpeterian economics and the Swedish growth school

Gunnar Eliasson

The four fundamentals of economics are interdependency, welfare, process and institutions. (Johan Åkerman, 1950)

Introduction

Austrian-Schumpeterian and Swedish economics share a more than century-long history of mutual intellectual development of a theoretical platform for understanding the dynamics of market economies.[1] Austrian-Schumpeterian economics took root both in Lund and in Stockholm, an intermediary in both places being Knut Wicksell. In Lund, Johan Åkerman took up the Schumpeterian challenge to the Walrasian static equilibrium model, as did his student there, Erik Dahmén. In doing so they departed from some of Schumpeter's own doctrine. Schumpeter (being a great admirer of Walras) often referred to Walrasian equilibrium as a benchmark for his analysis. In Stockholm the Austrian-Wicksellian influence mixed with the early Keynesian macro economics. The most outstanding result was the Stockholm school of economics,[2] whose best known representatives were Dag Hammarskjöld, Erik Lundberg, Gunnar Myrdal, Bertil Ohlin and Ingvar Svennilson.

Both Erik Dahmén and Ingvar Svennilson held influential positions at the *Industriens Utredningsinstitut* (IUI), where Austrian-Schumpeterian theory flourished early. In the close-to-industrial reality research environment of the IUI, innovative theorizing was encouraged by a board of directors composed solely of people from industry. The realistic assumptions of Schumpeterian theory also appealed to the IUI researchers. IUI research eventually developed into what has recently been termed 'the Swedish growth school (Johansson and Karlson, 2002). While the IUI unfortunately has turned conventional since the mid-1990s, the Schumpeterian theme has been taken over by the new Ratio institute.[3]

The path towards the Swedish growth school, however, was both long, winding and, not least, paradoxical. Even though the political centralist message built into Keynesian macro economics has more or less disappeared from the Swedish economic policy debate, the Austrian-Schumpeterian creative destruction paradigm is struggling to hold out against the even more centralist textbook message of the mathematically faultless, perfect competition Walras–Arrow–Debreu (WAD) model that currently dominates the US graduate teaching agenda in economics. It is symptomatic that the entrepreneur and the concept of tacit knowledge – both central concepts in this presentation – are conspicuously absent from the standard economics textbooks (Johansson, 2004). The story of Austrian-Schumpeterian economics in Sweden also illustrates how the economic policy agenda of the time influences the research agenda of economists and diverts attention away from understanding (the dynamics of an economy) toward theory structured for uncomplicated policy advice. The outstanding exception is Knut Wicksell, the premier Swedish economist of all times, who took on Austrian theory, and influenced the second-generation Austrian economists as well as the anglo-saxon economists, but unfortunately was not really understood until after his death.

The paradoxes
As it happened, the real father of Austrian and 'early Schumpeterian' economics, Carl Menger, was also one of the three fathers of marginalism, who, together with William Stanley Jevons and Leon Walras, over time tilted economics into the Walras–Arrow–Debreu (WAD) static equilibrium camp. WAD economics features 'frictionless' economic transactions that at no cost eliminate all economic mistakes by assumption. This is deeply paradoxical, since a key message of Carl Menger was that uncertainty is typical of the economic environment and that economic mistakes play a key role in economic development. As Wicksell (1924) points out in his review of the posthumously published revised version of Menger's *Grundsätze* (edited by his son, Karl Menger), Carl Menger managed to establish a school around his ideas, the Austrian school. The two best known disciples of that school, Friedrich von Wieser and Eugene von Böhm-Bawerk, however, very soon, and to the great disappointment of Menger (Alter, 1990, pp. 8, 14), began to modify Menger's original theory of value, making the concept of capital technical rather than economic, in what would now be called a neoclassical direction, 'the greatest error ever committed', to use Menger's own words.

Schumpeter's original notion of the innovator/entrepreneur and his forceful metaphor of *creative destruction* undoubtedly originate in Mengerian thinking about uncertainty, ignorance and error, even though Kirzner (1978), Knight (1921) and Streissler (1969) do not agree about the existence of a pivotal role for the entrepreneur in Menger's *Grundsätze*. Kirzner (1978) here argues that Menger's system with its focus on subjectivity, the critical role of knowledge and the prevalence of ignorance and error was a natural economic habitat for the entrepreneur, but that Menger missed the opportunity to define the role of an entrepreneur in his system.

To my mind entrepreneurship in the sense of unpredictable innovative change moved by much less than fully informed (read 'ignorant') actors, and business mistakes[4] figure both in Menger's and in Schumpeter's early writing, even though Joseph Schumpeter may not have been entirely consistent all the time.[5]

The second paradox is the intermediary role of Knut Wicksell, who introduced Austrian economics to Swedish economists. He also created an entirely new school of his own making (see *the cumulative process* and *the natural interest rate*, Eliasson, 1992), introduced a new type of invisible hand to organize dynamic market traffic, and in turn influenced the second-generation Austrian economists von Mises (1912, 1936) and von Hayek (1940) and, indirectly Kirzner, (1973 (see also Karlson, 2002)). Wicksell is labelled 'Austrian' in the old economics texts, not because he introduced disequilibrium economics into Sweden, but because he was the great interpreter of Austrian capital theory, i. e. of Böhm-Bawerk. In more recent economics texts, Knut Wicksell is rather reclassified as neoclassical, but then the unique disequilibrium features of his great theoretical contribution, the cumulative process, have been forgotten.

The two paradoxes probably depend on the verbal presentation of the different theoretical approaches, making it impossible to keep them distinctly apart. Menger disliked using mathematics. His position was that mathematics is a deductive science that cannot contribute much to *understanding* economic phenomena, understanding or *Verstehen* being more important than the analysis. He was strongly critical of the scientism of the anglo-saxon economists and their use of aggregates that had no causal relationship, an attitude that shows up as well in Schumpeter and even more strongly in the Swedish Schumpeterians Johan Åkerman and Erik Dahmén. The argument for Verstehen can be interpreted to mean that the clean deductive models of the marginalists have to be related to the real world. This is where the much more difficult art of understanding economics enters, namely when the symbolic language has to be related to observation. If you understand the restrictive assumptions of the analytical model, you can overcome that limitation and transfer the deductive analysis into empirical economic interpretation (Eliasson, 2002). Even though this is a reasonable position, since analysis will always have to be much more narrow-minded than broad-based reasoning (Eliasson, 1996), it is easy to see misunderstanding, confusion and academic antagonism develop when such reasoning is confronted with the clean models of mathematical economics. Wieser and Böhm-Bawerk cut out Menger's Aristotelian Essentialism and the Verstehen to make their notion of capital more objective (read 'technical') and compatible with the Walrasian model. This cleaned version is often called the Austrian school of economics, and this may be what Wicksell (1924) means. For Böhm-Bawerk, but not for Menger, value could now exist independently of the valuer.[6] Still, however, value according to the Austrian school was determined by (marginal) utility or demand and the Austrians never accepted the Marshallian idea of marginal costs being the determinant of prices (Böhm-Bawerk, 1894).[7]

There is also a third paradox involving Schumpeter himself and the different schools built around his 1911 *Theorie der Wirtschaftliche Entwicklung* and his 1942 *Capitalism, Socialism and Democracy.* The first and truly distinctive Austrian/Schumpeterian school formation in Sweden involved Knut Wicksell, Johan Åkerman and Erik Dahmén and eventually resulted in the Swedish growth school tradition. This tradition was clearly based on the early version of Schumpeter (1911) and implicitly rejected the notion of the exogenous static equilibrium of WAD theory by not being interested in the existence of such an equilibrium.[8] The later Schumpeter II school is centralist and built on the 1942 book and has reached Swedish technical universities by way of Chris Freeman (1974) and his Sussex group and the Nelson and Winter (1982) evolutionary modeling approach. In 1942, to quote Henriksson (2002), Schumpeter almost stumbled into Marxist thinking. Economic growth was now reduced to a linear consequence of technology and (by prior assumption) the state could play the role of the entrepreneur by subsidizing investments in R&D. The Schumpeter II approach with a direct linear technology-growth drive and a minimum of economics appealed to engineering school economists and appears in such concepts as the *national systems of innovation* of Lundvall (1992) in Aalborg, Denmark and Nelson (1993) and also, but in a less direct fashion, in Bo Carlsson's (1995) *technological systems.* Carlsson's analysis, however, was primarily focused on understanding and explaining the supply of innovations. The modern neoclassical R&D production functions of the so-called new growth theory come very close. Here innovative output is explained by knowledge production functions fed with R&D. As pointed out by Swedberg (1997), however, Schumpeter's theoretical structure seems to have appealed mostly to economic historians in Sweden, or economists taking a very long-term view of matters economic.

Knut Wicksell and the Austrian-Schumpeterian heritage
Knut Wicksell left deep Austrian impressions in the minds of economists both in Lund and in Stockholm. The impressions were, however, very different. Wicksell (1851–1926) began academic studies in mathematics at Uppsala University but changed (after a licentiate degree) to economics which was more in line with his interests in the acute problems of society. His radical public conduct, however, made him many enemies. He was no socialist and considered the labor theory of value of Marx all wrong. Nor

did Wicksell see the concentration of production to increasingly larger firms argued by Marx as a realistic prediction.[9] Even though Wicksell realized the enormous wealth-creating capacity of the capitalist organization of production, he was concerned with the negative sides of capitalism and advocated a third ideal way. Rather than being a dependent client of socialist governance he preferred seeing everybody as a small capitalist and possessing the means to be an independent individual (Wicksell, 1892). To express the same thing in modern terminology: only the capitalist organization of production is capable of producing sustainable growth in wealth on the order of magnitude witnessed in modern industrial economies. A welfare system (but not socialism) might, however, be needed to make the capitalist growth engine fair and politically acceptable.

Much of Wicksell's work in economics was focused on Austrian capital theory and Böhm-Bawerk and his attempts to introduce technology into the theory of production and the determination of value. Wicksell's most ingenious works were, however, *Geldzins and Guterpreise* (1898) and his *Lectures* (1901, 1906). *Geldzins und Guterpreise* was an early rendering of dynamic economic thinking with expectations and economic mistakes figuring importantly in the economic process. There, he formulated his famous *cumulative economic process*, generated by a capital market disequilibrium that was in turn moved by a real return to capital (read 'innovations') that was higher than the money market interest. Wicksell's important contribution was a total dynamical systems approach in which a monetary disequilibrium system was superimposed on the real economy. Wicksell's focus was on inflation, and he carried on his discussion on the basis of a fixed (given) production structure. He was nevertheless fast to grasp the significance of Böhm-Bawerk's analysis of the role of technology and production capital. Erik Dahmén (1980) in fact suggests that Wicksell's analysis of inflation could also be seen as a model of economic growth, driven (in Dahmén's interpretation) by Schumpeterian innovators who achieve a rate of return above the market rate of interest that makes them invest in new technology. Wicksell's disequilibrium idea was, however, too new and not understood by Böhm-Bawerk (see Schumpeter, 1954, p. 1118, footnote) who by then had lost track of the early Austrian economics.[10]

The distinction between Austrian-neoclassical and Austrian-disequilibrium economics comes out nicely in the intellectual dispute between Wicksell (1922, 1923) and Gustaf Åkerman (1921, 1922, 1923). The latter attempted to merge the two and to study how a changing, depreciable physical capital interacts in production with labor. This was a problem economists had stayed away from. Wicksell (1923, footnote, page 146) observed that production structures were normally assumed to be constant in price theory and vice versa; i.e. prices are assumed to be constant in production analysis. To allow both to change simultaneously is more difficult and should wait until both partial analyses had been carried out. Here Åkerman, therefore, stood alone to find his own ways. Apparently Wicksell thought that it could be done and that the mathematics needed to do it was available, but that the 'gymnasium mathematics' of Åkerman was not sufficient (Wicksell, 1923). The verbal arguments that followed were also parallel rather than converging, and one might say that this now classical problem has not yet been solved, despite efforts by neo-Keynesian theorists such as Robert Clower and others to introduce stocks into the flow model of Walras to free it from the restrictions of Say's law. In an Austrian-Schumpeterian-type model of general monopolistic competition with entry and exit and strategic behavior of firms, the model probably cannot be solved for an exogenous equilibrium (Eliasson, 1984, 1991a, 1996). Without this simultaneity there really is no theoretical foundation of macro analysis. Since endogenous growth is pushed by the constant existence of a pervasive disequilibrium and since the economy cannot operate in the neighborhood of that equilibrium, exogeneous equilibrium and the cumulative process are incompatible. Thus, even though Wicksell, technically speaking, also became a neoclassical capital theorist, with his cumulative disequilibrium process he retained more of the early Austrian thinking than did Böhm-Bawerk.

However, not until his Lectures (1901, 1906) did Wicksell go beyond Böhm-Bawerk and make the distinction between real, depreciable capital and monetary capital that allowed him to introduce the notion of investment mistakes, a theme later elaborated by both von Hayek (1935) and Erik Dahmén (1941) in his licentiate thesis. Wicksell's ideas were later picked up both by the Lund economist Johan Åkerman (a brother to Gustaf, see above) and by the economists of the Stockholm school, notably Gunnar Myrdal (1927, 1939) and Erik Lundberg (1937). At that time the ongoing depression weighed heavily on the economists' minds and Schumpeter (1928) had been studying the instability of the capitalist process that was later reformulated in his 1939 critical reaction to Keynes (1936). Wicksell's colleagues in Uppsala and in Stockholm were, however, cool to Wicksell's ideas. He was unable to get a chair in Uppsala and Stockholm and finally became professor in law and economics in Lund in 1901 and stayed there until his retirement in 1916, when he moved back to Stockholm. But his students in Lund were law students with a limited interest in economics. Wicksell was disappointed at not being able to find followers in Lund who were up to his wit. Back in Stockholm, however, he became the informal thesis advisor of Johan Åkerman. With Johan Åkerman and with the Stockholm school economists, Wicksell finally had serious followers, and since his work has been translated into English his reputation as one of the world's greatest economists has been steadily growing.

Carl Menger and Joseph Schumpeter were pivotal figures in Austrian Economics. Knut Wicksell was the pivotal figure in Swedish economics, and Wicksell's major contributions, that postdated Menger and predated Schumpeter, and influenced von Mises and von Hayek, very much reflected early Austrian thinking. Wicksell studied in Vienna in 1873 and sat in on Menger's lectures, that he, however, found both elementary and boring (Gårdlund, 1956). Over the years contacts between Wicksell and Menger appear to have been rare.[11] One would expect, nevertheless, that the subjective elements of Menger's value theory that his disciples had removed, and his emphasis on uncertainty, expectations and the absence of a determinable exogenous static equilibrium would somehow have carried over to Wicksell's cumulative process.[12] In his obituary of Menger (Wicksell, 1921) Wicksell, however, mentioned only Menger's contribution as probably the first father of marginal economic analysis and as a pioneer in capital theory.

Wicksell (1921) also observed that this time, and contrary to what is commonly the case, the idea of marginalism had not been in the air. Economists had been frustrated by the state of economic science, and 'turned to historical investigations' based on no theory. Marginalism came down suddenly on them as an enlightening experience which allowed new mathematical tools to be used, and, adds Wicksell (apparently referring to Menger's brief early practical experience as a civil servant), Menger is evidence of the old thesis that 'practitioners, when they correctly approach [a problem], if they are sufficiently talented often become the boldest and most abstract theoreticians'. However, Wicksell's (1924) review of the posthumously published Grundsätze (edited by Karl Menger) was not overenthusiastic. Wicksell argued that, for some incomprehensible reasons, earlier insights and important contributions from the 1871 edition had been removed, for instance concerning the origin of the interest (as compensation for waiting) that was one of the pillars of Austrian and Wicksellian economics.

Wicksell and Schumpeter probably never met. Schumpeter learned late about Wicksell and did not refer to him in his early works (1911, 1939). The reason may be (Henriksson, 2002) that Schumpeter at the time had worked out a complete intellectual structure. To work Wicksell's cumulative process into his growth cycle analysis would have required major rewriting, even though not necessarily major revision of his theory. When invited to participate in a Festschrift to Wicksell for his 70th birthday in 1921, Schumpeter declined, citing illness (Swedberg, 1997). Carl Menger, however, contributed a note in the form of a letter on the return to capital (Menger, 1921). On the other hand, Schumpeter's (1954) *History of Economic Analysis* labels Wicksell as the greatest of Swedish economists who was one of the four chief analytical performers of the period, after Walras and Marshall, but before the Austrians (1954, pp. 1082ff). Wicksell was in fact labeled the best formulator of the Austrian doctrine (ibid., p. 913) and was among the few who generously acknowledged professional predecessors (ibid., p. 872, footnote).

Structural analysis and the growth cycle

Johan Åkerman (1896–1982) was an early Schumpeterian economist in Lund. He took his degree at the Stockholm School of Economics. He then worked for several years for a company (ASEA) and spent several years at Harvard where he was influenced by Veblen and Mitchell. Back in Stockholm, Knut Wicksell (now retired) became his informal thesis adviser.

Åkerman defended his doctorate thesis in 1928 – two years after the death of Knut Wicksell – and became a professor in Lund. There he gave reading assignments of Schumpeter to those of his students, among them Erik Dahmén, who he thought were interested. At that time the Depression was the focus of economic analysis and the growth cycle a common theme among the economists. Knut Wicksell's early Austrian analysis was integrated into Johan Åkerman's writing, notably his analysis of cumulative economic developments, or let us call it 'evolutionary economic analysis'. Åkerman's first interest, however, was the dynamics of the business cycle, or rather the growth cycle in which business mistakes figured importantly as a natural element in long-run cyclical change (Åkerman, 1934). Here Åkerman became tied in with the great interest of the time of both Ragnar Frisch (1931, 1933) from Oslo, Knut Wicksell (1898) and Joseph Schumpeter (1928, 1939): the *growth cycle* and the flows of innovations that moved the long waves of business activity. While Schumpeter (1911) never seems to have been reviewed in Sweden, Schumpeter (1939) was by Erik Dahmén (1941). There, Dahmén emphasized that Schumpeter was wrong in believing that the equilibrium model is compatible with the existence of an entrepreneur, but expressed admiration for Schumpter's view that the business cycle is part and parcel of structural change or 'economic transformation'. Åkerman's causality concept, it should be noted, had already turned his economics into a process accompanied by constant structural change, and taken his analysis out of the intellectual confines of the static equilibrium model, so the Lund economists were intellectually well prepared to receive the Schumpeterian message, a positive attitude that Schumpeter himself did not reciprocate (see below). Johan Åkerman is consequently quoted as the father of the (Swedish) *structuralist school* (Pålsson Syll, 1995; Schön, 2000) and he was arguing the need to make institutions and culture an integral part of economics. Such broad approaches were not only incompatible with the nice pedagogics of static equilibrium, they also made for difficult reading. So Åkerman's writing, however relevant, has had difficulties getting a foothold in economic literature. Schumpeter met Åkerman in Stockholm but did not seem to have taken much notice. Åkerman regularly sent him his writings and, when asked to referee one of Åkerman's papers, Schumpeter did not do it favorably (Swedberg, 1997). This might explain why Åkerman does not quote Schumpeter very much in his later writings. Åkerman (1950) was, however, distinctly clear when he stated that the four fundamentals of economics had to be interdependence, welfare (value), process and institutions, thereby implying that modern conventional economics had lost sight of the last two and most difficult and important phenomena.

Development blocks and industrial transformation

Erik Dahmén (1916–2005) was Johan Åkerman's best known student. Dahmén began his studies in Lund in the 1930s and was stimulated by Åkerman both to read Schumpeter and to consider the early Austrian focus on ignorance and economic mistakes. Åkerman was also concerned about the negative influence of Keynesian macro analysis on economics in general and wanted (as well) to formulate a micro-based alternative to the Stockholm school model (Carlsson and Henriksson, 1991). Erik Dahmén's licentiate thesis (1942a) was an exercise in economic–structural analysis in the vein of Schumpeter (1939) with investment mistakes emerging explicitly because of the structural approach and, therefore, figuring importantly together with innovations behind the dynamics of the growth cycle. In the revised and much shortened version that appeared in *Ekonomisk Tidskrift* (Dahmén, 1942b), the transformation analysis of Dahmén's licentiate thesis was further refined into the notion of *development blocks*. Erik Dahmén here built a theoretical platform for industrial economics or industrial dynamics (Carlsson, 1987) research. Ingvar Svennilson, then the president of the recently (1939) founded IUI, asked Dahmén to come to Stockholm and continue his research and to look at the entry and exit of firms in particular. In his thesis, *Svenskt Industriellt Företagande* of 1950 (published in English in 1970 as *Entrepreneurial Activity and the Development of Swedish Industry, 1919–39*), structural tension in development blocs became part of this early industrial dynamic analysis of endogenous growth with a distinctly Schumpeterian resonance.

Dahmén's thesis was a massive empirical inquiry into the dynamics of technology supply as the mover of new industry formation that linked various industrial phenomena together into the architecture of the development bloc. His development bloc was physically defined and was designed to capture the cumulative industrial development around a 'generic' innovation such as the automobile engine (the Otto engine) and the automobile that created systemic scale economies. To become a useful transport vehicle you needed better roads and along the roads you needed gas stations. When this new transport innovation had been established, new configurations of urban organization were possible, and so on. Many path-breaking innovations require similar infrastructures of supporting services that take decades to develop, require large investments and eventually change our ways of producing and living. The exogenous technology supply drive was typical of Dahmén's early (1950) growth analysis where growth could be stimulated by demand.[13] The thesis also included the notion of transformation pressure ('*omvandlingstryck*') in the sense of Schumpeter's creative destruction. Much later Dahmén broadened this concept to include also the possibility that exogenous competition forces firms to innovate (endogenously) and raise productivity (see, for instance, Dahmén, 1980).

Dahmén's development bloc analysis set the stage for the IUI tradition of first defining an important and interesting empirical problem and then looking for and, whenever needed, developing the appropriate theoretical tools, and never refraining from large empirical efforts. Erik Dahmén was a promoter of one of the earliest and largest research efforts ever to collect data on new firm establishement (du Rietz, 1975, 1980). He has become known for criticizing the economists' narrow preoccupation with their tools and for restricting their attention, not to interesting economic problems but to problems where they can use the tools they happen to know. He has called the WAD economists of Sweden the 'intellectual prisoners of their tool shed'.

The IUI, being for a long time the only private research institute in social sciences in Sweden, with generous financial resources and a board staffed by high-level, active industrial people with an intellectual interest, was instrumental when it came to establishing a tradition of problem-oriented empirical research in economics in general, and in industrial economics in particular.

Erik Dahmén later became professor of economics at the Stockholm School of Economics and served for many years as an economic advisor to Marcus Wallenberg, the great entrepreneur, banker and industrialist of Sweden and for 25 years the chairman of the board of IUI.

The Stockholm school economic model

The Stockholm school model defines a second link to Knut Wicksell. Can history, say the business cycle, be looked at as drawings from a stationary process? You may then be falsely convinced that you understand the mechanisms that determine your economic environment, barring a random disturbance (Eliasson, 1992). You then face a lottery, the expected value of which you can learn by playing repeated games. Computable risk taking is your business. Posit, however, that this assumption is wrong and that you cannot look at entrepreneurship as the outcome of a lottery or a stationary process that remains stable over time. Suppose the parameters of the casino change every now and then because of factors outside your model and prevent you from learning. The Mengerian or early Schumpeterian entrepreneur is now exogenous to your model. In order to understand what is going on you have to endogenize the entrepreneur. The nature of your business risks should now be looked for in the transition from ex ante plans to ex post realizations. The *realization function* is a notion that originated in the thinking of the Stockholm school economists,[14] Wicksell being the creator, Myrdal, Lindahl, Svennilson, Lundberg in Stockholm and Lindahl in Lund and Uppsala representing the first generation, and Faxén in Stockholm the second generation (Eliasson, 1969; Palander, 1941; Petersson, 1987). In this context Gunnar Myrdal's (1927) thesis on the role of expectations in economics is particularly important, as well as his new rendering of the same theme in his *Monetary Equlibrium* (1939) which, as Palander (1941) put it, is Wicksell (1898), as Wicksell should have done it according to Myrdal, if he had understood as much as Myrdal now did.

When Dag Hammarskjöld and Erik Lundberg (1937) had introduced *sequential analysis* with the ex ante and ex post 'realization function' idea of Myrdal (1927, 1939) the Stockholm school had been established on the basis of Wicksellian (1898, 1906) disequilibrium economics. It is also interesting to observe how the Austrian-Wicksellian influence of disequilibrium economics coupled with uncertainty and ignorance versus understanding also integrated with American–Austrian economics as manifest in Frank Knight's (1921) distinction between uncertainty and risk. Myrdal struggled in his 1927 thesis to work uncertainty, as distinct from calculable risks, into his model. Even though he was not able to carry it all the way through, it was clear that the Austrian concept had now been made part of the Stockholm school model by way of the US. Karl-Olov Faxén's (1957) dissertation is particularly interesting. Faxén based his analysis on Svennilson's (1938) early micro firm approach to economic planning but placed the firm in an economic environment characterized by uncertainty, as distinct from calculable risks, and used von Neumann–Morgenstern game theoretical mathematics to analyse their strategic behavior. Even though Faxén attempted to use Nash's then very new method of equilibrium analysis he realized that exogenous equilibrium was not a realistic property of a dynamic model featuring strategic behavior among actors, and should not be attempted. (The main conclusion of Faxén, therefore, was that monetary policy could only be successful as a long-term stable monetary target, because in the medium term actors would learn the behavior of policy makers and take strategic positions to benefit: an early formulation of rational expectations, so to speak.) Genuine uncertainty, furthermore, made it impossible to formulate unique firm incentive functions and meaningless to assume that firms maximize profits. Faxén was, however, criticized by Bentzel (1957), the faculty appointed opponent for the dissertation, for failing to solve the aggregation problem under strategic firm behavior. Faxén's response was that, in a disequilibrium model with strategic positioning of firms, the aggregation problem was not analytically determinate. Under uncertainty there may not even be a stable macro economy. Today, he would add that the 'failure' of the Stockholm school rather was not to have come up with an evolutionary growth model (see further below). To better understand how firms formulated their strategies, Faxén argued that economists should conduct interviews with firms. Here, Petersson (1987, p. 180) even argues that we have a case of early Austrian *Verstehen*.

The distinction between risk and uncertainty has now been removed from the WAD model where the difference between ex ante and ex post is white noise that contains no information. Modern financial economics uses this assumption to establish an exogenous stochastic equilibrium. The entrepreneur faces a lottery with given odds. In the dynamic markets of Schumpeter (1911) and – to the extent innovators are explicit – the Menger–Wicksell Stockholm school model, innovators constantly enter and change the parameters of the game and turn the realization function into a non-stationary process. The business men now face uncertainty, as distinct from calculable risks and will attempt, using their intuition, to perceive transformations that allow them to compute and predict. They will all do it differently and all of them will be more or less mistaken. Under the Schumpeterian (1911), Wicksellian and Åkerman economic regimes, the realization process includes information that economic actors can learn from to upgrade their perceptions of the future, that is, to change the parameters of the distributions. In the WAD model such learning is excluded by assumption. There is nothing to learn. By making Schumpeter's (1911) unpredictable innovator/entrepreneur the agent that changes the parameters of the economic system and the moving force behind the systematic discrepancies arising out of the realization process, a connection was established between Wicksell and the Stockholm school economists, on the one hand, and Adam Smith, the early Austrian school and the early Joseph Schumpeter on the other. These early economists were not fully aware of the mathematical structure of this model, but we are now (Eliasson, 1992). But the unpredictability originating in the path dependency and the non-stationarity of the realization process effectively remove the possibility of ever achieving a state of full information in the economy. So even if the

Austrian-minded economists made some small formal mistakes and were not always distinctly clear in their formulations, their systematic academic endeavors have produced a body of dynamic understanding that defines a different Austrian/Schumpeterian lineage in the genealogy of economic doctrines which is still, unfortunately, dominated by variations on the WAD model (Eliasson, 2002). Schumpeter also appeared as a guest of honor at the Political Economy Club in Stockholm in May 1932 and left a deep impression on the there assembled Stockholm school economists, not least by outdoing this normally very eloquent group in elegantly articulated comments, in fact, to the extent (Henriksson, 1986) that Ingvar Svennilson (describing the event in a letter to Erik Lundberg), wondered if you would ever dare to read his works after this.

The sequential analysis of the Stockholm school economists, besides being a natural consequence of the Wicksellian heritage, may also be traced to Schumpeter, whom Erik Lundberg visited at Harvard in the early 1930s to discuss the theme of his thesis. Erik Lundberg also got a very appreciative letter from Schumpeter about his thesis and was given a positive mention in *The History of Economic Analysis* (1954) as a Keynesian before Keynes (p. 1085). The sequential analysis was also a first step in putting dynamics and growth into the Keynesian model, as later formalized in the Harrod (1939) growth model.

Schumpeter (1939) saw his analysis as an alternative to Keynes's business cycle analysis. Erik Dahmén reformulated it into a clear structural problem emphasizing the importance of the supply of innovations for economic growth. Here Ingvar Svennilson took on a more ambitious task, attempting to integrate Schumpeterian and Keynesian growth analysis, unfortunately falling between the two (the neoclassical and the economic historian) schools of research on economic growth that came to dominate the 1950s and the 1960s.

Svennilson's (1954) empirical problem was to explain why the most advanced economies at the beginning of the First World War (England, France and Germany) experienced much slower growth between the wars than before the first. To that end he integrated a short-term business cycle and a long-term growth perspective (using the Wicksellian notion of a cumulative process) with a structural change analysis. Svennilson's (1944) hypothesis, for a long time, had been that rapid production growth carries faster productivity growth because demand growth generates innovation. This is an early formulation of what has later come to be called 'Verdoorn's law' (Henriksson, 1990, p. 165). Svennilson's focus on such a 'demand driven' productivity advance probably confused his analysis and prevented him from seeing both sides of the dynamic: 'opportunities' and 'competitive pressure'.[15]

Neither Schumpeter (1939, I, p. 74) nor Dahmén (1950, pp. 74 ff) believed that such a demand pull innovation process carried any empirical significance. Even though Svennilson was a pioneer when it came to recognizing knowledge and education as critical factors behind economic growth and had a so-called 'Salter curve' formulated already in his 1944 study, his contributions were flushed out in the flow of neoclassical analyses during the post Second World War period. By playing down the possibility that increased competition might foster innovation and faster productivity advance, and that devaluations and inflation might reduce rather than stimulate growth, Svennilson gradually turned to conventional and neoclassical models during the 1960s, models in which such phenomena do not exist, and hence (Erixon, 2003), failed to leave a lasting influence on Swedish economics. This, however, was long after he had left the relevance-demanding environment of the IUI for academia. Svennilson, however, already at that time saw the great negative influence on economic growth of reducing competition by protecting inferior producers through subsidies to prevent unemployment.

IUI and the Swedish growth school: empirically founded theorizing
For several decades IUI had been the only research institute in Sweden engaged in large-scale industrial dynamics research. IUI had the resources and socially responsible industry leaders on its board were concerned that politicians knew too little about industrial reality and, therefore, were inclined to make uninformed policy decisions. At the IUI, research problems were identified in the reality of production. Since dynamic micro-based theory was lacking, IUI researchers had to formulate their own body of theory to organize their facts and their thinking.

After its foundation in 1939, IUI gradually became a plant school for young economists groomed in a different research environment than that of the regular universities. Resources were plentiful and doors were kept open for researchers to study the realities of production and markets. A key awareness of what was going on in production was reflected early in the many IUI studies. IUI was a pioneer addressing the intersection of technology and economics (Bentzel, Carlsson, Nabseth, Svennilson, Wallander) and of law and economics and the economics of institutions was on the research agenda long before the importance of these issues was understood in the Swedish university community. Industrial studies became a specialty of the IUI and Erik Höök's (1962) pioneering analysis of the public sector predated much of what has later come to be called public choice. IUI functioned as a private academy close to reality, producing empirical research and doctoral dissertations, increasingly emphasizing the role of the live entrepreneur and the necessity of a *micro foundation of endogenous* evolutionary *growth theory.* Above all, the need for new dynamic theory to organize the wealth of facts collected in the many IUI studies was understood early. As the previous discussion illustrates, however, obtaining a complete intellectual grasp of the full dynamics of a micro-based economic system is difficult. To capture both the demand pull and the competition push processes on economic development simultaneously you need a mathematically specified micro (firm)-based evolutionary theory of the entire economy that neither features price-taking firms nor assumes structures (quantities) to be fixed, i.e., does not impose exogenous equilibrium on the model.[16]

IUI therefore took steps in the late 1970s to develop a model that explicitly incorporated firm strategic behavior in dynamic markets and the experimental nature of economic dynamics. The ambition was to model a capitalist evolutionary growth process from the micro firm level and up, endogenizing aggregation over dynamic markets. The very notion of Schumpeterian creative destruction was no longer an empirical phenomenon only. It became an integral part of the understanding and modeling of the role of firms and entrepreneurship in endogenous growth (Eliasson, 1976, 1977, 1991b, Eliasson Johansson and Taymaz, 2002).[17] To emphasize the Schumpeterian approach and to honor the 100th anniversary of Schumpeter's birth, IUI also pioneered a conference with Schumpeterian themes in 1983. The conference proceedings were published in 1986 as *The Dynamics of Market Economies.* The theory of the *Experimentally Organized Economy* now became a guiding principle for research at the IUI.

The empirically specified micro-to-macro model developed at the Federation of Swedish Industries and the IUI (Eliasson, 1977) is a prototype of the experimentally organized economy. It was used to understand the post-oil crisis development of the Swedish economy (Carlsson *et al.,* 1979), and in Carlsson (1983) and Carlsson, Bergholm and Lindberg (1981) to study the macroeconomic effects of the Swedish industrial subsidy program to save employment temporarily. The model analysis was based on real firm data. By locking in resources in defunct shipyards with subsidies, notably skilled labor, factor supply was demonstrated to be depressed, factor prices increased and growth in other firms and new entry discouraged. Quantitatively, the model simulations demonstrated that the subsidy program could explain the period of almost complete stagnation at the macro manufacturing level that followed for more than ten years.

The IUI produced a large number of empirically based doctoral dissertations over the years and for many years was the largest supplier of candidates for chairs in economics at the universities. Economists with the IUI background of industrial dynamics were in demand both in industry and in the private and public bureaucracies. This was especially so when the

Swedish economy was beginning to lose steam after the oil crises of the 1970s. It became important to understand what was going on. With a series of complete dynamical systems analyses of the Swedish economy IUI (notably 1979, 1985 and 1993) stepped up its ambitions to understand what was going on and to advise on policy in competition with government proposals. What were the consequences for economic growth of inflation, large and growing tax wedges in the price system (Södersten and Lindberg, 1983), a dismal record of new firm establishment (Braunerhjelm, 1993), a lack of medium-sized firms (Johansson, 1997) and the industrial subsidy program (already mentioned)? The ambitions of the IUI to engage in research addressing these problems were reflected in the titles of the yearbooks of the institute, such as *The Firms in the Market Economy* (1979/80) and *The Economics of Institutions and Markets* (1986/7). During the 1970s, politicians increasingly demanded that business firms take responsibility for employment. At the same time a strong political movement was initiated by the central blue-collar labor union to take over ownership and management rights in the large industrial firms. This peculiar political demand for a switching of responsibilities to the incompetent and disinterested brought about a number of studies at the IUI aimed at clarifying the nature of competence needed to manage and innovate industrial firms successfully. Examples are Eliasson *et al.* (1990) on the *Knowledge Based Information Economy* and Pelikan (1993) on the negatively biased competence selection in politically controlled business organizations.

Bringing the live entrepreneur into economic theory, therefore, became a key ambition of research at IUI as well as departing intellectually from the centralist message of the WAD model. For the latter reason the Schumpeter II tradition never got established at the IUI.

Conclusions
Wicksell added analytical rigor and an Austrian evolutionary touch to Swedish economics. The Stockholm school economists took up the evolutionary theme but never managed to carry the idea on to an evolutionary growth model. Gradually, the exogenous static equilibrium approach of mathematical economics developed in the USA has taken over the teaching agenda at Western universities. It is clear in its implications and easy to teach, but its assumptions are of another world. By its prior assumptions this model features central government as the supreme solver of the welfare problems of its citizens. The Austrian-Schumpeterian (I,1911) evolutionary model is the exact antithesis to the neoclassical model in these respects and advises less rather than more central government intervention in the economy. Until recently the evolutionary economics theme was further developed in Sweden at the IUI, but the IUI was quite alone in that

ambition and Schumpeterian economics is currently struggling to survive in Sweden.

The Austrian-Schumpeterian (I) evolutionary model in its modern Swedish rendition of an experimentally organized economy carries a strong policy message: business decisions are always more or less in error, but so are also policy decisions. Policy making is extremely competence demanding, and would be understood as such if the voters acted as more demanding customers of policy. While the many business mistakes are part of the economic learning mechanisms in a capitalist market economy, bad policy carries a large negative long-term leverage on the economy. Hence, do not experiment at the national policy level, and keep ambitions low rather than high, because you are likely, as a policy maker, to be wrong and easily destructive. Such messages are not popular with politicians thriving, as they are, on large public budgets that make up the greater part of the resource flows in many industrial economies, as in Europe, and, hence, also indirectly influence research funding. The final paradox is puzzling. While the US economy is the advanced industrial economy most similar to the Austrian/Schumpeterian (1911) model, its economists have been instrumental in successfully developing and transferring centralist neoclassical themes throughout the academic community. Europe features less real economic dynamics but is the stronghold of evolutionary economics. Since Austrian-Schumpeterian economics of policy decisions will be synonymous with a healthy and growing economy, a strong presence of Austrian-Schumpeterian research in the academic community should at least be a positive economic signal.

Notes

1. This chapter has benefited greatly from discussions with Niclas Berggren, Bo Carlsson, Erik Dahmén, Lennart Erixon, Karl-Olof Faxén, Rolf Henriksson, Dan Johansson, Richard Johnsson, Nils Karlson, Lennart Schön and Richard Swedberg. Eric Nicander at the Lund University Library has been very helpful in providing me with copies of Wicksell's personal correspondence with Carl Menger.
2. Not to be confused with the Stockholm School of Economics, the business school in Stockholm.
3. A spinoff from the City University in Stockholm that cooperated with The Royal Institute of Technology (KTH) in organizing the 1996 International Joseph A. Schumpeter conference in Stockholm. Over a brief period three doctorate dissertations in the Swedish growth school tradition have also been defended at the KTH (Johansson, 2001; Jonason, 2001; Fridh, 2002).
4. This is also the position of Martin (1979) (as reported in Alter (1990, p. 16)) even though the entrepreneur is not being paid for carrying the risks, or rather the uncertainty associated with the lack of knowledge. For more on the role of ignorance in economic behavior, see Eliasson (2004).
5. Thus, for instance, the creative destruction process introduced, but not named, in 1911, is truly Mengerian in spirit, and not compatible with Schumpeter's didactic trick to illustrate the influence of the entrepreneur as a disturber of the Walrasian equilibrium by first placing the economy in static equilibrium. Static equilibrium does not exist in the

Mengerian-type model of Schumpeter (1911) (see Eliasson, 1984, 1992). A similar problem appears in Kirzner (1973) where the entrepreneur equilibrates the economy, but never really succeeds, because outside exogenous forces constantly change the equilibrium. With an endogenous entrepreneur and/or significant resource use being associated with market arbitrage the perceived equilibrium will constantly change endogenously because of the agents searching for it, and therefore be unreachable (Eliasson, 1991a).

6. For a more thorough discussion of this, see Johnsson (2003).
7. Or for that reason the market clearing or static equilibrium condition that marginal utilities equal marginal costs of the fully worked out WAD model. In static equilibrium entrepreneurial rents are eliminated and all markets cleared. Such a situation can be demonstrated never to be attainable in a truly Austrian model of the Experimentally Organized Economy. See below and Eliasson (1991b).
8. Note, however, the inconsistency in Schumpeter's analysis, mentioned in note 5.
9. Here Wicksell was already dissociating himself from the 'forthcoming' Schumpeter (1942).
10. This problem has returned again in neo-Keynesian analysis and attempts to overcome the restrictive price taking assumption of the competitive equilibrium model. Von Mises (1936) observes that Wicksell's attempt 'to rehabilitate the currency school was short lived', and makes a critical attempt himself. He observes that an artificially low interest rate maintained through credit expansion can only produce temporary results in the form of growth, but he does not discuss Wicksell's version of the cumulative process, where the positive difference between the return to investment and the money interest (the disequilibrium) can depend on a high return because of new technology.
11. In the Wicksell archives a letter from Menger dated 1893 exists certifying that Wicksell sat in on Menger's lectures in Vienna in 1888, and then nothing, except some correspondence between Wicksell and Menger in 1920 about a visit of Carl Menger's son Karl to Stockholm. Carl Menger spoke very positively of his son's intellectual merits.
12. Gårdlund (1956, ch. 6), however, reports no such influence.
13. Note, however, that Dahmén was also skeptical about the importance of demand.
14. Even though the term was coined by Modigliani and Cohen (1961). Modigliani and Cohen were, however, unaware of the Swedish school contribution, or – at least – they did not refer to it.
15. Despite the fact that he had formulated an embryo of the other (now missing) side already in 1939 (Svennilson, 1939). See also Henriksson (1990, pp. 93, 170).
16. Cf. the discussion between Wicksell and Gustaf Åkerman, and Faxén's arguments above.
17. Micro (firm)-based macro evolutionary modeling was started as a joint project between IBM Sweden, The University of Uppsala and the Federation of Swedish industries as early as 1974 (Eliasson, 1977). This project was taken over by IUI in 1977. It was recognized early that the tools chosen imposed intellectual restrictions on your thinking that influenced the analytical results. Therefore, the tools preferably should have an empirical micro foundation and possess the general evolutionary characteristics that we associate with reality. To understand, you should attempt to look at the same problem through different glasses ('intellectual filters'). For comparison, therefore, during a large part of the 1980s, IUI maintained three macro models parallel: the micro-to-macro model, a traditional Keynes/Leontief-type sector model and a highly aggregated monetary model. The three models gave different answers when asked the same questions. This not only illustrates the critical role of prior assumptions and guesses in economic analysis, but also created an awareness of new problems, at the time, in our own analysis of the Swedish economic situation that we would otherwise not have paid attention to.

Bibliography

Åkerman, Gustaf, 1921, Inflation, Penningmängd och Ränta, *Ekonomisk Tidskrift*, **9**, 143–62.
——, 1922, Inflation, Penningmängd och Ränta- ett genmäle, *Ekonomisk Tidskrift*, **24**, 5–9.
——, 1923, *Realkapital und Kapitalzins*, dissertation, Lund: Lund University.

Åkerman, Johan, 1928, *Om det Ekonomiska Livets Rytmik*, dissertation, Lund: Lund University.

——, 1932, *Industrialism och kultur*, Stockholm: Natur och Kultur.

——, 1934, *Konjunkturteoretiska problem*, Lund: Gleerup.

——, 1936, *Ekonomisk Kausalitet*, Lund: Gleerup.

——, 1950, Institutionalism, *Ekonomisk Tidskrift*, 1–14.

——, 1952a, Innovationer och kumulativa förlopp (Innovations and cumulative economic development), *Ekonomisk Tidskrift*, **54**, 185–202.

Alter, Max, 1990, *Carl Menger and the Origins of Austrian Economics*, New York: Westview Press.

Anderson, Thomas, Pontus Braunerhjelm, Bo Carlsson, Gunnar Eliasson, Stefan Fölster, Lars Jagren, Eugenia Kazamaki Otterstgen and Kent Rune Sjöholm, 1993, *Den Långa Vägen*, Stockholm: IUI.

Bentzel, Ragnar, 1957, ' "Recension" av Karl-Olof Faxén: Monetary and Fiscal Policy Under Uncertainty', *Ekonomisk Tidskrift*.

von Böhm-Bawerk, Eugen, 1894, Der Letzte Masstab der Güterwertes, English translation, 'The Ultimate Standard', *The Annals of the American Academy of Political and Social Science*, 1–60.

Braunerhjelm, Pontus, 1993, 'Nyetablering och Småföretagande i Svensk Industri' in Anderson *et al.* (eds), *Den Långa Vägen*, Stockholm: IUI.

Carlsson, Bo, 1987, Reflections on industrial dynamics – the challenges ahead, *International Journal of Industrial Organization*, **5**, 131–48.

——, 1983, Industrial subsidies in Sweden: macro-economic effects and an international comparison, *Journal of Industrial Economics*, **XXXII**(1), Sept., 9–14.

——, 1995 (ed.), *Technical Systems and Economic Performance: the Case of Factory Automation*, Boston/Dordrecht/London: Kluwer Academic Publishers.

Carlsson, Bo and Rolf Henriksson, 1991, *Development Blocs and Industrial Transformation*, Stockholm: IUI.

Carlsson, Bo, Fredrik Bergholm and Thomas Lindberg, 1981, *Industristödspolitiken och dess inverkan på samhällsekonomin*, Stockholm: IUI.

Carlsson, Bo, Erik Dahmén, Anders Grufman, Märtha Josefsson and Johan Örtengren, 1979, *Teknik och Industristruktur-70-talets ekonomiska kris i histrorisk belysning*, Stockholm: IUI and the Royal Swedish Academy of Engineering Sciencies (IVA).

Dahmén, Erik, 1941, revised edn of J. Schumpeter, *Business Cycles – a Theoretical, Historical and Statistical Analysis of the Capitalist Process*, 1939, *Statsvetenskaplig Tidskrift*, **44**.

——, 1942a, Ekonomisk Strukturanalys- begreppet felinvestering som konjunkturteoretiskt instrument, Licentiatavhandling, University of Lund.

——, 1942b, Ekonomisk strukturanalys: några synpunkter på den ekonomiska utvecklingens och konjunkturväxlingarnas problem, *Ekonomisk Tidskrift*, **44**(3), 177–94, English translation in Carlsson and Henriksson (1991).

——, 1950, *Svenskt Industriellt Företagande*, Stockholm: IUI.

——, 'Hur studera industriell Utveckling' in Dahmén and Eliasson (1980).

Dahmén, Erik and H. Gunnar Eliasson (eds), 1980, *Industriell Utveckling i Sverige. Teori och verklighet under ett sekel* (Industrial Development in Sweden. The Theory and Reality of a Century), Stockholm: IUI.

Day, Richard and H. Gunnar Eliasson (eds), 1986, *The Dynamics of Market Economies*, Stockholm/Amsterdam/London/New York/Tokyo: North-Holland & IUI.

Day, Richard, H. Gunnar Eliasson and Clas Wihlborg (eds), 1993, *The Markets for Innovation, Ownership and Control*, Stockholm/Amsterdam/London/New York/Tokyo: North-Holland & IUI.

du Rietz, Gunnar, 1975, *Etablering, nedläggning och industriell tillväxt i Sverige 1954–1970*, Stockholm: IUI.

——, 1980, *Företagsetableringen i Sverige under Efterkrigstiden*, Stockholm: IUI.

Eliasson, Gunnar, 1969, *The Credit Market, Investment Planning and Monetary Policy – an Econometric Study of Manufacturing Industries*, Stockholm: IUI.

——, 1976, *Business Economic Planning*, New York: John Wiley & Sons.

Eliasson, Gunnar, 1977, Competition and market processes in a simulation model of the Swedish Economy, *American Economic Review*, **67**(1), 277–81.

——, 1980, The firm in the market economy – 40 years of research at IUI, *The Firm in the Market Economy, IUI 40 years*, Stockholm: IUI.

——, 1984, Micro heterogeneity of firms and stability of growth, *Journal of Economic Behavior and Organization*, **5**(3–4), 249–98.

——, 1991a, Modelling the experimentally organized economy, *Journal of Economic Behavior and Organization*, **16**(1–2), 155–82.

——, 1991b, IUIs forskningsprogram inom Industriell Ekonomi, *50 Års forskning inom Industriell Ekonomi, IUI Yearbook 1989/90*, Stockholm: IUI.

——, 1992, 'Business competence, organizational learning, and economic growth – establishing the Smith–Schumpeter–Wicksell (SSW) connection, in Scherer-Perlman (eds), *Entrepreneurship*, Ann Arbor: University of Michigan Press.

——, 1996, *Firm Objectives, Controls and Organization*, Dordrecht/Boston/London: Kluwer Academic Publishers.

——, 2002, The 50 or so schools of industrial economics, mimeo, KTH, Indek, Stockholm.

——, 2004, 'Ignorant actors in the resource rich world of the knowledge based economy', paper prepared for the Schumpeter Conference in Milan, 9–13 June.

Eliasson, Gunnar, Dan Johansson and Erol Taymaz, 2002, Simulating the new economy, paper presented to the International Conference of the International Joseph A. Schumpeter Society, Florida, March; also in KTH TRITA, **14**, 2002, Stockholm.

Eliasson, Gunnar, Stefan Fölster, Thomas Lindberg, Tomas Pousette and Erol Taymaz, 1990, *The Knowledge Based Information Economy*, Stockholm: IUI and Telekon.

Erixon, Lennart, 2003, Att förena Keynes och Schumpeter, mimeo, Economics Department, University of Stockholm (April).

Faxén, Karl-Olof, 1957, *Monetary and Fiscal Policy under Uncertainty*, Stockholm: Almquist & Wiksell.

Freeman, Chris, 1974, *The Economics of Industrial Innovation*, Harmondsworth: Penguin.

Fridh, Ann-Charlotte, 2002, *Dynamics and Growth:The Health Care Industry*, Stockholm: KTH.

Frisch, Ragnar, 1931, Kritik av Johan Åkerman's avhandling 'Om det ekonomiska livets rytmik', *Statsvetenskaplig Tidskrift*, 281–300.

——, 1933, 'Propagating problems and impulse problems in dynamic economics', *Economic Essays in Honor of Gustav Cassel*, London: George Allan and Unwin.

Gårdlund, Torsten, 1956, *Knut Wicksell. Rebell i Det Nya Riket*, Stockholm: Bonniers.

Harrod, Roy F., 1939, An essay in dynamic theory, *Economic Journal*, **XLIX**(March), 14–33.

Henriksson, Rolf, 1986, The institutional base of the Stockholm school. The political economy club (1917–1951), *HES Bulletin*, **11**(1), Spring, 59–97.

——, 1990, *Som Edström Ville- Hur IUI blev till*, Stockholm: IUI.

——, 2002, Den Dahménska ansatsens tillkomst och dess ställning i den Schumpeterianska Tanketraditionen, in Johansson and Karlson (eds), *Den Svenska Tillvaxtskolan*, Stockholm: RATIO.

Höök, Erik, 1962 , *Den Offentliga Sektorns Expansion. En studie av de offentliga civila utgifternas utveckling åren 1913–58*, Stockholm: IUI.

IUI, 1979, *Att Välja 80-tal- IUIs Långtidsbedömning 1979*, Stockholm: IUI.

IUI, 1985, *Att Rätt Värdera 90-talet-IUIs Långtidsbedömning 1985*, Stockholm: IUI.

IUI, 1993, *Den Långa Vägen- den ekonomiska politikjens begränsnignar och möjligheter att föra Sverige ur 1990- talets kris*, Stockholm: IUI.

Johansson, Dan, 1997, *The Number and Size Distribution of Firms in Sweden and other European Countries*, Stockholm: Stockholm School of Economics.

——, 2001, *The Dynamics of Firm and Industry Growth – the Swedish Computer and Communications Industry*, Stockholm: KTH, Indek.

——, 2004, Entreprenören i Läroboken; förekomst, innebörd, konsekvens ('The entrepreneur in the textbook'), paper prepared for the FSF annual conference in Örebro, January. Published in English, 2004, as 'Economics without Entrepreneurship of Institutions: a vocabularly analysis of graduate textbooks', *Econ Journal Watch*, **1**(3), 515–38.

Johansson, Dan and Nils Karlson, 2002, *Den Svenska Tillväxtskolan- om den ekonomisak utvecklingens kreativa förstörelse*, Stockholm: RATIO.

Johnsson, Richard, 2003, 'Austrian' subjectivism vs. objectivism, Parts I & II, *The Free Radical*, **55** and **56**.

Jonason, Andreas, 2001, *Innovative Pricing*, Stockholm: KTH, Indek.

Karlson, Nils, 2002, *The State of State – an Inquiry into the Role of Invisible Hands in Politics and Civil Society*, New Brunswick: Transactions Press.

Keynes, John Maynard, 1936, *The General Theory of Employment, Interest and Money*, London: Macmillan.

Kirzner, Israel, M., 1973, *Competition and Entrepreneurship*, Chicago: University of Chicago Press.

——, 1978, The entrepreneurial role in Menger's system, *Atlantic Economic Journal*, **6**(3), 31–45.

Knight, F., 1921, *Risk, Uncertainy and Profit*, Boston: Houghton-Mifflin.

Lundberg, Erik, 1937, *Economic Expansion*, London: P.S. King & Sons.

Lundvall, Bengt-Åke, 1992, *National Systems of Innovation*, London: Pinter.

Martin, Dolores, T., 1979, Alternative views on Mengerian entrepreneurship, *History of Political Economy*, **11**(2), 271–85.

Menger, Carl, 1871, *Grundsätze der Volkwirtschaftlehere*, Vienna: Wilhelm Baumüller.

——, 1921, Zür Theorie des Capital Zinses, *Ekonomisk Tidskrift*, **XII** (Nationalekonomiska Studier tillägnade Professor Knut Wicksell), 87–8.

Modigliani, Franco and K.Cohen, 1961, *The Role of Anticipations and Plans in Economic Behavior*, Urbana: University of Illinois Press.

Myrdal, Gunnar, 1927, *Prisbildningsproblemet och föräderligheten*, Uppsala: Almquist & Wicksell.

——, 1939, *Monetary Equilibrium*, London: Hodge.

Nelson, Richard (ed.), 1993, *National Systems of Innovation: A Comparative Study*, Oxford: Oxford University Press.

Nelson, Richard and Sidney Winter, 1982, *An Evolutionary Theory of Economic Change*, Cambridge, MA: Harvard University Press.

Palander, Tord, 1941, Om 'Stockholmsskolans' begrepp och metoder. Metodologiska reflexioner kring Myrdals 'Monetary Equilibrium', *Ekonomisk Tidskrift*, **XLIII** (1), 88–143.

Pålsson-Syll, Lars, 1995, Den Strtukturanalytiska Skolan i Lund, Skrifter utgivna av ekonomisk-historiska föreningen, LXXIII, Department of Economic History, University of Lund, Lund.

Pelikan, Pavel, 1993, Evolution, Economic Competence, and the Market for Corporate Control in Day, Eliasson and Wihlborg (eds), *Markets for Innovation*, Stockholm: North-Holland/IUI.

Petersson, Jan, 1987, *Erik Lindahl och Stockholmsskolans Dynamiska Metod*, Lund: Lund Economic Studies.

Scherer, Frederic, and Mark Perlman (eds), 1992, *Entrepreneurship, Technological Innovation, and Economic Growth – Studies in the Schumpeterian Tradition*, Ann Arbor: University of Michigan Press.

Schön, Lennart, 2000, *En Modern Svensk Ekonomisk Historia – tillväxt och omvandling under två sekel*, Stockholm: SNS.

Schumpeter Joseph, A., 1911, *Theorie der Wirtschaftliche Entwicklung* (Schumpeter I), Cambridge: Harvard University Press.

——, 1939, *Business Cycles – a Theoretical, Historical and Statistical Analysis of the Capitalist Process*, vols I–II, 1st edn, New York: McGraw-Hill.

——, 1942, *Capitalism, Socialism and Democracy* (Schumpeter II), New York: Harper and Bros.

——, 1954, *History of Economic Analysis*, Oxford: Oxford University Press.

Streissler, Erich, 1969, Structural economic thought – on the significance of the Austrian school today, *Zeitschrift für nationalökonomie*, **29**, 237–66.

Svennilson, Ingvar, 1938, *Ekonomisk Planering*, Uppsala: Almqvist & Wicksell.

Svennilson, Ingvar, 1939, *Strukturella Inslag i den Senaste Årens Ekonomiska Utveckling*, Meddelanden från Konjunkturinstitutet, Ser B:1, Stockholm: Konjunkturinstitutet.

——, 1944, Industriarbetets Växande avkastning i belysning av svenska erfarenheter, *Studier i ekonomi och historia tillägnade Eli F. Hecdkscher på 65–årsdagen den 24 november 1944*, Uppsala: Almqvist & Wicksell.

——, 1954, *Growth and Stagnation in the European Economy*, Geneva: UN Economic Commission for Europe.

Södersten, Jan and Thomas Lindberg, 1983, *Skatt på Bolagskapital- Sverige i jämföresle med Storbritannien, USA och Västtyskland*, Stockholm: IUI.

Swedberg, Richard, 1997, Schumpeter in Sweden, *Scandinavian Economic History Review*, **45**, 113–30.

——, (ed.), 1998, *Knut Wicksell- Stridsskrifter och Saqmhällsekonomiska Analyser*, Ratio klassiker, Stockholm: City University Press.

von Hayek, Friedrich, 1935, Preiserwartungen, monetäre störungen und felinvestitionen, *Nationalökonomisk Tidskrift*, **73**.

——, 1940, *The Pure Theory of Capital*, London: Macmillan.

von Mises, Ludwig, 1912, *Theorie des Geldes und des Umlaufsmittal*, published in English, 1980, as *The Theory of Money and Credit*, Indianapolis: Bettina Bien Greaves.

——, 1936, 'The "Austrian" theory of the trade cycle', *The Austrian Theory of the Trade Cycle*, Auburn, Alabama: MISES Institute.

Wicksell, Knut, 1892, Den moderna arbetarrörelsen: strödda betraktelser, *Eskilstuna-Kuriren*, 14 and 21 July, 1, 11 and 18 August.

——, 1898, *Geldzins und Guterpreise*, Jena.

——, 1901, *Föreläsningar i Nationalekonomi*, Del 1; Teoretisk Nationalekonomi, Lund: Berlingske Boktryckeriet.

——, 1906, *Föreläsningar i Nationalekonomi: Del II Om pengar och krediter*, Stockholm: C.F. Fritzes Hofbokhandel.

——, 1911, Böhm-Bawerk's kapital teori och akritiken därav, *Ekonomisk Tidskrift*, 39–49.

——, 1920, Inflation, Penningmängd och Ränta, *Ekonomisk Tidskrift*, **10–11**, 167–71.

——, 1921, Carl Menger, *Ekonomisk Tidskrift*, **I–XI**, 113–18.

——, 1922, Svar till kand. Åkerman, *Ekonomisk Tidskrift*, **24**, 10–12.

——, 1923, Realkapital och kapitalränta, *Ekonomisk Tidskrift*, **5–6**, 145–80.

——, 1924, Mengers Grundsätze i ny upplaga, *Ekonomisk Tidskrift*, 1–10.

66 Experimental economics
Siegfried Berninghaus and Werner Güth

1 Introduction

At the beginning of the twenty-first century we can look back at half a century of experimental economics. Naturally the start was slow (although experimentation dates back much further in (social) psychology) but the finish is breathtaking. One has tried to implement economic and game-theoretical models as (laboratory) experiments, to test orthodox rationality theory (assuming that utilities are just material payoffs and beliefs correspond to chance moves), and to generalize the rational choice approach using behavioral concepts when narrowly defined orthodox theory produces misleading results.

Orthodox economics and game theory rely on what is commonly understood as 'perfect decision rationality' requiring unlimited cognitive and information processing capabilities. It is obvious that these requirements lie far beyond what human decision makers can accomplish. Another problem in applying orthodox theory is that it assumes the existence of individual cardinal utilities and subjective beliefs that can hardly ever be observed clearly, assuming that they exist at all. Of course, one may specify utilities by material payoffs such as profits (which can often be observed and measured, even in the field) and beliefs by objective probabilities whenever possible, but then the predictions, implied by rationality, are often not confirmed by experimental observations.

In what follows we begin by discussing decision-theoretical experiments. Regarding situations (involving) interpersonal strategic interaction, we reverse the natural chronological order somewhat by first reporting on experiments based on non-cooperative games. As in theory, experimental research of social conflicts was initially dominated by cooperative game experiments.

2 One-person decision making

Testing rationality experimentally in one-person games mainly involves testing (the axioms of) utility theory. There is probably no need to prove that human players will be unable to solve optimization tasks involving complex combinatorics. While people clearly differ in their capabilities, it is a fact of human existence that even the most capable among us encounter optimization problems which they cannot solve optimally. Let us therefore discuss three choice problems whose degree of difficulty differs greatly: dynamic optimization, risky choices, and dominance solvability in one-person games.

The simple dynamic choice problem (below) has an obvious solution (l, R, L). It shows that any discussion (see Bicchieri, 1989) of whether 'rationality' can be assumed at all decision nodes cannot be restricted to interpersonal strategic interaction. If agent 1 has to choose between L and R, an optimal choice R anticipates his/her own future rationality by preferring L over R. However, the fact that one must choose between L and R seems in itself to cast doubt on own rationality. A rational agent 1 would choose l (yielding the payoff of 3), and thus would never actually face the choice between L and R.

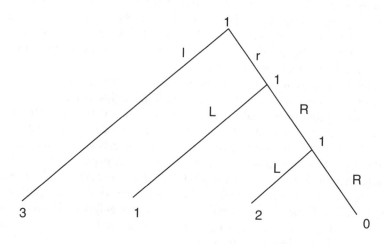

In more complex dynamic games, initial suboptimal choices are the rule rather than the exception. Such problems are more thoroughly studied in experimental (and cognitive) psychology. In experimental economics one tests the quantitative, or at least the qualitative, aspects of rational behavior, using models of intertemporal allocation behavior such as models of rational addiction (Becker and Murphy, 1988) or the so-called 'life-cycle-saving' models (see Anderhub and Güth, 1999, for a survey). Even the data generated by experienced participants clearly reveal that participants, if they behave at all systematically, rely on heuristics rather than backward induction (dynamic programming).

Most decision theory experiments focus on (axioms of) cardinal utilities where the experimental procedures vary widely: for example, from pure questionaires without monetary incentives to those where non-optimality leads to substantial losses. To some extent, it may be argued that deviations from optimal behavior should only be taken seriously (see Harrison, 1994) when they imply substantial losses (saliency). Although the theory of rational decision making does not offer any guidance here, the saliency requirement can be justified by the (uncontrolled and small) costs of optimizing, for example, the utility loss of deriving an optimal alternative. In simple cases, a participant is asked to choose between two simple lotteries of the form $L = (\underline{P}|w,\overline{P}|1 - w)$ with $0 \leq \underline{P} < \overline{P}$ and $0 < w < 1$ where sometimes (in cases of so-called 'compound lotteries') the monetary prizes $\underline{P}$ and $\overline{P}$ resulting with probability w, respectively $1 - w$, are replaced by lotteries. Comparing all these choices usually reveals that certain axioms of expected utility maximization are violated.

'Rationalizing' some apparent paradoxes by individual attitudes to risk can be excluded experimentally by applying the binary lottery technique. To show this, note that the cardinal utility of a participant is the probability $1 - w$ of winning times the utility $u(\overline{P})$ of the high prize $\overline{P}$ plus w times $u(\underline{P})$, the utility of the low prize $\underline{P}$ resulting with complementary probability w, i.e. $u(L) = (1 - w)u(\overline{P}) + wu(\underline{P})$. By setting $u(\underline{P}) = 0$ and $u(\overline{P}) = 1$ the utility $u(L) = 1 - w$ results: in other words, utility depends linearly on the experimental payoff variable $1 - w$ (implying risk neutrality). Thus specifying payoffs in such a way makes every participant risk-neutral. To justify this, participants need only prefer more $(\overline{P})$ over less $(\underline{P})$ money and obey the laws of probability calculus (since there are multiple chance moves).

When trying to observe experimentally how a lottery L is evaluated, one may rely on mechanisms rendering the truthful revelation of preferences as optimal: for example, in the sense that truthful revelation is the only undominated value statement. Let $[a, b] \subset IR$ be an interval with $a < b$ and $\phi(\cdot)$ a density over IR with $\phi(p) = 0$ for all $p \notin [a, b]$ and $\infty > \varphi(p) > 0$ for all $p \in [a, b]$. According to the random price mechanism (Becker, de Groot and Marshak, 1963) the price p, which one can receive or must pay, is randomly determined according to $\phi(\cdot)$. For a potential seller S the expected profit is $\int_l^b (p - v_s)d\phi(p)$ and for a potential buyer B it is $\int_a^l (v_B - p)d\phi(p)$, where v_i for $i = S, B$ with $a < v_i < b$ the value for the commodity under consideration.

The only decision variable is thus the price limit l, meaning that one only sells at prices $p \geq l$ and buys at prices $p \leq l$, respectively. Clearly, $l = v_i$ is the only undominated price limit, both for $i = S$ and $i = B$. Specifically, the optimal decision $l = v_i$ does not depend on a, b and $\phi(\cdot)$ as long as $a < v_i < b$ and the qualitative requirements for $\phi(\cdot)$ are satisfied. Nevertheless, experimentally observed choices l react to changes of a, b and $\phi(\cdot)$ and, very robustly, to whether one is in role S or B (endowment effect). Since dominant choices do not depend on risk attitudes, given true values v_i seems more a normative concept than a fact of life. Human decision makers do not rely on fully informed preferences. Instead they must generate their preferences by cognitively representing their decision environment, imagining how choices may affect their basic concerns, and so on. In the context of such a dynamic process, aspects which are strategically irrelevant may nevertheless become influential.

The consequences are that the normative concept of incentive compatibility may have little behavioral relevance or reliability. More generally, optimal mechanisms or institutions may perform relatively poorly. An institution that works best when all parties act rationally can itself induce non-rational behavior so that bad results can follow. One may wish to compare alternative mechanisms after replacing rational agents with more realistic ones, whose motivations may be context-dependent. This illustrates why orthodox theory has to be supplemented by a behavioral theory of decision making, whose formalization could be based on the (stylized) results of decision-making experiments.

3   Experimental results in strategic games

Some of the earliest experiments were based on markets that required an auctioneer (see Roth, 1995b, for a historical review). One may therefore be reluctant to view them as strategic game experiments. At the same time, simple games like 'prisoners' dilemma' games were studied experimentally. A solution concept for a given class of games (for example the class of finite games in normal form) is largely based on invariance or covariance with respect to certain classes of transformations, and thus partitions the class into *equivalence classes*. Two games from the same equivalence class are said to be strategically equivalent. Most solution concepts, for example, allow for positively affine utility transformations. Experimentally, one could try to induce transformations like this by changing the monetary payoffs appropriately. Differences like this, which are theoretically irrelevant, can nevertheless change participant behavior quite dramatically.

The situation can be even more ambiguous. Even if we do not transform a game at all but present (or *frame*) the same game differently, behavior may still react to the change (presentation/framing effects). In the case of a prisoners' dilemma game, where defection always leads to the same payoff advantage when compared to the cooperative strategy (i.e. regardless of what the other player chooses), one can *decompose* the same game in infinitely many ways. (Unlike a transformation, a decomposition does not affect the rules of the game.) This leads to a one-parameter family of decomposed games that are all identical to the same prisoners' dilemma game. Nonetheless, average cooperation rates react quite dramatically to decomposition (Pruitt, 1967).

More generally, a strategic game (regardless of whether modeled as a stage game, in extensive or normal form) does not seem to account for all determinants of behavior. On the other hand, as will be illustrated below, it may draw attention to subtle strategic details, such as the exact timing of decisions and specific information feedback, that are often neglected by experimental participants. It will therefore be necessary to supplement strategic equivalence with concepts of behavioral equivalence.

The prisoners' dilemma game, played once or repeatedly, has been a dominant paradigm of experimentation. Note that in an experiment a finite upper limit for the number of repetitions cannot be avoided, and should be commonly known. Therefore folk theorems do not apply, and mutual defection is the solution in repeated prisoners' dilemma games. Nevertheless, the robust results of many experiments are that players *cooperate in most rounds*, although they defect towards the end.

Cooperation, however, does not unravel altogether in the manner suggested by backward induction. Since participants try to avoid being preempted (meaning that their partner terminates cooperation earlier), they seem to be fully aware of the backward induction idea. Because of its detrimental consequences, however, they do not follow its recommendations but rather account for it only when the end of interaction is near.

Since folk theorems do not apply, this issue has posed quite a puzzle for game theorists, and has inspired the innovative *reputation approach* (other names are 'crazy perturbation' or 'gang of four': see Kreps *et al.*, 1982). The basic idea is to allow for (a little) incomplete information concerning another player's type: in repeated prisoners' dilemma games (s)he may be an unconditional cooperator (i.e. 'a bit crazy'). In this way one can try to build up the impression (the other's posterior probability) of being (confronting) an unconditional cooperator. Furthermore, the a priori probability of the other person being 'crazy' – necessary to justify initial cooperation – can be small when the number of iterations is large.

Although the reputation approach has been extremely successful (in the sense of inspiring a large literature), some qualitative aspects of reputation equilibria are supported only poorly, if at all, by experimental data. These include (a) the gradual decline in the probability of cooperation, leading to certain defection in the last period (some participants, for instance, cooperate in the last round), and (b) the specific mixing (the change of mixed strategies over time). Nevertheless, reputation equilibria illustrate how orthodox (game) theory can be enriched by paying attention to robust experimental findings. (Reputation equilibria do not question rationality itself, only the idea that rationality is clearly expected in participants.) Other applications concern signaling, trust, bargaining, and centipede games and, most of all, the classic paradigms of the industrial organization literature.

Repeated games are also the main playground for *tournament studies* (Axelrod, 1984). Here participants are invited to develop strategies (mostly through the medium of a computer) that then encounter each other in a 'tournament'. Usually participants learn about the varying successes of their strategies − often the only motivation for a participant is to achieve a high ranking which is thus only loosely related to the game payoff − and can try to improve them in the light of experience. These studies definitely lead participants to develop somewhat general behavioral plans (specifying what to do in all contingencies). They are also biased, however, in the sense that one's first aim is to ensure cooperation. If one were to expect such a drive towards cooperation in markets, even large markets with many pair-wise interactions, applying effective antitrust policies would be a hopeless task. In fact some experiments (e.g. Anderhub *et al.*, 2002) show that even very narrow markets may yield results closer to the competitive equilibrium than to the duopoly or cooperative solution (in one study, two duopolists interact over 60 rounds).

Another thoroughly explored topic is *strategic bargaining* (often referred to as the 'non-cooperative' approach to bargaining). Experimental studies mostly concentrated on very simple models of strategic bargaining, where the problem is less the difficulty of deriving the solution than that of accepting the behavior suggested by the solution, especially when it is unfair. In ultimatum bargaining experiments (Güth, Schmittberger and Schwarze, 1982) a positive sum p of money, the 'pie', can be distributed by (a) first allowing the proposer to decide on his/her offer o with $0 \leq o \leq p$ to the responder, who (b) can then either accept the offer o (so that the proposer gets $p - o$ and the responder o) or reject it (in which case both players get nothing).

Here the solution (assuming that both players only care about their own monetary payoffs) predicts that the proposer offers 0, or the smallest positive monetary unit, and that the responder accepts all (positive) offers. Typical and robust experimental findings (see Roth, 1995b, for a survey) are that (a) responders reject even substantial positive offers o in the range $0 < o < p/2$, which they apparently regard as unfair; and (b) proposers shy away from excessively low offers o: the most frequent (modal) offer is usually the equal split $o = p/2$. Slight doubts about the responder's rationality would not resolve the problem here. To justify the offer $o = p/2$ instead of $o = \varepsilon$ (with ϵ denoting the smallest positive unit of money) the proposer must be extremely risk-averse, or the responder probably irrational or 'crazy'. Furthermore, this would not explain why responders willingly reject positive offers. How did theorists react to this challenge? One possibility is to study related or richer game models, hoping that their experimental results are more informative about the reasons why proposers usually offer rather fair shares and responders are unwilling to accept meager offers. Actually one can generalize the ultimatum game by assuming that non-acceptance of the offer o implies the conflict payoff $\rho(p - o)$ for the proposer and λo for the responder with $0 \leq \rho, \lambda \leq 1$. The ultimatum game corresponds to $\rho = 0$ and $\lambda = 0$ whereas $\rho = 1$ and $\lambda = 1$ represent dictatorship (the responder has lost all veto power). Similarly, one can study $\rho = 1$ and $\lambda = 0$, the so-called 'impunity game' (see, for experimental studies of 'corner-point games', Bolton and Zwick, 1995, as well as Güth and Huck, 1997) but also 'interior games' like $0 < \rho = \lambda < 1$ (see Suleiman, 1996) or $0 < \rho = 1 - \lambda < 1$ (see Fellner and Güth, 2003). The general conclusion is that behavior strongly depends on how efficiently the responder can punish the proposer.

A more complex game may, for instance, try to combine the aspects of ultimatum bargaining and dictatorship. If one includes, for instance, a dummy player in addition to the proposer and the responder an ultimatum proposal would consist of two offers o_R and o_D with $o_R, o_D \geq 0$ and $o_R + o_D \leq p$ meaning that the proposer offers o_R to the responder R and o_D to the dummy D and wants to keep $p - o_R - o_D$ and that rejection by R implies zero profits for all (see Güth and van Damme, 1998; Brandstätter and Güth, 2002; Güth, Schmidt and Sutter, 2002; for experimental studies). The fact that (according to the results of Güth and van Damme, 1998) o_D was usually much smaller than o_R, and no rejection by R could be attributed to an embarrassingly low asymmetric o_D alone, seems to suggest that neither proposers nor responders have a strong intrinsic concern for fairness. They rather seem to care only for their own share (see, for a theoretical discussion, Bolton and Ockenfels, 1998).

Another escape route is to 'repair' the representation of the experimental situation: for example, by assuming that utilities depend not only on profits, but also on their distribution, or on a desire for reciprocity, or on what one participant thinks is expected by the other(s). These repairs do not allow questioning rationality, but only adjust the representation of the experimental situation (game fitting). The problem, of course, is that nearly all results can be 'saved' in this way, so 'repairs' should be at least reasonable and intuitive. For instance, it is obvious that we often care about the distribution of rewards, but when and why we do so already appears to be a cognitive result rather than a given.

A more recently developed escape route may be termed the 'throw out the baby with the bath water' approach. Inspired by the development of 'evolutionary theory' – which is based partly on evolutionary biology and partly revives an earlier research tradition of learning theories in psychology – this offers two alternative approaches. Either one denies cognition entirely (by assuming pre-programmed phenotypical behavior, as in orthodox evolutionary biology) or one restricts rationality more or less (in reinforcement or stimulus–response learning, for instance, one uses a strategy with higher probability than another simply because it yielded a higher payoff level in past plays). Initially behavior can take any form, but often the claim is that it will converge to equilibrium behavior. The most prominent evolutionary dynamics are the *replicator* dynamics. Other adaptation dynamics are *best-reply* dynamics, *reinforcement* or *stimulus–response learning*, and *imitation* processes. To determine the stable behavior one relies partly on static concepts (for example, evolutionarily stable strategies) instead of analyzing the (stable) rest points of adaptation over time.

This theoretical discussion, and progress in developing software packages for computerized experiments, has inspired a very new type of experiment. The same group of participants plays the same base game (e.g. a 2 $\times$2-bimatrix game) repeatedly with randomly changing partners. This research tradition is too recent to permit any general conclusions about how people adapt to past experiences, and how such path dependence is combined with undeniable strategic deliberations. One rather robust result is that behavior in two-person coordination games converges to strict equilibria, but not necessarily to the payoff-dominating strict equilibrium (see section 8 below). It is striking, however, to observe how closely theoretical exercises of adaptive dynamics and experimental studies are related to each other.

If the same simple game is played very frequently boredom might lead players to seek variety. In studies of robust learning (see Güth, 2002, for a selective account), where participants confront repeatedly a variety of related games instead of just one such game, this seems less likely, however.

A third reaction to the typical results of strategic game experiments is the 'bounded rationality approach', which denies all the givens of normative decision and game theory such as given strategy sets, given evaluations of plays, given Bayesian beliefs, and unlimited cognitive and information-processing capabilities.

When one makes decisions, and which options one considers, are often the first steps in one's deliberation process. Furthermore, no evaluation of the results is readily available. Instead one has to decide upon reasonable goals and assess their (relative) importance: for example, in order to satisfy multiple objectives. In case of conflicting concerns in ultimatum bargaining (for example, between the desire to be fair and to earn as much as possible as a proposer) one often avoids cognitive dissonance (Festinger, 1957) by suppressing one of the goals (perhaps by viewing the situation simply as a fair division task and offering $o = p/2$). Rather than forming Bayesian judgments as to how likely different possible offers o are accepted, a player will simply distinguish offers o (close to $o = p/2$) which are clearly acceptable and choose the lowest among those. Finally, explanations of experimental results should rely on the deliberations which human decision makers are likely to perform when confronting such a decision problem. (If theorists need months to derive the equilibrium, how should experimental participants derive it during an experiment?)

4   Alternating offer bargaining

The experimental results of ultimatum bargaining provoked a lively debate among game theorists as to whether or not orthodox game theory is just a normative exercise that has little value in application. As in decision tasks, the question is whether rationality explains experimental behavior (at least by experienced participants), or whether orthodox theory has to be supplemented by a behavioral theory: one which pays more attention to psychological ideas than to elegant axiomatic characterizations.

One typical reaction to striking experimental results is to ask how the results will change when the experimental setup is altered to some degree. In the case of ultimatum bargaining, it has been argued that fairness may matter less when parties are not limited to only one negotiation round for reaching an agreement. The guiding model for this line of experimental research is that of *alternating offer bargaining* (e.g. Rubinstein, 1982). In odd rounds t player 1 offers and player 2 responds; in even rounds t the roles are reversed. Agreement is achieved if an offer is accepted. Otherwise, one proceeds to the next round (except in the last round when non-acceptance means conflict, implying zero payoffs). Assume for example that T, the number of the last round, is a large odd integer (player 1 is the last proposer) and that the same 'pie' p can be divided, regardless of the round in which $t = 1, \ldots, T$ an agreement is achieved. Surprisingly, no such experiment has yet been explored (to the best of our knowledge). The solution outcome is, of course, the same as in the case $T = 1$. In an experiment, however, participants might learn from unsuccessful offers in earlier periods $t < T$ how issues of fairness matter. Yet the usual assumption in experimental studies has been that delaying agreement is costly (i.e. the risks posed by a shrinking 'pie').

There are now several experimental studies of alternating offer bargaining (see Güth, 1995, and Roth, 1995b, for surveys) which vary the time preferences involved (for example, in the form of equal or unequal discount factors) and the horizon (the maximum number of rounds). The latter is, of course, finite although one study (Weg and Rapoport, Felsenthal, 1990) tries to create an illusion of an infinite horizon. Another study (Güth, Ockenfels and Wendel, 1993) assumes that every periodic proposer can declare his or her offer to be an ultimatum, and that the 'pie' p is increasing instead of decreasing. As in a centipede experiment both participants here can gain by trusting (i.e. by not terminating early): this happens in nearly half of the plays, although this tendency could of course be exploited. The explanation of the 'centipede results' in terms of (expected) altruism (in the tradition of reputation equilibria: see McKelvey and Palfrey, 1992) cannot account for the increasing 'pie' results.

Whereas all these models rely on asymmetric bargaining rules, among the symmetrical bargaining models the so-called (Nash) 'demand game' has received the most attention (Nash, 1950, 1953). Here all parties simultaneously choose their demands, which are what they obtain whenever the vector of demands is feasible; otherwise they receive their conflict payoffs. An interesting study by Roth and Malouf, 1979, applies the binary lottery technique when studying demand bargaining (allowing, however, for several rounds of simultaneous demands). Parties can earn individual positive monetary prizes, and only bargain about the probability of winning their prize (with complementary probability, the other party wins its prize). What is varied systematically is the information available about the other's prize. When prize information is completely private, parties usually agree on equal winning probabilities. If both prizes are generally known, parties choose winning probabilities that equate their monetary expectations. This, of course, violates the axiom of independence with respect to affine utility transformations.

Owing to the usually large number of strict equilibria (all efficient vectors of demands exceeding conflict payoffs), participants in the demand game face an additional coordination problem which might justify introducing pre-play communication or more strategic possibilities; see section 7 below. The main findings are that the (Nash) bargaining solution maximizing the product of agreement dividends must be focal (e.g. as a corner point of a piecewise linear utility frontier) to be selected and that the (Nash) axioms, although normatively convincing, are behaviorally questionable. Experimentally, the monotonicity axiom (Kalai and Smorodinsky, 1975) is better supported. Other topics in experimental (non-cooperative) games, often related to strategic market games, can be found in handbooks and in introductions to experimental economics.

5   Characteristic function experiments

Experimental game theory, like orthodox game theory, was dominated at first by characteristic function models. Of course, it is not at all clear a priori how to implement a given characteristic function as an experiment (it is not, after all, a strategic game). The usual procedure is to permit free face-to-face communication and to let coalitions announce payoff agreements, which become binding if no coalition member withdraws within a certain number of minutes.

Given the usual heterogeneity in individuals' behavior, value concepts were rarely used, although they may become important in accounting experiments: among these, reward or cost allocation experiments (Mikula, 1973; Shapiro, 1975) may offer early, but (too) simple, precedents. But in most studies (see Sauermann (ed.), 1978a, 1978b) the well-known set solutions, like the core, internally, and externally stable sets, or the various bargaining sets, were tested, or new related concepts developed.

Robust results (see Selten and Uhlich, 1988; Sauermann (ed.), 1978a, 1978b) are that

- players in the same coalition obey the power structure (by granting a more powerful coalition member at least as much as a less powerful one);
- equal payoff distributions are frequently proposed, and often used as counter-proposals when trying to argue against a previous proposal; and
- coalitions smaller than the grand coalition are formed, even when they are inefficient.

Characteristic function experiments were not only performed by game theorists, but also by (social) psychologists. A typical situation is to rely on majority voting games $(w_1, . . ., w_n; m)$ where w_i with $0 \leq w_i \leq 1$ and $w_1 + . . . + w_n = 1$ denotes the voting share of player $i = 1, .., n$ and m with $1/2 \leq m \leq 1$, mostly $m = 0.5$, the majority level which a winning coalition S with $\Sigma_{i \in S} w_i > m$ must obtain. The characteristic function $v(\cdot)$ allowing for side payments assumes $v(S) = 1$ if S is winning and $v(S) = 0$ otherwise. In the case of $n = 3$, $m = 0.5$ and $w_1 = 0.49$, $w_2 = 0.39$, $w_3 = 0.12$ one has $v(\{i\}) = 0$ for $i = 1, 2, 3$, and $v(S) = 1$ for any coalition S with at least two members. Thus the power structure, as reflected by the winning coalitions, is completely symmetric despite the large differences in voting shares. In such a situation, experimentally observed payoff distributions are often influenced by both the power structure and the voting shares (see Komorita and Chertkoff, 1973).

Because of the dominance of strategic models in the industrial organization literature, characteristic function experiments became a less popular research topic. Since strategic models seem to account for every possible result without any serious restrictions on what to assume (see the discussion of 'repairs', above) there may, however, be a revival of characteristic function experiments for special situations where cooperative solutions are informative: for example, in the sense of a small, but non-empty core. The main advantage would be that such informative solutions do not depend on subtle strategic aspects that often are behaviorally irrelevant, although crucial to non-cooperative solution. An example is the sequential timing of moves in ultimatum bargaining whose characteristic function is, however, symmetrical in the sense of $v(\{i\}) = 0$ for both players i and $v(N) = p$ for the grand coalition N consisting of both players.

6 Macroeconomic experiments

The experience made with microeconomic experiments encouraged some economists to extend experimental investigations to *macroeconomic problems*. In this type of experiment individuals or small teams have to make decisions which have an impact on the macroeconomic performance of a stylized economy. The KRESKO game (Tietz, 1973) was one of the first attempts to conduct a macroeconomic experiment. The KRESKO economy is a macroeconomic model with five sectors (industrial sector, households, credit banks, the central bank, and the government) which are linked by five markets. The economic decision processes can be simulated by using rules of 'aspiration adaptation and balancing'.

In a KRESKO experiment there are three groups playing the roles of (1) the employers' association, (2) the labor union, and (3) the central bank. Employers' associations and trade unions bargain on the standard wage rate and the standard working hours weekly. The central bank player has to decide on ten monetary policy variables. Besides this, the central bank player is allowed to make suggestions on bargaining variables during bargaining sessions. After each bargaining round the macroeconomics consequences of the decisions are derived and announced.

The KRESKO project generated a lot of data which have partly been evaluated in sequel papers by Tietz and other authors (see Tietz and Weber, 1972; Tietz and Assmus, 1972). The main results of the project concern wage bargaining procedures. Tietz *et al.* investigate, for example, the determinants of concessions in wage bargaining by comparing their results with Zeuthen's bargaining theory (Zeuthen, 1930) and they analyze the role of aspiration levels (elicited by questionnaires for preparing decision behavior) in bargaining. Instead of experimenting further with rather complex macroeconomic models, experimental research after the KRESKO project focused on selected macroeconomic problems of which *wage bargaining* was one of the most popular topics. Although the motivation of such studies is to learn about macroeconomic relationships, they often employ a microeconomic setting (without providing a macroeconomic background).

7 Wage bargaining experiments

Several experiments on wage bargaining are concerned with the problem of *centralization in bargaining*. These experiments were motivated by empirical results of Calmfors and Driffill (1988) which seem to show that the degree of centralization of wage bargaining procedures in an economy has an impact on macroeconomic performance. Countries with a low level of centralization (e.g., USA, Canada) or a high level of centralization (e.g., Austria, Sweden) are characterized by low wage levels while countries with a moderate level of centralization (e.g., Germany) have high wage rates. The opposite relation holds for the degree of centralization and the unemployment level. Up to now a satisfactory theoretical explanation of this phenomenon is still missing. In a series of experiments on 'centralized vs. decentralized bargaining' (Berninghaus *et al.*, 2001; Berninghaus, Güth and Keser, 2002) it was investigated whether a tendency to centralized bargaining can be observed at all when trade unions have the choice to centralize.

We briefly review here some results of Berninghaus, Güth and Keser (2002). In these experiments there are three players, X, Y and Z. These players can negotiate either in a decentralized way or collectively. In decentralized bargaining, X negotiates with Z about the allocation of a 'pie' P_{XZ}, and, independently, Y negotiates with Z about the allocation of a 'pie' P_{YZ} ($= P_{XZ}$). In the case of collective bargaining, X and Y merge into a new player XY who then bargains with Z about the allocation of the total 'pie' P_{XYZ} ($= 2 P_{XZ}$). Whatever XY earns is equally divided between X and Y. Let i and j denote one of the two bargaining parties; that is, (i, j) is either (X, Z) or (Y, Z) or (XY, Z). A modified bargaining procedure of Nash (1950, 1953) is applied: each of the two parties $k = i, j$ chooses a *demand* D_k and a *bottom line* B_k with $P_{ij} \geq D_k \geq B_k \geq C_k$, where $C_k (\geq 0)$ denotes the *conflict payoff* of party k. Given the vector (D_i, B_i, D_j, B_j) of bargaining choices and the size of the 'pie' P_{ij}, a *demand agreement* is reached if $D_i + D_j \leq P_{ij}$, whereas a *bottom line agreement* is reached in the case of no demand agreement and $B_i + B_j \leq P_{ij}$. While both parties $k = i, j$ obtain their demand D_k in the case of a demand agreement, their profits are determined by their bottom lines B_k in the case of a bottom line agreement. If neither of these two agreements is achieved, the two parties end up in *conflict* with conflict payoffs C_k.[1]

Conflict payoffs C_k depend on the pairing (i, j), therefore we write $C_k(i, j)$. It is an essential assumption that $C_Y(Y, Z) > C_X(X, Z)$ holds, that is, Y is stronger than X.

To solve this game theoretically, note that the acceptance borders are the (only) essential strategic variables. Obviously, in an efficient equilibrium the bargaining parties must choose $B_i + B_j = P_{ij}$. To select a unique efficient equilibrium outcome as a benchmark solution one relies on the Nash bargaining solution, which maximizes the product of the dividends $(B_k - C_k)$ for $k = i, j$. For example, for the pair $(i, j) = (X, Z)$ we maximize $(B_X - C_X(XZ)) (B_Z - C_Z(XZ))$ subject to $B_X + B_Z = P_{XZ}$.

In this experimental study, a situation was considered, where the stronger party Y has no interest in forming XY. Therefore, condition $B^*_Y > B^*_{XY}/2$ had to be satisfied by the solution choices. Of the three players only X has positive incentives for centralizing. Our benchmark solution thus predicts decentralized bargaining. However, the experimental results show different behavior suggesting that 'centralization' helps. This might reflect a common experience or belief that one gains in strength by merging, based on factual or expected synergy. This sometimes finds expression in phrases like 'unity is strength' or, in German, 'Einigkeit macht stark'. Players also might view (the choice of) centralization as signaling, 'I am tough.'

It was observed in the experiments that in 51 per cent of the cases the stronger Y-players opt for collective bargaining, although it is not in their strategic interest: not only according to the theoretical benchmark solution, but also in the experiment (although this just fails significance), Y-players on average gain higher payoffs in decentralized than in collective bargaining. The decisions of collective bargaining made by Y-players might be influenced by some kind of inequality aversion with respect to the other players (Fehr and Schmidt, 1999; Bolton and Ockenfels, 2000). In collective bargaining, Z-players claim less than in decentralized bargaining. Thus, in collective bargaining Z-players gain significantly lower payoffs than in decentralized bargaining, their payoffs in collective bargaining still being higher than those of the X- or Y-players, however.[2] Demands and bottom lines are located around the equal split of the total 'pie' (not around equal dividends as supposed by the Nash bargaining solution). Obviously, fairness considerations similar to those observed in ultimatum bargaining experiments apply (see Roth, 1995b, for a survey). X- (and Y-) players who opt for collective bargaining claim (in collective bargaining) a larger share of the pie for themselves than those who opt for decentralized bargaining. This supports the common claim that by forming a coalition a bargaining side becomes more ambitious (*unity suggests strength!*), which, however, need not imply larger payoffs due to an increase of conflicts. Similar results could be derived in an experimental study by Berninghaus *et al.* (2001), in which a simplified framework has been used.[3]

Wage bargaining processes in industrialized countries are often accompanied by discussions about the 'true theory' on the impact of wage increases on macroeconomic performance. While trade union representatives emphasize the relevance of the so-called 'purchasing power argument', employers' representatives point to the 'labor cost argument' which predicts a decrease in aggregate investment when wage rates increase. The wage bargaining experiments by Kirstein, Ehrhart and Keser (2002) were motivated by this scenario. They modeled the problem as a two-person non-cooperative bargaining game in which the size of the 'pie' (gross national product) in the next round is affected by the bargaining result (division of the GNP) in the previous round. Purchasing power or wage cost arguments would require that the pie would only expand if the per period bargaining results (division of the GNP) would favor the workers or the employers. In one treatment of the experiments subjects were fully informed about the 'mathematical law of pie growth'. The 'variable pie size' bargaining process lasted 20 rounds. The experimental results show that subjects show a strong tendency towards 'equal division' although both bargaining partners suffer from significant welfare losses (induced by shrinking or stagnation of the pie). Only some periods before bargaining ends the bargaining partners gave up equal division in favor of divisions which maximize pie growth. Seen from a macroeconomic perspective this result is not very encouraging, for one cannot expect the outcome of wage bargaining processes to be in line with the true principles of economic growth (whatever these principles are).

8   Experiments on coordination games

During the past decade many experimental economists became interested in *coordination games*. By such games one can model interesting economic problems. In some stimulating papers (e.g., Bryant, 1983; Cooper and John, 1988; Cooper, 1999) the basic problems in coordination games were interpreted as problems of *macroeconomic market coordination* (with complementarities). Consider, for example, the problem of a 'big push' in less developed countries (see, e.g., Shleifer, Murphy and Vishny, 1989). It is characterized by a situation where all economic sectors with complementary products show large investment and innovation activities which result in maximal economic growth. If the investment decisions in the sectors are made independently of each other this situation can be regarded as a coordination game. As another well-known macroeconomic coordination problem, Bryant (1983) considered an 'input game' where different sectors producing complementary intermediate products choose their input for producing the macroeconomic product independently of each other. This game is characterized by multiple equilibria where the resulting output is determined by the minimum input level ('weakest link'). If all firms choose the lowest possible input level an unemployment equilibrium for the economy may arise.

A precise description of this strategic situation is the so called 'weakest link game'. This is a symmetric *n*-person game with a finite strategy set and payoff function

$$H(\sigma_i, \sigma_{-i}) = a \, min \, \{\sigma_1, \ldots \ldots, \sigma_n\} - b \, \sigma_i,$$

where $\sigma_i \in \Sigma$ denotes the strategy choice of player i and $\sigma_{-i} = (\sigma_1, \ldots \ldots, \sigma_{i-1}, \sigma_i + {}_1, \ldots \ldots, \sigma_n)$ denotes the strategy choice of i's opponents.

Furthermore, it is required that $a>b>0$ holds. According to Bryant (1983), one can interpret the weakest link game describing a joint production process in which each firm contributes a particular input level σ_i. Production is characterized by a Leontieff production function, and part of the output is supposed to be shared equally between the firms. After subtracting production costs $b\sigma_i$, the payoff of the game may be interpreted as firm i's profit. In experiments the strategy set is restricted to a finite subset of integers which represent different input levels. One can easily show that weakest link games have only symmetric equilibria which can be ranked according to their payoffs.

Experimental research on the weakest link game started with a stimulating study by Van Huyck, Battalio and Beil (1990) in which it was shown that players end up after a few periods at the minimum effort level, that is, at the worst equilibrium. The experimental design of this crucial experiment was characterized as follows: there were between 14 and 16 persons involved in ten fold repetitions of the weakest link base game. The strategy set was restricted to the natural numbers between 1 and 7. After each period, subjects were informed about the minimum input level as implied by all choices. No other information was disclosed.

Several later experimental studies show that the result obtained by Van Huyck, Battalio and Beil (in 1990) is remarkably robust. Strategic uncertainty among a 'large' number of players seems to be so important that players in a repeated weakest link game coordinate at best on the worst equilibrium. In the light of these results it seems hard to believe why such macroeconomic phenomena as the 'big push' or 'good equilibria' in commodity or labor markets should automatically come about when market participants decide independently of each other (like players in a normal form game).

After the publication of the basic results of Van Huyck, Battalio and Beil, many experimental researchers became attracted by this field. The direction of further research is to find an appropriate experimental design such that players in the repeated weakest link game automatically reach the best equilibrium. We present a brief survey of some selected results below.

Van Huyck, Battalio and Beil (1990) themselves found out that the **number of players** in the coordination game is an important determinant of equilibrium selection. In repeated two-person weakest link games coordination on the best equilibrium results occurred after few rounds. Obviously, with two players, strategic uncertainty about the opponent's strategy choice is significantly reduced.

Berninghaus and Ehrhart (1998) analyze the impact of the number of repetitions of a weakest link game on coordination failure. Their experimental results show that the number of repetitions actually has a significant impact. With an increasing number of repetitions, subjects show a significant tendency to coordinate on the best equilibria. One may hypothesize that players are more tolerant in coordination tasks when they expect more repetitions are yet to come. In a further study, Berninghaus and Ehrhart (2001) relax the original information assumption of Van Huyck, Battalio and Beil and show that an increasing 'degree' of information about the opponents' strategy choice (in the previous period) improves the equilibria on which players coordinate. For example, in the complete information treatment where each player is informed about the strategy choice of all the opponents (not only about the minimum input level) players show a clear tendency to coordinate on the best equilibrium.

Cooper *et al.* (1992a, 1992b) analyze the effects of unbinding preplay communication and the existence of outside options on equilibrium selection. If players can signal their action choice in the next period there is a clear preference for choosing the 'best' equilibrium. The same effect can be observed when players can choose between playing the coordination game or taking a certain amount of money (their outside option) instead. If the value of the outside option is between the best and worst equilibrium payoff a player can obtain in the coordination game, players who refuse the outside option signal their willingness to coordinate on the 'best' equilibrium (as suggested by forward induction; see Kohlberg and Mertens, 1986, for a theoretical underpinning).

The experiments by Cooper *et al.* are based on simple 2x2 coordination games (not on the weakest link games) in which the payoff dominant and the risk dominant equilibrium do not coincide.

9 Airwave auctions

Auctions have been an active field of experimentation (see Kagel, 1995, for a survey) which recently became an even hotter topic. The main reason for this were the so-called spectrum auctions which started in the 1990s in different countries. Several governments (USA, Australia, New Zealand) auctioned licenses to use the electromagnetic spectrum for personal communication: mobile telephones, two-way paging etc. The auctions conducted by the FCC (Federal Communications Commissions) were a great financial success which was acclaimed by the *New York Times* as the 'greatest auction in history'. It was not only a triumph for the FCC but also for game theory. The FCC has been advised by some leading game theorists[4] to choose an innovative form of auction and has over time tried out several alternative designs.

In contrast to selling a single item in traditional auction theory, which is now somewhat better understood, a general formal theory of the airwave auctions used in the previous decade by several governmental institutions is still missing. These auctions were designed as a simultaneous ascending multiple commodity auction. Only some selected aspects of these auctions have been analyzed formally (e.g. Cramton and Schwartz, 2000; Bolle and

Breitmoser, 2001). Although we do not have a satisfactory general theory the theoretical results obtained so far can at least strengthen our intuition for the design of further multiple commodity auctions.

Many spectrum auctions which have been conducted for allocating public rights to private firms used many elements of the FCC auctions, they even mimicked these rules completely. These stylized rules of the FCC can be summarized as follows (Cramton and Schwartz, 2000):

1. multiple individual licenses are sold simultaneously;
2. the auctions consist of multiple rounds and stop when no new bids are received on any license;
3. after each round all new bids and the respective identities of the bidders are disclosed;
4. objects are allocated to the highest bids, the winners have to pay for their bids;
5. one can only bid for single licenses, not for packages.

In all FCC-style auctions which have been conducted in Europe in 2000/2001 (in order to allocate the European UMTS spectra) the *simultaneous* multiple-rounds format was used. Why not use sequential auctions? Sequential auctions of the licenses can reveal information about the prices of later sold objects. This may reduce the winner's curse (it is often claimed that the financial success of some airwave auctions is the likely ruin of the bidding firms). However, in a sequential spectrum auction it may be difficult or even impossible to acquire a desired package of licenses, which may be important when the auctioned commodities exhibit some complementarities.

Multiple-round auctions are similar to infinitely repeated games with discount factors arbitrarily close to zero. From these games we know (Folk Theorem) that there exist collusive equilibria. Cramton and Schwartz (2000) show that participants in the FCC auctions indeed colluded.

Bidding for individual objects may be less appropriate when the values of the frequencies are interrelated. If a participant bids independently for the parts of a desired package he may only end up with a fraction of his desired package and may, therefore, not be able to benefit from spectrum complementarities. In a pioneering paper, Bernheim and Whinston (1986) analyzed auctions with multiple non-identical objects where participants could choose so-called 'combinatorial bids' (packages) and where all participants were completely informed. Under the same information assumption, Bolle and Breitmoser (2001) showed that with combinatorial bids one could reach efficient allocations of non-identical commodities.

Summarizing the discussion on FCC auctions so far, one can say that there is no (general) theory for spectrum auctions (see also Börgers and

Dustmann, 2002). Most theoretical inferences rely often on simplified assumptions which are necessarily made to cope with the complex auction forms which have actually been chosen by organizers of the spectrum auctions. In contrast to the vast body of theoretical and experimental literature on single object auctions there is only a small amount of literature on auctions with multiple but identical objects (e.g. Güth, 1986). And there are still fewer papers on auctions with multiple non-identical objects which are equivalent to spectrum auctions.

Concerning the experimental literature on spectrum auctions, the situation is even worse. We know of experiments in which the effects of several UMTS auction designs (Germany and the UK) have been tested (Ehrhart and Seifert, 2005). The main motivation of these experiments was to see which auction design works best for the market regulator, i.e. which works best in collecting revenues and allocating the licenses to those bidders who can make the best use of it. In the experiments a simplified version of the actually conducted auctions in Germany and the UK has been used. The principal idea of this auction design is that multiple objects (frequency spectra) are auctioned simultaneously. In every round a bidder can bid on any of the objects being offered. The auction ends when no new bid for any object is received.

In the experiment a private values setup was used. Participants were given a valuation function with a single value of each possible auction outcome. They had no information about the other bidders' valuations. In the German design in total seven bidders who participated in each session were classified with respect to their valuation function ('strong' bidders, 'weak' bidders). This particular ordering should reflect the difference in economic power (financial status, market share) between the firms which actually participated in the UMTS auctions. As in the actual German UMTS auction, participants could bid for two or three blocks out of a spectrum (of 12 identical blocks). Irrespective of one's type, in the German setup valuation depended on the number of blocks a bidder obtains and the number of bidders who are licensed, that is, who get at least two blocks by successful bidding. In the UK experimental setup there were two (identical) large licenses and three small licenses. Therefore, a bidder's valuation in the UK experiment consisted only of two numbers (the value of the large and the value of the small license). In contrast to the real UK auction, there was no restriction on which licenses participants were allowed to bid.

The German and the UK experiments were conducted by seven sessions each. The experimental results differed in the following selected points: the auctioneer collected larger revenues in the German design, and the average bidder surplus is significantly larger in the UK experiment whereas it is even (a bit) negative in the German experiment. In interpreting these results one has to be careful. The higher revenues in the German experiment might be generated exclusively by the negative surpluses of the relatively inexperienced bidders in the experiments. Furthermore, the outcomes of the real UMTS auctions could not be reproduced at all by the experiments and only in very few sessions could an efficient outcome be observed. More experimental studies on this topic seem to be necessary.

10   Where next for experimental economics?

Even if one is convinced that humans behave in ways other than those predicted by orthodox theory, it is still possible to learn a great deal from reasonable neoclassical repairs (which do not question rationality but only the representation of an experimental situation), so long as they are based on obvious motives, emotions etc. When a situation is relatively simple, so that even a boundedly rational participant can easily understand it, the 'rational choice' approach to explaining unexpected experimental results will often reflect how participants derive their decisions. The tradition of enriching models (fitting games to match earlier experimental results) and testing their solutions by new experiments will therefore continue.

On the other hand, more and more ideas from other social sciences, especially from cognitive and social psychology, will be imported into experimental and behavioral economics, since they are often mentioned (in 'think-aloud' studies, or in experiments with team players) by participants when asked to explain their deliberation processes. This line of research in experimental economics will still borrow its terminology, paradigms and (normative) benchmarks from orthodox theory but otherwise will rely on fundamentally different cognitive deliberations. One may prefer to accept satisficing outcomes rather than strive for optimal returns, and may sometimes be obliged (e.g. in small group situations) to obey social norms and conventions rather than exploit the own advantage to the full. This does not amount to a claim that *homo sapiens* is never rational or opportunistic. If a decision problem is simple enough, rational and boundedly rational behaviors will often coincide. Furthermore in certain situations, as on large markets, the prevailing behavior will be opportunistic simply because alternative behavior is strongly selected against (does not survive). Adopting the same behavior in small-group interactions, however, might lead to (social) isolation (ostracism).

Experimental results have suggested that observed behavior responds differently to subtle aspects than predicted by orthodox theory. This could revive the former tradition of characteristic function experiments, and of explanations rooted in cooperative game theory. Along these lines, the equal split in ultimatum bargaining could be due to the fact that this is the Shapley value, the kernel, or the nucleolus of its characteristic function.

Too large a solution set for a specific characteristic function, however, would not provide a clear benchmark. Therefore, if interest in characteristic function experiments is revived, we expect that it will be focused on cooperative games with small solution sets.

Finally, new policy problems such as how to set up airwave auctions will continuously bring about new research questions for experimental research, even when (as in airwave auctions) theory lags behind. As with test markets in marketing research experiments will often be an adequate means to generate reasonable expectations for the likely effects of institutional reforms. This could inspire the demand for experimentation. We do, however, also foresee likely frustration by what is accomplished in experimental economics. One often will experience that in the field certain aspects matter differently than in our usually very stylized experiments. Furthermore, as in the industrial organization and the evolutionary economics literature, there is such an abundance of studies with partly contrary results that one hardly can derive any guidance from such ambiguous findings. There is certainly also the possibility to 'frame' experiments in ways such that the 'desired results' will be observed.

Notes

1. The reason for splitting up the bargaining choice into demand and bottom line is that, although game theory does not account for this, it seems to help the parties to coordinate more easily on how to split the surplus. Behaviorally speaking, demands can aim at an efficient allocation, whereas bottom lines can be seen as a way to avoid conflict. Participants can also try to reach their higher aspirations by high demands and play safe using more modest bottom lines.
2. The theories by Fehr and Schmidt (1999) and Bolton and Ockenfels (2000) account for the desire to reduce this payoff advantage of Z-players. Whereas Fehr and Schmidt also allow that Y-players care for the well-being of players X, such a concern is ruled out by Bolton and Ockenfels.
3. This model allows for only two contracts.
4. A major role in designing the spectrum auctions has been played by game theorists like Milgrom, Wilson, McAffee, McMillan and Cramton.

Bibliography

Allais, M. (1953). Fondements d'une théorie positive des choix comportant un risque et critique des postulats et axiomes de L'Ecole Américaine, *Econometrica*, **40**, 257–332.

Anderhub, V. and Güth, W. (1999). On intertemporal allocation behavior: a selective survey of saving experiments, *Ifo-Studien*, **3**, 303–33.

Anderhub, V., Engelmann, D. and Güth, W. (2002). An experimental study of the repeated trust game with incomplete information, *Journal of Economic Behavior and Organization*, **48**, 197–216.

Anderhub, V., Güth, W., Kamecke, U. and Normann, H.-T. (2002). Capacity choices and price competition in experimental markets, *Experimental Economics*, **6**, 27–52.

Andreoni, J. (1988). Privately provided public goods in a large economy: the limits of altruism, *Journal of Public Economics*, **35**(1), 57–73.

Aumann, R. (1985). 'Repeated games', in G.R. Feiwel (ed.), *Issues in Contemporary Microeconomics and Welfare*, Albany, NY: State University of New York Press, pp. 209–42.

Aumann, R. (1995). Backward induction and common knowledge of rationality, *Games and Economic Behavior*, **8**, 6–19.

Aumann, R.J. and Maschler, M. (1964). 'The bargaining set for cooperative games', in M. Dresher, L.S. Shapley and A.W. Tucker (eds), *Advances in Game Theory*, Princeton, NJ: Princeton University Press, pp. 443–76 .

Axelrod, R. (1984). *The Evolution of Cooperation*, New York: Basic Books.

Becker, G.S. and Murphy, K.M. (1988). A theory of rational addiction, *Journal of Political Economy*, **96**, 675–700.

Becker, G.S., de Groot, M.H. and Marshak, J. (1963). An experimental study of some stochastic models for wagers, *Behavioral Science*, **8**, 199–202.

Bernheim, B.D. and Whinston, M.D. (1986). Menu auctions, resource allocation, and economic influence, *Quarterly Journal of Economics*, 1–31.

Berninghaus, S.K. and Ehrhart, K.-M. (1998). Time horizon and equilibrium selection in tacit coordination games: experimental results, *Journal of Economic Behavior and Organization*, **37**, 231–48.

Berninghaus, S.K. and Ehrhart, K.-M. (2001). Information and efficiency in coordination games: recent experimental results, in G. Debreu, W. Neuefeind, W. Trockel (eds), *Economic Essays*, New York: Springer, pp. 19–39.

Berninghaus, S.K., Güth, W. and Keser, C. (2002). Unity suggests strength: an experimental study of decentralized and collective bargaining, *Journal of Labour Economics*, **10**, 465–79.

Berninghaus, S.K., Güth, W., Lechler, R. and Ramser, H.-J. (2001). Decentralized versus collective bargaining: an experimental study, *International Journal of Game Theory*, **30**, 437–48.

Bicchieri, C. (1989). Self-refuting theories of strategic interaction: a paradox of common knowledge, *Erkenntnis*, **30**, 69–85.

Binmore K., Shaked, A. and Sutton, J. (1985). Testing noncooperative bargaining theory: a preliminary study, *American Economic Review*, **75**, 1178–80.

Bohm P., Lindén, J. and Sonnegard, J. (1997). Eliciting reservation prices: Becker–De Groot–Marschak mechanisms vs. markets, *Economic Journal*, **107**(443), 1079–89.

Bolle, F. and Breitmoser, Y. (2001). Spectrum auctions: how they should and how they should not be shaped, *Finanz Archiv*, **58**(3), 260–85.

Bolton, G. (1991). A comparative model of bargaining: theory and evidence, *American Economic Review*, **81**, 1096–136.

Bolton, G. and Ockenfels, A. (1998). An ERC-analysis of the Güth–van Damme game, *Journal of Mathematical Psychology*, **42**(2), 215–26.

Bolton, G. and Ockenfels, A. (2000). ERC: a theory of equity, reciprocity and competition, *American Economic Review*, **90**(1), 166–93.

Bolton, G. and Zwick, R. (1995). Anonymity versus punishment in ultimatum bargaining, *Games and Economic Behavior*, **10**, 95–121.

Börgers, T. and Dustmann, C. (2002). The British UMTs auction: a response to Klemperer and Schmidt, *Ifo Studien*, **48**, 121–2.

Brandstätter, H. and Güth, W. (2002). Personality in dictator and ultimatum games, *Central European Journal of Operations Research*, **3**(10), 191–215.

Bryant, J. (1983). A simple rational expectations Keynes-type model, *Quarterly Journal of Economics*, **97**, 525–9.

Bush, E. and Mosteller, F. (1955). *Stochastic Models for Learning*, New York: Wiley.

Calmfors, L. and Driffill, J. (1988). Bargaining structure, corporatism and macroeconomic performance, *Economic Policy*, **6**, 14–61.

Camerer, C. (1995). 'Individual decision making', in J.H. Kagel and A.E. Roth (eds), *Handbook of Experimental Economics*, Princeton, NJ: Princeton University Press, pp. 587–703.

Chamberlin, E.H. (1948). An experimental imperfect market, *Journal of Political Economy*, **56**, 95–108.

Cooper, R.W. (1999). *Coordination Games*, Cambridge: Cambridge University Press.

Cooper, R.W. and John, A. (1988). Coordinating coordination failures in Keynesian models, *Quarterly Journal of Economics*, **103**, 441–63.

Cooper, R.W., De Jong, D.V., Forsythe, R. and Ross, T.W. (1992a). Forward induction in coordination games, *Economics Letters*, **40**, 167–72.

Cooper, R.W., De Jong, D.V., Forsythe, R. and Ross, T.W. (1992b). Communication in coordination games, *Quarterly Journal of Economics*, **107**, 739–71.

Cournot, A.A. (1838). *Recherches sur les Principes Mathématiques de la Théorie des Richesses*, Paris: Hachette; English trans: *Researches into the Mathematical Principles of the Theory of Wealth*, New York: Macmillan, 1897.

Cramton, P. and Schwartz, J. (2000). Collusive bidding: lessons from the FCC spectrum auctions, *Journal of Regulatory Economics*, **17**, 229–52.

Davis, D.D. and Holt, C.A. (1993). *Experimental Economics*, Princeton, NJ: Princeton University Press.

Edgeworth, F.Y. (1881). *Mathematical Psychics: An Essay on the Application of Mathematics to the Moral Sciences*, London: Kegan.

Ehrhart, K. and Seifert, S. (2005). The design of the 3G license auctions in the UK and Germany, *German Economic Review*, **6**(2), May, 229–48.

Fehr, E. and Schmidt, K.M. (1999). A theory of fairness, competition and cooperation. *Quarterly Journal of Economics*, **114**, 817–68.

Fellner, G. and Güth, W. (2003). What limits escalation? Varying threat power in an ultimatum experiment, *Economics Letters*, **80**, 53–60.

Festinger, L. (1957). *A Theory of Cognitive Dissonance*, Stanford: Stanford University Press.

Fischbacher, U. (1999). Z-Tree: Zurich toolbox for readymade economic experiments, working paper no. 21, Institute for Empirical Research in Economics, University of Zurich.

Fouraker, L.E. and Siegel, S. (1963). *Bargaining Behavior*, New York: McGraw-Hill.

Friedman, D. and Sunder, S. (1994). *Experimental Methods: A Primer for Economists*, Cambridge: Cambridge University Press.

Gale, J.K., Binmore, G. and Samuelson, L. (1995). Learning to be imperfect: the ultimatum game, *Games and Economic Behavior*, **8**(1), 56–90.

Geanakoplos J., Pearce, D. and Stacchetti, E. (1989). Psychological games and sequential rationality, *Games and Economic Behavior*, **1**(1), 60–79.

Güth, W. (1986). Auctions, public tenders, and fair division games: an axiomatic approach, *Mathematical Social Sciences*, **11**, 283–94.

Güth, W. (1995). On ultimate bargaining – a personal review, *Journal of Economic Behavioural Organization*, **27**, 329–44.

Güth, W. (2002). 'Robust learning experiments', in F. Andersson and H. Holm (eds), *Experimental Economics: Financial Markets, Auctions, and Decision Making, Interviews and Contributions from the 20th Arne Ryde Symposium*, Lund University: Kluwer Academic Publishers.

Güth, W. and Huck, S. (1997). From ultimatum bargaining to dictatorship – an experimental study of four games varying in veto power, *Metroeconomica*, **48**, 262–79.

Güth, W. and van Damme, E. (1998). Information, strategic behavior, and fairness in ultimatum bargaining: an experimental study, *Journal of Mathematical Psychology*, **42**, 227–47.

Güth, W., Ockenfels, P. and Wendel, M. (1993). Efficiency by trust in fairness? Multiperiod ultimatum bargaining experiments with an increasing pie, *International Journal of Game Theory*, **22**, 51–73.

Güth, W., Schmidt, C. and Sutter, M. (2002). Bargaining outside the lab – a newspaper experiment of a three-person ultimatum game, forthcoming in *The Economic Journal*, 2007.

Güth, W., Schmittberger, R. and Schwarze, B. (1982). An experimental analysis of ultimatum bargaining, *Journal of Economic Behavior and Organization*, **3**(4), 367–88.

Güth, W., Ivanova-Stenzel, R., Königstein, M. and Strobel, M. (2003). Learning to bid – an experimental study of bid functions in auctions and fair division games, *The Economic Journal*, **113**, 477–94.

Hammerstein, P. and Selten, R. (1994). 'Game theory and evolutionary biology', in R.J. Aumann and S. Hart (eds), *Handbook of Game Theory, Vol. 2*, Amsterdam: Elsevier, pp. 928–93.

Harrison, G.W. (1994). Expected utility theory and the experimentalists, *Empirical Economics*, **19**, 223–53.

Henning-Schmidt, H. (1999). *Bargaining in a Video Experiment: Determinants of Boundedly Rational Behavior*, Lecture Notes in Economics and Mathematical Systems, 467, Berlin, Heidelberg, New York: Springer.

Hey, J.D. (1991). *Experiments in Economics*, Oxford: Blackwell.
Hoggatt, A.C. (1959). An experimental business game, *Behavioral Science*, **4**, 192–203.
Huck, S. and Oechssler, J. (1999). The indirect evolutionary approach to explaining fair allocations, *Games and Economic Behavior*, **28**, 13–24.
Huck, S., Normann, H.-T. and Oechssler, J. (1999). Learning in Cournot oligopoly: an experiment, *Economic Journal*, **109**, C80–C95.
Kagel, J.H. (1995), Auctions: a survey of experimental research, in J.H. Kagel and A.E. Roth (eds), *Handbook of Experimental Economics*, Princeton, NJ: Princeton University Press, pp. 501–35.
Kagel, J.H. and Roth, A.E. (1995). *Handbook of Experimental Economics*, Princeton, NJ: Princeton University Press.
Kahneman, D. and Tversky, A. (1986). Rational choice and the framing of decisions, *Journal of Business*, **59**(4), pt 2, 251–78.
Kahneman, D. and Tversky, A. (1992). Advances in prospect theory: cumulative representation of uncertainty, *Journal of Risk and Uncertainty*, **5**(4), 297–323.
Kalai, E. and Smorodinsky, M. (1975). Other solutions to Nash's bargaining problem, *Econometrica*, **43**, 513–18.
Kalish, G., Milnor, J.W., Nash, J.F. and Nering, E.D. (1954). 'Some experimental n-person games', in R.M. Thrall, C.H. Coombs and R.L. Davis (eds), *Decision Processes*, New York: Wiley, pp. 301–28.
Kirchsteiger, G. (1994). The role of envy in ultimatum games, *Journal of Economic Behavior and Organization*, **25**(3), 373–89.
Kirstein, A., Ehrhart, K-M. and Keser, C. (2002). Efficiency versus equity in bargaining: a theoretical and experimental analysis, Universität Karlsruhe, Institute WIOR, mimeo.
Kohlberg, E. and Mertens, J.-F. (1986). On the strategic stability of equilibria, *Econometrica*, **54**, 1003–38.
Komorita, S.S. and Chertkoff, J.M. (1973). A bargaining theory of coalition formation, *Psychological Review*, **80**, 149–62.
Kreps, D., Milgrom, P., Roberts, J. and Wilson, R.A. (1982). Rational cooperation in the finitely repeated prisoners' dilemma, *Journal of Economic Theory*, **27**, 245–52.
Maynard Smith, J. and Price, G.R. (1973). The logic of animal conflict, *Nature*, **246**, 15–18.
McKelvey, R.D. and Palfrey, T. (1992). An experimental study of the centipede game, *Econometrica*, **60**, 803–36.
Mikula, G. (1973). Gewinnaufteilungsverhalten in Dyaden bei variiertem Leistungsverhältnis, *Zeitschrift für Sozialpsychologie*, **3**, 126–33.
Modigliani, F. and Brumberg, R. (1954). Utility analysis and the consumption function: an interpretation of cross-section data, in K.K. Kurihara (ed.), *Post-Keynsian Economics*, New Brunswick, NJ: Rutgers University, pp. 388–436.
Nash, J.F. (1950). The bargaining problem, *Econometrica*, **18**, 155–62.
Nash, J.F. (1953). Two-person cooperative games, *Econometrica*, **21**, 128–40.
Nydegger, R.V. and Owen, G. (1975). Two person bargaining: an experimental test of the Nash axioms, *International Journal of Game Theory*, **3**, 239–349.
Peleg, B. and Tijs, S. (1996). The consistency principle for games in strategic forms, *International Journal of Game Theory*, **25**(1), 13–34.
Pruitt, D.G. 1967. Reward structure and cooperation: the decomposed prisoner's dilemma game, *Journal of Personality and Social Psychology*, **7**, 21–7.
Rabin, M. (1993). Incorporating fairness into game theory and economics, *American Economic Review*, **83**(5), 1281–302.
Rapoport, A. and Chammah, A.M. (1965). *Prisoner's Dilemma: A Study in Conflict and Cooperation*, Ann Arbor, MI: University of Michigan Press.
Roth, A.E. (1995a). 'Introduction to experimental economics', in J.H. Kagel and A.E. Roth (eds), *Handbook of Experimental Economics*, Princeton, NJ: Princeton University Press, pp. 3–109.
Roth, A.E. (1995b). 'Bargaining experiments', in J.H. Kagel and A.E. Roth (eds), *Handbook of Experimental Economics*, Princeton, NJ: Princeton University Press, pp. 253–348.
Roth, A.E. and Malouf, M.W.K. (1979). Game theoretic models and the role of information in bargaining, *Psychological Review*, **86**, 574–94.

Rubinstein, A. (1982). Perfect equilibrium in a bargaining model, *Econometrica*, **50**, 97–110.
Rubinstein, A. (1991). Comments on the interpretation of game theory, *Econometrica*, **59**, 909–24.
Sauermann, H. (1978a). *Bargaining Behavior, Contributions to Experimental Economics*, *Vol. 7*, Tübingen: Mohr.
Sauermann, H. (1978b). *Coalition – Former Behavior, Contributions to Experimental Economics*, *Vol. 8*, Tübingen: Mohr.
Sauermann, H. and Selten, R. (1959). Ein Oligopolexperiment, *Zeitschrift für die gesamte Staatswissenschaft*, **155**, 427–71; English trans: 'An experiment in oligopoly', in L. von Bartalanffy and A. Rapoport (eds), *General Systems Yearbook of the Society for General Systems Research*, **5**, Ann Arbor, MI: Society for General Systems Research, 1960, pp. 85–114.
Schmeidler, D. (1969). The nucleolus of a characteristic function game, *SIAM Journal of Applied Mathematics*, **17**, 1163–70.
Selten, R. and Stöcker, R. (1986). End behavior in sequences of finite prisoner's dilemma supergames: a learning theory approach, *Journal of Economic Behavior and Organization*, **7**(1), 47–70.
Selten, R. and Uhlich, G.R. (1988). Order of strength and exhaustivity as additional hypotheses in theories for three-person characteristic function games, in: *Bounded rational behavior in experimental games and markets: Proceedings of the Fourth Conference on Experimental Economics*, (Bielefeld, 21–25 September 1986), R. Tietz, W. Albers, R. Selten (eds), *Lecture Notes in Economics and Mathematical Systems*, **314**, 235–50, Berlin: Springer.
Shapiro, E.G. (1975). Effects of future interaction in reward allocation in dyads: equity or equality, *Journal of Personality and Social Psychology*, **31**, 873–80.
Shapley, L.S. (1953). A value for n-person games, in H.W. Kuhn and A.W. Tucker (eds), *Contributions to the Theory of Games II. Annals of Mathematical Studies Series*, **28**, Princeton, NJ: Princeton University Press, pp. 307–17.
Shleifer, A., Murphy, K.M. and Vishny, R. (1989). Industrialization and the big push, *Journal of Political Economy*, October, 1003–26.
Suleiman, R. (1996). Expectations and fairness in a modified ultimatum game, *Journal of Economic Psychology*, **17**, 531–54.
Taylor, P. and Jonker, L. (1978). Evolutionary stable strategies and game dynamics, *Mathematical Biosciences*, **40**, 145–56.
Tietz, R. (1973). Ein anspruchsanpassungsorientiertes Wachstums- und Konjunkturmodell (KRESKO), in H. Sauermann (ed.), *Beiträge zur experimentellen Wirtschaftsforschung IV*, Tübingen: J.C.B. Mohr, Paul Siebeck, pp. 267–88.
Tietz, R. and Assmus, V. (1972). Some experiences with regression analysis of the wage determination in the KRESKO-game, in H. Sauermann (ed.), *Beiträge zur experimentellen Wirtschaftsforschung IV*, Tübingen: J.C.B. Mohr, Paul Siebeck, pp. 300–304.
Tietz, R. and Weber, H.J. (1972). On the nature of the bargaining process in the KRESKO-game, in H. Sauermann (ed.), *Beiträge zur experimentellen Wirtschaftsforschung IV*, Tübingen: J.C.B. Mohr, Paul Siebeck, pp. 305–34.
Tirole, J. (1988). *The Theory of Industrial Organization*, Cambridge, MA: MIT Press.
Van Huyck, J., Battalio, R.C. and Beil, R.O. (1990). Tacit coordination games, strategic uncertainty and coordination failure, *American Economic Review*, **80**, 234–48.
von Neumann, J. and Morgenstern, O. (1944). *Theory of Games and Economic Behavior*, Princeton, NJ: Princeton University Press.
Weg E., Rapoport, A. and Felsenthal, D.S. (1990). Two-person bargaining behavior in fixed discounting factors games with infinite horizon, *Games and Economic Behavior*, **2**, 76–95.
Weibull, J.W. (1995). *Evolutionary Game Theory*, Cambridge, MA, London: MIT Press.
Zeuthen, F. (1930). *Problems of Monopoly and Warfare*, London: Routledge.

67 Complexity and the economy[*]
W. Brian Arthur

One theme that runs throughout Schumpeter's writings is that the economy is not in equilibrium: it is constantly forming and re-forming its structures. This theme has resurfaced recently in theoretical economics under the general heading of 'complexity'. Complexity economics explores not just 'solutions' to economic problems, but how these solutions form, and, as such, it could be called 'out-of-equilibrium' economics. Schumpeter would have felt at home in this new approach. And he would have recognized its emphasis on the emergence of patterns, perpetual novelty, and above all, process.

Let me start this survey of out-of-equilbrium economics by asking: what, in general, is complexity? There are many definitions and none is absolute. But common to all studies on complexity are systems with multiple elements adapting or reacting to the pattern these elements create. The elements might be cells in a cellular automaton, or ions in a spin glass, or cells in an immune system, and they may react to neighboring cells' states, or local magnetic moments, or concentrations of B and T cells – 'elements' and the 'patterns' they respond to vary from one context to another. But the elements adapt to the world (the aggregate pattern) they co-create. *Time* enters naturally here via adjustment and change: as the elements react, the aggregate changes, as the aggregate changes, elements react anew. Barring some asymptotic state or equilibrium reached, complex systems are systems in process, systems that constantly evolve and unfold over time. Thus complexity in the sciences is not a discipline. It is a movement that takes process seriously.

Why did the complexity movement come along in the late 1970s and early 1980s? The answer is simple. Generally, complex systems have no analytic 'solution'. The patterns that are in process of being formed are too complicated to be worked out analytically and hence are beyond analytic study. But with the computer we can get insight into the formation of patterns by directly simulating them, computing them and observing them as they form. Complexity as a movement came along in the late 1970s and early 1980s because at that time scientists got workstations.

Complex systems arise naturally in the economy. Economic agents, whether they are banks, consumers, firms, or investors, continually adjust their market moves, buying decisions, prices, and forecasts to the situation

[*] This chapter builds on an earlier article published in *Science* on April 2 1999, 284, 107–109.

these moves, decisions, prices or forecasts together create. But unlike ions in a spin glass which react dumbly to their local magnetic field, economic 'elements' (human agents) react with strategy and foresight by considering outcomes that *might* result as a consequence of behavior they *might* undertake. This adds a layer of complication to economics not experienced in physics or immunology.

Like most other sciences in pre-computer days, conventional economic theory chose not to study the unfolding of patterns its agents create, but rather to seek analytical solutions. To do this it needed to simplify its questions. Thus conventional theory asks what behavioral elements (actions, strategies, expectations) are consistent with the aggregate patterns these behavioral elements co-create. For example, general equilibrium theory asks: what prices and quantities of goods produced and consumed are consistent with (would pose no incentives for change to) the overall pattern of prices and quantities in the economy's markets? Game theory asks: what strategies, moves, or allocations are consistent with – would promote an optimal outcome for an agent (under some criterion) – given the strategies, moves, allocations his rivals might choose? Rational expectations economics asks: what forecasts (or expectations) are consistent with (are on average validated by) the outcomes these forecasts and expectations together create? Conventional economics thus studies patterns in behavioral *equilibrium*, patterns that would induce no further reaction. In the last few years, economists, at the Santa Fe Institute, Stanford, Wisconsin, MIT, Chicago, and other institutions, have begun to broaden this equilibrium approach by turning to the question of how actions, strategies or expectations might react in general to (might endogenously change with) the aggregate patterns these create (Anderson *et al.*, 1988; Arthur *et al.*, 1997). And so, this 'Santa Fe approach', or complexity approach, is not an adjunct to standard theory, but to theory at a more general level. It is out-of-equilibrium economics.

At this more general level, economic patterns sometimes simplify into a simple, homogeneous equilibrium; more often they are ever-changing, showing perpetually novel behavior and emergent phenomena. Let me illustrate perpetual novelty with a classic study of Kristian Lindgren (1991). Lindgren sets up a computerized tournament where strategies compete in randomly chosen pairs to play a repeated prisoner's dilemma game. Strategies that do well replicate and mutate. Ones that lose eventually die. Strategies can 'deepen' by using deeper memory of their past moves and their opponent's. A strategy's success of course depends on the current population of strategies, and so the elements here – strategies – in a sense react to, or change with, the competitive world they together create.

In his computerized tournament Lindgren discovered that the simple strategies in use at the start went unchallenged for some time. Tit-for-tat and other simple strategies dominated at the start. But then other, deeper strategies emerged that were able to exploit the mixture of these simple ones. In time, yet deeper strategies emerged to take advantage of those, and so on. If strategies got 'too smart' – too complicated – sometimes simple ones could exploit these. In this computer world of strategies, Lindgren found periods with very large numbers of diverse strategies in the population, and periods with few strategies; periods dominated by simple strategies, and periods dominated by deep strategies. But nothing ever settled down. In Lindgren's world, the set of strategies in use evolved and kept evolving in a world of perpetual novelty. This is unfamiliar to us in standard economics. Yet there is a realism about such dynamics with its unpredictable, emergent, and complicated sets of strategies. Chess play at the grand master level, for example, evolves over decades and never settles down. Lindgren's system is simple, yet it leads to a dynamic of endless unfolding and evolution. This is typical of complex system studies.

Positive feedbacks

The type of systems I have described, where elements react to the pattern the elements create, become interesting if they contain nonlinearities or positive feedbacks. To get some idea of how positive and negative feedback work, imagine a tray with water poured on it. First consider negative feedback: under gravity alone, the water flows away from any accumulation of water. And trivially a single, equilibrium water level is reached. A physicist would say that a single phase or single mode emerges: the equilibrium level of the water. This outcome is unique and perfectly predictable. Now let us add positive feedback. Take the same tray, polish it, and spread a thin film of water on it. Now surface tension – a form of positive feedback – becomes important. Under surface tension an agglomeration of water tends to attract neighboring molecules, so we have a mixture of positive and negative feedback of molecules attracting one another and flowing away from water. What happens? Droplets form. Do the experiment once and you get a pattern of droplets; do the experiment again and in all likelihood you get a different pattern of droplets, even though you are careful to start out with the same conditions. When there are positive feedbacks, small differences in temperature, small quantum effects, get magnified and change the outcome. It is therefore history dependent. It is also a pattern: it cannot be described by a single phase variable. It is not predictable. The presence of positive feedback leads to properties we associate with complexity.

In economics, positive feedback arises from increasing returns (Arthur, 1990a, 1994b). Standard economics usually assumes negative feedback, or diminishing returns, so as to ensure a unique, predictable equilibrium. If one firm gets too far ahead in the market, it runs into higher costs or some other negative feedback and the market is shared at a predictable, unique equilibrium. When we allow positive feedbacks or increasing returns, a different outcome arises. Suppose a new technology becomes available, nuclear power for example, in alternative versions *A* or *B* or *C* (light water, heavy water, gas-cooled, etc.) And suppose each technology improves as it becomes more adopted: there are increasing returns. Then if one technology gets far enough ahead it gains advantage and eventually may dominate. (In the nuclear case, light-water reactors almost completely dominate in the US.) Alternatively, consider the market for online services of a few years back, in which three major companies competed: Prodigy, CompuServe, and America Online. As each gained in membership base it could offer a wider menu of services as well as more members to share specialized hobby and chatroom interests with: there were increasing returns to expanding the membership base. Prodigy was first in the market, but by chance and strategy American Online got far enough ahead to gain an unassailable advantage. Today it dominates. Under different circumstances, another rival might have taken the market. Notice the properties here: a multiplicity of potential 'solutions'; the outcome actually reached is not predictable in advance; it tends to be locked in; it is not necessarily the most efficient economically; it is subject to the 'adoption path' taken; and, while the technologies may start equal, the outcome is asymmetrical. These properties have counterparts in nonlinear physics where similar positive feedbacks are present. What economists call multiple equilibria, non-predictability, lock-in, inefficiency, historical path dependence, and asymmetry, physicists call multiple meta-stable states, non-predictability, phase- or mode-locking, high-energy ground states, non-ergodicity, and symmetry breaking.

Increasing returns problems have been discussed in economics for a long time. A hundred years ago, in his *Principles*, Alfred Marshall (Marshall, 1891) noted that, if firms gain advantage as their market share increases, then 'the market goes to whichever firm first gets off to a good start'. But the conventional, static equilibrium approach gets stymied by indeterminacy: if there is a multiplicity of equilibria, how might one be reached? The process-oriented, complexity approach suggests a way to deal with this. In the actual economy, 'small random events' happen: in the technology case 'random' design improvements, word-of-mouth recommendations. Over time increasing returns magnifies the cumulation of such events to 'select' the outcome randomly. Thus increasing returns problems in economics are best seen as dynamic *processes* with random events and natural positive feedbacks, as nonlinear stochastic processes. This shift from a static outlook into a process orientation is common to complexity studies. Increasing returns problems are being studied intensively in market allocation theory (Arthur, 1994a), international trade theory (Helpman and Krugman, 1985), the evolution of technology choice (Arthur, 1989), economic geography (Arthur, 1990a; Krugman, 1991) and the evolution of patterns of poverty and segregation (Durlauf, 1997). The common finding that economic structures can crystal-lize around small events and lock-in is beginning to change policy in all these areas toward an awareness that governments should avoid both extremes of coercing a desired outcome or keeping strict hands off, and instead seek to push the system gently toward favored structures that can grow and emerge naturally. Not a heavy hand, not an invisible hand, but a nudging hand.

Expectational problems in economics

Once we adopt the complexity outlook, with its emphasis on the *formation* of structures rather than their given existence, problems involving prediction in the economy look different. The conventional approach asks what fore-casting model (or expectations) in a particular problem, if given and shared by all agents, would be consistent with (would be on average validated by) the actual time series this forecasting model would in part generate. This 'ratio-nal expectations' approach is valid, but it assumes that agents can somehow deduce in advance what model will work, and that everyone 'knows' that everyone knows to use this model (the *common knowledge* assumption.) What happens when forecasting models are not obvious and must be formed individually by agents who are not privy to the expectations of others?

Consider as an example my Bar or El Farol Problem (Arthur, 1994b). One hundred people must decide independently each week whether to show up at their favorite bar (*El Farol* in Santa Fe). The rule is that, if a person predicts that more that 60 (say) will attend, he will avoid the crowds and stay home; if he predicts fewer than 60 he will go. Of interest are how the bar-goers each week might predict the numbers showing up, and the result-ing dynamics of the numbers attending. Notice two features of this problem. Our agents will quickly realize that predictions of how many will attend depend on others' predictions of how many attend (because that determines their attendance). But others' predictions in turn depend on their predictions of others' predictions. Deductively there is an infinite regress, no 'correct' expectational model that can be assumed to be common knowledge, and from the agents' viewpoint, the problem is ill-defined. (This is true for most expectational problems, not just for this special case.) Second, and diabolically, any commonalty of expectations gets broken up: if all use an expectational model that predicts *few* will go, *all* will go, invalidating that model. Similarly, if all believe *most* will go, *nobody* will go, invalidating that belief. Expectations will be *forced* to differ.

In 1993, I modeled this situation by assuming that, as the agents visit the bar, they act inductively: they act as statisticians, each starting with a variety of subjectively chosen expectational models or forecasting hypotheses. Each

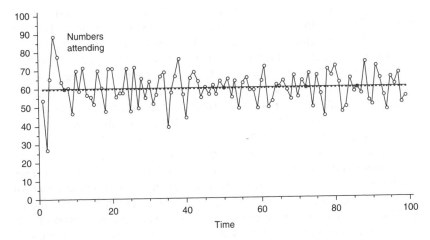

Figure 67.1   Bar attendance in the first 100 weeks

week they act on their currently most accurate model (call this their *active* predictor). Thus agents' beliefs or hypotheses compete for use in an *ecology* these beliefs create. Computer simulation (Figure 67.1) showed that the mean attendance quickly converges to 60. In fact, the predictors self-organize into an equilibrium pattern or 'ecology' in which, of the active predictors, on average 40 per cent are forecasting above 60, 60 per cent below 60. This emergent ecology is organic in nature. For, while the population of active predictors splits into this 60/40 average ratio, it keeps changing in membership forever. Why do the predictors self-organize so that 60 emerges as average attendance and forecasts split into a 60/40 ratio? Well, suppose 70 per cent of predictors forecast above 60 for a longish time, then on average only 30 people would show up. But then this would validate predictors that forecast close to 30, restoring the 'ecological' balance among predictions. Even though different predictors are used continually, over time the 40 per cent–60 per cent 'natural' combination becomes an emergent structure. As an expectational economy in miniature, the Bar Problem has become popular for study among physicists.

Financial markets
One important application of these ideas is in financial markets. Standard theories of financial markets assume rational expectations, that agents adopt uniform expectations (or forecasting models) that are on average validated by the prices these forecast (Lucas, 1978). The theory works well to first order, but it does not account for actual market 'anomalies' such as unexpected price bubbles and crashes, random periods of high and low volatility (price

variation), and the heavy use of technical trading (trades based on the recent history of price patterns). Holland, LeBaron, Palmer, Taylor and I (Arthur *et al.*, 1997) have created a model which relaxes rational expectations by assuming, as in the Bar Problem, that investors cannot assume or deduce expectations but must discover them. Our agents continually create and use multiple 'market hypotheses' – individual, subjective, expectational models – of what moves the market price and dividend within an artificial stock market on the computer. These 'investors' are individual, artificially intelligent computer programs that can generate and discard expectational 'hypotheses', and make bids or offers based on their currently most accurate of these. The stock price forms endogenously from the bids and offers of the agents, and thus ultimately from their expectations. So this market-in-the-machine is its own self-contained, simple, artificial financial world, like the bar, a 'mini-ecology' in which expectations compete in a world these expectations together create.

Within this computerized market, we found two phases or regimes. If parameters are set so that our artificial agents update their hypotheses slowly, the diversity of expectations collapses quickly into homogeneous rational expectation ones. The reason is that, if a majority of investors believes something close to the rational expectations forecast, then resulting prices will validate it, and deviant or mutant predictions that arise in the population of expectational models will be rendered inaccurate. Standard finance theory, under these special circumstances, is upheld. But if the rate of updating of hypotheses is turned up, the market undergoes a phase transition into a 'complex regime' and displays several of the 'anomalies' observed in real markets. It develops a rich 'psychology' of divergent beliefs that do not converge over time. Expectational rules such as 'If the market is trending up, predict a 1% price rise' that appear randomly in the population of hypotheses can become mutually reinforcing: if enough investors act on these, the price will indeed go up. Thus sub-populations of mutually reinforcing expectations arise, agents bet on these (therefore technical trading emerges) and this causes occasional bubbles and crashes. Our artificial market also shows periods of high volatility in prices followed randomly by periods of low volatility. This is because, if some investors 'discover' new, profitable hypotheses, they change the market slightly, causing other investors also to change *their* expectations. Changes in beliefs therefore ripple through the market in avalanches of all sizes, causing periods of high and low volatility. We conjecture that actual financial markets, which show exactly these phenomena, lie in this 'complex' regime.

Conclusion

After two centuries of studying equilibria – static patterns that call for no further behavioral adjustments – economists are beginning to study the general emergence of structures and unfolding of patterns in the economy. In the actual economy, agents continually adjust their behaviors to the aggregate 'pattern' these behaviors create. Economic theory has always recognized this, but until recently has simplified its approach to the identification of equilibrium states, where agents' behaviors are consistent with the aggregates these behaviors imply. In the last few years, economists have been turning to the wider question of how agents might continually respond endogenously to the patterns they create. Complexity economics is not a temporary adjunct to static economic theory, but theory at a more general, out-of-equilibrium level.

The approach is making itself felt in every area of economics: game theory (Lindgren, 1991; Young, 1993; Blume, 1997; Huberman and Glance, 1993); the theory of money and finance (Marimon *et al.*, 1990; Shubik, 1997; Brock *et al.*, 1995); learning in the economy (Sargent, 1993; Lane and Maxfield, 1997; Darley and Kauffman, 1997); economic history (North, 1997); the evolution of trading networks (Ioannides, 1997; Kirman, 1997; Tesfatsion, 1997); the stability of the economy (Bak *et al.*, 1993; Leijonhufvud, 1997); and political economy (Axelrod, 1986; Kollman *et al.*, 1997). It is helping us understand phenomena such as market instability, the emergence of monopolies, and the persistence of poverty in ways that will help us deal with these. And it is bringing an awareness that policies succeed better by influencing the natural processes of formation of economic structures than by forcing static outcomes.

When viewed in out-of-equilibrium formation, economic patterns sometimes simplify into a simple, homogeneous equilibrium of standard economics. More often they are ever-changing, showing perpetually novel behavior and yielding emergent phenomena. Complexity therefore portrays the economy, not as deterministic, predictable and mechanistic, but as process-dependent, organic and always evolving. It portrays the economy, in a word, as Schumpeterian.

References

Anderson, P., K.J. Arrow and D. Pines, (eds) (1988), *The Economy as an Evolving Complex System*, Reading, MA: Addison-Wesley.

Arthur, W.B. (1989), 'Competing technologies, increasing returns, and lock-in by historical events', *Economic Journal*, **99**, 116–31.

Arthur, W.B. (1990a), 'Silicon Valley locational clusters: when do increasing returns imply monopoly', *Mathematical Social Sciences*, **19**, 235–51.

Arthur, W.B. (1990b), 'Positive feedbacks in the economy', *Scientific American*, **262**, 92–9.

Arthur, W.B. (1994a), 'Inductive reasoning and bounded rationality', *American Economic Review*, **84**, 406–11.

Arthur, W.B. (1994b), *Increasing Returns and Path Dependence in the Economy*, Ann Arbor, MI: University of Michigan Press.

Arthur, W.B., J.H. Holland, B. LeBaron, R. Palmer and Paul Taylor (1997), *The Economy as an Evolving Complex System II*, Reading, MA: Addison-Wesley.

Axelrod, R. (1986), 'An evolutionary approach to norms', *American Political Science Review*, **80**, 1095–1111.
Bak, P., K. Chen, J. Scheinkman and M. Woodford (1993), 'Aggregate fluctuations from independent sectoral shocks: self-organized criticality in a model of production and inventory dynamics', *Ricerche Economiche*, **47**, 3–30.
Blume, L.E. (1997), 'Population games', in W.B. Arthur, S.N. Durlauf and D.A. Lane (eds), *The Economy as an Evolving Complex System II*, Reading, MA: Addison-Wesley, pp. 425–60.
Brock, W.A., P. de Lima, G.S. Maddala, H. Rao and H. Vinod (eds) (1995), *Handbook of Statistics 12: Finance*, Amsterdam: North-Holland.
Darley, V.M. and S.A. Kauffman (1997), 'Natural rationality', in W.B. Arthur, S.N. Durlauf and D.A. Lane (eds), *The Economy as an Evolving Complex System II*, Reading, MA: Addison-Wesley, pp. 425–60.
Durlauf, S.N. (1997), 'Statistical mechanics approaches to socioeconomic behavior', in W.B. Arthur, S.N. Durlauf and D.A. Lane (eds), *The Economy as an Evolving Complex System II*, Reading, MA: Addison-Wesley, pp. 129–68.
Helpman, E. and P.R. Krugman (1985), *Market Structure and Foreign Trade*, Cambridge, MA: MIT Press.
Huberman, B.A. and N.S. Glance (1993), 'Evolutionary games and computer simulations', *Proceedings of the National Academy of Science*, **90**, 7716–18.
Ioannides, Y.M. (1997), 'Evolution of trading structures', in W.B. Arthur, S.N. Durlauf and D.A. Lane (eds), *The Economy as an Evolving Complex System II*, Reading, MA: Addison-Wesley, pp. 129–68.
Kirman, A.P. (1997), 'The economy as an interactive system', in W.B. Arthur, S.N. Durlauf and D.A. Lane (eds), *The Economy as an Evolving Complex System II*, Reading, MA: Addison-Wesley, pp. 491–532.
Kollman, K., J.H. Miller, S.E. Page (1997), 'Computational political economy', in W.B. Arthur, S.N. Durlauf and D.A. Lane (eds), *The Economy as an Evolving Complex System II*, Reading, MA: Addison-Wesley, pp. 461–90.
Krugman, P.R. (1991), *Geography and Trade*, Cambridge, MA: MIT Press.
Lane, D.A. and R. Maxfield (1997), 'Foresight, complexity and strategy', in W.B. Arthur, S.N. Durlauf and D.A. Lane (eds), *The Economy as an Evolving Complex System II*, Reading, MA: Addison-Wesley, pp. 169–98.
Langton, C., C. Taylor, D.J. Farmer and R. Rasmussen (eds), *Artificial Life II*, Reading, MA: Addison-Wesley.
Leijonhufvud, A. (1997), 'Macroeconomics and complexity: inflation theory', in W.B. Arthur, S.N. Durlauf and D.A. Lane (eds), *The Economy as an Evolving Complex System II*, Reading, MA: Addison-Wesley, pp. 321–36.
Lindgren, K. (1991), 'Evolutionary phenomena, in simple dynamics', in Lindgren, K., C.G. Langton, C. Taylor, J.D. Farmer and S. Rasmussen (eds), *Artificial Life II*, Reading, MA: Addison-Wesley, pp. 295–312.
Lucas, R.E. Jr (1978), 'Asset prices in our exchange economy', *Econometrica*, **46**(6), 1429–45.
Marimon, R., E. McGrattan and T.J. Sargent (1990), 'Money as a medium of exchange in an economy with artificially intelligent agents', *Journal of Economic Dynamics and Control*, **14**(2), 329–73.
Marshall, A. (1891), *Principles of Economics*, 2nd edn, London: Macmillan.
North, D.C. (1997), 'Some fundamental puzzles in economic history development', in W.B. Arthur, S.N. Durlauf and D.A. Lane (eds), *The Economy as an Evolving Complex System II*, Reading, MA: Addison-Wesley, pp. 223–38.
Sargent, T.J. (1993), *Bounded Rationality in Macroeconomics*, Oxford: Clarendon Press.
Shubik, M. (1997), 'Time and money', in W.B. Arthur, S.N. Durlauf and D.A. Lane (eds), *The Economy as an Evolving Complex System II*, Reading, MA: Addison-Wesley, pp. 263–84.
Tesfatsion, L. (1997), 'How economists can get alive', in W.B. Arthur, S.N. Durlauf and D.A. Lane (eds), *The Economy as an Evolving Complex System II*, Reading, MA: Addison-Wesley, pp. 533–64.
Young, H.P. (1993), 'The evolution of conventions', *Econometrica*, **61**(1), 57–84.

68 Self-organization in economic systems
P.M. Allen

1 Introduction

In this chapter we shall set out a new understanding of economic processes that has emerged, and how this can be represented in mathematical terms allowing a much clearer view of what goes on in market places. Instead of supposing that the agents participating in an economic market know how to drive it to equilibrium, and what prices they need to choose for their goods so that the market 'clears', we shall try to see what really happens. We shall view the market place as the arena in which economic agents (people) can discover whether they can find products and accompanying strategies that can enable them to survive profitably in the context of the other producers, and of course, of consumers. We shall not assume that they already know what to produce and what strategy to use to sell it. In this way our mathematics will describe the self-organization of the market place as the result of different agents exploring possible products and strategies and discovering which ones do not work, and, happily for some, ones that do work. In this new view of economics coming out of complexity studies, the co-ordination that emerges from the market place is a process of self-organization resulting from the exploration and learning behaviours of the agents involved, who must attempt to find adequate strategies of product type and qualities, pricing and profitability to enable them to continue. They have to discover things by trying them out. The market place and the agents that interact within it are therefore learning systems in which some agents may never find adequate strategies, while others must work out how to up-date and modify their strategies in order to respond to the information that the market place gives them.

If we think about economic systems in general, then we see that they concern a changing number of agents who wish to live by making products that other consuming agents will buy. The question that matters for any potential producer is: what product can I make that I can sell at a sufficient profit to expand my production?

This is clearly a question that cannot be answered in the abstract. It depends on whether the producer can and does make a product that enough consumers consider sufficiently desirable that they will choose that product among others, and will pay a price large enough to give a profit and allow the continuation and expansion of production. In any real situation, the quality of the product and the costs of production that will be successful are difficult to estimate theoretically without actually trying them out. Similarly, the potential consumers will not necessarily know how much they are willing to pay for which product.

The market place is therefore the arena in which both producers and consumers can discover whether their beliefs are really true, and by exploration and experimentation what products, pricing strategies, sales techniques and consumer views are really viable. And this process of mutual learning – of co-evolution – is precisely what goes on in market places over time. This is market dynamics and evolution. It is patently absurd to suppose that people can know beforehand what range of products can be made and will be consumed, and in this way to jump instantaneously to economic equilibrium. General equilibrium theory in economics supposes that agents act as if they have perfect foresight about the best strategy to follow in any future state of the world (Radner, 1968). The proof of existence of equilibrium requires that each agent possesses an infinite amount of knowledge.

This is at the opposite extreme of an approach based on complexity, otherwise known as common sense, in which it is assumed that agents know almost nothing beforehand. However, they discover viable strategies by exploring the possibilities, and in responding to the feedback they get from the market place into which they are selling. It is this process of exploration and decay or reinforcement of possible behaviours that means that most things of interest in economics (as in life) are about the emergence of structure and organization over time as a result of self-transformation of the agents' knowledge and behaviour. It is self-organization in that it arises within a population of agents that are willing to explore and respond to what they discover.

2   Self-organization and evolution

The principles on which these new ideas rest are those coming from the natural sciences concerning the behaviour of open, non-linear systems (Nicolis and Prigogine, 1977; Haken, 1978). They showed that non-linear chemical reaction systems such as the Brusselator could, if driven out of equilibrium, exhibit self-organizing behaviour in which spatial, temporal and spatiotemporal patterns of reactants spontaneously appear.

In Figure 68.1 the presence of x and y in close proximity accelerated the production of more x and y and this non-linear systems model can create patterns of x and y in space and time as initially small differences of concentration are amplified. In this way chemical reactions were able to show how open systems, supplied with some flows of energy and/or matter, could, providing there were non-linear reactions involved, create structure and patterns spontaneously.

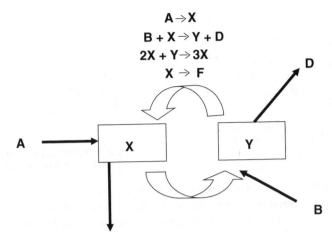

$$A \rightarrow X$$
$$B + X \rightarrow Y + D$$
$$2X + Y \rightarrow 3X$$
$$X \rightarrow F$$

Figure 68.1   A typical systems model allows for feedback interactions so that the rate of production of x and y is affected by the local density of x and y

But in thinking about economic self-organization, the question that we need to ask is whether the principles of self-organization that underlie the Brusselator are relevant to understanding economic markets. The first step that we can take is to look at the possibility of extending the chemical kinetics from molecules to animal populations. What differences would exist between chemical kinetics and population dynamics of real populations? Let us consider this by taking the following example. Consider an ecosystem, and let us attempt to model it using population dynamics. We can establish the different species that exist there, and then find out how many of each population there are. We can also, by sampling, find out which population eats which other population and calibrate the multiple plant/herbivore and predator/prey interactions. Now, once this is established, we can put the whole system of equations on a computer, and run it forward. What happens is shown in Figure 68.2.

This is a very important result. It means that although the model was calibrated on the real state of the ecosystem at time $t = 0$, it diverged from reality as time moved forward. The real ecosystem stayed complex, and indeed continued to adapt and change with its real environment while the mathematical representation of that reality simplified down to just a few species and interactions. This tells us that there is a problem with the mechanical representation of an ecosystem that did not really occur for chemical kinetics. Roughly speaking, chemical kinetics works, while the population dynamics of an ecosystem clearly does not. Why is this, and

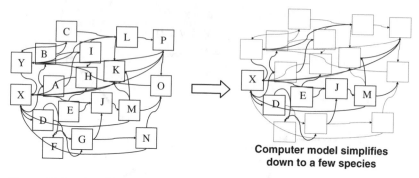

**Computer model simplifies
down to a few species**

*Figure 68.2   A calibrated ecosystem (populations and interaction
parameters) represented by the population dynamics of its
constituent species collapses when run forward in time*

what does it say about the problem that we want to address next, which is
that of interacting agents, in an economic system?

In order to understand what went wrong, we need to examine the
assumptions we made in formulating our equations of population dynamics. What happened is that the loops interactions of a real ecosystem
form parallel food chains, with cross connections and complications of
course, but essentially with each level feeding on the lower one, some
of these dying and others being eaten by the level above. The whole system
of food chains loops back through death and microorganisms that recycle
all the carbon and minerals. When we run the population dynamics with
the fixed birth, death capture and escape rates that we have found on
average in the real system (in analogy with chemical reaction rates), then
the food chain with the highest performance simply eliminates all the
others. In other words, selection between food chains operates and this
selects for the highest performing chain. The model therefore simplifies
down from the many parallel food chains present to a single, best performing chain. It is the 'survival of the fittest' – but clearly, this selective
collapse of the ecosystem is not what happens in reality. Therefore we need
to understand what is missing between the dynamic model and the original real system.

What is missing is the aspects that we have removed as the result of our
assumptions (see Figure 68.3):

- that we can establish a boundary for the 'system' under study, with
  the environment outside and the system inside;
- that we have adequate rules of classification to identify and name the
  components, or component type within the system;

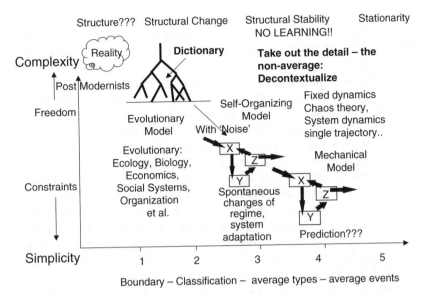

Figure 68.3   *This shows the results of successive simplifying assumptions that take us from a complex evolving system to its mechanical representation*

- that we can describe the behaviour of the current system in terms of its components or component types, and their interaction;
- that we can use the average rates of the discrete events that link the components.

The first two assumptions are really those that reflect the situation under study and the type of question that we want to answer. However, the third assumption is important because it considers the identity of the average individual of the population as fixed. For molecules that is very true, since one molecule is identical to another. However, for a biological population there is always a micro-diversity among the constituent individuals. We will have young and old individuals, shorter, taller, longer, fatter, darker, lighter and so on. This in itself already explains the failure of the ecosystem model in Figure 68.2. In the real ecosystem if the populations within one food chain suffer from pressure of the others, then it is the more vulnerable individuals, whoever they are, that suffer most. As a result, the overall performance of the remaining individuals is relatively better, giving rise to increased performance of the population on average, and creating an automatic corrective response to whatever is threatening the population. And this will be true for any and all of the populations within the ecosystem, so that we see that it is the internal micro-diversity of each species that leads to the resilience and persistence of real populations. The model in which this was replaced by average types simply fails to behave in the same way as the real system.

The fourth assumption of the list makes the noisy behaviour of a real system smooth, as we create the impression of a mechanical system dynamics in which the system will follow a single trajectory into the future. Instead of this, as shown in the Brusselator, in reality, even in the case of chemical kinetics, the real system can undergo instabilities and bifurcations leading to different possible structures and forms.

The final two assumptions are crucial as they replace the actual micro-diversity and events by their average. In chemistry, one molecule is very like another, and the only difference is their spatial location. Dissipative structures can create spatio-temporal patterns because of this. But populations of organisms differ in many possible ways, firstly in location, but also in age, size, strength, speed, colour etc. and so this means that, whenever a population, X, is being decreased by the action of some particular predator or environmental change, then the individuals that are most vulnerable will be the ones that 'go' first. Because of this the parameter representing the average death rate will actually change its value as the distribution within the population X increases the average 'resistance'. In other words, the whole system of populations has built in, through the internal diversities of its populations, a multiple set of self-regulatory processes that will automatically strengthen the weak, and weaken the strong. In the same way that reaction diffusion systems in chemistry can create patterns in space and time, so in this more complex system the dynamics will create patterns in the different dimensions of diversity that the populations inhabit. But neither we, nor the populations concerned, need to know what these dimensions are. It just happens as a result of evolutionary dynamics.

However, if we think now either of populations of x and y, or of agents x and y, then the feedback interaction operates quite differently. Running this 'system' either of populations x and y, or of agents x and y (with internal decisional mechanisms) is no longer just a question of getting more or fewer agents of type X and type Y. Each agent acts according to the set of rules and responses that constitute its decisional mechanism, and which experience has led to. But as the system runs, so the on-going experience can modify the decision making mechanisms. In a biological population, the micro-diversity hidden within the species and its average type will lead to adaptation and learning. Similarly, agents will use the on-going knowledge that they receive to change their decision rules and criteria. Some agents may revise their experience rapidly, others slowly, but for most of us the aim is to find internal rules and responses that lead to better outcomes.

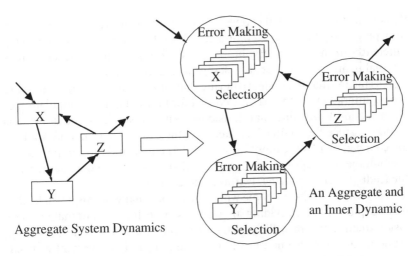

Figure 68.4 *The reality either of having populations interacting or agents with possible alternative internal structures means that running the system leads to multiple possible futures*

Now, we must envisage not just more or less x and y, but instead new x and new y as they try out new rules and criteria of action. This is qualitative evolution, not simply dynamics.

This brings out the essential temporal asymmetry that is perhaps not so evident in the systems model such as the Brusselator. When we draw a systems model involving feedback we fail to account properly for the fact that the feedback may change the *internal* structure of the node from which it comes. In the Brusselator the internal elements are molecules, and when they are of type x or y they are identical and are not changed by the presence of more or less x or y in their surroundings. However, when we are looking at an evolved, multi-level system, where the populations or agents x or y have actually got internal structure that gives them rules, criteria and responses, then this corresponds to their 'knowledge' or 'interpretive framework' of the world. Over time, therefore, as the system runs, the feedback selects among the internal diversity for the more successful types, thus changing the average behavioural parameters of the population, or for agents, modifies their 'knowledge' and leads to a different set of rules, criteria and responses corresponding to changed internal structure.

This means that the species or agent is now different because he now has information coming from the action taken at time t, and this new knowledge may lead to the agent trying out a different rule, criterion or response from that used previously. Therefore the agents present in the system, even if they start out as x, will evolve over time, and new types of x will come into play, introducing the combined effects for each agent of behaving differently from other x. Evolution is therefore present whenever there is internal memory or irreversible change inside the components.

This means that the system drawing that shows X interacting with Y and then Y interacting with X is only correct for molecules. For a population of X, or for an X with internal decision-making capabilities, the drawing is *incorrect*, since the feedback is later than the original action, and X and Y are changed by it. We cannot draw the interactions and the components in a simultaneous diagram, because the X that acts is not the X that receives the feedback. It is evolving, learning and changing.

What improves the outcome will persist, and what worsens it will lead to fresh explorations. Providing that agents have lots of alternative ideas inside them, and are willing to try them out, we will have a 'satisficing' (Simon, 1980) motor underneath our system. If an improvement works, it is retained and reinforced, but if it worsens then something else will be tried out. The whole system of agents will discover, in a changing world, how to co-evolve with their fellow agents, and with their wider environment. But it is this internal wealth of possible rules, criteria and responses as well as the willingness and freedom to try them out that leads to evolution. This is of course true, not just for economic markets, but for all social and ecological systems (Allen, 1976).

3   Self-organization and evolution in economics

In this section we shall consider the behaviour of systems containing agents whose primary concerns and motivations concern economic problem solving. In order to do this we shall describe an evolutionary market model inhabited by multiple agents managing firms. The agents will have bounded rationality and will survive if they succeed in finding strategies that produce goods and services that sufficient customers will buy to provide revenues greater than costs. In other words, the model will try to represent both sides of the market, supply and demand, instead of focusing on only one of these. It will also show us that what matters is not so much 'knowing' a good strategy, but having the capacity to succeed in finding a successful strategy and in adapting and learning as market conditions and competitors learn change over time.

Since the 'invisible hand' of Adam Smith, the idea of self-organization has been present in economic thought. However, economics happened to evolve in a very particular way, one that avoided serious reflection on dynamic processes, by transferring ideas from equilibrium physics as the basis for understanding. This led to classical and neoclassical economics that was strong on very general and rigorous theorems concerning completely artificial systems, but rather weak on dealing with reality in practice. Today, with the development of evolutionary complex systems and the arrival of computers able to 'run' systems instead of us having to solve them analytically, interest is burgeoning in complex systems simulations and modelling. And this can help us improve our quality of life and the functioning of our organizations and social institutions, by providing better knowledge for an integrated and dynamic reflection on possible policies and interventions, including the possible creative responses of agents that are affected. We need to understand how socio-economic systems 'work' and more particularly how they evolve. And this means that we need to 'understand' how the underlying causality of a current social situation is operating, and what the mechanical system predicts. But the difficulty with this approach is that it fails to recognize the essentially fluid nature of human behaviour, and the ability of actors to modify their previous habits in response to the new opportunities or constraints of the situation.

In several previous papers (Allen, 2001a, 2001b), it was shown how the creative interaction of multiple agents is naturally described by co-evolutionary, complex systems models in which both the agents, the structure of their interactions and the products and services that they exchange evolve *qualitatively*.

The subject of this chapter is the self-organization of economic systems and this is about how and whether agents learn about the system or market in which they operate, and both the importance and the limits to the effectiveness of that learning. Learning is about the acquisition of knowledge and this is about the development of an interpretive framework that can turn 'data' into 'information'. The interpretive framework however, only developed as the result of the confirmation or rejection of conjectures concerning possible associations, classifications and interactions within the situation considered. However, there is clearly some requirement of stationarity if this is to be at all cumulative. The present chapter will explore the issue of the limits to learning that characterize an evolving market place. In building the model the modeller is confronted with the problem of what knowledge an agent can have concerning the sales and revenue generation that will result from a given strategy. It may be clear that high-quality products will be bought by richer potential customers than poor and that, between two identical products, sales will be greater if a lower price is charged. But in reality, beyond this, the profits that can be made by an agent for a given strategy will depend on what strategies are being used by other agents and firms, and on the sensitivities of potential customers to these. Since all activity will start by investing in materials and wages in order to produce, this will show up as an initial loss. If the decision rule used by the agent is that of expanding production when profits are positive, and contracting when they are negative, then clearly, all firms will shut down as soon as they start. Because, however, in the real world, firms are in fact started and new products and services are developed it is obvious that the 'equation' governing the increase or decrease of production volume cannot be based on the actual profits made instantaneously.

This underlines what seems obvious after a little thought: agents must use a rule based on 'expected' profits to adjust their production volume. So firms moving into a new market area must be doing so because they 'expect' to make profits in the future. It is merely a matter of a delayed dynamic, whereby profits follow according to the expectations of the competing agents.

But this raises the vital question at the heart of this chapter: how much knowledge can an agent have about future, expected profits? If no firm ever went bankrupt then we might assume that considerable knowledge was present. However, the fact that most start-up firms fail within five years tells us something very important: they cannot calculate expected profits correctly, or else they would never go bankrupt. Clearly, what really happens is that agents adopt, and probably believe in, particular strategies of quality and mark-up, and some of them *discover* that their strategy does take them on a successful trajectory, and others that it does not.

We can better understand economic reality by using our model to explore strategies of 'learning' as agents can attempt to respond to their situation, either taking corrective action if they appear to be failing, or increasing their profits if the strategy appears to be working. The model can be used to explore learning strategies that can keep agents from bankruptcy, including changes in quality and mark-up, or alternatively deciding which other agent should be imitated.

The structure of each firm that is modelled is as shown in Figure 68.5. Inputs and labour are necessary for production, and the cost of these, added to the fixed and start-up costs, produce goods that are sold by sales staff who must 'interact' with potential customers in order to turn them into actual customers. The potential market for a product is related to its qualities and price, and although in this simple case we have assumed that customers all like the same qualities, they have a different response to the price charged. The price charged is made up of the cost of production (variable cost) to which is added a mark-up. The mark-up needs to be such that it will turn out to cover the fixed and start-up costs as well as the sales staff wages. Depending on the quality and price, therefore, there are different-sized potential markets coming from the different customer segments.

When customers buy a product, they cease to be potential customers for a time that is related to the lifetime of the product. For high-quality goods this may be longer than for low quality, but of course, many goods are bought in order to follow fashion and style rather than through absolute necessity. Indeed, different strategies would be required, depending on

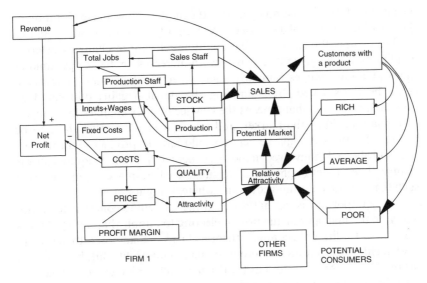

Figure 68.5   The evolutionary market model structure

whether or not this is the case, and so this is one of the many explorations that can be made with the model.

The model calculates the relative attractiveness of a product (of given quality and price) for a customer of a given type (poor, medium or rich). This results in a calculation of the 'potential market' for each firm at each moment, and the sales staff must interact with these potential customers in order to turn them into customers. When a sale is made, then the potential customer becomes a customer and disappears from the market for a time that depends on the product lifetime.

The revenue from the sales of a firm are used to pay the fixed and variable costs of production, and any profit can be used either to increase production or to decrease the bank debt if there is any. In this way, the firm tries to finance its growth and to avoid going near its credit limit. *If it exceeds its credit limit then it is declared bankrupt and closed down.* In order to continue the exploration of strategy space for successful 'business conjectures', the evolutionary model then replaces the failed firm with a new one, with new credit and a new strategy of price and quality. This either survives or fails in its turn. The model represents a kind of 'Darwinian' model of market evolution in which the random strategies that work remain, and those that do not are replaced by new, randomly chosen strategies.

In the model, interventions can be made at any time and different strategies can be tried out. Apart from the obvious ones concerning the quality and mark-up of the product, there is that of increasing the sales force and having an advertising campaign. Also the model allows the exploration of the possible impacts of increased R&D. In addition, the model could be used to explore the strategies that might be relevant to changing external conditions, as the general level of wealth increases or the age pyramid of the population changes. Similarly, some aspects of technology assessment could be investigated, by examining the possible gains that could be obtained, and over what time, as the new technology changes the competitive relationship in the market, and allows a larger market share to be tapped. But this extra market share would have to produce extra revenue over and above that involved in the investment and training required for the change. The model might therefore suggest where market densities were such that this was advantageous, and where it might not be.

A very important issue that arises in the modelling concerns the rationality of the manager of the firm in electing to adopt whatever strategy is chosen. In traditional economic theories firms are supposed to act, or to have acted, in such a way as to obtain maximum profit. But, here, we can see that, if we used the profit as the driving force for increased production, then the system could not start. *Every new action must start with an investment*, that is, with a negative profit. So, if firms do start production, and increase it, then this cannot be modelled by linking the increase in production to the profit at that time. Instead, we might say that it is driven by the *expected profit over some future time*. But how does a manager form his expectations? Probably a model of the kind that is being described here is way beyond what is usually used, and in any case, there is a paradox. In order to build this model, in order perhaps for managers to formulate their expectations, the model requires a representation of managers' expectations. But this is only a paradox if we believe that the model is about *prediction*. Really, it is about exploration, the exploration of how we think a market works, and so it is a part of a learning process, which may indeed lead participants to behave differently from the way that was supposed initially. Such an outcome would already be a triumph.

Despite this paradox, and the difficulty in knowing what is going to happen beforehand, firms do start up, production is increased, and economic sectors are populated with firms, so, even though there is this logical problem, obviously it does not worry participants in reality. Since bankruptcies obviously also occur, then we can be sure that the expectations that drive the investment process are not necessarily related to the real outcomes. In our model therefore we simply have assumed that managers want to expand to capture their potential markets, but are forced to cut production if sales fall. So they can make a loss for some time, providing that it is within their credit limit, but they much prefer to make a profit, and so attempt to increase sales, and to match production to this.

4   Market self-organization

The picture that emerges from this study of a dynamically self-organizing market sector model is that of the emergence of product niches. It is the economies and diseconomies of production and distribution that will determine the number, size and scale of these niches, and they will depend on the initial history of the market sector in question as a 'lock-in' evolves. However, as new technology appears, or as the rest of society evolves, new attributes can come into play for the products, although the effect and importance of these may be different when viewed by the producers as opposed to consumers.

A typical long-term simulation is shown in Figure 68.6. This shows the 2-D space of mark-up (%) and quality (Q), and the positions of the various firms. The rows at the top show the strategy, price, profit, present balance and sales of each firm, and the state of the market is shown at the lower left. The simulation shows us that using purely random initial beliefs about possible strategies and random 'relaunches' of failed firms leads to a fairly reasonable distribution of the firms in the space of 'possibilities' as well as to good levels of consumer satisfaction at the middle and rich end of the market.

The evolutionary model can be used to explore, not only the self-organization of the market with non-learning economic agents with particular business strategies, but also the effectiveness of different internal processes for modifying them in the light of experience: their *evolutionary or learning strategies*. We can discover resilient strategies that emerge from such systems, and in the case of particular market sectors suggest how the rules of learning can also evolve. In other words, by testing firms with different rates and types of response mechanism, we can move towards understanding not only the emergent 'behavioural rules' for firms, but also the rules about 'how to learn' these rules.

4.1   Self-organization: Darwinist strategies

The first method used for the 'relaunch' of new firms was to pick new strategies purely randomly, giving us a 'Darwinian' evolutionary model in which selection acted on random 'mutations'. Each firm is launched with a given, randomly chosen, profit margin and product quality. They are very simple agents, however, who carry on producing their products and trying to sell them unless they lose more than their credit limit and are closed down by the bank. This is a demonstration of simple self-organization of the market place, revealing an attractor of possible coherent patterns of behaviour for several firms – possible market niches. The model of Figure 68.6 has a kind of 'Darwinian' evolutionary mechanism that allows entrepreneurs to explore the 'possibility space' for products of this kind.

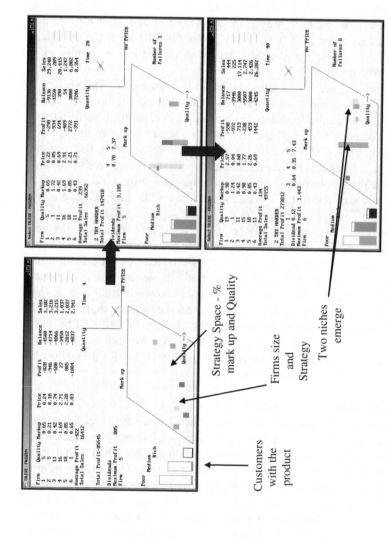

Figure 68.6   A typical evolutionary run where gradually the 'Darwinian' process discovers two fairly stable niches: around Q=11, % = 40 and Q = 18, % = 85

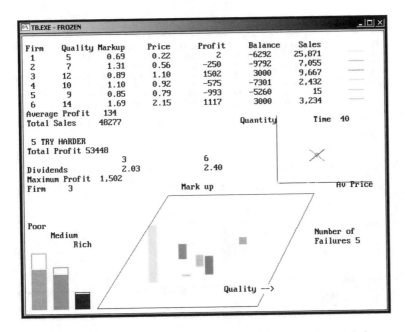

Figure 68.7 *The situation at t=40 uses 'Darwinian' learning and shows a typical evolution in which, in this case, firm 1 has survived, though it has never got into profit*

The pay-off achieved by any one firm or entrepreneur depends on the strategy (product quality and mark-up) used by the other entrepreneurs present (see Figure 68.7). The 'replacement' of firms that go bankrupt from a supply of willing new entrants makes this simulation Darwinian, because it implies a population of firms, and allows the market interactions to explore over time which strategies can *in reality* co-exist. Because there is an interdependence, the outcome of the process is both dependent on the initial random choices, and on the particular sequence of replacement firms, and their randomly chosen strategies.

4.2 A marginal learning strategy
The market model can now be used to examine the effects of a firm actively 'hill-climbing' in profit space by exploring systematically the gains or losses of higher or lower qualities, and higher or lower mark-ups. In this version of the model, a learning firm tests the 'reward' or 'costs' of changing the profit margin slightly, and also the quality. In this way, it senses the 'profit slope' and then decides to modify its behaviour by moving a small way up the slope. This is very successful for a firm as we see in Figure 68.8, where

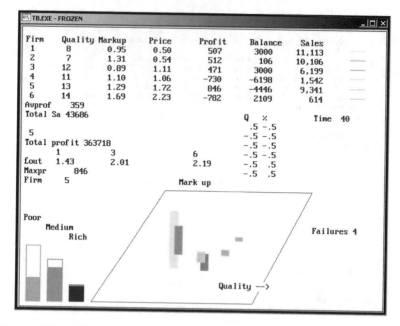

Figure 68.8   This is an identical simulation to that of Figure 68.7 except that here firm 1 tests the 'profit gradient' and moves Q and % accordingly up-hill; it does much better, making a profit and paying a dividend to investors

we see the effect of inserting the ability for firm 1 to 'hill-climb' while the others do not. Firm 1 rapidly moves into profit by climbing whatever gradient it encounters. It succeeds in paying a dividend to its investors.

The model can therefore demonstrate the improved probability of survival and of success on the part of a learning firm. The problem is, however, that as soon as a strategy can be seen to be successful, it has a tendency to be adopted by other agents. In the next case we look at the situation when all the firms adopt this learning strategy.

4.3   All firms use learning

If we allow all the firms to 'hill-climb', then their mutual interaction reduces the advantage of learning. However, fewer bankruptcies do occur (are necessary?) in order to discover this market structure. We see the 'limits to learning' in which the speed of learning and the frequency really matter and affect the ability to survive and prosper.

In Figure 68.9 the whole market evolution is different as all the firms 'hill-climb' in profit space, moving overall to higher qualities and higher mark-ups.

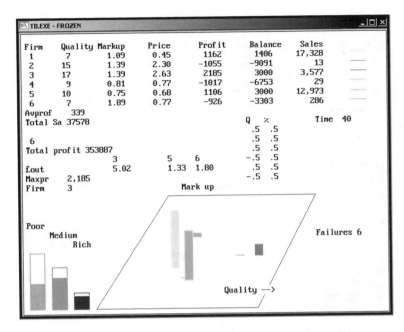

Figure 68.9   The whole market is completely different when all firms can 'hill-climb'; firm 1 does just get into profit but not enough to pay a dividend to investors

However, for several firms this very sophisticated strategy, involving careful testing of experimental variations in mark-up and quality, does not bring success. In that case, it becomes important to see what other strategies are possible, and whether they can result in better outcomes.

4.4   One loser imitating the winner

One such strategy is for a firm to monitor the market carefully and for it to adapt its production as rapidly as possible to copy whichever firm is currently making most profit. Obviously this might be hindered by patent laws and copyright but the model merely supposes that the quality Q and the percentage mark-up %, are perceived as being the same by the potential customers. The model then allows the imitator to move towards its target. Of course, it may not have the same economies of scale, but nevertheless its presence clearly increases competition at that point in strategy space, and changes the outcome for the market as a whole. In Figure 68.10 we see the result for an identical simulation to that of Figures 68.7 to 9, except that here firm 1 discovers which firm is most profitable and imitates their strategy.

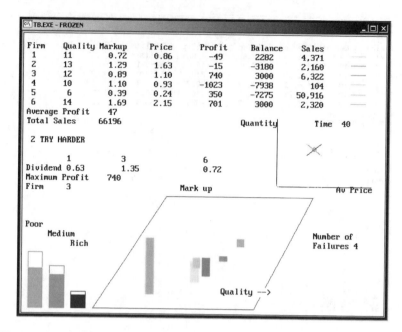

Figure 68.10   If firm 1 imitates whoever is currently winning, then this can lead to success; it is in the 'mid-range' niche and so will probably survive, having avoided a bankruptcy that occurred in Figure 68.7

This strategy can also emerge as a ploy to avoid bankruptcy. In Figure 68.7, firm 1 goes bankrupt at least once, whereas in the simulation of Figure 68.10 this does not happen. We see that the number of bankruptcies 'required' to shape the market varies for the different runs. For a 'Darwinian' strategy of Figure 68.7 it is five up to this point, and for Figures 68.8, 68.9 and 68.10 it is four, six and four, respectively.

4.5   Losers imitate winners

In the next simulation, we consider the impact of the idea of imitation of the firms making up the market. If firm 1 can avoid a pathway leading to bankruptcy, then it shows that it is a 'risk-reducing' strategy. Rather than taking the risk of finding out whether one's own, individual strategy will really work, it seems tempting to imitate whichever strategy is making maximum profit. At least the 'decision-maker' is not going to be alone, and obviously it must be a good strategy since it is already making more profit than any other. So the idea can be tested. What happens if all the players decide to imitate whoever is making the most profit? The answer is shown

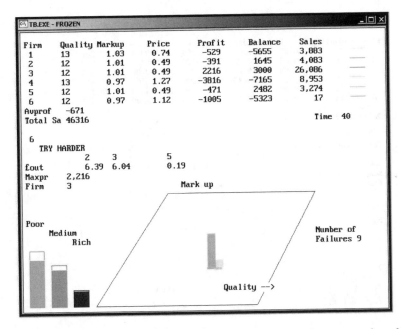

Figure 68.11   *If all the firms adopt the 'imitate a winner' strategy, then the*
outcome is bad: in trying to avoid risks, they actually
increase them (9 failures up to this point)

in Figure 68.11, which shows us that all the firms move to the same place
in strategy space, and in so doing increase the degree of competition that
they each feel. As a result, there are more bankruptcies (nine) than in any
of the other simulations.

What might have been a 'risk averse' strategy turns out to be the opposite. To imitate in a market of imitators is highly risky. In a further variant,
we can also examine the result of a single firm staying true to its own ideas
and making its own strategy of profit margin and quality, while the other
five all imitate the winner. Initially, the imitators often win, but, over time,
the greater degree of competition that their strategy leads to means that in
general it is the 'single' original firm that does better. Eventually, of course,
this leads to the others trying to imitate the 'loner' – but of course, the
founder of a strategy has had more time to gain economies of scale and has
an advantage that lasts.

4.6 Diverse learning strategies

In a previous paper concerning the emergence of different strategies among
fleets of fishing boats, it was shown that what mattered was that an ecology

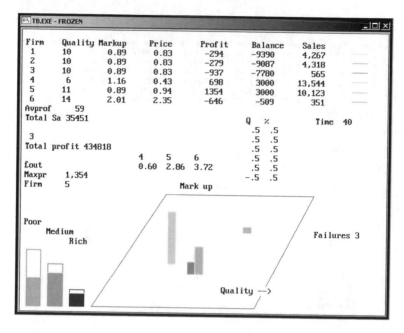

Figure 68.12   *The situation at* t *= 40 for a set of mixed strategies: firms 1*
to 3 imitate and firms 4 to 6 'hill-climb'; there are only 3
bankruptcies and good overall profits

of strategies emerged. Instead of having agents that are susceptible to adopting the same strategy, what really matters is that there should be real micro-diversity such that, whatever happens, there will be a diverse set of strategies being played out in the collective system. This is equivalent to insisting on the opposite of 'Best Practice'. In the next simulation of Figure (68.12) we see the outcome for a situation in which some firms imitate winners and others 'hill-climb'.

We see that it is not particularly successful for firm 1, but that it has actually produced an overall market structure that has been largest in total profits, and which has only suffered three bankruptcies. This introduces an interesting point about the different levels at which we can look at market evolution, that of the internal capabilities of firms and of their products, the strategy of one firm relative to the others and finally the overall outcome of the different capabilities and strategies adopted by participating firms. In some ways, for public policy what matters is the level of customer satisfaction, and the level of overall profit for the sector. In our accounting for overall costs we need to include that of bankruptcy, since every time that it occurs in our model, the social system, other firms and so on lose 10 000 units. In the real world the costs can be more devastating still to those involved and could even lead to a serious limitation on the willingness of actors to innovate.

We can examine the question as to the overall outcomes for the 'industry' of different strategies. In order to look at this, we have calculated the overall profits of the whole market, and we have included the costs of bankruptcies, in which, often, a loser takes trade away from others in an attempt to keep going, but eventually crashes with debts.

In Figure 68.13 we show the overall outcome for four different learning strategies: Darwinian (random strategies, no learning); Old Strategy (If profit less than half average, reduce %); 'Hill-Climbing'; 3–6 hill-climbers, 1–3 imitators. The comparative results for the overall profit profile for the market are shown in the figure. However, here we have also performed four different runs for different sequences of random numbers, implying simply a different sequence of chance events.

The important result that emerges is that, in general, hill-climbing in profit space is a good strategy, but a system that mixes this with some firms that imitate success seems even better. However, what is really significant is that the particular random sequence that seed 6 provides, and that of seed 5, differ remarkably in the overall outcomes. Seed 6 has high values for the industry with all strategies other than pure Darwinian. However, seed 5 only has value under one strategy. Indeed, using the Darwinian strategy, the value of the whole sector is still increasingly negative. This shows us that, for the same potential demand, for the same technology, the same strategies and the same interactions, chance can still allow great variation in market structures to emerge, some very favourable some very unfavourable, and this tells us that the 'structural attractors' of economic markets are diverse and of very different overall efficiency. The invisible hand seems to be highly capricious.

We can also use our model to study the problem of investment in innovation that increases productivity of a firm, but costs an investment, which must be recuperated before increased profits can be made. In this example, we see how investments in higher technology characterize the market evolution.

Having looked at the level of the market place, we can now look at the problem at the level below, inside the competing firms. How do they gain their capacities to produce and deliver products and services sufficiently effectively to survive?

5   Evolutionary multi-agent economic models

The previous sections demonstrate theoretically how micro-diversity in character space, tentative trials of novel concepts and activities, will lead to emergent objects and systems. However, it is still true that we cannot predict what they will be. Mathematically we can always solve a given set of equations to

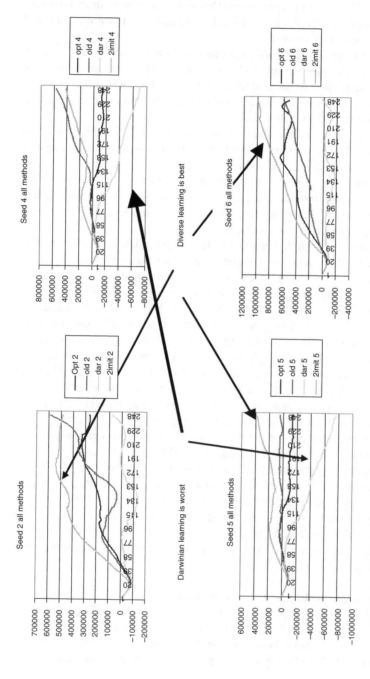

Figure 68.13 Hill-climbing in profit space is a good strategy, but a mix of this with imitation of success is best; however, luck (the random sequence) can lead to very different market outcomes, from highly profitable to only marginally so

find the values of the variables for an optimal performance. But we do not know *which* variables will be present, as we do not know what new 'concept' may lead to a new structural attractor, and therefore we do not know *which* equations to solve or optimize. The changing patterns of practices and routines that are observed in the evolution of firms and organizations can be looked at in exactly the same way as that of 'product' evolution above. We would see a 'cladistic diagram' (a diagram showing evolutionary history) showing the history of successive new practices and innovative ideas in an economic sector. It would generate an evolutionary history of both artifacts and the organizational forms that underlie their production (McKelvey, 1982, 1994; McCarthy, 1995; McCarthy, Leseure, Ridgeway and Fieller, 1997). Let us consider manufacturing organizations in the automobile sector. In order to improve the quality and the costs of the products that a firm can offer, it must evolve its own internal practices and knowledge so that it will have emergent capabilities that make it a difficult firm to beat. In this section we look at the internal evolution of a firm, in its changing ability to increase its competitivity and capabilities.

5.1 Automobile manufacturing

In this example, we examine how the internal structure of firms has evolved over time in this particular sector. Clearly, however, this is transferable to any other sector. It corresponds to examining how the characteristic internal features and characteristics have emerged over time within the industry.

Table 68.1   53 Characteristics of manufacturing organizations

Standardization of parts	1
Assembly time standards	2
Assembly line layout	3
Reduction of craft skills	4
Automation (machine-paced shops)	5
Pull production system	6
Reduction of lot size	7
Pull procurement planning	8
Operator-based machine maintenance	9
Quality circles	10
Employee innovation prizes	11
Job rotation	12
Large volume production	13
Mass subcontracting by sub-bidding	14
Exchange of workers with suppliers	15
Training through socialization	16
Proactive training programmes	17

Table 68.1   (continued)

Product range reduction	18
Automation (machine-paced shops)	19
Multiple subcontracting	20
Quality systems	21
Quality philosophy	22
Open book policy with suppliers	23
Flexible multifunctional workforce	24
Set-up time reduction	25
Kaizen change management	26
TQM sourcing	27
100% inspection sampling	28
U-shape layout	29
Preventive maintenance	30
Individual error correction	31
Sequential dependency of workers	32
Line balancing	33
Team Policy	34
Toyota verification of assembly line	35
Groups vs. teams	36
Job enrichment	37
Manufacturing cells	38
Concurrent engineering	39
ABC costing	40
Excess capacity	41
Flexible automation of product versions	42
Agile automation for different products	43
In-sourcing	44
Immigrant workforce	45
Dedicated automation	46
Division of labour	47
Employees are system tools	48
Employees are system developers	49
Product focus	50
Parallel processing	51
Dependence on written rules	52
Further intensification of labour	53

With these characteristics (see Figure 68.14) as our 'dictionary' we can also identify 16 distinct organizational forms:

- ancient craft system,
- standardized craft system,

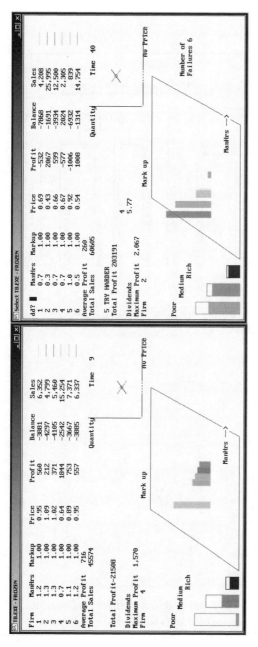

Figure 68.14   The early market has low productivity, and high labour content (a), but later after an evolution the productivity increases and labour requirements fall (b)

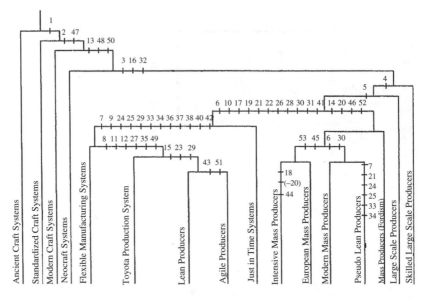

Source: McCarthy, Leseure, Ridgeway and Fieller (1997).

Figure 68.15   The cladistic diagram for automobile manufacturing organizational forms

- modern craft system,
- neocraft system,
- flexible manufacturing,
- toyota production,
- lean producers,
- agile producers,
- just in time,
- intensive mass producers,
- European mass producers,
- modern mass producers,
- pseudo lean producers,
- fordist mass producers,
- large-scale producers,
- skilled large-scale producers.

The evolutionary tree of Figure 68.15 can be deduced from cladistic theory, and this shows the probable sequence of events that led to the different possible organizational forms. However, in the spirit of complex systems thinking and that of the formation of networks, we want to consider the synergy

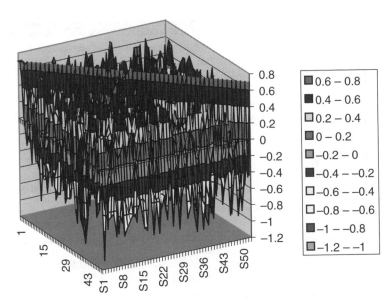

Figure 68.16   *The 53×53 matrix of pair interactions of the characteristic practices, which allows us to calculate the net attraction or conflict for any new practice, depending on which ones are present already*

or conflict that different *pairs of attributes* actually have. Instead of only considering the different list of characteristic features that constitute the different organizational forms, we also look at the pair-wise interactions between each pair of practices, in order to examine the role of 'internal coherence' in the organizational performance. In this 'complex systems' approach, a new practice can only invade an organization if it is not in conflict with the practices that already exist there. In other words, we are looking at 'organizations', not in terms of simply additive features and practices, but as mutually interactive 'complexes' of constituent factors.

From a survey of manufacturers (Baldwin, 2002) concerning the positive or negative interactions between the different practices, a matrix of pair interaction was constructed allowing us to examine the 'reasons' behind the emergent organizational forms, with successful forms arising from positive mutual interactions of constituent practices. This is shown in Figure 68.16.

We have then been able to develop an evolutionary simulation model, in which a manufacturing firm attempts to incorporate successive new practices at some characteristic rate. There is an incredible range of possible structures that can emerge, however, depending simply on the order in which they are tried. But, each time a new practice is adopted within an

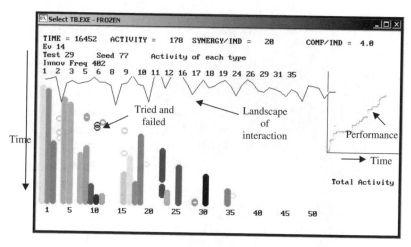

Figure 68.17   An evolutionary model tries to 'launch' possible innovative practices in a random order: if they invade, they change the 'invadability' of the new system

organization, it changes the 'invadability' or 'receptivity' of the organization for any new innovations in the future. This is a true illustration of the 'path-dependent evolution' that characterizes organizational change. Successful evolution is about the 'discovery' or 'creation' of highly synergetic structures of interacting practices.

In Figure 68.17 we see the changing internal structure of a particular organization as it attempts to incorporate new practices from those available. In the simulation, the number available start from the ancient craft practice on the left, and successively add the further 52 practices on the right. At each moment the organization can choose from the practices available at that time, and its overall performance is a function of the synergy of the practices that are tried successfully. We see cases where practice 4, for example, is tried several times and simply cannot invade. However, practice 9 is tried early on and fails, but does successfully invade at a later date. The particular emergent attributes and capabilities of the organization are a function of the particular combination of practices that constitute it.

The model starts off from a craft structure. New practices are chosen randomly from those available at the time and are launched as a small 'experimental' value of 5. Sometimes the behaviour declines and disappears, and sometimes it grows and becomes part of the 'formal' structure that then conditions which innovative behaviour can invade next.

Different simulations lead to different structures, and there are a very large number of possible 'histories' (see Figure 68.18). This demonstrates a

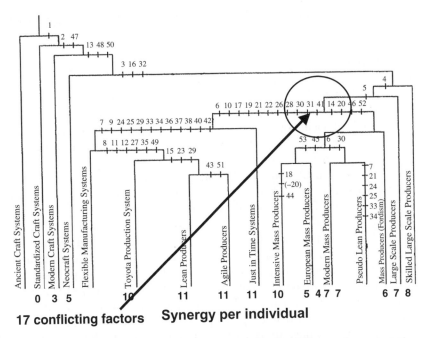

17 conflicting factors **Synergy per individual**

Figure 68.18 *Knowledge of the pair matrix for the different characteristics allows us to calculate the synergy/individual in the different organizations*

key idea in complex systems thinking. The explorations/innovations that are tried out at a given time cannot be logically or rationally deduced because their overall effects cannot be known ahead of time. Therefore, the impossibility of prediction gives the system 'choice'. In our simulation we mimic this by using a random number generator to actually choose what to try out, though in reality this would actually be promoted by someone who believes in this choice, and who will be proved right or wrong by experience, or in this case by our simulation. In real life there will be debate and discussion by different people in favour of one or another choice, and each would cite their own projections about the trade-offs and the overall effect of their choice. However, the actual success that a new practice meets with is pre-determined by the 'fitness landscape' resulting from the practices already present and what the emergent attributes and capabilities encounter in the market place. But this landscape will be changed if a new practice does successfully invade the system. The new practice will bring with it its own set of pair interactions, modifying the selection criteria for further change. So the pattern of what could then invade the system (if it were tried) has been changed by what has already invaded successfully. This is technically referred to as a 'path-dependent' process since the future evolutionary pathway is affected by that of the past.

Our results have already shown (Figure 68.18), that the evolution through the tree of forms corresponds to a gradual increase in overall 'synergy'. That is, the more modern structures related to 'lean' and to 'agile' organizations contain more 'positive' links and fewer 'negative' links per unit than the ancient craft systems and also the mass-producing side of the tree. In future research we shall also see how many different structures could have emerged, and start to reflect on what new practices and innovations may be available today for the future.

Our work also highlights a 'problem' with the acceptance of complex systems thinking for operational use. The theory of complex systems tells us that the future is not completely predictable because the system has some internal autonomy and will undergo path-dependent learning. However, this also means that the 'present' (existing data) cannot be proved to be a *necessary* outcome of the past, but only, hopefully, a *possible* outcome. So, there are perhaps so many possible structures for organizations to discover and render functional that the observed organizational structures may be 16 in several hundred that are possible. In traditional science the assumption was that 'only the optimal survive', and therefore that what we observe is an optimal structure with only a few temporary deviations from average. But selection is effected through the competitive interactions of the other players, and if they are different, catering to a slightly different market, and also suboptimal at any particular moment, then there is no selection force capable of pruning the burgeoning possibilities to a single, optimal outcome. Complexity tells us that we are freer than we thought, and that the diversity that this freedom allows is the mechanism through which sustainability, adaptability and learning occur.

This picture shows us that evolution is about the discovery and emergence of structural attractors (Allen, 2001b) that express the natural synergies and conflicts (the non-linearities) of underlying components. Their properties and consequences are difficult to anticipate and therefore require real explorations and experiments to be going on, based in turn on diversity of beliefs, views and experiences of freely acting individuals.

6   Economic and social self-organization

There are several important points about these examples. The first is that the models above are very simple, and the results very generic. They show us that, for a system of co-evolving agents with underlying micro-diversity and idiosyncrasy, we *automatically* obtain the emergence of structural attractors such as Figure 68.14. A structural attractor is the temporary emergence of a particular dynamical system of limited dimensions, from a much larger space of possible dynamical systems and dimensions. They also encompass and include the recent discussion concerning evolution as being not simply the effect of systems (agents, firms and markets) adapting to the environment – the action of selection – but also expressing the exaptations of Gould and Vrba (1982) in which essentially new dimensions of selection emerge over time, and the reasons why an organism, organization or market structure emerges is not the same as its current utility. So this is a recognition of path-dependent emergent evolution. We observe complex systems of interdependent behaviours whose attributes are on the whole synergetic. They have better performance than any single, pure homogeneous behaviour, but are less diverse than if all 'possible' behaviours were present. In other words, they show how an evolved entity will not have 'all possible characteristics' but will have some that fit together synergetically, and allow it to succeed in the context that it inhabits. They correspond to the emergence of hypercycles in the work of Eigen and Schuster, 1979, but recognize the importance of emergent collective attributes and dimensions. The structural attractor (or complex system) that emerges results from the particular history of search and accident that has occurred and is characteristic of the particular patterns, positive and negative interactions of the components that comprise it. In other words, a structural attractor is the emergence of a set of interacting factors that have mutually supportive, complementary attributes.

What are the implications of these structural attractors? First, search carried out by the 'error-making' diffusion in character space leads to vastly increased performance of the final object. Instead of a homogeneous system, characterized by intense internal competition and low symbiosis, the development of the system leads to a much higher performance, and one that decreases internal competition and increases synergy.

Second, the whole process leads to the evolution of a complex, a 'community' of agents whose activities, whatever they are, have effects that feed back positively on themselves and the others present. It is an emergent 'team' or 'community' in which positive interactions are greater than the negative ones.

Third, the diversity, dimensionality and attribute space occupied by the final complex are much greater than the initial homogeneous starting structure of a single population. However, it is much less than the diversity, dimensionality and attribute spaces that all possible populations would have brought to the system. The structural attractor therefore represents a reduced set of activities from all those possible in principle. It reflects the 'discovery' of a subset of agents whose attributes and dimensions have properties that provide positive feedback. This is different from a classical dynamic attractor that refers to the long-term trajectory traced by the given set of variables. Here, our structural attractor concerns the emergence of variables, dimensions and attribute sets that not only co-exist but actually are synergetic.

Finally, a successful and sustainable evolutionary system will clearly be one in which there is freedom and encouragement for the exploratory search process in behaviour space. Sustainability in other words results from the existence of a capacity to explore and change. This process leads to a highly co-operative system, where the competition per individual is low, but where loops of positive feedback and synergy are high. In other words, the free evolution of the different populations, each seeking its own growth, leads to a system that is more co-operative than competitive. The vision of a modern, free market economy leading to, and requiring, a cut-throat society where selfish competitivity dominates is shown to be false, at least in this simple case.

The most important point really is the generality of the model presented above. Clearly, this situation characterizes almost any group of humans: families, companies, communities and so on, but only if the exploratory learning is permitted will the evolutionary emergence of structural attractors be possible. If we think of an artifact, some product resulting from a design process, then there is also a parallel with the emergent structural attractor. A successful product or organization is one in which the 'bundling' of its different components creates emergent attributes and capabilities that assure the resources for its production and maintenance. However, the complication is that the emergent attributes and capabilities are not simply an additive effect of the components. If a change is made in the design of one component it will have multidimensional consequences for the emergent properties in different attribute spaces. Some may be made better and some worse. Our emergent structural attractor is therefore relevant to understanding what successful products and organizations are and how they are obtained. Clearly, a successful product is one that has attributes that are in synergy, and which lead to a high average performance. From all the possible designs and modifications we seek a structural attractor that has dimensions and attributes that work well together.

The structural evolution of complex systems in Figure 68.19 shows how explorations and perturbations lead to attempts to suggest modifications, and these lead sometimes to new 'concepts' and structural attractors that have emergent properties. The history of any particular product sector can then be seen as an evolutionary tree, with new types emerging and old types disappearing. But, in fact, the evolution of 'products' is merely an aspect of the larger system of organizations and of consumer lifestyles that also follow a similar, linked pattern of multiple co-evolution.

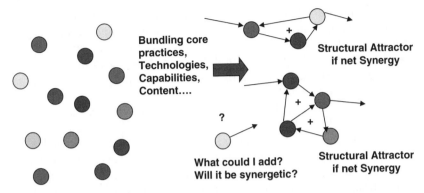

Figure 68.19   *On the left we have a 'dictionary' of possible core concepts, practices or ideas; these are 'bundled' on the right and if the different elements have synergy then the structure is successful*

7 Conclusions

The theory of complexity and the models described above show us the multi-level nature of socio-economic systems. Individuals with characteristic and developing skills and particularities form groups within companies, generating specific capabilities and also particular receptivities for possible future changes. The products and services that emerge from this are perceived by a segmented and heterogeneous population of potential consumers, who are attracted by the qualities of a particular product or service and the low price at which it is offered. This results in a market share and in changing volumes of activity for different firms. When volume increases, economies of scale occur and allow further price decreases and greater attractiveness for potential customers. However, debts can be cleared more quickly if higher prices are practised, and, since there is an interest rate in the model, paying off debt is also a way of reducing costs.

Basically, then, the competition between different quality and pricing strategies is subtle, as the true 'value' of a strategy cannot be seen at a particular moment, but instead is only apparent over time, as gradually market share or profits accumulate and investors can be paid a dividend. The important result from this multi-agent, complex systems simulation above is that, instead of showing us the optimal strategy for a firm, it tells us that there is no such thing. What will work for a company depends on the strategies being played by the others. The overall lesson is that it is better to be playing in a diverse market ecology than in one involving mainly imitation. So having a unique identity and product may seem 'risky', but it is better than simply packing into the same strategy as others. Coupled with having an individual product and strategy, it is an advantage to 'learn'. So exploring the landscape sufficiently to enable 'hill-climbing' in profit space is generally better than not doing it. However, it does not necessarily solve all problems because the pathway 'up-hill' can be blocked by other firms. In this case a more radical exploration is required with the possibility of a 'big jump' in the product and strategy space.

The model shows the limits to learning because firms may all conclude that they should all be 'learning' and 'hill-climbing'. This is amusing to watch in the simulations, because it is a bit like the 'boyds' simulations where there is a flocking motion as firms move up market (Q) and up mark-up space, and then start to try to spread out as a result of their competitive interactions. This still results in the failure of some firms, as we saw, and so simply 'hill-climbing' is not necessarily a solution. What is best is to have a different strategy from the others, and also to be able to move into new dimensions of quality and of product definition. This basically allows more space within which to be 'individual' and hence can allow more specialized niches to be created, and more diverse firms to co-exist.

The lower-level evolutionary model of section 4 shows us how firms explore possible functional innovations, and evolve capabilities that lead either to survival or to failure. They describe a divergent evolutionary diffusion into 'possibility space'. Each of these is then either amplified or diminished, depending on the 'performance' of the products or services provided, which depends on the internal trade-offs within them, on the synergies and conflicts that it encounters or discovers in its supply networks, retail structures and in the lifestyles of final consumers.

Similarly, at the level of the market place, firms with different strategies or capabilities also try to 'invade' and remain in the system. Exploratory changes lead to a divergent exploration of possibilities. New elements are amplified or diminished as a result of the dual selection processes operating on one hand 'inside them' in terms of the synergies and conflicts of their internal structures, and also 'outside them', in their revealing of synergy or conflict with their surrounding features in the market. So a new practice can 'invade' a system if it is synergetic with the existing structure, and this will then lead to either the reinforcement or the decline of that system in its environment if the modified system is synergetic or in conflict with its environment. Because of the difficulty of predicting both the emergent internal and external behaviours of a new action, the pay-off that will result from any given new action can therefore generally not be anticipated. It is this very ignorance that is a key factor in allowing any exploration at all. Either the fear of the unknown will stop innovation, or divergent innovations will occur even though the actors concerned do not necessarily intend this. Attempting to imitate another player can lead to quite different outcomes because either the internal structure or the external context is found to be different.

Throughout the economy, and indeed the social, cultural system of inter-acting elements and structures, we see a generic picture at multiple tempo-ral and spatial scales in which uncertainty about the future allows actions that are exploratory and divergent, which are then either amplified or sup-pressed by the way that this modifies the interaction with their environ-ment. Essentially, this fulfils the early vision of dissipative structures, in that their existence and amplification depend on 'learning' how to access energy and matter in their environment and on whether they can form a self-reinforcing loop of mutual advantage in which entities and actors in the environment wish to supply the resources required for the growth and maintenance of the system in question. In this way, structures emerge as multi-scalar entities of co-operative, self-reinforcing processes.

What we see is a theoretical framework that encompasses both the evo-lutionary and the resource-based theory of the firm. And, not only of the firm, but of the social and economic system as a whole. It is the complex systems dialogue between explorations of possible futures at one level, and the unpredictable effects of this at both the level below and the level above. There is a dialogue between the 'trade-offs' or 'non-linearities' affected inside and outside the particular level of exploration. But it is also true that all levels are exploring. Unless there is an imposition of rigid homogeneity up and down the levels of the system, there will necessarily be behavioural explorations due to internal diversity. In this way, multi-level systems are precisely the structures that can 'shield' the lower levels from instantaneous selection, and allow an exploratory drift to occur, that can generate enough diversity to eventually *discover* a new behaviour that will grow. Without the multiple levels, selection would act instantly, and there would be no chance to build up significant deviations from the previous behaviour.

This chapter sketches out an integrated theory of economic and social evolution. It suggests how different types of people channel their needs into particular patterns of demand for different products and services. These are delivered according to the non-linear interactions of synergy and conflict that lead to particular retailing structures, both expressing natural 'markets' and within that complementarities between product categories and lines. Products themselves exist as embodiments of attributes that are synergetic (internally coherent) clusters, and different product markets emerge natu-rally as a result of inherent conflicts between attributes. For example, a palmtop computer cannot have a really easy-to-use keyboard (under exist-ing design concepts) and so notebooks and laptops exist in a different market from palmtops. Similarly, toasters and telephones also occupy sep-arate markets because answering a call on a toaster/telephone can set your hair on fire. So again it is the 'complementarities and conflicts' of possible attributes that structure the space of possible product or service markets.

On the supply side, the capabilities of organizations, and the products and services that they create, are the result of a creative evolutionary process in which clusters of compatible practices and structures are built up, in the context of the others, and discover and occupy different niches. At each moment, it is difficult to know the consequences of adopting some new practice, such as 'best' practice, since the actual effect will depend on both the internal nature of the organization and its actual context and relationships it had developed. For this reason it is bound to be an exploratory, risky process to try new practices and new products. In the short term it will always be better simply to optimize what already exists, and not to risk engaging in some innovation. But, over time, without engaging in evolution, extinction becomes, not simply possible, but actually certain.

The synergies and conflicts of the supply network exhibit similar properties as new technologies provide possible opportunities and threats, and it may be necessary for new technologies and new knowledge to be adopted if extinction is to be avoided later. It is necessary to couple the driving potentials of 'human needs' to the products and services that are consumed to satisfy them, and the technologies, the structures and the organizations that form and evolve to create new responses to their changing embodiments. The whole system is an (imperfect) evolutionary, learning system in which people learn of different ways that they could spend their time and income, and what this may mean to them. Companies attempt to understand what customers are seeking, and how they can adapt their products and services to capture these needs. They attempt to find new capabilities and practices to achieve this, and create new products and services as a result. These call on new technologies and materials and cause evolution in the supply networks. Technological innovation, cultural evolution and social pressures all change the opportunities and possibilities that can exist, and also the desires and dreams of consumers and their patterns of choice and of consumption.

This supports the view of evolutionary economics driven by 'restless capitalism' (Metcalfe, 1998,1999) as of course not all good. This imperfect learning process means that decisions will tend to reflect the short-term positive performance of something with respect to the dimensions of which we are aware, but obviously, in a complex system, there will be all kinds of less obvious factors that are perhaps adversely affected, perhaps over the longer term, but even quite immediately. In other words, what we choose to do is dependent on 'what we are measuring', and so the system changes reflect our limited understanding of what will actually affect us. This is because our actions are based on our limited understanding and knowledge of the complex systems we inhabit. And their evolution therefore bears the imprints of our particular patterns of ignorance. So we may grab economic gain, by pushing 'costs' into the 'externalities', or we may seek rapid satisfaction from consuming some product that actually harms us, or our community, or our region, or the ozone and so on over the longer term.

In response to the question that this chapter addresses, whether economic systems move with nearly perfect knowledge or with very imperfect knowledge, we see that multi-agent simulations support the latter view. We cannot know how effective a particular strategy will be, because it will depend on the strategies practised by others, as well as on consumer tastes and needs. In addition, although having a learning strategy is better than not having one, it does not necessarily solve the problem, because either the hill-climbing path may be blocked by other firms or, more probably, they are all learning too. In effect, the successful working of the market requires underlying heterogeneity, both of potential consumers and of the agents on the supply side. Diverse strategies are required, and ones that are maintained even when some other strategy is working better. Fortunately, the evolutionary model of organizational forms shows us underlying reasons for the creation of such diversity. Since the future is not known there is an element of randomness in which new practice or innovation is tried. But there is an element of non-randomness as to whether, if tried, it can invade. If it does not fit the current internal practices, then it can not invade, but if it does, then it can. However, if it does invade, then it changes the 'receptivity' of the system to future innovations. So the fact of uncertainty about the future leads naturally to a divergent, branching evolution of possible structures, which then compete and co-operate, leading to a selection of a compatible subset, and creating a future that cannot be foreseen.

Acknowledgment

This work was supported by the ESRC NEXSUS Priority Network.

References

Allen, P.M., 1976, 'Evolution, population dynamics and stability', *Proceedings of the National Academy of Science*, **73**(3), 665–8.

Allen, P.M., 1993, 'Evolution: persistant ignorance from continual learning', in E. Day and P. Chen (eds), *Nonlinear Dynamics and Evolutionary Economics*, Oxford: Oxford University Press, pp. 101–12.

Allen, P.M., 1994, 'Evolutionary complex systems: models of technology change', in L. Leydesdorff and P. van den Besselaar (eds), *Chaos and Economic Theory*, London: Pinter.

Allen, P.M., 2001a, 'Knowledge, ignorance and the evolution of complex systems', in J. Foster and J.S. Metcalfe (eds), *Frontiers of Evolutionary Economics: Competition, Self-Organisation and Innovation Policy*, Cheltenham, UK and Northampton, MA, USA: Edward Elgar.

Allen, P.M., 2001b, A complex systems approach to learning, adaptive networks, *International Journal of Innovation Management*, **5**(2), June pp. 149–180 .

Baldwin, J.S., 2002, 'The complex cladistic evolution of manufacturing form', NEXUS conference on Evolutionary Processes, Offley Place, Hertfordshire, October.

Eigen, M. and Schuster, P., 1979, *The Hypercycle*, Berlin: Springer.

Gould, S.J. and Vrba, E., 1982, 'Exaptation, a missing term in the science of form', *Paleobiology*, **8**(1) Winter, 4–15.

Haken, H., 1978, *Synergetics – An Introduction*, Berlin: Springer.

McCarthy, I., 1995, 'Manufacturing classifications: lessons from organisational systematics and biological taxonomy', *Journal of Manufacturing and Technology Management – Integrated Manufacturing Systems*, **6**(6), 37–49.

McCarthy, I., Leseure, M., Ridgeway, K. and Fieller, N., 1997, 'Building a manufacturing cladogram', *International Journal of Technology Management*, **13**(3), 2269–96.

McKelvey, B., 1982, *Organizational Systematics*, Berkeley, CA: University of California Press.

McKelvey, B., 1994, 'Evolution and organizational science', in J. Baum and J. Singh (eds), *Evolutionary Dynamics of Organizations*, Oxford: Oxford University Press, pp. 314–26.

Metcalfe, J.S., 1998, *Evolutionary Economics and Creative Destruction*, London: Routledge.

Metcalfe, J.S., 1999, 'Restless capitalism, returns and growth in enterprise economics', CRIC, University of Manchester.

Nicolis, G. and Prigogine, I., 1977, *Self-organization in Nonequilibrium Systems*, New York: Wiley-Interscience.

Radner, R., 1968, 'Competitive equilibrium under uncertainty', *Econometrica*, **36**, 31–58.

Simon, H.A., 1980, 'The behavioral and social sciences, *Science*, **209**, 72–8.

69 Regional economics and economic geography from a neo-Schumpeterian perspective
Claudia Werker

1 Introduction

Whereas regions might differ considerably in terms of economic performance within the same country, regions in different countries might be quite similar. There are various explanations for differences and similarities, in particular differences or similarities in the industrial structure, in the endowment with production factors (including natural resources) and in historical events. This rather incomplete list already comprises two different kinds of factors that can explain differences and similarities of regional development and growth. On the one hand, there are static factors such as the endowment with production factors. On the other hand, there exist dynamic factors, such as historical events that change regional development and growth in time. Some factors even carry both elements. The industry structure, for instance, is a static factor when one looks at one point in time and a dynamic factor as it changes in time.

Analyses that consider static factors only describe and explain one stable situation concerning the economic performance of regions. In this case differences and similarities between regions remain. Changes in regional performance stem from dynamic processes and are at the core of neo-Schumpeterian analyses. Therefore, I start with the elements analyses need to include when looking into the issue of regional economics and economic geography from a neo-Schumpeterian perspective (section 2). In regional economics and economic geography factors, which cause accumulation or equal distribution of economic activities, are subsumed as agglomeration or deglomeration factors (section 3). Neo-Schumpeterian approaches use agglomeration and deglomeration factors to describe and explain regional development and growth in rather different ways. Three different strands of this research are shown in section 4. This chapter is limited to economic approaches. However, even most of the economics approaches carry substantial multidisciplinary elements and I will show that questions about dynamic processes in regional economics and economic geography can generally be best answered from a multidisciplinary perspective.

2   A neo-Schumpeterian perspective on regional economics and economic geography

Rather divergent streams in economics and related disciplines take a neo-Schumpeterian perspective. In economics, the neo-Schumpeterian view has been largely defined in opposition to mainstream economics. However, I will not concentrate on the differences between neo-Schumpeterian and mainstream economics but discuss the essential assumptions the divergent neo-Schumpeterian streams have in common – in particular in the context of regional economics and economic geography. At the micro level, neo-Schumpeterian approaches look at human behaviour as being determined by high uncertainty, because business persons, firms and so on cannot fully assess what outcome today's behaviour will have. Consequently, individual agents act under the constraint of bounded rationality, and their behaviour is derived from routines or rules of thumb (Nelson and Winter, 1982, p. 16). For this reason individual agents in similar situations show a variety of behaviour. However, selection mechanisms such as the market mechanism reduce this variety, because they determine which behaviour is successful and which is not.

The way selection mechanisms work feeds back into the way variety is created, because individual agents try to take the way selection mechanisms work into account (Metcalfe, 1995, p. 415). The selection mechanisms stem from formal and informal institutions within and outside the individual agents themselves in the form of legislation, contracts, habits and so on. Many institutions are developed in the course of interaction between individual agents. Others are created by the state. Thus processes of variety creation and reduction are complex and complicated. Moreover, chance elements, most notably unexpected historical events, interfere with these complex and complicated processes, so that uncertainty is at their very core and has to be faced by individual agents.

Generally speaking, regional economics and economic geography investigate the location of economic activities and the flows of production factors and products. From a neo-Schumpeterian perspective this research stream is concerned with the variety-enhancing and variety-reducing processes in regions: 'why regions differ in their ability to generate, imitate or apply new variety, and what are the economic and institutional structures through which a region can retain and even expand its competitive position' (Boschma and Lambooy, 1999, p. 412).

How neo-Schumpeterian approaches of regional economics and economic geography address this question about the sources of regional development and growth will be shown in the following.

3 Agglomeration and deglomeration factors

Regional development and growth as well as differences between regions originate from agglomeration and deglomeration factors. These factors can have static and dynamic effects. The static effects of agglomeration emerge from production factors and infrastructure as well as from possibilities to access markets and information (Malecki, 1997, p. 151). Dynamic effects of agglomeration can only emerge in time by interaction and cooperation between firms, research organizations and policy makers. Whereas agglomeration factors foster the regional concentration of economic activities, deglomeration factors lead to deconcentration as when, for instance, congestion makes concentration of even more economic activities in one region difficult and expensive. In the following I will show the static and in particular the dynamic aspects of infrastructure and production factors, of innovation and technological change as well as of regional supply and demand.

3.1 Infrastructure and production factors

Infrastructure comprises the governance structure of a region that is relevant for economic development and growth (cf. Howells, 1999, pp. 72f.; Malecki, 1997, pp. 14f.). To a large extent infrastructure is provided by the state. However, public–private intermediaries as well as the private sector also contribute to infrastructure. How important regional institutions are in comparison to national institutions largely depends on how the national state is organized. For instance, in countries such as Germany, with strong regional governments, regional institutions are crucial. One element of regional infrastructure is formal and informal institutions, which provide in particular selection mechanisms, e.g. written rules as well as habits. These institutions mirror the interests of different groups in the region and evolve over time. Another element of regional infrastructure is provided in the form of traffic as well as information and communication links. Traffic links do not only influence transportation costs of inputs and outputs of the production process but also determine how easily a region is accessible for visits to maintain contacts. The latter can partly be replaced by information and communication links, such as telephone and fax connections and e-mail – at least as long as face-to-face contacts are not inevitable. Traffic as well as information and communication links can lead to more or less regional concentration. Good traffic connections might make it possible for firms to co-locate in one region, e.g. because of shared R&D facilities, and sell their products all over the world at the same time. On the other hand, they also increase the mobility of production factors, e.g. labour. A third element of infrastructure is education and R&D facilities. These facilities provide knowledge about different technologies and innovation possibilities but also sustain and create human capital and absorptive capacities (Breschi and Lissoni, 2001, pp. 994–6). In this context policy makers as well as public–private intermediaries play a crucial role as they can serve as regional gatekeepers or brokers of knowledge, thereby complementing innovative agents and helping to diffuse knowledge. Education and R&D facilities can form agglomeration advantages, as they can lead to firms' decision to locate in the respective region. This closeness of location might then lead to agglomeration effects, e.g. the access to a much deeper and broader labour market, the sharing of research organizations and the easier diffusion of (tacit) knowledge.

Production factors in the classical sense are land, labour and capital. Originally they were looked at from a static perspective, i.e. differences in regional performance were explained by the endowment with these factors. However, it is more interesting to analyse production factors from a dynamic perspective, because only then is it possible to explain regional development and growth in time. The production factor land is usually fixed, with few exceptions, such as reclaiming land in the Ijselmeer in the north of the Netherlands. In contrast, the factor labour can change in time in two respects. First, it can grow if population is growing. Second, labour can be divided into unskilled labour of non-educated people and skilled labour, often also called human capital, that represents the knowledge embodied and accumulated in a person (Malecki, 1997, p. 33). Human capital can help to diffuse knowledge within the region – and outside if it is mobile (Breschi and Lissoni, 2001, pp. 991–4). Here, the depth and breadth of labour markets for skilled labour play a crucial role. The factor capital can also change in time as it can be accumulated into a capital stock like, for instance, a machinery park that is added to, replaced and renewed. Non-accumulable production factors like, for instance, land of a specific quality can lead to agglomeration effects as they can provide a regional advantage for production. These static factors lead to static agglomeration effects. In contrast, accumulable production factors can lead to dynamic agglomeration effects. If the production factors that can be accumulated, such as human capital and capital stock, are subject to increasing returns to scale, they may lead to dynamic agglomeration effects, as the accumulation of the production factors means that self-reinforcing processes are explaining a major part of regional development and growth as well as decreasing or increasing differences between regions.

3.2   Driving forces of innovation and technological change

The generation and selection of innovation drive dynamic processes of regions. Agents such as firms and R&D organizations, which revert to their own limited resources, generate innovations. Firms have acquired these limited resources over time by accumulating knowledge, capital stock and human capital. Innovative agents choose new knowledge, human capital and capital stock on the basis of what they have already accumulated. Knowledge is, for instance, usually chosen on the basis of already existing knowledge, because new knowledge can be much more easily understood if it fits what is already known (Nelson and Winter, 1982, pp. 247f.). As innovative agents have only limited resources to acquire new production factors, they try to use them as efficiently as possible. As a consequence, they usually follow a specific trajectory, and their heterogeneity is due not only to chance but also to the accumulation of production factors in the course of time (ibid., p. 99). Because of their heterogeneity, innovative agents offer different solutions for the same problem, thereby creating a variety of solutions. This variety of solutions is then confronted with the selection mechanisms in the form of institutions and routines (see section 3.1). For a long time innovation and technological change were seen as being supply-driven, until Schmookler (1966) hinted at the importance of the demand side for these phenomena. Nowadays it is clear that both sides play an important role, in particular when one looks at the feedback effects between the supply and demand side (cf. section 3.3).

3.3 Regional supply and regional demand

Regional supply and demand is a very important driving force of development and growth in a region. The endowment of a region with infrastructure and production factors influences the supply and the demand side within that region. Supply is to a certain extent manifested in the industrial structure of a region, because firms provide goods and services. In addition, firms might act as consumers as far as their inputs are concerned, thereby being a part of regional demand. Regional demand is of course also dependent on the private consumers in the region. When looking at the industry structure from the angle of *regional supply*, it is helpful to base this analysis on the product life cycle approach. Empirical evidence (e.g. Audretsch, 1995; Malerba and Orsenigo, 1997) suggests that, during their lifetime, industries pass through different stages. Models dealing with industrial life cycles (e.g. Voßkamp, 1999; Montobbio, 2002; Werker, 2003) hint at a number of stylized patterns related to (interlinked) characteristics of an industry that evolve over its life cycle. The first stages of product life cycles are characterized by the use of various combinations of production factors and by a lot of experimenting with different technological designs of a basic product. In contrast, more mature industries are characterized by standardized and efficient production processes. The industry structure of a region comprises mature and new industries. It has a substantial influence on regional development and growth, because mature and new industries contribute in different ways to the economic activities within regions in terms of use of production factors, of how to connect with other firms and research organizations and of how to generate innovation. Vernon (1966) provided a theory of the way production shifts from one region of the world to another according to the level of improvement of the technology used. Newly developed technologies are first introduced and brought to perfection in the most advanced regions. As soon as the technology is mature, production is located in less developed regions of the world to reduce labour costs. When the technology becomes automated, i.e. when a lot of capital and some human capital is needed, the production is relocated to the more developed regions of the world, as human capital and capital is easily available there. Vernon's approach may be connected to dynamic agglomeration and deglomeration effects at the regional level (see Boschma and Lambooy, 1999, p. 420). Agglomeration effects stem from increasing returns, as cumulative and self-reinforcing processes trigger the specialization of regions into high-tech and middle-tech regions. On the other hand, deglomeration effects in the form of knowledge diffusion play a role when the production is transferred from one region to another.

Regional demand can provide agglomeration effects for three reasons. First, transport costs might make production which is relatively close to the consumers advantageous. Second, regional markets are particularly attractive if they are large and firms can realize economies of scale and/or learning effects in their production. Third, regional demand can provide agglomeration effects if the market provides specific knowledge. This holds in particular for user–producer networks (cf. Lundvall, 1992) and all regions in which markets contain information about preferences of consumers earlier than in other regions. Producing in such a region is then an advantage for the producer and might lead to agglomeration effects, as other firms with their knowledge and human capital also tend to locate their firm or at least subsidiaries in this region.

4   Neo-Schumpeterian approaches in regional economics and economic geography

When one looks into the neo-Schumpeterian assumptions (section 2) it becomes clear that a combination of heterogeneous agents, informal and formal institutions as well as systemic forces drive regional development and growth. In the following, approaches are introduced that deal with the description and explanation of regional dynamic processes and that are based on neo-Schumpeterian assumptions. Sources of regional dynamic processes are agglomeration and deglomeration factors (section 3) that can be interpreted as regional sources of competitive advantage, which can be counter-balanced by deglomeration factors. This means that regional development and growth as well as differences between regions depend on the co-evolution of agglomeration and deglomeration factors. There exist manifold approaches of regional economics and economic geography. I will here concentrate on three major lines of analysis that are the closest linked to the neo-Schumpeterian perspective. First, I will present approaches that concentrate on the micro-behaviour of agents and that are usually carried out in the form of case studies. They can be found under different headings, such as regional clusters, industrial districts, learning regions and innovative milieu. Second, more systematic approaches that concentrate on structural and systemic elements and can be found under the headings of regional innovation systems or regional networks are introduced. Third, the most aggregated level of representing regional development and growth will be presented: regional growth theory.

4.1 Regional clusters, industrial districts, learning regions and innovative milieus

Generally speaking, regional clusters, industrial districts, learning regions and innovative milieus are describing and analysing similar phenomena, i.e. the regional concentration of small and medium-sized enterprises belonging to the same or vertically integrated industries (for an overview, see Boschma and Lambooy, 1999, pp. 414–16; Malecki, 1997, pp. 152–5). All these approaches are agent-centred and focus on elements like infrastructure and production factors that lead to competitive advantage because of the surrounding region, which transforms proximity into innovative activities and prosperity of the region. These elements can be a shared culture, a specific set of rules on how to maintain face-to-face contacts or trust. Here, the relationships between private innovative agents (mostly small and medium-sized enterprises) and the supporting non-private organizations, on the one hand, and soft factors, such as culture and habits, on the other hand are centre-stage. This strand of literature carries quite a number of multidisciplinary elements, as it is concerned not only with economic aspects but also with sociological, historical and geographical ones. It usually provides in-depth case studies of successful regions or at least of regions which are partly successful. A recent example of this strand of literature is the investigation of the New York City's Garment District (Rantisi, 2002). In this paper the neo-Schumpeterian forces behind the success of the New York women's wear industry are shown, in particular how the variety created in the co-evolution of high-class designers and mass production and the exchange of knowledge as well as the development of common institutions led to the ability to adapt to shifting competitive pressures.

4.2   Regional innovation systems and regional networks

The regional innovation systems approach – sometimes also connoted as the regional network approach – stems from the national innovation system approach (cf. Howells, 1999, pp. 70f.). It tries to provide a theoretical and empirical way to systematize success cases and non-success cases (see, e.g., Morgan, 2004). Nevertheless, the regional innovation system approach has a lot in common with the approaches described above (section 4.1). In particular, it also comprises the relationships between innovative agents, the supporting governmental and non-governmental organizations and the institutional setting. However, the regional innovation systems approach is much more concerned with structural elements of regions that eventually lead to innovation and prosperity. As with the national innovation systems approach (see, e.g., Howells, 1999), it looks into the institutional set-up of a region in order to identify key elements, for instance publicly funded research organizations and universities, but also norms, rules and formal legislation. Moreover, the regional innovation systems approach does not only concentrate on regional concentrations of small and medium-sized enterprises and supporting organizations but also looks into firms of other sizes as well as national and supranational players and regulations that play a role for the firms in the region. Moreover, although analyses of regional innovation systems often describe success stories of regions, they are not only concentrating on these but also try to find distinguishing elements between success and non-success stories.

One recent example of this approach is an investigation of networking within manufacturing in the metropolitan region of Vienna (Fischer and Varga, 2002). In this regional innovation system networking is much less common than expected and emerges in particular where vertical relationships are more important than horizontal ones, where industry–university linkages are important and where firms concentrate on earlier stages in the innovation process. In general, the sources of knowledge used by the firms turn out to be national and international to a large extent. This study clearly shows that not all elements of a region might be relevant for networking between innovative agents. Whereas the study by Fischer and Varga (2002) is mainly concerned with economic aspects, another example of this stream of research carries a number of multidisciplinary elements, because it is an analysis in the tradition of economic history using the regional innovation system approach and elements of regional industrial cluster analysis. Schwerin (2004) investigates the Clyde shipbuilding industry in the second half of the 19th century. He identifies overlapping channels of information exchange within the shipbuilders' network in the Clyde region and shows the importance of the link between the right 'mix' of formal and informal institutions, the geographical size and the evolution of the innovation system.

4.3 Regional economic growth theory

In contrast to the aforementioned approaches, regional economic growth theory looks at regional development and growth from a quite different angle. Its roots lie in economic growth theory. Innovation as the driving force behind growth processes as well as differences in such processes between countries is a widely investigated phenomenon at the national level. Similarly, regional economic growth theory puts together agglomeration and deglomeration factors in a theoretical framework to explain growth in regions and, in particular, differences in such growth. The starting point of these models in the neo-Schumpeterian tradition is the microfoundation in which heterogeneous agents with bounded rationality are modelled. These models were by and large fathered by Nelson and Winter (1982, pp. 206–45).

In regional growth theory, one important strand investigates the reasons for differences in growth. Here, the question is whether or not regions converge. An important deglomeration effect that leads to convergence between regions stems from technological knowledge that diffuses from advanced to less advanced regions. Important agglomeration factors that lead to divergence of regions are differences in knowledge generation or factors hindering knowledge diffusion. Regional growth theory is mainly concerned with economic factors but also includes some geographical aspects. One example of this literature is a simulation model, in which such knowledge spillovers explain regional growth (Caniëls and Verspagen, 2001). This model approximates the heterogeneity of agents by taking into consideration differences at the regional level. Here, knowledge generation and diffusion as well as borders between regions that hinder knowledge diffusion are centre-stage in explaining differences in regional growth.

5 Conclusions

Looking at regional economics and economic geography from a neo-Schumpeterian perspective means concentrating on (co-evolving) dynamic processes which explain regional development and growth (section 2). The agglomeration and deglomeration factors presented in section 3 are at the core of this kind of analysis. Which of these factors are highlighted depends on the respective approach chosen: the approaches presented in section 4 concentrate on economic effects, although most of them are multidisciplinary, as they contain geographical, sociological and historical elements. I could only give a brief sketch of the approaches which seemed to me most relevant in dealing with questions of regional development and growth from a neo-Schumpeterian perspective. As the neo-Schumpeterian perspective comprises heterodox approaches that often carry multidisciplinary elements, the range of studies is broader than depicted in this overview.

Regional economics and economic geography from a neo-Schumpeterian perspective are mostly concerned with co-evolving agglomeration and deglomeration processes that lead to regional development and growth. These processes are in their very core not purely economic, because elements like trust, reputation, historical events and geographical givens all play a role. Therefore, it seems most promising to combine elements from different disciplines in studies to provide truly multidisciplinary analyses. This will be particularly helpful in identifying how regions function and develop, what they have in common and how they differ from each other.

References

Audretsch, D.B. (1995): *Innovation and Industry Evolution*, Cambridge, MA (US), London (UK): MIT Press.

Boschma, R.A. and J.G. Lambooy (1999): Evolutionary economics and economic geography, *Journal of Evolutionary Economics*, **9**(4), 411–29.

Breschi, S. and F. Lissoni (2001): Knowledge spillovers and local innovation systems: a critical survey, *Industrial and Corporate Change*, **10**(4), 975–1002.

Caniëls, M.C.J. and B. Verspagen (2001): Barriers to knowledge spillovers and regional convergence in an evolutionary model, *Journal of Evolutionary Economics*, **11**, 307–29.

Fischer, M.M. and A. Varga (2002): Technological innovation and interfirm cooperation: an exploratory analysis using survey data from manufacturing firms in the metropolitan region of Vienna, *International Journal of Technology Management*, **24**(7/8), 724–42.

Howells, J. (1999): 'Regional systems of innovation', in D. Archibugi, J. Howells and J. Michie (eds), *Innovation Policy in a Global Environment*, Cambridge (UK), New York (US), Melbourne (AUS): Cambridge University Press.

Lundvall, B.-Å. (1992): 'User–producer relationships, national systems of innovation and internationalisation', in B.-Å. Lundvall (ed.), *National Systems of Innovation and Interactive Learning*, London: Pinter Publishers.

Malecki, E.J. (1997): *Technology and Economic Development. The Development of Local, Regional and National Competitiveness*, Harlow (UK): Addison Wesley Longman.

Malerba, F. and L. Orsenigo (1997): Technological regimes and sectoral patterns of innovative activities, *Industrial and Corporate Change*, **6**(1), 83–117.

Metcalfe, J.S. (1995): 'The economic foundations of technology policy: equilibrium and evolutionary perspectives', in P. Stoneman (ed.), *Handbook of the Economics of Innovation and Technological Change*, Oxford (UK), Cambridge, MA (US): Blackwell.

Montobbio, F. (2002): An evolutionary model of industrial growth and structural change, *Structural Change and Economic Dynamics*, **13**(4), 387–414.

Morgan, K. (2004): The exaggerated death of geography: learning, proximity and territorial innovation systems, *Journal of Economic Geography*, special issue on physical and organizational proximity in territorial innovation systems, ed. C. Werker, K. Morgan and C. Meister, **4**(1), 3–21.

Nelson, R.R. and S.G. Winter (1982): *An Evolutionary Theory of Economic Change*, Cambrige, MA (US), London (UK): The Belknap Press of Harvard University Press.

Rantisi, N.M. (2002): The local innovation system as a source of 'variety': openness and adaptability in New York City's Garment District, *Regional Studies*, **36**(6), 587–602.

Schmookler, J. (1966): *Invention and Economic Growth*, Cambridge, MA (US): Harvard University Press.

Schwerin, J. (2004): The evolution of the Clyde region's shipbuilding innovation system in the second half of the nineteenth century, *Journal of Economic Geography*, special issue on physical and organizational proximity in territorial innovation systems, ed. C. Werker, K. Morgan and C. Meister, **4**(1), 83–101.

Vernon, R. (1966): International investment and international trade in the product life cycle, *Quarterly Journal of Economics*, **80**, 190–207.

Voßkamp, R. (1999): Innovation, market structure and the structure of the economy: a micro-to-macro-model, *Economic Systems Research*, **11**, 213–31.

Werker, C. (2003): Market performance and competition: a product life cycle model, *Technovation*, **23**, 281–90.

70 A roadmap to comprehensive neo-Schumpeterian economics

Horst Hanusch and Andreas Pyka

In this, the concluding chapter of the *Elgar Companion to Neo-Schumpeterian Economics*, we want to give some indications of necessary future strands of research. Without doubt at the present stage of development, neo-Schumpeterian economics can contribute much to the understanding of the dynamic processes of the real side of an economy, as is impressively demonstrated in the contributions to this volume. One can even state that, without applying the neo-Schumpeterian perspective, the complex phenomena of economic development remain nebulous, as they are inaccessible to other schools in economics. In particular, neoclassical economics, with its orientation towards rational individuals and the price mechanism, which together are responsible for an efficient allocation of resources within a set of constraints, contrasts well with the neo-Schumpeterian perspective. Here, innovation has taken over the role of a central normative principle. Entrepreneurship and innovation are responsible for economic development by overcoming the limiting constraints, which are considered to be a datum in neoclassical economics. With innovation, also, true uncertainty as an essential characteristic of the future orientation of development processes enters all economic domains, leaving far behind the possibilities of analysis within the neoclassical framework of strict rationality.

However, at the present stage of development, neo-Schumpeterian economics is still far from offering a comprehensive theory of economic development. The contributions to this volume bear witness to the maturity of neo-Schumpeterian economics in the analysis of development and change in the real spheres of an economy. Technological innovations propelling industry dynamics and economic growth obviously are a major source of economic development, but technological innovations are not the only source, nor can industry development take place in a vacuum. Instead, development is accompanied and influenced by, and exerts influence on the monetary realms of an economy as well as the public sector. Admittedly, with respect to the stage of development of neo-Schumpeterian economics, the high degree of maturity does not hold for neo-Schumpeterian approaches aiming at financial markets and their development as well as on the public sector.

A comprehensive economic approach has to offer a consistent theory which encompasses all realms relevant to an improved understanding of the economic processes under investigation. This becomes even more pressing in cases in which the different realms are in close relation, influencing each other, which is very likely the case for economic development. In other words, a comprehensive understanding of economic development inevitably has to consider the co-evolutionary processes between the different economic domains.

In the following paragraphs, we argue that it is high time for neo-Schumpeterian economics to devote considerable attention to the role of the financial and public sectors with respect to economic development. In particular, we introduce the comprehensive neo-Schumpeterian approach as a theory composed of three pillars: one for the real side of an economy, one for the monetary side of an economy, and one for the public sector. Economic development then takes place in a co-evolutionary manner, pushed, hindered and even eliminated within these three pillars (Figure 70.1).

In order to understand the crucial co-evolutionary relationship, one has to consider the bracket encompassing all three pillars, namely their orientation towards the future which introduces uncertainty into the analysis. The relationships between the three pillars drive or hinder the development of the whole economic system in a non-deterministic way. Consider for example the case of the financial sector, exaggerating the developments taking place in

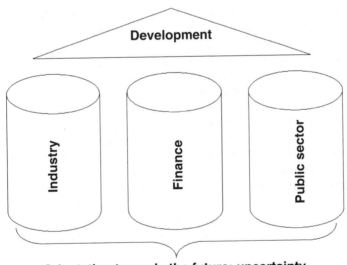

Figure 70.1   The three pillars of comprehensive neo-Schumpeterian economics

the real sector and leading to dangerous bubble effects, which might cause a breakdown of the whole economy. Or think of the case in which the public sector cannot cope with the overall economic development, and infrastructure, education and so on become the bottlenecks of system development.

In this light, the notion of innovation, i.e. the introduction of novelties, has to be seen as all-encompassing, covering not only scientific and technological innovation, but including also all institutional, organizational, social and political dimensions. Furthermore, besides this result-orientation of innovation, a process-orientation has to be considered, both because innovations are taking place in time and because of the co-evolutionary nature of economic development. Having in mind this understanding of innovation, a definition of neo-Schumpeterian economics may appear as follows:

> *Neo-Schumpeterian economics deals with dynamic processes causing qualitative transformation of economies driven by the introduction of innovation in their various and multifaceted forms and the related co-evolutionary processes.*

This definition includes the three characteristic features of neo-Schumpeterian economics as elaborated in the introductory chapter to this *Companion*, namely (i) qualitative change, affecting all levels and domains of an economy, (ii) punctuated equilibria i.e. periods of radical change followed by periods of smooth and regular development, and (iii) pattern formation: despite the true uncertainty, the processes to be observed are not completely erratic but spontaneously structuring.

With respect to the analysis of industry development, this might not sound new. However, according to our understanding, qualitative development is a ubiquitous phenomenon affecting not only industries but also the financial markets and the state. Furthermore, there is an important co-evolutionary relationship between these different domains, which constitutes a core part of neo-Schumpeterian economics.

Concerning the pillar of innovation-driven industry dynamics, we refer to the contributions of this *Companion*. With respect to the pillars of financial markets and the public sector, the following sections briefly outline the basic ideas. The final section of this concluding chapter synthesizes the three pillars of neo-Schumpeterian economics by introducing the concept of the *neo-Schumpeterian corridor* of economic development.

The role of finance in a neo-Schumpeterian economy

Schumpeter himself gives a first hint of the important role of the financial sector for economic development in his *Theory of Economic Development* of 1912. After the creative entrepreneur, the risk-taking banker is the second most important force behind economic dynamics. Indeed, the entrepreneur and the banker have to be considered as in a symbiotic relationship: the entrepreneur opens up the possibilities of investment for the banker, and the banker enables venturing possibilities for the entrepreneur.

In this respect, J.P. Morgan (1837–1913) – as a banker who also took active roles in real ventures such as the American railways – can be considered as an example par excellence of a Schumpeterian banker. Generally, one can claim that the major task for the financial sector as a whole has to be seen in the acquisition and supply of capital over time needed by firm actors for their entrepreneurial activities.

Keeping in mind the research objective of neo-Schumpeterian economics, it is difficult to distinguish between the evolution of the financial sector and its role and function in particular stages of development in capitalist economies. For this reason, we highlight the symbiotic and co-evolutionary relationships of the real and monetary sides by giving a brief overview of the most important developments, without the claim of being comprehensive.

The banker and the bank system turn out to be not sufficient in describing the prolific development of capitalistic economies. Besides banks, stock markets entered the scene and played an outstanding role for firms in their endeavors to acquire capital. The amount of capital needed to finance ventures in the new industrializing world since the end of the 18th century accelerated the diffusion of stock markets tremendously.

The mixture of bank and stock market financing was extended only recently by the emergence of private equity and venture capital firms. Basically, owing to the increased techno-economic opportunities within knowledge-based economies going hand in hand with strongly felt uncertainties of scientific and technological innovation, venture capitalists appeared as a blend of financial and technological knowledge focusing on acquiring capital for risky innovative start-up companies.

These developments obviously fulfil the requirements of neo-Schumpeterian economics as the financial sector's development follows the increasing and differentiating needs of the real sector and at the same time enable the development of the real sector. From a neo-Schumpeterian perspective, the future orientation of the finance sector is essential and can be traced back, on the one hand, of course, to the uncertainty of innovation processes. On the other hand, however, a major feature of knowledge creation and innovation is the extremely time-consuming nature of these processes. Both characteristics make a long-term orientation absolutely necessary. However, from this alliance between uncertainty and a long-term orientation, two threads, stemming from the financial sector, may be identified for neo-Schumpeterian development.

First, the actors in the financial markets are induced to shorten their time-horizons for decisions in order to reduce uncertainty. Consider, e.g., the most recent developments in financial markets, such as the introduction of obligatory quarterly reports etc., which might improve the possibilities of control, but at the same time severely damage the possibilities of long-run innovative commitment on the firm side.

Second, short-term signals of potential technological breakthroughs are misinterpreted in the financial sphere of an economy and cause a positive feedback within expectation formation. Such a development can lead to bubble effects in the financial markets and, finally, to a major collapse of the real sector

Of course, the future orientation of neo-Schumpeterian economics also makes it necessary to rethink the role of monetary policy and central banks. In monetarism and neoclassical economics, this role is clearly defined: it is the stability of consumer prices or low inflation rates which more or less defines the only benchmark for the policy of central banks. The main instruments to fight inflationary tendencies can then be seen in regulating the supply of money and liquidity and in fixing short-term interest rates. These instruments still remain important when we turn to the neo-Schumpeterian context. What changes, however, is the main goal of monetary policy. Besides, or even instead of, fighting consumer price inflation, the political support of growth and development in an economy or in a global economic area, for instance the European Union, takes center stage in strategic thinking, with severe consequences concerning the economic and political role of central banks, for instance the European Central Bank.

On the one hand, this means that the supply of money and liquidity should be intended above all to foster neo-Schumpeterian innovation dynamics, being the main source and the basis of modern growth and development. On the other hand, central banks continuously have to consider carefully the symbiotic relationship between the real and the financial spheres of an economy, as mentioned above. Because a policy of cheap liquidity, for instance, aimed initially at inducing and accelerating economic growth, may easily turn a regular neo-Schumpeterian development into a hyper-dynamic one, with the tendency to build up explosive bubbles on the financial, and (today, even more importantly) on the asset and energy markets. This might especially be the case when huge speculation oriented hedge funds enter the markets and try to maximize short-term profits.

In this case central banks, from a neo-Schumpeterian perspective, have the task of observing and controlling such inflationary tendencies. For modern economies, these tendencies may be increasingly important, compared to the ordinary consumer price inflation considered exclusively in the past. This argument is even stronger if one considers that neo-Schumpeterian dynamics, based on innovation, sooner or later will be accompanied by remarkable productivity gains, which very likely restrict consumer price inflation to a very moderate rate.

Summing up, we can state with Amendola and Gaffard (2005): 'The problem that central banks confronted with processes of change (and hence with innovation and growth) are really facing is to deal with financial constraints to impact on real constraints – the constraints that determine the evolution of the economy and hence what eventually happens to inflation – rather than the problem of credibility of their commitment to price stability.'

The public sector in neo-Schumpeterian economics

Our considerations of a neo-Schumpeterian theory of the public sector focus on the justification of the state and encompass a normative perspective in the sense of defining tasks for public activities as well as a positive–empirical perspective supposed to explain real developments.

The existence and necessity of a public sector can be explained within the neo-Schumpeterian approach again by the persistence and inevitability of uncertainty accompanying every kind of innovation. Schumpeter's notion of *creative destruction* in his 1942 book, *Capitalism, Socialism and Democracy*, hints at the two sides of the innovation coin: in every innovation process, we find winners and losers. Ex ante it is impossible to know who will win and who will lose the innovative game. Accordingly, the uncertainty of innovation processes throws a veil of ignorance over the economic actors. In this sense, the ideas of John Rawls' *Theory of Justice* (1971) can be transferred to the neo-Schumpeterian context. A society can agree on a *social contract* to deal with the peculiarities and imponderables of innovation processes. This social contract then has to be executed by a state authority. In the neo-Schumpeterian context, sure enough the social contract also applies to firm actors and entails both support for uncertain innovation activities as well as social responsibilities in the case of innovative success (see e.g. the contribution of Zoltan Acs in this volume).

The normative perspective of an economic theory of the state is supposed to guide the deviation and design of all public activities – encompassing public expenditures as well as public revenues – which in a neo-Schumpeterian context has to include the developmental potential of the economy. In this sense, basically all public interventions have to be scrutinized, as to whether they support or hinder the potential of economic development. Accordingly, for public activities, an orientation towards the future is postulated.

Two types of failure generally endanger this goal and can be considered the cardinal errors of economies: the first deals with the danger of discarding promising opportunities too soon, whereas the second deals with the possibility of staying too long on exhausted trajectories (Eliasson, 2000). In both cases, resources for future development are wasted, which calls for policy intervention. But why do economies and economic actors tend to these failures? The sources of potential failures are manifold, but again stem from the uncertainty underlying economic processes as well as the complex nature of novelties.

A first example is given by consumers' decisions concerning so-called 'merit wants' as introduced by Richard Musgrave (1958) in public finance. Because of the future orientation and the complex character as well as the high probability of positive spillover effects of merit wants, individuals tend to undervalue considerably their consumption as, e.g., in education, or to underinvest in respective activities, as, e.g. with respect to R&D. A future-oriented policy, therefore, has to consider these shortfalls, e.g. by improving the knowledge of economic actors concerning the benefits of the respective goods and activities and/or by supporting their consumption, use and production.

A second example deals with different and unbalanced speeds of development, which is symptomatic of dynamic innovation-driven processes. Creative destruction in a Schumpeterian sense is most often closely connected to the obsolescence of labor qualifications which might cause severe problems of mismatch unemployment on the labor markets: the new qualifications are not sufficiently available, whereas obsolete qualifications abound. From the neo-Schumpeterian economics perspective, this mismatch on labor markets demands not only an administrative design of labor policy, but also an active future-oriented or knowledge-based design. With respect to recent labor market policy designs, the Danish model implemented since the 1990s is a good example of such a future-oriented approach.

A third example for normatively defining the tasks of a neo-Schumpeterian policy stems from the interaction dimension and, in particular, deals with the increasing need for international policy coordination. Newly-emerging economic areas challenge international and supranational coordination of policy in order to benefit from developmental potentials resulting from larger economic areas. An illustrative example is given by the necessary balancing act between globalization and regionalization which the European Union has to manage after the recent Eastern enlargement. On the one hand, economies of scale due to growing markets and globalization are obviously targets of policy. On the other hand, international competitiveness strongly depends on specialization and differentiation: the creativity potential of larger economic areas is essentially fed by the exploitation of the heterogeneous endowments of the regions. Thus, specialization and differentiation are processes which take place at the regional levels of economic areas.

Whereas the above examples focus on the public expenditures side, the final example is taken from the domain of public revenues. Obviously, issues concerning the design of tax systems and the size of public deficits exert an enormous pressure on the development potential of an economy. Besides questions concerning the intergenerational distribution of burdens, questions of the sustainability of, e.g., the health and pension systems, as well as of the sustainable prerequisites of economic growth and development, arise. Consider, for example, the increasing life expectancies and demographic changes which are key issues in almost all industrialized countries and which demand new models of health insurance and pension systems. Or consider the international and interregional competition for industrial settlement, its impact on future development of nations and regions, and the role the design of tax systems plays in this competition. A future-oriented neo-Schumpeterian policy has to scrutinize whether the conditions generated by public activities allow for, or even open up, developmental potentials in the future. To refer to Isaac Newton and his famous quotation on the intellectual heritage of past generations, one can also state that a neo-Schumpeterian policy design has to allow future generations to say that they stand on the shoulders of giants and not those of dwarfs.

With respect to a positive–empirical approach of a neo-Schumpeterian theory of the state, which seeks to explain real developments, a promising starting point again comes from public finance and an empirical observation discussed for more than 100 years under the heading of *Wagner's Law* (Wagner, 1892). Adolph Wagner (1835–1917) formulated this law following empirical observations that the development of an industrialized economy is accompanied by an increasing absolute and relative share of public expenditures in GNP. According to Wagner, the reasons for the income elasticity above unity towards public goods are to be seen in the increasing importance of *law and power* issues as well as *culture and welfare* issues in industrializing and developing economies. This way, public dynamics are narrowly connected to neo-Schumpeterian dynamics, which demand higher qualities of public goods such as infrastructure, education, basic research and so on as a condition sine qua non for economic development.

To avoid either an unbounded growth of public activities, which Schumpeter (1950) himself labelled *the march into socialism*, or an increasing privatization of public goods, e.g., in the health and education sector (which goes hand in hand with an increasing uneven distribution of services, itself an obstacle to economic development) a policy recommendation of neo-Schumpeterian economics has to focus on adding a qualitative dimension to Wagner's quantitative dimension. This can be achieved only by taking seriously the normative requirement in the design of all public activities of the neo-Schumpeterian approach, namely their orientation towards future development. In the case of potential insane Wagnerian dynamics leading to an overall expansion of the public sector, neo-Schumpeterian policy design encompasses a strengthening of the absorptive capacities of consumers towards superior merit wants. This example illustrates the important co-evolutionary relationship between the different pillars of comprehensive neo-Schumpeterian economics which is the subject of the final section.

The neo-Schumpeterian corridor

A comprehensive Neo-Schumpeterian economic theory focusing on innovation-driven qualitative development has to offer theoretical concepts to analyze the various issues of all three pillars: industry dynamics, financial markets, and the public sector. Innovation and, as a consequence thereof, uncertainty, are ubiquitous phenomena characteristic of each of these pillars and are also intrinsically interrelated. An improved understanding of the development processes can only be expected when the co-evolutionary dimensions of the three pillars are taken into account. This is illustrated with the concept of a neo-Schumpeterian corridor, shown in Figure 70.2.

In a neo-Schumpeterian economics perspective, there exists only a narrow corridor for a prolific development of socio-economic systems. Profound neo-Schumpeterian development takes place in a narrow corridor between

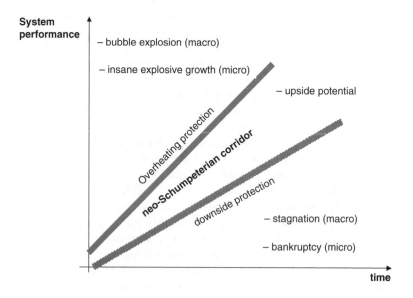

Figure 70.2   The neo-Schumpeterian corridor

the extremes of uncontrolled growth and exploding bubbles, on the one hand, and stationarity, i.e. zero growth and stagnancy, on the other hand. Economic policy in the sense of neo-Schumpeterian economics is supposed to keep the system in an *upside potential* including both *overheating protection*, i.e. on the macro-level bubble explosions and on the micro-level insane explosive growth, and *downside protection*, i.e. on the macro-level stagnation and on the micro-level bankruptcy.

A brief view of the economic history of different economies illustrates that the two threats – bubble explosion and stagnation – shape economic evolution. It emphasizes also the necessity to develop further comprehensive neo-Schumpeterian economics, in order to get a grip on the important co-evolutionary processes.

In the post-Second World War period, both Japan and Germany recovered extremely well in economic terms, whereas the United States increasingly lost ground. However, both countries fell out of the neo-Schumpeterian corridor (in opposite directions) whereas the United States returned to the corridor. What happened? In both Japan and Germany, specific institutional arrangements and organizational forms evolved after the Second World War which were not simple copies of the previous successful US system but instead proved to be relatively superior. In particular, one may stress the important meaning of the financial sectors designed for economic recovery and the overtaking of the Japanese and the German industrial sectors. In both cases, long-term relationships between industry and banks opposed the short-term character of these relationships within the US financial sector. This long-term commitment was extremely beneficial for economic development of large industries in this period of comparatively stable technological environments. In the same vein, labor markets and their institutions were oriented towards long-term relationships compared with hire-and-fire policies in the US, which served well to further productivity improvements.

But during the late 1970s and early 1980s, the German system could not cope with the new challenges coming from the information and communication technology revolution, as the starting event of the so-called 'knowledge-based' economies. Its institutions and organizational designs now proved to be too sedate, and its economy drifted upwards in the stagnation sector of Figure 70.2.

By the end of the 1980s and early 1990s, the Japanese economy had broken down and moved into a development period. today referred to as the decade of near-zero growth. The major reason w⌣ an overheating of the financial sector which led to speculative bubbles, which, after their bursting, affected the whole economy.

The American model, by contrast, was now regarded as the epitome of dynamism and entrepreneurship, and was seen as a guidepost for the 21st century. The US economy thus entered the neo-Schumpeterian corridor in the *new growth* period again. Since the early 1990s, a high rate of creation of technology-intensive firms, combined with a substantive rise in privately financed R&D, led to the emergence of world leading technology clusters such as the famous Silicon Valley and Route 121. Thus, economic development of the 1990s was characterized by high average growth rates, low unemployment and low inflation.

The historical examples illustrate the powerful economic dynamics shaping overall economic development and also illustrate further the explanatory power of the neo-Schumpeterian corridor, which allows an analysis of the underlying mechanisms. In this sense, we emphasize the important need to develop further the comprehensive neo-Schumpeterian economics approach in the directions outlined above. We are convinced that this *Companion* is a first step in this direction.

References

Amendola, M. and Gaffard, J.-L. (2005), *Out of Equilibrium*, New York: Oxford University Press.
Eliasson, G. (2000), 'The role of knowledge in economic growth', Royal Institute of Technology, Stockholm, TRITA-IEO-R 2000:17.
Musgrave, R.A. (1958), *The Theory of Public Finance*, New York: McGraw-Hill.
Rawls, J. (1971), *A Theory of Justice*, New York: Oxford University Press.
Schumpeter, J.A. (1912), *Theorie der wirtschaftlichen Entwicklung*, Leipzig: Duncker & Humblot.
Schumpeter, J.A. (1942), *Capitalism, Socialism, and Democracy*, New York: Harper and Bros.
Schumpeter, J.A. (1950), The march into socialism, *American Economic Review*, **40**, 446–56.
Wagner, A. (1892), *Grundlegung der politischen Ökonomie*, 3rd edn, part 1, vol. 1, Leipzig: Winter.

Index